CASES AND MATER
ON EMPLOYMENT

We work with leading authors to develop the
strongest educational materials in law,
bringing cutting-edge thinking and best
learning practice to a global market.

Under a range of well-known imprints, including
Longman, we craft high quality print and
electronic publications which help readers to understand
and apply their content, whether studying or at work.

To find out more about the complete range of our
publishing, please visit us on the World Wide Web at:
www.pearsoned.co.uk

CASES AND MATERIALS ON EMPLOYMENT LAW

THIRD EDITION

GWYNETH PITT

Professor of Law, Kingston University

PEARSON

Longman

Harlow, England • London • New York • Boston • San Francisco • Toronto
Sydney • Tokyo • Singapore • Hong Kong • Seoul • Taipei • New Delhi
Cape Town • Madrid • Mexico City • Amsterdam • Munich • Paris • Milan

Pearson Education Limited
Edinburgh Gate
Harlow
Essex CM20 2JE
England

and Associated Companies throughout the world

Visit us on the World Wide Web at:
www.pearsoned.co.uk

First published 1994
Second edition published 1998
Third edition published 2008

© Financial Times Professional Limited 1998
© Gwyneth Pitt 2008

ISBN: 978-0-582-47275-4

British Library Cataloguing-in-Publication Data
A catalogue record for this book is available from the British Library

Library of Congress Cataloging-in-Publication Data
Pitt, Gwyneth.
  Cases and materials on employment law / Gwyneth Pitt. — 3rd ed.
    p. cm.
  ISBN 978-0-582-47275-4
1. Labor laws and legislation—Great Britain—Cases. I. Title.
  KD3009.P57 2008
    344.4101—dc22

                                                2008018426

10 9 8 7 6 5 4 3 2 1
12 11 10 09 08

Typeset in 10/12pt Plantin by 35
Printed in Great Britain by Henry Ling Ltd, at the Dorset Press, Dorchester, Dorset.

The publisher's policy is to use paper manufactured from sustainable forests.

BRIEF CONTENTS

CONTENTS

Contents

Visit the *Cases and Materials on Employment Law, third edition* **mylawchamber** site at **http://www.mylawchamber.co.uk/pitt** to access:

● **Companion website support:** The site includes updates to major changes in the law to make sure you are ahead of the game, and weblinks to help you read more widely around the subject.

PREFACE

There are two main reasons for producing a collection of cases and materials. One is to develop students' skills in legal reasoning by getting them to sift out arguments and reasons from lengthy judgments. The other is to provide the reader with a portable library containing the most important primary materials. The latter remains the objective of this book. The aim is to tell the story of employment law through the primary materials selected, with commentary to link it all together and set up a framework for critique. As most students of employment law will also have access to a statute book, reproduction of statutory materials is limited to just those provisions which are essential for understanding the point at issue. While this book can be used as a vehicle for teaching employment law by the case method, or as a stand-alone account of the subject, it has been designed to function ideally as a companion to my textbook, *Employment Law*, 6th edition, published by Sweet & Maxwell in 2007.

There are definite advantages in having materials to hand in a casebook. Although a case extract takes longer to read than a summary of principles in a textbook, reading the judgments enables the reader to gain a far more nuanced understanding of the law than is possible with even the most sophisticated texts. Also, employment case law is often about interpreting legislation, and employment legislation is amended so frequently that a student reading a case in the reports might well have difficulty in marrying up the earlier incarnation of a statutory provision with its current form. An advantage of this collection is that it has been possible either to substitute the current references in the judgments or at least to provide cross-references to present legislative provisions. In the same vein, industrial tribunals are referred to as employment tribunals throughout and plaintiffs and applicants have become claimants. For any reader who finds it disconcertingly anachronistic to have Lord Denning referring to employment tribunals or Lord Atkin talking about claimants, I can only apologise.

It has been an unconscionably long time since the last edition of this book appeared. I am grateful to my publishers for their patience – or at least for concealing their impatience – and for treating me throughout with their usual courtesy, good humour and professionalism. All authors make much of the rate and scale of change in their subject area, but perhaps employment lawyers have one of the strongest claims for this. While the structure of this book remains the same as the last edition, there is little else that is unchanged. Among the most important recent legislative changes covered are the Equality Act 2006, the Transfer of Undertakings (Protection of Employment) Regulations 2006 and the Employment Equality (Age) Regulations 2006. Important recent decisions include *Cadman v Health and Safety Executive* on equal pay and *Robinson-Steele v R D Retail Services Ltd* on working time in the European Court of Justice; the important decision of the European Court of Human Rights on union freedom, *ASLEF v UK*, and the historic, hardly less significant decision of the House of Lords in *OBG* v *Allan*, reshaping the economic torts. The website which now accompanies the book will alert readers to changes as they happen.

The law is generally stated as at 1 February 2008. However, it has occasionally been possible to include later references – in particular, the important amendments made to equality law by the Sex Discrimination Act 1975 (Amendment) Regulations 2008.

This edition of the *Casebook* contains extracts from over 220 key cases in English and European law, as well as legislative extracts and excerpts from official Reports, Command Papers and other sources. It has been designed to be as complete a set of fundamental employment law materials as is possible in a book of this size. I hope that readers will find it interesting and useful.

Gwyneth Pitt
March 2008

ACKNOWLEDGEMENTS

We are grateful to the following for permission to reproduce copyright material:

Trade Union & Labour Relations (Consolidation) Act 1992; www.acas.org.uk, *ACAS Annual Report 2005/06, ACAS Code of Practice 2,3,* and *ACAS Code of Practice on Disciplinary and Grievance Procedures (2004); Equality Act 2006; The Industrial Tribunals Extension of Jurisdiction (England and Wales) Order 1994* and *Employment Tribunals Act 1996* (now the *Industrial Tribunals Act 1996); Employment Tribunals (Constitution and Rules of Procedure) Regulations 2004; Universal Declaration of Human Rights Act 1948, 1950; The Sex Discrimination Act 1975;* Race Relations Act *1976; Employment Equality (Sexual Orientation) Regulations 2003; Employment Equality (Religion or Belief) Regulations 2003; Employment Equality (Age) Regulations 2006; Disability Discrimination Act 1995; The Disability Discrimination (Meaning of Disability) Regulations 1996; Employment Rights Act 1996; Part-time workers (Prevention of Less Favourable Treatment) Regulations 2000, 2002; The Telecommunications (Lawful Business Practice) (Interception of Communications) Regulations 2000; Report of the Royal Commission on Trade Unions and Employers' Associations, 1965–1968* (Chairman: The Rt. Hon. Lord Donovan) Cmnd. 3623, 1968; *UK White Paper People, Jobs and Opportunity* Cmd 1810, Feb 1992; Government White Paper, *Fairness at Work,* Cm 3968, May 1998 outlined in *Employment Relations Act 1999* and *Employment Relations Act 1999; The Transnational Information and Consultation of Employees Regulations 1999* and *The Information and Consultation of Employees Regulations 2004; The Social Security Act 1986, The Trade Union Reform and Employment Rights Act 1993, The Maternity and Parental Leave etc. Regulations 1999, Green Paper Work and Parents: Competitiveness and Choice* Cmnd 5005, December 2000, *Employment Protection Act 1975, European Communities (Amendment) Act 1986, Work and Families Act 2006, Employment Act 1980, 2002* and *(Dispute Resolution) Regulations 2004;* Directgov details about Maternity Rights, Paternal Rights, Adoption Rights, Leave for care of dependants; *The Working Time Regulations 1998; Working Time Directive (2003/88/EC), The Equal Pay Act 1970 and Equal Pay Directive (75/117/EEC);* DTI consultation paper *(2001)* Department for Business Enterprise & Regulatory Reform; *The Transfer of Undertakings (Protection of Employment) Regulations 1981, 2006; UK White Paper Removing Barriers to Employment* Cm 655, March 1989 © Crown copyright 1968–2008 reproduced with permission of the Controller of Her Majesty's Stationery Office; cases from *The Law Reports; The Weekly Law Reports* and *The Industrial Cases Reports* copyright © The Incorporated Council of Law Reporting for England and Wales, Megarry House, 119 Chancery Lane, London WC2A 1PP; *Industrial Law Reports* reproduced with permission of IRS/Eclipse Group Limited; the law report *Stevenson Jordan & Harrison Ltd* v *Macdonald & Evans, [1952] 1 TLR 101 Court of Appeal* copyright © News International Syndication Ltd; *Employment*

Practices Code (2005) copyright © Information Commissioners Office; *CAC Guide to Statutory Recognition*, 2007 copyright © Central Arbitration Committee; *Spijkers v GebroedersBbenedik Abattoir CV (1986) 2 CMLR 296, European Court of Justice* and 'The closed shop' from *Labour and the Law* 2nd edition by Otto Kahn-Freund, 1977, copyright © Sweet & Maxwell Limited; *ILO Convention No 87* (1948) and *ILO Convention No 98* (1949) copyright © International Labour Organization.

In some instances we have been unable to trace the owners of copyright material and we would appreciate any information that would enable us to do so.

TABLE OF CASES

Page numbers in **bold** refer to pages where the cases are extracted.

TABLE OF STATUTES

Page numbers in **bold** refer to pages where the statutes are extracted.

TABLE OF STATUTORY INSTRUMENTS

Page numbers in **bold** refer to pages where the statutory instruments are extracted.

TABLE OF EU AND OTHER LEGISLATION

Page numbers in **bold** refer to pages where the legislation is extracted.

EU LEGISLATION

INTERNATIONAL CONVENTIONS, ETC.

TABLE OF ABBREVIATIONS

Acas	Advisory, Conciliation and Arbitration Service
Age Reg	Employment Equality (Age) Regulations 2006
ASLEF	Associated Society of Locomotive Engineers and Firemen
CAC	Central Arbitration Committee
CBI	Confederation of British Industry
CCSU	Council of Civil Service Unions
CCT	Compulsory Competitive Tendering
CEEP	European Centre of Enterprises with Public Participation and of Enterprises of General Economic Interest
CO	Certification Officer
COHSE	Confederation of Health Service Employees
CRE	Commission for Racial Equality
DDA	Disability Discrimination Act 1995
DDA 2005	Disability Discrimination Act 2005
Dispute Regulations	Employment Act 2002 (Dispute Resolution) Regulations 2004
EA 2002	Employment Act 2002
EAT	Employment Appeal Tribunal
EC	European Community
ECHR	European Convention on Human Rights
ECJ	European Court of Justice
ECtHR	European Court of Human Rights
EOC	Equal Opportunities Commission
EPA	Employment Protection Act 1975
EPCA	Employment Protection (Consolidation) Act 1978
EqA	Equality Act 2006
EqPA	Equal Pay Act 1970
ERA	Employment Rights Act 1996
ERelA 1999	Employment Relations Act 1999
ERelA 2004	Employment Relations Act 2004
ETA	Employment Tribunals Act 1996
ETUC	European Trade Union Federation
EU	European Union
EWC	European Works Council
GOQ	Genuine occupational qualification
GOR	Genuine occupational requirement
HRA	Human Rights Act 1998
HSWA	Health and Safety at Work etc Act 1974
ICE	Information and Consultation of Employees Regulations 2004
ILO	International Labour Organization

ITF	International Transport Workers' Federation
MPL	Maternity and Parental Leave etc Regulations 1999
NALGO	National Association of Local Government Officers
NATSOPA	National Society of Operative Printers Graphical and Media Personnel
NUJ	National Union of Journalists
NUM	National Union of Mineworkers
NUPE	National Union of Public Employees
NUR	National Union of Railwaymen
PCP	Provision, criterion or practice
RB Regs	Employment Equality (Religion or Belief) Regulations 2003
RIPA	Regulation of Investigatory Powers Act 2000
RMT	Rail Maritime and Transport Union
RPA	Redundancy Payments Act 1965
RRA	Race Relations Act 1976
SDA	Sex Discrimination Act 1975
SOGAT	Society of Graphical and Allied Trades 1982
SO Regs	Employment Equality (Sexual Orientation) Regulations 2003
TGWU	Transport and General Workers' Union
TICE	Transnational Information and Consultation of Empolyees Regulations 1999
TSSA	Transport and Salaried Staffs Association
TUC	Trades Union Congress
TULRA	Trade Union and Labour Relations Act 1974
TULRCA	Trade Union and Labour Relations (Consolidation) Act 1992
TUPE	Transfer of Undertakings (Protection of Employment) Regulations 1981
TUPE 2006	Transfer of Undertakings (Protection of Employment) Regulations 2006
TURERA	Trade Union Reform and Employment Rights Act 1993
UDHR	Universal Declaration of Human Rights
UNICE	Union of Industrial and Employers Confederations of Europe

1

INTRODUCTION

Employment law is one of the most dynamic and engaging subjects in the legal curriculum. All readers are, will be, or have been employees or employers at some point in their lives, and are bound therefore to find much within these covers which they can relate to their own experiences and help them to make sense of problems and issues. As a subject which above all is at the interface of law and politics, it is nearly impossible – and certainly undesirable – to study employment law without engaging at the same time with the political and social context of employment relations issues. Employment law reflects the changing nature of society and the global environment in which business operates in the twenty-first century. International labour law standards have their impact on British employment law but British membership of the European Union has reshaped the legal environment in the workplace most decisively, as will become evident in later chapters, especially in relation to equality law.

In this chapter, salient features of the British employment relations scene will be sketched as a foundation for what follows, and the sources of employment law will be identified and introduced. This brief section is intended to provide an underpinning for the discussion of the law and would repay initial reading. The rest of the chapter gives an account of the main institutions of employment law: the organisations and officials who have responsibilities in defined areas. It may be convenient to defer reading about many of these until they come into focus through a substantive law issue.

CHARACTERISTICS OF THE BRITISH EMPLOYMENT SCENE

In 2006 the labour force in the United Kingdom, including those seeking work, stood at 30.6 million. Of these, 1.68 million were unemployed; unemployment has remained around the 5 per cent mark since the turn of the century, although rising to 5.5 per cent in 2006. Of the nearly 29 million people in employment, just over 20 per cent were employed in the public sector. Having shrunk from 5.98 million in 1991 to 5.16 million by 1998, the numbers employed in the public sector have crept up again under the Labour administration in power since 1997 to stand at 5.85 million by 2006.

In 1971 nearly two-thirds of the workforce (62.9 per cent) were men and only just over one-third (37.1 per cent) were women. This position changed dramatically, especially in the 1970s and 1980s, to the position today where 54.2 per cent of those employed are men and 45.8 per cent are women. The increased participation of women has been driven in part by changes in social attitudes (encouraged by the equality legislation) and in part because one of the main areas of employment growth has been in the service sector, where women are more likely to be employed. More opportunities for part-time work and other flexible forms of working have also encouraged mothers to return to work and the evidence is that increasingly they are returning to work relatively soon after the birth of their children. Some 83 per cent of all part-time workers are women.

One demographic driver which, combined with legislative change, will have a more noticeable effect on the composition of the workforce in the future is the growing proportion of the population aged 50 or more. The 'old-age dependency ratio' is forecast to rise from 23.8 per cent in 2005 to 29.7 per cent in 2020, as the baby-boomers reach pension age and life expectancy continues to increase. This has led to initiatives to encourage workers to continue working for longer and the outlawing of age discrimination by the Employment Equality (Age) Regulations 2006 should help to facilitate this. As pension schemes have become less generous in recent years, especially to new entrants, and as the state pension age is being gradually equalised upwards to 65 for both men and women by 2020, there is a strong financial incentive for people to work up to and past pension age, so it is likely that the proportion of workers over 50 remaining in work will continue to grow. The era of employers encouraging workers to take early retirement in their 50s is over.

About 3.79 million workers in the United Kingdom are self-employed, with men here outnumbering women by 2.5 to 1. Self-employed workers constitute about 13 per cent of the whole workforce, a proportion which has seen a slight increase in the last four or five years. It should be remembered that self-employment is not always a positive choice: the biggest growth in the United Kingdom was in the 1980s and caused by the recession. While many self-employed people are genuine small-scale entrepreneurs, others may be effectively temporary employees, hiring themselves out to numerous employers in a more or less precarious fashion.

As to the kinds of business in which people are employed, the decline in traditional manufacturing continues apace, representing a little over 11 per cent of all jobs in 2006, while the service sector has increased to more than 82 per cent.

Trade union membership among British workers peaked at 13.3 million in 1979, but the anti-union measures of the Thatcher government led to this figure going into freefall. Even after eight years of a more sympathetic administration, by 2005 numbers were half this, at 6.68 million trade union members. This constitutes about 29 per cent of all workers. In general, older workers and those with longer service (factors which, of course, go together) have higher levels of union membership and unionism is growing among women although sliding among men. One reason for this is that more women are employed in the public sector. The differences in union membership between public and private sector workplaces are stark: 58.6 per cent of public sector workers were union members in 2005, against just 17.2 per cent of private sector workers.

The percentage of workers whose terms and conditions are bargained for collectively by trade unions is always higher than the percentage of workers who belong to trade unions, as collective agreements usually cover all workers in a particular workplace or section of a workplace, regardless of union membership. Thus 71 per cent of workers in the public sector were covered by collective agreements in 2005, against 20.9 per cent of private sector workers. Taken overall, this means that about 36 per cent of workers are covered by collective agreements, a percentage which has remained fairly constant for the past ten years. It would appear that the statutory recognition procedure (see Chapter 5) which compels employers to recognise unions for collective bargaining in certain situations, has not had a major effect on levels of union membership or collective bargaining coverage.

SOURCES OF EMPLOYMENT LAW

The pivotal relationship of employment law, that of employer and worker, is governed by contract. Thus the law of contract, which is essentially common law (meaning case law rather than statute law) is central to the study of employment law. Since the early 1960s, the contractual relationship between employers and employees has been transformed through legislative intervention. These statutory reforms have almost invariably been predicated on the existence of the contract of employment, however, and in situations where a statute is unclear or where there appears to be a gap in the law, it is still to the law of contract that courts and tribunals look to supply the deficiency.

Thus the primary sources for the study of employment law are an amalgam of case law and statute law. Two major consolidations mean that, today, the bulk of the statutory provisions relevant to the individual employment relationship are to be found in the Employment Rights Act 1996 (ERA) and the bulk of statute law applicable to trade unions is found in the Trade Union and Labour Relations (Consolidation) Act 1992 (TULRCA). There have been numerous reforms since then, but most of these have operated by amending the two main statutes. This means that it is essential to have an up-to-date version of them: these are found most conveniently in the collections of statutes emanating from the major legal publishers and the on-line legal information retrieval systems such as Lexis or Westlaw. Some specific areas of legal regulation are outside the two main statutes: equality law is dealt with in a number of separate enactments (see Chapter 2) and there are different sets of regulations covering such things as the National Minimum Wage, holidays and working time.

Cases based on employment law statutes are almost always heard in employment tribunals with a right of appeal to the Employment Appeal Tribunal (EAT). Employment tribunals are inferior courts and their decisions have no value as precedents. The Employment Appeal Tribunal has the same standing as the High Court and its decisions must be followed by employment tribunals. Different divisions of the EAT are not bound to follow each other's decisions, although they will usually try to do so for the sake of judicial comity. Employment tribunals have a limited jurisdiction over some matters arising on the termination of a contract of employment, but all other purely contractual claims go to the normal courts – the county court or the High Court, depending on how much is at stake.

Employment law has been substantially affected by the United Kingdom's membership of the European Community (EC) and the European Union (EU). Accession to the Treaty of Rome, the principal treaty constituting the EC, entails obligations to accept EU law and, where necessary, to change English law to be in accordance with it. English courts and tribunals have a duty to apply EU law, preferring it over English law in case of conflict and interpreting English law in accordance with EU law as far as possible. Thus EU treaties, directives, regulations and decisions, and decisions of the European Court of Justice (ECJ) on the interpretation of EU law, are also primary sources of employment law.

Other international treaties influence British law in a different way. The United Kingdom is a member of the International Labour Organization (ILO) and has ratified many ILO Conventions. These are treaties which should then be brought into effect in British law. A failure to do so will not result in court proceedings in the way that a failure to implement EU law can, but creates at the very least a strong moral and diplomatic pressure to conform. The ILO reports regularly on its members' compliance with their treaty obligations. The European Convention on Human Rights is also frequently relevant in an employment context. The Human Rights Act 1998 (HRA) made Convention rights enforceable directly by British courts and tribunals in two main ways. First, all courts and tribunals have a duty to interpret legislation consistently with the Convention, as far as possible (HRA s 3). Secondly, HRA s 6 places public authorities (including courts and tribunals) under an obligation to ensure that their actions are compatible with Convention rights. This means that workers employed by public authorities could bring claims related to employment based directly on Convention rights. Workers not employed by public authorities could not base a claim solely on a Convention right, but provided they can find a different jurisdictional basis on which to claim, relevant Convention rights will be taken into account in deciding their case.

Finally, there is a plethora of non-statutory materials available, both official and semi-official. Codes of Practice issued by competent authorities (such as Acas, the equality Commissions, the Health and Safety Commission or the Secretary of State) do not create legal obligations, but have to be taken into account by courts and tribunals wherever they are relevant to legal proceedings. In so far as failure to follow a Code of Practice may help to establish liability, there is a strong, if indirect, pressure to comply with them. In addition, all these bodies and others offer a range of guidance to the law, most of it available to be downloaded from their websites. Such guidance does not have the force of law and should always be read with this distinction in mind. The same goes for the Explanatory Notes which now accompany all new statutes and statutory instruments. These Notes are very useful for understanding what was intended to be achieved by the legislation, but they have no legal force and are certainly not binding on any court or tribunal to whom it falls to interpret the statutory provisions.

INSTITUTIONS OF EMPLOYMENT LAW

Advisory, Conciliation and Arbitration Service (Acas)

Trade Union and Labour Relations (Consolidation) Act 1992

247 (1) There shall continue to be a body called the Advisory, Conciliation and Arbitration Service (referred to in this Act as 'ACAS').

      (2) ACAS is a body corporate of which the corporators are the members of its Council.

      (3) Its functions, and those of its officers and servants, shall be performed on behalf of the Crown, but not so as to make it subject to directions of any kind from any Minister of the Crown as to the manner in which it is to exercise its functions under any enactment . . .

209 It is the general duty of ACAS to promote the improvement of industrial relations . . .

Comment

(1) Acas was established in 1974. It took over the conciliation, arbitration and advisory roles which had previously been carried out by the Department of Employment, and also the wider remit of monitoring and improving the institutions and procedures for the conduct of employment relations which had belonged to the Commission on Industrial Relations. Both the CBI and the TUC were agreed that there was a need for a conciliation and arbitration procedure that was independent of government, so that it would not be affected by government incomes policies in particular. Hence the importance of TULRCA s 247(3).

(2) Acas was put on a statutory footing by the Employment Protection Act 1975, although the provisions relating to it are now consolidated in TULRCA. Its constitution still reflects the tripartism which was a standard feature of the voluntary system of employment relations prevalent until the 1980s – that is, it is composed of an equal number of employer and employee representatives, balanced by an uneven number of independent members. Thus there is a chairperson (who may be part-time) and nine part-time members, of whom three represent employers, three represent employees and three are independent. The main change in recent years has been that since 1998, following the recommendations of the Nolan Report (Nolan, 1995) membership vacancies are filled following open competition rather than by appointment from interested bodies.

(3) Acas has five Regional Offices in England and one each in Wales and Scotland. Its work is carried out mainly in the regions by about 850 employees. In 2004/05 Acas was faced with a budget allocation for the next three years which saw its budget slashed by £1 million between 2005/06 and 2006/07 and a further £2 million in the following year. In real terms, of course, the cut is much greater. Inevitably this has led to Acas shedding staff, which may impact on its effectiveness.

(4) Under TULRCA s 209 Acas originally had a duty to 'encourage the extension of collective bargaining' – but this was abolished by TURERA in 1993. The extension of collective bargaining was definitely not encouraged under the Conservative administration of the time and the Labour administration from 1997 has not seen fit to restore this obligation. Acas itself states its mission statement (in its Annual Reports for 2004/05 and 2005/06) in the following terms:

5

Acas aims to improve organisations and working life through better employment relations. We provide up-to-date information, independent advice, high quality training and we work with employers and employees to solve problems and improve performance.

(5) In addition to its statutory functions, considered below, Acas carries out a great deal of training, especially for smaller employers, and publishes numerous guidance leaflets, most of which are also available on-line. Its website, www.acas.org.uk, is a useful source; among other things, its Annual Reports, which provide a wealth of information about Acas and its work, can be accessed from the website.

Advice

Trade Union and Labour Relations (Consolidation) Act 1992

213 (1) ACAS may, on request or otherwise, give employers, employers' associations, workers and trade unions such advice as it thinks appropriate on matters concerned with or affecting or likely to affect industrial relations.

(2) ACAS may also publish general advice on matters concerned with or affecting or likely to affect industrial relations.

Comment

(1) Acas carries out its advisory function in four main ways. First, it provides a telephone helpline service which anyone can use to raise general employment queries. In its Annual Report for 2005/06 Acas reported that it received over 900,000 calls, double the level of the 1990s. Secondly, it publishes information leaflets and guidance, increasingly making use of its website for this. Thirdly, it engages in workplace consultancy projects on a range of employment relations issues. Finally, it runs training sessions, conferences and seminars.

Conciliation

Trade Union and Labour Relations (Consolidation) Act 1992

210 (1) Where a trade dispute exists or is apprehended ACAS may, at the request of one or more parties to the dispute or otherwise, offer the parties to the dispute its assistance with a view to bringing about a settlement.

(2) The assistance may be by way of conciliation or by other means, and may include the appointment of a person other than an officer or servant of ACAS to offer assistance to the parties to the dispute with a view to bringing about a settlement.

(3) In exercising its functions under this section ACAS shall have regard to the desirability of encouraging the parties to a dispute to use any appropriate agreed procedures for negotiation or the settlement of disputes.

Comment

(1) While Acas does not have to wait to be asked to provide its conciliation services in collective disputes, the system is voluntary. Historically it derives from the Conciliation Act 1896, and the guiding principle is that the parties are encouraged to achieve a voluntary settlement first if possible.

(2) The collective conciliation service offered by Acas seems to be well regarded by both sides of industry. In 2005/06 Acas received 904 requests for assistance and reckoned that it had assisted resolution of the issues in over 91 per cent of these. About half of the cases concerned pay and terms and conditions of employment, and about one-fifth were concerned with union recognition.

(3) One of the most important aspects of Acas's work is individual conciliation where employment disputes have resulted in an application to an employment tribunal. Virtually all applications to employment tribunals are referred to Acas to see if the dispute can be settled without going as far as a tribunal hearing. This area of work has grown substantially over the years. In the last three years, the number of cases referred to Acas were:

2003/04	104,952
2004/05	86,816
2005/06	141,288

The dip in 2004/05 can probably be attributed to the introduction of the statutory dispute resolution procedures in that year (see Chapter 8) and some 30,000 extra claims in 2005/06 are multiple equal pay claims against public authorities (see Chapter 7). Nonetheless, the trend is remorselessly upwards.

(4) Between 70 per cent and 75 per cent of all claims are settled or withdrawn following Acas conciliation, showing the importance of its work in this area.

Arbitration

Trade Union and Labour Relations (Consolidation) Act 1992

212 (1)   Where a trade dispute exists or is apprehended ACAS may, at the request of one or more of the parties to the dispute and with the consent of all the parties to the dispute, refer all or any of the matters to which the dispute relates for settlement to the arbitration of –

(a)   one or more persons appointed by ACAS for that purpose (not being officers or employees of ACAS), or

(b)   the Central Arbitration Committee . . .

Comment

(1) Acas engages in both arbitration and mediation. The difference is explained in the Acas Annual Report for 2005/06.

Acas Annual Report 2005/06

Both arbitration and mediation involve an independent person giving direction to employer and workforce parties over the way in which they should settle their differences. These processes are, as always with Acas-provided assistance, entered into voluntarily by the parties, and the arbitrator or mediator is required to operate within the powers set down in the terms of reference agreed by all parties.

Arbitration is a process in which an independent person from the Acas panel considers the parties' positions in a dispute and decides the terms for settlement. The parties agree in advance to be bound by this decision.

Mediation means Acas assists parties involved in a dispute to find a mutually agreeable settlement. Usually the mediator will have powers to suggest a way forward and make formal recommendations. These recommendations are not binding, but parties are expected to seriously consider them as a basis for resolving the dispute. As well as providing arbitration or mediation in workplace disputes, Acas often works with parties to establish their own standing arrangements.

Comment

(1) There were only 57 requests for collective arbitration in 2005/06, which is about average for recent years. This contrasts with the much greater number of requests (904) for collective conciliation and shows parties' reluctance to commit themselves to accepting an arbitrator's award.

(2) Acas does not provide arbitrators from its own staff. Arbitrators are either drawn from a panel of independent arbitrators maintained by Acas or arbitration is provided through the Central Arbitration Committee (CAC).

(3) In 2001 Acas set up an individual Arbitration Scheme as an alternative to unfair dismissal proceedings. Provided both parties agree, 'simple' unfair dismissal claims (where there is no doubt that the employee is qualified to claim and has been dismissed) can be referred to an independent arbitrator. The arbitrator is required to:

> (i) have regard to general principles of fairness and good conduct in employment relations (including, for example, principles referred to in any relevant ACAS 'Disciplinary and Grievance Procedures' Code of Practice or 'Discipline and Grievances at Work' Handbook), instead of applying legal tests or rules (eg court decisions or legislation); (ii) apply EC law. (ACAS Arbitration Scheme Order 2004 para 17.)

This inherent uncertainty may explain why the Acas Arbitration Scheme has not been a success. In the five years since it was introduced, only 55 claims in total have been made under it.

Codes of practice

Trade Union and Labour Relations (Consolidation) Act 1992

199 (1) ACAS may issue Codes of Practice containing such practical guidance as it thinks fit for the purpose of promoting the improvement of industrial relations or for purposes connected with trade union learning representatives.

   (2) In particular, ACAS shall in one or more Codes of Practice provide practical guidance on the following matters –
- (a) the time off to be permitted by an employer to a trade union official in accordance with section 168 (time off for carrying out trade union duties);
- (b) the time off to be permitted by an employer to a trade union member in accordance with section 170 (time off for trade union activities); and
- (c) the information to be disclosed by employers to trade union representatives in accordance with sections 181 and 182 (disclosure of information for purposes of collective bargaining). . . .

   (4) ACAS may from time to time revise the whole or any part of a Code of Practice issued by it and issue that revised Code.

Comment

(1) In pursuance of its powers under this section Acas has issued three Codes of Practice. The current versions of these are: the *Code of Practice on Disciplinary and Grievance Procedures* (2004); the *Code of Practice on Disclosure of Information to Trade Unions for Collective Bargaining Purposes* (1997) and the *Code of Practice on Time Off for Trade Union Duties and Activities* (2003).

(2) Where Acas wishes to issue a Code of Practice, it must first publish a draft for consultation and consider any representations made to it. The draft must then be submitted to the Secretary of State for approval; if it is not approved, it goes no further, but reasons must be given. If the Secretary of State gives approval, the Code is laid before Parliament. Unless Parliament passes a resolution to the contrary within 40 days, the Code is brought into force by statutory instrument (TULRCA s 200).

Trade Union and Labour Relations (Consolidation) Act 1992

207 (1) A failure on the part of any person to observe any provision of a Code of Practice issued under this Chapter shall not of itself render him liable to any proceedings.

(2) In any proceedings before an employment tribunal or the Central Arbitration Committee any Code of Practice issued under this Chapter by ACAS shall be admissible in evidence, and any provision of the Code which appears to the tribunal or Committee to be relevant to any question arising in the proceedings shall be taken into account in determining that question.

(3) In any proceedings before a court or employment tribunal or the Central Arbitration Committee any Code of Practice issued under this Chapter by the Secretary of State shall be admissible in evidence, and any provision of the Code which appears to the court, tribunal or Committee to be relevant to any question arising in the proceedings shall be taken into account in determining that question.

Comment

(1) Acas is not the only body empowered to issue Codes of Practice. The previous equality commissions had, and the Equality and Human Rights Commission has, power to issue Codes of Practice in their fields and the Health and Safety Commission can issue Codes on health and safety issues.

(2) Under TULRCA s 203 the Secretary of State was given power to issue Codes containing 'such practical guidance as he thinks fit for the purpose (a) of promoting the improvement of industrial relations, or (b) of promoting what appear to him to be desirable practices in relation to the conduct by trade unions of ballots and elections or for purposes connected with trade union learning representatives'.

(3) Using this power, the Secretary of State has issued Codes of Practice on picketing, the closed shop and industrial action ballots. These were seen as such controversial areas that Acas was unwilling to risk its reputation for impartiality by drawing up a Code which would certainly be seen as partisan.

(4) There is further discussion of Acas in Towers and Brown (2000) and in Dickens and Neal (2006, ch 3).

Central Arbitration Committee (CAC)

Trade Union and Labour Relations (Consolidation) Act 1992

259 (1) There shall continue to be a body called the Central Arbitration Committee.

(2) The functions of the Committee shall be performed on behalf of the Crown, but not so as to make it subject to directions of any kind from any Minister of the Crown as to the manner in which it is to exercise its functions.

(3) ACAS shall provide for the Committee the requisite staff (from among the officers and servants of ACAS) and the requisite accommodation, equipment and other facilities.

Comment

(1) The CAC was established by the Employment Protection Act 1975. At that time it was constituted as a fairly small organisation within Acas, but it was a decision-making body with some weighty issues within its jurisdiction. First, the Employment Protection Act 1975 established a statutory recognition procedure under which trade unions could complain to the CAC about employers' refusal to recognise them. Secondly, under Sch 11 to the Employment Protection Act 1975, an application could be made to the CAC to order an employer to give terms and conditions to the workforce comparable to those pertaining generally in the trade or in the trade in that locality. This was to prevent unscrupulous employers undercutting collectively bargained levels of terms and conditions and was an extension of the Fair Wages Resolution procedure (requiring government contractors to pay fair wages).

(2) The recognition procedure was fairly disastrous in operation and was repealed by the Employment Act 1980 as one of the first acts of the incoming Conservative government. The Sch 11 wage-fixing machinery was anathema to a government committed to free market ideals: it was also repealed by the Employment Act 1980 and the Fair Wages Resolution followed it into oblivion in 1982.

(3) This left the CAC with just two limited functions: (a) to arbitrate on disputes referred under TULRCA s 212 (above p 7); and (b) to deal with complaints by recognised trade unions alleging failure by an employer to disclose information in accordance with TULRCA ss 181–185 (discussed in Chapter 5). Neither jurisdiction generated much activity: the voluntary arbitration procedure is virtually a dead letter and in 1998 there were only six requests for disclosure of information.

(4) All this changed when the Employment Relations Act 1999 introduced a new statutory recognition procedure and the CAC was once more put in charge of adjudicating disputes in relation to it. This is also discussed in Chapter 5. The new statutory recognition procedure has bedded in without the problems which dogged the 1975 procedure and, since June 2000, when it came into force, over 500 applications have been dealt with by the CAC with very little controversy. The Employment Relations Act 2004 extended the CAC's powers in various ways, in particular by giving it jurisdiction over complaints of unfair practices in relation to recognition ballots.

(5) The CAC's caseload on disclosure of information under TURLCA ss 181–185 remains tiny, with just ten applications in 2005/06, which is slightly higher than in each of the previous three years. Other statutory duties on employers to provide information to workers have been introduced in the last decade to comply with EU directives: the Transnational Information and Consultation of Employees Regulations 1999 (TICE);

10

the European Public Limited-Liability Company Regulations 2004 and the Information and Consultation of Employees Regulations 2004 (ICE). The CAC was also given jurisdiction over disputes relating to this legislation, which so far has also failed to give rise to many cases (four complaints in six years under TICE; none under the European Company Regulations and six under ICE in its first year of operation). Disclosure of information is dealt with in Chapter 5.

(6) It is evident from the CAC's Annual Reports of recent years (which are available on its website, www.cac.gov.uk) that it counts the lack of controversy about, and the few legal challenges to, its decisions as key indicators of its success. For further discussion of the role of the CAC, see Dickens and Neal (2006, ch 7) and Rideout (2002).

Certification Officer

Ever since they were recognised as lawful organisations in the nineteenth century, trade unions have been subject to a system of voluntary registration which was originally of importance merely in so far as it gave them certain tax advantages. The duty of checking that they were qualified to be on the register and of maintaining the register was placed first on the Registrar of Friendly Societies. The Industrial Relations Act 1971 created a new official, the Registrar of Trade Unions, to whom this duty was transferred. The unpopularity of the Industrial Relations Act with trade unions found a focus in a successful campaign to refuse to register under the Act. Thus, when it was repealed in 1974 it was felt necessary to create a new system and a new official – the Certification Officer.

From the mid-1980s to the 1990s, the Conservative government pursued a policy of intervening more and more in trade union affairs and, from having merely administrative duties, the Certification Officer gained investigatory powers and increasing judicial or quasi-judicial functions. His current duties and powers are outlined in the Certification Officer's Annual Report.

Annual Report of the Certification Officer 2005–2006

The functions of the Certification Officer are contained in the Trade Union and Labour Relations (Consolidation) Act 1992 (as amended) (referred to in this report as 'the 1992 Act' or 'the Act'). They include responsibility:

under Part I, Chapter I – for maintaining a list of trade unions and for determining the independence of trade unions;

under Part I, Chapter III – for dealing with complaints by members that a trade union has failed to maintain an accurate register of members or failed to permit access to its accounting records; for seeing that trade unions keep proper accounting records, have their accounts properly audited and submit annual returns; for the investigation of the financial affairs of trade unions; for ensuring that the statutory requirements concerning the actuarial examination of members' superannuation schemes are observed; and for dealing with complaints that a trade union has failed in its duty to secure that positions in the union are not held by certain offenders;

under Part I, Chapter IV – for dealing with complaints by members that a trade union has failed to comply with one or more of the provisions of the Act which require a trade union to secure that its president, general secretary and members of its executive are elected to those positions in accordance with the Act;

under Part I, Chapter VI – for ensuring observance by trade unions of the statutory procedures governing the setting up, operation and review of political funds; and for dealing with complaints about breaches of political fund rules or about the conduct of political fund ballots or the application of general funds for political objects;

under Part I, Chapter VII – for seeing that the statutory procedures for amalgamations, transfers of engagements and changes of name are complied with, and for dealing with complaints by members about the conduct of merger ballots;

under Part I, Chapter VIIA – for dealing with complaints by members that there has been a breach, or threatened breach of the rules of a trade union relating to the appointment, election or removal of an office holder; disciplinary proceedings; ballots of members other than in respect of industrial action; or relating to the constitution or proceedings of an executive committee or decision making meeting;

under Part II – for maintaining a list of employers' associations; for ensuring compliance with the statutory requirements concerning accounting records, annual returns, financial affairs and political funds; and for ensuring that the statutory procedures applying to amalgamations and transfers of engagements in respect of employers' associations are followed.

Comment

(1) The listing of independent trade unions is dealt with in Chapter 10 and the other topics in Chapter 11. For a discussion of the Certification Officer's role by the present Certification Officer, see Dickens and Neal (2006, ch 8).

(2) The Certification Officer's Annual Reports and decisions can be obtained from his website, www.certoffice.org.uk, together with useful guidance documents.

Commission for Equality and Human Rights

The Sex Discrimination Act 1975 and the Race Relations Act 1976 set up the Equal Opportunities Commission (EOC) and the Commission for Racial Equality (CRE) as administrative enforcement institutions with duties to eliminate discrimination and to promote equality of opportunity between men and women and between people of different racial groups. The idea was to create bodies which could monitor the efficacy of the law, make suggestions for its improvement and assist strategically in its enforcement, by such means as issuing codes of practice, assisting individuals in important cases and investigating industries or employers suspected of discriminatory practice.

When the Disability Discrimination Act 1995 was passed, commentators universally criticised the failure of the Conservative government to establish a similar enforcement body for disability, as the Act only set up a weak advisory body, the National Disability Council. This deficiency was remedied by the Disability Rights Commission Act 1999, instituting the Disability Rights Commission with powers which did not merely mirror those of the EOC and CRE, but went beyond them, drawing on their experience and also developments in enforcement mechanisms in Northern Ireland under the Fair Employment (Northern Ireland) Act 1989 (see now the Fair Employment and Treatment (Northern Ireland) Order 1998).

Some commentators have argued for some time that there should be a unified body dealing with all equality issues to avoid a fragmented and inconsistent approach to the problem of inequality (eg Hepple, Coussey and Choudhury, 2000). Once the Framework Employment Directive (2000/78/EC) mandated member states to outlaw discrimination on grounds of sexual orientation, religion or belief and age as well as the existing grounds, and in the light of the Human Rights Act 1998, which also came into force in 2000, the arguments for a single, integrated Commission became unstoppable. The Commission for Equality and Human Rights (CEHR) was set up by the Equality Act 2006 and took over the functions of the other Commissions from October 2007. One of its first decisions was to determine to call itself the Equality and Human Rights Commission, rather than by the title given in the Equality Act.

Equality Act 2006

3   The Commission shall exercise its functions under this Part with a view to encouraging and supporting the development of a society in which
(a)   people's ability to achieve their potential is not limited by prejudice or discrimination,
(b)   there is respect for and protection of each individual's human rights,
(c)   there is respect for the dignity and worth of each individual,
(d)   each individual has an equal opportunity to participate in society, and
(e)   there is mutual respect between groups based on understanding and valuing of diversity and on shared respect for equality and human rights.

8   (1)   The Commission shall, by exercising the powers conferred by this Part –
(a)   promote understanding of the importance of equality and diversity,
(b)   encourage good practice in relation to equality and diversity,
(c)   promote equality of opportunity,
(d)   promote awareness and understanding of rights under the equality enactments,
(e)   enforce the equality enactments,
(f)   work towards the elimination of unlawful discrimination, and
(g)   work towards the elimination of unlawful harassment.
(2)   In subsection (1) –
'diversity' means the fact that individuals are different,
'equality' means equality between individuals . . .

Comment

(1) By comparison with the constitution of the earlier Commissions, the statement of the Equality and Human Rights Commission's duties is striking in two ways. First, in the high aspirations expressed in the general duty in EqA s 3 and secondly, in the definition of equality. While the duty to promote equality is stated in terms of equality of opportunity, 'equality' is defined in EqA s 8 as 'equality between individuals', which could be read as at least including a focus on equality of outcome (see further Chapter 2).

(2) As well as taking over the functions of the other Commissions in relation to sex, race and disability, the Equality and Human Rights Commission has responsibility for the other grounds protected by the equality enactments (sexual orientation, religion or belief and age) and a range of parallel duties in relation to human rights (see EqA s 9).

(3) One of the big advantages of a single integrated Commission is that it should be in a far better position to deal with the problems of multiple discrimination. It is increasingly

recognised that membership of more than one protected group can produce its own special problems, which could not be dealt with effectively by single issue commissions. EqA s 10 specifically obligates the Commission to consider group issues, where groups can be defined by reference to any of the protected grounds.

(4) In order to carry out its duties, the Commission has a range of general powers: to provide information, advice, education and training; to undertake research, to make grants, to conduct inquiries and to issue Codes of Practice, which have to be taken into account by courts and tribunals in any proceedings where they are relevant (EqA ss 13–19). Inquiries under EqA s 16, which may relate to any of the Commission's duties under EqA ss 8–10 and which normally result in a report and recommendations, should be distinguished from investigations under EqA s 20. The power to carry out investigations is limited to situations where the Commission has a reasonable suspicion that a person has committed an act which is unlawful under the equality enactments and is part of the Commission's enforcement powers.

(5) This statutory distinction between inquiries and investigations codifies the position reached at common law by the House of Lords in *Re Prestige Group plc* (1984), where it was held that there could be no investigation of a named person without a reasonable belief that unlawful acts were being committed. That decision greatly inhibited the EOC's and CRE's use of the investigation power, because it was often impossible to form a reasonable belief without conducting an investigation first! The CRE came to believe that the threat of an investigation was more powerful as a means of getting an employer to address discrimination issues than actually instituting one, and this is reflected in the way the Equality and Human Rights Commission's enforcement powers have been enacted.

(6) If an investigation concludes that the person has committed an unlawful act, he may be given an 'unlawful act notice' (EqA s 21). This specifies what the unlawful act is and may require the person to prepare an action plan to avoid repetition or to take some other recommended action. If an action plan has been required, the employer must prepare a draft for approval within a specified timescale and, once approved, it will come into force six weeks later. Compliance with an unlawful act notice or an action plan can ultimately be enforced through the Commission making an application to an employment tribunal. Equally, an employer who is issued with an unlawful action notice has a right of appeal to an employment tribunal within six weeks.

(7) Alternatively, under EqA s 23, the Commission can agree not to pursue an investigation against an employer in return for the employer undertaking not to commit discriminatory actions and/or to engage in recommended actions – such as producing an action plan. Such an agreement will also be enforceable through the tribunal, and has advantages for both sides. The Commission can get the desired outcome without committing resources to an investigation; the employer is not taken to have admitted any unlawful act through entering an agreement and can avoid the potential shame of being found to have breached the equality enactments.

(8) The Commission's enforcement powers also extend to unlawful advertising, instructions and pressure to discriminate, where it alone has standing to bring proceedings (EqA s 25) and to the enforcement of the public sector equality duties in relation to race, gender and disability (see further below, p 39).

(9) Finally, as with the previous Commissions, the Equality and Human Rights Commission may provide legal assistance in relations to proceedings under the equality enactments – but not other legislation, such as the parental rights provided for in the Employment Rights Act 1996 Part VIII. The EOC and CRE adopted a policy of assisting only in strategically important cases and it is likely that the new Commission will do something similar.

Employment tribunals

Employment Tribunals Act 1996

1 (1) The Secretary of State may by regulations make provision for the establishment of tribunals to be known as employment tribunals.
. . .
2 Employment tribunals shall exercise the jurisdiction conferred on them by or by virtue of this Act or any other Act, whether passed before or after this Act.

Employment Tribunals Extension of Jurisdiction (England and Wales) Order 1994

3 Proceedings may be brought before an employment tribunal in respect of a claim of an employee for the recovery of damages or any other sum (other than a claim for damages, or for a sum due, in respect of personal injuries) if –
   (a) the claim is one to which [ETA s 3(2)] applies and which a court in England and Wales would under the law for the time being in force have jurisdiction to hear and determine;
   (b) the claim is not one to which article 5 applies; and
   (c) the claim arises or is outstanding on the termination of the employee's employment.
5 This article applies to a claim for breach of a contractual term of any of the following descriptions –
   (a) a term requiring the employer to provide living accommodation for the employee;
   (b) a term imposing an obligation on the employer or the employee in connection with the provision of living accommodation;
   (c) a term relating to intellectual property;
   (d) a term imposing an obligation of confidence;
   (e) a term which is a covenant in restraint of trade.
   In this article, 'intellectual property' includes copyright, rights in performances, moral rights, design right, registered designs, patents and trade marks.
10 An employment tribunal shall not in proceedings in respect of a contract claim, or in respect of a number of contract claims relating to the same contract, order the payment of an amount exceeding £25,000.

Comment

(1) Industrial tribunals (as they were originally called) were set up with very limited jurisdiction in 1964. Today, employment tribunals (as they were renamed by the Employment Rights (Dispute Resolution) Act 1998) have jurisdiction over almost all individual employment disputes based on over 70 statutory jurisdictions and hear thousands of cases every year. The Employment Tribunals Service Annual Report for 2003/04 showed that 22,433 cases were actually heard by tribunals in that year. Subsequent Annual Reports record the figures according to jurisdiction, and since

increasingly claims involve more than one jurisdiction, the number of actual cases heard cannot be calculated, but the scale of activity continues at least at similar levels. Employment tribunals sit all over the country and all through the year.

(2) The extension in 1994 of employment tribunal jurisdiction to claims for breach of contract arising out of termination of a contract of employment was momentous and met an important need: there was clear evidence that employees had been trying to use claims under the Wages Act 1986 as a way of getting claims for pay in lieu of notice and other contract claims in front of employment tribunals. However, the cap on claims at £25,000 has not been lifted since 1994, meaning that increasing numbers of potential claims may be excluded.

(3) Employment tribunals are usually composed of three members: a legally qualified chairperson, who is a barrister or solicitor of at least seven years' standing, and two lay members, drawn from each side of industry. All have an equal vote, so it is possible, and not at all unknown, for the lay members to outvote the chair. Since TURERA amendments in 1993 it has been possible for the tribunal chair to sit alone to hear certain kinds of case, and this jurisdiction was extended by the Employment Rights (Dispute Resolution) Act 1998 (see now the Employment Tribunals Act 1996 s 4). This was criticised by many as a purely cost-cutting measure which compromised the basic philosophy of employment tribunals as tripartite institutions with strong practical expertise in employment matters. The current President of Employment Tribunals has noted an increase in matters being heard by the tribunal chair sitting alone (Meeran, 2006).

(4) Tribunal procedure is governed by the Employment Tribunals (Constitution and Rules of Procedure) Regulations 2004. There have been substantial reforms since the turn of the century. This was partly in the interests of increased efficiency and cost-effectiveness, and informed by the Legatt Review (a review of all tribunals under the chairmanship of Sir Andrew Leggatt, which reported March 2001) and the recommendations of the Employment Tribunals Taskforce, set up October 2001, and partly because of the introduction of statutory dispute resolution procedures in the Employment Act 2002 (see further Chapter 8).

Employment Tribunals (Constitution and Rules of Procedure) Regulations 2004

3 (1) The overriding objective of these Regulations and the rules in Schedules 1, 2, 3, 4, 5 and 6 is to enable tribunals and chairmen to deal with cases justly.
  (2) Dealing with a case justly includes, so far as practicable –
    (a) ensuring that the parties are on an equal footing;
    (b) dealing with the case in ways which are proportionate to the complexity or importance of the issues;
    (c) ensuring that it is dealt with expeditiously and fairly; and
    (d) saving expense.
  (3) A tribunal or chairman shall seek to give effect to the overriding objective when it or he:
    (a) exercises any power given to it or him by these Regulations or the rules in Schedules 1, 2, 3, 4, 5 and 6; or
    (b) interprets these Regulations or any rule in Schedules 1, 2, 3, 4, 5 and 6.
  (4) The parties shall assist the tribunal or the chairman to further the overriding objective.

SCHEDULE 1

10 (1) Subject to the following rules, the chairman may at any time either on the application of a party or on his own initiative make an order in relation to any matter which appears to him to be appropriate. Such orders may be any of those listed in paragraph (2) or such other orders as he thinks fit. Subject to the following rules, orders may be issued as a result of a chairman considering the papers before him in the absence of the parties, or at a hearing . . .

Comment

(1) The rules of procedure for the vast majority of employment tribunal cases are set out in Schedule 1 to the Employment Tribunals (Constitution and Rules of Procedure) Regulations 2004. Rule 10 provides the tribunal chair with general case management powers – some 20 examples of possible orders are included in rule 10(2).

(2) The first stage of tribunal proceedings is for the claimant to submit her claim, which must now be on the prescribed form ET1. In addition to details of the claimant and respondent, rule 1(4) requires the claimant to state the details of the claim and, most importantly, whether or not the claimant has raised the subject matter of the claim with the respondent at least 28 days before submitting the claim. This is part of the statutory grievance procedure, discussed further below, p 385. As tribunal claims have to be brought within fairly short, strict time limits (usually within three months of a claim arising), and time continues to run if an improperly completed form is sent back for amendment, there is a greatly increased chance of claims being lost because they are out of time. This has led the EAT to advise tribunals to interpret the rules so as to avoid injustice wherever possible.

Richardson v U Mole Ltd [2005] ICR 1664
Employment Appeal Tribunal

The claimant's form had been rejected because he had not stated his employment status as required by rule 1(4), although that fact could be determined from other statements made in the claim. He was not able to remedy the defect within the time limit and so the employment tribunal rejected his claim.

BURTON J: '. . . In a number of cases which antedated the new Rules it was left uncertain as to whether requirements, either for originating applications or responses, were mandatory or directory or advisory and what the consequence would be of failing to comply with those requirements. The approach that was taken over many years by tribunals and by this appeal tribunal was that if parties failed to comply with requirements then the matter was best dealt with in most cases by accepting the application or the response as valid, and dealing with inadequacies by way of subsequent directions or applications for further information or further and better particulars. That system has now changed to introduce a clear test at the outset.

On the face of it the new Rules are extremely welcome, whereby there is a gateway to ensure that applications or responses kick off on a sensible and complete basis from the beginning, so that there is no need for subsequent clarifications. In the first instance, the secretary of employment tribunals and, in the second instance, the chairman are the guardians of those gateways . . . If, however, the result of the imposition of the gateway is not simply to point out

17

gaps which ought to be corrected, but to drive away a claimant so that, as, for example, in this case, it means that by the time the completely immaterial defect is corrected the claimant is out of time, then injustice is inevitably going to be done. I have no doubt that that is not, and if it were it should not be, the purpose of the Rules . . .'

. . . I have seen other examples, either waiting in the wings for appeal or being dealt with on our sift, where respondents have, by error, omitted, for example, in one case an address, resulting in their response being rejected and their being thus debarred from defending a claim. That is not an appropriate use of the Rules and in my judgment the better course is to construe the Rules in order to avoid such injustice . . .'

Comment

(1) The EAT held that in such a case it was open to the tribunal to review the decision to reject the claim and to reinstate it on the basis that the error was immaterial.

(2) When a claim has been properly submitted, it is copied to the respondent, who must respond within 28 days on the prescribed form ET3, and to Acas, who will assign a conciliation officer to help the parties to reach a settlement. In order to encourage parties to settle at an earlier stage, the 2004 Rules of Procedure introduced fixed conciliation periods, outside of which Acas would have no obligation to assist the parties (Sch 1, rule 22). The 'standard' conciliation period is 13 weeks from the date on which the claim is sent to the respondent, and applies to the vast majority of tribunal claims. The 'short' conciliation period is seven weeks and applies to claims for breach of contract, redundancy, deductions from wages and disputes over time off rights. There is no limit to the conciliation period in relation to claims under the equality enactments and for public interest disclosures.

(3) Failure by the respondents to reply within 28 days will lead to them being prevented from taking any further part in the proceedings and may result in a default judgment being made against them (Sch 1, rules 8, 9). Extensions to the time limit for response will only be entertained if made before the time limit has expired and giving reasons for the delay. It will then depend on whether the tribunal chair considers that it is just and equitable to extend the time limit (Sch 1, rule 4).

Employment Tribunals (Constitution and Rules of Procedure) Regulations 2004

SCHEDULE 1

14 (1) A chairman or a tribunal (depending on the relevant rule) may hold the following types of hearing –
(a) a case management discussion under rule 17;
(b) a pre-hearing review under rule 18;
(c) a Hearing under rule 26; or
(d) a review hearing under rule 33 or 36.
(2) So far as it appears appropriate to do so, the chairman or tribunal shall seek to avoid formality in his or its proceedings and shall not be bound by any enactment or rule of law relating to the admissibility of evidence in proceedings before the courts.
(3) The chairman or tribunal (as the case may be) shall make such enquiries of persons appearing before him or it and of witnesses as he or it considers appropriate and shall otherwise conduct the hearing in such manner as he or it considers most appropriate for the clarification of the issues and generally for the just handling of the proceedings . . .

Comment

(1) Case management discussions are defined in Sch 1, rule 17(1) as interim hearings, conducted by a tribunal chair, which are held in private and which can deal with matters of procedure and management of the proceedings.

(2) Pre-hearing reviews are also interim hearings, conducted in public either on the application of one of the parties or on the tribunal's initiative. They may be held to deal with preliminary matters (for example, whether an employee has sufficient continuous service to bring a claim of unfair dismissal) but, importantly, can also be used to consider whether some or all of the contentions of either party have any reasonable prospect of success. If the tribunal chair concludes that they do not, she can require the relevant party to pay a deposit of up to £500 as a condition of pursuing that claim (Sch 1, rule 20). If so, that tribunal chair will not take part in any subsequent proceedings, but the tribunal which does hear the claim will have access to her reasons *after* reaching its decision, and if they have rejected the contentions on substantially the same grounds, they will consider whether it is appropriate to make a costs or preparation time order against the party for pursuing the issue unreasonably. If so, the deposit will be used to defray the amount awarded (Sch 1, rule 47).

(3) While Sch 1, rule 14 makes it clear that the tribunal has discretion over its procedure and tribunal hearings are less formal than ordinary courts, in practice their proceedings do tend to follow normal court practice. In particular, although the rules of evidence need not be followed, tribunals do not like leading questions being asked, nor hearsay evidence being presented.

(4) Thus the case is usually opened by the party who has the burden of proof presenting her case and calling witnesses, who give evidence on oath or affirmation, for evidence in chief and cross-examination by the other side. After both sides have presented their evidence, they make closing statements and the tribunal retires to consider its decision.

Employment Tribunals (Constitution and Rules of Procedure) Regulations 2004

SCHEDULE 1

28 (1) Chairmen or tribunals may issue the following –
  (a) a 'judgment', which is a final determination of the proceedings or of a particular issue in those proceedings; it may include an award of compensation, a declaration or recommendation and it may also include orders for costs, preparation time or wasted costs;
  (b) an 'order', which may be issued in relation to interim matters and it will require a person to do or not to do something.
  (2) If the parties agree in writing upon the terms of any order or judgment a chairman or tribunal may, if he or it thinks fit, make such order or judgment.
  (3) At the end of a hearing the chairman (or, as the case may be, the tribunal) shall either issue any order or judgment orally or shall reserve the judgment or order to be given in writing at a later date.
  (4) Where a tribunal is composed of three persons any order or judgment may be made or issued by a majority; and if a tribunal is composed of two persons only, the chairman has a second or casting vote.

. . .

30 (1) A tribunal or chairman must give reasons (either oral or written) for any –
    (a) judgment; or
    (b) order, if a request for reasons is made before or at the hearing at which the order is made.

(2) Reasons may be given orally at the time of issuing the judgment or order or they may be reserved to be given in writing at a later date. If reasons are reserved, they shall be signed by the chairman and sent to the parties by the Secretary.

(3) Where oral reasons have been provided, written reasons shall only be provided –
    (a) in relation to judgments if requested by one of the parties within the time limit set out in paragraph (5); or
    (b) in relation to any judgment or order if requested by the Employment Appeal Tribunal at any time.

(4) When written reasons are provided, the Secretary shall send a copy of the reasons to all parties to the proceedings and record the date on which the reasons were sent. Written reasons shall be signed by the chairman.

(5) A request for written reasons for a judgment must be made by a party either orally at the hearing (if the judgment is issued at a hearing), or in writing within 14 days of the date on which the judgment was sent to the parties. This time limit may be extended by a chairman where he considers it just and equitable to do so.

(6) Written reasons for a judgment shall include the following information –
    (a) the issues which the tribunal or chairman has identified as being relevant to the claim;
    (b) if some identified issues were not determined, what those issues were and why they were not determined;
    (c) findings of fact relevant to the issues which have been determined;
    (d) a concise statement of the applicable law;
    (e) how the relevant findings of fact and applicable law have been applied in order to determine the issues; and
    (f) where the judgment includes an award of compensation or a determination that one party make a payment to the other, a table showing how the amount or sum has been calculated or a description of the manner in which it has been calculated.

Comment

(1) Costs are not normally awarded against the losing party in employment tribunal proceedings. There has always been a power to award costs where one party acted frivolously, vexatiously or unreasonably, but it was rarely exercised. Over the last 15 years, however, the power to award costs has been extended in the following ways.

(2) First, the grounds on which costs can be awarded have been extended over the years. Costs can be awarded in any situation where bringing or conducting proceedings has involved someone acting 'vexatiously, abusively, disruptively or otherwise unreasonably, or the bringing or conducting of the proceedings by the paying party has been misconceived' (Sch 1, rule 40(3)). Costs may also be awarded where proceedings have been adjourned because of a failure to provide evidence in respect of a claim for reinstatement or re-engagement, or where a party has not complied with a tribunal order or practice direction.

(3) Secondly, costs can now be awarded in respect of the conduct of the paying party's representative as well as the party herself.

(4) Thirdly, as costs orders can only be made in favour of a party who has been legally represented, there is now provision for a preparation time order to be made in favour of a party who has not been legally represented, but only for time spent by that party, his employees and other advisers in preparation before the hearing – not for the hearing itself. The grounds on which a preparation time order can be made mirror those of the costs order.

(5) Fourthly, the tribunal can make a 'wasted costs' order against the representative of any party (whether a legal representative or not) in respect of costs incurred as a result of an 'improper, unreasonable or negligent act or omission' by the representative (Sch 1, rule 48). This does not apply to unpaid representatives.

(6) The increased powers to take action because of what representatives have or have not done reflects a concern about standards in conducting proceedings where representation is no longer the preserve of qualified lawyers or experienced trade union representatives and where commercial organisations have increasingly become involved, especially representing employers. The Compensation Act 2006 gave ministerial powers to regulate claims management companies and, from April 2007, any commercial organisation providing advice or representation in relation to employment tribunal proceedings must be registered with the Claims Management Regulator. Such registration is conditional on the organisation complying with specified standards of conduct. Barristers and solicitors are exempt from such regulation, as are trade unions, charities and other voluntary organisations providing advice or assistance, such as Citizens' Advice Bureaux.

(7) The maximum amount of a costs or preparation time order was raised to a very substantial £10,000 in 2001, although it has remained at this level since then. Tribunals are instructed to have regard to the paying party's ability to pay in making any order – particularly important in unfair dismissal cases where a claimant may well still be unemployed by the time of the hearing. In 2005/06 costs awards were made in favour of 148 claimants and 432 respondents, with the average award being £2,256.

(8) Reviews of judgments and orders can be requested in accordance with Sch 1, rules 33 and 34. Additionally, either party has a right of appeal to the Employment Appeal Tribunal.

Employment Appeal Tribunal (EAT)

Employment Tribunals Act 1996

20 (1) The Employment Appeal Tribunal ('the Appeal Tribunal') shall continue in existence.

(2) The Appeal Tribunal shall have a central office in London but may sit at any time and in any place in Great Britain.

(3) The Appeal Tribunal shall be a superior court of record and shall have an official seal which shall be judicially noticed.

22 (1) The Appeal Tribunal shall consist of –

(a) such number of judges as may be nominated from time to time by the Lord Chief Justice, after consulting the Lord Chancellor, from the judges of the High Court and the Court of Appeal,

(b) at least one judge of the Court of Session nominated from time to time by the Lord President of the Court of Session, and

(c)   such number of other members as may be appointed from time to time by Her Majesty on the joint recommendation of the Lord Chancellor and the Secretary of State ('appointed members').

(2)   The appointed members shall be persons who appear to the Lord Chancellor and the Secretary of State to have special knowledge or experience of industrial relations either –

(a)   as representatives of employers, or

(b)   as representatives of workers (within the meaning of the Trade Union and Labour Relations (Consolidation) Act 1992).

(3)   The Lord Chief Justice shall appoint one of the judges nominated under subsection (1) to be the President of the Appeal Tribunal.

(3A) The Lord Chief Justice must not make an appointment under subsection (3) unless –

(a)   he has consulted the Lord Chancellor, and

(b)   the Lord President of the Court of Session agrees.

(4)   No judge shall be nominated a member of the Appeal Tribunal except with his consent.

(5)   The Lord Chief Justice may nominate a judicial office holder (as defined in section 109(4) of the Constitutional Reform Act 2005) to exercise his functions under this section.

(6)   The Lord President of the Court of Session may nominate a judge of the Court of Session who is a member of the First or Second Division of the Inner House of that Court to exercise his functions under subsection (3A)(b).

28   (1)   The Appeal Tribunal may sit, in accordance with directions given by the President of the Appeal Tribunal, either as a single tribunal or in two or more divisions concurrently.

(2)   Subject to subsections (3) to (5), proceedings before the Appeal Tribunal shall be heard by a judge and either two or four appointed members, so that in either case there is an equal number –

(a)   of persons whose knowledge or experience of industrial relations is as representatives of employers, and

(b)   of persons whose knowledge or experience of industrial relations is as representatives of workers.

(3)   With the consent of the parties, proceedings before the Appeal Tribunal may be heard by a judge and one appointed member or by a judge and three appointed members.

(4)   Proceedings on an appeal on a question arising from any decision of, or arising in any proceedings before, an employment tribunal consisting of the person mentioned in section 4(1)(a) alone shall be heard by a judge alone unless a judge directs that the proceedings shall be heard in accordance with subsections (2) and (3).

Comment

(1) As the EAT is a superior court of record, its decisions are capable of settling the law and constitute binding precedents for employment tribunals. Different divisions of the EAT are not bound to follow each other's decisions, although as a matter of judicial comity (and to avoid confusion for tribunals) they usually do so. It should be noted, however, that even in the EAT the judge may be outvoted by the lay members.

(2) The EAT's procedure is governed by the Employment Appeal Tribunal Rules 1993, as subsequently amended. Broadly, the EAT Rules 1993 mirror the procedures for employment tribunals, in particular including the overriding objective of dealing

with cases justly expressed in the same terms (EAT Rules rule 2A). Subject to the EAT Rules, the EAT has the right to regulate its own procedure (ETA s 30(3)) and has used that power to issue Practice Directions. The current Practice Direction 2004 superseded all earlier Practice Directions.

(3) The EAT deals mainly with appeals from employment tribunals, but it also hears appeals from certain decisions of the CAC (although not in relation to recognition of trade unions) and the Certification Officer. It is important to note that appeals to the EAT may only be made on a point of law (ETA s 21). What is a point of law is restrictively interpreted, essentially as a matter of policy to keep down the number of appeals. For example, in 2005/06 the EAT received 1,728 appeals, of which only 836 – fewer than half – were registered. This is a typical pattern. Many of those rejected will have been turned down because they did not disclose a point of law. This is a particular issue in relation to unfair dismissal and is discussed further in Chapter 8.

(4) Appeals from the EAT lie to the Court of Appeal on a point of law only, and may not proceed without leave from either the EAT or the Court of Appeal (ETA s 37).

The European Community (EC) and the European Union (EU)

Ever since the United Kingdom joined the EC in 1972, European Community law has been an important source of regulation in the field of employment law, mainly through provisions in the Treaty of Rome and directives issued by the European Council.

Treaty of Rome (Treaty establishing the European Community)

ARTICLE 94

The Council shall, acting unanimously on a proposal from the Commission and after consulting the European Parliament and the Economic and Social Committee, issue directives for the approximation of such laws, regulations or administrative provisions of the Member States as directly affect the establishment or functioning of the common market.

Comment

(1) In 1986 the Single European Act made provision for qualified majority voting on many issues, including health and safety, but excluding employment rights (see Treaty of Rome Art 95). This meant that it became possible for measures such as the Pregnant Workers Directive (92/85/EC) and the Working Time Directive (93/104/EC) to be passed as health and safety directives despite the opposition of the Conservative government in the United Kingdom, which would have vetoed them.

(2) In 1989, 11 of the then 12 member states adopted the Community Charter of the Fundamental Social Rights of Workers (usually known simply as 'the Social Charter'). This did not have legal force, but was a statement of the intent of the EC in relation to workers' rights. The one country which would not accept it was the United Kingdom.

(3) The Social Charter formed the basis for the Social Chapter which the other member states wanted to insert into the Treaty of Rome. This was blocked by the United Kingdom, with the result that the other states adopted it as a Protocol to the Maastricht

Treaty on European Union in 1992. Following the replacement of the Conservative government by a Labour government in 1997, the United Kingdom dropped its opt-out from the Social Chapter, which meant that it could be incorporated in the Treaty of Rome: the relevant provisions are Arts 136–145.

Treaty of Rome (Treaty establishing the European Community)

ARTICLE 136

The Community and the Member States, having in mind fundamental social rights such as those set out in the European Social Charter signed at Turin on 18 October 1961 and in the 1989 Community Charter of the Fundamental Social Rights of Workers, shall have as their objectives the promotion of employment, improved living and working conditions, so as to make possible their harmonisation while the improvement is being maintained, proper social protection, dialogue between management and labour, the development of human resources with a view to lasting high employment and the combating of exclusion.

To this end the Community and the Member States shall implement measures which take account of the diverse forms of national practices, in particular in the field of contractual relations, and the need to maintain the competitiveness of the Community economy.

They believe that such a development will ensue not only from the functioning of the common market, which will favour the harmonisation of social systems, but also from the procedures provided for in this Treaty and from the approximation of provisions laid down by law, regulation or administrative action.

ARTICLE 137

1   With a view to achieving the objectives of Article 136, the Community shall support and complement the activities of the Member States in the following fields:
   (a)   improvement in particular of the working environment to protect workers' health and safety;
   (b)   working conditions;
   (c)   social security and social protection of workers;
   (d)   protection of workers where their employment contract is terminated;
   (e)   the information and consultation of workers;
   (f)   representation and collective defence of the interests of workers and employers, including codetermination, subject to paragraph 5;
   (g)   conditions of employment for third-country nationals legally residing in Community territory;
   (h)   the integration of persons excluded from the labour market, without prejudice to Article 150;
   (i)   equality between men and women with regard to labour market opportunities and treatment at work;
   (j)   the combating of social exclusion;
   (k)   the modernisation of social protection systems without prejudice to point (c).
2   To this end, the Council:
   (a)   may adopt measures designed to encourage cooperation between Member States through initiatives aimed at improving knowledge, developing exchanges of information and best practices, promoting innovative approaches and evaluating experiences, excluding any harmonisation of the laws and regulations of the Member States;

(b) may adopt, in the fields referred to in paragraph 1(a) to (i), by means of directives, minimum requirements for gradual implementation, having regard to the conditions and technical rules obtaining in each of the Member States. Such directives shall avoid imposing administrative, financial and legal constraints in a way which would hold back the creation and development of small and medium-sized undertakings.

The Council shall act in accordance with the procedure referred to in Article 251 after consulting the Economic and Social Committee and the Committee of the Regions, except in the fields referred to in paragraph 1(c), (d), (f) and (g) of this Article, where the Council shall act unanimously on a proposal from the Commission, after consulting the European Parliament and the said Committees. The Council, acting unanimously on a proposal from the Commission, after consulting the European Parliament, may decide to render the procedure referred to in Article 251 applicable to paragraph 1(d), (f) and (g) of this Article . . .

Comment

(1) It will be seen that Art 137 extended the areas relating to employment law for which legislation could be passed by qualified majority voting (which is dealt with in Art 251). This is particularly important since enlargement of the EU in 2004 and 2007 to include twelve new member states, making 27 in all.

(2) Another innovation in the Social Chapter is the increased importance accorded to agreements resulting from dialogue between management and labour.

Treaty of Rome (Treaty establishing the European Community)

ARTICLE 138

1 The Commission shall have the task of promoting the consultation of management and labour at Community level and shall take any relevant measure to facilitate their dialogue by ensuring balanced support for the parties.
2 To this end, before submitting proposals in the social policy field, the Commission shall consult management and labour on the possible direction of Community action.
3 If, after such consultation, the Commission considers Community action advisable, it shall consult management and labour on the content of the envisaged proposal. Management and labour shall forward to the Commission an opinion or, where appropriate, a recommendation.
4 On the occasion of such consultation, management and labour may inform the Commission of their wish to initiate the process provided for in Article 139. The duration of the procedure shall not exceed nine months, unless the management and labour concerned and the Commission decide jointly to extend it.

ARTICLE 139

1 Should management and labour so desire, the dialogue between them at Community level may lead to contractual relations, including agreements.
2 Agreements concluded at Community level shall be implemented either in accordance with the procedures and practices specific to management and labour and the Member States or, in matters covered by Article 137, at the joint request of the signatory parties, by a Council decision on a proposal from the Commission.

   The Council shall act by qualified majority, except where the agreement in question contains one or more provisions relating to one of the areas for which unanimity is required pursuant to Article 137(2). In that case, it shall act unanimously.

Comment

(1) The extension of law-making powers to bodies representing both sides of industry was ground-breaking. The bodies which represent employers in the 'social dialogue' process are CEEP (the European Centre of Enterprises with Public Participation and of Enterprises of General Economic Interest) and UNICE (the Union of Industrial and Employers Confederations of Europe). The body representing workers is ETUC (the European Trade Union Federation).

(2) Directives aimed at protecting part-time workers and workers on fixed-term contracts have been adopted under this procedure (Part-time Work Directive (97/81/EC); Fixed-term Work Directive (99/70/EC)). However, the social partners were unable to reach agreement on provision of information to and consultation of workers, which ultimately required the Council to act (see Chapter 5 below), nor on the protection of agency workers.

(3) Member states have an obligation to change domestic law where this is necessary to implement EU law. Where this has not been done, the EC Commission can take proceedings against the member state in front of the European Court of Justice (ECJ). In addition, any individual who has been disadvantaged by the failure to implement the EU instrument may have a claim for damages against the national government (*Francovich* v *Italian Republic* (1992)).

(4) Where EU instruments have not been implemented by national legislation, it may be possible for a claimant to rely directly on the Treaty provision or directive in a national court. In *Van Gend en Loos* (1963) the ECJ held that a Treaty provision would have direct effect provided that it was clear and unconditional and did not require any legislative intervention in order to be implemented, and in *Van Duyn* v *Home Office* (1975) this doctrine was extended to directives. The doctrine is mainly limited to 'vertical' direct effect – meaning that it can be relied upon against the state and those institutions which can be regarded as 'emanations of the state', but not against private organisations. However, in *Defrenne* v *Sabena* (1976) the ECJ held that Art 141 of the Treaty of Rome (guaranteeing equal pay for men and women for equal work) had direct 'horizontal' effect as well as direct vertical effect – meaning that it could be relied on against a private organisation as well as an emanation of the state.

(5) EU law prevails over inconsistent British law, whether subsequent or prior to the EU rule (*Factortame* v *Secretary of State for Transport* (1989)). English courts and tribunals have an obligation to interpret English law in accordance with EU law as far as possible, whether or not the English law was made before or after the EU provision (*Marleasing SA* v *La Comercial Internacional de Alimentación* (1990)).

(6) It is possible for an interested party to check the compatibility of English legislation with EU law in national courts by way of judicial review proceedings: this was permitted by the House of Lords in *R* v *Secretary of State ex p EOC* (1994), where a declaration was granted to the effect that a statutory provision disadvantaging part-time workers was contrary to Art 141 of the Treaty of Rome. Where there is doubt as to the interpretation or applicability of EU law in proceedings before national courts, questions can be referred to the ECJ for an authoritative ruling. This can be done at any level, from an employment tribunal to the House of Lords. Once the ECJ has given guidance, the case is returned to the national court or tribunal which referred it for decision.

(7) The website for the European Union provides access to case law, official documents, legislation and a wealth of useful information sources: http:\\europa.eu.

International Labour Organization

Declaration of Philadelphia 1944

The General Conference of the International Labour Organization meeting in its 26th Session in Philadelphia, hereby adopts this 10 May 1944 the present Declaration of the aims and purposes of the International Labour Organization and of the principles which should inspire the policy of its Members.

I

- labour is not a commodity;
- freedom of expression and of association are essential to sustained progress;
- poverty anywhere constitutes a danger to prosperity everywhere;
- the war against want requires to be carried on with unrelenting vigour within each nation, and by continuous and concerted international effort in which the representatives of workers and employers, enjoying equal status with those of governments, join with them in free discussion and democratic decision with a view to the promotion of the common welfare.

Comment

(1) The International Labour Organization (ILO) was established as an organ of the League of Nations in 1919 at the Treaty of Versailles. It is charged with the duty of promoting fair working conditions in all countries. With the demise of the League of Nations after the Second World War and its replacement by the United Nations, the ILO was reconstituted as a tripartite agency of the UN with separate legal status. The constitution is still based on the original Treaty provisions and the above 'Declaration Concerning the Aims and Purposes of the International Labour Organization', better known as the Declaration of Philadelphia, appears as an Annex to the Constitution.

(2) The ILO works through international Treaties, Conventions or Recommendations agreed by two-thirds of the representatives of member states (there are 180 member states) at its Conferences. It is up to the Conference to decide whether a particular proposal should take the form of a Convention or a Recommendation. In general, those matters which are fairly non-controversial go into Conventions, but more radical proposals are put in a Recommendation. It is thus common to find a Convention and a Recommendation on the same subject emanating from the same conference.

(3) Representatives of member states undertake to bring any Conventions or Recommendations to the attention of their governments for consideration within a year of their being agreed. However, member states are not obliged to accept the requirements of these instruments unless they ratify them. On receiving a stipulated number of ratifications, the Convention or Recommendation comes into force and member states who have ratified it then come under an obligation to ensure that municipal (state) law conforms to it.

(4) In the case of non-ratification, there is nothing the ILO can do, except to call for reports from time to time on the subject covered by the instrument. It is not necessarily developing countries which refuse to ratify: the USA is notorious for having only

ever ratified seven Conventions and actually withdrew from membership of the ILO from 1977–80.

(5) If a state fails to comply with its obligations, the sanctions are essentially diplomatic: there is no court and there are no individual rights of redress. Governments must submit regular reports on their compliance with Conventions they have ratified and these are considered by the ILO's Committee of Experts, which reports annually, and can 'name and shame' states which are in breach of their obligations. Since states are only bound by Conventions which they have agreed to, it ought to be the case that they will comply – but this is not always borne out in practice.

(6) If a state no longer wishes to be bound by a Convention which it has ratified, it must give notice of withdrawal. The process is called denunciation. The state may not act in a manner contrary to the Convention until the notice period has expired. The United Kingdom gave notice in the mid-1980s to denounce the Minimum Wage-Fixing Machinery Convention No 26 so that it could pass the Wages Act 1986 restricting the powers and ambit of wages councils.

(7) In 1998 the ILO adopted a Declaration on Fundamental Principles and Rights at Work, reaffirming its commitment to core labour standards in four areas: freedom of association and collective bargaining; elimination of forced labour; abolition of child labour; and elimination of employment discrimination. This was a response to concerns raised by increasing globalisation and deregulation of trade.

(8) Further information about the ILO can be found on its website, www.ilo.org. See also Ewing (1994).

The Low Pay Commission

The Low Pay Commission was set up in 1997 to assist the new Labour government in realising its manifesto commitment to introducing the National Minimum Wage. It was put on a statutory footing by the National Minimum Wage Act 1998 and consists of a chair and eight commissioners. The following statement of its activities was taken from its website (www.lowpay.gov.uk) in 2007.

What We Do

The Low Pay Commission (LPC) is an independent statutory non departmental public body set up under the National Minimum Wage Act 1998 to advise the Government about the National Minimum Wage. Our permanent status was confirmed by Government in 2001 and we were given a remit for a programme of longer-term research. To enable us to advise and make our recommendations to Government, we undertake the following activities:

- Extensive research and consultation;
- Commission research projects;
- Analyse relevant data and actively encourage the Office of National Statistics to establish better estimates of the incidence of low pay;
- Carry out surveys of firms in low-paying sectors;
- Consultation with employers, workers and their representatives;
- Take written and oral evidence from a wide range of organisations; and
- Fact-finding visits throughout the UK to meet employers, employees and representative organisations.

Comment

(1) The National Minimum Wage was introduced in April 1999. Since then the Low Pay Commission has reported annually making recommendations to government for its increase and or extension to new groups of workers.

(2) The government is not bound to accept the recommendations of the Low Pay Commission, but so far has tended to do so. See Brown (2006).

REFERENCES AND FURTHER READING

W Brown (2006), 'The Low Pay Commission' in L Dickens and A C Neal (eds), *The Changing Institutional Face of British Employment Relations*, Kluwer Law International

Sir Michael Burton (2005), 'The Employment Appeal Tribunal October 2002–July 2005' 34 ILJ 273

T Choudhury (2006), 'The Commission for Equality and Human Rights: Designing the Big Tent' 13 *Maastricht Journal* 351

C O'Cinneide (2007), 'The Commission for Equality and Human Rights: a New Institution for New and Uncertain Times' 36 ILJ 141

L Dickens and A C Neal (eds) (2006), *The Changing Institutional Face of British Employment Relations*, Kluwer Law International

K Ewing (1994), *Britain and the ILO*, 2nd ed, Institute of Employment Rights

B Hepple, M Coussey and T Choudhury (2000), *Equality: A New Framework*, Hart Publishing

J K MacMillan (1999), 'Employment tribunals: philosophies and practicalities' 28 ILJ 33

G Meeran (2006), 'The Employment Tribunals' in L Dickens and A C Neal (eds), *The Changing Institutional Face of British Employment Relations*, Kluwer Law International

Nolan (1995) *First Report of the Committee on Standards in Public Life*, Cmnd 2850

R W Rideout (2002), 'What shall we do with the CAC?' 31 ILJ 1

B Towers and W Brown (eds) (2000), *Employee Relations in Britain: 25 Years of ACAS*, Blackwell

Acas, the Certification Officer, the CAC and the Equality and Human Rights Commission all issue Annual Reports, which are an invaluable source of information about their work and their perceptions of it.

Labour Market Trends (formerly *Employment Gazette*), published by the Office for National Statistics, supplies statistics and useful analyses of the British labour market

Resolving Employment Rights Disputes, Cm 2707 (1994)

Routes to Resolution, DTI Consultation Paper (2001)

2

EQUALITY LAW

Laws promoting equal treatment of individuals regardless of characteristics such as sex, race, disability, etc can be justified on a number of grounds. First, that these characteristics are irrelevant to a person's ability to perform a particular role; secondly, that it is unfair to treat someone less favourably by reason of an unalterable characteristic; and, thirdly, that equal respect for all citizens requires that no one should be treated less favourably because they are in some sense different from some other (favoured) person. These justifications have implications way beyond the labour market and the right not to be discriminated against on irrelevant grounds has been recognised in all major human rights treaties as a basic human right.

Universal Declaration of Human Rights 1948

ARTICLE 2

Everyone is entitled to all the rights and freedoms set forth in this Declaration, without distinction of any kind, such as race, colour, sex, language, religion, political or other opinion, national or social origin, property, birth or other status . . .

Comment

(1) See also the International Covenant on Civil and Political Rights 1996 Art 2(1) and the International Covenant on Economic, Social and Cultural Rights 1966 Art 2(2). Note that the list of grounds does not expressly include disability – but also that the final words indicate that the list is not exhaustive.

(2) The European Convention on Human Rights 1950 Art 14 is in similar terms, although it also includes 'association with a national minority'. Under the Human Rights Act 1998 (HRA), Convention rights are enforceable in the United Kingdom in two ways. Under HRA s 3 courts and tribunals have a duty to interpret legislation consistently with Convention rights if they possibly can, and under HRA s 6 public authorities (which include courts and tribunals) must ensure that their actions are compatible with Convention rights. However, this does not mean that Art 14 can thus be given effect in British courts, because all that Art 14 requires is that there should be no discrimination in relation to the enjoyment of the other Convention rights: it is not framed as a freestanding right for individuals to be free of discrimination. This would be achieved if the United Kingdom would ratify Protocol 12 to the ECHR, but so far the government has not even signed this Protocol, much less ratified it.

Charter of Fundamental Rights of the European Union

CHAPTER III – EQUALITY

Article 20   Equality before the law

Everyone is equal before the law.

Article 21   Non-discrimination

1   Any discrimination based on any ground such as sex, race, colour, ethnic or social origin, genetic features, language, religion or belief, political or any other opinion, membership of a national minority, property, birth, disability, age or sexual orientation shall be prohibited.
2   Within the scope of application of the Treaty establishing the European Community and of the Treaty on European Union, and without prejudice to the special provisions of those Treaties, any discrimination on grounds of nationality shall be prohibited.

Article 22   Cultural, religious and linguistic diversity

The Union shall respect cultural, religious and linguistic diversity.

Article 23   Equality between men and women

Equality between men and women must be ensured in all areas, including employment, work and pay.
The principle of equality shall not prevent the maintenance or adoption of measures providing for specific advantages in favour of the under-represented sex.
. . .

Article 26   Integration of persons with disabilities

The Union recognises and respects the right of persons with disabilities to benefit from measures designed to ensure their independence, social and occupational integration and participation in the life of the community.

Comment

(1) The Charter of Fundamental Rights of the European Union was adopted in 2000. It currently has no legal standing, but is important as an expression of the fundamental values of the European Union and it is likely to be treated as having persuasive authority by the ECJ. The draft EU Constitutional Treaty would have enshrined the Charter in the Constitution – but movement on the Constitution is currently stalled, following its rejection in referendums in France and the Netherlands in 2005.

(2) Note the breadth of the protected grounds in Art 21(1) – and note also that this is not an exhaustive list.

(3) While the Charter is not legally binding, at least at present, other EU law provisions do create legal obligations for member states.

Treaty of Rome (Treaty establishing the European Community)

ARTICLE 141

1   Each Member State shall ensure that the principle of equal pay for male and female workers for equal work or work of equal value is applied . . .

ARTICLE 13

1   Without prejudice to the other provisions of this Treaty and within the limits of the powers conferred by it upon the Community, the Council, acting unanimously on a proposal from the Commission and after consulting the European Parliament, may take appropriate action to combat discrimination based on sex, racial or ethnic origin, religion or belief, disability, age or sexual orientation . . .

Comment

(1) Art 141, containing the basic principle of equality for men and women, has been in the Treaty of Rome from the very beginning. It was inserted not so much because of concerns for fundamental values but because while some of the original six member states required equal terms for men and women, others did not. Those which had equal treatment laws feared that they would be disadvantaged in the Common Market because of lower labour costs in countries which allowed employers to pay women less than men.

(2) While the basic principle in Art 141(1) refers only to pay and is very briefly stated, it formed the springboard for the Equal Pay Directive (75/117/EEC), spelling out the equal terms obligation in more detail, and the Equal Treatment Directive (76/207/EEC), which made it clear that the principle of equality covered access to employment, access to employment benefits and termination of employment as well as the actual terms of employment.

(3) For many years equality between women and men was the only area where the EU had power to legislate, even though the problems of racism and xenophobia were well recognised and numerous policy initiatives were put into practice to try and address the issues. The big change came in the negotiations leading to the Treaty of Amsterdam 1997, which amended the Treaty of Rome to introduce what is now Art 13, giving power to legislate on wider grounds. This was swiftly followed by two directives in 2000. The Race Directive (2000/43/EC) required member states to outlaw discrimination on grounds of racial or ethnic origin, not only in the field of employment, but also in relation to social security, education, housing and access to goods and services, and had to be implemented by July 2003. The Framework Equal Treatment Directive (2000/78/EC) extended the principle of equality to discrimination on grounds of sexual orientation, religion or belief, disability and age – but only in the employment field. This had to be implemented by 2003 for sexual orientation and religion or belief, but member states were given until the end of 2006 to enact laws relating to disability and age.

(4) Thus the six protected grounds in EU and UK law are now as follows:

* sex;
* race;
* disability;
* sexual orientation;
* religion or belief;
* age.

(5) The development of equality law can be seen as having happened in more or less distinct historical phases. Thus, in the first phase, until the twentieth century, there was no legislative interference with the basic common law position that employers were free to contract with whoever they wanted, and thus free to discriminate on any grounds at all. The first legislative interventions were merely in the direction of removing certain

prohibitions which previously existed. The Catholic Emancipation Act 1829, finally putting Roman Catholics on an equal footing with Protestants for the first time since the Tudors, can be regarded as one of the early examples of this in relation to religion or belief and the Sex Disqualification (Removal) Act 1919 permitted women to enter professions (such as medicine and the law) from which they had previously been barred. But this did not mean that they could not still be treated less favourably on grounds of their sex.

(6) The second phase, from the 1960s to the 1990s, shows the law moving to a more interventionist position with the aim of preventing discrimination on certain limited grounds – basically, race and sex. In the case of sex discrimination, but not race discrimination, British law was bolstered and pushed forward by the legislation and case law of the European Community. The principal Acts which still govern sex and race equality law, the Equal Pay Act 1970, the Sex Discrimination Act 1975 and the Race Relations Act 1976, were passed at this time.

While the first statute relating to disability discrimination was passed in 1944, it had little effect since the quota system it imposed was never very effective. It was not until the Disability Discrimination Act 1995 that discrimination in employment on grounds of disability was addressed generally. The aim was to produce similar protection as for race and sex discrimination, but the concepts used were significantly different, and remain different today.

(7) The third phase can be seen as dating from the end of the 1990s, with critical events being the amendment of the Treaty of Rome in 1997, enabling the EU to legislate against discrimination on grounds other than sex; the Race Relations (Amendment) Act 2000, imposing a general race equality duty on public authorities, requiring them to promote equality of opportunity and good relations between persons of different racial groups, and the Equality Act 2006, creating the Commission for Equality and Human Rights, giving it positive duties to promote the values of equality and diversity and to encourage good practice, as well as introducing general gender equality and disability equality duties for public authorities.

(8) In the current, third phase, the law has moved on from simply trying to prevent unfavourable treatment on the protected grounds to a more ambitious project of striving for genuine equality of outcome for disadvantaged groups. This is why it seems more appropriate now to term this area of law 'equality law' rather than 'discrimination law'.

(9) At present, the law is still to be found in a wide variety of statutes and statutory instruments which differ from each other; differences which are sometimes niggly and unimportant and sometimes critical. The trend is towards convergence, which would bring about a welcome rationalisation and simplification of equality law. This can be seen in the gradual adoption of consistent concepts in EU directives, the most recent of which is the Recast Equal Treatment Directive 2006 (2006/54/EC), and in the moves in the United Kingdom towards a Single Equality Act, which was the subject of consultation in 2007.

SCOPE OF EQUALITY LAW

In this part we will look first at the categories of worker protected under equality law and then at what is covered under each of the protected grounds.

Categories of worker covered

Sex Discrimination Act 1975

82 (1) In this Act, unless the context otherwise requires – . . .
'employment' means employment under a contract of service or of apprenticeship or a contract personally to execute any work or labour, and related expressions shall be construed accordingly; . . .

Comment

(1) The same definition is used in RRA s 78. The newer equality legislation defines employment as 'employment under a contract of service or of apprenticeship or a contract personally to do any work': see DDA s 68; RB Regs reg 2(3); SO Regs reg 2(3); Age Regs reg 2(2). The meaning is the same.

Mirror Group Newspapers Ltd v *Gunning* [1986] ICR 145 Court of Appeal

The respondent's father held the distributorship for the appellant's newspapers, supplying over 90 shops in the Sheffield area. He wished to retire and for his daughter to take over. The appellant refused to renew the distributorship in her name and she alleged that this was on grounds of sex discrimination. The issue was whether they had denied her 'employment' as defined in SDA s 82.

OLIVER LJ: '. . . Enough has been said to demonstrate that Mr Stark [Mrs Gunning's father] was not "employed" by the appellants in any conventional sense of the word. He was simply an independent contractor with a franchise to purchase and distribute the appellants' goods. Mrs Gunning's case, however, rests upon the extended definition of "employment" in s.82(1) . . .

The first point is the pure point of law as to the correct meaning, as a matter of statutory interpretation, of the words "a contract personally to execute any work or labour". Here the primary division between the parties is as to the meaning of the word "any". Mr Alexander Irvine QC, on behalf of the appellants, contends that the court has to read the section in the light of the fact that what it is doing is providing an extension of the meaning of the word "employment" in its ordinary sense of a contract of employment or service, the essential condition of which is that the employee engages to provide his own work or skill in return for remuneration. There may be lacking other essential conditions, for instance, that of control by the other party to the contract, so that it does not qualify as a contract of service, but the essential concept is of a contract for the services of the "employee", the purpose of which is to make available to the other contracting party (the "employer") the services and skill of the contractor. An example would, for instance, be a contract for the painting of a portrait by an artist or the engagement of an actor, singer or dancer. Whilst it is true that the section uses the word "any" work or labour, Mr Irvine submits that this cannot sensibly be applied to include within the definition every contract which contains a stipulation of whatever minimal importance for the personal performance of some function. What is to be looked for is not simply a contractual obligation forming part of the larger whole to do something personally but a contract (ie a complete contract) personally to do work or labour. Only thus, he submits, can one give a sensible meaning to the word "any" . . . Thus, he submits, to qualify as a contract under the extended definition in s.82(1) the contract must be one the sole or dominant purpose of which is the execution of work or labour by the contracting party. A contract the purpose of which is to secure a result which is to be achieved by the employment of many does not become a contract personally to execute work or labour merely because the contracting party assumes an obligation to engage himself, in however small a way, in the carrying out of the contractual purpose.

As against this Mr Beloff QC, for the respondent, submits that nothing turns on the fact that the starting point is that the definition is an extension of the word "employment", which, he submits, in ordinary parlance merely means "work". He accepts that the court has to look for a positive contractual obligation of personal execution and not merely an underlying hope or expectation, even an expectation which is an inducing cause for entering into the contract at all. But if there is a contractual obligation to do anything active under the contract which can properly be described as "work or labour" the fact that this may be entirely undefined and subsidiary to the principal purpose of the contract is, he submits, irrelevant. He accepts that "any" does mean "of any kind" but it also embraces "of any extent", although he accepts, as I understand his argument, that the obligation has to be of such substantiality that it can be said to be a material term of the contract. What he suggests is, essentially, a two-stage inquiry: first, is there an obligation to do any work or labour at all personally? If so, then is that obligation sufficiently substantial to the contract as a whole to enable the tribunal properly to describe the contract as "a contract personally to execute work or labour" as opposed to a contract containing a minimal obligation for such execution? . . .

The arguments are closely balanced and indeed, on analysis, are probably not for practical purposes widely different in their results, since, as already mentioned, Mr Beloff does not contend that any obligation, however minimal, is sufficient to constitute a "contract" of the kind in question. On balance, however, for my part I am persuaded that the more natural and logical meaning is that contended for by Mr Irvine and expressed by Mr Scott in the Employment Appeal Tribunal. In my judgment, what is contemplated by the legislature in this extended definition is a contract the dominant purpose of which is the execution of personal work or labour, and I would allow the appeal on this ground, for quite clearly here the dominant purpose was simply the regular and efficient distribution of newspapers . . .'

(Balcombe LJ delivered a concurring judgment; Sir David Cairns agreed.)

Comment

(1) The distinction between employees and independent contractors is explored in detail in the next chapter. Much of employment law applies only to 'employees'. However, equality law has a much greater reach, including some independent contractors as long as personal service is the dominant purpose of the contract as here explained.

(2) In *Mingeley* v *Pennock* (2004) a taxi driver's claim for race discrimination was ruled inadmissible because his contract with the taxi firm did not require him to do any work at all: it was up to him if he chose to do so. In the absence of mutual obligations to provide and accept work, the Court of Appeal held that the arrangement could not be described as 'employment' for the purposes of RRA s 78. In passing Kay LJ noted that the search for the 'dominant purpose' of a contract could be elusive and that the test had its difficulties – but also held that it was too well established to be disregarded.

(3) The equality enactments all also provide that employment agencies may not discriminate in taking workers on to their books, nor may the clients with whom they place the workers. Similarly, partnerships may not discriminate on the protected grounds in offering, or in the terms on which they offer, partnerships, and there must be no discrimination against office-holders.

(4) There are some exceptions in relation to specific employments: these will be considered in relation to the scope of the protected grounds.

The protected grounds

In this section we will look at each of the protected grounds, except for disability, to see what exactly is covered and also where there are exceptions. As disability discrimination law is still significantly different from the law applying to the other grounds, it will be considered separately at the end of the chapter.

Race

Race Relations Act 1976

3 (1) In this Act, unless the context otherwise requires –

'racial grounds' means any of the following grounds, namely colour, race, nationality or ethnic or national origins;

'racial group' means a group of persons defined by reference to colour, race, nationality or ethnic or national origins, and references to a person's racial group refer to any racial group into which he falls.

(2) The fact that a racial group comprises two or more distinct racial groups does not prevent it from constituting a particular racial group for the purposes of this Act . . .

Comment

(1) While the RRA covers discrimination on grounds of nationality, the Race Directive (2000/43/EC) is narrower in scope. Art 2(1) states: 'the principle of equal treatment shall mean that there shall be no direct or indirect discrimination based on racial or ethnic origin.' No doubt discrimination on grounds of colour would be caught by this, but not discrimination on grounds of nationality. The omission is deliberate, since the EU still permits member states to treat non-EU nationals less favourably than EU nationals in certain respects.

(2) Unfortunately, the government decided to implement the Race Directive by making regulations under the authority of the European Communities Act 1972 rather than by introducing new primary legislation. This meant that they could not legislate for anything more than what was necessary to implement the Directive (although the Race Relations Act 1976 (Amendment) Regulations 2003 adopted the terminology, 'race or ethnic or national origins' in delimiting their scope). The result, as we will see, is that for some purposes colour and nationality are explicitly covered and for others they are not.

(3) In *BBC* v *Souster* (2001) the Court of Session held that nationality and national origin did not have to be defined exclusively in terms of citizenship, so that it was possible for an English broadcaster to claim under the RRA when he alleged that he had been overlooked in favour of a Scottish broadcaster on grounds of nationality. Compare also *Gwynedd CC* v *Jones* (1986), where it was held that the Welsh constituted a nation and an ethnic group.

(4) The most difficulty arising in relation to the definition is the concept of ethnic origin, considered in the next case.

Mandla v Dowell Lee [1983] ICR 385 House of Lords

An orthodox Sikh boy, required by the rules of his religion to wear a turban, was refused admission to an independent school, on the grounds that wearing a turban would breach the school's rules on uniform. The main issue before the House of Lords was whether Sikhs qualified as a racial group within the meaning of the RRA.

LORD FRASER: 'It is not suggested that Sikhs are a group defined by reference to colour, race, nationality or *national* origins. In none of these respects are they distinguishable from many other groups, especially those living, like most Sikhs, in the Punjab. The argument turns entirely upon whether they are a group defined by "*ethnic* origins". It is therefore necessary to ascertain the sense in which the word "ethnic" is used in the Act of 1976. We were referred to various dictionary definitions. The *Oxford English Dictionary* (1897 ed) gives two meanings of "ethnic". The first is "Pertaining to nations not Christian or Jewish; gentile, heathen, pagan". That clearly cannot be its meaning in the Act of 1976, because it is inconceivable that Parliament would have legislated against racial discrimination intending that the protection should not apply either to Christians or (above all) to Jews. Neither party contended that that was the relevant meaning for the present purpose. The second meaning given in the *Oxford English Dictionary* (1897 ed) was "Pertaining to race; peculiar to a race or nation; ethnological". A slightly shorter form of that meaning (omitting "peculiar to a race or nation") was given by the *Concise Oxford Dictionary* in 1934 and was expressly accepted by Lord Denning MR as the correct meaning for the present purpose. Oliver and Kerr LJJ also accepted that meaning as being substantially correct, and Oliver LJ said that the word "ethnic" in its popular meaning involved "essentially a racial concept – the concept of something with which the members of the group are born; some fixed or inherited characteristic". The respondent, who appeared on his own behalf, submitted that that was the relevant meaning of "ethnic" in the Act of 1976, and that it did not apply to Sikhs because they were essentially a religious group, and they shared their racial characteristics with other religious groups, including Hindus and Muslims, living in the Punjab . . .

For a group to constitute an ethnic group in the sense of the Act of 1976, it must, in my opinion, regard itself, and be regarded by others, as a distinct community by virtue of certain characteristics. Some of these characteristics are essential; others are not essential but one or more of them will commonly be found and will help to distinguish the group from the surrounding community. The conditions which appear to me to be essential are these: (1) a long shared history, of which the group is conscious as distinguishing it from other groups, and the memory of which it keeps alive; (2) a cultural tradition of its own, including family and social customs and manners, often but not necessarily associated with religious observance. In addition to those two essential characteristics the following characteristics are, in my opinion, relevant: (3) either a common geographical origin, or descent from a small number of common ancestors; (4) a common language, not necessarily peculiar to the group; (5) a common literature peculiar to the group; (6) a common religion different from that of neighbouring groups or from the general community surrounding it; (7) being a minority or being an oppressed or a dominant group within a larger community, for example a conquered people (say, the inhabitants of England shortly after the Norman conquest) and their conquerors might both be ethnic groups.

A group defined by reference to enough of these characteristics would be capable of including converts, for example, persons who marry into the group, and of excluding apostates. Provided a person who joins the group feels himself or herself to be a member of it, and is accepted by other members, then he is, for the purposes of the Act, a member. That appears to be consistent with the words at the end of section 3 (1): "references to a person's racial group refer to any racial group into which he falls". In my opinion, it is possible for a person to fall into a particular racial group either by birth or by adherence, and it makes no difference, so far as the Act of 1976 is concerned, by which route he finds his way into the group . . .

My Lords, I have attempted so far to explain the reasons why, in my opinion, the word "ethnic" in the Act of 1976 should be construed relatively widely, in what was referred to by

Mr Irvine as a broad, cultural/historic sense. The conclusion at which I have arrived by construction of the Act itself is greatly strengthened by consideration of the decision of the Court of Appeal in New Zealand (Richmond P, Woodhouse and Richardson JJ) in *King-Ansell* v *Police* (1979) . . . Richardson J said:

> "The real test is whether the individuals or the group regard themselves and are regarded by others in the community as having a particular historical identity in terms of their colour or their racial, national or ethnic origins. That must be based on a belief shared by members of the group."

And the same learned judge said:

> "a group is identifiable in terms of its ethnic origins if it is a segment of the population distinguished from others by a sufficient combination of shared customs, beliefs, traditions and characteristics derived from a common or presumed common past, even if not drawn from what in biological terms is a common racial stock. It is that combination which gives them an historically determined social identity in their own eyes and in the eyes of those outside the group. They have a distinct social identity based not simply on group cohesion and solidarity but also on their belief as to their historical antecedents."

My Lords, that last passage sums up in a way upon which I could not hope to improve the views which I have been endeavouring to express. It is important that courts in English-speaking countries should, if possible, construe the words which we are considering in the same way where they occur in the same context, and I am happy to say that I find no difficulty at all in agreeing with the construction favoured by the New Zealand Court of Appeal . . .

The respondent admitted, rightly in my opinion, that, if the proper construction of the word "ethnic" in section 3 of the Act of 1976 is a wide one, on lines such as I have suggested, the Sikhs would qualify as a group defined by ethnic origins for the purposes of the Act. It is, therefore, unnecessary to consider in any detail the relevant characteristics of the Sikhs. They were originally a religious community founded about the end of the 15th century in the Punjab by Guru Nanak, who was born in 1469. But the community is no longer purely religious in character. Their present position is summarised sufficiently for present purposes in the opinion of the learned judge in the county court in the following passage:

> "The evidence in my judgment shows that Sikhs are a distinctive and self-conscious community. They have a history going back to the 15th century. They have a written language which a small proportion of Sikhs can read but which can be read by a much higher proportion of Sikhs than of Hindus. They were at one time politically supreme in the Punjab."

The result is, in my opinion, that Sikhs are a group defined by a reference to ethnic origins for the purpose of the Act of 1976, although they are not biologically distinguishable from the other peoples living in the Punjab. That is true whether one is considering the position before the partition of 1947, when the Sikhs lived mainly in that part of the Punjab which is now Pakistan, or after 1947, since when most of them have moved into India . . .'

(Lord Templeman delivered a concurring judgment. Lords Edmund-Davies, Roskill and Brandon agreed with both.)

Comment

(1) This is the leading authority on this point. In practice most of the cases on this issue have been about whether members of particular religions can bring themselves within the definition of 'ethnic group' in order to bring a claim of discrimination. This may be

less of a problem in the employment field now, since discrimination on grounds of religion or belief is now separately protected. But there are still some differences between the protected grounds and there may still be advantages in suing under the RRA rather than the RB Regs.

(2) The other point to note is that whether or not a group passes the test has been treated as a question of fact rather than of law, meaning that it is difficult successfully to appeal an employment tribunal decision, as long as they have directed themselves in accordance with *Mandla* v *Dowell Lee*.

(3) With that qualification in mind, it may be noted that Jews (*Seide* v *Gillette Industries* (1980)) and gypsies (*CRE* v *Dutton* (1989)) have also been held to constitute ethnic groups for the purposes of the RRA, but not Rastafarians (*Dawkins* v *Department of the Environment* (1993)). In *Walker* v *Hussain* (1996) the EAT assumed that Muslims did not constitute an ethnic group, but the point was not argued.

The race equality duty

In 1999 the report of the Stephen Lawrence Inquiry was published. It examined the failures in the police investigation into the racially motivated murder of Stephen Lawrence in 1993 and concluded that one of the reasons was 'institutional racism', which it explained as a collective organisational failure to tackle unwitting racism in the police force in its day-to-day operations and implementation of its policies. To address this, the Race Relations (Amendment) Act 2000 amended the RRA to introduce a new, general race equality duty for all public authorities (RRA ss 71–71E). It is summarised in the CRE's Code of Practice on the general equality duty.

CRE *Code of Practice on the Duty to Promote Race Equality* (2002)

1.1   The Race Relations Act . . . places a general duty on a wide range of public authorities to promote race equality. This duty means that authorities (listed in appendix 1 of this code) must have due regard to the need to:
   (a)   eliminate unlawful racial discrimination;
   (b)   promote equality of opportunity; and
   (c)   promote good relations between people of different racial groups.

1.2   Most public authorities are bound by this duty. Many of them provide major public services, such as education or health. Some of them (for example professional representative organisations, such as the Royal College of Surgeons, or broadcasting authorities) are bound by this duty only so far as their public functions . . . are concerned.

1.3   The duty aims to make the promotion of race equality central to the way public authorities work. Promoting race equality will improve the way public services are delivered for everyone. In most cases, these authorities should be able to use their existing arrangements – such as those for policy making – to meet the duty's requirements. This should help to avoid any unnecessary or duplicated work.

Comment

(1) Full lists of the bodies who are subject to the general race equality duty are set out in RRA Sch 1A – which is extremely extensive. The three complementary aspects of the duty range from the negative prevention of discrimination to the positive promotion of equality. The Code recommends that public authorities carry out the duty by identifying which of their functions or policies are relevant to the duty, assessing whether they

meet the duty at present and making any necessary changes if not. Naturally, an ongoing monitoring process is also necessary.

(2) Most of the public authorities also have specific duties, which are intended to support them in carrying out the general duty. The two main specific duties are (a) to publish a race equality scheme, and (b) to comply with the employment duty. A race equality scheme is defined by the CRE as 'a timetabled and realistic plan, setting out an authority's arrangements for meeting the general and specific duties'. The employment duty entails monitoring all staff, and applicants for jobs, training or promotion, by racial group. In the case of employers with 150 or more employees, the monitoring should also involve collecting information by racial group as to numbers of staff receiving training, involved in disciplinary and grievance procedures, benefiting or suffering detriment through performance assessment procedures, and leaving employment. In all cases, the purpose of this is to see whether there are differences in the experiences of different racial groups, to explore the reasons for any differences uncovered and to deal with any unfairness or disadvantage that may surface as a result.

(3) Commenting on the general race equality duty, Hepple (2006) states:

> Unfortunately, many of the public sector schemes currently being implemented in respect of race equality, on the basis of CRE guidance, place too much emphasis on procedures and too little on outcomes. The result has been to generate a large amount of paperwork but, as yet, not much objective measurement of results.

As we will see, similar duties to promote equality have been passed in relation to gender and disability. It is to be hoped that they contribute to a different institutional culture, rather than just being a paper exercise.

Genuine occupational requirements (GOR)

Race Relations Act 1976

4A (1) In relation to discrimination on grounds of race or ethnic or national origins –
    (a) section 4(1)(a) or (c) does not apply to any employment; and
    (b) section 4(2)(b) does not apply to promotion or transfer to, or training for, any employment; and
    (c) section 4(2)(c) does not apply to dismissal from any employment;

where subsection (2) applies.

(2) This subsection applies where, having regard to the nature of the employment or the context in which it is carried out –
    (a) being of a particular race or of particular ethnic or national origins is a genuine and determining occupational requirement;
    (b) it is proportionate to apply that requirement in the particular case; and
    (c) either –
        (i) the person to whom that requirement is applied does not meet it, or
        (ii) the employer is not satisfied, and in all the circumstances it is reasonable for him not to be satisfied, that that person meets it.

Comment

(1) The reference in s 4A(1) to s 4 is a reference to the section which defines unlawful discrimination. Thus it is saying that discrimination is lawful where s 4A(2) applies.

(2) There have always been limited exceptional cases where less favourable treatment on racial grounds has been permitted. This general exception was introduced in 2003 as a result of the Race Directive (2000/43/EC) and therefore does not expressly cover discrimination on grounds of colour or nationality.

(3) Note that the GOR can apply to the context of the post as well as the functions of the post, allowing a rounded consideration of all relevant circumstances. Obviously it has to be genuine and not a sham. As to 'determining', the DTI Explanatory Notes on the RB Regs and SO Regs, which contain an exactly similar exception, state that this means it must be 'crucial to the post and not merely one of several important factors'. It must also be a 'requirement', which the same Notes explain as follows:

> A requirement is stronger than something which is merely a factor, a preference, or a qualification for the job – it is something which is essential for the person to be able to perform the functions of the job.

While the Explanatory Notes have no legal standing, in this instance they seem to capture accurately the meaning of the GOR definition. Case law on the meaning of 'requirement' when that was part of the definition of indirect discrimination may be relevant by analogy here, and defined the word in this way (see *Perera* v *Civil Service Commission (No 2)* (1982)).

(4) The concept of proportionality, which is fundamental in EU law, means that the requirement must be an appropriate and necessary means of achieving a legitimate aim. Thus employers should consider whether their aim could be met by some other means, or some lesser stipulation.

(5) Unlike the genuine occupational qualification, below, the GOR can apply to dismissal as well as appointment to a job or access to promotion and training. It may seem strange that if someone is initially qualified to do a job, a GOR can later be invoked to justify their dismissal, but see the CRE Code of Practice, Annex 1, for a plausible example.

(6) A job applicant may be unwilling to disclose his or her ethnic or national origin. This is why s 4A(2)(c)(ii) nonetheless permits the application of a GOR if the employer reasonably believes that the person does not meet it.

Genuine occupational qualifications (GOQ)

Race Relations Act 1976

5 (2) Being of a particular racial group is a genuine occupational qualification for a job only where –

  (a) the job involves participation in a dramatic performance or other entertainment in a capacity for which a person of that racial group is required for reasons of authenticity; or

  (b) the job involves participation as an artist's or photographic model in the production of a work of art, visual image or sequence of visual images for which a person of that racial group is required for reasons of authenticity; or

  (c) the job involves working in a place where food or drink is (for payment or not) provided to and consumed by members of the public or a section of the public in a particular setting for which, in that job, a person of that racial group is required for reasons of authenticity; or

(d)   the holder of the job provides persons of that racial group with personal services promoting their welfare, and those services can most effectively be provided by a person
of that racial group.

(3)   Subsection (2) applies where some only of the duties of the job fall within paragraph (a), (b),
(c) or (d) as well as where all of them do . . .

Comment

(1) The GOQ exception now applies only where RRA s 4A does not apply – ie, to discrimination on grounds of colour or nationality; although, as noted already, it is hard to
imagine a situation where discrimination on grounds of colour would not come within
race or ethnic origin. There is also an exception which allows discrimination on these
grounds for employment in a private household (RRA s 4(3)) and a complete exception
for seamen recruited abroad (RRA s 9).

(2) The GOQ exception was always interpreted narrowly by the courts – which in many
ways is entirely proper. However, it could get in the way of positive action measures, as
the GOR may also. The next extract illustrates the point.

Lambeth LBC v Commission for Racial Equality **[1990] ICR 768 Court of Appeal**

The council advertised the posts of group manager and assistant head of housing benefits in
its housing department, stating that the posts were open only to Afro-Caribbean and Asian
applicants. It argued that being of one of those racial groups was a genuine occupational
qualification for the job under RRA s 5(2)(d) because over half of the council's tenants were
of Afro-Caribbean or Asian origin and it had been decided that there was a need to make the
housing benefits system more sensitive to the needs and experiences of these communities.

BALCOMBE LJ: '. . . I am wholly unpersuaded that one of the two main purposes of the Race
Relations Act is to promote positive action to benefit racial groups. The purpose of the Act, as
stated in its long title, is "to make fresh provision with respect to discrimination on racial
grounds and relations between people of different racial groups", and the substance of the
operative Parts (I to IV) of the Act is to render acts of racial discrimination unlawful. It is true that
ss 35, 37 and 38 do allow for limited acts of positive discrimination which would otherwise be
unlawful, but that does not constrain us to give to s 5(2)(d) a meaning which its words do not
naturally bear. If s 5(2)(d) had been intended to provide for positive action in the particular field
to which it relates, one would have expected to find it grouped together with ss 35, 37 and 38,
rather than as the last paragraph in a group relating to dramatic performances (eg the casting
of "Othello") or restaurants (eg a Chinese take-away) where membership of a racial group is
required for reasons of authenticity.

The only other reported decision in which s 5(2)(d) has been considered is *Tottenham Green
Under Fives' Centre* v *Marshall* (1989), another decision of the appeal tribunal. In giving the judgment of the tribunal in that case, Wood J said:

"The purpose of the Act of 1976 is to eliminate discrimination on racial grounds, and in construing section 5 it is important not to give too wide a construction, which would enable it to
provide an excuse or cloak for undesirable discrimination; on the other hand where genuine
attempts are being made to integrate ethnic groups into society, too narrow a construction
might stifle such initiatives."

In their judgment in the present case, the EAT cited that passage and said that they saw no
reason to change their view of the purpose of the Act. I agree with this view. However, I should
make it clear that by doing so I express no view of the case for or against positive action in

favour of ethnic minorities in order to counter the effects of past discrimination; I confine my attention to the present meaning of the Act of 1976.

Finally, in this connection I would mention that, subject to the specified exceptions, any discriminatory advertisement is unlawful, even though the act of discrimination advertised might itself be lawful.

"Personal services promoting their welfare"
The services provided by Lambeth's housing benefits department undoubtedly promote the welfare of the recipients of those benefits, but the rest of the phrase is qualified by the word "personal". "Personal" is defined by the Oxford English *Dictionary* as:

> "Of, pertaining to, concerning or affecting the individual or self (as opposed, variously, to other persons, the general community, etc . . .); individual; private; one's own."

The use of the word "personal" indicates that the identity of the giver and the recipient of the services is important. I agree with the EAT when they say that the Act appears to contemplate direct contact between the giver and the recipient – mainly face-to-face or where there could be susceptibility in personal, physical contact. Where language or a knowledge and under-standing of cultural and religious background are of importance, then those services may be most effectively provided by a person of a particular racial group . . .

However, I also agree with the appeal tribunal that the decision in any particular case whether the holder of a particular job provides persons of a particular group with personal ser-vices promoting their welfare is a question of mixed law and fact, and that unless the employ-ment tribunal have come to a decision which is wrong in law, neither the appeal tribunal nor this court can interfere. The employment tribunal held that the holders of the jobs advertised, being managerial positions, did not provide personal services promoting the welfare of persons of a particular racial group. I can find no error of law in that decision. On this ground alone I would dismiss this appeal . . .

For the reasons already given I would dismiss this appeal. I would add one final point which counsel for the Commission conceded in the final paragraph of his skeleton argument. The recognition that the particular posts required knowledge and sensitivity of the particular prob-lems of an ethnic minority was a legitimate and laudable stance by the local authority. However, the method adopted to achieve the end was unlawful.'

(Mann LJ delivered a concurring judgment and Mustill LJ agreed.)

Comment

(1) Note that only the Commissions have power to take action in relation to discrim-inatory advertisements.

(2) Positive action is discussed further below (p 97).

Sex

Sex Discrimination Act 1975

2 (1) Section 1, and the provisions of Parts II and III relating to sex discrimination against women, are to be read as applying equally to the treatment of men, and for that purpose shall have effect with such modifications as are requisite.

(2) In the application of subsection (1) no account shall be taken of special treatment afforded to women in connection with pregnancy or childbirth.

. . .

3   (1)   In any circumstances relevant for the purposes of any provision of Part 2, a person discriminates against a person ('A') who fulfils the condition in subsection (2) if –

(a)   on the ground of the fulfilment of the condition, he treats A less favourably . . .

(2)   The condition is that the person is –

(a)   married, or

(b)   a civil partner . . .

Comment

(1) As SDA s 2 shows, the SDA adopts a symmetrical model of equality: although the Act is written in terms of discrimination against women, discrimination against men is just as unlawful.

(2) The SDA has always made discrimination against married people unlawful. This is essentially about preventing sex discrimination against women: at one time, women were frequently expected to resign or else were dismissed if they got married. As a result of the Civil Partnership Act 2004, putting same-sex couples who have entered a civil partnership on a par with married couples, the protection was extended to civil partners in December 2005.

(3) While no protection is expressly given to single people, Art 2(1) of the Equal Treatment Directive 1976 prohibits discrimination on grounds of 'marital or family status', so such discrimination could be actionable in EU law.

(4) As a result of the next case, sex discrimination protection was extended further.

P v S and Cornwall CC [1996] IRLR 347 European Court of Justice

The claimant was employed as a manager at an educational institution run by the council, and had been taken on as a male employee. She was dismissed when she indicated that she was to undergo a sex change operation. She claimed that this was a breach of the Equal Treatment Directive 1976, but the United Kingdom argued that transsexuals were not within its scope.

ADVOCATE-GENERAL'S OPINION: '. . . While it is quite true that the Directive prohibits any discrimination whatsoever on grounds of sex, it is equally indisputable that the wording of the principle of equal treatment which it lays down refers to the traditional man/woman dichotomy.

In order to ascertain whether the Directive can, as the employment tribunal suggests, be so interpreted as to cover discrimination against transsexuals too, it must, in any event, be determined in the first place whether the unfavourable treatment of transsexuals constitutes discrimination on grounds of sex. It will then be necessary to decide whether it is only dis-crimination between men and women which is covered by the expression "discrimination on grounds of sex" or, more generally, all unfavourable treatment connected with sex.

I shall start by calling to mind the proposition, which has ever stronger support in medical and scientific circles, that it is necessary to go beyond the traditional classification and recognise that, in addition to the man/woman dichotomy, there is a range of characteristics, behaviour and roles shared by men and women, so that sex itself ought rather to be thought of as a continuum. From that point of view it is clear that it would not be right to continue to treat as unlawful solely acts of discrimination on grounds of sex which are referable to men and women in the traditional sense of those terms, while refusing to protect those who are also treated unfavourably precisely because of their sex and/or sexual identity.

The argument just put forward, attractive as it is, requires a redefinition of sex which merits deeper consideration in more appropriate circles; consequently, this is not the path that I propose that the Court should follow. I fully realise that from time immemorial a person's sex has merely been ascertained, without need of the law to define it. The law dislikes ambiguities, and it is certainly simpler to think in terms of Adam and Eve.

Having said that, I regard as obsolete the idea that the law should take into consideration, and protect, a woman who has suffered discrimination in comparison with a man, or vice versa, but denies that protection to those who are also *discriminated against*, again by reason of sex, merely because they fall outside the traditional man/woman classification.

The objection is taken too much for granted, and has been raised on several occasions in these proceedings, that the factor of sex discrimination is missing, on the grounds that "female transsexuals" are not treated differently from "male transsexuals". In short, both are treated unfavourably, hence there can be no discrimination at all. A survey of the relevant case law confirms that point of view, albeit with some exceptions.

I am not convinced by that view. It is quite true that even if P had been in the opposite situation, that is to say changing from female to male, it is possible that she would have been dismissed anyway. One fact, however, is not just possible, but certain: P would not have been dismissed if she had remained a man.

So how can it be claimed that discrimination on grounds of sex was not involved? How can it be denied that the cause of discrimination was precisely, and solely, sex? To my mind, where unfavourable treatment of a transsexual is related to (or rather is caused by) a change of sex, there is discrimination by reason of sex or on grounds of sex, if that is preferred.

On this subject I cannot do other than recall that the prohibition of discrimination on grounds of sex is an aspect of the principle of equality, a principle which requires no account to be taken of discriminatory factors, principally sex, race, language and religion. What matters is that, in like situations, individuals should be treated alike.

Consequently, the principle of equality prohibits unequal treatment of individuals based on certain distinguishing factors, and these specifically include sex. This means that importance may not and must not be given to sex as such, so as to influence in one way or another the treatment afforded, for example, to workers. That is the reasoning on which my Opinion in *Kalanke* is based, in which, as I recall, I declared myself opposed to employment and promotion quotas for women, because I believe that the principle of non-discrimination on grounds of sex permits only those exceptions which, because they aim at attaining *substantive* equality, are justified by the objective of ensuring actual equality between persons.

In the present case, what is required is at least a rigorous application of the principle of equality so that, therefore, any connotations relating to sex and/or sexual identity cannot be in any way relevant. Moreover, in trying to justify their relevance, it would be very hard to argue, and in any event it has not been claimed, that the abilities and role of the person in question were adversely affected by her change of sex.

I must add that, for the purposes of this case, sex is important as a convention, a social parameter. The discrimination of which women are frequently the victims is not of course due to their physical characteristics, but rather to their role, to the image which society has of women. Hence the rationale for less favourable treatment is the social role which women are supposed to play and certainly not their physical characteristics. In the same way it must be recognised that the unfavourable treatment suffered by transsexuals is most often linked to a negative image, a moral judgment which has nothing to do with their abilities in the sphere of employment.

Such a situation is still less acceptable when the social change and scientific advances made in this area in recent years are taken into consideration. Whilst it is true, as I have already said, that transsexuals are in fact not very significant in statistical terms, it is equally true that for that very reason it is vital that they should have at least a minimum of protection. On this view, to maintain that the unfavourable treatment suffered by P was not on grounds of sex because it was due to her change of sex or else because in such a case it is not possible to speak of discrimination between the two sexes would be a quibbling formalistic interpretation and a betrayal of the true essence of that fundamental and inalienable value which is equality . . .'

JUDGMENT OF THE COURT: '. . . The United Kingdom and the Commission submit that to dismiss a person because he or she is a transsexual or because he or she has undergone a gender-reassignment operation does not constitute sex discrimination for the purposes of the Directive.

In support of that argument, the United Kingdom points out in particular that it appears from the order for reference that the employer would also have dismissed P if P had previously been a woman and had undergone an operation to become a man.

The European Court of Human Rights has held that "the term 'transsexual' is usually applied to those who, whilst belonging physically to one sex, feel convinced that they belong to the other; they often seek to achieve a more integrated, unambiguous identity by undergoing medical treatment and surgical operations to adapt their physical characteristics to their psychological nature. Transsexuals who have been operated upon thus form a fairly well defined and identifiable group" (*Rees* v *United Kingdom* (1986)).

The principle of equal treatment "for men and women" to which the Directive refers in its title, preamble and provisions means, as Articles 2(1) and 3(1) in particular indicate, that there should be "no discrimination whatsoever on grounds of sex".

Thus, the Directive is simply the expression, in the relevant field, of the principle of equality, which is one of the fundamental principles of Community law.

Moreover, as the Court has repeatedly held, the right not to be discriminated against on grounds of sex is one of the fundamental human rights whose observance the Court has a duty to ensure (see, to that effect, *Defrenne* v *Sabena (No 3)* (1978) and joined cases *Razzouk and Beydoun* v *Commission* (1984)).

Accordingly, the scope of the Directive cannot be confined simply to discrimination based on the fact that a person is of one or other sex. In view of its purpose and the nature of the rights which it seeks to safeguard, the scope of the Directive is also such as to apply to discrimination arising, as in this case, from the gender reassignment of the person concerned.

Such discrimination is based, essentially if not exclusively, on the sex of the person concerned. Where a person is dismissed on the ground that he or she intends to undergo, or has undergone, gender reassignment, he or she is treated unfavourably by comparison with persons of the sex to which he or she was deemed to belong before undergoing gender reassignment.

To tolerate such discrimination would be tantamount, as regards such a person, to a failure to respect the dignity and freedom to which he or she is entitled, and which the Court has a duty to safeguard.

Dismissal of such a person must therefore be regarded as contrary to Article 5(1) of the Directive, unless the dismissal could be justified under Article 2(2). There is, however, no material before the Court to suggest that this was so here.

It follows from the foregoing that the reply to the questions referred by the employment tribunal must be that, in view of the objective pursued by the Directive, Article 5(1) of the Directive precludes dismissal of a transsexual for a reason related to a gender reassignment . . .'

Comment

(1) Note the different ways in which the Advocate-General and the ECJ argue that this is discrimination on grounds of sex – and how they deal with the comparison issue (the argument that there is no sex discrimination because the council would have treated

male and female transsexuals equally unfavourably). How convincing do you find the reasoning?

(2) As a result of this decision, the SDA was amended to outlaw discrimination on grounds that someone 'intends to undergo, is undergoing or has undergone gender reassignment' (SDA s 2A). Gender reassignment is defined in SDA s 82 as follows:

> 'gender reassignment' means a process which is undertaken under medical supervision for the purpose of reassigning a person's sex by changing physiological or other characteristics of sex, and includes any part of such a process.

The requirement for medical supervision is presumably to enable there to be some certainty in identifying the difference, say, between someone who is cross-dressing and someone who is dressing as a member of the sex they are intending to change to as part of the process of undergoing gender reassignment. At the same time, the definition implicitly recognises that the process need not involve medical intervention.

(3) As *P* v *S and Cornwall CC* (1996) only involved direct discrimination, the government opted for a policy of minimum compliance in amending the SDA, so that only direct discrimination was made unlawful. It may be doubted whether this is in accordance with the spirit of the ECJ's decision in the case (see *Richards* v *Secretary of State for Work and Pensions* (2006)). This may be addressed as part of the 2007 consultation on the proposal for a Single Equality Act.

(4) The Gender Recognition Act 2004 s 9 provides that a person who has a full gender recognition certificate 'becomes for all purposes the acquired gender'. A full gender recognition certificate is issued by a Gender Recognition Panel once it is convinced that the applicant: (a) has the condition gender dysphoria; (b) has lived in the acquired gender for at least two years; and (c) intends to change sex permanently.

The gender equality duty

The Equality Act 2006 introduced SDA s 76A, imposing a general equality duty on public authorities from April 2007. It means that they must have due regard to the need to eliminate discrimination and harassment and to promote equality of opportunity between men and women. The general gender equality duty is similar in many ways to the race equality duty discussed above (p 39) – for example, public authorities must produce a gender equality scheme and action plan, and there are specific duties supporting the general duty. It is accepted that public authorities may choose to carry out their obligations by producing a single equality scheme to cover all three general duties (the third relates to disability). There are some differences, however. The EOC's Code of Practice on the gender equality duty (2006) explains the requirements of the duty and highlights some of the differences between it and the race equality duty.

Genuine occupational qualifications (GOQ)

Sex Discrimination Act 1975

7   . . .

(2)   Being a man is a genuine occupational qualification for a job only where –

(a)   the essential nature of the job calls for a man for reasons of physiology (excluding physical strength or stamina) or, in dramatic performances or other entertainment, for reasons of authenticity, so that the essential nature of the job would be materially different if carried out by a woman; or

(b)   the job needs to be held by a man to preserve decency or privacy because –

(i)   it is likely to involve physical contact with men in circumstances where they might reasonably object to its being carried out by a woman, or

(ii)   the holder of the job is likely to do his work in circumstances where men might reasonably object to the presence of a woman because they are in a state of undress or are using sanitary facilities; or

(ba)   the job is likely to involve the holder of the job doing his work, or living, in a private home and needs to be held by a man because objection might reasonably be taken to allowing to a woman –

(i)   the degree of physical or social contact with a person living in the home, or

(ii)   the knowledge of intimate details of such a person's life,

which is likely, because of the nature or circumstances of the job or of the home, to be allowed to, or available to, the holder of the job; or

(c)   the nature or location of the establishment makes it impracticable for the holder of the job to live elsewhere than in premises provided by the employer, and –

(i)   the only such premises which are available for persons holding that kind of job are lived in, or normally lived in, by men and are not equipped with separate sleeping accommodation for women and sanitary facilities which could be used by women in privacy from men, and

(ii)   it is not reasonable to expect the employer either to equip those premises with such accommodation and facilities or to provide other premises for women; or

(d)   the nature of the establishment, or of the part of it within which the work is done, requires the job to be held by a man because –

(i)   it is, or is part of, a hospital, prison or other establishment for persons requiring special care, supervision or attention, and

(ii)   those persons are all men (disregarding any woman whose presence is exceptional), and

(iii)   it is reasonable, having regard to the essential character of the establishment or that part, that the job should not be held by a woman; or

(e)   the holder of the job provides individuals with personal services promoting their welfare or education, or similar personal services, and those services can most effectively be provided by a man, or

(g)   the job needs to be held by a man because it is likely to involve the performance of duties outside the United Kingdom in a country whose laws or customs are such that the duties could not, or could not effectively, be performed by a woman, or

(h)   the job is one of two to be held –

(i)   by a married couple,

(ii)   by a couple who are civil partners of each other, or

(iii)   by a married couple or a couple who are civil partners of each other . . .

48

Comment

(1) The SDA used to contain a blanket exclusion for employment in a private household, such as still exists under RRA s 4(3) in relation to discrimination on grounds of colour or nationality. In *Commission of the EC* v *UK* (1984), some of these exclusions were successfully challenged as being in breach of the Equal Treatment Directive. As a result, the Sex Discrimination Act 1986 repealed the exclusion which formerly applied to employers with five or fewer employees and formulated the private household exemption more narrowly. In addition to the GOQs in s 7, the SDA makes special provision for the police, prison officers and ministers of religion (SDA ss 17–19).

(2) There is no general genuine occupational requirement exemption in the SDA, although it is included in the amended Equal Treatment Directive. The Government decided that the existing GOQ exception matched the GOR concept and that there should be no change to the familiar wording.

(3) There is a separate set of GOQs for transsexuals in SDA s 7B. These are:
- where the job holder may have to perform intimate physical searches pursuant to statutory powers;
- where the post is in a private household, on the same conditions as s 7(2)(ba);
- where the job involves living on the employer's premises and there could reasonably be objection, for purposes of decency and privacy, to someone undergoing gender reassignment sharing those facilities with either sex;
- where the job involves providing vulnerable individuals with personal services promoting their welfare and the employer reasonably believes that those services cannot be effectively provided by someone undergoing gender reassignment.

Note, however, that neither of the last two exceptions applies to someone who has completed the gender reassignment process.

(4) These exceptions do not apply to someone who has received a full gender recognition certificate under the Gender Recognition Act 2004. The status of at least the first exception is also in doubt following the House of Lords decision in *A* v *Chief Constable of West Yorkshire Police* (2003) that a transsexual person should be treated in all respects as belonging to the acquired sex and that the SDA could be properly interpreted to achieve this.

Sexual orientation

It might have been thought that the reasoning of the ECJ in *P* v *S and Cornwall CC*, with its high-flown references to fundamental human rights and dignity and freedom, might have been equally applicable to those suffering discrimination on grounds of their sexual orientation. However, it proved not to be the case. In *Grant* v *South West Trains Ltd* (1998) the ECJ held that it was not contrary to the Equal Treatment Directive for an employer to withhold travel concessions from the partner of a lesbian employee, although they were given to heterosexual partners, whether married or not. The House of Lords confirmed that the SDA would only offer protection to homosexuals if male and female homosexuals were treated differently in the joined appeals in *Macdonald* v *Advocate General for Scotland* and *Pearce* v *Governing Body of Mayfield School* (2003).

The position changed when sexual orientation was included as one of the grounds to be protected from discrimination in the Framework Employment Directive 2000. It was implemented in the United Kingdom by the Employment Equality (Sexual Orientation) Regulations 2003.

Employment Equality (Sexual Orientation) Regulations 2003

2 (1) In these Regulations, 'sexual orientation' means a sexual orientation towards –
   (a) persons of the same sex;
   (b) persons of the opposite sex; or
   (c) persons of the same sex and of the opposite sex.

Comment

(1) Note that the protection covers not only homosexuals, but also heterosexuals or bisexual people.

(2) The definition of discrimination in SO Regs reg 3 makes unlawful discrimination 'on grounds of sexual orientation' – which means it need not necessarily be the sexual orientation of the person who suffers the discrimination. This means (a) that a person who is discriminated against because of his or her association with a homosexual would be protected, and (b) a person who is discriminated against because of a belief about his or her sexual orientation, whether true or not, would be protected.

Genuine occupational requirements (GOR)

Regulation 7(2) of the SO Regs contains the standard genuine occupational requirement exception in parallel terms to the GOR exception in the RRA, discussed above, p 40. More controversial is the special exception contained in reg 7(3).

Employment Equality (Sexual Orientation) Regulations 2003

7 (3) This paragraph applies where –
   (a) the employment is for purposes of an organised religion;
   (b) the employer applies a requirement related to sexual orientation –
       (i)   so as to comply with the doctrines of the religion, or
       (ii) because of the nature of the employment and the context in which it is carried out, so as to avoid conflicting with the strongly held religious convictions of a significant number of the religion's followers; and
   (c) either –
       (i)   the person to whom that requirement is applied does not meet it, or
       (ii) the employer is not satisfied, and in all the circumstances it is reasonable for him not to be satisfied, that that person meets it.

Comment

(1) The compatibility of this exception with the Framework Employment Directive 2000 was challenged by a number of unions by way of judicial review. A particular concern was whether it might permit faith schools to discriminate against gay and lesbian teachers.

R (Amicus) v Secretary of State for Trade and Industry
[2004] IRLR 430 Queen's Bench Division

RICHARDS J: '. . . Regulation 7(3) was not included in the detailed draft regulations originally published for the purposes of consultation. It was added as a result of representations from the Churches, including in particular, it would seem, the Archbishops' Council of the Church of England . . .

The Government's position was explained in more detail by the Minister of State, Lord Sainsbury of Turville, in replying to the debate on the Regulations in the House of Lords on 17 June 2003:

"It became clear that with the regulations as [originally] drafted the Churches would have some difficulty upholding the doctrine and teaching of their faith in relation to particular posts . . . [W]e do not believe that these regulations should interfere with religious teachings or doctrine, nor do we believe it appropriate that doctrine should be the subject of litigation in the civil courts . . .

This is not a question of extreme positions. Article 4(1) of the European Directive is quite clear that religious considerations can be taken into account. What we are debating this evening is exactly where that line is drawn.

Under these circumstances I believe that Government need to take a lead – and we did that in preparing reg 7(3). It resolves the problem of interfering with doctrine and teachings while remaining consistent with the Directive. We believe that reg 7(3) is lawful because it pursues a legitimate aim of preventing interference with a religion's doctrine and teaching and it does so proportionately because of its narrow application to a small number of jobs and the strict criteria which it lays down . . .

When drafting reg 7(3) we had in mind a very narrow range of employment: ministers of religion, plus a small number of posts outside the clergy, including those who exist to promote and represent religion. The words on the page reflect our intentions . . .

First, this is no 'blanket exception'. It is quite clear that reg 7(3) does not apply to all jobs in a particular type of organisation. On the contrary, employers must be prepared to justify any requirement relating to sexual orientation on a case by case basis. The rule only applies to employment which is for the purposes of 'organised religion', not religious organisations. There is a clear distinction in meaning between the two. A religious organisation could be any organisation with an ethos based on religion or belief. However, employment for the purposes of an organised religion clearly means a job, such as a minister of religion, involving work for a church, synagogue or mosque.

A care home run by a religious foundation may qualify as a religious organisation, for example . . . but I believe that it would be very difficult under these regulations to show that a job of a nurse in a care home exists 'for the purposes of an organised religion'. I would say exactly the same in relation to a teacher at a faith school. Such jobs exist for the purposes of healthcare and education . . .

Regulation 7(3) does not stop there. Even if an employer can show that the job exists for the purposes of organised religion, and that is a significant hurdle, he may only apply a requirement related to sexual orientation if one of two further tests are met. In the first test the requirement must be applied to comply with the doctrines of the religion. We do not believe that that test would be met in relation to many posts. It would be very difficult for a church to argue that a requirement related to sexual orientation applied to a post of cleaner, gardener or secretary. Religious doctrine rarely has much to say about posts such as those.

If the first test is not met, what about the second? . . . Both elements have to be satisfied before the second test can be met. It is, therefore, a very strict test and one that will be met in very few cases. The position of a cleaner and librarian, which has been raised many times, has to be judged against those strict criteria. They are strict criteria and one cannot say in a specific case what the situation will be. In such cases one has to apply the criteria and see whether or not they are fulfilled . . ."

. . . The main question, as it seems to me, concerns the scope of the exception. If it had as wide a scope as was submitted by Mr Singh and Mr O'Neill [counsel for the unions], then it would be open to serious objection on the grounds that they put forward. But if it is as narrow in scope as contended for by Miss Carss-Frisk [counsel for the Secretary of State], the objection advanced loses much of its force. I think it clear from the Parliamentary material that the exception was intended to be very narrow; and in my view it is, on its proper construction, very narrow. It has to be construed strictly since it is a derogation from the principle of equal treatment; and it has to be construed purposively so as to ensure, so far as possible, compatibility with the Directive. When its terms are considered in the light of those interpretative principles, they can be seen to afford an exception only in very limited circumstances.

The fact that the exception applies, by reg 7(3)(a), only to employment "for purposes of an organised religion" is an important initial limitation. I accept Miss Carss-Frisk's submission that that is a narrower expression than "for purposes of a religious organisation", or the expression "where an employer has an ethos based on religion or belief", as used in the corresponding regulations relating to discrimination on grounds of religion or belief. I also accept the example she gave, that employment as a teacher in a faith school is likely to be "for purposes of a religious organisation" but not "for purposes of an organised religion".

The conditions in reg 7(3)(b) impose very real additional limitations. In my view the condition in reg 7(3)(b)(i), that the employer must apply the requirement "so as to comply with the doctrines of the religion", is to be read not as a subjective test concerning the motivation of the employer, but as an objective test whereby it must be shown that employment of a person not meeting the requirement would be incompatible with the doctrines of the religion. That is very narrow in scope. Admittedly the alternative in reg 7(3)(b)(ii) is wider; but even that is hemmed about by restrictive language. The condition must be applied "because of the nature of the employment and the context in which it is carried out" – which requires careful examination of the precise nature of the employment – "so as to avoid conflicting with the strongly held religious convictions of a significant number of the religion's followers". Again this is in my view an objective, not subjective, test. Further, the conflict to be avoided is with religious convictions, which must be strongly held; and they must be the convictions of a significant number of the religion's followers. This is going to be a very far from easy test to satisfy in practice.

The fact that reference is made to "a significant number" rather than to all or the majority of a religion's followers not only reflects the desirability of avoiding detailed statistical analysis, to which Lord Sainsbury referred in the Parliamentary debate, but also ensures that proper account is taken of the existence of differing bodies of opinion even within an organised religion. Sexual orientation is a matter on which some followers of a religion may hold stronger religious convictions than others. In my view it is legitimate to allow for the possibility of applying a relevant requirement even if the convictions in question are held only by a significant minority of followers . . .

Looking at reg 7(3) as a whole, and bearing in mind what I have said about its terms and the strict construction that they must be given, I take the view that the exception is a lawful implementation of Article 4(1) of the Directive.

The exception involves a legislative striking of the balance between competing rights . . .'

Comment

(1) Note the distinction discussed here between 'employment for the purposes of an organised religion' and employment by, or for the purposes of, a religious organisation, or an organisation with an ethos based on religion or belief. As we will see in the next section, organisations with an ethos based on religion or belief are allowed to discriminate on grounds of religion or belief – but not on grounds of sexual orientation.

(2) The result in the case was that the application for judicial review was rejected, the judge holding that the SO Regs were compatible with the Framework Employment Directive 2000. His opinion that teachers in a faith school would be employed for the purposes of a religious organisation (thus permitting religious discrimination under the RB Regs reg 7(3)), but not for the purposes of an organised religion (thus not permitting discrimination on grounds of sexual orientation) is persuasive, but strictly *obiter*. The point remains to be tested and cannot be regarded as free from doubt. For example, what if the teacher is employed to teach the religious doctrine, or is the head teacher and public persona of the school?

(3) It is interesting that the exception applies even if the objection is not based on religious doctrine but only on the strongly held religious convictions of a significant number of the religion's followers. Note that it is only the quantity, not the quality, of their beliefs which counts. So as long as there is a vocal minority faction within a religion who strongly believe that homosexuals cause earthquakes, it appears that a gay or lesbian can be denied employment as a minister, even if the religion itself does not espouse so bigoted or irrational a doctrine.

It must be recognised that a similarly worded exception has existed in the SDA since 1975 (SDA s 19), although it might be more contested if it were being proposed for the first time today. The important question, it is submitted, is whether discrimination in employment opportunities should be allowed just to avoid giving offence to one group of people (cf Allen and Moon, 2006).

Religion or belief

Employment Equality (Religion or Belief) Regulations 2003

2 (1) In these Regulations –
  (a) 'religion' means any religion,
  (b) 'belief' means any religious or philosophical belief,
  (c) a reference to religion includes a reference to lack of religion, and
  (d) a reference to belief includes a reference to lack of belief.

Comment

(1) The term 'religion or belief' is not defined in the Framework Employment Directive 2000. It was originally defined in the RB Regs as 'any religion, religious belief, or similar philosophical belief' – but this was criticised because it would only protect beliefs which were similar to religious beliefs. The government accepted that this criticism was justified and the Equality Act 2006 substituted the definition above.

(2) As we have seen, some religious groups, such as Jews and Sikhs, received protection as 'ethnic groups' under the Race Relations Act 1976. Discrimination on grounds of religious belief or political opinion has also been unlawful in Northern Ireland since

1976 (currently under the Fair Employment and Treatment (Northern Ireland) Order 1998).

(3) It is likely that there will be major questions for tribunals and courts to answer as to whether a particular religion or belief is protected. The Acas Guide to the RB Regs states:

> 1.1 **Religion or belief** is not explicitly defined in the Regulations. In most applications to a tribunal it will be clear what is or is not a religion or a similar belief. It will be for the tribunals and higher courts to decide where the issue is disputed. They may consider a number of factors when deciding what is a religion or similar belief. It is likely that they will consider things such as collective worship, a clear belief system, a profound belief affecting the way of life or view of the world. Employers should be aware that these Regulations extend beyond the more well known religions and faiths to include beliefs such as Paganism and Humanism. The Regulations also cover those without religious or similar beliefs.

This guidance pre-dates the amendment to the definition by the Equality Act 2006 and is therefore clearly too restrictive in relation to belief. In any case, it may be argued that elements such as collective worship and a clear belief system are too limited and reflect very much a Western, Judaeo-Christian concept of religion.

(4) It is probable that the case law of the European Court of Human Rights on Art 9 of the ECHR, which protects freedom of religion, may be influential. It is referred to in the DTI's Explanatory Notes on the RB Regs, which state:

> 11   The reference to 'religion' is a broad one, and is in line with the freedom of religion guaranteed by Article 9 ECHR. It includes those religions widely recognised in this country such as Christianity, Islam, Hinduism, Judaism, Buddhism, Sikhism, Rastafarianism, Baha'is, Zoroastrians and Jains. Equally, branches or sects within a religion can be considered as a religion or religious belief, such as Catholics or Protestants within the Christian church, for example. The European Court of Human Rights has recognised other collective religions including Druidism, the Church of Scientology, and the Divine Light Zentrum. The main limitation on what constitutes a 'religion' for the purposes of Article 9 ECHR, is that it must have a clear structure and belief system (see *X* v *UK* (1977)). Even if a belief does not constitute a religion for these purposes, it may constitute a 'similar philosophical belief' (see below).
>
> 12   The reference to 'religious belief' is also a broad one, in line with Article 9 ECHR. It may go further than simply a belief about adherence to a religion or its central articles of faith. It may include other beliefs founded in a religion, if they attain a certain level of cogency, seriousness, cohesion and importance, provided the beliefs are worthy of respect in a democratic society and are not incompatible with human dignity (see judgment of the European Court of Human Rights in *Campbell and Cosans* v *UK* (1982)).

Again, these notes pre-date the Equality Act amendment of the definition, but it may well be that the final proviso about beliefs should be taken on board by courts and tribunals. However, in considering the case law of the ECtHR, it has been pointed out that the Court has tended not to focus closely on whether or not a belief system should be regarded as a 'religion or belief' for the purposes of ECHR Art 9(1), but rather to concentrate on whether the limitations in Art 9(2) apply (see Evans, 2001). On these issues generally, see Pitt (2007).

Employment Equality (Religion or Belief) Regulations 2003

3   (1) For the purposes of these Regulations, a person ('A') discriminates against another person ('B') if –

(a) on the grounds of the religion or belief of B or of any other person except A (whether or not it is also A's religion or belief) A treats B less favourably than he treats or would treat other persons; or . . .

Comment

(1) The purpose of the slightly convoluted wording of reg 3(1)(a) is to make it clear that only discrimination on grounds of the *claimant's* religion or belief is protected, not the employer's. Thus, to use an example from the DTI's Explanatory Notes, if an employer with strong religious views rejected a job applicant because she was gay, that would be discrimination on grounds of sexual orientation, but not on grounds of religion or belief. And if an employer's religious views led her to consider sex outside marriage as immoral and therefore to refuse to employ someone known to engage in serial sexual liaisons, the job applicant would have no claim.

(2) As with sexual orientation, discrimination on grounds of being believed to have a particular religion or belief, or because of association with another person who has a particular religion or belief, is unlawful.

Genuine occupational requirements (GOR)

Regulation 7(2) of the RB Regs contains the standard genuine occupational requirement exception in parallel terms to the GOR exception in the RRA, discussed above, p 40. There is a particular GOR which applies only to religion or belief.

Employment Equality (Religion or Belief) Regulations 2003

7 (3) This paragraph applies where an employer has an ethos based on religion or belief and, having regard to that ethos and to the nature of the employment or the context in which it is carried out –
    (a) being of a particular religion or belief is a genuine occupational requirement for the job;
    (b) it is proportionate to apply that requirement in the particular case; and
    (c) either –
        (i) the person to whom that requirement is applied does not meet it, or
        (ii) the employer is not satisfied, and in all the circumstances it is reasonable for him not to be satisfied, that that person meets it.

Comment

(1) The extent of this exception may depend on how broadly the concept of an organisation with a religious ethos is interpreted (see Vickers, 2003). In *R (Amicus) v Secretary of State for Trade and Industry* (2004) Richards J indicated *obiter* that a faith school could be regarded as such an organisation. However, note the further conditions for this exception to apply. In the first case to reach the EAT, *Glasgow City Council v McNab* (2007), the post of principal teacher of pastoral care was held not to be within the exception, although it was arguable that principal teacher of guidance or religious education would be. Although a post providing pastoral care might also involve guidance, the EAT upheld the employment tribunal's view that provision of pastoral care involved wider duties, and if religious guidance needed to be provided, the school could call on another teacher to provide it.

(2) There is often a risk that protection against one kind of discrimination may bring about another. *R (Amicus)* v *Secretary of State for Trade and Industry* (2004) is a striking example of the possible clash of interests. Can you think of other areas where this could occur? See Elias and Coppel (2000) for one example.

Age

Employment Equality (Age) Regulations 2006

3 (1) For the purposes of these Regulations, a person ('A') discriminates against another person ('B') if –

    (a) on grounds of B's age, A treats B less favourably than he treats or would treat other persons, or

    (b) A applies to B a provision, criterion or practice which he applies or would apply equally to persons not of the same age group as B, but –

        (i) which puts or would put persons of the same age group as B at a particular disadvantage when compared with other persons, and

        (ii) which puts B at that disadvantage,

and A cannot show the treatment or, as the case may be, provision, criterion or practice to be a proportionate means of achieving a legitimate aim.

. . .

(3) In this regulation –

    (a) 'age group' means a group of persons defined by reference to age, whether by reference to a particular age or a range of ages; and

    (b) the reference in paragraph (1)(a) to B's age includes B's apparent age.

Comment

(1) Note that, unlike the parallel provisions on sexual orientation and religion or belief, the prohibition on age discrimination applies only where the individual suffers discrimination because of her own age, or age group.

(2) People may look older or younger than they actually are – hence the inclusion of apparent as well as actual age.

(3) There is a major difference between age discrimination and the other protected grounds – which is that even direct age discrimination is capable of being justified and thus allowed. Normally only indirect discrimination can be justified: the concepts of direct and indirect discrimination are considered in the next section of this chapter.

Exceptions

The usual GOR exception, discussed above in relation to race discrimination (p 40) also applies to age discrimination (Age Regs reg 8). The other, huge, exception which exists in relation to age discrimination is the law on retirement. It remains lawful, subject to certain conditions, to dismiss employees on the grounds that they have reached retirement age. As this is essentially about dismissal, it is discussed in Chapter 8.

There are three further special exceptions in the Age Regs. First, under reg 31 it remains lawful for the National Minimum Wage rate for younger workers to be less than the standard rate. Secondly, under reg 33, it remains lawful to pay enhanced redundancy payments which are more advantageous for older workers as long as they follow the pattern of the statutory redundancy scheme. The third exception permits length of service to be taken into account, subject to certain conditions.

Employment Equality (Age) Regulations 2006

32 (1) Subject to paragraph (2), nothing in Part 2 or 3 shall render it unlawful for a person ('A'), in relation to the award of any benefit by him, to put a worker ('B') at a disadvantage when compared with another worker ('C'), if and to the extent that the disadvantage suffered by B is because B's length of service is less than that of C.

(2) Where B's length of service exceeds 5 years, it must reasonably appear to A that the way in which he uses the criterion of length of service, in relation to the award in respect of which B is put at a disadvantage, fulfils a business need of his undertaking (for example, by encouraging the loyalty or motivation, or rewarding the experience, of some or all of his workers).

(3) In calculating a worker's length of service for these purposes, A shall calculate –

(a) the length of time the worker has been working for him doing work which he reasonably considers to be at or above a particular level (assessed by reference to the demands made on the worker, for example, in terms of effort, skills and decision making); or

(b) the length of time the worker has been working for him in total;

and on each occasion on which he decides to use the criterion of length of service in relation to the award of a benefit to workers, it is for him to decide which of these definitions to use to calculate their lengths of service.

Comment

(1) Length of service or seniority is frequently used as a factor for decision-making in employment. The most obvious example is the use of incremental salary scales, where employees progress by a point for each complete year of service. Length of service has also traditionally been a criterion taken into account in redundancy selection procedures, so that workers with less service are made redundant before longer-serving colleagues. Rather than make these practices completely unlawful, the Age Regs provide a compromise position: there is no need to justify discrimination on grounds of length of service where a period of five years or less is taken into account. However, an incremental scale which covers a period longer than five years will have to be justified.

(2) There may be some doubt as to the compatibility of reg 32 with the Equal Pay Directive 1975, in the light of the ECJ's decision in *Cadman* v *HSE* (2006), discussed below (p 326).

(3) One of the most important areas where length of service matters is in relation to pension entitlement. Although pension schemes are subject to the general principle of non-discrimination, most age-related rules and practices are expressly exempt.

THE CONCEPT OF DISCRIMINATION

There are four categories of activity which count as discrimination in British law. The most obvious kind is less favourable treatment because of one of the protected grounds: this is known as 'direct discrimination'. The second kind of discrimination appears to be neutral, in that the same rules are applied to everyone, but they have a greater adverse effect on the protected group than on other people: this is called 'indirect discrimination'. The third category was introduced to supplement the others, by protecting complainants and people who assist them from retaliatory action by the employer. This is 'victimisation'. The fourth category is harassment on one of the protected grounds. Harassment used to be recognised as an unlawful practice in British law as a kind of direct discrimination, but developments in EU law meant that it had to be introduced as a separate, freestanding category.

Broadly speaking, these concepts of discrimination work in the same way for all of the five protected grounds considered so far – disability discrimination proceeds on different lines, which is why it is dealt with separately at the end of this chapter. Because most of the case law to date has been in relation to the SDA and RRA, they figure more in the following discussion. Where there are differences in the concepts for different grounds, they are indicated.

Direct discrimination

Sex Discrimination Act 1975

1 (1) In any circumstances relevant for the purposes of any provision of this Act, other than a provision to which subsection (2) applies, a person discriminates against a woman if –
   (a) on the ground of her sex he treats her less favourably than he treats or would treat a man . . .

Race Relations Act 1976

1 (1) A person discriminates against another in any circumstances relevant for the purposes of any provision of this Act if –
   (a) on racial grounds he treats that other less favourably than he treats or would treat other persons;
   . . .

(2) It is hereby declared that, for the purposes of this Act, segregating a person from other persons on racial grounds is treating him less favourably than they are treated.

Comment

(1) In the USA for many years it was claimed that 'separate but equal' provision for black and white people did not infringe their civil rights. RRA s 1(2) puts it beyond doubt that deliberate segregation will amount to racial discrimination. There is no corresponding provision in the other equality enactments, presumably because the problem has never arisen.

(2) Note the important difference between the wording of these two sections: under the SDA, you can only complain of discrimination on grounds of your own sex. Under the RRA, it is possible to complain of being less favourably treated on racial grounds generally. This is a wider protection, as is shown by *Showboat* v *Owens* (1984), where a white manager of an amusement centre was held to have been treated less favourably on racial grounds when he was dismissed for refusing to obey an order to exclude young black men from the arcade (cf also *Weathersfield Ltd* v *Sargent* (1999)).

(3) The RB Regs (reg 3(1)(a)) and the SO Regs (reg 3(1)(a)) follow the same format as the RRA on this. The Age Regs (reg 3(1)(a)) are limited to less favourable treatment on grounds of one's own age, like the SDA.

(4) While the wider format of the RRA is generally applauded for giving a remedy in situations like that which arose in *Showboat* v *Owens* (1984), it is not entirely without problems, as the next case indicates.

Redfearn v *Serco Ltd* [2006] ICR 1367 Court of Appeal

The company provided transport services for people with physical and mental disabilities under contract to Bradford City Council. The majority of passengers were of Asian origin. The claimant had been employed as a bus driver. The company dismissed him when he was elected as a councillor for the British National Party. He claimed that this was less favourable treatment on racial grounds. The employment tribunal held that he had been dismissed on health and safety grounds, not on racial grounds.

MUMMERY LJ: '. . . A claim for race discrimination contrary to the Race Relations Act 1976, as amended was brought in the employment tribunal by a member of the British National Party ("BNP") against his former employer. According to its constitution the membership of the BNP is confined to white people and the BNP is:

> "wholly opposed to any form of integration between British and non-European peoples. It is therefore committed to stemming and reversing the tide of non-white immigration and to restoring, by legal changes, negotiation and consent, the overwhelmingly white makeup of the British population that existed in Britain prior to 1948."

. . . On 15 June Mr Redfearn was elected as a local councillor for the BNP. On 30 June 2004 Serco summarily dismissed him. It had received legal advice from group level (employment relations) to the effect that his employment would present a risk to the health and safety of its employees and passengers. It would give rise to considerable anxieties to passengers and their carers, who placed a great deal of trust in the drivers and escorts. It would potentially jeopardise Serco's reputation, possibly leading to the loss of its contract with the council . . .

Direct discrimination

Did the tribunal make an error of law in holding that the dismissal was not "on racial grounds" within the meaning of the 1976 Act?

The answer depends, first, on the construction of the 1976 Act and, secondly, on its application to the facts found by the tribunal. Regard must be had to the anti-discrimination purposes for which the legislation was enacted, the context of the direct discrimination provisions, the language in which those provisions were drafted and the consequences of adopting one possible interpretation of the expression "on racial grounds" rather than another possible interpretation. As the tribunals below appreciated, the decision of the Employment Appeal Tribunal (Browne-Wilkinson J presiding) in *Showboat* v *Owens* (1984) and the later authorities which have followed it, are very much in point: see *Weathersfield Ltd* v *Sargent* (1999) and *Carter* v *Ahsan* (unreported) (2004).

The cases demonstrate that discrimination "on racial grounds" is not confined to less favourable treatment on the ground of the colour or race *of the claimant*. It is accepted that A can be liable for discriminating against B on the ground of C's colour or race. In other words the racial characteristic of C, rather than that of B, the victim of the less favourable treatment, may be a racial ground of the less favourable treatment of B by A and therefore direct discrimination by A against B. If that were not so, cases plainly within the purposes of the 1976 Act would fall outside its scope. There is no reason in the policy of the 1976 Act or in its language why its provisions should not cover the case where the colour or race of the claimant and the respondent are the same, so that it is possible for a white person to discriminate against another white person on racial grounds where the difference in race is that between the discriminator and a third person, not between the discriminator and the person discriminated against.

Showboat Entertainment Centre v *Owens* (1984), following the earlier case of *Zarcynska* v *Levy* (1978), illustrates the point. Direct discrimination against an employee on racial grounds occurred when an employee was dismissed for disobeying his employer's unlawful instruction not to admit black customers to an entertainment centre. The black customers were not in fact treated less favourably, as the white employee refused to carry out the unlawful order to treat them less favourably. It was the white employee who was treated less favourably "on racial grounds" because he was dismissed for refusing to carry out his employer's racially discriminatory policy or practice to discriminate against others on racial grounds . . .

The difference between the parties was as to the ambit of the ratio of the *Showboat* case. Mr Bowers [counsel for the claimant] submitted that the employment tribunal had taken too narrow a view of the ratio of *Showboat*. He pointed to the width of the expression "on racial grounds" in the 1976 Act and he relied on passages in the judgment of *Showboat* to support the proposition that the expression "on racial grounds" covers any case in which the discriminator's less favourable act was "significantly informed by racial considerations or racial attitudes" or was "referable to race", or was taken on the basis of racial considerations or racial attitudes or associations, even if the race was that of a third party. The less favourable treatment of Mr Redfearn in this case (his dismissal) was, Mr Bowers argued, covered by the legislation, because it was significantly influenced by considerations of the Asian race of the customers and employees of Serco, with whom Mr Redfearn had contact during his employment. The health and safety grounds for dismissal relied on by Serco and accepted by the employment tribunal and the concerns expressed by UNISON to Serco were all associated with the Asian origin of the passengers in the buses and a significant number of Serco's employees and the actual or perceived attitudes of Mr Redfearn to race . . .

Mr Bowers accepted that, as a matter of causation, it would have to be shown that race was a substantial and effective cause of the act or decision that constituted less favourable treatment, but the employment tribunal had erred in ruling that a case such as this was outside the expression "on racial grounds" altogether, so that the causation stage was never reached. He pointed out that Serco's motive for acting as it did (to protect its customers and its workforce) was irrelevant to liability for race discrimination; that racial considerations did not have to be the sole reason for or influence on the treatment (see *Nagarajan* v *London Regional Transport* (1999)); and that the defence of justification (such as health and safety grounds) was not available in a case of direct discrimination (such as for industrial relations reasons: see *R* v *Commission for Racial Equality ex parte Westminster City Council* (1984)). As for the policy of the 1976 Act, he said that there was no warrant for confining it to the protection of ethnic minorities. Mr Redfearn was entitled to be protected from race discrimination as much as anyone else . . .

In my judgment, the ratio of *Showboat* advanced by Mr Bowers is far too wide. His citation of selected passages from the judgment must be read in the context of the judgment as a whole. His sweeping proposition is wrong in principle, is inconsistent with the purposes of the legislation and is unsupported by authority. His proposition covers cases that would produce consequences at odds with the legislative aim. Taken to its logical conclusion his interpretation of the 1976 Act would mean that it could be an act of direct race discrimination for an employer, who was trying to improve race relations in the workplace, to dismiss an employee, whom he discovered had committed an act of race discrimination, such as racist abuse, against a fellow employee or against a customer of the employer. I am confident that that is not the kind of case for which the anti-discrimination legislation was designed.

The essence of *Showboat* is that an employee who refuses to implement his employer's racially discriminatory policy is entitled to be protected from less favourable treatment under the 1976 Act. The use of the employee to implement the employer's racially discriminatory policy means that "racial grounds" operate directly in the less favourable treatment of the employee, whether the race or colour in question be that of the employee or that of a third party. Mr Bowers's proposition goes far wider so as to embrace cases in which the employer, far from seeking to implement a racially discriminatory policy contrary to the policy of the 1976 Act, is acting to eliminate race discrimination in accordance with the policy of the 1976 Act. According to Mr Bowers (subject to his points on causation and remedy) the employee would be entitled to receive the same protection under the 1976 Act from unfavourable treatment, such as dismissal, however racially discriminatory he was towards third parties contrary to his employer's instructions.

Mr Bowers's proposition turns the ratio of *Showboat* and the policy of the race relations legislation upside down. It would mean that any less favourable treatment brought about because of concern about the racist views or conduct of a person in a multi-ethnic workplace would constitute race discrimination . . .

In this case it is true that the circumstances in which the decision to dismiss Mr Redfearn was taken included racial considerations, namely the fact that Serco's customers were mainly Asian and that a significant percentage of the workforce was Asian. Racial considerations were relevant to Serco's decision to dismiss Mr Redfearn, but that does not mean that it is right to characterise Serco's dismissal of Mr Redfearn as being "on racial grounds". It is a non sequitur to argue that he was dismissed "on racial grounds" because the circumstances leading up to his dismissal included a relevant racial consideration, such as the race of fellow employees and customers and the policies of the BNP on racial matters. Mr Redfearn was no more dismissed "on racial grounds" than an employee who is dismissed for racially abusing his employer, a fellow employee or a valued customer. Any other result would be incompatible with the purpose of the 1976 Act to promote equal treatment of persons irrespective of race by making it unlawful to discriminate against a person on the grounds of race.

In my judgment, the employment tribunal was correct in law in deciding that Mr Redfearn was not dismissed "on racial grounds". The grounds of dismissal were not racial. They did not become racial grounds because Serco dismissed him in circumstances in which it wished to avoid the perceived detrimental effects of Mr Redfearn's membership of, and election to office representing, the BNP, which propagated racially discriminatory policies concerning non-white races who formed part of Serco's workforce and customer base.'

(Dyson LJ and Sir Martin Nourse agreed.)

Comment

(1) Had it been decided that this was a dismissal on racial grounds then, as Mummery LJ points out, this would result in the absurd situation that if an employer dismissed an employee for an act of racial harassment against another employee, the employee dismissed would be able to claim direct discrimination. And, of course, the harassed employee might equally have a claim, and certainly would if the employer did nothing about the harassment. But while the Court of Appeal has saved the legislation from falling into absurdity, is the legal reasoning convincing?

(2) The Court of Appeal relies heavily on the purpose of the legislation in reaching its conclusion. This is an interesting recognition that, although the legislation is framed in symmetrical terms (so that discrimination against a white person is equally unlawful as discrimination against a member of a minority racial group), it is actually meant to address the problem of discrimination against ethnic minorities in the United Kingdom.

The judgment also distinguishes between taking account of racial considerations and doing something 'on racial grounds': is this a valid distinction?

(3) It is worth noting that there was no complaint about the claimant's work or working relationships at the time of his dismissal. Had he been employed for more than a year, do you think that this would have been a fair dismissal?

(4) As Serco Ltd was a private organisation, albeit carrying out a function on behalf of a public authority, the Court of Appeal held that the Human Rights Act 1998 was not in point and the court was therefore saved from having to consider whether the claimant's right to freedom of thought, conscience and religion and freedom of expression had been infringed – but it is easy to think of situations where this might be an issue, raising the problem of competing rights.

(5) While it may be appropriate to take account of the purpose of the legislation, motive of the discriminator is not relevant, at least, not in the sense that a benign motive will save an employer from liability if in fact there is less favourable treatment on one of the protected grounds, as the next case shows.

James v Eastleigh Borough Council [1990] ICR 554
House of Lords

Mr and Mrs James were both aged 61. Because she had reached state pension age while he had not, she received free admission to the municipal swimming pool, but he had to pay 75p to get in.

LORD BRIDGE: '. . . At first glance this may seem to be a very trivial matter. But the truth is to the contrary. It is an important test case brought with the backing of the Equal Opportunities Commission in performance of their statutory functions under the Act. The phrase "pensionable age" is a term of art derived from the definition in section 27(1) of the Social Security Act 1975 where it means: "(a) in the case of a man, the age of 65; and (b) in the case of a woman, the age of 60". In this sense it not only governs the age at which persons can first qualify for their state pensions, but is also used as the basis on which men and women qualify for a variety of concessions to the elderly such as free or reduced travel and free prescriptions under the National Health Service. The commission's purpose in this litigation is to establish the principle for which they contend that in any sphere of activity in which discrimination on the ground of sex is prohibited by the Sex Discrimination Act 1975 the practice of denying to men between the ages of 60 and 65 benefits which are offered to women between those ages is unlawful unless it is authorised by other express statutory provisions . . .

In the Court of Appeal the case took an entirely new turn and the court found in favour of the council on a ground first raised in argument by the court themselves. It had been common ground in the county court that the concession offered by the council to persons of pensionable age was discriminatory in favour of women and against men under section 1 of the Sex Discrimination Act 1975. But the Court of Appeal held that the council's less favourable treatment of a man than a woman was not "on the ground of his sex" and that there had accordingly been no direct discrimination contrary to section 1(1)(a) . . .

The Vice-Chancellor summarised Mr Lester's submissions for the claimant as follows:

"Mr Lester, for the claimant, forcefully submitted that there is direct discrimination in this case. He submitted that discrimination is 'on the ground of' sex within section 1(1)(a) if the sex of the claimant is a substantial cause of the less favourable treatment. In this context, he says, the correct question is 'what would the position have been but for the sex of the claimant?' If the position would be different if the claimant's sex were different, that is direct discrimination."

I hope I do justice to the judgment if I recite only what seem to me to be the two essential passages rejecting these submissions as follows:

"In my judgment section 1(1)(a) is looking to the case where, subjectively, the defendant has treated the claimant less favourably because of his or her sex. What is relevant is the defendant's reason for doing an act, not the causative effect of the act done by the defendant.

There is a further objection to Mr Lester's construction of the section. If there is direct discrimination in every case where there is a substantial causative link between the defendant's treatment and the detriment suffered by the claimant as a result of his sex I can see no room for the operation of subsection (1)(b). In every case in which a sexually neutral condition in fact operates differentially and detrimentally to one sex as opposed to the other, the imposition of such condition would be a substantial cause of detriment to the claimant by reason of his or her sex, i.e. it would fall within Mr Lester's causation test and therefore constitute direct discrimination under subsection (1)(a). This plainly was not the intention of Parliament which was drawing a clear distinction between, on the one hand, those cases where the defendant expressly or covertly acts by reference to the sex of the claimant and, on the other, those cases where the defendant acted on grounds not expressly or covertly related to sex but his actions have caused a disparate impact as between the sexes."

The fallacy, with all respect, which underlies and vitiates this reasoning is a failure to recognise that the statutory pensionable age, being fixed at 60 for women and 65 for men, is itself a criterion which directly discriminates between men and women in that it treats women more favourably than men "on the ground of their sex". This was readily conceded by Mr Beloff [counsel for the council] and is indeed self-evident. It follows inevitably that any other differential treatment of men and women which adopts the same criterion must equally involve discrimination "on the ground of sex". As Mr Beloff was again constrained to concede, the council would certainly have discriminated directly in favour of women and against men on the ground of their sex if they had *expressly* made their concession of free entry to the swimming pool available to women aged 60 and to men aged 65. He submits that the availability of the statutory concept of pensionable age in the Social Security Act 1975 to denote the criterion on which the concession is based and the fact that pensionable age, although now discriminatory, will not necessarily always remain so, enables the council to escape the charge of direct discrimination "on the ground of sex". But this simply will not do. The expression "pensionable age" is no more than a convenient shorthand expression which refers to the age of 60 in a woman and to the age of 65 in a man. In considering whether there has been discrimination against a man "on the ground of his sex" it cannot possibly make any difference whether the alleged discriminator uses the shorthand expression or spells out its full meaning.

The Court of Appeal's attempt to escape from these conclusions lies in construing the phrase "on the ground of her sex" in section 1(1)(a) as referring subjectively to the alleged discriminator's "reason" for doing the act complained of. As already noted, the judgment had earlier identified the council's reason as "to give benefits to those whose resources would be likely to have been reduced by retirement" and "to aid the needy, whether male or female". But to construe the phrase, "on the ground of her sex" as referring to the alleged discriminator's reason in this sense is directly contrary to a long line of authority confirmed by your Lordships' House in *R v Birmingham City Council, ex parte Equal Opportunities Commission* (1989). In that case the council, as local education authority, was held to have discriminated against girls under section 1(1)(a). At the council's independent, single-sex grammar schools there were more places available for boys than girls. Consequently the council were obliged to set a higher pass mark for girls than boys in the grammar school entrance examination. In his speech, expressing the unanimous opinion of the House, Lord Goff of Chieveley said:

> "The first argument advanced by the council before your Lordship's House was that there had not been, in the present case, less favourable treatment of the girls on the grounds of sex. Here two points were taken. It was submitted . . . (2) that, if that burden had been discharged, it still had to be shown that there was less favourable treatment on grounds of sex, and that involved establishing an intention or motive on the part of the council to discriminate against the girls. In my opinion, neither of these submissions is well-founded . . . As to the second point, it is, in my opinion, contrary to the terms of the statute. There is discrimination under the statute if there is less favourable treatment on the ground of sex, in other words if the relevant girl or girls would have received the same treatment as the boys but for their sex. The intention or motive of the defendant to discriminate, though it may be relevant so far as remedies are concerned . . . is not a necessary condition of liability; it is perfectly possible to envisage cases where the defendant had no such motive, and yet did in fact discriminate on the ground of sex . . ."

Lord Goff's test, it will be observed, is not subjective, but objective. Adopting it here the question becomes: "Would the claimant, a man of 61, have received the same treatment as his wife but for his sex?" An affirmative answer is inescapable . . .

The question of indirect discrimination under section 1(1)(b) arises only where the "requirement or condition" applied by the alleged discriminator to a person of one sex is applied by him equally to a person of the other sex. Pensionable age cannot be regarded as a requirement or condition which is applied equally to persons of either sex precisely because it is itself discriminatory between the sexes. Whether or not the proportion of men of pensionable age resorting to the council's swimming pool was smaller than the proportion of women of pensionable age was quite irrelevant. Women were being treated more favourably than men because they attained the age to qualify for free admission five years earlier than men . . .'

(Lords Ackner and Goff delivered concurring speeches; Lords Griffiths and Lowry dissented.)

Comment

(1) Suppose that everything that was red was also round. Would the two qualities still be different? Would action taken on grounds of redness also be action taken on grounds of roundness? Is that the situation here?

(2) Note that since this case, state pension age is being gradually increased – upwards – to 65 for both men and women (Social Security Contributions and Benefits Act 1992 s 122, Pensions Act 1995 Sch 4, para 1). From 2024 it will be gradually raised to 68 (Pensions Act 2007).

(3) Suppose that the gender-based criterion affects no members of one group and only some members of the other group. Is action on the basis of this criterion direct discrimination? Pregnancy is an example of such a criterion: what happens if a woman is discriminated against because she is pregnant? This gave courts some difficulty, especially as SDA s 5(3) provides that a comparison of persons of different sex 'must be such that the relevant circumstances in the one case are the same, or not materially different, in the other'.

Webb v *EMO Air Cargo (UK) Ltd* **[1994] IRLR 482 European Court of Justice**

JUDGMENT OF THE COURT:

'1   By order of 26 November 1992, received at the Court on 4 February 1993, the House of Lords referred to the Court for a preliminary ruling under Article 177 of the EEC Treaty a question on the interpretation of [the Equal Treatment Directive 1976] on the implementation of the principle of equal treatment for men and women as regards access to employment, vocational training and promotion, and working conditions.

2   That question was raised in proceedings between Mrs Webb and EMO Air Cargo (UK) Ltd (hereinafter "EMO").

3   It appears from the order for reference that in 1987 EMO employed 16 persons. In June one of the four employees working in the import operations department, Mrs Stewart, found that she was pregnant. EMO decided not to wait until her departure on maternity leave before engaging a replacement whom Mrs Stewart could train during the six months prior to her going on leave. Mrs Webb was recruited with a view, initially, to replacing Mrs Stewart following a probationary period. However, it was envisaged that Mrs Webb would continue to work for EMO following Mrs Stewart's return. The documents before the Court show that Mrs Webb did not know she was pregnant when the employment contract was entered into.

4   Mrs Webb started work at EMO on 1 July 1987. Two weeks later, she thought that she might be pregnant. Her employer was informed of this indirectly. He then called her in to see him and informed her of his intention to dismiss her. Mrs Webb's pregnancy was confirmed a week later. On 30 July she received a letter dismissing her in the following terms: "You will recall that at your interview some four weeks ago you were told that the job for which you applied and were given had become available because of one of our employees becoming pregnant. Since you have only now told me that you are also pregnant I have no alternative other than to terminate your employment with our company."

5   Mrs Webb then brought proceedings before the employment tribunal, pleading direct discrimination on grounds of sex and, in the alternative, indirect discrimination . . .

14   The House of Lords found that the special feature of this case lay in the fact that the pregnant woman who was dismissed had been recruited precisely in order to replace, at least initially, an employee who was herself due to take maternity leave. The national court is uncertain whether it was unlawful to dismiss Mrs Webb on the ground of her pregnancy, or whether greater weight should be attached to the reasons for which she was recruited.

15   Taking the view that it should construe the applicable domestic legislation so as to accord with the interpretation of [the Equal Treatment Directive 1976], as laid down by the court, the House of Lords stayed proceedings and submitted the following question for a preliminary ruling:

> "Is it discrimination on grounds of sex contrary to Council Directive 76/207/EEC for an employer to dismiss a female employee ('the appellant') (a) whom he engaged for the specific purpose of replacing (after training) another female employee during the latter's forthcoming maternity leave, (b) when, very shortly after appointment, the employer discovers that the appellant herself will be absent on maternity leave during the maternity leave of the other employee, and the employer dismisses her because he needs the jobholder to be at work during that period, (c) had the employer known of the pregnancy of the appellant at the date of appointment, she would not have been appointed, and (d) the employer would similarly have dismissed a male employee engaged for this purpose who required leave of absence at the relevant time for medical or other reasons?"

16   As is apparent from the documents before the court, the question submitted for a preliminary ruling relates to a contract of employment concluded for an indefinite period.

17   According to article 1(1), the purpose of Directive 76/207 is to put into effect in the member states the principle of equal treatment for men and women as regards access to employment, including promotion, and vocational training and as regards working conditions.

18   Article 2(1) of Directive 76/207 states that "the principle of equal treatment shall mean that there shall be no discrimination whatsoever on grounds of sex either directly or indirectly by reference in particular to marital or family status". Under art 5(1), "application of the principle of equal treatment with regard to working conditions, including the conditions governing dismissal, means that men and women shall be guaranteed the same conditions without dis-crimination on grounds of sex".

19   As the court ruled in *Handels-og Kontorfunktionoererenes Forbund i Danmark v Dansk Arbejdsgiverforening* (1991) (the *Hertz* case) and confirmed in its judgment in *Habermann-Beltermann v Arbeiterwohlfahrt, Bezirksverband Ndb/Opf eV* (1994), the dismissal of a female worker on account of pregnancy constitutes direct discrimination on grounds of sex.

20   Furthermore, by reserving to member states the right to retain or introduce provisions which are intended to protect women in connection with "pregnancy and maternity", art 2(3) of Directive 76/207 recognises the legitimacy, in terms of the principle of equal treatment, first, of protecting a woman's biological condition during and after pregnancy and, second, of protecting the special relationship between a woman and her child over the period which follows pregnancy and childbirth (see the *Habermann-Beltermann* case and *Hoffmann v Barmer Ersatzkasse* (1984)).

21   In view of the harmful effects which the risk of dismissal may have on the physical and mental state of women who are pregnant, have recently given birth or are breastfeeding, includ-ing the particularly serious risk that pregnant women may be prompted voluntarily to terminate their pregnancy, the Community legislature subsequently provided, pursuant to art 10 of Council Directive 92/85/EEC of 19 October 1992 on the introduction of measures to encourage improvements in the safety and health at work of pregnant workers and workers who have recently given birth or are breastfeeding, for special protection to be given to women, by pro-hibiting dismissal during the period from the beginning of their pregnancy to the end of their maternity leave.

22   Furthermore, art 10 of Directive 92/85 provides that there is to be no exception to, or dero-gation from, the prohibition on the dismissal of pregnant women during that period, save in exceptional cases not connected with their condition.

23   The answer to the question submitted by the House of Lords, which concerns Directive 76/207, must take account of that general context.

24   First, in response to the House of Lords' inquiry, there can be no question of comparing the situation of a woman who finds herself incapable, by reason of pregnancy discovered very shortly after the conclusion of the employment contract, of performing the task for which she was recruited with that of a man similarly incapable for medical or other reasons.

25   As Mrs Webb rightly argues, pregnancy is not in any way comparable with a pathological condition, and even less so with unavailability for work on non-medical grounds, both of which are situations that may justify the dismissal of a woman without discriminating on grounds of sex. Moreover, in the *Hertz* case the court drew a clear distinction between pregnancy and illness, even where the illness is attributable to pregnancy but manifests itself after the mater-nity leave. As the court pointed out, there is no reason to distinguish such an illness from any other illness.

26   Furthermore, contrary to the submission of the United Kingdom, dismissal of a pregnant woman recruited for an indefinite period cannot be justified on grounds relating to her inability to fulfil a fundamental condition of her employment contract. The availability of an employee is necessarily, for the employer, a precondition for the proper performance of the employment contract. However, the protection afforded by Community law to a woman during pregnancy

and after childbirth cannot be dependent on whether her presence at work during maternity is essential to the proper functioning of the undertaking in which she is employed. Any contrary interpretation would render ineffective the provisions of Directive 76/207.

27   In circumstances such as those of Mrs Webb, termination of a contract for an indefinite period on grounds of the woman's pregnancy cannot be justified by the fact that she is prevented, on a purely temporary basis, from performing the work for which she has been engaged (see the *Habermann-Beltermann* case and the Advocate General's opinion in this case).

28   The fact that the main proceedings concern a woman who was initially recruited to replace another employee during the latter's maternity leave but who was herself found to be pregnant shortly after her recruitment cannot affect the answer to be given to the national court.

29   Accordingly, the answer to the question submitted must be that art 2(1) read with art 5(1) of Directive 76/207 precludes dismissal of an employee who is recruited for an unlimited term with a view, initially, to replacing another employee during the latter's maternity leave and who cannot do so because, shortly after recruitment, she is herself found to be pregnant . . .'

Comment

(1) *Webb* v *EMO* established that unfavourable treatment of a woman on grounds of her pregnancy was direct sex discrimination, even though there was no comparable male. In subsequent cases (eg *Gillespie* v *Northern Health and Social Services Board* (1996) and *Brown* v *Rentokil Ltd* (1998)), the ECJ developed this reasoning to the point of holding that pregnancy and maternity leave constitute a 'protected period', during which a woman is in a special position which is not comparable either to men or to women who are not pregnant. Unfavourable treatment of her during this protected period is direct sex discrimination, and comparison with how other workers would be treated is irrelevant – except in so far as it may provide evidence of whether the treatment complained of was indeed on this ground.

(2) Although the ECJ decision in *Webb* v *EMO* could have been read as indicating that only women recruited on indefinite, rather than fixed-term, contracts were protected (a point stressed when the case came back to the House of Lords in *Webb* v *EMO (No 2)* (1995)), later case law made it clear that the protection applied to any contract (*Tele Danmark* v *Brandt-Nielsen* (2001); *Jimenez Melgar* v *Ayuntamiento de Los Barrios* (2001)).

(3) Much of the heat went out of the pregnancy issue with the implementation of the Pregnant Workers Directive (92/85/EC), which made dismissal on grounds of pregnancy, childbirth or maternity leave automatically unfair. The Employment Relations Act 1999 extended this protection by making it unlawful to subject workers to any detriment on these grounds (ERA 1996 s 47C).

(4) The Equal Treatment Directive 1976 was amended by Directive 2002/73/EC in 2002 and under Art 2(7) of the Equal Treatment Directive as amended, less favourable treatment of a woman related to pregnancy or maternity leave was expressly stated to constitute discrimination. As a result, the SDA was amended by the Employment Equality (Sex Discrimination) Regulations 2005, introducing new SDA s 3A, which expressly states that discrimination on grounds of pregnancy or maternity leave is unlawful.

(5) This has not solved all the problems of comparison, however. SDA s 3A(1) defines direct discrimination on grounds of pregnancy as treating the woman 'less favourably than he [the employer] would treat her had she not become pregnant'. Thus it still involves comparison, albeit not with a man. The EOC challenged this in judicial review

proceedings, arguing that this did not correctly implement the Directive, because it meant that less favourable treatment of a woman on grounds of pregnancy would not be protected under s 3A if it was not possible to make a comparison with how she would have been treated if she had not been pregnant. The EOC successfully argued that the Directive required that any unfavourable treatment related to pregnancy or maternity leave should be protected, without any element of comparison being required (*EOC* v *Secretary of State for Trade and Industry* (2007)). As a result, the Sex Discrimination Act 1975 (Amendment) Regulations 2008 removed the comparison requirement in SDA s 3A.

(6) The whole discussion of pregnancy as a form of sex discrimination should indicate how slippery the concept of comparing like with like can be. The crucial question is: what are to be regarded as relevantly similar cases? The EU position on pregnancy is strong on pragmatism, but short on logic, as shown by the fact that the 'sick man' comparison has not been abandoned for all purposes: once outside the protected period comprising pregnancy plus maternity leave, a woman's absence for a pregnancy-related illness can be compared with a man's sickness absence and it will not be less favourable treatment to dismiss her where a man would have been dismissed for a similar amount of absence (counting only absence which does not fall within the protected period): *Hertz* v *Aldi Marked* (1991); *Brown* v *Rentokil Ltd* (1998).

(7) Another area where the comparison of relevantly like with like has caused problems is in relation to dress codes. If men can wear trousers, can women insist on wearing them too? If women are allowed to wear their hair long, why can't men? In *Smith* v *Safeway plc* (1996) the Court of Appeal held that:

> Rules concerning appearance will not be discriminatory because their content is different for men and women if they enforce a common principle of smartness or conventionality, and taken as a whole and not garment by garment or item by item, neither gender is treated less favourably in enforcing that principle.

This meant that it was not direct sex discrimination, in their opinion, to dismiss a male delicatessen assistant for refusing to cut his hair short while female delicatessen assistants only had to tie theirs back. But the apparent objectivity of this decision disguises the inherent value judgement: compare *McConomy* v *Croft Inns* (1992), where the Northern Ireland High Court considered that it was no longer unconventional for a man to wear an earring (see further Clayton and Pitt, 1997). In relation to discrimination on grounds of religion or belief, see *Azmi* v *Kirklees Metropolitan Borough Council* (2007).

Problems of proof

Proof of direct discrimination can be particularly difficult, especially at the stage of recruitment, where a claimant may not have relevant information about other candidates for a job. Tribunals can be reluctant to find that an employer has treated someone less favourably on the protected grounds, because of the moral stigma attached to such a finding. It is obviously the employer who has the best information about why one candidate was preferred over another, and such considerations led the EU in 1997 to pass a directive requiring that the burden of proof should shift to the employer in sex discrimination claims if the claimant could raise a *prima facie* case (Burden of Proof Directive (97/80/EC)). This was implemented by regulations inserting new s 63A in the SDA.

Sex Discrimination Act 1975

63A (1) This section applies to any complaint presented under section 63 to an employment tribunal.

(2) Where, on the hearing of the complaint, the complainant proves facts from which the tribunal could, apart from this section, conclude in the absence of an adequate explanation that the respondent –

  (a) has committed an act of discrimination or harassment against the complainant which is unlawful by virtue of Part 2 or section 35A or 35B, or

  (b) is by virtue of section 41 or 42 to be treated as having committed such an act of discrimination or harassment against the complainant,

the tribunal shall uphold the complaint unless the respondent proves that he did not commit, or, as the case may be, is not to be treated as having committed, that act.

Comment

(1) Comparable provisions for the other grounds are contained in the RRA s 54A, RB Regs reg 29, SO Regs reg 29 and Age Regs reg 37.

(2) Guidance on how tribunals and courts should now approach the burden of proof in direct discrimination cases was given by the EAT in *Barton* v *Investec Henderson Crosthwaite Securities* (2003) and refined by the Court of Appeal in *Igen Ltd* v *Wong* (2005).

Igen Ltd v *Wong* [2005] IRLR 258 Court of Appeal

PETER GIBSON LJ: '...

The revised Barton *guidance*

As this is the first time that the *Barton* guidance has been considered by this court, it may be helpful for us to set it out again in the form in which we approve it. In *Webster* v *Brunel University* [one of the cases joined in this appeal, referring to it in the EAT] Burton J refers to criticisms made of its prolixity. Tempting though it is to rewrite the guidance in a shorter form, we think it better to resist that temptation in view of the fact that in practice the guidance appears to be offering practical help in a way which most employment tribunals and EATs find acceptable. What is set out in the annex to this judgment incorporates the amendments to which we have referred and other minor corrections. We have also omitted references to authorities. For example, the unreported case referred to in para (6) of the guidance may be difficult for employment tribunals to obtain. We repeat the warning that the guidance is only that and is not a substitute for the statutory language.

Annex

(1) Pursuant to s 63A of the SDA, it is for the claimant who complains of sex discrimination to prove on the balance of probabilities facts from which the tribunal could conclude, in the absence of an adequate explanation, that the respondent has committed an act of discrimination against the claimant which is unlawful by virtue of Pt II or which by virtue of s 41 or s 42 of the SDA is to be treated as having been committed against the claimant. These are referred to below as "such facts".

(2) If the claimant does not prove such facts he or she will fail.

69

(3)   It is important to bear in mind in deciding whether the claimant has proved such facts that it is unusual to find direct evidence of sex discrimination. Few employers would be prepared to admit such discrimination, even to themselves. In some cases the discrimination will not be an intention but merely based on the assumption that "he or she would not have fitted in".

(4)   In deciding whether the claimant has proved such facts, it is important to remember that the outcome at this stage of the analysis by the tribunal will therefore usually depend on what inferences it is proper to draw from the primary facts found by the tribunal.

(5)   It is important to note the word "could" in s 63A(2). At this stage the tribunal does not have to reach a definitive determination that such facts would lead it to the conclusion that there was an act of unlawful discrimination. At this stage a tribunal is looking at the primary facts before it to see what inferences of secondary fact could be drawn from them.

(6)   In considering what inferences or conclusions can be drawn from the primary facts, the tribunal must assume that there is no adequate explanation for those facts.

(7)   These inferences can include, in appropriate cases, any inferences that it is just and equitable to draw in accordance with s 74(2)(b) of the SDA from an evasive or equivocal reply to a questionnaire or any other questions that fall within s 74(2) of the SDA.

(8)   Likewise, the tribunal must decide whether any provision of any relevant code of practice is relevant and if so, take it into account in determining such facts pursuant to s 56A(10) of the SDA. This means that inferences may also be drawn from any failure to comply with any relevant code of practice.

(9)   Where the claimant has proved facts from which conclusions could be drawn that the respondent has treated the claimant less favourably on the ground of sex, then the burden of proof moves to the respondent.

(10)   It is then for the respondent to prove that he did not commit, or, as the case may be, is not to be treated as having committed, that act.

(11)   To discharge that burden it is necessary for the respondent to prove, on the balance of probabilities, that the treatment was in no sense whatsoever on the grounds of sex, since "no discrimination whatsoever" is compatible with the Burden of Proof Directive.

(12)   That requires a tribunal to assess not merely whether the respondent has proved an explanation for the facts from which such inferences can be drawn, but further that it is adequate to discharge the burden of proof on the balance of probabilities that sex was not a ground for the treatment in question.

(13)   Since the facts necessary to prove an explanation would normally be in the possession of the respondent, a tribunal would normally expect cogent evidence to discharge that burden of proof. In particular, the tribunal will need to examine carefully explanations for failure to deal with the questionnaire procedure and/or code of practice.'

Comment

(1) The statutory questionnaire procedure referred to in propositions 7 and 13 is provided for in relation to all of the protected grounds. *King* v *Great Britain-China Centre* (1991) is an example of an employer's equivocal reply being used as evidence supporting an inference of discrimination.

(2) On the other hand, remember that it is still possible for employers to run the 'lousy employer' defence: that although the claimant was treated badly, this does not necessarily mean it was on one of the protected grounds, because the employer treats everyone badly (*Glasgow CC* v *Zafar* (1998); *Bahl* v *Law Society* (2004)).

(3) One of the biggest difficulties facing a rejected candidate is finding out about the other candidates: only with this information is it possible to form a judgement as to

whether you were unfairly passed over. However, much of this information is confidential. In *Science Research Council* v *Nassé* (1979) the House of Lords held that a claim of confidentiality should not necessarily defeat a claim for disclosure of documents. The test is whether or not the information is required to dispose fairly of the proceedings.

(4) Disclosure (formerly called 'discovery') will not be ordered if it would be oppressive. In *West Midlands PTE* v *Singh* (1988) Balcombe LJ said:

> Discovery may be oppressive in two respects. (1) It may require the provision of material not readily to hand which can only be made available with difficulty and at great expense . . . (2) It is also possible that the effect of discovery may be to require the party ordered to make discovery to embark on a course which will add unreasonably to the length and cost of the hearing.

This was said in relation to the provision of statistics. The issue in the case was the extent to which statistics could be regarded as having evidential value.

West Midlands Passenger Transport Executive v Singh
[1988] ICR 614 Court of Appeal

The claimant, a Sikh, had been employed as an inspector by the PTE since 1977. He applied for promotion to one of 13 senior inspector posts in 1985 but was rejected. He instituted proceedings for racial discrimination and sought disclosure of statistics relating to the ethnic origins, qualifications and experience of all 55 applicants for the posts and the documentation (anonymised) relating to the short-listing process. The employers agreed to this, but resisted a further request for similar information relating to all posts in broadly comparable grades from 1983 (when an equal opportunities policy had been adopted) to the end of 1985, when he applied for promotion. The Court of Appeal's decision was given by Balcombe LJ.

BALCOMBE LJ: '. . . The issue is whether evidence that a particular employer has or has not appointed any or many coloured applicants in the past is material to the question whether he has discriminated on racial grounds against a particular complainant; and whether discovery devoted to ascertaining the percentage of successful coloured applicants with successful white applicants should be ordered. Or as the Employment Appeal Tribunal put it in its judgment:

> "Assuming for the purpose of argument that no single coloured applicant who has applied over the last 18 months for a succession of these jobs has succeeded in obtaining them, is that fact in any way logically probative that in the instant application by the claimant there may be race discrimination? Put another way, is it open to an employment tribunal to draw an inference from a long history of unsuccessful applications by coloured applicants that an employer has adopted a discriminatory policy and has exercised it in the particular case . . ."

Direct discrimination involves that an individual is not treated on his merits but receives unfavourable treatment because he is a member of a group. Statistical evidence may establish a discernible pattern in the treatment of a particular group: if that pattern demonstrates a regular failure of members of the group to obtain promotion to particular jobs and to under-representation in such jobs, it may give rise to an inference of discrimination against the group. That is the reason why the Race Relations Code of Practice, which came into effect on 1 April 1984 . . . recommends ethnic monitoring of the workforce and of applications for promotion and recruitment, a practice adopted by the employers in their own organisation. Statistics obtained through monitoring are not conclusive in themselves, but if they show racial or ethnic imbalance or disparities, then they may indicate areas of racial discrimination.

If a practice is being operated against a group then, in the absence of a satisfactory explanation in a particular case, it is reasonable to infer that the claimant, as a member of the group, has himself been treated less favourably on grounds of race. Indeed, evidence of discriminatory treatment against the group in relation to promotion may be more persuasive of discrimination in the particular case than previous treatment of the claimant, which may be indicative of personal factors peculiar to the claimant and not necessarily racially motivated.

It has been a regular feature of cases conducted before employment tribunals in race discrimination cases for employers to give evidence that persons holding responsible positions include both white and non-white as demonstrating that they have a policy of non-discrimination and as providing evidence from which an employment tribunal could decide in a particular case that the particular claimant had not been discriminated against – see the judgment of the Employment Appeal Tribunal.

The validity of this practice, and its probative effect, has been approved by this court in *Owen and Briggs* v *James* (1982), approving a similar approach by the Employment Appeal Tribunal in that case. If evidence of a non-discriminatory attitude on the part of an employer is accepted as having probative force, as being likely to have governed his behaviour in the particular case, then evidence of a discriminatory attitude on his part may also have probative effect.

The suitability of candidates can rarely be measured objectively; often subjective judgments will be made. If there is evidence of a high percentage rate of failure to achieve promotion at particular levels by members of a particular racial group, this may indicate that the real reason for refusal is a conscious or unconscious racial attitude which involves stereotyped assumptions about members of that group.

Mr Beloff, for the employers, submitted that the statistical material ordered by the Employment Appeal Tribunal was not relevant, because it was not logically probative of the question in issue, namely whether the employers discriminated against the claimant on racial grounds when they denied him promotion in December 1985. The fact that the statistical evidence might show that the employers had between October 1984 and December 1985 rejected all coloured applicants for the post of traffic supervisor would not of itself prove racial discrimination; in every case there may have been good, non-racial, reasons for the rejection of the particular applicant. And, even if there had been racial discrimination by the employers on other occasions, it would not of itself prove racial discrimination against the claimant on this particular occasion. As a matter of strict logic both these propositions are true. Nevertheless, the courts do not apply so stringent a test in deciding on the relevance of material to be used as evidence. "Relevant (ie logically probative or disprobative) evidence is evidence which makes the matter which requires proof more or less probable": see *Reg* v *Kilbourne* (1973) per Lord Simon of Glaisdale, cited with approval by Lord Hailsham of St Marylebone in *Reg* v *Boardman* (1974); see also the dictum of Lord Wilberforce in *Reg* v *Boardman*, ". . . in judging whether one fact is probative of another, experience plays as large a place as logic".

A number of cases on "similar fact" evidence, in both the criminal and the civil field, were cited to us. We did not find these of assistance in answering the question with which we are faced. We are satisfied, for the reasons set out above, that the statistical material ordered is relevant to the issues in this case, in that (i) it may assist the claimant in establishing a positive case that treatment of coloured employees was on racial grounds, which was an effective cause for their, and his, failure to obtain promotion; (ii) it may assist the claimant to rebut the employers' contention that they operated in practice an equal opportunities policy which was applied in his case.'

(The case was remitted to the tribunal.)

Comment

(1) The 1984 race relations code of practice was replaced by the CRE's Code of Practice on Racial Equality in Employment 2005 (in force from April 2006). This still recommends monitoring, of course (see paras 3.25–3.35), as does the EOC's Code of Practice on Sex Discrimination, etc (1985) (paras 37–40).

(2) Public authorities which are subject to the Race Equality duty, the Gender Equality duty and the Disability Equality duty have a statutory obligation to monitor relevant statistics about the composition of their workforce and applicants for jobs.

Harassment

The concept of harassment did not appear in the original anti-discrimination legislation. Influenced by American jurisprudence, British law recognised sexual and racial harassment as forms of direct discrimination in the 1980s (*Porcelli* v *Strathclyde Regional Council* (1984); *De Souza* v *AA* (1986)). The stumbling blocks were showing that there had been adverse employment consequences for the claimant (frequently, this meant showing that distress caused by harassment amounted to a 'detriment' within the meaning of SDA s 6(2)(b) or RRA s 4(2)(c)), and, in the case of sexual harassment, getting over the problem of comparison with the treatment of a similarly situated real or hypothetical man. As with pregnancy, the idea of comparing sexual harassment of a woman with how the employer might have treated a man, or how a comparable man would have reacted, was highly artificial.

Following the Race Directive 2000, the Framework Employment Directive 2000 and amendment to the Equal Treatment Directive 1976 by Directive 2002/73/EC, it became necessary to introduce harassment as a freestanding head of discrimination. A difference in the formulation of the concept in the directives should be noted.

Equal Treatment Directive 76/207/EEC

2 (2) For the purposes of this Directive, the following definitions shall apply: . . .

— harassment: where an unwanted conduct related to the sex of a person occurs with the purpose or effect of violating the dignity of a person, and of creating an intimidating, hostile, degrading, humiliating or offensive environment,

— sexual harassment: where any form of unwanted verbal, non-verbal or physical conduct of a sexual nature occurs, with the purpose or effect of violating the dignity of a person, in particular when creating an intimidating, hostile, degrading, humiliating or offensive environment.

(3) Harassment and sexual harassment within the meaning of this Directive shall be deemed to be discrimination on the grounds of sex and therefore prohibited.

A person's rejection of, or submission to, such conduct may not be used as a basis for a decision affecting that person.

Race Directive 2000/43/EC

2 (3) Harassment shall be deemed to be discrimination within the meaning of paragraph 1, when an unwanted conduct related to racial or ethnic origin takes place with the purpose or effect of violating the dignity of a person and of creating an intimidating, hostile, degrading,

humiliating or offensive environment. In this context, the concept of harassment may be defined in accordance with the national laws and practice of the Member States.

Comment

(1) Article 2(3) of the Framework Employment Directive 2000 defines harassment on the other protected grounds in parallel terms to Art 2(3) of the Race Directive.

(2) The obvious difference here is that two forms of harassment are defined in the Equal Treatment Directive: 'harassment' *tout court* – often called 'sex-based harassment' in the literature, and 'sexual harassment'. This distinction is considered in relation to the new concept of harassment inserted in the SDA by the Employment Equality (Sex Discrimination) Regulations 2005.

Sex Discrimination Act 1975

4A (1) For the purposes of this Act, a person subjects a woman to harassment if –
   (a) he engages in unwanted conduct that is related to her sex or that of another person and has the purpose or effect –
      (i) of violating her dignity, or
      (ii) of creating an intimidating, hostile, degrading, humiliating or offensive environment for her,
   (b) he engages in any form of unwanted verbal, non-verbal or physical conduct of a sexual nature that has the purpose or effect –
      (i) of violating her dignity, or
      (ii) of creating an intimidating, hostile, degrading, humiliating or offensive environment for her, or
   (c) on the ground of her rejection of or submission to unwanted conduct of a kind mentioned in paragraph (a) or (b), he treats her less favourably than he would treat her had she not rejected, or submitted to, the conduct.
(2) Conduct shall be regarded as having the effect mentioned in sub-paragraph (i) or (ii) of subsection (1)(a) or (b) only if, having regard to all the circumstances, including in particular the perception of the woman, it should reasonably be considered as having that effect . . .

Comment

(1) Before these directives were implemented, British law had come to recognise two main forms of harassment: conduct which humiliated the recipient, and therefore violated her dignity (eg *Insitu Cleaning Co Ltd* v *Heads* (1995)), or conduct which created a hostile work environment for him or her, tainted by discrimination (eg *Porcelli* v *Strathclyde Regional Council* (1984)). However, the requirement of comparison with how a similarly situated man might be treated led to some narrowing of the hostile work environment concept (*Stewart* v *Cleveland Guest* (1994)), and in *Pearce* v *Governing Body of Mayfield School* (2003) the House of Lords denied that the use of gender-specific foul language would amount to discrimination on grounds of sex where it was clear that a man would have been subject to the same level of abuse (albeit with different terms being used). Thus in *Brumfitt* v *Ministry of Defence* (2005) a training officer used offensive and obscene language directed at both men and women in his audience, which the claimant found offensive and humiliating to her as a woman. But because he had treated men and women equally, there was no sex discrimination.

(2) Does the introduction of an independent concept of sex-based harassment which is deemed to constitute discrimination free the law from the comparison problem? As

originally worded, probably not. SDA s 4A(1)(a) was intended to incorporate the EU concept of sex-based harassment, but while that defines harassment as '*related to* the sex of *a* person', s 4A(1)(a) stated originally that it was something done to a woman '*on the grounds of her* sex'. In judicial proceedings brought by the EOC, the High Court held that this failed correctly to implement the directive, in that 'on the grounds of' suggested that there had to be a causative link between the claimant's sex and the harassing behaviour, which would require comparison with how someone of the opposite sex would have been treated, while the directive required only harassing conduct related to sex (*EOC* v *Secretary of State for Trade and Industry* (2007)). SDA s 4A(1)(a) was therefore amended by the Sex Discrimination Act 1975 (Amendment) Regs 2008 to the form shown on the previous page. This means that the harassing behaviour need only be connected to sex, not by reason of the claimant's sex. Provided the other requirements are fulfilled, it could even cover harassing behaviour where the claimant is not the person directly experiencing the harassment.

(3) Note that the definition of harassment in the directives suggests that it must have the purpose or effect of violating dignity *and* of creating a hostile atmosphere. British law had recognised either of these results as constituting harassment, and on the 'no-regression' principle (ie that EU law cannot be used to justify a reduction in existing protection) this remains the case, as is clear from the wording of the implementing legislation.

(4) The second concept of sexual harassment has no parallel among the other protected grounds: this is 'unwanted . . . conduct of a sexual nature'. In a 1993 European Commission Guide to implementing the then EC Code of Practice on sexual harassment, unwanted conduct of a sexual nature was described as follows:

> Physical conduct of a sexual nature means unwanted physical conduct ranging from unnecessary touching, patting or pinching or brushing against another employee's body, to assault and coercing sexual intercourse.
>
> Verbal conduct of a sexual nature can include unwelcome sexual advances, propositions or pressure for sexual activity; continued suggestions for social activity outside the workplace after it has been made clear that such suggestions are unwelcome; offensive flirtations; suggestive remarks, innuendoes or lewd comments. Such behaviour defines women's role as sexual objects rather than work colleagues.
>
> Non-verbal conduct of a sexual nature refers to the display of pornographic or sexually suggestive pictures, objects or written materials; leering, whistling, or making sexually suggestive gestures. These behaviours may make employees feel uncomfortable or threatened and undermine the position of a woman who seeks to deal with her fellow employees with professional dignity.

(5) SDA s 4A(1)(c) defines a third form of harassment, called 'quid pro quo' harassment in the USA. Note that this will also constitute discrimination even if the recipient submits to the conduct and possibly receives some employment benefit as a result. Again, there is no parallel for this in relation to the other protected grounds, presumably because it is only perceived as a problem in relation to sex.

(6) For all of the protected grounds, harassment is defined as conduct having 'the purpose *or effect*' of violating dignity or creating a hostile atmosphere (SDA s 4A(1)(a) above: the same formulation is used in the other equality enactments). This makes it clear that the subjective reaction of the recipient is relevant to whether or not conduct constitutes harassment. However, this is qualified by the proviso that it is only to be seen

as having that effect if it is reasonable to reach that conclusion. This is believed to embody the test already laid down in *Driskel* v *Peninsula Business Services Ltd* (2000).

(7) Note that harassment may also be actionable in other ways. The Protection from Harassment Act 1997 creates a criminal offence and civil wrong of harassment which, although aimed at stalkers, can be used in the workplace. In *Majrowski* v *Guy's and St Thomas's NHS Trust* (2006) the House of Lords held that an employer could be vicariously liable for harassment by an employee in contravention of that Act.

(8) Similarly, in *Waters* v *Commissioner of Police of the Metropolis* (2000) the House of Lords held that an employer could be liable in negligence where bullying or harassment in the workplace was foreseeable and the employer did not take steps to prevent it. Opinion is divided as to whether harassment ought to be linked to the protected grounds or seen as a separate wrong linked to other forms of bullying – what arguments do you think there are for or against each position?

Indirect discrimination

Sex Discrimination Act 1975

1 (2) In any circumstances relevant for the purposes of a provision to which this subsection applies, a person discriminates against a woman if –
. . .
   (b) he applies to her a provision, criterion or practice which he applies or would apply equally to a man, but –
      (i) which puts or would put women at a particular disadvantage when compared with men,
      (ii) which puts her at that disadvantage, and
      (iii) which he cannot show to be a proportionate means of achieving a legitimate aim
        . . .

Comment

(1) The general idea here is that facially neutral rules or practices which actually have a greater impact on one protected group rather than another ought to be prohibited, unless it can be shown that they serve a legitimate purpose which cannot be achieved in some other way. The concept is based on *Griggs* v *Duke Power Co* (1971), where the US Supreme Court held that application tests which screened out many more blacks than whites, and which were not job-related, constituted unlawful race discrimination.

(2) Implementing this seemingly straightforward idea has always given rise to difficulties, however. The first problem relates to identifying the barrier which it is more difficult for one group to surmount than another. The second relates (again) to the question of who is compared with whom. The third issue is deciding how much adverse impact has to be shown in order for it to be actionable, and the final problem is judging what level of need on the part of the employer should be taken to justify a discriminatory practice.

Provision, criterion or practice

British Airways plc v *Starmer* [2005] IRLR 863 Employment Appeal Tribunal

The claimant had been employed as a pilot by BA since 2001. In order to accommodate her childcare needs, she asked to reduce her hours to 50 per cent of full-time. BA refused to let her work less than 75 per cent of full-time hours and she challenged this as indirect discrimination, on the grounds that it is more difficult for women than men to work full-time. Was the employer's decision that she could not work half-time a provision, criterion or practice (PCP) applied to her?

BURTON J: '. . . The *provision, criterion or practice* ("PCP") there referred to [in SDA s 1(2)(b)] replaced, upon the amendment of the Act resulting from the Burden of Proof Directive (97/80/EC), the previous rubric of a "requirement or condition" in s 1(1)(b); but, by virtue of the "non-derogation" provision in Article 6 of the Burden of Proof Directive, the definition of a PCP will be at least as wide as to include anything that would previously have qualified as a requirement or condition . . .

[T]he tribunal records that in April 2003, "in response to the legislative changes providing employees with statutory rights to request flexible working in certain circumstances", a new scheme was introduced, which the tribunal found to accord with the statutory regime, entitled "Request for flexible working contract variation".

The actual making of the request is recorded in paragraph 29 of the judgment:

"The claimant made application for a contract variation to reduce her current working pattern from full-time to 50 per cent. Pursuant to that request, the claimant met with her manager on 16 March 2004. The decision, notified to the claimant in a letter dated 25 March 2004, was:

'The RTR board has considered your written request and your comments at the meeting. Having evaluated the possible impacts on you, your colleagues and BA at this time, I have decided that I am not able to grant your request for 50%, but I am able to agree a change for the alternative option of 75% contract starting January 2005.'"

The business reasons, as they were described, for the decision, were given on 1 April 2004, as paragraph 30 of the judgment records:

"The business reasons were under the headings of: Burden of additional costs; Inability to re-organise work among existing employees, detrimental effect on quality and performance; and inability to recruit extra employees."

This was, submits Mr Jeans [counsel for the employer], simply a one-off decision by the respondent to refuse permission to work on the terms which the claimant sought, namely 50%, and to state that the only basis upon which she could go part-time was to work 75%. Such decision, he submits, was not a PCP:

1) It was a one-off management decision, not applying generally to others. There was no pool to which it applied, nor anyone by reference to whom the detriment suffered by the claimant can be compared.
2) It was a discretionary decision relating to this particular claimant. Permission for 50% was given to two pilots, both captains, being one man and one woman, who were also part of the Airbus fleet at London Heathrow, and to 21 people, being 10 men (seven captains and three first officers) and 11 women (nine captains and two first officers) in the entire flight operations crew of the respondent. In the respondent's reply to the claimant's request for written answers relating to the questionnaire under the Act, served prior to the hearing, it was said that, by reference to the records kept in respect of formal requests for 50% part-time working under the right to request policy in the period 1 December 2003 to 30 November 2004, there had been two applications by men, both of which were refused and five by women, one of which was accepted, three rejected and one withdrawn . . .

However, Mr Cavanagh QC [counsel for the claimant] points to the judgment of Sedley LJ, with which the rest of the Court of Appeal agreed, in *Allonby* v *Accrington College* (2001):

"It is for the claimant to identify the requirement or condition which she seeks to impugn. These words are not terms of art: they are overlapping concepts and are not to be narrowly construed: see *Clarke* v *Eley (IMI) Kynoch* (1982). If the claimant can realistically identify a requirement or condition capable of supporting her case, as Ms Allonby did here to the employment tribunal's satisfaction, it is nothing to the point that her employer can with equal cogency derive from the facts a different and unobjectionable requirement or condition."

It is the PCP upon which the claimant relies which must be tested. Was the employment tribunal entitled to regard the decision of the respondent relating to the applicant, in response to her application for part-time working, as a PCP?

Mr Cavanagh QC submits that there is no support in the statutory language for Mr Jeans QC's submission that a one-off discretionary decision cannot be a PCP, that it is inconsistent with the spirit of the legislation, that there is no authority for it . . .

We are satisfied that it was a PCP:

1)   The decision that, if the claimant was to go part-time it must be at 75% and not 50%, was a requirement or a condition or a provision. If it is a requirement or condition then, by virtue of Article 6 of the Burden of Proof Directive, it must also be a provision. It may not be a criterion or a practice, but it is quite plain that these three words or alternatives are not cumulative, and it is enough if it is a provision. It need not have been imposed/applied by the respondent, as its decision was a discretionary one, but it was. The suggestion that a condition or requirement meant an "absolute bar" was "correctly not pursued" before the Employment Appeal Tribunal in *Chief Constable of Avon & Somerset Constabulary* v *Chew* (2001), per Charles J. It is plain that a practice or a criterion can allow for exceptions to be made, and it seems to us a fortiori that a provision, which does not carry with it any similar inference of being universally applicable, certainly carries no contrary implication. Any suggestion that a similar concept to the eiusdem generis rule might be applicable so as to seek to construe a provision as being similar to, as opposed to alternative to and different from, criterion or practice, a contention which was in any event not in terms put forward by Mr Jeans QC, is plainly ousted by the need to construe provision by reference to requirement or condition, which carry within them no possible such inference.

2)   There is, as Mr Cavanagh QC submitted, no authority for the proposition that a PCP cannot be one-off, or that it cannot involve a discretionary decision (indeed the passage in Charles J's judgment referred to above can be said to be authority to the contrary in relation to the latter proposition). Mr Cavanagh QC points to a similar argument put forward by Mr Jeans QC in *Allonby*, which did not find favour and which, at any rate in that case, was specifically rejected by Ward LJ, albeit in relation to a submission he was there making in relation to a requirement or condition that was not, on its face, one-off (being a requirement or condition that an employee, in order to acquire continuous employment, had to have been employed effectively full-time):

"Mr Jeans QC submits that the college was not applying to her any requirement or condition but merely implementing a decision about the way in which to run its business. He submits that the indirect discrimination provisions are addressed to cases where, for example, an employer stipulates that certain criteria must be met in order that a person can be appointed to a post, eg the erstwhile minimum height required to work in the police force, or a requirement that a person have a degree in a particular subject. He submits the law should not be contorted so that every commercial decision can be described as applying a requirement or condition. The tribunal rejected that submission dealing with the problem of good business reasons under the issue of justifiability. It concluded: 'the changes namely the requirement that hourly paid contract workers would in future only be employed through ELS was the application of a requirement or condition'.

In my judgment, they were fully entitled so to regard it. The reality is that the college told its former employee that it was no longer willing to accept her back as a part-time lecturer unless she came either on a full-time basis or through ELS. Although the imposition of that threshold may well have been the implementation of a commercial decision forced upon it by changes in the law, it none the less was a threshold for her to cross and it was in that sense a requirement or condition which they applied to her when considering upon what terms she would be permitted to resume her teaching. I see no error in their approach and like Sedley LJ and Gage J I reject Mr Jeans's submissions." . . .

In our judgment there is no necessity for the impugned PCP actually to apply, or be applied, to others, as would for example be the case if it were the 2,000-hour threshold that was in issue in this case, as it is not. What is required in order to test the question of whether the PCP is discriminatory or not is to extrapolate it to others; ie the reference under s 1(2)(b) is not simply to a "provision . . . which he applies equally to a man" but also to one which he "would apply equally to a man" . . .

In our judgment the best way for an employer to avoid the problem which may be caused by a one-off PCP is to establish and operate a non-discriminatory and/or justifiable generally applicable PCP. That is what the respondent sought to introduce by way of the 2,000-hour threshold, three months or so after, and, it seems, as a direct result of, the problem caused by and for this claimant . . .'

Comment

(1) As Burton J points out, before amendment resulting from the Burden of Proof Directive (97/80/EC), the claimant had to show that there was a 'requirement or condition' applied to him or her having an exclusionary effect. This was interpreted as meaning that the criterion challenged had to be an 'absolute bar' to recruitment to the post or access to some other employment benefit (*Perera* v *Civil Service Commission (No 2)* (1982) and *Meer* v *Tower Hamlets LBC* (1988), both cases on race discrimination). This interpretation was widely criticised in that it allowed employers to exclude women or minorities by expressing discriminatory preferences, provided they were not described as absolutely necessary attributes.

(2) An interesting facet of this case is that Burton J refers approvingly to an unreported EAT case, *Chief Constable of Avon & Somerset Constabulary* v *Chew* (2001), as authority for the proposition that this interpretation of 'requirement or condition' should not have been applied in sex discrimination claims, on the basis that it was inconsistent with the Equal Treatment Directive 1976. This point is still of some importance, because the newer definition of indirect discrimination in SDA s 1(2)(b) applies only to discrimination in the employment field. The former definition, to be found in SDA s 1(1)(b), still applies where discrimination in fields such as education or the supply of goods and services is alleged – but this is beyond the scope of this book.

(3) Note the judge's point in this case that any rule which would have counted as a 'requirement or condition' under the old law must count at least as a 'provision' under the new definition, since otherwise the non-regression principle of EU law would be infringed: this is the principle that implementation of a directive cannot be used to

reduce levels of protection already existing in the law of a member state (see Art 6 of the Burden of Proof Directive (97/80/EC)). In numerous cases on the previous definition it was held that employer policies disadvantaging part-time workers consti- tuted *prima facie* indirect sex discrimination, because they could be seen as requiring a woman to work full-time in order to access a benefit or avoid a detriment (eg *Clarke* v *Eley (IMI) Kynoch* (1982); *Home Office* v *Holmes* (1984); *R* v *Secretary of State for Employment ex parte EOC* (1994)).

(4) The central question in this case was whether a one-off decision could be described as a provision, criterion or practice. The arguments put forward are cogent; however, it does raise the question as to whether there is now any difference in practice between the duty to avoid unjustified indirect discrimination and the duty (which currently exists only in relation to disability discrimination) to make reasonable accommodation for an employee's needs. This point might have been addressed on appeal, but the case was settled shortly before it was due to be heard by the Court of Appeal.

(5) The decision may at least be taken as indicating that the legislation is likely to be interpreted fairly widely on this point, with the greatest focus likely to be on whether the practice can be justified.

(6) The definition of indirect discrimination in SDA s 1(2)(b) is repeated in relation to the other protected grounds (see RRA s 1A; RB Regs reg 3(1)(b); SO Regs reg 3(1)(b); Age Regs 3(1)(b)) – but note that RRA s 1A does not expressly cover discrimination on grounds of colour or nationality, for which the old definition in RRA s 1(1)(b) con- tinues to apply.

Proving adverse impact

SDA s 1(2)(b)(i) states that adverse impact occurs where the employer applies a provision, criterion or practice 'which puts or would put women at a particular dis- advantage when compared with men' and the same formulation is used in the other equality enactments. It was not always so. The original formulation in the SDA and RRA required proof that the *proportion* of women, or of people of the same racial group who could comply with the requirement was *considerably smaller* than the pro- portion of men, or people from other racial groups who could comply with it. This comparison is still required in relation to claims of indirect sex discrimination in fields outside employment and indirect race discrimination on grounds of colour and nationality. The difficulties of that approach are well illustrated by an early EAT decision.

Price v Civil Service Commission [1983] ICR 428 Employment Appeal Tribunal

The claimant applied for a job in the civil service. The further particulars for the post said that applicants should be aged between $17\frac{1}{2}$ and 28. She was 35. She claimed that the age limit indirectly discriminated against women, who were frequently out of the labour market looking after young children between those ages.

PHILLIPS J: '... The argument [in the employment tribunal] went further, and was that since the number of women and the number of men in the population is not widely different it was impossible to say that the proportion of women who can comply with the age condition was considerably smaller than the proportion of men, because all men and all women had equal opportunity to comply with it. In paragraph 11 of the decision the employment tribunal put it like this:

"We have unanimously decided that Mr Howard's submission on behalf of the [Civil Service Commission] must be upheld on both grounds. We are of the view that the only requirement or condition was that applicants should be between the specified age groups. Since the claimant conceded that the proportion of women within these groups was not considerably smaller than the proportion of men we are of the view that this concession is fatal to her case. In so far as the statistics are concerned, as Mr Howard submitted, no one can really say whether these women with children really wanted a job or chose to stay at home. If one takes the up-to-date statistics provided by the [Civil Service Commission] we find that indeed more women than men applied for . . . executive officer than men. If they could apply for those posts then it follows that they could have applied for any other kind of job. It is also worthwhile recording that during 1976 53.7% of women were accepted as against 46.3% of men."

The appeal tribunal are not in agreement. Mr Alderton accepts this conclusion, and would dismiss the appeal. The majority take a different view, which is set out in the remainder of this judgment and which is theirs alone.

The employment tribunal further decided that the statistics produced in evidence did not establish to their satisfaction why it was that fewer women applied for posts than men, and whether it was not that they chose not to do so, rather than that they were prevented from doing so. They were also impressed by the fact that during 1976, according to statistics produced of applications for executive officers, of those accepted 53.7 per cent were women as against 46.3 per cent who were men. We do not regard this last point as significant, since the complaint is not that over the whole range of appointment between $17\frac{1}{2}$ and 28 years fewer women were successful than men, but that the age bar at 28 was more disadvantageous to women than to men . . .

Knowledge and experience suggest that a considerable number of women between the mid-twenties and the mid-thirties are engaged in bearing children and in minding children, and that while many find it possible to take up employment many others, while desiring to do so, find it impossible, and that many of the latter as their children get older find that they can follow their wish and seek employment. This knowledge and experience is confirmed by some of the statistical evidence produced to the employment tribunal (and by certain additional statistical evidence put in by consent of the parties on the hearing of the appeal). This demonstrates clearly that the economic activity of women with at least one Advanced Level falls off markedly about the age of 23, reaching a bottom at about the age of 33 when it climbs gradually to a plateau at about 45.

Basing ourselves on this and other evidence, we should have no hesitation in concluding that our own knowledge and experience is confirmed, and that it is safe to say that the condition is one which it is in practice harder for women to comply with than it is for men. We should be inclined to go further and say that there are undoubtedly women of whom it may be properly said in the terms of SDA section 1(1)(b)(i) that they "cannot" comply with the condition, because they are women; that is to say because of their involvement with their children. But this is not enough to enable the claimant to satisfy the requirements of sub-para (i). The difficulty we have is in saying whether the proportion of women who can comply with the condition is *considerably smaller* than the proportion of men who can comply with it. It follows from what we have said earlier that we do not agree with the approach of the employment tribunal to this question, and it follows that there has never been a finding of fact based on the evidence correctly approached and interpreted.

At one stage of the hearing we thought that it might be in order for us to make a finding ourselves on the basis of the evidence given to the employment tribunal, together with that put in by consent on the hearing of the appeal. At the end of the day we have come to the conclusion that we ought not to do so. The difficulty is that most of the evidence is statistical, and is of a kind which needs to be analysed and interpreted, since it is designed for other purposes, and it is not entirely easy to draw relevant conclusions. We think it *does* confirm the likelihood that women are put into difficulties by the condition, and that there are women who would wish to apply to be an executive officer and could do so in, say, their thirties, but cannot do so in their late twenties. The difficulty is to quantify this in the terms of a "considerably smaller" result. We find that it would be unsafe for us to reach a conclusion without having had the benefit of hearing the statistician give evidence and be subjected to cross-examination on the proper analysis and inferences to be drawn from the statistics.

Accordingly we propose to allow the appeal and to remit the case to be heard afresh, bearing in mind the terms of this judgment and such guidance as we have been able to give. It may perhaps be helpful to mention one other matter. The employment tribunal, in their decision, rightly pointed out that when considering s 1(1)(b)(i) and considering the proportion of women and the proportion of men, it may be proper to consider as the "pool" of women or men available for the purpose something less than total female and male population. We agree with that, though, as we have pointed out, the employment tribunal itself in the present case proceeded on the footing that it was appropriate to take into account the whole population, male and female respectively. We doubt whether that was the right approach, though we do not wish to lay down a proposition binding on the employment tribunal which will hear the remitted case. It seems to us, as at present advised, that there would be a good deal in the present case for saying that the appropriate "pool" is that of qualified men and qualified women as the case may be . . .'

Comment

(1) Note that three separate pools for comparison were proposed in this case: which do you think was appropriate? What would happen if there were no available statistics for the groups to be compared?

(2) Disagreements about appropriate pools for comparison are common and tribunals have frequently struggled to make sense of statistical evidence. The problem was compounded by the EAT's suggestion in *Kidd* v *DRG Ltd* (1985) that the choice of pool was a question of fact for the tribunal, which could therefore not easily be reopened on appeal. However, in *Allonby* v *Accrington & Rossendale College* (2001) Sedley LJ sounded 'a strong note of caution' about this approach. He said:

> I would prefer to characterise the identification of the pool as a matter neither of discretion nor of fact-finding but of logic . . . Logic may on occasion be capable of producing more than one outcome, especially if two or more conditions or requirements are in issue. But the choice of pool is not at large.

The issue was also extensively canvassed by members of the House of Lords in *Rutherford* v *Secretary of State for Trade and Industry* (2006), although their Lordships disagreed about which comparisons were appropriate and the significance of the statistical differences, perhaps providing the perfect demonstration of the problems of the statistical approach to adverse impact.

(3) As a result of the Burden of Proof Directive (97/80/EC) the test for indirect sex discrimination in employment was changed in October 2001, so that it was defined as application of a provision, criterion or practice 'which is such that it would be to the *detriment* of a *considerably larger proportion* of women than of men' (emphasis added). The reference to a 'considerably larger' proportion rather than a 'considerably smaller' one seemed to make no difference in practice. The innovation was that, although the formulation still invited comparison, it no longer focused on the claimant's ability or otherwise to comply with the provision.

(4) This change was short-lived, however, because in the meantime a different definition of indirect discrimination had been introduced for race discrimination (except for colour and nationality) by the Race Directive (2000/43/EC) and for religion or belief, sexual orientation and age by the Framework Employment Directive (2000/78/EC). In 2002 the Equal Treatment Amendment Directive (2002/73/EC) followed suit and the same definition was applied to sex discrimination in the employment field. It was introduced as SDA s 1(2)(b) in the form extracted above (p 76) with effect from 1 October 2005.

(5) What this means is that now, for all of the protected grounds currently under consideration, what has to be shown is that the provision, criterion or practice puts the complainant's group 'at a particular disadvantage' compared with the comparator group. Thus an element of comparison is still required, and statistical differences may still be one way of showing disadvantage, but the aim of the change is to make it easier to show adverse impact, and it is clear that other kinds of evidence will also be permissible.

(6) The question of compliance has come back in with the new definition, in that it must be shown that the claimant is herself put at a disadvantage. When this was considered in relation to the former formulation (whether or not the claimant 'could comply' with the excluding provision), the House of Lords adopted a practical approach to the question.

Mandla v *Dowell Lee* [1983] ICR 385 House of Lords

LORD FRASER: '. . . *"Can comply"*
   It is obvious that Sikhs, like anyone else, "can" refrain from wearing a turban, if "can" is construed literally. But if the broad cultural/historic meaning of ethnic is the appropriate meaning of the word in the Act of 1976, then a literal reading of the word "can" would deprive Sikhs and members of other groups defined by reference to their ethnic origins of much of the protection which Parliament evidently intended the Act to afford to them. They "can" comply with almost any requirement or condition if they are willing to give up their distinctive customs and cultural rules. On the other hand, if ethnic means inherited or unalterable, as the Court of Appeal thought it did, then "can" ought logically to be read literally. The word "can" is used with many shades of meaning. In the context of section 1(1)(b)(i) of the Act of 1976 it must, in my opinion, have been intended by Parliament to be read not as meaning "can physically", so as to indicate a theoretical possibility, but as meaning "can in practice" or "can consistently with the customs and cultural conditions of the racial group". The latter meaning was attributed to the word by the Employment Appeal Tribunal in *Price* v *Civil Service Commission* (1978), on a construction of the parallel provision in the Sex Discrimination Act 1975. I agree with their construction of the word in that context. Accordingly I am of opinion that the "No turban" rule was not one with which the second appellant could, in the relevant sense, comply . . .'

Comment

(1) It seems virtually certain that the 'in practice rather than in theory' approach will also be used in judging whether or not someone is actually put at a disadvantage by an indirectly discriminatory provision, criterion or practice.

Justification

Even if a provision, criterion or practice is more disadvantageous to one group rather than another, the employer will have a defence if it can show that it is 'a proportionate means of achieving a legitimate aim'. The test used to be whether the employer could show that it was justifiable, and it is likely that the term 'justification' will continue to be used. The more precise language of the current formulation in the equality enactments derives from the landmark ECJ decision in *Bilka-Kaufhaus* v *Weber von Hartz* (1987), discussed and extracted in Chapter 7 (p 329).

Hardys & Hansons plc v *Lax* [2005] IRLR 726 Court of Appeal

The claimant was employed as a retail recruitment manager for a brewery before she went on maternity leave. She asked if she could work part-time when she returned, but this was refused on the grounds that the employer needed a full-time worker for operational reasons. Her claim that this was indirect discrimination on grounds of sex was upheld by an employment tribunal, which felt that the employer had exaggerated the difficulties in allowing her job to be done on a part-time or job-share basis. The employer appealed on the basis that the tribunal should not have substituted its decision for that of the employer and that, in effect, a 'range of reasonable responses' test should have been applied, so that if their decision was reasonable, it should be regarded as justified even if another employer might have accommodated the woman's request. The Court of Appeal dismissed the employer's appeal.

PILL LJ: '... For the respondent, Mr Langstaff QC submits that the requirement that the employer justify the scheme objectively does not permit the margin of discretion or range of reasonable responses for which Mr Clarke [counsel for the employer] contends. Mr Langstaff accepts that, if another possible scheme is unreasonable, the employer is justified in not adopting it. He accepts that the test does not require the employer to establish that the measure complained of was "necessary" in the sense of being the only course open to him. There is, however, it is submitted, no room for the introduction into this test of the band of reasonable responses which a reasonable employer would adopt which is available to an employer in cases of unfair dismissal (*Foley* v *Post Office* (2000)). It is for the employment tribunal to weigh the real needs of the undertaking, expressed without exaggeration, against the discriminatory effect of the employer's proposal. The proposal must be objectively justified and proportionate.

Section 1(2)(b)(ii) requires the employer to show that the proposal is justifiable irrespective of the sex of the person to whom it is applied. It must be objectively justifiable (*Barry* v *Midland Bank* (1999)) and I accept that the word "necessary" used in *Bilka-Kaufhaus* v *Weber von Hartz* (1987) is to be qualified by the word "reasonably". That qualification does not, however, permit the margin of discretion or range of reasonable responses for which the appellants contend. The presence of the word "reasonably" reflects the presence and applicability of the principle of proportionality. The employer does not have to demonstrate that no other proposal is possible. The employer has to show that the proposal, in this case for a full-time appointment, is justified objectively notwithstanding its discriminatory effect. The principle of proportionality requires the tribunal to take into account the reasonable needs of the business. But it has to make its own judgment, upon a fair and detailed analysis of the working practices and business considerations involved, as to whether the proposal is reasonably necessary. I reject the appellants' submission (apparently accepted by the EAT) that, when reaching its conclusion, the employment tribunal needs to consider only whether or not it is satisfied that the employer's views are within the range of views reasonable in the particular circumstances.

The statute requires the employment tribunal to make judgments upon systems of work, their feasibility or otherwise, the practical problems which may or may not arise from job sharing in a particular business, and the economic impact, in a competitive world, which the restrictions impose upon the employer's freedom of action. The effect of the judgment of the employment tribunal may be profound both for the business and for the employees involved. This is an appraisal requiring considerable skill and insight. As this court has recognised in *Allonby* (2001) and in *Cadman* v *HSE* (2004), a critical evaluation is required and is required to be demonstrated in the reasoning of the tribunal. In considering whether the employment tribunal has adequately performed its duty, appellate courts must keep in mind, as did this court in *Allonby* and in *Cadman*, the respect due to the conclusions of the fact finding tribunal and the importance of not overturning a sound decision because there are imperfections in presentation. Equally, the statutory task is such that, just as the employment tribunal must conduct a critical evaluation of the scheme in question, so must the appellate court consider critically whether the employment tribunal has understood and applied the evidence and has assessed fairly the employer's attempts at justification.

The power and duty of the employment tribunal to pass judgment on the employer's attempt at justification must be accompanied by a power and duty in the appellate courts to scrutinise carefully the manner in which its decision has been reached. The risk of superficiality is revealed in the cases cited and, in this field, a broader understanding of the needs of business will be required than in most other situations in which tribunals are called upon to make decisions . . .'

(Gage and Thomas LJJ agreed.)

Comment

(1) This decision was made by reference to the second definition of indirect sex discrimination, but the discussion of proportionality indicates a focus on the EU test and it is submitted that the same reasoning would be applied in relation to the current definition.

(2) In *Cross* v *British Airways* (2005) the EAT held that the cost implications of a decision are relevant in relation to the justification of indirect discrimination, although the cost of avoiding indirect discrimination would not on its own constitute sufficient justification. But perhaps this would be a matter of degree.

Victimisation

Race Relations Act 1976

2 (1) A person ('the discriminator') discriminates against another person ('the person victimised') in any circumstances relevant for the purposes of any provision of this Act if he treats the person victimised less favourably than in those circumstances he treats or would treat other persons, and does so by reason that the person victimised has –

(a)   brought proceedings against the discriminator or any other person under this Act; or

(b)   given evidence or information in connection with proceedings brought by any person against the discriminator or any other person under this Act; or

(c)   otherwise done anything under or by reference to this Act in relation to the discriminator or any other person; or

(d)   alleged that the discriminator or any other person has committed an act which (whether or not the allegation so states) would amount to a contravention of this Act,

or by reason that the discriminator knows that the person victimised intends to do any of those things, or suspects that the person victimised has done, or intends to do, any of them.

(2)   Subsection (1) does not apply to treatment of a person by reason of any allegation made by him if the allegation was false and not made in good faith.

Comment

(1) Victimisation is similarly defined in the other equality enactments: SDA s 4, RB Regs reg 4, SO Regs reg 4 and Age Regs reg 4.

(2) The test for victimisation looks similar in many ways to that for direct discrimination. However, as the following case shows, they are subtly different.

Chief Constable of West Yorkshire Police v Khan [2001] IRLR 830 House of Lords

The claimant, who was of Indian origin, was a detective sergeant in the West Yorkshire police force. Over a period of 11 years he applied on several occasions for promotion to the rank of detective inspector. All these applications were unsuccessful and he eventually decided that this was because of his race. He therefore instituted a claim for direct race discrimination against the Chief Constable, as the responsible officer. While this was pending, he applied for a detective inspector post in the Norfolk police force. That force approached the West Yorkshire force for a reference. The West Yorkshire force refused to give a reference because it might prejudice the outstanding tribunal proceedings. The claimant argued that this constituted victimisation.

LORD NICHOLLS: '. . . The primary object of the victimisation provisions in s 2 is to ensure that persons are not penalised or prejudiced because they have taken steps to exercise their statutory rights or are intending to do so. The structure of s 2 is similar to the structure of s 1(1)(a), but with an important difference. Racial discrimination, in s 1(1)(a), is discrimination on the grounds of race. Discrimination by victimisation, in s 2, is discrimination on one of the grounds, colloquially known as the protected acts, described in s 2 . . .

Difficulties have arisen in the application of this definition of victimisation and the like definition in s 4 of the Sex Discrimination Act 1975. The difficulties have been most apparent in cases where the employer's impugned conduct was his response to a protected act but he was not racially or gender motivated. I must first refer briefly to the principal authorities. They are illustrative of the problems.

The authorities

In *Kirby* v *Manpower Services Commission* (1980) an employee at a job centre was demoted because he had disclosed confidential information about possible contraventions of the race relations legislation. The Employment Appeal Tribunal held this was not victimisation within s 2. Slynn J, delivering the judgment of the tribunal, said that the relevant question was whether the employers had treated the complainant less favourably than they would have treated someone in their employment who gave away confidential information whatever its kind. So Mr Kirby's claim failed, because the Manpower Services Commission would have treated in the same way any employee who gave away confidential information whatever its nature.

Aziz v Trinity Street Taxis Ltd (1988) was a decision of the Court of Appeal, comprising Slade, Neill and Mann LJJ. Mr Aziz was a member of a taxi drivers' association. He collected evidence with a view to pursuing a racial discrimination claim against the association, by secretly recording conversations with other members. He was expelled for doing so, and he brought a victimisation claim. Slade LJ, delivering the judgment of the court, disapproved the test applied in Kirby's case. He held that by expelling Mr Aziz the association had treated him less favourably than other members. But, to constitute victimisation, the motive which caused the alleged discriminator to treat the complainant less favourably than others must be a motive consciously connected with the race relations legislation. Mr Aziz's claim therefore failed, because the fact that the recordings were made by reference to the Act had not influenced the association in expelling Mr Aziz. Any member who made undisclosed recordings of conversations relating to the activities of the association in a controversial context would have been treated in the same way.

Next, in order of time, is the decision of the Court of Appeal in the present case. Lord Woolf MR held (2000) that Sgt Khan had been treated less favourably by being refused a reference. It was necessary to compare the way other employees in relation to whom a reference was requested would normally be treated with the way Sgt Khan was treated. Further, Sgt Khan was treated less favourably by reason of having done a protected act. If it had not been for the proceedings brought under the Act a reference would have been provided.

Finally, in *Brown v TNT Express Worldwide (UK) Ltd* (2001) the employee requested an afternoon off work to consult his advisor about a racial discrimination claim he had brought against his employer. The claim was due for hearing in an employment tribunal the following week. The employer refused permission, although requests for time off for personal reasons were normally granted. Despite this, the employee left work to keep his appointment, whereupon he was dismissed. Mr Brown's victimisation claim succeeded. The Court of Appeal, comprising Peter Gibson and Mantell LJJ and Sumner J, rejected the employer's contention that the appropriate comparator was an employee who had brought proceedings against the employer but not under the 1976 Act.

Victimisation

(1) The relevant circumstances

Victimisation occurs when, in any circumstances relevant for the purposes of any provision of the Act, a person is treated less favourably than others because he has done one of the protected acts. Thus, the definition of victimisation has, essentially, three ingredients. The first is "in any circumstances relevant for the purposes of any provision of this Act". This is a reference to circumstances in respect of which discrimination is unlawful under the Act. For instance, under s 4(2) it is unlawful for an employer to discriminate against an employee by dismissing him. If an employee brings a victimisation claim based on his dismissal, the relevant circumstances are his dismissal by his employer. In the present case Sgt Khan is treated as employed by the chief officer of police of West Yorkshire (see s 16 of the Act). The relevant circumstances are that, while employed, Sgt Khan requested a reference when seeking new employment and his request was refused.

(2) Less favourable treatment

The second ingredient in the statutory definition calls for a comparison between the treatment afforded to the complainant in the relevant respect with the treatment he affords, or would afford, to other persons "in those circumstances".

As appears from my summary of the authorities, different views have emerged on the correct way to identify the "others", or the comparators or control group, as they are usually known. One approach is that, to continue with my example, if an employee is dismissed the control group comprises the other employees. The complainant was less favourably treated because he was dismissed and they were not. There may be good reasons for this difference in treatment but, on this approach, that is a matter to be taken into account at the third stage when considering why the employer afforded the employee less favourable treatment. This was the approach adopted in *Aziz's* case. It was the approach adopted at all levels in the present case. Sergeant Khan was treated less favourably than other employees, because references are normally provided on request and Sgt Khan was refused a reference. It was also the approach adopted in *Brown's* case.

The other approach is that when considering whether a complainant was treated less favourably there should be factored into the comparison features which make the situation of the complainant and the control group fairly comparable. The control group should be limited to employees who have not done the protected act but whose circumstances, in the material respects, are fairly comparable . . .

There are arguments in favour of both approaches. On the whole I see no sufficient reason for departing from the former approach, adopted by Slade LJ in *Aziz's* case. The statute is to be regarded as calling for a simple comparison between the treatment afforded to the complainant who has done a protected act and the treatment which was or would be afforded to other employees who have not done the protected act.

Applying this approach, Sgt Khan was treated less favourably than other employees. Ordinarily West Yorkshire provides references for members of the force who are seeking new employment.

(3) "by reason that"

Contrary to views sometimes stated, the third ingredient ("by reason that") does not raise a question of causation as that expression is usually understood. Causation is a slippery word, but normally it is used to describe a legal exercise. From the many events leading up to the crucial happening, the court selects one or more of them which the law regards as causative of the happening. Sometimes the court may look for the "operative" cause, or the "effective" cause. Sometimes it may apply a "but for" approach. For the reasons I sought to explain in *Nagarajan v London Regional Transport* (1999), a causation exercise of this type is not required either by s 1(1)(a) or s 2. The phrases "on racial grounds" and "by reason that" denote a different exercise: why did the alleged discriminator act as he did? What, consciously or unconsciously, was his reason? Unlike causation, this is a subjective test. Causation is a legal conclusion. The reason why a person acted as he did is a question of fact.

A situation, closely comparable to that in the present case, arose in *Cornelius v University College of Swansea* (1987). This was a decision of the Court of Appeal, comprising Donaldson MR, and Fox and Bingham LJJ. Like the present case, *Cornelius'* case concerned steps taken by employers to preserve their position pending the outcome of proceedings. A college declined to act on an employee's transfer request or to operate their grievance procedure while proceedings under the 1975 Act, brought by the employee against the college, were still awaiting determination. Giving the only reasoned judgment, Bingham LJ said:

"There is no reason whatever to suppose that the decisions of the Registrar and his senior assistant on the claimant's requests for a transfer and a hearing under the grievance procedure were influenced in any way by the facts that the claimant had brought proceedings or that those proceedings were under the Act. The existence of proceedings plainly did influence their decisions. No doubt, like most experienced administrators, they recognised the risk of acting in a way which might embarrass the handling or be inconsistent with the outcome of current proceedings. They accordingly wished to defer action until the proceedings were over. But that had . . . nothing whatever to do with the claimant's conduct in bringing proceedings under the Act. There is no reason to think that their decision would have been different whoever had brought the proceedings or whatever their nature, if the subject matter was allied. If the appellant was victimised, it is not shown to have been because of her reliance on the Act."

Two strands are discernible in this passage. One strand is that the reason why the officers of the college did not act on the claimant's two requests was the existence of the pending proceedings, as distinct from the claimant's conduct in bringing the proceedings. They wished to defer action until the proceedings were over. The second strand is that the college decisions had nothing to do with the claimant's conduct in bringing proceedings against the college under the 1975 Act. The decisions would have been the same, whatever the nature of the proceedings, if the subject matter had been allied to the content of the employee's requests.

Mr Hand QC, for Sgt Khan, submitted that *Cornelius'* case was wrongly decided. I do not agree. Employers, acting honestly and reasonably, ought to be able to take steps to preserve their position in pending discrimination proceedings without laying themselves open to a charge of victimisation. This accords with the spirit and purpose of the Act. Moreover, the statute accommodates this approach without any straining of language. An employer who conducts himself in this way is not doing so because of the fact that the complainant has brought discrimination proceedings. He is doing so because, currently and temporarily, he needs to take steps to preserve his position in the outstanding proceedings. Protected act (a) ("by reason that the person victimised has – (a) brought proceedings against the discriminator . . . under this Act") cannot have been intended to prejudice an employer's proper conduct of his defence, so long as he acts honestly and reasonably. Acting within this limit, he cannot be regarded as discriminating by way of victimisation against the employee who brought the proceedings . . .'

(Lords Mackay, Hoffmann and Scott delivered concurring speeches. Lord Hutton agreed with Lords Nicholls and Hoffmann.)

Comment

(1) Members of the House of Lords here showed themselves acutely aware of the no-win situation for the employer in this case if they had upheld the victimisation claim. However, is it really appropriate to use a subjective test of the employer's reason in this situation when it is clear that a but-for test of causation is to be used in direct discrimination cases? Are the purposes and wording of the two pieces of legislation so different as to justify this approach?

(2) In *Derbyshire* v *St Helens MBC* (2007) the House of Lords held that whether an alleged act of victimisation was serious enough to be actionable should be judged by the effects on a reasonable employee rather than by what the employer intended. In that case, the council had managed to settle a major equal pay claim involving over 500 women by offering a lump sum to be divided amongst them. However, 39 women refused the settlement and continued their claims. The council then wrote to all the women indicating that dire consequences would ensue if the claims were successful – in particular, that there would be bound to be job losses. The claimants felt that they were being pressurised to give up their claims and argued that it was victimisation. The House of Lords agreed.

Employers' liability

Race Relations Act 1976

32 (1) Anything done by a person in the course of his employment shall be treated for the purposes of this Act (except as regards offences thereunder) as done by his employer as well as by him, whether or not it was done with the employer's knowledge or approval.

(2) Anything done by a person as agent for another person with the authority (whether express or implied, and whether precedent or subsequent) of that other person shall be treated for the purposes of this Act (except as regards offences thereunder) as done by that other person as well as by him.

(3) In proceedings brought under this Act against any person in respect of an act alleged to have been done by an employee of his it shall be a defence for that person to prove that he took such steps as were reasonably practicable to prevent the employee from doing that act, or from doing in the course of his employment acts of that description.

Comment

(1) The comparable provisions in the other equality enactments are: SDA s 41, RB Regs reg 22, SO Regs reg 22 and Age Regs reg 25.

(2) Originally, tribunals used a test of vicarious liability imported from the law of tort in assessing whether an employee's action was 'in the course of employment'. However, in the next case, the Court of Appeal held that a different approach was needed.

Jones v *Tower Boot Co Ltd* [1997] IRLR 168 Court of Appeal

WAITE LJ: 'In April 1992 a 16-year-old boy started work at the employers' shoe factory, as a last operative. He was of mixed ethnic parentage and was joining a workforce which had not previously employed anyone of ethnic minority origin. From this outset he was subjected by fellow-employees to harassment of the gravest kind. He was called by such racially offensive names as "chimp" and "monkey". A notice had been stuck on his back reading "Chipmonks are go". Two employees whipped him on the legs with a piece of welt and threw metal bolts at his head. One of them burnt his arm with a hot screwdriver, and later the same two seized his arm again and tried to put it in a lasting machine, where the burn was caught and started to bleed again. Unable to endure this treatment, the boy left the job after four weeks. He made a complaint against the employers of racial discrimination, contending that his fellow-employees had subjected him to a discriminatory detriment on racial grounds under s 4(2)(c) of the Race Relations Act 1976 ("racial harassment"), for which the employers were responsible by virtue of s 32(1) of the Act as representing acts done by the employees in the course of their employment. The employers sought to resist the claim on the ground that the relevant acts had been outside the scope of the employees' employment; or on the alternative ground that all reasonably practicable steps to avoid them for the purposes of s 32(3) ("the reasonable steps defence") had been taken.

On appeal to the Employment Appeal Tribunal the employers did not challenge the employment tribunal's primary findings of fact as to the treatment given to the complainant or the finding that such treatment amounted to racial harassment. Nor was any challenge directed to the employment tribunal's finding that the reasonable steps defence had not been made out. The sole ground of appeal was that the employment tribunal had been wrong to regard the racial harassment as having been "done by a person in the course of his employment" for the purposes of s 32(1). The Employment Appeal Tribunal (Buckley J, Mrs Boyle and Mr Blyghton) were divided on that issue. The majority (the judicial chairman and Mrs Boyle) regarded this ground of appeal as being made out. They stated their reasons thus:

"That phrase ['the course of employment'] has, and had at the time the draftsman penned s 32, a well-established meaning in law. We would have seen no reason not to adopt that meaning in the present context, in any event. Since it has been adopted by other decisions of this tribunal and by the Court of Appeal, see *Irving* v *The Post Office* (1987), we shall certainly do so.

We were referred to *Bracebridge Engineering* v *Darby* (1990) by Mr Whitmore on behalf of Mr Jones. That case conveniently cites *Aldred* v *Nacanco* (1987) in which the Court of Appeal quoted the well-known statement of principle set out in *Salmond on Torts* 18th edition at page 437 . . . The nub of the test is whether the unauthorised wrongful act of the servant is so connected with that which he was employed to do as to be a mode of doing it. That has to be judged by reference to all the circumstances of the case. Applying that test to the facts of this case we cannot, by any stretch of the imagination, see how the acts complained of by Mr Jones, including deliberate branding with a hot screwdriver and whipping, could be described as an improper mode of performing authorised tasks. With respect, the employment tribunal cannot have applied the law correctly and paragraph 9 of the reasons illustrates that. In answer to [counsel for the employers] Mr Buckhaven's submission that the acts were outside the scope of employment the tribunal held – 'if we accept the breadth of Mr Buckhaven's submission . . . no act carried out by an employee can become the liability of the employer unless it was expressly authorised'. We presume the tribunal must have been referring to acts of the type in question, that is, acts such as assault not usually regarded as modes of carrying out employment tasks, otherwise the comment makes no sense. But to hold that an act is in the course of employment on this basis is to rewrite the accepted legal test. In any event, *Bracebridge* itself illustrates how such an act, in that case an indecent assault, could be in the course of employment. We are bound to say *Bracebridge* seems to stretch the test to its limit but the explanation for the decision clearly lies in the fact that the perpetrators were, at the time, involved in disciplinary supervision. That was not so in the present case and we conclude that Mr Jones's fellow-employees were not acting in the course of employment and their misdeeds cannot be laid at the door of [the employers] by reason of s 32(1)."

The minority view was summed up by Mr Blyghton in these words:

"One has to ask the question: 'Under what circumstances could a claim for racial discrimination succeed if it could be held that such actions do not occur in the course of employment?' The very strict common-law principles of vicarious liability were not intended to be rigidly applied in such cases; hence the code of practice."

In this appeal the claimant, with the backing of the Commission for Racial Equality, submits that Mr Blyghton was right and the majority was wrong. He does not base that claim (as he might have done) on the narrow objection that even if the majority was right in regarding the acts of physical assault as being outside the conventional tortious test for vicarious liability, they failed to consider whether the verbal abuse stood in a different category. He bases it (as in my opinion he is fully entitled to do) upon a challenge to the entire notion that the words "in the course of his employment" in s 32(1) are to be given a restricted meaning which would limit them to instances where the impugned conduct on the part of the employee would attract tortious liability to the employer under the common-law doctrine of vicarious liability.

The issue on this appeal

The effect of that challenge is to require an answer to this question. When an employment tribunal is considering whether for the purposes of s 32(1) any conduct complained of does or does not amount to a "thing done by a person in the course of his employment", is the tribunal bound to answer that by reference to:

(a) the words "course of employment" in the sense in which they are employed in everyday speech; or
(b) the principles laid down by case law for the establishment of vicarious liability by an employer for the torts committed by an employee during the course of his employment?

That is an issue of widespread importance. The fact that the mechanism of the relevant sections of the Race Relations Act is matched exactly by corresponding provisions in the Sex Discrimination Act 1975 means that the issue needs to be resolved in relation to all acts of harassment on the grounds of race or sex which occur in an employment context.

The governing principles of statutory construction

Two principles are in my view involved. The first is that a statute is to be construed according to its legislative purpose, with due regard to the result which it is the stated or presumed intention of Parliament to achieve and the means provided for achieving it ("the purposive construction"); and the second is that words in a statute are to be given their normal meaning according to general use in the English language unless the context indicates that such words have to be given a special or technical meaning as a term of art ("the linguistic construction"). It will be convenient to deal with those separately.

The purposive construction

The legislation now represented by the Race and Sex Discrimination Acts currently in force broke new ground in seeking to work upon the minds of men and women and thus affect their attitude to the social consequences of difference between the sexes or distinction of skin colour. Its general thrust was educative, persuasive, and (where necessary) coercive. The relief accorded to the victims (or potential victims) of discrimination went beyond the ordinary remedies of damages and an injunction – introducing, through declaratory powers in the court or tribunal and recommendatory powers in the relevant Commission, provisions with a proactive function, designed as much to eliminate the occasions for discrimination as to compensate its victims or punish its perpetrators. These were linked to a code of practice of which courts and tribunals were to take cognisance. Consistently with the broad front on which it operates, the legislation has traditionally been given a wide interpretation – see for example *Savjani* v *IRC* (1981) where Templeman LJ said of the Race Relations Act:

"... the Act was brought in to remedy a very great evil. It is expressed in very wide terms, and I should be slow to find that the effect of something which is humiliatingly discriminatory in racial matters falls outside the ambit of the Act."

Since the getting and losing of work, and the daily functioning of the workplace, are prime areas for potential discrimination on grounds of race or sex, it is not surprising that both Acts contain specific provisions to govern the field of employment. Those provisions are themselves wide-ranging – as is evidenced, for example, by the inclusion of contract workers without employee status within the scheme of the legislation. There is no indication in the Act that by dealing specifically with the employment field Parliament intended in any way to limit the general thrust of the legislation.

A purposive construction accordingly requires s 32 of the Race Relations Act (and the corresponding s 41 of the Sex Discrimination Act) to be given a broad interpretation. It would be inconsistent with that requirement to allow the notion of the "course of employment" to be construed in any sense more limited than the natural meaning of those everyday words would allow.

The linguistic construction

Mr Buckhaven's [counsel for the employer] argument is attractively simple. Vicarious liability is a doctrine of tortious liability which has been applied by the common law to the employment context. Part Three of the Race Relations Act applies expressly to discrimination in the employment field. The two fields are the same. Words and phrases that have acquired a familiar and particular meaning through case law applied to employers' liability in the former context must therefore have been intended by Parliament to have the same meaning when applied to employers' liability in the latter context.

Mr Allen QC [counsel for the claimant], while acknowledging that there is a broad conceptual similarity between the employers' responsibility that applies in both contexts, submits that substantial differences emerge when vicarious liability in tort is analysed and contrasted with the statutory scheme of which s 32 forms part. The employer's authority, for example, is a crucial element in vicarious liability in tort – as evidenced by the statement in *Salmond* (20th edition) in paragraph 21.5 that:

> "A master is not responsible for a wrongful act done by his servant unless it is done in the course of his employment. It is deemed to be so done if it is either (1) a wrongful act authorised by the master, or (2) a wrongful and unauthorised way of doing some act authorised by the master."

That is to be contrasted with the position under s 32(1) of the Race Relations Act, where all actions by a person in the course of employment are attributed to the employer "whether or not . . . done with the employer's knowledge or approval". Mr Allen points to other distinctions, such as the greater range of remedies available under the statute (including damages for injury to feelings) than those available in tort against an employer at common law and the total absence from the concept of vicarious liability in tort of any provision corresponding to the reasonable steps defence under s 32(3).

I am persuaded that Mr Allen's submission is to be preferred, and that there is here no sufficient similarity between the two contexts to justify, on a linguistic construction, the reading of the phrase "course of employment" as subject to the gloss imposed on it in the common law context of vicarious liability.

The position apart from authority

Both approaches to statutory construction therefore lead to the same interpretation. But even more compelling, in my view is the anomaly which would result (as the minority member Mr Blyghton pointed out) from adopting any other interpretation. Mr Buckhaven accepts (indeed in his written argument he relies upon) the fact that an inevitable result of construing "course of employment" in the sense for which he contends will be that the more heinous the act of discrimination, the less likely it will be that the employer would be liable. That, he argues, is all to the good. Parliament must have intended the liability of employers to be kept within reasonable bounds.

I would reject that submission entirely. It cuts across the whole legislative scheme and underlying policy of s 32 (and its counterpart in sex discrimination), which is to deter racial and sexual harassment in the workplace through a widening of the net of responsibility beyond the guilty employees themselves, by making all employers additionally liable for such harassment, and then supplying them with the reasonable steps defence under s 32(3) which will exonerate the conscientious employer who has used his best endeavours to prevent such harassment, and will encourage all employers who have not yet undertaken such endeavours to take the steps necessary to make the same defence available in their own workplace . . .

Conclusion

It would be particularly wrong to allow racial harassment on the scale that was suffered by the complainant in this case at the hands of his workmates – treatment that was wounding both emotionally and physically – to slip through the net of employer responsibility by apply to it a common-law principle evolved in another area of the law to deal with vicarious responsibility for wrongdoing of a wholly different kind. To do so would seriously undermine the statutory scheme of the Discrimination Acts and flout the purposes which they were passed to achieve.

The tribunals are free, and are indeed bound, to interpret the ordinary, and readily under-standable, words "in the course of employment" in the sense in which every layman would understand them. This is not to say that when it comes to applying them to the infinite variety of circumstance which is liable to occur in particular instances – within or without the work-place, in or out of uniform, in or out of rest-breaks – all laymen would necessarily agree as to the result. That is what makes their application so well suited to decision by an industrial jury. The application of the phrase will be a question of fact for each employment tribunal to resolve, in the light of the circumstances presented to it, with a mind unclouded by any parallels sought to be drawn from the law of vicarious liability in tort.

I, too, would allow the appeal and restore the order of the employment tribunal.'

(McCowan LJ delivered a concurring judgment and Potter LJ agreed.)

Comment

(1) A high standard of vicarious liability is considered necessary, since it would be too easy otherwise for employers to deny responsibility for discriminatory practices in the workplace. The Court of Appeal's rejection of the common law concept of vicarious liability in this case was vitally important in maintaining this. While Waite LJ's decision focuses particularly on harassment, the principles apply to all forms of discrimination.

(2) Note that under RRA s 32(3) and the corresponding provisions in the other equal-ity enactments, an employer has a defence if it has taken all reasonably practicable steps to prevent discrimination taking place. The best way that employers can protect them-selves from discrimination claims is to have an effective equal opportunities policy, properly promulgated among the workforce – see *Balgobin* v *Tower Hamlets LBC* (1987); *Canniffe* v *East Riding of Yorkshire Council* (2000).

(3) Where the employer is held liable for the acts of employees, those employees can also be sued under the legislation. However, if the acts are not in the course of employ-ment, there is no way of suing the employees under the discrimination legislation, although there may be alternative claims. In *Jones* v *Tower Boot*, for example, the per-petrators could have been liable for a number of torts and crimes on the facts.

(4) Can the employer ever be held responsible for the actions of third parties who commit acts of discrimination against employees (eg, customers of the employer)? Following the EAT's decision in *Burton v De Vere Hotels* (1996), it was thought that they could. The law changed when the issue went to the House of Lords.

Pearce v *Governing Body of Mayfield Secondary School*
[2003] IRLR 512 House of Lords

The claimant was a lesbian teacher who was hounded out of her job by the homophobic abuse she received from pupils at the school. She eventually had to take early retirement on grounds of stress. She claimed that this was sex discrimination, because of the gender-specific nature of much of the name-calling, and also that the school was responsible for the actions of the pupils. The House of Lords unanimously held that this was not sex discrimination, but nonetheless went on to consider the issue of the school's liability for the actions of non-employees.

LORD NICHOLLS: '... This issue concerns an additional hurdle Ms Pearce would have to cross if her claim were to be successful. Her claim is against the school as her employer. But the campaign of abuse mounted against her was a campaign by pupils of the school, not by members of the school staff. So Ms Pearce is not assisted by s 41(1) of the Sex Discrimination Act. This provides that, subject to the defence set out in s 41(3), acts done by an employee in the course of his employment are to be treated as done also by his employer. Nor were the pupils acting as agents of the school, so as to give rise to liability under s 41(2).

Mr Emmerson QC [counsel for the employee] sought, nevertheless, to fix the school with liability. The school, he submitted, could and should have taken steps to shield Ms Pearce. Its failure to do so constituted sex discrimination. Reliance was placed on the decision of the Employment Appeal Tribunal in *Burton v De Vere Hotels Ltd* (1996). In the present case the employment tribunal accepted this submission.

This submission, although not calling for decision, raises a point of some general importance. In *Burton v De Vere Hotels Ltd* two black waitresses, clearing tables in the banqueting hall of a hotel, were the butt of racist and sexist jibes made by a guest speaker entertaining the assembled all-male company at a private dinner party. The Employment Appeal Tribunal held that the employer of the waitresses had racially discriminated against the waitresses. Had the assistant managers in charge for the evening been properly instructed, the two young women would not have suffered embarrassment. They could, and should, have been withdrawn from the room.

This is not a satisfactory decision. Lindsay J, sitting as the President of the Employment Appeal Tribunal, has said the decision may be "vulnerable": see *Hussain v HM Prison Service* (2002). Viewed in the broadest terms, the *Burton* decision has much to commend it. There is, surely, everything to be said in favour of a conclusion which requires employers to take reasonable steps to protect employees from racial or sexual abuse by third parties. But is a failure to do so "discrimination" by the employer? Where the *Burton* decision is, indeed, vulnerable is that it treats an employer's inadvertent failure to take such steps as discrimination even though the failure had nothing to do with the sex or race of the employees. In this crucially important respect the decision gives insufficient heed to the statutory discrimination provisions. An essential element of "direct" sex discrimination by an employer is that, on the grounds of sex, the employer treats the employee less favourably than he treats or would treat an employee of the opposite sex. Similarly with "direct" racial discrimination: the "less favourable treatment" comparison is an essential ingredient of the statutory wrong: see s 1(1)(a) of the Race Relations Act 1976. Unless the employer's conduct satisfies this "less favourable treatment" test, the employer is not guilty of direct sex or racial discrimination. In making this comparison acts of persons for whose conduct an employer is vicariously responsible are to be attributed to the employer. It is otherwise in respect of acts of third parties for whose conduct the employer is not vicariously liable.

With this in mind, the reasoning in the *Burton* decision is unsatisfactory in two important respects. First, the tribunal proceeded on the basis that harassment which is race specific in form is itself less favourable treatment on racial grounds. In the case of racial harassment of a black person there is no need to show that a white person would have been treated differently. Counsel's concession on this point was based on an apparently widespread misinterpretation of the decision in *Strathclyde Regional Council* v *Porcelli* (1986). This is a point I have already discussed.

Secondly, the harassment in *Burton* was committed by third parties for whose conduct the employer was not vicariously responsible. Despite this, the tribunal seems to have proceeded on the basis that the racial harassment of the waitresses by the speaker and some of the guests constituted discrimination on the part of the employer, and that the only issue left outstanding on the appeal, if the discrimination claim were to succeed, was whether the employers had by active or passive conduct subjected the waitresses to racial harassment by the speaker and the offending guests. This cannot be right. In order to succeed the two Caribbean waitresses had to prove discrimination by their employer.

On the sole outstanding issue before the tribunal Smith J said:

"The employment tribunal should ask themselves whether the event in question was something which was sufficiently under the control of the employer that he could, *by the application of good employment practice*, have prevented the harassment or reduced the extent of it. If such is their finding, then the employer has subjected the employee to the harassment" [emphasis added].

This decision, I have to say, seems to have proceeded on altogether the wrong footing. "Subjecting" an employee to "detriment" is one of the circumstances in which it is unlawful for an employer to "discriminate" against an employee: s 4(2)(c) of the Race Relations Act 1976. Thus s 4(2)(c) is not satisfied unless the conduct constituted "discrimination". To constitute "discrimination" the definitions in ss 1 or 2 of the Act must be met.

(Lords Hope, Hobhouse, Scott and Rodger delivered concurring opinions.)

Comment

(1) The House of Lords' decision on employers' liability for the acts of third parties was strictly *obiter*, but it was clear that *Burton* v *De Vere Hotels* could no longer be regarded as good law. Thus the possibility of holding an employer directly liable for a failure to protect employees from discriminatory behaviour by third parties was closed off.

(2) This issue was also canvassed in *EOC* v *Secretary of State for Trade and Industry* (2007), although ultimately the EOC conceded that the directive did not stipulate that employers should be liable for the acts of third parties. Burton J nonetheless expressed the view that employers should be liable in these circumstances – and this was accepted by the Government. The Sex Discrimination Act 1975 (Amendment) Regulations 2008 introduced the following new provisions into the SDA.

Sex Discrimination Act 1975

6 (2A) It is unlawful for an employer, in relation to employment by him at an establishment in Great Britain, to subject to harassment –
    (a)   a woman whom he employs, or
    (b)   a woman who has applied to him for employment.

(2B)   For the purposes of subsection (2A), the circumstances in which an employer is to be treated as subjecting a woman to harassment shall include those where –

(a)   a third party subjects the woman to harassment in the course of her employment, and

(b)   the employer has failed to take such steps as would have been reasonably practicable to prevent the third party from doing so.

(2C)   Subsection (2B) does not apply unless the employer knows that the woman has been subject to harassment in the course of her employment on at least two other occasions by a third party.

(2D)   In subsections (2B) and (2C), 'third party' means a person other than –

(a)   the employer, or

(b)   a person whom the employer employs,

and for the purposes of those subsections it is immaterial whether the third party is the same or a different person on each occasion.

Comment

(1) The employer's liability in these circumstances is limited by reference to the concept of reasonable practicability. No doubt it will be easier to make the employer liable in situations like *Burton* v *De Vere* and *Pearce* v *Mayfield School* where the employer has a high degree of control over the work surroundings. It might be harder where the employee's job is performed elsewhere than on the employer's premises: bus drivers and traffic wardens, for example.

(2) Devising and implementing an equal opportunities policy may not be sufficient to discharge the employer's duty to take reasonably practicable steps to prevent harassment (as it usually does for the purposes of RRA s 32(2), above, p 90, and the equivalent provisions in the other equality enactments). Employers will no doubt need to post notices, or make it clear by other means, to customers and other third parties that harassment will not be tolerated – backed up with effective action.

(3) Note that SDA s 6(2C) makes it very important that employees should report all third party acts of harassment as soon as possible and ensure that the information is recorded, since the legislation adopts a 'three strikes and you're out' approach to the employer's knowledge.

Positive action and positive discrimination

The terms 'positive action' and 'positive discrimination' are often used as if they are interchangeable. However, it is helpful, and more accurate, to distinguish between them. In this book, 'positive discrimination' is used for the situation where one candidate is preferred over another, better-qualified candidate, because of the first candidate's membership of a disadvantaged group. This is usually unlawful in UK law. The term 'positive action' is used for measures taken to promote employment opportunities for members of disadvantaged groups or where one group is under-represented compared with others in a particular area of employment. This is generally lawful.

Sex Discrimination Act 1975

48   (1)   Nothing in Parts II to IV shall render unlawful any act done by an employer in relation to particular work in his employment, being an act done in, or in connection with –

97

(a) affording his female employees only, or his male employees only, access to facilities for training which would help to fit them for that work, or

(b) encouraging women only, or men only, to take advantage of opportunities for doing that work,

where at any time within the twelve months immediately preceding the doing of the act there were no persons of the sex in question among those doing that work or the number of persons of that sex doing the work was comparatively small.

(2) Nothing in section 12 shall render unlawful any act done by an organisation to which that section applies in, or in connection with –

(a) affording female members of the organisation only, or male members of the organisation only, access to facilities for training which would help to fit them for holding a post of any kind in the organisation, or

(b) encouraging female members only, or male members only, to take advantage of opportunities for holding such posts in the organisation,

where at any time within the twelve months immediately preceding the doing of the act there were no persons of the sex in question among persons holding such posts in the organisation or the number of persons of that sex holding such posts was comparatively small . . .

Comment

(1) SDA s 47 contains a parallel exception for training bodies and equivalent provisions are to be found in the other equality enactments. Note that they allow preference to be given only in relation to training places – not in relation to appointment or promotion to jobs. The idea is to assist members of under-represented groups to get into a position where they may be the best person for the job – but not to give them preference for a job on grounds of their group membership.

(2) This is an illustration of the symmetrical approach of British discrimination law. Note that positive action is allowed in relation to disability (below, p 109). Direct discrimination is also allowed on grounds of age, as long as it is a proportionate means of achieving a legitimate aim (Age Regs reg 3(1)); whether this would permit positive discrimination has yet to be seen.

(3) Positive discrimination is permitted to a much greater extent by EU law.

Treaty of Rome

ARTICLE 141

4   With a view to ensuring full equality in practice between men and women in working life, the principle of equal treatment shall not prevent any Member State from maintaining or adopting measures providing for specific advantages in order to make it easier for the under-represented sex to pursue a vocational activity or to prevent or compensate for disadvantages in professional careers.

Comment

(1) Until amendment by the Equal Treatment Amendment Directive (2002/73/EC), which came into force in 2005, the Equal Treatment Directive (76/207/EEC) stated that: 'This Directive shall be without prejudice to measures to promote equal opportunity for men and women, in particular by removing existing inequalities which affect women's opportunities in the areas referred to in Article 1(1).' It was thought that Art 141(4) of the Treaty of Rome, added by the Treaty of Amsterdam and in force from

1 May 1999, permitted a greater degree of positive discrimination. However, this seems doubtful in the light of the next case.

Abrahamsson v *Fogelqvist* [2000] IRLR 732 European Court of Justice

The issue was whether it was lawful to appoint a woman to a university professorship in preference to a better-qualified man in pursuance of a statutory regulation on universities designed to promote equality between men and women. The regulation provided that where one sex was under-represented, a candidate belonging to the under-represented sex who possessed sufficient qualifications for the post had to be chosen in preference to a better-qualified candidate of the opposite sex. This was subject to a proviso that 'Positive discrimination must, however, not be applied where the difference between the candidates' qualifications is so great that such application would give rise to a breach of the requirement of objectivity in the making of appointments'.

JUDGMENT OF THE COURT: '. . . It is to be noted at the outset that, by its questions, the national court seeks to ascertain whether Article 2(1) and (4) of the Equal Treatment Directive [NB all references in this judgment are to the Directive before amendment] preclude national legislation, such as the Swedish legislation at issue in the main proceedings, which provides, in the sector of higher education, for positive discrimination in recruitment in favour of candidates of the underrepresented sex.

Interpretation of Article 141(4) EC, which concerns measures of that kind, would not assist in determining the main proceedings unless the Court were to consider that Article 2 of the Directive precludes national legislation of the kind there at issue.

Next, Article 1(1) of the Directive is intended to put into effect in the Member States the principle of equal treatment for men and women as regards, in particular, access to employment, including promotion, and to vocational training. Under Article 2(1) of the Directive, that principle implies that all discrimination based directly or indirectly on sex must be abolished.

However, by virtue of Article 2(4), the Directive does not preclude measures to promote equal opportunity for men and women, in particular by removing existing inequalities which affect women's opportunities in the areas referred to in Article 1(1).

Finally, in its judgment in *Badeck and others* the Court held that a measure which is intended to give priority in promotion to women in sectors of the public service where they are under-represented must be regarded as compatible with Community law

- where it does not automatically and unconditionally give priority to women when women and men are equally qualified, and
- where the candidatures are the subject of an objective assessment which takes account of the specific personal situations of all candidates.

THE FIRST QUESTION

The issue raised by the first question is whether Article 2(1) and (4) precludes national legislation, such as the Swedish legislation at issue in the main proceedings, under which a candidate for a public post who belongs to the underrepresented sex and possesses sufficient qualifications for that post must be chosen in preference to a candidate of the opposite sex who would otherwise have been appointed, where this is necessary to secure the appointment of a candidate of the underrepresented sex and the difference between the respective merits of the candidates is not so great as to give rise to a breach of the requirement of objectivity in making appointments.

In contrast to the national legislation on positive discrimination examined by the Court in its *Kalanke* (1995), *Marschall* (1998) and *Badeck* (2000) judgments, the national legislation at issue in the main proceedings enables preference to be given to a candidate of the underrepresented sex who, although sufficiently qualified, does not possess qualifications equal to those of other candidates of the opposite sex.

As a rule, a procedure for the selection of candidates for a post involves assessment of their qualifications by reference to the requirements of the vacant post or of the duties to be performed.

In *Badeck*, cited above, the Court held that it is legitimate for the purposes of that assessment for certain positive and negative criteria to be taken into account which, although formulated in terms which are neutral as regards sex and thus capable of benefiting men too, in general favour women. Thus, it may be decided that seniority, age and the date of last promotion are to be taken into account only in so far as they are of importance for the suitability, qualifications and professional capability of candidates. Similarly, it may be prescribed that the family status or income of the partner is immaterial and that part-time work, leave and delays in completing training as a result of looking after children or dependants in need of care must not have a negative effect.

The clear aim of such criteria is to achieve substantive, rather than formal, equality by reducing de facto inequalities which may arise in society and, thus, in accordance with Article 141(4) EC, to prevent or compensate for disadvantages in the professional career of persons belonging to the underrepresented sex.

It is important to emphasise in that connection that the application of criteria such as those mentioned above must be transparent and amenable to review in order to obviate any arbitrary assessment of the qualifications of candidates.

As regards the selection procedure at issue in the main proceedings, it does not appear from the relevant Swedish legislation that assessment of the qualifications of candidates by reference to the requirements of the vacant post is based on clear and unambiguous criteria such as to prevent or compensate for disadvantages in the professional career of members of the underrepresented sex.

On the contrary, under that legislation, a candidate for a public post belonging to the underrepresented sex and possessing sufficient qualifications for that post must be chosen in preference to a candidate of the opposite sex who would otherwise have been appointed, where that measure is necessary for a candidate belonging to the underrepresented sex to be appointed.

It follows that the legislation at issue in the main proceedings automatically grants preference to candidates belonging to the underrepresented sex, provided that they are sufficiently qualified, subject only to the proviso that the difference between the merits of the candidates of each sex is not so great as to result in a breach of the requirement of objectivity in making appointments.

The scope and effect of that condition cannot be precisely determined, with the result that the selection of a candidate from among those who are sufficiently qualified is ultimately based on the mere fact of belonging to the underrepresented sex, and that this is so even if the merits of the candidate so selected are inferior to those of a candidate of the opposite sex. Moreover, candidatures are not subjected to an objective assessment taking account of the specific personal situations of all the candidates. It follows that such a method of selection is not such as to be permitted by Article 2(4) of the Directive.

In those circumstances, it is necessary to determine whether legislation such as that at issue in the main proceedings is justified by Article 141(4) EC.

In that connection, it is enough to point out that, even though Article 141(4) EC allows the Member States to maintain or adopt measures providing for special advantages intended to prevent or compensate for disadvantages in professional careers in order to ensure full equality between men and women in professional life, it cannot be inferred from this that it allows a selection method of the kind at issue in the main proceedings which appears, on any view, to be disproportionate to the aim pursued.

100

The answer to the first question must therefore be that Article 2(1) and (4) of the Directive and Article 141(4) EC preclude national legislation under which a candidate for a public post who belongs to the underrepresented sex and possesses sufficient qualifications for that post must be chosen in preference to a candidate of the opposite sex who would otherwise have been appointed, where this is necessary to secure the appointment of a candidate of the underrepresented sex and the difference between the respective merits of the candidates is not so great as to give rise to a breach of the requirement of objectivity in making appointments.

THE SECOND QUESTION

By its second question, the national court seeks to ascertain whether Article 2(1) and (4) of the Directive also precludes such national legislation where the latter applies only to procedures for the filling of a predetermined number of posts or to posts created as part of a specific programme of a particular higher educational institution allowing the application of positive discrimination measures.

As to that, the mere fact of restricting the scope of a positive discrimination measure of the kind in point here is not capable of changing its absolute and disproportionate nature.

The answer to the second question must therefore be that Article 2(1) and (4) of the Directive and Article 141(4) EC also preclude national legislation of that kind where it applies only to procedures for filling a predetermined number of posts or to posts created as part of a specific programme of a particular higher educational institution allowing the application of positive discrimination measures.

THE THIRD QUESTION

By its third question, the national court seeks to ascertain whether Article 2(1) and (4) of the Directive preclude a rule of national case law under which a candidate belonging to the underrepresented sex may be granted preference over a competitor of the opposite sex provided that the candidates possess equivalent or substantially equivalent merits.

On that point, it is enough to say that, as indicated above, such a rule must be regarded as compatible with Community law where the candidatures are subjected to an objective assessment which takes account of the specific personal situations of all the candidates.

The answer to the third question must therefore be that Article 2(1) and (4) of the Directive does not preclude a rule of national case law under which a candidate belonging to the underrepresented sex may be granted preference over a competitor of the opposite sex, provided that the candidates possess equivalent or substantially equivalent merits, where the candidatures are subjected to an objective assessment which takes account of the specific personal situations of all the candidates.

THE FOURTH QUESTION

By its fourth question, the national court seeks to ascertain whether the answer to the first, second and third questions would differ according to whether the national legislation concerns the selection of candidates for posts of a lower level or posts of a higher level.

As to that, Community law does not in any way make application of the principle of equal treatment for men and women concerning access to employment conditional upon the level of the posts to be filled.

The answer to the fourth question must therefore be that the question whether national rules providing for positive discrimination in the making of appointments in higher education are lawful cannot depend on the level of the post to be filled . . .'

Comment

(1) The tenor of the judgment suggests that Art 141(4) is unlikely to be seen as adding much to the previous position. Note that since amendment of the Equal Treatment Directive (76/207/EEC) in 2002, the provision in relation to positive discrimination is now to be found in Art 2(8), which now simply says that: 'Member States may maintain or adopt measures within the meaning of Article 141(4) of the Treaty with a view to ensuring full equality in practice between men and women.'

(2) The position in EU law appears to be that any law giving automatic preference to women over men will not be allowed (*Kalanke* v *Freie Hansestadt Bremen* (1995), *Abrahamsson*), but that rules which provide for a preference but (a) weigh all the circumstances relevant to the candidates, and (b) allow for flexibility so that men are not excluded in all circumstances are permissible (*Marschall* v *Land Nordrhein-Westfalen* (1998), *Badeck* (2000), *Lommers* v *Minister van Landbouw, Natuurbeheer en Visserij* (2002)).

(3) Article 5 of the Race Directive (2000/43/EC) states:

> With a view to ensuring full equality in practice, the principle of equal treatment shall not prevent any Member State from maintaining or adopting specific measures to prevent or compensate for disadvantages linked to racial or ethnic origin.

Article 7(1) of the Framework Employment Directive (2000/78/EC) makes similar provision in relation to religion or belief, sexual orientation and age.

(4) There is no indication that the United Kingdom is likely to avail itself of the opportunity to permit some measure of positive discrimination.

REMEDIES

Sex Discrimination Act 1975

65 (1) Where an employment tribunal finds that a complaint presented to it under section 63 is well-founded the tribunal shall make such of the following as it considers just and equitable –

   (a) an order declaring the rights of the complainant and the respondent in relation to the act to which the complaint relates;

   (b) an order requiring the respondent to pay to the complainant compensation of an amount corresponding to any damages he could have been ordered by a county court or by a sheriff court to pay to the complainant if the complaint had fallen to be dealt with under section 66;

   (c) a recommendation that the respondent take within a specified period action appearing to the tribunal to be practicable for the purpose of obviating or reducing the adverse effect on the complainant of any act of discrimination to which the complaint relates . . .

Comment

(1) There are parallel provisions in the other equality enactments: RRA s 56, RB Regs reg 30, SO Regs reg 30 and Age Regs reg 38.

Compensation

Marshall v Southampton and South West Hants AHA (No 2)
[1993] IRLR 445 European Court of Justice

In the first *Marshall* case, the ECJ held that it was a breach of the Equal Treatment Directive (76/207/EEC) to force Ms Marshall to retire at 60 while men could continue to work until they were 65. At that time the maximum compensation for discrimination was the same as the maximum compensatory award for unfair dismissal: £6,250. An employment tribunal awarded her a sum larger than the statutory limit and included interest on the award, on the basis that this was required by Art 6 of the Equal Treatment Directive. At that time, Art 6 stated:

> 'Member States shall introduce . . . such measures as are necessary to enable all persons who consider themselves wronged by failure to apply to them the principle of equal treatment . . . to pursue their claims by judicial process . . .'

The House of Lords referred the issue to the ECJ.

JUDGMENT OF THE COURT: '. . . Article 6 of the Directive puts Member States under a duty to take the necessary measures to enable all persons who consider themselves wronged by discrimination to pursue their claims by judicial process. Such obligation implies that the measures in question should be sufficiently effective to achieve the objective of the Directive and should be capable of being effectively relied upon by the persons concerned before national courts . . . In the event of discriminatory dismissal contrary to Article 5(1) of the Directive, a situation of equality could not be restored without either reinstating the victim of discrimination or, in the alternative, granting financial compensation for the loss and damage sustained.

Where financial compensation is the measure adopted in order to achieve the objective indicated above, it must be adequate, in that it must enable the loss and damage actually sustained as a result of the discriminatory dismissal to be made good in full in accordance with the applicable national rules.

The first and second questions

In its first question, the House of Lords seeks to establish whether it is contrary to Article 6 of the Directive for national provisions to lay down an upper limit on the amount of compensation recoverable by a victim of discrimination.

In its second question, the House of Lords asks whether Article 6 requires (a) that the compensation for the damage sustained as a result of the illegal discrimination should be full and (b) that it should include an award of interest on the principal amount from the date of the unlawful discrimination to the date when compensation is paid.

The Court's interpretation of Article 6 as set out above provides a direct reply to the first part of the second question relating to the level of compensation required by that provision.

It also follows from that interpretation that the fixing of an upper limit of the kind at issue in the main proceedings cannot, by definition, constitute proper implementation of Article 6 of the Directive, since it limits the amount of compensation a priori to a level which is not necessarily consistent with the requirement of ensuring real equality of opportunity through adequate reparation for the loss and damage sustained as a result of discriminatory dismissal.

With regard to the second part of the second question relating to the award of interest, suffice it to say that full compensation for the loss and damage sustained as a result of discriminatory dismissal cannot leave out of account factors, such as the effluxion of time, which may in fact reduce its value. The award of interest, in accordance with the applicable national rules, must therefore be regarded as an essential component of compensation for the purposes of restoring real equality of treatment.

Accordingly, the reply to be given to the first and second questions is that the interpretation of Article 6 of the Directive must be that reparation of the loss and damage sustained by a person injured as a result of discriminatory dismissal may not be limited to an upper limit fixed a priori or by excluding an award of interest to compensate for the loss sustained by the recipient of the compensation as a result of the effluxion of time until the capital sum awarded is actually paid.

The third question

In its third question, the House of Lords seeks to establish whether a person who has been injured as a result of discriminatory dismissal may rely, as against an authority of the State acting in its capacity as employer, on Article 6 of the Directive in order to contest the application of national rules which impose limits on the amount of compensation recoverable by way of reparation.

It follows from the considerations set out above as to the meaning and scope of Article 6 of the Directive, that that provision is an essential factor for attaining the fundamental objective of equal treatment for men and women, in particular as regards working conditions, including the conditions governing dismissal, referred to in Article 5(1) of the Directive, and that, where, in the event of discriminatory dismissal, financial compensation is the measure adopted in order to restore that equality, such compensation must be full and may not be limited a priori in terms of its amount.

Accordingly, the combined provisions of Article 6 and Article 5 of the Directive give rise, on the part of a person who has been injured as a result of discriminatory dismissal, to rights which that person must be able to rely upon before the national courts as against the State and authorities which are an emanation of the State . . .'

Comment

(1) As a result of this case the limit on compensation for both sex and race discrimination was lifted and provision was made for interest on awards. The same has always applied in relation to the other protected grounds.

(2) Discrimination is treated as a statutory tort and so damages are awarded on the same principles as for other torts, with the aim of putting the claimant in the position in which she would have been but for the unlawful conduct (*Ministry of Defence* v *Wheeler* (1998)). In *Essa* v *Laing* (2004) the Court of Appeal held that all loss flowing directly from a discriminatory act was recoverable, regardless of whether it was foreseeable.

(3) The equality enactments specifically provide that compensation can be awarded for injury to feelings caused by discriminatory acts.

Vento v *Chief Constable of West Yorkshire* [2003] IRLR 102 Court of Appeal

The claimant, a former probationary police officer, was awarded £257,844 for sex discrimination, including £65,000 for injury to feelings (including £15,000 aggravated damages) and £9,000 for psychiatric damage. The judgment of the court (Mummery, Ward and Jonathan Parker LJJ) was given by Mummery LJ.

MUMMERY LJ: '. . . This is the first time for many years that the Court of Appeal has had the opportunity to consider the appropriate level of compensation for injury to feelings in discrimination cases. Some decisions in the employment tribunal and in the Appeal Tribunal have resulted in awards of substantial sums for injury to feelings, sometimes supplemented by compensation for psychiatric damage and aggravated damages. Cases were cited to the court in which employment tribunals had, as in this case, awarded compensation for injury to feelings (plus aggravated damages) larger than the damages separately awarded for psychiatric injury, and totalling well in excess of £20,000. The court was shown the decision of an employment tribunal in a race discrimination case awarding the sum of £100,000 for injury to feelings, plus aggravated damages of £25,000: *Virdi* v *Commissioner of Police of the Metropolis* (2007). (This pales into insignificance in comparison with the reported award in 1994 by a Californian jury of $7.1m to a legal secretary for sexual harassment, and even with the subsequent halving of that sum on appeal.)

Compensation of the magnitude of £125,000 for non-pecuniary damage creates concern as to whether some recent tribunal awards in discrimination cases are in line with general levels of compensation recovered in other cases of non-pecuniary loss, such as general damages for personal injuries, malicious prosecution and defamation. In the interests of justice (social and individual), and of predictability of outcome and consistency of treatment of like cases (an important ingredient of justice) this court should indicate to employment tribunals and practitioners general guidance on the proper level of award for injury to feelings and other forms of non-pecuniary damage . . .

It is self-evident that the assessment of compensation for an injury or loss, which is neither physical nor financial, presents special problems for the judicial process, which aims to produce results objectively justified by evidence, reason and precedent. Subjective feelings of upset, frustration, worry, anxiety, mental distress, fear, grief, anguish, humiliation, unhappiness, stress, depression and so on and the degree of their intensity are incapable of objective proof or of measurement in monetary terms . . .

Although they are incapable of objective proof or measurement in monetary terms, hurt feelings are none the less real in human terms. The courts and tribunals have to do the best they can on the available material to make a sensible assessment, accepting that it is impossible to justify or explain a particular sum with the same kind of solid evidential foundation and persuasive practical reasoning available in the calculation of financial loss or compensation for bodily injury. In these circumstances an appellate body is not entitled to interfere with the assessment of the employment tribunal simply because it would have awarded more or less than the tribunal has done. It has to be established that the tribunal has acted on a wrong principle of law or has misapprehended the facts or made a wholly erroneous estimate of the loss suffered. Striking the right balance between awarding too much and too little is obviously not easy . . .

In *HM Prison Service* v *Johnson*, Smith J reviewed the authorities on compensation for non-pecuniary loss and made a valuable summary of the general principles gathered from them. We would gratefully adopt that summary. Employment tribunals should have it in mind when carrying out this challenging exercise. In her judgment on behalf of the Appeal Tribunal, Smith J said:

"(i)   Awards for injury to feelings are compensatory. They should be just to both parties. They should compensate fully without punishing the tortfeasor. Feelings of indignation at the tortfeasor's conduct should not be allowed to inflate the award.

(ii)   Awards should not be too low, as that would diminish respect for the policy of the anti-discrimination legislation. Society has condemned discrimination and awards must ensure that it is seen to be wrong. On the other hand, awards should be restrained, as excessive awards could, to use the phrase of Sir Thomas Bingham MR, be seen as the way to 'untaxed riches'.

(iii) Awards should bear some broad general similarity to the range of awards in personal injury cases. We do not think that this should be done by reference to any particular type of personal injury award, rather to the whole range of such awards.

(iv)   In exercising their discretion in assessing a sum, tribunals should remind themselves of the value in everyday life of the sum they have in mind. This may be done by reference to purchasing power or by reference to earnings.

(v)   Finally, tribunals should bear in mind Sir Thomas Bingham's reference to the need for public respect for the level of awards made." . . .

At the end of the day this court must first ask itself whether the award by the employment tribunal in this case was so excessive as to constitute an error of law. That was the conclusion of the Appeal Tribunal and it is clearly right. The totality of the award for non-pecuniary loss is seriously out of line with the majority of those made and approved on appeal in reported Employment Appeal Tribunal cases. It is also seriously out of line with the guidelines compiled for the Judicial Studies Board and with the cases reported in the personal injury field where general damages have been awarded for pain, suffering, disability and loss of amenity. The total award of £74,000 for non-pecuniary loss is, for example, in excess of the JSB Guidelines for the award of general damages for moderate brain damage, involving epilepsy, for severe post-traumatic stress disorder having permanent effects and badly affecting all aspects of the life of the injured person, for loss of sight in one eye, with reduced vision in the remaining eye, and for total deafness and loss of speech. No reasonable person would think that that excess was a sensible result. The patent extravagance of the global sum is unjustifiable as an award of compensation. It is probably explicable by the understandable strength of feeling in the tribunal and as an expression of its condemnation of, and punishment for, the discriminatory treatment of Ms Vento . . .

Guidance

Employment tribunals and those who practise in them might find it helpful if this court were to identify three broad bands of compensation for injury to feelings, as distinct from compensation for psychiatric or similar personal injury.

(i)   The top band should normally be between £15,000 and £25,000. Sums in this range should be awarded in the most serious cases, such as where there has been a lengthy campaign of discriminatory harassment on the ground of sex or race. This case falls within that band. Only in the most exceptional case should an award of compensation for injury to feelings exceed £25,000.

(ii)   The middle band of between £5,000 and £15,000 should be used for serious cases, which do not merit an award in the highest band.

(iii)   Awards of between £500 and £5,000 are appropriate for less serious cases, such as where the act of discrimination is an isolated or one-off occurrence. In general, awards of less than £500 are to be avoided altogether, as they risk being regarded as so low as not to be a proper recognition of injury to feelings.

There is, of course, within each band considerable flexibility, allowing tribunals to fix what is considered to be fair, reasonable and just compensation in the particular circumstances of the case.

The decision whether or not to award aggravated damages and, if so, in what amount must depend on the particular circumstances of the discrimination and on the way in which the complaint of discrimination has been handled.

Common sense requires that regard should also be had to the overall magnitude of the sum total of the awards of compensation for non-pecuniary loss made under the various headings of injury to feelings, psychiatric damage and aggravated damage. In particular, double recovery should be avoided by taking appropriate account of the overlap between the individual heads of damage. The extent of overlap will depend on the facts of each particular case.

Result

For these reasons, we allow the appeal and the cross-appeal against the decision of the Employment Appeal Tribunal, restore the figure for financial loss, substitute for the decision of the employment tribunal the sum of £18,000 for injury to feelings, plus £5,000 for aggravated damages, and leave the damages for psychiatric injury at £9,000.'

Comment

(1) This decision was in 2003. Those using it for guidance should seek an appropriate inflationary uplift on these figures.

Recommendations

A recommendation can be made in addition to a declaration and an award of compensation. However, the power of tribunals to make recommendations has been interpreted fairly strictly.

North West Thames RHA v *Noone* [1988] ICR 813 Court of Appeal

The claimant was a Sri Lankan doctor who had worked in England, specialising in pathology, for many years. She applied for a post as a consultant microbiologist with the health authority, but was not appointed. The employment tribunal found that this was on grounds of race. As well as awarding compensation, the employment tribunal wished to make a recommendation to the effect that the next time a vacancy for a consultant microbiologist occurred, it should not be advertised, so that Noone would in all likelihood be the only candidate.

Under statutory regulations applying to the appointments of consultants to positions in the National Health Service, all consultants posts had to be advertised, although the Secretary of State had power to dispense with this requirement.

MAY LJ: '. . . What is sought in this appeal in lieu of the recommendation made by the employment tribunal in November 1985 is in effect a recommendation that the authority should seek the Secretary of State's dispensation from the advertisement requirement when next a vacant consultant microbiologist post arises. In those circumstances, as Mrs Smith put it in the course of her argument before us today, that would mean that the complainant in whose favour we have found discrimination made out, should have an advantage in seeking appointment to the vacant post. Without the advertisement the field would be limited to her and, as was accepted in the course of the argument, to anybody else who, without an advertisement, heard of the vacancy and was minded to apply for it. But without the advertisement one can see that the field of those seeking the vacant post would be smaller than it might have been had the post been advertised. Of course that always proceeds on the premise, first, that the Secretary of State agreed to the request of the local authority to dispense with the advertising requirement . . . If he does not, then nothing happens at all. The position is precisely the same as it would be without any recommendation.

In my judgment, however, the proposed recommendation for which the appellant seeks an order on this appeal is subject to one fundamental objection, in addition to a number of others into which I do not propose to go. The fundamental objection is this, that any such recommendation would set at nought the statutory procedure set out for the benefit of the National Health Service, the various professions concerned in that service, the public and others qualified for the vacant post, for making that particular consultant appointment, and on that ground alone, which is, as I think, fundamental, I for my part would dismiss this appeal insofar as I have indicated it relates to the third type of relief under s 56(1)(c) of the Race Relations Act 1976 . . .'

Comment

(1) This does not amount to saying that a tribunal could never recommend that the next vacancy be offered to the claimant, because there were special rules applicable here. However, in *British Gas* v *Sharma* (1991) the EAT struck down such a recommendation saying that it would be positive discrimination and could amount to direct discrimination against other applicants. Leaving aside the fact that, if the post was not advertised, there would probably be no other applicants, the argument is misconceived, for there is no general requirement that employers should advertise posts. Suppose I employ 20 workers in my factory; as a favour to a friend, I promise her that I will offer the next vacancy to her unemployed child. Would that be contrary to discrimination law? Are anyone else's rights infringed?

(2) The wording of the equality enactments does not seem to preclude a tribunal making a recommendation of this kind, which might seem to many to be the most appropriate kind of compensation for discrimination which has cost someone a post. It is unfortunate that the trend seems to be running against this.

(3) In *Irvine* v *Prestcold Ltd* (1981) a tribunal recommended that the claimant should be promoted to the next vacancy, or alternatively should be paid the difference in salary between the two posts until she was promoted to that or an equivalent post. This was overturned on appeal, both because the recommendation should be limited to a 'specified period' and because any compensation for pecuniary loss should be the subject of a compensation award, not a recommendation.

DISABILITY DISCRIMINATION

The Disability Discrimination Act 1995 came into force in December 1996, replacing the Disabled Persons (Employment) Act 1944 and attempting for the first time to provide comprehensive protection against discrimination for people with disabilities in fields such as education, transport, and the supply of goods and services, as well as employment. Although discrimination on grounds of disability had not traditionally been prohibited by treaties on human rights, it was the denial of civil liberties inherent in the previous position which provided the mainspring for the movement which led to the DDA. It took its inspiration from the campaign in the USA which led to the influential Americans with Disabilities Act 1990.

In 1999 the government set up the Disability Rights Task Force to advise it on reforms to the legislation. In addition, the Framework Employment Directive (2000/78/EC) included disability among the protected grounds and made some reform to the DDA essential. The reforms required to comply with the Directive were carried out by the Disability Discrimination Act 1995 (Amendment) Regulations 2003. Reforms based on the recommendations of the Task Force and the Disability Rights Commission were contained in the Disability Discrimination Act 2005. Both pieces of legislation mainly operate by amending the DDA 1995.

In addition to the principal Act, to understand disability equality law it is also necessary to have recourse to the DRC's Code of Practice on Employment and

Occupation (2004) and the Statutory Guidance on the Definition of Disability (2006) issued by the Secretary of State for Work and Pensions.

Scope

Like the other equality enactments, the DDA applies not only to employees but also to anyone having a contract personally to do any work (DDA s 68). Originally, employers with fewer than 20 workers were exempt from the Act, an exception which was much criticised, since most people with disabilities work for small organisations. The exception was abolished in 2004, along with specific exemptions which formerly applied to the police, barristers, the prison service and the fire service.

Unlike the other equality enactments, the DDA is asymmetrical: it prohibits discrimination against people with disabilities, but does not make it unlawful to give *more* favourable treatment to disabled people. This recognises that this may be necessary to achieve substantive equality.

Definition of disability

Disability Discrimination Act 1995

1 (1) Subject to the provisions of Schedule 1, a person has a disability for the purposes of this Act and Part III of the 2005 Order if he has a physical or mental impairment which has a substantial and long-term adverse effect on his ability to carry out normal day-to-day activities.
(2) In this Act and Part III of the 2005 Order 'disabled person' means a person who has a disability.
2 (1) The provisions of this Part and Parts II to 4 and 5A and Part III of the 2005 Order apply in relation to a person who has had a disability as they apply in relation to a person who has that disability . . .

Comment

(1) Note that the Act covers mental impairments as well as physical impairments. Mental impairments include mental illness and learning disabilities. The previous limitation, that a mental illness had to be 'clinically well-recognised' before it could count as a disability, was removed by DDA 2005. It is clear that depression can constitute a disability, if it is sufficiently severe and long-lasting (eg *Kapadia* v *Lambeth LBC* (2000); see also the Statutory Guidance paras A3–A9).

(2) According to the Statutory Guidance, a 'substantial' effect is one which is more than 'minor' or 'trivial', and factors such as the time taken to do something, or the way in which it is done are among the things to be taken into account in deciding how substantial an effect is (Statutory Guidance paras B1–B21).

(3) In the case of progressive illnesses, the effects may not at first be substantial, or there may be periods of remission. For that reason, DDA Sch 1, para 8 provides that people with these illnesses are to receive the protection of the Act as soon as the illness manifests itself in *any* adverse effect on their normal day-to-day activities, even if it is not at that stage a substantial effect. However, the Disability Rights Task Force noted that people often suffer discrimination from the moment of their diagnosis with a progressive condition, even if it has no effect at all. As a result, Sch 1, para 6A

was added, which states that a person diagnosed with cancer, HIV infection or multiple sclerosis (but not other progressive conditions, such as muscular dystrophy) is deemed to be a disabled person at once.

(4) DDA Sch 1, para 6 provides that where an impairment *would* have a substantial effect were it not for its being treated or corrected, it is to be treated as if it had the effect without the treatment, for the purposes of judging whether a person is disabled. This makes sense: an employer might well discriminate against someone with epilepsy, say, even though it has no effects on the person at all because it is controlled by medication. This is sometimes called a 'deduced effect'.

(5) A 'long-term effect' is defined by DDA Sch 1, para 2 as capable of lasting for 12 months or more, or the rest of the claimant's life, although its severity may vary over time.

(6) 'Normal day-to-day activities' are exhaustively defined by DDA Sch 1, para 4 as involving mobility; manual dexterity; physical co-ordination; continence; ability to lift, carry or move everyday objects; speech, hearing or eyesight; memory or ability to con-centrate, learn or understand; perception of the risk of personal danger. Note that it is enough if the disability has a substantial long-term effect on *one* of these. The concept is extensively discussed, with examples, in section D of the Statutory Guidance.

(7) English law is clear that someone whose disability prevents them from working at their usual occupation but does not interfere with 'normal day-to-day activities' is not a disabled person for the purposes of the DDA. However, in *Chacón Navas* v *Eurest Colectivades SA* (2006) the ECJ defined disability as 'a limitation which results in par-ticular from physical, mental or psychological impairments and which hinders the participation of the person concerned in professional life'. This has the potential to be both wider than, and narrower than, the English definition.

(8) Note that the effect of DDA s 2 is that a person with a past disability will be treated as a disabled person. This is because employers are apt to discriminate against people with a history of disabling conditions, even if they no longer suffer from them.

(9) The Disability Discrimination (Meaning of Disability) Regulations 1996 refine the definition further.

Disability Discrimination (Meaning of Disability) Regulations 1996

3 (1) Subject to paragraph (2) below, addiction to alcohol, nicotine or any other substance is to be treated as not amounting to an impairment for the purposes of the Act.

(2) Paragraph (1) above does not apply to addiction which was originally the result of administration of medically prescribed drugs or other medical treatment.

4 (1) For the purposes of the Act the following conditions are to be treated as not amount-ing to impairments –

(a) a tendency to set fires,

(b) a tendency to steal,

(c) a tendency to physical or sexual abuse of other persons,

(d) exhibitionism, and

(e) voyeurism.

(2) Subject to paragraph (3) below for the purposes of the Act the condition known as seasonal allergic rhinitis shall be treated as not amounting to an impairment.

(3) Paragraph (2) above shall not prevent that condition from being taken into account for the purposes of the Act where it aggravates the effect of another condition.

5   For the purposes of paragraph 3 of Schedule 1 to the Act a severe disfigurement is not to be treated as having a substantial adverse effect on the ability of the person concerned to carry out normal day-to-day activities if it consists of –
(a)   a tattoo (which has not been removed), or
(b)   a piercing of the body for decorative or other non-medical purposes, including any object attached through the piercing for such purposes.

Meaning of discrimination

The DDA used to cover two main forms of discrimination only: less favourable treatment for a reason related to disability, and failure to comply with a duty to make reasonable adjustments. An employer had a potential defence of justification in relation to both. This had to be changed as a result of the Framework Employment Directive (2000/78/EC), principally to introduce a concept of direct discrimination for which no defence would be possible. With harassment and victimisation, which have always been unlawful under the DDA, there are now five forms of unlawful disability discrimination.

Direct discrimination

Disability Discrimination Act 1995

3A   (5)   A person directly discriminates against a disabled person if, on the ground of the disabled person's disability, he treats the disabled person less favourably than he treats or would treat a person not having that particular disability whose relevant circumstances, including his abilities, are the same as, or not materially different from, those of the disabled person.

Comment

(1) The former concept of less favourable treatment because of disability has now been split into the separate concepts of direct discrimination and disability-related discrimination. For direct discrimination, the disability must be an effective cause (although not necessarily the only cause) of the less favourable treatment. Once again, the way the comparison is to be carried out is critical. To use an example from the DRC *Code of Practice on Employment and Occupation*, if an employee's disability causes him to be off work for six months and he is dismissed as a result, the comparison should be with another employee requiring the same amount of leave, but not because of that disability. If the employer would dismiss anyone who was away for six months, that is not direct discrimination on grounds of disability (although it may be disability-related discrimination: see below).

(2) In reality, the most likely situation where direct discrimination on grounds of disability is likely to occur is where an employer makes stereotypical assumptions about the capabilities of a disabled person – for example, assuming that someone with a history of mental illness cannot be appointed to a highly responsible job. Such an assumption would not be made about someone without that disability, and so it would constitute direct discrimination.

(3) Note that there is no defence to direct discrimination: DDA s 3A(4).

Disability-related discrimination

Disability Discrimination Act

3A (1) For the purposes of this Part, a person discriminates against a disabled person if –
   (a) for a reason which relates to the disabled person's disability, he treats him less favourably than he treats or would treat others to whom that reason does not or would not apply, and
   (b) he cannot show that the treatment in question is justified . . .
(3) Treatment is justified for the purposes of subsection (1)(b) if, but only if, the reason for it is both material to the circumstances of the particular case and substantial . . .

Comment

(1) It is enough for disability-related discrimination if the less favourable treatment is for some reason related to the disability – it need not be caused by it. This also means that it can occur even if the employer is unaware of the disability (*Heinz* v *Kenrick* (2000)).

(2) The comparison in this situation should be with someone to whom the disability-related reason does not apply. Thus, taking the example already used, if an employee is dismissed because of six months' absence attributable to his disability, the appropriate comparison is with someone to whom that reason – the six months' absence – does not apply. Fairly obviously, the disabled employee would have been treated less favourably than such a person (cf *Clark* v *Novacold* (1999)). The issue would then shift to a consideration of whether or not the treatment was justified.

(3) The issue of justification is therefore crucial in relation to this form of discrimination.

Jones v *Post Office* [2001] IRLR 384 Court of Appeal

The claimant had worked for the Post Office since 1977. His job involved driving a mail delivery van. In 1979 he was diagnosed as diabetic, but his condition was dealt with by diet and tablets until 1997, when he suffered a heart attack. Thereafter he needed insulin treatment. The Post Office at first stopped him driving altogether, as it was their policy not to allow people using insulin to drive for safety reasons. They then reinstated him, but limited his driving duties to two hours a day. This was clearly less favourable treatment for a reason related to disability: the issue was whether it was justified.

PILL LJ: '. . . Upon a consideration of the wording of [DDA s 3A(3)] in context, I conclude that the employment tribunal are confined to considering whether the reason given for the less favourable treatment can properly be described as both material to the circumstances of the particular case and substantial. The less favourable treatment in the present case is the limit upon the hours of driving. The reason given for it is the risk arising from longer periods of driving. The respondent obtained what are admitted to be suitably qualified and expert medical opinions. Upon the basis of those opinions, the respondent decided that the risk was such as to require the less favourable treatment. In order to rely on [s 3A(3)] it is not enough for the employer to assert that his conduct was reasonable in a general way; he has to establish that the reason given satisfies the statutory criteria. The respondent asserts in this case that the risk arising from the presence of diabetes is material to the circumstance of the particular case and is substantial. Where a properly conducted risk assessment provides a reason which is on its face both material and substantial, and is not irrational, the tribunal cannot substitute its own appraisal. The employment tribunal must consider whether the reason meets the statutory

112

criteria; it does not have the more general power to make its own appraisal of the medical evidence and conclude that the evidence from admittedly competent medical witnesses was incorrect or make its own risk assessment.

The present problem will typically arise when a risk assessment is involved. I am not doubting that the employment tribunal is permitted to investigate facts, for example as to the time-keeping record of the disabled person or as to his rate of productivity, matters which would arise upon some of the illustrations given in the Code of Practice. Consideration of the statutory criteria may also involve an assessment of the employer's decision to the extent of considering whether there was evidence on the basis of which a decision could properly be taken. Thus if no risk assessment was made or a decision was taken otherwise than on the basis of appropriate medical evidence, or was an irrational decision as being beyond the range of responses open to a reasonable decision-maker (a test approved by Sir Thomas Bingham MR in a different context in *R* v *Ministry of Defence ex parte Smith* (1996)), the employment tribunal could hold the reason insufficient and the treatment unjustified.

The tribunal cannot, however, in my judgment, conclude that the reason is not material or substantial because the suitably qualified and competently expressed medical opinion, on the basis of which the employer's decision was made, was thought by them to be inferior to a different medical opinion expressed to them. Moreover, a reason may be material and substantial within the meaning of the section even if the employment tribunal would have come to a different decision as to the extent of the risk. An investigation of the facts by the tribunal will often be required, but it cannot go to the extent of disagreeing with a risk assessment which is properly conducted, based on the properly formed opinion of suitably qualified doctors and produces an answer which is not irrational. This constraint limits the power of tribunals to provide relief to disabled employees, but in my view it follows from the wording of the section, which requires consideration of the reason given by the employer, and recognises the importance of the employer's responsibility for working practices.

The limited function of the employment tribunal may in some circumstances place them in a situation which is less than straightforward procedurally. However, it is not one with which they are unfamiliar. It is different but not very different from the task employment tribunals have to perform in cases of unfair dismissal. In *Post Office* v *Foley* (2000), it was held in this court that, in applying the law of unfair dismissal in s 98 of the Employment Rights Act 1996, tribunals should continue to adopt the "band or range of reasonable responses" approach to the issue of the reasonableness or unreasonableness of a dismissal as expounded in *Iceland Frozen Foods Ltd* v *Jones* (1982). Under that section, the tribunal's task is to consider the reasonableness of the employer's response and, under the present section, it is to consider the materiality and substantiality of his reason. In both cases, the members of the tribunal might themselves have come to a different conclusion on the evidence, but they must respect the opinion of the employer, in the one case if it is within the range of reasonable responses and in the other if the reason given is material and substantial . . .'

ARDEN LJ: '. . . [Section 3A(3)] uses the words "material" and "substantial". In my judgment, those words cover different subject matter. "Material" denotes the quality of the connection which must exist between, on the one hand, the employer's reason for discriminating against the employee and, on the other hand, the circumstances of the particular case. The circumstances of the particular case may include those of both the employer and employee (*Baynton* v *Saurus Ltd* (1999)). Under s 5(3), this connection must be "material" . . .

The second requirement in [s 3A(3)] is that the reason should be "substantial". This means, in my judgment, that the reason which the employer adopted as his ground for discrimination must carry real weight and thus be of substance. However, the word "substantial" does not mean that the employer must necessarily have reached the best conclusion that could be reached in the light of all known medical science. Employers are not obliged to search for the Holy Grail. It is sufficient if their conclusion is one which on a critical examination is found to have substance. Thus a reason which on analysis is meretricious would not be a "substantial" reason. It would fail to meet the test in [s 3A(3)] . . .'

(Kay LJ delivered a concurring judgment. The case was remitted to the employment tribunal.)

Comment

(1) There are two important points in these judgments. First, Arden LJ indicates that the test of what is 'material' and 'substantial' is not particularly demanding, although it is said to be objective. Secondly, as Pill LJ makes clear, a tribunal should approach the employer's decision rather as they do for unfair dismissal, recognising that in any particular situation, there may be a 'range of reasonable responses', and an employer is not to be judged wrong just because the tribunal would have acted differently. This test is controversial: see the discussion in Chapter 8 (p 390).

(2) This decision was made before the DDA was amended in 2005, but there is no significant difference in wording in relation to the justification defence. Similarly, it refers to an earlier version of the Code of Practice. The current 2004 Code is far more extensive than the earlier version. However, in relation to justification, it states:

> This is an objective test. 'Material' means that there must be a reasonable strong connection between the reason given for the treatment and the circumstances of the particular case. 'Substantial' means, in the context of justification, that the reason must carry real weight and be of substance. (para 6.3)

Thus the Code largely adopts the language used by Arden LJ.

(3) The question must be whether this standard of justification is too low to be compatible with what is required by the Framework Employment Directive (2000/78/EC). The test of objective justification used in the directive is the same for all the protected grounds, and requires that the employer's decision should be an appropriate and necessary means of achieving a legitimate aim. While the test in *Jones* v *Post Office* was approved by a later Court of Appeal in *Williams* v *J Walter Thompson* (2005), this was still on the original version of the Act and this point was not argued.

Duty to make reasonable adjustments

Disability Discrimination Act 1995

3   (2)   For the purposes of this Part, a person also discriminates against a disabled person if he fails to comply with a duty to make reasonable adjustments imposed on him in relation to the disabled person.
4   (1)   Where –
   (a)   a provision, criterion or practice applied by or on behalf of an employer, or
   (b)   any physical feature of premises occupied by the employer,
places the disabled person concerned at a substantial disadvantage in comparison with persons who are not disabled, it is the duty of the employer to take such steps as it is reasonable, in all the circumstances of the case, for him to have to take in order to prevent the provision, criterion or practice, or feature, having that effect.

114

(2)   In subsection (1), 'the disabled person concerned' means –

(a)   in the case of a provision, criterion or practice for determining to whom employment should be offered, any disabled person who is, or has notified the employer that he may be, an applicant for that employment;

(b)   in any other case, a disabled person who is –

(i)   an applicant for the employment concerned, or

(ii)   an employee of the employer concerned.

(3)   Nothing in this section imposes any duty on an employer in relation to a disabled person if the employer does not know, and could not reasonably be expected to know –

(a)   in the case of an applicant or potential applicant, that the disabled person concerned is, or may be, an applicant for the employment; or

(b)   in any case, that that person has a disability and is likely to be affected in the way mentioned in subsection (1).

Comment

(1) Thus DDA s 4A defines the duty to make reasonable adjustments – stating when it arises and what it entails – and s 3A(2) states that it will be disability discrimination if the employer fails to comply with such a duty.

(2) This form of disability discrimination cuts across the others and is frequently a separate head of claim in relation to the same facts. In this way, disability discrimination is different from the other protected grounds, where the facts usually give rise to only one form of discrimination.

(3) Note that the duty is owed to individuals: the employer's duty is not to try and make the workplace disability-proof, but to accommodate the needs of disabled employees or job applicants. It follows from this that the employer only has the duty in relation to job applicants if they disclose that they are disabled and have particular needs (cf *Ridout* v *T C Group* (1998)).

Disability Discrimination Act 1995

18B   (1)   In determining whether it is reasonable for a person to have to take a particular step in order to comply with a duty to make reasonable adjustments, regard shall be had, in particular, to –

(a)   the extent to which taking the step would prevent the effect in relation to which the duty is imposed;

(b)   the extent to which it is practicable for him to take the step;

(c)   the financial and other costs which would be incurred by him in taking the step and the extent to which taking it would disrupt any of his activities;

(d)   the extent of his financial and other resources;

(e)   the availability to him of financial or other assistance with respect to taking the step;

(f)   the nature of his activities and the size of his undertaking;

(g)   where the step would be taken in relation to a private household, the extent to which taking it would –

(i)   disrupt that household, or

(ii)   disturb any person residing there.

(2)   The following are examples of steps which a person may need to take in relation to a disabled person in order to comply with a duty to make reasonable adjustments –

(a)   making adjustments to premises;

(b)   allocating some of the disabled person's duties to another person;

   (c)   transferring him to fill an existing vacancy;

   (d)   altering his hours of working or training;

   (e)   assigning him to a different place of work or training;

   (f)   allowing him to be absent during working or training hours for rehabilitation, assessment or treatment;

   (g)   giving, or arranging for, training or mentoring (whether for the disabled person or any other person);

   (h)   acquiring or modifying equipment;

   (i)   modifying instructions or reference manuals;

   (j)   modifying procedures for testing or assessment;

   (k)   providing a reader or interpreter;

   (l)   providing supervision or other support . . .

Comment

(1) The guidance in DDA s 18B is amplified at length in the DRC Code of Practice on Employment and Occupation, which provides a wealth of practical examples.

(2) In *Kenny* v *Hampshire Constabulary* (1999) it was held that the duty to make reasonable adjustments did not extend to provision of personal assistance to an employee to enable him to work. In *Archibald* v *Fife Council* (2004) the House of Lords held that it could be a reasonable adjustment to redeploy a worker who had become disabled in a grade higher than the one she previously held after retraining without requiring her to go through a competitive interview.

Harassment and victimisation

Harassment was introduced as a freestanding ground of disability discrimination in the 2003 amendments to the DDA to comply with the Framework Employment Directive. It is defined by DDA s 3B in the same way as for the other equality enactments, and the discussion above should be referred to (p 73).

Victimisation has always been unlawful under DDA s 55. Again, it is defined in parallel terms to the other equality enactments and readers are referred to the earlier discussion (p 85).

Enforcement and remedies

Disability discrimination claims are litigated in employment tribunals in the usual way, with the same range of remedies available as under the other equality enactments (above, p 102). While the CRE and EOC could assist litigants in cases of importance and also had independent enforcement powers, this was not the case for the National Disability Council, the body originally set up by the DDA. It had a purely advisory role, and this downgrading of disability discrimination by comparison with the other grounds was strongly resented by groups lobbying for the rights of people with disabilities. The Labour government set up the Disability Rights Commission in 1999 as a body corresponding to the EOC and CRE. It is now replaced by the Equality and Human Rights Commission, along with the other Commissions. However, as it had not been in existence so long, and because of strong lobbying to the effect that disabled rights might be marginalised, it was agreed that a separate sub-committee on disability would continue at least for the first few years.

REFERENCES AND FURTHER READING

R Allen and G Moon (2006), 'Dignity Discourse in Discrimination Law: a Better Route to Equality' 6 *European Human Rights Law Review* 610

L Barmes (2007), 'Constitutional and Conceptual Complexities in UK Implementation of the EU Harassment Provisions' 36 ILJ 446

M Bell (2002), *Anti-Discrimination Law and the European Union*, OUP

L Clarke (2005), 'Harassment, Sexual Harassment, and the Employment Equality (Sex Discrimination) Regulations 2005' 35 ILJ 161

G Clayton and G Pitt (1997), 'Dress Codes and Freedom of Expression' 1 *European Human Rights Law Review* 52

H Collins (2003), 'Discrimination, equality and social inclusion' 66 MLR 16

M Connolly (2006), *Discrimination Law*, Sweet & Maxwell

B Doyle (2008), *Disability Discrimination: Law and Practice*, 6th ed, Jordan Publishing

P Elias and J Coppel (2000), 'Freedom of Expression and Freedom of Religion: some thoughts on the *Glenn Hoddle* case' in J Beatson and Y Cripps (eds), *Freedom of Expression and Freedom of Information*, CUP

E Ellis (2005), *EC Anti-Discrimination Law*, OUP

C Evans (2001), *Freedom of Religion under the European Convention on Human Rights*, OUP

S Fredman (2002), *Discrimination Law*, OUP

B Hepple (2006), 'The Equality Commissions and the Future Commission for Equality and Human Rights' in L Dickens and A C Neal (eds), *The Changing Institutional Face of British Employment Relations*, Kluwer Law International

C McCrudden (1998), 'Merit principles' 18 OJLS 543

H Meenan (ed) (2007), *Equality Law for an Enlarged Europe*, CUP

H Oliver (2004), 'Sexual Orientation Discrimination: Perceptions, Definitions and Genuine Occupational Requirements' 33 ILJ 1

G Pitt (2007), 'Religion or belief: aiming at the right target?' in H Meenan (ed) *Equality Law for an Enlarged Europe*, CUP

M Sargeant (2006), 'The Employment Equality (Age) Regulations 2006: a Legitimisation of Age Discrimination in Employment' 35 ILJ 209

D Schiek (2002), 'A New Framework on Equal Treatment of Persons in EC Law' *European Law Journal* 290

L Vickers (2003), 'Freedom of Religion and the Workplace: the *draft* Employment Equality (Religion or Belief) Regulations 2003' 32 ILJ 23

L Vickers (2006), 'Is all harassment equal? The case of religious harassment' [2006] CLJ 579

See also the journal, *Equal Opportunities Review*, published fortnightly, which is a valuable source of news and comment.

Visit **http://www.mylawchamber.co.uk/pitt** to access live web updates and web links to extend your knowledge of Employment Law.

3

EMPLOYMENT STATUS

In Chapter 2 we saw that the equality enactments protect anyone who has or seeks a contract personally to execute any work or labour. Contracts for personal labour must now be subdivided to distinguish between workers providing personal service under a *contract of employment* (called employees) and workers providing work on a *self-employed* basis (called independent contractors). The second category can be further subdivided into those who count as 'workers' for the purposes of legislative protection and those who do not. Finally, there may be a category of workers providing personal service who are neither employees nor independent contractors.

Why are these distinctions made? There are six main reasons. First, certain terms are implied by law into employees' contracts of employment. Secondly, most statutory protection rights (such as the right to claim unfair dismissal) are reserved to employees. Thirdly, liability for tax and National Insurance contributions is different for employees and self-employed workers. Fourthly, and relatedly, only employees are eligible for many social security benefits. Fifthly, an employer has a higher duty of care to employees than to independent contractors. Conversely, and finally, the employer is responsible for actions of employees in the course of their employment, but not usually for the actions of independent contractors.

EMPLOYEES AND INDEPENDENT CONTRACTORS

Who is an employee?

Employment Rights Act 1996

230

(1) In this Act 'employee' means an individual who has entered into or works under (or, where the employment has ceased, worked under) a contract of employment.
(2) In this Act 'contract of employment' means a contract of service or apprenticeship, whether express or implied, and (if it is express) whether it is oral or in writing.

Comment

(1) Note that for statutory purposes a contract of apprenticeship is to be treated as a contract of employment. This means, for example, that an apprentice who is not kept on at the end of his training period has the right to claim redundancy or unfair dismissal (though see *North East Coast Shiprepairers Ltd* v *Secretary of State* (1978)). In *Flett* v *Matheson* (2006) the Court of Appeal extended the traditional concept of apprenticeship to cover a typical tripartite modern apprenticeship programme where the training

was mainly provided at college and the employer was essentially providing work experience. The test was how far the arrangement displayed the features classically associated with an apprenticeship contract: that the main aim was to learn a skill; a lengthy period of training was involved, and the employer's power to dismiss was restricted.

(2) Apart from clarifying the status of apprentices, the statutory definitions of 'employee' and 'contract of employment' are not very helpful, as they give no indication of how a contract of service is to be identified. The answer must be found at common law, and various factors to be taken into account can be identified from the extracts which follow.

Yewens v Noakes (1880) 6 QBD 530 Court of Appeal

BRAMWELL LJ: 'A servant is a person subject to the command of his master as to the manner in which he shall do his work.'

Walker v Crystal Palace Football Club [1910] 1 KB 87 Court of Appeal

COZENS-HARDY MR: 'The question in this appeal is whether the particular respondent here, who has been party to a written form of agreement, is a workman entitled to compensation under the Workmen's Compensation Act. The man in question is a professional football player. The present appellants are the Crystal Palace Football and Athletic Club Ltd. Amongst their objects as provided by the memorandum of association is this: "To promote the game of football and to establish games and to maintain a team of football players either professional or amateur or partly of the one and partly the other" . . .

Now, that being the relation between the parties, the agreement is in these terms: "The club hereby agrees to engage the said G Walker from 1 May 1908 until 30 April 1909 for the purpose of playing football with the Crystal Palace Football Club Ltd provided always and it is hereby agreed and declared that the said G Walker shall not . . . ;" and then there is a limitation that the man shall not be a publican or reside in a public-house or take part in professional running or any other sport without the consent in writing of the club. First of all the club agrees to engage the man. Then what does the man do? "The said G Walker hereby agrees to serve the club for the purpose and period aforesaid and not to engage himself to play football for any other person or club during the said period", and at the expiration of that period the club is to have the first offer to re-engage his services. Then in consideration of such service the club agrees to pay the man so much per week, and the man agrees that he will during the period aforesaid "play in all matches when required by the club and will keep himself temperate, sober, and in good playing form and attend regularly to training and observe the training and general instructions of the club and do all that may by the club be deemed necessary to fit himself as an efficient football player and will in all respects conform to the rules and laws of the Football Association". Then there is a proviso that if the man refuses or neglects "to play in club matches when required as aforesaid or if he shall refuse or neglect to obey the training and general instructions of the club he shall pay to the club a sum not exceeding five pounds as liquidated damages".

Before going further it is right to say that the regulations or instructions there referred to are also in print, and it is quite clear, without going through those regulations in detail, that the man agrees to devote his whole time, to attend regularly on certain days and hours, not merely for the purpose of playing, but for the purpose of training, and there are a number of detailed regulations which the man is bound to observe and comply with . . .

It has been argued before us very forcibly by Mr Russell [counsel for the football club] that there is a certain difference between an ordinary workman and a man who contracts to exhibit and employ his skill where the employer would have no right to dictate to him in the exercise of that skill; e.g., the club in this case would have no right to dictate to him how he should play football. I am unable to follow that. He is bound according to the express terms of his contract to obey all general directions of the club, and I think in any particular game in which he was engaged he would also be bound to obey the particular instructions of the captain or whoever it might be who was the delegate of the authority of the club for the purpose of giving those instructions. In my judgment it cannot be that a man is taken out of the operation of the Act simply because in doing a particular kind of work which he is employed to do, and in doing which he obeys general instructions, he also exercises his own judgment uncontrolled by anybody. I think this appeal must be dismissed.

FARWELL LJ: 'I agree. The appellants . . . say there is no contract of service with an employer because the football player is at liberty to exercise his own initiative in playing the game. That appears to me to be no answer. There are many employments in which the workman exercises initiative, but he may or may not be bound to obey the directions of his employer when given to him. If he has no duty to obey them, it may very well be that there is no service, but here not only is the agreement by the player that he will serve, but he also agrees to obey the training and general instructions of the club. I cannot doubt that he is bound to obey any directions which the captain, as the delegate of the club, may give him during the course of the game – that is to say, any direction that is within the terms of his employment as a football player . . .'

(Fletcher Moulton LJ delivered a concurring judgment.)

Comment

(1) The element of control remains important, even though it has long been recognised that the employer may only control the arrangements under which work is done rather than the work itself.

(2) Note the importance of this factor in relation to agency workers, below p 135.

Stevenson Jordan & Harrison Ltd v *Macdonald & Evans*
[1952] 1 TLR 101 Court of Appeal

DENNING LJ: '. . . [This case] raises the troublesome question: What is the distinction between a contract of service and a contract for services? The test usually applied is whether the employer has the right to control the manner of doing the work. Thus in *Collins* v *Herts CC* (1947), Hilbery J said:

> "The distinction between a contract for services and a contract of service can be summarised in this way: In the one case the master can order or require what is to be done, while in the other cases, he can not only require what is to be done but how it shall be done."

But in *Cassidy* v *The Ministry of Health* (1951) Somervell LJ pointed out that that test is not universally correct. There are many contracts of service where the master cannot control the manner in which the work is to be done, as in the case of a captain of a ship. Somervell LJ went on to say that "One perhaps cannot get much beyond this 'Was the contract a contract of service within the meaning which an ordinary person would give under the words?'." I respectfully agree. As my Lord has said it is almost impossible to give a precise definition of the distinction. It is often quite easy to recognise a contract of service when you see it, but very difficult to say wherein the difference lies. A ship's master, a chauffeur, and a reporter on the staff of a newspaper are all employed under a contract of service; but a ship's pilot, a taxi-man, and a newspaper contributor are employed under a contract for services. One feature which seems to me to run through the instances is that, under a contract of service, a man is employed as part of the business and his work is done as an integral part of the business: whereas under a contract for services his work, although done for the business, is not integrated into it but is only accessory to it.'

Comment

(1) The 'integration' or 'organisation' test propounded by Lord Denning in *Stevenson Jordan & Harrison Ltd* v *MacDonald & Evans* was intended to overcome the deficiencies of the 'control' test. However, today it may frequently be misleading, if not useless. It has become increasingly common for businesses to outsource parts of their operation, rather than having the function performed by employees. One of the reasons for this is that it saves them the overheads and potential liabilities associated with having employees. The function is still as necessary and integral as ever it was. An example might be a road haulage company subcontracting the maintenance of its vehicles rather than having its own garage and mechanics. Clearly, the maintenance of the lorries would continue to be integral to the road haulage business, but the workers carrying it out would not be employees.

Market Investigations v Minister of Social Security
[1969] 2 QB 173 High Court, Queen's Bench

The company was involved in market research. In addition to its permanent staff, it employed interviewers to carry out over 8,000 interviews a year. These interviewers worked as and when they were called upon. The issue was whether they were employees of the company, in which case the company was liable to pay National Insurance contributions on their behalf. The contract of one interviewer was used as a test case and it was held that they were employees.

COOKE J: '. . . I think it is fair to say that there was at one time a school of thought according to which the extent and degree of the control which B was entitled to exercise over A in the performance of the work would be a decisive factor. However, it has for long been apparent that an analysis of the extent and degree of such control is not in itself decisive. Thus in *Collins* v *Hertfordshire County Council* (1947) it had been suggested that the distinguishing feature of a contract of service is that the master can not only order or require what is to be done but also how it shall be done. The inadequacy of this test was pointed out by Somervell LJ in *Cassidy* v *Ministry of Health* (1951) when he referred to the case of a certified master of a ship. The master may be employed by the owners under what is clearly a contract of service, and yet the owners have no power to tell him how to navigate his ship. As Lord Parker CJ pointed out in *Morren* v *Swinton and Pendlebury Borough Council* (1965), when one is dealing with a professional man, or a man of some particular skill and experience, there can be no question of an employer telling him how to do the work; therefore the absence of control and direction in that sense can be of little, if any, use as a test . . .

In *United States of America* v *Silk* (1947) the question was whether certain men were "employees" within the meaning of that word in the Social Security Act, 1935. The judges of the Supreme Court decided that the test to be applied was not "power of control, whether exercised or not, over the manner of performing service to the undertaking", but whether the men were employees "as a matter of economic reality".

The observations of Lord Wright, of Denning LJ and of the judges of the Supreme Court suggest that the fundamental test to be applied is this: "Is the person who has engaged himself to perform these services performing them as a person in business on his own account?". If the answer to that question is "Yes", then the contract is a contract for services. If the answer is "No" then the contract is a contract of service. No exhaustive list has been compiled and perhaps no exhaustive list can be compiled of considerations which are relevant in determining that question, nor can strict rules be laid down as to the relative weight which the various considerations should carry in particular cases. The most that can be said is that control will no doubt always have to be considered, although it can no longer be regarded as the sole determining factor; and that factors, which may be of importance, are such matters as whether the man performing the services provides his own equipment, whether he hires his own helpers, what degree of financial risk he takes, what degree of responsibility for investment and management he has, and whether and how far he has an opportunity of profiting from sound management in the performance of his task.

The application of the general test may be easier in a case where the person who engages himself to perform the services does so in the course of an already established business of his own; but this factor is not decisive, and a person who engages himself to perform services for another may well be an independent contractor even though he has not entered into the contract in the course of an existing business carried on by him . . .'

Comment

(1) The multi-factor test propounded here requires tribunals to consider all relevant information, implying that no particular factor will necessarily be decisive. The focus of Cooke J's test is on distinguishing genuinely independent entrepreneurs from those who are economically dependent on one employer. It emphasises the realities of the situation and the worker's degree of subordination to the employer in practice.

(2) Cooke J's formulation was approved by the Privy Council in *Lee v Chung* (1990) and has been cited frequently ever since. However, even more influential has been another High Court decision of around the same time, also using the multi-factor test, but with a different emphasis.

Ready Mixed Concrete v Minister for Pensions and National Insurance
[1968] 2 QB 497 Queen's Bench Division

This was a test case as to whether over 700 drivers who delivered concrete for the company were self-employed or not. The Ministry argued that they were employees and that the company should therefore be making National Insurance contributions in respect of them. The company (and the drivers) argued that they were self-employed.

The company had introduced a scheme for the delivery of concrete to customers using a fleet of owner-drivers. The drivers bought the trucks on hire purchase from Ready Mixed. They were painted in company colours and adapted to carry the Ready Mixed concrete-mixing unit. The trucks had to be available whenever required by the company and could not be used for any other purposes. The drivers were allowed to appoint a substitute driver, provided that such a driver was acceptable to the company; however, the company retained the right to require the owner-driver to operate the truck himself. While working, the owner-driver had to wear the company uniform, comply with all company rules and carry out all reasonable orders from any competent employee of the company 'as if he were an employee of the company', as it said in the contract.

The owner-drivers had to maintain and operate the trucks at their own expense, but the company could specify repairs to be carried out and could require the work to be done at a garage it nominated. They were paid by results, a combination of distance travelled and amounts carried, but were guaranteed an annual minimum wage. The contract itself stated expressly that the drivers were independent contractors.

MCKENNA J: '. . . I must now consider what is meant by a contract of service.

A contract of service exists if these three conditions are fulfilled. (i) The servant agrees that, in consideration of a wage or other remuneration, he will provide his own work and skill in the performance of some service for his master. (ii) He agrees, expressly or impliedly, that in the performance of that service he will be subject to the other's control in a sufficient degree to make that other master. (iii) The other provisions of the contract are consistent with its being a contract of service.

I need say little about (i) and (ii).

As to (i). There must be a wage or other remuneration. Otherwise there will be no consideration, and without consideration no contract of any kind. The servant must be obliged to provide his own work and skill. Freedom to do a job either by one's own hands or by another's is inconsistent with a contract of service, though a limited or occasional power of delegation may not be: see Atiyah's *Vicarious Liability in the Law of Torts* (1967) pp 59 to 61 and the cases cited by him.

As to (ii). Control includes the power of deciding the thing to be done, the way in which it shall be done, the means to be employed in doing it, the time when and the place where it shall be done. All these aspects of control must be considered in deciding whether the right exists in a sufficient degree to make one party the master and the other his servant. The right need not be unrestricted.

"What matters is lawful authority to command so far as there is scope for it. And there must always be some room for it, if only in incidental or collateral matters." (*Zuijs* v *Wirth Brothers Proprietary Ltd* (1955)).

To find where the right resides one must look first to the express terms of the contract, and if they deal fully with the matter one may look no further. If the contract does not expressly provide which party shall have the right, the question must be answered in the ordinary way by implication.

The third and negative condition is for my purpose the important one, and I shall try with the help of five examples to explain what I mean by provisions inconsistent with the nature of a contract of service.

(i) A contract obliges one party to build for the other, providing at his own expense the necessary plant and materials. This is not a contract of service, even though the builder may be obliged to use his own labour only and to accept a high degree of control: it is a building contract. It is not a contract to serve another for a wage, but a contract to produce a thing (or a result) for a price.

(ii) A contract obliges one party to carry another's goods, providing at his own expense everything needed for performance. This is not a contract of service, even though the carrier may be obliged to drive the vehicle himself and to accept the other's control over his performance: it is a contract of carriage.

(iii) A contract obliges a labourer to work for a builder, providing some simple tools, and to accept the builder's control. Notwithstanding the obligation to provide the tools, the contract is one of service. That obligation is not inconsistent with the nature of a contract of service. It is not a sufficiently important matter to affect the substance of the contract.

(iv) A contract obliges one party to work for the other, accepting his control, and to provide his own transport. This is still a contract of service. The obligation to provide his own transport does not affect the substance. Transport in this example is incidental to the main purpose of the contract. Transport in the second example was the essential part of the performance.

(v) The same instrument provides that one party shall work for the other subject to the other's control, and also that he shall sell him his land. The first part of the instrument is no less a contract of service because the second part imposes obligations of a different kind: (*Amalgamated Engineering Union* v *Minister of Pensions and National Insurance* (1963)).

I can put the point which I am making in other words. An obligation to do work subject to the other party's control is a necessary, though not always a sufficient, condition of a contract of service. If the provisions of the contract as a whole are inconsistent with its being a contract of service, it will be some other kind of contract, and the person doing the work will not be a servant. The judge's task is to classify the contract (a task like that of distinguishing a contract of sale from one of work and labour). He may, in performing it, take into account other matters besides control . . .'

(The judge held that the owner-driver was an independent contractor performing a contract of carriage with the company.)

Comment

(1) McKenna J's formulation of the basic requirements for a contract of service has also been cited with approval by higher courts over the years. It has been particularly influential when atypical working relationships, such as those of casual workers or agency workers, are being considered, as we will see (below, p 130).

(2) Note that the employing company in this case was in some ways having its cake and eating it: for example, the owner-drivers could employ a substitute driver – but the company retained a right of veto and could insist on the owner-driver personally operating the truck. Is that a requirement for personal service or not?

(3) 'Substitution clauses', which require the worker to provide a substitute if he is unwilling or unable to work, have been held to be inconsistent with a finding that there is a contract of service because they negate the obligation to give personal service (*Express & Echo* v *Tanton* (1999); *Staffordshire Sentinel Newspapers* v *Potter* (2004) – but contrast *MacFarlane* v *Glasgow City Council* (2001)). However, the EAT has recently held that if the clause applies only where the worker cannot work (rather than chooses not to), then it is not inconsistent with the contract of employment obligation to give personal service (*James* v *Redcats* (2007)).

(4) Another factor in this case was the 'label' given by the parties themselves to their relationship. What weight should be given to this?

Ferguson v John Dawson & Partners (Contractors) Ltd
[1976] IRLR 346 Court of Appeal

MEGAW LJ: 'On April 19, 1972, the claimant, Mr Michael Joseph Ferguson, fell some 15 feet from a flat roof on which he was working. He suffered serious injuries. He claimed damages for breach of statutory duty from the defendants.

The action was heard by Boreham J at Leeds. On July 28, 1975, the judge gave judgment for the claimant for £30,387.88, including interest. The defendants appeal on issues as to liability. There is no appeal as to the amount of damages . . .

I turn to the other issue. Was the claimant employed by the defendants? For the claimant it is submitted that he was employed by the defendants under a contract of service. For the defendants it is contended that the contract was a contract for services, and therefore the defendants were not under a statutory duty to him to provide a guard for the working place. For if it were a contract for services the claimant would not have been "employed" by the defendants; and in the circumstances of this accident reg 3(1)(a) of the Construction (Working Places) Regulations 1966 [see now the Construction (Health, Safety and Welfare) Regulations 1996] would not have brought reg 28(1) into effect so as to impose on the defendants a duty towards the claimant. Regulation 28(1) of the Construction (Working Places) Regulations 1966 [see now the Construction (Health, Safety and Welfare) Regulations 1996] is brought into operation only in relation to "the falling or slipping of persons" (which this accident was) so far as the requirements of that regulation "affect . . . any workman employed by him": "him", here, being the defendants. Regulation 3(1)(b) has a wider scope as regards the persons who are under the duty; but it is confined to "the falling of materials and articles".

It is conceded by the defendants that if the claimant was employed under a contract of service, they were, subject only to the issue as to "appreciable time", under a duty to the claimant; they failed to carry out that duty; and that failure was the cause of the accident. But, say the defendants, the claimant was employed under a contract for services: he was "self-employed"; he owed a statutory duty to himself to take the statutory precautions (*Smith* v *George Wimpey & Co Ltd* (1972)). It was for him, under the regulations, not for the defendants, to ensure that the guardrail was erected. The defendants were under no such duty.

What is the basis for that contention? The judge accepted the evidence given by Mr Murray, the defendants' site agent, as to the circumstances in which the claimant came to work for the defendants in January 1972, some three months before the accident happened. The evidence was simply this: the claimant came with four other Irishmen, already working for the defendants, and he asked, or perhaps one of his friends asked, if he could "come along". Mr Murray's evidence is: "I said he could start on Monday and that was it. But I did inform him there were no cards; we were purely working as a lump labour force." . . .

Mr Murray accepted that he was responsible for "hiring and firing". In other words, as between the defendants and the workmen, including the claimant, he, Mr Murray, could dismiss them. There would be no question of his being able to determine a contract between the defendants and a sub-contractor. He could move men from site to site, if he was so minded; and, in support of the existence of that contractual right on behalf of the defendants, he gave instances of having done so. If tools were required for the work, it was for the defendants to provide them. Again, as confirmation of that contractual obligation, Mr Murray gave evidence of instances where the claimant had required tools for the work which he had been required to do, and the defendants had provided them. It was for Mr Murray to tell the workmen, including the claimant, what particular work they were to do: "I tell him what to take and what to do". The centurion in St Matthew's gospel says to the man under him "Do this, and he doeth it". The man under him is a servant, not an independent contractor. All these things are in relation to the contractual relationships existing. "I tell him what to do", and he does it on Mr Murray's instructions because, when legal analysis has to be applied, it is a term of the contract that the claimant shall carry out the defendants' instructions what to do when they tell him to do it. The men, including the claimant, were employed on an hourly basis. The money paid to them would be correctly described as "a wage".

In my judgment, on the tests laid down in the authorities, all of this indicates beyond doubt that the reality of the relationship was employer and employee – a contract of service. I do not propose to lengthen this judgment by examining afresh the criteria, so fully discussed in so many cases. The judge, as I have already said, based himself on the judgment of MacKenna J in *Ready Mixed Concrete (South East) Ltd* v *Minister of Pensions and National Insurance* (1968). Another judgment which I have found very helpful is that of Cooke J in *Market Investigations Ltd* v *Minister of Social Security* (1969).

My own view would have been that a declaration by the parties, even if it be incorporated in the contract, that the workman is to be, or is to be deemed to be, self-employed, an independent contractor, ought to be wholly disregarded – not merely treated as not being conclusive – if the remainder of the contractual terms, governing the realities of the relationship, show the relationship of employer and employee. The Roman soldier would not have been a self-employed labour only sub-contractor because of any verbal exchange between him and the centurion when he enlisted. I find difficulty in accepting that the parties, by a mere expression of intention as to what the legal relationship should be, can in any way influence the conclusion of law as to what the relationship is. I think that it would be contrary to the public interest if that were so, for it would mean that the parties, by their own whim, by the use of a verbal formula, unrelated to the reality of the relationship, could influence the decision on whom the responsibility for the safety of workmen, as imposed by statutory regulations, should rest . . .'

(Browne LJ agreed that the claimant was an employee. Lawton LJ dissented.)

Massey v *Crown Life Insurance Co* [1978] ICR 590 Court of Appeal

LORD DENNING MR: '. . . What was the position of Mr Massey? He was the manager of the Ilford branch of the insurance company. For a couple of years, from 1971 to 1973, the company treated him as though he were a servant. They gave him a memorandum under [ERA s 1]. They paid him wages; and, before paying him, they deducted the tax, they deducted the stamp, and they deducted graduated pension contributions from the amount they paid him. Further, they had a pension scheme of their own and he had to make contributions towards his pension. Being regarded as a servant, he was taxed for his income tax payments under Schedule E.

But then in 1973 Mr Massey went to his accountant who advised him to change his relationship with his employers. The accountant said: "I think you would be much better off if you so arranged your affairs as to be self-employed instead of being a servant. Then you will come under Schedule D instead of Schedule E." That is what was proposed. Instead of wages subject to deductions, the company would pay him the full amount each week but they would not deduct tax or national insurance contributions or anything like that. He would get the full amount. It would be for him to account for tax to the Inland Revenue under Schedule D.

He went to the company and told them: "I have been advised by my accountants to change over to Schedule D. Will you agree?" They said: "Oh, yes; we are agreeable." So it was put through. It was done in this way. Instead of being called "Mr John L Massey", he was called "John L Massey and Associates". It was really just the same man under another name. He registered that new name under the Registration of Business Names Act 1916. With that new name he entered into a new agreement with the company. So far as his duties were concerned, the agreement was in almost identical terms as the previous one. As a result of that new agreement, Mr Massey said he was no longer a servant, he was an independent contractor. He was therefore liable to be taxed under Schedule D. The position was placed before the Inland Revenue, and the Inland Revenue seem to have thought it was all right . . .

In November 1975 Mr Massey was dismissed. Thereafter he said: "I want to claim for unfair dismissal." A claim for unfair dismissal was quite admissible if he was employed by the company under a contract of service, but not if he was employed under a contract for services. So here he was claiming as a servant whereas, for the last two years, he had been paid on the basis that he was an independent contractor.

The law, as I see it, is this: if the true relationship of the parties is that of master and servant under a contract of service, the parties cannot alter the truth of that relationship by putting a different label on it. If they should put a different label on it, and use it as a dishonest device to deceive the revenue, I should have thought it was illegal and could not be enforced by either party and they could not get any advantage out of it – at any rate not in any case where they had to rely on it as the basis of a claim: see *Alexander* v *Rayson* (1936). An arrangement between two parties to put forward a dishonest description of their relationship so as to deceive the revenue would clearly be illegal and unenforceable.

On the other hand, if their relationship is ambiguous and is capable of being one or the other, then the parties can remove that ambiguity, by the very agreement itself which they make with one another . . .

I would only say a word about the recent case of *Ferguson* v *John Dawson & Partners (Contractors) Ltd* (1976). That case turned on its facts. Boreham J held that the real relationship of the parties was that of master and servant and that they had put the wrong label on it by regarding him as working on "the lump". The majority of this court accepted that view. But Lawton LJ thought that the partners had deliberately put the right label on their relationship. The man was on "the lump". He had had all the benefits of it by avoiding tax. It was contrary to public policy that, when he had had an accident, he could throw over that relationship and claim that he was only a servant.

In most of these cases, I expect that it will be found that the parties do deliberately agree for the man to be "self-employed" or "on the lump". It is done especially so as to obtain the tax benefits. When such an agreement is made, it affords strong evidence that that is the real relationship. If it is so found, the man must accept it. He cannot afterwards assert that he was only a servant.

In the present case there is a perfectly genuine agreement entered into at the instance of Mr Massey on the footing that he is self-employed. He gets the benefit of it by avoiding tax deductions and getting his pension contributions returned. I do not see that he can come along afterwards and say it is something else in order to claim that he has been unfairly dismissed. Having made his bed as being self-employed, he must lie on it. He is not under a contract of service.

I agree entirely with the employment tribunal and with the Employment Appeal Tribunal that he does not qualify to claim for unfair dismissal in this case, and I would dismiss the appeal.'

(Lawton LJ delivered a concurring judgment. Eveleigh LJ agreed with both judgments.)

Lane v Shire Roofing Co Ltd [1995] IRLR 493 Court of Appeal

The claimant suffered serious head injuries when he fell off his ladder while tiling the roof of a porch at a domestic house. Had scaffolding been provided, he would have had a safer platform from which to work. He alleged negligence on the part of the company for failing to provide him with scaffolding to do the job.

HENRY LJ: 'The next question is whether the respondents owed to the claimant the common law or statutory duty of an employer to his employees, or whether the appellant when doing that job was acting as an independent contractor. When it comes to the question of safety at work, there is a real public interest in recognising the employer/employee relationship when it exists, because of the responsibilities that the common law and statutes such as the Employers' Liability (Compulsory Insurance) Act 1969 places on the employer.

The judge was to find that the appellant was not an employee, but was an independent contractor. In that event the appellant would have been responsible for his own safety; the respondent would have owed him no duty of care, and would have had no responsibility (statutory or at common law) for the safety of the work done by the appellant. That was the context in which the question was asked.

We were taken through the standard authorities on this matter: *Readymix Concrete (South East) Ltd v Minister of Pensions and National Insurance* (1968); *Market Investigations Ltd v Minister of Social Security* (1969); and *Ferguson v John Dawson & Partners (Contractors) Ltd* (1976), to name the principal ones. Two general remarks should be made. The overall employment background is very different today (and was, though less so, in 1986) than it had been at the time when those cases were decided. First, for a variety of reasons there are more self-employed and fewer in employment. There is a greater flexibility in employment, with more temporary and shared employment. Second, there are perceived advantages for both workman and employer in the relationship between them being that of independent contractor. From the workman's point of view, being self-employed brings him into a more benevolent and less prompt taxation regime. From the employer's point of view, the protection of employee's rights contained in the employment protection legislation of the 1970s brought certain perceived dis-incentives to the employer to take on full-time long-term employees. So even in 1986 there were reasons on both sides to avoid the employee label. But, as I have already said, there were, and are, good policy reasons in the safety at work field to ensure that the law properly categorises between employees and independent contractors.

That line of authority shows that there are many factors to be taken into account in answer-ing this question, and, with different priority being given to those factors in different cases, all depends on the facts of each individual case. Certain principles relevant to this case, however, emerge.

First, the element of control will be important: who lays down what is to be done, the way in which it is to be done, the means by which it is to be done, and the time when it is done? Who provides (ie hires and fires) the team by which it is done, and who provides the material, plant and machinery and tools used?

But it is recognised that the control test may not be decisive – for instance, in the case of skilled employees, with discretion to decide how their work should be done. In such cases the question is broadened to whose business was it? Was the workman carrying on his own busi-ness, or was he carrying on that of his employers? The American Supreme Court, in *United States of America* v *Silk* (1947), asks the question whether the men were employees "as a mat-ter of economic reality". The answer to this question may cover much of the same ground as the control test (such as whether he provides his own equipment and hires his own helpers) but may involve looking to see where the financial risk lies, and whether and how far he has an opportunity of profiting from sound management in the performance of his task (see *Market Investigations* v *Minister of Social Security*, supra).

And these questions must be asked in the context of who is responsible for the overall safety of the men doing the work in question. Mr Whittaker, of the respondents, was cross-examined on these lines and he agreed that he was so responsible. Such an answer is not decisive (though it may be indicative) because ultimately the question is one of law, and he could be wrong as to where the legal responsibility lies (see *Ferguson* v *Dawson*, supra).

The facts that the judge had to consider were as follows. The appellant was a builder/roofer/carpenter who had since 1982 traded as a one-man firm, PJ Building. He had obtained self-employed fiscal status, with a right to the 714 tax exemption certificates issued by the Inland Revenue. As a one-man firm he solicited work through advertisements, and when engaged by clients would of course be responsible for estimating, buying in materials, and mat-ters of that kind. But that work had dried up. His public liability insurance had lapsed. At the time he answered the respondents' advertisement he was usually working for others.

The respondent company (which was the corporate manifestation of its proprietor, Mr Whittaker) was a newly established roofing contractor. It was in its early days of trading, and Mr Whittaker did not wish to take on too many long-term employees – he considered it prudent and advantageous to hire for individual jobs. In September of 1986 he obtained a large roofing sub-contract in Marlow. He advertised for men to work that contract. The appellant answered that advertisement, and was employed by him at the daily rate of £45. He started work on that job at some time in September. It seems, though the evidence is not entirely clear on this, that that job was nearly over when, at the respondents' request, he left that job to do the Sonning Common porch re-roofing job. As he had been promised no work from the respondents after the Marlow job, it is right to consider the question whether he was an employee in the context of the Sonning Common job.

The building contract in relation to that job had been entered into by the respondents, through Mr Whittaker, and the householders, Mr and Mrs Bird, for an agreed price of £389 (plus VAT). (As will be seen, the economic realities of that price were that if, to do it safely, scaffolding had to be hired and erected, the job would be loss-making to the respondents.)

128

Mr Whittaker then visited the site with the appellant, agreed to pay him an all-in fee of £200 for the job, and discussed (as we shall see) with him what was necessary in the way of plant (using that phrase to embrace ladders, scaffolds and trestles) to do the job. And Mr Whittaker accepted in cross-examination that it was his responsibility to supply aids such as scaffolds and trestles. Had two men been employed on that job, Mr Whittaker would have provided the other. The appellant brought to that job all his personal roofing and carpentry tools (including a slate cutter) but of course he provided no materials or plant. He brought his own ladder.

The judge's reasons for finding that the appellant was an independent contractor, not an employee, were these:

"The defendant company (which was really Mr Whittaker's company) had only been in operation for six months and it would obviously be of advantage to him to be able to enter into contracts with other people for specific works without having a continuous payroll for those parts. I consider it important that the claimant himself had his own genuine roofing business, so that he was a roofing specialist, and he had the benefit of 714 certificates so that he could pay his own tax and was paid gross. He continued with that system while he was working on contracts for the defendant company. I note that the claimant was obviously capable of working without supervision and that Mr Whittaker relied upon him to do so, although it seems that Mr Whittaker was subsequently rather disappointed with the quality of the claimant's work and subsequently thought that the claimant had more experience with clay tiles than the artificial slates which he was using on the final contract. There was no guarantee given by Mr Whittaker of continuing work for the defendant, no provision for notice or dismissal and, as pointed out by Mr Matthews, that would have been unnecessary if this was genuine sub-contracting work, because each job had to be taken on its own and there was no guarantee that the claimant would be employed thereafter, though both the claimant and Mr Whittaker were obviously anticipating that further jobs would arise which Mr Whittaker could give to the claimant. In all the circumstances, therefore, I find that the claimant was an independent contractor throughout the time that he was working for the defendant company and in particular, of course, on the contract in question at the Birds's."

Each of those four reasons given by the judge would apply equally to the work being done under a short-term single job contract of employment. All of them concentrate on what Mr Whittaker wanted, and not on whose business it was. Mr Matthews, for the respondents, rightly distinguishes between a *Ferguson* v *Dawson* situation, where an employer engages men on "the lump" to do labouring work (where the men are clearly employees, whatever their tax status may be), and when a specialist sub-contractor is employed to perform some part of a general building contract. That team or individual clearly will be an independent contractor. He submits that the appellant in this case falls somewhere in between. With that I would agree, but would put this case substantially nearer "the lump" than the specialist sub-contractor. Though the degree of control that Mr Whittaker would use would depend on the need he felt to supervise and direct the appellant (who was just someone answering the advertisement) the question "Whose business was it?" in relation to the Sonning Common job could only in my judgment be answered by saying that it was the respondents' business and not the appellant's. In my judgment, therefore, they owed the duties of employers to the appellant. Consequently, for my part I would find that the first ground of appeal against the judge's judgment succeeds . . .'

(Auld and Norse LJJ agreed.)

Comment

(1) *Lane* v *Shire Roofing* seems to mark a decisive shift in the approach to this issue. What reasons are put forward for suggesting that the question of whether Lane was an

employee or not should be more closely scrutinised in this situation than in others? Are either or both of these reasons convincing, in your opinion? (See McKendrick (1996).)

(2) It is notable that this case adopts the test as stated by Cooke J in *Market Investigations* v *Minister of Social Security* – is the person in question a person in business on his own account? However, as already noted, where atypical workers are concerned, the more legalistic approach of *Ready Mixed Concrete* v *MPNI* has been more influential.

Casual workers

Fluctuating demand may lead an employer to rely heavily on workers who are not permanently employed. Seasonal work, such as fruit-picking, is an obvious example, but demand varies considerably in the hotel and catering industry, retail and other service areas, and in quite a lot of manufacturing or technically-focused businesses too. Many homeworkers also fall into this category of regular, but not permanent, workers. Are they employees? The problem is that while they expect to be given work and the employer expects to have work for them, there is no legal obligation on the employer to offer them work, nor on them to accept.

O'Kelly v *Trusthouse Forte* [1984] QB 90 Court of Appeal

The banqueting division of the company employed only 34 permanent staff at Grosvenor House in London, relying on staffing functions with casual staff who were drafted in for each occasion. Some of these were more casual than others: the claimants in the case were on a list of about 100 'regular casuals' who were given preference when work was available. In addition there was another list of about 200–300 other casual staff who were used less frequently. The claimants claimed that they had been unfairly dismissed for trade union activities. This is an exceptional situation where unfair dismissal may be claimed without the necessity for one year's continuous employment. The issue in the case was therefore whether the 'regular casuals' were employees. The factors taken into account by the employment tribunal were quoted in the judgment of Ackner LJ.

ACKNER LJ: '. . . In making their assessment, the employment tribunal took into account the following factors which they considered consistent with a contract of employment:

(a) The claimants provided their services in return for remuneration for work actually performed. They did not invest their own capital or stand to gain or lose from the commercial success of the functions organised by the banqueting department. (b) They performed their work under the direction and control of [the company]. (c) When the casual workers attended at functions they were part of [the company's] organisation and for the purpose of ensuring the smooth running of the business they were represented in the staff consultation process. (d) When working they were carrying on the business of [the company]. (e) Clothing and equipment were provided by [the company]. (f) The applicants were paid weekly in arrear and were paid under deduction of income tax and social security contributions. (g) Their work was organised on the basis of a weekly rota and they required permission to take time off from rostered duties. (h) There was a disciplinary and grievance procedure. (i) There was holiday pay or an incentive bonus calculated by reference to past service.

The following additional factors in the relationship the employment tribunal considered were not inconsistent with the contract of employment:

(j) The claimants were paid for work actually performed and did not receive a regular wage or retainer. The method of calculating entitlement to remuneration is not an essential aspect of the employment relationship. (k) Casual workers were not remunerated on the same basis as permanent employees and did not receive sick pay and were not included in [the company's] staff pension scheme and did not receive the fringe benefits accorded to established employees. There is, however, no objection to employers adopting different terms and conditions of employment for different categories of employee (e.g. different terms for manual and managerial staff). (l) There were no regular or assured working hours. It is not a requirement of employment that there should be "normal working hours": see [ERA ss 88–89]. (m) Casual workers were not provided with written particulars of employment. If it is established that casual workers are employees there is a statutory obligation to furnish written particulars.

The following factors were considered by the employment tribunal to be inconsistent with a contract of employment:

(n) The engagement was terminable without notice on either side. (o) The claimants had the right to decide whether or not to accept work, although whether or not it would be in their interest to exercise the right to refuse work is another matter. (p) [The company] had no obligation to provide any work. (q) During the subsistence of the relationship it was the parties' view that casual workers were independent contractors engaged under successive contracts for services. (r) It is the recognised custom and practice of the industry that casual workers are engaged under a contract for services . . .'

SIR JOHN DONALDSON MR: '. . . In the instant appeal the employment tribunal directed itself to:

"consider all aspects of the relationship, no single factor being in itself decisive and each of which may vary in weight and direction, and having given such balance to the factors as seems appropriate, to determine whether the person was carrying on business on his own account."

This is wholly correct as a matter of law and it is not for this court or for the appeal tribunal to re-weigh the facts.

The employment tribunal then concluded that there was no contract of employment extending over a series of engagements. This conclusion was based upon an evaluation of the large number of factors set out in their reasons, but it is clear that the majority attached great importance to the fact that, as they saw it, there was no mutuality of obligation and that in the industry casual workers were not regarded as working under any overall contract of employment.

The appeal tribunal refused to interfere with this conclusion and in my judgment they were right to do so. So far as mutuality is concerned, the "arrangement," to use a neutral term, could have been that the company promised to offer work to the regular casuals and, in exchange, the regular casuals undertook to accept and perform such work as was offered. This would have constituted a contract. But what happened in fact could equally well be attributed to market forces. Which represented the true view could only be determined by the tribunal which heard the witnesses and evaluated the facts. Again, although how the industry and its casual workers regarded their status is not directly material, any generally accepted view would be part of the contractual matrix and so indirectly material, although in no way decisive. This again was a matter for the employment tribunal.

Although I, like the appeal tribunal, am content to accept the employment tribunal's conclusion that there was no overall or umbrella contract, I think that there is a shorter answer. It is that giving the claimants' evidence its fullest possible weight, all that could emerge was an umbrella or master contract *for*, not *of*, employment. It would be a contract to offer and

131

accept individual contracts of employment and, as such, outside the scope of the unfair dismissal provisions.

This leaves the question of whether the claimants entered into individual contracts of employment on each occasion when they worked for the company and it is here that the appeal tribunal and the employment tribunal parted company. The appeal tribunal dealt with this aspect of the matter by saying:

"For whatever reason, the employment tribunal have not dealt with the point, nor have they weighed the factors bearing on the question: 'was each contract for services?' in the same careful way in which they weighed those factors when looking at the nature of an overall contract of employment. In our judgment, the mere assertion by the employment tribunal that it was a succession of contracts for services entered into by independent contractors cannot stand as good in law in the absence of any reason for that conclusion. We must therefore consider the point and reach our own decision on it."

This, in my judgment, does less than justice to the decision of the employment tribunal. It had weighed the relevant factors governing the relationship between the parties with great care in the course of determining whether any umbrella contract was one of employment or for the provision of services. It had rejected the umbrella contract on the grounds that there was no contract at all, but it had also concluded:

"the applicants were in business on their own account as independent contractors supplying services and are not qualified for interim relief because they were not employees who worked under a contract of employment."

This, unless erroneous in law, was wholly sufficient reason for holding that the individual contracts, which clearly existed, were contracts for the provision of services . . .'

(Ackner and Fox LJJ delivered concurring judgments.)

Comment

(1) In a case like this, it seems that there could be three possibilities:
  (a) that there is no global or umbrella contract to offer work (or to accept), but that there is a contract when the worker is actually at work (sometimes called 'the specific engagement'), and it is a contract of employment;
  (b) as in (a), but the individual contracts or specific engagements when the worker is actually at work are not contracts of employment;
  (c) that the work takes place within the overall framework of a contract, and this global or umbrella contract (sometimes called 'the general engagement') is a contract of employment.

(2) The Court of Appeal in *O'Kelly* considers that the tribunal thought that the situation fell within (b), contrary to the view of the EAT, and upholds that decision. The Master of the Rolls also expresses the view that even if there were a global contract, it would not be a contract *of* employment.

(3) In *Clark* v *Oxfordshire HA* (1998), where the claimant was a 'bank nurse' – effectively, on call to be offered work whenever the health authority had a temporary need – the Court of Appeal held that there was no global contract of employment, because of the lack of mutual obligation, but the case was remitted to the tribunal to consider whether the individual assignments could be regarded as falling within category (a). Similarly, in *Cornwall CC* v *Prater* (2006) the Court of Appeal held that the numerous

short contracts held by a home tutor with the council over a ten-year period were all contracts of employment and could be linked together by the continuity provisions (below, p 148) to entitle her to claim continuous employment throughout that time.

(4) Possibility (c) was held to be the best fit for the facts in *Airfix Footwear Ltd* v *Cope* (1978) and *Nethermere (St Neots) Ltd* v *Gardiner* (1984). Both of these may have started out as category (a) situations, but had gone on for so long (seven years in *Airfix*, three years in *Nethermere*) that the arrangement had changed its nature. In *Nethermere (St Neots) Ltd* v *Gardiner*, which concerned homeworkers doing the same work as factory workers, albeit on an ostensibly casual basis, Stephenson LJ said:

> I cannot see why well founded expectations of continuing homework should not be hardened or refined into enforceable contracts by regular giving and taking of work over periods of a year or more, and why outworkers should not thereby become employees under contracts of service like those doing similar work at the same rate in the factory.

(5) As many statutory employment protection rights (such as the right to claim unfair dismissal) depend on establishing periods of continuous employment, casual workers are often trying to establish a global contract, as in *Airfix* and *Nethermere*. This means trying to show ongoing mutual obligations between the parties.

Carmichael v National Power plc [1999] ICR 1226 House of Lords

The two claimants worked for the Central Electricity Generating Board (CEGB) as guides showing parties round the Blyth Power Stations in Northumberland. They tested their employment status by claiming to be entitled to a written statement of their terms and conditions of employment – a right reserved to employees.

The claimants worked when required for more than six years, latterly doing as much as 25 hours a week. However, the work was 'on a casual as required basis'. The Court of Appeal held that this meant that the employer had an obligation to offer them a reasonable amount of such work as was available and that they had a corresponding obligation to accept a reasonable amount of such work. Thus they did have an ongoing contract of employment. The employer appealed.

LORD IRVINE LC: '. . . On 15 November 1988 the CEGB invited applications "for the posts of Station Guides". "Successful candidates" would be required to: "Supervise parties of visitors on pre-selected tour routes around the power station site"; as well as explain and answer questions on the various parts of the plant; and give a short presentation about the CEGB and how electricity is made and transmitted. They were also to be given "full training". The invitation continued: "Employment will be on a casual as required basis and payment will be at the rate of 376.56 pence per hour, being the minimum of Band I of the NJIC Agreement." . . .

The employment tribunal held that their case "founders on the rock of absence of mutuality", that is that when not working as guides, they were in no contractual relationship of any kind with the CEGB.

The tribunal made this finding on the basis of (a) the language of the March 1989 documentation; (b) the way in which it had been operated; and (c) the evidence of the parties as to how it had been understood. For reasons I will amplify later, this was in my judgment the correct approach. In substance the tribunal held that the documents did no more than provide a framework for a series of successive ad hoc contracts of service or for services which the parties might subsequently make; and that when they were not working as guides they were not in any contractual relationship with the CEGB. The parties incurred no obligations to provide or accept work but at best assumed moral obligations of loyalty in a context where both recognised that the best interests of each lay in being accommodating to the other. . . .

133

In my judgment it would only be appropriate to determine the issue in these cases solely by reference to the documents in March 1989, if it appeared from their own terms and/or from what the parties said or did then, or subsequently, that they intended them to constitute an exclusive memorial of their relationship. The employment tribunal must be taken to have decided that they were not so intended but constituted one, albeit important, relevant source of material from which they were entitled to infer the parties' true intention, along with the other objective inferences which could reasonably be drawn from what the parties said and did in March 1989, and subsequently.

The documents contained no provisions governing when, how, or with what frequency guide work would be offered; there were no provisions for notice of termination on either side; the sickness, holiday and pension arrangements for regular staff did not apply; nor did the grievance and disciplinary procedures. Significantly, as Kennedy LJ in his dissenting judgment with which I agree emphasised, in 1994, for example, Mrs Carmichael was not available for work on 17 occasions nor Mrs Leese on eight. No suggestion of disciplining them arose. The objective inference is that when work was available they were free to undertake it or not as they chose . . . In my judgment, therefore, the employment tribunal was well entitled to infer from the March 1989 documents, the surrounding circumstances and how the parties conducted themselves subsequently that their intention neither in 1989 nor subsequently was to have their relationship regulated by contract whilst Mrs Leese and Mrs Carmichael were not working as guides. The employment tribunal correctly concluded that their case "founders on the rock of absence of mutuality". I repeat that no issue arises as to their status when actually working as guides. . . .

For all these reasons I would allow this appeal and reinstate the employment tribunal's reserved decision . . .'

(Lords Goff, Jauncey and Browne-Wilkinson agreed. Lord Hoffmann delivered a concurring speech.)

Comment

(1) Note that although the House of Lords holds that there is no global contract of employment, Lord Irvine expresses no view as to their status when actually working.

(2) The decision can be contrasted with *Wilson* v *Circular Distributors Ltd* (2006) where an 'area relief manager' whose job was to stand in when the regular managers were sick or on holiday was held by the EAT to have an ongoing contract of employment, notwithstanding the fact that there was no guarantee of regular work under the contract and the contract specified that he was not entitled to any payment when there was no work for him. The EAT construed the contract as meaning that he had an obligation to work when the work was made available to him, and therefore that the employer had a corresponding obligation to give him work when it was available.

(3) The documentation of the agreement between the parties, and whether or not it is intended to be an exhaustive record of their agreement can be important, as *Carmichael* v *National Power plc* indicates. As with the label the parties give to their relationship, merely stating that the documents contain the entire agreement will not prevent a court or tribunal deciding that other evidence is necessary to ascertain the parties' intentions. But if the documents do contain the entire agreement, and this negatives a contract of employment, workers will not be able to adduce other evidence to show that the reality was different in some way: cf *Stevedoring & Haulage Services Ltd* v *Fuller* (2001).

(4) Another point which comes across clearly in these cases is the difficulty of attacking the original decision of an employment tribunal on the status of the contract. This

is because the issue is classified as a question of fact rather than a question of law. Unfortunately, this means that different tribunals could reasonably come to different conclusions on very similar facts but yet there could be no appeal from their decisions (compare *Nethermere (St Neots) Ltd* v *Gardiner* with *O'Kelly* v *Trusthouse Forte*, for example). This kind of inconsistency is undesirable (see further, Pitt, 1985).

Agency workers

The employment status of temporary or agency workers gives particular problems, because they usually contract with the agency on the basis that the agency does not guarantee to find them work and they are not bound to accept assignments which are offered. Thus if they try to claim that they are employees of the agency, they face the problem of mutual obligation, as with casual workers, and also the problem that they are not under the control of the agency in doing their day-to-day work.

However, the agency worker does not look much like the employee of the agency's client, the end-user, either. The problem here is that the agency worker and the end-user will have no direct contractual relationship: the end-user contracts as a client with the agency.

Montgomery v *Johnson Underwood Ltd* [2001] IRLR 269 Court of Appeal

The claimant was placed in a post as a part-time receptionist with a company called Orenstein & Kopple Ltd by the respondent employment agency. She worked there for over two years, but then the company told the agency to remove her, because they were unhappy about her use of the telephone for private calls. The agency then terminated its relationship with her. She sued both the agency and the end-user company for unfair dismissal. Was she the employee of either organisation?

An employment tribunal held that she was an employee of the agency, but not of the end-user. The EAT upheld this decision, although only because the lay members outvoted the judge. The agency appealed and so the only issue in the Court of Appeal was whether she was an employee of the agency.

BUCKLEY J: 'I consider the safest starting point to be the oft-quoted passage of McKenna J in *Ready Mixed Concrete (South East) Ltd* v *Minister of Pensions and National Insurance* (1968) [extracted above, p 122] . . . For my part, I regard the quoted passage from *Ready Mixed Concrete* as still the best guide and as containing the irreducible minimum by way of legal requirement for a contract of employment to exist. It permits tribunals appropriate latitude in considering the nature and extent of "mutual obligations" in respect of the work in question and the "control" an employer has over the individual. It does not permit those concepts to be dispensed with altogether. As several recent cases have illustrated, it directs tribunals to consider the whole picture to see whether a contract of employment emerges. It is though important that "mutual obligation" and "control" to a sufficient extent are first identified before looking at the whole . . .

I am satisfied that the tribunal's approach to these two essential ingredients of a contract of employment was wrong in law.

Mr de Mello [counsel for the claimant] submitted that "control" could be found by virtue of clause 5 of the standard conditions applicable to Mrs Montgomery. That condition reserved to JU the right to terminate her "service" if she failed to perform with the degree of technical and professional skill to be anticipated. He submitted that clause should be read with clause 4 of the terms and conditions between JU and the client, O&K. That clause simply provides that JU

135

will make every effort to meet the client's reasonable requirements by ensuring a reasonable standard of skill and integrity and reliability from their temporary workers. Without more, I would not be inclined to regard those clauses alone as amounting to "sufficient control". But that is not really in point because the tribunal here made a very clear finding of fact concerning the lack of control which I have quoted above. It is not open to this court to go behind such a clear finding which in my view is fatal to the tribunal's decision that Mrs Montgomery was employed by JU . . .

Charles J [dissenting in the EAT] held that the tribunal took into account an irrelevant consideration by having regard to the actual length of Mrs Montgomery's service with O&K. It is true that the tribunal did not explain clearly what if any inference they drew from this fact but to my mind it does have some potential relevance. For example, it suggests that the parties had come to accept that the assignment had a degree of permanence. It might be considered as lending some support to Mrs Montgomery's evidence that she was at the outset looking for a position of some permanence. In *Carmichael*, it seems to me that both the Lord Chancellor and Lord Hoffmann encouraged tribunals to take a realistic view of circumstances generally. The Lord Chancellor referred to subsequent words and events as a legitimate source from which inferences might be drawn as to the parties' intentions . . .

For my part, I would accept that an offer of work by an agency, even at another's workplace, accepted by the individual for remuneration to be paid by the agency, could satisfy the requirement of mutual obligation. I put it no higher because it would be necessary to look at the circumstances carefully and realistically. It may, for example, be more difficult to find that necessary mutuality in a very short assignment as opposed to one which was or had become more permanent. Since I have reached the conclusion that I have on "control", I prefer to say no more on this aspect of the matter, particularly as it was not really explored before the tribunal . . .

Finally, I would observe that there appears to be considerable uncertainty concerning the status of individuals who find work through employment agencies. This is apparent from the remarks of both the tribunal and the EAT. Their view seems to be shared by those in the agency business. Mrs Johnson, a director of JU, said in evidence before the tribunal:

"Temps are not employed by the clients nor by us. We are not allowed to treat them as self-employed. I do not know what their status is. No one in the agency business knows the answer. They're in limbo."

I agree with the passage in the EAT's judgment in which they comment on this uncertainty:

"It follows that, in line with the comment made by the employment tribunal . . . it seems to us that it would be sensible for the relevant government department and Parliament to give further consideration to the position of employment agencies, their clients and the individuals who work for such clients on the introduction of the agency . . . Continued confusion about whether there exists any protection at all in certain cases against unfair dismissal assists nobody."

I would allow this appeal and hold that Mrs Montgomery was not employed by JU.'

(Longmore and Brooke LJJ delivered concurring judgments.)

Comment

(1) Lack of control is thus seen as crucial in holding that the agency could not be regarded as the temporary worker's employer in this case – an issue barely raised in the earlier Court of Appeal decision, *McMeechan* v *Secretary of State for Employment* (1997),

where an agency was held to be the worker's employer in relation to one specific assignment. See also *Bunce* v *Postworth Ltd* (2005).

(2) In a trilogy of recent cases the Court of Appeal raised the possibility of the agency worker being regarded as the employee of the end-user on the basis of an *implied* contract of employment. In *Franks* v *Reuters Ltd* (2003) the case was remitted to the employment tribunal on the basis that it had erred in not considering this possibility, and in *Dacas* v *Brook Street Bureau* (2004) the Court of Appeal dismissed the worker's claim against the agency but stated that she could well have had a claim against the end-user. Finally, in *Cable & Wireless plc* v *Muscat* (2006), it was held that the agency worker was the end-user's employee, on the basis of an implied contract of employment. The reasoning supporting these developments is best expressed in *Dacas* v *Brook Street Bureau*.

Dacas v *Brook Street Bureau* [2004] ICR 1437 Court of Appeal

The claimant had been working as a cleaner supplied by the respondent employment agency to Wandsworth Borough Council. She had worked at a hostel run by the council for over four years when they asked the agency to remove her. The agency terminated its relationship with her and the claimant sued both the agency and the council for unfair dismissal. An employment tribunal held that she did not have a contract of employment with either organisation. She only appealed against the finding that she was not the agency's employee. The EAT allowed her appeal and held that she was an employee of the agency. The agency appealed. The Court of Appeal asked for Wandsworth Borough Council to be joined as a party to the appeal.

MUMMERY LJ: '. . . The real problem for the tribunals is the application of the basic legal requirements to the case where an employment agency is interposed between the applicant and the end-user and where the functions normally found in a single employing entity are re-distributed between two entities, each of which denies that it is the employer. Thus, while the end-user is the real and immediate recipient of the work done by the claimant, the employment agency is made responsible for paying remuneration to the claimant and for arranging other benefits usually associated with employment, such as sick leave and holiday pay. If there were no interposed employment agency there would be no doubt that, even in the absence of an express contract, Mrs Dacas worked under a contract of service with the council: it was managing and controlling work done by her in the mutual expectation that she would be paid for what she was told to do and had in fact done. So what difference does the presence of the employment agency really make to the status of Mrs Dacas? Does it mean that, although working under the daily control of the council, she was an employee of Brook Street, who supplied her services to the council? Or does it mean that she was not an employee of anyone?

. . .

It is legitimate to have regard to the fact, if it be the case, that a series or number of transactions are intended to operate in combination with one another or are ingredients of a wider transaction intended as a whole.

This means that, in ascertaining the overall legal effect of the triangular arrangements on the status of Mrs Dacas, the employment tribunal should not focus so intently on the express terms of the written contracts entered into by Brook Street with Mrs Dacas and the council that it is deflected from considering finding facts relevant to a possible implied contract of service between Mrs Dacas and the council in respect of the work actually done by her exclusively for the council at its premises and under its control, until it took the initiative in terminating that arrangement. The formal written contracts between Mrs Dacas and Brook Street and between Brook Street and the council relating to the work to be done by her for the council may not tell the whole of the story about the legal relationships affecting the work situation. They do not, as a matter of law, necessarily preclude the implication of a contract of service between Mrs Dacas and the council. There may be evidence of a pattern of regular mutual contact of a transactional character between Mrs Dacas and the council, from which a contract of service may be implied by the tribunal. I see no insuperable objection in law to a combination of transactions in the triangular arrangements, embracing an express contract for services between Mrs Dacas and Brook Street, an express contract between Brook Street and the council and an implied contract of service between Mrs Dacas and the council, with Brook Street acting in certain agreed respects as an agent for Mrs Dacas and as an agent for the council under the terms of the express written agreements.

I approach the question posed by this kind of case on the basis that the outcome, which would accord with practical reality and common sense, would be that, if it is legally and factually permissible to do so, the claimant has a contract, which is not a contract of service, with the employment agency, and that the claimant works under an implied contract, which is a contract of service, with the end-user and is therefore an employee of the end-user with a right not to be unfairly dismissed. The objective fact and degree of control over the work done by Mrs Dacas at West Drive over the years is crucial. The council in fact exercised the relevant control over her work and over her. As for mutuality of obligation, (a) the council was under an obligation to pay for the work that she did for it and she received payment in respect of such work from Brook Street, and (b) Mrs Dacas, while at West Drive, was under an obligation to do what she was told and to attend punctually at stated times. As for dismissal, it was the council which was entitled to take and in fact took the initiative in bringing to an end work done by her at West Drive. But for the council's action she would have continued to work there as previously. It is true that the obligations and the power to dismiss were not contained in an express contract between Mrs Dacas and the council. The fact that the obligations were contained in express contracts made between Mrs Dacas and Brook Street and between Brook Street and the council does not prevent them from being read across the triangular arrangements into an implied contract and taking effect as implied mutual obligations as between Mrs Dacas and the council . . .'

(Sedley LJ delivered a concurring judgment. Munby J dissented.)

Comment

(1) Following the approval of this approach by a differently constituted Court of Appeal in *Cable & Wireless plc* v *Muscat* (2006), numerous claims by agency workers against end-users were lodged with tribunals. In 2007 the EAT began a fightback, with different divisions paying lip-service to the need to consider the possibility of an implied contract between the worker and the end-user while strongly opining that such an implication would very rarely be appropriate (*James* v *Greenwich LBC* (2007); *Cairns* v *Visteon* (2007)).

(2) When *James* v *Greenwich LBC* (2008) was appealed to the Court of Appeal, not only was the EAT's decision upheld, but the reasoning was expressly approved. Mummery LJ, giving the main judgment, entertainingly denied any difference between the Court of Appeal and the EAT approaches to these cases.

(3) The EC Commission put forward a proposal for a Temporary Workers Directive in 2002, which would essentially have required agency workers to be treated no less favourably than comparable permanent employees of the end-user. However, it failed to win agreement in the Council of Ministers and has been stalled since shelved in 2005.

(4) Some legislation, notably the National Minimum Wage Act 1998 and the Working Time Regulations 1998, is expressly extended to agency workers.

'Workers'

Employment Rights Act 1996

230   . . .

(3) In this Act 'worker' . . . means an individual who has entered into or works under (or, where the employment has ceased, worked under) –

(a) a contract of employment, or

(b) any other contract, whether express or implied and (if it is express) whether oral or in writing, whereby the individual undertakes to do or perform personally any work or services for another party to the contract whose status is not by virtue of the contract that of a client or customer of any profession or business undertaking carried on by the individual . . .

Comment

(1) This is similar to the definitions used in the equality enactments to identify people 'in employment' to whom those enactments apply. The difference is that the equality enactments only refer to an undertaking to perform work personally – they do not contain the proviso about clients or customers of a profession or business undertaking.

(2) The status of 'worker' has become increasingly important as quite a lot of new statutory employment protection rights have been extended to 'workers' rather than just employees. The principal ones are:

- Protection from deductions from wages (ERA Part II).
- Protection for whistleblowers (ERA ss 43A–43L).
- Working Time Regulations 1998.
- National Minimum Wage Act 1998.
- Right to be accompanied in disciplinary and grievance proceedings (ERelA 1999 ss 10–13).
- Part-time Workers (Prevention of Less Favourable Treatment) Regulations 2000.

(3) The meaning of the term 'worker' was considered by the EAT in the next case.

Cotswold Developments Construction Ltd v *Williams*
[2006] IRLR 181 Employment Appeal Tribunal

LANGSTAFF J: '. . . The distinction is not that between employee and independent contractor. The paradigm case falling within the proviso to [ERA s 230(3)(b)] is that of a person working within one of the established professions: solicitor and client, barrister and client, accountant, architect etc. The paradigm case of a customer and someone working in a business undertaking of his own will perhaps be that of the customer of a shop and the shop owner, or of the customer of a tradesman such as a domestic plumber, cabinet maker or portrait painter who commercially markets services as such. Thus viewed, it seems plain that a focus upon whether the purported worker actively markets his services as an independent person to the world in general (a person who will thus have a client or customer) on the one hand, or whether he is recruited by the principal to work for that principal as an integral part of the principal's operations, will in most cases demonstrate on which side of the line a given person falls . . .'

Comment

(1) Note that the status of 'worker' still requires personal service, and so is apt to be defeated by a substitution clause, as in *Express & Echo* v *Tanton* (1999).

Part-time workers

Many employment protection rights depend on having been employed for a certain period of time (see Continuity of Employment, below, p 148). At one time this meant that part-time workers were disadvantaged, because unless they worked for at least eight hours a week they were excluded from nearly all statutory employment protection rights, and if they worked fewer than 16 hours a week, they had to fulfil a longer continuity requirement than full-time workers. In 1995 this law was successfully challenged by the EOC. In *R v Secretary of State for Employment ex parte EOC* (1994) the House of Lords held that making it more difficult for part-timers to qualify for statutory protection constituted indirect sex discrimination, because most part-time workers are women. Regulations were passed in 1995 to remove this discrimination.

Meanwhile, at EU level various issues around atypical work had been referred to the 'social partners' (representative bodies of management and workers) in the wake of commitments in the Community Charter on the Fundamental Social Rights of Workers, point 7 of which states:

> The completion of the internal market must lead to an improvement in the living and working conditions of workers in the European Community. This process must result from an approximation of these conditions while the improvement is being maintained, as regards in particular the duration and organisation of working time and forms of employment other than open-ended contracts, such as fixed-term contracts, part-time working, temporary work and seasonal work.

This resulted in the Part-time Work Directive (97/81/EC), implemented in the United Kingdom by the Part-time Workers (Prevention of Less Favourable Treatment) Regulations 2000. Its background is explained in government guidance to the Regulations.

Part-time workers: The law and best practice – a detailed guide for employers and part-timers

URN No 02/1710 (DTI)

REASONS FOR THE LEGISLATION

Less-favourable treatment of part-time workers is not widespread in the UK. However, where it does occur, it can affect a variety of terms and conditions, including pay, pensions, holidays and training.

It was partly in order to combat these residual cases of less-favourable treatment across the EU that the Part-time Work Directive was drawn up. The Directive aims to end less favourable treatment of part-timers in order to support the development of a flexible labour market, by encouraging the greater availability of part-time employment, and increasing the quality and range of jobs which are considered suitable for part-time work or job-sharing.

The Directive was negotiated at the European level by representatives of public and private-sector employers' associations and the European TUC (the 'social partners'). The UK was represented by the CBI and TUC, both of whom approved the agreement. The Government also supported the proposals. The Government has implemented the Directive in the UK by way of regulations and guidance in order to take account of the specific nature of the British labour market. This will ensure that it is effective whilst not imposing unnecessary burdens on business.

Comment

(1) Not all part-time workers would necessarily agree with the opening statement in this extract. In practice, the Part-time Workers (Prevention of Less Favourable Treatment) Regulations 2000 can only address the issue of less favourable treatment of part-time workers – not the other aim of the directive, of improving the quality and availability of part-time work.

(2) As with the equality enactments, the issue of comparison is critical here. It is dealt with in reg 2.

Part-Time Workers (Prevention of Less Favourable Treatment) Regulations 2000

2   (1)   A worker is a full-time worker for the purpose of these Regulations if he is paid wholly or in part by reference to the time he works and, having regard to the custom and practice of the employer in relation to workers employed by the worker's employer under the same type of contract, is identifiable as a full-time worker.

(2)   A worker is a part-time worker for the purpose of these Regulations if he is paid wholly or in part by reference to the time he works and, having regard to the custom and practice of the employer in relation to workers employed by the worker's employer under the same type of contract, is not identifiable as a full-time worker.

(3)   For the purposes of paragraphs (1), (2) and (4), the following shall be regarded as being employed under different types of contract –
   (a)   employees employed under a contract that is not a contract of apprenticeship;
   (b)   employees employed under a contract of apprenticeship;
   (c)   workers who are not employees;
   (d)   any other description of worker that it is reasonable for the employer to treat differently from other workers on the ground that workers of that description have a different type of contract.

(4)   A full-time worker is a comparable full-time worker in relation to a part-time worker if, at the time when the treatment that is alleged to be less favourable to the part-time worker takes place –
   (a)   both workers are –
      (i)   employed by the same employer under the same type of contract, and
      (ii)   engaged in the same or broadly similar work having regard, where relevant, to whether they have a similar level of qualification, skills and experience; and
   (b)   the full-time worker works or is based at the same establishment as the part-time worker or, where there is no full-time worker working or based at that establishment who satisfies the requirements of sub-paragraph (a), works or is based at a different establishment and satisfies those requirements.

Matthews v *Kent and Medway Towns Fire Authority* [2006] ICR 365 House of Lords

This was a test case on behalf of more than 12,000 retained (ie, part-time) firefighters, who wanted to gain access to the same occupational pension scheme and certain other benefits as full-time firefighters. There were two main issues: first, were they employed on 'the same type

141

of contract', as required by reg 2(4)(a), and secondly, if so, were they engaged in 'the same or broadly similar work'?

LORD HOPE: '. . . Directions as to the situations in which full-time and part-time workers are to be regarded as being employed under different types of contract for the purposes of regula-tion 2(4) are given in regulation 2(3). A list is given in [paragraphs (a)–(c)] of [three] kinds of employee or worker whose contracts are to be regarded as of a different type. It follows that, where both workers are employed under contracts that answer to the description given in the same paragraph, they are both to be regarded as employed under the same type of contract for the purposes of regulation 2(4). They are workers as between, assuming that the other requirements of regulation 2(4) are satisfied, it is not permissible for the employer to discrim-inate unless he can justify this on objective grounds under regulation 5(2)(b).

It is agreed that retained firefighters and whole-time firefighters are both employed under a contract that is neither for a fixed term nor a contract of apprenticeship. This is a type of con-tract of the kind described in paragraph (a). There is however one other paragraph in regulation 2(3) that has to be considered. [Paragraph (d)] adds to the list "any other description of worker that it is reasonable for the employer to treat differently from other workers on the ground that workers of that description have a different type of contract". There is a difference of opinion among your Lordships as to whether the Court of Appeal were right to hold that retained firefighters were employees of the type described in paragraph (a), not workers of the descrip-tion given in [paragraph (d)]. The question is one of construction. What does [paragraph (d)] mean, when its words are construed according to their ordinary meaning in the context of the regulation read as a whole, having regard to the purpose of the regulation? This is a question of general public importance too. The answer that is given to it will affect all part-time workers who seek the protection of the 2000 Regulations, not just retained firefighters.

It is convenient to look first at the purpose of regulation 2(3). As its opening words make clear, its function is to provide a definition of what are to be regarded as different types of con-tract for the purposes of paragraphs (1), (2) and (4) of the regulation, all of which direct atten-tion to the question whether workers are employed by the employer under the same type of contract. Clause 3(2) of the Framework Agreement annexed to Council Directive 97/81/EC defines the term "comparable full-time worker" for the purposes of the agreement as a full-time worker in the same establishment having the same type of employment contract or relation-ship who is engaged in the same or a similar work/occupation, due regard being given to other considerations which may include seniority and qualification/skills. This is the clause in the Framework Agreement to which regulation 2(4) gives effect.

There is no separate definition in clause 3 of the Framework Agreement of what is meant by the expression "the same type of contract". But one can derive from the way clause 3(2) is framed that the question whether a full-time worker is employed under the same type of con-tract as a part-time worker is to be approached broadly, having regard to the purpose of the agreement set out in clause 1. This is to provide for the removal of discrimination against part-time workers and to improve the quality of part-time work, to facilitate the development of part-time work on a voluntary basis and to contribute to the flexible organisation of working time in a manner which takes into account the needs of employers and workers. The use of the word "type" fits in with this approach. When one thinks of a type of person or a type of car, for ex-ample, one looks for a broad characteristic that separates one type from another. One ignores the many variations and differences within each type and looks instead for something that brings them all together within the same category. An over-precise view as to what makes one type of contract different from another would tend to undermine the purpose of the agreement.

The wording of the first [three] paragraphs of regulation 2(3) adopts this approach. The descriptions that are given here are broad. They do not suggest that a contract can be treated as being of a different type from another just because the terms and conditions that it lays down are different. Nor do they suggest that a contract can be treated as being of a different type just because the employer chooses to treat workers of a particular type differently. The underlying purpose seems to be to ensure that it is not left to the employer to decide whether or not to treat persons falling within the same category differently. On the contrary he is not permitted to discriminate between them if they fall within the same category, assuming that the other parts of regulation 2(4) are satisfied, unless he can justify the different treatment on objective grounds under regulation 5(2). By listing the various categories in the way it does, it suggests that all that one needs to do in order to satisfy the requirements of regulation 2(4)(a)(i) is to find that both workers are employed under contracts that fit into one or other of the [three] listed categories. The question is whether [paragraph (d)] departs from this approach. Does it add something new, or does it require one to revisit the previous categories?

In my opinion the wording of [paragraph (d)] suggests that it is adding something new. In its opening words it refers to "any *other* description of worker" (my emphasis). These words, on their own, seem to indicate that we are being asked here to examine a type of worker who is different from any of those previously mentioned. It then goes on to qualify the opening words. But it does so in a way that does not take anything away from the initial impression that we are dealing here with a type of worker, or perhaps various types of workers, who are different from those previously mentioned.

[Paragraph (d)] tells us that we are dealing now with any other description of worker that it is reasonable for the employer to treat differently from other workers, "on the ground that workers of that description have a different type of contract". It is the fact that they have a type of contract which is different from other types of contract that enables the employer to treat them differently, if it is reasonable for him to do so. This wording also permits workers of several different descriptions to be treated differently from each other on this ground under this paragraph. It is the fact that they have a different type of contract, not that the terms and conditions of their employment are different, that enables the employer to treat them differently from other workers. The breadth of the meaning to be given to the expression "type of contract" is indicated by the categories mentioned in the preceding paragraphs, which are defined broadly in a way that allows for a wide variety of different terms and conditions within each category. This protects the part-time worker from terms and conditions that treat him less favourably in comparison with those that apply to full-time workers in the same category unless the difference of treatment can be objectively justified.

Everyone agrees that it is difficult to think of a type of contract which is different from those mentioned elsewhere in the list. But I do not think that this prevents [paragraph (d)] from being treated as adding something new to the list which will not be reached if a worker falls into one or other of the previous categories. It is sufficient to say, to give it some meaning, that it is there to fill any gaps that may have been left, as a long stop or residual category. The list as a whole makes it unnecessary to carry out the kind of fact-finding exercise that my noble and learned friend Lord Mance envisages. Its purpose, after all, is simply to identify in a broad and simple fashion the types of contract that enable workers to be treated as comparable workers for the purpose of applying the less favourable treatment rules that Part II of the 2000 Regulations identifies.

For these reasons, and those given by Baroness Hale with which I entirely agree, I would hold that the Court of Appeal were right on this point. This makes it necessary to consider whether the other part of the definition in regulation 2(4)(a)(ii) is also satisfied. Are retained firefighters and whole-time firefighters engaged in "the same or broadly similar work", having regard to whether they have a similar level of qualification, skills and experience? . . .

The key passages in the tribunal's decision . . . referred . . . to their conclusions of fact about the particular methods of working of the retained fire fighter service and the way the whole operation had been geared to focus the working duties of the retained fire fighter substantially on the emergency call-out fire-fighting role. They then said that it was not in dispute that the fire fighting role was the central and most important job function of the retained fire fighter and a major part of the job role of the whole-time fire fighter. But they also found that there were measurable additional job functions which were carried out by whole-time firefighters. On that ground alone they held that the job of the whole-time fire fighter was a "fuller wider job" than that of the retained fire fighter.

The tribunal found that, because of entry standards, probationary standards, probationary training and ongoing training, there were material differences in the level of qualification and skills between the retained fire fighter and the whole-time fire fighter. As for experience, they found that retained firefighters who put in a large number of hours could develop this characteristic to an impressive level. They set out their overall conclusion putting together the fuller wider role and the higher level of qualification and skills. They held that the retained fire fighter could not establish comparability with his full-time counterpart.

It seems to me that there is a weakness in the way the tribunal dealt with differences in the level of qualification and skills between the two kinds of worker. It would not be right to subject the tribunal's reasoning to an unduly critical analysis, especially in view of their assurance that they did in the end stand back and look at the whole picture. But I think their reasons show that they failed to appreciate that the question whether the two kinds of worker had a similar level of qualification, skills and experience was relevant only in so far as it bore on the exercise of assessing whether the work that they were actually engaged in was the same or broadly similar. They did not ask themselves whether these characteristics showed that they were each contributing something different to that work. They treated the fact that there were differences in the levels of skills and experience as an additional factor leading to the conclusion that comparability could not be established, without assessing the extent to which these differences affected the work that the two different kinds of worker were actually engaged in . . .

I am not confident however that the tribunal gave sufficient weight to the extent to which the work on which both groups of firefighters were engaged was "the same" work. The painstaking way in which they addressed themselves to the various differences was a necessary and admirable reaction to the way the evidence was presented and the issues were argued before them. But it led them to concentrate on the differences and not to assess the weight that ought to be given to the similarities. Their conclusion that the job of the whole-time fire fighter was a fuller wider job than that of the retained fire fighter was not, as they appear to have thought, the end of the exercise. They still had to address the question posed by the statute which was whether, notwithstanding the fact that the job of the whole-time fire fighter was a fuller and wider job, the work on which both groups were engaged could nevertheless be described as broadly similar . . .'

BARONESS HALE: '. . . The work which they do must be looked at as a whole, taking into account both similarities and differences. But the question is not whether it is different but whether it is the same or broadly similar. That question has also to be approached in the context of regulations which are inviting a comparison between two types of worker whose work will almost inevitably be different to some extent.

In making that assessment, the extent to which the work that they do is *exactly the same* must be of great importance. If a large component of their work is exactly the same, the question is whether any differences are of such importance as to prevent their work being regarded overall as "the same or broadly similar". It is easy to imagine workplaces where both full- and part-timers do the same work, but the full-timers have extra activities with which to fill their time. This should not prevent their work being regarded as the same or broadly similar overall. Also of great importance in this assessment is the importance of the same work which they do to the work of the enterprise as a whole. It is easy to imagine workplaces where the full-timers do the more important work and the part-timers are brought in to do the more peripheral tasks: the fact that they both do some of the same work would not mean that their work was the same or broadly similar. It is equally easy to imagine workplaces where the full-timers and part-timers spend much of their time on the core activity of the enterprise: judging in the courts or complaints-handling in an ombudsman's office spring to mind. The fact that the full-timers do some extra tasks would not prevent their work being the same or broadly similar. In other words, in answering that question particular weight should be given to the extent to which their work is in fact the same and to the importance of that work to the enterprise as a whole. Otherwise one runs the risk of giving too much weight to differences which are the almost inevitable result of one worker working full-time and another working less than full-time . . .'

(Lord Nicholls agreed with Lord Hope and Baroness Hale. Lords Carswell and Mance dissented. The case was remitted to the employment tribunal to consider whether the work was broadly similar, in the light of this guidance.)

Comment

(1) This is an immensely important decision. The claimants had lost on both points in the tribunal, EAT and Court of Appeal and it looked in consequence as if the impact of the Part-time Workers Regulations would be limited. However, the broad approach adopted by the majority of the House of Lords on both points paves the way for a purposive interpretation to be adopted and gives a clear signal that employers need to address differential treatment as a matter of urgency.

(2) Note that the Part-time Workers (Prevention of Less Favourable Treatment) Regulations 2000 reg 2(3) originally contained six categories of contract, because it also included fixed-term contracts. When the Fixed-term Employees (Prevention of Less Favourable Treatment) Regulations 2002 were passed, this regulation was amended to remove these references – but this was after proceedings in this case had begun.

(3) It remains the case that less favourable treatment of part-time workers may also constitute indirect sex discrimination. The virtue of Part-time Workers Regulations is that it is not necessary to show that one sex is disadvantaged. On the other hand, these Regulations do require an actual comparator.

(4) The phrase, 'the same or broadly similar work', is almost identical to the formulation used in the Equal Pay Act – but they are not identical and Baroness Hale warned against assuming that they would be interpreted in exactly the same way.

Fixed-term contracts

Most contracts of employment are indefinite, meaning that at the time of contracting, neither party knows at what point in the future the contract will terminate. This uncertainty is dealt with by providing that either party will have a right to terminate by giving notice. However, there may be situations where an employer has a genuine short-term need for an employee for a specific period of time. It may be for a project with a limited lifespan, or to cover the absence of another employee, or because of a short-term increase in demand. But because statutory employment protection rights depend on building up periods of continuous employment and many contractual benefits are available only to employees and are also enhanced through length of service (eg pension rights, incremental salary scales) an employee on a fixed-term contract could be in a precarious position. It became clear that many employers used fixed-term employees as a way of obtaining the benefits of flexibility in the same way that they might use casual workers or agency workers – to give them a pool of disposable workers in respect of whom they would not incur the costs and responsibilities of permanent employees.

The dangers of this in relation to redundancy and unfair dismissal were always recognised and guarded against (see below, p 365). As part of the EU initiative discussed above in relation to part-time workers, issues surrounding the use of fixed-term contracts were referred to the social partners, resulting in the Fixed-term Work Directive (99/70/EC), mainly implemented in the United Kingdom by the Fixed-term Employees (Prevention of Less Favourable Treatment) Regulations 2002.

EC Council Directive 99/70/ concerning the framework agreement on fixed-term work concluded by ETUC, UNICE and CEEP (the Fixed-term Work Directive)

ANNEX

General considerations

4.   Whereas in its opinion on the proposal for a Directive on part-time work, the European Parliament invited the Commission to submit immediately proposals for directives on other forms of flexible work, such as fixed-term work and temporary agency work;
5.   Whereas in the conclusions of the extraordinary summit on employment adopted in Luxembourg, the European Council invited the social partners to negotiate agreements to 'modernise the organisation of work, including flexible working arrangements, with the aim of making undertakings productive and competitive and achieving the required balance between flexibility and security' . . .

The Signatory Parties have agreed the following
Purpose (clause 1)

The purpose of this framework agreement is to:
(a)   improve the quality of fixed-term work by ensuring the application of the principle of non-discrimination;
(b)   establish a framework to prevent abuse arising from the use of successive fixed-term employment contracts or relationships.

Fixed-Term Employees (Prevention of Less Favourable Treatment) Regulations 2002

1(2) . . .
   "fixed-term contract" means a contract of employment that, under its provisions determining how it will terminate in the normal course, will terminate –
   (a)   on the expiry of a specific term,
   (b)   on the completion of a particular task, or
   (c)   on the occurrence or non-occurrence of any other specific event other than the attainment by the employee of any normal and bona fide retiring age in the establishment for an employee holding the position held by him,
   and any reference to "fixed-term" shall be construed accordingly; . . .

146

2 (1) For the purposes of these Regulations, an employee is a comparable permanent employee in relation to a fixed-term employee if, at the time when the treatment that is alleged to be less favourable to the fixed-term employee takes place,

(a) both employees are –
   (i) employed by the same employer, and
   (ii) engaged in the same or broadly similar work having regard, where relevant, to whether they have a similar level of qualification and skills; and
(b) the permanent employee works or is based at the same establishment as the fixed-term employee or, where there is no comparable permanent employee working or based at that establishment who satisfies the requirements of sub-paragraph (a), works or is based at a different establishment and satisfies those requirements.

(2) For the purposes of paragraph (1), an employee is not a comparable permanent employee if his employment has ceased.

3 (1) A fixed-term employee has the right not to be treated by his employer less favourably than the employer treats a comparable permanent employee –
   (a) as regards the terms of his contract; or
   (b) by being subjected to any other detriment by any act, or deliberate failure to act, of his employer.

(2) Subject to paragraphs (3) and (4), the right conferred by paragraph (1) includes in particular the right of the fixed-term employee in question not to be treated less favourably than the employer treats a comparable permanent employee in relation to
   (a) any period of service qualification relating to any particular condition of service,
   (b) the opportunity to receive training, or
   (c) the opportunity to secure any permanent position in the establishment.

(3) The right conferred by paragraph (1) applies only if –
   (a) the treatment is on the ground that the employee is a fixed-term employee, and
   (b) the treatment is not justified on objective grounds.

(4) Paragraph (3)(b) is subject to regulation 4.

(5) In determining whether a fixed-term employee has been treated less favourably than a comparable permanent employee, the pro rata principle shall be applied unless it is inappropriate.

(6) In order to ensure that an employee is able to exercise the right conferred by paragraph (1) as described in paragraph (2)(c) the employee has the right to be informed by his employer of available vacancies in the establishment.

(7) For the purposes of paragraph (6) an employee is 'informed by his employer' only if the vacancy is contained in an advertisement which the employee has a reasonable opportunity of reading in the course of his employment or the employee is given reasonable notification of the vacancy in some other way.

4 (1) Where a fixed-term employee is treated by his employer less favourably than the employer treats a comparable permanent employee as regards any term of his contract, the treatment in question shall be regarded for the purposes of regulation 3(3)(b) as justified on objective grounds if the terms of the fixed-term employee's contract of employment, taken as a whole, are at least as favourable as the terms of the comparable permanent employee's contract of employment.

(2) Paragraph (1) is without prejudice to the generality of regulation 3(3)(b).

Comment

(1) It should be noted that these Regulations apply to employees only (the protection for part-timers extends to 'workers').

(2) The definition of a comparable permanent employee is similar to that used in the Part-time Workers (Prevention of Less Favourable Treatment) Regulations 2000, but note the differences.

(3) The other purpose of the directive – preventing abuse through the use of successive fixed-term contracts – is dealt with by reg 8, which places an upper limit for successive fixed-term contracts of four years, after which the employee is treated as a permanent employee.

(4) There are exceptions to this position. First, an initial fixed-term contract can be for any period: it is only if there is a renewal which takes the whole period beyond four years that reg 8 kicks in. Secondly, the four-year period can be exceeded if the employer can show objective justification for continuing it as a fixed-term contract.

(5) It would not enhance the position of fixed-term employees if the employer was to avoid renewing their contracts just before the four years was up in order to prevent them from being treated as permanent employees. In part to allow for this danger, a further exception is that the four-year period can be varied by collective or workforce agreement. It should be noted that the prohibition on less favourable treatment was held not to be infringed by an employer ensuring that any fixed-term contract did not exceed 51 weeks, thus preventing fixed-term employees gaining rights to claim unfair dismissal (*Webley* v *Department for Work and Pensions* (2005)).

CONTINUITY OF EMPLOYMENT

So far in this chapter we have seen the difficulties faced by atypical workers such as casual and agency workers in establishing that they are employed under a contract of employment. Even if they can show that they are working under a contract of employment while at work, they may still fail to qualify for statutory employment protection rights if they are held to be working under a series of separate contracts. This is because many rights depend on having completed a period of *continuous* employment: for example, one year for unfair dismissal and two years for redundancy.

Employment Rights Act 1996

210 . . .

(4)   Subject to sections 215 to 217, a week which does not count in computing the length of a period of continuous employment breaks continuity of employment.

(5)   A person's employment during any period shall, unless the contrary is shown, be presumed to have been continuous.

212 (1)   Any week during the whole or part of which an employee's relations with his employer are governed by a contract of employment counts in computing the employee's period of employment.

(3)   Subject to subsection (4), any week (not within subsection (1)) during the whole or part of which an employee is –

(a)   incapable of work in consequence of sickness or injury,

(b)   absent from work on account of a temporary cessation of work, [or]

(c)   absent from work in circumstances such that, by arrangement or custom, he is regarded as continuing in the employment of his employer for any purpose,

counts in computing the employee's period of employment.

(4)   Not more than twenty-six weeks count under subsection (3)(a) between any periods falling under subsection (1).

216   (1)   A week does not count under section 212 if during the week, or any part of the week, the employee takes part in a strike.

(2)   The continuity of an employee's period of employment is not broken by a week which does not count under this Chapter . . . if during the week, or any part of the week, the employee takes part in a strike . . .

(3)   The continuity of an employee's period of employment is not broken by a week if during the week, or any part of the week, the employee is absent from work because of a lock-out by the employer . . .

Comment

(1) As there is no longer any minimum hours stipulation for building up continuity of employment, the only requirement is that there should be a contract of employment in existence (ERA s 212(1)) during the week in question. Note that this does not mean that the employee must have attended for work.

(2) Special provision is made for strikes and lock-outs in ERA s 216. They will not break continuity, provided that the employee goes back to work for the employer afterwards, but time when the employee is on strike will not count towards their continuous service. This is intended to place the law in a neutral position between the interests of employer and employees. For the purposes of computing continuity, there is a definition of 'strike' and 'lock-out' in ERA s 235.

(3) Note the importance of the exceptions in ERA s 212(3): this provides for continuity to be preserved *even when no contract is in existence* – provided that the gap is not more than 26 weeks and the absence is for one of the reasons in s 212(3)(a)–(c).

(4) If an employee is absent from work through sickness or injury, the contract of employment normally continues and ERA s 212(3)(a) is not necessary. However, there may be exceptional cases where the contract has been terminated for this reason but the employee does recover and go back to work for the same employer. Continuity is preserved as long as the period without a contract is not more than 26 weeks.

(5) Casual workers often seek to rely on the 'temporary cessation of work' exception to preserve their continuity of employment between contracts. Clearly there is a lot of room for disagreement about how temporary a break is. Guidance was given by the House of Lords in the next case.

Ford v *Warwickshire County Council* [1983] ICR 273 House of Lords

The appellant was a teacher who had been employed on a series of fixed-term contracts for the school year over an 8-year period. The contracts would begin in September and finish in July. In July 1979 she was told that she would not be given a contract for the next school year and she claimed redundancy and unfair dismissal. The case went to the House of Lords on the preliminary issue of whether she had a sufficient period of continuous employment to be able to claim.

LORD DIPLOCK: '. . . My Lords, since [ERA s 212(3)] only applies to an interval of time between the coming to an end of one contract of employment and the beginning of a fresh contract of employment, the expression "absent from work", where it appears in [ERA s 212(3)(b) and (c)] must mean not only that the employee is not doing any actual work for his employer but that there is no contract of employment subsisting between him and his employer that would entitle the latter to require him to do any work. So in this context the phrase "the employee is ... absent from work on account of a temporary cessation of work" as descriptive of a period of time, as it would seem to me, must refer to the interval between (1) the date on which the employee who would otherwise be continuing to work under an existing contract of employment is dismissed because for the time being his employer has no work for him to do, and (2) the date on which work for him to do having become again available he is re-engaged under a fresh contract of employment to do it; and the words "on account of a temporary cessation of work" refer to the reason why the employer dismissed the employee, and make it necessary to inquire what the reason for the dismissal was. The fact that the unavailability of work had been foreseen by the employer sufficiently far in advance to enable him to anticipate it by giving to the employee a notice to terminate his contract of employment that is of sufficient length to satisfy the requirements of [ERA s 86] (which may be as long as 12 weeks) cannot alter the reason for the dismissal or prevent the absence from work following on the expiry of the notice from being "on account of a temporary cessation of work" . . .

From the fact that there is no work available for the employee to do for the employer during the whole of the interval between the end of one fixed-term contract of employment and the beginning of the next, and that this was the reason for his non-employment during that interval, it does not necessarily follow that the interval constitutes a "temporary cessation of work". In harmony with what this House held in *Fitzgerald* v *Hall, Russell & Co Ltd* (1970), [ERA s 212(3)(b)], in cases of employment under a succession of fixed-term contracts of employment with intervals in between, requires one to look back from the date of the expiry of the fixed-term contract in respect of the non-renewal of which the employee's claim is made over the whole period during which the employee has been intermittently employed by the same employer, in order to see whether the interval between one fixed-term contract and the fixed-term contract that next preceded it was short in duration relative to the combined duration of those two fixed-term contracts during which work had continued; for the whole scheme of the Act appears to me to show that it is in the sense of "transient", ie, lasting only for a relatively short time, that the word "temporary" is used in [ERA s 212(3)(b)]. So, the continuity of employment for the purposes of the Act in relation to unfair dismissal and redundancy payments is not broken unless and until, looking backwards from the date of the expiry of the fixed-term contract on which the employee's claim is based, there is to be found between one fixed-term contract and its immediate predecessor an interval that cannot be characterised as short relatively to the combined duration of the two fixed-term contracts. Whether it can be so characterised is a question of fact and degree and so is for decision by an employment tribunal rather than by the Employment Appeal Tribunal or an appellate court of law . . .

My Lords, as I indicated at the outset, the length of successive fixed-term contracts on which part-time lecturers are employed and the intervals between them vary considerably with the particular course that the part-time lecturer is engaged to teach; so it by no means follows that a similar concession would be made or would be appropriate in each of their cases. It also follows from what I have said that successive periods of seasonal employment of other kinds under fixed-term contracts, such as employment in agriculture during harvest-time or in hotel work during the summer season, will only qualify as continuous employment if the length of the period between two successive seasonal contracts is so short in comparison with the length of the season during which the employee is employed as properly to be regarded by the employment tribunal as no more than a *temporary* cessation of work in the sense that I have indicated.'

(The appeal was allowed. Lord Brightman delivered a concurring speech and Lords Keith, Roskill and Brandon agreed with both.)

Comment

(1) Note from this that not only must the absence be temporary, judged with hindsight according to the duration of the whole relationship, but the reason for the absence must be a temporary cessation of work. If there was work available, continuity will not be preserved even if the employee's absence was only temporary (*Byrne* v *Birmingham City DC* (1987)).

(2) It is puzzling to see how an employee can be regarded as absent from work by arrangement or custom but continuing in employment, although there is no contract of employment in existence, as the next case illustrates.

Curr v *Marks & Spencer plc* [2003] ICR 443 Court of Appeal

The employee was a manager with 17 years' service. When she was about to return from maternity leave following the birth of her third child, she was encouraged by the company to take part in a new career break scheme instead. This allowed her to leave the company for four years, with a guaranteed right to return to a similar job at a similar level. She had to resign at the end of her maternity leave, but she was required to stay in touch by working for the company for at least two weeks during each year of the career break. In fact she worked for five separate periods totalling more than one year during the break. Five years after she returned from the career break she was made redundant. The company argued that the career break had interrupted her continuous employment. She argued that it should be regarded as an absence where, by arrangement or custom, she was to be regarded as having continued in their employment.

PETER GIBSON LJ: '. . . The clear purpose of ERA s 212(3) was to extend what was meant by continuous employment under a contract of employment to include certain periods where there was no employment under a contract of employment if the specified conditions were satisfied. Thus if an employee during a week not within ERA s 212(1) is incapable of work in consequence of sickness or injury or is absent from work on account of a temporary cessation of work, that week is nevertheless to count in computing the employee's period of employment (ERA s 212 (3)(a) and (b)). Similarly a week in which the conditions of ERA s 212(3)(c) are satisfied will so count. But the ex-employee (who is included in the definition of "employee") must, by arrangement (which can, but need not, be a contract) or custom, be regarded by both the employer and the ex-employee as continuing in the employment of the employer for any purpose in that week. The parties might, for example, agree that for pension purposes the ex-employee is to be treated during the child break as continuing in the employment of the employer. But there must be a mutual recognition by the arrangement that the ex-employee, though absent from work, nevertheless continues in the employment of the employer. Without there being a meeting of minds by the arrangement that both parties regard the ex-employee as continuing in that employment for some purpose, ERA s 212(3)(c) will not be satisfied. Further, unless in every week of the child break the ex-employee is so regarded there will be a break in the continuity of employment . . .

The question whether Mrs Curr was regarded as continuing in the employment of M&S for any purpose falls to be answered by a consideration of all the circumstances, and in particular the terms of the two letters of 16 November 1990 and what she was told by Miss Johnstone [the company's personnel manager] before agreeing to accept the child break. I, of course, accept that ERA s 212(3) proceeds on the basis that there is no contract of employment for any week in question, but that does not remove the force of the clear emphasis on the bringing to an end of the previous employment. Mrs Curr was required to resign and that carried all the financial consequences of such cesser of employment. She was given her P45. She even had to repay her house purchase loan forthwith. Whilst paragraph 11 of the second letter refers to the personnel manager discussing the effect the child break would have on her staff benefits, we know from the employment tribunal's findings that she was told that she would lose all staff benefits during the child break, and we know that her pension was frozen.

In my judgment by the agreement constituted by Mrs Curr accepting the terms and conditions of the child break she was not regarded as continuing in the employment of M&S for any purpose. The terms and conditions conferred on her the option to be re-employed in a management post at the end of the child break, provided she satisfied the specific conditions (such as passing a medical examination), and many of the provisions of the second letter are directed to facilitating that re-employment. But it was only an option, which she was free not to exercise. During the child break it was expressly provided that she was to be unpaid. True it is that she was required to serve a minimum of 2 weeks a year and was entitled to be paid for such service, but that was subject to the qualification that the time and pattern of hours had to be mutually convenient. It was not specified where she would work or what her work or her pay would be. It is also true that contact would be maintained through her line/personnel manager, but that manager was not given any power of control over her. The prohibition against undertaking any form of paid employment was made subject to prior consultation with that manager. It was not a prohibition against so undertaking in the absence of consent from the manager, and so long as Mrs Curr consulted the manager she was free to work elsewhere.

The majority of the appeal tribunal do not appear to have recognised that the emphasis in the terms and conditions of the second letter on re-employment at the end of the child break serves to show that she was not regarded as continuing in employment during the child break. I therefore cannot accept that the option conferred on Mrs Curr to be re-employed shows that she was regarded as continuing in employment for the purpose of re-engagement. Nor can I accept that it was for the purpose of working in the interim that she was regarded as continuing in employment. On the contrary: provision was made for her to work a minimum of two weeks each year, but until that happened and only while it happened would she be in temporary paid employment. Otherwise the period of the child break was to be unpaid. As for the purpose of restricting Mrs Curr from taking up other employment, it was not an effective restriction and I do not understand how an attempt to restrict her entails the conclusion that she was mutually regarded as continuing in the employer's employment.

Accordingly on this aspect of the appeal I reach the clear conclusion that the employment tribunal was fully entitled to find no arrangement within ERA s 212(3)(c) and that the majority of the EAT were wrong in their conclusion to the contrary . . .'

(Clarke and Scott Baker LJJ delivered concurring judgments.)

Comment

(1) The question remains, in what situations will you be regarded as continuing in employment, even though there is no contract of employment in existence?

(2) It has been argued that the trend towards the greater use of atypical workers has the effect of shifting the risks associated with the enterprise from the employer to the worker (see Collins, 1990). Would you agree? If so, is it a fair allocation of risk?

REFERENCES AND FURTHER READING

H Collins (1990), 'Independent Contractors and the Challenge of Vertical Disintegration to Employment Protection Law' 10 OJLS 353
L Dickens (1992), *Whose Flexibility? Discrimination and equality issues in atypical work*, Institute of Employment Rights

M Freedland (2003), *The Personal Employment Contract*, OUP

M Freedland (2006), 'From the contract of employment to the personal work contract' 35 ILJ 1

J Kenner (1999), 'Statement or contract? Some reflections on the EC Employee Information (Contract or Employment Relationship) Directive after *Kampelmann*' 28 ILJ 205

E McKendrick (1996), 'Who is an employee? A contextual approach?' 25 ILJ 136

G Pitt (1985), 'Law, Fact and Casual Workers' 101 LQR 217

Visit **http://www.mylawchamber.co.uk/pitt**
to access live web updates and web links to extend
your knowledge of Employment Law.

 mylawchamber

4

THE CONTRACT OF EMPLOYMENT

FORMATION

No particular formalities are required for making a contract of employment. It is usual, however, for the process of offer and acceptance to follow after a recruitment procedure, which normally begins with an advertisement, continues with a consideration of written applications and the drawing up a shortlist, followed by a selection process which still usually centres on a panel interviewing applicants. Applicants are generally asked for the names of someone who may be approached to give a reference, and the present or former employer is the most obvious person.

This can create something of a problem for an employee, especially if there are reasons for suspecting that the former employer may not be wholly favourable. First, employers have no general obligation to give references about employees at all. Secondly, the applicant has no right to see a copy of the reference which is sent. Although this is 'personal data' within the meaning of the Data Protection Act 1998 s 1, references are expressly excepted by Sch 7, para 1 to the Act. If successful in getting the job, the employee could then ask to see the reference as part of the personal data held by the employer, but the Data Protection Act 1998 s 7(4) states that access should not be given to data which identifies a third party unless that party consents. Thus a reference given by a referee who has expressed a desire for it to remain confidential should not be disclosed. (See further the Information Commissioner's Code on Employment Practices (2005).) Thirdly, even if a reference contains defamatory matter which is untrue, the referee will not be liable provided that the reference was only published to the person with an interest in seeing it (the prospective new employer) and provided that the statements were not made maliciously: ie, the reference attracts qualified privilege. What about a damaging reference which is given negligently?

Spring v Guardian Assurance plc [1994] IRLR 460 House of Lords

Until his dismissal in July 1989, Spring had been employed as sales director and office manager by Corinium, the third defendants in the case. Corinium were authorised agents for the sale of Guardian Assurance insurance policies, and Spring was authorised as a representative for their sale in accordance with the rules of the then statutory regulatory authority, LAUTRO.

After his dismissal, Spring tried to set up his own business selling Scottish Amicable policies. LAUTRO rules required insurance companies to take up references on potential representatives, and also instructed insurance companies giving references to make full and frank disclosure of relevant matters.

154

Scottish Amicable therefore approached Guardian Assurance for a reference. It was drawn up by a Guardian Assurance compliance officer who had no personal knowledge of Spring. She relied on information given to her by his former boss, who disliked him and had been responsible for his dismissal, and two other company officials. The reference, which impugned Spring's honesty and stated that he had been involved in serious mis-selling, was aptly described by the trial judge as 'the kiss of death' to his career in the insurance industry.

It was found that the reference was inaccurate and that those giving the information on which it was based had acted negligently, although not maliciously. Spring sued Guardian Assurance. Did the company owe him a duty of care?

LORD WOOLF: '. . . I am able, from the outset, to focus on the important issues of principle to which this appeal gives rise. They are:

1. Whether a person who suffers loss as a result of being the subject of an inaccurate reference is ever able to recover damages for that loss in an action for negligence or whether he is confined to seeking damages for defamation or injurious falsehood. (The difference in practice between an action for negligence and an action for defamation or injurious falsehood is that in an action based on defamation or injurious falsehood it will be necessary to establish that the person responsible for giving the reference was motivated by malice, while in the case of an action based on negligence it will be sufficient to establish that it was due to a lack of care in ascertaining the facts on which the reference is based on the part of the person giving the reference or those for whom he is responsible.)

2. Whether, in the appropriate circumstances, in a contract for service or services a term can be implied requiring an employer to exercise due care in the preparation of a reference relating to a person who is, or has been, in his service.

I do not consider that it is of any significance whether Mr Spring was employed by or acting under a contract for services with Corinium. Certain of the documents suggest he was self-employed and the judge held he was acting under a contract for services. However, this is wholly inconsistent with the nature of his role with the company, which was that of sales director (designate) and office manager. However, whether he was a servant or self-employed, his activities in selling insurance policies would be as a company representative, subject to the LAUTRO rules; and the person who was responsible for compiling the reference, Mrs Debra Lee-Moore, had delegated to others the task of collecting the information on which the reference was based. As a matter of convenience, I will treat him as an employee, but it should be appreciated that my views would be the same if he was acting under a contract for services . . .

THE CLAIM BASED ON NEGLIGENCE

The claim here is in respect of economic loss. Before there can be a duty owed in respect of economic loss, it is now clearly established that it is important to be able to show foreseeability of that loss, coupled with the necessary degree of proximity between the parties. It is also necessary to establish that in all the circumstances it is fair, just and reasonable for a duty to be imposed in respect of the economic loss. Deferring for the moment consideration of the consequences of there being possible alternative causes of action of defamation and injurious falsehood and the related public policy considerations, there can really be no dispute that Mr Spring can establish the necessary foreseeability and proximity.

It is clearly foreseeable that if you respond to a request for a reference by giving a reference which is inaccurate, the subject of the reference may be caused financial loss. Where the reference is required by a prospective employer, the loss will frequently result from a failure to obtain that employment. The prospect of such loss is considerably increased if the reference relates to an applicant, like Mr Spring, for a position as a company representative in an industry which is subject to a rule which is in equivalent terms to rule 3.5. of the LAUTRO rules. That rule provides:

> "(1) A person shall not be appointed as a company representative of a member unless the member has first taken reasonable steps to satisfy itself that he is of good character and of the requisite aptitude and competence, and those steps shall . . . include . . . taking up of references relating to character and experience.
>
> (2) A member which receives an inquiry for a reference in respect of a person whom another member or appointed representative is proposing to appoint shall make full and frank disclosure of all relevant matters which are believed to be true to the other member or the representative."

His Honour Judge Lever, at first instance, accepted Mr Spring's counsel's description of the reference as being "the kiss of death" to Mr Spring's career in insurance. This was the inevitable consequence of the reference. The reference related to a time and was based upon events which occurred while Mr Spring was working for Corinium and was engaged in selling policies issued by Guardian. The relationship between Mr Spring and the respondents could hardly be closer. Subject to what I have to say hereafter, it also appears to be uncontroversial that if an employer, or former employer, by his failure to make proper inquiries, causes loss to an employee, it is fair, just and reasonable that he should be under an obligation to compensate that employee for the consequences. This is the position if an employer injures his employee physically by failing to exercise reasonable care for his safety and I find it impossible to justify taking a different view where an employer, by giving an inaccurate reference about his employee, deprives an employee, possibly for a considerable period, of the means of earning his livelihood. The consequences of the employer's carelessness can be as great in the long term as causing the employee a serious injury . . .

. . .

In *Hedley Byrne* v *Heller* (1963) their Lordships extended the circumstances giving rise to a duty of care so as to protect the recipient from an inaccurate reference in those situations where the relationship between the person giving and receiving the reference is "'equivalent to contract,' that is, where there is an assumption of responsibility in circumstances in which, but for the absence of consideration, there would be a contract." In such a situation it is necessary to distinguish "between social and professional relationships and between those which are of a contractual character and those which are not." It may also "be material to consider whether the adviser is acting purely out of good nature or whether he is getting his reward in some indirect form" (*per* Lord Devlin). Applying that guidance to the different situation of the relationship between the person giving and the person who is the subject of the reference, it is immediately clear that a distinction can be drawn between cases where the subject of the reference is an employee (I use that term hereafter to include a person engaged on a contract for services as well as a contract of service) or an ex-employee and where the relationship is social and has never been contractual. In the latter situation all that the person who is the subject of the reference may be able to rely on is the fact that the referee gave the reference. That I can well understand may not be considered sufficient to create the required degree of proximity. The proximity would be closer to that in *Hedley Byrne*, if the reference had been given by a purely social acquaintance at the request of the subject of the reference. While the request may or may not be sufficient to create the required proximity it can still be distinguished from the present class of case. Here the relationship is of a different order because there is or has been a contract of employment or for services. Of course the period which elapses between the end of the engagement and the giving of the reference is capable of reducing the degree of proximity.

In addition, the relationship is one where the employer should, as I have already indicated, appreciate that the terms of any reference which he gives could materially affect the ability of the subject of the reference to find alternative employment. Furthermore, in a contemporary employment context it is appropriate to regard the employer as obtaining an indirect benefit from giving a reference. Employers in industry, commerce and the professions are all dependent on the reciprocity which exists among employers as to the giving of references on prospective recruits. Without that reciprocity recruitment of staff would be more difficult. It would also directly affect an employer's ability to recruit staff if it became known that he was not prepared to assist those he had previously engaged by giving them references. Employees are unlikely to regard as attractive employment at the end of which they would find themselves without a reference.

The duty imposed by the LAUTRO rules is not for the protection of employees. It is for the protection of the public. An employee cannot therefore rely on the rules directly. However, they nonetheless demonstrate the importance now attached in the insurance industry to references being given and obtained. To be of value they need to be full, frank and, by implication, accurate references.

Finally, no difficulty is created by the fact that before the reference was given the employment had come to an end. Mr Spring was dismissed on 26 July 1989 and the reference which has resulted in these proceedings was the consequence of his seeking an appointment as a representative almost immediately thereafter on 2 August 1989. The reference was sent on 21 November 1989 and, as Judge Lever said, "the inevitable happened." Mr Spring was rejected first by Scottish Amicable and then by two other insurance companies. This all occurred within a reasonable time of the employment ending.

I therefore now turn to examine the two factors which make the issues in this case difficult to resolve. The first of those factors is the existence of the alternative causes of action in defamation and injurious falsehood which are available to a person in Mr Spring's position who believes he has been caused damage by an inaccurate reference. (I will treat both those alternative causes of action under the heading of defamation since it is their common characteristic that to succeed a claimant must prove malice which creates the difficulty.) The second factor is closely related to the first. It is the public policy consequences which would follow from there being a remedy in negligence.

THE DEFAMATION ISSUE

There would be no purpose in extending the tort of negligence to protect the subject of an inaccurate reference if he was already adequately protected by the law of defamation. However, because of the defence of qualified privilege, before an action for defamation can succeed (or, for that matter, an action for injurious falsehood) it is necessary to establish malice. In my judgment the result of this requirement is that an action for defamation provides a wholly inadequate remedy for an employee who is caused damage by a reference which due to negligence is inaccurate. This is because it places a wholly disproportionate burden on the employee. Malice is extremely difficult to establish. This is demonstrated by the facts of this case. Mr Spring was able to establish that one of his colleagues, who played a part in compiling the information on which the reference was based, had lied about interviewing him, but this was still insufficient to prove malice. Without an action for negligence the employee may, therefore, be left with no practical prospect of redress, even though the reference may have permanently prevented him from obtaining employment in his chosen vocation.

If the law provided a remedy for references which are inaccurate due to carelessness this would be beneficial. It would encourage the adoption of appropriate standards when preparing references. This would be an important advantage as frequently an employee will be ignorant that it is because of the terms of an inaccurate reference, of the contents of which he is unaware, that he is not offered fresh employment.

The availability of a remedy without having to prove malice will not open the floodgates. In cases where the employee discovers the existence of the inaccurate reference, he will have a remedy if, but only if, he can establish, instead of malice, that the reason for the inaccuracy is the default of the employer, in the sense that he has been careless. To make an employer liable for an inaccurate reference, but only if he is careless, is, I would suggest, wholly fair. It would balance the respective interests of the employer and employee. It would amount to a development of the law of negligence which accords with the principles which should control its development. It would, in addition, avoid a rather unattractive situation continuing of a recipient of a reference, but not the subject of a reference, being able to bring an action for negligence. It would also recognise that while both in negligence and defamation it is the untrue statement which causes the damage, there is a fundamental difference between the torts. An action for defamation is founded upon the inaccurate terms of the reference itself. An action for negligence is based on the lack of care of the author of the reference . . .

PUBLIC POLICY

. . . It is obviously in accord with public policy that references should be full and frank. It is also in accord with public policy that they should not be based upon careless investigations. In the case of references for positions of responsibility this is particularly important. That is confirmed by the LAUTRO rules. It has also to be accepted that some referees may be more timid in giving full and frank references if they feel there is a risk of their being found liable for negligence. However, there is already such a possible liability in respect of a negligently favourable reference, so all that needs to be considered is the possible adverse consequences of a negligently unfavourable reference. For reasons to which I have already referred I consider there is little practical likelihood of no reference at all being given nowadays. Certainly this could not happen in the case of appointments to which the LAUTRO rules apply.

However, the real issue is not whether there would be any adverse effect on the giving of references. Rather the issue is whether the adverse effects, when balanced against the benefits which would flow from giving the subject a right of action, sufficiently outweigh the benefits to justify depriving the subject of a remedy unless he can establish malice. In considering this issue it is necessary to take into account contemporary practices in the field of employment; the fact that nowadays most employment is conditional upon a reference being provided. There are also the restrictions on unfair dismissal which mean that an employee is ordinarily not capable of being dismissed except after being told of what is alleged against him and after he has been given an opportunity of giving an explanation. There is also the widespread practice, especially in the Civil Service, of having annual reports which the subject is entitled to see – which practice, apparently even in an ongoing employment situation, is not defeated by any lack of candour. There is now an openness in employment relationships which did not exist even a few years ago.

There is also the advantage, already referred to, of it being appreciated that you cannot give a reference which could cause immense harm to its subject without exercising reasonable care.

A further consideration mentioned by the President is the undesirability of infringing freedom of speech. This is a consideration at least as important to the common law as it is under the international conventions by which it is also protected. Here it is necessary to bear in mind that, as is the case with all fundamental freedoms, the protection is qualified and not absolute. Freedom of speech does not necessarily entitle the speaker to make a statement without exercising reasonable care. Freedom of speech has to be balanced against the equally well recognised freedom both at common law and under the conventions that an individual should not be deprived of the opportunity of earning his livelihood in his chosen occupation. A development of the law which does no more than protect an employee from being deprived of employment as a result of a negligent reference would fully justify any limited intrusion on freedom of speech.

When I weigh these considerations I find that public policy comes down firmly in favour of not depriving an employee of a remedy to recover the damages to which he would otherwise be entitled as a result of being a victim of a negligent reference.

Under this head there remains to be considered whether it is preferable for the law in this area to be developed by Parliament or by the courts. It is an area of law where previous decisions of the courts have already clearly identified the tests which should be applied in deciding whether the law should be developed. It is also an area where a case-by-case approach is particularly appropriate and so as happened in *Hedley Byrne*, it appears to me desirable for the courts to provide the remedy which I believe is clearly required . . .'

(The employee's appeal was allowed. Lords Slynn and Lowry delivered concurring speeches. Lord Goff concurred, but based his decision only on the *Hedley Byrne* duty rather than the wider duty of care. Lord Keith dissented.)

Comment

(1) Note the statement that the duty of care is the same whether or not the subject of the reference is an employee or an independent contractor.

(2) Do employers have an obligation to give references, according to Lord Woolf? Are there any situations where the provider of a reference would not owe a duty of care to the subject of the reference?

(3) What policy reasons are identified as relevant to the decision? Do you agree with the judge's assessment of them?

(4) In subsequent cases it has been held that the duty of an employer giving a reference is to ensure that the reference does not give an unfair or misleading impression overall (*Bartholomew* v *Hackney LBC* (1999)). Thus, a reference containing entirely true statements could still be unfair if it does not give the full picture (cf *TSB Bank plc* v *Harris* (2000)).

(5) Under the Rehabilitation of Offenders Act 1974 s 4(2) a referee has a duty not to mention any spent conviction or ancillary circumstances; the referee will be protected from any legal liability in such a case. However, by regulation there are a number of exceptions to this basic position.

WRITTEN STATEMENT OF TERMS

Employment Rights Act 1996

1 (1) Where an employee begins employment with an employer, the employer shall give to the employee a written statement of particulars of employment.
  (2) The statement may (subject to section 2(4)) be given in instalments and (whether or not given in instalments) shall be given not later than two months after the beginning of the employment.
  (3) The statement shall contain particulars of –
      (a) the names of the employer and employee,
      (b) the date when the employment began, and

    (c)   the date on which the employee's period of continuous employment began (taking into account any employment with a previous employer which counts towards that period)

(4)   The statement shall also contain particulars, as at a specified date not more than seven days before the statement (or the instalment containing them) is given, of –

    (a)   the scale or rate of remuneration or the method of calculating remuneration,

    (b)   the intervals at which remuneration is paid (that is, weekly, monthly or other specified intervals),

    (c)   any terms and conditions relating to hours of work (including any terms and conditions relating to normal working hours),

    (d)   any terms and conditions relating to any of the following –

        (i)   entitlement to holidays, including public holidays, and holiday pay (the particulars given being sufficient to enable the employee's entitlement, including any entitlement to accrued holiday pay on the termination of employment, to be precisely calculated),

        (ii)   incapacity for work due to sickness or injury, including any provision for sick pay, and

        (iii)   pensions and pension schemes,

    (e)   the length of notice which the employee is obliged to give and entitled to receive to terminate his contract of employment,

    (f)   the title of the job which the employee is employed to do or a brief description of the work for which he is employed,

    (g)   where the employment is not intended to be permanent, the period for which it is expected to continue or, if it is for a fixed term, the date when it is to end,

    (h)   either the place of work or, where the employee is required or permitted to work at various places, an indication of that and of the address of the employer,

    (j)   any collective agreements which directly affect the terms and conditions of the employment including, where the employer is not a party, the persons by whom they were made, and

    (k)   where the employee is required to work outside the United Kingdom for a period of more than one month –

        (i)   the period for which he is to work outside the United Kingdom,

        (ii)   the currency in which remuneration is to be paid while he is working outside the United Kingdom,

        (iii)   any additional remuneration payable to him, and any benefits to be provided to or in respect of him, by reason of his being required to work outside the United Kingdom, and

        (iv)   any terms and conditions relating to his return to the United Kingdom . . .

Comment

(1) The requirement to give employees a written statement of their principal terms and conditions of employment has existed in some form since 1963. It has been extended over the years, most significantly by TURERA in 1993 to give effect to the EU Directive on the Proof of the Employment Relationship (91/533/EEC).

(2) Although the employer has two months in which to provide the statement, the employee actually becomes entitled to it after one month of employment: ERA s 198.

(3) In case of dispute between the parties, what is the legal status of the written statement?

Status of the written statement

System Floors v *Daniel* [1981] IRLR 475 Employment Appeal Tribunal

The employer disputed the starting date in the employee's written statement.

BROWNE-WILKINSON P: '. . . The first issue is whether the employment tribunal was right in holding that the statement was a contract and fell within the decision of the Court of Appeal in *Gascol Conversions Ltd* v *Mercer* (1974). The statement was served under the statutory provisions now included in ss 1 to 4 of the [Employment Rights Act 1996]. Under [ERA s 1(3)], an employer is required, in a statement which must be served under that section, to specify the date when the employment began.

There is some authority as to the effect of the statutory particulars of the terms of employment. In *Turriff Construction Ltd* v *Bryant* (1967) the Divisional Court had to consider for the purposes of redundancy payment what effect was to be given to the number of hours worked specified in a statutory statement. Speaking of the statutory predecessor of [ERA s 1], Lord Parker, giving the decision of the Court, said this:

> "It is of course quite clear that the statement made pursuant to s 4 of the Act is not a contract. It is not even conclusive evidence of the terms of a contract."

Again, the Divisional Court in *Parkes Classic Confectionery Ltd* v *Ashcroft* (1973) overruled the decision of an employment tribunal which had held that where the terms of the contract of employment had been varied, but the employer had failed to serve particulars of the changes in the terms in accordance with what is now [ERA s 4], the employer was not entitled to rely on the varied contract. The Divisional Court held that notwithstanding the failure to serve the necessary statutory statement and notwithstanding that that might be a criminal offence, there was nothing in the Act to provide that a change of contractual terms should be ineffectual between the parties merely because the employer had failed to give written notice of the change.

It seems to us, therefore, that in general the status of the statutory statement is this. It provides very strong *prima facie* evidence of what were the terms of the contract between the parties, but does not constitute a written contract between the parties. Nor are the statements of the terms finally conclusive: at most, they place a heavy burden on the employer to show that the actual terms of contract are different from those which he has set out in the statutory statement.

Against that background we turn to consider the decision of the Court of Appeal in *Gascol Conversions Ltd* v *Mercer* which was the basis of the employment tribunal's decision in this case. In that case there was an agreed variation in the terms on which the employees were engaged. When the Industrial Relations Act 1971 came into operation the employer became bound to give a written statement of particulars, and in pursuance of that obligation the employer sent a new contract of employment to each of their men. Each man was given a copy to keep, and he was required to sign a document in these terms: "I confirm receipt of a new contract of employment dated 25.2.72, which sets out as required under the Industrial Relations Act 1971 the terms and conditions of my employment." Mr Mercer signed such document. The Court of Appeal held that in those circumstances the document constituted a binding written contract and that accordingly no evidence was admissible to show that the terms of the contract were otherwise. In our view that case does not cover the present case. In that case Mr Mercer had signed a document which he confirmed was a new contract of employment and that it set out the terms and conditions of his employment. The Court of Appeal treated that as being a contract in writing, as indeed it was, having been signed by both parties. But in the case of an ordinary statutory statement served pursuant to the statutory obligation, the document is a unilateral one merely stating the employer's view of what those terms are. In the absence of an acknowledgement by the parties that the statement is itself a contract and that the terms are correct (such as that contained in the *Mercer* case), the statutory statement does not itself constitute a contract in writing.

In the present case, all that Mr Daniel did was to sign an acknowledgement that he had received the statement. In no sense did he sign it as a contract or acknowledge the accuracy of the terms in it. We therefore think that the employment tribunal erred in law in treating the date of commencement mentioned in the statement as decisive because it was a contractual term. In our view the statement is no more than persuasive, though not conclusive, evidence of the date of commencement.'

Comment

(1) The difference between *System Floors* v *Daniel* and *Gascol Conversions* v *Mercer* lies in the nature of the document signed. Do you think that the relevance of the form of documentation was necessarily appreciated by the parties at the time of signing?

(2) What if no written statement is given, or the employee disputes its accuracy? Under ERA s 11 the employee may apply to an employment tribunal, which has power to determine the particulars which ought to have been included, or to amend inaccurate particulars.

(3) In *Mears* v *Safecar Security Ltd* (1982) the Court of Appeal suggested that if no particulars had been included on a specific issue, and if there was no evidence of what the parties had agreed on it, then the employment tribunal should 'invent' the relevant particulars 'by deciding which term fits best with all the circumstances of the case, which may be getting near to deciding what is a reasonable term, or a term which, to quote the employment tribunal's decision, "would be sensible if the parties had in fact agreed it"' (*per* Stephenson LJ). This surprising encouragement to judicial creativity has since been disapproved in a Court of Appeal decision.

Eagland v *British Telecommunications plc* [1992] IRLR 323 Court of Appeal

PARKER LJ: '. . . There is in the passage which I have read from *Mears* v *Safecar Security Ltd* clearly an indication, albeit *obiter*, by Lord Justice Stephenson, with whom Lord Justice O'Connor and Sir Stanley Rees agreed, that the tribunal is under a statutory duty to invent terms if there are no materials upon which they can say a term could be found to be agreed expressly or by implication or by the general conduct of the parties. It is to be noted that in that passage Lord Justice Stephenson does not distinguish between mandatory terms and non-mandatory terms. The terms with which we are concerned in this case are all non-mandatory terms. With respect to the Lord Justice, I have no hesitation in saying that, so far as non-mandatory terms are concerned, the tribunal have no power to include any such terms. What they would have power to do – but it is a wholly different matter – is to say that, because the contract turned out to be a contract of employment, it was a necessary legal incident of that contract that the ordinary requirements of such a relationship be included. But the requirements of such a relationship do not include disciplinary rules, pension, sick pay or holiday pay and in my judgment they have no power to impose upon an employer any such terms if it be the fact, as it undoubtedly was, that either it had been agreed that there should be no pension, sick pay, holiday pay, or disciplinary rules, or the matter had not been agreed at all. The wording of the section makes it perfectly plain, as indeed must be the case at common law, that there may be no such terms and there is nothing in any section of the Act which empowers or requires the tribunal to impose upon the parties terms which had not been agreed when the statute recognises that it may be the case that no such terms have been agreed.

So far as mandatory terms are concerned, it may be difficult to see how the matter can ever arise, subject only to this. There may be a case where there is, for example, no provision as to the length of notice. In such a case the tribunal would in my view have power to conclude that there must be reasonable notice. It may also have power to decide, as would a court of law, the length of such notice, which would be a question of fact. But I do not consider that even in mandatory cases the tribunal have power to impose on parties terms which have not been agreed.

This may be piling *obiter* upon *obiter*, since my conclusion is that, quite apart from the guidance, the appeal must fail on the facts, the tribunal having concluded the matter in a manner which in my judgment cannot be faulted. But it is undesirable that there should remain in the authorities guidance which appears to me to have been arrived at without paying any attention to the distinction between mandatory and non-mandatory terms and when the guidance was given without argument on the point. We have in this Court heard argument on the point and it is therefore desirable that we should correct the matter in so far as it is possible . . .'

Comment

(1) As Parker LJ points out, not only were Stephenson LJ's remarks in *Mears v Safecar Security Ltd* (1982) *obiter*, but so were his remarks in *Eagland*. However, there is general acceptance that this is a correct statement of the law.

(2) Another possible course of action for a dissatisfied employee is shown by the next case.

W A Goold (Pearmak) Ltd v *McConnell* [1995] IRLR 516
Employment Appeal Tribunal

The company had a wholesale jewellery business and employed the two claimants as sales representatives on a salary and commission basis. Following financial difficulties a new managing director was taken on to reorganise and improve the business. Changes introduced to the payment system resulted in a substantial drop in the claimants' take-home pay and they sought to discuss this with management.

Their own manager did nothing about it, and approaches to the new managing director got a negative response. Finally, they attempted to get an interview with the company chairman, but were told that any appointment had to be made through the managing director. They resigned and claimed unfair dismissal. The claim depended on their being able to show that the company had committed a fundamental breach of contract.

MORISON J: '. . . The employment tribunal asked itself the right question, namely, and I quote:

"Whether the [employers] were in such serious breach of their obligations under the contracts of employment as to entitle the [employees] to leave as they did."

They noted that neither man was provided with a written statement of the terms and conditions of his employment, which would have specified the method of pursuing a grievance. In his written statement, which was admitted in evidence, the employers' chairman said he was well-known to see any employee who has a grievance or other problem. As the tribunal noted, the employees tried to speak to the chairman, but were rebuffed. The tribunal was of the view that any grievance procedure should have incorporated within it some kind of time limit, so as to ensure that grievances were nipped in the bud. In the absence of any grievance procedure in the contract of employment, the employees' grievances, instead of being considered and dealt with promptly, were allowed to fester in an atmosphere of prevarication and indecision. The employment tribunal concluded, and I quote:

"We think that this failure by the [employers] amounted to a breach of contract."

. . . It seems to us quite clear that the breach of contract identified by the employment tribunal related to the way the employees' grievances were dealt with. Their process of reasoning was that Parliament requires employers to provide their employees with written particulars of their employment in compliance with the statutory requirements. Section 3(1) of the [Employment Rights Act 1996] provides that the written statement required under s 1 of the Act shall include a note specifying, by description or otherwise, to whom and in what manner the employee may apply if he is either dissatisfied with any disciplinary decision or has any other grievance, and an explanation of any further steps in the grievance procedure. It is clear therefore, that Parliament considered that good industrial relations requires employers to provide their employees with a method of dealing with grievances in a proper and timeous fashion. This is also consistent, of course, with the codes of practice. That being so, the employment tribunal was entitled, in our judgment, to conclude that there was an implied term in the contract of employment that the employers would reasonably and promptly afford a reasonable opportunity to their employees to obtain redress of any grievance they may have. It was in our judgment rightly conceded at the employment tribunal that such could be a breach of contract.

Further, it seems to us that the right to obtain redress against a grievance is fundamental for very obvious reasons. The working environment may well lead to employees experiencing difficulties, whether because of the physical conditions under which they are required to work, or because of a breakdown in human relationships, which can readily occur when people of different backgrounds and sensitivities are required to work together, often under pressure.

There may well be difficulties arising out of the way that authority and control is exercised – sometimes by people who themselves have insufficient experience and training to exercise such power wisely . . .'

(The EAT upheld the tribunal's finding that they had been unfairly dismissed.)

Comment

(1) There is now a statutory grievance procedure which must be followed before employees can bring tribunal proceedings against their employer (see below, p 385).

(2) Under the Employment Act 2002 s 38, if an employer fails to provide a written statement, the employment tribunal should award the employee between two and four weeks' pay. However, this is not a freestanding right: it applies only if the employee (a) is bringing proceedings in the tribunal on some other ground, and (b) is successful in those proceedings. It is not clear why the remedy should be limited in this way.

Variation of the contract

Employment Rights Act 1996

4 (1) If, after the material date, there is a change in any of the matters particulars of which are required by sections 1 to 3 to be included or referred to in a statement under section 1, the employer shall give to the employee a written statement containing particulars of the change . . .

 (3) A statement under subsection (1) shall be given at the earliest opportunity and, in any event, not later than –

 (a) one month after the change in question . . .

Comment

(1) While ERA s 4 requires notification of changes, it does not give the employer the authority to change the contract unilaterally.

Burdett-Coutts v Hertfordshire County Council
[1984] IRLR 91 High Court, Queen's Bench

KENNETH JONES J: 'In about 1982 the defendants, the Hertfordshire County Council, were minded to reduce the incomes of certain of their employees who have been referred to as "the dinner ladies". Six of those dinner ladies now appear as claimants in this action. Let me say immediately that I am not concerned to inquire in any way into the reasonableness or unreasonableness of either the defendants or of the claimants, or of the representatives of the union who were seeking to safeguard the claimants' interests; I am concerned solely with the contractual relationship between the claimants and the defendants.

What the claimants say very shortly is that the defendants have broken the contracts of employment which they have entered into with the claimants and, by reason of that breach, the claimants are entitled to damages taking the form of arrears of wages and a declaration that the defendants were not entitled lawfully to act as they have done in this case . . .

What . . . happened was that the defendants wrote to each of these ladies a letter . . . This letter is central to the whole of this case and I propose to read much of it. It is dated 5.1.83. The significance of that date is that it was at least 12 weeks before 31.3.83. The letter continues:

"Dear Madam,
Amendment of contract of service – general kitchen assistant.
    I refer to my letters of 8 and 19.10.82 concerning the proposals made by the Education Committee for changes in the working arrangements of school meal staff and mid-day supervisory assistants. In adopting these proposals the Committee were concerned to seek to maintain the school meals service and to avoid the redundancies which other courses of action would have involved. Consultation with the appropriate unions have not resulted in any changes in the proposals and it is now necessary for me to give you detailed notice of the variations in your contract of service. As you know, your appointment as a general kitchen assistant is subject to such terms and conditions determined by the National Joint Council, and Essex and Hertfordshire Provincial Local Authority Services as are adopted by the County Council from time to time, together with such other terms as the County Council may from time to time lay down. I am now writing to inform you that these terms and conditions of service will be amended by the County Council from 31.3.83 as follows."

There are then set out details of the amendments which relate to (a) rates of pay and meals entitlement, (b) the working week year, (c) payment of wages. I can summarise all those detailed amendments by saying that they each involve, and were designed to involve, a reduction in the pay of the employees. The letter continues:

"This letter is the formal notice of these changes in your contract of service which take effect on 31.3.83. I do hope you will understand why the County Council have to change your conditions of service as set out above, as a means of preserving both the school meals service and employment. I hope you will continue in the school meals service."

That letter was signed by the County Education Officer.

Mr Pardoe [counsel for the employer] does not suggest that the County Council was in any way entitled to make these amendments to the contract of service within the terms of the document containing the terms and conditions of employment. He submits, with great clarity, that this letter properly construed is a letter giving notice to the addressee of the termination of her employment on 31.3.83 and offering to re-employ her with effect from that date on the new terms set out in that letter.

There can, of course, be no doubt whatsoever that what was in the mind of the County Education Officer was that all his dinner ladies should continue with their jobs and should accept a reduction in their wages. It may be that he was not concerned primarily with the precise method as to which that way to be carried out. Put another way, this was a letter written not by a lawyer but by a layman.

Mr Higgs, on behalf of the claimants, say that that is not the correct interpretation to be put upon this letter and this letter, although in practical terms is offering the employee the choice of accepting a reduction in pay or leaving, looked at properly it is an attempt by the defendant unilaterally to vary the terms of the contracts of employment. As such it amounted to a fundamental breach of that contract which had the effect of repudiating the contract and putting the employee in the position where she could either refuse to accept that repudiation, or she could have accepted it and left.

I am bound to say that, in reading this letter, I can see nowhere within it any words which can be construed as giving notice to the employee to terminate her employment. The words of the letter are clear beyond a peradventure. It is giving "detailed notice of the variations in your contract of service". It is informing the addressee that these terms and conditions will be amended by the County Council. The letter is expressed to be "formal notice of these changes in your contract of service". Those words are apt, and apt only, to describe an attempt by the employer to vary unilaterally the terms of the contract of employment. Of course it was present in the author's mind that the addressee may fall into line and be content to carry on at a reduced wage, or that they may prefer to leave, so he understandably ended his letter by saying, "I hope you will continue in the school meals service"; but it is stretching words beyond meanings they are capable of bearing to say that the letter having given notice of termination of employment that was an offer of re-employment. I have therefore come to the conclusion that the defendants sought to repudiate the contracts of employment.

What happened afterwards was that these ladies allowed 31 March to pass and stayed at their posts, taking the lower sums which were paid to them. Mr Pardoe relies upon that activity by the employees as being an acceptance of the new contract of employment which he says was offered in the letter. Since I have held that there was no such offer in the letter, then there is no occasion for me to consider whether the conduct of these ladies constituted an acceptance of such an offer. But the argument could have been put in a slightly different way and have the same effect in the end; that these ladies, by implication, have waived their right to treat the contract as having been brought to an end and have, as I say, by implication after that entered into some fresh contract. I cannot accept that that is a true construction to put on their activities because it has been made abundantly clear to the defendants from a date prior to 31.3.83 that they were not in any way prepared to accept the new terms, or amendments, which had been put forward by the defendants . . .

What is the position? In my judgment the defendants have sought unilaterally to impose amendments to the contracts of employment here. By so doing they are in breach of those contracts and have repudiated them. The claimant, faced with the choice which every innocent party to a contract has, has not accepted that repudiation but is standing on the original contract and saying, as she is entitled to say, "I can now recover the total wages which should have been paid to me under the original contract".

Accordingly, I give judgment in this case for the arrears of wages and return of excess monies as claimed . . . I also find that the claimants, each of them, are entitled . . . to a declaration that the defendants sought . . . to vary unilaterally the terms of the claimants' contract of employment, and that they were not entitled in law so to do.'

Comment

(1) The case illustrates the point that variation of a contract requires the agreement of both parties. However, what if the construction argued for by the council had been

accepted by the court? Would the dismissals have been fair? This must depend on the circumstances. In 1991 Rolls Royce announced that it would dismiss its 34,000-strong workforce and offer them new contracts, essentially because the company wanted to impose a wage freeze which would have been a breach of contract. The outcry was such that the company backed down and the legality of its action was never tested. But some commentators thought that the employees would have had a good claim for redundancy and/or unfair dismissal (see, eg, McGlyne, 1991).

(2) There is also a risk that, the more time goes on, the more likely it becomes that a court may hold that the employees' conduct in continuing to work is only explicable in terms of their having accepted the new contract, even if they are maintaining that they are working under protest. This is in effect what happened in *Henry* v *London General Transport Services Ltd* (2002), where employees objected to a new rota system introduced without their agreement. However, they operated the new system for two years, while continuing to argue that they were not bound to. The Court of Appeal held that this issue should be remitted to the employment tribunal, while indicating their own strong view that this conduct had to be seen as an affirmation of the contract.

(3) Having said that, there is also established authority that in some circumstances a unilateral variation may be held not to have been accepted even though the employee made no protest when presented with the new terms.

Jones v *Associated Tunnelling* [1981] IRLR 477 Employment Appeal Tribunal

J started working for the company in 1964. From 1969 he was employed at the Ham Heath Colliery, about 12 miles from his home. When work at that colliery ceased in 1980 his employers sought to move him to another colliery which was a similar distance from his home. J claimed that they had no right to move him and that he was redundant. The employers relied on an express mobility clause that had been notified to him in updated versions of his written statement of terms and conditions in 1973 and 1976. J had never objected that these were inaccurate and the employers therefore claimed that he had acquiesced in the variation.

BROWNE-WILKINSON P: 'We therefore reach the conclusion that we are entitled to hold, and do hold, that the right term to imply into Mr Jones's contract from the outset was that he could be required to work at any place within reasonable daily commuting distance from his home . . .

It is therefore not necessary for us to reach any concluded view as to whether the employment tribunal was right in holding that, even if under the original contract Mr Jones's place of work could not be changed, by continuing to work without objection Mr Jones must be taken to have assented to a variation in his terms of employment including the introduction of the mobility clause. However, since the case may go further and the Court of Appeal may take a different view on the implied term, we must state our reservations about the employment tribunal's view on such variations. The statutory "statement of terms and conditions of employment" is not itself a contract but merely contains the employer's statement of what has previously been agreed. As such, the first of such statements to be issued is often compelling evidence of what terms have in fact been agreed. But where there are two or more statements which are not in identical terms, the later statement can only be evidence of an agreed variation of the original terms. Such variation may be either express or implied. If, as in the present case, there is no evidence of any oral discussion varying the original terms, the fact that a statement of terms and conditions containing different terms has been issued cannot be compelling evidence of an express oral variation. The most that can be said is that by continuing to work without objection after receiving such further statement, the employee may have impliedly agreed to the variation recorded in the second statement or is estopped from denying it.

In our view, to imply an agreement to vary or to raise an estoppel against the employee on the grounds that he has not objected to a false record by the employers of the terms actually agreed is a course which should be adopted with great caution. If the variation relates to a matter which has immediate practical application (eg, the rate of pay) and the employee continues to work without objection after effect has been given to the variation (eg, his pay packet has been reduced) then obviously he may well be taken to have impliedly agreed. But where, as in the present case, the variation has no immediate practical effect the position is not the same. It is the view of both members of this tribunal with experience in industrial relations (with which the Chairman, without such experience, agrees) that it is asking too much of the ordinary employee to require him either to object to an erroneous statement of his terms of employment having no immediate practical impact on him or be taken to have assented to the variation. So to hold would involve an unrealistic view of the inclination and ability of the ordinary employee to read and fully understand such statements.

Even if he does read the statement and can understand it, it would be unreaslistic of the law to require him to risk a confrontation with his employer on a matter which has no immediate practical impact on the employee. For those reasons, as at present advised, we would not be inclined to imply any assent to a variation from mere failure by the employee to object to the unilateral alteration by the employer of the terms of employment contained in a statutory statement . . .'

Comment

(1) It was important in this case that the purported variation had not been drawn to employees' attention and that it was contained in a revised version of the written statement only. This reasoning has frequently been applied since: see, for example, *Aparau* v *Iceland Frozen Foods* (1996). Contrast, however, *Crédit Suisse Asset Management* v *Armstrong* (1996), where changes introduced in a handbook which described itself as contractual were held to be binding on employees who were investment fund managers, 'men of experience and sophistication' who were used to dealing with complex contractual documentation.

(2) Note that, in this judgment, Browne-Wilkinson P again stressed the difference between a written statement, as the employer's version of what has been previously agreed, and a written contract, which would itself create the rights and duties between the parties.

CUSTOM AND PRACTICE

Sagar v *Ridehalgh* [1931] 1 Ch 310 Court of Appeal

The claimant was employed by the defendant company as a weaver. He sued when one shilling was deducted from his wages for bad work. The employers claimed that they were entitled to make deductions for bad work, either because this was the longstanding practice in their mill, or because it was customary in the Lancashire cotton weaving trade.

LAWRENCE LJ: '. . . The employers based their contention on two alternative grounds, either that the established practice of making reasonable deductions for bad work in the defendants' mill was incorporated into the claimant's contract of service by reason of his having agreed to be employed upon the same terms as the other weavers in that mill or else that the general usage of making reasonable deductions for bad work prevailing in the cotton weaving trade of

Lancashire was so well known and understood that every weaver engaging in that trade must be taken to have entered upon his employment on the footing of that usage.

As regards the first of these grounds, it is clearly established by the evidence of Mr George Ridehalgh that the practice of making reasonable deductions for bad work has continuously prevailed at the defendants' mill for upwards of thirty years, and that during the whole of that time all weavers employed by the defendants have been treated alike in that respect. The practice was, therefore, firmly established at the defendants' mills when the claimant entered upon his employment there. Further, I think that it is clear that the claimant accepted employment in the defendants' mill on the same terms as the other weavers employed at that mill . . . Although I entirely agree with the learned judge in finding it difficult to believe that the claimant did not know of the existence of the practice at the mill, I think that it is immaterial whether he knew of it or not, as I am satisfied that he accepted his employment in the same terms as to deductions for bad work as the other weavers at the mill.

In the result I have come to the conclusion that the practice of making reasonable deductions for bad work prevailing at the defendants' mill was incorporated in the claimant's contract of service.

Further, I am of opinion that the second ground is also established by the evidence, namely, that the practice in the defendants' mill is in accordance with the general usage of making reasonable deductions for bad work prevailing in the weaving trade of Lancashire, which usage, in the absence of any stipulation to the contrary, would be incorporated into every contract of service as a weaver in a Lancashire cotton mill without special mention. This usage seems to me to receive recognition in the Joint Rules for the Settlement of Trade Disputes appended to the Uniform List of Prices (to which rules both the claimant and the defendants were subject) inasmuch as rule 4 expressly provides that in the case of an underpayment by the employer of the Uniform List of Prices, where the employer either admits the underpayment or refuses to consent to an inspection of the work, the workman is to be at liberty to take whatever action he thinks fit without the necessity of bringing the matter before either the Local or Central Employers Committee . . .

Farwell J [the judge at first instance] has held that the usage is not a good usage because it is neither universal nor reasonable nor certain, and accordingly, does not comply with the tests laid down in *Devonald* v *Rosser & Sons* (1906). If I am right in thinking that the claimant's contract of service incorporated the established practice at the defendants' mill, the question whether the general usage in the trade is good or bad does not arise, but, as I may be wrong on this point, and as the question has been fully argued and dealt with by the learned judge in his judgment, I think it right that I should shortly express my views upon it. In the first place, it is to be noticed that in *Hart* v *Riversdale Mill Co* (1928) the justices found that "deductions for bad work are, and have been for many years, the usage and custom in the cotton weaving trade of Lancashire, and have always been, and are, an incident of a weaver's contract of service, and have always been and are taken into account in calculating the correct wages". The Court of Appeal decided that this usage was not illegal under the Truck Acts and gave effect to it. This decision is binding both on Courts of first instance and on this Court, and, in my opinion, covers the present case . . .

In the next place, I am of opinion that the usage is not, as held by the learned judge, unreasonable. The deductions are not arbitrary deductions at the will and pleasure of the employers; they are limited to cases where there has been bad work, and they are limited to an amount which does not exceed the actual or estimated damage or loss occasioned to the employer by the act or omission of the workman. The workman is free to prove that his work was good and that no deduction ought to be made, or to prove that any particular deduction exceeds the amount of the actual or estimated damage or loss to the employer . . . The ground upon which the learned judge held that the usage was bad for uncertainty is because the amount of the deductions for bad work is left to the discretion of the employers, and because the maximum amount of such deductions is the actual loss occasioned to the employers, which could not in most cases be ascertained until after the payment of the wages. In the first place, I think it is clear that the maximum amount of the deduction is not merely the actual but also the estimated loss occasioned to the employer, and that the workman is free to dispute the accuracy of such actual or estimated loss. In the next place, a trade usage allowing an employer to make deductions for bad work at his discretion not exceeding a certain defined limit does not, in my opinion, render the usage uncertain. It would be altogether unreasonable if the usage were to make certain definite deductions in every case. There are degrees of negligence and it is reasonable that employers should not exact the full amount of the loss occasioned to them in every case. From a business point of view there is no uncertainty about such a usage. A Lancashire weaver knows, and has for very many years past known, precisely what his position was as regards deductions for bad work on accepting employment in a Lancashire mill. There would be no uncertainty in his mind on this point as to the effect of his engagement . . .'

(Lord Hanworth MR and Romer LJJ delivered concurring judgments.)

Comment

(1) Note the three criteria used by the court for deciding whether or not a customary terms should be recognised.

(2) A customary practice must start somewhere, either with the employer or with the employees. If it is the employer, note the qualification suggested by the EAT in *Duke* v *Reliance Systems* (1982):

> A policy adopted by management unilaterally cannot become a term of the employees' contracts on the grounds that it is an established custom and practice unless it is at least shown that the policy has been drawn to the attention of the employees or has been followed without exception for a substantial period.

(3) Today the requirement to provide employees with a written statement of their main terms and conditions means that it must be fairly unlikely that a customary term will be invoked (although see *Henry* v *London General Transport Services Ltd* (2002) where this was a central argument). It is also interesting to note that the definition of a part-time worker in the Part-time Workers (Prevention of Less Favourable Treatment) Regulations 2000 is in terms of the employer's custom and practice (see reg 2).

(4) In the next case, employees who tried to rely on a right to perform work according to their customary methods had a rather different axe to grind.

Cresswell v *Board of Inland Revenue* [1984] 2 All ER 713
High Court, Chancery Division

The Inland Revenue wanted to computerise all its PAYE operations. The claimant employees and their union feared that the new technology would lead to job losses. Having failed to get assurances from the Inland Revenue that there would be no compulsory redundancies as a result of the computerisation, they refused to co-operate with it, claiming *inter alia* that it was a term of their contracts that they could not be required to carry out tasks except in the manner that they had habitually been carried out by custom and practice.

WALTON J: '. . . I now turn straight away to a consideration of the main point on which counsel for the claimants relied. He put his case in this way, that although it is undoubtedly correct that an employer may, within limits, change the manner in which his employees perform the work which they are employed to do, there may be such a change in the method of performing the task which the employee was recruited to perform proposed by the employer as to amount to a change in the nature of the job. This would mean that the employee was being asked to perform work under a wholly different contract and this cannot be done without his consent . . .

It is a very fine line from counsel's submissions to the submission that employees have a vested right to preserve their working obligations completely unchanged as from the moment when they first begin work. This cannot surely, by any stretch of the imagination, be correct. That it is not so is very clearly shown by *O'Neill* v *Merseyside Plumbing Co Ltd* (1973). In that case the employee had entered the services of his employer in 1947 and remained (apart from absence for national service) in their employment until 1972. Throughout all that time he worked as a gas fitter, i.e., for something approaching a quarter of a century. Then his employers directed him to work at a hospital site as a general plumber and he refused on the ground that he was incompetent to perform the plumbing work required. He submitted that the purported transfer to work of a different kind from that to which he was accustomed made him redundant. He claimed redundancy and the hearing in the National Industrial Relations Court was on an appeal by him from an employment tribunal. The court held that the crucial question to ask was whether he was employed as a plumber or as a specialist gas fitter; in other words, what were his terms of employment? What was it that he was employed to do? For if he was employed as a general plumber then, although he had always previously worked as a gas fitter "the employers were plainly entitled to require him to do other forms of plumbing work and the cause of his dismissal was quite simply that he refused to do that which he was required to do under his contract of employment" . . .

Granted that down to the present the work of each of these three grades has been done manually, with pen, paper and pocket calculator, if the employer changes this so as largely to remove the necessity to use pen and paper but requires the person concerned to use a computer instead, or in some cases in addition, is the nature of the job thereby fundamentally changed? I do not think that the drawing of parallels with other situations really assists because, at the end of the day, it is the precise impact which is made by the computerisation programme on the day-to-day work of these three grades which is in question. However there is, I think, one important point. When dealing with other examples counsel for the claimants made the point that the requirements of the employer might be such that the employee was genuinely unable to comply therewith. He instanced, for example, a typist engaged on audio typing who might be unable, with the best will in the world, to re-adapt as a word processor. What then?

That kind of case can be left to be dealt with when it arises, although *O'Neill's* case, already cited, would certainly not suggest that if the employee had been originally engaged as a typist simpliciter there would really be much doubt about the matter.

But there can really be no doubt as to the fact that an employee is expected to adapt himself to new methods and techniques introduced in the course of his employment (*cf North Riding Garages Ltd* v *Butterwick* (1967)). Of course, in a proper case the employer must provide any necessary training or retraining. I think the probable answer to counsel's point is simply that it will, in all cases, be a question of pure fact whether the retraining involved the acquisition of such esoteric skills that it would not be reasonable to expect the employee to acquire them. In an age when the computer has forced its way into the school room and where electronic games are played by schoolchildren in their own homes as a matter of everyday occurrence, it can hardly be considered that to ask an employee to acquire basic skills as to retrieving information from a computer or feeding such information into a computer is something in the slightest esoteric or, even nowadays, unusual.

In any event in the present case one remarkable feature, comparable to that of the dog which did not bark in the night, is that from first to last in all the voluminous evidence put in by the claimants, there is no suggestion whatsoever that the claimants themselves, or anybody else in

any similar category in all the 14 districts covered by the present scheme, found any real difficulty in accepting the necessary instruction in the use of COP1 and putting it into practice as
they had been doing for some little time at the end of last year.

Whatever the change in working methods may be it is one which, of course with proper
instruction (which I think the employer must be under a duty to provide and which has, of
course, been provided in the present case), the three grades concerned have, one and all, taken
in their stride . . .'

Comment

(1) Usually changes in working methods will be introduced by agreement with the
workforce, their agreement being secured by offering consideration for it, such as higher
wages. This case arose because of a failure to agree in the collective bargaining process.

(2) How extensive should the duty of adaptability be? Should it make a difference if the
employee *cannot* adapt rather than *will not* adapt?

TERMS IMPLIED AT COMMON LAW

The common law, meaning the law created by judges, is an important source of
employment obligations. Courts have decided that certain terms are to be regarded
as part of every contract of employment as a necessary incident of the relationship
of employer and employee. Implied terms can be overridden by express agreement
to the contrary, but this is comparatively rare. There is also an increasing body of
opinion that, in some circumstances, implied terms can be used to control the
application of express terms of the contract.

The advantage of common law implied terms is their flexibility: judges can adapt
the law to take account of changing circumstances. The disadvantage is that the law
may become more uncertain as a result. Employees may further feel that judges are
more likely to exercise their creativity in favour of employers rather than workers
– a point worth bearing in mind while considering the extracts which follow. The
terms implied at common law are commonly expressed as being duties of the
employer and employee.

Duty to provide work?

Probably the most fundamental duty of the employer is the duty to pay wages.
The aspect of that duty considered here is whether it is enough if the employer
pays wages, or must she also provide work for the employee to perform?

Turner v *Sawdon* [1901] 2 KB 653 Court of Appeal

The claimant was taken on as a sales representative by the defendants for a period of four years
on a fixed annual salary. After two years the defendants withdrew his authority to act, although
they were willing to continue paying his salary. He sued for breach of contract.

A L SMITH MR: '. . . The action is by a man who was in the employment of the defendants,
and it was not brought for wages, because it is clear that the defendants were always ready and
willing to pay all that was due under the contract. The real question which the claimant thought
to raise, and which was raised, was whether beyond the question of remuneration there was a

172

further obligation on the masters that, during the period over which the contract was to extend, they should find continuous, or at least some, employment for the claimant. In my opinion such an action is unique – that is an action in which it is shewn that the master is willing to pay the wages of his servant, but is sued for damages because the servant is not given employment. In *Turner v Goldsmith* (1891) the wages were to be paid in the form of commission, and that impliedly created a contract to find employment for the servant. This contract is different, being to employ for wages which are to be paid at a certain rate per year. I do not think this can be read otherwise than as a contract by the master to retain the servant, and during the time covered by the retainer to pay him wages under such a contract. It is within the province of the master to say that he will go on paying the wages, but that he is under no obligation to provide work. The obligation suggested is said to arise out of the undertaking to engage and employ the claimant as their representative salesman. It is said that if the salesman is not given employment which allows him to go on the market his hand is not kept in practice, and he will not be so efficient a salesman at the end of the term. To read in an obligation of that sort would be to convert the retainer at fixed wages into a contract to keep the servant in the service of his employer in such a manner as to enable the former to become *au fait* at his work. In my opinion, no such obligation arose under this contract, and it is a mistake to stretch the words of the contract so as to include in what is a mere retainer an obligation to employ the plaintiff continuously for the term of his service . . .'

(Vaughan Williams and Stirling LJJ delivered concurring judgments.)

Devonald v *Rosser* [1906] 2 KB 728 Court of Appeal

The claimant worked as a rollerman in the defendants' tinplate works. He was paid by the piece, meaning that he had no fixed salary but was paid according to the amount of work he produced. His contract stipulated that either party had to give a month's notice to terminate.

Because of a downturn in trade, the defendants closed the works and two weeks later gave him a month's notice. He claimed damages for breach of an implied agreement to give him work to do during this six-week period. The defendants argued that as he was a piece worker, if he did no work, he was not entitled to any pay. They denied the existence of any implied term to provide him with work.

LORD ALVERSTONE CJ: '. . . In this case I am of opinion that Jelf J [the judge at first instance] came to a perfectly right conclusion, but I wish to add a few observations of my own in confirmation of his view. I entirely agree with Mr Bailhache [counsel for the employers] that the implication which is to be drawn from this contract is one which, to use the language of Bowen LJ in *The Moorcock* (1889) is raised "from the presumed intention of the parties with the object of giving to the transaction such efficacy as both parties must have intended that at all events it should have", that "what the law desires to effect by the implication is to give such business efficacy to the transaction as must have been intended at all events by both parties who are business men". I am content to accept that test in deciding whether or not this contract involves the implication which is necessary to enable the claimant to recover. Now, in order to determine that question, the only facts that are material to be considered are that the claimant was in the defendants' regular employment, that he was paid by piece work, and that he was employed upon the terms of a rule which provides that "No person regularly employed shall quit or be discharged from these works without giving or receiving twenty-eight days' notice in writing, such notice to be given on the first Monday of any calendar month." I put out of consideration rule 11, as to the workmen being employed on other than their own special work in case of emergency, as it is not necessary to rely upon it, but in my opinion there is nothing in it which contradicts the implication which, to my mind, is involved in the language of the former rule. No distinction in principle can be drawn between wages by time and wages by piece. Piece work is only a method of ascertaining the amount of the wages which is to be paid to the workman. What, then, is the obligation of the employers under such a contract as the present? On the one hand we must consider the matter from the point of view of the employers who I agree will under ordinary circumstances desire to carry on their works at a profit, though not necessarily at a profit in every week, for it is matter of common knowledge that masters have frequently to run their mills for weeks and months together at a loss in order to keep their business together and in hopes of better times. On the other hand, we have to consider the position of the work-man. The workman has to live; and the effect of the defendants' contention is that if the master at any time found that his works were being carried on at a loss, he might at once close down his works and cease to employ his men, who, even if they gave notice to quit the employ-ment, would be bound to the master for a period of at least twenty-eight days during which time they would be unable to earn any wages at all. I agree with Jelf J that that is an unreasonable contention from the workman's point of view. In my opinion the necessary implication to be drawn from this contract is at least that the master will find a reasonable amount of work up to the expiration of a notice given in accordance with the contract. I am not prepared to say that that obligation is an absolute one to find work at all events, for the evidence shewed that it was subject to certain contingencies, such as breakdown of machinery and want of water and mater-ials. But I am clearly of opinion that it would be no excuse to the master, for non-performance of his implied obligation to provide the workman with work, that he could no longer make his plates at a profit either for orders or for stock. It is to be observed that the question how the works are to be carried on, whether they are going to work short or full time, or whether for stock or current orders, is a matter which rests entirely in the hands of the master. The men have absolutely nothing to say to it . . .'

(Jelf J and Sir Gorell Barnes agreed.)

Collier v *Sunday Referee Publishing Co* [1940] 2 KB 647 High Court, King's Bench

The claimant was engaged for two years as chief sub-editor of the *Sunday Referee*, a news-paper. When his contract still had more than a year to run the publication was sold to new owners, who ceased to publish it. They continued to pay him, as long as he came into the office at certain times in case they wanted him to do anything. He stopped doing this, they stopped paying him and he sued for breach of contract.

ASQUITH J: '. . . The claimant argues that by ceasing to publish the *Sunday Referee* the defendants disabled themselves from performing further their contractual obligation, which was to employ him as chief sub-editor of that newspaper. The defendants contend that they were not bound to provide the claimant with work, but merely to continue to pay his salary, retaining the right to call on him to do work for them; that they did continue to pay his salary until November, 1939, but that at that time the claimant finally repudiated his alleged obligation to work for them when required so to do; and that the contract of service, alive until then, was ter-minated by such repudiation, and with it went any obligation on their part to pay further salary.
It is true that a contract of employment does not necessarily, or perhaps normally, oblige the master to provide the servant with work. Provided I pay my cook her wages regularly she can-not complain if I choose to take any or all of my meals out. In some exceptional cases there is an obligation to provide work. For instance, where the servant is remunerated by commission, or where (as in the case of an actor or singer) the servant bargains, among other things, for pub-licity, and the master, by withholding work, also withholds the stipulated publicity: see, for instance, *Marbé* v *George Edwardes (Daly's Theatre) Ltd* (1928) but such cases are anomalous, and the normal rule is illustrated by authorities such as *Lagerwall* v *Wilkinson, Henderson &*

Clarke Ltd (1899) and *Turner* v *Sawdon* (1901) , where the claimants (a commercial traveller and a salesman respectively, retained for a fixed period and remunerated by salary) were held to have no legal complaint so long as the salary continued to be paid, notwithstanding that owing to their employers' action they were left with nothing to do. The employers were not bound to supply work to enable the employee, as the phrase goes, to "keep his hand in", or to avoid the reproach of idleness, or even to make a profit out of a travelling allowance. In such a case there is no breach of contract, but the result is much the same as if there had been, because in either event the claimant is entitled to a sum or sums which are measured *prima facie* by the amount of salary in respect of the unexpired period of service.

I do not hold that in the present case there was in the contract of employment an implied stipulation for publicity and an obligation to provide work for the purpose of providing publicity.'

(The claimant's case was ultimately successful on the different ground that he was an office-holder and the defendants were in breach of contract by destroying the office.)

Comment

(1) The extracts above illustrate the traditional view on whether there is a duty to provide work. However, the story would not be complete without reference to the one-judge campaign of Lord Denning to create a general right to work – usually in order to supply what in his eyes was some deficiency in existing rules. The apotheosis of this approach is his judgment in *Langston* v *AUEW* (1974).

Langston v AUEW [1974] ICR 180 Court of Appeal

The claimant, who was employed by Chrysler UK, refused to belong to the defendant trade union, as was his right under the legislation of the time. Rather than risk a confrontation with the union if they let him work, or attract heavy penalties if they dismissed him, Chrysler UK paid him his wages, but instructed him to stay away from the workplace. He sued the union for inducing a breach of his contract of employment. The case came to the Court of Appeal on the preliminary point of whether the employers were in fact in breach of contract by paying his wages but not allowing him to work.

LORD DENNING MR: '. . . In the second place, Mr Harvey [counsel for Chryslers] suggested that there was no evidence of breach of contract. This was based on the fact that Chryslers had not dismissed Mr Langston. They had only suspended him from work. And they had paid him full wages. So it was said there was no breach of contract. In this regard we were referred to *Collier* v *Sunday Referee Publishing Co* (1940) where Asquith J said:

"It is true that a contract of employment does not necessarily, or perhaps normally, oblige the master to provide the servant with work. Provided I pay my cook her wages regularly, she cannot complain if I choose to take any or all of my meals out."

Asquith J went on to refer to two cases where a commercial traveller and a salesman –

"were held to have no legal complaint so long as the salary continued to be paid, notwithstanding that, owing to the action of their respective employers, they were left with nothing to do. The employer was not bound to provide work to enable the employee [as the phrase goes] to "keep his hand in", avoid the reproach of idleness, or even make a profit out of travelling allowances."

That was said 33 years ago. Things have altered much since then. We have repeatedly said in this court that a man has a right to work, which the courts will protect: see *Nagle* v *Feilden* (1966) and *Hill* v *C A Parsons & Co Ltd* (1972). I would not wish to express any decided view, but simply state the argument which could be put forward for Mr Langston. In these days an employer, when employing a skilled man, is bound to provide him with work. By which I mean that the man should be given the opportunity of doing his work when it is available and he is ready and willing to do it. A skilled man takes a pride in his work. He does not do it merely to earn money. He does it so as to make his contribution to the well-being of all. He does it so as to keep himself busy, and not idle. To use his skill, and to improve it. To have the satisfaction which comes of a task well done. Such as Longfellow attributed to *The Village Blacksmith*:

> "Something attempted, something done,
> Has earned a night's repose."

The Code of Practice [1972, repealed 1991] contains the same thought. It says, at paragraph 9:

> ". . . management should recognise the employee's need to achieve a sense of satisfaction in his job and should provide for it so far as practicable."

A parallel can be drawn in regard to women's work. Many a married woman seeks work. She does so when the children grow up and leave the home. She does it, not solely to earn money, helpful as it is: but to fill her time with useful occupation, rather than sit idly at home waiting for her husband to return. The devil tempts those who have nothing to do.

To my mind, therefore, it is arguable that in these days a man has, by reason of an implication in the contract, a right to work. That is, he has a right to have the opportunity of doing his work when it is there to be done. If this be correct, then if any person knowingly induces the employer to turn the man away – and thus deprive him of the opportunity of doing his work – then that person induces the employer to break his contract. It is nonetheless a breach, even though the employer pays the man his full wages. So also when fellow workers threaten to walk out unless a man is turned off the job, they threaten to induce a breach of contract. At any rate, the man who is suspended has a case for saying that they have induced or threatened to induce the employer to break the contract of employment . . .'

(Cairns and Stephenson LJJ concurred that this was an arguable point, so that the case should proceed to a full trial.)

Comment

(1) This is not a masterpiece of legal reasoning. Quite apart from the views expressed about women's work (dated even in 1974), Lord Denning omits to mention that he gave the principal judgment in the two cases he cites as supporting his view, so to use them as authority is rather to pull himself up by his bootstraps. In any case, there is no reference to a right to work in *Hill* v *Parsons*, where Lord Denning, discussing the situation of an employee whose contract was kept alive during the notice period, actually said: 'If the company did not want him to come to work, the court would not order the company to give him work.'

(2) Following the Court of Appeal's decision on the preliminary point, the case returned to the National Industrial Relations Court for a decision on the substance. The NIRC decided that Langston was really a piece worker and therefore entitled to be given work within the principle of *Devonald* v *Rosser*.

(3) Thus in general, the orthodox position has been that there is no right to work, except in the two exceptional cases mentioned by Asquith J in *Collier* v *Sunday Referee*. However, although in that case Asquith J denied any duty to provide work in order that the employee should be able 'to keep his hand in', a third exception along these lines is now being recognised.

William Hill Organisation Ltd v Tucker [1998] IRLR 313 Court of Appeal

The employee was a senior dealer who had been given the task of introducing the new business of spread betting to the organisation. Although his contract required him to give six months' notice, he attempted to resign on one month's notice in order to join a competitor organisation. The employer wanted to hold him to the six-month notice period, but told him not to come to work during that time. He argued that the employer was in breach of contract in not giving him work while he was employed, which released him from his obligations under the contract.

MORRITT LJ: 'When an employee has given notice to determine his contract of employment, may his employer, whilst continuing to pay his remuneration, insist that he stays away from work for the duration of the notice period, colloquially known as sending him on garden leave? It is not disputed that he may do so if there is an express contractual term to that effect. The issue on this appeal is whether, in the absence of such a term, William Hill Organisation Ltd ("the employer"), was entitled to do so in the circumstances of this case . . .

For the employer, it was submitted that there was no general right to work whether or not the employee was skilled. It was accepted that such a right may be implied in cases where the provision of work furthers the career of the employee or enables him to earn remuneration. It was also accepted that an employer might not capriciously deny to an employee work which was reasonably available. It was suggested that the decided cases might now be rationalised by reference to the implied obligation on both parties to a contract of employment to refrain from conduct likely to damage or destroy the mutual trust and confidence each is entitled to have in the other: *Malik* v *Bank of Credit and Commerce International SA* (1997).

For Mr Tucker, two propositions were advanced, a narrow proposition and a broad one. The narrow proposition was that an employee appointed to a particular and unique position may not be excluded from that position in the absence of his consent or a term in the contract entitling the employer so to do. The broad proposition was that it is a guiding principle (not a universal rule) when construing a contract of employment that the employee's interest in doing his job, as well as being paid his salary, is now recognised; in particular in the case of skilled workers and others who benefit from practising their skills either because their remuneration depends on it or because their career prospects would be thereby advanced. It was accepted that in the case of each proposition it is necessary to construe the contract in the light of its own surrounding circumstances.

We were referred to many more authorities than were drawn to the judge's attention and have had greater opportunity than he did to consider the implications and effect of these rival submissions. I mention that because neither party appears to support the broad proposition, which I have quoted, on which the judge founded his decision. Neither side suggests that there is "a right to work" having any source other than the contract of employment. Moreover the submissions for each side are inconsistent with the existence of rights and obligations arising from the status of employer and employee as explained by Lord Steyn in *Malik* v *Bank of Credit and Commerce International SA* (1997). Thus it is common ground that the solution to the problem must be found from the terms of the contract between the employer and Mr Tucker. I agree. One proposition which is clearly demonstrated by all the cases to which we were referred is that the question whether there is a "right to work" is one of construction of the particular contract in the light of its surrounding circumstances.

The issue is most clearly expressed in the judgment of Stirling LJ in *Turner* v *Sawdon & Co* (1901) in a passage expressly approved by the House of Lords in *Herbert Clayton and Jack Waller Ltd* v *Oliver* (1930). He said:

"It is an agreement by which the defendants agreed to engage and employ the claimant, and the claimant agreed to devote the whole of his time to their service. The question is, What is

177

the meaning of the word 'employ' as used in this agreement? It seems to me clear, and if authority be required we find it in the case of *Emmens* v *Elderton* (1853), that the word 'employ' is capable of two meanings – to retain in service, or to give actual work to be done by the person employed. There are many cases in which the nature of the work to be done shews which of these meanings should be adopted. Take the case of a medical man engaged for a term at a fixed payment. No one would say that employment must be found for him. On the other hand, in the case of an actor who accepts an engagement, it may be an important consideration with him to have an opportunity of displaying his abilities before the public, and it may be that there is an implied obligation on the part of the master to afford such an opportunity: *Fechter* v *Montgomery* (1863). So in the case of a commission agent, to which reference has been made. The term 'employ' being one with a flexible meaning, I feel the force of the argument that the claimant was to be employed in the capacity of sales-man to serve and solicit orders, and so there should be a correlative duty on the employers to give him the opportunity of doing this."

In more recent times the same point was made by Sir John Donaldson in *Langston* v *AUEW (No 2)* (1974). He said:

"In our judgment, the crucial question to be asked is, 'What is the consideration moving from the employers under the contract of employment?' In the case of theatrical performers, it is a salary plus the opportunity of becoming better known. Thus a failure to pay the salary pro-duces a partial failure of the consideration and thus a breach of contract. But so does the cancellation of the performance, even if the salary is paid: see *Herbert Clayton and Jack Waller* v *Oliver* (1930). Similarly, the consideration in a commission or piece work contract of employment is the express obligation to pay an agreed rate for work done plus the implied obligation to provide a reasonable amount of work: see *Devonald* v *Rosser & Sons* (1906). In a contract for the employment of one who needs practice to maintain or develop his skills, the consideration will include an obligation to pay the salary or wage, but it may also extend to an obligation to provide a reasonable amount of work. The complainant's work as a spot welder may have been in the 'skilled' category, but we do not think that he needs practice in order to maintain his skills. There are, however, other cases in which the sole consider-ation moving from the employer is the obligation to pay a wage. An example is provided by *Turner* v *Sawdon & Co* (1901)."

. . .

In *Provident Financial Group* v *Hayward* (1989), there was a specific term absolving the employer from providing any work so that the question of construction did not arise. But in the context of the exercise of the discretion of the court as to how long to impose the restraint Dillon LJ observed: "The employee has a concern to work and a concern to exercise his skills. That has been recognised in some circumstances concerned with artists and singers who depend on publicity, but it applies equally, I apprehend, to skilled workmen and even to chartered accountants." Though it did not arise in that case, Taylor LJ recognised that the employee would be concerned if in the period of restraint his skill was likely to atrophy.

It is important to appreciate the limits to the obligation for which Mr Tucker contends. It is not suggested that there is an obligation to find work if there is none to be done or none which can be done with profit to the employer. Nor does he contend that the employer is bound to allocate work to him in preference to another employee if there is not enough for both of them. He submits that if the job is there to be done and the employee was appointed to do it and is ready and willing to do so, then the employer must permit him to do so. He submits, by refer-ence to the analogy of the cook given by Asquith J in *Collier* v *Sunday Referee Publishing Co Ltd* (1940), that though that judge was not bound to eat the food his cook provided he was not entitled to put another cook in her kitchen. So, likewise in this case, he submits, the employer is not entitled to exclude Mr Tucker from the post to which they appointed him; the work is there to be done and it is the obligation of the employer to permit Mr Tucker to do it unless, which there is not, there is a provision in the contract absolving the employer from that obligation.

For my part, I accept that the contract of employment in this case can and should be construed as giving rise to such an obligation on the part of the employer. First, the post of senior dealer was a specific and unique post. It is not in dispute that Mr Tucker was asked by the employer in August 1994 to investigate what was involved in setting up a spread betting business. After considering the product of his researches, the employer decided to extend its operations into that field. Mr Tucker was the only senior dealer. There were juniors below him and a manager above him but he was the person appointed to conduct this new and specialised business. No doubt every employment nowadays has a title and job description which make it sound specific and unique but I have no doubt that the post to which Mr Tucker was appointed merited that description both in substance as well as form. Secondly, the skills necessary to the proper discharge of such duties did require their frequent exercise. Though it is not a case comparable to a skilled musician who requires regular practice to stay at concert pitch I have little doubt that frequent and continuing experience of the spread betting market, what it will bear and the subtle changes it goes through, is necessary to the enhancement and preservation of the skills of those who work in it.

Both those considerations arise from the surrounding circumstances in which the contract falls to be construed. But, thirdly, when one turns to the terms of the contract, there are further considerations pointing to the same conclusion. Not only does the contract provide for the hours and days of work so as to fill the normal working week, it specifically imposes on the employee the obligation to work those hours necessary to carry out his duties in a full and professional manner. If the work is available, it is inconsistent with that provision if the employee is entitled or bound to draw the remuneration without doing the work. To my mind, that consideration is unaffected by the provision that the duties of members of staff are as assigned by the employer or by individual managers. Not only is it followed immediately by a further stipulation requiring all staff to work such hours as are necessary for the proper performance of their duties but, in this case, the post of senior dealer in the spread betting business itself involved a broad assignment of duties. But the absence of an obligation on the employer, as contended for by Mr Tucker, would be contrary to two express terms. The first is that appearing under the heading "Training and development". In that part of the staff handbook, the employer declares that:

"The most important asset in any business is its employees and the [employer] is prepared to invest in its staff to ensure that they have every opportunity to develop their skills."

The second is the express power of suspension, to which I have already referred, which is limited to cases where more time is required to investigate serious allegations of breach of discipline or security. If the employer were to be entitled to keep its employee in idleness, the investment in its staff might be as illusory as the limited power of suspension would be unnecessary.

For these reasons I conclude that, on the proper construction of this contract of employment, the employer was under an obligation to permit Mr Tucker to perform the duties of the post to which it had appointed him in accordance with his contract as well during the period of his notice as before it was given.'

(Stuart-Smith and Robert Walker LJJ agreed with Morritt LJ.)

Comment

(1) Note that the idea of a general right to work is not accepted here. At most, the Court of Appeal states that the employer may not, in certain circumstances, withhold work which is available.

(2) The various reasons for holding that it was a breach of contract to withhold work in the circumstances of this case are interesting: which would have most applicability to other kinds of employee?

(3) The effect of holding that the employer was in breach of contract was that the employee was able to accept the breach and thus bring his contract of employment to an end at once – thus releasing him to go and work for a rival firm immediately. However, the employer could have prevented this by having an express term allowing the employee to be put on 'garden leave' during his notice period.

Duty to respect the employee's privacy?

European Convention on Human Rights

ARTICLE 8: RIGHT TO RESPECT FOR PRIVATE AND FAMILY LIFE

1 Everyone has the right to respect for his private and family life, his home and his correspondence.
2 There shall be no interference by a public authority with the exercise of this right except such as is in accordance with the law and is necessary in a democratic society in the interests of national security, public safety or the economic well-being of the country, for the prevention of disorder or crime, for the protection of health or morals, or for the protection of the rights and freedoms of others.

Halford v *United Kingdom* [1997] IRLR 471 European Court of Human Rights

Alison Halford was appointed as Assistant Chief Constable of Merseyside Police in 1983, thus becoming the most senior policewoman in the country. In the next seven years she made eight applications for the post of Deputy Chief Constable which were unsuccessful. She alleged that this was because the Chief Constable of Merseyside Police was blocking her approval by the Home Office, on grounds of sex discrimination.

She began sex discrimination proceedings against Merseyside Police. She alleged that calls from her office telephone in connection with these proceedings were intercepted by her employers and she claimed that this was a breach of ECHR, Art 8. Convention rights were not enforceable in the UK until the Human Rights Act 1998 came into force in 2000, so her claim went to the European Court of Human Rights.

JUDGMENT OF THE COURT: '. . .

1 APPLICABILITY OF ARTICLE 8 TO THE COMPLAINT RELATING TO THE OFFICE TELEPHONES

The applicant argued and the Commission agreed that conversations made on the telephones in Ms Halford's office at Merseyside Police Headquarters fell within the scope of "private life" and "correspondence" in Article 8(1), since the Court in its case law had adopted a broad construction of these expressions (see, for example, *Klass* v *Germany* (1978), *Huvig* v *France* (1990), *Niemietz* v *Germany* (1992) and *A* v *France* (1994)).

The Government submitted that telephone calls made by Ms Halford from her workplace fell outside the protection of Article 8, because she could have had no reasonable expectation of privacy in relation to them. At the hearing before the Court, counsel for the Government expressed the view that an employer should in principle, without the prior knowledge of the employee, be able to monitor calls made by the latter on telephones provided by the employer.

In the Court's view, it is clear from its case law that telephone calls made from business premises as well as from the home may be covered by the notions of "private life" and "correspondence" within the meaning of Article 8(1) (See *Klass* v *Germany* (1978), *Malone* v *United Kingdom* (1985), *Huvig* v *France* (1990), and, *mutatis mutandis, Niemietz* v *Germany* (1992)).

There is no evidence of any warning having been given to Ms Halford, as a user of the internal telecommunications system operated at the Merseyside Police Headquarters, that calls made on that system would be liable to interception. She would, the Court considers, have had a reasonable expectation of privacy for such calls, which expectation was moreover reinforced by a number of factors. As Assistant Chief Constable she had sole use of her office where there were two telephones, one of which was specifically designated for her private use. Furthermore, she had been given the assurance, in response to a memorandum, that she could use her office telephones for the purposes of her sex discrimination case.

For all of the above reasons, the Court concludes that telephone conversations made by Ms Halford on her office telephones fell within the scope of the notions of "private life" and "correspondence" and that Article 8 was therefore applicable to this part of the complaint . . .'

Comment

(1) The European Court of Human Rights further held that her right had been interfered with by a public authority and awarded her compensation.

(2) While the ECtHR held that employees have an expectation of privacy at work, it is also implied that there may be no breach if an employer warns employees that their calls may be intercepted.

(3) At the time of this case there was no law specifically covering interception of communications on private communications systems. The law has now changed as a result of the Regulation of Investigatory Powers Act 2000 (RIPA), passed partly because of the developments in human rights law and partly to implement the EU Telecommunications and Data Protection Directive (97/66/EC). The RIPA makes it *prima facie* a criminal offence to intercept communications on either public or private communications systems, and provides for civil liability as well. However, in relation to employment, this strong position is diluted considerably by the exceptions permitted under the Lawful Business Practice Regulations.

Telecommunications (Lawful Business Practice) (Interception of Communications) Regulations 2000 – Explanatory Note

These Regulations authorise certain interceptions of telecommunication communications which would otherwise be prohibited by section 1 of the Regulation of Investigatory Powers Act 2000. To the extent that the interceptions are also prohibited by Article 5.1 of Directive 97/66/EC, the authorisation does not exceed that permitted by Articles 5.2 and 14.1 of the Directive.

The interception has to be by or with the consent of a person carrying on a business (which includes the activities of government departments, public authorities and others exercising statutory functions) for purposes relevant to that person's business and using that business's own telecommunication system.

Interceptions are authorised for—

monitoring or recording communications—

to establish the existence of facts, to ascertain compliance with regulatory or self-regulatory practices or procedures or to ascertain or demonstrate standards which are or ought to be achieved (quality control and training),

in the interests of national security (in which case only certain specified public officials may make the interception),

to prevent or detect crime,

to investigate or detect unauthorised use of telecommunication systems or,

to secure, or as an inherent part of, effective system operation;

monitoring received communications to determine whether they are business or personal communications;

monitoring communications made to anonymous telephone helplines.

Interceptions are authorised only if the controller of the telecommunications system on which they are effected has made all reasonable efforts to inform potential users that interceptions may be made.

The Regulations do not authorise interceptions to which the persons making and receiving the communications have consented: they are not prohibited by the Act.

Comment

(1) The Explanatory Note to the Regulations has no legal force, but it provides a useful and accurate summary of the position.

(2) Where the employer monitors employees to gather information, there must be compliance with the Data Protection Act 1998. Forms of monitoring which involve interception of communications must comply with RIPA and the Data Protection Act. The Information Commissioner's Employment Practices Code (2005), Part 3 and Supplementary Guidance on the Employment Practices Code (2005), Part 3 provide useful practical advice, which stresses the importance of respecting workers' privacy. These are the core principles laid down in the Employment Practices Code:

Employment Practices Code (2005)

3.1 THE GENERAL APPROACH TO MONITORING

Core principles

- It will usually be intrusive to monitor your workers.
- Workers have legitimate expectations that they can keep their personal lives private and that they are also entitled to a degree of privacy in the work environment.
- If employers wish to monitor their workers, they should be clear about the purpose and satisfied that the particular monitoring arrangement is justified by real benefits that will be delivered.
- Workers should be aware of the nature, extent and reasons for any monitoring, unless (exceptionally) covert monitoring is justified.
- In any event, workers' awareness will influence their expectations.

Duty to maintain mutual trust and confidence

Recognition of such a duty, applicable to both employer and employee, has developed over the last 30 years. The extracts which follow chart its development.

Post Office v *Roberts* [1980] IRLR 347 Employment Appeal Tribunal

A senior official wrote a bad report on the employee, judging her to be unfit for promotion. This was written without proper consideration of the employee's record, and led to her being refused a transfer to another branch, although the true reason for this refusal was not made known to her until some time later. When she found out, she left and claimed unfair dismissal. An employment tribunal found that she had been constructively dismissed and that it was unfair.

TALBOT J: '. . . The final point of complaint made by Mr Carr [counsel for the employer] is that the employment tribunal's finding of a breach of the obligation of mutual trust and confidence is erroneous, in that the conduct relied upon was incapable in law of amounting to a repudiation. In this respect the main burden of his submission was that, for the obligation of mutual trust and confidence to be destroyed, there must be deliberate conduct or bad faith in the appraisal reports. Though there was a finding that Mr O'Keefe had failed to discharge his responsibilities it was not deliberate and it was not in bad faith. To support this submission Mr Carr cited a number of authorities: the first was *Isle of Wight Tourist Board* v *Coombes* (1976). In that case the respondent had been a personal secretary to the appellant's director and in the course of an argument that director had spoken to another employee about her, saying that she was an "intolerable bitch on a Monday morning". The Employment Appeal Tribunal held that the relationship between the director and his personal secretary must be one of complete confidence and they must trust and respect each other, that in calling his secretary a "bitch" the employer's director had shattered that relationship. Thus, they confirmed the employment tribunal's decision that there had been a constructive dismissal.

We do not find in that decision any hint of the need for the conduct to be deliberate and intentional or prompted by bad faith.

The next case was *Courtaulds Northern Textiles Ltd* v *Andrew* (1979). Again this was a case where words had been spoken in an argument. The words spoken by the assistant manager of the respondent were "You can't do the bloody job anyway". Again the Employment Appeal Tribunal, in this case Arnold J presiding, referred to the implied term of the contract of employment that "the employers will not without proper reason and cause conduct themselves in a manner calculated or likely to destroy or seriously damage the relationship of confidence and trust between the parties". That part of the headnote is borne out in the judgment. We will read the latter part of that dictum, where Arnold J said:

> "We think that, thus phrased, the implied term (as regards 'calculated') extends only to an obligation not to conduct themselves in such a manner as is intended, although not intended by itself, to destroy or seriously damage the relationship in question."

. . . The next authority was *FC Gardner Ltd* v *Beresford* (1978). In substance, the complaint in that appeal was that there had been no increase in pay for two years. Phillips J, giving the judgment of the Employment Appeal Tribunal, referred to the obligation on an employer not to behave arbitrarily, capriciously, or inequitably in matters of remuneration. Certainly, we can see no complaint about that; that is absolutely right. But that is not this case. In the headnote (and this is borne out by the judgment) it is stated:

> "On the other hand, if there was evidence to support a finding that the employers were deliberately singling the respondent out for special treatment inferior to that given to everybody else and that they were doing it arbitrarily, capriciously and inequitably, that might well lead the employment tribunal to say that she had a good claim even under the new test for constructive dismissal."

Again we fail to see why that plain and sensible dictum applied to the question of remuneration states a general principle that applies to cases of the kind with which we are dealing.

Then there was the authority of *Robinson* v *Crompton Parkinson Ltd* (1978). In that appeal Kilner Brown J referred to this obligation of mutual trust and confidence. He said, in his judgment:

"It seems to us, although there is no direct authority to which we have been referred, that the law is perfectly plain and needs to be re-stated so that there shall be no opportunity for confusion in the future. In a contract of employment, and in conditions of employment, there has to be mutual trust and confidence between master and servant. Although most of the reported cases deal with the master seeking remedy against a servant or former servant for acting in breach of confidence or in breach of trust, that action can only be upon the basis that trust and confidence is mutual. Consequently where a man says of his employer, 'I claim that you have broken your contract because you have clearly shown you have no confidence in me, and you have behaved in a way which is contrary to that mutual trust which ought to exist between master and servant,' he is entitled in those circumstances, it seems to us, to say that there is conduct which amounts to a repudiation of the contract."

In stating that principle, in our view Kilner Brown J does not set out any requirement that there should be deliberation, or intent, or bad faith.

Finally, there are very important words in a part of the judgment in *Palmanor Ltd* v *Cedron* (1978), the words appearing in the judgment of Slynn J. It is a short quotation and reads as follows:

"It seems to us that in a case of this kind the Tribunal is required to ask itself the question whether the conduct was so unreasonable that it really went beyond the limits of the contract. We observe that in the course of the argument on behalf of the employee, it was submitted that the treatment that he was accorded was a repudiation of the contract." . . .'

(The employer's appeal against the finding of unfair dismissal was dismissed.)

Woods v WM Car Services [1981] ICR 666 Employment Appeal Tribunal

The claimant was employed as chief secretary and accounts clerk. Following a take-over of the business, the new employers first put pressure on her to take a drop in salary, then to work longer hours, both of which she refused. Then they dropped the word 'chief' from her title and gave her additional duties. She left and claimed unfair dismissal.

BROWNE-WILKINSON J: '. . . In our view it is clearly established that there is implied in a contract of employment a term that the employers will not, without reasonable and proper cause, conduct themselves in a manner calculated or likely to destroy or seriously damage the relationship of confidence and trust between employer and employee: *Courtaulds Northern Textiles Ltd* v *Andrew* (1979). To constitute a breach of this implied term, it is not necessary to show that the employer intended any repudiation of the contract: the tribunals' function is to look at the employer's conduct as a whole and determine whether it is such that its effect, judged reasonably and sensibly, is such that the employee cannot be expected to put up with it: see *BAC* v *Austin* (1978) and *Post Office* v *Roberts* (1980). The conduct of the parties has to be looked at as a whole and its cumulative impact assessed: *Post Office* v *Roberts*.

We regard this implied term as one of great importance in good industrial relations . . .'

(The EAT upheld the decision of the employment tribunal that, on the facts of this case, there was in fact no fundamental breach of contract. The Court of Appeal dismissed the employee's appeal.)

Lewis v Motorworld Garages Ltd [1986] ICR 157 Court of Appeal

In November 1981 the employee was demoted without warning, lost his office and had his pay structure altered detrimentally. This was a fundamental breach of contract by the employer, but the employee elected to affirm the contract by continuing to work. Over the next months the employee was persistently and unfairly criticised and threatened with dismissal. The employer purported to give him a final warning in August 1982. This was the last straw: the employee left and claimed unfair dismissal.

GLIDEWELL LJ: '. . . The principles to be found in the relevant authorities can, I believe, be summarised as follows:

(1)   In order to prove that he has suffered constructive dismissal, an employee who leaves his employment must prove that he did so as the result of a breach of contract by his employer, which shows that the employer no longer intends to be bound by an essential term of the contract: see *Western Excavating (ECC) Ltd* v *Sharp* (1978).

(2)   However, there are normally implied in a contract of employment mutual rights and obligations of trust and confidence. A breach of this implied term may justify the employee in leaving and claiming he has been constructively dismissed: see *Post Office* v *Roberts* (1980) and *Woods* v *WM Car Services (Peterborough) Ltd* (1981) *per* Browne Wilkinson J.

(3)   The breach of this implied obligation of trust and confidence may consist of a series of actions on the part of the employer which cumulatively amount to a breach of the term, though each individual incident may not do so. In particular in such a case the last action of the employer which leads to the employee leaving need not itself be a breach of contract; the question is, does the cumulative series of acts taken together amount to a breach of the implied term? (See *Woods* v *WM Car Services (Peterborough) Ltd*.) This is the "last straw" situation.

(4)   The decision whether there has been a breach of contract by the employer so as to constitute constructive dismissal of the employee is one of mixed law and fact for the employment tribunal. An appellate court, whether the Employment Appeal Tribunal or the Court of Appeal, may only overrule that decision if the employment tribunal has misdirected itself as to the relevant law or has made a finding of fact for which there is no supporting evidence or which no reasonable tribunal could make: see *Pedersen* v *Camden LBC (Note)* (1981) and *Woods* v *WM Car Services (Peterborough) Ltd* (1982) both in the Court of Appeal, applying the test laid down in *Edwards* v *Bairstow* (1956).

     This case raises another issue of principle which, so far as I can ascertain, has not yet been considered by this court. If the employer is in breach of an express term of a contract of employment, of such seriousness that the employee would be justified in leaving and claiming constructive dismissal, but the employee does not leave and accepts the altered terms of employment: and if subsequently a series of actions by the employer might constitute together a breach of the implied obligation of trust and confidence: is the employee then entitled to treat the original action by the employer which was a breach of the express terms of the contract as a part – the start – of the series of actions which, taken together with the employer's other actions, might cumulatively amount to a breach of the implied terms? In my judgment the answer to this question is clearly "yes".'

(Ackner and Neill LJJ delivered concurring judgments. The case was remitted to a different employment tribunal for rehearing.)

Comment

(1) It will be noted that all these cases in the EAT, and eventually the Court of Appeal, where the implied term was adumbrated and developed, were cases of unfair dismissal – specifically, constructive dismissal. If a contract of employment is terminated through the employee resigning, the situation will only be construed as a dismissal if the

resignation was caused by the employer's fundamental breach of contract (see further below, p 366). Hence the development of this 'portmanteau' term, which allows a great variety of bad behaviour by an employer to be packed neatly under the general heading of a term whose breach will be categorised as fundamental. There is no end to the possible actions which could be attacked on this ground, as the cases discussed in the extracts illustrate.

(2) The implied reciprocal duty to maintain mutual trust and confidence may have developed in the context of constructive dismissal claims, but it has moved on since. The landmark decision of the House of Lords in the next case admitted the possibility of an action for damages for its breach.

Malik v Bank of Credit and Commerce International
[1997] IRLR 462 House of Lords

LORD NICHOLLS: 'My Lords,

This is another case arising from the disastrous collapse of Bank of Credit and Commerce International SA (BCCI) in the summer of 1991. Thousands of people around the world suffered loss. Depositors lost their money, employees lost their jobs. Two employees who lost their jobs were Mr Raihan Nasir Mahmud and Mr Qaiser Mansoor Malik. They were employed by BCCI in London. They claim they lost more than their jobs. They claim that their association with BCCI placed them at a serious disadvantage in finding new jobs. So in March 1992 they sought to prove for damages in the winding up of BCCI. The liquidators rejected this "stigma" head of loss in their proofs. Liability for notice money and statutory redundancy pay was not in dispute.

Mr Mahmud had worked for the bank for 16 years. At the time of his dismissal he was manager of the bank's Brompton Road branch. Mr Malik was employed by the bank for 12 years. His last post was as the head of deposit accounts and customer services at BCCI's Leadenhall branch. On 3 October 1991 they were both dismissed by the provisional liquidators, on the ground of redundancy.

Mr Mahmud and Mr Malik appealed to the court against the liquidators' decision on their proofs. The registrar directed the trial of a preliminary issue: whether the applicants' evidence disclosed a reasonable cause of action or sustainable claim for damages. The Judge, Evans-Lombe J, gave a negative answer to this question. So did the Court of Appeal, comprising Glidewell, Morritt and Aldous LJJ.

Before this House, as in the courts below, the issue is being decided on the basis of an agreed set of facts. The liquidators do not admit the accuracy of these facts, but for the purpose of this preliminary issue it is being assumed that the bank operated in a corrupt and dishonest manner, that Mr Mahmud and Mr Malik were innocent of any involvement, that following the collapse of BCCI its corruption and dishonesty became widely known, that in consequence Mr Mahmud and Mr Malik were at a handicap on the labour market because they were stigmatised by reason of their previous employment by BCCI, and that they suffered loss in consequence.

In the Court of Appeal and in your Lordships' House the parties were agreed that the contracts of employment of these two former employees each contained an implied term to the effect that the bank would not, without reasonable and proper cause, conduct itself in a manner likely to destroy or seriously damage the relationship of confidence and trust between employer and employee. Argument proceeded on this footing, and ranged round the type of conduct and other circumstances which could or could not constitute a breach of this implied term. The submissions embraced questions such as the following: whether the trust-destroying conduct must be directed at the employee, either individually or as part of a group; whether an employee must know of the employer's trust-destroying conduct while still employed; and whether the employee's trust must actually be undermined. Furthermore, and at the heart of this case, the submissions raised an important question on the damages recoverable for breach of the implied term, with particular reference to the decisions in *Addis* v *Gramophone Co Ltd* (1909) and *Withers* v *General Theatre Corp Ltd* (1933).

A dishonest and corrupt business

These questions are best approached by focusing first on the particular conduct of which complaint is made. The bank operated its business dishonestly and corruptly. On the assumed facts, this was not a case where one or two individuals, however senior, were behaving dishonestly. Matters had gone beyond this. They had reached the point where the bank itself could properly be identified with the dishonesty. This was a dishonest business, a corrupt business.

It is against this background that the position of an innocent employee has to be considered. In my view, when an innocent employee of the bank learned the true nature of the bank's business, from whatever source, he was entitled to say: "I wish to have nothing more to do with this organisation. I am not prepared to help this business, by working for it. I am leaving at once." This is my intuitive response in the case of all innocent employees of the business, from the most senior to the most junior, from the most long serving to the most recently joined. No one could be expected to have to continue to work with and for such a company against his wish.

This intuitive response is no more than a reflection of what goes without saying in any ordinary contract of employment, namely, that in agreeing to work for an employer the employee, whatever his status, cannot be taken to have agreed to work in furtherance of a dishonest business. This is as much true of a doorkeeper or cleaner as a senior executive or branch manager.

An implied obligation

Two points can be noted here. First, as a matter of legal analysis, the innocent employee's entitlement to leave at once must derive from the bank being in breach of a term of the contract of employment which the employee is entitled to treat as a repudiation by the bank of its contractual obligations. That is the source of his right to step away from the contract forthwith.

In other words, and this is the necessary corollary of the employee's right to leave at once, the bank was under an implied obligation to its employees not to conduct a dishonest or corrupt business. This implied obligation is no more than one particular aspect of the portmanteau, general obligation not to engage in conduct likely to undermine the trust and confidence required if the employment relationship is to continue in the manner the employment contract implicitly envisages.

Second, I do not accept the liquidators' submission that the conduct of which complaint is made must be targeted in some way at the employee or a group of employees. No doubt that will often be the position, perhaps usually so. But there is no reason in principle why this must always be so. The trust and confidence required in the employment relationship can be undermined by an employer, or indeed an employee, in many different ways. I can see no justification for the law giving the employee a remedy if the unjustified trust-destroying conduct occurs in some ways but refusing a remedy if it occurs in others. The conduct must, of course, impinge on the relationship in the sense that, looked at objectively, it is likely to destroy or seriously damage the degree of trust and confidence the employee is reasonably entitled to have in his employer. That requires one to look at all the circumstances.

Breach

The objective standard just mentioned provides the answer to the liquidators' submission that unless the employee's confidence is actually undermined there is no breach. A breach occurs when the proscribed conduct takes place: here, operating a dishonest and corrupt business. Proof of a subjective loss of confidence in the employer is not an essential element of the breach, although the time when the employee learns of the misconduct and his response to it may affect his remedy . . .

Continuing financial losses

Exceptionally, however, the losses suffered by an employee as a result of a breach of the trust and confidence term may not consist of, or be confined to, loss of pay and other premature termination losses. Leaving aside injured feelings and anxiety, which are not the basis of the claim in the present case, an employee may find himself worse off financially than when he entered into the contract. The most obvious example is conduct, in breach of the trust and confidence term, which prejudicially affects an employee's future employment prospects. The conduct may diminish the employee's attractiveness to future employers.

The loss in the present case is of this character. BCCI promised, in an implied term, not to conduct a dishonest or corrupt business. The promised benefit was employment by an honest employer. This benefit did not materialise. Proof that Mr Mahmud and Mr Malik were handicapped in the labour market in consequence of BCCI's corruption may not be easy, but that is an assumed fact for the purpose of this preliminary issue.

There is here an important point of principle. Are financial losses of this character, which I shall call "continuing financial losses", recoverable for breach of the trust and confidence term? This is the crucial point in the present appeals. In my view, if it was reasonably foreseeable that a particular type of loss of this character was a serious possibility, and loss of this type is sustained in consequence of a breach, then in principle damages in respect of the loss should be recoverable.

In the present case the agreed facts make no assumption, either way, about whether the appellants' handicap in the labour market was reasonably foreseeable by the bank. On this there must be scope for argument. I would not regard the absence of this necessary ingredient from the assumed facts as a sufficient reason for refusing to permit the former employees' claims to proceed further.

The contrary argument of principle is that since the purpose of the trust and confidence term is to preserve the employment relationship and to enable that relationship to prosper and continue, the losses recoverable for breach should be confined to those flowing from the premature termination of the relationship. Thus, a breach of the term should not be regarded as giving rise to recoverable losses beyond those I have described as premature termination losses. In this way, the measure of damages would be commensurate with, and not go beyond, the scope of the protection the trust and confidence term is intended to provide for the employee.

This is an unacceptably narrow evaluation of the trust and confidence term. Employers may be under no common law obligation, through the medium of an implied contractual term of general application, to take steps to improve their employees' future job prospects. But failure to improve is one thing, positively to damage is another. Employment, and job prospects, are matters of vital concern to most people. Jobs of all descriptions are less secure than formerly, people change jobs more frequently, and the job market is not always buoyant. Everyone knows this. An employment contract creates a close personal relationship, where there is often a disparity of power between the parties. Frequently the employee is vulnerable. Although the underlying purpose of the trust and confidence term is to protect the employment relationship, there can be nothing unfairly onerous or unreasonable in requiring an employer who breaches the trust and confidence term to be liable if he thereby causes continuing financial loss of a nature that was reasonably foreseeable. Employers must take care not to damage their employees' future employment prospects, by harsh and oppressive behaviour or by any other form of conduct which is unacceptable today as falling below the standards set by the implied trust and confidence term . . .'

Comment

(1) The most dramatic feature of the decision in this case is that it showed a way of getting round the limitation on damages for wrongful dismissal set out by the House of Lords in *Addis* v *Gramophone Co Ltd* (1909). This aspect of the case is considered below (p 345).

(2) Lord Steyn noted that this was the first time that the implied duty to maintain mutual trust and confidence had been considered by the House of Lords. He commented:

> The evolution of the implied term of trust and confidence is a fact. It has not yet been indorsed by your Lordships' House. It has proved a workable principle in practice. It has not been the subject of adverse criticism in any decided cases and it has been welcomed in academic writings. I regard the emergence of the implied obligation of mutual trust and confidence as a sound development.

(3) Note in particular the discussion of the parameters of the implied term in Lord Nicholls's speech, and the decisions reached.

(4) Lord Nicholls here refers to the duty to maintain mutual trust and confidence as a 'portmanteau obligation'. It has been suggested that it might in time swallow up the other specific duties, which could be regarded as facets of this general obligation.

Duty to obey lawful and reasonable orders

Laws v London Chronicle [1959] 1 WLR 698 Court of Appeal

The claimant was employed on the advertising staff of the company. She attended a meeting where there was an argument between D, the advertising manager, and B, chairman and managing director of the company. D left the room, telling her to go with him. B told her to stay. She went, and was dismissed without notice as a result. Dismissal without notice is justifiable if the employee has committed a fundamental breach of contract.

LORD EVERSHED MR: '. . . it is the corner-stone of Mr Stable's case [counsel for the employer] that there was in truth nothing that a self-respecting employer could do but to dismiss summarily: for here was an order given – "Stay where you are" – and disobeyed. Mr Stable cited authority – of antiquity, but none the less of respectability – to show (as he contends) that disobedience of any order that is lawful entitles the employer to dismiss the servant summarily. In *Turner* v *Mason* (1845) a domestic servant – quite deliberately, because she had made a request which was rejected – absented herself during a certain night when she should have been on duty; and her plea of justification was that her mother was desperately ill – though it is not clear that she so informed her employer. She was dismissed; and the Court of Queen's Bench affirmed the view that the dismissal was justified. I will not read the judgments of Parke CB and Barons Alderson and Rolfe: but it would in my judgment be going too far to say that any of those judges laid it down as a proposition of law that every act of disobedience of a lawful order must entitle the employer to dismiss. I think that cannot be extracted from the judgments; and I am satisfied that it is too narrow a proposition as one of law.

The law to be applied is stated (for example) in the paragraphs of Halsbury's Laws of England, 3rd ed, Vol 25, at pp 485 and 486, to which Mr Stable referred us in reply; and I will cite a sentence or two as a foundation to what follows. "Wilful disobedience to the lawful and reasonable order of the master justifies summary dismissal." Then, a little later, "Misconduct, inconsistent with the due and faithful discharge by the servant of the duties for which he was engaged, is good cause for his dismissal, but there is no fixed rule of law defining the degree of misconduct which will justify dismissal." Later, again, "There is good ground for the dismissal of a servant if he is habitually neglectful in respect of the duties for which he was engaged." And in one of the footnotes on that page there is a further statement, in reference to *Edwards* v *Levy* (1860), observing that in that case "it was pointed out that a single instance if insolence in the case of a servant in such a position as that of a newspaper critic would hardly justify dismissal".

To my mind, the proper conclusion to be drawn from the passages which I have cited and the cases to which we were referred is that, since a contract of service is but an example of contracts in general, so that the general law of contract will be applicable, it follows that the question must be – if summary dismissal is claimed to be justifiable – whether the conduct complained of is such as to show the servant to have disregarded the essential conditions of the contract of service. It is, no doubt, therefore, generally true that wilful disobedience of an order will justify summary dismissal, since wilful disobedience of a lawful and reasonable order shows a disregard – a complete disregard – of a condition essential to the contract of service, namely, the condition that the servant must obey the proper orders of the master and that, unless he does so, the relationship is, so to speak, struck at fundamentally . . .'

(Lord Jenkins and Willmer LJ agreed with Lord Evershed MR.)

On the facts, the court held that the special circumstances surrounding her single act of disobedience indicated that she had not shown an intention not to comply with the contract and had therefore not committed a fundamental breach of contract.

Comment

(1) An order is not lawful and reasonable if it requires the employee to do something outside the terms of his contract. Many employment disputes arise because it is not clear whether compliance with an order from management is within the employee's contract or not, as the next case shows.

O'Brien v *Associated Fire Alarms Ltd* [1968] 1 WLR 1916 Court of Appeal

This was a claim for redundancy payments: the redundancy aspects of this case are dealt with below, p 444.

SALMON LJ: '. . . These three men all lived close to Liverpool, and they had each been employed for many years by the respondents. During the whole time that they were so employed, they had worked in and around Liverpool. Each night they went home after the day's work was done. The time came when the work in and around Liverpool tended to diminish, but there was work that required to be done in Barrow. The men were ordered to go and do this work in Barrow. They refused. As a result of their conduct in refusing to go to Barrow, the employers dismissed them.

Now clearly, if under the contract of employment the employers were entitled to order them to go to Barrow and they refused to go there, the employers would be entitled to dismiss them . . .

The employment tribunal, in the course of its very careful decision, came to the conclusion that it was an implied term of the contract of employment that these men could be ordered to work in any part of the area controlled from the company's Liverpool office. That area ran from Whitehaven in the north down to mid-Wales in the south. It was a very large area, and Barrow was undoubtedly within it. Barrow was about 150 miles from Liverpool and the jobs which the employees were ordered to do there would have entailed their being away from home for about 13 weeks.

Whether a term should be implied into a contract is a question of law. Whether the implication should be made in law no doubt depends on the facts. In my view there were no facts proved in evidence from which it was permissible for the tribunal to draw the inference in law that it was a term of the men's employment that they could be asked to work anywhere within what I have referred to as the area controlled from the company's Liverpool office . . .

I would have thought that as the material circumstances in which these contracts of employment were entered into are shrouded in mystery, it is permissible, if one is seeking to reconstruct the contract, to look at what happened while the men were being employed. The fact is that never during all the years in which they worked for the respondents were they ever asked to work anywhere except in the conurbation of Liverpool or those parts of Cheshire which they could reach from their homes so that they returned to their homes every night. This, of course, would be by no means conclusive about the terms of their employment if there were any evidence the other way, but it is all that there is as to where they could be required to work. This indicates (and there is nothing to the contrary) that what they were doing during the years of their employment was all that they could be required to do in accordance with the terms of their employment. There is no evidence that the terms of their employment gave the company the power to order them to do anything else . . .'

(Lord Denning MR and Edmund Davies LJ delivered concurring judgments.)

Comment

(1) It makes sense for employers to include requirements of flexibility and mobility expressly in the contract if they are needed, and to provide the information in permanent form to employees, as is now required by ERA s 1. This should head off disputes of this kind.

Morrish v Henly's Ltd [1973] ICR 482 National Industrial Relations Court

SIR HUGH GRIFFITHS: '. . . For nearly four years the employee had been employed as a stores driver, and he drove one vehicle all the time. It was his duty to draw diesel oil for the vehicle as and when it was required. On the morning of August 2 he drew five gallons of diesel oil from one of his employers' forecourt pumps and recorded that upon a document called a monthly fuel invoice. He entered on that document the date, the number of the vehicle, the amount and grade of fuel, and he signed it. Next day he drew another five gallons but when he went to record it on the invoice he discovered that the figure of five gallons he had entered on the previous day had been altered to seven. He changed it back to five. Later that day he found that the entry had again been altered to seven, and again he changed it to five. Still later he saw that a further entry had been made which showed that on August 2 two gallons of diesel had been drawn by the vehicle he was driving on that day, and that entry was signed by the manager, Mr. Wilkes. The employee had by that time learned that the manager had made the previous alterations to his figure of five, and so, after crossing out the number of his vehicle against the entry of two gallons, he went to see the manager. A heated interview ensued. The manager explained that there was no suggestion that the employee had in fact drawn seven gallons and not five gallons, but that there was a deficiency of two gallons in the forecourt pumps and the alteration was merely to cover that deficiency and the forecourt staff. The employee was not willing to have an entry recorded which showed that two gallons of diesel had been put into the vehicle which he was driving, when that was not in fact the case, even if it was against the signature of the manager. The manager told him that, as he would not accept his instructions to leave the record showing two gallons attributed to that vehicle, he had no alternative but to give him notice; and that he did. On those facts the tribunal held that the employee had been unfairly dismissed.

The employers contended that, as there was evidence before the tribunal that it was a common practice to alter the records in that way to cover deficiencies, it was unreasonable of the employee to object, and he should have accepted the manager's instructions. Accordingly, his refusal to do so was an unreasonable refusal to obey an order, which justified dismissal.

We cannot accept this submission. It involves the proposition that it is an implied term of an employee's contract of service that he should accept an order to connive at the falsification of one of his employers' records. The proposition only has to be stated to be seen to be untenable. In our view, the employee was fully entitled to refuse to be in any way party to a falsification of that record and the tribunal were manifestly right in holding that he had been unfairly dismissed . . .'

Duty to co-operate

We have seen that employees have a duty to obey lawful and reasonable orders (*Laws* v *London Chronicle*, p 189), that to some extent they must be prepared to adapt (*Cresswell* v *Board of Inland Revenue*, p 170) and that they have a duty to maintain mutual trust and confidence (*Malik* v *BCCI*, p 186). It is perhaps not surprising, therefore, that it is now argued that employees have a positive duty to co-operate with their employer. This has potentially wide implications.

Ticehurst v British Telecommunications plc [1992] IRLR 219 Court of Appeal

In the course of a pay dispute, the Society of Telecoms Executives (STE) instructed members to withdraw goodwill, essentially meaning that they should do nothing outside their existing contracts. After some months, BT announced that it would no longer accept non-co-operation and that any employee not prepared to sign an undertaking to work normally would be sent home and not paid. The claimant, who had been sent home without pay, claimed her lost wages. It was conceded that, apart from refusing to give the required undertaking, no action or omission on her part amounting to a breach of her contract could be established.

The judgment of the court was given by Ralph Gibson LJ.

RALPH GIBSON LJ: '. . . The instruction of 21 October 1989 informed members that the industrial action centred on a withdrawal of goodwill and that the slogan of members should be: "Say no first, ask questions later."

On 16 November 1989 the report to members from STE included the observation that "members are taking an increasingly rigid view of what withdrawal of goodwill means" and members were asked to "examine their work carefully to see in what areas members might still be extending goodwill". It was repeated that the guiding motto should be "Say no first, ask questions later". The suggestion was made that when confronted with anything which might come within the scope of the STE action each member, after considering (*inter alia*) whether it formed part of his or her job description, should consider how much choice he or she had in how to do it and which option would cause the most inconvenience . . .

The instructions continued:

"Many managers make use of the 'quiet period' between Christmas and New Year to catch up on backlogs of work. You should not. If you are obliged to be present at work during that period, concentrate on the items listed in (5) below.
You should from now on ensure that you:
(a) Apply for all vacancies for which you might be qualified.
(b) Apply for your pension benefit statement.

(c) Request that *Telecom Today* and other company mailings be sent to you at work rather than at home. Continue to request it until complied with.

(d) Apply for all relevant training courses, and insist on receiving a syllabus in advance of attending . . .

(e) Seek information on the terms of local bonus schemes. Do not be satisfied with less than full details of qualifications for and levels of payment.

(f) Take adequate meal breaks away from your desk – or, if possible, off-site.

(g) Take your responsibilities seriously, particularly such peripheral activities as chargeship of buildings. Ensure you have all safety and security instructions which might possibly have relevance to your duty, and that you read, fully understand and apply them.

(h) Observe strictly BT's 'clear desk' policy . . . and ensure that you leave adequate time at the end of the day to do so properly."

Under the heading "Total Quality Management", the instructions continued:

"While continuing to endorse its principles, do not cooperate with any project not specifically agreed with the STE . . ."

Then, under "Changes of Practice or Procedure", the instructions were:

"No new practices or procedures should be accepted unless specifically agreed by the STE."

and:

"Do not work with or to any consultants or contractors unless their use has been specifically agreed with the STE." . . .

The analysis which I respectfully find most apt to define the relevant duties of Mrs Ticehurst under her contract of employment as a manager employed by BT, is that stated by Buckley LJ [in *Secretary of State* v *ASLEF (No 2)* (1972)], namely "an implied term to serve the employer faithfully within the requirements of the contract". It is, I think, consistent with the judgments of Lord Denning and Roskill LJ. It was not suggested that there is any express term in the contract of employment of Mrs Ticehurst, or anything else in the general circumstances of this case, which would make it wrong to imply such a term into her contract. It is, in my judgment, necessary to imply such a term in the case of a manager who is given charge of the work of other employees and who therefore must necessarily be trusted to exercise her judgment and discretion in giving instructions to others and in supervising their work. Such a discretion, if the contract is to work properly, must be exercised faithfully in the interests of the employers.

Next, it seems to me clear that participation by Mrs Ticehurst in the concerted action of withdrawal of goodwill, as it was devised and carried out by STE and the members, would constitute a breach of that term if Mrs Ticehurst was intending to continue to participate in it. For example, a manager who intends, when opportunity offers, to consider how much choice she has in performing any task within those listed by STE and then to choose that which would cause the most inconvenience to her employers, is intending, in my judgment, to break her obligation to serve her employers faithfully. Similarly, the doing of the other acts listed . . . above, not from a genuine intention or interest but so as to cause disruption, would be a breach of that obligation. In addition to those acts by Mrs Ticehurst herself, she was intending after 12 April (if she was intending to continue in the action of the withdrawal of goodwill) to continue, as a committee member of the Stone branch of STE, to advise and encourage other members of STE at

Stone to carry on that action by herself distributing STE documents and by being available to answer questions of members by telephone. Her name and telephone number were included in documents distributed by the Stone branch committee for that purpose.

I do not accept the submission of Mr Elias [counsel for Mrs Ticehurst] that there can be no breach of the implied term for faithful service unless the intended disruption of BT's undertaking was achieved by the action taken, whether to the extent of rendering the business unmanageable or to some other level of disruption. The term is breached, in my judgment, when the employee does an act, or omits to do an act, which it would be within her contract and the discretion allowed to her not to do, or to do, as the case may be, and the employee so acts or omits to do the act, not in honest exercise of choice or discretion for the faithful performance of her work but in order to disrupt the employer's business or to cause the most inconvenience that can be caused. We need not consider the position which would arise if the ill-intentioned course of conduct is shown to have had no significant consequences adverse to the employer and to be incapable of causing any such adverse consequences in future. This action by way of withdrawal of goodwill did have adverse consequences . . . and the fact that STE was asserting that the effect of the action was greater than that in fact achieved does not cause the conduct not to have been a breach of contract.'

Comment

(1) The judgment of Buckley LJ in *Secretary of State* v *ASLEF (No 2)* is extracted on p 579.

(2) On this analysis, the duty to co-operate is another facet of the duty of fidelity. The Court of Appeal's decision here is in one sense wider than in *Secretary of State* v *ASLEF (No 2)*, in that it holds conduct to be a breach even where there is no allegation that any specific duty of the employee has been performed wrongly or has been neglected. However, it may also be construed more narrowly, in that the court places emphasis on her managerial role and the discretion that it entails.

(3) Would it be right to draw a distinction between employees with a high degree of discretion as to how they carry out their work (who generally have correspondingly higher salaries) and employees with virtually no discretion, holding that the former, but not the latter, have an implied duty to co-operate with their employer?

Duty of fidelity

In common with other agents, employees owe a duty of fidelity to their employers. This means that they must at all times show good faith in their dealings with the employer and on the employer's behalf. Specific aspects of the duty of fidelity warrant separate consideration.

Secret profits

Boston Deep Sea Fishing and Ice Co v Ansell
(1888) 39 ChD 339 Court of Appeal

The defendant was managing director of the claimant company until his dismissal for failing to have the fishing smacks properly repaired and for overcharging for repairs. At the trial it was found that these allegations were unsubstantiated; however, by that time the company had discovered that some months previously the defendant had received a commission from a shipbuilder on a contract he had arranged on behalf of the company for the construction of new boats.

BOWEN LJ: '. . . In the present instance we have first of all to consider what was done by the managing director, and, in the next place, if we find that the managing director has taken and received a commission behind the back of his company and without the knowledge of his company, and kept it, we have to pronounce our opinion upon the question of whether or not in law that is an ample reason for his dismissal.

Now with regard to the facts relating to Earle's Shipbuilding Company, they stand beyond all dispute. The managing director has received a profit, and he has received a profit which was unknown to his own employers. How does that bear upon the condition which is implied in every contract of service or agency such as his – the condition that he will faithfully and truly discharge his duty towards his employer, and that if he does not so discharge it, the employer is to be at liberty to elect whether he will determine the service, or in spite of the fault continue the erring servant in his employ? . . .

There may be cases where the breach of confidence and good faith towards the master would not arise from a simple isolated act, but would be founded on the accumulation and repetition of such acts, but those classes of cases are not cases of fraud at all, they are cases of isolated acts which, if they occurred singly, would not, in themselves, amount to a violation of the confidential relation or breach of the faithful service which the servant is bound to render. In that class of cases it is perfectly proper to consider whether on the whole the conduct of the servant has been such as to amount to a breach of confidence, and if it has not, then the master will not be justified in the dismissal. In such cases you might leave to the jury to consider whether there had been such an accumulation, or such a repetition of the acts, as to give a ground for the determination of service; but in cases where the character of the isolated act is such as of itself to be beyond all dispute a violation of the confidential relation, and a breach of faith towards the master, the rights of the master do not depend on the caprice of the jury, or of the tribunal which tries the question. Once the tribunal has found the fact – has found that there is a fraud and breach of faith – then the rights of the master to determine the contract follow as matter of law.

Now, there can be no question that an agent employed by a principal or master to do business with another, who, unknown to that principal or master, takes from that other person a profit arising out of the business which he is employed to transact, is doing a wrongful act inconsistent with his duty towards his master, and the continuance of confidence between them. He does the wrongful act whether such profit be given to him in return for services which he actually performs for the third party, or whether it be given to him for his supposed influence, or whether it be given to him on any other ground at all; if it is a profit which arises out of the transaction, it belongs to his master, and the agent or servant has no right to take it, or keep it, or bargain for it, or to receive it without bargain, unless his master knows it. It is said if the transaction be one of very old date, that in some way deprives the master of his right to treat it as a breach of faith. As the Lord Justice has pointed out, the age of the fraud may be a reason in the master's mind for not acting on his rights; but it is impossible to say that because a fraud has been concealed for six years, therefore the master has not a right when he discovers it to act upon his discovery, and to put an end to the relation of employer and employed with which such fraud was inconsistent. I, therefore, find it impossible to adopt Mr Justice Kekewich's view, or to come to any other conclusion except that the managing director having been guilty of a fraud on his employers was rightly dismissed by them, and dismissed by them rightly even though they did not discover the fraud until after they had actually pronounced the sentence of dismissal . . .'

(Cotton and Fry LJJ delivered concurring judgments.)

Comment

(1) While this case involved the managing director of a company – the most senior employee – it is clear that the duty is not confined to directors but applies to every employee.

(2) In this case the reason relied on first by the company for dismissing him was inadequate but they were allowed to rely instead on a reason discovered *after* he had been dismissed. The importance of this point will be seen later in the discussion of unfair dismissal (cf *W Devis* v *Atkins & Sons* (1976) p 408).

(3) Recent cases restating this point include *Neary* v *Dean of Westminster* (1999) and *Tesco Stores Ltd* v *Pook* (2004).

Disclosure of misconduct

Bell v *Lever Bros* [1932] AC 161 House of Lords

B and S were appointed chairman and vice-chairman respectively of Niger Company, a subsidiary of Lever Bros, for a fixed period of five years. At a point when their contracts still had almost two years to run, Lever Bros arranged to sell the company; they therefore entered compensation agreements with B and S to pay them £50,000 for the loss of their contracts of employment. It later transpired that B and S had been using their position and inside knowledge to deal in the same goods as the company on their own account, making a profit of £1,360. 'No defence can be offered for this piece of misconduct', said Lord Atkin. 'The appellants were acting in a business in which their employers were concerned; their interests and their employers' conflicted; they were taking a secret advantage out of their employment, and committing a grave breach of duty both to Levers and to the Niger Company. The jury have found that had the facts been discovered during the service, Levers could and would have dismissed them, and no objection can be taken to this finding.'

However, the facts were not discovered at the time, only afterwards. Lever Bros claimed back the compensation and an amount equivalent to the secret profits they had made. There was no argument but that the latter sum should be disgorged. The issue was whether the compensation should be returned. At this time, juries commonly sat in civil cases to make findings of fact. The jury here found as a fact that at the time they negotiated their 'golden parachutes' with Lever Bros, the employees did not have in mind their earlier misconduct and that therefore they were not guilty of fraudulent misrepresentation.

The main issue in the case was whether the compensation agreements were void for mistake – a point on which this case is the leading authority. The issue for us, however, is whether the compensation agreements could be set aside on the ground that the employees were in breach of duty in failing to disclose their misconduct. By a 3–2 majority, the House of Lords held that they were not.

LORD ATKIN: '. . . It now becomes necessary to deal with the second point of the claimants – namely, that the contract of March 19, 1929, could be avoided by them in consequence of the non-disclosure by Bell of his misconduct as to the cocoa dealings. Fraudulent concealment has been negatived by the jury; this claim is based upon the contention that Bell owed a duty to Levers to disclose his misconduct, and that in default of disclosure the contract was voidable. Ordinarily the failure to disclose a material fact which might influence the mind of a prudent contractor does not give the right to avoid the contract. The principle of *caveat emptor* applies outside contracts of sale. There are certain contracts expressed by the law to be contracts of the utmost good faith, where material facts must be disclosed; if not, the contract is voidable.

Apart from special fiduciary relationships, contracts for partnership and contracts of insurance are the leading instances. In such cases the duty does not arise out of contract; the duty of a person proposing an insurance arises before a contract is made, so of an intending partner. Unless this contract can be brought within this limited category of contracts *uberrimae fidei* it appears to me that this ground of defence must fail. I see nothing to differentiate this agreement from the ordinary contract of service; and I am aware of no authority which places contracts of service within the limited category I have mentioned. It seems to me clear that master and man negotiating for an agreement of service are as unfettered as in any other negotiation. Nor can I find anything in the relation of master and servant, when established, that places agreements between them within the protected category. It is said that there is a contractual duty of the servant to disclose his past faults. I agree that the duty in the servant to protect his master's property may involve the duty to report a fellow servant whom he knows to be wrongfully dealing with that property. The servant owes a duty not to steal, but, having stolen, is there superadded a duty to confess that he has stolen? I am satisfied that to imply such a duty would be a departure from the well established usage of mankind and would be to create obligations entirely outside the normal contemplation of the parties concerned. If a man agrees to raise his butler's wages, must the butler disclose that two years ago he received a secret commission from the wine merchant; and if the master discovers it, can he, without dismissal or after the servant has left, avoid the agreement for the increase in salary and recover back the extra wages paid? If he gives his cook a month's wages in lieu of notice can he, on discovering that the cook has been pilfering the tea and sugar, claim the return of the month's wages? I think not. He takes the risk; if he wishes to protect himself he can question his servant, and will then be protected by the truth or otherwise of the answers.'

(Lord Blanesburgh and Lord Thankerton delivered concurring speeches. Viscount Hailsham and Lord Warrington of Clyffe dissented.)

Sybron Corporation v *Rochem Ltd* [1983] ICR 801 Court of Appeal

Roques was employed as manager of the European zone of Sybron, an American chemicals company. He was party to a conspiracy in which he and other senior employees of Sybron secretly set up competing companies, including Rochem Ltd, to which they diverted contracts and opportunities which should have gone to Sybron. Roques's fraud was not discovered until after he had been permitted to take early retirement with pension and insurance benefits which Sybron now sought to recover. It was argued for Roques that, following *Bell* v *Lever Bros*, he was under no duty to disclose his misconduct. After quoting a passage from Lord Atkin's speech in that case, reproduced above, Stephenson LJ continued as follows.

STEPHENSON LJ: '. . . So there again, what that judge is saying about the duty to report a fellow servant is linked to the question of a duty to report his own wrongdoing, but it is I think significant that Lord Atkin is agreeing that the duty of a servant to protect his master's property "may involve the duty to report a fellow servant whom he knows to be wrongfully dealing with that property", although Lord Atkin was of the firm view that the servant had no such duty to report his own wrongful conduct. It is, as I have already indicated, puzzling that it never seems to have occurred to counsel or to any of the many judges who dealt with *Bell* v *Lever Bros Ltd*, that they might have to consider the duty of Bell to report Snelling's misconduct, or Snelling's duty to report Bell's.

But the question was not there considered, let alone decided, and there is the direct authority of a decision of this court, in a case in which *Bell* v *Lever Bros Ltd* was considered, that there is in certain circumstances a duty to report the misconduct of fellow servants. That case is *Swain* v *West (Butchers) Ltd* (1936). There the claimant was employed for a term of five years as a general manager of the defendant company. His contract of service provided, *inter alia*, that he would do all in his power to promote, extend and develop the interests of the company. The managing director gave the claimant certain unlawful orders, which orders the claimant carried out. The matter came to the notice of the chairman of the board of directors who, in an interview with the claimant, told the claimant that if he gave conclusive proof of the managing director's dishonesty he would not be dismissed. The claimant duly supplied the information required and was then dismissed, the defendants alleging fraud and dishonesty. The claimant did not deny the allegations, but he brought an action for breach of contract and wrongful dismissal on the grounds that under the terms of a verbal agreement between the claimant and the chairman it was not open to the defendants to rely upon information given by the claimant relating to his own fraud and dishonesty. It was held that it was the claimant's duty, as part of his contract of service, to report to the board of directors any acts which were not in the interests of the company; that there was therefore no consideration for the alleged verbal agreement and the defendant company was not prevented from relying upon the information received from the claimant . . .

It follows from that decision, which is consistent with *Bell v Lever Bros Ltd* and is binding upon us, that there is no general duty to report a fellow-servant's misconduct or breach of contract; whether there is such a duty depends on the contract and on the terms of employment of the particular servant. He may be so placed in the hierarchy as to have a duty to report either the misconduct of his superior, as in *Swain v West (Butchers) Ltd*, or the misconduct of his inferiors, as in this case. Mr Munby [counsel for Rochem] will not have it that Mr Roques's "No. 2" was subordinate to Mr Roques, or that the other managers involved in the conspiracy were his subordinates or inferiors; but on this point I agree with Walton J [the judge at first instance] and I refer, again without apology and with approval, to the way in which he put the matter in his judgment below:

> "I do not think that there is any general duty resting upon an employee to inform his master of the breaches of duty of other employees; the law would do industrial relations generally no great service if it held that such a duty did in fact exist in all cases. The duty must, in my view, depend upon all the circumstances of the case, and the relationship of the parties to their employer and *inter se*. I think it would be very difficult to have submitted, with any hope of success, that Messrs Bell and Snelling, having been appointed to rescue the affairs of their employers' African subsidiary in effect jointly, ought to have denounced each other."

That is a reference to the finding that Messrs Bell and Snelling were according to the report of the case in the House of Lords, in joint management and therefore one was not subordinate to the other. Walton J goes on:

> "However, where there is an hierarchical system, particularly where the person in the hierarchy whose conduct is called into question is a person near the top who is responsible to his employers for the whole of the operation of a complete sector of the employers' business – here the European zone – then in my view entirely different considerations apply. That the principle of disclosure extends at least as far as I think it extends (and perhaps further, but that is of no consequence for present purposes) has been decided once and for all, so far as this court is concerned, by *Swain v West (Butchers) Ltd*, a decision of the Court of Appeal. *Bell v Lever Bros Ltd* was very much in the forefront of everybody's mind in that case, but none of the Lords Justices thought it had any bearing on the case before them."

After reading, pretty well in full, the judgment of Greene LJ, from which I have read extracts, Walton J went on:

> "This judgment has, if I may respectfully say so, the great merit of common sense. A person in a managerial position cannot possibly stand by and allow fellow servants to pilfer the

198

company's assets and do nothing about it, which is really what Mr Munby's submissions would come to when applied to the present type of case. Certainly at all events where the misconduct is serious and the servant is not discharged immediately it must be quite obvious that, as part of his duties generally, the senior employee is under a duty to report what has happened as soon as he finds out, and further to indicate which steps (if any) he has taken to prevent a repetition thereof.

Of course, this all depends upon the duties of the relevant employee under his contract of service. In the present case there was a well-recognised reporting procedure, whereunder the zone controller, Mr Roques, was expected to make reports as to the state of matters in his zone every month. It may possibly be argued that in such a case the duty to report was not an immediate duty but one to be fulfilled at the next reporting date; so be it, because even if this is correct no such report was ever made by Mr Roques to his superiors.

I therefore reach the not very surprising conclusion that Mr Roques was under a duty to report all he knew about the misdeeds of his subordinate employees, commencing with those of Mr Bove, as soon as he found out about them, and that he did not do so, deliberately and fraudulently, because he was one of the conspirators himself. The duty which lay upon him was, I repeat, not a duty to report his own misdeeds – this may well be regarded as negatived by *Bell* v *Lever Bros Ltd* – but to report those of his fellow conspirators."

Sorry as I am for Mrs Roques, I am happy to find that the law is not so outrageous as to enable Mr Roques to keep the £13,000. What Mr Roques did disentitled him, and I am afraid his wife, from keeping the money, and the claimants are entitled to the declaration and orders for which they have asked, against these two defendants . . .'

(Fox and Kerr LJJ delivered concurring judgments.)

Comment

(1) While there is no general implied duty to disclose one's own misconduct, it has been suggested since *Bell* v *Lever Bros* that developments in the law of directors' duties mean that directors, or at least managing directors, should be regarded as having such a duty. In *Item Software (UK) Ltd* v *Fassihi* (2004) the Court of Appeal held that a company director could be liable in damages for failure to disclose his own wrongdoing and in *Tesco Stores Ltd* v *Pook* (2004) this principle was held to apply also to a senior manager.

(2) Would the duty to disclose other employees' misconduct apply to the supervisor of a workshop aware of falsification of time sheets by her subordinates? Would it apply to a personnel manager aware that the sales manager (of equal status) was cheating on expenses? Should it?

(3) The strong culture against telling tales seems to be behind Walton J's remark that a general duty to inform 'would do industrial relations generally no great service'. Is there anything that an employer not happy with this situation can do?

(4) Does it make sense to have a duty in certain circumstances to disclose someone else's misconduct but not your own?

Nottingham University v *Fishel* [2000] ICR 1462 High Court, Queen's Bench

The claimant was a clinical embryologist, internationally renowned for his work in the field of *in vitro* fertilisation. He was employed by the university as director of an infertility unit. During the period of his employment Dr Fishel frequently worked at clinics abroad, for which he

199

was paid on top of his full-time university salary. He should have got his employer's express permission for this, but he did not do so, although the university was aware of the outside work he was doing. He also used other university staff to help him and did not get permission for this either. After he resigned following a dispute over his pay the university sought an account of the profits he had made from his outside work, or alternatively, damages for breach of contract and for breach of fiduciary duty.

ELIAS J: '. . . Mr Dutton [counsel for the university] has advanced a further argument that the employee's duty of loyalty and good faith obliged Dr Fishel to inform the university that he was being paid for his outside work. The argument then is that, had the university been aware of the opportunity to do outside work, it would have sought to do it itself. In my view the premise is wrong. I do not think that as a general principle an employee is bound to inform his employer if and when he is doing outside work in breach of his contract. Mr Dutton relies upon the case of *Neary* v *Dean of Westminster* (1999) in which Lord Jauncey, sitting as special commissioner appointed to hear the case on behalf of Her Majesty the Queen as Visitor, held that in the circumstances of that case the employee in question was in breach of the duty of trust and confidence in failing to inform the Abbey authorities of certain activities he was conducting on his own behalf. However, in that case Lord Jauncey clearly considered that the employee had taken advantage of his position as organist at the Abbey for his own benefit. In other words, the duty to inform the Abbey authorities arose because Dr Neary had used his position to earn secret profits; he ought to have accounted for these to his employers in the absence of full disclosure and consent. It is similarly contended in this case that Dr Fishel was a fiduciary who abused his position for his own benefit. I consider that issue later in this judgment. If that is right, then it may be said that by acting in secret Dr Fishel has both acted in breach of his fiduciary duty and in breach of contract. But the contractual claim then adds nothing to the fiduciary claim. Absent the fiduciary obligation, the employee is not obliged to disclose the fact that he has earned sums from third parties. Indeed, were he to be so obliged, this would circumvent the well-established rule in *Bell* v *Lever Brothers Ltd* (1932) that employees are not obliged to disclose their own past misconduct or breaches of contract. (It might conceivably be said in this case that Dr Fishel was obliged to disclose the wrongdoing of his fellow embryologists, in accordance with authorities such as *Swain* v *West (Butchers) Ltd* (1936) and *Sybron Corpn* v *Rochem Ltd* (1983), even if this also involved revealing his own wrongdoing. However, the case was not put on this basis, and furthermore I do not believe that Dr Fishel perceived the other embryologists to be committing misconduct. I doubt whether the principle applies in such circumstances.) . . .

Fiduciary duties

A major allegation in this case is that Dr Fishel acted in breach of his fiduciary duties. In particular, it is alleged that by working abroad for reward, and by profiting from the work done by embryologists under his control, he acted in breach of the conflict of duty and interest rule, which prohibits him from pursuing his own interests when he is duty bound to advance the interests of his employer; the conflict of duty and duty rule, which prevents him from placing himself in a situation where he owes a duty to another which is inconsistent with undivided duty of loyalty which he owes to his employer; and the obligation not to make a secret profit by misusing his position to exploit opportunities which came to him in his position as employee. This raises the question to what extent, if at all, Dr Fishel is subject to such duties. It also involves a consideration of whether he received fully informed consent from the university, for if he did there will be no fiduciary liability.

Establishing fiduciary obligations: the legal principles

What then are the underlying principles which enable the court to determine whether or not fiduciary obligations arise? Lord Millett, writing extra-judicially, has identified three distinct categories of relationship (see his article "Equity's Place in the Law of Commerce" 114 LQR 214 (1998)). Two of them have no application in this case. These are first, where the obligations arise out of the fact that one party is in a position of influence over another; and second, where they arise from the fact that one is in receipt of information imparted in confidence by the other. Employees frequently fall into this latter category, because their work will often involve their being made privy to trade or business secrets of their employer. But although the existence of the employment relationship explains why the employee comes to be in possession of such information, and the contract of employment will define the purposes for which such information may be used, the employment relationship itself in such cases is really only incidental to the imposition of the fiduciary duties. As the Court of Appeal noted in *AG* v *Blake* (1998), this fiduciary obligation of confidence often arises in the course of another fiduciary relationship but it is not derived from it. It is for this reason that the obligation of confidence can continue to subsist even when the employment relationship, and any fiduciary duties arising out of it, has terminated.

The third category identified by Lord Millett, and described by him as the most important, is as follows:

"[it] is the relationship of trust and confidence. Such a relationship arises whenever one party undertakes to act in the interests of another, or where he places himself in a position where he is obliged to act in the interests of another. The core obligation of a fiduciary of this kind is the obligation of loyalty."

In *Bristol and West Building Society* v *Mothew* (1998) he elaborated on this analysis, and identified the duties which classically arise from such a fiduciary relationship:

"A fiduciary is someone who has undertaken to act for or on behalf of another in a particular matter in circumstances which give rise to a relationship of trust and confidence. The distinguishing obligation of a fiduciary is the obligation of loyalty. The principal is entitled to the single-minded loyalty of his fiduciary. This core liability has several facets. A fiduciary must act in good faith; he must not make a profit out of his trust; he must not place himself in a position where his duty and his interest may conflict; he may not act for his own benefit or the benefit of a third person without the informed consent of his principal. This is not intended to be an exhaustive list, but it is sufficient to indicate the nature of fiduciary obligations. They are the defining characteristics of the fiduciary."

It is vital to recognise that although the key feature identified is the obligation of loyalty, that has a precise meaning, namely the duty to act in the interests of another. This is the fundamental feature which, in this category of relationship at least, marks out the relationship as a fiduciary one . . .

Employees as fiduciaries

It is important to recognise that the mere fact that Dr Fishel is an employee does not mean that he owes the range of fiduciary duties referred to above. It is true that in *Blake* Lord Woolf, giving judgment for the Court of Appeal, said that the employer-employee relationship is a fiduciary one. But plainly the court was not thereby intending to indicate that the whole range of fiduciary obligations was engaged in every employment relationship. This would be revolutionary indeed, transforming the contract of employment beyond all recognition and transmuting contractual duties into fiduciary ones. In my opinion, the court was merely indicating that circumstances may arise in the context of an employment relationship, or arising out of it, which, when they occur, will place the employee in the position of a fiduciary. In *Blake* itself, as I have indicated, it was the receipt of confidential information. There are other examples. Thus every employee is subject to the principle that he should not accept a bribe and he will have to account for it (and possibly any profits derived from it) to his employer. Again, as Fletcher-Moulton LJ observed in *Coomber* v *Coomber* (1911), even an errand boy is obliged to bring back my change, and is in fiduciary relations with me. But his fiduciary obligations are limited and arise out of the particular circumstances, namely that he is put in a position where he is obliged to account to me for the change he has received. In that case the obligation arises out of the employment relationship but it is not inherent in the nature of the relationship itself.

As these examples all illustrate, simply labelling the relationship as fiduciary tells us nothing about which particular fiduciary duties will arise. As Lord Browne-Wilkinson has recently observed:

> ". . . the phrase 'fiduciary duties' is a dangerous one, giving rise to a mistaken assumption that all fiduciaries owe the same duties in all circumstances. This is not the case" (*Henderson* v *Merrett Syndicates Ltd* (1995)).

This is particularly true in the employment context.

The employment relationship is obviously not a fiduciary relationship in the classic sense. It is to be contrasted with a number of other relationships which can readily and universally be recognised as "fiduciary relationships" because the very essence of the relationship is that one party must exercise his powers for the benefit of another. Trustees, company directors and liquidators classically fall into this category which Dr Finn, in his seminal work on fiduciaries, has termed "fiduciary offices". (See P D Finn, *Fiduciary Obligations* (1977).) As he has pointed out, typically there are two characteristics of these relationships, apart from duty on the office holder to act in the interests of another. The first is that the powers are conferred by someone other than the beneficiaries in whose interests the fiduciary must act; and the second is that these fiduciaries have considerable autonomy over decision making and are not subject to the control of those beneficiaries.

By contrast, the essence of the employment relationship is not typically fiduciary at all. Its purpose is not to place the employee in a position where he is obliged to pursue his employer's interests at the expense of his own. The relationship is a contractual one and the powers imposed on the employee are conferred by the employer himself. The employee's freedom of action is regulated by the contract, the scope of his powers is determined by the terms (express or implied) of the contract, and as a consequence the employer can exercise (or at least he can place himself in a position where he has the opportunity to exercise) considerable control over the employee's decision-making powers.

This is not to say that fiduciary duties cannot arise out of the employment relationship itself. But they arise not as a result of the mere fact that there is an employment relationship. Rather they result from the fact that within a particular contractual relationship there are specific contractual obligations which the employee has undertaken which have placed him in a situation where equity imposes these rigorous duties in addition to the contractual obligations. Where this occurs, the scope of the fiduciary obligations both arises out of, and is circumscribed by, the contractual terms; it is circumscribed because equity cannot alter the terms of the contract validly undertaken. The position was succinctly expressed by Mason J in the High Court of Australia in *Hospital Products Ltd* v *United States Surgical Corporation* (1985) as follows:

> "That contractual and fiduciary relationships may coexist between the same parties has never been doubted. Indeed, the existence of a basic contractual relationship has in many situations provided a foundation for the erection of a fiduciary relationship. In these

situations it is the contractual foundation which is all-important because it is the contract that regulates the basic rights and liabilities of the parties. The fiduciary relationship, if it is to exist at all, must accommodate itself to the terms of the contract so that it is consistent with, and conforms to, them. The fiduciary relationship cannot be superimposed upon the contract in such a way as to alter the operation which the contract was intended to have according to its true construction."

The problem of identifying the scope of any fiduciary duties arising out of the relationship is particularly acute in the case of employees. This is because of the use of potentially ambiguous terminology in describing an employee's obligations, which use may prove a trap for the unwary. There are many cases which have recognised the existence of the employee's duty of good faith, or loyalty, or the mutual duty of trust and confidence – concepts which tend to shade into one another. As I have already indicated, Lord Millett has used precisely this language when describing the characteristic features which trigger fiduciary obligations. But he was not using the concepts in quite the same sense as they tend to be used in the employment field. Lord Millett was applying the concepts of loyalty and good faith to circumstances where a person undertakes to act solely in the interests of another. Unfortunately, these concepts are frequently used in the employment context to describe situations where a party merely has to take into consideration the interests of another, but does not have to act in the interests of that other . . .

Accordingly, in analysing the employment cases in this field, care must be taken not auto-matically to equate the duties of good faith and loyalty or trust and confidence, with fiduciary obligations. Very often in such cases the court has simply been concerned with the question whether the employee's conduct has been such as to justify summary dismissal, and there has been no need to decide whether the duties infringed, properly analysed, are contractual or fidu-ciary obligations. As a consequence, the two are sometimes wrongly treated as identical: see eg *Neary* v *Dean of Westminster* (1999) where the mutual duty of trust and confidence was described as constituting a "fiduciary relationship".

Accordingly, in determining whether a fiduciary relationship arises in the context of an employment relationship, it is necessary to identify with care the particular duties undertaken by the employee, and to ask whether in all the circumstances he has placed himself in a position where he must act solely in the interests of his employer. It is only once those duties have been identified that it is possible to determine whether any fiduciary duty has been breached . . .'

Comment

(1) The court held that Dr Fishel was not in breach of any fiduciary duty to his employer by accepting work abroad, since this was not work which he should have been seeking on behalf of the university, and the fact that he was paid for it did not alter the position. He did act in breach of his contract of employment, because he did not get permission to do the outside work, but the court held that it was no breach of his duty of loyalty and good faith not to disclose this breach to his employer.

(2) The court did hold, however, that Dr Fishel put himself in a position of potential conflict of interest by employing other university staff, whose manager he was, to assist him and that this was a breach of his fiduciary duty: to this limited extent the university was entitled to an account of profits. Note, however, Elias J's doubts as to whether the duty to disclose another's wrongdoing would apply in these circumstances.

(3) This decision provides strong arguments against treating employees as fiduciaries in general.

Competition

When your working day is finished, you are free to do whatever you want, and what you do is none of your employer's business. True or false?

Hivac Ltd v *Park Royal Scientific Instruments Ltd* [1946] Ch 169 Court of Appeal

The claimant company had a virtual monopoly in the manufacture of miniature valves. Discovering that some of their employees were doing similar work for a competitor, the defendant company, in their spare time, the claimant sought an injunction to stop the defendant employing these workers.

LORD GREENE MR: '. . . It has been said on many occasions that an employee owes a duty of fidelity to his employer. As a general proposition that is indisputable. The practical difficulty in any given case is to find exactly how far that rather vague duty of fidelity extends. Prima facie it seems to me on considering the authorities and the arguments that it must be a question on the facts of each particular case. I can very well understand that the obligation of fidelity, which is an implied term of the contract, may extend very much further in the case of one class of employee than it does in others. For instance, when you are dealing, as we are dealing here, with mere manual workers whose job is to work five and a half days for their employer at a specific type of work and stop their work when the hour strikes, the obligation of fidelity may be one the operation of which will have a comparatively limited scope. The law would, I think, be jealous of attempting to impose on a manual worker restrictions, the real effect of which would be to prevent him utilizing his spare time. He is paid for five and a half days in the week. The rest of the week is his own, and to impose upon a man, in relation to the rest of the week, some kind of obligation which really would unreasonably tie his hands and prevent him adding to his weekly money during that time would, I think, be very undesirable. On the other hand, if one has employees of a different character, one may very well find that the obligation is of a different nature. A manual worker might say: "You pay me for five and a half days' work. I do five and a half days work for you. What greater obligation have I taken upon myself? If you want in some way to limit my activities during the other day and a half of the week, you must pay me for it." In many cases that may be a very good answer. In other cases it may not be a good answer because the very nature of the work may be such as to make it quite clear that the duties of the employee to his employer cannot properly be performed if in his spare time the employee engages in certain classes of activity . . .

Anything that I say on this matter stands, of course, to be varied and corrected when the full facts are known, but prima facie it appears to me the question we have to consider resolves itself into these elements. First of all, what was done here was done in the spare time of the employees. That leads to this: we have to consider what implication, if any, needs to be read into the contract of service with regard to the employee's use of his spare time. Does that implication in any way restrict him, or, rather (which is the practical question here) did that implication make it a breach of duty on his part to do what he did, with the consequential result that the defendants, in persuading the employees to do what they did, procured a breach of contract? I think the judgment of Maugham LJ in *Wessex Dairies Ltd* v *Smith* (1953) which is quite deliberately placed by him on a broad ground, does lead to this. Although the case before him was concerned with an employee who had done certain things in his employer's time, I cannot find that in his reasoning that was regarded as an essential part of the offence. I cannot read the judgment as meaning that if the roundsman had on a Saturday afternoon, when his work was over, gone round to all these customers and canvassed them, he would have been doing something he was entitled to do. It would be a curious result if, quite apart from making use of the list of customers or his special knowledge or anything of that kind, he could set himself during his spare time deliberately to injure the goodwill of his master's business by trying to get his customers to leave him. Then again the question here is not a question of getting the customers to leave the business but a question of building up a rival in business to the prejudice of the goodwill of the employer's business.

I am not ashamed to confess that in the course of the argument my mind has fluctuated considerably on this question. As I see it, the court stands in a sense between Scylla and Charybdis, because it would be most unfortunate if anything we said, or any other court said, should place an undue restriction on the right of the workman, particularly a manual workman, to make use of his leisure for his profit. On the other hand, it would be deplorable if it were laid down that a workman could, consistently with his duty to his employer, knowingly, deliberately and secretly set himself to do in his spare time something which would inflict great harm on his employer's business. I have endeavoured to raise the questions in the way that they appeal to me and, on the best consideration I can give to the matter, I think that the claimants are prima facie right in this case . . .'

(Morton LJ delivered a concurring judgment; Bucknill LJ agreed.)

Comment

(1) This defines the scope of the employee's *implied* duty while still employed. It is open to the employer to prevent employees working in competition by use of an appropriate express term. However, restraining ex-employees is more difficult, as the term may be struck down as being in unlawful restraint of trade. This topic is outside the scope of this book: see Pitt (2007).

(2) An intention to leave and set up in competition is not in itself a breach of the duty of fidelity: *Laughton* v *Bapp Industrial Supplies* (1986). Contrast *Lancashire Fires* v *S A Lyons* (1997).

(3) One of the issues in this case was the possible leakage of confidential information to the competitor. The duty not to disclose confidential information is another aspect of the duty of fidelity.

Confidential information

An employee has an implied duty not to disclose confidential information. This applies to some extent to ex-employees also. The greatest difficulty is establishing what is confidential information.

Faccenda Chicken v *Fowler* [1986] ICR 297 Court of Appeal

Fowler had been employed as sales manager by the claimant company and had established a system whereby sales staff delivered fresh chickens to customers from refrigerated vans. He left and set up in competition, employing a number of other sales staff who were also former employees of the claimant. They all knew the names and addresses of the claimant company's customers, the routes taken by the vans and when they called, the customers' regular require-ments and the prices charged. The claimants argued that this package of sales information was confidential information and that Fowler and the other former employees should be restrained from using it. Neill LJ delivered the judgment of the court. Look for the definition of three kinds of information; the factors which suggest that information is confidential and the difference between the duty of an employee and an ex-employee.

NEILL LJ: 'In these two appeals it will be necessary to consider the interaction of three sep-arate legal concepts. (1) The duty of an employee during the period of his employment to act with good faith towards his employer: this duty is sometimes called the duty of fidelity. (2) The duty of an employee not to use or disclose after his employment has ceased any confidential information which he has obtained during his employment about his employer's affairs. (3) The prima facie right of any person to use and to exploit for the purpose of earning his living all the skill, experience and knowledge which he has at his disposal, including skill, experience and knowledge which he has acquired in the course of previous periods of employment . . .

In the course of his submissions in support of the appeal Mr Dehn [counsel for Faccenda] took us on an instructive and valuable tour of many of the cases dealing with the law of confidence in the context of the relationship between employer and employee and also referred us to some of the cases on restrictive covenants.

It is not necessary, however, for us for the purpose of this judgment to travel this ground again. It is sufficient to set out what we understand to be the relevant principles of law. Having considered the cases to which we were referred, we would venture to state these principles:

(1) Where the parties are, or have been, linked by a contract of employment, the obligations of the employee are to be determined by the contract between him and his employer: *cf Vokes Ltd v Heather* (1945).

(2) In the absence of any express term, the obligations of the employee in respect of the use and disclosure of information are the subject of implied terms.

(3) While the employee remains in the employment of the employer the obligations are included in the implied term which imposes a duty of good faith or fidelity on the employee. For the purposes of the present appeal it is not necessary to consider the precise limits of this implied term, but it may be noted: (a) that the extent of the duty of good faith will vary according to the nature of the contract (see *Vokes Ltd v Heather*); (b) that the duty of good faith will be broken if an employee makes or copies a list of the customers of the employer for use after his employment ends or deliberately memorises such a list, even though, except in special circumstances, there is no general restriction on an ex-employee canvassing or doing business with customers of his former employer: see *Robb v Green* (1895) and *Wessex Dairies Ltd v Smith* (1935).

(4) The implied term which imposes an obligation on the employee as to his conduct after the determination of the employment is more restricted in its scope than that which imposes a general duty of good faith. It is clear that the obligation not to use or disclose information may cover secret processes of manufacture such as chemical formulae (*Amber Size and Chemical Co Ltd v Menzel* (1913)), or designs or special methods of construction (*Reid & Sigrist Ltd v Moss and Mechanism Ltd* (1932)), and other information which is of a sufficiently high degree of confidentiality as to amount to a trade secret.

  The obligation does not extend, however, to cover all information which is given to or acquired by the employee while in his employment, and in particular may not cover information which is only "confidential" in the sense that an unauthorised disclosure of such information to a third party while the employment subsisted would be a clear breach of the duty of good faith. This distinction is clearly set out in the judgment of Cross J in *Printers & Finishers Ltd v Holloway* (1965) where he had to consider whether an ex-employee should be restrained by injunction from making use of his recollection of the contents of certain written printing instructions which had been made available to him when he was working in his former employers' flock printing factory. In his judgment he said:

"In this connection one must bear in mind that not all information which is given to a servant in confidence and which it would be a breach of his duty for him to disclose to another person during his employment is a trade secret which he can be prevented from using for his own advantage after the employment is over, even though he has entered into no express covenant with regard to the matter in hand. For example, the printing instructions were handed to Holloway to be used by him during his employment exclusively for the claimants' benefit. It would have been a breach of duty on his part to divulge any of the contents to a stranger while he was employed, but many of these instructions are not really 'trade secrets' at all. Holloway was not, indeed, entitled to take a copy of the instructions away with him; but in so far as the instructions cannot be called 'trade secrets' and he carried them in his head, he is entitled to use them for his own benefit or the benefit of any future employer."

The same distinction is to be found in *E Worsley & Co Ltd* v *Cooper* (1939) where it was held that the defendant was entitled, after he had ceased to be employed, to make use of his knowledge of the source of the paper supplied to his previous employer. In our view it is quite plain that this knowledge was nevertheless "confidential" in the sense that it would have been a breach of the duty of good faith for the employee, while the employment subsisted, to have used it for his own purposes or to have disclosed it to a competitor of his employer.

(5)   In order to determine whether any particular item of information falls within the implied term so as to prevent its use or disclosure by an employee after his employment has ceased, it is necessary to consider all the circumstances of the case. We are satisfied that the following matters are among those to which attention must be paid:

(a)   The nature of the employment. Thus employment in a capacity where "confidential" material is habitually handled may impose a high obligation of confidentiality because the employee can be expected to realise its sensitive nature to a greater extent than if he were employed in a capacity where such material reaches him only occasionally or incidentally.

(b)   The nature of the information itself. In our judgment the information will only be protected if it can properly be classed as a trade secret or as material which, while not properly to be described as a trade secret, is in all the circumstances of such a highly confidential nature as to require the same protection as a trade secret eo nomine. The restrictive covenant cases demonstrate that a covenant will not be upheld on the basis of the status of the information which might be disclosed by the former employee if he is not restrained, unless it can be regarded as a trade secret or the equivalent of a trade secret: see, for example, *Herbert Morris Ltd* v *Saxelby* (1916) *per* Lord Parker of Waddington and *Littlewoods Organisation Ltd* v *Harris* (1977) *per* Megaw LJ.

We must therefore express our respectful disagreement with the passage in Goulding J's judgment where he suggested that an employer can protect the use of information in his second category, even though it does not include either a trade secret or its equivalent, by means of a restrictive covenant. As Lord Parker of Waddington made clear in *Herbert Morris Ltd* v *Saxelby* (1916) in a passage to which Mr Dehn drew our attention, a restrictive covenant will not be enforced unless the protection sought is reasonably necessary to protect a trade secret or to prevent some personal influence over customers being abused in order to entice them away . . .

It is clearly impossible to provide a list of matters which will qualify as trade secrets or their equivalent. Secret processes of manufacture provide obvious examples, but innumerable other pieces of information are *capable* of being trade secrets, though the secrecy of some information may be only short-lived. In addition, the fact that the circulation of certain information is restricted to a limited number of individuals may throw light on the status of the information and its degree of confidentiality.

(c)   Whether the employer impressed on the employee the confidentiality of the information. Thus, though an employer cannot prevent the use or disclosure *merely* by telling the employee that certain information is confidential, the attitude of the employer towards the information provides evidence which may assist in determining whether or not the information can properly be regarded as a trade secret. It is to be observed that in *E Worsley & Co Ltd* v *Cooper* (1939) Morton J attached significance to the fact that no warning had been given to the defendant that "the source from which the paper came was to be treated as confidential".

(d) Whether the relevant information can be easily isolated from other information which the employee is free to use or disclose. In *Printers & Finishers Ltd* v *Holloway* (1965) Cross J considered the protection which might be afforded to information which had been memorised by an ex-employee. He put on one side the memorising of a formula or a list of customers or what had been said (obviously in confidence) at a particular meeting, and continued:

> "The employee might well not realise that the feature or expedient in question was in fact peculiar to his late employer's process and factory; but even if he did, such knowledge is not readily separable from his general knowledge of the flock printing process and his acquired skill in manipulating a flock printing plant, and I do not think that any man of average intelligence and honesty would think that there was anything improper in his putting his memory of particular features of his late employer's plant at the disposal of his new employer."

For our part we would not regard the separability of the information in question as being conclusive, but the fact that the alleged "confidential" information is part of a package and that the remainder of the package is not confidential is likely to throw light on whether the information in question is really a trade secret.

These then are the principles of law which we consider to be applicable to a case such as the present one. We would wish to leave open, however, for further examination on some other occasion the question whether additional protection should be afforded to an employer where the former employee is not seeking to earn his living by making use of the body of skill, knowledge and experience which he has acquired in the course of his career, but is merely selling to a third party information which he acquired in confidence in the course of his former employment . . .

We find ourselves unable to accept Mr Dehn's submissions either as to the information about prices or as to the sales information as a whole. We can well appreciate that in certain circumstances information about prices can be invested with a sufficient degree of confidentiality to render that information a trade secret or its equivalent. The price put forward in a tender document is an obvious example. But there may be many other cases where the circumstances show that a price or prices are matters of great importance and highly confidential.

Information about the price to be charged for a new model of a car or some other product or about the prices negotiated, for example, for various grades of oil in a highly competitive market in which it is known that prices are to be kept secret from competitors occur to us as providing possible further instances of information which is entitled to protection as having the requisite degree of confidentiality.

But in the present case the following factors appear to us to lead to the clear conclusion that neither the information about prices nor the sales information as a whole had the degree of confidentiality necessary to support the claimants' case. We would list these factors as follows. (1) The sales information contained some material which the claimants conceded was not confidential if looked at in isolation. (2) The information about the prices was not clearly severable from the rest of the sales information. (3) Neither the sales information in general, nor the information about the prices in particular, though of some value to a competitor, could reasonably be regarded as plainly secret or sensitive. (4) The sales information, including the information about prices, was necessarily acquired by the defendants in order that they could do their work. Moreover, as the judge observed in the course of his judgment, each salesman could quickly commit the whole of the sales information relating to his own area to memory. (5) The sales information was generally known among the van drivers who were employees, as were the secretaries, at quite a junior level. This was not a case where the relevant information was restricted to senior management or to confidential staff. (6) There was no evidence that the claimants had ever given any express instructions that the sales information or the information about prices was to be treated as confidential. We are satisfied that, in the light of all the matters set out by the judge in his judgment, neither the sales information as a whole nor the information about prices looked at by itself fell within the class of confidential information which an employee is bound by an implied term of his contract of employment or otherwise not to use or disclose after his employment has come to an end.

Accordingly these appeals must be dismissed.'

Comment

(1) While the duty not to disclose confidential information is usually seen as a duty of employees, it is worth noting that in an appropriate case it may apply to the employer. In *Dalgliesh* v *Lothian and Borders Police Board* (1991) the Court of Session Outer House thought it probable that the Police Board would be in breach of such a duty if it disclosed the names and addresses of its employees to the Lothian Regional Council, thus enabling the council to identify public employees who had failed to pay the community charge (poll tax). See also the discussion of privacy above, p 180.

(2) Most cases about the abuse of confidential information come up in the same context as *Faccenda Chicken* v *Fowler*, where the ex-employee has set up in competition or has gone to work for a competitor. However, there is another situation where employees may be tempted to disclose confidential information: where they want to go public on wrongdoing by their employer.

Whistleblowing

The term 'whistleblower' was coined in the USA for employees or ex-employees who reveal damaging information about their employers. At common law there was a recognised, but slightly unclear exception to the general duty that confidential information should not be disclosed, which was that disclosure could be justified where it was in the public interest. The uncertainty related to the scope of 'public interest'. In the 1980s and 1990s there were a number of high-profile business scandals which could have been prevented if employees had been encouraged to reveal wrongdoing, or at least been protected if they did make damaging revelations. This led to the passage of the Public Interest Disclosure Act 1998, now consolidated as ERA ss 43A–43L.

Essentially, the way this works is to make it automatically unfair to dismiss a worker, or to subject him or her to a detriment, for making a 'protected disclosure', provided that the worker complies with the conditions laid down in the Act. These relate to the subject matter of the disclosure; to whom it is disclosed; and the bona fides of the whistleblower.

Employment Rights Act 1996

43B (1) In this Part a 'qualifying disclosure' means any disclosure of information which, in the reasonable belief of the worker making the disclosure, tends to show one or more of the following –

(a) that a criminal offence has been committed, is being committed or is likely to be committed,

(b) that a person has failed, is failing or is likely to fail to comply with any legal obligation to which he is subject,

(c) that a miscarriage of justice has occurred, is occurring or is likely to occur,

(d) that the health or safety of any individual has been, is being or is likely to be endangered,

(e) that the environment has been, is being or is likely to be damaged, or

(f) that information tending to show any matter falling within any one of the preceding paragraphs has been, or is likely to be deliberately concealed.

(2) For the purposes of subsection (1), it is immaterial whether the relevant failure occurred, occurs or would occur in the United Kingdom or elsewhere, and whether the law applying to it is that of the United Kingdom or of any other country or territory . . .

43C (1) A qualifying disclosure is made in accordance with this section if the worker makes the disclosure in good faith –

(a) to his employer, or

(b) where the worker reasonably believes that the relevant failure relates solely or mainly to –

(i) the conduct of a person other than his employer, or

(ii) any other matter for which a person other than his employer has legal responsibility,

to that other person.

(2) A worker who, in accordance with a procedure whose use by him is authorised by his employer, makes a qualifying disclosure to a person other than his employer, is to be treated for the purposes of this Part as making the qualifying disclosure to his employer.

Comment

(1) Note that it is not necessary for the worker to be correct that some form of misconduct has taken place: the test is honest and reasonable belief (*Babula* v *Waltham Forest College* (2007)).

(2) Requiring the worker to make the disclosure to the person responsible for the wrongdoing may be expecting him to show just a bit too much moral fibre. However, ss 43D–43F provide that the worker is also protected if the disclosure is to a legal adviser; to a Minister of the Crown (where the employer is publicly appointed); or to an appropriate prescribed body (bodies such as the Audit Commission and the Health and Safety Executive are prescribed in the Public Interest Disclosure (Prescribed Persons) Order 1999).

(3) There is also a limited permission to disclose in other cases.

Employment Rights Act 1996

43G (1) A qualifying disclosure is made in accordance with this section if –

(a) the worker makes the disclosure in good faith,

(b) he reasonably believes that the information disclosed, and any allegation contained in it, are substantially true,

(c) he does not make the disclosure for purposes of personal gain,

(d) any of the conditions in subsection (2) is met, and

(e) in all the circumstances of the case, it is reasonable for him to make the disclosure.

(2) The conditions referred to in subsection (1)(d) are –

    (a) that, at the time he makes the disclosure, the worker reasonably believes that he will be subjected to a detriment by his employer if he makes a disclosure to his employer or in accordance with section 43F,

    (b) that, in a case where no person is prescribed for the purposes of section 43F in relation to the relevant failure, the worker reasonably believes that it is likely that evidence relating to the relevant failure will be concealed or destroyed if he makes a disclosure to his employer, or

    (c) that the worker has previously made a disclosure of substantially the same information –

        (i) to his employer, or

        (ii) in accordance with section 43F.

(3) In determining for the purposes of subsection (1)(e) whether it is reasonable for the worker to make the disclosure, regard shall be had, in particular, to –

    (a) the identity of the person to whom the disclosure is made,

    (b) the seriousness of the relevant failure,

    (c) whether the relevant failure is continuing or is likely to occur in the future,

    (d) whether the disclosure is made in breach of a duty of confidentiality owed by the employer to any other person,

    (e) in a case falling within subsection (2)(c)(i) or (ii), any action which the employer or the person to whom the previous disclosure in accordance with section 43F was made has taken or might reasonably be expected to have taken as a result of the previous disclosure, and

    (f) in a case falling within subsection (2)(c)(i), whether in making the disclosure to the employer the worker complied with any procedure whose use by him was authorised by the employer.

(4) For the purposes of this section a subsequent disclosure may be regarded as a disclosure of substantially the same information as that disclosed by a previous disclosure as mentioned in subsection (2)(c) even though the subsequent disclosure extends to information about action taken or not taken by any person as a result of the previous disclosure.

Comment

(1) It will be seen from this that disclosure to a 'red-top' tabloid newspaper (or even a pink broadsheet) in return for a large cheque is unlikely ever to be a protected disclosure.

(2) The requirement that the worker making the disclosure should be acting in good faith applies generally. In *Street* v *Derbyshire Unemployed Workers' Centre* (2004) a worker who was dismissed for making allegations against a colleague which she honestly believed to be true was held to be outside the protection of the Act because she held a grudge against this colleague. Should motive really be relevant?

(3) The number of claims under this legislation has risen every year since its introduction, with over 1,000 claims in 2005/06.

REFERENCES AND FURTHER READING

L Barmes (2004), 'The Continuing Conceptual Crisis in the Common Law of the Contract of Employment' 67 MLR 435

D Brodie (1998), 'Beyond exchange: the new contract of employment' 27 ILJ 79

D Brodie (2001), 'Legal coherence and the employment revolution' 117 LQR 604

M Ford (2002), 'Two conceptions of worker privacy' 31 ILJ 135

B Hepple (1981), 'A Right to Work?' 10 ILJ 65

D Lewis (2005), 'Providing rights for whistleblowers' 34 ILJ 239

Lindsay J (2001), 'The implied term of trust and condence' 30 ILJ 1

J McGlyne (1991), 'A technical hitch' 141 NLJ 705

H Oliver (2002), 'Email and Internet Monitoring in the Workplace: information privacy and contracting-out' 31 ILJ 321

G Pitt (1995), 'Rights and Employee Rights: the case of free speech' in C Gearty and A Tomkins (eds), *Understanding Human Rights*, Mansell

G Pitt (2007), *Employment Law*, 6th ed, Sweet & Maxwell, p 121

L Vickers (2002), *Freedom of Speech and Employment*, OUP

5

COLLECTIVE BARGAINING

What is collective bargaining? Let us start by looking at a definition taken from the Donovan Commission Report in 1968. A Royal Commission chaired by Lord Donovan was set up in 1965 to review the law relating to industrial relations. It carried out a comprehensive programme of research, so that its report constitutes an authoritative survey of law and industrial relations in the United Kingdom at that time.

In the following extract, note the different levels of bargaining, the overlap between them and the distinction between substantive and procedural collective agreements.

Report of the Royal Commission on Trade Unions and Employers' Associations 1965–1968 (the Donovan Commission) Cmnd 3623

31 The relationship between trade unions and employers' associations arises principally in the process of negotiating and applying collective agreements, and the rules established by these agreements form a considerable part of the framework within which managers and workers deal with each other. 'Collective bargain' is a term coined by Beatrice Webb to describe an agreement concerning pay and conditions of work settled between trade unions on the one hand and an employer on the other. Thus it covers any negotiations in which employees do not negotiate individually, and on their own behalf, but do so collectively through representatives.

32 The best-known type of collective agreement in this country is the industry-wide agreement (a more precise term than 'national agreement'). This is an agreement between an employers' association (or in some instances two or more associations) and a trade union (or, more commonly, two or more unions or a federation of unions) which is intended to operate throughout an industry. Where industry-wide bargaining is practised the resulting agreements can be classified into substantive agreements, which deal with matters such as rates of pay, hours of work, overtime rates and holiday arrangements, and procedural agreements dealing with the procedures for reaching substantive agreements and for dealing with disputes which may arise in the establishments within the industry. Substantive agreements and disputes procedures are almost invariably written down and often printed in a handbook of agreements for the industry. Some industries have agreed formal constitutions for joint bodies at industry level which meet regularly to deal with such matters as negotiating or amending substantive agreements. Where they exist, these constitutions are generally included in the handbooks. Other industries prefer to rely on arranging *ad hoc* meetings for negotiating and revising substantive agreements.

33 Some large corporations which do not belong to employers' associations negotiate their own substantive and procedural agreements with the unions. A few of these agreements, like that of the Ford Motor Company, operate throughout the undertaking and cover more

workers than many industry-wide agreements. Some of the major oil companies, on the other hand, negotiate separate agreements for each of their refineries. In a few instances, including the National Coal Board, an agreement with a single corporation is also an industry-wide agreement.

34 Companies in membership of employers' associations (usually called 'federated' companies) may negotiate agreements with unions representing their employees to supplement industry-wide agreements, either substantive or procedural, but such agreements are relatively rare. More commonly bargaining to supplement industry-wide agreements takes place between managers and representatives of particular groups of workers. In a company possessing two or more factories it is normal for managers in each factory to deal separately with representatives of groups of their own workers. This type of bargaining we refer to as 'workplace bargaining'. In some instances workers are represented by full-time trade union district officials in workplace bargaining. More commonly, however, their spokesmen are representatives chosen from among themselves, usually called 'shop stewards', and full-time officials are called in only where managers and shop stewards cannot reach agreement. Many of these agreements affect only one group of workers in a single shop, and may be settled between a shop steward and a foreman or departmental manager. This is 'workshop' or 'shop floor' bargaining. Most industry-wide disputes procedures give some guidance on the conduct of workplace bargaining, although in practice this guidance is not strictly observed.

35 Workplace agreements may be written down, but are rarely collected together into a single coherent document. Many of them, especially shop floor agreements, are oral. These oral agreements are difficult to distinguish from 'custom and practice'. This is the body of customary forms of behaviour among groups of workers which managers have permitted to grow up and are therefore assumed to accept. Examples of matters widely covered by custom and practice are 'tea-breaks' and tasks reserved for members of a given craft. These customs play an important part in shop floor industrial relations, and some have their origin in oral agreements.

36 The pay and conditions of an individual employee may therefore be the result of collective bargains struck at one or more (even, conceivably, all) of the foregoing levels.

Comment

(1) For employees, the advantage of collective bargaining is that the combined power of many employees can even up the otherwise unequal bargaining position between employer and worker. What is in it for the employer?

Kahn-Freund's Labour and the Law 3rd ed 1983, edited P Davies and M Freedland, p 69

... it is not difficult to summarise the purposes of collective bargaining: by bargaining collectively with organised labour, management seeks to give effect to its legitimate expectation that the planning of production, distribution, etc, should not be frustrated through interruptions of work. By bargaining collectively with management, organised labour seeks to give effect to its legitimate expectations that wages and other conditions of work should be such as to guarantee a stable and adequate form of existence and as to be compatible with the physical integrity and moral dignity of the individual, and also that jobs should be reasonably secure. This definition is not intended to be exhaustive. It is intended to indicate (and this is important for the law) that the principal interest of management in collective bargaining has always been the maintenance of industrial peace over a given area and period, and that the principal interest of labour has always been the creation and the maintenance of certain standards over a given area and period, standards of distribution of work, of rewards, and of stability of employment.

Comment

(1) Traditionally, therefore, the trade-off has been that the employer can expect that no industrial action will take place without procedures laid down in collective agreements being carried out first. The agreement is seen as an industrial peace treaty.

(2) Because of the contribution of collective bargaining to orderly industrial relations, the policy of successive governments and therefore of the law was that the process should be encouraged. However, the policing of collective agreements was not seen as the law's business.

Report of the Royal Commission on Trade Unions and Employers' Associations 1965–1968 (the Donovan Commission) Cmnd 3623

39 Until recent times it was a distinctive feature of our system of industrial relations that the State remained aloof from the process of collective bargaining in private industry. It left the parties free to come to their own agreement. It imposed some, but few, restrictions on the right of employees to strike or of employers to resort to a lock-out. The parties to the collective agreement themselves rarely intend that their bargain shall be a legally enforceable contract, but rather that it shall be binding in honour only. The law goes out of its way to provide that such bargains between employers' associations and trade unions shall not be directly enforceable.

40 This abstentionist attitude has reflected a belief that it is better in the long run for the law to interfere as little as possible in the settlement of questions arising between employers and workmen over pay and conditions of work. Parliament has long been committed to the view that the best means of settling such questions is voluntary collective bargaining and has equipped Governments in various ways to support, assist and promote collective bargaining.

41 One example of support for collective agreements is the Fair Wages Resolution of the House of Commons. The first was passed in 1891, and the Resolution at present in force was adopted in 1946. Its basic purpose is to ensure that employers engaged on Government contracts do not give their employees terms and conditions inferior to those established generally. Other examples are the Terms and Conditions of Employment Act 1959, under which an employer may be required under certain conditions to observe terms and conditions not less favourable than those established for his trade or industry by collective bargaining; and the statutory obligation placed on the boards of nationalised industries to seek agreement with trade unions over the establishment of negotiating machinery for settling terms and conditions of work for their employees.

Comment

(1) The Donovan Commission concluded that collective bargaining needed reform because the overlap between national agreements and local arrangements led to considerable confusion. However, overall they remained convinced that voluntary collective bargaining was the best policy for orderly industrial relations.

(2) As well as the two measures of state support mentioned in the extract, collective bargaining was also encouraged by the wages council system (designed, among other things, to foster collective bargaining in low-paid industries with low levels of unionisation) and through government-provided conciliation and arbitration systems. In 1975

the Labour government extended this support further, in particular by providing a legal mechanism for trade unions to demand recognition from an unwilling employer.

(3) All this changed with the arrival of the Conservative administration of Mrs Thatcher in 1979. During the 1980s many of the legislative supports for collective bargaining were dismantled. The Fair Wages Resolution was rescinded in 1983 (which required the government first to denounce ILO Convention 94 in 1982). The Employment Act 1980 abolished the procedure for extension of terms and conditions to other employers and the statutory recognition procedure. The powers of wages councils were cut drastically by the Wages Councils Act 1986 and TURERA abolished them altogether. TURERA also repealed the duty of Acas to promote collective bargaining. The attitude of the Conservative government towards collective bargaining was made clear in its policy documents of the time.

People, Jobs and Opportunity Cm 1810 (1992) (White Paper)

4.3   In the 1960s and 1970s, the way in which pay was determined for the great majority of employees ran counter to the objectives of rewarding individual effort and performance, and increasing job opportunities and choice through the operation of a more efficient labour market. The combination of centralised, industry-wide collective bargaining and Government policies to limit the growth of earnings by imposing uniform 'pay limits' resulted in a strong trend towards identical pay increases, regardless of individual employees' contributions to the organisations for which they worked.

4.4   Since 1979 the Government has taken a series of steps to reverse this damaging trend. In the first place, pay determination has been freed from Government interference through the discredited mechanism of past 'incomes policies'. Secondly, . . . the Government, through its employment legislation, has provided effective protection for employers and employees alike against the abuses of trade union power which created such an imbalance of bargaining power in the 1970s: employers are now free to decide for themselves whether or not to recognise and negotiate with trade unions, just as employees are now free to decide for themselves whether or not to join a trade union. Thirdly, the Government has taken specific steps to encourage the spread of profit-related pay. Finally it has set an example, as an employer, in taking initiatives to move pay determination away from centralised collective bargaining and make it more responsive to local needs.

4.5   As a result, the 1980s have seen a number of important developments:
- there has been a marked decline in the number of people whose pay is determined by national collective agreements. Data from the New Earnings Survey shows that the coverage of major national collective agreements dropped substantially – from 47 per cent in 1983 to 34 per cent in 1991. Moreover, those covered by such agreements did relatively worse than those who were not covered. In 1983 those covered earned £3 a week more than those who were not covered. By 1991 the picture was reversed, with those covered earning £7.50 a week less than those who were not.
- there is an increasing trend to move away from collective bargaining altogether: external research suggests that by 1990 some 42 per cent of the workforce was not covered, either directly or indirectly, by collective bargaining; more and more companies are negotiating pay on an individual basis with each of their employees on the basis of relevant skills and performance;
- even where collective bargaining persists, pay determination has become increasingly decentralised to local level; there are now much greater regional variations in pay within organisations where previously employees were paid at the same rate regardless of differences in labour market conditions;

- new forms of performance pay, merit pay and other incentives such as employee share ownership and profit-sharing are becoming more widespread at all levels. A recent study found that 47 per cent of companies surveyed used performance related pay for all their white collar workers and 30 per cent had an element of merit pay for manual workers;
- there has been a widening in skill differentials after reaching a low-point in the mid 1970s. For instance, the average pay of foremen and technicians has risen from around 30 per cent above the skilled rate in 1976 to about 50 per cent above in 1990.

4.6 These are all valuable and healthy developments. They mean that pay determination is increasingly responsive to individual effort. Furthermore, they are making an important contribution to improving the effective operation of the labour market on which the expansion of job opportunities and choice crucially depends. It is, therefore, essential that these developments should be built upon in the 1990s.

The way forward for the 1990s

4.7 The Government will be ready to take further action, as necessary, to remove any obstacles to these developments and to stimulate progress in such areas as profit-related pay. It will continue to encourage employers to move away from traditional, centralised collective bargaining towards methods of pay determination which reward individual skills and performance; respond to the wish of individual employees to negotiate their own terms and conditions of employment; and take full account of business circumstances.

Comment

(1) As this demonstrates, the policy of the Conservative government was firmly to discourage collective bargaining in favour of individualised contracts and greater variations in terms and conditions. Various initiatives to achieve this are mentioned in the extract. Profit-related pay was introduced by the 1986 budget and was meant to give workers the opportunity to earn tax-free payments based on the profitability of their company. The idea was that they would therefore have a direct interest in the success of the organisation and would be motivated to work harder. In fact, it became simply a way of paying employees without paying tax, and was phased out in 2000.

(2) Performance-related pay, or merit pay systems still persist in many organisations. The idea here is that individuals are rewarded according to their personal contribution, again as a means of improving motivation. However, such systems require an awful lot of time and effort (on the part of employees as well as management) to operate and some studies have shown that they can have a demotivating effect. Employees who are not rated highly may feel that their contribution is undervalued and that others have been unduly rewarded, causing jealousies and deterioration in relationships between colleagues. As appraisals are usually carried out by line managers, there are dangers of subjectivity and favouritism, resulting in inconsistent applications and the risk of unlawful discrimination – as we will see in Chapter 7.

(3) At the same time that government policy in the United Kingdom was moving away from collective bargaining, the trend at EC level was in the opposite direction. The Single European Act of 1986 added what are now Arts 138 and 139 to the Treaty of Rome (extracted above, p 25) which gave the European Commission the task of promoting consultation of management and labour at Community level and of facilitating dialogue between them. Compare this with the former duty of Acas to promote collective bargaining – abolished by TURERA. The social partners – European organisations

representing both sides of industry – must be consulted before proposals about social policy (including employment law) are submitted and if the social partners reach agreement on social policy initiatives, their agreements can be given legislative force. To date, three directives, the Parental Leave Directive (96/34/EC), the Part-time Work Directive (97/81/EC)) and the Fixed-term Work Directive (99/70/EC) have been adopted under this procedure.

(4) This is one area of employment law where the policy of the Labour government which came to power in 1997 broke decisively with the previous administration.

Fairness at Work Cm 3968 (1998) (White Paper)

COLLECTIVE RIGHTS

4.1 Individual rights provide the essential underpinning of effective working relationships. Individuals seek and obtain jobs, and agree employment contracts with their employer. Individual employees have the right to expect fair treatment at work, and decent employment standards. Most employers recognise this. Individual employees also have the responsibility to work diligently and to the best of their ability to fulfil their part of the employment contract. Most employees recognise this. Employers and employees value individual success, individual achievement and individual ambition. Good employers have in place a range of policies and practices for their employees designed to ensure that individuals are able to make the maximum contribution they can to the success of the enterprise.

4.2 But individual contracts of employment are not always agreements between equal partners. Good employers and employees recognise that there is a basic justification in terms of fairness at work for fair representation of all employees. Collective representation of individuals at work can be the best method of ensuring that employees are treated fairly, and it is often the preferred option of both employers and employees.

4.3 Collective representation can help achieve important business objectives, including good communication. It can facilitate negotiation on terms and conditions without preventing the recognition of good individual performance. Representatives who are respected by other employees can help employers to explain the company's circumstances and the need for change. Collective representation can give employees a more effective voice in discussion with employers by drawing on a wide range of expertise and experience in the company . . .

4.6 Employers and employees now have available a wide range of representational mechanisms. Many employers and employees choose representational methods not involving trade unions, which achieve good employment relations. The role of trade unions in centralised collective bargaining on pay and conditions has declined, reflecting decentralised decision-taking in many organisations.

4.7 But many equally successful British companies and organisations operate with employers and employees selecting trade unions to act as their main means of representation. Of the 50 largest UK companies, 44 recognise trade unions. Trade unions can make the task of forging effective partnerships easier for employers and employees. In recent years they have changed to reflect change in business. Many trade unions now focus much more strongly on working with management to develop a flexible, skilled and motivated workforce. Trade unions can be a force for fair treatment, and a means of driving towards innovation and partnerships . . .

4.10 The Government accepts the importance of voluntary choices, and believes that mutually-agreed arrangements for representation, whether involving trade unions or not, are the best ways for employers and employees to move forward. Where agreements are reached voluntarily, they are most likely to be successful and suited to the needs of the enterprise.

4.11 However, there will be occasions where employees want the benefit of representation at work, but are unable to secure agreement to it from their employer. The Government believes strongly that these will form a very small minority of cases, and that even then the prospects of voluntary agreement must be exhaustively examined. But as part of setting in place minimum standards, **the Government will bring forward legislation to provide for representation and recognition where a majority of the relevant workforce wants it.** The prime purpose of this is to offer greater protection and security at work for the vulnerable. The extent of trade union growth and organisation is dependent on trade unions being able to convince employers and employees of their value – how much help they can bring to the success of an enterprise for employers, and how much active support they can offer employees. Where trade unions are able to demonstrate value to employers they are more likely to be recognised, and where they are able to demonstrate value to employees they are more likely to win members.

Comment

(1) Note the emphasis on partnership, drawing on the philosophy behind the social dialogue at EU level. This draws on the unitary approach to employment relations, which holds that the interests of employers and employees are essentially aligned. The pluralist approach holds that, on the contrary, there is an inevitable conflict between the interests of management and labour. Which do you think is correct?

(2) The statutory recognition procedure, referred to here, was introduced by the Employment Relations Act 1999 and is considered later in this chapter.

(3) Collective agreements remain the main source of terms and conditions for over a third of all employees. In law, this raises the question of how terms in an agreement between a trade union and an employer can affect a third party, namely the employee, who may not even be a member of the union. As between the employer and the trade union, the issue is whether either side can enforce the agreement if the other side wants to renege. These questions will be considered next.

COLLECTIVE AGREEMENTS AND THE INDIVIDUAL EMPLOYEE

It is a basic principle of contract law that agreements are binding only on the parties who make the agreement: this is the doctrine of privity of contract. Even if a contract is made for the benefit of a third party, the third party cannot (usually) enforce it. So if a trade union and an employer were to agree that employees' pay should be increased by 3 per cent, the employees could not sue to enforce that agreement. In fact, as we will see, collective agreements are hardly ever binding contracts even between the employers and trade unions who are parties to them. Yet everyone knows that the collective agreement is intended to have legal effects. How can this be translated into law?

Union as agent

Can it be argued that the union negotiates the collective agreement as agent for its members? If so, that could bring them into direct contractual relations with the employer. Since we think of the union as acting on behalf of the workers, this initially seems an attractive proposition. There are two difficulties, however. First, by no stretch of the imagination could the union be regarded as acting as the agent of workers who do not belong to the union – yet collective agreements typically apply to all the workers in a bargaining unit, whether they are union members or not. Secondly, it is unrealistic to suppose that simply by joining a union, members intend to give it virtually unlimited authority to enter agreements on their behalf.

Burton Group Ltd v *Smith* [1977] IRLR 351 Employment Appeal Tribunal

The issue was whether notice to a trade union had been received by the union as agent for its member.

ARNOLD J: '. . . There is no reason at all why, in a particular case, union representatives should not be the agents of an employee to make a contract, or to receive a notice, or otherwise effect a binding transaction on his behalf. But that agency so to do does not stem from the mere fact that they are union representatives and that he is a member of the union; it must be supported in the particular case by the creation of some specific agency, and that can arise only if the evidence supports the conclusion that there was such an agency. It is sufficient to say that in this case there was no evidence before the Tribunal of the existence of such an agency . . .'

Comment

(1) This correctly states the law on this matter. Examples of the union being held to be the agent of the members include *Edwards* v *Skyways* (1964) and *Harris* v *Richard Lawson Autologistics Ltd* (2002).

(2) Where membership alone has been argued to create an agency relationship, it has usually been rejected: *Holland* v *London Society of Compositors* (1924); *NUGSAT* v *Albury Bros* (1979). Note, however, *Chappell* v *Times Newspapers* (1975), where Lord Denning went so far as to interpret a union's strike notice to the employer as notice given on behalf of the workers that they were repudiating their contracts of employment! Fortunately, this was an *obiter dictum*.

Incorporation into individual contracts

Since the agency argument will operate only in very limited circumstances, the usual question is whether or not the collective agreement has become incorporated into the individual employee's own contract of employment. If so, then the term can be enforced by and against the individual like any other contract term. The simplest case is where the incorporation of the collective agreement is expressly agreed between the parties.

Marley v *Forward Trust Group Ltd* [1986] ICR 891 Court of Appeal

The company decided to close its Bristol office, where the claimant was employed, and to redeploy him to London. Under a collective agreement between the employers and the trade union, ASTMS, employees redeployed in a redundancy situation were allowed six months in which to assess the suitability of the new job, and could opt instead for redundancy terms if they were unhappy. Having tried the new job for two months, the claimant decided to take redundancy instead. The company argued that the terms of the collective agreement were not binding.

DILLON LJ: '. . . When the employee's contract of employment was taken over by the respondents, Forward Trust Group Limited, in December 1981, possibly as a result of a group reconstruction or a takeover of the previous employer, he was given a letter which made it plain that the terms and conditions of his employment were being published in a new personnel manual. When, in June 1983, he was promoted to field supervisor operating from the south west regional head office of the employers, the particulars of his terms of employment set out again and again that details were contained in various sections of the personnel manual. One of these sections was section A10, and section A10 provides categorically that redundancies will be handled in accordance with the procedure outlined in section A25 of the personnel manual. Section A25 sets out the terms of the collective agreement between the respondents and the trade union ASTMS, to which Lawton LJ has referred. It sets it out verbatim and that includes the clause 11: "This agreement is binding in honour only and it is not intended to give rise to any legal obligation." That may, no doubt, have been so as between the employers and the union, but the terms of the agreement are incorporated into the personnel manual in section A25 and they must have legal effect thereby as terms of the contract between the employee and the employers.

I, therefore, am unable to accept the conclusion of the employment tribunal and of the Employment Appeal Tribunal that clause 11 prevented the employee enforcing those terms. If there was a redundancy situation he was entitled to the benefit of the terms set out in section A25 in relation to a redundancy situation . . .'

(Lawton LJ delivered a concurring judgment and Woolf LJ agreed.)

Comment

(1) Here there was a double incorporation. The employee's contract incorporated the personnel manual, and the personnel manual incorporated the collective agreement.

(2) The collective agreement contained a term (clause 11) to the effect that it was not intended to be a legally binding agreement as between the union and the employer. While not strictly necessary (see below), this kind of provision is not uncommon. The collective agreement had been reproduced verbatim in the personnel manual, hence the argument that the term saying that it was not binding was also incorporated. That argument, which would involve a paradox of the Cretan liar variety, was sensibly rejected by the court.

(3) It is a consequence of the non-binding nature of collective agreements that either the union or the employer can terminate them at any time. What effect does this have on individual employees?

Robertson v British Gas [1983] ICR 351 Court of Appeal

British Gas appealed against a decision that they were liable to pay arrears of pay to the employee under an incentive bonus scheme. The incentive bonus scheme had been contained in a collective agreement and had undergone some variation over the years. British Gas had terminated the collective agreement containing the latest version at the end of 1981.

The employee relied on his letter of appointment, which stated, 'Incentive bonus conditions will apply . . .', as incorporating entitlement into his contract of employment. His written statement of terms and conditions of employment said, 'Any payment which may, from time to time, become due in respect . . . of incentive bonuses . . . will be calculated in accordance with the rules of the scheme in force at the time.' The letter of appointment and the written statement are the two sets of contractual documents referred to by the judge.

221

KERR LJ: '. . . Turning to the two sets of contractual documents in this case, and without distinguishing between them, it seems to me to be clear that both of them were designed to operate in the context of some agreed collective scheme concerning bonus payments, with conditions (in the case of the first document) and rules in force (in the case of the second document), whose terms are to be treated as incorporated into the individual contracts evidenced by these documents. Both of them proceed on the basis that there will be an incentive bonus and that its amount and the terms governing it are to be found in an agreed collective scheme in force from time to time. Such an agreement was in force at the time when both these documents came into existence, and from time to time the terms of the scheme were thereafter varied by some further collective agreement between the trade union side and the employer's side. I agree with Mr Sedley's [counsel for the employee] submission that, when the terms of the collective agreements were varied by consent between the two sides, then the new terms clearly became incorporated into the individual contracts of employment. But what does not follow, in my view, is that the contracts of the individual workmen can be varied by some unilateral variation or abrogation or withdrawal from the collective agreement by either side.

It is true that collective agreements such as those in the present case create no legally enforceable obligation between the trade union and the employers. Either side can withdraw. But their terms are in this case incorporated into the individual contracts of employment, and it is only if and when those terms are varied collectively by agreement that the individual contracts of employment will also be varied. If the collective scheme is not varied by agreement, but by some unilateral abrogation or withdrawal or variation to which the other side does not agree, then it seems to me that the individual contracts of employment remain unaffected. This is another way of saying that the terms of the individual contracts are in part to be found in the agreed collective agreements as they exist from time to time, and, if these cease to exist as collective agreements, then the terms, unless expressly varied between the individual and the employer, will remain as they were by reference to the last agreed collective agreement incorporated into the individual contracts.

In the present case this construction is reinforced by the fact that, although it looks from the documents as though the incentive bonus scheme is merely one small part of the total terms of the individual contracts of employment, it provides in fact an integrated and general framework for a very large number of the mutual rights and obligations of the parties. Indeed, it becomes virtually impossible to determine what the full terms of these individual contracts of employment are if you once take away the agreed collective scheme for an incentive bonus as an integral part of these contracts.

For all these reasons I have no doubt that the judge came to the right conclusion, and I would equally dismiss this appeal.'

(Ackner LJ delivered a concurring judgment and Sir David Cairns agreed.)

Comment

(1) What if the contractual documents had said something like, 'any incentive scheme will be subject to the collective agreement in force for the time being'? Would the employer have been excused liability after terminating the agreement? See *Cadoux v Central Regional Council* (1986) and *Airlie v City of Edinburgh DC* (1996).

(2) This case illustrates the major problem likely to arise in the context of express incorporation: what precisely has been incorporated? For another example, see *Gascol Conversions v Mercer* (1974), where the issue was whether a local agreement which had in fact been acted on took precedence over a national collective agreement.

(3) Where there has been no express incorporation of the terms of a collective agreement, it may be possible to rely instead on implied incorporation. That is, the circumstances

may indicate that the collective agreement should be treated as incorporated into the contract of employment. This is essentially a question of fact.

Alexander v Standard Telephones & Cables Ltd (No 2)
[1991] IRLR 286 Queen's Bench Division

Faced with the need to make 112 redundancies, the company, after consultation with the relevant trade unions, selected on the basis of several criteria: length of service, skill, aptitude, performance, attendance record and approach to work. Two groups of employees thereby selected for redundancy challenged the lawfulness of their dismissals. These were cable operators, of whom Mr Alexander was representative ('the *Alexander* action'), and maintenance workers, of whom Mr Wall was representative ('the *Wall* action').

HOBHOUSE J: '. . . The various claimants dispute that they were lawfully dismissed. They make no complaint about the conduct of the consultation procedures that were gone through prior to their dismissal, nor do they complain about their selection for dismissal if the criteria adopted by the company were the proper criteria. Nor do they say in these actions that they were unfairly dismissed. What the claimants say is that the company was only entitled to select employees for compulsory redundancy on the basis of seniority, or as it is commonly known, "last in first out". If that criterion had been applied they would not have been selected for dismissal; they were among the more senior employees. They say that it was a requirement of the collective agreements between the company and the relevant union or unions covering the maintenance workers and the cable operators that selection for redundancy should be on the basis of seniority alone and they further say that provision of each collective agreement was incorporated into their individual contracts of employment. Accordingly each claimant says that his dismissal was wrongful and in breach of contract from the defendant company . . .

The so-called "normative effect" by which it can be inferred that provisions of collective agreements have become part of individual contracts of employment is now well recognised in employment law (see, for example, *Harvey on Industrial Relations and Employment Law*). However, serious difficulties still arise because the principle still has to be one of incorporation into the individual contracts of employment and the extraction of a recognisable contractual intent as between the individual employee and his employer. The mere existence of collective agreements which are relevant to the employee and his employment does not include a contractual intent (see for example per Ackner LJ, *Robertson v British Gas* (1983)). The contractual intent has to be found in the individual contract of employment and very often the evidence will not be sufficient to establish such an intent in a manner which satisfies accepted contractual criteria and satisfies ordinary criteria of certainty. Where the relevant subject-matter is one of present day-to-day relevance to the employer and employee, as for example wage rates and hours of work, the continuing relationship between employer and employee, the former paying wages and providing work, the latter working and accepting wages, provides a basis for inferring such a contractual intent. Where, as in the case of redundancy, the situation is one which does not have daily implications but only arises occasionally the inference will be more difficult to sustain. Here, there had not previously been any question of compulsory redundancies. There was no previously tested position by which a local custom could be demonstrated, nor was there any previous situation involving any of the relevant individuals, or for that matter any other employees of the defendants from which it could be inferred as a matter of individual contractual intent, that individual contracts of employment were to include as a matter of contractual right and obligation selection for redundancy on the seniority principle. It must be borne in mind that although the present claimants would be the beneficiaries of the application of such a principle, by a parity of reasoning there would be other employees who would be disadvantaged. Similarly, there is no necessity to infer an intention to incorporate since collective agreements have a function and value of their own which exists wholly independently of any individual contract of employment (see, for example, the reasoning of the Judicial Committee in *Young* v *Canadian Northern Railway* (1931)) . . .

The principles to be applied can therefore be summarised. The relevant contract is that between the individual employee and his employer; it is the contractual intention of those two parties which must be ascertained. In so far as that intention is to be found in a written document, that document must be construed on ordinary contractual principles. In so far as there is no such document or that document is not complete or conclusive, their contractual intention has to be ascertained by inference from the other available material including collective agreements. The fact that another document is not itself contractual does not prevent it from being incorporated into the contract if that intention is shown as between the employer and the individual employee. Where a document is expressly incorporated by general words it is still necessary to consider, in conjunction with the words of incorporation, whether any particular part of that document is apt to be a term of the contract; if it is inapt, the correct construction of the contract may be that it is not a term of the contract. Where it is not a case of express incorporation, but a matter of inferring the contractual intent, the character of the document and the relevant part of it and whether it is apt to form part of the individual contract is central to the decision whether or not the inference should be drawn.

In the present cases I have concluded that the wording of the only document directly applicable to the individual claimants, the statutory statements, is not sufficient to effect an express incorporation of the provisions relating to redundancy in the collective agreements: accordingly it is a matter of considering whether or not to *infer* that the selection procedures and the principle of seniority have been incorporated into the individual contracts of employment and this has to be decided having regard to the evidence given and an evaluation of the character of the relevant provisions in the collective agreements. . . .'

Comment

(1) See also *Henry* v *London General Transport Services Ltd* (2002), where the Court of Appeal held that a collective agreement was capable of being incorporated into individual contracts of employment by custom and practice.

(2) In *Alexander (No 2)* the judge considered that the evidence did not support an inference of incorporation because the relevant part of the collective agreement was not apt for incorporation. This brings us to the remaining issue: can the whole of a collective agreement be regarded as incorporated, and so enforceable by an individual employee?

What terms are incorporated?

Young v Canadian Northern Railway Company [1931] AC 83 Privy Council

The appellant was made redundant in contravention of a collective agreement ('Wage Agreement No 4') which provided that selection for redundancy should be on the basis of 'last in, first out' – the seniority principle. The advice of the Privy Council (the members of the panel being Viscount Dunedin, Lords Blanesburgh, Tomlin and Russell and Anglin CJ) was given by Lord Russell.

LORD RUSSELL: '. . . There can be no doubt upon the evidence that in fact, the provisions of Wage Agreement No 4 were applied by the railway company to all its employees in its locomotive and car department. One extract from the evidence of the general manager (Mr Tisdale) makes this clear: "(A.) I understand your question to be this: Is the agreement that was negotiated between the railway companies and Division 4 applicable to all the men in the shop? (Q.) Yes? (A.) The answer is Yes."

Their Lordships, however, are unable to treat these matters as establishing contractual liability by the railway company to the appellant. The fact that the railway company applied the agreement to the appellant, is equally consistent with the view that it did so, not because it was bound contractually to apply it to him, but because as a matter of policy it deemed it expedient to apply it to all.

If the conduct of the railway company in applying the provisions of the agreement to the appellant could be explained only by the existence of a contractual obligation to the appellant so to do, it would be not only permissible, but necessary to hold that the existence of the contractual obligation had been established. In the circumstances, however, of the present case, their Lordships find themselves unable so to decide.

But the matter does not quite rest there. When Wage Agreement No 4 is examined, it does not appear to their Lordships to be a document adapted for conversion into or incorporation with a service agreement, so as to entitle master and servant to enforce *inter se* the terms thereof. It consists of some 188 "rules", which the railway companies contract with Division No 4 to observe. It appears to their Lordships to be intended merely to operate as an agreement between a body of employers and a labour organisation by which the employers undertake that as regards their workmen, certain rules beneficial to the workmen shall be observed. By itself it constitutes no contract between any individual employee and the company which employs him. If an employer refused to observe the rules, the effective sequel would be, not an action by any employee, not even an action by Division No 4 against the employer for specific performance or damages, but the calling of a strike until the grievance was remedied. . . .'

(The employee's appeal failed.)

Alexander v *Standard Telephones & Cables Ltd (No 2)* [1991] IRLR 286 Queen's Bench Division

Faced with the need to make 112 redundancies, the company, after consultation with the relevant trade unions, selected on the basis of several criteria: length of service, skill, aptitude, performance, attendance record and approach to work. Two groups of employees thereby selected for redundancy challenged the lawfulness of their dismissals. These were cable operators, of whom Mr Alexander was representative ('the *Alexander* action'), and maintenance workers, of whom Mr Wall was representative ('the *Wall* action').

HOBHOUSE J: '. . . In the case *National Coal Board* v *National Union of Mineworkers* (1986), to which some individual employees were also parties, Scott J reviewed the authorities on incorporation. In that case there was an express provision in the individual contracts of employment that the employees' "wages and conditions of service shall be regulated by and subject to such national, district and pit agreements as are for the time being in force". The question was the application of that clear contractual intent; the question in the action therefore was: what was the extent of the resultant incorporation? He drew a distinction which was derived from the argument of Mr Dehn before him.

"He seeks, however, to draw a distinction between the terms of a collective agreement which are of their nature apt to become enforceable terms of an individual's contract of employment and terms which are of their nature inapt to become enforceable by individuals. Terms of collective agreements fixing rates of pay, or hours of work, would obviously fall into the first category. Terms . . . dismissing an employee also would fall into the first category. But conciliation agreements setting up machinery designed to resolve by discussions between employers' representatives and union representatives, or by arbitral proceedings, questions arising within the industry, fall, submitted Mr Dehn, firmly in the second category.

The terms of conciliation schemes are not intended to become contractually enforceable by individual workers whether or not referred into the individual contracts of employment . . .

A collective agreement between an employer and a union providing machinery for collective bargaining and for resolving industrial disputes may be of very great importance to each and every worker in the industry. But it is not likely to be an agreement intended to be legally enforceable as between employer and union, and it is almost inconceivable to my mind that it could have been intended to become legally enforceable at the suit of an individual worker. In the procedures laid down by the 1946 Scheme, for instance, no part is played by an individual mineworker. The machinery is designed to be invoked and operated either by the NCB or by the NUM with the co-operation of the other. It simply does not lend itself at all to enforceability at the suit of an individual mineworker."

Therefore, even in a case which involved wide express words of incorporation the court considered it necessary to look at the content and character of the relevant parts of the collective agreement in order to decide whether or not they were incorporated into the individual contracts of employment . . .

Turning to the collective agreements themselves it is convenient to take the *Wall* agreement first. It expressly states that it is a "procedure" agreement. Thus, on a simplistic application of the language of Scott J, one would conclude that it was not apt to be incorporated. However, it is of course necessary to examine the character of the agreement and its relevant parts more closely before reaching a conclusion. It is undoubtedly primarily a policy document applicable to the relationship between the unions and the company. It also is specifically concerned with procedure. Thus the third clause under the heading "Joint consultation" lays down a procedure and it is within that scheme that individuals are to be selected for compulsory redundancy. Indeed, all the first five clauses of the agreement are clearly inappropriate for application to or incorporation in individual contracts of employment.

Clauses 7 to 10 are also inapt for such incorporation. The reference to temporary workers is merely to exclude them from the scope of the agreement. The re-employment clause merely says that the company will give consideration to re-employment, at a later date, of employees made compulsorily redundant; this is neither expressed as a contractual obligation nor could it form part of a present contract of employment. As regards transfer allowances the clause contemplates that the company may make offers of employment in another division of the company to some individuals as an alternative to redundancy and states that if such an offer should be made it will include assistance in making the transfer. This again is not apt to be a term of an existing contract of employment as it involves the choice of the company to make an offer and it is only from the making of that offer and its acceptance that any individual right can subsequently arise. As regards the provision relating to employees who leave early, it merely provides that employees will normally be required to observe their contractual obligations under their contracts of employment; therefore again it is not apt for incorporation.

In this context, where none of the other clauses of the collective agreement are apt to be incorporated into the individual contract of employment, it would require some cogent indication in clause 6 [dealing with selection for redundancy] that it was to have a different character and to be incorporated into the individual contracts of employment. The claimants' submissions gain nothing from the context within which clause 6 is to be found; indeed the context strongly detracts from their case. The first part of clause 6 is a statement of policy – looking for volunteers, giving priority to employees taking early retirement or affected by ill-health. Likewise paragraph 6.2 is again expressed in policy terms having regard to inter-union relationships and to the requirements of the company's on-going business; it is stated to be "the mutual objective". Whilst this again is not inconsistent with giving paragraph 6.1 contractual effect, it does detract from that implication. Paragraph 6.1, the critical paragraph, is expressed in terms which are

226

capable of giving rise to individual rights. It says that selection for compulsory redundancy "will be made on the basis of service" within the relevant group. Therefore the claimants can reasonably argue that as individuals they are entitled, on account of their seniority, not to be selected. However, I consider that the wording of paragraph 6.1 is too weak, when considered in the context in which it occurs in clause 6 itself and within the context and consultation scheme of the procedure agreement as a whole, to support the inference of incorporation. Clear and specific express words of incorporation contained in a primary contractual document could displace this conclusion, but on any view the wording of the statutory statements in the present case do not suffice.

It follows that the *Wall* claimants' case of breach of contract must fail. They cannot establish the contractual right under their individual contracts of employment which they need in order to succeed in their action for damages for breach of contract against the defendants . . .'

Comment

(1) The judge dismissed the *Alexander* action for similar reasons.

(2) In *Marley* v *Forward Trust* (1986) the court proceeded on the basis that the redundancy agreement was incorporated into the individual's contract of employment without any discussion of the point which arose here. However, the relevant issue there was not the method of selection. Again, in *Lee* v *GEC Plessey* (1993) a provision for the payment of enhanced severance pay in a collective agreement was held to be apt for incorporation, and in *Airlie* v *City of Edinburgh DC* (1996), where the employees' written statements expressly incorporated the collective agreement, the EAT in Scotland rejected the argument that this did not incorporate all parts of it, even though some clauses were clearly inapt.

(3) The approach of Hobhouse J to the issue of what terms should be incorporated was approved by the Court of Appeal in *Kaur* v *MG Rover Group Ltd* (2005), another case notable for the court's minute examination of the terms of the collective agreement. It may be doubted whether such a technical approach is appropriate for a document which is not intended to be a contract. In *Kaur*, the Court of Appeal held that a commitment in the collective agreement (expressly incorporated in the employee's contract) to the effect that there would be no compulsory redundancies (in capital letters) was intended only to convey the employer's hope that this would be so.

(4) The amount of discretion available to a court in deciding whether or not terms of a collective agreement are apt for incorporation means that at best, there is a high degree of uncertainty in this area, and at worst, *carte blanche* for courts to decide what they think is reasonable on a subjective and inconsistent basis. It is interesting to note how many of these cases have related to collective agreements dealing with redundancy. It is submitted that the criteria for selection for redundancy so closely affect individuals that such provisions ought to be regarded as suitable for incorporation – but it must be admitted that the weight of authority is the other way.

No-strike clauses

At the beginning of this chapter we noted that one of the advantages for an employer in recognising unions for collective bargaining is the promotion of industrial peace. Today some employers, especially foreign companies investing in the United Kingdom, want collective agreements which do not merely require procedures to be followed before industrial action is instituted, but which prohibit industrial action altogether. As this is a significant inroad on employees' freedom of action, it is subject to statutory safeguard.

Trade Union and Labour Relations (Consolidation) Act 1992

180 (1) Any terms of a collective agreement which prohibit or restrict the right of workers to engage in a strike or other industrial action, or have the effect of prohibiting or restricting that right, shall not form part of any contract between a worker and the person for whom he works unless the following conditions are met.

(2) The conditions are that the collective agreement –

    (a) is in writing,

    (b) contains a provision expressly stating that those terms shall or may be incorporated in such a contract,

    (c) is reasonably accessible at his place of work to the worker to whom it applies and is available for him to consult during working hours, and

    (d) is one where each trade union which is a party to the agreement is an independent trade union;

and that the contract with the worker expressly or impliedly incorporates those terms in the contract.

(3) The above provisions have effect notwithstanding anything in section 179 and notwithstanding any provision to the contrary in any agreement (including a collective agreement or a contract with any worker).

Comment

(1) If workers take part in a strike or other industrial action despite a no-strike clause having been incorporated into their contracts of employment, they will be no worse off than they would be if there were no such clause. As we will see (Chapter 12), almost all industrial action involves a breach of contracts of employment, for which workers may be liable in damages. The damages would not be increased because of the existence of the no-strike clause and courts cannot order workers to return to work. Whether or not their dismissal for taking part in such action would be lawful or unfair is also unaffected by a no-strike clause.

(2) Suppose that a collective agreement required the employer to be given a period of notice longer than that provided for by statute before workers engaged in industrial action. Would this be a term suitable for inclusion in individual contracts?

ENFORCEABILITY BETWEEN UNION AND EMPLOYER

As indicated in the extract from the Donovan Report (p 215), collective agreements have traditionally been regarded as unenforceable in law. This view is now enshrined in TULRCA s 179.

Trade Union and Labour Relations (Consolidation) Act 1992

179 (1) A collective agreement shall be conclusively presumed not to have been intended by the parties to be a legally enforceable contract unless the agreement –

    (a) is in writing, and

    (b) contains a provision which (however expressed) states that the parties intend that the agreement shall be a legally enforceable contract.

(2) A collective agreement which does satisfy those conditions shall be conclusively presumed to have been intended by the parties to be a legally enforceable contract . . .

Comment

(1) In a seminal judgment in *Ford* v *AUEFW* (1969) Geoffrey Lane J held that collective agreements were not legally binding because the parties did not intend to create legally binding relations, referring specifically to the views of Kahn-Freund and the Donovan Commission.

(2) The advantage seen by some in making collective agreements legally enforceable is that strikes on matters covered by the agreement would be unlawful so long as the agreement remained in force. This is certainly how it works in some countries, such as the USA. However, note that it is possible to have a no-strike clause in contracts of employment without having a legally enforceable collective agreement, and also that a legally enforceable collective agreement need not contain a no-strike clause. Furthermore, even if a 'peace obligation' is included, it will probably not prevent strikes about matters outside the agreement (see Lewis, 1990).

(3) As the reason for non-enforceability is the intention of the parties, it is difficult to see how legislation could change the position. A statute cannot force people to enter contracts if they do not want to. When the Industrial Relations Act 1971 attempted to make collective agreements legally binding, the result was a rash of disclaimers inserted into agreements, usually known by their acronym, TINA LEA (This Is Not A Legally Enforceable Agreement). The Industrial Relations Act was repealed by TULRA 1974, when the forerunner of TULRCA s 179 was passed. The Conservative Government of the 1980s considered more than once whether the law should be changed to 'encourage' employers and unions to enter legally enforceable agreements (see the Green Paper, *Industrial Relations in the 1990s* Cm 1602 (1991) Chapter 8). The advantages claimed were not only the 'peace obligation' but also that it would bring the United Kingdom into line with most of the rest of Europe and North America, and would be easier for foreign companies investing in the United Kingdom to understand.

(4) It is, of course, possible for foreign investors to insist on legally binding collective agreements, and some made this a condition of recognising unions at new plants. Peace obligations were often, but not always, included. Another feature of this development was the insistence on 'single union deals'. To avoid the confusion and delay inherent in having to negotiate with many trade unions (in *Ford* v *AUEFW* (1969) the company recognised 19 unions) companies began to offer recognition to only one union, representing all grades of worker.

(5) These developments took place against a background of voluntary collective bargaining, meaning that it was up to the employer to decide whether or not to recognise the union. Things have changed on this front since the introduction of the statutory recognition procedure by the Employment Relations Act 1999. We turn now to the question of recognition.

RECOGNITION OF TRADE UNIONS

Recognition of trade unions means recognition by an employer for the purposes of collective bargaining. If the employer refuses to recognise the union, its influence will be limited and therefore there will be little advantage for employees in belonging to it. Hence it is extremely important to trade unions that they should achieve recognition.

Trade Union and Labour Relations (Consolidation) Act 1992

178   (1)   In this Act 'collective agreement' means any agreement or arrangement made by or on behalf of one or more trade unions and one or more employers or employers' associations and relating to one or more of the matters specified below; and 'collective bargaining' means negotiations relating to or connected with one or more of those matters.

(2)   The matters referred to above are –

(a)   terms and conditions of employment, or the physical conditions in which any workers are required to work;

(b)   engagement or non-engagement, or termination or suspension of employment or the duties of employment, of one or more workers;

(c)   allocation of work or the duties of employment between workers or groups of workers;

(d)   matters of discipline;

(e)   a worker's membership or non-membership of a trade union;

(f)   facilities for officials of trade unions; and

(g)   machinery for negotiation or consultation, and other procedures, relating to any of the above matters, including the recognition by employers or employers' associations of the right of a trade union to represent workers in such negotiation or consultation or in the carrying out of such procedures.

(3)   In this Act 'recognition', in relation to a trade union, means the recognition of the union by an employer, or two or more associated employers, to any extent, for the purpose of collective bargaining; and 'recognised' and other related expressions shall be construed accordingly.

Comment

(1) Where a trade union is recognised within the meaning of s 178 it qualifies for certain useful rights: the right to disclosure of information for collective bargaining (TULRCA s 181, dealt with later in this chapter); the right to appoint a safety representative and to be consulted over health and safety matters (Health and Safety at Work Act 1974 s 2); the right to consultation over redundancies and transfers of undertakings (TULRCA s 188 and TUPE 2006 reg 13) and the right to time off for its members and officials (TULRCA ss 168, 170).

(2) Note that the subject matter for collective bargaining defined in s 178(2) is the same as the definition of matters which may properly be regarded as giving rise to a trade dispute within the meaning of TULRCA s 244(1) (see below, p 623). It is also important to note that this is a much wider range of matters than those on which an employer can be compelled to negotiate under the statutory recognition procedure.

(3) The reference to recognition 'to any extent' in s 178(3) means that a union can be recognised for the purposes of s 178 for only some of the matters listed in subsection (2) and still count as recognised under this section. In *NUGSAT v Albury Bros* (1979) the Court of Appeal accepted that recognition need not be express but could be implied from the parties' conduct, although also stating that very clear evidence of such an intention would be necessary.

(4) It is important to understand the difference between voluntary recognition in terms of TULRCA s 178 and recognition under the statutory recognition procedure. Voluntary recognition gives the employer freedom to decide which union(s) to recognise, in respect of which group of workers and in relation to what subject matter. There is no requirement, as there is under the statutory recognition procedure, for the union to be independent (the meaning of 'independent trade union' is discussed in

Chapter 10, p 529). There is no procedure to follow and, crucially, it is also open to the employer to withdraw from the agreement by derecognising the union at any time. Under the statutory procedure, all these things are regulated, as we will see.

The statutory recognition procedure

The statutory recognition procedure was presaged in the *Fairness at Work* White Paper, as we saw at the beginning of this chapter. There was a precedent: the Employment Protection Act 1975 first established a statutory recognition procedure, set out in just six sections of the Act, whereby unions could refer a recognition request to Acas. Acas was supposed to investigate and then make a recommendation. If the employer refused to accept a recommendation in favour of recognition, the sanction was that the CAC could make an award of improved terms and conditions for employees.

A major flaw in that procedure was revealed in the bitter dispute over recognition at the Grunwick photo processing laboratory in west London in 1977, where the employer scuppered an Acas investigation into the wishes of the workforce by the simple (and lawful) expedient of denying them access to the premises and refusing to give them information that would allow them to contact the workers in other ways. The company then successfully challenged the resulting Acas recommendation for recognition on the grounds that the majority of the workforce had not been consulted (*Grunwick* v *ACAS* (1978)).

The Grunwick dispute was the highest profile example of a challenge to Acas under the recognition procedure, but there were a number of others and the procedure was generally accepted to have failed. Even trade union protests were muted when it was repealed by the incoming Conservative government in the Employment Act 1980.

If the 1975 statutory recognition procedure was insufficiently thought through and too brief to cover all eventualities, the same certainly cannot be said of the current procedure, which was introduced by the Employment Relations Act 1999, and is to be found as Sch A1 to TULRCA 1992. It runs to something over 200 paragraphs, covering more than 70 pages of the statute book – and is thus not reproduced here! In addition to TULRCA Sch A1, reference should also be made to the Trade Union Recognition (Method of Collective Bargaining) Order 2000, the Recognition and Derecognition Ballots (Qualified Persons) Order 2000 and the *Code of Practice on Access and Unfair Practices during Recognition and Derecognition Ballots* (2005). The current statutory recognition procedure is operated by the CAC, and their Guidance on the Statutory Recognition Procedure (2007) is an essential tool in understanding the system.

Scope of the statutory recognition scheme

Applications for recognition can only be made by independent trade unions (Sch A1, para 6) and to employers who have at least 21 workers (Sch A1, para 7). 'Worker' is defined in accordance with TULRCA s 296 as including not only employees, but also those who work under a contract personally to perform work for another party who is not a professional client of the worker. In *R (BBC)* v *CAC*

(2003) the issue was whether freelance cameramen and women who provided material for the BBC's Natural History Unit were doing so as 'workers' or whether they were professionals providing services to a client. The High Court quashed a CAC decision that it was necessary to be able to identify a regulatory body before people could be regarded as 'professionals' – but a later CAC held that the cameramen and women were 'workers' for the purposes of s 296.

Trade Union and Labour Relations (Consolidation) Act 1992

SCHEDULE A1

3 (3) References to collective bargaining are to negotiations relating to pay, hours and holidays; but this has effect subject to sub-paragraph (4).

(4) If the parties agree matters as the subject of collective bargaining, references to collective bargaining are to negotiations relating to the agreed matters; and this is the case whether the agreement is made before or after the time when the CAC issues a declaration, or the parties agree, that the union is (or unions are) entitled to conduct collective bargaining on behalf of a bargaining unit.

Comment

(1) The fact that statutory recognition is limited to pay, hours and holidays, unless the parties agree a wider range of issues, is seen by trade unions as one of the weaknesses of the legislation. Unions were particularly keen that training should be included in the list. The compromise reached on this position is that under TULRCA s 70A, employers must consult over training with unions which have statutory recognition at least once every six months. But although the employer is enjoined to 'take account' of the union's comments or suggestions, this can hardly be enforced in practice.

(2) The Employment Relations Act 2004 introduced TULRCA Sch A1, para 171A, which clarifies that negotiations over pay do not include negotiations over pensions. That paragraph also gives the Secretary of State power to amend the list of matters which can be topics for collective bargaining under the statutory procedure.

Compulsory recognition

Application to the CAC

The first step in the recognition process is for the union to make a formal written request for recognition to the employer, identifying the workers (ie, 'the bargaining unit') in respect of whom it seeks recognition. The employer must respond within ten days. If the employer is willing to negotiate, the parties have 20 days or such longer period as they agree in which to do it.

If either the employer refuses the request or no agreement is reached by the end of the negotiating period, the union may apply to the CAC, sending a copy of its application to the employer. The CAC then decides whether or not the application is admissible. The main hurdle for the union to surmount at this stage is to show that it has sufficient support.

Trade Union and Labour Relations (Consolidation) Act 1992

SCHEDULE A1

36 (1) An application . . . is not admissible unless the CAC decides that –
   (a) members of the union (or unions) constitute at least 10 per cent of the workers con-
        stituting the relevant bargaining unit, and
   (b) a majority of the workers constituting the relevant bargaining unit would be likely to
        favour recognition of the union (or unions) as entitled to conduct collective bargaining
        on behalf of the bargaining unit . . .

Comment

(1) Unions normally demonstrate that they have the required 10 per cent membership by providing a list of members to the case manager – the CAC official assigned to the application. This is to preserve the members' privacy vis-à-vis the employer, since they might otherwise feel vulnerable to retaliatory action. Evidence of majority support may be a petition, or 'pledge cards' submitted by workers. The CAC has a general power to require the parties to submit further evidence if it wishes at any stage.

(2) Note that the application for recognition may be made by more than one union – provided that they can demonstrate that they are willing to co-operate and will take part in single table bargaining if the employer so wishes (Sch A1, para 37(2)). However, if more than one union submits competing applications in respect of the same workers (and any overlap of bargaining units will be so construed), none of the applications will be admissible.

(3) An application is also inadmissible if another independent union is already recognised, as the next case dramatically illustrates.

R (on the application of the National Union of Journalists) v Central Arbitration Committee [2006] IRLR 53 Court of Appeal

In 2003 the NUJ was negotiating with Mirror Group Newspapers (MGN) seeking recognition in respect of journalists in the sports division, where it represented more than 50 per cent of the journalists. Out of the blue, MGN signed a recognition agreement with the British Association of Journalists, a union formed as a breakaway from the NUJ in the early 1990s, giving the BAJ exclusive rights to negotiate for journalists in the sports division. The BAJ had only one member in the sports division. The CAC held that the NUJ's application for recognition was inadmissible because the BAJ was already recognised in respect of those workers. The NUJ's application for judicial review of that decision was dismissed by the High Court and the NUJ appealed.

BUXTON LJ: '. . . We are concerned in this case with [TULRCA Sch A1] paragraph 35, which renders certain such applications inadmissible and therefore outwith the jurisdiction of the CAC. Paragraph 35(1) reads as follows:

"An application . . . is not admissible if the CAC is satisfied that there is already in force a collective agreement under which a union is (or unions are) recognised as entitled to conduct collective bargaining on behalf of any workers falling within the relevant bargaining unit . . ."

233

. . . [T]he CAC indicated that it was very far from satisfied about the outcome that its application of paragraph 35 had produced. It said this:

> "Nevertheless, we should like to put on record our firm belief that the exclusionary rule contained in paragraph 35 has not achieved justice in this case. The employer has been able to defeat what are in all probability the wishes of a majority of the relevant workforce by the simple expedient of concluding a voluntary recognition agreement with a wholly unrepresentative union. It may be said that the principle of avoiding CAC adjudication upon inter-union disputes was regarded by Parliament as more important than the principle of providing collective bargaining where a majority of the appropriate workforce desire it. Even accepting that, we think this case displays a lacuna in the legislation. Were the BAJ a non-independent trade union, which it is not, its recognition by the company could be challenged under Part VI of the Schedule. Were the BAJ affiliated to the Trades Union Congress, which it is not, the NUJ could have recourse to the procedures of the TUC to bring about a resolution of the issues raised by the case. Since the BAJ is independent but not affiliated, the defeated majority union has no avenue of potential redress, once it is excluded from the statutory recognition process. This seems to us highly unsatisfactory."

But the nub of the matter, as the CAC recognised in those two passages, was that once the union with which the employer had concluded the agreement was indeed an independent union (as there is no doubt that the BAJ is), then the CAC had, and this court has, to apply the wording of the scheme including paragraph 35. Before the CAC and before the judge a range of matters were argued in relation to the proper construction of paragraph 35. But before us the argument came down to an argument about the meaning of the words "already in force" in that paragraph . . .

Against that background I turn to the question of construction: what is meant by the agreement being "already in force"? As a matter of normal legal or contractual understanding, I would think that an agreement is "in force" when it can be shown to be binding on the parties to it. No one has been able to point to any authoritative, or indeed any, exposition of the meaning of this phrase in general contractual practice, nor have the court's own researches revealed anything of that sort. But that, in my estimation, is straightforwardly what contract lawyers would understand by the statement that an agreement was in force . . .

Mr Hendy [counsel for the NUJ] said to us that "in force" meant more than that there was simply an agreement. That agreement must be reasonably capable of being operated and have reasonable prospects of being so operated.

That formulation and the points listed in Mr Hendy's skeleton argument, to which he said the CAC should have had regard, comes in my view very close, at least in this case, to suggesting that the agreement was in fact a sham. When pressed on that point I did not understand Mr Hendy to resile from such a contention, at least in the sense of saying that it was known that the agreement would never work.

But whatever arguments that were or were not put to them, it is clear that the CAC were very unenthusiastic indeed about this agreement, and alert to the possibilities of paragraph 35 being misused. They heard evidence from the people who made the agreement, and they were best placed to determine (and I have no doubt that if they thought it justified would have determined) whether or not that agreement was a sham. There is no basis on which this court can make such a finding or come near to doing so.

Once it is agreed, or at least accepted, that the agreement is genuine, albeit being used to an end that paragraph 35 did not envisage, the additional requirements argued for by Mr Hendy simply cannot stand up. As the CAC held, there may come a time when failure to act or impossibility cause the agreement to collapse or force a tribunal to say that it has collapsed. But unless the possibility of the agreement operating is simply not believed in by the parties to it, and as we have seen the CAC did not so find, it is wrong as a matter of contract, or indeed as a matter of logic, to say that an agreement does not come into present force simply on the basis of doubts about its future viability . . .

All that the CAC was looking for, and all that it needed to look for, was an earnest desire to work within the agreement; not evidence that any of its specific provisions had in fact been carried out. Granted that the agreement was in existence, the evidence that the parties had dealt according to any of its terms, even if those were not the terms that gave it its status as a collective agreement, was in my judgement sufficient to show that the written agreement, genuinely signed up to, was not merely a piece of paper.

I would therefore uphold the CAC and the judge on this part of the case.'

(Latham LJ and Sir Martin Nourse agreed.)

Comment

(1) Would you agree with the CAC's conclusion that this case shows a lacuna in the legislation?

(2) Note the CAC's reference to the BAJ's status as an independent trade union. If it were non-independent, its recognition could have been attacked under Sch A1, Part VI; if it were then derecognised, the NUJ's application could have gone ahead. But in the actual circumstances of the case, the result of the BAJ being recognised was to bar an application from any other independent trade union.

(3) If an application is unsuccessful at this stage, it may not be renewed for three years in respect of the same, or substantially the same bargaining unit (Sch A1, paras 39–41). This is to prevent the possibility of vexatious repeated applications.

(4) If the application is successful, there are three main possibilities:

(a) The employer and union agree on recognition and exit the procedure: this is called 'semi-voluntary recognition' by the CAC and is discussed below.
(b) The CAC moves to consider whether the proposed bargaining unit is appropriate.
(c) If the parties are agreed on the bargaining unit, the CAC moves to consider whether recognition should be ordered, or whether there should be a ballot.

The bargaining unit

Trade Union and Labour Relations (Consolidation) Act 1992

SCHEDULE A1

19B (1) This paragraph applies if the CAC has to decide whether a bargaining unit is appropriate for the purposes of paragraph 19(2) or (3) or 19A(2) or (3).
(2) The CAC must take these matters into account –
    (a) the need for the unit to be compatible with effective management;
    (b) the matters listed in sub-paragraph (3), so far as they do not conflict with that need.
(3) The matters are –
    (a) the views of the employer and of the union (or unions);
    (b) existing national and local bargaining arrangements;
    (c) the desirability of avoiding small fragmented bargaining units within an undertaking;

(d) the characteristics of workers falling within the bargaining unit under consideration and of any other employees of the employer whom the CAC considers relevant;

(e) the location of workers.

(4) In taking an employer's views into account for the purpose of deciding whether the proposed bargaining unit is appropriate, the CAC must take into account any view the employer has about any other bargaining unit that he considers would be appropriate.

(5) The CAC must give notice of its decision to the parties.

Comment

(1) The Employment Relations Act 2004 amended Sch A1, para 19 to make it clear that the CAC should first consider whether the bargaining unit proposed by the union is appropriate (giving statutory force to the Court of Appeal's decision in *R (Kwik-Fit Ltd) v CAC* (2002)). If it considers it is not, it must decide itself what the appropriate bargaining unit is, taking into account the matters listed in para 19B.

(2) To facilitate this, para 18A stipulates that the employer must provide information about numbers, categories and location of workers in the union's proposed bargaining unit within five working days of being notified that the union's application has been accepted as admissible.

Should there be a ballot?

The next question for the CAC is whether it should order a ballot in the bargaining unit, to see if the workforce wants the union to represent them, or simply to order recognition. As the union has to establish that it has majority support (although only 10 per cent membership) in the bargaining unit as a condition of its application being held to be admissible, it might be thought that a ballot would be unnecessary. In practice, it depends firstly on whether the union has a majority of members in the bargaining unit.

Trade Union and Labour Relations (Consolidation) Act 1992

SCHEDULE A1

22 (1) This paragraph applies if . . .

(b) the CAC is satisfied that a majority of the workers constituting the bargaining unit are members of the union (or unions).

(2) The CAC must issue a declaration that the union is (or unions are) recognised as entitled to conduct collective bargaining on behalf of the workers constituting the bargaining unit.

(3) But if any of the three qualifying conditions is fulfilled, instead of issuing a declaration under sub-paragraph (2) the CAC must give notice to the parties that it intends to arrange for the holding of a secret ballot in which the workers constituting the bargaining unit are asked whether they want the union (or unions) to conduct collective bargaining on their behalf.

(4) These are the three qualifying conditions –

(a) the CAC is satisfied that a ballot should be held in the interests of good industrial relations;

(b) the CAC has evidence, which it considers to be credible, from a significant number of the union members within the bargaining unit that they do not want the union (or unions) to conduct collective bargaining on their behalf;

   (c)   membership evidence is produced which leads the CAC to conclude that there are doubts whether a significant number of the union members within the bargaining unit want the union (or unions) to conduct collective bargaining on their behalf.

(5)   For the purposes of sub-paragraph (4)(c) membership evidence is –

   (a)   evidence about the circumstances in which union members became members;

   (b)   evidence about the length of time for which union members have been members, in a case where the CAC is satisfied that such evidence should be taken into account.

Comment

(1) This lays down a basic rule that majority representation leads to automatic recognition – but immediately qualifies it by opening up the possibility for having a ballot in some circumstances. Originally, it was intended that recognition would be automatic if a majority of workers in the bargaining unit belonged to the union. However, the CBI lobbied hard for ballots even in these circumstances. The resulting compromise is contained in para 22. Concerns that para 22(3) would lead to a situation where balloting became the norm have not been borne out: the CAC Annual Report for 2006/07 shows that since the scheme came into force, recognition has been ordered without a ballot in 74 cases and ballots ordered in 143 cases (the figures do not indicate in how many of these cases the union had majority membership). If the union has less than a majority membership in the bargaining unit, a ballot will always be held (Sch A1, para 23).

(2) Both employers and unions have expressed concerns about the other side using dubious tactics to influence the decision as to whether to ballot. Unions may claim that employees have been 'leaned on' to write letters or otherwise indicate that they do not wish the union to represent them; employers may feel that the union has artificially boosted its numbers by offering discounted or even free membership to workers in the bargaining unit. These are the sorts of things the CAC may take into account.

(3) Once a ballot has been ordered, the possibilities for an acrimonious campaign, with employees caught in the crossfire, escalate. In the light of the experience of the first few years of the statutory procedure, the Employment Relations Act 2004 attempted to stem this by prohibiting certain kinds of unfair practices.

Trade Union and Labour Relations (Consolidation) Act 1992

SCHEDULE A1

27A   (1)   Each of the parties . . . must refrain from using any unfair practice.

(2)   A party uses an unfair practice if, with a view to influencing the result of the ballot, the party –

   (a)   offers to pay money or give money's worth to a worker entitled to vote in the ballot in return for the worker's agreement to vote in a particular way or to abstain from voting,

   (b)   makes an outcome-specific offer to a worker entitled to vote in the ballot,

   (c)   coerces or attempts to coerce a worker entitled to vote in the ballot to disclose –

      (i)   whether he intends to vote or to abstain from voting in the ballot, or

      (ii)   how he intends to vote, or how he has voted, in the ballot,

   (d)   dismisses or threatens to dismiss a worker,

   (e)   takes or threatens to take disciplinary action against a worker,

(f)   subjects or threatens to subject a worker to any other detriment, or

(g)   uses or attempts to use undue influence on a worker entitled to vote in the ballot.

(3)   For the purposes of sub-paragraph (2)(b) an 'outcome-specific offer' is an offer to pay money or give money's worth which –

(a)   is conditional on the issuing by the CAC of a declaration that –

    (i)   the union is (or unions are) recognised as entitled to conduct collective bargaining on behalf of the bargaining unit, or

    (ii)   the union is (or unions are) not entitled to be so recognised, and

(b)   is not conditional on anything which is done or occurs as a result of the declaration in question . . .

Comment

(1) To avoid the sorts of problems that arose in *Grunwick* v *ACAS* (1978), Sch A1, para 26 imposes five duties on the employer. These are:

(a)   to co-operate generally in the holding of the ballot;

(b)   to allow the union reasonable access to the workers;

(c)   to provide the CAC with the names and addresses of workers in the bargaining unit;

(d)   to refrain from offering workers inducements not to attend meetings organised by the union; and

(e)   not to take, or threaten, retaliatory action against any workers attending such meetings.

(2) In addition to the detailed rules in Sch A1, access to workers during the period of recognition ballots is governed by the *Code of Practice on Access and Unfair Practices during Recognition and Derecognition Ballots* (2005).

(3) The ballot must be conducted by a qualified independent person (QIP), as laid down in the Recognition and Derecognition Ballots (Qualified Persons) Order 2000. The costs of the ballot are shared equally between the union and the employer. Like other industrial relations ballots, this must be secret, but unusually, need not be fully postal: the CAC can order a workplace ballot, or part-postal ballot.

(4) To win the ballot, the union must get not only a majority voting in favour, but that majority must also constitute at least 40 per cent of the workers in the bargaining unit (Sch A1, para 29(3)). This makes it a very high hurdle: it means that if a worker does not bother to vote, she or he will count as a vote against. The CAC's Annual Report for 2006/07 shows that, of 143 ballots under the statutory procedure to date, unions have failed to achieve the necessary majority in 55. Do you think that there is any justification for requiring a special majority for recognition to be ordered?

Recognition

If the ballot result is in favour of recognition, the CAC must declare that the union is recognised and the parties then have 30 days in which to agree the method of collective bargaining – effectively, the procedural collective agreement (TULRCA Sch A1, paras 29, 30). If they are unable to do so, the CAC can impose a method in accordance with the Trade Union Recognition (Method of Collective Bargaining) Order 2000.

The employer is then legally bound to negotiate with the union: but the legislation does not stipulate that they must reach agreement, or even that the negotiations must be 'with a view to reaching agreement' (the formula used in other statutory consultation requirements). The rationale for this is that there is no such requirement where voluntary collective bargaining takes place, and the purpose of the statutory recognition procedure was only to put unions in the same position as a union voluntarily recognised by the employer. There is no sanction, such as existed under the 1975 statutory recognition procedure, whereby the employees can be awarded better terms and conditions. Thus it is open to employers to 'go through the motions' without actually agreeing to anything.

Semi-voluntary recognition

The parties can opt out of the statutory procedure at any time if they make their own 'agreement for recognition'. This is dealt with in TULRCA Sch A1, Part II, where it is called 'voluntary recognition', but because this might cause confusion with the true form of voluntary recognition which occurs where an employer agrees to recognise a union without reference to the statutory recognition procedure, the CAC describes it as 'semi-voluntary' recognition in its Guidance on Statutory Recognition, and that term is adopted here too.

Trade Union and Labour Relations (Consolidation) Act 1992

SCHEDULE A1

56 (1) The employer may not terminate an agreement for recognition before the relevant period ends.

(2) After that period ends the employer may terminate the agreement, with or without the consent of the union (or unions).

(3) The union (or unions) may terminate an agreement for recognition at any time, with or without the consent of the employer.

(4) Sub-paragraphs (1) to (3) have effect subject to the terms of the agreement or any other agreement of the parties.

(5) The relevant period is the period of three years starting with the day after the date of the agreement.

Comment

(1) This illustrates the difference between semi-voluntary recognition (an 'agreement for recognition') and genuine voluntary recognition which takes place outside the statutory procedure. It remains the case that outside the statutory procedure, the employer is free to derecognise the union at any time. But an agreement for recognition made in the context of an agreed exit from the statutory procedure is binding on the employer for three years.

(2) Note that after three years, the employer is free to derecognise without further ado. This contrasts with the position where recognition was ordered by the CAC. We turn, finally, to that issue.

Derecognition

Derecognition under the statutory procedure can occur in three situations, summarised in the CAC's Guide to the procedure.

CAC Guide to Statutory Recognition (2007)

12.5 Part IV (derecognition where recognition was achieved following a ballot): applies where an employer, or worker seeks to derecognise a union which was recognised under Part I. Statutory derecognition can only take place three years or more after recognition was granted. The employer can ask the union to end recognition arrangements and if the union does not agree, the employer can apply to the CAC asking for an end to the bargaining arrangement. The CAC conducts tests similar to the Part I admissibility tests in reverse, and the question is settled by a ballot. A worker or workers in the bargaining unit can apply to the CAC for an end to the bargaining arrangements. The employer can also apply for derecognition on the grounds that the entire workforce has fallen below 21. The CAC has produced a Guide to Part IV.

12.6 Part V (derecognition where recognition was achieved without a ballot): This applies where the union was granted recognition under Part I or Part III without a ballot. The differences from Part IV are that only the employer can make use of this Part of the Schedule and the test for accepting the employer's application is whether fewer than half the workers in the bargaining unit are members of the union. As with Part IV, the question of derecognition is settled by a ballot. Again the employer cannot apply for three years after recognition was granted.

12.7 Part VI (derecognition where the union is not independent): If a non-independent union is voluntarily recognised for collective bargaining purposes, a worker or workers within the bargaining unit can apply to the CAC to have the bargaining arrangements ended. While the workers concerned can be backed by another union, that union cannot itself use this route. Again the CAC applies some initial tests of admissibility, attempts to help the employer, union and worker to end the bargaining arrangements and arranges a ballot to take place if necessary. This process has to be halted if the non-independent union obtains a certificate of independence. The main difference between this route and Parts IV and V is that, under Part VI, a worker can apply any time after recognition was granted – there is no need to wait for three years.

12.8 Part VII (loss of independence): If a union recognised under Part I of the Schedule loses its certificate of independence, then statutory recognition ceases.

Conclusion

At the end of the 1970s, trade union membership was at its highest and around 70 per cent of the workforce were reckoned to be covered by collective bargaining. That coverage declined markedly in the 1980s and 1990s, when government policy favoured individualised contracts and discouraged collective bargaining. A recent DTI report estimated that by 2005, only 35.3 per cent of all employees were covered by collective agreements – and that percentage masks a huge difference between the public and private sectors. While over 70 per cent of public sector employees are still covered by collective agreements, this applies to only just over 20 per cent of private sector employees.

Has the statutory recognition scheme had any real impact on this position? The number of applications to the CAC for recognition has varied between 57 and 118 per year, with a peak occurring in 2003/04. There were 64 applications in 2006/07 and there now seems to be a fairly stable flow, rather than a declining trend. The CAC estimates that it ordered recognition for collective bargaining in respect of 23,000 workers in the first five years of operation of the statutory recognition scheme. While important for them, this is a very small percentage of the working population.

INFORMATION AND CONSULTATION

In order to bargain effectively, trade unions need information about the employer's business. Thus when the original statutory recognition procedure was introduced in 1975, a duty to disclose certain kinds of information to recognised trade unions was also introduced. It survived the repeal of that procedure in 1980 and is now to be found in TULRCA ss 181–185.

Dialogue between management and workers is at the heart of the 'social partnership' model of employment relations which is fundamental to EU social policy discussed earlier in this chapter. In other countries in the European Union employees have long been consulted and taken part in decision-making, through their representation on works councils or even through worker-directors on the boards of companies. Thus it is not surprising to find that many of the requirements in British law for employers to consult with their employees came about as a result of EU initiatives. These include consultation over redundancies and transfers, dealt with in Chapter 9, but also two general consultation duties, which are discussed here.

Disclosure of information under TULRCA

Trade Union and Labour Relations (Consolidation) Act 1992

181 (1) An employer who recognises an independent trade union shall, for the purposes of all stages of collective bargaining about matters, and in relation to descriptions of workers, in respect of which the union is recognised by him, disclose to representatives of the union, on request, the information required by this section.

In this section and sections 182 to 185 'representative', in relation to a trade union, means an official or other person authorised by the union to carry on such collective bargaining.

(2) The information to be disclosed is all information relating to the employer's undertaking which is in his possession, or that of an associated employer, and is information –

(a) without which the trade union representatives would be to a material extent impeded in carrying on collective bargaining with him, and

(b) which it would be in accordance with good industrial relations practice that he should disclose to them for the purposes of collective bargaining . . .

182 (1) An employer is not required by section 181 to disclose information –

(a) the disclosure of which would be against the interests of national security, or

(b) which he could not disclose without contravening a prohibition imposed by or under an enactment, or

(c) which has been communicated to him in confidence, or which he has otherwise obtained in consequence of the confidence reposed in him by another person, or

(d) which relates specifically to an individual (unless that individual has consented to its being disclosed), or

(e) the disclosure of which would cause substantial injury to his undertaking for reasons other than its effect on collective bargaining, or

(f) obtained by him for the purpose of bringing, prosecuting or defending any legal proceedings.

In formulating the provisions of any Code of Practice relating to the disclosure of information, ACAS shall have regard to the provisions of this subsection.

(2) In the performance of his duty under section 181 an employer is not required –

(a) to produce, or allow inspection of, any document (other than a document prepared for the purpose of conveying or confirming the information) or to make a copy of or extracts from any document, or

(b) to compile or assemble any information where the compilation or assembly would involve an amount of work or expenditure out of reasonable proportion to the value of the information in the conduct of collective bargaining.

Comment

(1) The reason that this was not repealed when the original statutory recognition procedure was repealed in 1980 was that the duty to disclose information is triggered by recognition. Thus an employer who did not want to disclose information could simply avoid the duty by refusing to recognise the union.

(2) In any case, note that TULRCA s 182 sets out numerous exceptions to the duty to disclose, one of the most controversial of which is the last – where the cost of assembling the information would be out of proportion to its value (in whose eyes?).

(3) There is an Acas *Code of Practice on Disclosure of Information to Trade Unions for Collective Bargaining Purposes* (1998), which gives guidance on the kinds of information that should be disclosed.

Acas Code of Practice 2

DISCLOSURE OF INFORMATION TO TRADE UNIONS FOR COLLECTIVE BARGAINING PURPOSES (1998)

11 Collective bargaining within an undertaking can range from negotiations on specific matters arising daily at the workplace affecting particular sections of the workforce, to extensive periodic negotiations on terms and conditions of employment affecting the whole workforce in multi-plant companies. The relevant information and the depth, detail and form in which it could be presented to negotiators will vary accordingly. Consequently, it is not possible to compile a list of items that should be disclosed in all circumstances. Some examples of information relating to the undertaking which could be relevant in certain collective bargaining situations are given overleaf:

(i) *Pay and benefits:* principles and structure of payment systems; job evaluation systems and grading criteria; earnings and hours analysed according to work-group, grade, plant, sex, out-workers and homeworkers, department or division, giving, where appropriate, distributions and make-up of pay showing any additions to basic rate or salary; total pay bill; details of fringe benefits and non-wage labour costs.

(ii) *Conditions of service:* policies on recruitment, redeployment, redundancy, training, equal opportunity, and promotion; appraisal systems; health, welfare and safety matters.

(iii) *Manpower:* numbers employed analysed according to grade, department, location, age and sex; labour turnover; absenteeism; overtime and short-time; manning standards; planned changes in work methods, materials, equipment or organisation; available manpower plans; investment plans.

(iv) *Performance:* productivity and efficiency data; savings from increased productivity and output, return on capital invested; sales and state of order book.

(v) *Financial:* cost structures; gross and net profits; sources of earnings; assets; liabilities; allocation of profits; details of government financial assistance; transfer prices; loans to parent or subsidiary companies and interest charged.

12 These examples are not intended to represent a check list of information that should be provided for all negotiations. Nor are they meant to be an exhaustive list of types of information as other items may be relevant in particular negotiations.

Comment

(1) If a trade union considers that an employer is in breach of this duty to disclose information, it may make a complaint to the CAC. The CAC may refer the matter to Acas for conciliation or may proceed to hear and determine the complaint (as it will also do if conciliation fails). Where the CAC upholds the complaint, it will specify the information which should have been disclosed and a timetable for its disclosure (TULRCA s 183).

(2) If the employer still refuses to disclose the information, the union must complain again to the CAC and may also bid for certain improvements to be included in the employees' terms and conditions of employment. If the CAC finds the further complaint to be well founded, it makes a declaration to that effect and may also award the improvements requested (TULRCA ss 184–185). In effect, the employer is treated as having impeded the collective bargaining process, and the sanction is not to force disclosure, but to give the workforce the kinds of improvements to their working conditions, which could perhaps have been expected to result from proper collective bargaining.

(3) The Acas Code does not of itself impose any legal obligation to disclose information, nor does failure to observe the Code render anyone liable; however, the Code must be taken into account where relevant in any proceedings before the CAC.

(4) Since the turn of the century, the number of complaints to the CAC under this jurisdiction has been small – between six and eleven per year. Many are settled voluntarily with CAC or Acas assistance and few declarations are necessary.

(5) Shareholders in companies get regular information, including financial information, about the company via its annual report. Although employees have no right to receive similar information, employers increasingly make some version of the annual report available to them too. Under the Companies Act 1985 Sch 7, para 11, companies with more than 250 employees must include in the annual report a statement of action that has been taken during the year to make arrangements providing employees systematically with information on matters of concern to them as employees, consulting them or their representatives on a regular basis so that the views of employees can be taken into account in making decisions which are likely to affect their interests, encouraging their involvement in the company's performance through an employees' share scheme or by some other means, and achieving a common awareness of the financial and economic factors affecting the performance of the company.

European Works Councils

European Works Council Directive (94/45/EC)

ARTICLE 1: OBJECTIVE

1 The purpose of this Directive is to improve the right to information and to consultation of employees in Community-scale undertakings and Community-scale groups of undertakings.

2 To that end, a European Works Council or a procedure for informing and consulting employees shall be established in every Community-scale undertaking and every Community-scale group of undertakings, where requested in the manner laid down in Article 5(1), with the purpose of informing and consulting employees under the terms, in the manner and with the effects laid down in this Directive.

ARTICLE 2: DEFINITIONS

1 For the purposes of this Directive:
   (a) 'Community-scale undertaking' means any undertaking with at least 1,000 employees within the Member States and at least 150 employees in each of at least two Member States;
   (b) 'group of undertakings' means a controlling undertaking and its controlled undertakings;
   (c) 'Community-scale group of undertakings' means a group of undertakings with the following characteristics:
   – at least 1,000 employees within the Member States,
   – at least two group undertakings in different Member States, and
   – at least one group undertaking with at least 150 employees in one Member State and at least one other group undertaking with at least 150 employees in another Member State; . . .
   (f) 'consultation' means the exchange of views and establishment of dialogue between employees' representatives and central management or any more appropriate level of management . . .

Comment

(1) The recitals in the preamble to this directive refer to the 'transnationalisation' of business through cross-border mergers, takeovers, joint ventures and the like, and the consequent need to inform and consult representatives of employees 'if economic activities are to develop in a harmonious fashion'. How compelling is this argument, in your view?

(2) Although this issue was referred to the social partners, they were unable to agree a proposal. The directive was therefore drawn up by the Commission and was adopted by all the member states with the exception of the United Kingdom under the Social Chapter Protocol attached to the Treaty of European Union. It therefore did not apply to the United Kingdom when it was passed, although many British companies were affected by it through their operations in other EU states and some chose to act in accordance with it anyway, in case the stance of the United Kingdom changed. This was sensible, as the Labour government elected in 1997 withdrew its opt-out and the European Works Council Directive was extended to the United Kingdom by Directive 97/74/EC and had to be implemented by December 1999.

(3) The directive was implemented in the United Kingdom by the Transnational Information and Consultation of Employees Regulations 1999 (TICE). However, transnational enterprises which already had a procedure for informing and consulting employees on transnational issues before the deadline for implementation of the original directive (22 September 1996) were exempt from the requirements of TICE. This was the main reason for British companies concluding such agreements even when the directive did not apply to the United Kingdom.

(4) Obligations under TICE are not automatic: they are triggered only when a request is made by at least 100 employees or their representatives from at least two different establishments in at least two different member states (TICE reg 9). When this happens, management has six months in which to set up a special negotiating body (SNB).

Transnational Information and Consultation of Employees Regulations 1999

11 The special negotiating body shall have the task of determining, with the central management, by written agreement, the scope, composition, functions, and term of office of a European Works Council or the arrangements for implementing an information and consultation procedure.

Comment

(1) The special negotiating body consists of between three and seventeen members, including at least one representative from each member state in which the company operates, elected or appointed from the workforce.

(2) Note that the SNB need not conclude that there should be a European Works Council: they may decide instead that there should be some other kind of information and consultation procedure (TICE reg 17). If so, there must be some provision for representatives to meet together to discuss the information they receive.

(3) If the SNB cannot reach agreement, or fails to do so within three years of its being set up, the fall-back arrangements in the Schedule to TICE apply instead. These are highly prescriptive, so there is some incentive for management to reach agreement with employee representatives to avoid this.

(4) Curiously, although the TICE Regulations go into great detail about the procedure for setting up an EWC, there is almost nothing in the main part of the Regulations about the subject matter on which information should be provided or consultation take place. Thus TICE reg 17 stipulates a number of conditions for the composition and procedure of EWCs but says only that if the parties agree instead on an information and consultation procedure, 'the information conveyed . . . shall relate in particular to transnational questions which significantly affect the interests of the employees' (reg 17(5)(b)). However, the fall-back procedure contained in the Schedule to TICE indicates the sort of information and consultation which is envisaged.

Transnational Information and Consultation of Employees Regulations 1999

SCHEDULE

6 (1) The competence of the European Works Council shall be limited to information and consultation on the matters which concern the Community-scale undertaking or

Community-scale group of undertakings as a whole or at least two of its establishments or group undertakings situated in different Member States.

(2) In the case of a Community-scale undertaking or Community-scale group of under-takings falling within regulation 5(1)(b) or 5(1)(c), the competence of the European Works Council shall be limited to those matters concerning all of its establishments or group under-takings situated within the Member States or concerning at least two of its establishments or group undertakings situated in different Member States.

7 (1) Subject to paragraph 8, the European Works Council shall have the right to meet with the central management once a year in an information and consultation meeting, to be informed and consulted, on the basis of a report drawn up by the central management, on the progress of the business of the Community-scale undertaking or Community-scale group of under-takings and its prospects.

(2) The central management shall inform the local managements accordingly.

(3) The information and consultation meeting shall relate in particular to the structure, eco-nomic and financial situation, the probable development of the business and of production and sales, the situation and probable trend of employment, investments, and substantial changes concerning organisation, introduction of new working methods or production processes, trans-fers of production, mergers, cut-backs or closures of undertakings, establishments or important parts thereof, and collective redundancies.

8 (1) Where there are exceptional circumstances affecting the employees' interests to a considerable extent, particularly in the event of relocations, the closure of establishments or undertakings or collective redundancies, the select committee or, where no such committee exists, the European Works Council shall have the right to be informed. It shall have the right to meet in an exceptional information and consultation meeting, at its request, the central man-agement, or any other more appropriate level of management within the Community-scale undertaking or group of undertakings having its own powers of decision, so as to be informed and consulted on measures significantly affecting employees' interests.

Comment

(1) Under TICE reg 24, information need not be disclosed if it would 'seriously harm the functioning of, or would be prejudicial to, the undertaking or group of undertakings concerned', according to objective criteria. In case of dispute over this, the CAC has jurisdiction.

(2) It is possible for management to disclose information to representatives in confidence, in which case the obligation of confidence is permanent (TICE reg 23). Employees who act as representatives at any stage of the setting up or operation of an EWC of information and consultation procedure are entitled to paid time off to carry out their duties (TICE regs 25–27) and are protected from detriment or dismissal in relation to carrying out their duties (TICE regs 28–32).

(3) The emphasis on procedure in the directive and the TICE Regulations and the corresponding lack of focus on content is arguably symbolic. The European Works Councils initiative has barely had any effect on workers in multinational companies and an ETUC report estimated that only about one-third of affected companies had been asked by employees to set up an EWC. One reason for this may be that employees fre-quently regard their fellow employees in other countries as competitors for jobs and investment, rather than as colleagues with a common interest.

NATIONAL CONSULTATION

Building on the European Works Council Directive and the general philosophy of social partnership, the EU Commission proposed a directive which would impose a general obligation to consult with employees in 1998. It was blocked for some while by a coalition of four member states, led by the United Kingdom. In 2001 the other three countries dropped their objections and the United Kingdom reluctantly followed suit. Thus the Information and Consultation Directive (2002/14/EC) was agreed by the European Parliament and Council in 2002 and implemented in the United Kingdom by the Information and Consultation of Employees Regulations 2004 (ICE).

The ICE Regulations came into force in April 2005, at that stage covering undertakings with at least 150 employees. In April 2006 they were extended to undertakings with at least 100 employees, and since April 2007, have applied to undertakings with at least 50 employees. Like the TICE Regulations, the procedure is started by a request from a specific proportion of employees (ICE reg 7), unless there is already a pre-existing agreement in place (ICE reg 8).

Stewart v *Moray Council* [2006] IRLR 592 Employment Appeal Tribunal

ELIAS J: '*The context*

The Information and Consultation of Employees Regulations 2004 impose obligations on employers of large workforces to put in place arrangements to ensure that employees are informed and consulted on a wide range of business, employment and restructuring issues. The Regulations are intended to give effect to European Directive 2002/14/EC which established a general framework for informing and consulting employees in the European Union. The Regulations came into force on 6 April 2005.

The Regulations set out a complex structure for securing the rights conferred on the employees. The employer is not under an automatic duty to set up or reach an agreement on information and consultation arrangements. The employer may initiate a negotiating process even in the absence of any interest shown by the employees, but is only obliged to do so if there is a request by at least 10% of the employees in an undertaking (subject to a minimum of 15 employees and a maximum of 2,500): reg 7. Once that request is made, the employer must undertake negotiations to seek to reach an agreement on information and consultation arrangements pursuant to reg 14, unless he seeks to challenge the validity of the request under reg 13 or to test support for the request under reg 8.

The Regulations set out in terms how the employer is to conduct the negotiations to establish such an agreement (regs 14 and 15), and they also identify the conditions which any such agreement must meet (reg 16). In the absence of an agreement successfully being negotiated, there is a default position, what is termed in the Regulations the "standard information and consultation provisions" (reg 18). This involves the employer informing or consulting elected employee information and consultation representatives (reg 20).

However, the Government's intention was that these Regulations should permit a certain amount of flexibility in the way in which the arrangements were made, and to support agreements voluntarily established. To that end, it is provided in reg 8 that where at the date of a request there are already agreements in place (termed "pre-existing agreements") which meet certain minimum standards identified in the Regulations, then the employer is not automatically required to undertake negotiations to reach an information and consultation agreement merely at the request of 10% of the employees. That obligation arises only if 40% of the employees request that such negotiations should take place. In circumstances where the relevant pre-existing agreements are in place, the employer, if requested by employees constituting between 10% and 40% of the employees in the workforce, may – not must – hold a ballot in which the employees are given the opportunity to say whether they support the request for a negotiated agreement to be made. If in that ballot the request for a negotiated agreement is supported by at least 40% of the employees and by a majority of those voting, then the employer must take appropriate steps to seek to enter into the negotiated agreement. But if not, then he is entitled to continue to operate the pre-existing agreements and to give effect to the objectives of the Directive in that way.

In this case a percentage of employees between 10 and 40% did make a request for a negotiated agreement and the council wished to hold a ballot to determine whether or not there was sufficient support among the workforce to require it to seek to make a negotiated agreement. The pre-condition for that, as we have indicated, is that the pre-existing agreements have to meet certain requirements. The council alleged that they did, but Mr Stewart submitted that they did not. The procedure for determining that conflict is for the employee to make a complaint to the Central Arbitration Committee under reg 10. It is then for that committee to determine whether the relevant conditions have been satisfied or not. There is an appeal from the CAC on a point of law to the Employment Appeal Tribunal pursuant to section 21 of the Employment Tribunals Act 1996 . . .

The CAC decision

The CAC set out the context in which this issue arose. Mr Stewart is an employee of the Moray Council ("the council"). It was accepted that over 500 employees requested the council to initiate negotiations to reach an agreement under the Regulations, which number is between 10 and 40% of the council's employees. The council notified Mr Stewart that it intended to hold a ballot in accordance with reg 8(2). It submitted that there were three pre-existing agreements for the purposes of the Regulations. These were: the Framework Local Regulation and procedure agreement; the Moray Council officer trade union group agreement; and a protocol for consultation with trade unions. The framework agreement was for teachers and the officer trade union group agreement was for all other staff including chief officers. The protocol related to the latter agreement, applying to all consultations with non-teaching staff representatives.

The council submitted that these agreements, taken together, satisfied the provisions of reg 8(1). Each was in writing; taken together they covered all the employees of the undertaking in the sense that each employee was within one of the groups of workers in respect of whom the agreement was made; they had been agreed by the relevant trade unions which represented a majority of the workforce; and they provided for the procedure for giving information to employees or their representatives and to seek their views on such information.

Mr Stewart contended that these agreements were quite inadequate to meet the requirements of reg 8. He conceded that they were in writing but submitted that they failed to comply with the other requirements. His principal argument was that these three agreements were simply agreements with the relevant trade unions; they provided for consultation with the trade union representatives and there was no procedure for ensuring that the interests of non-unionists would be taken into consideration. It was, he submitted, misleading to say that the agreements covered all the employees of the undertaking. The union officials did not act so as to represent the interest of any non-union employees; their concern was with their trade union members. Moreover, he submitted that under the officer trade union group constitution, full time officers who are not employees could attend meetings whereas employees who were not union members could not.

Nor had these agreements been approved by the employees. The non-members had had no opportunity to approve or reject these agreements at all. These agreements were negotiated without any reference to non-members or their interests whatsoever. There had been no separate endorsement by the employees as a whole.

The CAC considered these submissions. They found for the council on the specific matters relied upon by Mr Stewart but they concluded nonetheless that the agreements failed to comply with the fourth condition set out in reg 8, in that one of them, namely the framework agreement relating to teachers, did not set out how the employer was to give information to the employees or their representative and seek their views on that information . . .

In our judgment the CAC did not err in law. It is true that reg 8(1) is not as clearly formulated as it might be. For example, if one says that each of the requirements of reg 8(1) must be met by each agreement then, on a literal interpretation, in the case of multiple agreements each would have to cover all the employees. Plainly that cannot be right. The point of multiple agreements is that cumulatively they cover all employees but different agreements will cover different groups of employees.

However, whilst recognising that no construction is wholly without difficulty, in our opinion it is tolerably clear that whereas reg 8(1)(b) has to be met by the agreements read together, each of the other requirements has to be met by each individual agreement. It is not good enough for merely one of the agreements to do so even if it covers the majority of the employees or a substantial proportion of them. In our judgment this is supported by the following considerations. First, reg 8 refers to "each of the agreements" where there is more than one pre-existing agreement; they are not treated as merely parts of one overall pre-existing agreement. Reg 2 then in turn defines a pre-existing agreement as one where each of the conditions of reg 8(1)(a) to (d) are satisfied. It follows, in our view, that each must satisfy each of those conditions (subject to the point we have made about para (b)).

Second, there is no justification in the language of the regulation itself to suggest that it is sufficient for the conditions to be met only by agreements covering the majority of the employees or a substantial proportion of them. It is not a legitimate reading of this Regulation to read in any such limitation, and the definition of a pre-existing agreement in reg 2 tells against it.

Third, the purpose of the provision seems to us to be consistent with it being construed so as to enable the employer to test whether or not the employees support the request for an information and consultation arrangement only when all the employees are subject to agreements which meet the conditions. After all, the effect of the ballot may be to defeat the right to have the statutory procedures at all and to leave the voluntary pre-existing arrangements in place. In those circumstances one might expect that if the existing arrangements are to be given priority, the minimum standards set down in reg 8 (whatever they might require) should at least apply to all employees.

It follows that the appeal itself fails. The CAC were right to find that reg 8(1)(d) was not satisfied with respect to one of the pre-existing agreements . . .'

Comment

(1) The first part of this decision provides a useful summary of the purpose and structure of the ICE Regulations. The case also illustrates a problem to which ICE may give rise: the potential destabilisation of existing information, consultation and bargaining arrangements. Unlike the provisions for consultation over redundancies, transfers and health and safety, the ICE Regulations (and TICE Regulations) do not give primacy to the trade union channel. In this case, the council clearly had longstanding arrangements with trade unions (as is common in public sector organisations) – but because one of these agreements was defective in the level of detail it gave about how employees would

be informed or consulted, the council was unable to rely on the 'pre-existing agreement' let-out and was compelled to begin new negotiations under ICE reg 7.

(2) The employee cross-appealed on the CAC's rejection of his argument that the agreements did not cover all employees because they were made with unions on behalf of union members and had not been put to the approval of all employees in any sort of ballot. The EAT upholds the approach of the CAC that as collective agreements cover all employees in a bargaining unit, not just union members, the agreements should be taken to cover all employees. This seems right. However, the point as to whether or not the agreements were appropriately approved by the relevant employees was left open. It is an important issue which may well arise for future decision.

(3) As with the TICE Regulations, the ICE Regulations focus more on the format for initiating and implementing a procedure than on the subject matter for consultation. If the parties cannot reach an agreement on a method for information and consultation, fall-back arrangements ('the standard information and consultation provisions') in ICE Regs 18–20 will apply. This indicates the subject matter which would be normal in such a procedure.

Information and Consultation of Employees Regulations 2004

20 (1) Where the standard information and consultation provisions apply pursuant to regulation 18, the employer must provide the information and consultation representatives with information on –

    (a) the recent and probable development of the undertaking's activities and economic situation;

    (b) the situation, structure and probable development of employment within the undertaking and on any anticipatory measures envisaged, in particular, where there is a threat to employment within the undertaking; and

    (c) subject to paragraph (5), decisions likely to lead to substantial changes in work organisation or in contractual relations, including those referred to in –

        (i) sections 188 to 192 of the Trade Union and Labour Relations (Consolidation) Act 1992; and

        (ii) regulations 13 to 16 of the Transfer of Undertakings (Protection of Employment) Regulations 2006.

    (2) The information referred to in paragraph (1) must be given at such time, in such fashion and with such content as are appropriate to enable, in particular, the information and consultation representatives to conduct an adequate study and, where necessary, to prepare for consultation.

    (3) The employer must consult the information and consultation representatives on the matters referred to in paragraph (1)(b) and (c) . . .

21 The parties are under a duty, when negotiating or implementing a negotiated agreement or when implementing the standard information and consultation provisions, to work in a spirit of co-operation and with due regard for their reciprocal rights and obligations, taking into account the interests of both the undertaking and the employees.

Comment

(1) Note the requirement that parties should work in a 'spirit of co-operation' – this may be difficult to enforce in practice.

(2) The possible danger of destabilising existing arrangements with recognised trade unions has already been mentioned. However, employers who do not recognise unions

are equally exercised that the requirement to consult over a wide range of issues affecting the workforce could draw them almost imperceptibly into full-blown collective bargaining.

REFERENCES AND FURTHER READING

B Bercusson (2002), 'The European social model comes to Britain' 31 ILJ 20

A Bogg (2006), 'Politics, Community, Democracy: Appraising CAC Decision-Making in the First Five Years' 35 ILJ 245

M Carley and M Hall (2000), 'The implementation of the European Work Councils Directive' 29 ILJ 103

R Lewis (1990), 'Strike-free deals and pendulum arbitration' 28 BJIR 28

B Simpson (2000), 'Trade union recognition and the law, a new approach' 29 ILJ 193

Lord Wedderburn (1997), 'Consultation and collective bargaining in Europe: success or ideology?' 26 ILJ 1

Lord Wedderburn (2000), 'Collective bargaining or legal enactment: the 1999 Act and union recognition' 29 ILJ 1

6

STATUTORY EMPLOYMENT PROTECTION RIGHTS

While voluntary collective bargaining was seen for most of the twentieth century as the prime method of equalising the bargaining position between employers and workers, it was recognised that on its own it was often not enough. There are always industries where the workforce is transient or fragmented and where effective unionisation is difficult.

In the 1960s employees were given certain basic protections by statute, such as the right to a written statement of their main terms and conditions of employment and the right to compensation if dismissed for redundancy. In 1971 the Industrial Relations Act introduced the important right to claim unfair dismissal. However, the mid-1970s saw a move to a different style of legislation which impinged to a much greater extent on the ongoing day-to-day relationship of employer and employee. The Sex Discrimination Act 1975 and Race Relations Act 1976 can be seen as examples of this, but many of the rights to be considered in this chapter came about because of the Employment Protection Act 1975.

Much of the impetus for these rights came from the informal 'Social Contract' between the Labour government of the day and the TUC. The idea was that unions should show restraint in their pay demands in return for receiving a legislative guarantee of certain positive rights. The principal individual rights introduced by the Employment Protection Act 1975 related to maternity, guaranteed pay for certain kinds of lay-off and a range of time off rights linked to particular duties or activities. They are now mainly found in the Employment Rights Act 1996.

During the 1990s the European Union became an important source of employment protection rights. This was partly through legislation, following the agreement on the Social Charter in 1989, and partly through case law of the ECJ, especially in relation to women's rights during pregnancy and maternity leave. While the United Kingdom opted out of the Social Charter (until 1997), the fact that health and safety measures could be agreed by qualified majority voting meant that employment protection could be extended despite opposition from the then Conservative government. Thus the Pregnant Workers Directive (92/85/EEC) extended women's rights during pregnancy and maternity leave, the Parental Leave Directive (96/34/EC) gave both parents a right to leave and the Working Time Directive (93/104/EC) (now replaced by 2003/88/EC) limited working hours and gave rights to rest periods and paid annual leave.

The Labour administration in power from 1997 made 'family-friendly' policies one of the main planks of its strategy, aiming to 'create a society where being a good parent and a good employer are not in conflict' (DTI, 2000). This led to further extensions of rights to leave for family responsibilities.

FAMILY RIGHTS

Family rights fall into five main categories:

- Maternity rights.
- Parental rights.
- Paternity rights.
- Rights for adoptive parents.
- Leave for care of dependants.

Most of these rights are contained in fairly extensive and technical legislation, much of it in statutory instruments, which it would be of limited use to reproduce here. What follows is, first, a timeline, showing the development of these rights, and then a table summarising the present position.

Timeline: the development of family rights

Date	Rights	Explanation
1975	*Employment Protection Act:* women with 2 years' continuous employment qualified for: • Maternity pay: 6 weeks at 90% gross pay • Maternity leave: right to return to former job after six months – subject to complex notice requirements • Dismissal on grounds of pregnancy automatically unfair – subject to exceptions	Part of a package of positive statutory employment protection rights resulting from the 'Social Contract' between employers and trade unions
1980	*Employment Act 1980:* Time off for ante-natal care introduced	Figures show UK has one of the worst records for perinatal deaths among industrialised nations
1986	*Single European Act:* EU assumes power to legislate on employment law issues and qualified majority voting is introduced for some other issues, including health and safety	Agreed to – surprisingly – by the Conservative administration headed by Margaret Thatcher
1986	*Social Security Act 1986:* Duty to provide SMP shifted from the state to the employer. Total maternity pay period now 18 weeks	To reduce administrative costs: previously both employer and state had to administer maternity payments
1991	*Dekker v VJV Centrum* (ECJ) *Hertz v Aldi Marked* (ECJ)	ECJ rules that discrimination on grounds of pregnancy is sex discrimination, but retains 'sick man' comparison for treatment outside the protected period of pregnancy and maternity leave

253

Date	Rights	Explanation
1992	***Pregnant Workers Directive*** (92/85/EEC) • Member states to provide employees with a right to 14 weeks' maternity leave paid at rate of statutory sick pay • No more than one year's service to be required to qualify for this • Dismissal on grounds of pregnancy or maternity leave to be prohibited	Passed by majority vote as a health and safety measure, despite UK opposition
1993	***Trade Union Reform and Employment Rights Act:*** • Dismissal or detriment on grounds of pregnancy, childbirth, maternity rights automatically unfair: no qualifying period of employment • Right to 14 weeks' leave introduced regardless of period of service, paid at same rate as SSP	Implementation of the Pregnant Workers Directive
1996	***Parental Leave Directive*** (96/34/EC) • Three months' unpaid leave for each parent • No more than one year's service to be required to qualify for this • Right to leave for urgent family reasons	Agreed by the social partners in accordance with the Social Policy Protocol – BUT not applicable to the UK, as it had opted out of this
1997	***Treaty of Amsterdam***: UK ends opt out; Social Policy Protocol included in Treaty of Rome and directives (such as Parental Leave Directive) extended to UK	May 1997: Labour administration replaces Conservative administration
1999	***Employment Relations Act; Maternity and Parental Leave etc Regulations*** Extension of ordinary maternity leave and SMP from 14 weeks to 18 weeks Simplification of notice requirements Additional maternity leave available after only one year's service Protection against detriment for exercise of family rights introduced Parental leave introduced Time off for dependant care introduced	First implementation of 'family-friendly' policies, in line with government's stated policy in the White Paper, *Fairness at Work* (1998: Cm 3968)
2000	***Work and Parents: Competitiveness and Choice*** (Cm 5005)	Green Paper with options for extension of rights, in particular paternity and adoption leave
2002	***Employment Act*** Extension of maternity leave to one year in total Further simplification of notice requirements Introduction of paid paternity and adoption leave	Further implementation of family-friendly policies: EA 2002 gives power to amend MPL Regs and make regulations for new rights

Date	Rights	Explanation
2003	Extension of ordinary maternity leave and SMP from 18 weeks to 26 weeks	Amendments to MPL
2006	**Work and Families Act** No qualifying period of employment for additional maternity leave from April 2007 SMP entitlement raised from 26 weeks to 39 weeks Right to request flexible working extended to carers for older or infirm dependants	Further implementation of family-friendly policies; power to extend SMP to one year included in the Act

Family rights: the present position

Rights	Conditions	Source
Maternity rights *Time off for ante-natal care* Paid time off to attend an ante-natal appointment with doctor, nurse, etc No qualifying period of employment	Employee to provide written proof of appointment if requested. Employer must not refuse time off unreasonably	ERA s 55
Statutory Maternity Pay (SMP): 90% of usual gross pay for 6 weeks ('the higher rate') Rate equivalent to Statutory Sick Pay (SSP) for 33 weeks ('the lower rate') (£117.18 per week in 2008)	Employee must have 26 weeks of continuous employment by the 15th week before the expected week of childbirth (EWC)	Social Security Contributions and Benefits Act 1992 Part XII and associated regulations
Maternity Allowance (MA) Rate equivalent to lower rate SMP (£117.18 per week in 2008) or 90% of average earnings if lower Payable for 39 weeks	Worker must have worked and made National Insurance contributions in 26 out of the 66 weeks before EWC Worker need not have worked for same employer and may have been self-employed	Social Security Contributions and Benefits Act 1992 ss 35, 35A and associated regulations
Statutory maternity leave Ordinary maternity leave 26 weeks' leave Contractual rights (except for pay) continue	No qualifying period of employment	ERA s 71 Maternity and Parental Leave, etc Regulations 1999, as amended

Rights	Conditions	Source
	By 15th week before EWC, employee must inform employer of pregnancy, expected date of childbirth and expected date of commencing maternity leave	
	Employer must then give employee notice of date when maternity leave ends	
Additional maternity leave 26 weeks' leave Contractual rights mainly suspended, except those relating to good faith	No qualifying period of employment	ERA s 73 Maternity and Parental Leave, etc Regulations 1999, as amended
Parental rights		
Parental leave 13 weeks of unpaid leave for each parent, to be taken between the child's birth and fifth birthday (18 for children with disabilities)	One-year qualifying period of employment Must be taken as a full week at a time Cannot be transferred between parents	ERA s 76 Maternity and Parental Leave, etc Regulations 1999, as amended
Flexible working Parents of children under 6 (or 18 if disabled) may request flexible working arrangements	26-week qualifying period of employment Employer bound at least to hold a meeting to discuss the proposal and give a right of appeal against refusal. Time limits apply for arranging meetings Refusal only on one of the nine grounds in ERA s 80G	ERA s 80F Flexible Working (Procedural Requirements) Regulations 2002 Flexible Working (Eligibility, Complaints and Remedies) Regulations 2002
Paternity rights		
Paternity leave Right for father (or mother's partner) to take two weeks leave within 8 weeks of the child's birth	26 weeks of continuous employment by the 14th week before the EWC Must comply with notice requirements	ERA s 80A Paternity and Adoption Leave Regulations 2002
Statutory Paternity Pay (SPP) Right to SPP during the paternity leave period, payable at rate equivalent to lower rate SMP (£117.18 pw in 2008)		Social Security Contributions and Benefits Act 1992 and associated regulations

Rights	Conditions	Source
Adoption rights		
Adoption leave Right for adopter (or one of adopting couple) to take adoption leave equivalent to ordinary and additional maternity leave	As per maternity leave, above	ERA ss 75A, 75B Paternity and Adoption Leave Regulations 2002
The other partner may qualify for leave equivalent to paternity leave	As per paternity leave, above	
Adoption pay Right to pay equivalent to SMP and SPP	As per SMP and SPP – except no higher rate of SMP applies	Social Security Contributions and Benefits Act 1992 and associated regulations
Leave for care of dependants		
Leave for dependants' care Right to reasonable unpaid time off for care of dependants in specified circumstances	Dependant must be within definition in ERA s 57A(3)–(5) Circumstances must be within ERA s 57A(1) Employee to give notice as soon as reasonably practicable Employer must not refuse time off unreasonably	ERA s 57A
Flexible working Right to request flexible working arrangements to care for a dependant	As per parental leave right for flexible working above	Work and Families Act 2006 amending ERA s 80F and Flexible Working (Eligibility, Complaints and Remedies) Regulations 2002

Comments

(1) In *Gillespie* v *Northern Health and Social Services Board* (1996) the ECJ held that it was not a breach of Art 141 of the Treaty of Rome not to give women full pay during maternity leave. The Court's reasoning was that a woman who was on maternity leave was in a unique position which could not be compared with either a man or woman who was working. Once again, there is some manipulation of the concept of comparison in this argument.

(2) The employee's right to SMP is freestanding and does not depend on her having an intention to return to work. Some employers provide contractual maternity pay at a higher level, which may be dependent on the employee returning to work for a specified period of time. While there is no right to SMP for any week during which the employee works for the employer, the Work and Families Act 2006 makes provision for the

employee to undertake up to ten days' work ('keeping in touch' days) during maternity leave without jeopardising her rights to maternity pay or maternity leave.

(3) While the employee is generally free to choose the date on which maternity leave will start (and most women leave it as late as possible, so as to maximise the period of leave after the baby is born), there are two situations in which the start of maternity leave is brought forward automatically. The first is if the birth is before the start date – in which case, maternity leave begins immediately from the birth. The second is if the employee is absent for a pregnancy-related illness at any time after the fourth week before birth is due: this again triggers the start of the maternity leave period. This is to prevent women from taking sick leave rather than maternity leave at this late stage, which they may prefer since (a) it is likely to be paid at the full contractual rate, and (b) it will not eat into their maternity leave period.

(4) Now that additional maternity leave is not dependent on any qualifying period of service, the main difference between it and ordinary maternity leave is that during add- itional maternity leave the employee will not be entitled to contractual benefits such as use of a company car or inclusion in a private health scheme. From 5 October 2008 this distinction will disappear as a result of the Sex Discrimination Act 1975 (Amendment) Regulations 2008. Thereafter employers will have to provide contractual benefits dur- ing additional maternity leave and to count this period towards continuous service for qualifying for contractual benefits.

(5) Notice requirements in relation to statutory maternity leave have been greatly sim- plified over recent years. No notice need be given of her intention to take additional maternity leave after ordinary maternity leave, nor of her intention to return to work at the notified end of ordinary or additional maternity leave. Only if the employee wishes to return early must she give notice: the requirement is to give eight weeks' notice of her new return date – and the employer is not entitled to postpone it.

(6) At the end of statutory maternity leave the employee is usually entitled to return to her former post as if she had not been away. There is an exception if it is not reason- ably practicable (for a reason other than redundancy) to let her have her old job back and she has been offered a suitable alternative which either she has accepted or else has unreasonably refused (Maternity and Parental Leave, etc Regulations 1999 reg 20(7)). If her post has become redundant while she is on statutory maternity leave, the employee is entitled to be offered any suitable alternative vacancy (ahead of other poten- tially redundant employees).

(7) Employers may have more flexible arrangements than those stipulated in the Maternity and Parental Leave, etc Regulations 1999, but if there is no collective agree- ment or workforce agreement in place, the model scheme in Sch 2 to the Regulations applies. The problems of the inflexibility of the one week minimum leave requirement are well illustrated by *Rodway v South Central Trains* (2005).

(8) The biggest drawback of the right to request flexible working is that the employer's obligation is only to consider it: a complaint can be made to an employment tribunal only if the employer has either not followed the procedure correctly or reached a decision based on incorrect facts. The remedy is also limited: a tribunal can award a maximum of eight weeks' pay, subject to the statutory maximum (£2,640 in 2008).

(9) While the right to paternity leave and pay is currently very limited, the Work and Families Act 2006 gives the Secretary of State power to make regulations allowing

fathers to take the second six months of maternity leave instead of mothers. This would be unpaid, but the idea is that the father would be entitled to any rights to pay that the mother would have had.

(10) In *Qua* v *John Ford Morrison* (2003) the EAT held that leave for care of dependants covered making arrangements in the immediate crisis when a child fell sick, but not to the ongoing need to care for him: the employee should have taken normal leave or parental leave for that purpose. Similarly, in *Forster* v *Cartwright Black* (2004), leave on the death of a dependant was held to be intended for things such as funeral arrangements – but not coming to terms with the bereavement emotionally.

(11) Subjecting an employee to any detriment during employment for any of the family rights gives the employee a right to complain to an employment tribunal. Dismissal or selection for redundancy on any of these grounds is automatically unfair and there is no qualifying period of employment for this.

GUARANTEE PAYMENTS AND SUSPENSION ON MEDICAL GROUNDS

Employment Rights Act 1996

28 (1) Where throughout a day during any part of which an employee would normally be required to work in accordance with his contract of employment the employee is not provided with work by his employer by reason of –

(a) a diminution in the requirements of the employer's business for work of the kind which the employee is employed to do, or

(b) any other occurrence affecting the normal working of the employer's business in relation to work of the kind which the employee is employed to do,

the employee is entitled to be paid by his employer an amount in respect of that day.

(2) In this Act a payment to which an employee is entitled under subsection (1) is referred to as a guarantee payment.

Comment

(1) The purpose of the guarantee payment and suspension on medical grounds provisions is to give some kind of wage to employees laid off work through no fault of their own. Note that ERA s 28 does not give employers a right to lay off workers: they may only do this if they have a contractual right to do so. Otherwise, it would be a fundamental breach of contract by the employer (see p 344).

Even if the contract does permit the employer to lay off workers temporarily, to prevent excessive use of this power the ERA provides that an employee can leave and claim a redundancy payment under certain conditions (see p 459).

(2) The right to claim a guarantee payment is not particularly generous. It is limited to a maximum of five days in any three-month period, and is subject to an upper limit which was only £20.40 gross per day in 2008 (ERA s 31). Employers who have their own arrangements for lay-off payments can opt out of the statutory scheme as long as their schemes are at least equally beneficial, and quite a number of employers have done so.

(3) The interplay between this and entitlement to jobseeker's allowance is also worth noting. Jobseeker's allowance (which is paid at a similar level to the maximum guarantee payment) is payable after three days of unemployment. Thus the overall effect is

broadly to shift the burden of paying to the employer instead of the state for the first five days. The only real benefit to the employee is that she gets paid for the first three days that she is out of work. But if the lay-off persists beyond five days, she will have to wait three more days before becoming entitled to unemployment benefit, so this advantage may be marginal.

(4) If the employer fails to make a guarantee payment, the employee can complain to an employment tribunal (ERA s 34).

(5) Under ERA s 64, an employee has a right to up to 26 weeks' pay where an employer has to shut down the business temporarily to meet health or safety requirements in accordance with specified enactments. In the absence of any contractual right to suspend without pay in these circumstances the employee would remain entitled to pay at the usual rate. However, if the employer does have the power to suspend without pay, these provisions afford some measure of income protection to the employees.

(6) At present, the enactments specified in ERA s 64(3) are:

- Control of Lead at Work Regulations 1980.
- Ionising Radiations Regulations 1999.
- Control of Substances Hazardous to Health Regulations 1988.

(7) As with guarantee payments, the remedy for an employee is a claim within three months to an employment tribunal, which can order payment (ERA s 70).

TIME OFF RIGHTS

A range of rights to time off work for particular reasons was introduced by the Employment Protection Act 1975. The rights introduced since then, the right to time off for ante-natal care and the right to time off for dependant care, have been discussed above, under Family Rights. The right to time off to look for work in a redundancy situation is discussed with the other redundancy provisions (p 460). This section covers the right to time off for trade union duties and activities, for safety representatives and for public duties.

Time off for trade union duties and activities

Paid time off

Trade Union and Labour Relations (Consolidation) Act 1992

168 (1) An employer shall permit an employee of his who is an official of an independent trade union recognised by the employer to take time off during his working hours for the purpose of carrying out any duties of his, as such an official, concerned with –
   (a) negotiations with the employer related to or connected with matters falling within section 178(2) (collective bargaining) in relation to which the trade union is recognised by the employer, or
   (b) the performance on behalf of employees of the employer of functions related to or connected with matters falling within that provision which the employer has agreed may be so performed by the trade union, or

    (c)   receipt of information from the employer and consultation by the employer under section 188 (redundancies) or under the Transfer of Undertakings (Protection of Employment) Regulations 2006, or

    (d)   negotiations with a view to entering into an agreement under regulation 9 of the Transfer of Undertakings (Protection of Employment) Regulations 2006 that applies to employees of the employer, or

    (e)   the performance on behalf of employees of the employer of functions related to or connected with the making of an agreement under that regulation.

    (2)   He shall also permit such an employee to take time off during his working hours for the purpose of undergoing training in aspects of industrial relations –

    (a)   relevant to the carrying out of such duties as are mentioned in subsection (1), and

    (b)   approved by the Trades Union Congress or by the independent trade union of which he is an official.

    (3)   The amount of time off which an employee is to be permitted to take under this section and the purposes for which, the occasions on which and any conditions subject to which time off may be so taken are those that are reasonable in all the circumstances having regard to any relevant provisions of a Code of Practice issued by ACAS.

    (4)   An employee may present a complaint to an employment tribunal that his employer has failed to permit him to take time off as required by this section.

169   (1)   An employer who permits an employee to take time off under section 168 or 168A shall pay him for the time taken off pursuant to the permission . . .

Comment

(1) There is no qualifying period of service for this right. However, it is subject to the important limitation that it applies only where the trade union has the status of recognised trade union (see Chapter 5, p 229).

(2) The right is limited by the fact that it must be connected with matters falling under TULRCA s 178(2), which contains a definition of collective bargaining. The list of matters in s 178(2) is identical to s 244(1) (subject matter of a trade dispute), which is extracted on p 623. The Acas *Code of Practice No 3 on Time Off for Trade Union Duties and Activities* etc (2003) gives examples.

ACAS *Code of Practice No 3 on Trade Union Duties and Activities (including Guidance on Time Off for Union Learning Representatives)* (2003)

EXAMPLES OF TRADE UNION DUTIES

11   Subject to the recognition or other agreement, trade union officials should be allowed to take reasonable time off for duties concerned with negotiations or, where their employer has agreed, for duties concerned with other functions related to or connected with:

    (a)   terms and conditions of employment, or the physical conditions in which workers are required to work. Examples could include:
- pay
- hours of work
- holidays and holiday pay
- sick pay arrangements
- pensions
- learning and training needs
- equal opportunities

- notice periods
- the working environment
- operation of digital equipment and other machinery;

(b) engagement or non-engagement, or termination or suspension of employment or the duties of employment, of one or more workers. Examples could include:
- recruitment and selection policies
- human resource planning
- redundancy and dismissal arrangements;

(c) allocation of work or the duties of employment as between workers or groups of workers. Examples could include:
- job grading
- job evaluation
- job descriptions
- flexible working practices
- family friendly policies;

(d) matters of discipline. Examples could include:
- disciplinary procedures
- arrangements for representing trade union members at internal interviews
- arrangements for appearing on behalf of trade union members, or as witnesses, before agreed outside appeal bodies or employment tribunals;

(e) trade union membership or non-membership. Examples could include:
- representational arrangements
- any union involvement in the induction of new workers;

(f) facilities for officials of trade unions. Examples could include any agreed arrangements for the provision of:
- accommodation
- equipment
- names of new workers to the union;

(g) machinery for negotiation or consultation and other procedures. Examples could include arrangements for:
- collective bargaining
- grievance procedures
- joint consultation
- communicating with members
- communicating with other union officials also concerned with collective bargaining with the employer.

12 The duties of an official of a recognised trade union must be connected with or related to negotiations or the performance of functions both in time and subject matter. Reasonable time off may be sought, for example, to:
- prepare for negotiations
- inform members of progress
- explain outcomes to members
- prepare for meetings with the employer about matters for which the trade union has only representational rights.

Comment

(1) In addition to being connected with one of these matters, the right to paid time off is further restricted in that it must be related to matters in respect of which the employer actually recognises the union, which may be a narrower range of issues than those

above. For example, where recognition is ordered under the statutory recognition procedure, it can relate only to pay, hours of work and holidays.

(2) Whether any particular preparatory act or advisory meeting is sufficiently proximate to negotiations with the employer to attract the right to paid time off is essentially a question of fact: see *British Bakeries (Northern) Ltd* v *Adlington* (1989) and *London Ambulance Service* v *Charlton* (1992).

(3) Lay union officials may also qualify for paid time off under ERelA s 10, where they accompany a worker to a disciplinary or grievance hearing (see p 378). This right exists regardless of whether the employer recognises the union.

(4) As a result of amendment by the Employment Act 2002, Union Learning Representatives also have a right to reasonable paid time off to carry out their duties as stipulated in TULRCA s 168A. Union Learning Representatives are union officials whose role is to promote training in the workplace among their co-workers. They may not necessarily have any other official union capacity. Practical guidance on this is included in the Acas *Code of Practice No 3 on Time Off for Trade Union Duties and Activities* etc (2003).

(5) Where paid time off for trade union duties is unreasonably refused, the remedy is to apply to the employment tribunal within three months of the refusal. In situations where the employee has been refused the time off altogether, the tribunal awards whatever it considers to be just and equitable 'having regard to the employer's default in failing to permit time off to be taken by the employee and to any loss sustained by the employee which is attributable to the matters complained of' (TULRCA s 172(2)). In *Skiggs* v *South West Trains Ltd* (2005) the EAT held that a tribunal was wrong to make no award of compensation just because the employee had not lost any pay, pointing out that this would normally be the case where an employer refused to allow the employee to take time off. The case was remitted for the tribunal to take account of the employer's default, as per s 172(2).

(6) Where the employee has had the time off, but the employer refuses to pay, the tribunal will obviously award the lost wages as part of the compensation. One problem which often arises is whether the employer is liable to pay wages where the employee is carrying out trade union duties, but not during normal working hours.

Kuratorium für Dialyse v *Lewark* [1996] IRLR 637 European Court of Justice

The employee worked four days a week for the employer. When elected to the staff council, she went on a one-week training course, with her employer's consent. Although the course lasted for five days, the employer only paid her for her usual four days. The employee argued that this was a breach of Art 141 of the Treaty of Rome and of the Equal Pay Directive 1975, on the grounds that the employer was thus treating part-time employees less favourably than full-time employees (who would get full pay for time spent on the course), and that this amounted to sex discrimination because the vast majority of part-time workers are women.

JUDGMENT OF THE COURT: '. . . It must be observed first of all that legal concepts and definitions established or laid down by national law cannot affect the interpretation or binding force of Community law, or, consequently, the scope of the principle of equal pay for men and women laid down in [Article 141] of the Treaty and in the Directive and developed by the Court's case law (see the judgments in *Arbeiterwholfahrt der Stadt Berlin e V* v *Bötel* (1992) and *Hoekstra* v *Bestuur der Bedrijfsvereniging voor Detail-handel* (1964).

Secondly, as the Court has consistently held, the concept of pay within the meaning of [Art 141] of the Treaty comprises any consideration, whether in cash or in kind, whether immediate or future, provided that the worker receives it, albeit indirectly, in respect of his employment from his employer, and irrespective of whether the worker receives it under a contract of employment, by virtue of legislative provisions or on a voluntary basis (see the judgments in *Bötel* and in *Barber* v *Guardian Royal Exchange Assurance Group* (1990)).

As the Court held in *Bötel*, although compensation such as that at issue in the main proceedings does not derive as such from the contract of employment, it is nevertheless paid by the employer by virtue of legislative provisions and under a contract of employment. Staff council members must necessarily be employees of the undertaking, to be able to serve on that undertaking's staff council.

It follows that compensation received for losses of earnings due to attendance at training courses imparting the information necessary for performing staff council functions must be regarded as pay within the meaning of [Art 141], since it constitutes a benefit paid indirectly by the employer by reason of the existence of an employment relationship.

The German Government also considers, as does the referring court, that the legislation in question does not cause any difference in treatment between staff council members working part time and those working full time, since they all have the same protection against losses of earnings incurred through attending training courses.

The Court held in joined cases *Stadt Lengerich* v *Helmig and others* (1995) that there is unequal treatment whenever the overall pay of full-time employees is higher than that of part-time employees for the same number of hours worked on the basis of an employment relationship.

In the present case, it is indisputable that where training courses necessary for performing staff council functions are organised during the full-time working hours in force in the undertaking but outside the individual working hours of part-time workers serving on those councils, the overall pay received by the latter is, for the same number of hours worked, lower than that received by the full-time workers serving on the same staff councils.

Nor can it be objected that the time spent by staff council members on such training courses is not a direct consequence of the existence of a contract of employment, since it is sufficient for that time to be spent by reason of the existence of an employment relationship, which is indeed the case, as was found in paragraphs 22 and 23 in connections with the concept of pay.

Since a difference in treatment has been found to exist, it follows from settled case law that, if it were the case that a much lower proportion of women than men work full time, the exclusion of part-time workers from certain benefits would be contrary to [Art 141] of the Treaty where, taking into account the difficulties encountered by women workers in working full time, that measure could not be explained by factors excluding any discrimination on grounds of sex (judgments in *Jenkins* v *Kingsgate (Clothing Productions) Ltd* (1981) and in *Bilka-Kaufhaus GmbH* v *Weber von Hartz* (1987)).

According to the order for reference, the official employment and social statistics show that at the end of June 1991 93.4% of all part-time workers were women and 6.6% were men. The Landesarbeitsgericht considered that in view of that very great difference between the numbers of men and women working part time, it was to be supposed that the proportion of men and women working part time among staff council members was at least similar.

As those figures have not been disputed, it must be considered that the application of legislative provisions such as those at issue in the main proceedings in principle causes indirect discrimination against women workers, contrary to [Art 141] of the Treaty and to the Directive.

It would be otherwise only if the difference of treatment found to exist was justified by objective factors unrelated to any discrimination based on sex. On this point, the Court held in *Bötel*, cited above, that it remained open to the Member State to prove that the legislation was justified by such factors.

However, although in preliminary-ruling proceedings it is for the national court to establish whether such objective factors exist in the particular case before it, the Court of Justice, which has to provide the national court with helpful answers, may provide guidance based on the documents before the national court and on the written and oral observations which have been submitted to it, in order to enable the national court to give judgment (see the judgment in *Secretary of State for Social Security* v *Thomas* (1993)).

The German Government considers that, assuming that there is a proven difference of treatment, it is justified by the principle that staff council members are not paid, which is intended to ensure their independence. The unpaid and honorary nature of staff council functions and the principle that they must not confer any benefit or entail any disadvantage have the purpose of ensuring staff council members' independence from both internal and external pressures.

It is also apparent from the order for reference in the present case that the Bundesarbeitsgericht considers that the German legislature's wish to place the independence of staff councils above financial inducements for performing staff council functions, as expressed in the provisions at issue, is an aim of social policy.

Such a social policy aim appears in itself to be unrelated to any discrimination on grounds of sex. It cannot be disputed that the work of staff councils does indeed play a part in German social policy, in that the councils have the task of promoting harmonious labour relations within undertakings and in their interest. The concern to ensure the independence of the members of those councils thus likewise reflects a legitimate aim of social policy.

If a Member State is able to show that the measures chosen reflect a legitimate aim of its social policy, are appropriate to achieve that aim and are necessary in order to do so, the mere fact that the legislative provision affects far more women workers than men cannot be regarded as a breach of Article 119 (see the judgments in *De Weerd and others* (1994) and in *Megner and Scheffel* (1995).

However, it should be noted that, as the Court held in *Bötel*, legislation such as that at issue is likely to deter workers in the part-time category, in which the proportion of women is undeniably preponderant, from performing staff council functions or from acquiring the knowledge necessary for performing them, thus making it more difficult for that category of worker to be represented by qualified staff council members.

In the light of all those considerations and taking into account the possibility of achieving the social policy aim in question by other means, the difference in treatment could be justified from the point of view of [Art 141] of the Treaty and of the Directive only if it appeared to be suitable and necessary for achieving that aim. It is for the national court to ascertain whether that is so in the present case.

Consequently, where the category of part-time workers includes a much higher number of women than men, the prohibition of indirect discrimination in the matter of pay, as set out in [Art 141] and in the Directive, precludes national legislation which, not being suitable and necessary for achieving a legitimate social policy aim, has the effect of limiting to their individual working hours the compensation which staff council members employed on a part-time basis are to receive from their employer for attending training courses which impart the knowledge necessary for serving on staff councils and are held during the full-time working hours applicable in the undertaking but which exceed their individual part-time working hours, when staff council members employed on a full-time basis receive compensation for attendance at the same courses on the basis of their full-time working hours . . .'

Comment

(1) This decision suggests that the EAT's decision in *Manor Bakeries* v *Nazir* (1996), that payments to union officials attending a union conference were not within the equal pay principle, was wrong. This was also the view of a later EAT in *Davies* v *Neath Port Talbot County BC* (1999) (part-time worker elected as union safety representative entitled to pay at the full-time rate when attending a full-time training course). If TULRCA s 169 was inconsistent with this, the EAT held that it should be set aside to that extent.

(2) This issue is not addressed directly by the Part-time Workers (Prevention of Less Favourable Treatment) Regulations 2000, with the government guidance accompanying those regulations confined to recommending that training should be scheduled as far as possible so that part-timers are able to attend. It is probable that the same result would be reached under these Regulations, and their main advantage is probably that they make it easier for a male part-timer to sue.

(3) Similar problems can arise for shift workers, whose union duties may well be performed outside their normal working hours. In *Ryford Ltd* v *Drinkwater* (1996) it seemed to be accepted that a night worker was entitled to be paid where he had missed a night shift in order to get some sleep so as to be able to attend a daytime meeting. However, in *Hairsine* v *Hull CC* (1992), where an employee who worked evening shifts took time off in the evening to make up for a day he had spent at a training course, it was held that he was not entitled to be paid for it. The difference seems to be in relation to how far it was necessary for the worker to take the time off.

(3) It is possible for the tribunal to find that a union official is not entitled to be paid for a particular period of time off work – but was entitled to the time off as unpaid time off for trade union activities. This is considered next.

Unpaid time off

Trade Union and Labour Relations (Consolidation) Act 1992

170   (1)   An employer shall permit an employee of his who is a member of an independent trade union recognised by the employer in respect of that description of employee to take time off during his working hours for the purpose of taking part in –
   (a)   any activities of the union, and
   (b)   any activities in relation to which the employee is acting as a representative of the union.

   (2)   The right conferred by subsection (1) does not extend to activities which themselves consist of industrial action, whether or not in contemplation or furtherance of a trade dispute
. . .

   (3)   The amount of time off which an employee is to be permitted to take under this section and the purposes for which, the occasions on which and any conditions subject to which time off may be so taken are those that are reasonable in all the circumstances having regard to any relevant provisions of a Code of Practice issued by ACAS.

   (4)   An employee may present a complaint to an employment tribunal that his employer has failed to permit him to take time off as required by this section . . .

Comment

(1) The omitted part of this section, s 170(2A)–(2C), provides a right to unpaid time off to access the services of a Union Learning Representative.

(2) The right to unpaid time off for trade union members is also limited to situations where the union is recognised. Examples of the kinds of activities covered are given in the Acas Code.

ACAS *Code of Practice No 3 on Trade Union Duties and Activities (including Guidance on Time Off for Union Learning Representatives)* (2003)

30   The activities of a trade union member can be, for example:
- attending workplace meetings to discuss and vote on the outcome of negotiations with the employer
- meeting full-time officials to discuss issues relevant to the workplace
- voting in union elections.

31   Where the member is acting as a representative of a recognised union, activities can be, for example, taking part in:
- branch, area or regional meetings of the union where the business of the union is under discussion
- meetings of official policy making bodies such as the executive committee or annual conference
- meetings with full-time officials to discuss issues relevant to the workplace.

Comment

(1) Although the right is to unpaid time off only, the Acas Code para 34 states: 'Nevertheless, employers may want to consider payment in certain circumstances, for example, to ensure that workplace meetings are fully representative.'

(2) It is not surprising to find that taking part in industrial action is not something for which the employer must allow time off. However, it is not always easy to distinguish between what is a union activity and what is industrial action. This problem has received most attention where an employer has dismissed a union member for what the member claims is a protected union activity (see p 496). Note also para 49 of the Acas Code:

49   Employers and unions have a responsibility to use agreed procedures to settle problems and avoid industrial action. Time off may therefore be permitted for this purpose particularly where there is a dispute. There is no right to time off for trade union activities which themselves consist of industrial action. However, where an official is not taking part in industrial action but represents members involved, normal arrangements for time off with pay for the official should apply.

(3) Another problem is to define the line between trade union activity and political activity. Similar debates are encountered in deciding whether industrial action has occurred in the context of a trade dispute or a political dispute. The following decision is not wholly satisfactory, as the claimant refused to give evidence himself or to call any witnesses.

Luce v Bexley LBC [1990] ICR 591 Employment Appeal Tribunal

When the Bill which eventually became the Education Reform Act 1988 was going through Parliament, the Bexley division of the National Union of Teachers sought permission for six teachers to have a day's paid leave to attend a lobby of Parliament. The council refused and the claimant, one of the teachers involved, claimed that this was a contravention of TULRCA s 170. The employment tribunal held that a Parliamentary lobby was not a union activity within the meaning of the section.

WOOD J: '. . . In the present case, however, the tribunal decided against the claimant on the first issue and went no further. What then can we indicate which may be helpful to tribunals in approaching the phrase "any activities of an appropriate trade union of which the employee is a member"? First, and most importantly, we are satisfied that the issue is ultimately one of degree and therefore one of fact. This must be left to the good sense and experience of the employment tribunal which is entitled to look at all the circumstances. Second, although we do not consider that the phrase should be understood too restrictively, we are satisfied that it cannot have been the intention of Parliament to have included any activity of whatever nature. The whole context of the phrase is within the ambit of the employment relationship between that employee and that employer and that trade union. Quite apart from the overall consider-ations which we have expressed above, this seems to be emphasised by the provisions of [TULRCA s 173(1)]. The time off is during the employee's normal working hours for which he would be contractually bound. Thus is seems to us that in a broad sense the activity should be one which is in some way linked to that employment relationship, *ie* between that employer, that employee and that trade union.

The ACAS Code of Practice 3, Time Off for Trade Union Duties and Activities (1977) [now 2003] offers some support to this approach at the start of paragraph 8. This section of the code is entitled "General consideration for time off arrangements" and the first sentence of that paragraph reads,

> "The general purpose of the statutory provisions on time off for trade union duties and activ-ities is to aid and improve the conduct of industrial relations."

We are satisfied that the decision of the schools subcommittee was far too sweeping without further consideration of the details of each case and is not justified. Lobbying is the presentation of arguments intended to persuade a Member of Parliament to vote in a particular way on a particular issue. It is to be contrasted with an approach which is in essence based upon mere protest.

The reasoning of the employment tribunal can be found in the following passages of its decision:

> "18 . . . [TULRCA ss 168–170] confer rights to time off for limited purposes only and we regard it as inconceivable that it was intended that the rights to time off given to ordinary trade union members should be entirely unlimited in purpose and should extend to, for example, activities with purely political or ideological ends. In relation to such activities, [s 170(3)], which requires consideration to be given to the purpose of the time off, would, in our view, put the employer in a particularly invidious position.
> "20 In our view, the terms 'trade union activity' and 'trade union activities' are to be construed as they are commonly understood when used to describe the purpose of time off, that is, as encompassing activities usually associated with trade unions and peculiarly within their province. Paragraph (a) of [TULRCA s 170(1)] applies to such activities when they are carried out or organised by a trade union itself. But, in addition, a trade union member may seek time off for 'trade union activities' even though his or her trade union does no more than send representatives to a particular body, for example, if the employee is the union's representative on the committee of an industrial training board. Although the trade union activity in such a case is not that of the union itself, it is nevertheless caught by paragraph (b) of [TULRCA s 170(1)].
> "21 We take the view that, so construed, the term 'trade union activities' covers a very broad range of activity and that there is much force in Mr Davies' [claimant's trade union representative] submission that the examples of trade union activity given in paragraphs 21

and 22 of the Code of Practice are too narrow. We do not exclude the possibility that some activities directed at Parliament may fall within the scope of [TULRCA s 170]. For example, a trade union may have developed, in the ordinary course of its work for its members, specialised technical knowledge relevant to a measure before Parliament concerned with health and safety at work. We consider that representations to Parliament arising out of the union's expertise concerning such a measure might well fall within the scope of [s 170]. In our view, however, time off to attend a lobby of Parliament intended to convey only political or ideological objections to proposed legislation cannot be regarded as time off for the purpose of taking part in 'trade union activity' as that term is commonly understood, even if the legislation is of vital concern to the members of the union concerned."

The employment tribunal were constrained to make their findings of the nature and purpose of the proposed activity upon the very limited evidence proffered by the claimant and did so in the terms to which we have referred. Despite the able arguments of Mr Clayton [solicitor for the claimant] we are not satisfied that the tribunal erred in law in their approach to the problems before them, and their conclusions were fully justified upon the evidence before them . . .'

Comment

(1) While the action failed in this case, it seems that some lobbying can count as a trade union activity.

(2) References to specific paragraphs in the Acas Code of Practice No 3 refer to the 1977 version. The general purpose of the provisions is now stated in para 3 rather than para 8 and refers to improving 'the effectiveness of relationships between employers and trade unions' rather than 'the conduct of industrial relations'. While this may make it sound like the mission statement for Relate, the meaning is probably unchanged. The examples of activities which used to be in paras 21 and 22 of the 1977 Code are considerably expanded in the present Code, as per the extract above (p 267).

(3) The biggest question is probably 'how much time off is reasonable?' But since this will depend on so many variables, no simple answer can be given. The issue is addressed to some extent in sections 4 and 5 of the Code of Practice, which indicates many of the considerations and recommends unions and employers to reach prior agreement on amounts of time off, the purposes for which it can be taken and the procedure for requesting it.

Time off for safety representatives

Under the authority of the Health and Safety at Work etc Act 1974, the Safety Representatives and Safety Committees Regulations 1977 were made.

Safety Representatives and Safety Committees Regulations 1977

3 (1) For the purposes of section 2(4) of the 1974 Act, a recognised trade union may appoint safety representatives from amongst the employees in all cases where one or more employees are employed by an employer by whom it is recognised.

(2) Where the employer has been notified in writing by or on behalf of a trade union of the names of the persons appointed as safety representatives under this Regulation and the group or groups of employees they represent, each such safety representative shall have the functions set out in Regulation 4 below.

(3) A person shall cease to be a safety representative for the purposes of these Regulations when –

(a) the trade union which appointed him notifies the employer in writing that his appointment has been terminated; or

(b) he ceases to be employed at the workplace but if he was appointed to represent employees at more than one workplace he shall not cease by virtue of this sub-paragraph to be a safety representative so long as he continues to be employed at any one of them; or

(c) he resigns.

(4) A person appointed under paragraph (1) above as a safety representative shall so far as is reasonably practicable either have been employed by his employer throughout the preceding two years or have had at least two years experience in similar employment.

4 (1) In addition to his function under section 2(4) of the 1974 Act to represent the employees in consultations with the employer under section 2(6) of the 1974 Act (which requires every employer to consult safety representatives with a view to the making and maintenance of arrangements which will enable him and his employees to cooperate effectively in promoting and developing measures to ensure the health and safety at work of the employees and in checking the effectiveness of such measures), each safety representative shall have the following functions:–

(a) to investigate potential hazards and dangerous occurrences at the workplace (whether or not they are drawn to his attention by the employees he represents) and to examine the causes of accidents at the workplace;

(b) to investigate complaints by any employee he represents relating to that employee's health, safety or welfare at work;

(c) to make representations to the employer on matters arising out of sub-paragraphs (a) and (b) above;

(d) to make representations to the employer on general matters affecting the health, safety or welfare at work of the employees at the workplace;

(e) to carry out inspections in accordance with Regulations 5, 6 and 7 below;

(f) to represent the employees he was appointed to represent in consultations at the workplace with inspectors of the Health and Safety Executive and of any other enforcing authority;

(g) to receive information from inspectors in accordance with section 28(8) of the 1974 Act; and

(h) to attend meetings of safety committees where he attends in his capacity as a safety representative in connection with any of the above functions;

but, without prejudice to sections 7 and 8 of the 1974 Act, no function given to a safety representative by this paragraph shall be construed as imposing any duty on him.

(2) An employer shall permit a safety representative to take such time off with pay during the employee's working hours as shall be necessary for the purposes of –

(a) performing his functions under section 2(4) of the 1974 Act and paragraph (1)(a) to (h) above;

(b) undergoing such training in aspects of those functions as may be reasonable in all the circumstances having regard to any relevant provisions of a code of practice relating to time off for training approved for the time being by the Health and Safety Commission under section 16 of the 1974 Act.

In this paragraph 'with pay' means with pay in accordance with Schedule 2 to these Regulations.

Comment

(1) In 1994 the ECJ decided that consultation over redundancies and transfers was inadequate where representation was only possible through recognised trade unions (*EC Commission v UK* (1994)). It therefore became clear that statutory provisions for employee safety representatives which applied only where there was a trade union were also inadequate and that change was necessary. However, in line with the then Conservative government's policy of 'no gold-plating' when forced to introduce Community directives, it was decided not to take the straightforward course of extending the 1977 Regulations but instead to introduce new regulations which constituted a minimum compliance with the Framework Health and Safety Directive (89/391/EEC). Under the Health and Safety (Consultation with Employees) Regulations 1996, workplaces without a recognised trade union have a right to elect safety representatives, but their role is more limited than that of union-appointed safety representatives.

(2) In accordance with the directive, protection from detriment or dismissal for exercise of their functions was also introduced for both kinds of safety representatives (see ERA ss 44 and 100). The protection also applies to employer-appointed safety representatives, or any employee who acts in good faith in circumstances where either there is no safety representative or where it is not practicable to contact the proper person.

(3) The right to time off for union-appointed safety representatives is explained further by the Health and Safety Commission's Codes of Practice, *Safety Representatives and Safety Committees* (1978) and *Time Off for the Training of Safety Representatives* (1978). There are no corresponding codes for other employee safety representatives.

Time off for public duties

Employment Rights Act 1996

50 (1) An employer shall permit an employee of his who is a justice of the peace to take time off during the employee's working hours for the purpose of performing any of the duties of his office.

(2) An employer shall permit an employee of his who is a member of –

(a) a local authority,

(b) a statutory tribunal,

(c) a police authority established under section 3 of the Police Act 1996 or the Metropolitan Police Authority,

(d) an independent monitoring board for a prison or a prison visiting committee,

(e) a relevant health body,

(f) a relevant education body,

(g) the Environment Agency or the Scottish Environment Protection Agency, or

(h) Scottish Water or a Water Customer Consultation Panel,

to take time off during the employee's working hours for the purposes specified in subsection (3).

(3) The purposes referred to in subsection (2) are –

(a) attendance at a meeting of the body or any of its committees or sub-committees, and

(b) the doing of any other thing approved by the body, or anything of a class so approved, for the purpose of the discharge of the functions of the body or of any of its committees or sub-committees, and

(c) in the case of a local authority which are operating executive arrangements –
  (i) attendance at a meeting of the executive of that local authority or committee of that executive; and
  (ii) the doing of any other thing, by an individual member of that executive, for the purposes of the discharge of any function which is to any extent the responsibility of that executive.

(4) The amount of time off which an employee is to be permitted to take under this section, and the occasions on which and any condition subject to which time off may be so taken, are those that are reasonable in all the circumstances having regard, in particular, to –
  (a) how much time off is required for the performance of the duties of the office or as a member of the body in question, and how much time off is required for the performance of the particular duty,
  (b) how much time off the employee has already been permitted under this section or sections 168 and 170 of the Trade Union and Labour Relations (Consolidation) Act 1992 (time off for trade union duties and activities), and
  (c) the circumstances of the employer's business and the effect of the employee's absence on the running of that business . . .

Comment

(1) The remedy for an employee denied time off is to complain to an employment tribunal. One of the purposes of this was to bring about a wider representation of the community on public bodies. There is no code of practice on this, and an attempt by an employment tribunal to supply the deficiency came to grief in the following case.

Corner v *Buckinghamshire County Council*
[1978] ICR 836 Employment Appeal Tribunal

The employee, a teacher, was permitted 15 days a year to carry out his duties as a magistrate. He wanted more time and brought an action claiming that he had not been permitted reasonable time off. The employment tribunal, balancing the needs of the employer against the needs of the employee, considered that a reasonable compromise would be to give the employee 19 days' leave, but stipulating that all leave beyond the first ten days should be unpaid. Both sides appealed.

SLYNN J: '. . . The employee's submission is that the employment tribunal did not have the jurisdiction or the power to impose that condition as a part of their award. On behalf of the employers it is said that the sole power of an employment tribunal . . . is to make a declaration that a complaint that an employer has failed to permit an employee to take time off is well-founded, and in a suitable case to make an award of compensation, but that it is not open to the tribunal to go beyond that. In this case, apparently it is agreed by both parties that there really was no discussion or issue about the number of days which might be taken unpaid. The employers said, quite simply, "15 and no more". The employee said, "I need more". Accordingly, it was open to the tribunal to say that there had been a refusal on the part of the employers to grant the employee time to carry out his duties as a justice of the peace. The question really is whether the employment tribunal can go beyond that. It may be that in a suitable case, as is here accepted on behalf of the employers, that in considering whether there has been a refusal to grant time, the employment tribunal can look at the conditions subject to which an employer is prepared to grant time off (including conditions relating to pay) and could say that the conditions imposed by an employer were such that they really amounted to a refusal to allow time to be taken. But this was not a matter which arose before this tribunal, and we all accept the submission of the employers and the employee, that it is not within the power of the employment tribunal to do more than to make the declaration whether or not there has been a failure to permit the employee to take time off. The tribunal, as we understand it, does not have power to impose conditions upon the parties as to the way in which the time off shall be granted. It is not for the tribunal to re-write the terms of service between the employer and the employee. They may be able to consider whether the conditions are reasonable in deciding whether there has been a refusal but, in our judgment, beyond that, they are not empowered to go.

We, accordingly, uphold the submission made here both by the employee and by the employers that the tribunal did not have jurisdiction to impose the condition in paragraph 21 of their decision, and that condition is deleted from their decision.'

Comment

(1) It is perhaps unfortunate that a tribunal cannot decide what is reasonable if the parties cannot agree; however, there has been little litigation on this section, so presumably there are few problems in practice.

(2) It is not specified in ERA s 50 that the time off must be paid. Interestingly, Slynn J here suggests *obiter* that a failure to pay wages could conceivably be regarded as amounting to a refusal of time off.

LIMITS ON WORKING TIME

Until the Working Time Regulations 1998 came into force, there were no universal legislative provisions dealing with working time and holidays in the United Kingdom. Since the nineteenth century, there had been limitations on the employment of women and children in factories and mines, and the wages councils which operated in various low-paid industries during most of the twentieth century stipulated minimum periods of leave, among other things.

So it may well have continued, had not the European Union stepped in, with the Working Time Directive (93/104/EC). This was passed as a health and safety measure under Article 137 of the Treaty of Rome, meaning that the unanimous consent of member states was not required. Otherwise it would not have passed, because the Conservative government of the time would most certainly not have agreed to it. Indeed, the United Kingdom challenged the legality of the directive, arguing that it was really about terms and conditions of employment and thus should not have been passed without unanimous agreement. This was rejected by the ECJ in *United Kingdom v Council of the European Union* (1997) and the Working Time Regulations finally limped on to the statute book two years after the due implementation date in 1998. They have subsequently been amended several times, partly in response to revisions to the directive. In 2003 the original directive was repealed and replaced by the consolidated Working Time Directive (2003/88/EC), which came into force in August 2004.

The Working Time Regulations do three main things. First, they lay down limits on working time. Secondly, they require workers to be given rest breaks. Thirdly, they stipulate minimum paid annual leave entitlements. Before looking at each of these, we need to identify the workers who come within this statutory protection.

Scope

Working Time Regulations 1998

2 (1) In these Regulations –

. . .

'worker' means an individual who has entered into or works under (or, where the employment has ceased, worked under) –

(a) a contract of employment; or

(b) any other contract, whether express or implied and (if it is express) whether oral or in writing, whereby the individual undertakes to do or perform personally any work or services for another party to the contract whose status is not by virtue of the contract that of a client or customer of any profession or business undertaking carried on by the individual;

and any reference to a worker's contract shall be construed accordingly . . .

Comment

(1) The Regulations give protection to 'workers' rather than just employees. The definition in reg 2 is the same as that in ERA s 230(3) discussed above (p 139). It is clear that some self-employed workers can come within this (*Redrow Homes (Yorkshire) Ltd* v *Wright* (2004)). Agency workers and trainees are expressly included (regs 36 and 42) and there is no qualifying period of service.

(2) Workers in the transport industry were excluded from the original directive, because of their unusual working patterns. However, the Horizontal Amending Directive (2000/34/EC) gave power to extend the Working Time Directive generally, and specific directives were then passed to give protection to seafarers and workers in the road transport and aviation industries. Rail transport was already covered.

(3) There was originally an exception, introduced at the behest of the United Kingdom, for doctors in training. However, they have been brought within the Regulations since 2004. Their position is still exceptional, in that their maximum working hours could average 58 per week until July 2007 and then 56 per week until July 2009. Workers in the armed forces and emergency services are generally outside the protection of the Regulations.

The 48-hour week

The basic rule, set out in reg 4 of the Working Time Regulations and reflecting Art 6 of the directive, is that *average* working hours should not exceed 48 per week. As the average is measured over a 17-week period (and can be over as long as a year by agreement) in practice, this means that workers can still be required to work well above 48 hours a week for quite lengthy periods of time.

One of the biggest issues in relation to this provision is to decide what counts as 'working time'.

Working Time Directive (2003/88/EC)

ARTICLE 2

For the purposes of this Directive, the following definitions shall apply:

(1) 'working time' means any period during which the worker is working, at the employer's disposal and carrying out his activity or duties, in accordance with national laws and/or practice; . . .

Sindicato de Médicos de Asistencia Pública (SIMAP) v *Consellaria de Sanidad y Consumo de la Generalidad Valenciana* [2000] IRLR 845 European Court of Justice

This was an action brought by SIMAP, the union representing doctors in the Spanish public health service, against the responsible regional ministry, challenging the way in which the working time of doctors was calculated. In addition to their regular 40-hour working week, doctors working in primary care teams also had to do substantial on-call time. One group had to be on call from the end of one working day until the beginning of the next, at least once every 11 days. Under the relevant legislation, only that part of the on-call time when they actually worked was counted as part of their working time. The national court referred the question of whether this was compatible with the directive and, in particular, whether it made any difference if they were required to be on call at the health centre or if they were only required to be contactable if needed.

JUDGMENT OF THE COURT: '. . . By questions 2(a) to 2(c), 3(a), 3(b) and 4(c), which it is appropriate to consider together, the national court seeks essentially to determine whether time spent on call by doctors in primary care teams, whether they are required to be present in the health centre or merely contactable, must be regarded as working time or as overtime within the meaning of Directive [2003/88/EC].

It must be borne in mind that that Directive defines working time as any period during which the worker is working, at the employer's disposal and carrying out his activity or duties, in accordance with national laws and/or practice. Moreover, in the scheme of the Directive, it is placed in opposition to rest periods, the two being mutually exclusive.

In the main proceedings, the characteristic features of working time are present in the case of time spent on call by doctors in primary care teams where their presence at the health centre is required. It is not disputed that during periods of duty on call under those rules, the first two conditions are fulfilled. Moreover, even if the activity actually performed varies according to the circumstances, the fact that such doctors are obliged to be present and available at the workplace with a view to providing their professional services means that they are carrying out their duties in that instance.

That interpretation is also in conformity with the objective of Directive [2003/88/EC] which is to ensure the safety and health of workers by granting them minimum periods of rest and adequate breaks ([fifth] recital in the preamble to the Directive). It is clear, as the Advocate General emphasises in point 35 of his Opinion, that to exclude duty on call from working time if physical presence is required would seriously undermine that objective.

As the Advocate General also states in point 37 of his Opinion, the situation is different where doctors in primary care teams are on call by being contactable at all times without having to be at the health centre. Even if they are at the disposal of their employer, in that it must be possible to contact them, in that situation doctors may manage their time with fewer constraints and pursue their own interests. In those circumstances, only time linked to the actual provision of primary care services must be regarded as working time within the meaning of Directive [2003/88/EC].

As regards the question whether time spent on call may be regarded as overtime, although Directive [2003/88/EC] does not define overtime, which is mentioned only in Article 6, relating to the maximum length of the working week, the fact remains that overtime falls within the concept of working time for the purposes of the Directive, which draws no distinction according to whether or not such time is spent within normal hours of work.

The answer to questions 2(a) to 2(c), 3(a), 3(b) and 4(c) is therefore that time spent on call by doctors in primary healthcare teams must be regarded in its entirety as working time, and where appropriate as overtime, within the meaning of Directive [2003/88/EC] if they are required to be present at the health centre. If they must merely be contactable at all times when on call, only time linked to the actual provision of primary care services must be regarded as working time. . . .'

Comment

(1) In addition to holding that on-call time at the employer's premises is working time, the ECJ makes two important points: first, that overtime is part of working time; and, secondly, that working time and rest breaks are mutually exclusive concepts.

(2) In *SIMAP* doctors on call at the health centre were expected to be ready at all times to render service if required. Thus in *Landeshauptstadt Kiel v Jaeger* (2003) a German court referred the question of whether on-call time counted as working time for junior hospital doctors who were provided with a bedroom at the hospital and allowed to sleep if they were not actually needed. The ECJ held that this, too, was working time.

(3) In *Dellas v Premier Ministre* (2006) on-call night duty for teachers in special residential schools in France was discounted, so that the first nine hours counted as only three hours of working time, and thereafter every hour counted as half-an-hour. Again, the ECJ held that this was incompatible with the definition of working time in the directive. However, in *Vorel v Nemocnice Český Krumlov* (2007), a reference from the Czech Republic, where a doctor challenged the practice of paying on-call time at only 20 per cent of the full-time rate unless actual work was performed, the ECJ held that there was no contravention of the Working Time Directive. The ECJ said:

> Directives 93/104 and 2003/88 do not prevent a Member State applying legislation on the remuneration of workers and concerning on-call duties performed by them at the workplace which makes a distinction between the treatment of periods in the course of which work is actually done and those during which no actual work is done, provided that such a system wholly guarantees the practical effect of the rights conferred on workers by the said directives in order to ensure the effective protection of their health and safety.

This would seem to provide a way out for employers otherwise compelled to remunerate workers at the usual rate during on-call time, although in the United Kingdom, this would be subject to the National Minimum Wage Act 1998.

The opt-out

Workers can individually choose to opt out of the 48-hour limit, provided that they agree to this in writing. This is permitted by Art 22 of the Working Time Directive. This derogation, included in the directive at the insistence of the United Kingdom, is highly controversial. Unions argue that employees are vulnerable to pressure to agree to the opt-out and may find it difficult in practice to assert their right to work no more than the 48-hour average. Employers argue that employees should be free to choose to work extra hours and that workers themselves want this freedom.

The opt-out was included in the original directive for a limited period of time initially and came up for review in 2003. Proposals from the European Commission to phase it out over a period of years were rejected by the Council of Ministers in 2006, so it continues for the time being.

Night workers

A 'night worker' is defined in reg 2 of the Working Time Regulations as someone 'who, as a normal course, works at least three hours of his daily working time during night time'. Such workers are subject to the further protection that their daily working hours should not exceed eight in any 24-hour period, averaged over 17 weeks.

In *R* v *Attorney General (Northern Ireland) ex parte Burns* (1999) the High Court in Northern Ireland held that an employee who worked nights one week in every three was a night worker within the meaning of the Regulations. The test was whether she regularly worked nights, not whether the majority of her work was done at night.

Rest breaks

Working Time Regulations 1998

10   (1)   A worker is entitled to a rest period of not less than eleven consecutive hours in each 24-hour period during which he works for his employer.

(2)   Subject to paragraph (3), a young worker is entitled to a rest period of not less than twelve consecutive hours in each 24-hour period during which he works for his employer.

(3)   The minimum rest period provided for in paragraph (2) may be interrupted in the case of activities involving periods of work that are split up over the day or of short duration.

11   (1)   Subject to paragraph (2), a worker is entitled to an uninterrupted rest period of not less than 24 hours in each seven-day period during which he works for his employer.

(2)   If his employer so determines, a worker shall be entitled to either –

(a)   two uninterrupted rest periods each of not less than 24 hours in each 14-day period during which he works for his employer; or

(b)   one uninterrupted rest period of not less than 48 hours in each such 14-day period, in place of the entitlement provided for in paragraph (1) . . .

12   (1)   Where a worker's daily working time is more than six hours, he is entitled to a rest break.

(2)   The details of the rest break to which a worker is entitled under paragraph (1), including its duration and the terms on which it is granted, shall be in accordance with any provisions for the purposes of this regulation which are contained in a collective agreement or a workforce agreement.

(3)   Subject to the provisions of any applicable collective agreement or workforce agreement, the rest break provided for in paragraph (1) is an uninterrupted period of not less than 20 minutes, and the worker is entitled to spend it away from his workstation if he has one . . .

Comment

(1) A young worker is someone over compulsory school age but under the age of 18. Their entitlements to rest breaks are a little more generous than for adult workers. Note that weekly rest is additional to daily rest.

(2) While the 48-hour limit is mandatory (subject to exceptions such as the opt-out), the rest break regulations provide an *entitlement* for workers. The DTI Guidance to the Working Time Regulations therefore stated that: 'employers must make sure that workers can take their rest, but are not required to make sure that they do take their rest.' In *Commission of the EC* v *UK* (2006) the ECJ upheld a complaint that the negative way in which this was expressed might make it less likely that workers would be encouraged to use their entitlements, although the Court did not think that the directive put employers under an obligation to ensure that workers took their breaks. The upshot was only that the guidance was changed to remove the second clause of the sentence.

Annual leave

Working Time Regulations 1998

13   (1) Subject to paragraph (5), a worker is entitled to four weeks' annual leave in each leave year . . .
        (9) Leave to which a worker is entitled under this regulation may be taken in instalments, but –
        (a) it may only be taken in the leave year in respect of which it is due, and
        (b) it may not be replaced by a payment in lieu except where the worker's employment is terminated.
13A   (1) Subject to regulation 26A and paragraphs (3) and (5), a worker is entitled in each leave year to a period of additional leave determined in accordance with paragraph (2).
        (2) The period of additional leave to which a worker is entitled under paragraph (1) is –
        (a) in any leave year beginning on or after 1st October 2007 but before 1st April 2008, 0.8 weeks;
        (b) in any leave year beginning before 1st October 2007, a proportion of 0.8 weeks equivalent to the proportion of the year beginning on 1st October 2007 which would have elapsed at the end of that leave year;
        (c) in any leave year beginning on 1st April 2008, 0.8 weeks; . . .

Comment

(1) In practice, the provision for a minimum of four weeks' paid annual leave had the greatest impact on working people of any of the provisions of the Working Time Regulations – as well as generating the largest number of legal challenges.

(2) The extension of paid leave entitlement in reg 13A was introduced by regulations made under the Work and Families Act 2006. For workers working a standard five-day week, this means an extra eight days in total and is meant in effect to give workers bank and public holidays in addition to the basic four-week period.

(3) Note that part-time workers are entitled to leave on a pro rata basis – so someone who works only two days a week would get eight days' leave under reg 13, as the equivalent to four weeks off work.

(4) Originally the Regulations contained a 13-week qualifying period for this right, but this was successfully challenged in the ECJ by the Broadcasting, Entertainment, Cinematographic and Theatre Union, many of whose members work on very short-term contracts (*R* v *Secretary of State ex parte BECTU* (2001)). This gave employers some difficulties about how to make paid leave arrangements for casual and temporary workers on short-term contracts. The solution adopted by many was to include an element of holiday pay in the hourly rate of pay (giving the worker what was called a 'rolled-up' rate). In some cases this was genuinely an increased hourly rate. Other employers simply redesignated their existing hourly rate as a rolled-up rate. The compatibility of this with the directive was tested in the next case.

Robinson-Steele v *R D Retail Services Ltd; Clarke* v *Frank Staddon Ltd; Caulfield* v *Hanson Clay Products Ltd* [2006] IRLR 386 European Court of Justice

These joined appeals all concerned temporary workers who had been paid 'rolled-up' holiday pay. The Court of Appeal held that this was permissible; the Scottish Court of Session thought it was not. The question was referred to the ECJ.

Article 7 of the Working Time Directive states:

(1)   Member States shall take the measures necessary to ensure that every worker is entitled to paid annual leave of at least four weeks in accordance with the conditions for entitlement to, and granting of, such leave laid down by national legislation and/or practice.

(2)   The minimum period of paid annual leave may not be replaced by an allowance in lieu, except where the employment relationship is terminated.

JUDGMENT OF THE COURT: '. . . By those questions the referring courts are asking, in essence, whether Article 7 of the Directive precludes payment for minimum annual leave within the meaning of that provision from being made in the form of part payments staggered over the corresponding annual period of work and paid together with the remuneration for work done, rather than in the form of a payment in respect of a specific period during which the worker actually takes leave.

In that regard, it must be stated that there is no provision in the Directive which lays down expressly the point at which the payment for annual leave must be made.

Under Article 7(1) of the Directive, the Member States are to take the measures necessary to ensure that every worker is entitled to paid annual leave of at least four weeks in accordance with the conditions for entitlement to, and granting of, such leave laid down by national legislation and/or practice.

The fixing of the point at which the payment for annual leave must be made comes within those conditions.

In that regard, the Member States must ensure that the detailed national implementing rules take account of the limits flowing from the Directive itself.

The Directive treats entitlement to annual leave and to a payment on that account as being two aspects of a single right. The purpose of the requirement of payment for that leave is to put the worker, during such leave, in a position which is, as regards remuneration, comparable to periods of work.

Accordingly, without prejudice to more favourable provisions under Article 15 of the Directive, the point at which the payment for annual leave is made must be fixed in such a way that, during that leave, the worker is, as regards remuneration, put in a position comparable to periods of work.

Furthermore, account must be taken of the fact that, under Article 7(2) of the Directive, the minimum period of paid annual leave may not be replaced by an allowance in lieu, except where the employment relationship is terminated. That prohibition is intended to ensure that a worker is normally entitled to actual rest, with a view to ensuring effective protection of his health and safety (see, to that effect, *R* v *Secretary of State ex parte BECTU* (2001) and *Merino Gómez* v *Continental Industrias del Caucho* (2004)).

A regime such as that referred to by the questions at issue may lead to situations in which, without the conditions laid down in Article 7(2) of the Directive being met, the minimum period of paid annual leave is, in effect, replaced by an allowance in lieu.

It is appropriate to add that Article 7 of the Directive is not one of the provisions from which the Directive expressly allows derogations (see *BECTU*). Therefore, it does not matter whether such a regime of paid annual leave is or is not based on a contractual arrangement.

It follows from all the foregoing considerations that the reply to the first question referred in each of cases C-131/04 and C-257/04 and to the fourth question referred in case C-257/04 must be that Article 7 of the Directive precludes the payment for minimum annual leave within the meaning of that provision from being made in the form of part payments staggered over the corresponding annual period of work and paid together with the remuneration for work done, rather than in the form of a payment in respect of a specific period during which the worker actually takes leave . . .'

Comment

(1) The ECJ has interpreted the requirements of Art 7 strictly, recognising that if workers are not actually paid during the leave period, they are less likely to take the leave.

(2) In *Federatie Nederlandse Vakbeweging* v *Staat der Nederlanden* (2006) the Dutch trade union federation challenged advice from the relevant Ministry which said that annual leave could be carried over from one year to the next, and that it could then either be taken as leave or exchanged for payment in lieu. The ECJ held that this was a breach of Art 7, which is clear that leave entitlement can only be exchanged for payment in lieu when the employment relationship is terminated.

Sunday working

The Sunday Trading Act 1994 allowed shops to open on Sundays, following years of fierce debate. A major argument against allowing this was concern that shop workers would be compelled to work on Sundays. Therefore, the Sunday Trading Act provided protection whereby workers (except those recruited specifically to work on Sundays) have a right to opt out of Sunday working on giving three months' notice to their employer. The relevant statutory provisions are now to be found in ERA ss 36–43.

Shop workers who were already employed when this came into force (25 August 1994) have the status of 'protected' shop workers, and cannot be required to work on Sundays. Both protected and opted-out shop workers have remedies if they suffer any detriment for not working on Sundays, and dismissal or selection for redundancy on this ground is automatically unfair.

REFERENCES AND FURTHER READING

DTI (2000), *Work and Parents: Competitiveness and Choice*, CM 5005

S Evans and R Lewis (1987), 'Anti-Union Discrimination: Practice, Law and Policy' 16 ILJ 88

A McColgan (2000), 'Family friendly frolics? The Maternity and Parental Leave etc Regulations 1999' 29 ILJ 125

Visit **http://www.mylawchamber.co.uk/pitt**
to access live web updates and web links to extend
your knowledge of Employment Law.

7

EQUAL PAY

The Equal Pay Act 1970 was passed to address part of the problem of discrimination against women at work. At one time it was regarded as quite acceptable to pay a woman less than a man doing exactly the same work and employers openly set a man's rate and a woman's rate for the job. Although the TUC supported the principle of equal pay as long ago as 1888, this did not translate into practical action. When the Equal Pay Act was passed, the average wage of full-time female workers was less than two-thirds that of full-time male workers.

Support for the basic principle of equality can be found in numerous international treaties and in ILO Convention No 100. However, in practice, the most important treaty obligation is that in the Treaty of Rome.

Treaty of Rome (Treaty establishing the European Community)

ARTICLE 141

1 Each Member State shall ensure that the principle of equal pay for male and female workers for equal work or work of equal value is applied.
2 For the purpose of this article, 'pay' means the ordinary basic or minimum wage or salary and any other consideration, whether in cash or in kind, which the worker receives directly or indirectly, in respect of his employment, from his employer.

   Equal pay without discrimination based on sex means:
   (a) that pay for the same work at piece rates shall be calculated on the basis of the same unit of measurement;
   (b) that pay for work at time rates shall be the same for the same job.
3 The Council, acting in accordance with the procedure referred to in Article 251, and after consulting the Economic and Social Committee, shall adopt measures to ensure the application of the principle of equal opportunities and equal treatment of men and women in matters of employment and occupation, including the principle of equal pay for equal work or work of equal value.
4 With a view to ensuring full equality in practice between men and women in working life, the principle of equal treatment shall not prevent any Member State from maintaining or adopting measures providing for specific advantages in order to make it easier for the underrepresented sex to pursue a vocational activity or to prevent or compensate for disadvantages in professional careers.

Comment

(1) In *Defrenne* v *SABENA (No 2)* (1976) the ECJ held that this article had direct horizontal and vertical effect, meaning that it could be relied upon by an individual in

English courts and tribunals even if the national legislation intended to give it effect was defective or inconsistent with it. In relation to terms and conditions of employment it is amplified by the Equal Pay Directive 1975 (75/117/EEC).

Equal Pay Directive (75/117/EEC)

ARTICLE 1

The principle of equal pay for men and women outlined in Article 119 of the Treaty, hereinafter called 'principle of equal pay', means, for the same work or for work to which equal value is attributed, the elimination of all discrimination on grounds of sex with regard to all aspects and conditions of remuneration.

In particular, where a job classification system is used for determining pay, it must be based on the same criteria for both men and women and so drawn up as to exclude any discrimination on grounds of sex.

ARTICLE 2

Member States shall introduce into their national legal systems such measures as are necessary to enable all employees who consider themselves wronged by failure to apply the principle of equal pay to pursue their claims by judicial process after possible recourse to other competent authorities.

ARTICLE 3

Member States shall abolish all discrimination between men and women arising from laws, regulations or administrative provisions which is contrary to the principle of equal pay.

ARTICLE 4

Member States shall take the necessary measures to ensure that provisions appearing in collective agreements, wage scales, wage agreements or individual contracts of employment which are contrary to the principle of equal pay shall be, or may be declared, null and void or may be amended . . .

Comment

(1) In *Jenkins* v *Kingsgate* (1981) the ECJ held that Art 1 of the Equal Pay Directive 1975 merely explains and does not extend Art 141, meaning that a claimant can rely on it directly in equal pay proceedings in British courts and tribunals.

(2) Although we tend to talk about 'equal pay', it is actually a shorthand way of referring to equal terms and conditions of employment generally between men and women. Thus the Equal Treatment Directive 1976 is also relevant to this area, although in *Gillespie* v *Northern Health and Social Services Board* (1996) the ECJ held that the Equal Treatment Directive and the Equal Pay Directive were mutually exclusive: they cannot both apply to the same set of facts. The Recast Equal Treatment Directive (2006/54/EC) brings the two directives together and is to be implemented by August 2009, but this will not change the substantive position.

(3) The Equal Pay Act 1970 was not passed in order to implement the Equal Pay Directive, but was considered to be sufficient to implement EC law and to need only slight amendment when the United Kingdom joined the EC. This has not always

proved to be the case in practice, as we will see. Thus consideration of British equal pay legislation must include reference to EU law, both as an aid to interpretation and as a standard against which British law should be tested.

(4) Although passed in 1970, the Equal Pay Act was not brought into force until 29 December 1975 – the date on which the Sex Discrimination Act 1975 came into force. This was so that employers would not react to a requirement to give women equal terms to men by simply refusing to employ women. The five-year lead-in also gave employers due warning of what was required and ample time to sort out their payment systems and equalise terms for men and women before the legislation came into force.

CLAIMS FOR EQUAL PAY

While the Equal Pay Act 1970 was passed in order to address discrimination against women, it is in fact symmetrical in design, like the SDA, so men can claim equal terms with women as well as women claiming equal terms with men. It operates by deeming an 'equality clause' to be included in every contract of employment, providing that any terms in a woman's contract which are less favourable than those in the comparator man's contract (or which do not appear at all in the woman's contract) are to be equalised (EqPA s 1(1), (2)). There are three situations in which an equality clause can be relied upon; each will be considered in turn.

Like work

The first situation where equal pay can be claimed is –

Equal Pay Act 1970

1 . . .

  (2) . . .

  (a) where the woman is employed on like work with a man in the same employment . . .

. . .

  (4) A woman is to be regarded as employed on like work with men if, but only if, her work and theirs is of the same or a broadly similar nature, and the differences (if any) between the things she does and the things they do are not of practical importance in relation to terms and conditions of employment; and accordingly in comparing her work with theirs regard shall be had to the frequency or otherwise with which any such differences occur in practice as well as to the nature and extent of the differences.

Capper Pass Ltd v Lawton [1977] ICR 83 Employment Appeal Tribunal

PHILLIPS J: '. . . The employee worked as a cook in the kitchen from which the directors of the employers, and their guests, were served. She sought equality of treatment with Mr Smith and Mr Brattan, who were employed as assistant chefs in the kitchen serving the canteen at the employers' factory. She was the only cook in her kitchen. She had to provide lunch for between 10 and 20 persons per day, and the kitchen was of an appropriate semi-domestic sort. Mr Smith and Mr Brattan worked as assistant chefs under a head chef and between them provided 350 meals a day in six sittings: two for breakfast, two for lunch, and two for tea. The kitchen in which they worked was on an appropriate non-domestic scale. The facts upon which the complaint had to be decided were not in dispute, and, as the employment tribunal said, it was a question of how to interpret them.

284

It is not necessary for the purposes of this judgment to set out the whole of the facts and circumstances. During the course of the argument Mr Bradley, for the employers, summarised the main differences between the work done by the employee and that done by Mr Smith and Mr Brattan under five heads, as follows: (i) the employee was the directors' cook, cooking on a domestic scale. The others were cooks in an industrial canteen. (ii) She worked a 40-hour week. The others worked a 45½-hour week, and one Saturday in three. (iii) She did not have to prepare food in advance on a large scale. They did. (iv) She only cooked lunch; they cooked breakfast, lunch and tea in two sittings; and (v) she was not answerable to a head chef, and to that extent might be admitted to have greater authority. She was answerable to the catering manager; they were answerable to the head chef. As against this, when the catering manager was on holiday the head chef deputised for him, so that one of the assistant chefs had to take over the head chef's functions, and similarly, when the head chef was on holiday, one of them had to take his place . . .

The vital provision in determining whether a woman is employed on like work with a man is to be found in section 1(4), and we think that it may be helpful to say something about the proper approach to that provision.

It is obviously difficult, in an Act intended to prevent discrimination between men and women in terms and conditions of employment, to define the test which is to be applied in determining whether discrimination exists. It is easy to talk in general terms but very hard to lay down a clear test which can be applied satisfactorily in practice. One can see that it would be possible to prescribe tests of varying degrees of severity. The least favourable from a woman's point of view would be to require equality of treatment when men and women are doing the *same work*. More favourable would be to require equality where the work done by the man and woman, although different, was of *equal value*. The Act has chosen a middle course. Equality of treatment is required where the woman is employed on "like work" with the man. And "like work" is work which is of the *same* nature as, or of a broadly *similar* nature to, the man's work.

In cases of dispute this test, imposed by section 1(4), requires the employment tribunal to make a comparison between the work done by the woman and the work done by the man. It is clear from the terms of the subsection that the work need not be of the *same* nature in order to be like work. It is enough if it is of a similar nature. Indeed, it need only be broadly similar. In such cases where the work is of a broadly similar nature (and not of the *same* nature) there will necessarily be differences between the work done by the woman and the work done by the man. It seems clear to us that the definition requires the employment tribunal to bring to the solution of the question, whether work is of a broadly similar nature, a broad judgment. Because, in such cases, there will be such differences of one sort or another it would be possible in almost every case, by too pedantic an approach, to say that the work was not of a like nature despite the similarity of what was done and the similar kinds of skill and knowledge required to do it. That would be wrong. The intention, we think, is clearly that the employment tribunal should not be required to undertake too minute an examination, or be constrained to find that work is not like work merely because of insubstantial differences.

It seems to us that in most cases the inquiry will fall into two stages. *First*, is the work of the same, or, if not, "of a broadly similar" nature? This question can be answered by a general consideration of the type of work involved, and of the skill and knowledge required to do it. It seems to us to be implicit in the words of subsection (4) that it can be answered without a minute examination of the detail of the differences between the work done by the man and the work done by the woman. But, *secondly*, if on such an examination the answer is that the work is of a broadly similar nature, it is then necessary to go on to consider the detail and to inquire whether the differences between the work being compared are of "practical importance in relation to terms and conditions of employment". In answering that question the employment tribunal will be guided by the concluding words of the subsection. But again, it seems to us, trivial differences, or differences not likely in the real world to be reflected in the terms and conditions of employment, ought to be disregarded. In other words, once it is determined that work is of a broadly similar nature it should be regarded as being like work unless the differences are plainly of a kind which the employment tribunal in its experience would expect to find reflected in the terms and conditions of employment. This last point requires to be emphasised. There seems to be a tendency, apparent in some of the decisions of employment tribunals cited to us, and in some of the arguments upon the hearing of this appeal, to weigh up the differences by reference to such questions as whether one type of work or another is or is not suitable for women, or is the kind of work which women can do, or whether the differences are important, and so on. These are not the tests prescribed by the Act. The only differences which will prevent work which is of a broadly similar nature from being "like work" are differences which in practice will be reflected in the terms and conditions of employment . . .'

Comment

(1) Applying this test to the facts, the EAT held that the tribunal had been correct in holding that Ms Lawton was entitled to equal pay. Note that this meant that she should get the same hourly rate, not the same overall pay.

(2) This was the first case to reach the EAT on the meaning of like work. Its liberal approach to the interpretation of that phrase was subsequently endorsed by the Court of Appeal.

Dugdale v Kraft Foods Ltd [1977] ICR 48 Employment Appeal Tribunal

Four women employed as quality control inspectors claimed parity with the six male quality control inspectors who worked with them, but who received a higher basic wage. The women worked morning and afternoon shifts. The men worked these shifts, but also night shifts and Sunday mornings. The night shifts were compulsory for the men, once every three weeks, but they received a shift allowance of more than 25 per cent of the basic wage for this. The Sunday morning shifts were optional, but all the men chose to work them. At that date, women were prevented by statute from working at night unless the employer obtained a specific exemption to allow it.

The employment tribunal held that the work of the men and women was similar, but that working at night constituted a difference of such magnitude that the women could not be said to be employed on like work with the men.

PHILLIPS J: '. . . To summarise, it seems to us on the admitted facts to be clear that the female employees' work (or certainly Mrs Dugdale's) and that of the male quality control inspectors was of the same or a broadly similar nature, and that the question, then, was whether the differences between the things which the female employees did and the things which the men did were of practical importance in relation to terms and conditions of employment. This involves a consideration of two separate matters: (1) the fact that the male quality control inspectors unlike the female employees worked at night and on Sunday morning, and (2) the nature of the work which they did on those occasions. It is not clear to us that the employment tribunal in reaching its decision distinguished between these two matters.

It appears to us to be necessary to decide, as a matter of the construction of s 1(4), whether the first of these matters, ie the fact of doing work at a different time, falls within the words "the things she does and the things they do". To simplify the question by an example: take a factory in which a simple repetitive process of assembly takes place, employing men and women engaged on identical work. Suppose that the men did, but the women did not, work at night and on a Sunday morning doing the same work. Undoubtedly, the women's work and the men's work would be of the same or a broadly similar nature. Prima facie, therefore, they would be employed on "like work". Does the fact that the men work at night and on Sunday morning, and the women do not, constitute a difference between the things which the women do and the things which the men do? It may be that either view is possible. A man, if asked what he does, might reply, "I assemble radio components", or he might reply, "I assemble radio components on the night shift". We have come to the conclusion that, in the context of the Equal Pay Act 1970 (as amended), the mere time at which the work is performed should be disregarded when considering the differences between the things which the woman does and the things which the man does. Were it not so, the Act could never apply in cases where it must obviously have been intended to apply, where the men doing the same work are engaged on a night shift . . .

It does not seem to us that this interpretation of section 1(4) would lead to any unfairness; rather the reverse. Where the work done is the same, and the only difference is the time at which it is done, the men will be compensated for the extra burden of working at night or on Sundays by the shift payment or premium. There seems to be no reason why the women should not have equality of treatment in respect of the basic wage, or in respect of the day shift payment (if any). In a case in which the men are not paid a shift payment or premium for night working or Sunday working, but are paid at an enhanced basic wage to reflect their readiness to work at nights or on Sundays, there seems to us to be no reason why, in giving effect to the equality clause in accordance with s 1(2)(a)(i), the terms in the women's contract as to remuneration should not be so modified as to take account of the fact that the men do, and they do not, work at nights or on Sunday . . .'

Comment

(1) The case was remitted to the employment tribunal because it had not given sufficient consideration to whether the work done by the men on the night shift or on Sunday mornings was different from the work done on the day shifts. For a case where the added responsibility which came from working a permanent night shift without a supervisor being available *was* held to be a difference of practical importance, see *Thomas* v *NCB* (1987).

(2) What is to stop an employer getting round the decision in *Dugdale* v *Kraft Foods* by paying a massive premium for night shifts worked by men? In such a case, the claimant would have to lead evidence to show that the premium was excessive. In *NCB* v *Sherwin* (1978) the EAT noted that 'the percentage taken to represent the differential properly attributed to night work is often of the order of 20 per cent', and also said:

> . . . the disadvantage of working at night or at other inconvenient times can be compensated by an additional night shift premium, or other appropriate arrangement; but there is no reason why the person, usually the man, should receive by way of remuneration a sum which is greater than necessary to recognise the fact that he works at night, or at other inconvenient times; and if he does there is no reason why the woman should not be remunerated to the extent of the excess.

(3) Most restrictions on women's working hours, including night work, were removed by the Sex Discrimination Act 1986.

Shields v E Coomes (Holdings) Ltd [1978] ICR 1159 Court of Appeal

LORD DENNING MR: 'E Coomes (Holdings) Ltd are bookmakers, alias turf accountants. They have 90 betting shops, 60 of them in south-east London, and the remaining 30 in south coast towns, such as Ramsgate, where they have five. In 81 of the shops they have two counter-hands, who are both women. But in nine of the shops one of the counterhands is a man, and the other is a woman. The reason why they have a man in those nine is because they are situated in areas where the company anticipate there may be trouble from customers and others: and a man is needed to cope with it, if it arises. One of these nine shops is in Sussex Street, Pimlico. The employment tribunal describes it:

> "The company has a policy of employing some male counterhands at each of those nine shops, not only as a possible deterrent to attack or forcible entry or other trouble, but also to ensure that, if trouble arises then physical help shall be available on the spot to repel it until such time as the police are given an opportunity of arriving . . ."

The tribunal describes how the company took over this shop in 1973. They were told that trouble had been experienced there before they took over, but they had not themselves had any trouble in their three years of ownership. The company said that this period of calm has been ensured by employing suitable male personnel, particularly on the counter where he was read-ily visible. The man was especially important when the shop is opened in the mornings as a cover or precaution against illegal entry when the opening of the shop makes it most vulner-able to attack. The man was needed, too, from time to time when cash had to be transported to and from their shop and other shops or head office.

Those findings make it clear that, at those nine shops in troublesome areas, the man fills a protective role. He does the same work at the counter as the woman counterhand. He takes the bets and receives and pays out the money. But, in his protective role, he works longer hours. He has to be at the shop when it is opened and most vulnerable, whereas the woman comes half-an-hour later. He is required to work a basic week of 37$\frac{1}{2}$ hours a week as compared with a woman counterhand who does 32$\frac{1}{2}$ hours.

Now here is the point: at 81 shops in trouble-free areas, the counterhands are all women and receive 92p per hour. But at the nine shops in troublesome areas the man counterhand is paid £1.06 per hour, and the woman 92p per hour. . . .

In this case the woman and the man were employed on work of a broadly similar nature. They were both counterhands. There were several differences between the things she did and the things which he did; for instance, he started at opening time and worked longer hours; but this did not, by itself, warrant a difference in the "rate for the job". He carried cash from shop to shop or to head office. But this difference was, by itself, "not of practical importance". The one difference of any significance between them was that the man filled a protective role. He was a watchdog ready to bark and scare off intruders. This difference, when taken with the others, amounted to differences which the majority of the employment tribunal found were "real and existing and of practical importance". Accepting this finding, I do not think these differ-ences could or did affect the "rate for the job". Both the woman and the man worked alongside one another hour after hour, doing precisely the same work. She should, therefore, receive the same hourly rate as he. It is rather like the difference between a barman and a barmaid. They do the same work as one another in serving drinks. Each has his or her own way of deal-ing with awkward customers. Each is subject to the same risk of abuse or unpleasantness. But, whichever way each adopts in dealing with awkward customers, the job of each, as a job, is of equivalent rating. Each should, therefore, receive the same "rate for the job". It comes within s 1(4) as "like work".

It would be otherwise if the difference was based on any special personal qualification that he had; as, for instance, if he was a fierce and formidable figure, trained to tackle intruders. Then there might be a variation such as to warrant a "wage differential" under s 1(3). But no such special personal qualification is suggested. The only difference between the two jobs is on the ground of sex. He may have been a small nervous man, who could not say "boo to a goose".

She may have been as fierce and formidable as a battle-axe. Such differences, whatever they were, did not have any relation to the terms and conditions of employment. They did not affect the "rate for the job".

I confess, however, that I have felt great difficulty in overcoming the finding of the employment tribunal that the differences, especially the protective role of the man, were "real and existing and of practical importance". I thought for some time that this protective role should be rewarded by some additional bonus or premium. But my difficulties on this score have been resolved by giving supremacy to Community law. Under that law it is imperative that "pay for work at time rates shall be the same for the same job" (article 141); and that all discrimination on the ground of sex shall be eliminated with regard to all aspects and conditions of remuneration: see Council Directive 75/117/EEC article 1. The differences found by the majority of the employment tribunal are all based on sex. They are because he is a man. He only gets the higher hourly rate because he is a man. In order to eliminate all discrimination, there should be an equality clause written into the woman's contract.

I would, therefore dismiss the appeal.'

BRIDGE LJ: '. . . The matter falls for decision, as already stated, under s 1 of the Equal Pay Act. In comparing the claimant's position with that of her fellow counterhand, Mr Rolls, three possible questions fell to be answered, as they would in any case where a woman claims an equality clause by virtue of employment on like work with a man under s 1(2)(a). First, was their work of the same or a broadly similar nature? Secondly, if so, were any differences between the things she did and the things he did (regard being had to the frequency, nature and extent of such differences) of practical importance in relation to terms and conditions of employment? These first two questions arise under section 1(4) which defines like work. The legal burden of proving that she is employed on like work with a man rests on the woman claimant. But if the first question is answered in her favour, an evidential burden of showing differences of practical importance rests upon the employers. The third question under section 1(3) arises only if the woman has established that she is employed on like work with a man. Can the employer then prove that any variation between the woman's contract and the man's is genuinely due to a material difference (other than the difference of sex) between her case and his? If so, her claim to an equality clause is defeated . . .'

(Bridge LJ and Orr LJ concurred in holding that the claimant was entitled to equal pay.)

Comment

(1) The three-stage approach to like work cases set out by Bridge LJ is a helpful way of dealing with these cases. The third stage, the genuine material factor defence, is considered later in this chapter.

(2) On situations where it is alleged that the men have additional responsibilities see also *Electrolux v Hutchinson* (1977).

(3) The emphasis in these cases is very much on what the employees actually do, rather than what they might do. It would seem to follow, therefore, that if the men had skills and qualifications for their protective role, but did not actually have to exercise them in practice, the women would still have a like work claim. It should be noted that in *Angestelltenbetriebsrat der Wiener Gebietskrankenkasse v Wiener Gebietskrankenkasse* (1999) the ECJ held that graduate psychologists and medical doctors providing psychotherapy services were not doing similar work because of their different training and qualifications, which would mean that the two groups would draw upon knowledge and expertise derived from their distinct disciplines, although ostensibly providing the same

service. This may be an area where UK law is stricter than EU law in its approach to what is the same or broadly similar work. It is possible for people doing the same job but with different levels of qualifications or training to be remunerated at different rates, but this is usually done at Bridge LJ's third stage – considering whether or not there is a genuine material factor distinguishing the cases.

Eaton Ltd v *Nuttall* [1977] ICR 272 Employment Appeal Tribunal

The claimant was employed as one of six production schedulers, who were responsible for ordering materials to ensure that the production process proceeded smoothly. She earned £45.38 per week and claimed equal pay with a male production scheduler who earned £51.88 per week.

PHILLIPS J: '. . . We turn now to the case as it proceeded before the employment tribunal and to the point put forward in the notice of appeal. This matter is dealt with in para 7 of the employment tribunal's reasons. It is there stated:

> "So far as [the claimant] is concerned it is suggested by the [employers] that the work she does involves a different and less degree of responsibility from that involved in the work done by the male production schedulers. The test by which this suggested difference in degree of responsibility is established is by gravity of consequence in the event of an error and we unanimously reject that as being the proper test for responsibility. The proper test is whether or not the same function is done with the same degree of competence; if it is, then the responsibility is the same."

Mr Turner [counsel for the employee] suggested that in this passage the employment tribunal were not rejecting responsibility as being always irrelevant but holding that in the circumstances of this case it was of no importance. We do not read the decision in this way, and it seems clear to us that the employment tribunal were saying that it is always irrelevant to see whether the acts done by the woman and the man, albeit the same, may have very different consequences if badly done. The contention in the present case was that, whereas the claimant looked after 2,400 items up to a value of £2.50, Mr Biddle looked after 1,200 items of a value from £5 to £1,000, so that an error by him was likely to have far more serious consequences.

In our judgment the employment tribunal came to a wrong conclusion on this point. Several decisions of the appeal tribunal have said that in applying s 1(4) of the Act the most important point to consider is what the woman does and what the man does, but we do not think that it is right to disregard the circumstances in which they do it, any more than it would be right to do so when applying s 1(5); and the circumstances in which a job is carried out would commonly be taken into account in an evaluation study. Thus in *Waddington* v *Leicester Council for Voluntary Service* (1977), when considering s 1(4), we said that it was wrong to ignore the responsibility for supervision taken by the woman and not by the man albeit that in the circumstances of that case it was difficult to pin-point particular acts done in performance of the duty to supervise. In earlier cases we have tried to discourage employment tribunals from applying s 1(4) too narrowly, and this we strongly endorse; and we should expect them to act in that way when considering such matters as responsibility. Nonetheless this is a job aspect highly regarded by all groups of employers and employees alike, and we would think it not only unacceptable, but also wrong, to ignore it as a factor properly to be taken into account. The sort of situation where we think that the existence of a factor such as responsibility, in the case of one only of two persons whose work is being compared, might truly be decisive is where it can be seen to put one into a different grade from the other. For example, suppose two book-keepers working side by side doing, so far as actions were concerned, almost identical work, where on an examination of the importance of the work done it could be seen that one was a senior book-keeper and another a junior book-keeper. Such distinctions between two employees are often easy to spot in practice but difficult to distinguish only in the terms of what each of them does. That is the sort of case where we think that the existence of the factor of responsibility might be crucial. Accordingly we came to the conclusion that the employment tribunal misdirected itself on this point . . .'

(The case was remitted to a different employment tribunal for rehearing.)

Work rated as equivalent under a job evaluation scheme

Equal Pay Act 1970

1   . . .
   (2) . . .
      (b)   where the woman is employed on work rated as equivalent with that of a man in the same employment . . .

. . .

   (5)   A woman is to be regarded as employed on work rated as equivalent with that of any men if, but only if, her job and their job have been given an equal value, in terms of the demand made on a worker under various headings (for instance effort, skill, decision), on a study undertaken with a view to evaluating in those terms the jobs to be done by all or any of the employees in an undertaking or group of undertakings, or would have been given an equal value but for the evaluation being made on a system setting different values for men and women on the same demand under any heading.

Comment

(1) Job evaluation studies permit the comparison of jobs involving entirely different duties. Given the persistence of *de facto* job segregation in many parts of the labour market between 'women's jobs' and 'men's jobs', which means that in many cases there is no man employed on like work with whom a woman could compare in a like work claim, job evaluation is an extremely important tool in achieving equal pay for women.

(2) A job evaluation study normally compares all jobs across an organisation. There is no single accepted method of carrying them out, nor a foolproof one. The main methods were conveniently summarised in *Eaton Ltd* v *Nuttall*. (The judge refers to an Acas Guide which has since been superseded.)

Eaton Ltd v *Nuttall* [1977] ICR 272 Employment Appeal Tribunal

PHILLIPS J:
'APPENDIX
As not all concerned are familiar with job evaluation, we set out below a note on the principal methods (*see*: ACAS Guide No 1).
   Job ranking.   This is commonly thought to be the simplest method. Each job is considered as a whole and is then given a ranking in relation to all other jobs. A ranking table is then drawn up and the ranked jobs grouped into grades. Pay levels can then be fixed for each grade.

Paired comparisons.   This is also a simple method. Each job is compared as a whole with each other job in turn and points (0, 1 or 2) awarded according to whether its overall importance is judged to be less than, equal to or more than the other. Points awarded for each job are then totalled and a ranking order produced.

Job classification.   This is similar to ranking except that it starts from the opposite end; the grading structure is established first and individual jobs fitted into it. A broad description of each grade is drawn up and individual jobs considered typical of each grade are selected as "benchmarks". The other jobs are then compared with these benchmarks and the general description and placed in their appropriate grade.

Points assessment.   This is the most common system in use. It is an analytical method, which, instead of comparing whole jobs, breaks down each job into a number of factors – for example, skills, responsibility, physical and mental requirements and working conditions. Each of these factors may be analysed further. Points are awarded for each factor according to a predetermined scale and the total points decide a job's place in the ranking order. Usually, the factors are weighted so that, for example, more or less weight may be given to hard physical conditions or to a high degree of skill.

Factor comparison.   This is also an analytical method, employing the same principles as points assessment but using only a limited number of factors, such as skill, responsibility and working conditions. A number of "key" jobs are selected because their wage rates are generally agreed to be "fair". The proportion of the total wage attributable to each factor is then decided and a scale produced showing the rate for each factor of each key job. The other jobs are then compared with this scale, factor by factor, so that a rate is finally obtained for each factor of each job. The total pay for each job is reached by adding together the rates for its individual factors.'

Bromley v H & J Quick Ltd [1988] ICR 623 Court of Appeal

The employers carried out a job evaluation study, essentially by using the paired comparison method. The female claimants claimed that the job evaluation study was invalid and that their work was of equal value to that of male comparators who had been ranked higher.

DILLON LJ: '. . . It is clear from the decision of the European Court in *Rummler* v *Dato Druck GmbH* (1987) that the consideration of any job, and of the qualities required to perform that job, under a job evaluation study must be objective. See especially paragraphs 13 and 14, where it is said:

> "13 It follows that the principle of equal pay requires essentially that the nature of the work to be carried out be considered objectively. Consequently, the same work or work to which equal value is attributed must be remunerated in the same manner whether it is carried out by a man or by a woman. Where a job classification system is used in determining remuneration, that system must be based on criteria which do not differ according to whether the work is carried out by a man or by a woman and must not be organised, as a whole, in such a manner that it has the practical effect of discriminating generally against workers of one sex.
>
> 14 Consequently, criteria corresponding to the duties performed meet the requirements of article 1 of the Directive where those duties by their nature require particular physical effort or are physically heavy. In differentiating rates of pay, it is consistent with the principle of non-discrimination to use a criterion based on the objectively measurable expenditure of effort necessary in carrying out the work or the degree to which, reviewed objectively, the work is physically heavy."

The approach of English law to the construction of s 1(5) appears to be in line with the European law approach: see *Eaton Ltd* v *Nuttall* (1977) where Phillips J said:

"It seems to us that subsection (5) can only apply to what may be called a valid evaluation study. By that, we mean a study satisfying the test of being thorough in analysis and capable of impartial application . . . One which does not satisfy that test, and requires the management to make a subjective argument concerning the nature of the work before the employee can be fitted into the appropriate place in the appropriate salary grade, would seem to us not to be a valid study for the purpose of subsection (5)."

The same judge made observations to the same effect in *England* v *Bromley London Borough Council* (1978). One has to be a little careful, however, in considering what is meant by "objective" since, so far as the evidence in the present case goes, there are no universally accepted external criteria available for measuring how much of a factor or quality is involved in a particular job or for measuring what relative weights ought to be attached to different factors or qualities involved, to differing extents, in various jobs. Every attempt at job evaluation will, as the expert witnesses seem to have agreed, inevitably at some stages involve value judgments, which are inherently to some extent subjective or "felt fair" . . .

What s 1(5) does require is, however, a study undertaken with a view to evaluating jobs in terms of the demand made on a worker under various headings, for instance effort, skill and decision. To apply that to s 2A(2)(a) it is necessary, in my judgment, that both the work of the woman who had made application to the employment tribunal and the work of the man who is her chosen comparator should have been valued in such terms of demand made on the worker under various headings. Mr Lester [counsel for the claimants] submitted that the method used on undertaking a study within s 1(5) must necessarily be analytical, a word he used in the sense of describing the process of dividing a physical or abstract whole into its constituent parts to determine their relationship or value. Sir Ralph Kilner-Brown criticised the use of the word analytical as a gloss on the section. In my judgment, the word is not a gloss, but indicates conveniently the general nature of what is required by the section, viz. that the jobs of each worker covered by the study must have been valued in terms of the demand made on the worker under various headings. . . .'

(The Court of Appeal held unanimously that the job evaluation study in this case was invalid.)

Comment

(1) In this case, the employer was trying to use the fact that the women's jobs had been rated lower than the men's as a defence to an equal value claim brought by the female employees. The equal value claim is discussed in the next section.

(2) While it is not a requirement to involve trade unions or other worker representatives in the design and execution of a job evaluation study, nor to provide a right of appeal against grading, it obviously makes sense in employment relations terms to do these things. Involving employees' representatives also helps to establish the validity of the job evaluation study.

(3) In order for an employee to be able to rely on a job evaluation study to claim equal pay, it must be shown that the study is complete, in the sense of having been agreed by the parties. In *O'Brien* v *Sim-Chem Ltd* (1980), the study had been agreed, and rated the women's jobs in the same grade as the men's, but had not been implemented because of government pay policy. It was held that the women were entitled to equal pay.

However, in *Arnold* v *Beecham Group* (1982), the study had been carried out, but was not acceptable to the employer, the trade union, nor most of the workers covered by it. It was held that it could not be relied on.

(4) Note Dillon LJ's warning that job evaluation is not an exact science. Value judgments come into play at several points: deciding the criteria in the first place, deciding how the criteria should be weighted against each other, and in assessing job duties against the criteria. It is important to ensure that there is no unconscious discrimination in favour of one sex in choice of criteria and their weighting. For example, a criterion of physical effort may well favour male workers, whereas a criterion of manual dexterity may favour women. In *Rummler* v *Dato-Druck GmbH* (1987) the ECJ was faced with the difficult question whether, in assessing the effort associated with a job, it was appropriate to class it as 'heavy' if it would be heavy for an average woman, even if not for an average man. The danger of using one sex as the benchmark and thus arriving at a discriminatory result is clear. The answer of the ECJ, quoted in the judgment of Dillon LJ above, was expanded as follows:

Rummler v *Dato-Druck GmbH* [1987] ICR 774 European Court of Justice

'*Questions 2 and 3*

18 It appears from the wording of these questions and from the grounds of the order of reference that the national court wishes in substance to know whether, in the event that the criteria of muscle demand or muscular effort and of the heaviness of the work are compatible with Council Directive (75/117/EEC), the fact that in determining to what extent work requires an effort or is demanding or heavy regard is had to the degree to which the work requires an effort or is demanding or heavy for women workers satisfies the requirements of the directive.

19 The defendant argues that regard must be had only to the objective nature of the work to be carried out and the objectively measurable demands that it makes.

20 The United Kingdom adds that to use an absolute level of muscular effort or an absolute degree of heaviness of the work, which in fact amounts to using male points of reference, can constitute no more than indirect discrimination, which is not prohibited by [Article 141 of the Treaty of Rome] in so far as it is based on objectively justifiable grounds. Such grounds exist where an employer must, in order to attract workers to and retain them in a specific job, set the rate of pay for that job in accordance with the particular effort required by it.

21 The Commission considers that in this regard the directive contains no general legal principle, so that national courts are not precluded from basing themselves mainly or exclusively on female values if the principle of non-discrimination so requires in order to avoid discrimination against women.

22 The answer to questions 2 and 3, seen in those terms, follows from what has already been said in answer to question 1, this is to say that nothing in the directive prevents the use in determining wage rates of a criterion based on the degree of muscular effort objectively required by a specific job or the objective degree of heaviness of the job.

23 The directive lays down the principle of equal pay for equal work. It follows that the work actually carried out must be remunerated in accordance with its nature. Any criterion based on values appropriate only to workers of one sex carries with it a risk of discrimination and may jeopardise the main objective of the directive, equal treatment for equal work. That is true even of a criterion based on values corresponding to the average performance of workers of the sex considered to have less natural ability for the purposes of that criterion,

for the result would be another form of pay discrimination: work objectively requiring greater strength would be paid at the same rate as work requiring less strength.

24 The failure to take into consideration values corresponding to the average performance of female workers in establishing a progressive pay scale based on the degree of muscle demand and muscular effort may indeed have the effect of placing women workers, who cannot take jobs which are beyond their physical strength, at a disadvantage. That difference in treatment may, however, be objectively justified by the nature of the job when such a difference is necessary in order to ensure a level of pay appropriate to the effort required by the work and thus corresponds to a real need on the part of the undertaking: see *Bilka-Kaufhaus GmbH* v *Weber von Hartz* (1987). As has already been stated, however, a job classification system must, in so far as the nature of the tasks in question permits, include other criteria which serve to ensure that the system as a whole is not discriminatory.

25 The answer to the second and third questions must therefore be that it follows from Council Directive (75/117/EEC) that (a) the criteria governing pay-rate classification must ensure that work which is objectively the same attracts the same rate of pay whether it is performed by a man or a woman; (b) the use of values reflecting the average performance of workers of one sex as a basis for determining the extent to which work makes demands or requires effort or whether it is heavy constitutes a form of discrimination on grounds of sex, contrary to the directive; (c) in order for a job classification system not to be discriminatory as a whole, it must, in so far as the nature of the tasks carried out in the undertaking permits, take into account criteria for which workers of each sex may show particular aptitude . . .'

Comment

(1) Does this answer the question posed? If so, is it a satisfactory answer?

(2) Very few claims for equal pay are based on job evaluation studies. It is more likely that a claimant will seek to attack the job evaluation study as being defective in some way, in order to clear the way for an equal value claim. Note that if a tribunal rules that a job evaluation study is defective, it cannot compel the employer to carry out a new study, still less can it substitute its judgment of what the outcome should have been (*England* v *Bromley LBC* (1978)).

(3) If jobs have been rated unequally under a valid job evaluation study, a female employee would simply have to accept her rating. If the study is held to be invalid, it means that she can choose her own comparator(s) and mount a claim for work of equal value.

(4) By the same token, the main incentive for employers to carry out job evaluation studies is to head off claims for work of equal value, to be looked at next.

Work of equal value

Enabling women to compare their jobs with men in different jobs is crucial to reducing the pay gap, because it allows them to break out of labour market segregation and challenge undiscussed assumptions about the relative value of men's work and women's work. However, the drawback of the Equal Pay Act 1970, as originally drafted, was that it was completely up to the employer whether or not to carry out a job evaluation study, and there was no mechanism to compel this to happen. It is hardly surprising, therefore, that statistics on equal pay claims between

1976 and 1983 show that over 90 per cent were brought under the like work provisions, and also that the total number of claims dropped substantially from 1,742 in 1976 to a mere 35 in 1983. This indicated that it did not take long for most anomalies arising where men and women did similar work to be ironed out, and it was not possible for more fundamental problems to be addressed because of the limitation on claims for work rated as equivalent following a job evaluation study.

In 1982 the EC Commission successfully sued the United Kingdom on the ground that UK legislation on equal pay contravened Art 141 and the Equal Pay Directive (*EC Commission* v *UK* (1982)). As a result, the Equal Pay (Amendment) Regulations 1983 were passed to introduce a third situation where equal pay could be claimed.

Equal Pay Act 1970

1   . . .
   (2)   . . .
      (c)   where a woman is employed on work which, not being work in relation to which paragraph (a) or (b) above applies, is, in terms of the demands made on her (for instance under such headings as effort, skill and decision), of equal value to that of a man in the same employment . . .

Comment

(1) Note that an equal value claim is expressed to be available only where one of the other two claims cannot be brought. This seemed to open up a considerable hole in the scheme until it was plugged by the House of Lords.

Pickstone v *Freemans plc* [1988] ICR 697 House of Lords

LORD KEITH: '. . . In the present case the respondent, Mrs Pickstone, who is employed by the appellant employers as a "warehouse operative," claims that her work as such is of equal value with that of a man, Mr Phillips, who is employed in the same establishment as a "checker warehouse operative", and who is paid £4.22 per week more than she is paid. However, it happens to be the fact that one man is employed in the establishment as a warehouse operative doing the same work as Mrs Pickstone. The employers maintain that the existence of this fact precludes Mrs Pickstone from claiming equal pay with Mr Phillips under section 1(2)(c) of the Act of 1970, as amended, notwithstanding that she may be performing work of equal value with his and notwithstanding that the difference in pay may be the result of discrimination on grounds of sex.

This argument is based on the words in paragraph (c) "not being work in relation to which paragraph (a) or (b) above applies". The employers say that the work on which Mrs Pickstone is employed is work to which paragraph (a) applies because it is like work with a man in the same employment, namely the one male warehouse operative. So Mrs Pickstone's work does not qualify under paragraph (c).

The question is whether the exclusionary words in paragraph (c) are intended to have effect whenever the employers are able to point to some man who is employed by them on like work with the woman claimant within the meaning of paragraph (a) or work rated as equivalent with hers within the meaning of paragraph (b), or whether they are intended to have effect only where the particular man with whom she seeks comparison is employed on such work. In my opinion the latter is the correct answer. The opposite result would leave a large gap in the equal work provision, enabling an employer to evade it by employing one token man on the same work as a group of potential women claimants who were deliberately paid less than a group of men employed on work of equal value with that of the women. This would mean that the United Kingdom had failed yet again fully to implement its obligations under [Article 141] of the Treaty and the Equal Pay Directive, and had not given full effect to the decision of the European Court in *Commission of the European Communities* v *United Kingdom of Great Britain and Northern Ireland* (1982).

It is plain that Parliament cannot possibly have intended such a failure. The draft Regulations of 1983 were presented to Parliament as giving full effect to the decision in question. The draft Regulations were not subject to the Parliamentary process of consideration and amendment in Committee, as a Bill would have been. In these circumstances and in the context of section 2 of the European Communities Act 1972 I consider it to be entirely legitimate for the purpose of ascertaining the intention of Parliament to take into account the terms in which the draft was presented by the responsible Minister and which formed the basis of its acceptance. The terms in which it was presented to the House of Commons are set out in the speech of my noble and learned friend Lord Templeman. Much the same was said before the House of Lords. There was no suggestion that the exclusionary words in paragraph (c) were intended to apply in any other situation than where the man selected by a woman complainant for comparison was one in relation to whose work paragraph (a) or paragraph (b) applied. It may be that, in order to confine the words in question to that situation, some necessary implication falls to be made into their literal meaning. The precise terms of that implication do not seem to me to matter. It is sufficient to say that the words must be construed purposively in order to give effect to the manifest broad intention of the maker of the Regulations and of Parliament. I would therefore reject the employers' argument.

In the circumstances it is unnecessary to consider the ground upon which the Court of Appeal found in favour of the respondents, namely that [Art 141] was directly enforceable in such a way as to enable their claim to be supported irrespective of the true construction of the Regulations of 1983.

My Lords, for these reasons and those given by my noble and learned friends Lord Templeman and Lord Oliver of Aylmerton, I would dismiss the appeal.'

LORD TEMPLEMAN: 'My Lords, the appellants, Freemans Plc ("the employers") conduct a mail order business. The respondents are five women who work for the employers as "warehouse operatives"; their basic weekly wage is £77.66. Mr Phillips is a man who works for the employers as a "checker warehouse operative"; his basic weekly wage is £81.88. The respondents assert that the work carried out by the respondents is equal in value to the work of Mr Phillips in terms of the demands, effort, skill and decision-making involved. The respondents say that the difference of £4.22 between the respondents' pay and the pay of Mr Phillips is due to the difference of sex; the respondents are paid less because they are women. The respondents complained to an employment tribunal that they were the victims of sex discrimination, contrary to the provisions of the Equal Pay Act 1970 and contrary to Community law. When the complaints of the respondents came before the tribunal, investigation might have shown that there was no discrimination, that the work of Mr Phillips was of greater value than the work of the respondents or that for some other reason the difference between the pay of Mr Phillips and the pay of the respondents was not due to the difference of sex. By agreement between the parties however, the employment tribunal was asked to decide a preliminary point of law which is the subject of this appeal on assumed facts. The assumptions are that the respondents are factually correct in their complaint; that the work of the respondents is equal in value to the work of Mr Phillips; that the respondents are paid £4.22 less on the grounds of difference of sex and for no other reason; that, in short, the respondents are the victims of discrimination. It is unlawful under British law and under Community law for an employer to discriminate against a woman by paying her less than a man if the work of the woman is the same as or is equal in value to the work of the man. Nevertheless, the employers contend that under British law and under Community law, the respondents have no right to or, alternatively, no remedy for the discrimination which on the assumed facts is practised by the employer against the respondents and in favour of Mr Phillips. The employers' argument is based on the fact that it so happens that one of the employers' warehouse operatives is a man, doing the same work as the respondents. According to the employers this fact makes all the difference. The respondents are entitled to complain if they are discriminated against by reason of the fact that they are not paid the same as the man who does the same work. Therefore, it is argued, the respondents are not entitled to complain if they are discriminated against by reason of the fact that they are not paid the same as Mr Phillips who does work of equal value. The employers admit that if there were 15 warehouse operators and all the warehouse operators were women, paid £77.66, for work equal in value to the work of 10 checker warehouse operatives, all men, paid £81.88 and the difference was due to difference in sex, the respondents would be entitled to an increase in pay of £4.22. But the employers claim that if there were 14 women warehouse operatives, one male warehouse operative, and 10 checker warehouse operatives the respondents would be obliged to rest content with £77.66 and would have no remedy for the admitted discrimination based on difference in sex. The employment tribunal and the Employment Appeal Tribunal accepted the argument of the employers. The Court of Appeal (Purchas and Nicholls L JJ and Sir Roualeyn Cumming-Bruce) decided that under Community law the respondents had an enforceable right on the assumed facts to equal pay with Mr Phillips for work of equal value. The employers appeal to this House . . .

The draft of the Regulations of 1983 was not subject to any process of amendment by Parliament. In these circumstances the explanations of the Government and the criticisms voiced by Members of Parliament in the debates which led to approval of the draft Regulations provide some indications of the intentions of Parliament. The debate on the draft Regulations in the House of Commons which led to their approval by Resolution was initiated by the Under Secretary of State for Employment who, in the reports of the House of Commons for 20 July 1983 said:

"The Equal Pay Act allows a woman to claim equal pay with a man . . . if she is doing the same or broadly similar work, or if her job and his have been rated equal through job evaluation in effort, skill and decision. However, if a woman is doing different work from a comparable man, or if the jobs are not covered by a job evaluation study, the woman has at present no right to make a claim for equal pay. This is the gap, identified by the European Court, which we are closing . . ."

In the course of his speech, the Minister outlined the procedure which will apply if a claim is made under paragraph (c) in the following words:

"Under the amending Regulations which are the subject of this debate, an employee will be able to bring a claim for equal pay with an employee of the opposite sex working in the same employment on the ground that the work is of equal value. When this happens, conciliation will first be attempted, as in all equal pay claims. If conciliation is unsuccessful, the employment tribunal will take the following steps. First, it will check that the work is not in fact so similar that the case can be heard under the current Act. Secondly, it will consider whether the jobs have already been covered by a job evaluation scheme and judged not to be of equal value. If this is the case, the claim may proceed only if the original job evaluation scheme is shown to have been sexually discriminatory. Having decided that the case should proceed, the tribunal will first invite the parties to see if they can settle the claim voluntarily. If not, the tribunal will consider whether to commission an independent expert to report on the value of the jobs. It will not commission an expert's report if it feels that it is unreasonable to determine the question of value – for example, if the two jobs are quite obviously of unequal value. Nor . . . will it commission an expert's report if the employer shows at this stage that inequality in pay is due to material factors other than sex discrimination . . .".

Thus it is clear that the construction which I have placed upon the Regulations corresponds to the intentions of the Government in introducing the Regulations. In the course of the debate in the House of Commons, and in the corresponding debate in the House of Lords, no one suggested that a claim for equal pay for equal work might be defeated under the Regulations by an employer who proved that a man who was not the subject of the complaint was employed on the same or on similar work with the complainant. The Minister took the view, and Parliament accepted the view, that paragraph (c) will only apply if paragraphs (a) and (b) are first held by the tribunal not to apply in respect of the work of the woman and the work of the man with whom she seeks parity of pay. This is also the only view consistent with Community law.

In *von Colson and Kamann* v *Land Nordrhein-Westfalen* (1984) the European Court of Justice advised that in dealing with national legislation designed to give effect to a Directive:

"3. . . . It is for the national court to interpret and apply the legislation adopted for the implementation of the Directive in conformity with the requirements of Community law, in so far as it is given discretion to do so under national law."

In *Duke* v *Reliance Systems Ltd* (1988) this House declined to distort the construction of an Act of Parliament which was not drafted to give effect to a Directive and which was not capable of complying with the Directive as subsequently construed by the European Court of Justice. In the present case I can see no difficulty in construing the Regulations of 1983 in a way which gives effect to the declared intention of the Government of the United Kingdom responsible for drafting the Regulations and is consistent with the objects of the EEC Treaty, the provisions of the Equal Pay Directive and the rulings of the European Court of Justice. I would dismiss the appeal.'

(Lord Oliver delivered a concurring speech; Lords Brandon and Jauncey agreed with all three.)

Comment

(1) This is an important decision on substantive equal pay law, establishing as it does that a woman may choose another man with whom to compare for equal value notwithstanding that there is a man who does the same work as her. However, it is almost more interesting for the approach of the House of Lords to the interpretation of English and European law, especially the willingness of the House to construe national legislation so as to accord with EU law. These issues are well discussed in Hepple and Byre (1989).

(2) A woman will be precluded from claiming that her work is of equal value with a man's if a valid job evaluation study has been carried out which applies to them both and ranks their jobs unequally. In *Dibro Ltd* v *Hore* (1990) the EAT held that this applied even where the employer only instituted the job evaluation study after the woman had submitted her equal value claim.

(3) The procedure for bringing an equal value claim as outlined by the Under-Secretary of State, quoted in the speech of Lord Templeman, has been subject to some amendment over the years in an attempt to speed up equal value claims, which can be notoriously long-winded. The present procedure is contained in EqPA s 2A together with the Employment Tribunals (Equal Value) Rules of Procedure contained in Sch 6 to the

Employment Tribunal (Constitution and Rules of Procedure) Regulations 2004 (hereafter referred to as the Equal Value Rules of Procedure).

Procedure for bringing an equal value claim

The procedure is complex and best understood if broken down into a number of stages.

Stage 0

As with most other employment tribunal proceedings, the claimant's claim on form ET1 is sent to Acas, who can try and help the parties to reach a conciliated settlement of the issue. If conciliation is unsuccessful, the process moves to Stage 1.

Stage 1

Equal Pay Act 1970

2A (1) Where on a complaint or reference made to an employment tribunal under section 2 above, a dispute arises as to whether any work is of equal value as mentioned in section 1(2)(c) above the tribunal may either –

(a) proceed to determine that question; or

(b) require a member of the panel of independent experts to prepare a report with respect to that question;

(1A) Subsections (1B) and (1C) below apply in a case where the tribunal has required a member of the panel of independent experts to prepare a report under paragraph (b) of subsection (1) above.

(1B) The tribunal may –

(a) withdraw the requirement, and

(b) request the member of the panel of independent experts to provide it with any documentation specified by it or make any other request to him connected with the withdrawal of the requirement.

(1C) If the requirement has not been withdrawn under paragraph (a) of subsection (1B) above, the tribunal shall not make any determination under paragraph (a) of subsection (1) above unless it has received the report.

. . .

(4) In this section a reference to a member of the panel of independent experts is a reference to a person who is for the time being designated by the Advisory, Conciliation and Arbitration Service for the purposes of that paragraph as such a member, being neither a member of the Council of that Service nor one of its officers or servants.

Comment

(1) This initial hearing is referred to in the Equal Value Rules of Procedure as a Stage 1 hearing. Originally, tribunals had the option at this hearing of dismissing the claim if it had no hope of success, or referring it to an independent expert. However, much of the delay inherent in equal value claims lay with the length of time it took to get the independent expert's report. Thus in 1996 the rules were amended so that the tribunal had the further possibility of moving to determine the issue itself without reference to an independent expert. EqPA s 2A was further amended from October 2004 by the addition of subsections (1A)–(1C) so as to allow the tribunal to take the case back from the independent expert, again in order to deal with problems caused by delays in getting the final report.

(2) Another reform in 2004 was the introduction of an indicative timetable, to try and ensure that cases are heard within a reasonable time.

Employment Tribunals (Constitution and Rules of Procedure) Regulations 2004

SCHEDULE 6

ANNEX

The indicative timetable

Claims *not* involving an independent expert		Claims involving an independent expert
Claim		Claim
↓		↓
28 days		28 days
↓		↓
Response		Response
↓		↓
3 weeks		3 weeks
↓		↓
Stage 1 equal value hearing		Stage 1 equal value hearing
↓		↓
		10 weeks
↓		↓
		Stage 2 equal value hearing
↓		↓
		[8 weeks]
↓		↓
		Independent expert's report
18 weeks		
↓		↓
		4 weeks
↓		↓
		written questions
↓		↓
		8 weeks
↓		↓
Hearing		Hearing
Total 25 weeks		Total 37 weeks

Comment

(1) Independent experts are appointed in the majority of equal value cases. It remains to be seen how successful the changes to procedure introduced in 2004 will be in speeding up these claims.

(2) Under the Equal Value Rules of Procedure r 4, at the Stage 1 hearing the tribunal should set a date for the next hearing, having regard to the indicative timetable. If an independent expert has been appointed, this will be a Stage 2 hearing. Rule 5 sets out a series of standard orders which the tribunal should make which are designed to try and get the

parties to clarify the issues in writing. In particular, the parties are required to produce a *joint* statement, within 56 days (eight weeks) of the Stage 1 hearing, of the following:

- the job descriptions of the claimant and her comparator(s);
- the facts which the parties agree are relevant to the equal value question;
- the points on which they disagree – with a summary of the reasons for their disagreement.

The independent expert can be asked to assist in this fact-finding stage.

Stage 2

Employment Tribunals (Constitution and Rules of Procedure) Regulations 2004

SCHEDULE 6

7 . . .

(3) At the stage 2 equal value hearing the tribunal shall make a determination of facts on which the parties cannot agree which relate to the question and shall require the independent expert to prepare his report on the basis of facts which have (at any stage of the proceedings) either been agreed between the parties or determined by the tribunal (referred to as 'the facts relating to the question').

(4) At the stage 2 equal value hearing the tribunal shall:

(a) subject to rule 8 and having regard to the indicative timetable, make the standard orders for the stage 2 equal value hearing as set out in rule 8;

(b) make any orders which it considers appropriate;

(c) fix a date for the Hearing, having regard to the indicative timetable.

(5) Subject to paragraph (6), the facts relating to the question shall, in relation to the question, be the only facts on which the tribunal shall rely at the Hearing . . .

Comment

(1) Rule 8 says that the tribunal should set a date for the independent expert's report to be received. That report must be based on the facts as agreed by the parties and/or determined by the tribunal, and no others.

(2) It became common practice for parties, especially employers, to commission reports by their own experts to pit against that of the independent expert, if it was unfavourable to their case. This again contributed to the length and expense of equal value proceedings. This is now restricted by rule 11:

- First, parties have to have the tribunal's permission to call expert evidence.
- Secondly, any report has to be disclosed to all the other parties at least 28 days before the hearing. It should be disclosed on the same date as the independent expert's report – to minimise the chances of parties' experts tailoring their reports to the contents of that of the independent expert.
- Thirdly, if more than one party wants to submit expert evidence on an issue, the tribunal can require them to appoint a single joint expert. This is more likely to occur where parties are on the same side – for example, a claim by a group of employees that they should be receiving equal pay.

(3) Following receipt of the independent expert's report (and the reports of any other experts) a 12-week period is allowed for the parties and any of the experts to submit written questions about their reports to any of the experts, and for them to reply in writing.

Stage 3

The final stage is the substantive hearing of the equal value claim (or 'the Hearing' as it is styled in the Equal Value Rules of Procedure).

Employment Tribunals (Constitution and Rules of Procedure) Regulations 2004

SCHEDULE 6

9 (1) In proceedings in relation to which an independent expert has prepared a report, unless the tribunal determines that the report is not based on the facts relating to the question, the report of the independent expert shall be admitted in evidence in those proceedings.

(2) If the tribunal does not admit the report of an independent expert in accordance with paragraph (1), it may determine the question itself or require another independent expert to prepare a report on the question.

(3) The tribunal may refuse to admit evidence of facts or hear argument as to issues which have not been disclosed to the other party as required by these rules or any order made under them, unless it was not reasonably practicable for the party to have so complied.

Comment

(1) The independent expert's report usually has a conclusion that the jobs compared are or are not of equal value. In *Tennants Textile Colours* v *Todd* (1989) the Northern Ireland Court of Appeal held that accepting the report into evidence did not commit the tribunal to accepting its conclusion – although it would be unusual for the tribunal not to do so.

(2) While the powers of the tribunal have been strengthened to enable it to take a proactive role in progressing equal value claims, it remains the case that it is a complex procedure. The emphasis in the latest version of the Rules on reducing the issues to writing in advance make it less and less likely that an unrepresented claimant could have any real hope of successfully prosecuting a claim.

(3) In 1993 the EOC requested the European Commission to consider taking infringement proceedings against the United Kingdom on the grounds that the procedure for equal value claims was so cumbersome and time-consuming that it amounted to a denial of claimants' rights under Art 2 of the Equal Pay Directive 1975, quoted above p 283. The Commission declined to take action. Since then, the Equal Value Rules of Procedure have been amended several times. It remains to be seen whether the 2004 amendments have any real effect on the length of time taken to deal with equal value cases.

'In the same employment'

Claims for discrimination in terms and conditions of employment on any of the protected grounds other than sex would allow a comparison with a hypothetical comparator. It would be possible to argue, for example, that an employee from a different ethnic group would have been paid more than the claimant. This is not so in relation to sex discrimination in relation to the terms and conditions of employment. The claimant has to identify an *actual* comparator (or more than one) of the opposite sex. And EqPA s 1(2) lays down a further restriction: the comparator must be 'in the same employment' as the claimant.

This raises three issues: the employment status of the claimant; the meaning of 'in the same employment', and the choice of comparator.

Employment status

Equal Pay Act 1970

1 (6) Subject to the following subsections, for purposes of this section –

    (a) 'employed' means employed under a contract of service or of apprenticeship or a contract personally to execute any work or labour, and related expressions shall be construed accordingly;

Allonby v *Accrington & Rossendale College* [2004] IRLR 224
European Court of Justice

The claimant had been employed as an hourly-paid part-time lecturer by the college on a series of fixed-term contracts for six years. Because changes in the law meant that the college would have to give part-time staff the same rights as full-time staff, including pension entitlements, the college decided not to renew the contracts of the part-time staff but to employ them instead through an agency, so that they would not be employees of the college. The claimant and other part-timers registered with the agency, ELS, and were thereafter treated as self-employed. This led to their income being reduced and their exclusion from such benefits as sick pay and pension entitlement. The Teachers' Superannuation Scheme (TSS), to which she had formerly belonged, was open only to employees.

The claimant argued, among other things, that she should be entitled to be a member of the pension scheme. The Court of Appeal referred this and other questions to the ECJ.

JUDGMENT OF THE COURT: '. . . Second, the Court of Appeal raises the question whether Ms Allonby may, on the basis of Article 141 EC, claim access to the TSS. It explains in that connection that, in the context of her employment with ELS, Ms Allonby, having only a contract for services, has no access to the TSS . . .

In order to answer this question, it is necessary, first, to interpret the concept of worker within the meaning of Article 141(1) EC, second, to determine precisely the category of persons who may be included in the comparison and, third, to examine the consequences of possible incompatibility of the condition at issue with that provision.

The concept of worker within the meaning of Article 141(1) EC

The criterion on which Article 141(1) EC is based is the comparability of the work done by workers of each sex (see, to that effect, *Defrenne (No 3)* (1978)). Accordingly, for the purpose of the comparison provided for by Article 141(1) EC, only women and men who are workers within the meaning of that article can be taken into consideration.

In that connection, it must be pointed out that there is no single definition of worker in Community law: it varies according to the area in which the definition is to be applied (*Martinez Sala* (1998)).

The term worker within the meaning of Article 141(1) EC is not expressly defined in the EC Treaty. It is therefore necessary, in order to determine its meaning, to apply the generally recognised principles of interpretation, having regard to its context and to the objectives of the Treaty.

According to Article 2 EC, the Community is to have as its task to promote, among other things, equality between men and women. Article 141(1) EC constitutes a specific expression of the principle of equality for men and women, which forms part of the fundamental principles protected by the Community legal order (see, to that effect, *Deutsche Post* (2000)). As the Court held in *Defrenne (No 2)* (1976), the principle of equal pay forms part of the foundations of the Community.

Accordingly, the term worker used in Article 141(1) EC cannot be defined by reference to the legislation of the Member States but has a Community meaning. Moreover, it cannot be interpreted restrictively.

For the purposes of that provision, there must be considered as a worker a person who, for a certain period of time, performs services for and under the direction of another person in return for which he receives remuneration (see, in relation to free movement of workers, in particular *Lawrie-Blum* (1986) and *Martinez Sala* (1998)).

Pursuant to the first paragraph of Article 141(2) EC, for the purpose of that article, pay means the ordinary basic or minimum wage or salary and any other consideration, whether in cash or in kind, which the worker receives directly or indirectly, in respect of his employment, from his employer. It is clear from that definition that the authors of the Treaty did not intend that the term worker, within the meaning of Article 141(1) EC, should include independent providers of services who are not in a relationship of subordination with the person who receives the services (see also, in the context of free movement of workers, *Meeusen* (1999)).

The question whether such a relationship exists must be answered in each particular case having regard to all the factors and circumstances by which the relationship between the parties is characterised.

Provided that a person is a worker within the meaning of Article 141(1) EC, the nature of his legal relationship with the other party to the employment relationship is of no consequence in regard to the application of that article (see, in the context of free movement of workers, *Bettray* (1989) and *Raulin* (1992)).

The formal classification of a self-employed person under national law does not exclude the possibility that a person must be classified as a worker within the meaning of Article 141(1) EC if his independence is merely notional, thereby disguising an employment relationship within the meaning of that article.

In the case of teachers who are, vis-à-vis an intermediary undertaking, under an obligation to undertake an assignment at a college, it is necessary in particular to consider the extent of any limitation on their freedom to choose their timetable, and the place and content of their work. The fact that no obligation is imposed on them to accept an assignment is of no consequence in that context (see to that effect, in relation to free movement of workers, *Raulin*) . . .

In view of the foregoing considerations, the answer to the first part of part (b) of the second question must be that, in the absence of any objective justification, the requirement, imposed by State legislation, of being employed under a contract of employment as a precondition for membership of a pension scheme for teachers is not applicable where it is shown that, among the teachers who are workers within the meaning of Article 141(1) EC and fulfil all the other conditions for membership, a much lower percentage of women than of men is able to fulfil that condition. The formal classification of a self-employed person under national law does not change the fact that a person must be classified as a worker within the meaning of that article if his independence is merely notional . . .'

Comment

(1) The EU usually leaves it to member states to decide which workers come within the scope of directives and in English law, they are usually applied only to employees. The equality enactments apply to a wider category, as stated in EqPA s 1(6)(a) – but still require a contract between the worker and the employer. However, the effect of *Allonby* is that, for the purposes of sex discrimination law at least, including equal pay, the net

must be cast wider. As will be seen from the judgment, the crucial element is the 'relationship of subordination'. The lack of a direct contractual nexus between the claimant and the college was held not to be fatal to finding that she was a worker to whom Art 141 applied.

'The same employment'

Equal Pay Act 1970

1 (6) Subject to the following subsections, for purposes of this section –
. . .

   (c) two employers are to be treated as associated if one is a company of which the other (directly or indirectly) has control or if both are companies of which a third person (directly or indirectly) has control, and men shall be treated as in the same employment with a woman if they are men employed by her employer or any associated employer at the same establishment or at establishments in Great Britain which include that one and at which common terms and conditions of employment are observed either generally or for employees of the relevant classes.

Comment

(1) Two separate issues have been raised in relation to this provision. The first is whether this definition of 'the same employment' is consonant with EU law on this point. The second is over the meaning of 'common terms and conditions' where the woman wants to compare herself with a man at a different establishment.

(2) In relation to the first issue, in *Defrenne* v *Sabena (No 2)* (1976) the ECJ stated that the principle of equal pay applied to the work of men and women 'which is carried out in the same establishment or service, whether private or public'. This led to the argument that it was not necessarily limited to employees working for the same employer, an argument which was successful in *Scullard* v *Knowles* (1996), where a cross-employer comparison was allowed in relation to employees of separate regional educational councils across the United Kingdom which were all funded by the Department of Employment.

The issue was referred to the ECJ in the next case.

Lawrence v *Regent Office Care Ltd* [2002] IRLR 822 European Court of Justice

The claimants were 447 women employed to perform catering and cleaning functions for North Yorkshire County Council. Most of them had originally done this work as direct employees of the council. However, following a compulsory competitive tendering exercise, the work was outsourced to various outside contractors. The women's contracts of employment were automatically transferred to these new employers under TUPE.

When they worked directly for the council, the women's jobs had been rated as being of equal value to those of various groups of male manual workers. Following the transfer, the contractors employed them on lower rates of pay than these male workers. The women claimed that they should have equal terms with the men who were still employed by the council. The Court of Appeal referred to the ECJ the question of whether the women, although employed by private contractors, could nonetheless compare themselves with men employed by the council.

JUDGMENT OF THE COURT: '. . . In order to reply to the first question, it should be noted at the outset that Article 141(1) EC lays down the principle that equal work or work of equal value must be remunerated in the same way, whether it is performed by a man or a woman.

As the Court held in *Defrenne (No 2)* (1976), that principle, which is a particular expression of the general principle of equality which prohibits comparable situations from being treated differently unless the difference is objectively justified, forms part of the foundations of the Community (see *Brunnhofer* (2001)) . . .

Three features distinguish the present case. First, the persons whose pay is being compared work for different employers, that is to say, on the one hand, the council and, on the other, the respondent undertakings. Second, the work which the appellants perform for those undertakings is identical to that which some of them performed for the council before the transfer of undertakings. Finally, that work has been recognised as being of equal value to that performed by the chosen comparators employed by the council and continues to be so recognised . . .

There is, in this connection, nothing in the wording of Article 141(1) EC to suggest that the applicability of that provision is limited to situations in which men and women work for the same employer. The Court has held that the principle established by that article may be invoked before national courts, in particular in cases of discrimination arising directly from legislative provisions or collective labour agreements, as well as in cases in which work is carried out in the same establishment or service, whether private or public (see, inter alia, *Defrenne (No 2)* (1976); *Macarthys v Smith* (1980); and *Jenkins v Kingsgate* (1981)).

However, where, as in the main proceedings here, the differences identified in the pay conditions of workers performing equal work or work of equal value cannot be attributed to a single source, there is no body which is responsible for the inequality and which could restore equal treatment. Such a situation does not come within the scope of Article 141(1) EC. The work and the pay of those workers cannot therefore be compared on the basis of that provision.

In view of all of the foregoing, the answer to the first question must be that a situation such as that in the main proceedings, in which the differences identified in the pay conditions of workers of different sex performing equal work or work of equal value cannot be attributed to a single source, does not come within the scope of Article 141(1) EC . . .'

Comment

(1) In this case the ECJ recognises the very important principle that Art 141 comparisons need not be confined to a single employer – but only if the differences between the pay and conditions of the woman and her comparator can be attributed to a single source.

(2) It appears from *Scullard v Knowles* (1996) that the Equal Pay Act can be interpreted in accordance with this position (see also *South Ayrshire Council v Morton* (2002)).

(3) The 'single source' test meant that the claimants in *Lawrence* actually lost their claims. It also prevented the claimant in *Allonby v Accrington & Rossendale College* (2004) from being able to claim equal terms with a male colleague directly employed by the college. Although she was employed in the same establishment as him, albeit as a self-employed agency worker, the differences in their terms were held by the ECJ not to be attributable to the same source. It was true that what the college paid the agency affected what the agency paid the claimant, but this was not regarded as sufficient to satisfy the test. What is unsatisfactory about both cases is that the ECJ does not take account of the context; most importantly, the facts that the claimants in both cases had formerly been directly employed in the comparator organisation, and that their

new employment arrangements had been entered into as a way of saving on employment costs.

(4) The single source test has also been used in the opposite sense, to say that even where employees are employed by the same employer, they cannot compare across establishments or departments if their terms and conditions are actually settled separately (see *Robertson* v *DEFRA* (2005) and *Armstrong* v *Newcastle upon Tyne NHS Trust* (2006)).

(5) This brings us to the second issue: where a woman is employed by the same employer as a male comparator, but at a different establishment, EqPA s 1(6) allows a comparison if there are 'common terms and conditions' across the two. What does this mean?

British Coal Corporation v *Smith* [1996] IRLR 404 House of Lords

1,286 women employed as canteen workers at 47 different establishments claimed equal pay with 150 male surface mineworkers and clerical staff at 14 different establishments. British Coal argued that common terms and conditions did not apply across the establishments because, while national bargaining was used to settle most terms, some things, such as entitlement to concessionary coal and incentive bonuses, were left to local bargaining. Thus surface mineworkers and clerical workers at different establishments did not have exactly the same terms and conditions.

LORD SLYNN: '. . . The real question, however, is what is meant by "common terms and conditions of employment" and between whom do such terms and conditions have to be common?

It is plain and it is agreed between the parties that the woman does not have to show that she shares common terms and conditions with her comparator, either in the sense that all the terms are the same, since necessarily his terms must be different in some respect if she is to show a breach of the equality clause, or in regard to terms other than that said to constitute the discrimination.

It is accepted by the corporation that for the purposes of this appeal, as between the different establishments, common terms and conditions do in any event apply to the two classes of claimants, canteen workers and cleaners. What therefore has to be shown is that the male comparators at other establishments and at her establishment share common terms and conditions. If there are no such men at the claimant's place of work then it has to be shown that like terms and conditions would apply if men were employed there in the particular jobs concerned.

The corporation contends that the claimants can only succeed if they can show that common terms and conditions were observed at the two establishments for the relevant classes in the sense that they apply "across the board"; in other words, the terms and conditions of the comparators (eg surface mineworkers) are "common in substantially all respects" for such workers at her pit and at the places of employment of the comparators. This in effect means that all the terms and conditions must be common, ie the same, subject only to de minimis differences.

The claimants reject this and contend that it is sufficient if there is a broad similarity of terms rather than that they are strictly coterminous.

Your Lordships have been referred to a number of dictionary definitions of "common" but I do not think that they help. The real question is what the legislation was seeking to achieve. Was it seeking to exclude a woman's claim unless, subject to de minimis exceptions, there was complete identity of terms and conditions for the comparator at his establishment and those which applied or would apply to a similar male worker at her establishment? Or was the legislation seeking to establish that the terms and conditions of the relevant class were sufficiently similar for a fair comparison to be made, subject always to the employer's right to establish a "material difference" defence under s 1(3) of the 1970 Act?

If it was the former then the woman would fail at the first hurdle if there was any difference (other than a de minimis one) between the terms and conditions of the men at the various establishments since she could not then show that the men were in the same employment as she was. The issue as to whether the differences were material so as to justify different treatment would then never arise.

I do not consider that this can have been intended. The purpose of requiring common terms and conditions was to avoid it being said simply "a gardener does work of equal value to mine and my comparator at another establishment is a gardener". It was necessary for the claimant to go further and to show that gardeners at other establishments and at her establishment were or would be employed on broadly similar terms. It was necessary, but it was also sufficient. . . .

If, as I consider, the terms and conditions do not have to be identical, but on a broad basis to be substantially comparable, then it seems to me that the employment tribunal did not err in law in the way it directed itself and there was clearly material on which it could base its finding that the claimants and their comparators were in the same employment. On this issue, accordingly, in my view, the claimants' cross-appeal succeeds . . .'

(Lords Keith, Browne-Wilkinson, Steyn and Hoffmann agreed with Lord Slynn.)

Comment

(1) This continues the liberal approach to 'common terms and conditions' set out in the House of Lords' earlier decision in *Leverton* v *Clwyd CC* (1989).

Choice of comparator

Macarthys Ltd v *Smith* [1980] ICR 672 European Court of Justice

S was taken on as stockroom manager by the company at a salary of £50 per week. She discovered that her male predecessor in the post, who had left some four months earlier, had been paid £60 per week. There was no one else in a similar post with whom she could compare, so she claimed equal pay with her predecessor. The Court of Appeal took the view that the wording of the Equal Pay Act meant that the woman and her male comparator had to be employed at the same time. They referred the case to the ECJ for answers to the following questions. First, whether the principle of equal pay was confined to situations where the man and woman were contemporaneously employed. Secondly, if it was not, did the woman have to identify an actual male to compare with, or could she seek comparison with how a (hypothetical) man would have been treated.

JUDGMENT OF THE COURT: '. . .
9   According to the first paragraph of [Art 141] the member states are obliged to ensure and maintain "the application of the principle that men and women should receive equal pay for equal work."
10   As the court indicated in *Defrenne* v *Sabena* (1976), that provision applies directly, and without the need for more detailed implementing measures on the part of the Community or the member states, to all forms of direct and overt discrimination which may be identified solely with the aid of the criteria of equal work and equal pay referred to by the article in question.

Among the forms of discrimination which may be thus judicially identified, the court mentioned in particular cases where men and women receive unequal pay for equal work carried out in the same establishment or service.

11   In such a situation the decisive test lies in establishing whether there is a difference in treatment between a man and a woman performing "equal work" within the meaning of [Art 141]. The scope of that concept, which is entirely qualitative in character in that it is exclusively concerned with the nature of the services in question, may not be restricted by the introduction of a requirement of contemporaneity.

12   It must be acknowledged, however, that, as the Employment Appeal Tribunal properly recognised, it cannot be ruled out that a difference in pay between two workers occupying the same post but at different periods in time may be explained by the operation of factors which are unconnected with any discrimination on grounds of sex. That is a question of fact which it is for the court or tribunal to decide.

13   Thus the answer to the first question should be that the principle that men and women should receive equal pay for equal work, enshrined in [Art 141] of the EEC Treaty, is not confined to situations in which men and women are contemporaneously doing equal work for the same employer.

14   The second question put by the Court of Appeal and expressed in terms of alternatives concerns the framework within which the existence of possible discrimination in pay may be established. This question is intended to enable the court to rule upon a submission made by the employee and developed by her before the European Court of Justice to the effect that a woman may claim not only the salary received by a man who previously did the same work for her employer but also, more generally, the salary to which she would be entitled were she a man, even in the absence of any man who was concurrently performing, or had previously performed, similar work. The employee defined this term of comparison by reference to the concept of what she described as "a hypothetical male worker."

15   It is clear that the latter proposition, which is the subject of question 2 (a), is to be classed as indirect and disguised discrimination, the identification of which, as the court explained in *Defrenne* v *Sabena* (1976), implies comparative studies of entire branches of industry and therefore requires, as a prerequisite, the elaboration by the Community and national legislative bodies of criteria of assessment. From that it follows that, in cases of actual discrimination falling within the scope of the direct application of [Art 141], comparisons are confined to parallels which may be drawn on the basis of concrete appraisals of the work actually performed by employees of different sex within the same establishment or service.

16   The answer to the second question should therefore be that the principle of equal pay enshrined in [Art 141] applies to the case where it is established that, having regard to the nature of her services, a woman has received less pay than a man who was employed prior to the woman's period of employment and who did equal work for the employer.

17   From the foregoing it appears that the dispute brought before the national court may be decided within the framework of an interpretation of [Art 141] of the Treaty alone. In those circumstances it is unnecessary to answer the questions submitted in so far as they relate to the effect and to the interpretation of Council Directive (75/117/EEC) . . .'

Comment

(1) The Equal Pay Act 1970 was not amended in the light of this decision, but it is obviously incumbent on courts and tribunals to interpret the Act so as not to include a requirement of contemporaneity. In suitable cases, it may be possible for a woman to compare herself with a successor who receives higher pay than she did (*Diocese of Hallam* v *Connaughton* (1996)).

(2) A major problem for a woman in identifying suitable comparators is that she has no statutory right to gain information about the terms and conditions of her male colleagues. It is true that once she has mounted a claim she will be entitled to disclosure of documents, but it is axiomatic that disclosure will not be made for the purposes of a 'fishing expedition' and so she will have to have adduced sufficient evidence to make out a decent case first. Her trade union may be able to be of assistance, but note the limitations on disclosure of information to trade unions discussed above (p 241).

(3) Getting information about other employees' terms and conditions is generally easier in the public sector, where this information is more transparent, than in the private sector (where some employers actually forbid employees to disclose their pay to other employees). However, there can be dangers in choosing too many comparators, as Lord Bridge pointed out in *Leverton* v *Clwyd CC*.

Leverton v *Clwyd County Council* [1989] ICR 33 House of Lords

The claimant was employed by the council as a nursery nurse, working 32½ hours per week and having all school holidays (some 70 days a year) off. After obtaining disclosure of the contracts of 200 other council staff, she chose 11 male comparators, all of whom worked at different establishments from her and who had significantly higher annual salaries. All council employees were employed on terms and conditions of employment derived from a national collective agreement known as 'the Purple Book'. The House of Lords therefore held that there were common terms and conditions across the different establishments, so her claims that her work was of equal value with theirs could go ahead.

LORD BRIDGE: '... I cannot leave this case without adding a word about the procedure involved in equal value claims under section 1(2)(c) of the Act of 1970. If such a claim is referred to an expert under section 2A, the expert's job evaluation and the subsequent procedural steps which follow the presentation of his report under the special rules of procedure governing equal value claims ... will involve a lengthy, elaborate and, I apprehend, expensive process. The larger the number of comparators whose jobs have to be evaluated, the more elaborate and expensive the process is likely to be. Here, as already mentioned, the appellant spread her net very widely by claiming equality with eleven comparators. But, by the time the case reached the House, your Lordships were told that, if her appeal succeeded, she would only seek a reference to an expert in relation to four of the original comparators. This only goes to show what a lot of time and money would have been wasted if the matter had proceeded on a reference to an expert with respect to all the 11 comparators. I do not in any way criticise the employment tribunal in this case for deciding ... that they could not be satisfied that there were no reasonable grounds for determining her work to be of equal value with any one of the comparators. But I think that employment tribunals should, so far as possible, be alert to prevent abuse of the equal value claims procedure by applicants who cast their net over too wide a spread of comparators. To take an extreme case, a claimant who claimed equality with A who earns £X and also with B who earns £2X could hardly complain if an employment tribunal concluded that her claim of equality with A itself demonstrated that there were no reasonable grounds for her claim of equality with B. That said, however, it is right to point out that an employer's most effective safeguard against oppressive equal value claims is to initiate his own comprehensive job evaluation study under section 1(5) which, if properly carried out, will afford him complete protection ...'

(Lord Templeman delivered a concurring speech. Lords Griffiths, Ackner and Goff agreed with Lord Bridge.)

THE 'GENUINE MATERIAL FACTOR' DEFENCE

Equal Pay Act 1970

1   (3)   An equality clause falling within subsection (2)(a), (b) or (c) above shall not operate in relation to a variation between the woman's contract and the man's contract if the employer proves that the variation is genuinely due to a material factor which is not the difference of sex and that factor –

   (a)   in the case of an equality clause falling within subsection (2)(a) or (b) above, must be a material difference between the woman's case and the man's; and

   (b)   in the case of an equality clause falling within subsection (2)(c) above, may be such a material difference.

Comment

(1) This most important defence explains why it is that not everyone doing the same job gets the same pay. Most workers expect that factors such as seniority, merit or qualifications will also be taken into account, and present management orthodoxy, with its emphasis on performance-related pay, would be impossible if workers had to be paid the same for the same job.

(2) The onus is clearly on the employer to prove that the genuine material factor accounts for the variation in terms. While it is frequently said that this defence takes account of the 'personal equation' – the real differences between individuals – it is now well recognised that things which are capable of constituting a genuine material factor are wider than this.

(3) In considering the validity of a defence under EqPA s 1(3), regard must be had to the statement of the ECJ in *Bilka-Kaufhaus GmbH* v *Weber von Hartz* (1987) that:

> It is for the national court, which has sole jurisdiction to make findings of fact, to determine whether and to what extent the grounds put forward by the employer to explain the adoption of a pay practice which applies independently of a worker's sex but in fact affects more women than men may be regarded as objectively justified economic grounds.

It is clear from this that if a genuine material factor has an indirectly discriminatory effect on one sex, it must be objectively justified in order to be valid. There has been a long debate as to whether in fact the law should go further and demand that all genuine material factors should be objectively justified. Those who argue for this do so on the basis that once a *prima facie* claim for equal pay has been established, it means in effect that there is *prima facie* sex discrimination. If there is *prima facie* sex discrimination, then if it is direct, it cannot be justified and the woman should win. If it is indirect, it can only be allowed if it is objectively justified – which goes beyond finding merely that it has occurred for non-discriminatory reasons. The point is considered in the next case.

Strathclyde Regional Council v *Wallace* [1998] IRLR 146 House of Lords

LORD BROWNE-WILKINSON: 'My Lords, in this case the appellants, all of whom are unpromoted women teachers employed by the respondents, advance a claim to equal pay under the Equal Pay Act 1970. Their claim is based on the fact that, although they do the same work as a "principal teacher", they are paid at a lower rate. Each of the female applicants has selected a male comparator who is a principal teacher employed by the respondents and claims equality of pay with such comparator . . .

The structure of what are known as promoted posts in schools was laid down originally in the Schools (Scotland) Code 1956, and revised by a Scottish Office Education Department circular in 1972 and SED Staffing Standard in 1987. That structure permits the appointment of one head teacher in each school, with a number of lower grades of promoted posts, the number in each school depending upon a number of factors. The possible grades are deputy head teacher, assistant head teacher, principal teacher, assistant principal teacher, and senior teacher . . .

The particular circumstances which obtain within each school determine the number of promoted posts to which appointment can be made in that school, ie the number of vacancies for promoted appointment. In a significant number of schools in the region (in particular, those in which the nine appellants were employed) conditions were such that there was a requirement for the work of a principal teacher to be done, but the application of the relevant rules to the school did not permit the appointment of a principal teacher to do such work. In other words, there was no available vacancy. In that situation the appellants and doubtless other teachers found themselves in the position of doing the work of a principal teacher without having been promoted to that grade and without receiving the salary . . .

Finally, I must state an agreed fact of the greatest importance. The disparity in pay between the appellants and principal teachers has nothing to do with gender. Of the 134 unpromoted teachers who claimed to be carrying out the duties of principal teachers, 81 were men and 53 women. The selection by the appellants in this case of male principal teachers as comparators was purely the result of a tactical selection by these appellants: there are male and female principal teachers employed by the respondents without discrimination. Therefore the objective sought by the appellants is to achieve equal pay for like work regardless of sex, not to eliminate any inequalities due to sex discrimination. There is no such discrimination in the present case. To my mind it would be very surprising if a differential pay structure which had no disparate effect or impact as between the sexes should prove to be unlawful under the Equal Pay Act 1970. The preamble to that Act describes its purpose as being "An Act to prevent discrimination, as regards terms and conditions of employment, between men and women" . . .

If the words of EqPA s 1(3) are read without reference to authority they do not present any great difficulty in this case. The subsection provides a defence if the employer shows that the variation between the woman's contract and the man's contract is "genuinely" due to a factor which is (a) material and (b) not the difference of sex. The requirement of genuineness would be satisfied if the employment tribunal came to the conclusion that the reason put forward was not a sham or a pretence. For the matters relied upon by the employer to constitute "material factors" it would have to be shown that the matters relied upon were in fact causally relevant to the difference in pay, ie that they were significant factors. Finally, the employer had to show that the difference of sex was not a factor relied upon. This final point is capable of presenting problems in other cases. But in the present case it presents none: there is no suggestion that the matters relied on were in any way linked to differences in sex.

If that approach had been adopted by the employment tribunal, this case would have been straightforward. The five factors summarised by the employment tribunal were undoubtedly genuine reasons for there being a difference between the pay of the appellants and that of principal teachers. They were also significant and causally relevant factors leading to that disparity. They did not relate to sex in any way. Therefore, on the straightforward application of the section the respondents have established a sub-s (3) defence. There is nothing in the words of the subsection which requires the employer to "justify" the factors giving rise to this disparity by showing that there was no way in which the employer could have avoided such disparity if he had adopted other measures.

How then did the employment tribunal come to mislead itself by introducing into the case the concept of "justification"?

313

The answer is that they wrongly thought that the authorities demanded such justification in every case where an employer seeks to establish a sub-s (3) defence whereas, on a proper reading, the question of justification only arises where a factor relied upon is gender discriminatory. Although in the present case there is no question of gender discrimination, the authorities are in such a state of confusion that it is desirable for your Lordships to seek to establish the law on a clear and sound basis.

To establish a sub-s (3) defence, the employer has to prove that the disparity in pay is due to a factor "which is not the difference of sex", ie is not sexually discriminatory. The question then arises "what is sexually discriminatory"? Both the Sex Discrimination Act 1975 and [Art 141] of the EC Treaty recognise two types of sex discrimination. First, there is direct discrimination, ie a detriment suffered by women which they would not have suffered but for being women. Second, there is indirect discrimination, ie a detriment suffered by a class of individuals, men and women alike, but the class is such that a substantially larger number of women than men suffer the detriment. The classic example of indirect discrimination is a policy under which part-time workers, whether male or female, are paid less than full-time workers. There are many more women than men who are part-time workers. Accordingly, such a policy applied to part-time workers is indirectly discriminatory against women.

Under the Sex Discrimination Act 1975, direct sexual discrimination is always unlawful. But, both under the Sex Discrimination Act 1975 and under [Art 141], indirect discrimination is not unlawful if it is "justified": see the Sex Discrimination Act 1975, s 1(1)(b)(ii) and *Bilka-Kaufhaus GmbH* v *Weber von Hartz* (1987). Indirect discrimination can be "justified" if it is shown that the measures adopted by the employers which cause the adverse impact on women "correspond to a real need on the part of the [employers], are appropriate with a view to achieving the objectives pursued and are necessary to that end": see *Rainey* v *Greater Glasgow Health Board* (1987).

The cases establish that the Equal Pay Act 1970 has to be construed so far as possible to work harmoniously both with the Sex Discrimination Act 1975 and [Art 141]. All three sources of law are part of a code dealing with unlawful sex discrimination: see *Shields* v *E Coomes (Holdings) Ltd* (1978) and *Garland* v *British Rail Engineering Ltd* (1982). It follows that the words "not the difference of sex" where they appear in s 1(3) of the Equal Pay Act 1970 must be construed so as to accord with the Sex Discrimination Act 1975 and [Art 141], ie an employer will not be able to demonstrate that a factor is "not the difference of sex" if the factor relied upon is sexually discriminatory whether directly or indirectly. Further, a sexually discriminatory practice will not be fatal to a sub-s (3) defence if the employer can "justify" it applying the test in the *Bilka-Kaufhaus* case . . .

From what I have said, it is apparent that in considering s 1(3) of the Equal Pay Act 1970, the only circumstances in which questions of "justification" can arise are those in which the employer is relying on a factor which is sexually discriminatory. There is no question of the employer having to "justify" (in the *Bilka* sense) all disparities of pay. Provided that there is no element of sexual discrimination, the employer establishes a sub-s (3) defence by identifying the factors which he alleges have caused the disparity, proving that those factors are genuine and proving further that they were causally relevant to the disparity in pay complained of . . .

Mr Pannick QC, for the appellants, submitted that the employment tribunal were right to consider whether the factors relied upon (even though not gender related) "justified" the disparity in pay. He submitted that for a factor to be a "material" factor within sub-s (3) it had to be demonstrated that the matters relied upon unavoidably led to the disparity in pay: the employment tribunal was throughout engaged upon a consideration of whether the factors were "material" in that sense. I cannot accept that submission. The words of the subsection indicate no requirement of such a justification inherent in the use of the words "material factor". It has long been established by the decision of this House in *Rainey* v *Greater Glasgow Health Board*

(1987) that a factor is material if it is "significant and relevant", a test which looks to the reason why there is a disparity in pay not whether there is an excuse for such disparity. To my mind decisively, if one were to accept Mr Pannick's submission that would be to turn the Equal Pay Act into a "fair wages" Act requiring the elimination of disparity in wages even though such disparity had nothing to do with sex discrimination. As I have said, the preamble to the Act renders such an argument impossible.

In my judgment the law was correctly stated by Mummery J, giving the judgment of the Employment Appeal Tribunal in *Tyldesley* v *TML Plastics Ltd* (1996), in which he followed and applied the earlier Employment Appeal Tribunal decisions in *Calder* v *Rowntree Mackintosh Confectionery Ltd* (1992) and *Yorkshire Blood Transfusion Service* v *Plaskitt* (1994). The purpose of s 1 of the Equal Pay Act 1970 is to eliminate sex discrimination in pay not to achieve fair wages. Therefore, if a difference in pay is explained by genuine factors not tainted by discrimination that is sufficient to raise a valid defence under sub-s (3): in such a case there is no further burden on the employer to "justify" anything. However, if the factor explaining the disparity in pay is tainted by sex discrimination (whether direct or indirect) that will be fatal to a defence under sub-s (3) unless such discrimination can be objectively justified in accordance with the tests laid down in the Bilka and Rainey cases . . .'

(Lords Steyn, Hoffmann, Hope and Clyde agreed with Lord Browne-Wilkinson.)

Comment

(1) If the 53 unpromoted women teachers in this case had been successful, the 81 unpromoted men could then have claimed parity with them. What do you think of Lord Browne-Wilkinson's argument that, if all differences had to be justified, this would convert the Equal Pay Act into a Fair Wages Act?

(2) The House of Lords restated this position in *Glasgow City Council* v *Marshall* (2000). An argument that this was inconsistent with the ECJ's decision in *Brunhofer* (2001), which some commentators read as requiring objective justification in all cases, was accepted by the EAT in *Sharp* v *Caledonia Group Services* (2006), but rejected by the Court of Appeal in the later case of *Armstrong* v *Newcastle upon Tyne NHS Trust* (2006).

(3) This means that there is no limit on the factors which can be relied on for this defence (in *Yorkshire Blood Transfusion Service* v *Plaskitt* (1994) it was an error by the employer). However, there are some fairly well-recognised categories of material factor, which will be looked at in turn.

Market forces

Rainey v Greater Glasgow Health Board [1987] ICR 129 House of Lords

In 1980 it was decided to establish a prosthetic fitting service within the National Health Service in Scotland. Some prosthetists were recruited from the National Health Service and were paid according to appropriate NHS scales; however, because it was not possible to recruit enough from this source, 20 prosthetists, all men, were recruited directly from the private sector.

In order to make the job attractive to them, these direct recruits were allowed to keep their former terms and conditions of employment and existing negotiating procedure. This meant that in 1980 the claimant, a female prosthetist subject to NHS scales, earned £4,773 pa, whereas a man recruited from the private sector earned £6,680. There were no plans to phase out this differential, and by the time her equal pay claim was heard by an employment tribunal in 1983, their salaries were £7,295 and £10,085 respectively: the gap was actually getting bigger. It was accepted that they were employed on like work. The employer argued that market forces compelled them to pay the privately-recruited prosthetists at a higher rate and that this constituted a genuine material difference. The House of Lords agreed.

LORD KEITH: '... The main question at issue in the appeal is whether those circumstances are capable in law of constituting, within the meaning of section 1(3) of the Act of 1970, "a material difference (other than the difference of sex) between her case and his."

Counsel for the appellant argued that nothing can constitute such a difference which is not related to the personal circumstances of the two employees, such as their respective skills, experience or training. Reliance was placed upon the decision of the Court of Appeal in *Clay Cross (Quarry Services) Ltd* v *Fletcher* (1978). In that case a woman sales clerk was employed at a lower wage than a male sales clerk who had been engaged at a later date. The employers relied, as being the material difference between her case and his, on the circumstance that the male clerk had been the only suitable applicant for the post and that he had refused to accept it unless he was paid the same wage as he had received in his previous job. The Employment Appeal Tribunal had accepted this as discharging the onus on the employers under section 1(3) of the Act of 1970, but their decision was reversed by the Court of Appeal. Lord Denning MR said:

"The issue depends on whether there is a material difference (other than sex) between her case and his. Take heed to the words 'between her case and his'. They show that the tribunal is to have regard to *her* and to *him* – to the personal equation of the woman as compared to that of the man – irrespective of any extrinsic forces which led to the variation in pay. As I said in *Shields* v *E Coomes (Holdings) Ltd* (1978), section 1(3) applies when 'the personal equation of the man is such that he deserves to be paid at a higher rate than the woman'. Thus the personal equation of the man may warrant a wage differential if he has much longer length of service, or has superior skill or qualifications; or gives bigger output or productivity; or has been placed, owing to downgrading, in a protected pay category, vividly described as 'red-circled'; or to other circumstances personal to him in doing his job. But the tribunal is not to have regard to any extrinsic forces which have led to the man being paid more. An employer cannot avoid his obligations under the Act by saying: 'I paid him more because he asked for more', or 'I paid her less because she was willing to come for less'. If any such excuse were permitted, the Act would be a dead letter. Those are the very reasons why there was unequal pay before the statute. They are the very circumstances in which the statute was intended to operate. Nor can the employer avoid his obligations by giving the reasons why he submitted to the extrinsic forces. As for instance by saying: 'He asked for that sum because it was what he was getting in his previous job', or, 'He was the only applicant for the job, so I had no option'. In such cases the employer may beat his breast, and say: 'I did not pay him more because he was a man. I paid it because he was the only suitable person who applied for the job. Man or woman made no difference to me'. Those are reasons personal to the employer. If any such reasons were permitted as an excuse, the door would be wide open. Every employer who wished to avoid the statute would walk straight through it."

Lawton LJ said:

"What does section 1(3) in its context in both the Equal Pay Act 1970 and the Sex Discrimination Act 1975 mean? The context is important. The overall object of both Acts is to ensure that women are treated no less favourably than men. If a woman is treated less favourably than a man there is a presumption of discrimination which can only be rebutted in the sphere of employment if the employer brings himself within section 1(3). He cannot do so merely by proving that he did not intend to discriminate. There are more ways of discriminating against women than by deliberately setting out to do so: see section 1(1)(b) of the Sex Discrimination Act 1975. If lack of intention had provided a lawful excuse for variation, section 1(3) would surely have been worded differently. The variation must have been genuinely due to (that is, caused by) a material difference (that is, one which was relevant and real) between – and now come the important words – her case and his. What is her case? And what is his? In my judgment, her case embraces what appertains to her *in* her job, such as the qualifications she brought to it, the length of time she has been in it, the skill she has acquired, the responsibilities she has undertaken and where and under what conditions she has to do it. It is on this kind of basis that her case is to be compared with that of the man's. What does not appertain to her job or to his are the circumstances in which they came to be employed. These are collateral to the jobs as such."

In my opinion these statements are unduly restrictive of the proper interpretation of section 1(3). The difference must be "material," which I would construe as meaning "significant and relevant", and it must be between "her case and his". Consideration of a person's case must necessarily involve consideration of all the circumstances of that case. These may well go beyond what is not very happily described as "the personal equation", i.e. the personal qualities by way of skill, experience or training which the individual brings to the job. Some circumstances may on examination prove to be not significant or not relevant, but others may do so, though not relating to the personal qualities of the employee. In particular, where there is no question of intentional sex discrimination whether direct or indirect (and there is none here) a difference which is connected with economic factors affecting the efficient carrying on of the employer's business or other activity may well be relevant . . .'

[Lord Keith then discussed the decisions of the ECJ in *Jenkins* v *Kingsgate (Clothing Productions) Ltd* (1981) and *Bilka-Kaufhaus* v *Weber von Hartz* (1986). Referring to the latter, he continued:]

'. . . It therefore appears that the European Court has resolved the doubts expressed by Browne-Wilkinson J in *Jenkins* v *Kingsgate (Clothing Productions) Ltd* (1981) and established that the true meaning and effect of [Art 141] in this particular context is the same as that there attributed to section 1(3) of the Act of 1970 by the Employment Appeal Tribunal. Although the European Court at one point refers to "economic" grounds objectively justified, whereas Browne-Wilkinson J speaks of "economic or other reasons", I consider that read as a whole the ruling of the European Court would not exclude objectively justified grounds which are other than economic, such as administrative efficiency in a concern not engaged in commerce or business.

The decision of the European Court on [Art 141] must be accepted as authoritative and the judgment of the Employment Appeal Tribunal on section 1(3) of the Act of 1970, which in my opinion is correct, is in harmony with it. There is now no reason to construe section 1(3) as conferring greater rights on a worker in this context than does [Art 141] of the Treaty. It follows that a relevant difference for purposes of section 1(3) may relate to circumstances other than the personal qualifications or merits of the male and female workers who are the subject of comparison . . .'

(Lords Brandon, Griffiths, MacKay and Goff agreed with Lord Keith.)

Comment

(1) Market forces can operate in the opposite way – to depress the pay of workers as well as to raise it. *Strathclyde Regional Council* v *Wallace* (1998) is an example of this. In this context, note *Benveniste* v *University of Southampton* (1989), where the EAT held

317

that once the financial exigency, which had been a genuine material factor justifying lower pay for a woman at the time of her appointment, had eased, she was entitled to equal pay.

(2) Consider the arguments of the Court of Appeal in *Clay Cross* v *Fletcher* (1978), extensively quoted here by Lord Keith. Do you find them persuasive at all? Many commentators criticised the decision in *Rainey* on the grounds that to allow a defence of market forces will result in the perpetuation of unequal pay for women. This is because market forces generally have the effect of putting women at the lower end of the pay scale for any job, because they are likely to be valued less, and that work done predominantly by women is consistently undervalued by comparison with work undertaken predominantly by men. This issue was considered by the ECJ in the next case.

Enderby v *Frenchay Health Authority* [1994] ICR 112 European Court of Justice

JUDGMENT OF THE COURT:
'1   By order of 30 October 1991, received by the Court of Justice on 17 April 1992, the Court of Appeal of England and Wales, pursuant to [Art 234 of the EC Treaty], referred for a preliminary ruling questions concerning the interpretation of [Art 141] of the Treaty, enshrining the principle of equal pay for men and women.
2   Those questions were referred in the context of proceedings brought by Dr Pamela Enderby, against the Frenchay Health Authority and the Secretary of State for Health concerning the difference in pay between two jobs within the National Health Service.
3   The claimant, who is employed as a speech therapist by the health authority, considers that she is a victim of sex discrimination due to the fact that at her level of seniority within the National Health Service, namely, chief 3, members of her profession, which is overwhelmingly a female profession, are appreciably less well paid than members of comparable professions in which, at an equivalent professional level, there are more men than women. In 1986, she brought proceedings against her employer before an employment tribunal, claiming that her annual pay was only £10,106 while that of a principal clinical psychologist and of a grade 3 principal pharmacist, jobs which were of equal value to hers, was £12,527 and £14,106 respectively.
4   The claimant's claim was dismissed by the employment tribunal and then, on appeal, by the appeal tribunal. The employment tribunal considered that the differences in pay were the result of structures specific to each profession, and in particular the separate collective bargaining arrangements, which were not discriminatory. The appeal tribunal also considered that the differences were not attributable to discrimination. It held further that it had been established that the state of the employment market played some part in the difference in pay between speech therapists and pharmacists and that that was enough to justify the whole of the difference between those two professions.
5   On appeal, the Court of Appeal, considering that the outcome of the proceedings depended on the interpretation of [Art 141] of the Treaty, decided to refer questions to the Court of Justice for a preliminary ruling. In the statement of facts in its order, the Court of Appeal defined the job of principal speech therapist as "job A" and that of principal pharmacist as "job B", and assumed for the purpose of the present proceedings that those two different jobs were of equal value. It then asked the following questions:

"(1)   Does the principle of equal pay enshrined in [Art 141 of the Treaty of Rome] require the employer to justify objectively the difference in pay between job A and job B?
(2)   If the answer to question (1) is in the affirmative can the employer rely as sufficient justification for the difference in pay upon the fact that the pay of jobs A and B respectively have been determined by different collective bargaining processes which (considered

separately) do not discriminate on grounds of sex and do not operate so as to disadvantage women because of their sex?

(3) If the employer is able to establish that at times there are serious shortages of suitable candidates for job B and that he pays the higher remuneration to holders of job B so as to attract them to job B but it can also be established that only part of the difference in pay between job B and job A is due to the need to attract suitable candidates to job B, (a) is the whole of the difference of pay objectively justified, or (b) is that part but only that part of the difference which is due to the need to attract suitable candidates to job B objectively justified, or (c) must the employer equalise the pay of jobs A and B on the ground that he has failed to show that the whole of the difference is objectively justified?"

. . .

The third question

24   In its third question, the Court of Appeal wishes to know to what extent – wholly, in part or not at all – the fact that part of the difference in pay is attributable to a shortage of candidates for one job and to the need to attract them by higher salaries can objectively justify that pay differential.

25   The court has consistently held that it is for the national court, which has sole jurisdiction to make findings of fact, to determine whether and to what extent the grounds put forward by an employer to explain the adoption of a pay practice which applies independently of a worker's sex but in fact affects more women than men may be regarded as objectively justified economic grounds: *Bilka-Kaufhaus GmbH* v *Weber von Hartz* (1987) and *Nimz* v *Freie und Hansestadt Hamburg* (1991)). Those grounds may include, if they can be attributed to the needs and objectives of the undertaking, different criteria such as the worker's flexibility or adaptability to hours and places of work, his training or his length of service: see *Handels-og Kontorfunk-tionærernes Forbund i Danmark* v *Dansk Arbejdsgiverforening* (1991) [the *Danfoss* case].

26   The state of the employment market, which may lead an employer to increase the pay of a particular job in order to attract candidates, may constitute an objectively justified economic ground within the meaning of the case law cited above. How it is to be applied in the circum-stances of each case depends on the facts and so falls within the jurisdiction of the national court.

27   If, as the question referred seems to suggest, the national court has been able to deter-mine precisely what proportion of the increase in pay is attributable to market forces, it must necessarily accept that the pay differential is objectively justified to the extent of that proportion. When national authorities have to apply Community law, they must apply the principle of proportionality.

28   If that is not the case, it is for the national court to assess whether the role of market forces in determining the rate of pay was sufficiently significant to provide objective justification for part of all of the difference.

29   The answer to the third question, therefore, is that it is for the national court to determine, if necessary by applying the principle of proportionality, whether and to what extent the shortage of candidates for a job and the need to attract them by higher pay constitutes an objectively justified economic ground for the difference in pay between the jobs in question . . .'

Grading structures and collective bargaining

An employer's grading structure could be the outcome of a job evaluation study – in which case we have seen that a woman would not be able to claim parity with a man in a higher grade unless she argued that the study itself was discriminatory. Alternatively, it may be the product of collective bargaining, where the employer recognises a trade union, or it may be unilaterally imposed.

In the first case, to reach the Court of Appeal on EqPA s 1 it was held that, provided the grading scheme was implemented in good faith, it could constitute a genuine material difference justifying unequal pay (*National Vulcan Engineering Insurance Group Ltd* v *Wade* (1978). This principle was later extended to situations where the reason for the difference was the fact that the man and the woman were subject to different grading schemes, or separate collective bargaining structures (see *Rainey*, above, and *Reed Packaging* v *Boozer* (1988)). As usual, however, this must be considered in the context of European Union law.

Handels-og Kontorfunktionærernes Forbund i Danmark v *Dansk Arbejdsgiverforening (acting for Danfoss)* ('the *Danfoss* case') [1991] ICR 74 European Court of Justice

Employees of Danfoss were paid individual supplements to their basic wages according to a collective agreement. The first set of supplements were on the basis of the worker's skill, independence, responsibility and quality of work. The second set of supplements were on the basis of training and length of service.

A study of 157 workers over a period of four years revealed that on average men earned 6.85 per cent more than women. The scheme was challenged as being in breach of Art 141 and the Equal Pay Directive 1975.

JUDGMENT OF THE COURT:
'. . . 10   It is apparent from the documents before the court that the issue between the parties in the main proceedings has its origin in the fact that the system of individual supplements applied to basic pay is implemented in such a way that a woman is unable to identify the reasons for a difference between her pay and that of a man doing the same work. Employees do not know what criteria in the matter of supplements are applied to them and how they are applied. They know only the amount of their supplemented pay without being able to determine the effect of the individual criteria. Those who are in a particular wage group are thus unable to compare the various components of their pay with those of the pay of their colleagues who are in the same wage group.

11   In those circumstances the questions put by the national court must be understood as asking whether the Equal Pay Directive must be interpreted as meaning that where an undertaking applies a system of pay which is totally lacking in transparency, it is for the employer to prove that his practice in the matter of wages is not discriminatory, if a female worker establishes, in relation to a relatively large number of employees, that the average pay for women is less that that for men.

12   In that respect it must first be borne in mind that in *Commission* v *France* (1988) the court condemned a system of recruitment characterised by a lack of transparency as being contrary to the principle of equal access to employment on the ground that the lack of transparency prevented any form of supervision by the national courts.

13   It should next be pointed out that in a situation where a system of individual pay supplements which is completely lacking in transparency is at issue, female employees can establish differences only so far as average pay is concerned. They would be deprived of any effective means of enforcing the principle of equal pay before the national courts if the effect of adducing such evidence was not to impose upon the employer the burden of proving that his practice in the matter of wages is not in fact discriminatory.

14   Finally, it should be noted that under article 6 of the Equal Pay Directive member states must, in accordance with their national circumstances and legal systems, take the measures necessary to ensure that the principle of equal pay is applied and that effective means are available to ensure that it is observed. The concern for effectiveness which thus underlies the Directive means that it must be interpreted as implying adjustments to national rules on the burden of proof in special cases where such adjustments are necessary for the effective implementation of the principle of equality.

15   To show that his practice in the matter of wages does not systematically work to the disadvantage of female employees the employer will have to indicate how he has applied the criteria concerning supplements and will thus be forced to make his system of pay transparent . . .'

The court in reply to the questions submitted to it by the industrial arbitration board by order of 12 October 1987, hereby rules:

Council Directive (75/117/EEC) on the approximation of the laws of the member states relating to the application of the principle of equal pay for men and women must be interpreted as meaning:

1   Where an undertaking applies a system of pay which is totally lacking in transparency, it is for the employer to prove that his practice in the matter of wages is not discriminatory, if a female worker establishes, in relation to a relatively large number of employees, that the average pay of women is less than that for men.

2   Where it appears that the application of criteria for additional payments such as mobility, training or length of service of the employee works systematically to the disadvantage of female employees, the employer may justify recourse to the criterion of mobility if it is understood as referring to adaptability to variable hours and varying places of work, by showing that such adaptability is of importance for the performance of the specific tasks entrusted to the employee, but not if that criterion is understood as covering the quality of the work done by the employee; the employer may justify recourse to the criterion of training by showing that such training is of importance for the performance of the specific tasks entrusted to the employee; the employer does not have to provide special justification for recourse to the criterion of length of service.'

Enderby v *Frenchay Health Authority* [1994] ICR 112 European Court of Justice

The facts of the case are given above, p 318. The second question referred to the Court deals with the issue of collective bargaining.

JUDGMENT OF THE COURT:

'. . . *The second question*

20   In its second question, the Court of Appeal wishes to know whether the employer can rely as sufficient justification for the difference in pay upon the fact that the rates of pay of the jobs in question were decided by collective bargaining processes which, although carried out by the same parties, are distinct and which, considered separately, have no discriminatory effect.

21   As is clear from article 4 of Council Directive (75/117/EEC) on the approximation of the laws of the member states relating to the application of the principle of equal pay for men and women, collective agreements, like laws, regulations or administrative provisions, must observe the principle enshrined in [Art 141] of the Treaty.

22   The fact that the rates of pay at issue are decided by collective bargaining processes conducted separately for each of the two professional groups concerned, without any

discriminatory effect within each group, does not preclude a finding of prima facie discrimination where the results of those processes show that two groups with the same employer and the same trade union are treated differently. If the employer could rely on the absence of discrimination within each of the collective bargaining processes taken separately as sufficient justification for the difference in pay, he could, as the German Government pointed out, easily circumvent the principle of equal pay by using separate bargaining processes.

23   Accordingly, the answer to the second question is that the fact that the respective rates of pay of two jobs of equal value, one carried out almost exclusively by women and the other predominantly by men, were arrived at by collective bargaining processes which, although carried out by the same parties, are distinct, and, taken separately, have in themselves no discriminatory effect, is not sufficient objective justification for the difference in pay between those two jobs . . .'

Comment

(1) What may be gleaned from these cases is that while separate bargaining structures may *explain* differences in pay, they do not necessarily *justify* them. Thus if it is shown that the pay structures arrived at through collective bargaining have an adverse impact on women compared with men, they will require objective justification in order to be accepted as constituting a genuine material difference. There is also a strong push towards transparency, both as to the reasons for differences in pay for work of equal value and as to how the system is applied. As the *Danfoss* case shows, lack of transparency will be construed against the employer.

(2) In the last few years there has been a huge slew of equal pay litigation involving public sector organisations, focused on the north-east of England, arising from collective bargaining structures which historically favoured male groups of workers, in particular by giving them bonuses and allowances which were not available to predominantly female groups. It was accepted in the late 1990s that the pay system was discriminatory and work began on introducing a single pay structure for all workers – but the existing bonus and allowance systems were left in place. Groups of women successfully challenged many of these on the basis of a denial of equal pay and it was clear that separate bargaining processes did not constitute an acceptable material difference.

(3) If separate bargaining structures result in unequal pay, but there is no evidence that the bargaining structures are tainted by sex discrimination, (ie, they do not have an adverse impact on women), there is no need for the employer to justify them: *Glasgow City Council* v *Marshall* (2000). So, how much disparity has to be shown before an adverse impact is established? This will usually be a question of fact for the employment tribunal, but it is worth noting that in *Bailey* v *Home Office* (2005) the Court of Appeal held that objective justification was required where the advantaged group was predominantly male and the disadvantaged group contained a significant number of women, even if they did not constitute a majority.

Performance-related pay

Employers may pay workers wholly or partly by results: commission on sales, payments by the piece and payments dependent on reaching specific targets are all forms of this. Can such a system constitute a genuine material factor justifying unequal pay for men and women?

Specialarbejdforbundet I Danmark v Dansk Industri (acting for Royal Copenhagen) ('the *Royal Copenhagen* case') [1995] IRLR 648 European Court of Justice

JUDGMENT OF THE COURT: '. . . Royal Copenhagen is a ceramics producer employing some 1,150 workers, 40% men and 60% women, in the manufacture of such products. Its employees may be divided into three groups: turners, who use a variety of techniques to mould the porcelain clay mass; painters, who decorate the products; and unskilled workers, who are engaged in operating the kilns, sorting and polishing, transport within the factory and so forth.

The turners' group consists of some 200 persons and the painters' group 453 persons. Those groups may in turn be divided into a number of subgroups, such as, within the first group, automatic-machine operators, who man machines which automatically mould ceramic products, and, within the second, blue-pattern painters, who decorate the products by brush, and ornamental-plate painters, who spray-paint ornamental plates which already have a pattern and then remove the paint from certain parts of the pattern with a sponge.

All these employees are covered by the same collective agreement, under which they are in principle paid on a piecework basis, that is to say, the level of their pay is wholly or partially dependent on their output. They may however opt to be paid a fixed hourly rate which is the same for all the groups. In practice, approximately 70% of the turners and 70% of the painters are paid by the piece: their pay consists of a fixed element, paid as a basic hourly wage, and a variable element, paid by reference to the number of items produced.

The group of automatic-machine operators paid by the piece comprises 26 persons, all men, and accounts for approximately 18% of all turners paid by the piece. The group of blue-pattern painters paid by the piece comprises 156 persons, 155 women and 1 man, and accounts for approximately 49% of the group of painters paid by the piece. The group of ornamental-plate decorators paid by the piece comprises 51 persons, all women, and accounts for approximately 16% of the group of painters paid by the piece.

In April 1990, the average hourly pay of the automatic-machine operators paid by the piece was DKR 103.93, including a fixed element of DKR 71.69, with the highest earner receiving DKR 118 per hour and the lowest earner DKR 86 per hour. During the same period, the average hourly pay of the blue-pattern painters paid by the piece was DKR 91, including a fixed element of DKR 57, with the highest earner receiving DKR 125 per hour and the lowest DKR 72 per hour, and the average hourly pay of the ornamental-plate decorators paid by the piece was DKR 116.20, including a fixed element of DKR 35.85, with the highest earner receiving DKR 159 per hour and the lowest DKR 86 per hour.

The Specialarbejderforbundet considered that Royal Copenhagen was infringing the requirement of equal pay because the average hourly piecework pay of the group of blue-pattern painters, all but one of whom were women, was less than that of the group of automatic-machine operators, all of whom were men. It brought proceedings before the Faglige Voldgiftsret of Copenhagen, seeking an order that Royal Copenhagen acknowledge that the blue-pattern painters perform work of equal value to that of the automatic-machine operators and bring the average hourly piecework pay of the former up to the level of that of the latter . . .

The first question

The national court's first question asks whether [Art 141] of the Treaty and the Directive apply to piecework pay schemes in which pay depends entirely or in large measure on the individual output of each worker.

[Art 141], by stating expressly in subparagraph (a) of its [second] paragraph that equal pay without discrimination based on sex means that pay for the same work at piece rates is to be calculated on the basis of the same unit of measurement, itself provides that the principle of equal pay applies to piecework pay schemes.

Moreover the Court has already held that [Art 141] prohibits any discrimination with regard to pay as between men and women, whatever the system which gives rise to such inequality (*Barber* v *Guardian Royal Exchange Assurance Group* (1990)).

That conclusion is borne out by the first paragraph of Article 1 of the Equal Pay Directive, which provides that the principle of equal pay for men and women means the elimination of all discrimination on grounds of sex "with regard to all aspects and conditions of remuneration".

The reply to the first question should accordingly be that [Art 141] of the Treaty and the Directive apply to piecework pay schemes in which pay depends entirely or in large measure on the individual output of each worker . . .

It follows from paragraph 12 of this judgment that in a piecework pay scheme the principle of equal pay requires that the pay of two groups of workers, one consisting predominantly of men and the other predominantly of women, is to be calculated on the basis of the same unit of measurement.

Where the unit of measurement is the same for two groups of workers carrying out the same work or is objectively capable of ensuring that the total individual pay of workers in the two groups is the same for work which, although different, is considered to be of equal value, the principle of equal pay does not prohibit workers belonging to one or the other group from receiving different total pay if that is due to their different individual output.

It follows that in a piecework pay scheme the mere finding that there is a difference in the average pay of two groups of workers, calculated on the basis of the total individual pay of all the workers belonging to one or the other group, does not suffice to establish that there is discrimination with regard to pay.

It is for the national court, which alone is competent to assess the facts, to decide whether the unit of measurement applicable to the work carried out by the two groups of workers is the same or, if the two groups carry out work which is different but considered to be of equal value, whether the unit of measurement is objectively capable of ensuring that their total pay is the same. It is also for that court to ascertain whether a pay differential relied on by a worker belonging to a group consisting predominantly of women as evidence of sex discrimination against that worker compared with a worker belonging to a group consisting predominantly of men is due to a difference between the units of measurement applicable to the two groups or to a difference in individual output.

The Court has, however, held (*Enderby* v *Frenchay Health Authority* (1994)) that the burden of proof, which is normally on the worker bringing legal proceedings against his employer with a view to removing the discrimination of which he believes himself to be the victim, may be shifted when that is necessary to avoid depriving workers who appear to be the victims of dis-crimination of any effective means of enforcing the principle of equal pay. Thus in particular where an undertaking applies a system of pay which is wholly lacking in transparency, it is for the employer to prove that his practice in the matter of wages is not discriminatory if a female worker establishes, in relation to a relatively large number of employees, that the average pay for women is less than that for men (*Handels-og Kontorfunktionaerernes Forbund i Danmark* v *Dansk Arbejdsgiverforening ("Danfoss")* (1989)). Similarly, where significant statistics disclose an appreciable difference in pay between two jobs of equal value, one of which is carried out almost exclusively by women and the other predominantly by men, so that there is a prima facie case of sex discrimination, [Art 141] of the Treaty requires the employer to show that that difference is based on objectively justified factors unrelated to any discrimination on grounds of sex (*Enderby*, cited above).

Admittedly, in a piecework pay scheme such a prima facie case of discrimination does not arise solely because significant statistics disclose appreciable differences between the average pay of two groups of workers, since those differences may be due to differences in individual output of the workers constituting the two groups.

If however, in a system such as that in the main proceedings where the individual pay taken into account in calculating the average pay of the two groups of workers consists of a variable element depending on each worker's output and a fixed element differing according to the group of workers concerned (fourth question, paragraph (e)), it is not possible to identify the factors which determined the rates or units of measurement used to calculate the variable element in the pay (fourth question, paragraph (g)), the objective of not depriving workers of any effective means of enforcing the principle of equal pay may require the employer to bear the burden of proving that the differences found are not due to sex discrimination.

It is for the national court to ascertain whether, in the light in particular of those factors and the extent of the differences between the average pay of the two groups of workers, the conditions for so shifting the burden of proof are satisfied in the main proceedings. If so, it will be open to the employer for example to demonstrate that the pay differentials are due to differences in the choice by the workers concerned of their rate of work (fourth question, paragraph (c)) and to rely on major differences between total individual pay within each of those groups (fourth question, paragraph (d)).

The reply to the second question in conjunction with paragraphs (c), (d), (e) and (g) of the fourth question should accordingly be that the principle of equal pay set out in [Art 141] of the Treaty and Article 1 of the Directive means that the mere finding that in a piecework pay scheme the average pay of a group of workers consisting predominantly of women carrying out one type of work is appreciably lower than the average pay of a group of workers consisting predominantly of men carrying out another type of work to which equal value is attributed does not suffice to establish that there is discrimination with regard to pay. However, where in a piecework pay scheme in which individual pay consists of a variable element depending on each worker's output and a fixed element differing according to the group of workers concerned it is not possible to identify the factors which determined the rates or units of measurement used to calculate the variable element in the pay, the employer may have to bear the burden of proving that the differences found are not due to sex discrimination . . .'

Comment

(1) The general message is that payment systems which result in women overall receiving less than men overall are suspect, and will require the employer to produce objective justification for any differences. However, note that this is dependent on their jobs being adjudged to be of equal value in the first place.

(2) Note also that performance-related factors which are said to constitute a genuine material difference must actually exist. *Redcar & Cleveland Borough Council* v *Bainbridge* (2007), one of the north-east public sector equal pay cases, is a good example of this. It was a claim by a large number of female caterers and cleaners for parity with predominantly male gardeners, refuse collectors and street sweepers. All the jobs had been rated as of equal value under a job evaluation scheme and they were all paid at the same basic rate. However, the gardeners and refuse collectors got a productivity bonus worth 36–40 per cent extra per week, and the street sweepers got an attendance allowance of around £34 per week. It was held that only the refuse collectors' bonuses genuinely resulted in increased productivity. The bonuses and allowances paid to the gardeners and street sweepers no longer served any genuine purpose and were thus not genuine material factors justifying their higher pay.

Length of service

Length of service, or seniority, has long been a factor used to establish pay differentials: very many employers use incremental scales, sometimes with as many as 15 or 20 points, whereby staff progress to a higher point for every year of service. However, as women frequently have interrupted patterns of service, it could be argued that this is indirectly discriminatory on grounds of sex. In the *Danfoss* case, above p 320, the ECJ specifically said that the use of length of service as a criterion did not require special justification. The point was considered more fully by the ECJ in the next case.

Cadman v *Health and Safety Executive* [2006] ICR 1623
European Court of Justice

JUDGMENT OF THE COURT: '. . . The applicant is employed by the respondent. Since she has been working for that body the pay system has been altered several times. Before 1992 the system was incremental, that is to say that each employee received an annual increase until he reached the top of the pay scale for his grade. In 1992, the HSE introduced a performance-related element so that the amount of the annual increment was adjusted to reflect the employee's individual performance. Under this system high performing employees could reach the top of the scale more quickly. Following the introduction in 1995 of a long-term pay agreement, annual pay increases were set in accordance with the award of points called "equity shares" linked to the employee's performance. That change had the effect of decreasing the rate at which pay differentials narrowed between longer-serving and shorter-serving employees on the same grade. Finally, in 2000, the system was altered again to enable employees lower down the pay bands to be paid larger annual increases and, therefore, to progress more quickly through the pay band.

In June 2001, the applicant lodged an application before the Manchester employment tribunal based on the Equal Pay Act 1970. At the date of her claim, she had been engaged as a band 2 inspector, a managerial post, for nearly five years. She took as comparators four male colleagues who were also band 2 inspectors.

Although they were in the same band as the applicant, those four persons were paid substantially more than her. In the financial year 2000/01 the applicant's annual salary was £35,129, while the corresponding figures paid to her comparators were £39,125, £43,345, £43,119 and £44,183.

It is common ground that at the date of the claim lodged at the employment tribunal the four male comparators had longer service than Mrs Cadman, acquired in part in more junior posts.

The employment tribunal held that under section 1 of the Equal Pay Act 1970 the term in the applicant's employment contract relating to pay should be modified so as not to be less favourable than that in the employment contracts of her four comparators.

The respondent appealed to the Employment Appeal Tribunal against that decision. That tribunal held, first, that in the light of the judgment in *Danfoss* (1991), where unequal pay arose because of the use of length of service as a criterion, no special justification was required. It held, secondly, that even if such justification were required, the employment tribunal had erred in law when considering justification.

By notice of appeal of 4 November 2003, the applicant appealed against the decision of the Employment Appeal Tribunal to the Court of Appeal.

The Court of Appeal states that the differentials in pay relied on by the applicant in support of her action are explained by the structure of the pay system, as the respondent applies a system of pay increases which, in one way or another, reflects and rewards length of service.

Since women in pay band 2 and generally in the relevant part of the HSE's workforce have on average shorter service than men, the use of length of service as a determinant of pay has a disproportionate impact on women.

The Court of Appeal states that evidence submitted by the intervener, the Equal Opportunities Commission, and accepted by all the parties to the dispute, shows that in the United Kingdom and throughout the European Union the length of service of female workers, taken as a whole, is less than that of male workers. The use of length of service as a determinant of pay plays an important part in the continuing, albeit slowly narrowing, gap between female and male workers.

In that regard, the Court of Appeal is uncertain whether the case-law of the Court has departed from the finding in *Danfoss* that "the employer does not have to provide special justification for recourse to the criterion of length of service . . .".

By its first and second questions, which it is appropriate to examine together, the national court asks essentially whether, and if so in what circumstances, Article 141 EC requires an employer to provide justification for recourse to the criterion of length of service as a determinant of pay where use of that criterion leads to disparities in pay between the men and women to be included in the comparison . . .

Recourse to the criterion of length of service

In *Danfoss*, the court, after stating that it is not to be excluded that recourse to the criterion of length of service may involve less advantageous treatment of women than of men, held that the employer does not have to provide special justification for recourse to that criterion.

By adopting that position, the court acknowledged that rewarding, in particular, experience acquired which enables the worker to perform his duties better constitutes a legitimate objective of pay policy.

As a general rule, recourse to the criterion of length of service is appropriate to attain that objective. Length of service goes hand in hand with experience, and experience generally enables the worker to perform his duties better.

The employer is therefore free to reward length of service without having to establish the importance it has in the performance of specific tasks entrusted to the employee.

In the same judgment, the court did not, however, exclude the possibility that there may be situations in which recourse to the criterion of length of service must be justified by the employer in detail.

That is so, in particular, where the worker provides evidence capable of giving rise to serious doubts as to whether recourse to the criterion of length of service is, in the circumstances, appropriate to attain the above-mentioned objective. It is in such circumstances for the employer to prove that that which is true as a general rule, namely that length of service goes hand in hand with experience and that experience enables the worker to perform his duties better, is also true as regards the job in question.

It should be added that where a job classification system based on an evaluation of the work to be carried out is used in determining pay, it is not necessary for the justification for recourse to a certain criterion to relate on an individual basis to the situation of the workers concerned. Therefore, if the objective pursued by recourse to the criterion of length of service is to recognise experience acquired, there is no need to show in the context of such a system that an individual worker has acquired experience during the relevant period which has enabled him to perform his duties better. By contrast, the nature of the work to be carried out must be considered objectively (*Rummler* v *Dato-Druck* (1987)).

It follows from all of the foregoing considerations, that the answer to the first and second questions referred must be that Article 141 EC is to be interpreted as meaning that, where recourse to the criterion of length of service as a determinant of pay leads to disparities in pay, in respect of equal work or work of equal value, between the men and women to be included in the comparison, (i) since, as a general rule, recourse to the criterion of length of service is appropriate to attain the legitimate objective of rewarding experience acquired which enables the worker to perform his duties better, the employer does not have to establish specifically that recourse to that criterion is appropriate to attain that objective as regards a particular job, unless the worker provides evidence capable of raising serious doubts in that regard; (ii) where a job classification system based on an evaluation of the work to be carried out is used in deter- mining pay, there is no need to show that an individual worker has acquired experience during the relevant period which has enabled him to perform his duties better . . .'

Comment

(1) The case now returns to the Court of Appeal for decision in the light of this advice. One interesting point will be whether the men's extra service in lower grade jobs will be accepted as relevant to their performance in their current posts.

(2) We saw in Chapter 2 that length of service also discriminates on grounds of age – but that this is allowed to some extent by the Age Regs reg 32 (above p 57). There may be some question as to whether reg 32 is in accordance with EU law as stated in *Cadman*. Regulation 32 exempts an employer from the need to justify using length of service as a criterion if the period is not more than five years; and beyond five years, it may yet be justified if it 'fulfils a business need of his undertaking (for example, by encouraging the loyalty or motivation, or rewarding the experience, of some or all of his workers)'.

Red-circling

A job evaluation study, or any other review of grading systems, may result in some jobs being graded lower than they were before. In these circumstances, the employees are usually left on their existing wage (higher than others in the same grade) for a protected period or the differential is gradually phased out over a period of time. The employees placed in this protected category are thus singled out, or 'red- circled'. Another common situation where red-circling is used is where an employee who has become unable to do his (usually his) existing job is given lower grade work, but at his former salary level (eg *Methven* v *Cow Industrial Polymers* (1980)).

It has long been accepted that this amounts to a genuine material difference, as long as the reason for the red-circling is not itself discriminatory.

Snoxell v Vauxhall Motors Ltd
[1977] ICR 700 Employment Appeal Tribunal

Until 1971 the company had separate pay grades for men and women, even for exactly the same jobs. In 1971 they introduced an amended structure which was open to men and women. It was agreed that one of the male grades in the past had been given too high a status and so it was assimilated to a lower grade, but those in it (all men, of course) were red-circled. Two women claimed equal pay, arguing that the reason that they were not also red-circled was because, as women, they did not have the opportunity to join the higher grade before 1971.

PHILLIPS J: '. . . Mr Lester [counsel for the claimants] submitted that section 1(3) is not a general escape clause designed to enable employers to phase in equal pay gradually; that was provided for in the Equal Pay Act 1970 itself which did not come into operation until December 29, 1975, five years after it was enacted. Nor, he submitted, could reliance be placed on section 1(3) where the facts said to constitute the difference other than sex could be shown to have their origin in sex discrimination. Thus in the present case, although the immediate cause of the discrimination lay in the fact that the male inspectors were red circled whereas Miss Snoxell and Mrs Davies were not, and although they were red circled in order to preserve their status for reasons unconnected with sex, it was necessary to look to see why Miss Snoxell and Mrs Davies were not also within the red circle. The answer was that, because they were women, they were not able to enter grade X2, and so did not qualify. Thus at the root of the difference relied on lay sex discrimination, and it would be contrary to the purpose and intent of the Equal Pay Act 1970 to allow such an answer to the claim.

Mr Grabiner [counsel for the employer] submitted that the reason for the red circling of the male inspectors had nothing to do with sex discrimination, but was intended merely to preserve their status, and that it was not brought into existence to discriminate against women. If there had been no red circle, he submitted, all the men and the women would have been paid the same. The difference for the purpose of section 1(3) was the formation of the red circle. The substantive cause of the discrimination, he submitted, was the formation of the red circle, and it was the effective cause. Thus there was no discrimination, and a good answer to the claim was available to Vauxhall under section 1(3).

Putting these arguments side by side it can be seen that the solution depends on whether, in analysing the history of the difference in treatment of Miss Snoxell and Mrs Davies on the one hand and the red circle male inspectors on the other, one stops at the moment of the formation of the red circle or looks further back to see why Miss Snoxell and Mrs Davies were not within it. The arguments presented to us have, not surprisingly, considered questions of causation, and it has been said that the inability of Miss Snoxell and Mrs Davies to join the red circle was, or was not, the effective cause of the current variation in the terms of their contracts of employment. It seems to us that this earlier discrimination can be said to be an effective cause of the current variation . . .'

(It was held that the women were entitled to equal pay.)

Part-time working

Bilka Kaufhaus GmbH v Weber von Hartz
[1987] ICR 110 European Court of Justice

JUDGMENT OF THE COURT

'. . . *The first question*

24   In the first of its questions the national court asks whether a staff policy pursued by a department store company excluding part-time employees from an occupational pension scheme constitutes discrimination contrary to [Art 141] where that exclusion affects a far greater number of women than men.

25   In order to reply to that question reference must be made to the judgment of 31 March 1981 in *Jenkins* v *Kingsgate (Clothing Productions) Ltd*.

26   In that judgment the court considered the question whether the payment of a lower hourly rate for part-time work than for full-time work was compatible with [Art 141].

27   Such a practice is comparable to that at issue before the national court in this case: Bilka does not pay different hourly rates to part-time and full-time workers, but it grants only full-time

workers an occupational pension. Since, as was stated above, such a pension falls within the concept of pay for the purposes of the second paragraph of [Art 141] it follows that, hour for hour, the total remuneration paid by Bilka to full-time workers is higher than that paid to part-time workers.

28   The conclusion reached by the court in its judgment of 31 March 1981 is therefore equally valid in the context of this case.

29   If, therefore, it should be found that a much lower proportion of women than of men work full-time, the exclusion of part-time workers from the occupational pension scheme would be contrary to [Art 141] of the Treaty where, taking into account the difficulties encountered by women workers in working full-time, that measure could not be explained by factors which exclude any discrimination on grounds of sex.

30   However, if the undertaking is able to show that its pay practice may be explained by objectively justified factors unrelated to any discrimination on grounds of sex there is no breach of [Art 141].

31   The answer to the first question referred by the national court must therefore be that [Art 141 of the EC Treaty] is infringed by a department store company which excludes part-time employees from its occupational pension scheme, where that exclusion affects a far greater number of women than men, unless the undertaking shows that the exclusion is based on objectively justified factors unrelated to any discrimination on grounds of sex.

Question 2(a)

32   In its second question the national court seeks in essence to know whether the reasons put forward by Bilka to explain its pay policy may be regarded as "objectively justified economic grounds", as referred to in the judgment of 31 March 1981, where the interests of undertakings in the department store sector do not require such a policy.

33   In its observations Bilka argues that the exclusion of part-time workers from the occupational pension scheme is intended solely to discourage part-time work, since in general part-time workers refuse to work in the late afternoon and on Saturdays. In order to ensure the presence of an adequate workforce during those periods it was therefore necessary to make full-time work more attractive than part-time work, by making the occupational pension scheme open only to full-time workers. Bilka concludes that on the basis of the judgment of 31 March 1981 it cannot be accused of having infringed [Art 141].

34   In reply to the reasons put forward to justify the exclusion of part-time workers Mrs Weber von Hartz points out that Bilka is in no way obliged to employ part-time workers and that if it decides to do so it may not subsequently restrict the pension rights of such workers, which are already reduced by reason of the fact that they work fewer hours.

35   According to the Commission, in order to establish that there has been no breach of [Art 141] it is not sufficient to show that in adopting a pay practice which in fact discriminates against women workers the employer sought to achieve objectives other than discrimination against women. The Commission considers that in order to justify such a pay practice from the point of view of [Art 141] the employer must, as the court held in its judgment of 31 March 1981, put forward objective economic grounds relating to the management of the undertaking. It is also necessary to ascertain whether the pay practice in question is necessary and in proportion to the objectives pursued by the employer.

36   It is for the national court, which has sole jurisdiction to make findings of fact, to determine whether and to what extent the grounds put forward by an employer to explain the adoption of a pay practice which applies independently of a worker's sex but in fact affects more women than men may be regarded as objectively justified economic grounds. If the national court finds

that the measures chosen by Bilka correspond to a real need on the part of the undertaking, are appropriate with a view to achieving the objectives pursued and are necessary to that end, the fact that the measures affect a far greater number of women than men is not sufficient to show that they constitute an infringement of [Art 141].

37   The answer to question 2(a) must therefore be that under [Art 141] a department store company may justify the adoption of a pay policy excluding part-time workers, irrespective of their sex, from its occupational pension scheme on the ground that it seeks to employ as few part-time workers as possible, where it is found that the means chosen for achieving that objective correspond to a real need on the part of the undertaking, are appropriate with a view to achieving the objective in question and are necessary to that end . . .'

Comment

(1) In *Jenkins* v *Kingsgate* (1981) evidence was given that about 90 per cent of all part-time workers are women. The proportion has not changed substantially since then, although there are different patterns in different industries. Therefore, terms which are disadvantageous to part-time workers will indirectly discriminate against women. According to the ECJ this does not prevent part-time working from being a genuine material difference, subject to the need for objective justification.

(2) The Equal Pay Act 1970 does not expressly adopt the concept of indirect discrimination. Hence the importance of the ECJ's decision in *Jenkins* v *Kingsgate* (1981), which made it clear that it must be read so as to include the concept.

(3) In *Kowalska* v *Freie und Hansestadt Hamburg* (1990) the ECJ held that exclusion of part-timers from the employer's redundancy payments scheme was indirect discrimination contrary to Art 141 and the Equal Pay Directive 1975. It was held that the women should receive pro rata payments according to the number of hours worked. Similarly, in *Rinner-Kühn* v *FWW Spezial-Gebäudereinigung GmbH* (1989) the ECJ held that German legislation excluding part-time workers from the right to receive sick pay from their employers required objective justification. Largely on the strength of these decisions, the EOC successfully challenged the exclusion of workers working fewer than 16 hours a week from the right to claim redundancy payments or unfair dismissal: see *R* v *Secretary of State for Employment ex parte EOC* (1994).

(4) As we saw in Chapter 3, the Part-time Work Directive (97/81/EC), implemented in the United Kingdom by the Part-time Workers (Prevention of Less Favourable Treatment) Regulations 2000, now makes discrimination against part-time workers independently unlawful, unless it can be justified. The possibility of a claim based on the SDA or EqPA remains important, however.

WHAT IS EQUALISED?

Hayward v Cammell Laird Shipbuilders Ltd (No 2)
[1988] ICR 464 House of Lords

Julie Hayward, employed as a cook by Cammell Laird, brought the first equal value claim in the country when in 1984 she claimed that her work was of equal value with male painters, thermal insulation engineers and joiners employed by the company. An employment tribunal held that her work was of equal value to theirs and that the company could not rely on the genuine material difference defence between her case and theirs because they had made it clear at the beginning that they were not relying on that defence and they could not change their minds.

There was a further hearing as to the form of relief that she should receive. The employers here sought to argue that what should be compared was the overall job packages of the employees. While her basic pay was lower than that of the men, she had better terms in relation to sickness, holidays, paid meal breaks and benefits in kind. Taken overall, the employers argued that although her basic pay was £25 per week less than theirs, she was actually £11 per week better off than them!

LORD MACKAY: '... I deal first with the issue between the parties arising on the United Kingdom legislation to which I have referred. The issue is whether in terms of the Equal Pay Act 1970, as amended, the woman who can point to a term of her contract which is less favourable than a term of a similar kind in the man's contract is entitled to have that term made not less favourable irrespective of whether she is as favourably treated as the man when the whole of her contract and the whole of his contract are considered, as the appellant submits, or whether, although she shows that a particular term of her contract is less favourable to her than a term of a similar kind in the man's contract, her claim can nevertheless be defeated if it is shown that the terms of her contract considered as a whole are not less favourable to her than the terms of the man's contract considered as a whole, as the respondents submit.

No authority dealing with this question was referred to in the argument before your Lordships. There is no definition of the word "term" in the legislation. In that situation I am of opinion that the natural meaning of the word "term" in this context is a distinct provision or part of the contract which has sufficient content to make it possible to compare it from the point of view of the benefits it confers with a similar provision or part in another contract. For example, Miss Hayward was employed on her accepting terms set out in a letter to her from the respondents which includes the following:

> "We can offer you a position on our staff as a cook at a salary of £5,165 per annum. The base rate on which overtime is based is £4,471 . . ."

There is a provision in the letter setting out the normal hours of work, providing that the overtime payment shall be plain time rate plus a third (two-thirds on Saturday and Sunday).

The corresponding provision with regard to basic pay in the men's contracts is less specific and refers to a national agreement from which the rate of wages to be paid weekly in arrears is to be determined. Overtime payments are to be determined also in accordance with the national agreement.

It appears to me that it would be natural to compare the appellant's basic salary as set out in her contract with the basic salary determined under the men's contracts. I think it would be natural to treat the provision relating to basic pay as a term in each of the contracts.

However, one has to take account of the hours to be worked in order to earn this money and I think this consideration points to the importance of the provision in question being one which is capable of being compared from the point of view of the benefit it confers with a corresponding provision in another contract to see whether or not it is more beneficial than that provision. Accordingly, I am of opinion that the natural application of the word "term" to this contract is that it applies for example, to the basic pay, and that the appropriate comparison is with the hourly rate of basic pay . . .'

LORD GOFF: '. . . Now I fully appreciate that this construction of section 1(2) will always lead, where the section is held to apply, to enhancement of the relevant term in the woman's contract. Likewise, it will in the converse case lead to enhancement of the relevant term in the man's contract. This appears to me to be the effect of the philosophy underlying the sub-section. I also appreciate that this may, in some cases, lead to what has been called mutual enhancement or leap-frogging, as terms of the woman's contract and the man's contract are both, so to speak, upgraded to bring them into line with each other. It is this effect which was found to be so offensive by both the Employment Appeal Tribunal and the Court of Appeal. They viewed with dismay the possibility of equality being achieved only by mutual enhancement, and not by an overall consideration of the respective contractual terms of both the man and the woman, at least in relation to a particular subject matter such as overall remuneration, considering that mutual enhancement transcended the underlying philosophy of the 1970 Act and that it could have a profoundly inflationary effect.

To these fears there are, I consider, two different answers on two different levels. The first answer is that given by Mr Lester, for the appellant, which is that the employer must, where he can, have recourse to s 1(3). I, for my part, see great force in this argument . . .

This brings me to my second answer, which is that, if the construction of section 1(2) which I prefer does not accord with the true intention of Parliament, then the appropriate course for Parliament is to amend the legislation to bring it into line with its true intention. In the meanwhile, however, the decision of your Lordships' House may have the salutary effect of drawing to the attention of employers and trade unions the absolute need for ensuring that the pay structures for various groups of employees do not contain any element of sex discrimination, direct or indirect, because otherwise section 1(3) will not be available to mitigate the effects which section 1(2), in its present form, is capable of producing on its own.

For these reasons, I would allow the appeal.'

(Lords Bridge, Brandon and Griffiths agreed with Lords Mackay and Goff. The case was remitted to the employment tribunal for determination accordingly.)

Comment

(1) It is no longer open to Parliament to adopt the second solution proposed by Lord Goff to the problem of leap-frogging, because the approach requiring the equalisation of each different element of the remuneration package was explicitly endorsed by the ECJ in *Barber* v *Guardian Royal Exchange* as can be seen from the last part of the next extract.

(2) The precise ambit of a 'term' of the contract continues to give rise to difficulty. In *Degnan* v *Redcar & Cleveland BC* (2005), part of the north-east public sector equal pay litigation, the issue was whether female workers doing work of equal value to and getting the same basic pay as three groups of male workers could claim the bonuses and allowances which they got. If so, the women could claim the best bonus arrangement and the best attendance allowance, and would end up with a wage higher than any of the male groups (although the men, of course, would then be entitled to claim parity with the women). The Court of Appeal avoided this result by holding that the men's pay should be viewed as an amalgam of basic pay and bonuses or allowances, which could then be reduced to a notional hourly rate, to which the women would then be entitled. In other words, they treated it as a situation where there was one 'term' governing pay, rather than separate terms for basic pay and bonuses. Is this compatible with *Hayward* and *Barber*, do you think?

Equal pay

Barber v Guardian Royal Exchange
[1990] ICR 616 European Court of Justice

Mr Barber was made compulsorily redundant in 1980 at the age of 52. Under the company's severance terms, men aged 55 and women aged 50 got an immediate pension on redundancy, plus a small lump sum. Men aged under 55 and women aged under 50 had to wait until normal pension age for their pensions, but got a higher lump sum. Overall, the first option was more beneficial. If Barber had been a woman aged 52, he would have had an immediate pension, hence his claim, which the Court of Appeal referred to the ECJ.

JUDGMENT OF THE COURT:

'. . . The first question

10   In its first question the Court of Appeal seeks to ascertain, in substance, whether the benefits paid by an employer to a worker in connection with the latter's compulsory redundancy fall within the scope of [Art 141] of the Treaty and the Equal Pay Directive or within the scope of the Equal Treatment Directive.

11   The court has consistently held (see, in particular, *Jenkins* v *Kingsgate (Clothing Productions) Ltd* (1981)) that the first of those two Directives, which is designed principally to facilitate the application of the principle of equal pay outlined in [Art 141] of the Treaty, in no way alters the content or scope of that principle as defined in the latter provision. It is therefore appropriate to consider, in the first place, whether [Art 141] applies in circumstances such as those of this case.

12   As the court has held, the concept of pay, within the meaning of the second paragraph of [Art 141], comprises any other consideration, whether in cash or in kind, whether immediate or future, provided that the worker receives it, albeit indirectly, in respect of his employment from his employer (see, in particular, *Garland* v *British Rail Engineering Ltd* (1982)). Accordingly, the fact that certain benefits are paid after the termination of the employment relationship does not prevent them from being in the nature of pay, within the meaning of [Art 141] of the Treaty.

13   As regards, in particular, the compensation granted to a worker in connection with his redundancy, it must be stated that such compensation constitutes a form of pay to which the worker is entitled in respect of his employment, which is paid to him on termination of the employment relationship, which makes it possible to facilitate his adjustment to the new circumstances resulting from the loss of his employment and which provides him with a source of income during the period in which he is seeking new employment.

14   It follows that compensation granted to a worker in connection with his redundancy falls in principle within the concept of pay for the purposes of [Art 141] of the Treaty.

15   At the hearing, the United Kingdom argued that the statutory redundancy payment fell outside the scope of [Art 141] of the Treaty because it constituted a social security benefit and not a form of pay.

16   In that regard it must be pointed out that a redundancy payment made by the employer, such as that which is at issue, cannot cease to constitute a form of pay on the sole ground that, rather than deriving from the contract of employment, it is a statutory or ex gratia payment.

17   In the case of statutory redundancy payments it must be borne in mind that, as the court held in its judgment in *Defrenne* v *Sabena* (1976), [Art 141] of the Treaty also applies to discrimination arising directly from legislative provisions. This means that benefits provided for by law may come within the concept of pay for the purposes of that provision

18   Although it is true that many advantages granted by an employer also reflect considerations of social policy, the fact that a benefit is in the nature of pay cannot be called in question

where the worker is entitled to receive the benefit in question from his employer by reason of the existence of the employment relationship.

19   In the case of ex gratia payments by the employer, it is clear from the *Garland* case that [Art 141] also applies to advantages which an employer grants to workers although he is not required to do so by contract.

20   Accordingly, without there being any need to discuss whether or not the Directive on Equal Treatment is applicable, the answer to the first question must be that the benefits paid by an employer to a worker in connection with the latter's compulsory redundancy fall within the scope of the second paragraph of [Art 141], whether they are paid under a contract of employment, by virtue of legislative provisions or on a voluntary basis.

The second question

21   In view of the answer given to the first question, the second question must be understood as seeking in substance to ascertain whether a retirement pension paid under a contracted-out private occupational scheme falls within the scope of [Art 141] of the Treaty, in particular where that pension is awarded in connection with compulsory redundancy.

22   It must be pointed out in that regard that in its judgment in *Defrenne v Belgian State* (1971) the court stated that consideration in the nature of social security benefits is not in principle alien to the concept of pay. However, the court pointed out that this concept, as defined in [Art 141], cannot encompass social security schemes or benefits, in particular retirement pensions, directly governed by legislation without any element of agreement within the undertaking or the occupational branch concerned, which are compulsorily applicable to general categories of workers.

23   The court noted that those schemes afford the workers the benefit of a statutory scheme, to the financing of which workers, employers and possibly the public authorities contribute in a measure determined less by the employment relationship than by considerations of social policy.

24   In order to answer the second question, therefore, it is necessary to ascertain whether those considerations also apply to contracted-out private occupational schemes such as that referred to in this case.

25   In that regard it must be pointed out first of all that the schemes in question are the result either of an agreement between workers and employers or of a unilateral decision taken by the employer. They are wholly financed by the employer or by both the employer and the workers without any contribution being made by the public authorities in any circumstances. Accordingly, such schemes form part of the consideration offered to workers by the employer.

26   Secondly, such schemes are not compulsorily applicable to general categories of workers. On the contrary, they apply only to workers employed by certain undertakings, with the result that affiliation to those schemes derives of necessity from the employment relationship with a given employer. Furthermore, even if the schemes in question are established in conformity with national legislation and consequently satisfy the conditions laid down by it for recognition as contracted-out schemes, they are governed by their own rules.

27   Thirdly, it must be pointed out that, even if the contributions paid to those schemes and the benefits which they provide are in part a substitute for those of the general statutory scheme, that fact cannot preclude the application of [Art 141]. It is apparent from the documents before the court that occupational schemes such as that referred to in this case may grant to their members benefits greater than those which would be paid by the statutory scheme, with the result that their economic function is similar to that of the supplementary schemes which exist in certain member states, where affiliation and contribution to the statutory scheme is compulsory and no derogation is allowed. In its judgment in *Bilka-Kaufhaus*

GmbH v *Weber von Hartz* (1987) the court held that the benefits awarded under a supplementary pension scheme fell within the concept of pay, within the meaning of [Art 141].

28 It must therefore be concluded that, unlike the benefits awarded by national statutory social security schemes, a pension paid under a contracted-out scheme constitutes consideration paid by the employer to the worker in respect of his employment and consequently falls within the scope of [Art 141] of the Treaty.

29 That interpretation of [Art 141] is not affected by the fact that the private occupational scheme in question has been set up in the form of a trust and is administered by trustees who are technically independent of the employer, since [Art 141] also applies to consideration received indirectly from the employer.

30 The answer to the second question submitted by the Court of Appeal must therefore be that a pension paid under a contracted-out private occupational scheme falls within the scope of [Art 141] of the Treaty.

The third and fifth questions

31 In these questions the Court of Appeal seeks in substance to ascertain, in the first place, whether it is contrary to [Art 141] of the Treaty for a man made compulsorily redundant to be entitled only to a deferred pension payable at the normal pensionable age when a woman in the same position receives an immediate retirement pension as a result of the application of an age condition that varies according to sex in the same way as is provided for by the national statutory pension scheme. Secondly, the Court of Appeal wishes to ascertain, in substance, whether equal pay must be ensured at the level of each element of remuneration or only on the basis of a comprehensive assessment of the consideration paid to workers.

32 In the case of the first of those two questions thus formulated, it is sufficient to point out that [Art 141] prohibits any discrimination with regard to pay as between men and women, whatever the system which gives rise to such inequality. Accordingly, it is contrary to [Art 141] to impose an age condition which differs according to sex in respect of pensions paid under a contracted-out scheme, even if the difference between the pensionable age for men and that for women is based on the one provided for by the national statutory scheme.

33 As regards the second of those questions, it is appropriate to refer to the judgments in *Commission* v *France* (1988) and in *Handels-og Kontorfunktionærernes Forbund i Danmark* v *Dansk Arbejdsgiverforening* (1991) [the *Danfoss* case] in which the court emphasised the fundamental importance of transparency and, in particular, of the possibility of a review by the national courts, in order to prevent and, if necessary, eliminate any discrimination based on sex.

34 With regard to the means of verifying compliance with the principle of equal pay, it must be stated that if the national courts were under an obligation to make an assessment and a comparison of all the various types of consideration granted, according to the circumstances, to men and women, judicial review would be difficult and the effectiveness of [Art 141] would be diminished as a result. It follows that genuine transparency, permitting an effective review, is assured only if the principle of equal pay applies to each of the elements of remuneration granted to men or women.

35 The answer to the third and fifth questions submitted by the Court of Appeal must therefore be that it is contrary to [Art 141] of the Treaty for a man made compulsorily redundant to be entitled to claim only a deferred pension payable at the normal pensionable age when a woman in the same position is entitled to an immediate retirement pension as a result of the application of an age condition that varies according to sex in the same way as is provided for by the national statutory pension scheme. The application of the principle of equal pay must

be ensured in respect of each element of remuneration and not only on the basis of a comprehensive assessment of the consideration paid to workers . . .'

Comment

(1) Of a number of ECJ decisions giving a wide meaning to the term 'pay', this case was
a landmark. At a stroke it rendered redundant most of the Occupational Social Security
Directive (86/378/EC) which was designed to equalise the terms of employers' pension
schemes, by holding that these benefits were 'pay' and therefore required equalisation
under Art 141.

(2) Immediately following the *Barber* decision it was unclear if, and how far, the decision had retrospective effect. The pensions industry was not slow to warn of catas-
trophe should a wide interpretation be adopted. In *Ten Oever* (1993) the ECJ held that
equal pension benefits were payable only in respect of periods of employment after 17
May 1990 (the date of the *Barber* judgment). This was the most restrictive possible
interpretation of *Barber*, but accorded with the agreement reached by EU member states
and recorded in the second Protocol to the Treaty of Maastricht. *Ten Oever* also made
clear that benefits for widows and widowers of pensioners were also within the principle of equality.

(3) In *Smith* v *Avdel* (1994) and *Van den Akker* v *Stichting Shell Pensioenfonds* (1994) the
ECJ further held that retirement ages could be equalised upwards without infringing
Art 141. However, both men and women had to be given the benefit of the most
generous terms in any transitional period.

(4) It was already clear from *Bilka-Kaufhaus* v *Weber von Hartz* (1987) that Art 141
covered access to pension schemes, so that exclusion of part-time workers would be
unlawful indirect sex discrimination unless the employer could provide objective
justification for the inequality. In *Vroege* v *NCV Institut voor Volkhuisvesting* (1994) and
Fisscher v *Voorhuis Hengelo* (1994) the ECJ held that the access rights of part-timers
could be backdated to 1976 (when Art 141 was first held to be directly effective in
Defrenne v *Sabena*) and that there was no minimum hours requirement for these rights.

(5) These decisions led to a flood of claims by part-timers in the United Kingdom.
However, they ran into two problems. First, the Equal Pay Act had a six-month limitation period on bringing claims – so women who had left their employment, often some
years previously, looked to be excluded. Secondly, there was a two-year limit on backdating claims, which appeared drastically to reduce their value. The issue as to whether
these limitations were in accordance with EU law was referred to the ECJ by the House
of Lords. In *Preston* v *Wolverhampton Healthcare NHS Trust* (2000) (which actually
involved 22 test cases affecting many hundreds of workers) the ECJ held that the six-
month limitation period could be upheld, in that it did not make it too difficult for
women to enforce their rights under EU law. However, on backdating, it held that the
two-year limit was in breach of the EU law requirement that there should be effective
remedies. This was in accordance with their earlier decision on another United
Kingdom reference, *Levez* v *Jennings* (1999). When this case came back to the national
court, the EAT held that the appropriate time limit should be six years, by analogy with
other claims for breach of contract (*Levez* v *Jennings (No 2)* (2000)).

(6) As a result of these decisions, the Equal Pay Act 1970 (Amendment) Regulations
2003 were passed, amending the EqPA to this effect (see EqPA ss 2ZA and 2ZB).

REFERENCES AND FURTHER READING

S Fredman (1996), 'The Poverty of Equality: Pensions and the ECJ' 25 ILJ 91

B Hepple and A Byre (1989), 'EEC labour law in the United Kingdom' 18 ILJ 129

A Lester and D Rose (1991), 'Equal Value Claims and Sex Bias in Collective Bargaining' 20 ILJ 163

A McColgan (1997), *Just Wages for Women*, Clarendon Press

C McCrudden (1996), 'Third Time Lucky? The Pensions Act 1995 and Equal Treatment in Occupational Pensions' 25 ILJ 28

Visit **http://www.mylawchamber.co.uk/pitt**
to access live web updates and web links to extend
your knowledge of Employment Law.

8

DISCIPLINE AND DISMISSAL

Termination of a contract of employment may be a breach of contract by either party. Like any other claim for breach of contract, the aggrieved party may sue the other in the High Court or county court. Additionally, since 1994, many such claims can also be made in employment tribunals. It is fairly rare for an employer to sue an employee who leaves: the employer will usually regard it as more trouble than it is worth and will direct effort into finding a replacement instead. It is the employee who is most likely to want to sue for termination in breach of contract. In the employment context, this is called an action for wrongful dismissal and it will be considered first in this chapter.

Since 1965 employees have received some negative protection from the disaster of dismissal through statutory measures. They are described as 'negative protection' because they do not on the whole actually prevent dismissal: instead, they stipulate that in certain circumstances the employee should receive a remedy, usually monetary compensation. The first statutory measure was the Redundancy Payments Act 1965. Claims for redundancy payments are considered in Chapter 9. The second, and more important, was the action for unfair dismissal, introduced by the Industrial Relations Act 1971. This will be considered secondly in this chapter.

WRONGFUL DISMISSAL

An employee can only claim for wrongful dismissal if the employer's termination of the contract was in breach. There is no breach of contract if *either* the employer gave adequate notice to terminate *or* if the employer terminated in the face of a fundamental breach of contract by the employee.

Notice

Employment Rights Act 1996

86 (1) The notice required to be given by an employer to terminate the contract of employment of a person who has been continuously employed for one month or more –
  (a) is not less than one week's notice if his period of continuous employment is less than two years,
  (b) is not less than one week's notice for each year of continuous employment if his period of continuous employment is two years or more but less than twelve years, and
  (c) is not less than twelve weeks' notice if his period of continuous employment is twelve years or more.

(2)   The notice required to be given by an employee who has been continuously employed for one month or more to terminate his contract of employment is not less than one week.

Comment

(1) These are *minimum* periods of notice. If the contract stipulates a longer period, either party can sue if it is not given. Information about notice to be given on either side is one of the matters which must be included in the written statement of particulars given to the employee (ERA s 1(4)(e), above, p 160).

(2) Giving pay in lieu of notice is regarded as being as good as giving notice: if it is accepted that the employee has no right to work then her only entitlement is to be paid. Hence pay for the notice period is as good as having notice. Compare *Devonald* v *Rosser* (1906), above, p 173.

(3) The requirement at common law is that both parties should give *reasonable* notice to terminate the contract. In *Hill* v *C A Parsons Ltd* (1972) the Court of Appeal held that reasonable notice for a chartered engineer with 35 years' service was six months: however, this was a rather unusual case. The court was anxious to keep his contract in existence until the Industrial Relations Act 1971 came into force so that Hill, who had been dismissed for refusing to join a trade union, would be able to claim unfair dismissal and the union's insistence on a closed shop arrangement would have become unlawful. Thus the decision has rarely been relied on since, although it is also relevant to the possibilities of enforcing the contract (discussed below, p 357) because it treats the employer's notice as invalid in some circumstances.

(4) A fixed-term contract (or contract for a limited term) may contain a provision for termination by notice, even though this may seem inconsistent with the concept of a contract lasting for a specific period (*Dixon* v *BBC* (1978); *Allen* v *National Australia Group Europe Ltd* (2004)).

(5) Contracts of apprenticeship cannot be terminated lawfully by giving reasonable notice. Both parties are committed for the specified training period and the employer can only terminate for good cause, usually specified in the agreement. For a discussion of the kinds of arrangement which can constitute apprenticeship in modern employment conditions, see *Flett* v *Matheson* (2006).

Justified summary dismissal

Dismissal without notice or with inadequate notice is called summary dismissal. If it is not justified by an adequate reason, it will constitute wrongful dismissal.

Disobedience to a lawful and reasonable order is a prime example of conduct justifying summary dismissal: see *Laws* v *London Chronicle* (1959) above, p 189. This is why taking industrial action is almost always a fundamental breach of contract and would justify summary dismissal at common law. What else justifies summary dismissal?

Sinclair v *Neighbour* [1967] 2 QB 279 Court of Appeal

The claimant had been employed for about a month as manager of one of the defendant's betting shops. He borrowed £15 from the till – putting in an IOU – to place a bet at a different betting shop. The following day (the bet having been successful) he returned the money to the till. When the defendant heard about the incident, he summarily dismissed the claimant.

SELLERS LJ: '. . . This case turns on the attitude which the employer could properly take to that conduct. It seems that the employee not infrequently used to telephone to the employer. He said he did it too often and so he did not think he would do it again over this matter. He took the money without asking. He thought that, if he had asked, the employer might have lent him the money for some purposes, but that if he had told him it was for betting the employer would not have agreed. He would not have permitted it. In my view, whether such taking of the money would have resulted in a conviction for larceny or for dishonest misappropriation of the money does not arise. On these facts a jury might have taken the view that they would not convict. But whether it is to be described as dishonest misconduct or not, I do not think matters. Views might differ. It was sufficient for the employer if he could, in all the circumstances, regard what the employee did as being something which was seriously inconsistent – incompatible – with his duty as the manager in the business in which he was engaged.

To take money out of the till in such circumstances is on the face of it incompatible and inconsistent with his duty. Some people might well say that to take money out of the till, when the employee knew that if he had asked if he could do it for the purpose which he might have had to disclose it would have been refused, is dishonest conduct. The question for this court to decide is whether, in the circumstances of this case, it was conduct which in its nature justified the employer instantly dismissing the employee.

I think that it was. Counsel referred to some of the cases. I do not think that I need refer to them further. The whole question is whether that conduct was of such a type that it was inconsistent, in a grave way – incompatible – with the employment in which he had been engaged as a manager.

There was an aggravating feature, I think, in that there were in the office two others, including one boy who was only some 18 or 19 years of age who had said something about borrowing money out of the till, and it was said that it had been done before. On a new manager coming in, I should have thought that the one thing that was incumbent on him was to keep the till inviolate. The practice of taking money out of the till in that way, as all who have had experience in criminal courts know, can lead to endless trouble.

On the short facts of this case, and applying the law as I understand it, I would not hesitate to say that the dismissal was justified. I would allow the appeal accordingly.'

SACHS LJ: '. . . It is well-established law that a servant can be instantly dismissed when his conduct is such that it not only amounts to a wrongful act inconsistent with his duty towards his master but is also inconsistent with the continuance of confidence between them. That was said by Bowen LJ, in his classic judgment in *Boston Deep Sea Fishing and Ice Co v Ansell*.

Here we have a case where the manager of a betting shop, responsible for the conduct of the shop and of the other employees there, quite deliberately takes out of the till money for his own personal purposes, in circumstances which he knew quite well his employer if asked would not so permit.

To state those facts quite simply seems to me enough to make plain that here indeed there was beyond a peradventure misconduct of a type which justified instant dismissal; and I agree with the judge's view where he uses the adjectives "utterly reprehensible" and "improper" in regard to that conduct . . .'

(Davies LJ delivered a concurring judgment.)

Wilson v Racher [1974] ICR 428 Court of Appeal

The claimant was employed as head gardener by the defendant. On a Sunday afternoon, the defendant called him over and wrongly and aggressively accused him of various derelictions of duty. An argument developed and the claimant was provoked into swearing obscenely at his employer, who responded by summarily dismissing him.

EDMUND DAVIES LJ: '. . . *Pepper* v *Webb*, a case which Mr Connell [counsel for the employer] seemed to regard as affording some measure of support for his argument, appears to me, on the other hand, to do nothing of the kind. In that case also the claimant was a gardener, but there was a history of complaints of insolence and inefficiency from time to time. The culminating incident was when the employer asked the claimant what arrangements he had made in relation to a greenhouse in his absence during the weekend. The claimant said: "I couldn't care less about your bloody greenhouse or your sodding garden", and walked away. Harman LJ there said,

> "Now what will justify an instant dismissal? – something done by the employee which impliedly or expressly is a repudiation of the fundamental terms of the contract; and in my judgment if ever there was such a repudiation this is it. What is the gardener to do? He is to look after the garden and he is to look after the greenhouse. If he does not care a hoot about either then he is repudiating his contract. That is what it seems to me the claimant did, and I do not see, having done that, that he can complain if he is summarily dismissed. It is said on his behalf that one act of temper, one insolent outburst, does not merit so condign a punishment. But this, according to the defendant, his employer, and I think rightly on the evidence, was the last straw. He had been acting in a very unsatisfactory way ever since April."

And this was an incident which had occurred in June. That the Court were there having regard not simply to the last incident of June 10 in isolation, but to the whole history, appears also from the other judgments, Russell LJ, for example, saying:

> "I entirely agree that, against the background of what the claimant's counsel must admit the deputy county court judge found or assumed to be quite a number of disobediences and a certain amount of insolence, it must be taken as conduct repudiatory of the contract justifying summary dismissal."

The present case, too, has to be looked at against the whole background. On the judge's findings, here was a competent, diligent and efficient gardener who, apart from one complaint of leaving a ladder against a yew tree, had done nothing which could be regarded as blameworthy by any reasonable employer. Here, too, was an employer who was resolved to get rid of him; an employer who would use every barrel in the gun that he could find, or thought available; and an employer who was provocative from the outset and dealt with the claimant in an unseemly manner. The claimant lost his temper. He used obscene and deplorable language. He was therefore deserving of the severest reproof. But this was a solitary occasion. Unlike *Pepper* v *Webb*, there was no background either of inefficiency or of insolence. The claimant tried to avert the situation by walking away, but he was summoned back and the defendant continued his gadfly activity of goading him into intemperate language. Such are the findings of the county court judge.

In those circumstances, would it be just to say that the claimant's use of this extremely bad language on a solitary occasion made impossible the continuance of the master and servant relationship, and showed that the claimant was indeed resolved to follow a line of conduct which made the continuation of that relationship impossible? The judge thought the answer to that question was clear, and I cannot say that he was manifestly wrong. On the contrary, it seems to me that the parties could have made up their differences. The claimant apologised to

Wrongful dismissal

Mrs Racher. There are no grounds for thinking that if the defendant had given him a warning that such language would not be tolerated, and further, if he had manifested recognition that he himself had acted provocatively, the damage done might well have been repaired and some degree of harmony restored. Perhaps there was such instinctive antipathy between the two men that the defendant would, nevertheless, have been glad to get rid of the claimant when October 23, 1972 arrived.

In my judgment, in the light of the findings of fact the learned judge arrived at a just decision. That is not to say that language such as that employed by the claimant is to be tolerated. On the contrary, it requires very special circumstances to entitle a servant who expresses his feelings in such a grossly improper way to succeed in an action for wrongful dismissal. But there were special circumstances here, and they were of the defendant's own creation. The claimant, probably lacking the educational advantages of the defendant, and finding himself in a frustrating situation despite his efforts to escape from it, fell into the error of explosively using this language. To say that he ought to be kicked out because on this solitary occasion he fell into such grave error would, in my judgment, be wrong. I am not persuaded that the judge was in error in holding that ... it was wrongful dismissal, and that the claimant was entitled to the damages awarded. I would therefore be for dismissing the appeal.'

(Cairns and James LJJ concurred.)

Acas *Code of Practice on Disciplinary and Grievance Procedures* (2004)

56 Employers should inform employees of the likely consequences of breaking disciplinary rules. In particular, they should list examples of acts of gross misconduct that may warrant summary dismissal.

57 Acts which constitute gross misconduct are those resulting in a serious breach of contractual terms and are best decided by organisations in the light of their own particular circumstances. However, examples of gross misconduct might include:

- theft or fraud;
- physical violence or bullying;
- deliberate and serious damage to property;
- serious misuse of an organisation's property or name;
- deliberately accessing internet sites containing pornographic, offensive or obscene material;
- serious insubordination;
- unlawful discrimination or harassment;
- bringing the organisation into serious disrepute;
- serious incapability at work brought on by alcohol or illegal drugs;
- causing loss, damage or injury through serious negligence;
- a serious breach of health and safety rules; and
- a serious breach of confidence.

Comment

(1) The Acas *Code of Practice on Disciplinary and Grievance Procedures* is strictly only relevant to unfair dismissal claims – but in practice it is influential in dismissal law more generally.

(2) Gross misconduct is an evolving concept: in *Denco Ltd* v *Joinson* (1991) the EAT suggested that unauthorised access to the employer's computer system was probably to be regarded as the kind of offence that any employee should realise would be treated as

343

gross misconduct. However, they also suggested that employers should make their rules clear and post copies near all terminals. The Acas Code, para 54, states: 'It is unlikely that any set of rules will cover all possible disciplinary issues, but rules should normally cover . . . misuse of company facilities (for example email and internet).'

(3) In considering what offences justify summary dismissal, refer back to the discussion of the implied duties of the employee under the contract in Chapter 4. In general, breach of the implied duties will be regarded as a fundamental breach of contract justifying summary dismissal. In fact, many of the decisions establishing implied terms under the contract arose as claims for wrongful dismissal.

(4) In particular, note that in *Boston Deep Sea Fishing* v *Ansell* (1888) (above, p 194) conduct discovered only *after* the dismissal was held to justify the termination. This should be contrasted with the position for unfair dismissal (cf *W Devis* v *Atkins & Sons* (1976), below, p 408).

(5) An employer who is entitled to dismiss an employee for breach of contract may not substitute the lesser penalty of suspension without pay unless the right to suspend is incorporated into the employee's contract of employment (expressly or impliedly) (*Hanley* v *Pease* (1915); *Four Seasons Healthcare Ltd* v *Maughan* (2005)). See also the Acas Code, para 25.

(6) Suspension on full pay is not usually a breach of contract (see the discussion of the right to work, above, p 172) and is recommended by the Acas Code, para 35 as a way of giving time to investigate serious offences. However, it is important that it is not abused or seen as a disciplinary measure (cf *Gogay* v *Herts CC* (2000)).

Damages for wrongful dismissal

Addis v *Gramophone Co Ltd* [1909] AC 488 House of Lords

The claimant was manager of the defendant's business in Calcutta, paid by a mixture of salary and commission. The contract allowed him to be dismissed on six months' notice. The defendant gave him notice, but then prevented him from working out his notice period and earning any commission during that period. A jury awarded him £600 for wrongful dismissal and £340 for loss of commission.

LORD LOREBURN LC: 'As to the damages of £600 for wrongful dismissal a variety of controversies arose. Did what happened entitle the claimant to treat the breach of contract as a wrongful dismissal? If yes, then did he elect to treat the contract of service as still continuing? Was it open to the defendants to raise the point having regard to the pleadings and the amendments to the pleadings, and the way the case was conducted at the trial, and the contents of the notice of appeal to the Court of Appeal? A subsidiary dispute was raised as to the way in which the case had been in fact conducted at the trial, as to which eminent counsel did not agree. A further controversy ensued, whether the £600 was intended to include salary for the six months, or merely damages because of the abrupt and oppressive way in which the claimant's services were discontinued, and the loss he sustained from the discredit thus thrown upon him. And, finally, a question of law was argued, whether or not such damages could be recovered in law.

My Lords, it is difficult to imagine a better illustration of the way in which litigation between exasperated litigants can breed barren controversies and increase costs in a matter of itself simple enough.

To my mind it signifies nothing in the present case whether the claim is to be treated as for wrongful dismissal or not. In any case there was a breach of contract in not allowing the claimant to discharge his duties as manager, and the damages are exactly the same in either view. They are, in my opinion, the salary to which the claimant was entitled for the six months between October 1905 and April 1906 together with the commission which the jury think he would have earned had he been allowed to manage the business himself. I cannot agree that the manner of dismissal affects these damages. Such considerations have never been allowed to influence damages in this kind of case. An expression of Lord Coleridge CJ has been quoted as authority to the contrary[1]. I doubt if the learned Lord Chief Justice so intended it. If he did I cannot agree with him.

If there be a dismissal without notice the employer must pay an indemnity; but that indemnity cannot include compensation either for the injured feelings of the servant, or for the loss he may sustain from the fact that his having been dismissed of itself makes it more difficult for him to obtain fresh employment. The cases relating to a refusal by a banker to honour cheques when he has funds in hand have, in my opinion, no bearing. That class of case has always been regarded as exceptional. And the rule as to damages in wrongful dismissal, or in breach of contract to allow a man to continue in a stipulated service, has always been, I believe, what I have stated. It is too inveterate to be now altered, even if it were desirable to alter it.

Accordingly I think that so much of the verdict of £600 as relates to that head of damages cannot be allowed to stand. As there is an additional dispute how much of it does relate to that head of damages, the best course will be to disallow the £600 altogether, and to state in the order that claimant is entitled to be credited, in the account which is to be taken, with salary from October 1905, to April 1906 . . .'

[1] "The claimant by reason of his being dismissed during his apprenticeship with a slur on his character naturally would experience a greater difficulty in getting employment elsewhere": Lord Coleridge CJ in *Maw v Jones* (1890).

(Lords James, Atkinson, Gorell and Shaw agreed. Lord Collins dissented.)

Comment

(1) This important decision stated the basic rule that compensation for wrongful dismissal is limited to monies which the employee would have been entitled to during the notice period and nothing more. The justification for this is that since the employer could at any time terminate the contract lawfully by giving notice or pay in lieu of notice, this is all that the employee has lost through being wrongfully dismissed.

(2) Despite assaults on the citadel, the principle in *Addis* v *Gramophone Co* remained untouched for nearly 80 years, until the landmark decision of the House of Lords in *Malik* v *BCCI*.

Malik v Bank of Credit and Commerce International
[1997] IRLR 462 House of Lords

The employees, who were made redundant after the bank collapsed, claimed that their association with BCCI placed them at a serious disadvantage in finding new employment in the financial services industry. The House of Lords held that by carrying on a dishonest and corrupt business an employer would be in breach of the implied term not to act in such a way as to damage or destroy the relationship of mutual trust and confidence between employer and employee. This aspect of the case is considered above, p 186. Having found that this would be a breach, what were the remedies?

LORD NICHOLLS: '. . .

Remedies: (1) acceptance of breach as repudiation

The next step is to consider the consequences which flow from the bank being in breach of its obligation to its innocent employees by operating a corrupt banking business. The first remedy of an employee has already been noted. The employee may treat the bank's conduct as a repudiatory breach, entitling him to leave. He is not compelled to leave. He may choose to stay. The extent to which staying would be more than an election to remain, and would be a waiver of the breach for all purposes, depends on the circumstances.

I need say no more about waiver in the present case. The assumed facts do not state whether the appellants first learned of the corrupt nature of BCCI after their dismissal on 3 October 1991, or whether they acquired this knowledge earlier, in the interval of three months between the appointment of the provisional liquidators on 5 July 1991 and 3 October 1991. If anything should turn on this, the matter can be investigated further in due course.

In the nature of things, the remedy of treating the conduct as a repudiatory breach, entitling the employee to leave, can only avail an employee who learns of the facts while still employed. If he does not discover the facts while his employment is still continuing, perforce this remedy is not open to him. But this does not mean he has no remedy. In the ordinary course breach of a contractual term entitles the innocent party to damages.

Remedies: (2) damages

Can an employee recover damages for breach of the trust and confidence term when he first learns of the breach after he has left the employment? The answer to this question is inextricably bound up with the further question of what damages are recoverable for a breach of this term. In turn, the answer to this further question is inextricably linked with one aspect of the decision in *Addis* v *Gramophone Co Ltd* . . .

Addis v Gramophone Co Ltd

Against this background I turn to the much discussed case of *Addis* v *Gramophone Co Ltd*. Mr Addis, it will be recalled, was wrongfully and contumeliously dismissed from his post as the defendant's manager in Calcutta. At trial he was awarded damages exceeding the amount of his salary for the period of notice to which he was entitled. The case is generally regarded as having decided, echoing the words of Lord Loreburn LC, that an employee cannot recover damages for the manner in which the wrongful dismissal took place, for injured feelings or for any loss he may sustain from the fact that his having been dismissed of itself makes it more difficult for him to obtain fresh employment. In particular, *Addis* is generally understood to have decided that any loss suffered by the adverse impact on the employee's chances of obtaining alternative employment is to be excluded from an assessment of damages for wrongful dismissal: see, for instance, *O'Laoire* v *Jackel International Ltd (No 2)* (1991), following earlier authorities; in Canada, the decision of the Supreme Court in *Vorvis* v *Insurance Corporation of British Columbia* (1989); and, in New Zealand, *Vivian* v *Coca-Cola Export Corporation* (1984); *Whelan* v *Waitaki Meats Ltd* (1991), where Gallen J disagreed with the decision in *Addis*, and *Brandt* v *Nixdorf Computer Ltd* (1991).

For present purposes I am not concerned with the exclusion of damages for injured feelings. The present case is concerned only with financial loss. The report of the facts in *Addis* is sketchy. Whether Mr Addis sought to prove that the manner of his dismissal caused him financial loss over and above his premature termination losses is not clear beyond a peradventure. If he did, it is surprising that their Lordships did not address this important feature more specifically. Instead there are references to injured feelings, the fact of dismissal of itself, aggravated damages, exemplary damages amounting to damages for defamation, damages being compensatory and not punitive, and the irrelevance of motive. The dissenting speech of Lord Collins was based on competence to award exemplary or vindictive damages.

However, Lord Loreburn LC's observations were framed in quite general terms, and he expressly disagreed with the suggestion of Lord Coleridge CJ in *Maw* v *Jones* (1890), to the effect that an assessment of damages might take into account the greater difficulty which an apprentice dismissed with a slur on his character might have in obtaining other employment. Similarly general observations were made by Lord James of Hereford, Lord Atkinson, Lord Gorell and Lord Shaw of Dunfermline.

In my view these observations cannot be read as precluding the recovery of damages where the manner of dismissal involved a breach of the trust and confidence term and this caused financial loss. *Addis* v *Gramophone Co Ltd* was decided in the days before this implied term was adumbrated. Now that this term exists and is normally implied in every contract of employment, damages for its breach should be assessed in accordance with ordinary contractual principles. This is as much true if the breach occurs before or in connection with dismissal as at any other time.

This approach would accord, in its result, with the approach adopted by courts and tribunals in unfair dismissal cases when exercising the statutory jurisdiction, currently limited to a maximum of £11,300, to award an amount of compensation which the court or tribunal considers "just and reasonable" in all the circumstances. Writing on a clean slate, the courts have interpreted this as enabling awards to include compensation in respect of the manner and circumstances of dismissal if these would give rise to a risk of financial loss by, for instance, making the employee less acceptable to potential employers: see sections 123 and 124 of the Employment Rights Act 1996 and *Norton Tool Co Ltd* v *Tewson* (1972).

I do not believe this approach gives rise to artificiality. On the contrary, the trust and confidence term is a useful tool, well established now in employment law. At common law damages are awarded to compensate for *wrongful* dismissal. Thus, loss which an employee would have suffered even if the dismissal had been after due notice is irrecoverable, because such loss does not derive from the wrongful element in the dismissal. Further, it is difficult to see how the mere fact of wrongful dismissal, rather than dismissal after due notice, could of itself handicap an employee in the labour market. All this is in line with *Addis*. But the manner and circumstances of the dismissal, as measured by the standards of conduct now identified in the implied trust and confidence term, may give rise to such a handicap. The law would be blemished if this were not recognised today. There now exists the separate cause of action whose absence Lord Shaw of Dunfermline noted with "a certain regret": see *Addis* v *Gramophone Co Ltd* (1909). The trust and confidence term has removed the cause for his regret . . .

Conclusion

For these reasons I would allow these appeals. The agreed set of assumed facts discloses a good cause of action. Unlike the courts below, this House is not bound by the observations in *Addis* v *Gramophone Co Ltd* regarding irrecoverability of loss flowing from the manner of dismissal, or by the decision in *Withers* v *General Theatre Corporation Ltd* (1933).

I add some cautionary footnotes, having in mind the assumed facts in the present case. First, when considering these appeals I have been particularly conscious of the potential difficulties which claims of this sort may present for liquidators. I am conscious that the outcome of the present appeals may be seen by some as opening the door to speculative claims, to the detriment of admitted creditors. Claims of handicap in the labour market, and the other ingredients of the cause of action now under consideration, may give rise to lengthy and costly investigations and, ultimately, litigation. If the claims eventually fail, liquidators may well be unable to recover their costs from the former employees. The expense of liquidations, and the time they often take, are matters already giving rise to concern. I am aware of the dangers here, but it could not be right to allow "floodgates" arguments of this nature to stand in the way of claims which, as a matter of ordinary legal principle, are well founded. After all, if the former employee's claim is well founded in fact as well as in law, he himself is a creditor and ought to be admitted as such.

Secondly, one of the assumed facts in the present case is that the employer was conducting a dishonest and corrupt business. I would like to think this will rarely happen in practice. Thirdly, there are many circumstances in which an employee's reputation may suffer from his having been associated with an unsuccessful business, or an unsuccessful department within a business. In the ordinary way this will not found a claim of the nature made in the present case, even if the business or department was run with gross incompetence. A key feature in the present case is the assumed fact that the business was dishonest or corrupt.

Finally, although the implied term that the business will not be conducted dishonestly is a term which avails all employees, proof of consequential handicap in the labour market may well be much more difficult for some classes of employees than others. An employer seeking to employ a messenger, for instance, might be wholly unconcerned by an applicant's former employment in a dishonest business, whereas he might take a different view if he were seeking a senior executive.'

Comment

(1) Thus the House of Lords here allows employees to claim damages, not for the manner of their dismissal, but for the employer's breach of the implied term of mutual trust and confidence.

(2) As the case went to the House of Lords on an agreed set of hypothetical facts, testing whether or not the claim disclosed a recognised cause of action, the result meant only that the employees could go ahead with their claim. Whether they were successful or not depended on whether they could prove the relevant facts. In *BCCI v Ali (No 3)* (2002) five test cases were selected from among 369 claims by employees for stigma damages. The Court of Appeal upheld the finding of the trial judge that the employees had proved the employer's breach of duty, but the claims failed because they had not established that this blighted their prospects of fresh employment.

(3) Lord Nicholls's speech is an interesting example of the techniques of legal reasoning used by a court which does not wish to follow an earlier decision. First, it is suggested that the earlier court did not have this particular point in mind. Secondly, he points out that the situation has changed: the implied term did not exist at the time of *Addis*. Thirdly, it is morally right to take this position. Fourthly, there is a fleeting and indirect reference to the Practice Statement of 1966 which allows the House of Lords to depart from its own decisions in certain circumstances. Finally, he implies that the decisions will barely have any effect beyond the facts of this specific case. Where a court knows full well that it is extending the law, there is a tendency to try and confine the principle by reference to the specific fact pattern occurring. In practice, as might have been expected, courts were quickly faced with numerous claims for damages on the basis of breach of mutual trust and confidence.

Gogay v *Hertfordshire County Council* [2000] IRLR 703 Court of Appeal

The appellant was a residential care worker employed in a home for children in local authority care. A child living in the home who had been the victim of serious sexual abuse by her parents developed an obsession with the claimant, to the knowledge of staff, and behaved in a sexually provocative way towards her. The claimant found the situation stressful, sought help and had some time off work as a result.

Her managers initially expressed their support for her. However, a review meeting concluded that the child had made allegations of sexual abuse against the claimant, as a result of which she was immediately suspended on full pay to allow an investigation to take place. This came as a bolt from the blue given the reassurances she had been given.

Following a one-week investigation, the claimant was cleared of any suspicion of abuse and reinstated. However, by then she was ill and unable to return to work at the home. She eventually had to give up work because of clinical depression, a 'substantial and significant cause' of which was the suspension. The trial judge awarded her £26,000 by way of damages and the employer appealed.

LADY HALE J: '. . . The issue in this case is whether the defendant local authority acted reasonably in suspending the claimant from her post in a residential home while they investigated the circumstances surrounding a child living in that home. The investigation concluded that there was no case to answer, but the claimant suffered psychiatric illness and loss of earnings as a result of her suspension . . .

The point in this case is not whether the local authority should have conducted some inquiries. Clearly it had to do so . . . The point in this case, as I have already said more than once, is whether the local authority should have suspended the claimant in the way that it did simply because such inquiries were being made.

For the reasons given earlier, it does not follow that a staff member should be suspended simply because inquiries . . . are being made. There is always a separate decision to be taken about the implications for staff. It is not alleged that the decision was in breach of the express terms of the claimant's contract of employment. It remains to be considered, however, whether the authority's actions in this case were in breach of the implied term of confidence and trust.

The implied term of confidence and trust

It is now well settled that there is a mutual obligation implied in every contract of employment, not, without reasonable and proper cause, to conduct oneself in a manner likely to destroy or seriously damage the relationship of confidence and trust between employer and employee.

. . . Did the authority's conduct in this case amount to a breach of this implied term? The test is a severe one. The conduct must be such as to destroy or seriously damage the relationship. The conduct in this case was not only to suspend the claimant, but to do so by means of a letter which stated that "the issue to be investigated is an allegation of sexual abuse made by a young person in our care". Sexual abuse is a very serious matter, doing untold damage to those who suffer it. To be accused of it is also a serious matter. To be told by one's employer that one has been so accused is clearly calculated seriously to damage the relationship between employer and employee. The question is therefore whether there was "reasonable and proper cause" to do this.

In my judgment, there clearly was not . . . The difficulty was in determining what, if anything, [the child] was trying to convey. It warranted further investigation. But to describe it as an "allegation of sexual abuse" is putting it far too high. A close reading of the records coupled with further inquiries of the therapist were needed before it could be characterised as such.

Furthermore there was then a need to consider carefully what to do about the member of staff concerned . . . Miss Sinclair argues that transfer was impossible because all the people in their care are vulnerable. But that leaves out of account the particular circumstances in this case. It is difficult to accept that there is no other useful work to which the claimant might not have been transferred for the very short time that it ought to have taken to make the further inquiries needed. It is equally difficult to accept that some other step might not have been con-templated, such as a short period of leave. In any event, given the timescale involved, what was the rush?

The authority's own guidelines point out that "child sexual abuse rarely needs to be responded to as a crisis, but calls for a cool, clear and structured response". Instead what happened here was an immediate "knee-jerk" reaction . . .

On analysis, therefore, the actions of the local authority towards the claimant in this case were indeed in breach of its implied obligation not without reasonable and proper cause to act in a way which seriously damaged the relationship of confidence and trust between them. But in reaching this conclusion, I would not want local authorities to feel in any way inhibited in mak-ing the inquiries which they feel appropriate to safeguard the children in their care. Nor should there be any doubt that if there is a conflict between the interests of a child in their care and the interests of an employee, the interests of the child should prevail. But the employee is entitled to something better than the "knee-jerk" reaction which occurred in this case.

Damages

Miss Sinclair argues that, even if there were such a breach, the claimant would not be entitled to compensation for her depressive illness and resulting inability to do residential care work. There is clear authority for the proposition that general damages cannot be awarded for frus-tration, mental distress or injured feelings arising from an employer's breach of the implied term of confidence and trust: see *Bliss* v *South East Thames Regional Health Authority* (1985) hold-ing that the principle laid down in *Addis* v *Gramophone Co Ltd* (1909) applied to this breach as it did to wrongful dismissal; and *French* v *Barclays Bank plc* (1998), affirming that proposition despite other observations of the House of Lords in *Malik* v *BCCI* (1997).

Malik, of course, was not concerned with injured feelings but with financial loss, usually referred to as stigma damage, resulting from the employer's breach of contract. Both Lord Nicholls (with whom Lord Goff and Lord MacKay agreed) and Lord Steyn (with whom Lord Goff, Lord MacKay and Lord Mustill agreed) held that such damages could be recovered for breach of this implied term. In so far as *Addis* v *Gramophone Co* was thought to be authority to the contrary, it was a departure from the normal principle that damages for financial loss, including loss of reputation, were recoverable in contract, and should not be applied to a breach of the implied term.

There is, however, a clear distinction between frustration, mental distress and injured feel-ings, on the one hand, and a recognised psychiatric illness on the other. In *Page* v *Smith* (1996), the House of Lords held (by a majority) that once it was established that the defendant was under a duty of care to avoid causing personal injury to the claimant, it mattered not whether the injury sustained was physical, psychiatric or both. The cases limiting the ambit of liability in tort for psychiatric injury to secondary victims did not apply to primary victims to whom a duty of care not to cause personal injury was established. As Lord Lloyd of Berwick observed,

"In an age when medical knowledge is expanding fast, and psychiatric knowledge with it, it would not be sensible to commit the law to a distinction between physical and psychiatric injury, which may already be somewhat artificial, and may soon be altogether outmoded . . ."

In my judgment, that is correct. There is all the difference in the world between hurt, upset and injury to feelings, for which in general the law does not provide compensation whether in con-tract or (with certain well defined exceptions) in tort, and a recognised psychiatric illness . . .

I would therefore hold such damages recoverable unless constrained by authority to the contrary . . . The complaint here relates to a suspension, which manifestly contemplates the continuation of the employment relationship. The clear import of *Malik* is that the ambit of *Addis* should be confined. There are in this case two differences from *Addis*: first, this was not a dismissal, and secondly, this was psychiatric illness rather than hurt feelings. In my judgment, therefore, the judge was right to award damages for both the financial loss and the non-pecuniary damage resulting from the claimant's illness.'

(May and Peter Gibson LJJ agreed.)

Johnson v *Unisys Ltd* [2001] IRLR 279 House of Lords

The appellant had been employed by the defendant company for over 20 years, rising to become a director. He suffered from work-related stress over the years and the employers were aware of his psychological vulnerability. In January 1994 some unspecific allegations of misconduct were made against him and he was summarily dismissed in breach of the company's disciplinary procedure. As a result of his dismissal he developed a serious psychiatric illness.

Johnson claimed successfully for unfair dismissal and was awarded the maximum compensatory award possible at that time – £11,000. In these proceedings he sued his employer for breach of contract and negligence, alleging that they had broken the implied term to maintain mutual trust and confidence by the way they had treated him. He claimed over £400,000 in loss of earnings.

LORD HOFFMANN: 'On 11 August 1997 Mr Johnson commenced an action in the Milton Keynes County Court against Unisys for damages at common law. He claimed alternatively for breach of contract or negligence. In his re-amended particulars of claim, he alleged that his dismissal was in breach of various implied terms of his contract of employment. The main one was that the employer would not without reasonable cause conduct itself in a manner calculated and likely to destroy or seriously damage the relationship of trust and confidence between itself and the employee. The existence of this implied term in a contract of employment has recently been affirmed by the House of Lords in *Malik* v *Bank of Credit and Commerce International SA* (1997). It is commonly called the implied term of trust and confidence. He also pleaded various other implied terms; for example, that the company would not, without reasonable cause, do anything which would injure his physical or mental health, harm his professional development and so forth. But the alleged breach of all these terms lies in the fact that he was dismissed without a fair hearing and in breach of the company's disciplinary procedure.

Mr Johnson says that in consequence of the manner and the fact of his dismissal, he suffered a mental breakdown. He became depressed, attempted suicide and started to drink heavily. In 1994 he spent five months in a mental hospital and since then has occasionally had to be re-admitted. His family life has suffered and despite over 100 applications, he has been unable to find work. He is 52 and considers it unlikely that he will find remunerated work again. He says that severe damage of this kind was reasonably foreseeable by Unisys because during the period before his redundancy in 1987 it was known to persons whose knowledge should be attributed to the company that he was under stress and at risk of suffering psychological injury. The alternative claim in tort is based upon the allegation that Unisys owed him a duty of care because it ought reasonably to have foreseen that such injury was likely to result from dismissing him in the way it did . . .

My Lords, the first question is whether the implied term of trust and confidence upon which Mr Johnson relies, and about which in a general way there is no real dispute, or any of the other implied terms, applies to a dismissal. At common law the contract of employment was regarded by the courts as a contract like any other. The parties were free to negotiate whatever terms they liked and no terms would be implied unless they satisfied the strict test of necessity applied to a commercial contract. Freedom of contract meant that the stronger party, usually the employer, was free to impose his terms upon the weaker. But over the last 30 years or so, the nature of the contract of employment has been transformed. It has been recognised that a person's employment is usually one of the most important things in his or her life. It gives not only a livelihood but an occupation, an identity and a sense of self-esteem. The law has changed to recognise this social reality. Most of the changes have been made by Parliament. The Employment Rights Act 1996 consolidates numerous statutes which have conferred rights upon employees. European law has made a substantial contribution. And the common law has adapted itself to the new attitudes, proceeding sometimes by analogy with statutory rights.

The problem lies in extending or adapting any of these implied terms to dismissal. There are two reasons why dismissal presents special problems. The first is that any terms which the courts imply into a contract must be consistent with the express terms. Implied terms may supplement the express terms of the contract but cannot contradict them. Only Parliament may actually override what the parties have agreed. The second reason is that judges, in developing the law, must have regard to the policies expressed by Parliament in legislation. Employment law requires a balancing of the interests of employers and employees, with proper regard not only to the individual dignity and worth of the employees but also to the general economic interest. Subject to observance of fundamental human rights, the point at which this balance should be struck is a matter for democratic decision. The development of the common law by the judges plays a subsidiary role. Their traditional function is to adapt and modernise the common law. But such developments must be consistent with legislative policy as expressed in statutes. The courts may proceed in harmony with Parliament but there should be no discord.

My Lords, I shall consider first the problem posed by the express terms of the contract. In developing the implied term of trust and confidence and other similar terms applicable to the continuing employment relationship, the courts were advancing across open country. No express provision that BCCI would be entitled to conduct a fraudulent business . . . stood in their way. But the employer's right to dismiss the employee is strongly defended by the terms of the contract . . .

. . . In *Malloch* v *Aberdeen Corporation* (1971) Lord Reid said:

> "At common law a master is not bound to hear his servant before he dismisses him. He can act unreasonably or capriciously if he so chooses but the dismissal is valid. The servant has no remedy unless the dismissal is in breach of contract and then the servant's only remedy is damages for breach of contract."

The action for wrongful dismissal could therefore yield no more than the salary which should have been paid during the contractual period of notice. In the present case Mr Johnson's letter of engagement referred to Terms and Conditions of Employment contained in the company's Employee Handbook, which stipulated expressly that "The company reserves the right to make payment in lieu of notice". Unisys exercised that right.

My Lords, in the face of this express provision that Unisys was entitled to terminate Mr Johnson's employment on four weeks' notice without any reason, I think it is very difficult to imply a term that the company should not do so except for some good cause and after giving him a reasonable opportunity to demonstrate that no such cause existed . . .

On the other hand, I do not say that there is nothing which, consistently with such an express term, judicial creativity could do to provide a remedy in a case like this. In *Wallace* v *United Grain Growers Ltd* (1997) [a Canadian case] McLachlin J (in a minority judgment) said that the courts could imply an obligation to exercise the power of dismissal in good faith. That did not mean that the employer could not dismiss without cause. The contract entitled him to do so. But in so doing, he should be honest with the employee and refrain from untruthful, unfair or insensitive conduct. He should recognise that an employee losing his or her job was exceptionally vulnerable and behave accordingly. For breach of this implied obligation, McLachlin J would have awarded the employee, who had been dismissed in brutal circumstances, damages for mental distress and loss of reputation and prestige.

My Lords, such an approach would in this country have to circumvent or overcome the obstacle of *Addis* v *Gramophone Co Ltd*, in which it was decided that an employee cannot recover damages for injured feelings, mental distress or damage to his reputation, arising out of the manner of his dismissal. Speaking for myself, I think that, if this task was one which I felt called upon to perform, I would be able to do so. In *Malik* v *Bank of Credit and Commerce International SA* Lord Steyn said that the true ratio of *Addis's* case was that damages were recoverable only for loss caused by a breach of contract, not for loss caused by the manner of its breach. As McLachlin J said in the passage I have quoted, the only loss caused by a wrongful dismissal flows from a failure to give proper notice or make payment in lieu. Therefore, if wrongful dismissal is the only cause of action, nothing can be recovered for mental distress or damage to reputation. On the other hand, if such damage is loss flowing from a breach of another implied term of the contract, *Addis's* case does not stand in the way. That is why in *Malik's* case itself, damages were recoverable for financial loss flowing from damage to reputation caused by a breach of the implied term of trust and confidence.

In this case, Mr Johnson says likewise that his psychiatric injury is a consequence of a breach of the implied term of trust and confidence, which required Unisys to treat him fairly in the procedures for dismissal. He says that implied term now fills the gap which Lord Shaw of Dunfermline perceived and regretted in *Addis's* case by creating a breach of contract additional to the dismissal itself.

It may be a matter of words, but I rather doubt whether the term of trust and confidence should be pressed so far. In the way it has always been formulated, it is concerned with preserving the continuing relationship which should subsist between employer and employee. So it does not seem altogether appropriate for use in connection with the way that relationship is terminated. If one is looking for an implied term, I think a more elegant solution is McLachlin J's implication of a separate term that the power of dismissal will be exercised fairly and in good faith. But the result would be the same as that for which Mr Johnson contends by invoking the implied term of trust and confidence. As I have said, I think it would be possible to reach such a conclusion without contradicting the express term that the employer is entitled to dismiss without cause.

I must however make it clear that, although in my opinion it would be jurisprudentially possible to imply a term which gave a remedy in this case, I do not think that even if the courts were free of legislative constraint (a point to which I shall return in a moment) it would necessarily be wise to do so. It is not simply an incremental step from the duty of trust and confidence implied in *Malik* v *Bank of Credit and Commerce International SA*. The close association between the acts alleged to be in breach of the implied term and the irremovable and lawful fact of dismissal give rise to special problems. So, in *Wallace* v *United Grain Growers Ltd* the majority rejected an implied duty to exercise the power of dismissal in good faith. Iacobucci J said that such a step was better left to the legislature. It would be "overly intrusive and inconsistent with established principles of employment law" . . .

It follows, my Lords, that if there was no relevant legislation in this area, I would regard the question of whether judges should develop the law by implying a suitable term into the contract of employment as finely balanced. But now I must consider the statutory background against which your Lordships are invited to create such a cause of action . . .

My Lords, this statutory system for dealing with unfair dismissals was set up by Parliament to deal with the recognised deficiencies of the law as it stood at the time of *Malloch* v *Aberdeen Corporation*. The remedy adopted by Parliament was not to build upon the common law by creating a statutory implied term that the power of dismissal should be exercised fairly or in good faith, leaving the courts to give a remedy on general principles of contractual damages. Instead, it set up an entirely new system outside the ordinary courts, with tribunals staffed by a majority of lay members, applying new statutory concepts and offering statutory remedies. Many of the new rules, such as the exclusion of certain classes of employees and the limit on the amount of the compensatory award, were not based upon any principle which it would have been open to the courts to apply. They were based upon policy and represented an attempt to balance fairness to employees against the general economic interests of the community. And I should imagine that Parliament also had in mind the practical difficulties I have mentioned about causation and proportionality which would arise if the remedy was unlimited. So Parliament adopted the practical solution of giving the tribunals a very broad jurisdiction to award what they considered just and equitable but subject to a limit on the amount.

In my opinion, all the matters of which Mr Johnson complains in these proceedings were within the jurisdiction of the employment tribunal. His most substantial complaint is of financial loss flowing from his psychiatric injury which he says was a consequence of the unfair manner of his dismissal. Such loss is a consequence of the dismissal which may form the subject-matter of a compensatory award . . .

Part X of the Employment Rights Act 1996 therefore gives a remedy for exactly the conduct of which Mr Johnson complains. But Parliament had restricted that remedy to a maximum of £11,000, whereas Mr Johnson wants to claim a good deal more. The question is whether the courts should develop the common law to give a parallel remedy which is not subject to any such limit.

My Lords, I do not think that it is a proper exercise of the judicial function of the House to take such a step. Judge Ansell, to whose unreserved judgment I would pay respectful tribute, went in my opinion to the heart of the matter when he said:

> "there is not one hint in the authorities that the . . . tens of thousands of people that appear before the tribunals can have, as it were, a possible second bite in common law and I ask myself, if this is the situation, why on earth do we have this special statutory framework? What is the point of it if it can be circumvented in this way? . . . it would mean that effectively the statutory limit on compensation for unfair dismissal would disappear."

I can see no answer to these questions. For the judiciary to construct a general common law remedy for unfair circumstances attending dismissal would be to go contrary to the evident intention of Parliament that there should be such a remedy but that it should be limited in application and extent.'

(Lord Bingham and Lord Millett agreed with Lord Hoffmann; Lord Nicholls concurred on the statutory policy point. Lord Steyn dissented on these points, but would have dismissed the appeal on other grounds.)

Comment

(1) Note that two arguments are relied on here: an argument of legal principle and an argument based on policy – are they equally compelling?

(2) The maximum compensatory award at the time that these proceedings started was £11,000, a figure which had not kept pace with inflation and meant that employees did not have to be very high earners before they could find that a maximum award would not be enough to compensate them fully for their loss of employment. In 1999 the maximum was raised substantially to £50,000 and it has since been uprated in line with the

retail prices index. It stood at £63,000 in 2008. Nonetheless, this would come nowhere near the sort of sums claimed by Johnson in this case.

(3) *Johnson* v *Unisys Ltd* was felt to have left the law in an uncertain state as to when damages could be claimed for breach of the implied duty of mutual trust and confidence. It tends to treat the continuing employment relationship and dismissal as if they were entirely distinct, whereas there will normally be some procedural lead-up to the dismissal. Further guidance was given in two joined appeals to the House of Lords in 2004.

Eastwood v *Magnox Electric plc; McCabe* v *Cornwall County Council* [2004] IRLR 733 House of Lords

Both cases went to the House of Lords on the preliminary issue of whether the claims disclosed a cause of action, if the facts they alleged could be proved. The facts were therefore assumed for the purpose of the hearing. Both cases involved employees dismissed following lengthy, flawed, disciplinary proceedings.

The alleged facts in *Eastwood* v *Magnox* were that the first claimant's manager had a longstanding grudge against him and sought to find or manufacture evidence as a basis for disciplinary proceedings against him. The second claimant (Williams), a colleague who refused to give a false statement against Eastwood, was then threatened with the same treatment. The four-month period leading up to the disciplinary hearing following which Williams was dismissed was described as a campaign to undermine and demoralise him. He developed a depressive illness as a result. Eastwood's disciplinary hearing had to be postponed because he was suffering from a depressive illness brought on by the situation. He was dismissed six months later. Williams won an unfair dismissal claim, following which the employer reached a financial agreement with both men to settle their unfair dismissal claims. In this action, they claimed damages for breach of contract and negligence.

In *McCabe* v *Cornwall CC* the claimant was a teacher who was suspended following allegations that he had behaved inappropriately to female pupils. It took six months before the school governors held a disciplinary hearing, at which they decided to give him a final warning. He appealed, and four months later the appeal hearing was held and a decision to dismiss him was substituted. He appealed again, as allowed by the contract, and it took more than two years before his appeal was heard and rejected. He won a claim for unfair dismissal and was awarded the maximum compensatory award. He claimed damages for breach of contract, negligence and breach of statutory duty, alleging that the botched way the disciplinary proceedings had been conducted and the dismissal had caused him psychiatric injury.

LORD NICHOLLS: '. . .

The boundary line

Identifying the boundary of the "*Johnson* exclusion area", as it has been called, is comparatively straightforward. The statutory code provides remedies for infringement of the statutory right not to be *dismissed* unfairly. An employee's remedy for unfair dismissal, whether actual or constructive, is the remedy provided by statute. If before his dismissal, whether actual or constructive, an employee has acquired a cause of action at law, for breach of contract or otherwise, that cause of action remains unimpaired by his subsequent unfair dismissal and the statutory rights flowing therefrom. By definition, in law such a cause of action exists independently of the dismissal.

In the ordinary course, suspension apart, an employer's failure to act fairly in the steps leading to dismissal does not of itself cause the employee financial loss. The loss arises when the employee is dismissed and it arises by reason of his dismissal. Then the resultant claim for loss falls squarely within the *Johnson* exclusion area.

Exceptionally this is not so. Exceptionally, financial loss may flow directly from the employer's failure to act fairly when taking steps leading to dismissal. Financial loss flowing from suspension is an instance. Another instance is cases such as those now before the House, when an employee suffers financial loss from psychiatric or other illness caused by his pre-dismissal unfair treatment. In such cases the employee has a common law cause of action which precedes, and is independent of, his subsequent dismissal. In respect of his subsequent dismissal he may of course present a claim to an employment tribunal. If he brings proceedings both in court and before a tribunal he cannot recover any overlapping heads of loss twice over.

If identifying the boundary between the common law rights and remedies and the statutory rights and remedies is comparatively straightforward, the same cannot be said of the practical consequences of this unusual boundary. Particularly in cases concerning financial loss flowing from psychiatric illnesses, some of the practical consequences are far from straightforward or desirable. The first and most obvious drawback is that in such cases the division of remedial jurisdiction between the court and an employment tribunal will lead to duplication of proceedings. In practice there will be cases where the employment tribunal and the court each traverse much of the same ground in deciding the factual issues before them, with attendant waste of resources and costs.

Second, the existence of this boundary line means that in some cases a continuing course of conduct, typically a disciplinary process followed by dismissal, may have to be chopped artificially into separate pieces. In cases of constructive dismissal a distinction will have to be drawn between loss flowing from antecedent breaches of the trust and confidence term and loss flowing from the employee's acceptance of these breaches as a repudiation of the contract. The loss flowing from the impugned conduct taking place before actual or constructive dismissal lies outside the *Johnson* exclusion area, the loss flowing from the dismissal itself is within that area. In some cases this legalistic distinction may give rise to difficult questions of causation in cases such as those now before the House, where financial loss is claimed as the consequence of psychiatric illness said to have been brought on by the employer's conduct before the employee was dismissed. Judges and tribunals, faced perhaps with conflicting medical evidence, may have to decide whether the fact of dismissal was really the last straw which proved too much for the employee, or whether the onset of the illness occurred even before he was dismissed.

The existence of this boundary line produces other strange results. An employer may be better off dismissing an employee than suspending him. A statutory claim for unfair dismissal would be subject to the statutory cap, a common law claim for unfair suspension would not. The decision of the Court of Appeal in *Gogay* v *Hertfordshire County Council* (2000) is an example of the latter. Likewise, the decision in *Johnson's* case means that an employee who is psychologically vulnerable is owed no duty of care in respect of his dismissal although, depending on the circumstances, he may be owed a duty of care in respect of his suspension.

It goes without saying that an inter-relation between the common law and statute having these awkward and unfortunate consequences is not satisfactory. The difficulties arise principally because of the cap on the amount of compensatory awards for unfair dismissal. Although the cap was raised substantially in 1998, at times tribunals are still precluded from awarding full compensation for a dismissed employee's financial loss. So, understandably, employees and their legal advisers are seeking to side-step the statutory limit by identifying elements in the events preceding dismissal, but leading up to dismissal, which can be used as pegs on which to hang a common law claim for breach of an employer's implied contractual obligation to act fairly. This situation merits urgent attention by the government and the legislature.

The present cases

It follows from what is set out above that I would dismiss the appeal in Mr McCabe's case and allow the appeals of Mr Eastwood and Mr Williams. In the case of all three men the assumed facts constitute causes of action which accrued before the dismissals. They disclose reasonable causes of action which should proceed to trial.'

(Lords Hoffmann, Rodger and Brown agreed with Lord Nicholls. Lord Steyn agreed with the result and suggested that *Johnson* v *Unisys* should be reconsidered.)

Comment

(1) The disadvantages of the current approach are clearly spelt out in the speech of Lord Nicholls. The one-man campaign by Lord Steyn to grasp the nettle and depart from *Addis* v *Gramophone Co Ltd* has so far been received by his colleagues with a deafening silence: none so much as commented on his arguments either in this case or in *Johnson* v *Unisys Ltd*.

(2) For further criticism of the position post-*Johnson*, see the readings referred to by Lord Steyn: Barmes (2004); Brodie (2001); Collins (2001); Deakin and Morris (2001, pp 410–11, 418–19); Freedland (2003, pp 162–7, 303–5, 342–5, 362–4); Hepple and Morris (2002).

(3) One of the interesting facets of this case is that it illustrates a situation where the common law claim for breach of contract would potentially result in higher compensation than an unfair dismissal claim. This is rarely the case. Apart from those situations where damages may be forthcoming for breach of the implied term of trust and confidence, the only employees for whom pay in lieu of notice is likely to be substantial are those who are on fixed-term contracts with no provision for early termination on giving notice and/or who have a substantial package of additional benefits, such as private health insurance, share options, company car, etc. When Sven-Göran Eriksson's contract as the manager of the England football team, originally set to last until 2008, was terminated in 2006, his compensation was conservatively estimated at £2.5 million. See *Horkulak* v *Cantor Fitzgerald International* (2004) for an example from the financial services industry.

Enforcing the contract of employment

Another approach to the deficiencies of the action for wrongful dismissal is to seek an order which will to some extent enforce adherence to the contract of employment rather than accept a dismissal in breach.

Irani v *Southampton and South West Hampshire Health Authority*
[1985] ICR 590 Chancery Division

The employee was an ophthalmologist who worked part-time at a hospital run by the authority. His contract therefore incorporated National Health Service terms and conditions ('the blue book') which contained a procedure dealing with disputes between employees (section 33) and a disciplinary procedure (section 40).

The employee quarrelled with the consultant ophthalmologist and the dispute escalated. Instead of following the procedures in the blue book, the authority used an *ad hoc* procedure and decided that the employee's contract should be terminated. This was because, although they had no complaints about the employee's work, the authority thought that he and the consultant ophthalmologist could no longer work together. The employee brought an action for declarations that the dismissal was unlawful and that the procedure should have been followed, and an injunction to prevent the dismissal taking effect until the proper procedure had been implemented.

WARNER J: '. . . Mr Clifford [counsel for the employer] put forward as his primary submission that there was a clear rule that the court would not grant specific performance of a contract of employment or, in general, grant an injunction to restrain a breach of it and that there were no special circumstances here which would justify my granting an injunction the effect of which would be to compel the defendant authority to continue to employ Mr Irani until the trial or at all events until it had in the meantime completed the procedure under section 33.

The authorities that have been cited to me in the course of the argument evince three schools of thought among the judiciary as to the effect of the wrongful dismissal of a servant. Those three schools of thought are represented by the three members of the Court of Appeal in *Gunton v Richmond-upon-Thames LBC* (1980). Shaw LJ belonged to what I think is the old school, which holds that a wrongful dismissal constitutes a repudiation of the contract of employment and one which, exceptionally, brings the contract to an end even though it is not accepted by the other party to the contract, that is to say the employee. That was described during the argument before me as the "unilateralist" view. Buckley LJ took the opposite view that a contract of employment is no exception to the general rule that a repudiation of a contract by one party does not bring the contract to an end unless that repudiation is accepted by the other party. That has been described in the argument before me as the "acceptance" view. Brightman LJ took what seems to be a middle view, namely that the effect of the wrongful dismissal was to terminate the status or relationship of master and servant but not every provision of the contract.

In *R v East Berkshire Health Authority ex parte Walsh* (1984) May LJ expressed his agreement with the view of Browne-Wilkinson J as President of the Employment Appeal Tribunal in *Robert Cort & Son Ltd v Charman* (1981) that "this difficult question of the effect of an unaccepted wrongful dismissal is still unresolved". It was common ground between Mr Harwood-Stevenson [counsel for the employee] and Mr Clifford that it would be right for me to leave it unresolved despite a powerfully reasoned judgment of Sir Robert Megarry V-C in *Thomas Marshall (Exports) Ltd v Guinle* (1978) in which he came down firmly in favour of the acceptance view. I was urged by both counsel to leave the resolution of that question for the purposes of the present case to the trial judge.

Mr Clifford's submission was that, even if the acceptance view was correct, I should apply the clear rule of this court that it would not grant specific performance of a contract of employment or in general grant an injunction to restrain a breach of such a contract. He submitted that *Hill v CA Parsons & Co Ltd* (1972) was the only case where that rule had been departed from to the extent of the court granting an injunction to compel an employer to continue employing an employee whom he had dismissed, that that case, as was emphasised in the case itself and in subsequent authorities, was quite exceptional and that the considerations underlying it did not apply here. I shall come to *Hill v CA Parsons & Co Ltd* in a moment but I think that I must approach the relevant authorities with the reasons for the general rule on which Mr Clifford relied in mind. They were expressed by Geoffrey Lane LJ in *Chappell v Times Newspapers Limited* (1975) where he said:

> "Very rarely indeed will a court enforce, either by specific performance or by injunction, a contract for services, either at the behest of the employers or of the employee. The reason is obvious: if one party has no faith in the honesty or integrity or the loyalty of the other, to force him to serve or to employ that other is a plain recipe for disaster."

It is not the case here that the defendant authority has no faith in the honesty or integrity or loyalty of Mr Irani . . .

I think the true position here is that the defendant authority would be willing to continue employing Mr Irani were it not for the fact that they are convinced that his and Mr Walker's continued employment are incompatible.

Mr Clifford more happily, I think, expressed the distinction between this case and the *Parsons* case in this way. He said that in the *Parsons* case the defendant fought the case because it was in fear of what the trade union might do if it did not, whereas here the defendant is fighting the case because it genuinely wants to be rid of Mr Irani. But, to revert to what I said earlier when I quoted from the judgment of Geoffrey Lane LJ in *Chappell* v *Times Newspapers Ltd* (1975), it remains the fact that the defendant authority has perfect faith in the honesty, integrity and loyalty of Mr Irani.

Turning to Megarry J's second reason for the decision in the *Parsons* case, it seems to me that there is a comparable reason here. In the *Parsons* case, Mr Hill was seeking the protection of the Industrial Relations Act. Here Mr Irani is seeking the protection of section 33 of the blue book to which he is entitled if the circumstances are appropriate.

Thirdly, as Mr Harwood-Stevenson has pointed out, this is a case – and I anticipate now on what I shall have to say in a moment about some subsidiary submissions of Mr Clifford – where damages would not be an adequate remedy . . .'

Comment

(1) This judgment highlights the two main obstacles to granting employees orders which would effectively allow them to enforce the contract of employment. First, the idea that specific performance, or an injunction amounting to specific performance, should not be granted in relation to contracts involving personal service. Secondly, that a dismissal in breach of contract cannot be prevented anyway, because the employer's action brings the contract to an end regardless of whether or not the employee accepts the situation.

(2) So far as the first issue is concerned, this case is typical of a number where temporary injunctions have been granted. The fact that the employer retains confidence in the employee has been treated as crucial in any situation where the employee is seeking reinstatement, although not necessarily where the aim is to force the employer to carry out a disciplinary procedure properly (see *Gryf-Lowczowski* v *Hinchingbrooke Healthcare NHS Trust* (2006)). It is questionable whether it is also a condition that the claimant should not be seeking anything more than a temporary order to maintain the status quo while the proper procedure is carried out. This has usually been the case: see, eg, *Powell* v *Brent LBC* (1988) and *Boyo* v *Lambeth LBC* (1994). However, a permanent injunction was granted in *Jones* v *Gwent CC* (1992).

(3) So far as the second issue is concerned, the arguments of Megarry V-C which follow seem unanswerable.

Thomas Marshall (Exports) Ltd v *Guinle* [1978] ICR 905 Chancery Division

In this case, it was the employee who was trying to argue that his own fundamental breach of contract (competing with the employer in breach of an express term of the contract) had brought the contract to an end even though his resignation was not accepted by the employer. He hoped in this way to be free to continue his competing business.

MEGARRY V-C: 'Mr. Hutchison [counsel for the employee] accepted that the general rule was that a contract was not determined merely by the wrongful repudiation of it by one party, and that it was for the innocent party to decide whether to treat the contract as having determined or as continuing in existence. That rule, however, did not apply to contracts of employment, for they were subject to a special exception. Under the exception, any contract of employment could at any time be brought to an end by either party repudiating it. This exception, however, was itself subject to an exception, and that was where despite the repudiation the mutual confidence between the parties remained unimpaired. In that exceptional case the normal rule for contracts still applied, and the contract remained in being unless the innocent party elected to treat the repudiation as terminating it . . .

At least one thing is plain, and that is that the authorities on the point are in a far from satisfactory state. Let me say at the outset that I have great difficulty in accepting the view that contracts of employment are an exception to the general rule for repudiation, and that they are terminated forthwith by the repudiation, whether or not the innocent party elects to accept it as doing this. Indeed, Mr Hutchison was unable to contend that such a doctrine was right, and in order to make his proposition viable he had to narrow it to a substantial degree. Let me attempt to summarise the matter.

First, there will usually be a wide range of acts and omissions which will constitute a repudiation of a contract, whether for service or otherwise. In addition to an outright refusal to perform the contract, there are many other acts and omissions which can amount to a repudiation which will entitle the innocent party to treat the contract as being at an end. Such acts or omissions may consist either of a fundamental breach of the contract or the breach of a fundamental term of it . . . If cases of master and servant are an exception from the rule that an unaccepted repudiation works no determination of the contract, and instead are subject to what I have called the doctrine of automatic determination, the result would be that many a contract of employment would be determined forthwith upon the commission of a fundamental breach, or a breach of a fundamental term, even though the commission of this breach was unknown to the innocent party, and even if, had he known, he would have elected to keep the contract in being.

. . . In order to avoid difficulties such as these, Mr Hutchison reformulated the doctrine of automatic determination. He said that in master and servant cases a breach of contract amounting to a repudiation did not forthwith determine the contract unless the party breaking the contract intended to bring the contract to an end. This, of course, is a very substantial narrowing of the doctrine as stated in the cases. It also emphasises the shift in intention. Whereas for contracts in general it is the innocent party who decides whether the contract is to continue or come to an end, for master and servant it is the guilty party who has the choice, or at least the initial choice; for presumably if the wrongdoer sought to keep the contract alive, the innocent party would then be able to elect nevertheless to treat it as having come to an end.

It is plain that some such narrowing and reformulation of the doctrine is necessary if absurd results are to be avoided. It is also plain that nothing in the cases which have been put before me point to such a reformulation. It also produces a result which seems to me to be far from just. Why should a person who makes a contract of service have the right at any moment to put an end to his contractual obligations? No doubt the court will not decree specific performance of the contract, nor will it grant an injunction which will have the effect of an order for specific performance: but why should the limitation of the range of remedies for the breach invade the substance of the contract? Why should it deprive the innocent party of any right to elect how to treat the breach, except, perhaps, in remainder and subject to the wrongdoer's prior right of election?

Second, it is difficult, if not impossible, to reconcile the doctrine of automatic determination with a number of authorities which, for the most part, do not appear to have been cited in any of the cases that I have mentioned. I need say no more about *Boston Deep Sea Fishing* v *Ansell* (1888), but I must refer to some others. Johanna Wagner contracted to sing for a period for Benjamin Lumley, and not to sing for anyone else. She then agreed to sing for someone else for a larger sum, but Lord St Leonards LC granted an injunction to restrain her from doing so: *Lumley* v *Wagner* (1852) . . . Bette Davis, the film actress, entered into a contract with a film company for a period, agreeing to render her exclusive services as an actress to that company, and not during that period to render any services for any other stage or motion picture production or business. During the period of the contract the actress refused to be bound by it, and contracted with a third person to appear as a film artist. At the trial of the action Branson J granted an injunction which restrained the actress from rendering services in any motion picture or stage production for anyone save the film company: *Warner Brothers Pictures Incorporated* v *Nelson* (1937) . . .

Apart from the citation of *Lumley* v *Wagner* in *Hill* v *C A Parsons & Co Ltd* (1972), none of these authorities seem to have been considered in any of the recent cases on automatic determination that I have mentioned. Yet if the doctrine of automatic determination is good law, all that Johanna Wagner . . . and Bette Davis had to do was to say that their contracts were at an end, and so they were free from the contractual restrictions that applied while their employment continued. The claims to an injunction would thus have failed instead of succeeding . . .'

Comment

(1) This position has been accepted in relation to constructive dismissal: see *London Transport Executive* v *Clarke* (1981) (below, p 372), but remains for definitive decision at common law. The House of Lords expressly left the point open in *Rigby* v *Ferodo Ltd* (1988).

(2) Employees of public authorities, if they are able to show a sufficient 'statutory underpinning' of their contracts of employment, may be able to challenge dismissal through an action for judicial review: see, for example, *McLaren* v *Home Office* (1990). However, even if a contract of employment in the public sector is regulated at least in part by statute, the tendency is to treat the employment relationship as a private law matter, limiting the availability of public law remedies such as judicial review (*R* v *East Berks AHA ex parte Walsh* (1984)).

UNFAIR DISMISSAL

Royal Commission on Trade Unions and Employers' Associations 1965–1968 (the Donovan Commission) Cmnd 3623

521   In the eye of the law employer and employee are free and equal parties to the contract of employment. Hence, either employer or employee has the right to bring the contract to an end in accordance with its terms. Thus, an employer is legally entitled to dismiss an employee whenever he wishes and for whatever reason, provided only that he gives due notice. At common law he does not even have to reveal his reason, much less to justify it.

522   An employee has protection at common law against 'wrongful dismissal', but this protection is strictly limited; it means that if an employee is dismissed without due notice he can claim the payment of wages he would have earned for the period of notice. From this payment will be deducted any amount which he earned (or through his fault failed to earn) during the period of notice. Beyond this, the employee has no legal claim at common law, whatever hardship he suffers as a result of his dismissal. Even if the way in which he is

dismissed constitutes an imputation on his honesty and his ability to get another job is correspondingly reduced he cannot – except through an action for defamation – obtain any redress (see the decision of the House of Lords in *Addis* v *Gramophone Co*) . . .

524   In practice of course many employees enjoy much greater security against dismissal than is implied in the law. Many employers dislike having to dismiss employees and do so only with reluctance when they feel that there is no alternative. Some employers have introduced formal procedures designed to ensure that employees are not dismissed without an opportunity to get their case reconsidered at a higher level, and in many well-organised industries trade unions can take up a dismissal which they think unjust through an agreed disputes procedure. Sometimes additional factors may have some influence, such as an acute shortage of labour or the possibility that action which seemed arbitrary would provoke a strike.

525   There is nevertheless a very general feeling, shared by employers as well as trade unions, that the present situation is unsatisfactory, and it was reflected in the submissions of many who gave evidence to us. In 1964 the Government announced that they accepted Recommendation No 119 on Termination of Employment adopted by the International Labour Organisation in 1963 and would discuss the provision of procedures to give effect-ive safeguards against arbitrary dismissal with representatives or employers and trade unions. The Minister of Labour's National Joint Advisory Council subsequently set up a committee to examine dismissals and dismissal procedures. The committee's report was published in 1967, and the committee drew particular attention to a number of points about procedures in Great Britain as compared with the position in some other countries (see paragraph 121 of *Dismissal Procedures* published by HMSO in 1967). They pointed out that in law employees are in general protected only against dismissal without due notice, there being no legal protection against being dismissed unfairly or without good reason. Provision by employers of a formal procedure for the handling of dismissals is not very common and is usually only found in large concerns, and this is particularly serious because the great majority of grievances about dismissals are bound to be matters dealt with within the individual concern. Disputes procedures laid down by industry-wide agreements have limitations; for example the delays in their operation may mean that a dismissed worker often takes another job and the case lapses without his grievance having been properly thrashed out. In less highly organised sectors of employment there may be no disputes procedure and an employee may have no effective redress against dismissal. Finally, with rare exceptions employees have no right of appeal to an independ-ent person or body.

526   We share in full the belief that the present situation is unsatisfactory. In practice there is usually no comparison between the consequences for an employer if an employee terminates the contract of employment and those which will ensue for an employee if he is dismissed. In reality people build much of their lives around their jobs. Their incomes and prospects for the future are inevitably founded in the expectation that their jobs will continue. For workers in many situations dismissal is a disaster. For some workers it may make inevitable the breaking up of a community and the uprooting of homes and families. Others, and particularly older workers, may be faced with the greatest difficulty in getting work at all. The statutory provision for redundancy goes some way to recognise what is really at stake for an employee when his job is involved, but it is no less at stake if he is being dismissed for alleged incompetence or for misconduct than if he is being dismissed for redundancy. To this it is no answer that good employers will dismiss employees only if they have no alternative. Not all employers are good employers. Even if the employer's intentions are good, is it certain that his subordinates' intentions are always also good? And even when all concerned in management act in good faith, are

they always necessarily right? Should their view of the case automatically prevail over the employee's?

527 The passage we refer to above in the report of the committee on dismissals draws attention to the unsatisfactory situation in less highly organised sectors of employment. Elsewhere in this report we recommend measures to promote the growth of collective bargaining machinery on sound lines and in particular that any stipulation in a contract of employment that an employee should not belong to a trade union should by law be made void and of no effect. Clearly however the protection given by this enactment will be far from complete so long as it is open to an employer to dismiss an employee because he exercises his right to join a trade union or because, having joined, he takes a part in legitimate trade union activities. It is just where organisation is weak that the danger that this could happen is greatest.

528 From the point of view of industrial peace, it is plain also that the present situation leaves much to be desired. In the period 1964–1966 some 276 unofficial strikes took place each year on average as a result of disputes about whether individuals should or should not be employed, suspended or dismissed. The committee on dismissals analysed stoppages – whether official or unofficial – arising out of dismissals *other than redundancies* over this period and found that there were on average 203 a year. It can be argued that the right to secure a speedy and impartial decision on the justification for a dismissal might have averted many of these stoppages, though some cases would no doubt still have occurred where workers were taking spontaneous action to try to prevent a dismissal being given effect.

529 For all these reasons we believe it urgently necessary for workers to be given better protection against unfair dismissal.

Comment

(1) The Donovan Commission's proposals led to a right to claim unfair dismissal being included in the Industrial Relations Act 1971. The broad outlines of the law have remained much the same ever since. The present provisions are to be found in the Employment Rights Act 1996 Part X.

(2) Not every worker has the right to claim unfair dismissal, and in case of doubt, the burden of proof is on the worker to establish that she is entitled to claim. The main conditions are first, that the claimant must be an employee (ERA s 94: see Chapter 3), and secondly, that except for automatically unfair dismissals, the claimant must have been employed for one year (ERA s 108(1)).

(3) In addition, certain categories of worker are excluded from the right to claim: the police; share fishermen and Crown employees where the relevant minister has issued an excepting certificate on grounds of national security. Employees working abroad may exceptionally be covered, provided that their employment has sufficient connection with the UK: see *Lawson* v *Serco Ltd* (2006). Members of the armed forces may now claim unfair dismissal, but not under ERA s 100 (health and safety grounds) nor certain other specific grounds.

(4) It is possible for workers covered by a dismissals procedure agreed between employers and independent trade unions to be contracted out of the statutory scheme, but only if the voluntary procedure is at least as advantageous as the statutory scheme. There are no such contracted-out procedures at present. Since 2001, individual employees and employers have also had the option of having a dispute settled via the Acas Arbitration

Scheme rather than through unfair dismissal proceedings, but hardly any cases have gone along this route.

(5) Finally, if there is any dispute on the matter, it is for the employee to prove that she was dismissed.

The meaning of dismissal

Under ERA s 95 three kinds of termination of the contract of employment will count as dismissal and therefore as the foundation for a claim for unfair dismissal. Each will be examined in turn.

Termination with or without notice

Employment Rights Act 1996

95   (1)   . . . an employee is dismissed by his employer if . . .
          (a)   the contract under which he is employed is terminated by the employer (whether with or without notice) . . .

Comment

(1) The fact that it is largely irrelevant for the purposes of an unfair dismissal claim whether or not notice to terminate was given marks a major distinction from the common law action for wrongful dismissal.

(2) Difficulties in relation to dismissal under this head are only likely to arise if non-technical and perhaps equivocal language is used which the parties understand differently.

Tanner v Kean [1978] IRLR 110 Employment Appeal Tribunal

The employee had been instructed not to use the company van outside working hours and had been lent £275 by the employer to buy a car. On discovering that the employee was still using the van for his part-time job at a country club, the employer lost his temper, swore at the employee and said, 'That's it, you're finished with me.' When the employee claimed for unfair dismissal, the employer denied that he had been dismissed.

PHILLIPS J: 'In the present case the words are those set out in paragraph 1 of the Reasons: "What's my fucking van doing outside; you're a tight bastard. I've just lent you £275 to buy a car and you are too tight to put juice in it. That's it; you're finished with me." Part of the circumstances were that that was said in a country club to which Mr Tanner had taken the firm's van, and where he acted as a part-time doorman and had met Mr Kean, his employer. It seems to us – and although they do not say so, no doubt it seemed to the tribunal – that those words, in all the circumstances of the case, were not as a matter of law in one category or the other; in other words, whether what was said constituted a dismissal depended on all the circumstances of the case. In our judgment the test which has to be applied in cases of this kind is along these lines. Were the words spoken those of dismissal, that is to say, were they intended to bring the contract of employment to an end? What was the employer's intention? In answering that a relevant, and perhaps the most important, question is how would a reasonable employee, in all circumstances, have understood what the employer intended by what he said and did? Then in most of these cases, and in this case, it becomes relevant to look at the later events following the utterance of the words and preceding the actual departure of the employee. Some care, it seems to us, is necessary in regard to later events, and it might be put, we think, like this: that later events, unless relied on as themselves constituting a dismissal, are only relevant to the extent that they throw light on the employer's intention; that is to say, we would stress, his intention at the time of the alleged dismissal. A word of caution is necessary because in considering later events it is necessary to remember that a dismissal or resignation, once it has taken effect, cannot be unilaterally withdrawn. Accordingly, as it seems to us, later events need to be scrutinised with some care in order to see whether they are genuinely explanatory of the acts alleged to constitute dismissal, or whether they reflect a change of mind. If they are in the former category they may be valuable as showing what was really intended . . .'

(The EAT held that the tribunal had not misdirected itself in holding on the facts that there had been no dismissal.)

Comment

(1) It is worth noting that if an employer swears at an employee, it could be grounds for the employee to leave and claim constructive dismissal: see below.

(2) Similar considerations are relevant where an employee has apparently resigned in anger (see below).

Expiry of a limited-term contract without renewal

Employment Rights Act 1996

95 (1) . . . an employee is dismissed by his employer if . . .

     (b) he is employed under a limited-term contract and that contract terminates by virtue of the limiting event without being renewed under the same contract

     . . .

235 (2A) For the purposes of this Act a contract of employment is a "limited-term contract" if –

     (a) the employment under the contract is not intended to be permanent, and

     (b) provision is accordingly made in the contract for it to terminate by virtue of a limiting event.

     (2B) In this Act, "limiting event", in relation to a contract of employment means –

     (a) in the case of a contract for a fixed-term, the expiry of the term,

     (b) in the case of a contract made in contemplation of the performance of a specific task, the performance of the task, and

     (c) in the case of a contract which provides for its termination on the occurrence of an event (or the failure of an event to occur), the occurrence of the event (or the failure of the event to occur).

Comment

(1) Expiry of a limited-term contract is included in the definition of dismissal because otherwise there would be a major loophole in unfair dismissal protection. It would be possible for an employer to put staff on relatively short fixed-term contracts and then make entirely arbitrary decisions about whether or not to re-engage them, and the employee who was not kept on would have no redress, because technically there would have been no termination by the employer.

(2) Non-renewal does not mean that the dismissal is unfair: only that there has been a dismissal, so that the employee has the possibility of claiming for unfair dismissal. Its fairness or unfairness will depend on the reasons for non-renewal.

(3) To protect employers from having to defend unmeritorious claims where the fixed-term contract had been used for a genuine short-term need, it used to be possible for employers to get employees to waive their rights to claim unfair dismissal or redundancy. This, of course, opened the way for exactly the abuse described in (1) above. The possibility of seeking waivers of unfair dismissal rights was therefore abolished by the Employment Relations Act 1999. Following the EU Directive on Fixed-term Work in 1999 (99/70/EC), the Fixed-term Employees (Prevention of Less Favourable Treatment) Regulations 2002 were passed (see above, p 146) which abolished the waiver of redundancy rights.

(4) The original wording of ERA s 95(1)(b) referred to 'fixed-term contracts', which were defined by the courts as contracts with a definite finishing date, whether or not they could be lawfully terminated by giving notice before that date (*Wiltshire CC v NATFHE and Guy* (1980)). This excluded contracts to carry out a particular task, or for a particular purpose. As a result of the Fixed-term Work Directive, these contracts are now included in the wider definition of a limited-term contract in ERA s 235, above.

(5) It had already been held at common law that contracts purporting to terminate automatically on the happening of a particular event would be treated as dismissal, in order to prevent avoidance of the requirements of the ERA: *Igbo v Johnson Matthey* (1986).

Constructive dismissal

Employment Rights Act 1996

95 (1) . . . an employee is dismissed by his employer if . . .

> (c) the employee terminates the contract under which he is employed (with or without notice) in circumstances in which he is entitled to terminate it without notice by reason of the employer's conduct.

Western Excavating v Sharp [1978] QB 761 Court of Appeal

LORD DENNING MR: 'Mr Sharp was only employed by the China-Clay Co for 20 months. He left of his own accord. Yet he has been awarded £658 as compensation for unfair dismissal. There seems something wrong about that award. What is it?

To fill in the details, he started work with the company on July 9, 1974. One of the terms was that, if he worked extra time, he could have time off in lieu. One day in Feburary 1976 he wanted to play a card game for a team. He asked the foreman for three hours off. The foreman said that he could not have it that afternoon as there was a lot of work to be done. But Mr Sharp took it off and played his game of cards. Next morning – Friday, February 27, 1976 – the foreman dismissed him, giving him two weeks' notice for failing to carry out a reasonable order. The employee appealed to a panel set up by the company under its disciplinary procedure. On March 5, 1976 the panel allowed his appeal, saying:

> "Having considered all the evidence presented to us, we are of the unanimous decision that the dismissal be withdrawn, as there was room for confusion the way the situation was left, but having regard to the seriousness of what has happened, we substitute the dismissal with five working days' suspension without pay."

Thus the employee lost five days' pay. He does not dispute the justice of the panel's decision. But it left him in financial difficulties. He was living with a woman who was, in modern terminology, his "common law wife" and their two children. His take-home pay was £42.40 a week. He had no savings, but he had holiday pay accrued to him of £117.17 net.

As a result of the five days' loss of pay, he had no money to pay his household expenses. He went to the social security and was given £6.45. But that was not enough to carry on. So he went to his employers. He asked for an advance on his accrued holiday pay. He was told, quite correctly, that it was against company policy to pay holiday pay unless the holiday was itself actually taken. He then asked for a loan. He said he wanted £40. The welfare officer told him that the company could not make him a loan to that extent. The welfare officer suggested that Mr Sharp should see him again to discuss the details. That did not satisfy the employee. He said: "If the company cannot help me, I must sort it out myself. I shall have to obtain my holiday pay." That is just what he did. He went to see the workshop manager, and said: "I don't want to leave, but circumstances force me to do so. I am leaving and want my holiday pay now." So on March 11, 1976 he picked up his holiday pay of £117.17 and left. He went straight off to the employment tribunal and claimed compensation for unfair dismissal . . .

[ERA s 95(1)(c)] has given rise to a vast body of case law as to what comes within it. It is spoken of as "constructive dismissal". It has given rise to a problem on which there has been a diversity of views among chairmen of employment tribunals and among the judges of the Employment Appeal Tribunal. On July 28, 1977 the Employment Appeal Tribunal attempted to settle these differences in *Wetherall (Bond St, W1) Ltd* v *Lynn* (1978); but they were unsettled again by the discovery of some *obiter dicta* in this court in *Turner* v *London Transport Executive* (1977). This led the Employment Appeal Tribunal on October 4, 1977 to think that they ought to follow those *obiter dicta* and to give guidance accordingly. It is to be found in their decision in *Scott* v *Aveling Barford Ltd* (1978). But this guidance was expressed to be given as an interim measure pending an authoritative statement of the law by the Court of Appeal or the Court of Session.

It is with diffidence that we approach the task. The rival tests are as follows:

The contract test

On the one hand, it is said that the words of [ERA s 95(1)(c)] express a legal concept which is already well settled in the books on contract under the rubric "discharge by breach". If the employer is guilty of conduct which is a significant breach going to the root of the contract of employment, or which shows that the employer no longer intends to be bound by one or more of the essential terms of the contract, then the employee is entitled to treat himself as discharged from any further performance. If he does so, then he terminates the contract by reason of the employer's conduct. He is constructively dismissed. The employee is entitled in those circumstances to leave at the instant without giving any notice at all or, alternatively, he may give notice and say he is leaving at the end of the notice. But the conduct must in either case be sufficiently serious to entitle him to leave at once. Moreover, he must make up his mind soon after the conduct of which he complains: for, if he continues for any length of time without leaving, he will lose his right to treat himself as discharged. He will be regarded as having elected to affirm the contract.

The unreasonableness test

On the other hand, it is said that the words of [ERA s 95(1)(c)] do not express any settled legal concept. They introduce a new concept into contracts of employment. It is that the employer must act reasonably in his treatment of his employees. If he conducts himself or his affairs so unreasonably that the employee cannot fairly be expected to put up with it any longer, the employee is justified in leaving. He can go, with or without giving notice, and claim compensation for unfair dismissal.

It would seem that this new concept of "unreasonable conduct" is very similar to the concept of "unfairness" as described in TULRA 1974 Sched 1 para 6(8) [see now ERA s 98(4)] which says:

> ". . . the determination of the question whether the dismissal was fair or unfair, having regard to the reason shown by the employer, shall depend on whether the employer can satisfy the tribunal that in the circumstances (having regard to equity and the substantial merits of the case) he acted reasonably in treating it as a sufficient reason for dismissing the employee."

Those who adopt the unreasonableness test for dismissal say quite frankly that it is the same as the "unreasonableness" test for fairness. That was the view taken by Megaw LJ in *Turner* v *London Transport Executive*. He said:

> "So far as (c) is concerned, in my judgment, the wording of this sub-paragraph is not a wording which involves, or implies, the same concept as the common law concept of fundamental breach of a contract resulting in its unilateral repudiation and acceptance of that unilateral repudiation by the innocent party. The employer's 'conduct' here is employer's conduct to be adjudged by the employment tribunal by the criteria which they regard as right and fair in respect of a case in which the issue is whether or not there has been 'unfair' dismissal."

Previous cases

The only previous case in the Court of Appeal on the words is *Marriott* v *Oxford and District Co-operative Society Ltd (No 2)* (1970). It was under the Redundancy Payments Act 1965. Subparagraph (c) did not apply because it only applied where the employee terminated his contract *without* notice; whereas Marriott had terminated it *with* notice. So this court put it on sub-paragraph (a). But since the amendment to the wording of sub-paragraph (c), it would have been more properly brought under sub-para (c). It was not really an (a) case; but we had to stretch it a bit. It was not the employer who terminated the employment. It was the employee; and he was entitled to do so by reason of the employer's conduct.

All the other cases are in the Employment Appeal Tribunal. We have studied them all, but I hope I will be excused from going through them.

The result

In my opinion the contract test is the right test. My reasons are as follows. (i) The Act itself draws a distinction between "dismissal" in [ERA s 95(1)(c)] and "unfairness" in [ERA s 98(4)]. If Parliament intended that same test to apply, it would have said so. (ii) "Dismissal" in [ERA s 95(1)(c)] goes back to "dismissal" in the Redundancy Payments Act 1965. Its interpretation should not be influenced by [ERA s 98(4)] which was introduced first in 1971 in the Industrial Relations Act 1971. (iii) [ERA s 95(1)(c)] uses words which have a legal connotation, especially the words "entitled" and "without notice". If a non-legal connotation were intended, it would have added "justified in leaving at once" or some such non-legal phrase. (iv) [ERA s 95(1)(a) and 95(1)(c)] deal with different situations. [ERA s 95(1)(a)] deals with cases where the employer himself terminates the contract by dismissing the man with or without notice. That is, when the employer says to the man: "You must go". [ERA s 95(1)(c)] deals with the cases where the employee himself terminates the contract by saying: "I can't stand it any longer. I want my cards." (v) The new test of "unreasonable conduct" of the employer is too indefinite by far. It has led to acute difference of opinion between the members of tribunals. Often there are majority opinions. It has led to findings of "constructive dismissal" on the most whimsical grounds. The Employment Appeal Tribunal tells us so. It is better to have the contract test of the common law. It is more certain: as it can well be understood by intelligent laymen under the direction of a legal chairman. (vi) I would adopt the reasoning of the considered judgment of the Employment Appeal Tribunal in *Wetherall (Bond St, W1)* v *Lynn* (1978):

> "Parliament might well have said, in relation to whether the employer's conduct had been reasonable having regard to equity and the substantial merits of the case, but it neither laid down that special statutory criterion or any other. So, in our judgment, the answer can only be, entitled according to law, and it is to the law of contract that you have to look."

(vii) The test of unreasonableness gives no effect to the words "without notice". They impose a legal test which no test of "unreasonableness" can do.

Conclusion

The present case is a good illustration of a "whimsical decision". Applying the test of "unreasonable conduct", the employment tribunal decided by a majority of two to one in favour of the employee. All three members of the Employment Appeal Tribunal would have decided in favour of the employer, but felt that it was a matter of fact on which they could not reverse the employment tribunal. So, counting heads, it was four to two in favour of the employers, but yet the case was decided against them – because of the test of "unreasonable conduct".

If the contract test had been applied, the result would have been plain. There was no dismissal, constructive or otherwise, by the employers. The employers were not in breach at all. Nor had they repudiated the contract at all. The employee left of his own accord without anything wrong done by the employers. His claim should have been rejected. The decision against the employers was most unjust to them. I would allow the appeal accordingly.'

(Lawton and Eveleigh LJJ agreed.)

Comment

(1) Lord Denning's argument is compelling as a matter of statutory interpretation; however, many commentators have argued for a reasonableness test (was the employee justified in leaving?) rather than a contractual test (was the employer in fundamental breach of contract?) See, for example, Hepple (1986, pp 79–83); Collins (1992a, pp 44–5).

(2) At the same time, there is a strong view that reasonableness has come in through the back door, through the development of the implied term of mutual trust and confidence. The evolution of this implied term was tracked in Chapter 4 (pp 182–189), where the point was made that almost all the cases dealing with it were cases where employees were claiming that they had been constructively dismissed. The argument goes that if employers behave unreasonably, even though it is not possible to point to a specific breach of contract, they may be found to have acted in such a way as to undermine mutual trust and confidence – and that will be a fundamental breach of contract.

(3) Note that, since the introduction of the Statutory Grievance Procedure in 2004 (below, p 385) a claim for constructive dismissal cannot be made to an employment tribunal before the claimant has complied with that procedure, which in most cases means setting out the grievance in writing and then waiting 28 days before initiating a claim.

(4) A resignation which is not a response to a fundamental breach of contract by the employer will not constitute dismissal. Nor will other modes of termination of the contract which fall outside the statutory definition. These will be examined next.

Resignation and termination by mutual agreement

Sheffield v Oxford Controls Co Ltd [1979] ICR 396 Employment Appeal Tribunal

Sheffield was employed as a director of the defendant company, in which he also held shares. The majority of the shares were held by his co-director and the co-director's wife. Sheffield's wife, who also worked for the company, had a dispute with the co-director's wife and was threatened with dismissal as a result. In an acrimonious discussion, Sheffield threatened to resign if his wife was dismissed. He was asked how much he wanted to go, and eventually a figure of £10,000 was agreed upon. It seems that it was also made clear to him that if he did not resign he would be dismissed. Sheffield agreed to go in return for the payment, but later brought an action for unfair dismissal claiming that he had been forced to resign.

ARNOLD J: '. . . The principle of law has been stated in a number of cases. So far as we know we have been referred to all of them. They start with *East Sussex County Council v Walker* (1972) in the National Industrial Relations Court. That was a case about a school cook. What had happened there was that the cook was invited to resign; that it was indicated to her that her contract was to be terminated and that such determination should be brought about by her own letter of resignation; and that she wrote a letter of resignation. Those are the only relevant facts. Giving the judgment of the court, Brightman J said:

> "In our judgment, if an employee is told that she is no longer required in her employment and is expressly invited to resign, a court of law is entitled to come to the conclusion that, as a matter of commonsense, the employee was dismissed within the meaning of what was then s 3 of the Redundancy Payments Act 1965."

That being a case in fact about a redundancy payment, since the reason why the cook was invited to resign was that she had become redundant. Then the judge went on:

> "Suppose that the employer says to the employee, 'Your job is finished; I will give you the opportunity to resign. If you don't you'll be sacked.' How, we would ask, is it possible to reach a conclusion other than that the employment is being terminated by the employer even though the employee takes the first and more respectable alternative of signing a letter of resignation rather than being the recipient of a letter of dismissal? We feel that in such circumstances there really can be no other conclusion than that the employer terminated the contract."

. . . So, we find that there was the sort of threat which is referred to in the decided cases; and the question is, what is the legal consequence of that finding?

The employment tribunal concludes, in the course of their reasons, that as a result of what they describe as the shameful treatment meted out to the employee and Mrs Sheffield by the Raisons, the employee was, at the stage at which he initialled the heads of agreement, prepared to bow out of the industry in which they were all engaged "and the heads of agreement represent the terms upon which he was prepared to agree to terminate his employment with the company". The employment tribunal support that by the observation:

> "Mrs Sheffield was not prepared to resign as she had been asked to do until he [Mr Sheffield] had agreed terms satisfactory to himself but directly he had, and had initialled the heads of agreement, she signed her resignation letter."

It is plain, we think, that there must exist a principle, exemplified by the four cases to which we have referred, that where an employee resigns and that resignation is determined upon by him because he prefers to resign rather than to be dismissed (the alternative having been expressed to him by the employer in the terms of the threat that if he does not resign he will be dismissed), the mechanics of the resignation do not cause that to be other than a dismissal. The cases do not in terms go further than that. We find the principle to be one of causation. In cases such as that which we have just hypothesised, and those reported, the causation is the threat. It is the existence of the threat which causes the employee to be willing to sign, and to sign, a resignation later or to be willing to give, and to give, the oral resignation. But where that willingness is brought about by other considerations and the actual causation of the resignation is no longer the threat which has been made but is the state of mind of the resigning employee, that he is willing and content to resign on the terms which he has negotiated and which are satisfactory to him, then we think there is no room for the principle to be derived from the decided cases. In such a case he resigns because he is willing to resign as the result of being offered terms which are to him satisfactory terms on which to resign. He is no longer impelled or compelled by the threat of dismissal to resign, but a new matter has come into the history, namely that he has been brought into a condition of mind in which the threat is no longer the operative factor of his decision; it has been replaced by the emergence of terms which are satisfactory. Therefore we think that the finding that the employee had agreed to terms upon which he was prepared to agree to terminate his employment with the employers – terms which were satisfactory to him – means that there is no room for the principle and that it is impossible to upset the conclusion of the tribunal that he was not dismissed.'

Comment

(1) Whether or not the employee left because of the threat of dismissal or because of an inducement will be finely balanced at times, and will usually be treated as a question of fact for the employment tribunal.

(2) The position with termination 'by mutual agreement' is much the same. The question will be whether the agreement was genuine – and this will depend on whether the employee simply agreed in order to avoid being dismissed, or whether she received an inducement which caused her to agree.

(3) As we will see, the definition of dismissal for the purpose of redundancy claims is the same as for unfair dismissal. In the case of voluntary redundancies, it was held in the unusual circumstances of *Birch* v *University of Liverpool* (1985) that the termination was by mutual agreement (the employees had received a very good severance package which was stated to include any statutory redundancy entitlement). Similarly, in *AGCO Ltd* v *Massey Ferguson Pension Trust Ltd* (2003) the Court of Appeal held that voluntary redundancies were not 'at the request of the employer' but could be regarded as a kind of mutually agreed termination. However, usually this situation will count as dismissal, even if there are enhanced severance payments. The employee is to be taken as having volunteered to be dismissed, not to have resigned.

(4) As with dismissal by an employer, if an employee speaks ambiguous words of resignation, or says in anger that she is leaving, the issue is what was intended by the words, and whether a reasonable employer would have understood them as being a termination of the contract (see *Sovereign House Security* v *Savage* (1989)).

(5) Also by analogy with the concept of dismissal, at one time it was argued that tribunals should recognise a concept of 'constructive resignation', which should not count as dismissal. This was dealt with definitively in the next case.

London Transport Executive v *Clarke* [1981] ICR 355 Court of Appeal

TEMPLEMAN LJ: 'The first question raised by this appeal is whether a contract of employment was terminated by the respondent employee, Mr Clarke, or by the appellant employers, London Transport Executive. If the contract was terminated by the employee within the meaning of [ERA s 95] then he is not entitled to claim compensation for unfair dismissal. If the contract was terminated by the employers, then compensation is payable unless the employers have proved that Mr Clarke was fairly dismissed.

The employee absented himself from work for seven weeks without leave and it is agreed that by his conduct he repudiated his contract of employment. After he had been absent for four weeks, the employers took him off their books of employees and wrote to him to say so. The question is whether the contract of employment was terminated by the employee's conduct or by the employers' acceptance of his conduct as a repudiation of the contract.

The general rule is that a repudiated contract is not terminated unless and until the repudiation is accepted by the innocent party: see *Boston Deep Sea Fishing & Ice Co* v *Ansell* (1888).

That case itself illustrates that contracts of employment cannot provide a general exemption to that rule because it would be manifestly unjust to allow a wrongdoer to determine a contract by repudiatory breach if the innocent party wished to affirm the contract for good reason. Thus in *Thomas Marshall* v *Guinle* (1978), which contains a full discussion of principles and of the conflicting authorities, a contract of employment was repudiated by the employee. The court could not enforce specific performance of the contract for personal services, but Sir Robert Megarry VC enforced against the wrongdoing employee at the behest of the innocent employer who had not accepted the repudiation a confidentiality and non-competition obligation which was only effective during the continuance of the contract. Repudiation cannot determine a contract of service or any other contract while there exists a reason and an opportunity for the innocent party to affirm the contract.

Mr Scrivener, who appeared for the employers, argued that a contract of employment was an exception to the general rule that a repudiated contract is only determined by the acceptance and not by the repudiation. If there was no exception at common law, there is at any rate, he argued, an exception for the purposes of the [ERA] so that a worker can determine a contract of employment by repudiating that contract. It is plain from the Act that an employer can determine a contract by the employer's breaches of contract, which give good reason for the worker to leave the employment, whether the worker gives notice or not; the conduct of the employer produces constructive dismissal, which by [ERA s 95(1)(c)] constitutes a termination of the contract of employment by the employer. Similarly, says Mr Scrivener, although the Act does not expressly so provide, a worker who walks out or commits some similar breach of contract which is so fundamental that it amounts to a repudiation of the contract on his part is guilty of self-dismissal and in these circumstances it is the worker who terminates the contract and not the employer who can only stand helplessly by.

I can see no reason why a contract of employment or services should be determined by repudiation and not by the acceptance of repudiation. The argument has little practical importance at common law. The only difference which would exist at common law between self-dismissal and accepted repudiation is that self-dismissal would determine the contract when the worker walked out or otherwise committed a repudiatory breach of the contract whereas accepted repudiation determines the contract when the employer expressly or impliedly gives notice to the worker that the employer accepts the repudiation and does not wish to affirm the contract. But, in practice, at common law self-dismissal and acceptance of repudiation in contracts of service are usually simultaneous both being implied rather than express where affirmation of the contract would be meaningless; in any event, they involve similar consequences in almost all cases. A difficulty, however, arises under the [ERA] if Mr Scrivener's argument of a special category of determination of a contract by self-dismissal is correct. When a worker commits a breach of contract, neither he nor the employer nor in the final analysis the employment tribunal may be entirely clear whether the breach is repudiatory or not. Whatever the nature of the breach, the worker may seek expressly or impliedly to persuade the employer to affirm the contract and to allow the worker to continue in or resume his employment. If the employer does not allow the worker to continue or resume his employment, then if Mr Scrivener is right an employment tribunal must first decide whether the worker's breach of contract is repudiatory or not. If the breach of contract is so fundamental as to be repudiatory of the contract, then the tribunal must decide whether the repudiatory act is of a special kind which amounts to self-dismissal. If these matters are decided in favour of the employer, then the tribunal is not authorised to consider whether in the circumstances the refusal of the employer to affirm the contract and to allow the worker to continue or resume employment is fair or unfair unless, despite the finding of self-dismissal, the worker is able to establish conduct on the part of the employer which converts self-dismissal into constructive dismissal. If the tribunal decide that the breach of contract by the worker was not repudiatory or if the tribunal decide that the repudiatory breach was not of the special kind which amounts to self-dismissal, then they must conclude that the contract was terminated by the employer and they must then consider whether the employer satisfies the onus of proving that the termination of the contract which amounts to dismissal was in fact fair dismissal.

These complications arise, and only arise, if there is grafted on to the old common law rule that a repudiated contract is only terminated by acceptance, an exception in the case of contracts of employment. In my view any such exception is contrary to principle, unsupported by authority binding on this court and undesirable in practice. If a worker walks out of his job and does not thereafter claim to be entitled to resume work, then he repudiates his contract and the employer accepts that repudiation by taking no action to affirm the contract. No question of unfair dismissal can arise unless the worker claims that he was constructively dismissed. If a worker walks out of his job or commits any other breach of contract, repudiatory or otherwise, but at any time claims that he is entitled to resume or to continue his work, then his contract of employment is only determined if the employer expressly or impliedly asserts and accepts repudiation on the part of the worker. Acceptance can take the form of formal writing or can take the form of refusing to allow the worker to resume or continue his work. Where the contract of employment is determined by the employer purporting to accept repudiation on the part of the worker, the tribunal must decide whether the worker has been unfairly dismissed.

In my judgment, the acceptance by an employer of repudiation by a worker who wishes to continue his employment notwithstanding his repudiatory conduct constitutes the determination of the contract of employment by the employer; the employer relying on the repudiatory conduct of the worker must satisfy the tribunal in the words of [ERA s 98(4)] that in the circumstances, having regard to equity and the substantial merits of the case, the employer acted reasonably in treating the repudiatory conduct as sufficient reason for accepting repudiation and thus determining the contract.

In the present case the employee absented himself for seven weeks for what he no doubt considered was a good reason. The employers considered that the employee absented himself for a bad reason. After one month had elapsed the employers decided not to allow the employee to resume his work if and when he reported back and they wrote to the employee informing him of their decision. The employers thereby determined the employee's contract of employment and the question for the tribunal was whether he had been unfairly dismissed. . . .'

(Dunn LJ agreed; Lord Denning MR dissented.)

Comment

(1) This decision is so clearly right, it is surprising to find that there were conflicting EAT decisions before it settled the matter. One of the major features of unfair dismissal law is that a dismissal may be unfair even though the employer would have been justified in dismissing at common law, and vice versa. Had the concept of constructive resignation or self-dismissal been accepted, then the opportunity for tribunals to review the fairness of numbers of dismissals on grounds of misconduct would have been in doubt, for employers would have been able to argue that the misconduct was a fundamental breach and thus a self-dismissal.

(2) There are certain situations which at common law would either terminate the contract of employment automatically or operate as a frustrating event for which special provision is made by statute. First, where a company is dissolved, or an employer who is an individual dies, for the purposes of redundancy law the employee will be treated as having been dismissed and may be entitled to a redundancy payment (ERA s 136(5); see Chapter 9). Secondly, where a partnership is dissolved either through the death or retirement of a partner, the employee will be deemed to have been dismissed for redundancy unless taken on by the successors to the original partnership (ERA s 139(4)).

Frustration

The final situation to be considered where the contract of employment may be terminated without it counting as a dismissal for the purposes of unfair dismissal is frustration. This is a common law doctrine applicable to all kinds of contracts and it provides that where a contract becomes impossible to perform without the fault of either party, then both parties are discharged from further obligations under the contract.

Poussard v *Spiers and Pond* (1876) 1 QBD 410 Divisional Court

Madame Poussard was engaged to sing the principal female part in an opera at the Criterion Theatre. She was taken ill during the rehearsal period and was therefore unable to attend the final rehearsals or to perform on the opening night. The producers arranged for a substitute to cover the part on the basis that if the substitute was called on to perform on the opening night, she would then be given the engagement for the rest of the scheduled performances.

Mme Poussard had recovered sufficiently to perform by the fifth performance, but by that time the substitute had been promised all the performances. Her husband, who was also her agent, therefore brought this action alleging that the producers were in breach of contract.

The judgment of the court (Blackburn, Quain and Field JJ) was delivered by Blackburn J.

BLACKBURN J: '... We think that, from the nature of the engagement to take a leading, and, indeed, the principal female part (for the prima donna sang her part in male costume as the Prince de Conti) in a new opera which (as appears from the terms of the engagement) it was known might run for a longer or shorter time, and so be a profitable or losing concern to the defendants, we can, without the aid of the jury, see that it must have been of great importance to the defendants that the piece should start well, and consequently that the failure of the claimant's wife to be able to perform on the opening and early performances was a very serious detriment to them.

This inability having been occasioned by sickness was not any breach of contract by the claimant, and no action can lie against him for the failure thus occasioned. But the damage to the defendants and the consequent failure of consideration is just as great as if it had been occasioned by the claimant's fault, instead of by his wife's misfortune . . .

Now, in the present case, we must consider what were the courses open to the defendants under the circumstances. They might, it was said on the argument before us (though not on the trial), have postponed the bringing out of the piece till the recovery of Madame Poussard, and if her illness had been a temporary hoarseness incapacitating her from singing on the Saturday, but sure to be removed by the Monday, that might have been a proper course to pursue. But the illness here was a serious one, of uncertain duration, and if the claimant had at the trial suggested that this was the proper course, it would, no doubt, have been shewn that it would have been a ruinous course; and that it would have been much better to have abandoned the piece altogether than to have postponed it from day to day for an uncertain time, during which the theatre would have been a heavy loss.

The remaining alternatives were to employ a temporary substitute until such time as the claimant's wife should recover; and if a temporary substitute capable of performing the part adequately could have been obtained upon such a precarious engagement on any reasonable terms, that would have been a right course to pursue; but if no substitute capable of performing the part adequately could be obtained, except on the terms that she should be permanently engaged at higher pay than the claimant's wife, in our opinion it follows, as a matter of law, that the failure on the claimant's part went to the root of the matter and discharged the defendants.

We think, therefore, that the fifth question put to the jury, and answered by them in favour of the defendants, does find all the facts necessary to enable us to decide as a matter of law that the defendants are discharged . . .'

Comment

(1) This was a contract for services rather than a contract of employment: however, it is taken as the original authority for the proposition that the doctrine of frustration can apply to contracts of employment. If a contract is discharged in this way, then it is not terminated by either party and there is no dismissal for the purposes of an unfair dismissal claim.

(2) There are two main situations in which it is commonly claimed that the contract of employment is frustrated: first, where the employee is prevented from performing through illness or accident (as in *Poussard* v *Spiers & Pond*), and secondly, where the employee has been sentenced to a term of imprisonment. In relation to illness, guidance was given in the following case.

Egg Stores Ltd v *Leibovici* [1977] ICR 260 Employment Appeal Tribunal

An employee of 15 years' standing was injured in a road accident and was unfit to work for five months. He received sick pay for the first two months. When he asked to return to work the employers refused, because they had got a replacement for him. He claimed unfair dismissal, but the employers argued that they had not dismissed him, but that the contract had been frustrated.

PHILLIPS J: '. . . it is obvious from this and other cases that the doctrine of frustration causes considerable difficulties. Accordingly, it may not be out of place if we add a word or two by way of assistance to the employment tribunal which will have to decide the matter, and possibly to other employment tribunals in other cases.

In general, we would adopt and endorse the statement of the law by Sir John Donaldson in the National Industrial Relations Court in *Marshall* v *Harland & Wolff Ltd* (1972). It should be stressed (as is explained in that case, and as we have already stated in this judgment) that for frustration to be established it is not necessary to be able to show that the employers have taken some action in respect of it. The contract is terminated automatically by the event giving rise to frustration.

That being said, there is no doubt that difficulties in applying the doctrine do occur in the case of those contracts of employment which can be determined at short notice. In the case of a fixed-term contract of substantial length, no question can arise of the employer's terminating the contract and the doctrine of frustration is necessary if it has become impossible for the employee to continue to perform the contract. In the case of short-term periodic contracts of employment different considerations apply. Subject to the provisions of the [ERA], the employer can terminate the contract of employment at short notice, and, if he does so, the only question will be whether in the circumstances such dismissal was unfair. This will usually turn on the question whether the time has been reached when the employer cannot be expected to wait any longer before permanently filling the absent employee's post. *Marshall* v *Harland & Wolff Ltd*, though of great value as a general statement of the law, perhaps does not deal in practical terms with the questions which will arise when frustration is considered in respect of such short-term periodic contracts. The question to be decided is summarised in that case in these words:

> "The question is and remains: 'Was the employee's incapacity, looked at before the pur-ported dismissal, of such a nature, or did it appear likely to continue for such a period, that further performance of his obligations in the future would either be impossible or would be a thing radically different from that undertaken by him and accepted by the employer under the agreed terms of his employment?'"

That is helpful, but one needs to know in what kind of circumstances can it be said that further performance of his obligations in the future will be impossible? It seems to us that an important question to be asked in cases such as the present – we are not suggesting that it is the only question – is: "has the time arrived when the employer can no longer reasonably be expected to keep the absent employee's post open for him?" It will thus be seen that the sort of question which has to be considered when it is being decided whether a dismissal in such circumstances was unfair, and that which has to be considered when deciding whether the con-tract has been frustrated, are not dissimilar. For this reason, though we think that the employ-ment tribunal was wrong in what it stated in paragraph 10 about the consequences of the failure of the employers to take steps to terminate the employee's employment, we are not saying that in deciding whether a contract of employment has been frustrated it is irrelevant to consider what action the employer has taken or considered. Often it will be extremely relevant to note that the employer has not thought it right to dismiss the absent employee. The reason may be that he does not think that a sufficient length of time has elapsed to make it a proper course to take. If so, that view, represented by his failure to take action, will be one (but not the only) fact to be taken into consideration in deciding whether the contract has been frustrated.

It is possible to divide into two kinds the events relied upon as bringing about the frustration of a short-term periodic contract of employment. There may be an event (eg a crippling acci-dent) so dramatic and shattering that everyone concerned will realise immediately that to all intents and purposes the contract must be regarded as at an end. Or there may be an event, such as illness or accident, the course and outcome of which is uncertain. It may be a long pro-cess before one is able to say whether the event is such as to bring about the frustration of the contract. But there *will* have been frustration of the contract, even though at the time of the event the outcome was uncertain, if the time arrives when, looking back, one can say that at some point (even if it is not possible to say precisely when) matters had gone on so long, and the prospects for the future were so poor, that it was no longer practical to regard the contract as still subsisting. Among the matters to be taken into account in such a case in reaching a decision are these: (1) the length of the previous employment; (2) how long it had been expected that the employment would continue; (3) the nature of the job; (4) the nature, length and effect of the illness or disabling event; (5) the need of the employer for the work to be done, and the need for a replacement to do it; (6) the risk to the employer of acquiring obligations in respect of redundancy payments or compensation for unfair dismissal to the replacement employee; (7) whether wages have continued to be paid; (8) the acts and the statements of the employer in relation to the employment, including the dismissal of, or failure to dismiss, the employee; and (9) whether in all the circumstances a reasonable employer could be expected to wait any longer.'

(The case was remitted to a different tribunal for rehearing.)

Comment

(1) It will be seen that the guidance for judging whether an employer has unfairly dismissed an employee on grounds of illness is very similar to this, which raises the question of whether it is appropriate to use the doctrine of frustration at all in relation to this kind of situation. The arguments against treating this as a non-dismissal are the same as the arguments against allowing a concept of constructive resignation: namely, that it deprives the tribunal of an opportunity of reviewing the employer's decision (which is effectively what it is). Hence some commentators have argued that common law concepts such as frustration should not be used in interpreting a statutory labour code (see, for example, Hepple (1986); Collins (1992, pp 44–5)). However, such arguments were rejected by the Court of Appeal in *Notcutt* v *Universal Equipment* (1986).

(2) Despite *Notcutt* v *Universal Equipment*, cases in recent years show courts reluctant to find the contract of employment has been frustrated by the employee's absence: see, for example, *Villella* v *MFI* (1999), *Four Seasons Healthcare* v *Maughan* (2005) and *Gryf-Lowczowski* v *Hinchingbrooke Healthcare NHS Trust* (2006).

(3) A frustrating event is defined as one which occurs without the fault of either party. But a sentence of imprisonment which prevents an employee fulfilling her contract must involve fault on her part: does this mean that the contract is not frustrated?

Note that if this seemingly logical argument were accepted, it would mean that the employee would be better off through having been at fault in relation to the ending of the contract than if she had not been at fault. For if the contract was genuinely frustrated, she would not be able to bring an unfair dismissal claim, but if she can successfully argue that she was at fault, she must have been dismissed through the employer refusing to hold the contract open.

(4) It was largely because of this 'affront to common sense' that when the Court of Appeal was faced with this question in *FC Shepherd & Co Ltd* v *Jerrom* (1986), the judges held that the contract was capable of being frustrated by a term of imprisonment.

Procedural requirements before dismissal

We will see shortly that the concept of 'unfairness' in unfair dismissal has a technical meaning which does not always cohere with what we might think of as fair or unfair in ordinary parlance. But, as in other areas of law, it is possible to distinguish two major elements of just treatment: whether the outcome is actually fair to the parties (substantive justice) and whether the decision has been arrived at in a fair manner (procedural justice). Some elements of procedural justice are now statutory requirements and an employer who does not comply with them before reaching a decision to dismiss an employee may find that the dismissal is unfair for that reason alone. These requirements will therefore be considered before looking at the concept of fairness in detail.

The right to be accompanied

Employment Relations Act 1999

10 (1) This section applies where a worker –
   (a) is required or invited by his employer to attend a disciplinary or grievance hearing, and
   (b) reasonably requests to be accompanied at the hearing.

(2A) Where this section applies, the employer must permit the worker to be accompanied at the hearing by one companion who –
   (a) is chosen by the worker; and
   (b) is within subsection (3).

(2B) The employer must permit the worker's companion to –
   (a) address the hearing in order to do any or all of the following –
      (i) put the worker's case;
      (ii) sum up that case;
      (iii) respond on the worker's behalf to any view expressed at the hearing;
   (b) confer with the worker during the hearing.

(2C) Subsection (2B) does not require the employer to permit the worker's companion to –
   (a) answer questions on behalf of the worker;
   (b) address the hearing if the worker indicates at it that he does not wish his companion to do so; or
   (c) use the powers conferred by that subsection in a way that prevents the employer from explaining his case or prevents any other person at the hearing from making his contribution to it.

(3) A person is within this subsection if he is –
   (a) employed by a trade union of which he is an official within the meaning of sections 1 and 119 of the Trade Union and Labour Relations (Consolidation) Act 1992,
   (b) an official of a trade union (within that meaning) whom the union has reasonably certified in writing as having experience of, or as having received training in, acting as a worker's companion at disciplinary or grievance hearings, or
   (c) another of the employer's workers. . . .

Comment

(1) Note that this right applies to workers, not just employees, defined in ERelA 1999 s 13 as including agency workers and home workers. Guidance on the right is given in section 3 of the Acas *Code of Practice on Disciplinary and Grievance Procedures* (2004).

(2) Subsections (2A)–(2C) were added by ERelA 2004 to clarify the scope of the companion's role. A fellow worker cannot be compelled to act as a companion, but if she does, she is entitled to time off with pay to carry out the role and will be protected from retaliatory action from the employer by way of detriment or dismissal for performing it.

(3) Failure to allow a worker to be accompanied gives rise to an independent right to complain to a tribunal, resulting in an award of up to two weeks' pay (ERelA 1999 s 11(3)).

(4) The main question that arises in relation to the right to be accompanied is, to what hearings does it apply?

Acas *Code of Practice on Disciplinary and Grievance Procedures* (2004)

WHAT IS A DISCIPLINARY HEARING?

97 For the purposes of this right, disciplinary hearings are defined as meetings that could result in:
   - a formal warning being issued to a worker (ie a warning that will be placed on the worker's record);
   - the taking of some other disciplinary action (such as suspension without pay, demotion or dismissal) or other action; or
   - the confirmation of a warning or some other disciplinary action (such as an appeal hearing).

98 The right to be accompanied will also apply to any disciplinary meetings held as part of the statutory dismissal and disciplinary procedures. This includes any meetings held after an employee has left employment.

99 Informal discussions or counselling sessions do not attract the right to be accompanied unless they could result in formal warnings or other actions. Meetings to investigate an issue are not disciplinary hearings. If it becomes clear during the course of such a meeting that disciplinary action is called for, the meeting should be ended and a formal hearing arranged at which the worker will have the right to be accompanied.

WHAT IS A GRIEVANCE HEARING?

100 For the purposes of this right, a grievance hearing is a meeting at which an employer deals with a complaint about a duty owed by them to a worker, whether the duty arises from statute or common law (for example contractual commitments).

101 For instance, an individual's request for a pay rise is unlikely to fall within the definition, unless a right to an increase is specifically provided for in the contract or the request raises an issue about equal pay. Equally, most employers will be under no legal duty to provide their workers with car parking facilities, and a grievance about such facilities would carry no right to be accompanied at a hearing by a companion. However, if a worker were disabled and needed a car to get to and from work, they probably would be entitled to a companion at a grievance hearing, as an issue might arise as to whether the employer was meeting its obligations under the Disability Discrimination Act 1995.

102 The right to be accompanied will also apply to any meetings held as part of the statutory grievance procedures. This includes any meetings after the employee has left employment.

Comment

(1) In *Heathmill Multimedia Asp Ltd* v *Jones* (2003) the EAT held that a meeting to tell employees that they were to be made redundant was not a disciplinary hearing within the meaning of ERelA 1999 s 10. See also *London Underground Ltd* v *Ferenc-Batchelor* (2003) (meeting resulting in an 'informal oral warning' to be recorded on the employee's file was a disciplinary hearing) and *Skiggs* v *South West Trains Ltd* (2005).

(2) Employers will no doubt heave a sigh of relief that grievances about car parking facilities are not within the statutory definition.

Statutory dispute resolution procedures

Routes to Resolution DTI consultation paper (2001)

1.2   Employers and employees inevitably, at times, disagree over issues in the workplace and disputes arise. This consultation paper is about disputes between employers and individual employees. Such disputes generally arise where an individual is aggrieved by a management decision or incident in the workplace or when they feel they have been treated unfairly.

1.3   In most businesses, employment disputes do not escalate into a claim to an employment tribunal. Only 20% of workplaces have had a tribunal claim made against them in the last five years. But there is worrying evidence that employees are increasingly resorting to litigation to sort out workplace disputes. Sixty four per cent of applications to employment tribunals come from employees who have not attempted to resolve the problem directly with their employer in the first instance. But equally 60% of small employers who are facing a tribunal claim have no internal disciplinary or grievance procedures.

1.4   Claims to tribunals have trebled since 1990. This could be the tip of the iceberg. Only 15–25% of disputes which involve a breach of legal rights are believed to go to a tribunal. The reasons for the increases in tribunal claims are complex. It is suggested both that the higher levels of stress arising from increasing competitive pressures and an increased propensity to take legal action are the trends which underlie the increase. Certainly the increase has been across older employment tribunal jurisdictions such as unlawful deductions from wages and unfair dismissal, as well as coming from the introduction of new legislation such as the Working Time Regulations.

　　　...

1.7   Recourse to litigation as a first resort to solve workplace disputes is neither good for business nor the individual. Tribunal cases create uncertainty and stress for both parties. By the time the hearing is reached, it is common for the employment relationship to have broken down irretrievably. The remedies which may be most eagerly sought, such as an apology or moving a harasser to another post, are not available from the legal process.

1.8   For individuals, career prospects are damaged. Half of tribunal applicants report lower status or lower paid employment after taking their case to tribunal. Twenty three per cent are unemployed at the end of the case.

1.9   For employers, scarce management time is lost as well as the costs of defending the case. The average cost to the employer of each application is around £2,000, but this varies widely depending on the complexity of the case and the amount of advice and representation the employer seeks. In addition, recruiting a new employee typically costs £3,500. This does not take into account the investment made in training, which is lost if a skilled employee leaves the workplace. Workplace relations, employee morale and the organisation's reputation as an employer also suffer. In a tight labour market, the effect of the latter could be significant, even if the case is successfully defended.

1.10   These problems can be reduced through better dispute handling in the workplace, and greater focus on conciliation, ahead of litigation. Employment tribunals should take their proper place as the backstop to enforce individual employment rights.

Comment

(1) This extract from the government's 2001 consultation paper on individual employment dispute resolution gives a clear flavour of the driving force behind it: essentially, to reduce costs. While the opening chapter emphasises costs to the employer and (to some extent) employee, the report later points out that the cost of running the Employment Tribunal Service was £51.7 million at that date.

(2) The solution decided on was to introduce statutory dismissal and disciplinary procedures and statutory grievance procedures which parties would be required to use. The procedures were outlined in the Employment Act 2002 and further detail was given in the Employment Act 2002 (Dispute Resolution) Regulations 2004. The procedures came into force in October 2004 and quickly became universally unpopular.

Statutory dismissal and disciplinary procedures

Employment Act 2002

SCHEDULE 2

Part 1 Dismissal and Disciplinary Procedures

Chapter 1 Standard Procedure

Step 1: statement of grounds for action and invitation to meeting
1 (1) The employer must set out in writing the employee's alleged conduct or characteristics, or other circumstances, which lead him to contemplate dismissing or taking disciplinary action against the employee.
(2) The employer must send the statement or a copy of it to the employee and invite the employee to attend a meeting to discuss the matter.

Step 2: meeting
2 (1) The meeting must take place before action is taken, except in the case where the disciplinary action consists of suspension.
(2) The meeting must not take place unless—
   (a) the employer has informed the employee what the basis was for including in the statement under paragraph 1(1) the ground or grounds given in it, and
   (b) the employee has had a reasonable opportunity to consider his response to that information.
(3) The employee must take all reasonable steps to attend the meeting.
(4) After the meeting, the employer must inform the employee of his decision and notify him of the right to appeal against the decision if he is not satisfied with it.

Step 3: appeal
3 (1) If the employee does wish to appeal, he must inform the employer.
(2) If the employee informs the employer of his wish to appeal, the employer must invite him to attend a further meeting.
(3) The employee must take all reasonable steps to attend the meeting.
(4) The appeal meeting need not take place before the dismissal or disciplinary action takes effect.
(5) After the appeal meeting, the employer must inform the employee of his final decision.

381

Comment

(1) This is the standard, three-step procedure which must be applied to those disciplinary proceedings within the purview of the statutory dismissal and disciplinary procedures. Not all dismissals and not all disciplinary action is covered.

(2) The categories which are not covered are set out in the Dispute Regulations.

Employment Act 2002 (Dispute Resolution) Regulations 2004

2 Interpretation

(1) . . .

"relevant disciplinary action" means action, short of dismissal, which the employer asserts to be based wholly or mainly on the employee's conduct or capability, other than suspension on full pay or the issuing of warnings (whether oral or written) . . .

4 Dismissals to which the dismissal and disciplinary procedures do not apply

(1)   Neither of the dismissal and disciplinary procedures applies in relation to the dismissal of an employee where –
  (a)   all the employees of a description or in a category to which the employee belongs are dismissed, provided that the employer offers to re-engage all the employees so dismissed either before or upon the termination of their contracts;
  (b)   the dismissal is one of a number of dismissals in respect of which the duty in TULRCA s 188 (duty of employer to consult representatives when proposing to dismiss as redundant a certain number of employees) applies;
  (c)   at the time of the employee's dismissal he is taking part in –
    (i)   an unofficial strike or other unofficial industrial action, or
    (ii)   a strike or other industrial action (being neither unofficial industrial action nor protected industrial action), unless the circumstances of the dismissal are such that, by virtue of TULRCA s 238(2), an employment tribunal is entitled to determine whether the dismissal was fair or unfair;
  (d)   the reason (or, if more than one, the principal reason) for the dismissal is that the employee took protected industrial action and the dismissal would be regarded, by virtue of TULRCA s 238A(2), as unfair for the purposes of ERA Part 10;
  (e)   the employer's business suddenly ceases to function, because of an event unforeseen by the employer, with the result that it is impractical for him to employ any employees;
  (f)   the reason (or, if more than one principal reason) for the dismissal is that the employee could not continue to work in the position which he held without contravention (either on his part or on that of his employer) of a duty or restriction imposed by or under any enactment; or
  (g)   the employee is one to whom a dismissal procedures agreement designated by an order under ERA s 110 applies at the date of dismissal; or
  (h)   the reason (or, if more than one, the principal reason) for the dismissal is retirement of the employee (to be determined in accordance with ERA ss 98ZA to 98ZF).

Comment

(1) The exclusion of suspension on full pay and warnings from the requirement to follow the procedure was controversial, but justified by the government on the basis that the statutory procedures are meant to be minimum procedures only. It should also be

noted that if the employer fails to follow the statutory procedure in relation to disciplinary action short of dismissal the employee has no independent remedy. So far, the government has decided against exercising the power in the Employment Act 2002 s 30 to incorporate the procedures into the contract of employment.

(2) There is a modified, two-step procedure which applies where the dismissal has already taken place. However, an employer can only get away with using it if compliant with the following conditions (Dispute Regulations reg 3(2)):

- it is a summary dismissal on grounds of misconduct;
- the employer dismissed the employee at the time of becoming aware of the misconduct, or immediately thereafter;
- it was a justified summary dismissal;
- it was reasonable in the circumstances to dismiss the employee before making further enquiries.

This last condition means that the use of the modified procedure will rarely be acceptable. As the Acas Code of Practice says: 'It is a core principle of reasonable behaviour that employers should give employees the opportunity of putting their case at a disciplinary meeting before deciding whether to take action' (para 36).

(3) If an employer dismisses an employee in breach of the statutory dismissal and disciplinary procedure, the dismissal is automatically unfair (ERA s 98A(1)). The employee is entitled to a basic award of at least four weeks' pay (unless this would result in injustice to the employer) (ERA s 120(1A), (1B)). Furthermore, the compensatory award will be increased by between 10 and 50 per cent (EA 2002 s 31).

(4) If the statutory procedure is not followed and this is due to the employee's fault, her compensation if she wins the unfair dismissal case will be reduced by between 10 and 50 per cent.

(5) Guidance on compliance with the statutory procedure was given by an Employment Appeal Tribunal presided over by its President in the next case.

Alexander v *Bridgen Enterprises Ltd* [2006] IRLR 422 Employment Appeal Tribunal

The company needed to take drastic action to deal with financial problems. It was decided that ten welders would have to be made redundant. Selection criteria were drawn up and the welders were scored against each of them. The two appellants in this case got the lowest scores. The welders were sent a letter saying that their jobs were at risk and calling them to a 'consultation meeting' on 12 January at which the criteria were outlined to them. On 21 January there was a further meeting at which the appellants were told that they had been selected for redundancy. Only as they left that meeting were they given a document detailing their scores against the criteria. They argued that their dismissals were automatically unfair because the employer had failed to comply with the statutory dismissal and disciplinary procedures.

ELIAS J: '. . . The issue, therefore, is what information ought to be provided to an employee in order for the employer to comply with the statutory obligation. In answering that question, it seems to us that there are three matters in particular which should inform the answer, although they do not all point in the same direction.

First, the purpose of these statutory procedures is to seek to prevent the matter going to an employment tribunal if possible by providing the opportunity for differences to be resolved internally at an earlier stage: see the observations in *Canary Wharf Management Ltd* v *Edebi* (2006). Hence the reason why these procedures apply at the stage when dismissals are still only proposed and before they have taken effect. However, to achieve that purpose the information to be provided must be at least sufficient to enable the employee to give a considered and informed response to the proposed decision to dismiss.

Second, these procedures are concerned only with establishing the basic statutory minimum standard. It is plainly not the intention of Parliament that all procedural defects should render the dismissal automatically unfair with the increased compensation that such a finding attracts. They are intended to apply to all employers, large and small, sophisticated and unsophisticated. They are not intended to impose all the requirements breach of which might, depending on the circumstances, render a dismissal unfair. This suggests that the bar for compliance with these procedures should not be set too high.

Third, we think that it is relevant to bear in mind that once the statutory procedures have been complied with, employers are thereafter provided with a defence for failing to comply with fuller procedural safeguards if they can show that the dismissal would have occurred anyway even had such procedures been properly followed. This factor, in our view, militates against allowing the bar for the statutory procedures being set too low.

It must be emphasised that the statutory dismissal procedures are not concerned with the reasonableness of the employer's grounds, nor the basis of those grounds, in themselves. It may be that the basis for a dismissal is quite misconceived or unjustified, or that the employer has adopted inappropriate or vague criteria, or acted unreasonably in insisting on dismissing in the light of the employee's response. These are of course highly relevant to whether the dismissal is unfair, but it is irrelevant to the issue whether the statutory procedures have been complied with. The duty on the employer is to provide the ground for dismissal and the reasons why he is relying on that ground. At this stage, the focus is on what he is proposing to do and why he proposing to do it, rather than how reasonable it is for him to be doing it at all.

Taking these considerations into account, in our view, the proper analysis of the employer's obligation is as follows. At the first step the employer merely has to set out in writing the grounds which lead him to contemplate dismissing the employee, together with an invitation to attend a meeting. At that stage, in our view, the statement need do no more than state the issue in broad terms. We agree with Mr Barnett [counsel for the employer] that at Step 1 the employee simply needs to be told that he is at risk of dismissal and why. In a conduct case this will be identifying the nature of the misconduct in issue, such as fighting, insubordination or dishonesty. In other cases it may require no more than specifying, for example, that it is lack of capability or redundancy. That is consistent, we think, with the approach which this Tribunal has adopted in relation to grievance procedures in *Canary Wharf Management Ltd* v *Edebi* and other cases. Of course, most employers will say more than this brief statement of grounds, but compliance with the statutory minimum procedure is in our view met by a limited written statement of that nature.

It is at the second step that the employer must inform the employee of the basis for the ground or grounds given in the statement. This information need not be reduced into writing; it can be given orally. The basis for the grounds are simply the matters which have led the employer to contemplate dismissing for the stated ground or grounds. In the classic case of alleged misconduct this will mean putting the case against the employee; the detailed evidence need not be provided for compliance with this procedure, but the employee must be given sufficient detail of the case against him to enable him properly to put his side of the story. The fundamental elements of fairness must be met.

In redundancy dismissals the issue is more difficult, not least because there are two stages in the process. First, the employer has to decide that he is going to implement dismissals on the ground of redundancy. That is a decision which will generally be taken independently of the particular employees to be selected. Thereafter, absent at least sufficient volunteers, there will need to be the second stage at which particular employees are selected and compulsorily dismissed.

We reject Mr Barnett's submission that the only information to be given is that identifying why the decision to effect redundancies has been taken. That is too restrictive an approach and would undermine the protection which the procedures are intended to give to employees. In our judgment, the reference in Step 2 to "the basis for including in the statement . . . the ground or grounds given in it" requires that an explanation is given as to why the employer is contemplating dismissing that particular employee. It is, after all, the contemplated dismissal of the specific employee which is in issue and may lead to tribunal proceedings, not just the decision that certain jobs will have to go. In a redundancy context, that will involve providing information as to both why the employer considers that there is, to put it colloquially, a redundancy situation and also why the employee is being selected. The latter is, in practice, likely to be far more important to an employee than the former. In general, employees will not individually be in a position to make any cogent observations about an employer's conclusion that redundancy is necessary, although sometimes the information provided may raise a question as to whether redundancy is the genuine reason for the dismissal. But more pertinently, the employee will want to make representations about his own selection and, of course, he will be in the best position to make observations about that . . .

In our judgment in order to comply with the statutory provisions an employer should provide to the employee not only the basic selection criteria which have been used, but also the employee's own assessment. That will give the employee an opportunity to make representations not only about whether the criteria are justified and appropriate but also, more importantly, whether the marking given to him in respect of any particular criterion is arguably unjust, and why. It may be that he can correct some obvious factual error, such as being attributed with a disciplinary record he does not have, or what appears to be a rogue mark on one of the criterion, apparently wholly out of line with his work performance. His response will be difficult to formulate, and very much in a vacuum, without this information . . .

Analysing the case in that way, we are satisfied that there was not here the requisite compliance . . . each of these appellants ought to have had, in our view, his own particular assessment. He ought to have been able to make a considered response to the information bearing directly on his own situation so as to correct errors and make representations about particular aspects. In this case the assessment was not given until the employees were leaving the meeting on the 21 January, but by then their fate was already determined. That was, in our view, too late to amount to compliance with Step 2 . . .

For those reasons, our view is that this dismissal was automatically unfair, being in breach of the standard dismissal and disciplinary procedure.'

Statutory grievance procedures

Employment Act 2002

SCHEDULE 2

Part 2 Grievance Procedures

Chapter 1 Standard Procedure

Step 1: statement of grievance
6   The employee must set out the grievance in writing and send the statement or a copy of it to the employer.

Step 2: meeting

7 (1)   The employer must invite the employee to attend a meeting to discuss the grievance.

(2)   The meeting must not take place unless –

(a)   the employee has informed the employer what the basis for the grievance was when he made the statement under paragraph 6, and

(b)   the employer has had a reasonable opportunity to consider his response to that information.

(3)   The employee must take all reasonable steps to attend the meeting.

(4)   After the meeting, the employer must inform the employee of his decision as to his response to the grievance and notify him of the right to appeal against the decision if he is not satisfied with it.

Step 3: appeal

8 (1)   If the employee does wish to appeal, he must inform the employer.

(2)   If the employee informs the employer of his wish to appeal, the employer must invite him to attend a further meeting.

(3)   The employee must take all reasonable steps to attend the meeting.

(4)   After the appeal meeting, the employer must inform the employee of his final decision.

Comment

(1) 'Grievance' is defined in the Dispute Regulations reg 2 as 'a complaint by an employee about action which his employer has taken or is contemplating taking in relation to him' (and 'action' is defined as including an omission). Note that this is a different definition of grievance from that in ERelA 1999 s 13(5) for the purposes of the right to be accompanied.

(2) To achieve the government's aim of reducing tribunal proceedings by making sure employees raise their complaints with the employer before making a tribunal claim, EA 2002 s 32 actually prevents employees from bringing tribunal proceedings (not just for unfair dismissal, but for virtually any employment-related complaint) without first having gone through the statutory grievance procedure. This is an unprecedented restriction. After all, a constructive dismissal claim can only be brought if the employer has committed a fundamental breach of contract. Why should an innocent party have to go through this procedure before exercising their rights?

(3) It is obvious that the requirement to set out the grievance in writing will be a deterrent for many workers against bringing proceedings, and also that it will be a trap for the unwary. There is a modified, two-step procedure which operates if the employment has ended without the grievance having being raised, or without the grievance procedure having been completed. It consists of the employee setting out the nature and basis for the grievance in writing and the employer responding in writing – but this only applies if both parties agree (in writing) to use it. As it will be a clear indication that the employee is intending to bring tribunal proceedings, it is unlikely that many employers will agree.

(4) So what happens if an employee leaves employment, wants to claim constructive dismissal and has not followed the statutory grievance procedure? After all, the limitation period for tribunal claims is usually three months. If a claimant finds that the claim is returned by the tribunal office because he has not gone through the grievance procedure, will he not risk running out of time if he has to write a letter to the employer and wait 28 days?

All is not lost. In these circumstances, the three-month time limit is automatically extended by three months. Indeed, as long as the employee submits a grievance letter under Step 1 of the procedure to the employer within one month of when the original time limit would have expired, the time limit is automatically extended by three months even if there has been no communication with the tribunal office (Dispute Regulations reg 15).

(5) So far the EAT has shown itself astute to the danger that the statutory grievance procedure may be a barrier to claimants and has interpreted the Dispute Regulations liberally. Thus it has been held sufficient for Step 1 where the grievance was raised in a letter of resignation (*Shergold* v *Fieldway Medical Centre* (2006)), a solicitor's letter (*Mark Warner Ltd* v *Aspland* (2006)) or a written request for flexible working which was turned down (*Commotion Ltd* v *Rutty* (2006)). The liberal approach is evident in the guidance given by the President of the EAT in the next case.

Canary Wharf Management Ltd v Edebi [2006] IRLR 416
Employment Appeal Tribunal

ELIAS J: '. . . First, the timing of the grievance. There is no maximum time limit prior to the lodging of the claim to the tribunal in which the grievance must have been raised. There is the minimum period of 28 days which must be allowed for the employer to deal with it and go through the relevant procedures, but no maximum period. That is not to say, however, that the act of raising a complaint months or years prior to lodging the tribunal claim will necessarily constitute the appropriate raising of the grievance. The grievance must be extant. If it can no longer properly be said to be an outstanding grievance, perhaps because it was apparently satisfactorily dealt with or because the employee has not pursued it in circumstances where it may properly be inferred that he no longer wishes to have it determined, then it will be necessary for the employee to raise the complaint again in written form.

Second, the form of the grievance. There is considerable flexibility about that . . .

Third, the content. The contrast between the standard and the modified procedure highlights an important feature of the way in which the complaint must be made under the former. As we have noted, there is no obligation to set out the basis of the claim. It is enough, therefore, that the employee identifies the complaint. The need to substantiate that with some evidence to justify it arises under the standard procedure at the second stage where the employee has to inform the employer what is the basis of the grievance. The only requirement, as ERelA 2002 s 32(2) makes plain, is that the complaint to the employer must be essentially the same complaint that is subsequently advanced before the tribunal . . .

Comment

(1) While this shows a welcome desire to avoid technicality, it also reveals further difficulties for the claimant negotiating the statutory grievance procedure: the complaint must not be too remote in time from the proceedings (which led to one of the employee's claims being disallowed in the case) and the complaint to the tribunal must be substantially the same as the grievance raised.

(2) The statutory grievance procedures are generating a fair amount of case law in their own right, which is hardly what was intended. However, more worrying is the information that in the first year of operation, 10 per cent of claims to tribunals were disallowed because the claimant had not been through the statutory grievance procedure – and that fewer than half of these were resubmitted.

(3) As with the statutory dismissal and disciplinary procedures, if the standard grievance procedure is not followed properly because of the employee's fault, then any

award of compensation will be reduced by between 10 and 50 per cent. If the procedure is not completed because of the employer's fault, the employee's award will be increased by between 10 and 50 per cent.

(4) The statutory dispute resolution procedures were found in practice to be technical, cumbersome, difficult to interpret and more likely to generate tribunal hearings than to encourage resolution of problems at workplace level. The Secretary of State commissioned a report into options for improving dispute resolution at the end of 2006 and the resulting report in March 2007 recommended the radical remedy of abolishing them altogether. Implicitly recognising that the statutory procedures had been a failure, the government accepted this surprising, but universally welcomed, proposal. The Employment Bill passing through Parliament in 2008 when this book went to press provided for the abolition of the statutory dispute resolution procedures and their replacement by a more general discretion for tribunals to make adjustments to awards where one party has failed to follow the recommendations of a statutory code of practice.

The fair reasons for dismissal

Employment Rights Act 1996

98   (1)   In determining for the purposes of this Part whether the dismissal of an employee is fair or unfair, it is for the employer to show –
   (a)   the reason (or, if more than one, the principal reason) for the dismissal, and
   (b)   that it is either a reason falling within subsection (2) or some other substantial reason of a kind such as to justify the dismissal of an employee holding the position which the employee held.

(2)   A reason falls within this subsection if it –
   (a)   relates to the capability or qualifications of the employee for performing work of the kind which he was employed by the employer to do,
   (b)   relates to the conduct of the employee,
   (ba)   is retirement of the employee,
   (c)   is that the employee was redundant, or
   (d)   is that the employee could not continue to work in the position which he held without contravention (either on his part or on that of his employer) of a duty or restriction imposed by or under an enactment.

(2A)   Subsections (1) and (2) are subject to sections 98ZA to 98ZF.

(3)   In subsection (2)(a) –
   (a)   'capability', in relation to an employee, means his capability assessed by reference to skill, aptitude, health or any other physical or mental quality, and
   (b)   'qualifications', in relation to an employee, means any degree, diploma or other academic, technical or professional qualification relevant to the position which he held.

(3A)   In any case where the employer has fulfilled the requirements of subsection (1) by showing that the reason (or the principal reason) for the dismissal is retirement of the employee, the question whether the dismissal is fair or unfair shall be determined in accordance with section 98ZG.

(4)   In any other case where the employer has fulfilled the requirements of subsection (1), the determination of the question whether the dismissal is fair or unfair (having regard to the reason shown by the employer) –
   (a)   depends on whether in the circumstances (including the size and administrative resources of the employer's undertaking) the employer acted reasonably

or unreasonably in treating it as a sufficient reason for dismissing the employee, and

(b)   shall be determined in accordance with equity and the substantial merits of the case . . .

Comment

(1) Note that there are two elements in deciding whether a dismissal is unfair or not: whether the reason for it came within one of the six specified categories, and if so, whether the employer acted reasonably in making the decision to dismiss. The burden of proof used to be on the employer for both elements. Since 1980, however, while the employer is still charged with proving the reason for the dismissal and that it comes within one of the six categories, the burden of proof with regard to reasonableness is neutral.

(2) In *Abernethy* v *Mott Hay and Anderson* (1974) Cairns LJ said:

> A reason for the dismissal of an employee is a set of facts known to the employer, or it may be of beliefs held by him, which cause him to dismiss the employee. If at the time of the dismissal the employer gives a reason for it, that is no doubt evidence . . . but it does not necessarily constitute the real reason.

It is thus open to the tribunal to find that the actual reason for dismissal is something other than what the employer said it was.

(3) The existence of the 'some other substantial reason' category in ERA s 98(1)(b) means that it is rarely the case that an employer cannot show a reason, or principal reason falling within one of the six categories, although a recent example would be *ASLEF* v *Brady* (2006).

(4) Apart from making a claim for unfair dismissal an employee has an independent right to ask the employer to provide information in writing as to what was the reason for the dismissal. The employer must respond within two weeks, or can be ordered to pay the employee two weeks' pay (ERA s 92).

(5) The employer may sometimes specify that the reason falls into more than one category, or may be unsure as to which category the reason is in. It is fairly common for under-performance to be categorised as either incapability or misconduct, and in the case of business restructuring resulting in job losses, the reason may be either redundancy or other economic reasons falling into the 'some other substantial reason' category. This is permissible, although it may have repercussions in judging the reasonableness of the decision, as different considerations may apply to different categories of reason (see *Trico-Folberth* v *Devonshire* (1989), for example).

(6) In practice, cases rarely turn on whether or not a potentially fair reason for dismissal has been established. The battleground is reasonableness. Before looking at what is reasonable in relation to each of the categories, there is a prior issue: how far can a tribunal go in overturning an employer's decision? And relatedly, in what circumstances can an appeal court or tribunal interfere with the employment tribunal's decision?

Iceland Frozen Foods Ltd v *Jones* [1983] ICR 17 Employment Appeal Tribunal

BROWNE-WILKINSON J: '. . . Since the present state of the law can only be found by going through a number of different authorities, it may be convenient if we should seek to summarise the present law. We consider that the authorities establish that in law the correct approach for the employment tribunal to adopt in answering the question posed by [ERA s 98(4)] is as follows: (1) the starting point should always be the words of [ERA s 98(4)] themselves; (2) in applying the section an employment tribunal must consider the reasonableness of the employer's conduct, not simply whether they (the members of the employment tribunal) consider the dismissal to be fair; (3) in judging the reasonableness of the employer's conduct an employment tribunal must not substitute its decision as to what was the right course to adopt for that of the employer; (4) in many, though not all, cases there is a band of reasonable responses to the employee's conduct within which one employer might reasonably take one view, another quite reasonably take another; (5) the function of the employment tribunal, as an industrial jury, is to determine whether in the particular circumstances of each case the decision to dismiss the employee fell within the band of reasonable responses which a reasonable employer might have adopted. If the dismissal falls within the band the dismissal is fair: if the dismissal falls outside the band it is unfair . . .'

Comment

(1) This useful summary of the principles developed in the case law highlights two crucial points by which an employment tribunal must be guided. First, the greatest sin that a tribunal can commit is to hold that an employer was unreasonable because they would not have dismissed the employee in the same circumstances. This is defensible, for if that were the standard, it would simply amount to substituting one subjective opinion (that of the tribunal) for another (that of the employer) – whereas the use of the term 'reasonableness' implies an objective test.

(2) More controversial, however, is the second point. The 'band of reasonable responses' doctrine, classically stated by Lord Denning in *British Leyland (UK) Ltd* v *Swift* (1981), holds that a dismissal is not unfair unless the tribunal is convinced that other employers would not have dismissed in these circumstances. The idea is that reasonable people in possession of the same information may yet reach different conclusions. Therefore, the fact that one reasonable employer would have let the employee off with a warning, say, does not mean that another employer who dismisses the employee on the same facts is necessarily unreasonable.

(3) This means that the employer will only be acting unreasonably in dismissing if her decision lies wholly outside the range of reasonable responses to the case in hand. This gets uncomfortably close to adopting a test which would categorise the employer's decision as unreasonable only if no reasonable employer would have acted in that way, although the EAT in Scotland denied that it amounted to this in *Rentokil* v *Mackin* (1989). However, it is clear that the band of reasonable responses test gives a lot of scope to the managerial prerogative. As Collins argues persuasively, the balance is tilted in favour of the employer because tribunals are now encouraged to ask whether the employer has acted *un*reasonably, whereas the statute asks whether the employer's decision was reasonable (see Collins, 1992, pp 37–40).

(4) These arguments prevailed sufficiently for the then outgoing President of the EAT, Morison J, to suggest in *Haddon* v *Van den Bergh Foods* (1999) that the test was likely to lead tribunals to find dismissals unfair only if the employer's decision could be characterised as perverse. He implied that it should not be used. This caused some uproar, the test having been frequently cited with approval in the Court of Appeal. An expedited appeal in *HSBC* v *Madden* (2000) gave the Court of Appeal the opportunity to reaffirm the band of reasonable responses test and the brief period of heresy was over.

(5) If anything, the test is now more entrenched than ever. In *Sainsbury's Supermarkets Ltd* v *Hitt* (2003) the Court of Appeal held that the band of reasonable responses test applied not only to the decision whether or not to dismiss, but also to the adequacy of the employer's investigation of the employee's misconduct, and, indeed, to all aspects of the question of whether the employee was reasonably dismissed (see below, p 404).

(6) Debate has also raged over how far the EAT should be able to interfere with the decision of an employment tribunal. Appeals to the EAT lie on a question of law only (ETA s 21). This in itself is a limiting factor, as a narrow view is taken of what constitutes a question of law (see *O'Kelly* v *Trusthouse Forte*, above p 130). The decision that a dismissal is fair or unfair involves drawing inferences from facts, but on the basis of a knowledge and understanding of law. Thus it could be argued that it is essentially a factual decision, or that it is essentially legal (in that it cannot be done if you do not know the law) or a mixture of the two. What is certain, however, is that from the point of view of appeals, it counts as a question of fact. This means that simply arguing that the employment tribunal reached the wrong decision is not acceptable as grounds of appeal. The position is summarised and illustrated in the next case.

Piggott Bros v *Jackson* [1991] IRLR 309 Court of Appeal

Employees at the employers' factory began to suffer soreness and irritation from fumes given off by a consignment of PVC and some were off sick for several weeks. The employers took advice from the Health and Safety Executive and improved ventilation, and although the cause of the problem was not identified, they were satisfied that there was no continuing danger to employees. The employees, however, were not reassured, and they refused to work with the material. After attempts to persuade them to reconsider had failed, they were dismissed.

An employment tribunal found that the dismissals were unfair. The EAT allowed the employers' appeal and substituted a finding that the dismissals were fair. The employees appealed to the Court of Appeal, arguing that the EAT should not have interfered with the employment tribunal's decision.

LORD DONALDSON MR: '. . . There are, however, three categories of case where it is the duty of the EAT to interfere. They are stated by Lord Donaldson MR in *British Telecommunications plc* v *Sheridan* (1990) as follows:

"The Employment Appeal Tribunal can indeed interfere if it is satisfied that the employment tribunal has misdirected itself as to the applicable law, or if there is no evidence to support a finding of fact, since the absence of evidence to support a finding of fact has always been regarded as a pure question of law. It can also interfere if the decision is perverse, as has been explained by May LJ in *Neale* v *Hereford & Worcester CC* (1986)."

This last is an allusion to the now very familiar sentence:

"Deciding these cases is the job of employment tribunals and when they have not erred in law neither the appeal tribunal nor this Court should disturb their decision unless one can say in effect 'My goodness that was certainly wrong'."

I accept, as I must, the exposition of May LJ. Indeed, it has the added authority of, I think, being derived, albeit expressed in more homely terms, from the speech of Lord Diplock in *R* v *Secretary of State for Foreign and Commonwealth Affairs ex parte Council of Civil Service Unions* (1985) where he said that a decision which was plainly wrong could found an application for judicial review and that it was no longer necessary to resort to Viscount Radcliffe's explanation in *Edwards* v *Bairstow* (1956) of irrationality as raising an inference of an unidentifiable mistake of law.

Nevertheless, it is an approach which is not without its perils. A finding of fact which is unsupported by *any* evidence clearly involves an error of law. The tribunal cannot have directed itself, as it should, that findings of fact need *some* evidence to support them. The danger in the approach of May LJ is that an appellate court can very easily persuade itself that, as it would certainly not have reached the same conclusion, the tribunal which did so was "certainly wrong". Furthermore, the more dogmatic the temperament of the judges concerned, the more likely they are to take this view. However, this is a classic non sequitur. It does not matter whether, with whatever degree of certainty, the appellate court considers that it would have reached a different conclusion. What matters is whether the decision under appeal was a permissible option. To answer that question in the negative in the context of employment law, the EAT will almost always have to be able to identify a finding of fact which was unsupported by *any* evidence or a clear self-misdirection in law by the employment tribunal. If it cannot do this, it should re-examine with the greatest care its preliminary conclusion that the decision under appeal was not a permissible option and has to be characterised as "perverse" . . .

In my judgment the employment tribunal were holding that the employers could reasonably have been expected to do more with a view to obtaining a definitive answer than they did and that, in the light of the employees' reasonable fears for their own health, until more had been done and either an answer had emerged or it had become clear that nothing further could be done, it was not reasonable to dismiss the employees. What the EAT was doing was to decide that no reasonable employer could be expected to do more than rely upon the Health and Safety Executive. That was not a decision for it.

I have no idea whether I would have reached the same conclusion as the employment tribunal, particularly as I do not know what evidence was given by the employees as to the extent and basis of their fears, but that is in any event irrelevant. I can see no possible grounds for holding that no reasonable employment tribunal, properly directing itself, could have reached such a conclusion and accordingly cannot and would not hold its decision to be perverse . . .

I would allow the appeal and restore the decision of the employment tribunal.'

(Nicholls and Stuart-Smith LJJ agreed.)

Comment

(1) The Court of Appeal also held that if the decision of the employment tribunal had been perverse, the proper course would have been for the EAT to remit the case for rehearing rather than making its own finding.

Procedural fairness

We have seen that a failure to follow the statutory dismissal and disciplinary procedures will make a dismissal automatically unfair. However, these procedures lay down minimum standards only. Other norms of procedural fairness derive from the case law and (in the case of capability and conduct) from the Acas *Code of Practice on Disciplinary and Grievance Procedures* (2004). What happens if an employer fails to follow these norms? Does this make the dismissal unfair? Is it open to the employer to argue that no amount of procedural fairness would have made any difference to the decision to dismiss the employee? The answer can only be understood by examining some history.

Polkey v *AE Dayton Services Ltd* [1988] AC 344 House of Lords

The company employed four van drivers, including the claimant. It was decided to replace the four drivers with two van salespeople. Only one of the existing drivers was thought capable of carrying out the sales function as well as the driving function, so the other three were made redundant. The first Polkey knew of any of this was when he was called into the office, told that he was redundant with immediate effect and sent home. There was no warning, consultation or discussion with the three beforehand. The employment tribunal, however, considered that the outcome would have been no different even if the employer had followed the requirements of a fair procedure, so they held that the dismissal was fair. Polkey's appeal reached the House of Lords.

LORD MACKAY LC: '. . . This appeal raises an important question in the law of unfair dismissal. Where an employment tribunal has found that the reason for an applicant's dismissal was a reason of a kind such as could justify the dismissal and has found that there has been a failure to consult or warn the applicant in accordance with the code of practice, should the tribunal consider whether, if the employee had been consulted or warned before dismissal was decided upon, he would nevertheless have been dismissed? . . .

The tribunal in the present case was bound by a stream of authority applying the so-called *British Labour Pump* principle: *British Labour Pump Co Ltd* v *Byrne* (1979). Browne-Wilkinson J in *Sillifant* v *Powell Duffryn Timber Ltd* (1983) thus described the principle:

> "even if, judged in the light of the circumstances known at the time of dismissal, the employer's decision was not reasonable because of some failure to follow a fair procedure yet the dismissal can be held fair if, on the facts proved before the employment tribunal, the employment tribunal comes to the conclusion that the employer could reasonably have decided to dismiss if he had followed a fair procedure."

It is because one of its statements is contained in *British Labour Pump Co Ltd* v *Byrne* that it has been called the *British Labour Pump* principle although it did not originate in that decision. In *Sillifant's* case the Employment Appeal Tribunal were urged to hold that the principle was unsound and not to give effect to it. After referring to the cases which introduced this principle, namely *Charles Letts & Co Ltd* v *Howard* (1976), a decision relating only to compensation, *Lowndes* v *Specialist Heavy Engineering Ltd* (1977), *British United Shoe Machinery Co Ltd* v *Clarke* (1978) and the *British Labour Pump* case itself, Browne-Wilkinson J continued:

> "Apart therefore from recent Court of Appeal authority and the *Lowndes* case, the *British Labour Pump* principle appears to have become established in practice without it being appreciated that it represented a fundamental departure from both basic principle and the earlier decisions. If we felt able to do so we would hold that it is wrong in principle and undesirable in its practical effect. It introduces just that confusion which *Devis* v *Atkins* was concerned to avoid between the fairness of the dismissal (which depends solely upon the reasonableness of the employer's conduct) and the compensation payable to the employee (which takes into account the conduct of the employee whether known to the employer or not). In our judgment, apart from the authority to which we are about to refer, the correct approach to such a case would be as follows. The only test of the fairness of a dismissal is the reasonableness of the employer's decision to dismiss judged at the time at which the dismissal takes effect. An employment tribunal is not bound to hold that any procedural failure by the employer renders the dismissal unfair: it is one of the factors to be weighed by the employment tribunal in deciding whether or not the dismissal was reasonable within [ERA s 98(4)]. The weight to be attached to such procedural failure should depend upon the circumstances known to the employer at the time of dismissal, not on the actual consequence of such failure. Thus in the case of a failure to give an opportunity to explain, except in the

rare case where a reasonable employer could properly take the view on the facts known to him at the time of dismissal that no explanation or mitigation could alter his decision to dismiss, an employment tribunal would be likely to hold that the lack of 'equity' inherent in the failure would render the dismissal unfair. But there may be cases where the offence is so heinous and the facts so manifestly clear that a reasonable employer could, on the facts known to him at the time of dismissal, take the view that whatever explanation the employee advanced it would make no difference: see the example referred to by Lawton LJ in *Bailey* v *BP Oil (Kent Refinery) Ltd* (1980). Where, in the circumstances known at the time of dismissal, it was not reasonable for the employer to dismiss without giving an opportunity to explain but facts subsequently discovered or proved before the employment tribunal show that dismissal was in fact merited, compensation would be reduced to nil. Such an approach ensures that an employee who could have been fairly dismissed does not get compensation but would prevent the suggestion of 'double standards' inherent in the *British Labour Pump* principle. An employee dismissed for suspected dishonesty who is in fact innocent has no redress: if the employer acted fairly in dismissing him on the facts and in the circumstances known to him at the time of dismissal the employee's innocence is irrelevant. Why should an employer be entitled to a finding that he acted fairly when, on the facts known and in the circumstances existing at the time of dismissal, his actions were unfair but which facts subsequently coming to light show did not cause any injustice? The choice in dealing with [ERA s 98(4)] is between looking at the reasonableness of the employer or justice to the employee. *Devis* v *Atkins* shows that the correct test is the reasonableness of the employer: the *British Labour Pump* principle confuses the two approaches."

I gratefully adopt that analysis. The Employment Appeal Tribunal, however, went on to hold that they were bound by the decision of the Court of Appeal in *W & J Wass Ltd* v *Binns* (1982) which held that the *British Labour Pump* principle is good law . . .

The employment tribunal asked themselves the wrong question when they applied the *British Labour Pump* principle. It is not apparent what their answer would have been if they had asked themselves the correct question. In my opinion the proper course is to remit this case to a new employment tribunal for consideration in the light of your Lordships' judgment. The respondents must bear the appellant's costs in the Court of Appeal and in this House.'

LORD BRIDGE: 'My Lords, I have had the advantage of reading in draft the speech of my noble and learned friend the Lord Chancellor and I agree with it. I add some short observations of my own because of the importance of the case.

Employers contesting a claim of unfair dismissal will commonly advance as their reason for dismissal one of the reasons specifically recognised as valid by [ERA s 98(2)(a), (b) or (c)]. These, put shortly, are: (a) that the employee could not do his job properly; (b) that he had been guilty of misconduct; (c) that he was redundant. But an employer having prima facie grounds to dismiss for one of these reasons will in the great majority of cases not act reasonably in treating the reason as a sufficient reason for dismissal unless and until he has taken the steps, conveniently classified in most of the authorities as "procedural", which are necessary in the circumstances of the case to justify that course of action. Thus, in the case of incapacity, the employer will normally not act reasonably unless he gives the employee fair warning and an opportunity to mend his ways and show that he can do the job; in the case of misconduct, the employer will normally not act reasonably unless he investigates the complaint of misconduct fully and fairly and hears whatever the employee wishes to say in his defence or in explanation or mitigation; in the case of redundancy, the employer will normally not act reasonably unless he warns and consults any employees affected or their representative, adopts a fair basis on which to select for redundancy and takes such steps as may be reasonable to avoid or minimise redundancy by redeployment within his own organisation. If an employer has failed to take the appropriate procedural steps in any particular case, the one question the employment tribunal is not permitted to ask in applying the test of reasonableness posed by [ERA s 98(4)] is the hypothetical question whether it would have made any difference to the outcome if the appropriate procedural steps had been taken. On the true construction of [ERA s 98(4)] this question is simply irrelevant. It is quite a different matter if the tribunal is able to conclude that the employer himself, at the time of dismissal, acted reasonably in taking the view that, in the exceptional circumstances of the particular case, the procedural steps normally appropriate would have been futile, could not have altered the decision to dismiss and therefore could be dispensed with. In such a case the test of reasonableness under [ERA s 98(4)] may be satisfied . . .'

(Lords Keith, Ackner and Brandon agreed.)

Comment

(1) As can be seen from Lord Mackay's speech, the 'no-difference' rule (or the *British Labour Pump* principle) held sway from the end of the 1970s until this decision. It meant that the importance for employers of following appropriate procedures was diminished because they would frequently be able to argue that following a fair procedure would not have made any difference to the ultimate decision to dismiss.

(2) In this landmark decision, the House of Lords indicate the problems with the 'no-difference' rule and reject it as inconsistent with principle as well as unjust to employees. The effect of *Polkey* was a renewed emphasis on the importance of using correct procedures in relation to all kinds of dismissals. However, note the point that the 'no-difference' principle was relevant to compensation. Polkey finally settled his claim for £5,000 – but it was the sort of case where he could have been awarded nothing even though the dismissal was unfair.

(3) The issue was re-opened in the government consultation exercise which preceded the Employment Act 2002.

Routes to Resolution DTI consultation paper (2001)

3.21 Having established a firm foundation of basic standards in management of disputes, there is a case for looking again at the balance between principle (whether a dismissal is for a fair reason) and procedure (whether an employer acts reasonably in carrying it out) in the assessment of unfair dismissal claims. Although the essential features of unfair dismissal legislation have been unchanged since its introduction, case law has substantially affected this balance and has shifted over the years. At present, the effect of a 1987 House of Lords judgement (*Polkey v A E Dayton Services Ltd*) is that an otherwise fair dismissal – because it was reasonable for the employer to dismiss the employee for one of the potentially fair reasons allowed by the legislation – becomes unfair if the employer fails to follow their procedures in carrying out the dismissal. Previously it was open to the tribunals to find, if a dismissal was substantively fair, that it remained a fair dismissal even if the employer had not followed proper procedures – provided that following them made no difference to the outcome.

3.22 An employee whose dismissal is found to have been unfair on procedural grounds alone will receive minimal compensation if the procedural failing subjected him to no real injustice. But this may not be much consolation to the employer, who has had to devote resources to defending the case and may feel that he has been 'found guilty' for an unimportant reason. As a result, many employers claim that the present state of the law encourages employees to make claims, and allows them to succeed, for trivial reasons.

3.23 Even a partial return to a position in which procedural failings could be disregarded would be a significant shift in the development of unfair dismissal legislation. The Government would welcome views, however, on whether a fairer balance between principle and procedure would be provided by allowing tribunals to disregard procedural mistakes beyond the minimum procedural actions set out earlier in this Chapter [ie the statutory dispute resolution procedures], if they would have made no difference to the outcome and the dismissal was otherwise fair.

Comment

(1) Not surprisingly, business lobbied strongly to get the *Polkey* rule changed and their arguments were accepted by the government. The Employment Act 2002 amended the Employment Rights Act 1996 to insert a new section.

Employment Rights Act 1996

98A (2) Subject to subsection (1), failure by an employer to follow a procedure in relation to the dismissal of an employee shall not be regarded for the purposes of section 98(4)(a) as by itself making the employer's action unreasonable if he shows that he would have decided to dismiss the employee if he had followed the procedure.

Comment

(1) ERA s 98A(1) is the subsection which makes dismissal in breach of the statutory dismissal and disciplinary procedure automatically unfair.

(2) Thus ERA s 98A(2) operates as a statutory reversal of the *Polkey* principle. In the first cases to reach the EAT a divergence of view has emerged as to how far it goes. In *Alexander v Bridgen Enterprises Ltd* (2006) the EAT chaired by its President, Elias J, expressed the view that it applied to all kinds of procedural steps. However, in *Mason v Governing Body of Ward End Primary School* (2006) a different division of the EAT held that it applied only if there was an identifiable procedure which had not been followed in some respect. It seems likely that the former view will prevail, but the point awaits decision.

(3) How important now are the procedural requirements developed in the case law in relation to the different categories of fair reasons for dismissal? This cannot be answered authoritatively at this stage, but it is submitted that they remain important because in many situations it will not be possible for an employer to say that the decision would be the same if a fair procedure had been used. This is particularly the case for capability and conduct dismissals, although it may be less true in relation to warnings and consultation before redundancy (the issue in *Polkey v Dayton Services*). It must also be remembered that tribunals are mandated to take account of the Acas *Code of Practice on Disciplinary and Grievance Procedures* where applicable (TULRCA s 207).

(4) In what follows, procedural as well as substantive fairness will be examined in relation to each of the categories of potentially fair reason. However, it must be borne in mind that the outcomes of specific cases could be different if they occurred today, in the light of ERA s 98A(2).

Capability or qualifications

This category is set out in ERA s 98(2)(a), (3) (above p 388). It covers two separate situations: cases where the employee is sick or injured and for that reason incapable of work, and cases of incompetence.

Links & Co Ltd v *Rose* [1991] IRLR 353 Court of Session

The employee had worked at the company's snooker centre for six years. He suffered two heart attacks in August 1987 and remained unfit for work until April 1988 when he was dismissed. An employment tribunal held that the dismissal was unfair because of the lack of warning or consultation with the employee before the decision was taken.

LORD McCLUSKEY: '. . . The tribunal had been referred to a speech by Lord Bridge of Harwich in *Polkey* v *AE Dayton Services* (1987) containing an *obiter* passage which the tribunal considered afforded a clear indication as to the approach to be taken. As that dictum was also referred to by the Employment Appeal Tribunal and was the subject of some analysis in the submissions before us it should be quoted in full. It is as follows:

> "Employers contesting a claim of unfair dismissal will commonly advance as their reason for dismissal one of the reasons specifically recognised as valid by [ERA s 98(2)(a), (b) and (c)]. These, put shortly, are: (a) that the employee could not do his job properly; (b) that he had been guilty of misconduct; (c) that he was redundant. But an employer having prima facie grounds to dismiss for one of these reasons will in the great majority of cases not act reasonably in treating the reason as a sufficient reason for dismissal unless and until he has taken the steps, conveniently classified in most of the authorities as 'procedural', which are necessary in the circumstances of the case to justify the course of action. Thus in the case of incapacity, the employer will normally not act reasonably unless he gives the employee fair warning and an opportunity to mend his ways and show that he can do the job . . ."

The first two sentences of that passage, which were not quoted by the tribunal, indicate that his Lordship was intending to indicate what the duty of employers was in relation to dismissal for a reason recognised as valid by paragraph (a) or (b) or (c) of [ERA s 98(2)]. The tribunal, having quoted the latter part of that passage, stated:

> "In accordance with our findings in fact which show . . . that there was no warning or opportunity as envisaged by Lord Bridge, the employers must therefore be held to have dismissed the claimant unfairly in that they did not act reasonably in treating the reason as a sufficient reason for the dismissal in that they disregarded the steps described by Lord Bridge above."

. . . The law in relation to the duty of an employer who is considering dismissing an employee on the grounds of ill health, being ill health which appears to be such as to incapacitate the employee from performing the duties attached to his position, is not in dispute between the parties. We were referred to two cases where the employer's duty is described. It is sufficient to quote them. In the first, *East Lindsey District Council* v *Daubney* (1977), Phillips J said:

> "There have been several decisions of the Appeal Tribunal in which consideration has been given to what are the appropriate steps to be taken by an employer who is considering the dismissal of an employee on the ground of ill health. *Spencer* v *Paragon Wallpapers Ltd* (1976) and *David Sherratt Ltd* v *Williams* (1977) are examples. It comes to this. Unless there are wholly exceptional circumstances, before an employee is dismissed on the ground of ill health it is necessary that he should be consulted and the matter discussed with him, and that in one way or another steps should be taken by the employer to discover the true medical position. We do not propose to lay down detailed principles to be applied in such cases, for what will be necessary in one case may not be appropriate in another. But if in every case employers take such steps as are sensible according to the circumstances to consult the employee and to discuss the matter with him, and to inform themselves upon the true medical position, it will be found in practice that all that is necessary has been done. Discussions and consultation will often bring to light facts and circumstances of which the employers were unaware, and which will throw new light on the problem."

In the second case, *Taylorplan Catering (Scotland) Ltd* v *McInally* (1980), Lord McDonald said:

"There is no doubt that in the normal case a measure of consultation is expected of an employer before he decides to dismiss an employee for ill health. Apart from considerations of general courtesy the reason for this is to secure that the situation can be weighed up, balancing the employer's need for the work to be done on the one hand, against the employee's need for time to recover his health on the other."

It does not appear to us that the passage in the speech of Lord Bridge in *Polkey* is in any way inconsistent with these earlier cases. Lord Bridge was plainly addressing himself generally to cases of incapacity; that is clear from his reference to [ERA s 98(2)(a)]. It is true that the concept of "fair warning and an opportunity to mend his ways" is not one which can be applied readily to a situation where the ill health which has rendered the employee unfit for the work he has been doing is of such a character that it is likely to be permanent. But it is easy enough to envisage cases in which an employee's incapacity might result from ill health which in turn flowed directly from some circumstance within the control of the employee himself. It might be, for example, that his ill health took the form of obesity and that with reasonable dieting he could cure his condition and restore his capacity to do the job. Another example would be one where the physical incapacity to perform the work could be remedied by a simple operation which the employee was, for no apparent reason, neglecting to take. It would be easy to multiply examples but it is not necessary to do so. Lord Bridge, in any event, qualified his remarks in this passage by the adverb, "normally". Accordingly the relevant law appears to us to be that stated by Phillips J and Lord McDonald in the passages quoted. It follows, in our opinion, that an employment tribunal, in approaching the question as to whether the employer acted fairly or unfairly must determine, as a matter of fact and judgment, what consultation if any was necessary or desirable in the known circumstances of the particular case, what consultation, if any, in fact took place, and whether or not that consultation process was adequate in all the circumstances. If it was not adequate the dismissal will be unfair, as explained by Lord Bridge . . .'

(The court decided to remit the case to a fresh tribunal.)

Comment

(1) Dialogue with the employee remains important as a matter of good employment relations practice. However, cases where the employee's medical condition is known to render it practically impossible for her to resume her job are the sort of situations where it is likely that the reinstatement of the no-difference rule in ERA s 98A(2) may have an impact.

(2) This must be balanced against a further consideration: if the employee has a long-term medical incapability, this may constitute a disability within the meaning of the Disability Discrimination Act 1995. This puts a premium on the employer finding out what the true position is, because ignorance of the employee's disability may not excuse the employer from liability if she is treated less favourably on that account (see above, p 112).

(3) Absent an express clause in the contract, an employer cannot generally require an employee to undergo a medical examination (*Bliss* v *SE Thames RHA* (1987)). Furthermore, under the Access to Medical Reports Act 1988 an employee has the right to see any medical report drawn up for her employer and can refuse to allow it to be sent to the employers. However, if the employers' genuine attempts to inform themselves about

the state of the employee's health are frustrated by the employee's actions, the employers will probably be found to have acted reasonably if they go ahead with dismissal.

(4) It is not clear that the right to be accompanied applies where the employer is considering dismissal of an employee for ill-health incapability (see the definition of a disciplinary hearing above, p 379). Obviously it would be good practice to permit the employee to be accompanied, but she might not have a cause of action if the employer refused.

(5) A problem frequently faced by employers is the situation where an employee has a poor attendance record caused by a variety of minor illnesses of short-term duration. The proper approach in such a case may be more like a disciplinary procedure, as the EAT pointed out in the next case.

International Sports Co Ltd v *Thomson* [1980] IRLR 340
Employment Appeal Tribunal

The claimant was absent for about 25 per cent of her working time during the last 18 months of her employment. Medical certificates covering the different periods revealed numerous ailments – dizzy spells, anxiety and nerves, bronchitis, virus infections, cystitis, althruigra of the knee, dyspepsia and flatulence – the last two accounting for a month's absence just before she was dismissed.

The employers had an agreement with the trade union that absence levels above 8 per cent were unsatisfactory, and accordingly she was given a series of warnings over the last year of her employment. Before dismissing her, the employers reviewed the medical evidence, but the company doctor concluded that there was no point in examining her as all the illnesses were of a transitory nature and had nothing in common.

WATERHOUSE J: '. . . It must be stressed that *Williamson* v *Alcan (UK) Ltd* (1977) and the earlier decisions followed in that judgment were all cases of incapability relating to ill-health. The employment tribunal, in the present case, appears to have regarded those principles as applicable to all cases in which an employee is persistently absent on grounds of ill-health. We are unable to accept that as a correct proposition of law. In the *Williamson* case, the employee was still disabled by a slipped disc when he was dismissed. In *Spencer* v *Paragon Wallpapers Ltd* (1976) there was again continuing disability with back trouble, and in *East Lindsey District Council* v *Daubney* (1977) the employee had been continuously disabled following a stroke. Here, however, the employers did not purport to dismiss the employee on the ground of incapability. They were concerned with the impact of an unacceptable level of intermittent absences due to unconnected minor ailments.

In such a case, it would be placing too heavy a burden on an employer to require him to carry out a formal medical investigation and, even if he did, such an investigation would rarely be fruitful because of the transient nature of the employee's symptoms and complaints. What is required, in our judgment, is, first, that there should be a fair review by the employer of the attendance record and the reasons for it; and, second, appropriate warnings, after the employee has been given an opportunity to make representations. If then there is no adequate improvement in the attendance record, it is likely that in most cases the employer will be justified in treating the persistent absences as a sufficient reason for dismissing the employee. It is to be noted, in the instant case, that the appellants did seek medical advice before they made the decision, and we can see no ground for criticism of the quality of that advice or of the appellants' acceptance of it. Accordingly, there was no chronic illness for them to investigate. Moreover, if the appellants had investigated the dyspepsia and flatulence further, they would no doubt have reached the conclusion that the symptoms should have been cured very quickly by a simple diet, which was the tribunal's own finding . . .'

(The EAT allowed the employer's appeal and substituted a finding that the dismissal was not unfair.)

Comment

(1) In this case the EAT considered that the facts indicated a dismissal on grounds of conduct rather than capability. While it may be appropriate to use a quasi-disciplinary procedure in this sort of case, it is submitted that it is still properly to be regarded as dismissal for incapability unless the employer is prepared to stigmatise the reasons for the absenteeism as malingering rather than as genuine illness. Most employers are not prepared to do this, provided that they can get rid of the employee on some other ground, because it escalates the matter by effectively accusing the employee of dishonesty, even if they secretly believe that the illnesses are not genuine. An alternative way of dealing with this is simply to stipulate that absenteeism above a certain level is not acceptable whatever the reason.

(2) The interface between dismissals for incapability and misconduct is blurred also in relation to incompetence.

Winterhalter Gastronom Ltd v *Webb* [1973] ICR 245
National Industrial Relations Court

The employee was sales director of a company selling dishwashers. Sales were poor and the company lost money in its first full year of operation. While this was a concern to the three directors and the owner of the holding company, nothing was said to the effect that the employee would lose his job unless sales improved. However, in July 1972 he was asked to resign because of this. He refused, but was dismissed a month later. The employment tribunal held the dismissal to be unfair because there had been no warning as recommended by the Acas Code of Practice.

SIR HUGH GRIFFITHS: '. . . as Mr Webb in his capacity as sales director was responsible for sales and knew the deplorable state of the sales, he must have appreciated that if they did not improve his job was in peril. Thus, argues Mr Sedley [counsel for the employer], with all these facts at his disposal and bearing in mind his capacity as a director, warning was neither necessary nor could it serve any useful purpose. Mr Sedley went so far as to submit that a warning can never be appropriate when the reason for dismissing a man is lack of capability. Warning, he says, is appropriate in the case of misconduct, because it lies within the man's own powers to rectify his conduct but not his capability. We do not agree. There are many situations in which a man's apparent capabilities may be stretched when he knows what is demanded of him; many do not know they are capable of jumping the five-barred gate until the bull is close behind them. No doubt there may be cases in which giving warning to a director would be neither necessary nor achieve any useful purpose. But, each case must depend upon its own particular facts and it is, in the view of this court, quite impossible to say as a matter of law that there can never be circumstances in which it is necessary to give a warning to a director before dismissing him . . .'

(The employer's appeal was dismissed.)

Comment

(1) It was argued in this case that the version of the Acas Code then in force should not apply to capability dismissals because it was only aimed at misconduct. The argument was rejected by the NIRC. The current Acas Code makes it clear that it is intended to apply to under-performance as well as misconduct. It says, in para 2:

> Disciplinary procedures may also be used where employees don't meet their employer's expectations in the way they do their job. These cases, often known as unsatisfactory performance (or capability), may require different treatment from misconduct, and disciplinary procedures should allow for this.

(2) It must be remembered that cases turn on their facts and cannot be seen as providing hard and fast precedents. It is not always the case that warnings have to be given in incompetence cases: it may be pointless, because there is no way that the employee can change (as in *Dunning* v *Jacomb* (1973)), and in some cases, if the employee is senior, it may be felt that he should realise that his performance is not satisfactory.

(3) Once a warning has been given, then of course the employee must be permitted a reasonable period in which to show improvement. What is reasonable will depend on the nature of the job.

(4) Another important factor in incompetence cases is the adequacy of the training and support given to the employee. If the employee has a qualification which means that she should be able to carry out a particular kind of work, the employer is not required to retrain her, but often companies will expect to have to train their workers for the jobs they want them to do.

(5) Where the job involves a lot of responsibility, one mistake may be sufficient grounds for dismissal, as in *Alidair* v *Taylor* (1978), where a pilot was dismissed after landing his plane badly and damaging it when there were no adverse conditions. The Court of Appeal in that case stated that the test was whether the employer could show that they had honestly lost faith in the employee's ability and that they had reasonable grounds for that belief.

(6) Usually, however, the response to under-performance should follow the advice of the Acas *Code on of Practice Disciplinary and Grievance Procedures* (2004).

Acas *Code of Practice on Disciplinary and Grievance Procedures* (2004)

12 If informal action does not bring about an improvement, or the misconduct or unsatisfactory performance is considered to be too serious to be classed as minor, employers should provide employees with a clear signal of their dissatisfaction by taking formal action.

FORMAL ACTION

Inform the employee of the problem

13 The first step in any formal process is to let the employee know in writing what it is they are alleged to have done wrong. The letter or note should contain enough information for the individual to be able to understand both what it is they are alleged to have done wrong and the reasons why this is not acceptable. If the employee has difficulty reading, or if English is not their first language, the employer should explain the content of the letter or note to them orally. The letter or note should also invite the individual to a meeting at which the problem can be discussed, and it should inform the individual of their right to be

accompanied at the meeting (see section 3). The employee should be given copies of any documents that will be produced at the meeting . . .

First formal action – unsatisfactory performance

19 Following the meeting, an employee who is found to be performing unsatisfactorily should be given a written note setting out:
  • the performance problem;
  • the improvement that is required;
  • the timescale for achieving this improvement;
  • a review date; and
  • any support the employer will provide to assist the employee.
20 The employee should be informed that the note represents the first stage of a formal procedure and that failure to improve could lead to a final written warning and, ultimately, dismissal. A copy of the note should be kept and used as the basis for monitoring and reviewing performance over a specified period (eg six months).

Conduct

Acas *Code of Practice on Disciplinary and Grievance Procedures* (2004)

53 When making rules, the aim should be to specify those that are necessary for ensuring a safe and efficient workplace and for maintaining good employment relations.
54 It is unlikely that any set of rules will cover all possible disciplinary issues, but rules normally cover:
  • bad behaviour, such as fighting or drunkenness;
  • unsatisfactory work performance;
  • harassment or victimisation;
  • misuse of company facilities (for example email and internet);
  • poor timekeeping;
  • unauthorised absences; and
  • repeated or serious failure to follow instructions.
55 Rules should be specific, clear and recorded in writing. They also need to be readily available to employees, for instance on a noticeboard or, in larger organisations, in a staff handbook or on the intranet. Management should do all they can to ensure that every employee knows and understands the rules, including those employees whose first language is not English or who have trouble reading. This is often best done as part of an induction process.
. . .
58 Disciplinary procedures should not be seen primarily as a means of imposing sanctions but rather as a way of encouraging improvement amongst employees whose conduct or performance is unsatisfactory. Some organisations may prefer to have separate procedures for dealing with issues of conduct and capability. Large organisations may also have separate procedures to deal with other issues such as harassment and bullying.
59 When drawing up and applying procedures employers should always bear in mind the requirements of natural justice. This means that employees should be given the opportunity of a meeting with someone who has not been involved in the matter. They should be informed of the allegations against them, together with the supporting evidence, in advance of the meeting. Employees should be given the opportunity to challenge the allegations before decisions are reached and should be provided with a right of appeal.

60   Good disciplinary procedures should:
  • be put in writing;
  • say to whom they apply;
  • be non-discriminatory;
  • allow for matters to be dealt [with] without undue delay;
  • allow for information to be kept confidential;
  • tell employees what disciplinary action might be taken;
  • say what levels of management have the authority to take disciplinary action;
  • require employees to be informed of the complaints against them and supporting evidence, before a meeting;
  • give employees a chance to have their say before management reaches a decision;
  • provide employees with the right to be accompanied;
  • provide that no employee is dismissed for a first breach of discipline, except in cases of gross misconduct;
  • require management to investigate fully before any disciplinary action is taken;
  • ensure that employees are given an explanation for any sanction; and
  • allow employees to appeal against a decision.

Comment

(1) As noted already, the Code does not have the force of law, but must be taken into account by tribunals in judging the fairness or unfairness of dismissal for misconduct. See also paras 56–57 on gross misconduct, above, p 343.

(2) While the attributes of 'good' procedures are outlined in para 60 of the Code, it must be remembered that misconduct dismissals are one of the main categories where employers may be able to argue that they would still have decided to dismiss the employee if they had followed the procedure (ERA s 98A(2)). Much will depend on how far tribunals are prepared to speculate. For example, if an employer fails to investigate whether an employee actually committed some act of misconduct which the employee disputes, but an investigation *might* have revealed that the employee did it – how far should the employment tribunal go in conjecturing what sort of investigation the employer would have been likely to carry out? It is submitted that in these circumstances, any uncertainty should be construed against the employer, given the clear advice in the Acas Code and the longstanding acceptance that this is good practice.

British Home Stores Ltd v Burchell [1980] ICR 303 Employment Appeal Tribunal

The employee had been dismissed because the employers believed that she was fiddling on the staff discount purchase scheme.

ARNOLD J: '. . . The case is one of an increasingly familiar sort in this tribunal, in which there has been a suspicion or belief of the employee's misconduct entertained by the employers, it is on that ground that dismissal has taken place, and the tribunal then goes over that to review the situation as it was at the date of dismissal. The central point of appeal is what is the nature and proper extent of that review. We have had cited to us, we believe, really all the cases which deal with this particular aspect in the recent history of this tribunal over the three or four years; and the conclusions to be drawn from the cases we think are quite plain. What the tribunal have to decide every time is, broadly expressed, whether the employer who discharged the employee on the ground of the misconduct in question (usually, though not necessarily, dishonest conduct) entertained a reasonable suspicion amounting to a belief in the guilt of the employee of that misconduct at that time. That is really stating shortly and compendiously what is in fact more than one element. First of all, there must be established by the employer the fact of that belief; that the employer did believe it. Secondly, that the employer had in his mind reasonable grounds upon which to sustain that belief. And thirdly, we think, that the employer, at the stage at which he formed that belief on those grounds, at any rate at the final stage at which he formed that belief on those grounds, had carried out as much investigation into the matter as was reasonable in all the circumstances of the case. It is the employer who manages to discharge the onus of demonstrating those three matters, we think, who must not be examined further. It is not relevant, as we think, that the tribunal would themselves have shared that view in those circumstances. It is not relevant, as we think, for the tribunal to examine the quality of the material which the employers had before them, for instance to see whether it was the sort of material, objectively considered, which would lead to a certain conclusion on the balance of probabilities, or whether it was the sort of material which would lead to the same conclusion only upon the basis of being "sure" as it is now said more normally in a criminal context, or, to use the more old-fashioned term, such as to put the matter "beyond reasonable doubt". The test, and the test all the way through, is reasonableness; and certainly, as it seems to us, a conclusion on the balance of probabilities will in any surmisable circumstance be a reasonable conclusion . . .'

Comment

(1) Note that the issue is whether the employers were reasonable in reaching their conclusion on the facts as they appeared at the time of the decision to dismiss. Whether or not the employee is in fact guilty of the misconduct is beside the point so far as unfair dismissal is concerned. Dismissed employees frequently find this difficult to accept and say that they want to take tribunal proceedings 'to clear my name'.

(2) This approach, with the three requirements of honest belief, reasonable grounds for the belief, and a reasonable investigation, was expressly endorsed by the Court of Appeal in *Weddel* v *Tepper* (1980). While being developed specifically in the context where an employee is suspected of a criminal offence, it is appropriate also in any situation where there is doubt as to what actually occurred. The following caveats should, however, be noted.

Boys and Girls Welfare Society v *McDonald* [1996] IRLR 129
Employment Appeal Tribunal

JUDGE CLARK: '. . .

THE TEST OF REASONABLENESS

One starting point is the oft-cited *"Burchell* test". *British Home Stores Ltd* v *Burchell* (1980) was decided by this Appeal Tribunal (Sir John Arnold presiding) on 20 July 1978. Although earlier reported in the Industrial Relations Law Reports it came to prominence after being cited with approval by the Court of Appeal in *Weddel & Co* v *Tepper* (1980), see per Stephenson LJ and Cumming-Bruce LJ. The decision in *Burchell* was consequently published as a Note following the report of *Weddel* in the Industrial Cases Reports and has since come to be regarded as the leading authority on [ERA s 98(4)].

. . .

Whilst accepting unreservedly the importance of that test, we consider that a simplistic application of the test in each and every conduct case raised a danger of employment tribunals falling into error in the following respects.

(1) The burden of proof

Burchell itself was decided on the provisions of TULRA Sched 1 para 6(8), which provided that the question of reasonableness:

> ". . . shall depend on whether the employer can satisfy the tribunal that in the circumstances (having regard to equity and the substantial merits of the case) he acted reasonably in treating it as a sufficient reason for dismissing the employee."

That wording was reproduced in the Employment Protection (Consolidation) Act 1978 (EPCA) as originally drafted.

The amendment to EPCA s 57(3) effected by s 6 of the Employment Act 1980 produced the following wording:

> ". . . The determination of the question whether the dismissal was fair or unfair, having regard to the reason shown by the employer, shall depend on whether in the circumstances . . . the employer acted reasonably or unreasonably in treating it as a sufficient reason for dismissing the employee; and that question shall be determined in accordance with equity and the substantial merits of the case."

[The test in ERA s 98(4) is to the same effect, although expressed slightly differently.]

Thus, as a result of the 1980 amendment it was no longer necessary for the employer to satisfy the tribunal that it had acted reasonably. The burden of proof on the employer was removed. The question was now a "neutral" one for the employment tribunal to decide.

The risk that by following the wording of Sir John Arnold's test in *Burchell* a tribunal may fall into error by placing the onus of proof on an employer to satisfy it as to reasonableness is not confined to employment tribunals. In *Post Office (Counters) Ltd* v *Heavey* (1989), this Appeal Tribunal, presided over by Wood J, reviewed the legislative history and observed:

> "As the Court of Appeal has indicated on many occasions, the correct direction for an employment tribunal to give themselves is to use the actual wording of the statute, and to remind themselves that there is no burden of proof on either party. A 'neutral' issue is indeed strange to those brought up with our adversarial system. It is not for the employer 'to show', nor for the tribunal 'to be satisfied' – each of which expressions indicate the existence of a burden of proof."

In the next paragraph of the judgment, Wood J acknowledges that it is all too easy to fall into the trap of applying the wrong burden of proof, as the Appeal Tribunal did in *Inner London Education Authority* v *Gravett* (1988) . . .

(2) Universal application of the Burchell *test*

Setting aside the question of onus of proof, it is apparent that the threefold *Burchell* test is appropriate where the employer has to decide a factual contest. The position may be otherwise where there is no real conflict on the facts. In *Royal Society for the Protection of Birds* v *Croucher* (1984), a decision of the Employment Appeal Tribunal presided over by Waite J, the employee was suspected of dishonesty in relation to reimbursement of private petrol use by way of false expenses claims. He admitted the offences but said by way of mitigation that on earlier occasions he had omitted to claim genuine expenses. The employment tribunal, applying the *Burchell* test, concluded that the employer had failed to carry out sufficient investigation and that the dismissal was unfair. On appeal the Employment Appeal Tribunal held that the employee having admitted the misconduct, there was little scope for further investigation and reversed the employment tribunal's finding of unfairness. Waite J said:

"It is difficult to escape the impression that the source of error in the present case may have been their evident view that the test in *British Home Stores Ltd* v *Burchell* was one which fell to be applied automatically whenever reasonableness was in issue, at all events in cases of dishonesty, for the purposes of assessing whether a dismissal had been fair under [ERA s 98(4)]. The *Burchell* case, it will be remembered, was a case which concerned instances in which there has been a suspicion or belief of the employee's misconduct entertained by the employers.

Here there was no question of suspicion or of questioned belief: there the dishonest conduct was admitted. There was very little scope, therefore, for the kind of investigation to which this Appeal Tribunal was referring in *Burchell's* case; investigation, that is to say, designed to confirm suspicion or clear up doubt as to whether or not a particular act of misconduct has occurred. So we think that this may perhaps be another case where an employment tribunal has fallen into error by a misplaced and artificial emphasis upon the guidelines in the *Burchell* case, something to which this Appeal Tribunal had recent occasion to refer in *Lintafoam (Manchester) Ltd* v *Fletcher* (1984).

We repeat what we said then. The *Burchell* case remains, in circumstances akin to those that there were there under consideration, a most useful and helpful guideline; but it can never replace the soundness of an appraisal of all the circumstances of each particular case viewed in the round in the way that [ERA s 98(4)] requires them to be viewed."

(3) The range of reasonable responses test

It should always be remembered that at the conclusion of the threefold test in *Burchell*, Sir John Arnold observed that it is the employer who manages to discharge the onus of demonstrating those three matters who must not be examined further. Leaving aside the onus of proof, we do not understand Sir John Arnold to be saying that the converse is necessarily true; that is to say, an employer who fails one or more of the three tests is, without more, guilty of unfair dismissal. In *British Leyland (UK) Ltd* v *Swift* (1981) the Court of Appeal formulated the range of reasonable responses test. Lord Denning MR said this:

". . . It must be remembered that in all these cases there is a band of reasonableness, within which one employer might reasonably take one view: another quite reasonably take a different view. One would quite reasonably dismiss the man. The other would quite reasonably keep him on. Both views may be quite reasonable. If it was quite reasonable to dismiss him, then the dismissal must be upheld as fair: even though some other employers may not have dismissed him."

. . .'

Comment

(1) This is a timely reminder that the *Burchell* test, like most guidelines, is not to be followed slavishly. It is always necessary to consider whether it is appropriate in the circumstances.

(2) In fact, this is accentuated further in the next case, which stresses that the range of reasonable responses test applies also to the level of investigation carried out.

Sainsbury's Supermarkets Ltd v *Hitt* [2003] ICR 111 Court of Appeal

The employee was accused of stealing a box of razor blades which were found concealed in his locker. He denied theft and pointed out that other employees had keys which fitted his locker and could have planted them there. It was common ground that the employee had had the opportunity to take the blades and also that only one other employee was present in the store at the time who had a key fitting the locker. A statement was taken from this employee, who stated that he had not gone to the part of the store where the blades were stolen on that day. Following a disciplinary hearing, the employee was dismissed for gross misconduct.

MUMMERY LJ: '. . . It is now necessary to consider, first, the reasoning of the majority in the employment tribunal and, secondly, the effect upon that reasoning of the decision of the Court of Appeal in *HSBC* v *Madden* (2000). The reasoning of the majority was that the investigation by Sainsburys of Mr Hitt was flawed and was inadequate. The majority were of the view that Mr Hitt's claim that someone else had put the razor blades into his locker was not adequately investigated. In the view of the majority, Sainsburys should have investigated all the employees in the Barnstaple store at the relevant time to identify those who had a key fitting Mr Hitt's locker and, within that category, those who could have been in the warehouse at the relevant time. In the view of the majority, there had also been inadequate investigation of the whereabouts of Mr Tucker at the relevant time to eliminate the possibility that he had planted the blades in Mr Hitt's locker. The conclusion was that all of these matters should have been the subject of a full and thorough investigation carried out by Sainsburys 'before it labelled [Mr Hitt] a thief for the rest of his life' . . .

Conclusion

I am unable to agree either with the decision of the majority of the employment tribunal or with the decision of the Employment Appeal Tribunal. There is no doubt that the appeal from the employment tribunal raises a question of law. That question is whether that tribunal applied the correct legal test to decide whether Mr Hitt was unfairly dismissed for a conduct reason. The test applied by the majority in the employment tribunal and, I also think, by the dissenting chairman was that laid down by the EAT in *Midland Bank* v *Madden* (2000). Applying that test, the majority considered that the investigation was not reasonable. They arrived at that conclusion by substituting their own opinion as to what was a reasonable and adequate investigation, instead of applying, as was required by the Court of Appeal in the subsequent decision reversing the Employment Appeal Tribunal's decision in *Madden's* case, the objective standard of the reasonable employer as to what was a reasonable investigation.

The employment tribunal were understandably faced with a confusing state of the law as between, on the one hand, the long established approach laid down by Arnold J in the Employment Appeal Tribunal in *British Home Stores Ltd* v *Burchell* (1980) and, on the other hand, the more recent decisions of the EAT in *Haddon* v *Van den Bergh Foods Ltd* (1999) and *Midland Bank plc* v *Madden* (2000). I had hoped that that confusion would have been removed by the subsequent decision of the Court of Appeal on the appeal in *Foley* v *Post Office* and *HSBC* v *Madden* (2000), and that it had been made clear in the judgments that it was necessary to apply the objective standards of the reasonable employer to *all* aspects of the question whether the employee had been fairly and reasonably dismissed. Unfortunately, it appears that the law has not been made as clear as it should have been, since experienced members of the Employment Appeal Tribunal have in this case interpreted what was said in *Madden's* case, in relation to the objective standards of reasonableness and the range of reasonable responses test, as not applying to the question whether an investigation into the alleged or suspected misconduct was reasonable in the circumstances of the case.

In my judgment, the Appeal Tribunal have not correctly interpreted the impact of the decision of the Court of Appeal in *Madden's* case. The range of reasonable responses test (or, to put it another way, the need to apply the objective standards of the reasonable employer) applies as much to the question whether the investigation into the suspected misconduct was reasonable in all the circumstances as it does to the reasonableness of the decision to dismiss for the conduct reason.

If the correct approach is taken to the application of the test laid down by the Court of Appeal to the facts of this case, the only conclusion which a reasonable tribunal could reach is that the investigation in this case was reasonable in all the circumstances. The position is that the employment tribunal's decision was legally flawed by the application of the wrong test. If one looks at the findings of fact, the position is as stated by the chairman in his dissenting conclusions. The investigation carried out by Sainsburys was not for the purposes of determining, as one would in a court of law, whether Mr Hitt was guilty or not guilty of the theft of the razor blades. The purpose of the investigation was to establish whether there were reasonable grounds for the belief that they had formed, from the circumstances in which the razor blades were found in his locker, that there had been misconduct on his part, to which a reasonable response was a decision to dismiss him. The uncontested facts were that the missing razor blades were found in Mr Hitt's locker and that he had had the opportunity to steal them in the periods of his absence from the bakery during the time they went missing. Investigations were then made, both prior to and during the period of an adjournment of the disciplinary proceedings, into the question whether, as Mr Hitt alleged, someone else had planted the missing razor blades in his locker. In my judgment, Sainsburys were reasonably entitled to conclude, on the basis of such an investigation, that Mr Hitt's explanation was improbable. The objective standard of the reasonable employer did not require them to carry out yet further investigations of the kind which the majority in the employment tribunal in their view considered ought to have been carried out . . .'

(Ward and Jonathan Parker LJJ agreed.)

Comment

(1) While an employer should not be expected to carry out a quasi-police investigation and to find proof beyond reasonable doubt, is it not a little worrying that the Court of Appeal says here that the purpose of the investigation need not be aimed at establishing the employee's guilt or innocence, but at finding whether there are reasonable grounds for the employer's belief in his guilt?

(2) It is important to note that in judging whether or not the employer acted reasonably, it is the state of the employer's knowledge at the time of the dismissal which is at issue.

Devis v Atkins [1977] AC 931 House of Lords

The respondent had been employed as manager of the company's abattoir. Despite repeated instructions to buy animals directly from farmers, he persisted in buying animals through dealers. He was dismissed with pay in lieu of notice and an *ex gratia* payment of £6,000. He claimed that his dismissal was unfair. At the tribunal hearing the employers attempted to introduce evidence that he had been taking a secret commission from the dealers, as they had discovered after he left. The tribunal refused to admit this evidence and held that his dismissal was unfair because he had not received a warning before he was dismissed. The employers' appeal was dismissed by the High Court and the Court of Appeal.

VISCOUNT DILHORNE: 'They [the employers] not unnaturally resent the stigma which results from the tribunal's decision. In this appeal they do not challenge that decision on the evidence the tribunal heard, but they say the tribunal erred in refusing to hear evidence of the respondent's conduct which came to their knowledge after his dismissal and so in preventing them from establishing that the respondent was guilty of gross misconduct of such a character that, if they had had that information at the time and had acted on it, his dismissal would not have been unfair. In an action for damages for wrongful dismissal an employer can rely as justifying the dismissal on information only acquired after the dismissal: see *Boston Deep Sea Fishing and Ice Co* v *Ansell* (1888); *Cyril Leonard & Co* v *Simo Securities Trust Ltd* (1971). Why then should they not do so when the question at issue is, was the respondent unfairly dismissed? If they cannot do so, it must follow that a dishonest employee who up to the time of his dismissal has successfully concealed his dishonesty may succeed in obtaining a decision that his dismissal was unfair which, apart from reflecting on his employers, may assist him in obtaining other employment when, if the full facts had been known at the time of his dismissal, that would have been fully justified . . .

Reverting now to TULRA Sched 1 para 6(8) [the predecessor of ERA s 98(4)], it is to be observed that the paragraph does not require the tribunal to consider whether the complainant in fact suffered any injustice by being dismissed. If it had, then I see no reason to suppose that evidence subsequently discovered of the complainant's misconduct would not have been relevant to that question and admissible. The onus is on the employer to show what the reason was ([ERA s 98(1)(a)]) and that it was a reason falling within [ERA s 98(2)] or some other substantial reason of a kind such as to justify the dismissal of an employee holding the position which that employee held. In this case the employers' reason fell within [ERA s 98(2)] as it related to the conduct of the respondent.

Then para 6(8) requires the determination of the question whether the dismissal was unfair "having regard to the reason shown by the employer" to depend on whether in the circumstances the employer had acted "reasonably in treating it as a sufficient reason for dismissing the employee".

"It" must refer to the reason shown by the employer and to the reason for which the employee was dismissed. Without doing very great violence to the language I cannot construe this paragraph as enabling the tribunal to have regard to matters of which the employer was unaware at the time of dismissal and which therefore cannot have formed part of his reason or reasons for dismissing an employee.

Paragraph 6(8) appears to me to direct the tribunal to focus its attention on the conduct of the employer and not on whether the employee in fact suffered any injustice. If in the tribunal's view the employer has failed to satisfy it that he acted reasonably in treating the reason shown to be the reason for the dismissal as a sufficient reason for that dismissal, the conclusion will be that the dismissal was unfair . . .'

(On these grounds, the House of Lords also considered that the after-discovered information could not be taken into account and dismissed the employers' appeal.)

Comment

(1) At this time the law on unfair dismissal was contained in TULRA Sch 1. Paragraph 6(8) was not in exactly the same terms as ERA s 98(4), but the differences are not material for the issue in hand.

(2) At least three members of the House of Lords expressed some concern at their conclusion in this case, because at that time there was an irreducible minimum basic award equivalent to two weeks' pay in any case where a dismissal was found to be unfair. It was felt that this could amount to a 'rogues' charter' in situations where employees had successfully concealed their misdeeds while still employed. The rules were later changed so that, in such a case, the employee can be awarded nothing.

It will be remembered that a dismissal in breach of the statutory dismissal and disciplinary procedure is automatically unfair, regardless of the merits of the case, and the employee should receive a minimum of four weeks' pay (ERA s 120(1A)). No doubt with cases like *Devis* v *Atkins* in mind, this does not apply if it 'would result in injustice to the employer' (ERA s 120(1B)).

(3) The principle of this case is not affected by the no-difference rule in ERA s 98A(2). However, in judging what the employer knew at the time of the dismissal, the tribunal must also take account of what the employer would have known if the omitted procedural step had been carried out.

(4) The tribunal considered that the dismissal was unfair in this case because the employee had not received a warning. The old Acas Code used to include a three-step warning procedure (oral, written, final written warning). The new Code is more circumspect.

Acas *Code of Practice on Disciplinary and Grievance Procedures* (2004)

18 Examples of actions the employer might choose to take are set out in paragraphs 19–25 [see above, p 343]. It is normally good practice to give employees at least one chance to improve their conduct or performance before they are issued with a final written warning. However, if an employee's misconduct or unsatisfactory performance – or its continuance – is sufficiently serious, for example because it is having, or is likely to have, a serious harmful effect on the organisation, it may be appropriate to move directly to a final written warning. In cases of gross misconduct, the employer may decide to dismiss even though the employee has not previously received a warning for misconduct.

Comment

(1) It has also been held that a warning need not be given if it is clear that it will make no difference to the employee's conduct (*Retarded Children's Aid Society* v *Day* (1978)).

(2) Warnings should be disregarded after a specified period. The Code suggests six months for a first warning and 12 months for a final warning (paras 22 and 24). Where a period is stipulated, the employer is likely to be found to have acted unfairly if it takes account of the warning beyond that period (*Bevan Ashford* v *Malin* (1995); *Diosynth Ltd* v *Thomson* (2006)).

(3) What happens if an employee receives a warning for one kind of misconduct and then commits a different kind of misconduct? Must the procedure start again?

Auguste Noel Ltd v *Curtis* [1990] ICR 604 Employment Appeal Tribunal

The company supplied cheese to the wholesale market. The claimant, who had been employed as a delivery driver, was dismissed in March 1988 for mistreatment of two cheeses. He had received a warning in October 1987 for a noisy altercation with two other employees and another warning in February 1988 for failure to complete worksheets properly. The employment tribunal held that his dismissal was unfair because the previous warnings were not relevant to the misconduct for which he was dismissed and he had not received any warnings for cheese abuse.

WOOD J: '. . . Mr Sutcliffe [representing the company] makes a second criticism of that passage. He submits that the tribunal were wrong to say that the prior warnings were irrelevant because they did not refer to the same type of activity as that for which Mr Curtis was dismissed. He has referred us to what seems to be the only authority which he or Mr David Chalk, for the respondents, have been able to find on the issue of the relevance of warnings which is *Stein* v *Associated Dairies Ltd* (1982). This was a decision of this Court sitting in Edinburgh under the chairmanship of Lord MacDonald. The facts in that case were that on 9 April 1981 Mr Stein had received a final warning for some action which did not relate to bad time-keeping. On the following day, having just received that final warning, Mr Stein was 67 minutes late for work. He had previously accumulated periods of lateness which had justified entries in the disciplinary books.

The tribunal dismissed Mr Stein's allegation of unfair dismissal and had awarded £100 expenses against him. His appeal was dismissed. Lord MacDonald indicated that the tribunal were perfectly entitled to take into account the prior final warning albeit that it was not necessarily for the same type of conduct that was involved in that for which the dismissal was decided . . .

Looking at the situation which can exist in an industrial context, it seems to the industrial members sitting with me – and indeed I would respectfully agree – that it can very rarely be said, if ever, that warnings are irrelevant to the consideration of an employer who is considering dismissal. The mere fact that the conduct was of a different kind on those occasions when warnings were given does not seem to us to render them irrelevant. It is essentially a matter of balance, of doing that which is fair and just in the circumstances and an employer is entitled to consider the existence of the warnings. He is entitled to look at the substance of the complaint on each of those occasions, how many warnings there have been, the dates and the period of time between those warnings and indeed all the circumstances of the case. It is quite impossible to lay down any rules nor is it desirable. However, it does seem to us that those are matters which an employer is entitled to take into account and to look at.

In the present case under appeal there is in our judgment an error in law because the tribunal have decided that because the behaviour was not of the same nature or kind as that which had been the subject of the warnings, "therefore" those warnings were irrelevant to the situation which had to be considered by the employer. It seems us that is an error of law. It is a wrong approach and it follows that the reasoning here must be considered flawed.'

(The EAT remitted the case to a fresh tribunal.)

Comment

(1) The statutory dismissal and disciplinary procedure requires employees to be given the opportunity to appeal against a disciplinary decision. What if information about other kinds of misconduct come to light during the appeal? Is this information acquired after dismissal, which should therefore be disregarded in the light of *W Devis* v *Atkins & Sons* (1976)?

West Midlands Co-operative Society Ltd v *Tipton* [1986] ICR 192 House of Lords

The employee had an appalling attendance record. He received clear warnings that he would be dismissed if it did not improve. There was no improvement, and ultimately he was summarily dismissed. The employers then refused to hear his appeal against dismissal, in breach of the agreed contractual procedure. An employment tribunal found the dismissal unfair because of the refusal to entertain his appeal. This was upheld by the EAT but reversed by the Court of Appeal.

LORD BRIDGE: '. . . The appeal raises a question of considerable importance in industrial relations law. A substantial body of case law, based on decisions of the Employment Appeal Tribunal, a specialist court of great expertise in this field, supports the view that where an employer's reason for dismissing an employee has been examined in the course of an appeal under an agreed internal disciplinary procedure and that appeal has been dismissed, the employment tribunal may take into account the evidence which was available for consideration

411

by the employer on the appeal in determining whether the employer acted reasonably or unreasonably in treating his reason for dismissing the employee as sufficient. If this view is right, it would follow that the employer's denial to the employee of an opportunity to prosecute a domestic appeal to which he was contractually entitled could, by itself, justify a finding of unfair dismissal. Conversely, if the Court of Appeal were right in this case, it would follow that in every case where there has been a domestic appeal the employment tribunal must put on blinkers and consider only whether the employer acted reasonably in his original decision to dismiss, notwithstanding that when he rejected the employee's domestic appeal and thereby affirmed the decision to dismiss him he may have been acting quite unreasonably in the light of the further information presented to him in the course of the appeal.

. . . I can see nothing in the language of the statute to exclude from consideration in answering question (3) "in accordance with equity and the substantial merits of the case" evidence relevant to show the strength or weakness of the real reason for dismissal which the employer had the opportunity to consider in the course of an appeal heard pursuant to a disciplinary procedure which complies with the statutory Code of Practice. The apparent injustice of excluding, in relation to this question, misconduct of the employee which is irrelevant to the real reason for dismissal is mitigated, as I have earlier pointed out, by the provisions relating to compensation in such a case. But there is nothing to mitigate the injustice to an employee which would result if he were unable to complain that his employer, though acting reasonably on the facts known to him when he summarily dismissed the employee, acted quite unreasonably in maintaining his decision to dismiss in the face of mitigating circumstances established in the course of the domestic appeal procedure which a reasonable employer would have treated as sufficient to excuse the employee's offence on which the employer's real reason for the dismissal depended. Adopting the analysis which found favour in *J Sainsbury Ltd* v *Savage* (1981), if the domestic appeal succeeds the employee is reinstated with retrospective effect; if it fails the summary dismissal takes effect from the original date. Thus, in so far as the original dismissal and the decision on the domestic appeal are governed by the same consideration, *sc.* the real reason for dismissal, there is no reason to treat the effective date of termination as a watershed which separates the one process from the other. Both the original and the appellate decision by the employer, in any case where the contract of employment provides for an appeal and the right of appeal is invoked by the employee, are necessary elements in the overall process of terminating the contract of employment. To separate them and to consider only one half of the process in determining whether the employer acted reasonably or unreasonably in treating his real reason for dismissal as sufficient is to introduce an unnecessary artificiality into proceedings on a claim of unfair dismissal calculated to defeat, rather than accord with, the "equity and the substantial merits of the case" and for which the language of the statute affords no warrant.

This is the conclusion I should reach as a matter of construction, taking due account of the decision in the *Devis* case, if there were no other authority to guide me. But the conclusion is powerfully reinforced by the series of decisions of the Employment Appeal Tribunal, to which I have earlier referred, with which it is in full accord. The relevant cases are *Rank Xerox (UK) Ltd* v *Goodchild* (1979); *Quantrill* v *Eastern Counties Omnibus Co Ltd* (1980); *National Heart and Chest Hospitals Board of Governors* v *Nambiar* (1981); *Sillifant* v *Powell Duffryn Timber Ltd* (1983) and *Greenall Whitley plc* v *Carr* (1985). I need only quote certain key passages from the judgments.

In *National Heart and Chest Hospitals Board of Governors* v *Nambiar* (1981) Waterhouse J said:

"In this context it is necessary to distinguish the case where an employee is dismissed for reason A and evidence at an internal appeal invalidates reason A but demonstrates that a different reason B would justify dismissal. It is clear that in such circumstances the original dismissal ought not to stand and the employer must look at the matter afresh in order to decide whether a later dismissal on the new information is appropriate. In the more usual case, however, where the employer confirms the decision to dismiss for reason A, following the appeal, we consider that it is right for an employment tribunal to look at the information that came to light in the course of the appeal.

The date of the decision to dismiss and the principal reason for it are established before an internal appeal, but an employment tribunal has to consider whether the employer can satisfy them that, in the words of [ERA s 98(4)]: 'in the circumstances (having regard to equity and the substantial merits of the case) he acted reasonably in treating it as a sufficient reason for dismissing the employee'. In our judgment these are words of broad application and we suggest that our interpretation does not do violence to the language. When an internal appeal body decides or recommends that a dismissal shall stand, it has to consider whether the reason is sufficient to justify confirmation of the dismissal in the light of any new information about it as well as the information available to the employer when the original decision was made; and it would be artificial to exclude the new material from consideration by an employment tribunal adjudicating upon a decision to dismiss that the employer has confirmed."

. . . A dismissal is unfair if the employer unreasonably treats his real reason as a sufficient reason to dismiss the employee, either when he makes his original decision to dismiss or when he maintains that decision at the conclusion of an internal appeal. By the same token, a dismissal may be held to be unfair when the employer has refused to entertain an appeal to which the employee was contractually entitled and thereby denied to the employee the opportunity of showing that, in all the circumstances, the employer's real reason for dismissing him could not reasonably be treated as sufficient. There may, of course, be cases where, on the undisputed facts, the dismissal was inevitable, as for example where a trusted employee, before dismissal, was charged with, and pleaded guilty to, a serious offence of dishonesty committed in the course of his employment. In such a case the employer could reasonably refuse to entertain a domestic appeal on the ground that it could not affect the outcome. It has never been suggested, however, that this was such a case.

I would accordingly allow the appeal . . .'

(Lords Roskill, Brandon, Brightman and Mackay agreed.)

Comment

(1) Note the relevance of this issue also for determining the date at which the dismissal is held to have taken place. This is important because the limitation period for lodging an unfair dismissal claim is only three months from the effective date of termination.

(2) In *Westminster CC v Cabaj* (1996) the EAT held that a dismissal was unfair because the employee's appeal was heard by only two people instead of three, as stipulated in his contract. The Court of Appeal reversed this, holding that even though the procedural failure was also a breach of contract, this did not make the dismissal necessarily unfair. The case was remitted on the issue of whether the procedural failure prevented the employee getting a fair hearing (and now, whether it would have made a difference to the employer's decision to dismiss).

(3) The misconduct for which an employee is dismissed will usually be something done at work. However, it is possible for conduct outside the workplace to constitute a fair reason for dismissal.

Acas *Code of Practice on Disciplinary and Grievance Procedures* (2004)

Criminal charges or convictions not related to employment

43   If an employee is charged with, or convicted of, a criminal offence not related to work, this is not in itself reason for disciplinary action. The employer should establish the facts of the case and consider whether the matter is serious enough to warrant starting the disciplinary procedure. The main consideration should be whether the offence, or alleged offence, is one that makes the employee unsuitable for their type of work. Similarly, an employee should not be dismissed solely because they are absent from work as a result of being remanded in custody.

Comment

(1) Because of the 'range of reasonable responses' doctrine, an employer has some degree of latitude in deciding whether or not an offence is relevant to the employee's duties: see *Mathewson* v *R B Wilson Dental Laboratory Ltd* (1988), for example.

(2) How far unacceptability to other employees should be relevant is moot: under ERA s 107, pressure taking the form of a threat to engage in industrial action is to be disregarded in assessing whether a dismissal is fair. See the discussion by Watt (1992).

Retirement

Until the Employment Equality (Age) Regulations 2006 came into force in October 2006, employees who were over the age of 65 or had reached their employer's normal retirement age, if earlier, had no rights to claim unfair dismissal. This was blatant age discrimination and had to change as a result of the Framework Employment Directive (2000/78/EC), which required EU member states to prohibit discrimination on grounds of age, among other things (see Chapter 2, above).

To deal with the issue of retirement and unfair dismissal the Age Regs brought about one of the biggest changes in unfair dismissal law since its introduction in 1971, by adding a sixth general ground on which a dismissal could be regarded as fair: retirement.

Employment Equality (Age) Regulations 2006

30
(1)   This regulation applies in relation to an employee within the meaning of ERA s 230(1), a person in Crown employment, a relevant member of the House of Commons staff, and a relevant member of the House of Lords staff.
(2)   Nothing in Part 2 or 3 shall render unlawful the dismissal of a person to whom this regulation applies at or over the age of 65 where the reason for the dismissal is retirement.
(3)   For the purposes of this regulation, whether or not the reason for a dismissal is retirement shall be determined in accordance with ERA sections 98ZA to 98ZF.

Comment

(1) Absent this regulation, dismissal by way of retirement would be unlawful age discrimination. However, provided that the dismissal of an employee who is aged 65 or more is for 'retirement', then it is not age discrimination. Whether or not it is unfair

dismissal (which is a separate question) is governed by new ss 98ZA–98ZH inserted into the ERA by the Age Regs (confusingly, *between* ERA s 98 and ERA s 98A).

(2) Note that reg 30(2) means that if an employee aged under 65 is dismissed by reason of retirement, there is potential for an age discrimination claim. It is only if an employer has a normal retirement age below 65 which is justified in the sense of being a proportionate means of meeting a legitimate aim that the reason for dismissal will be regarded as 'retirement' for the purposes of unfair dismissal law, and not as age discrimination (ERA ss 98ZA, 98ZE). In practice, there are hardly any employers who could justify having a normal retirement age of below 65, so it is likely that this will become the norm.

(3) Broadly, the scheme of the legislation means that an employer can still compel employees to retire at 65 without facing unfair dismissal claims, provided that they follow the procedure laid down in the Age Regs Sch 6 (which allows an employee to make a request to stay on). Age Concern has challenged the compatibility of this with the Framework Employment Directive in a case referred to the ECJ in December 2006. In *Palacios de la Villa* v *Cortefiel Servicios* (2007) the ECJ held that Spanish law providing for compulsory retirement required objective justification – but that this was made out on the facts.

(4) The first question is whether the employee's contract has been terminated by reason of retirement, as defined in ERA ss 98ZA–98ZF. If not, the general law of unfair dismissal will apply to the dismissal. In this context, it is worth noting also that the former exclusion in the ERA which prevented people over 65 (or their employer's normal retiring age, if earlier) from claiming unfair dismissal was repealed by the Age Regs.

(5) If the employer has put forward retirement as the reason for the dismissal, but the tribunal holds that it is not by reason of retirement as so defined, it is quite likely that the dismissal will be unfair, either because the employer has failed to discharge the burden of showing a potentially fair reason (ERA s 98(1)) or because, in all probability, the employer will not have followed the statutory dismissal and disciplinary procedure (which does not apply to 'retirement' dismissals, but applies if the dismissal is not for 'retirement'), meaning that it will be automatically unfair under ERA s 98A(1). Depending on what the reason for the dismissal is found to be, it may also be age discrimination.

(6) Before looking at which situations count as retirement, it is necessary to define 'intended date of retirement' and 'normal retirement age', as these concepts are vital to the definition.

Employment Rights Act 1996

98ZH   In sections 98ZA to 98ZG –
. . . 'intended date of retirement' means the date which, by virtue of paragraph 1(2) of Schedule 6 of the 2006 Regulations, is the intended date of retirement in relation to a particular dismissal;
'normal retirement age', in relation to an employee, means the age at which employees in the undertaking who hold, or have held, the same kind of position as the employee are normally required to retire.

Comments

(1) Thus the 'intended date of retirement' means a date notified to the employee in compliance with the procedure in the Age Regs. It implies that the employer is potentially on course for dismissing the employee fairly by reason of retirement.

(2) In *Waite* v *GCHQ* (1983) the House of Lords had to construe the meaning of 'normal retiring age' for the purposes of the former exclusion of people over normal retiring age from the right to claim unfair dismissal. They held that 'normal' was not the same as 'usual' and that the test should be, what was the reasonable expectation of employees in the claimant's position? This would usually be retirement at the contractual retirement age, but if there was evidence that this was departed from in practice, then some other age might be established as the normal retiring age. It seems likely that a similar approach will be taken in relation to this definition.

(3) ERA ss 98ZA–98ZH make provision for three categories of dismissal. First, those which do *not* count as retirement, even though that may have been the employer's intention. Secondly, those which will be deemed as retirement and only for that reason, even though the employee may think it was for some other reason. Thirdly, those which may or may not be for retirement.

(4) The following situations do *not* count as 'retirement':

- dismissal before 65 where there is no normal retirement age (ERA s 98ZA);
- dismissal before 65 where there is a normal retirement age below 65 which is not justified under the Age Regs (ERA s 98ZE(2));
- dismissal before normal retirement age, where there is a normal retirement age (ERA s 98ZC);
- dismissal before the intended date of retirement (ERA ss 98ZB(3), (4); 98ZD(3), (4); 98ZE(5), (6)).

(5) In the following situations, retirement will be deemed to be the only reason for the dismissal and any other reason will be disregarded:

- Where the employee is at or above the age of 65, there is no normal retirement age, but the employer follows the Sch 6 procedure and dismisses the employee on the intended date of retirement (ERA s 98ZB(2)).
- Where there is a normal retirement age of 65 or above, the employer follows the Sch 6 procedure and dismisses the employee on the intended date of retirement (ERA s 98ZD(2)).
- Where there is a normal retirement age below 65 which is justified under the Age Regs (unlikely, as noted already), the employer follows the Sch 6 procedure and dismisses the employee on the intended date of retirement (ERA s 98ZE(4)).

(6) In the following situations, the tribunal will have to decide whether the dismissal is by reason of retirement or not:

- Where there is no normal retirement age, the employee is at or above the age of 65 at the date of dismissal, but the employer has not notified the employee in accordance with the requirements of the Sch 6 procedure (ERA s 98ZB(5))
- Where there is a normal retirement age of 65 or above and the employee is at or above that age at the date of dismissal, but the employer has not notified the employee in accordance with the requirements of the Sch 6 procedure (ERA s 98ZD(5)).
- Where there is a normal retirement age below 65 which is justified under the Age Regs, the employee is at or above that age at the date of dismissal, but the employer has not notified the employee in accordance with the requirements of the Sch 6 procedure (ERA s 98ZE(7)).

(7) In making that decision, tribunals must have regard to ERA s 98ZF.

Employment Rights Act 1996

98ZF

(1)   These are the matters to which particular regard is to be had in accordance with section 98ZB(5), 98ZD(5) or 98ZE(7) –

(a)   whether or not the employer has notified the employee in accordance with paragraph 4 of Schedule 6 to the 2006 Regulations;

(b)   if the employer has notified the employee in accordance with that paragraph, how long before the notified retirement date the notification was given;

(c)   whether or not the employer has followed, or sought to follow, the procedures in paragraph 7 of Schedule 6 to the 2006 Regulations.

(2)   In subsection (1)(b) 'notified retirement date' means the date notified to the employee in accordance with paragraph 4 of Schedule 6 to the 2006 Regulations as the date on which the employer intends to retire the employee.

98ZG

(1)   This section applies if the reason (or principal reason) for a dismissal is retirement of the employee.

(2)   The employee shall be regarded as unfairly dismissed if, and only if, there has been a failure on the part of the employer to comply with an obligation imposed on him by any of the following provisions of Schedule 6 to the 2006 Regulations –

(a)   paragraph 4 (notification of retirement, if not already given under paragraph 2),

(b)   paragraphs 6 and 7 (duty to consider employee's request not to be retired),

(c)   paragraph 8 (duty to consider appeal against decision to refuse request not to be retired).

Comment

(1) It will be clear that compliance with the procedure in Sch 6 of the Age Regs is crucial for the employer, and this will be looked at next.

(2) The effect of ERA s 98ZF is that if the employer fails to comply with some aspects of that procedure, all will not necessarily be lost. As long as the employer tries to remedy the defects, it is possible that the tribunal might excuse the lapse by allowing the dismissal to count as a retirement. Presumably, this will depend on how serious the lapse is in the first place and what steps the employer takes to remedy the defect.

(3) However, even if the reason for dismissal is retirement, it will be automatically unfair if the employer fails to comply with the aspects of the procedure listed in ERA s 98ZG.

Employment Equality (Age) Regulations 2006

SCHEDULE 6: DUTY TO CONSIDER WORKING BEYOND RETIREMENT

Duty of employer to inform employee

2   (1)   An employer who intends to retire an employee has a duty to notify the employee in writing of –

(a)   the employee's right to make a request; and

(b)   the date on which he intends the employee to retire,

not more than one year and not less than six months before that date.

(2) The duty to notify applies regardless of –

    (a) whether there is any term in the employee's contract of employment indicating when his retirement is expected to take place,

    (b) any other notification of, or information about, the employee's date of retirement given to him by the employer at any time, and

    (c) any other information about the employee's right to make a request given to him by the employer at any time.

. . .

Continuing duty to inform employee

4 Where the employer has failed to comply with paragraph 2, he has a continuing duty to notify the employee in writing as described in paragraph 2(1) until the fourteenth day before the operative date of termination.

Statutory right to request not to retire

5 (1) An employee may make a request to his employer not to retire on the intended date of retirement.

(2) In his request the employee must propose that his employment should continue, following the intended date of retirement –

    (a) indefinitely,

    (b) for a stated period, or

    (c) until a stated date;

and, if the request is made at a time when it is no longer possible for the employer to notify in accordance with paragraph 2 and the employer has not yet notified in accordance with paragraph 4, must identify the date on which he believes that the employer intends to retire him.

(3) A request must be in writing and state that it is made under this paragraph.

(4) An employee may only make one request under this paragraph in relation to any one intended date of retirement and may not make a request in relation to a date that supersedes a different date as the intended date of retirement by virtue of paragraph 3(3) or 10(3)(b).

(5) A request is only a request made under this paragraph if it is made –

    (a) in a case where the employer has complied with paragraph 2, more than three months but not more than six months before the intended date of retirement, or

    (b) in a case where the employer has not complied with paragraph 2, before, but not more than six months before, the intended date of retirement.

An employer's duty to consider a request

6 An employer to whom a request is made is under a duty to consider the request in accordance with paragraphs 7 to 9.

Meeting to consider request

7 (1) An employer having a duty under paragraph 6 to consider a request shall hold a meeting to discuss the request with the employee within a reasonable period after receiving it.

(2) The employer and employee must take all reasonable steps to attend the meeting . . .

(6) The employer shall give the employee notice of his decision on the request as soon as is reasonably practicable after the date of the meeting . . .

(7) A notice given under sub-paragraph (6) shall –
  (a) where the decision is to accept the request, state that it is accepted and –
    (i) where the decision is that the employee's employment will continue indefinitely, state that fact, or
    (ii) where the decision is that the employee's employment will continue for a further period, state that fact and specify the length of the period or the date on which it will end,
  (b) where the decision is to refuse the request, confirm that the employer wishes to retire the employee and the date on which the dismissal is to take effect,

and, in the case of a notice falling within paragraph (b), and of a notice referred to in paragraph (a) that specifies a period shorter than the period proposed by the employee in the request, shall inform the employee of his right to appeal.

(8) All notices given under this paragraph shall be in writing and be dated.

Appeals

8 (1) An employee is entitled to appeal against –
  (a) a decision of his employer to refuse the request, or
  (b) a decision of his employer to accept the request where the notice given under paragraph 7(6) states as mentioned in paragraph 7(7)(a)(ii) and specifies a period shorter than the period proposed by the employee in the request,

by giving notice in accordance with sub-paragraph (2) as soon as is reasonably practicable after the date of the notice given under paragraph 7(6).

(2) A notice of appeal under sub-paragraph (1) shall set out the grounds of appeal.

(3) The employer shall hold a meeting with the employee to discuss an appeal within a reasonable period after the date of the notice of appeal.

(4) The employer and employee must take all reasonable steps to attend the meeting . . .

Comment

(1) The employee has a right to be accompanied to the meeting – but only by a fellow worker, not a permanent trade union official (Sch 6, para 9: contrast the right to be accompanied under ERelA 1999 s 10, above, p 378). If the employer denies her the right, she may complain to an employment tribunal, which can award her up to two weeks' pay (Sch 6, para 12).

(2) Note that the employer's duty is only to consider the request and then communicate the decision to the employee. It is not even necessary to give reasons for the decision, much less to justify it. Hence the fear that employers will merely go through the motions but not actually give serious consideration to altering any decision to retire an employee.

(3) Under Sch 6, para 11 an employee has an independent right of complaint to an employment tribunal if the employer fails to notify her in accordance with the time limits in para 2. If the tribunal upholds the complaint it must award such compensation as it considers just and equitable, subject to a maximum of eight weeks' pay.

Redundancy

An employee of at least two years' standing who is made redundant will be entitled to a redundancy payment. Thus redundancy is a fair reason for dismissal, provided that it is handled reasonably. Advice on how to handle redundancies was contained in the 1972 Industrial Relations Code of Practice, but this was repealed in 1991, since when there has been no code of practice covering this area. However, the interpretation of reasonableness in relation to redundancy has brought back the concepts of good practice in this area.

Williams v *Compair Maxam Ltd* [1982] ICR 156 Employment Appeal Tribunal

The company, which had about 200 employees, was in dire financial straits. The recognised trade union was informed that redundancies would be necessary and that some of these would be compulsory because there were insufficient volunteers. However, the union was not consulted about the criteria to be used, nor given the names of those to be made compulsorily redundant in advance. In fact, the way it was carried out was that the three managers of the different departments were told to 'pick a team' of those who needed to be retained in their department to keep the company viable. The others were made redundant. The employees thus selected for redundancy were given no prior warning. They sued for unfair dismissal.

BROWNE-WILKINSON J: '. . . In law therefore the question we have to decide is whether a reasonable tribunal could have reached the conclusion that the dismissal of the claimants in this case lay within the range of conduct which a reasonable employer could have adopted. It is accordingly necessary to try to set down in very general terms what a properly instructed employment tribunal would know to be the principles which, in current industrial practice, a reasonable employer would be expected to adopt. This is not a matter on which the chairman of this Appeal Tribunal feels that he can contribute much, since it depends on what industrial practices are currently accepted as being normal and proper. The two lay members of this Appeal Tribunal hold the view that it would be impossible to lay down detailed procedures which all reasonable employers would follow in all circumstances: the fair conduct of dismissals for redundancy must depend on the circumstances of each case. But in their experience, there is a generally accepted view in industrial relations that, in cases where the employees are represented by an independent union recognised by the employer, reasonable employers will seek to act in accordance with the following principles:

1   The employer will seek to give as much warning as possible of impending redundancies so as to enable the union and employees who may be affected to take early steps to inform themselves of the relevant facts, consider possible alternative solutions and, if necessary, find alternative employment in the undertaking or elsewhere.

2   The employer will consult the union as to the best means by which the desired management result can be achieved fairly and with as little hardship to the employees as possible. In particular, the employer will seek to agree with the union the criteria to be applied in selecting the employees to be made redundant. When a selection has been made, the employer will consider with the union whether the selection has been made in accordance with those criteria.

3   Whether or not an agreement as to the criteria to be adopted has been agreed with the union, the employer will seek to establish criteria for selection which so far as possible do not depend solely upon the opinion of the person making the selection but can be objectively checked against such things as attendance record, efficiency at the job, experience, or length of service.

4   The employer will seek to ensure that the selection is made fairly in accordance with these criteria and will consider any representations the union may make as to such selection.

5   The employer will seek to see whether instead of dismissing an employee he could offer him alternative employment.

The lay members stress that not all these factors are present in every case since circumstances may prevent one or more of them being given effect to. But the lay members would expect these principles to be departed from only where some good reason is shown to justify such departure. The basic approach is that, in the unfortunate circumstances that necessarily attend redundancies, as much as is reasonably possible should be done to mitigate the impact on the work force and to satisfy them that the selection has been made fairly and not on the basis of personal whim . . .

We must add a word of warning. For the purpose of giving our reasons for reaching our exceptional conclusion that the decision of the employment tribunal in this case was perverse, we have had to state what in our view are the steps which a reasonable and fair employer at the present time would seek to take in dismissing unionised employees on the ground of redundancy. We stress two points. First, these are not immutable principles which will stay unaltered for ever. Practices and attitudes in industry change with time and new norms of acceptable industrial relations behaviour will emerge. Secondly the factors we have stated are *not* principles of law, but standards of behaviour. Therefore in future cases before this Appeal Tribunal there should be no attempt to say that an employment tribunal which did not have regard to or give effect to one of these factors has misdirected itself in law. Only in cases such as the present where a genuine case for perversity on the grounds that the decision flies in the face of commonly accepted standards of fairness can be made out, are these factors directly relevant. They are relevant only as showing the knowledge of industrial relations which the industrial jury is to be assumed as having brought to bear on the case they had to decide.

For the reasons that we have stated, we allow the appeal and substitute a finding that the four claimants were unfairly dismissed. We will remit the case to a differently constituted tribunal to assess the compensation.'

Comment

(1) This is one of the classic 'guidance' cases from the EAT, and it should be remembered that the Court of Appeal has frequently warned against this tendency and stressed that there should be no gloss on the words of the statute. Also, some reliance was placed on the 1972 Industrial Relations Code of Practice in the decision, which has now been repealed. However, despite these caveats, the principles of good practice are widely accepted and can obviously be used also where there is no recognised trade union.

(2) Employers have a statutory duty to consult over multiple redundancies and over transfers of undertakings: this is dealt with in Chapter 9.

(3) Note the emphasis on fair selection, through identification of objective criteria, objectively and fairly applied. The decision refers to length of service as one of these, and traditionally this has been a criterion favoured by trade unions because it is completely objective. However, as it obviously favours older workers, its use is likely to constitute indirect discrimination on grounds of age, unless it can be justified as a proportionate means of achieving a legitimate aim. This is likely to make it less attractive to employers, who tend in any case to prefer selection methods which make an assessment of workers' performance. This case illustrates the importance of being clear about how the 'best' workers will be identified for retention.

(4) Failure to give adequate warnings or to consult with affected employees has hitherto been a ground on which a redundancy dismissal can be found to be unfair – which is what happened in *Polkey* v *Dayton Services* (1988) (above, p 393). However, this is likely to be affected by the '*Polkey* reversal' in ERA s 98A(2). An employer is very likely to be able to say, for example, that the decision to dismiss the employees for redundancy would not have been altered by giving them plenty of warning.

(5) The final category of redundancy dismissals which have often been held to be unfair are those where there has been a failure to try and find alternative employment for the employee.

Vokes Ltd v *Bear* [1974] ICR 1 National Industrial Relations Court

SIR HUGH GRIFFITHS: 'On December 1 1969 the employee commenced employment with the employers as works manager at a salary of £ 3,000 a year, plus a company car and a company house for which he paid a very low rent. By December 1972 he was 47 years of age with a daughter at university, three sons of school age and his salary had been increased to £ 4,000 per annum. In that month the employers were taken over by the Tilling Group. After the takeover the Tilling Group sent the managing director of one of their other companies to investigate their new acquisition the employer company. He was elected to the board and took over as chief executive. He came to the conclusion that the management was top heavy and would have to be pruned. He indicated this in general terms at a meeting of management at which the employee was present at the beginning of February. The employee did not, however, think that his job was at risk; he thought he had an important role to play in the future development of the company under its new ownership, and it was not unreasonable that he should have thought this as he had been actively engaged in future planning.

It came therefore as a profound shock to him when on March 2 he was called into the chief executive's office, told that he was redundant, asked to leave forthwith and not to return to the company premises during working hours. He was paid his redundancy payment of £180, three months' salary in lieu of notice and allowed to use the car for eight weeks and the house for three months. We have not seen any written contract he may have had with the employers but in the absence of such a contract this would appear to be the bare minimum to which he would be entitled at common law. By no stretch of imagination could they be described as generous severance terms.

No attempt whatever had been made by the chief executive or anyone else within the company or the Tilling Group to see if this middle aged family man could be employed somewhere else within the group. He was given no real warning that he might be dismissed and before the blow fell no assistance whatever to find alternative employment . . .

Having decided that the employee was dismissed by reason of redundancy the tribunal then turned to consider whether nevertheless his dismissal was unfair by virtue of the provisions of [ERA s 98(4)]. The tribunal held that it was unfair because no attempt whatever had been made to see if the employee could have been fitted into some other position in the group before he was dismissed. The evidence showed that the Tilling Group consisted of some 300 companies and there was evidence that at least one of those companies was advertising for persons to fill senior management positions shortly after Mr Bear's dismissal. The Tilling Group apparently had no centralised machinery for providing services to all the companies in the group and it was argued before the tribunal and before this court that in all the circumstances it would have been impracticable to have made any enquiries within the group to see if there was another position that the employee might fill. The tribunal would have none of this argument. They said:

> "We do not think that such enquiries were impracticable. We think that some enquiries should have been made to see whether it was possible to help someone like the employee whose services had proved satisfactory to his employers in every respect. We think the employers' failure to consider the question of finding some other position for the employee in the group made the dismissal unfair."

We find ourselves in full agreement with the way in which the tribunal expressed themselves. It would have been the simplest of matters to have circulated an enquiry through the group to see if any assistance could be given to the employee in the very difficult circumstances in which he would shortly find himself . . .'

Comment

(1) This case is a good illustration of the sort of situation where the employer could be expected to make an effort to find alternative employment. Clearly, it will depend on the size and resources of the organisation in each case.

(2) In addition to these general grounds of unfairness, selection for redundancy will be automatically unfair if it is for one of the reasons discussed below for which dismissal would be automatically unfair.

Breach of statute

Where continued employment would be in breach of statute, it will be fair to dismiss the employee provided that the employer acts reasonably. Thus, where a particular qualification is necessary for a job (such as passing examinations for solicitors or accountants) an employee who fails may be fairly dismissed – although it may be reasonable to let them have another chance first (see, for example, *Sutcliffe and Eaton Ltd* v *Pinney* (1977)).

'Some other substantial reason'

The final category of fair reason is not really a category at all. It can embrace a variety of reasons which are not taken up elsewhere, and its boundaries are unlimited.

Hollister v *National Farmers' Union* [1979] ICR 542 Court of Appeal

The claimant was employed as a group secretary by the union in Cornwall. Group secretaries received a small salary from the union and gained most of their income through commission on insurance sold to members through an associated insurance company. For historical reasons, the arrangements in Cornwall were different from the rest of the country and the group secretaries were not so well off. It was finally decided to bring them into line with the rest of the country, which involved various changes to their contractual arrangements. The tribunal found that most conditions were as good or better than before, but pension arrangements were not as good. The claimant refused to accept the new arrangements and so his contract was terminated. He sued for unfair dismissal.

LORD DENNING MR: '. . . The question which is being discussed in this case is whether the reorganisation of the business which the National Farmers' Union felt they had to undertake in 1976, coupled with Mr Hollister's refusal to accept the new agreement, was a substantial reason of such a kind as to justify the dismissal of the employee. Upon that there have only been one or two cases. One we were particularly referred to was the case of *Ellis* v *Brighton Co-operative Society Ltd* (1976), where it was recognised by the court that reorganisation of business may on occasion be a sufficient reason justifying the dismissal of an employee. They went on to say:

> "Where there has been a properly consulted-upon reorganisation which, if it is not done, is going to bring the whole business to a standstill, a failure to go along with the new arrangements may well – it is not bound to, but it may well – constitute 'some other substantial reason'."

Certainly, I think, everyone would agree with that. But in the present case Arnold J expanded it a little so as not to limit it to where it came absolutely to a standstill but to where there was some sound, good business reason for the reorganisation. I must say I see no reason to differ from Arnold J's view on that. It must depend on all the circumstances whether the reorganisation was such that the only sensible thing to do was to terminate the employee's contract unless he would agree to a new arrangement. It seems to me that that paragraph may well be satisfied, and indeed was satisfied in this case, having regard to the commercial necessity of rearrangements being made and the termination of the relationship with the Cornish Mutual, and the setting up of a new relationship via the National Farmers' Union Mutual Insurance Society Ltd. On that rearrangement being made, it was absolutely essential for new contracts to be made with the existing group secretaries: and the only way to deal with it was to terminate the agreements and offer them reasonable new ones. It seems to me that that would be, and was, a substantial reason of a kind sufficient to justify this kind of dismissal . . .'

(Eveleigh LJ and Sir Stanley Rees agreed with Lord Denning that the dismissal in these circumstances was fair.)

Comment

(1) This authority has frequently been relied on in relation to restructuring of organisations as well as for variations to individuals' contracts. It can be quite difficult to explain to employees how come they have to abide by the terms of the contract while they cannot hold their employers to the agreed terms.

(2) Obviously, employers will have genuine needs to reorganise, particularly in difficult financial situations. But how far is it fair to pass this on to the workforce? In *St John of God (Care Services) Ltd* v *Brooks* (1992) a hospital run by a charity was faced with the need to make massive cuts in order to stay open. They proposed that paid holidays should be reduced, overtime rates abolished, the generous sick pay arrangements reduced to the statutory minimum and removal of the guarantee to link pay scales to national pay scales in future. Employees who refused the new contracts were dismissed. An employment tribunal found the dismissals unfair, in that this was not an offer which a reasonable employer could expect the workforce to accept. The EAT held that this was the wrong test: the question was whether the decision to dismiss was fair or unfair, judged in all the circumstances pertaining at that time. The case was therefore remitted to the tribunal. However, it provides a fairly extreme example of what may occur. Should dismissals be fair in these circumstances, bearing in mind that this will not count as a redundancy situation?

(3) Customer pressure has also been accepted as constituting some other substantial reason. However, the emphasis on justice to the employee is important, since the reason for the customer's reaction cannot be scrutinised by a tribunal in the same way as an employer's decision to dismiss (cf *Dobie* v *Burns International Security Services* (1984)). By the same token, a personality clash or unacceptability to other employees may constitute some other substantial reason (see *Treganowan* v *Knee* (1975) and *Perkin* v *St George's Healthcare NHS Trust* (2005), for example). However, note the point made in Comment (2) above, p 414.

(4) Expiry of a fixed-term or limited-term contract without renewal where the employer has a genuine short-term need has also been held to be some other substantial reason (*Terry* v *East Sussex CC* (1976)) and ERA s 106 provides that where a temporary replacement is taken on to cover the job of someone on maternity leave or someone

absent for a medical suspension, their termination will be regarded as being for some other substantial reason as long as the short-term nature of their engagement was notified to them in writing when they were taken on. However, as no general unfair dismissal obligations are assumed until the employee has been employed for a year, this does not arise frequently in practice. Dismissal in connection with the transfer of an undertaking which has been justified by an economic, technical or organisational reason will be treated as being either for redundancy or for some other substantial reason, by virtue of the Transfer of Undertakings (Protection of Employment) Regulations 2006 (see Chapter 9). All such dismissals must still be tested against the standard of reasonableness.

Automatically unfair dismissals

Certain kinds of reason for dismissal will be treated as automatically unfair. Where this applies, the employee does not have to have been continuously employed for one year before claiming. The categories have expanded over the years, partly as a result of EU directives as well as developments in government policy. There is some evidence from recent tribunal statistics that employees dismissed with less than one year's service are exercising considerable creativity in attempting to frame their claims under one of these headings. The main categories of automatically unfair reason are as follows:

- Dismissal in connection with family rights (see Chapter 6).
- Dismissal for refusal to do shop work or betting work on a Sunday (ERA s 101).
- Dismissal in connection with the Working Time Regulations 1998 (see Chapter 6).
- Dismissal of an employee trustee of a pension scheme (ERA s 102).
- Dismissal of employee representatives for consultation (see Chapter 9).
- Dismissal for making a protected disclosure (see Chapter 4).
- Dismissal contrary to the National Minimum Wage Act 1998 or the Tax Credits Act 1999 (ERA ss 104A, 104B).
- Dismissal for taking part in protected industrial action (see Chapter 12).
- Dismissal for trade union membership reasons (see Chapter 10).
- Dismissal on health and safety grounds.
- Dismissal for asserting a statutory right.

Most of these are dealt with elsewhere, as indicated. The last two categories are considered here.

Dismissal on health and safety grounds

Employment Rights Act 1996

100 (1) An employee who is dismissed shall be regarded for the purposes of this Part as unfairly dismissed if the reason (or, if more than one, the principal reason) for the dismissal is that –

   (a) having been designated by the employer to carry out activities in connection with preventing or reducing risks to health and safety at work, the employee carried out (or proposed to carry out) any such activities,

(b) being a representative of workers on matters of health and safety at work or member of a safety committee –
(i) in accordance with arrangements established under or by virtue of any enactment, or
(ii) by reason of being acknowledged as such by the employer,
the employee performed (or proposed to perform) any functions as such a representative or a member of such a committee,

(ba) the employee took part (or proposed to take part) in consultation with the employer pursuant to the Health and Safety (Consultation with Employees) Regulations 1996 or in an election of representatives of employee safety within the meaning of those Regulations (whether as a candidate or otherwise),

(c) being an employee at a place where –
(i) there was no such representative or safety committee, or
(ii) there was such a representative or safety committee but it was not reasonably practicable for the employee to raise the matter by those means,
he brought to his employer's attention, by reasonable means, circumstances connected with his work which he reasonably believed were harmful or potentially harmful to health or safety,

(d) in circumstances of danger which the employee reasonably believed to be serious and imminent and which he could not reasonably have been expected to avert, he left (or proposed to leave) or (while the danger persisted) refused to return to his place of work or any dangerous part of his place of work, or

(e) in circumstances of danger which the employee reasonably believed to be serious and imminent, he took (or proposed to take) appropriate steps to protect himself or other persons from the danger.

(2) For the purposes of subsection (1)(e) whether steps which an employee took (or proposed to take) were appropriate is to be judged by reference to all the circumstances including, in particular, his knowledge and the facilities and advice available to him at the time.

(3) Where the reason (or, if more than one, the principal reason) for the dismissal of an employee is that specified in subsection (1)(e), he shall not be regarded as unfairly dismissed if the employer shows that it was (or would have been) so negligent for the employee to take the steps which he took (or proposed to take) that a reasonable employer might have dismissed him for taking (or proposing to take) them.

Comment

(1) As explained in the next extract, this section was introduced in order to comply with the EU Framework Directive on Health and Safety (89/391/EEC).

(2) In general, it has been interpreted liberally: see, for example, *Goodwin* v *Cabletel* (1997); *Harvest Press* v *McCaffrey* (1999) and *Masiak* v *City Restaurants (UK) Ltd* (1999).

(3) Note that ERA s 100(d) actually allows employees to down tools if they reasonably believe that there is an imminent danger. This could be risky. If a tribunal takes a different view of the facts, they could be taking part in unofficial industrial action, putting themselves at risk of being dismissed without any remedy.

Balfour Kilpatrick Ltd v *Acheson* [2003] IRLR 683 Employment Appeal Tribunal

The employers provided electrical services on major construction sites. They had 240 employees on one particular site which became waterlogged because of prolonged and exceptionally heavy rainfall. The men complained that their clothes were soaking and they had concerns about working in standing water with electricity. Rats had been seen on the site and they were also worried about the risk of Weil's disease (a water-borne disease from rats' urine) from working in standing water. They asked to go home for the rest of the day. When this request was refused, they left anyway. Matters were not resolved over the next two days and the employers finally responded by dismissing all of them. The employees claimed that their actions fell within ERA s 100(1)(c) and 100(1)(d) and so the dismissals were automatically unfair. The employment tribunal held that s 100(1)(d) did not apply, because there was no serious and imminent danger at the time of the dismissals. This finding was not appealed. The tribunal found that their behaviour did come within s 100(1)(c), however. The employers appealed.

ELIAS J: '. . . The genesis of s 100 is to be found in the Framework Health and Safety Directive (89/391/EEC) on the introduction of measures to encourage improvements in the safety and health of workers at work . . . Article 8(4) deals amongst other matters with the evacuation of workers facing serious and imminent danger. It is as follows:

> "Workers who, in the event of serious, imminent and unavoidable danger, leave their workstation and/or a dangerous area may not be placed at any disadvantage because of their action and must be protected against any harmful and unjustified consequences, in accordance with national laws and/or practices."

. . . Article 11 deals with consultation and participation of workers. There is a duty to consult and allow workers and/or their representatives to take part in discussions on all questions relating to health and safety at work. Article 11(4) provides that workers and their representatives should not be placed at a disadvantage because of exercising their respective rights conferred upon them by the directive.

The obligations cast on workers are found in art 13. Article 13(2)(d) provides in terms that workers must

> "immediately inform the employer and/or the workers with specific responsibility for the safety and health of workers of any work situation they have reasonable grounds for considering represents a serious and immediate danger to safety and health and of any shortcomings in the protection arrangements."

Section 100 is only one of a number of provisions which together implement the directive. It does, however, implement the employment protection aspects of the directive. It is mirrored by a very similar provision in s 44 of the ERA which gives protection to workers and their representatives from detrimental action short of dismissal . . .

. . . Mr Linden [counsel for the employer] correctly noted that s 100(1)(c) requires that it is only if there is no safety representative or safety committee, or if it is not practicable for the employee to raise matters by those means, that he can use alternative means to bring to the employer's attention health and safety concerns. He submits with considerable force that that was not the question the tribunal asked itself. It did not consider whether it was reasonably practicable to use a safety representative; rather it asked whether it was reasonable for the men to use the representatives Mr Campbell and Mr Thompson [their trade union representatives].

. . . We accept that Mr Linden is right about that. It is impossible in our view to suggest otherwise. It may as a tribunal found to have been reasonable – perhaps even more reasonable – to express their concerns to the union representatives and the safety representatives. But that is not on the face of it what the section requires should be done.

427

However, in our view that is not the end of the matter. There is something highly artificial about a contention that when drawing matters of serious and imminent concern to the employer, the employees must concern themselves with the appropriate route whereby that information is conveyed. In the practical world, we cannot believe that any employer would criticise an employee for informing him of imminent health and safety risks, whether directly or through any other means of communication. The important thing is that the message is communicated quickly and succinctly. Moreover, in art 13(2)(d) of the Directive, which we have reproduced above, it is provided in terms that workers must "immediately inform the employer" of serious and immediate dangers to health and safety. If and in so far as there is a conflict between the Directive and ERA s 100(1)(c) then we must so far as we can construe the section compatibly with the Directive. We consider that there is no difficulty in doing that: in our view it would be possible to insert at the end of s 100(1)(e) the words "or to communicate these circumstances by any appropriate means to the employer". That would in turn restrict, in our view, the scope of 100(1)(c). It may be there are better ways of achieving the same result. What we are clear about, however, is that an employee exercising his obligations under art 13 of the Directive – and we emphasise that they are obligations – cannot conceivably be lawfully dismissed under English law on that account.

Accordingly, although we accept that the tribunal did not ask the right question in relation to s 100(1)(c), we are satisfied that nonetheless the employees were entitled to raise their concerns through the union representatives . . .

Were the matters being brought to employer's attention?

The argument here is that it is impossible to say that taking industrial action amounts to bringing to the employer's attention the potentially harmful risks to health and safety. The attention was drawn to the employer through the channel of the union representatives, and the taking of concerted and collected action did not in any way constitute the drawing attention of the concerns at all. What it was doing was drawing attention to the seriousness to which the workers viewed these matters, coupled with a desire to seek to compel the employers to do something about them. Mr Linden also submitted that it would be absurd to say that taking industrial action could conceivably be reasonable means within the meaning of s 100(1)(c), particularly when it constituted unlawful industrial action under domestic law. Moreover, it would be conflating the distinct provisions in subsections (c) and (d) to say that action taken under (d) could also fall within (c).

. . . We accept the appellant's submissions on this point. It seems to us that that even with a liberal construction of the subsection, it is not possible to say that taking industrial action could be reasonable means of bring the employer's attention to health and safety concerns. Nor could it amount to "informing" within the meaning of art 13(2)(g) of the Directive. We accept that there may be circumstances where communication can be by action rather than words, although this must be exceptional. For example, an employee may point out a hazard to his employer who is some distance away from him. We would also accept that the fact that the matter falls under one provision of ERA s 100 would not in itself preclude it from being protected by another. In our judgment, however, the concept of informing the employer cannot extend to taking industrial action to impress upon him the gravity of the issue as perceived by the employees. That is, in truth, part of the process of industrial warfare when the attempted negotiations to resolve the impasse have broken down.

That is not to say that employees may not be perfectly justified in resolving to take industrial action in an appropriate case to seek to put pressure on the employer to concede to what they consider to be wholly reasonable and justified health and safety concerns. However, as the law stands, such action cannot lawfully be taken without a ballot, save where the action is taken by employees together who are exercising their rights in s 100(1)(d). We fully appreciate that in this case the workers were deeply concerned that if the matter went through the usual procedural channels, as the employer was asserting should be the case, then it could take many months for the issue to be resolved. That was hardly a satisfactory resolution for a short-term problem generating real health and safety concerns. But we cannot remedy the weakness of the law in other respects to protect action by these employees by giving what, in our judgment, would be a wholly artificial and unrealistic construction of subsection (c).

The result is, therefore, that these workers are not protected under the automatically unfair provisions of s 100(1)(c) . . .'

Comment

(1) This in turn resulted in most of the workers being unable to bring an unfair dismissal claim because for members of one of the two unions it was 'unofficial industrial action' (see below, p 589) and even for the others, who could potentially claim, most were ruled out because they had less than one year's employment.

(2) Note the EAT's extension of the protection in ERA s 100(1)(c), in order to ensure its compatibility with the Framework Health and Safety Directive.

(3) ERA s 100 is complemented by ERA s 44, which protects employees from suffering any detriment short of dismissal on these grounds.

Dismissal for asserting a statutory right

Employment Rights Act 1996

104 (1) An employee who is dismissed shall be regarded for the purposes of this Part as unfairly dismissed if the reason (or, if more than one, the principal reason) for the dismissal is that the employee –

    (a) brought proceedings against the employer to enforce a right of his which is a relevant statutory right, or

    (b) alleged that the employer had infringed a right of his which is a relevant statutory right.

(2) It is immaterial for the purposes of subsection (1) –

    (a) whether or not the employee has the right, or

    (b) whether or not the right has been infringed;

but, for that subsection to apply, the claim to the right and that it has been infringed must be made in good faith.

(3) It is sufficient for subsection (1) to apply that the employee, without specifying the right, made it reasonably clear to the employer what the right claimed to have been infringed was . . .

Comment

(1) This was introduced on the back of ERA s 100 – the argument being that employees should not risk dismissal for exercising any individual rights, not just health and safety rights. However, there is no corresponding protection for detriment short of dismissal.

(2) This is comparable to the non-victimisation provisions in the equality enactments – but there is one big difference. The equality enactments extend protection to other employees who assist a co-worker who is claiming unlawful discrimination. There is no specific protection here for an employee assisting another employee to assert a statutory right.

Remedies for unfair dismissal

Reinstatement and re-engagement

Employment Rights Act 1996

114　(1)　An order for reinstatement is an order that the employer shall treat the complainant in all respects as if he had not been dismissed.

　　(2)　On making an order for reinstatement the tribunal shall specify –

　　　　(a)　any amount payable by the employer in respect of any benefit which the complainant might reasonably be expected to have had but for the dismissal (including arrears of pay) for the period between the date of termination of employment and the date of reinstatement;

　　　　(b)　any rights and privileges (including seniority and pension rights) which must be restored to the employee, and

　　　　(c)　the date by which the order must be complied with.

　　(3)　If the complainant would have benefited from an improvement in his terms and conditions of employment had he not been dismissed, an order for reinstatement shall require him to be treated as if he had benefited from that improvement from the date on which he would have done so but for being dismissed.

. . .

115　(1)　An order for re-engagement is an order, on such terms as the tribunal may decide, that the complainant be engaged by the employer, or by a successor of the employer or by an associated employer, in employment comparable to that from which he was dismissed or other suitable employment. . . .

Comment

(1) Reinstatement and re-engagement are categorically stated to be the first remedies which should be considered; however, they are rarely awarded: the figure has remained constant at about 1 per cent of cases proceeding to a hearing. Explanations for this vary, but it seems that the remedy is sought by very few claimants, because they fear victimisation if they return to work for the employer.

(2) Re-employment should not be ordered against the wishes of the employee. Apart from that, there are two limiting factors: whether it is practicable for the employer to reinstate or re-engage the employee, and whether it would be just to order re-employment, if the employee caused or contributed to some extent to his dismissal (ERA s 116). Under ERA s 116(5), the fact that an employer has taken on a permanent replacement for the dismissed employee is not to be taken to make reinstatement impracticable unless either it was not practicable to cover the work in any other way or a reasonable time had passed without the employee indicating that he would be seeking this remedy.

(3) Where an employer fails to comply with a reinstatement order, the tribunal makes an additional award of between 13 and 26 weeks' pay – unless the employer can show that it was not practicable to comply with the order. Employers thus get two chances to argue impracticability (see *Port of London Authority* v *Payne* (1994)).

Compensation

In general, compensation is made up of two elements: a basic award and a compensatory award. If an employer fails to comply with a re-employment order, an additional award is made as well. In the case of certain kinds of automatically unfair dismissal there are minimum levels of award: these are mentioned in relation to those grounds.

The basic award (ERA s 119)

The basic award is calculated according to a fixed mathematical formula:

$$\frac{\text{Years of}}{\text{service}} \times \frac{\text{Week's}}{\text{pay}} \times \frac{\text{Multiplier}}{(\frac{1}{2} \text{ or } 1 \text{ or } 1\frac{1}{2})}$$

Comment

(1) Years of service refers to *complete* years of service, up to a maximum of 20.

(2) Week's pay refers to gross pay, but is limited to a maximum figure which is uprated annually in line with the retail prices index. It stood at £330 in 2008.

(3) The multiplier depends on age: employees get half a week's pay for every year in which they were aged under 22, one week's pay for every year in which they were aged between 22 and 41, and one and a half weeks' pay for every year in which they were aged 41 or more. The maximum in 2008 was therefore £9,900. Note that a redundancy payment is calculated in the same way.

(4) The basic award can be reduced by a percentage fixed by the tribunal on three grounds. First, where the employee has unreasonably refused an offer of reinstatement (but not re-engagement) from the employer. Secondly, where the conduct of the employee makes it just and equitable to reduce the award. This refers to any conduct before the dismissal, even if the employer does not discover it until afterwards. This takes care of the problem noted in *W Devis* v *Atkins & Sons* (1976): if the employer dismisses unfairly, but later discovers grounds which would have justified the dismissal, the employee is entitled to a decision that the dismissal was unfair, but may well find that the compensation is reduced by 100 per cent because of her blameworthy conduct.

Thirdly, if the dismissal is for redundancy and the employee is awarded, or has already been paid, a redundancy payment, this will be deducted from the basic award to avoid double compensation.

The compensatory award

Employment Rights Act 1996

123 (1) Subject to the provisions of this section and sections 124, 124A and 126, the amount of the compensatory award shall be such amount as the tribunal considers just and equitable in all the circumstances having regard to the loss sustained by the complainant in consequence of the dismissal in so far as that loss is attributable to action taken by the employer . . .

Comment

(1) Between 1972 and 1999 the value of the maximum compensatory award in real terms slipped considerably, because it was not uprated in line with inflation or prices. In 1999 it stood at only £11,300. In its 1998 White Paper, *Fairness at Work* (Cm 3968) the government proposed to scrap the maximum limit altogether. It was persuaded not to do so, largely because it might make it harder to settle disputes before they got to the tribunal (because it would be difficult to quantify the value of a claim). The maximum

limit on the compensatory award was, however, raised substantially, to £50,000. It is now uprated annually by reference to the retail price index and stood at £63,000 in 2008.

(2) While the statutory formulation appears to leave tribunals with a high degree of discretion in calculating compensation, in fact fairly detailed rules have been developed through the case law. The starting point is the decision of the National Industrial Relations Court in an early appeal on the subject. They refer to the equivalent provisions to ERA s 123, which at that time were contained in the Industrial Relations Act 1971.

Norton Tool Co Ltd v *Tewson* [1972] ICR 501
National Industrial Relations Court

SIR JOHN DONALDSON: '. . . In our judgment, the common law rules and authorities on wrongful dismissal are irrelevant. That cause of action is quite unaffected by the 1971 Act which has created an entirely new cause of action, namely, the "unfair industrial practice" of unfair dismissal. The measure of compensation for that statutory wrong is itself the creature of statute and is to be found in the Act of 1971 and nowhere else. But we do not consider that Parliament intended the court or tribunal to dispense compensation arbitrarily. On the other hand, the amount has a discretionary element and is not to be assessed by adopting the approach of a conscientious and skilled cost accountant or actuary. Nevertheless, that discretion is to be exercised judicially and on the basis of principle.

The court or tribunal is enjoined to assess compensation in an amount which is just and equitable in all the circumstances, and there is neither justice nor equity in a failure to act in accordance with principle. The principles to be adopted emerge from section 116 of the Industrial Relations Act 1971 [now ERA s 123]. First, the object is to compensate, and compensate fully, but not to award a bonus, save possibly in the special case of a refusal by an employer to make an offer of employment in accordance with the recommendation of the court or a tribunal. Secondly, the amount to be awarded is that which is just and equitable in all the circumstances, having regard to the loss sustained by the complainant. "Loss", in the context of [ERA s 123], does not include injury to pride or feelings . . .

In these circumstances, and in the light of the request of the parties to which we have already referred, we shall substitute our own award. In our judgment the employee is entitled to compensation in the sum of £375. This sum we regard as just and equitable in all the circumstances having regard to the loss sustained by him. That loss falls to be considered under the following heads.

(a) Immediate loss of wages

The Contracts of Employment Act 1963, as amended by the Industrial Relations Act 1971, entitles a worker with more than ten years' continuous employment to not less than six weeks' notice to terminate his employment [now 12 weeks for 12 years: see ERA s 86]. Good industrial practice requires the employer either to give this notice or pay six weeks' wages in lieu. The employee was given neither. In an action for damages for wrongful, as opposed to unfair, dismissal he could have claimed that six weeks' wages, but would have had to give credit for anything which he earned or could have earned during the notice period. In the event he would have had to give credit for what he earned in the last two weeks, thus reducing his claim to about four weeks' wages. But if he had been paid the wages in lieu of notice at the time of his dismissal, he would not have had to make any repayment on obtaining further employment during the notice period. In the context of compensation for unfair dismissal we think that it is appropriate and in accordance with the intentions of Parliament that we should treat an employee as having suffered a loss insofar as he receives less than he would have received in accordance with good industrial practice. Accordingly, no deduction has been made for his earnings during the notice period. We have no information as to whether the £25.60 per week is a gross or a take-home figure. The relevant figure is the take-home pay since this and not the gross pay is what he should have received from his employer. However, neither party took this point and we have based our assessment of this head of loss on six weeks at £25.60 per week or £153.60. The employee drew £3 unemployment benefit for a short period, but we were not asked to make any deduction for this and have not done so. Finally, we have taken no account of the extent to which the employee's income tax liability may be reduced by his period of unemployment, since we consider that the sums involved will be small and that such a calculation is inappropriate to the broad, common sense assessment of compensation which Parliament contemplated in the case of unfair dismissal of a man earning the employee's level of wages.

(b) Manner of dismissal

As the employee secured employment within four weeks of his dismissal and we have taken full account of his loss during this period, we need only consider whether the manner and circumstances of his dismissal could give rise to any risk of financial loss at a later stage by, for example, making him less acceptable to potential employers or exceptionally liable to selection for dismissal. There is no evidence of any such disability and accordingly our assessment of the compensation takes no account of the manner of his dismissal. This took place during a heated exchange of words between him and one of the directors.

(c) Future loss of wages

There is no evidence to suggest that the employee's present employment is any less secure than his former employment, and we have therefore taken no account of possible future losses due to short-time working, lay-off or unemployment, apart from loss of rights in respect of redundancy and unfair dismissal which are considered separately below.

(d) Loss of protection in respect of unfair dismissal or dismissal by reason of redundancy

These losses may be more serious. So long as the employee remained in the employ of the employers he was entitled to protection in respect of unfair dismissal. He will acquire no such rights against his new employers until he has worked for them for two years [now one year: see ERA s 108(1)]. Accordingly, if he is unfairly dismissed during that period his remedy will be limited to claiming damages for wrongful dismissal which are unlikely to exceed six week's wages and may be less. Furthermore, on obtaining further employment he will be faced with starting a fresh two-year period. This process could be repeated indefinitely so that he was never again protected in respect of unfair dismissal. Whilst it is impossible for us to quantify this loss, which must be much affected by local conditions, we think that we shall do the respondent no injustice if we include £20 in our assessment on account of it.

The loss of rights under the Redundancy Payments Act 1965 [now ERA Part XI] is much more serious . . .'

Comment

(1) Immediate loss of wages refers to the net benefits which the employee would have received: it can therefore include overtime payments where overtime is regularly worked. The statement that no deduction should be made to take account of anything earned by the employee during her notice period must be read subject to the general principle that the award is intended to compensate and that the employee must mitigate

her loss. It has therefore been modified occasionally where the employee would other-wise be over-compensated by application of this rule.

(2) State benefits received by the employee are ignored by the tribunal in assessing loss up to the time of the tribunal hearing; the employer will be required to pay that part of the award back to the state under the recoupment regulations (Employment Protection (Recoupment of Jobseeker's Allowance and Income Support) Regulations 1996). The recoupment regulations do not apply where the parties themselves settle compensation, and so the employer can make a saving by agreeing a private settlement if found liable. This is facilitated by most tribunals, who often adjourn proceedings after deciding liability so that the parties can reach an agreement.

(3) Amounts awarded under the rubric of future loss cannot be quantified precisely if the employee has not found another job. Tribunals are often criticised for taking too optimistic a view of the employee's chances of re-employment at a similar level to the job she has lost.

(4) As well as wages, the loss of any other benefits received by virtue of the occupation must be compensated. This includes such things as use of a company vehicle, private health insurance, subsidised meals or accommodation, tips, share options and so on. An extremely important matter under this heading is the employee's occupational pension entitlement.

(5) At the time of this decision there was no basic award for unfair dismissal, only a compensatory award. Hence the reference at the end of the extract to the seriousness of the loss of redundancy rights. It was because of the fact that that accrued service entitlement was lost through an unfair dismissal that the basic award (calculated like a redundancy payment) was introduced. However, it remains the case that an employee will not be protected from unfair dismissal until she has completed one full year and will have no redundancy rights until two years are up. A small conventional sum continues to be awarded to reflect this – probably in the region of £250.

(6) Note the statement in the decision that the manner of the dismissal and the fact that it might make it harder to get another job could be taken into account (contrast wrong-ful dismissal, *Addis* v *Gramophone Co* above, p 344). However, the NIRC held that injury to feelings or general distress was not compensatable. This was put in doubt by an *obiter* comment of Lord Hoffmann in *Johnson* v *Unisys Ltd* (2001).

Johnson v *Unisys Ltd* [2001] IRLR 279 House of Lords

(The facts are given in the extract above, p 349.)

LORD HOFFMANN: '. . . In my opinion, all the matters of which Mr Johnson complains in these proceedings were within the jurisdiction of the employment tribunal. His most substantial complaint is of financial loss flowing from his psychiatric injury which he says was a conse-quence of the unfair manner of his dismissal. Such loss is a consequence of the dismissal which may form the subject matter of a compensatory award. The only doubtful question is whether it would have been open to the tribunal to include a sum by way of compensation for his dis-tress, damage to family life and similar matters. As the award, even reduced by 25%, exceeded the statutory maximum and had to be reduced to £11,000, the point would have been aca-demic. But perhaps I may be allowed a comment all the same. I know that in the early days of the National Industrial Relations Court it was laid down that only financial loss could be com-pensated: see *Norton Tool Co Ltd* v *Tewson* (1973) . . . It was said that the word "loss" can only mean financial loss. But I think that is too narrow a construction. The emphasis is upon the tribunal awarding such compensation as it thinks just and equitable. So I see no reason why in an appropriate case it should not include compensation for distress, humiliation, damage to reputation in the community or to family life . . .'

Comment

(1) As might be expected, this set off a storm of speculation and cases were quickly brought testing whether or not compensation for distress was recoverable as part of the compensatory award. The issue was settled by the House of Lords in *Dunnachie v Kingston-upon-Hull CC* (2004).

Dunnachie v *Kingston-upon-Hull City Council* [2004] IRLR 727 House of Lords

LORD STEYN: '. . . The observation of Lord Hoffmann was an obiter dictum. It presents no obstacle to the House now considering the matter in depth.

While in no way determinative of the point of construction before the House, the way in which the Norton Tool case has been acted on since it was decided in 1972 is of some relevance. In practice it has been consistently applied at all levels.

. . .

With the solitary exception of a critical note in 1991 on the *Norton Tool* case by Professor Hugh Collins ("The Just and Equitable Compensatory Award" (1991) 20 ILJ 201) I am not aware of any academic criticism of this decision. A contemporary case note described the decision in the *Norton Tool* case that loss does not include injury to pride or feelings as eminently sensible (see Bruce Reynolds "Compensation for unfair dismissal" (1973) 36 MLR 424).

. . .

Professor Neil MacCormick in *Legal Reasoning and Legal Theory* (1995), wrote:

"In a democratic constitution, it is the elected Parliament which must enact new laws; whether or not all the members of the legislature have the least idea of the contents of clauses of Bills, the least unsuccessful way of securing that the will of elected legislators will prevail will be to take the words enacted by them at their face value and so far as possible apply them in accordance with their plain meaning. In so far as Governments effectively control the business of Parliament, they are then at least put to the necessity of making exactly explicit the policies for which they solicit Parliamentary approval in legislation. And the ordinary citizen will be able to take statutes at their face value."

As he explains elsewhere Professor MacCormick had in mind a plain meaning of words read in their contextual setting. A statute does not always yield such a plain meaning. Sometimes arguments of principle must be considered and a balance of consequential arguments must be struck. But in the present case the citation is in point. Read in context the word "loss" has a plain meaning which excludes non-economic loss. It does not cover injury to feelings. It is to be contrasted with s 66(4) of the Sex Discrimination Act 1975, s 57(4) of the Race Relations Act 1976 and s 8(4) of the Disability Discrimination Act 1995 which all expressly provide for compensation for injury to feelings.

It can readily be accepted that the words "loss" in varying contexts may have wider and narrower meanings. But that proposition is of no legal interest. The question before the House is the meaning of the word "loss" in s 116(1) of the 1971 Act. If properly construed it was restricted to economic loss, the re-enactment of the statutory formula in 1996 must bear the same meaning. It is not a case in which the ambulatory consequences of the always speaking canon of construction has any role to play. Nothing that happened since 1971 could justify giving to the statutory formula a meaning it did not originally bear.

. . .

It may be of some assistance to imagine a Parliamentary draftsman, faced in 1971 with a departmental brief to prepare a bill which would make provision for compensation for financial loss as well as for a *solatium* for injury to feelings. Such instructions could have been given pursuant to the recommendation in 1968 of the Royal Commission that the remedy for unfair dismissal should include compensation for "injured feelings and reputation" (Cmnd 3623). Is it conceivable that a Parliamentary draftsman would have provided for the two radically different remedies by the rolled-up wording of s 116(1)? Intuitively, I regard it as implausible that if such a policy decision had been made the technique of providing simply for compensation for "loss" would have been adopted.

For all these reasons I would hold that the plain meaning of the word loss in s 123(1) excludes non-economic loss . . .'

(Lords Nicholls, Hoffmann, Rodgers and Brown agreed with Lord Steyn.)

Comment

(1) This puts the point beyond further argument. It would require statutory amendment to allow for this head of compensation to be recognised.

(2) Note that the compensatory award is also subject to reduction on account of the employee's conduct.

(3) While the maximum possible award for general unfair dismissal in 2008 was £72,900, most claimants do not get anything like this. The median compensatory award in 2004–5 was only £3,476, suggesting that lifting the limit substantially in 1999 has not had as great an effect as might have been expected.

REFERENCES AND FURTHER READING

L Barmes (2004), 'The continuing conceptual crisis in the common law of the contract of employment' 67 MLR 435

D Brodie (2001), 'Legal coherence and the employment revolution' 117 LQR 604

H Collins (1992), *Justice in Dismissal: the Law of Termination of Employment*, Clarendon Press

H Collins (2001), 'Claim for unfair dismissal' (note) 30 ILJ 305

S Deakin and G Morris (2001), *Labour Law*, 3rd ed, Butterworths

L Dickens, M Jones, B Weekes, M Hart (1985), *Dismissed*, Basil Blackwell

P Elias (1981) 'Fairness in Unfair Dismissal: Trends and Tensions' 10 ILJ 201

K Ewing (1989), 'Job Security and the Contract of Employment' 18 ILJ 217

M Freedland (2003), *The Personal Employment Contract*, OUP

B Hepple (1986), 'Restructuring employment rights' 15 ILJ 69

B Hepple and G Morris (2002), 'The Employment Act 2002 and the crisis of individual employment rights' 31 ILJ 245

G Pitt (1993), 'Justice in Dismissal: a Reply to Hugh Collins' 22 ILJ 251

R A Watt (1992), 'HIV, discrimination, unfair dismissal and pressure to dismiss' 21 ILJ 280

Visit **http://www.mylawchamber.co.uk/pitt**
to access live web updates and web links to extend
your knowledge of Employment Law.

9

REDUNDANCY AND TRANSFERS OF UNDERTAKINGS

In the 1960s the overstaffing of British industry was seen as a major problem. Today, the need to reduce staff costs in order for the business to survive and to have the flexibility necessary to respond quickly to technological developments or market pressures are major reasons for shedding workers. Problems of this kind need not always result in dismissals: retraining and redeployment, reduced recruitment, early retirement, abolition of overtime, reduction in hours and even short-time working are examples of other measures which can be utilised. However, it is often the case that at some point workers will lose their jobs involuntarily.

By the mid-1960s a number of trade unions had concluded severance agreements with employers, providing for procedures to be followed and payments to be received when workers were made redundant. The Redundancy Payments Act 1965 institutionalised and spread the practice of compensating employees thrown out of work, building on what had happened in some sectors as a result of collective bargaining.

Lloyd v *Brassey* [1969] 2 QB 98 Court of Appeal

LORD DENNING MR: '. . . As this is one of our first cases on the Redundancy Payments Act 1965, it is as well to remind ourselves of the policy of this legislation. As I read the Act, a worker of long standing is now recognised as having an accrued right in his job; and his right gains in value with the years. So much so that, if the job is shut down, he is entitled to compensation for loss of the job – just as a director gets compensation for loss of office. The director gets a golden handshake. The worker gets a redundancy payment. It is not unemployment pay. I repeat "not". Even if he gets another job straightaway, he nevertheless is entitled to full redundancy payment. It is, in a real sense, compensation for long service. No man gets it unless he has been employed for at least two years by the employer; and then the amount of it depends solely on his age and length of service . . .'

Comment

(1) The main purpose of providing for compensation in case of redundancy was to sweeten the pill of job loss, in the hope of making redundancy situations more acceptable to employees and trade unions. The result is that the focus of trade union reaction to the announcement of redundancies has shifted from outright opposition and an attempt to get the decision reversed to negotiation about the terms on which the redundancies will be carried out.

(2) The law relating to redundancy has not changed substantially since 1965. It is now consolidated in Part XI of the Employment Rights Act 1996. Between 1965 and 1972, when the action for unfair dismissal became available to sacked employees, a redundancy payment was the only statutory remedy available on dismissal, and so the cases from that period involve employees claiming to be redundant while the employers argue that the dismissal was for some other reason. However, as compensation levels for unfair dismissal are distinctly higher than redundancy payments, since 1972 it is more common to find cases where the employer is the one arguing that the dismissal was for redundancy while the employee claims that it was for a different reason – and unfair. This should be borne in mind in reading the first section of this chapter, dealing with the law of redundancy.

(3) This is another area where EU law has had a considerable effect. One thrust has been in the area of handling redundancies and transfers of businesses, insisting on more transparency in the provision of information to the workforce and consultation with representatives of employees. This is dealt with in the third section of this chapter.

(4) The other major EU development was the attempt to give workers the right to 'follow' their jobs into any new, merged business. Many redundancies come about as a result of mergers as markets consolidate and seek efficiencies through having larger units with fewer workers. In 1977 the EU passed a directive to give workers rights to keep their jobs wherever possible in these circumstances. This was enacted in English law through the Transfer of Undertakings (Protection of Employment) Regulations 1981. These have now been replaced by the Transfer of Undertakings (Protection of Employment) Regulations 2006 (TUPE 2006), and will be considered in the second section of this chapter.

REDUNDANCY

Entitlement to claim

The categories of worker entitled to claim redundancy are the same as for unfair dismissal, except that the police are also included (see p 363). Most importantly, they must be employees and the qualification period for redundancy is longer than for unfair dismissal: they must be able to show that they have two years' continuous employment to qualify for a redundancy payment. As with unfair dismissal, the burden of proof is on the claimant if there is any dispute as to whether the qualifying conditions have been met or whether the employee was dismissed. The definition of 'dismissal' for the purpose of a redundancy claim is found in ERA s 136. It is cast in the same terms as ERA s 95 and interpreted in the same way: on this, see pp 364–377 above. A particular problem in redundancy cases is presented where the employer, following good employment relations practice, gives the workforce as much notice as possible of impending redundancies and employees want to leave for other jobs ahead of the final shutdown.

Doble v *Firestone Tyre and Rubber Co Ltd* [1981] IRLR 300
Employment Appeal Tribunal

The company announced in November that it would be closing its Brentford plant on 15 February, and that staff would receive redundancy notices to expire on that date as they became due. The staff were only entitled to statutory minimum periods of notice, so the dates on which they had to be given notice varied according to their length of service. The claimant employee left early, and then claimed a redundancy payment. The employers argued that he had not been dismissed.

WATERHOUSE J: '. . . The broad submission made by counsel for the appellants is that that announcement constituted a notice of dismissal because a document of this kind amounts to notice of dismissal if either the date on which an individual employee's contract will be terminated is specified in the document or the announcement contains material from which that state can be identified with precision. In support of that proposition the appellant has relied principally upon the oft-cited judgment of Widgery J (as he then was) in *Morton Sundour Fabrics Ltd v Shaw* (1966).

That case establishes that there can be no notice of dismissal unless the document relied upon specifies the actual date of termination of an individual employee's contract or the date can be ascertained precisely from the document. It is necessary to stress, however, that the finding by the Divisional Court in that case was that there was no such identifiable date in the document and that, therefore, the argument that there had been a dismissal could not be upheld. What the Divisional Court did not decide was that, if a document of this kind does indicate a date on which a factory is to close, or even when an individual employee's employment is likely to be terminated, the necessary conclusion is that there has been a dismissal or notice of dismissal. On the contrary, Widgery J, in dealing with one branch of the argument put forward on behalf of the appellant in that case, said:

"It seems to me that however one looks at this case, the employee has the perfectly secure right if he thinks fit to wait until his contract is determined, to take his redundancy payment, and then see what he can do in regard to obtaining other employment. If he does, and one can appreciate that there may be compelling reasons, choose to leave his existing employment before the last minute in order to look for a new job before the rush of others competing with him comes, then that is up to him. The effect of the employer's warning is not in any way to derogate from his statutory rights but to give him an alternative which, if he is so minded, he can accept."

That was a helpful warning to employees who are faced with the kind of dilemma that faced the appellant in the present case, and it is perhaps unfortunate that the learned judge's words have not been more widely publicised.

Looking at the facts of the instant case, we are fully satisfied that the employment tribunal were right to conclude that there was no dismissal; indeed, the conclusion was an inescapable one from the history that we have related.

The first reason for that conclusion is that we do not accept the argument that the date when this appellant's contract of employment was to be terminated was specified in the document or that it was ascertainable with precision therefrom. The passages that we have cited indicated that discussions were to take place and that the implementation of any necessary redundancies was to be a matter of consultation and review as the discussions progressed. It is unnecessary to cite all the relevant material but there was express reference to the fact that consultations were to take place with union representation in order to determine the selection for redundancy. Later in the statement it was said that it was planned to maintain production until 15.2.80, but that was not stated to be a final decision and the question whether any employees might be made redundant before 15.2.80 was still open to discussion, because the statement referred only to the "present" intention of the respondents at the time of the announcement; their plans would be kept under constant review. Again, the announcement stated that individual notices of termination of employment would be issued at appropriate times to those employees who were selected for redundancy. It seems to us quite impossible therefore to say that this statement resolved, so to speak, the position of the individual appellant and we cannot infer that it fulfilled even the first requirement considered by the Divisional Court in the *Morton Sundour Fabrics* case.

The second major reason for rejecting the argument on behalf of the appellant is that we do not consider that this statement to employees could be construed as a notice to individual employees in any event. It was not a statement directed to individual employees: it was handed to branch secretaries of the unions at the beginning of the consultation process in pursuance of s 99 of the Employment Protection Act 1975 [see now TULRCA s 188], and it was circulated by the branch secretaries for information to their own members. When the notices mentioned in the statement were issued later, they were individual notices addressed to the employees concerned and handed to them by departmental managers or other senior employees of the respondents.

The decision of the employment tribunal on the interpretation of the statement of 14.11.79 was, therefore, correct and we are unable to uphold the appellant's arguments . . .'

Comment

(1) In so far as the purpose of the redundancy legislation is to ease the process of downsizing by making employees more willing to accept redundancy, it seems counter-productive to take such a strict approach to the giving of notice. The message for employees is to hang on at all costs until notice is actually given.

(2) Where notice has actually been given to an employee, she may give notice to leave early and yet retain the right to a redundancy payment. Provision for this is made by ERA s 142 – but it contains traps for the unwary. First, the employee's notice must be given in the 'obligatory period', which is that period of notice to which she is entitled by statute. Thus if, under her contract, she is entitled to, and given, three months' notice, but her statutory entitlement would only be five weeks, she must give notice during the last five weeks in order to leave early and keep her redundancy payment. Secondly, the employer is not bound to accept the situation and can serve a counter-notice, requiring the employee to stay to the end of the notice period. If she then insists on going early, it will be up to an employment tribunal to decide what part, if any, of her redundancy payment she should receive.

(3) Assuming that a dismissal is admitted or proved, the next stage is to consider whether it was for redundancy. ERA s 163(2) is relevant here, and its importance is dramatically illustrated by the case following it.

Employment Rights Act 1996

163 (1) Any question arising under this Part as to –
    (a) the right of an employee to a redundancy payment, or
    (b) the amount of a redundancy payment,
shall be referred to and determined by an employment tribunal.
(2) For the purposes of any such reference, an employee who has been dismissed by his employer shall, unless the contrary is proved, be presumed to have been so dismissed by reason of redundancy.

Willcox v Hastings [1987] IRLR 298 Court of Appeal

Willcox and Lane both worked as the only employees in a small business owned and operated by Willcox's father. Willcox senior sold the business to Mr and Mrs Hastings, who both intended to work in the business. This meant that the new owners required one fewer employee – a redundancy reason. They also wanted to bring their son into the business, so in fact they actually dismissed both Willcox and Lane. Replacing one employee with their son was not a redundancy reason. Both Willcox and Lane claimed redundancy payments, but the employment tribunal could not decide which one had been dismissed by reason of redundancy. It therefore held that neither was entitled to a redundancy payment.

SIR JOHN DONALDSON MR: '. . . Two people were dismissed. Two people had to be dismissed because there was a reduction in the requirements of the business to the extent of one employee, and another employee had to make way for the proprietor's son. That is uncontroverted. They [the employment tribunal] then go on to say, "There is no way in which we can decide which reason operated in respect of which employee. We are simply left with two employees leaving the service of the employer and two reasons, each of which could have been the cause of the departure of one such employee. In those circumstances, we just do not know. Maybe both operated on each. We just do not know." Had they then added in the presumption, they must, as I think, have reached the conclusion that the employer had failed to rebut it. As is accepted by Mr Marr-Johnson, appearing for the employers, each case has to be looked at individually. This is not a bulk application. Mr Lane is entitled to say on the findings of the employment tribunal, "They do not know whether I was dismissed wholly or mainly on account of redundancy. Therefore I am entitled to rely on the presumption." Mr Willcox junior is similarly able to say, "They do not know. I can rely on the presumption."

It is an unsatisfactory feature of this particular case that the Solomonic answer is without doubt that there should be one redundancy payment to be divided between the two claimants. It is an injustice if neither claimant can claim a redundancy payment. It is an injustice to the employers if they have to pay two redundancy payments. But we have to administer the law as it is, and, in my judgment, if the presumption in [ERA s 163(2)] is brought into account, as it does not appear to have been brought into account by the employment tribunal, then these two claimants succeed.

I would allow the appeal accordingly.'

(Nourse and Glidewell LJJ agreed.)

The definition of redundancy

Two situations count as redundancy under the legislation. They may loosely be described as (a) dealing with the shutdown of a business (or part of it) and (b) dealing with overstaffing.

Cessation of business

Employment Rights Act 1996

139 (1) For the purposes of this Act an employee who is dismissed shall be taken to be dismissed by reason of redundancy if the dismissal is wholly or mainly attributable to –
(a) the fact that his employer has ceased, or intends to cease –
(i) to carry on the business for the purposes of which the employee was employed by him, or
(ii) to carry on that business in the place where the employee was so employed . . .

Moon v *Homeworthy Furniture (Northern) Ltd* [1977] ICR 117
Employment Appeal Tribunal

KILNER BROWN J: '. . . The appeal raises a novel and important issue under the new legislation.

It was a case where a complete factory was closed down and the whole of the work force made redundant. Mr Stephenson, counsel for the employees, made it plain at the outset that there was a challenge to the validity of the redundancy process and that there was not a genuine redundancy situation. There was no suggestion that it was a contrived redundancy in any sinister sense but that the applicants did not accept that it was justifiable to say that the factory was not economically viable. Broadly put, they considered that it was unfair to the work force to close down the factory, unfair to declare redundancy and therefore dismissals resulting therefrom must also be unfair.

With admirable perspicacity the chairman of the employment tribunal recognised the inherent difficulties in this line of argument. He inquired how far the employment tribunal could go into policy decisions of a board of directors on trading and economic matters. He had in mind, and kept in mind, that the definition of redundancy was to be found in [ERA s 139(1)]. Redundancy arises where in fact the employer has ceased or intends to cease to carry on business or where there is a reduced requirement of labour. However, in order to determine the scope of the inquiry and to delineate the area of the evidence it was agreed to call a director of the employers, Mr Bullard, to give evidence as to what had happened and why it had happened and he was cross-examined along the lines of the general views and beliefs of the work force. One thing emerged with clarity and that was that there was a history of unhappy industrial relations, an involvement of trade union representatives on a local and national level, and an enlistment of the services of the local Member of Parliament. It is obvious, therefore, that when matters have reached this sort of pitch nothing that the employers did would be likely to be acceptable and a trading decision would be regarded as a cloak for an industrial relations decision. As a result of Mr Bullard's evidence it must have seemed plain to most people that there were genuine economic problems. It was still not accepted by the employees that they were sufficiently genuine to oust all political or industrial reasons. Nevertheless one common factor emerged and that was that, whatever the rights and wrongs of the original and persistent labour troubles, the economic difficulties both preceded and succeeded the labour difficulties. It was a classic instance of the age old problem as to whether or not the chicken or the egg came first. The irrelevance and futility of the question is matched only by the irrelevance and futility of the answer . . .

There are no reported decisions on the critical issue in the present case. The cases referred to under the previous jurisdiction concern the application of a redundancy situation on the grounds of unfair operation of redundancy notices either by method or by selection. In *Ram* v *Midland Motor Cylinder Co Ltd* Sir Hugh Collins, in the National Industrial Relations Court, said:

> "Although it is an unlikely situation the court does not exclude the possibility of a redundancy dismissal being unfair albeit it was because a particular works was closed."

Those remarks may well have had significance under the Industrial Relations Act 1971, and in any event were made in passing and merely touching upon a hypothetical situation unlikely to arise. We are now faced with such a situation in reality, unhampered and unsupported by any authority.

After the evidence of Mr Bullard was given, the chairman of the employment tribunal with acute cogency asked Mr Stephenson whether or not he accepted that there was a cessation of work and therefore a closure. With integrity and common sense Mr Stephenson conceded the point. Technically, therefore, a redundancy situation was proved up to the hilt. But Mr

442

Stephenson hung on to his proposition that if the reason of redundancy was relied on it ought to be open to challenge the declaration of redundancy on its merits . . .

Notwithstanding the care and the ability with which Mr Stephenson put his case, we are unable to criticise the way in which the chairman handled the matter or to find fault with his reasoning. However we would prefer to put the matter on a much broader and, in our view, more important basis.

The employees were and are seeking to use the employment tribunal and the Employment Appeal Tribunal as a platform for the ventilation of an industrial dispute. This appeal tribunal is unanimously of the opinion that if that is what this matter is all about then it must be stifled at birth, for it was this imaginary ogre which brought about the demise of National Industrial Relations Court. TULRA 1974 has taken away all powers of the courts to investigate the rights and wrongs of industrial disputes and we cannot tolerate any attempt by anybody to go behind the limits imposed on employment tribunals.

The result is therefore that whether this appeal is considered upon the basis on which it was argued or on the more fundamental basis of jurisdiction, the decision of the employment tribunal was right and there could not and cannot be any investigation into the rights and wrongs of the declared redundancy. There are no grounds for finding any error of law and the appeals are dismissed . . .'

Comment

(1) The unwillingness of tribunals to get drawn into anything which might look political is clearly demonstrated here, as is their equal unwillingness to usurp the managerial prerogative. It is open to employees claiming unfair dismissal, as these were, to argue that the real reason for their dismissal was something other than what the employer claims. However, it seems that if the employer has gone as far as closing down, an objectively verifiable fact, then there can be no going behind the reason.

(2) The position is less clear where the closure is partial and the issue is whether the business has ceased 'in the place where the employee was so employed'. Many employees will have express mobility clauses in their contracts; even if not express, there may be an implied mobility term. In such a situation, is it open to either the employer or the employee to argue that it is not a true redundancy because the contract permits the employee to be moved to another place of work which has not shut down?

High Table Ltd v *Horst* [1997] IRLR 513 Court of Appeal

The employer provided catering services to firms in the City of London. The three claimants had worked for a number of years as waitresses at Hill Samuel until being dismissed in 1993. The reason given by the employer was redundancy: following a reduction in the catering services required by Hill Samuel, they were no longer needed at that venue. They argued that they were not redundant because there was an express mobility clause in their contracts, so they could have been deployed elsewhere. Thus, they contested the reason put forward by the employer and claimed that their dismissals were unfair.

PETER GIBSON LJ: '. . . Before us two main issues have emerged. The first is whether [ERA s 139(1)] imposes a contractual test, as contended for by Mr O'Dempsey [counsel for the employees], or a primarily factual test, as contended for by Mr Underwood [counsel for the employers], to determine "the place where the employee was so employed". The second is whether the reasons given by the employment tribunal were adequate.

. . .

Mr O'Dempsey pointed out that in [ERA s 139(1)] the word "employed", not "worked", was used and he submitted that it connotes "employed under the contract of employment". He said that, in the context of the subsection and having regard to the definitions of "employee" and "employer", the question, what is the place where the employee was so employed, *i.e.* by the employer, must be determined by reference to the contract of employment; if the contract contains a mobility clause, allowing the employer to require the employee to work elsewhere, "'the place where the employee was so employed" extends to every place where the employee may be required to work. He sought to rely on the decision of this court in *Mumford v Boulton and Paul (Steel Construction) Ltd* (1971) as supporting the contractual test. In that case, a steel constructor worked for many years for his employer in and around London. When his employer required him to go to a site 77 miles from London, the employee refused. His employer dismissed him, claiming that he was in breach of contract in refusing. It was held that, because he had been employed on terms that only required him to work in and around London, he had not repudiated his contract but was dismissed for redundancy. But the reasoning of this court which relied on the terms of the contract went only to the question whether the employee was bound to obey the requirement to work out of the London area. None of it was directed to the question, what was the place where the employee was employed by the employer, and it is important to have in mind that, under [ERA s 163(2)], "an employee who has been dismissed by his employer shall, unless the contrary is proved, be presumed to have been so dismissed by reason of redundancy". The contrary was not proved. That decision does not assist Mr O'Dempsey.

I would add that *O'Brien v Associated Fire Alarms Ltd* (1968) was decided by this court in a similar way. Again, the question was whether employees (of a contract electricity firm) who had been employed for some years in jobs within commuting distance of their homes, and who refused the employer's requirement to work further afield, were in breach of contract justifying dismissal. Again, it was in that context that the terms of contract were considered. This court implied a term that the employees' area of work was within commuting distance of their homes and concluded that the employees were not in breach of contract and so the presumption under [ERA s 163(2)] applied. Salmon LJ specifically referred to, but found it unnecessary to decide, "the rather difficult point as to whether the words . . . 'the place where the employee was so employed' refer to the place where the employee actually worked or to the place where, under his contract of employment, the employee could be required to work".

. . .

Mr Underwood submitted that what he called a "plain words" construction of the statute was appropriate, the words "the place where he was so employed" clearly referring to the place where the employee actually worked and not where in theory the employer could require the employee to work. He relied in particular on the decision of the Employment Appeal Tribunal in *Bass Leisure Ltd v Thomas* (1994). In that case the employee was based at Coventry, but in the contract of employment the employer reserved the right to relocate the employee. When the employer closed its Coventry depot, the employee was expected to operate from a different location 20 miles away. After an unsuccessful trial, she left her employment and claimed a redundancy payment. The Employment Appeal Tribunal upheld the employment tribunal's finding that she was entitled to that payment. Judge John Hicks QC, in a judgment which I have found most helpful, considered the language of [ERA s 139(1)] and said:

> "We begin with the obvious but nevertheless important point that the question 'Where is X employed?' is on the fact of it a factual question. Indeed, where there is no contractual term – express or implied – requiring mobility, we do not see how it can be answered other than factually; that is to say as being equivalent to 'Where does X work?'

It is arguable that that is all that needs to be said, but for ourselves we should not be disposed to maintain that contractual provisions are irrelevant, or that 'Where does X work?' is always an adequate paraphrase. The use of the words 'so employed', relating back to the phrase 'employed by [the employer]', directs attention to the relationship between the parties, and the definite article in 'the place' suggests a certain fixity which tends against equating the place of employment with, for instance, each location of a peripatetic 'place of work' successively. Without needing to consider or decide whether the parties could arbitrarily define the 'place where the employee is employed' in terms outside the limits of the objective realities, we see no reason why there cannot be valid and effective contractual terms, express or implied, evidencing or defining the place of employment and its extent within those limits, so that (for example) the place where a steel erector is employed could be the area within which he can be required to attend at construction sites to perform his duties. That is supported by the fact that the preposition before the expression to be construed is 'in' not 'at'.

A construction which looks beyond those bounds and treats the 'place where the employee is employed' as including any place where he or she can contractually be required to work, whatever the nature of the term under which that requirement is imposed, whatever the limits to be observed, and whatever the conditions to be complied with before the power to impose it can be exercised, seems to us to raise substantial difficulties."

And a little later:

"We appreciate that if a distinction such as we have recognised is drawn between different types of contractual provision there will be debatable borderline cases, but that simply reflects the infinite variety of factual situations and contractual terms, and the difficulty of applying to them a statutory test which requires the identification of a unique 'place where the employee was . . . employed'.

It seems clear to us that the references to 'the place where [the employee] was . . . employed' in [ERA s 139(1)(a) and (b)] require that the location and extent of that 'place' be ascertainable, whether or not the employee is in fact to be required to move, and therefore before any such requirement is made (if it is) and without knowledge of the terms of any such requirement, or of the employee's response, or of whether any conditions upon the making of such a requirement have been complied with."

The judge carefully reviewed the authorities, finding particular assistance in the decision of the Divisional Court (Lord Parker CJ, Diplock LJ and Ashworth J) in *McCulloch v Moore* (1968). There the existence of a mobility clause had been held not to prevent an employee, who had worked for his employer in Sussex and whose work there had come to an end, but who declined the employer's offer of employment elsewhere, from being entitled to a redundancy payment. The judge chose not to follow *Sutton v Revlon Overseas Corporation* (1973) and *UK Atomic Energy Authority v Claydon* (1974) and concluded that the place where the employee was employed for the purposes of [ERA s 139(1)] "is to be established by a factual inquiry, taking into account the employee's fixed or changing place or places of work and any contractual terms which go to evidence or define the place of employment and its extent, but not those (if any) which make provision for the employee to be transferred to another."

I am in broad agreement with this interpretation of the statutory language. The question it poses – where was the employee employed by the employer for the purposes of the business? – is one to be answered primarily by a consideration of the factual circumstances which obtained until the dismissal. If an employee has worked in only one location under his contract of employment for the purposes of the employer's business, it defies common sense to widen the extent of the place where he was so employed, merely because of the existence of a mobility clause. Of course, the refusal by the employee to obey a lawful requirement under the contract of employment for the employee to move may constitute a valid reason for dismissal, but the issues of dismissal, redundancy and reasonableness in the actions of an employer should be kept distinct. It would be unfortunate if the law were to encourage the inclusion of mobility clauses in contracts of employment to defeat genuine redundancy claims. Parliament has recognised the importance of the employee's right to a redundancy payment. If the work of the employee for his employer has involved a change of location, as would be the case where the nature of the work required the employee to go from place to place, then the contract of employment may be helpful to determine the extent of the place where the employee was employed. But it cannot be right to let the contract be the sole determinant, regardless of where the employee actually worked for the employer. The question what was the place of employment is one that can safely be left to the good sense of the employment tribunal.

In my judgment, a remission on the first issue is not justified. It is plain that for all of the employees the place where they were employed by the employers was Hill Samuel and that there was a redundancy situation there which caused the employees to be dismissed . . .'

(Hobhouse and Evans LJJ agreed.)

Comment

(1) This case provides a useful review of the competing authorities and the debate around the contractual test and the factual test. The Court of Appeal makes an important extension of the concept of redundancy by coming down in favour of the factual approach to deciding what is the place of work. Of course, the effect of holding that it was redundancy was to the disadvantage of the employees because it defeated their unfair dismissal claims.

(2) What if the employer had asked the employees to move somewhere else because of the reduction of work at Hill Samuel and they had refused and asked for a redundancy payment? Would this result in a dismissal for refusal to obey a lawful and reasonable order, or would it be dismissal for redundancy? This converse situation is similar to what happened in *O'Brien* v *Associated Fire Alarms* (1968) (extracted above, p 190) and *Mumford* v *Bolton and Paul* (1971), but in both of those cases it was held that any mobility clause did not cover what was being asked by the employer. But what if it did?

(3) The question is not clearly answered here, because the point did not arise in that fashion. However, if the factual test is to be adopted, then this suggests that the situation should still be regarded as redundancy, despite the mobility clause, and it is submitted that the tenor of the judgment supports this conclusion. Thus, if an employer tells an employee to move, pursuant to a mobility clause in the contract, and the employee is dismissed for refusing, it may now be necessary to ask why the employer was making the employee move. If the reason is because of a reduction of work at that workplace, the employee would appear to be entitled to a redundancy payment. This may come as a surprise to the employer, who may well think it is simply a dismissal for misconduct.

(4) All of this must be read in the light of ERA s 141, which provides that an employee will not be entitled to a redundancy payment if she unreasonably refuses an offer of suitable alternative employment (see below, p 454). An offer of the same or similar work in a different place is very likely to be a suitable alternative.

Surplus labour

Employment Rights Act 1996

139 (1) For the purposes of this Act an employee who is dismissed shall be taken to be dismissed by reason of redundancy if the dismissal is wholly or mainly attributable to –

. . .

    (b) the fact that the requirements of that business –
        (i) for employees to carry out work of a particular kind, or
        (ii) for employees to carry out work of a particular kind in the place where the employee was employed by the employer,
      have ceased or diminished or are expected to cease or diminish.

Delanair Ltd v *Mead* [1976] ICR 522 Employment Appeal Tribunal

The company manufactured car heaters for Fords. A lengthy strike at Fords in 1974 led to knock-on problems for the company, resulting in decreased demand and severe financial difficulties. It was therefore decided that it was necessary to reduce the number of employees by 10 per cent and to alter working methods so that the work could be carried out by fewer people. The claimant was an electronics engineer who was the lamb chosen for sacrifice from his department, where one employee had to go. He successfully claimed at an employment tribunal that this was not a redundancy and that his dismissal was unfair. The employers appealed.

CUMMING-BRUCE J: '. . . It is submitted by Mr Irvine on behalf of the employers that the employment tribunal have applied the wrong test and have confused the diminution of work of a particular kind with the diminution of the requirement of the business for employees to carry out such work. It is clear that those two concepts differ in important respects, because the volume of work may remain the same though the requirement of the business for employees to carry it out has diminished. There are two obvious examples: (1) when a new machine is introduced which enables the same volume of work to be carried out by fewer men; (2) where there is over-manning such that on reorganisation of duties or terms and conditions of work the same volume of work is carried out by a slimmed down work force. Mr Irvine submits that this case illustrates a third example, namely where for reasons of economy the employers introduce a new structure of management and supervision, and so reallocate duties that the same volume of work is carried out without the requirement of a foreman/supervisor to organise and oversee its performance. That such reallocation of duties may give rise to dismissal by reason of redundancy is illustrated by *Sutton* v *Revlon Ltd* (1973) and *Scarth* v *Economic Forestry Ltd* (1973). As Sir Hugh Griffiths said in the latter case,

"... the fallacy ... is to equate the requirement to achieve an end with the requirement ... of the business to have employees in order to achieve the end."

... Mr Newman submits that the crucial finding is the conclusion:

"We find that the principal reason for the employee's dismissal was a managerial decision to reduce the number of monthly paid staff in order to save money, and we hold that his dismissal was unfair."

He submits that it is not open to a company which needs to save money to dismiss a man and claim that the reason is redundancy without attempting to decide whether the requirement of the company for that man's work has in fact diminished or is expected in the future to diminish . . .

The relevant question of fact for determination is whether the employers have shown that the decision to dispense with the services of a foreman/electrician in the maintenance department was the result of an appraisal of the requirement of the business for employees to carry out that work. If such an appraisal was made and a decision taken that the work formerly done by the employee could be redistributed over the remaining staff, that reallocation of his work brought about his dismissal on the grounds of redundancy. On the other hand, if a decision was taken that a monthly paid worker had to be dismissed somewhere in the business irrespective of the question whether it was practical to redistribute his work over the remaining staff, such dismissal was on the grounds of economy without such regard to the requirements of the business for employees to carry out the particular type of work as to constitute redundancy within the meaning given in [ERA s 139(1)(b)]. We accept the criticism made by Mr Irvine of the test apparently applied by the employment tribunal. On its face it was the wrong test, as the employment tribunal concentrated upon the question whether there had been a diminution in the type of work and not upon the question whether the requirement of the business for employees to carry out the type of work had diminished . . .'

(The EAT remitted the case for rehearing in the light of this advice.)

Comment

(1) Employees often feel that they are not really redundant when they see their work distributed among other people, and to some extent this decision seems to go along with that. However, it has been criticised on the ground that it involves going into the *motive* for the decision to make do with fewer staff, rather than the *fact* that this is what has been decided. If management has taken this decision, then the business's requirements for employees has diminished.

(2) In considering this argument, however, it must also be borne in mind that in an unfair dismissal claim – as this was, and where the issue is most likely to arise – the employer has to establish the true reason for the dismissal. This does invite an examination of motives. At the very least, the employers will have to convince the employment tribunal that they were in a state of financial exigency and were not simply using an excuse to get rid of a particular employee.

(3) In a later decision, another EAT has explained *Delanair Ltd* v *Mead* as follows:

> The distinction taken in *Delanair* was between a decision merely to reduce the workforce without considering any redistribution of work and hence requirement for the staff; and the case where the employer did assess the situation, did decide that there was a requirement for less staff, and in particular for the employee concerned; in which case there was a redundancy.

(*Association of University Teachers* v *University of Newcastle* (1987)).

(4) The employee may not be better off by persuading the tribunal that this was a situation of economising rather than redundancy. If the former, it is likely that it will be held to be a dismissal for 'some other substantial reason' and could be fair (see above, p 423). If so, the employee will not even get a redundancy payment.

Johnson v Nottinghamshire Combined Police Authority
[1974] ICR 170 Court of Appeal

LORD DENNING MR: 'Miss Johnson and Mrs Dutton were employed as clerks at a police station in Nottinghamshire. They had been so employed for over 20 years, each of them. Their hours of work were 9.30 am to 5 pm or 5.30 pm on five days of the week – Monday to Friday, inclusive. They typed reports. They filed papers. They did accounts. They answered the telephone. Before they arrived, a police officer was on duty answering the telephone, and so forth. Likewise after they left.

In 1972 the police authorities determined to reorganise the system. They wished to release police officers from the office work and put them on to the police work for which they had been trained. They proposed that the two ladies should work on separate shifts. One should work from 8 am to 3 pm for six days in the week. The other should work from 1 pm to 8 pm on those six days. Then the next week they would change over. Making allowance for meal times, this would mean a 38 hour week, which was the same number of hours as they had been working before. Their actual work would be just the same as before, but at different hours.

The ladies were offered the new hours. Each refused to accept them. Each had good reason for her refusal. She could not fit in the new hours with her duties in her home; whereas previously she had been able to do so. As each refused the new hours, the police authorities gave them due notice to terminate their employment on August 11 1972. They left. The police authority appointed two other ladies who were ready to do the new hours and accepted the employment.

The two ladies whose employment had been terminated claimed redundancy payments. The employment tribunal rejected their claim. On appeal, the National Industrial Relations Court did likewise. The ladies now appeal to this court.

The case raises directly the meaning of the words "work of a particular kind" . . .

Typical of redundancy situations are these. There may be a recession in trade so that not so many men are needed. There may be a change in the kind of work done, as from wood to fibre glass, so that woodworkers are no longer needed (see *Hindle* v *Percival Boats Ltd* (1969)). The business may be no longer profitable so that the employer has to cut down somewhere. Or, he may be overstaffed. The employer may meet such a situation by dispensing with the services of some of the men: or alternatively he may lower the wages: or put men on part-time. If he does it by making a change in the terms and conditions of employment, it is due to a redundancy situation. Those who lose or leave their work in consequence are entitled to redundancy payments.

It is often difficult to know whether the employer's proposals are due to a redundancy situation or not. But at this point the statute comes in to help the employee by providing that he is presumed to be dismissed by reason of redundancy: see [ERA s 163(2)]. So in all the cases where there is a change in the terms and conditions of employment, it is for the employer to prove that it was done for efficiency, and not so as to meet a redundancy situation.

It remains to apply these principles to a change in hours of work. It is a change in the terms and conditions of employment. It does not automatically give rise to a right to redundancy payments. If the employer proves that it was due to a reorganisation so as to achieve more efficient working, the man is not entitled to redundancy payments. The decision of the Industrial Court in Scotland in *Blakely* v *Chemetron Ltd* (1972) was, I think, correct.

A change in the hours of work is very different from a change in the place of employment. The statute expressly provides that if the requirements for employees at "the place" cease or diminish, there is a redundancy situation: see [ERA s 139(1)(b)]. But it says nothing of the like effect as to "hours" of work. If the employers require the same number of employees as before – for the same tasks as before – but require them at different hours, there is no redundancy situation. If the change in hours is unfair to a particular employee, in the situation in which she finds herself, it might give rise to a claim for unfair dismissal under the Industrial Relations Act 1971; but it does not give rise to a redundancy payment.

In the present case the police authorities proved that the change in the hours of work was not due to a redundancy situation, but to a reorganisation in the interests of efficiency. The same work was done by the ladies afterwards as it was before. But they did it at different hours. I think that the employment tribunal and the Industrial Court were quite right. I would dismiss the appeal.'

(Cairns and Stephenson LJJ agreed.)

Robinson v *British Island Airways Ltd* [1978] ICR 304 Employment Appeal Tribunal

Before the reorganisation of the company the claimant had been the flight operations manager, responsible to the general manager operations and traffic (Mr Owen), who was himself responsible to the general manager. Under the reorganisation, the post of general manager operations and traffic was replaced by a post of operations manager and the post of flight operations manager was abolished. The holder of the new post had to have a pilot's licence, which ruled out Mr Owen. The claimant was judged unsuitable for the new post, so both he and Mr Owen were made redundant. He claimed that it was unfair dismissal.

PHILLIPS J: '. . . Cases concerning redundancy arising out of a re-organisation always cause difficulties. Certain passages in some of the judgments in *Johnson* v *Nottinghamshire Combined Police Authority* (1974) and *Lesney Products & Co Ltd* v *Nolan* (1977), have been taken as suggesting that if a dismissal has been caused by a re-organisation the reason for the dismissal cannot be redundancy. We do not think that this is the meaning of the passages, or what was intended. In truth a re-organisation may or may not end in redundancy; it all depends on the nature and effect of the re-organisation. In *Johnson* v *Nottinghamshire Combined Police Authority* there was no redundancy because in the opinion of the Court of Appeal the change in the hours of work involved in that case did not change the particular kind of work being carried on. In *Lesney Products & Co Ltd* v *Nolan* there was no redundancy because on the correct analysis of the facts (it was in the analysis of the facts that the appeal tribunal and the employment tribunal were in error) there was no cessation or diminution of the requirement for employees to carry out work of a particular kind. The number of employees, and the nature of the work, remained the same, and all that changed was the ability to earn overtime. What has to be done in every case is to analyse the facts and to match the analysis against the words of [ERA s 139]. In doing this it is of no assistance to consider whether as a matter of impression there was or was not a "redundancy situation". The question is whether the definition is satisfied . . .

There is no doubt that Captain Robinson was dismissed. To what was his dismissal attributable? It seems to us that the work done by the flight operations manager was of a "particular kind" and that the work done by the general manager operations and traffic was of a "particular kind", and that each kind was different from the other. It seems to us that the work done by the operations manager was of a "particular kind" and of a kind different from that done by the general manager operations and traffic and different from that done by the flight operations manager. Thus in our judgment it can truly be said that the dismissal of the employee was attributable to the fact that the requirements of the business for employees to carry out work of a particular kind had ceased or diminished and that each was redundant.

If this were wrong, we should be inclined to say that the circumstances constituted "some other substantial reason of a kind such as to justify the dismissal of an employee holding the position which that employee held". It seems to us that where there is a genuine re-organisation which has dislodged an employee who cannot be fitted into the re-organisation it must be open to the employer to dismiss him. But we prefer to think that in those circumstances he will usually be redundant, and thus entitled to a redundancy payment . . .'

Comment

(1) These cases illustrate some of the difficulties in applying the statutory definition. The fact that it emphasises the work to be done rather than the job package of the employee results in situations like *Johnson* or *Lesney Products* not constituting redundancy, which seems rather hard on the employees. What is particularly surprising is the apparent conclusion that dismissing more senior workers for people who can be paid less is not redundancy, nor, seemingly, unfair dismissal.

(2) How different does the new job have to be before one can say that the employee who did the old job is redundant? In some ways, it is difficult to reconcile *Robinson* v *British Island Airways* with *North Riding Garages* v *Butterwick*.

North Riding Garages v *Butterwick* [1967] 2 QB 56 Queen's Bench Divisional Court

The employee had been employed at the garage for 30 years, becoming workshop manager. As the staff was small, he spent quite a lot of time actually working as a mechanic repairing cars. In 1965 new owners took over, who put more emphasis on the sales side of the business. This involved him in more paperwork, which he was not good at. They introduced new methods, which he had trouble adapting to. After eight months they dismissed him and he claimed that he was redundant. The employers argued that he had been dismissed for inefficiency and incompetence. An employment tribunal held that it was dismissal for redundancy.

WIDGERY J: '. . . It is, we think, important to observe that a claim under [ERA s 139(1)(b)] is conditional upon a change in the requirements of the business. If the requirement of the business for employees to carry out work of a particular kind increases or remains constant no redundancy payment can be claimed by an employee, in work of that kind, whose dismissal is attributable to personal deficiencies which prevent him from satisfying his employer. The very fact of dismissal shows that the employee's services are no longer required by his employer and that he may, in a popular sense, be said to have become redundant, but if the dismissal was attributable to age, physical disability or inability to meet his employer's standards he was not dismissed on account of redundancy within the meaning of the Act. For the purpose of this Act an employee who remains in the same kind of work is expected to adapt himself to new methods and techniques and cannot complain if his employer insists on higher standards of efficiency than those previously required; but if new methods alter the nature of the work required to be done it may follow that no requirement remains for employees to do work of the particular kind which has been superseded and that they are truly redundant. Thus, if a motor manufacturer decides to use plastics instead of wood in the bodywork of his cars and dismisses his woodworkers, they may well be entitled to redundancy payments on the footing that their dismissal is attributable to a cessation of the requirement of the business for employees to carry out work of a particular kind, namely, woodworking.

If one looks at the primary facts disclosed by the evidence in this case it is difficult to see what is the particular kind of work in which a requirement for employees has ceased or diminished. The vehicle workshop remained, as did the requirement for a workshop manager, and we do not understand the tribunal to have found that the volume of repair work had diminished to such an extent as to make the respondent's dismissal wholly or mainly attributable to that fact. The only possible conclusion which appears to us to have been open to the tribunal on the evidence was that the respondent was dismissed because he could not do his job in accordance with the new methods and new standards required by the appellants.

The tribunal seems to base its decision on the fact that a requirement for a workshop manager "of the old type" had ceased. This is probably a reference to the fact that the respondent had been required by the appellants to estimate costs, which the former owner had done for himself, but the mere fact that a reorganisation has transferred this work to the respondent does not show that the requirement of the business for employees to do this, or any other, kind of work has diminished. The only possible relevance of this evidence would be to show that the volume of repair work had been run down to such an extent that the respondent could no longer occupy his whole time in it, but the tribunal, on the totality of the evidence, does not seem to take that view.

We think that the tribunal has fallen into error by applying the wrong test in that they have not looked at the overall requirements of the business but at the allocation of duties between individuals. It is irrelevant that the duties of the new manager are not identical with the duties formerly undertaken by the respondent if the overall requirements of the business are unchanged.

    The court will accordingly allow the appeal and remit the matter to the tribunal to enable the hearing to be continued in the light of this opinion.'

Comment

(1) Would you agree that it is difficult to see a distinction between this case and *Robinson* v *British Island Airways*? One contrast is that here the employer wanted the employee to do the new job, unlike *Robinson*, but that should not make a difference: in theory, what is being tested is the objective issue of whether there is a redundancy within the statutory definition.

(2) It does look as if the flexibility permitted works in favour of the managerial pre-rogative. That is, if management forms the view that, following reorganisation, the employee is unsuitable for the new job, that will be accepted by the employment tribunal, who will find that the employee is redundant. But if management decides to give the employee the new job, the employee will be unable to argue that it involves such differences from her previous job that she is in fact redundant (in the context of tech-nological change, see also *Cresswell* v *Board of Inland Revenue* (1984) above, p 170.

(3) Finally, it is worth noting that at the time of *Robinson* v *British Island Airways*, employers were relatively willing to declare employees as redundant, even in borderline cases, because they could get back half of what they paid out by way of a statutory redundancy payment from the state Redundancy Fund. That rebate system was abolished in 1989, which may have led to employers taking a more rigorous approach.

(4) One rule of thumb which is implicit in these cases is that, where there is an overall reduction in staff, this tends to indicate that there is indeed a redundancy. However, this should not be assumed too readily: it is not always the case.

(5) What if the job which the employee has been doing disappears, but there is other work available which the employee could be required to do under the terms of his contract? Can it be said in these circumstances that the employee is not redundant?

Murray v *Foyle Meats Ltd* [1999] ICR 827 House of Lords

The two claimants had been employed in an abattoir. Their job titles were 'meat plant oper-atives', but in fact they worked virtually all the time in one of the two halls. (The workplace consisted of two halls and a loading bay.) When the 'line' on which they worked was closed down, the employer made them redundant. They argued that it was not redundancy because there was a flexibility clause in their contracts under which they could be asked to do any job in the workplace (all employees were employed on these terms). Therefore, as the employer had not proved the reason for their dismissals was what it had claimed it was, the dismissals should be found to be unfair. Having lost in the tribunal and the Northern Ireland Court of Appeal, the employees appealed to the House of Lords.

LORD IRVINE LC: '. . . The claimants say the company chose to engage all its employees on similar terms. "Requirements . . . for employees to carry out work of a particular kind" meant "requirements for employees contractually engaged to carry out work of a particular kind." In this respect, no distinction could be made between those who worked in the slaughter hall and those who worked elsewhere. It was therefore wrong of the company to select for redundancy solely from those who normally worked in the slaughter hall. It should have selected from every-one working under the same contract of employment.

My Lords, the language of [ERA s 139(1)(b)] is in my view simplicity itself. It asks two ques-tions of fact. The first is whether one or other of various states of economic affairs exists. In this case, the relevant one is whether the requirements of the business for employees to carry out work of a particular kind have diminished. The second question is whether the dismissal is attributable, wholly or mainly, to that state of affairs. This is a question of causation. In the present case, the tribunal found as a fact that the requirements of the business for employees to work in the slaughter hall had diminished. Secondly, they found that that state of affairs had led to the applicants being dismissed. That, in my opinion, is the end of the matter.

This conclusion is in accordance with the analysis of the statutory provisions by Judge Peter Clark in *Safeway Stores plc* v *Burrell* (1997) and I need to say no more than that I entirely agree with his admirably clear reasoning and conclusions. But I should, out of respect for the sub-missions of Mr Morgan for the claimants, say something about the earlier cases which may have encouraged a belief that the statute had a different meaning.

In *Nelson* v *British Broadcasting Corporation* (1977) Mr Nelson was employed by the BBC under a contract which required him to perform any duties to which he might be assigned. In fact he worked for the General Overseas Service broadcasting to the Caribbean. In 1974 the BBC reduced its services to the Caribbean, as a result of which Mr Nelson's services in that capacity were no longer required. When he refused alternative employment, he was dismissed on grounds of redundancy. The employment tribunal concluded that he had been dismissed for redundancy, apparently on the grounds that a term could be implied into Mr Nelson's contract of employment that he should carry out work on Caribbean programmes. The Court of Appeal rightly rejected the implication of such a term. But they went on to hold that Mr Nelson was therefore not redundant. This was wrong. Whatever the terms of Mr Nelson's contract, it was open to the tribunal to find that he had been dismissed because the BBC's requirements for work on Caribbean programmes had diminished. This was a question of fact.

The basis for the fallacy is to be found in the judgment of Brandon LJ in *Nelson* v *British Broadcasting Corporation (No 2)* (1980), when Mr Nelson's case came again before the Court of Appeal. He said that Mr Nelson had been right in law in maintaining that "because the work which he was employed to do continued to exist, he was not redundant . . .". In saying this Brandon LJ appears to have meant that because Mr Nelson was employed to do any work to which he might be assigned with the BBC and because the BBC was still carrying on business, he could not be redundant. In my opinion this cannot be right. The fact was that the BBC's requirements for employees in the General Overseas Service in general and for Caribbean broadcasts in particular had diminished. It must therefore have been open to the tribunal to decide that Mr Nelson's dismissal was attributable to that state of affairs. Of course, the BBC did not necessarily have to respond in that way. They could, for example, have transferred Mr Nelson to broadcasts which were still being maintained at full strength (say, to West Africa) in the place of a less experienced employee and made the latter redundant instead. In that case, it would have been open to the tribunal to find that the other employee had been dismissed on account of redundancy. (Compare *Safeway Stores plc* v *Burrell*.) In each case, the factual question of whether the dismissal was "attributable" to the statutory state of affairs is one for the tribunal.

The judgments in the two *Nelson* cases have caused understandable difficulty for employ-ment tribunals. They have been treated as authority for what has been called the "contract test", which requires consideration of whether there was a diminution in the kind of work for which, according to the terms of his contract, the employee had been engaged. I give one example. In *Pink* v *White and White & Co (Earls Barton) Ltd* (1985) Mr Pink was engaged to work in a shoe factory as a "making and finishing room operative". In practice, he did more specialised work as sole layer/pre-sole fitter. Because of a reduction in demand, the employer's requirements for making and finishing room operatives in general diminished, but their need for sole layers and pre-sole fitters remained the same. Nevertheless, they selected Mr Pink for redundancy, apparently because he had been absent for lengthy periods and the employer had had to train someone else to do his work while he was away. The argument before the Employment Appeal Tribunal turned on whether the "contract test" ought to be applied (*i.e.* did the company need less employees of the kind specified in Mr Pink's contract), in which case he was redundant, or the "function test" (did it need less employees to do the kind of work he was actually doing), in which case he was not. It held that it was bound by *Nelson v British Broadcasting Corporation* (1977) to apply the contract test and held that Mr Pink was redundant. I have no doubt that on its facts the case was rightly decided, but both the contract test and the function test miss the point. The key word in the statute is "attributable" and there is no reason in law why the dismissal of an employee should not be attributable to a diminution in the employer's need for employees irrespective of the terms of his contract or the function which he performed. Of course the dismissal of an employee who could perfectly well have been redeployed or who was doing work unaffected by the fall in demand may require some explanation to establish the necessary causal connection. But this is a question of fact, not law.

For these reasons, I would dismiss the appeal.'

(Lord Clyde delivered a concurring speech. Lords Hoffmann and Jauncey agreed with both and Lord Slynn agreed with Lord Irvine.)

Comment

(1) This typically robust analysis by Lord Irvine has the advantage of simplifying and clarifying the law – although at the expense of ignoring the qualifying words in ERA s 139(1)(b), which refer to the diminution of the business's requirements for work *of a particular kind*.

(2) This approach also settles the argument about 'bumping', where one employee's job is redundant, but she is moved to a different post and that postholder is the one dismissed. This would now clearly be redundancy (see the example given by Lord Irvine in relation to *Nelson* v *BBC*). Obviously, it could also be unfair dismissal, depending on the reasons for the employer's retention of the employee whose job had disappeared in preference to the one whose job continued (see above, p 419).

(3) Lord Irvine's analysis raises another issue, however. If the employee's regular job disappears and he or she is directed to do other work which is within the terms of his or her contract, can the employee decline and claim a redundancy payment? Consider the analogy with *High Table Ltd* v *Horst* (1997) above, p 443. However, it could be argued that this would simply be dismissal for refusal to obey a lawful order. This is buttressed by the provisions which deny redundancy payments to employees who refuse an offer of suitable alternative employment.

Offer of suitable alternative employment

Employment Rights Act 1996

141 (1) This section applies where an offer (whether in writing or not) is made to an employee before the end of his employment –

    (a) to renew his contract of employment, or

(b) to re-engage him under a new contract of employment,

with renewal or re-engagement to take effect either immediately on, or after an interval of not more than four weeks after, the end of his employment.

(2) Where subsection (3) is satisfied, the employee is not entitled to a redundancy payment if he unreasonably refuses the offer.

(3) This subsection is satisfied where –

    (a) the provisions of the contract as renewed, or of the new contract, as to –

        (i) the capacity and place in which the employee would be employed, and

        (ii) the other terms and conditions of his employment,

would not differ from the corresponding provisions of the previous contract, or

    (b) those provisions of the contract as renewed, or of the new contract, would differ from the corresponding provisions of the previous contract but the offer constitutes an offer of suitable employment in relation to the employee . . .

Comment

(1) Note that there are two separate questions here: first, whether the employment offered is suitable; and, secondly, whether the employee acted unreasonably in refusing it. The first suggests an objective examination of the offer, while the second permits consideration of the personal equation; however, in *Spencer* v *Gloucestershire CC* (1985) the Court of Appeal pointed out that many of the factors relevant to both questions are the same and that in practice it may be difficult, and perhaps not desirable, to attempt to draw a line between them. An example of the kind of reasoning used is found in the next case.

Taylor v *Kent CC* [1969] 2 QB 560 Queen's Bench Divisional Court

The claimant had been headmaster of a boys' school which was merged with a girls' school. He was not appointed to head the new institution and his appointment was therefore terminated. He was offered a post as one of a pool of mobile teachers to be sent out to schools as and when required, with his salary to remain the same. He declined. The council opposed his claim for a redundancy payment on the ground of his refusal to accept this offer.

LORD PARKER CJ: '. . . Let me say at once, suitability is almost entirely a matter of degree and fact for the tribunal, and not a matter with which this court would wish to or could interfere, unless it was plain that they had misdirected themselves in some way in law, or had taken into consideration matters which were not relevant for the purpose. It is to be observed that so far as age was concerned, so far as qualifications were concerned, so far as experience was concerned, they negative the suitability of this offer, because he is going to be put into a position where he has to go where he is told at any time for short periods, to any place, and be put under a headmaster and assigned duties by him.

The only matter which can be put against that as making this offer suitable is the guarantee of salary under Scale Q. One would think, speaking for myself, that for a headmaster of this experience, he would think an offer which, while guaranteeing him the same salary, reduced his status, was quite unsuitable. To go to quite a different sphere of activity, a director under a service agreement of a company is offered on dismissal a job as a navvy, and it is said: but we will guarantee you the same salary as you have been getting. I should have thought such an offer was plainly unsuitable . . .

But for my part I feel that the tribunal have here misdirected themselves in law as to the meaning of "suitable employment". I accept, of course, that suitable employment is as is said: suitable employment in relation to the employee in question. But it does seem to me here that by the words "suitable employment", suitability means employment which is substantially equivalent to the employment which has ceased. RPA s 2(3) [broadly equivalent to ERA s 141(3)(a)] which I read at the beginning is dealing with the case where the fundamental terms are the same, and then no offer in writing is needed, but when they differ, then it has to be put in writing and must be suitable. I for my part think that what is meant by "suitable" in relation to the employee means conditions of employment which are reasonably equivalent to those under the previous employment, not the same, because then subsection (2) would apply, but it does not seem to me that by "suitable employment" is meant employment of an entirely different nature, but in respect of which the salary is going to be the same. Looked at in that way, it seems to me that there could be only one answer in this case, and that is that this man was being asked to do something utterly different: as I have said, just as if a director under a service agreement with a company was being asked to do a workman's job, albeit at the same salary . . .'

(Melford Stevenson and Willis JJ agreed.)

Comment

(1) The importance of equivalent status and skills as well as equivalent salary is here stressed. Other relevant factors are whether or not retraining will be necessary – and how likely it is that the employee will be able to retrain successfully; travelling time and distance (cf *O'Brien* v *Associated Fire Alarms* (1968)); domestic circumstances, and whether it is necessary for the employee to relocate. If it is, how far the employer is prepared to assist will also be relevant.

(2) Much the same sort of things will be relevant to the question of whether the employee acted reasonably in refusing the offer.

Thomas Wragg & Sons Ltd v *Wood* [1976] ICR 313 Employment Appeal Tribunal

The employee, who was aged 56, had been given notice of redundancy on 24 October which would expire on 6 December. He found another job to start the following Monday. On 5 December he received an offer of alternative employment from his employer, which he refused.

LORD MCDONALD: '. . . The short point for decision, therefore, is whether or not the employee acted unreasonably in refusing the employers' offer of alternative employment, which indeed was the course which he adopted.

The tribunal have taken the view that the employee did not act unreasonably in refusing that offer. Reasons for so concluding are summarised in their decision, in the following terms:

> "The tribunal feels that [the employee], having committed himself to the new job, and having all the fears of a man of 56 who faces unemployment, and having received the offer not too late but . . . as late in the day as within 24 hours of the expiration of his notice, was not unreasonable in refusing the offer and, consequently, he succeeds in his claim."

Counsel for the employers argued to us that this reason involved three factors and that two of these factors, as matter of law, should not be considered. The three factors were: first, that the respondent had committed himself to accept a new job; secondly, that one of his reasons for refusing the employers' offer was fear of unemployment in the future in a contracting industry; and thirdly, the lateness of the offer of alternative employment.

So far as the second and third of those factors are concerned, counsel for the employers argued that those fell to be discounted completely as they were not factors which, in law, should be considered. In connection with the fears of the employee that he would or might become redundant in the near future if he accepted the employers' offer of re-engagement, our attention was directed to *James & Jones* v *National Coal Board* (1969). That was a case in which it was certainly held that it was unreasonable on the part of employees to refuse an offer of re-engagement simply because they considered that the industry was a contracting one and that their futures were not assured. There does not appear to have been any other factor, such as the acceptance on their part of another job elsewhere, or any other consideration which fell to be taken into account; and in that situation an employment tribunal took the view that the refusal was not reasonable. We do not, however, extract from that case the proposition that the situation in a particular industry may not be a factor which, together with others, could properly be taken into account in deciding whether or not the refusal as reasonable.

So far as the lateness of the offer is concerned, it was argued that if the statute had intended that this should be a factor falling to be taken into account in assessing reasonableness, it would have said so. On the contrary, the statute lays down a time limit and the offer was made within that time limit, albeit very late in the day. We would accept that if this was the only single factor which an employee relied upon to justify his refusal to accept an offer, and if no other factor existed, that would not be sufficient; but we do not consider that it is a matter which automatically falls to be ignored, if other considerations exist and, in particular, if the employee, as here, has sought and gained alternative employment and has accepted an offer of such alternative employment from another employer.

Accordingly the two factors which have been criticised by counsel for the employers as being wholly irrelevant as matters of law are not, in our view, irrelevant to that extent. They are factors which we consider can be taken into account, provided other factors also exist.

It is clear in the present case that a third factor does exist and it is one which counsel for the employers accepted may competently be taken into account, although he argued that standing by itself it would not suffice. That factor, of course, is the acceptance by the employee of different employment before the expiry of his notice of dismissal. Our attention in this connection was directed to *McNulty* v *T Bridges & Co Ltd* (1966). It was stated in that case that the fact that an employee accepts the offer of employment outside his employer's company, before an offer of alternative employment by that company was made, does not necessarily mean that his refusal of the company's offer is to be treated as reasonable. We would not quarrel with that proposition, but it is very clearly a factor which is to be taken into account when considering the element of reasonableness, and that is stated in terms in the decision of the tribunal in that particular case.

In the case with which we are concerned today, this third factor is in our opinion one of great importance. The employee obviously acted with some diligence and was successful in obtaining other employment which was due to commence at the termination of his employment with the employer. In our opinion, in doing so he acted very sensibly and very reasonably. Faced at the end of his period of notice with the sudden offer of re-engagement by his employers, we consider that he did not act unreasonably in refusing that offer, having regard to the fact that he had already engaged himself in this other job.

Accordingly we consider that the tribunal did not err in law in approaching the matter as they did, namely, considering all three factors as a whole rather than considering each in isolation. For these reasons, therefore, we dismiss the appeal.'

Trial periods

Under ERA s 138, where the employer offers the employee alternative employment which is different from her previous job, the employee has a four-week trial period in the new post without prejudice to her redundancy claim. If, during this four-week period, either the employee decides for any reason to leave, or the employer dismisses her, the termination will be treated as a dismissal on the date the original contract ended, for the reason for which that contract ended (ie, redundancy).

This means that by opting to try a new job the employee has not waived her claim for a redundancy payment (or even, perhaps, for unfair dismissal). It may be felt that four weeks is a rather short period in which to judge a new job. However, the statutory period has been interpreted strictly (see, eg, *Benton* v *Sanderson Keyser* (1989)). In the next case, the possibility of extending it by adding a common law trial period was canvassed.

Turvey v *C W Cheney & Son Ltd* [1979] ICR 341 Employment Appeal Tribunal

MS P SMITH: '. . . The four employees in this case were employed as polishers by C W Cheyney & Son Ltd, the employers. In May 1977, following a decline in the trade, work in the polishing department where they worked had diminished and was about to cease. The employees were so informed on June 1 and each was offered a job in a different department.

From the notes of evidence at the employment tribunal it appears that three of the four employees said that they would take the different jobs they were offered on trial; that is to say, they did not at once make a new contract or renew the contract of employment by agreeing to the variation in its terms, namely that they should work in a different job which under their existing contract the company could not require them to do. The evidence of the fourth suggests (though the note shows that this aspect of the problem was not fully explored) that she worked at the new job with an implied reservation that she was doing so, like the other three, on trial.

All worked in the new jobs for more than four weeks and then, finding that the new jobs did not suit them, left of their own accord. All applied to the employment tribunal for redundancy payments. The basis of their applications was that the company's action in informing them that there would be no more work for them in the polishing department (the only work which the company was entitled as a matter of contract to require them to do) amounted to a repudiation of their contracts of employment; that in the circumstances they were entitled to treat their contracts as at an end themselves and did so; and that accordingly by the operation of [ERA s 136(1)(c)] they were to be treated as having been dismissed by the employers . . .

It is clear law that where one party to a contract acts in such a way as to show he no longer intends to be bound, the other party can decide at his option whether or not to treat the contract as at an end. Moreover he does not necessarily have to make up his mind at once but is entitled to a reasonable time in which to do so.

The application of this common law principle to contracts of employment is illustrated in *Shields Furniture Ltd* v *Goff* (1973), where Brightman J said that the mere fact that an employee started to work under the terms of a new contract offered him by the employer did not constitute an acceptance of the new contract so that he must be regarded as having made up his mind not to rely on the repudiation of the old contract. You have to see whether the employee is accepting the new contract by his conduct, or whether he is giving it a try to see whether he will accept it or not.

If, as in this case with the three employees, the employee says that he is giving it a trial, clearly he has not accepted the new contract simply by doing that. If having started by expressly giving it a trial he goes on working under the new terms without any more being said about it, the time will come when a reasonable time for making up his mind has expired, and he will be taken to have made a new contract or renewed the old one with variations, and he will no longer be able to rely on [ERA s 136(1)(c)] and say: "You dismissed me". Each case will depend on its own facts, and it will be for the employment tribunal to say whether or not, on the facts which it finds, a new contract has been made or the old contract has been renewed with

Redundancy

variations. Since the answer must vary with the circumstances we will call the period which at common law the employee has to make up his mind period X . . .'

Comment

(1) This makes it clear that the common law trial period may be longer than the statutory trial period, although whether it was in this particular case was not decided. The EAT remitted the case for rehearing in the light of their decision.

Lay-off and short-time working

Employment Rights Act 1996

147 (1) For the purposes of this Part an employee shall be taken to be laid off for a week if –

    (a) he is employed under a contract on terms and conditions such that his remuneration under the contract depends on his being provided by the employer with work of the kind which he is employed to do, but

    (b) he is not entitled to any remuneration under the contract in respect of the week because the employer does not provide such work for him.

  (2) For the purposes of this Part an employee shall be taken to be kept on short-time for a week if by reason of a diminution in the work provided for the employee by his employer (being work of a kind which under his contract the employee is employed to do) the employee's remuneration for the week is less than half a week's pay.

Comment

(1) An employee who is laid off or kept on short-time for four consecutive weeks, or any six weeks in a 13-week period, may leave and claim a redundancy payment (ERA s 148). However, ERA ss 148–149 contain conditions for the exercise of the right, in terms of notice and counter-notice, which render this course of action potentially dangerous for an unrepresented employee, as failure to comply strictly with the rules will result in forfeiture of the right to claim a redundancy payment.

(2) Remember that it will be a fundamental breach of contract if the employer lays off workers or puts them on short-time without paying them their full wages unless there is an express or implied term in the contract permitting this.

Calculation of the redundancy payment

Employment Rights Act 1996

162 (1) The amount of a redundancy payment shall be calculated by –

    (a) determining the period, ending with the relevant date, during which the employee has been continuously employed,

    (b) reckoning backwards from the end of that period the number of years of employment falling within that period, and

    (c) allowing the appropriate amount for each of those years of employment.

  (2) In subsection (1)(c) 'the appropriate amount' means –

    (a) one and a half weeks' pay for a year of employment in which the employee was not below the age of forty-one,

459

(b)   one week's pay for a year of employment (not within paragraph (a)) in which he was not below the age of twenty-two, and

(c)   half a week's pay for each year of employment not within paragraph (a) or (b).

(3)   Where twenty years of employment have been reckoned under subsection (1), no account shall be taken under that subsection of any year of employment earlier than those twenty years . . .

Comment

(1) This is the same as the method for calculating the basic award for unfair dismissal compensation and the maximum payment in 2008 is the same: £9,900 (£330 × 30).

(2) There is in-built age discrimination in this – but it is permitted under the Employment Equality (Age) Regulations 2006. The former exclusion of years of service below the age of 18 has been removed, as has the exclusion of employees over retirement age from the right to claim.

(3) A redundancy payment may be reduced, or even extinguished, if the employee takes part in industrial action or is dismissed for misconduct while on notice of dismissal for redundancy (ERA s 140).

(4) In the event of the employer being insolvent (which is a common cause of redundancy), the payment will be met from the National Insurance Fund administered by the Secretary of State for Business, Enterprise and Regulatory Reform.

Time off to look for work

Employment Rights Act 1996

52 (1) An employee who is given notice of dismissal by reason of redundancy is entitled to be permitted by his employer to take reasonable time off during the employee's working hours before the end of his notice in order to –

(a)   look for new employment, or

(b)   make arrangements for training for future employment.

(2)   An employee is not entitled to take time off under this section unless, on whichever is the later of –

(a)   the date on which the notice is due to expire, and

(b)   the date on which it would expire were it the notice required to be given by section 86(1),

he will have been (or would have been) continuously employed for period of two years or more.

(3)   For the purposes of this section the working hours of an employee shall be taken to be any time when, in accordance with his contract of employment, the employee is required to be at work.

Comment

(1) This seemingly generous provision is qualified by the fact that the maximum payment is two days' pay! However, the employee may be entitled to more time than this, depending on what is judged to be reasonable.

TRANSFERS OF UNDERTAKINGS

The sale of a business from one owner to another frequently results in workers of one or both business undertakings becoming redundant, since one of the main reasons for mergers or acquisitions is to achieve economies of scale. In the run-up to and aftermath of an acquisition or merger there is frequently a period of restructuring and rationalisation, which again can mean that employees lose their jobs. Until EU law became involved, employees who were dismissed in these circumstances were usually entitled to a redundancy payment from their former employer, depending on their length of service.

EU policy aims to safeguard employees in the takeover situation by providing them with a right to follow their jobs into the new business. Thus the Acquired Rights Directive (77/187/EEC) stated, in essence, that when a business was transferred within the terms of the directive, contracts of employment were automatically transferred from the old business ('the transferor') to the new business ('the transferee'). The title of the directive expressed the underlying principle that workers should be regarded as having acquired rights to their jobs through their service to the employer.

Although passed in 1977, the Acquired Rights Directive was unpopular with both the main political parties at the time and was not implemented until the Transfer of Undertakings (Protection of Employment) Regulations 1981 (TUPE) – three years later than it should have been. Even then, because of a restricted definition of which transfers it applied to, it would be true to say that it did not have much effect through most of the 1980s.

Towards the end of that decade, a series of ECJ decisions made it obvious that the TUPE regulations were too restrictive and did not implement the directive properly. Some amendments were carried out by TURERA and the case law exploded, mainly because of uncertainty around the basic concept of a 'relevant transfer' – that is, a transfer to which the Regulations applied. This uncertainty existed at EU level also. In 1998 the Acquired Rights Directive was revised, to take account of some of the ECJ case law, and a consolidated version was produced in 2001 (the Acquired Rights Directive (2001/23/EC)). Once again, it took much longer than it should have done for reform of the British regulations to be carried out. New Transfer of Undertakings (Protection of Employment) Regulations 2006 (TUPE 2006) were finally brought in to replace completely the 1981 Regulations with effect from April 2006.

The government's aims in producing TUPE 2006 are set out in the Consultation Document which preceded (by five years!) the legislation.

Transfer of Undertakings (Protection of Employment) Regulations 1981
Government Proposals for Reform – Detailed Background Paper
(URN 01/1158 September 2001)

12   The Government considers that the TUPE Regulations are based on a positive principle – the coupling of flexibility for business with fairness for employees. If made to work effectively, they should assist the smooth management of necessary change, in both the private sector and the public, by securing the interests and commitment of the employees

affected. They should promote a co-operative, partnership approach toward business restructuring and public sector modernisation. They should help create a level playing field in the business acquisitions market and the business services sector. They should give everyone a stake in improving labour market flexibility and competitiveness.

13   The Government's underlying aim in amending the Regulations is to ensure that they operate effectively for all those whose interests depend on them: the employers and contractors whose businesses they help shape; the clients and local authorities who use them as a framework for contracting; and the employees whose rights they safeguard. The Government believes that the revision of the EC Directive has provided a much sounder basis for securing this than would otherwise have been the case.

14   The scope of the legislation is the most extensively debated and litigated aspect of the current Regulations. Ideally, everyone should know where they stand, so that employers can plan effectively in a climate of fair competition and affected employees are protected as a matter of course. In the past, however, this has not always been the case.

Comment

(1) This shows a conversion in government thinking to the benefits of TUPE. As noted in the final paragraph quoted, the scope of the legislation – identification of which transfers it applies to – has been the most difficult area. This will be considered first.

What is a transfer of an undertaking?

Transfer of Undertakings (Protection of Employment) Regulations 2006

3   (1)   These Regulations apply to –
     (a)   a transfer of an undertaking, business or part of an undertaking or business situated immediately before the transfer in the United Kingdom to another person where there is a transfer of an economic entity which retains its identity;
     (b)   a service provision change . . .
     (2)   In this regulation 'economic entity' means an organised grouping of resources which has the objective of pursuing an economic activity, whether or not that activity is central or ancillary.

Comment

(1) Note that the requirement of transfer to another person means that the Regulations do not cover the takeover of a business which is effected through a sale of shares in the business. As a company is distinct in law from its members, the identity of the employer in such a situation remains the same: the company. In the Consultation Document extracted above, the government stated expressly that it did not 'intend to apply the legislation to completely new areas such as takeovers by share transfer (in which the identity of the employer and the rights and obligations of the parties to the employment relationship remain legally unchanged)' (para 17). This has drawn criticism, because if control of a company passes to new owners, it is very likely that there will be significant changes to employment conditions, yet the Regulations will not apply.

(2) The definition of 'economic entity' is in exactly the same terms as Art 1(1)(b) of the Acquired Rights Directive 2001 (2001/23/EC), which was itself effectively a codification

of ECJ jurisprudence on this point. In *Süzen* v *Zehnacker* (1997) the ECJ held that 'in certain labour-intensive sectors a group of workers engaged in a joint activity on a permanent basis may constitute an economic entity' – ie, the organised grouping of resources can consist of human resources only.

(3) In *Rygaard* v *Strø Mølle* (1996) the ECJ held that the directive applied only to the transfer of a stable economic entity whose activity was not limited to performing one specific works contract, implying a need for some element of permanence or continuity. This requirement does not appear expressly in the directive or in TUPE 2006, but as the directive states its aim as clarification of the law rather than as an alteration of it, previous ECJ case law remains relevant and it is likely that the element of stability will continue to be required.

(4) In general, what is being looked for is the business, or part of it, being run in other hands. The guidance given by the ECJ in the important early case, *Spijkers* v *Gebroeders Benedik*, continues to be a good starting point for this.

Spijkers v *Gebroeders Benedik Abattoir CV* [1986] 2 CMLR 296
European Court of Justice

The claimant had been employed as assistant manager at an abattoir owned by Colaris. At the end of December 1982, Colaris sold the land, slaughterhouse premises and other offices to Benedik. By that stage, Colaris had ceased to carry on its commercial activity and there was no longer any goodwill in the business; Colaris was declared insolvent the following March.

Benedik began to operate an abattoir at the premises from February 1983, so there was a gap in trading. While Benedik took on all the former Colaris employees except Spijkers and one other, it did not take over the customers of Colaris. The Dutch court asked the ECJ whether or not the Acquired Rights Directive (77/187/EC) applied in these circumstances.

JUDGMENT OF THE COURT: '. . . [8]   Mr Spijkers submits that there is a transfer of an undertaking within the meaning of Article 1(1) of Directive 77/187 if the means of production and activities of the enterprise are transferred as a unit by one owner to another, and that it is unnecessary to decide whether, at the date of the transfer, the transferor's activities were interrupted or whether the goodwill (circle of customers and brand image) had already disappeared. [9]   The Dutch and British Governments, as well as the Commission, consider on the other hand that the existence or otherwise of a transfer of an undertaking within the meaning described above must be assessed in the light of all the circumstances of the transaction in question such as the transfer or otherwise of tangible (buildings, movables, stocks) and intangible assets (know-how, goodwill), the nature of the activities and the cessation or not, as the case may be, of those activities at the date of transfer. However, none of these factors is decisive on its own.
[10]   In this connection the British Government and the Commission suggest that the essential criterion of the concept should be determined by reference to whether the transferee is given possession of an undertaking which is still in existence and the activities of which he can continue, or at least activities of the same type. The Dutch Government emphasises that, having regard to the social objective of the directive, the concept of transfer assumes that the transferor's activities are actually continued by the transferee in the framework of the same undertaking.
[11]   The last-mentioned view should be accepted. It appears from the general structure of Directive 77/187 and the wording of Article 1(1) that the directive aims to ensure the continuity of existing employment relationships in the framework of an economic entity, irrespective of a

change of owner. It follows that the decisive criterion for establishing the existence of a transfer within the meaning of the directive is whether the entity in question retains its identity.

[12]   Consequently it cannot be said that there is a transfer of an enterprise, business or part of a business on the sole ground that its assets have been sold. On the contrary, in a case like the present, it is necessary to determine whether what has been sold is an economic entity which is still in existence, and this will be apparent from the fact that its operation is actually being continued or has been taken over by the new employer, with the same economic or similar activities.

[13]   To decide whether these conditions are fulfilled it is necessary to take account of all the factual circumstances of the transaction in question, including the type of undertaking or business in question, the transfer or otherwise of tangible assets such as buildings and stocks, the value of intangible assets at the date of transfer, whether the majority of the staff are taken over by the new employer, the transfer or otherwise of the circle of customers and the degree of similarity between activities before and after the transfer and the duration of any interruption in those activities. It should be made clear, however, that each of these factors is only a part of the overall assessment which is required and therefore they cannot be examined independently of each other.

[14]   The factual appraisal which is necessary to establish whether there is or is not a transfer as defined above is a matter for the national court, taking account of the detailed interpretation which has been given.

[15]   For these reasons the answers to the questions referred to the Court should be that Article 1(1) of Directive 77/187 must be interpreted to the effect that the expression "transfer of an undertaking, business or part of a business to another employer" envisages the case in which the business in question retains its identity. In order to establish whether or not such a transfer has taken place in a case such as that before the national court, it is necessary to consider whether, having regard to all the facts characterising the transaction, the business was disposed of as a going concern, as would be indicated *inter alia* by the fact that its operation was actually continued or resumed by the new employer, with the same or similar activities . . .'

Comment

(1) TUPE 2006 reg 3(4)(a) makes it clear that the Regulations apply to 'public and private undertakings engaged in economic activities whether or not they are operating for gain'. The original TUPE Regulations in 1981 excluded transfers of undertakings which were not in the nature of a commercial venture. It became clear from cases such as *Dr Sophie Redmond Stichting* v *Bartol* (1992) that this was not compatible with the directive and the qualification was repealed in 1993. The new Regulations positively state that transfers of not-for-profit and public sector undertakings are covered.

(2) That said, TUPE 2006 reg 3(5) states that an 'administrative reorganisation of public administrative authorities or the transfer of administrative functions between public administrative authorities is not a relevant transfer'. Thus the reallocation of responsibilities between different government departments which has been a frequent occurrence in the Labour administration of recent years would usually not be covered. However, in 2000 the government issued a Code of Practice ('the Cabinet Office Guidelines on Staff Transfers in the Public Sector') designed to give employees protection in these circumstances and has indicated that it will continue to apply this.

(3) The biggest change in TUPE 2006 is its express inclusion of service provision changes.

Transfer of Undertakings (Protection of Employment) Regulations 2006

3   (1)   These Regulations apply to –

. . .

   (b)   a service provision change, that is a situation in which –
   (i)   activities cease to be carried out by a person ('a client') on his own behalf and are carried out instead by another person on the client's behalf ('a contractor');
   (ii)   activities cease to be carried out by a contractor on a client's behalf (whether or not those activities had previously been carried out by the client on his own behalf) and are carried out instead by another person ('a subsequent contractor') on the client's behalf; or
   (iii) activities cease to be carried out by a contractor or a subsequent contractor on a client's behalf (whether or not those activities had previously been carried out by the client on his own behalf) and are carried out instead by the client on his own behalf,
   and in which the conditions set out in paragraph (3) are satisfied.

. . .

   (3)   The conditions referred to in paragraph (1)(b) are that –
   (a)   immediately before the service provision change –
   (i)   there is an organised grouping of employees situated in Great Britain which has as its principal purpose the carrying out of the activities concerned on behalf of the client;
   (ii)   the client intends that the activities will, following the service provision change, be carried out by the transferee other than in connection with a single specific event or task of short-term duration; and
   (b)   the activities concerned do not consist wholly or mainly of the supply of goods for the client's use.

Comment

(1) During the 1980s, business strategists adopted the idea that businesses would be more efficient if they concentrated on their core business and outsourced everything else (captured in such slogans as 'Stick to the knitting!'). Thus it became commonplace for activities such as catering services, cleaning and security, as well as ancillary or supporting parts of the business, to be 'contracted-out' to other businesses. The concept was embraced by the Conservative government of the 1980s, which passed the Local Government Act 1988 requiring local authorities to identify activities which could be put out to tender on a regular basis to see whether they could be performed more economically by the private sector. Many other public bodies, such as schools and hospitals, were strongly encouraged to engage in a similar process.

(2) The process of compulsory competitive tendering (CCT) necessarily implied that at two- or three-year intervals the supplier of services might change. Of course, where the contracted-out services involved the provision of labour and virtually nothing else, the only way one supplier can provide services more cheaply than another is either by paying their workers less or else by requiring the same amount of work from fewer people.

(3) But if the Acquired Rights Directive applied to this situation, it meant that the new supplier had to take on the employees of the former supplier *on the same terms and conditions* as they enjoyed before. This seemed to frustrate the purpose of the exercise and

the then Conservative government made strenuous efforts to get the directive altered, but without success.

(4) There followed a series of cases in the ECJ and domestic courts which, frankly, left the law in something of a mess. It became difficult to predict whether particular contracting-out arrangements (or changes in service provision) would be regarded as subject to TUPE or the directive. While no change was made to the Acquired Rights Directive in this regard, the government took the major step in TUPE 2006 of going beyond the requirements of EU law and applying TUPE 2006 to a change in service provision as well as a transfer of an undertaking.

(5) This is effected by TUPE 2006 reg 3(1)(b). Note that it covers a first contracting-out arrangement, a change in contractors following re-tendering (sometimes called a 'second generation transfer) and contracting-in, where the business brings a function back in-house.

(6) Note the three conditions for the Regulations applying: (i) an organised grouping of employees assigned to the activity; (ii) the activity is not intended to be short-term; and (iii) the main purpose of the contract is the provision of a service rather than the supply of goods.

Effect of a transfer on contracts of employment

Transfer of Undertakings (Protection of Employment) Regulations 2006

4   (1) Except where objection is made under paragraph (7), a relevant transfer shall not operate so as to terminate the contract of employment of any person employed by the transferor and assigned to the organised grouping of resources or employees that is subject to the relevant transfer, which would otherwise be terminated by the transfer, but any such contract shall have effect after the transfer as if originally made between the person so employed and the transferee.

(2) Without prejudice to paragraph (1), but subject to paragraph (6), and regulations 8 and 15(9), on the completion of a relevant transfer –

(a) all the transferor's rights, powers, duties and liabilities under or in connection with any such contract shall be transferred by virtue of this regulation to the transferee; and

(b) any act or omission before the transfer is completed, of or in relation to the transferor in respect of that contract or a person assigned to that organised grouping of resources or employees, shall be deemed to have been an act or omission of or in relation to the transferee.

(3) Any reference in paragraph (1) to a person employed by the transferor and assigned to the organised grouping of resources or employees that is subject to a relevant transfer, is a reference to a person so employed immediately before the transfer, or who would have been so employed if he had not been dismissed in the circumstances described in regulation 7(1), including, where the transfer is effected by a series of two or more transactions, a person so employed and assigned or who would have been so employed and assigned immediately before any of those transactions.

(4) Subject to regulation 9, in respect of a contract of employment that is, or will be, transferred by paragraph (1), any purported variation of the contract shall be void if the sole or principal reason for the variation is –

(a)   the transfer itself; or

(b)   a reason connected with the transfer that is not an economic, technical or organisational reason entailing changes in the workforce.

(5)   Paragraph (4) shall not prevent the employer and his employee, whose contract of employment is, or will be, transferred by paragraph (1), from agreeing a variation of that contract if the sole or principal reason for the variation is –

(a)   a reason connected with the transfer that is an economic, technical or organisational reason entailing changes in the workforce; or

(b)   a reason unconnected with the transfer.

(6)   Paragraph (2) shall not transfer or otherwise affect the liability of any person to be prosecuted for, convicted of and sentenced for any offence.

(7)   Paragraphs (1) and (2) shall not operate to transfer the contract of employment and the rights, powers, duties and liabilities under or in connection with it of an employee who informs the transferor or the transferee that he objects to becoming employed by the transferee.

(8)   Subject to paragraphs (9) and (11), where an employee so objects, the relevant transfer shall operate so as to terminate his contract of employment with the transferor but he shall not be treated, for any purpose, as having been dismissed by the transferor.

(9)   Subject to regulation 9, where a relevant transfer involves or would involve a substantial change in working conditions to the material detriment of a person whose contract of employment is or would be transferred under paragraph (1), such an employee may treat the contract of employment as having been terminated, and the employee shall be treated for any purpose as having been dismissed by the employer.

(10)   No damages shall be payable by an employer as a result of a dismissal falling within paragraph (9) in respect of any failure by the employer to pay wages to an employee in respect of a notice period which the employee has failed to work.

(11)   Paragraphs (1), (7), (8) and (9) are without prejudice to any right of an employee arising apart from these Regulations to terminate his contract of employment without notice in acceptance of a repudiatory breach of contract by his employer.

. . .

11   (2)   'employee liability information' means –

(a)   the identity and age of the employee;

(b)   those particulars of employment that an employer is obliged to give to an employee pursuant to section 1 of the 1996 Act;

(c)   information of any –

  (i)   disciplinary procedure taken against an employee;

  (ii)   grievance procedure taken by an employee,

  within the previous two years, in circumstances where the Employment Act 2002 (Dispute Resolution) Regulations 2004 apply;

(d)   information of any court or tribunal case, claim or action –

  (i)   brought by an employee against the transferor, within the previous two years;

  (ii)   that the transferor has reasonable grounds to believe that an employee may bring against the transferee, arising out of the employee's employment with the transferor; and

(e)   information of any collective agreement which will have effect after the transfer, in its application in relation to the employee, pursuant to regulation 5(a).

Comment

(1) Regulation 4 is the heart of the protection for employees, providing for their contracts of employment to be transferred automatically to the new employer. At common

law, contracts of employment could not be automatically transferred: see *Nokes* v *Doncaster Amalgamated Collieries* (1940), where the point was expressed forcibly by Lord Atkin:

> My Lords, I confess it appears to me astonishing that, apart from overriding questions of public welfare, power should be given to a court or to anyone else to transfer a man without his knowledge, and possibly against his will, from the service of one person to the service of another. I had fancied that ingrained in the personal status of a citizen under our laws was the right to choose for himself whom he would serve, and that this right of choice constituted the main difference between a servant and a serf . . .

(2) This position is preserved by reg 4(7), which states that there is no transfer if an employee objects to being transferred. However, in such a situation, reg 4(8) provides that the termination of the employee's contract does not count as 'dismissal' – meaning that the employee will be unable to claim unfair dismissal or even a redundancy payment.

(3) There is an exception to this in reg 4(9), if the transfer would lead to a change in working conditions to the material disadvantage of the employee, even if not actually constituting a breach of contract. In such a situation, the employee will be treated as having been dismissed for the purposes of claiming unfair dismissal or redundancy, but not wrongful dismissal (reg 4(10)). If the change results in a repudiatory breach of contract by the employer, the employee will have the usual rights to claim constructive or wrongful dismissal (reg 4(11)).

(4) The reference to the transfer of 'all rights, powers, duties and liabilities' now contained in reg 4(2) has been held to include liability for discrimination claims arising before the transfer (*DJM International* v *Nicholas* (1996)) and liability for personal injury claims (*Bernadone* v *Pall Mall Services* (1999)). To assist the transferee in assessing potential liabilities, TUPE 2006 reg 11 requires the transferor to supply 'employee liability information' to the transferee, as defined in reg 11(2).

(5) The reference in reg 4(3) to people who would have been employed immediately before the transfer if they had not been dismissed deals with the problem of the employer who might sack employees just before transferring the business, often at the transferee's behest, so that the transferee would not have to take them on. In *Secretary of State* v *Spence* (1986) the Court of Appeal held that TUPE could not apply to that situation, because the employees were not employed 'immediately before' the transfer – meaning the split second before the transfer took place. In *Litster* v *Forth Dry Dock* (1989) the House of Lords dealt with the obvious unfairness of this situation by a purposive interpretation of TUPE, reading into the Regulations the extra phrase which is now expressly included in TUPE 2006 reg 4(3).

(6) Regulation 4(4), (5) gives legislative effect to the *obiter* view of the House of Lords in *Wilson* v *St Helens BC* (1997) that a variation of the contracts of employees transferred should be permitted if it is justified by an economic, technical or organisational reason. Some commentators doubt that this is compatible with the ECJ's decision in *Foreningen af Arbejdsledere i Danmark* v *Daddy's Dance Hall* (1988), which said that any variation in connection with a transfer would be void. However, both EU law and TUPE 2006 allow employees to be dismissed in these circumstances (see below, p 470), so it seems reasonable to allow them to agree a change in terms to avoid dismissal.

(7) There is one major exception in relation to the transfer of the employee's existing terms and conditions. TUPE 2006 reg 10 states that pension rights are not transferred.

Beckmann v Dynamco Whicheloe Macfarlane Ltd
[2003] ICR 50 European Court of Justice

The claimant had been employed in the NHS on Whitley Council terms and conditions. These provided that employees who were made redundant over the age of 50 would qualify for generous early retirement benefits: an immediate pension, lump sum payments enhanced according to length of service and compensation payments for the fact that benefits were reduced through being retired early. The claimant was transferred to the defendants in 1995 and made redundant two years later. She claimed that she was still entitled to the benefits of the Whitley Council scheme. The employer argued that this was a pension entitlement and had therefore not transferred because of the exclusion of rights to 'old-age, invalidity or survivors' benefits' in what is now Art 3(4) of the Acquired Rights Directive (2001/23/EC). The High Court referred the issue to the ECJ.

JUDGMENT OF THE COURT: '. . . An arrangement such as that under section 46 of the General Whitley Council conditions of service, provides, *inter alia* in the event of a certain form of dismissal, for an early retirement pension together with payments to enhance that benefit.

Given the general objective, of safeguarding the rights of employees in the event of transfers of undertakings, pursued by [the Acquired Rights Directive (2001/23/EC)] when it provides, in [Art 3(1) and (3)], for transfer to the transferee of the transferor's rights and obligations arising from a contract of employment, from an employment relationship or collective agreement, the exception to that rule provided for by [Art 3(4)] must be interpreted strictly.

That exception can therefore apply only to the benefits listed exhaustively in that provision and they must be construed in a narrow sense.

In that connection, it is only benefits paid from the time when an employee reaches the end of his normal working life, as laid down by the general structure of the pension scheme in question, and not benefits paid in circumstances such as those in point in the main proceedings (dismissal for redundancy), that can be classified as old-age benefits, even if they are calculated by reference to the rules for calculating normal pension benefits.

The answer to the first question must therefore be that early retirement benefits and benefits intended to enhance the conditions of such retirement, paid in the event of dismissal to employees who have reached a certain age, such as the benefits at issue in the main proceedings, are not old-age, invalidity or survivors' benefits under supplementary company or inter-company pension schemes within the meaning of [Art 3(4) of the Acquired Rights Directive (2001/23/EC)] . . .'

Comment

(1) This is in line with the ECJ's jurisprudence on the meaning of 'pay' for the purposes of Art 141 of the Treaty of Rome on equal pay. In the United Kingdom, it is of great importance to employers who have taken on groups of employees from parts of the public sector during the move towards the privatisation of public services. In addition, the Cabinet Office Guidelines on Staff Transfers in the Public Sector (2000) require transferees to offer transferred employees pension benefits which are broadly comparable to those they would have had if they had stayed in the public sector.

(2) More generally, the Pensions Act 2004 and the Transfer of Employment (Pension Protection) Regulations 2005 provide some protection for any employees transferred after April 2005. If the transferor made contributions to an occupational pension scheme applying to the categories of employee transferred, the transferee must offer the

employees the option of belonging either to an occupational pension scheme or a stake-holder pension scheme to which the transferee contributes. The standards such schemes must meet are dealt with in detail in the Transfer of Employment (Pension Protection) Regulations 2005. It will be noted that this falls short of requiring the transferee to offer comparable benefits to their previous employer, but it is certainly better than the whole-sale exclusion which used to obtain.

Dismissal connected with the transfer

Transfer of Undertakings (Protection of Employment) Regulations 2006

7 (1) Where either before or after a relevant transfer, any employee of the transferor or the transferee is dismissed, that employee shall be treated for the purposes of Part X of the 1996 Act (unfair dismissal) as unfairly dismissed if the sole or principal reason for his dismissal is –

(a) the transfer itself; or

(b) a reason connected with the transfer that is not an economic, technical or organisa-tional reason entailing changes in the workforce.

(2) This paragraph applies where the sole or principal reason for the dismissal is a reason connected with the transfer that is an economic, technical or organisational reason entailing changes in the workforce of either the transferor or the transferee before or after a relevant transfer.

(3) Where paragraph (2) applies –

(a) paragraph (1) shall not apply;

(b) without prejudice to the application of section 98(4) of the 1996 Act (test of fair dismissal), the dismissal shall, for the purposes of sections 98(1) and 135 of that Act (reason for dismissal), be regarded as having been for redundancy where section 98(2)(c) of that Act applies, or otherwise for a substantial reason of a kind such as to justify the dismissal of an employee holding the position which that employee held . . .

Comment

(1) TUPE 2006 reg 7 complements reg 4 by providing employees with a remedy if they are dismissed (by either transferor or transferee) in connection with the transfer. Such a dismissal is automatically unfair unless the employer can show that it was for an 'economic, technical or organisational reason' (often called 'an ETO reason') entailing changes in the workforce. This expression is lifted from Art 4(1) of the Acquired Rights Directive (2001/23/EC) and is not defined in the legislation. Where the dismissal is for an ETO reason, it may count as redundancy or as 'some other substantial reason' justifying dismissal. In either case, it may still be unfair if the employer has not acted reasonably as required by ERA s 98(4).

(2) The following case is still the leading authority on what constitutes an 'economic, technical or organisational reason entailing changes in the workforce'.

Berriman v *Delabole Slate Ltd* [1985] ICR 546 Court of Appeal

The business in which the claimant was employed as a quarryman was transferred to the respondent company. They wanted to harmonise the employees' conditions of employment with their own workforce, and this meant reducing the amount of guaranteed basic pay that the claimant received. He refused the offer and left, claiming unfair dismissal.

BROWNE-WILKINSON LJ: '. . . The combined effect of these regulations and the [Employment Rights Act 1996] is as follows. On the transfer of a business, the employees of the transferor become the employees of the transferee. An employee has the right to treat himself as constructively dismissed by any detrimental change in his working conditions (regulation 5(5) [see now TUPE 2006 reg 4(9)]) but the question whether his dismissal is fair is dealt with by regulation 8 [see now TUPE 2006 reg 7]. Under regulation 8(1) [see now TUPE 2006 reg 7(1)], if any employee is dismissed in connection with the transfer, the dismissal is unfair unless the reason or principal reason for dismissing the employee is an "economic, technical or organisational reason entailing changes in the workforce". In this event the case is taken out of the automatic unfairness provisions of regulation 8(1) [see now TUPE 2006 reg 7(1)] and the employer is treated as having demonstrated some other potentially fair reason for his dismissal thereby satisfying the requirements of [ERA s 98(1)]. The question will still remain whether, in the circumstances of the particular case, the dismissal of that employee was in fact fair for the purposes of [ERA s 98(4)].

Applying those provisions to the present case, the first question was whether the employee was constructively dismissed by the employers' attempt to impose on him a lower guaranteed wage. The employment tribunal held that he was constructively dismissed and the employers did not challenge this finding in the appeal tribunal. The next question was whether the employers' reason for dismissing the employee was the transfer of the undertaking to the employers or a reason connected with it so as to bring the case within regulation 8(1) [see now TUPE 2006 reg 7(1)]. The employment tribunal held that it was and that accordingly the dismissal was rendered unfair by regulation 8(1) [see now TUPE 2006 reg 7(1)]. The next question was whether the case was taken out of the automatic unfairness provision by regulation 8(2) [see now TUPE 2006 reg 7(2), (3)] in that the employers' reason or principal reason for dismissing Mr Berriman was an "economic, technical or organisational reason entailing changes in the workforce". The employment tribunal held that the employers' reason for dismissal was such a reason, but the appeal tribunal reversed them on this point holding that, although the reason for dismissal was an economic, technical or organisational reason, such reason did not "entail changes in the workforce". Finally, the employment tribunal decided that the dismissal of the employee was fair within the meaning of [ERA s 98(4)]. That finding was challenged before the appeal tribunal who did not decide the point: there is no respondent's notice raising the point before us.

The only point we have to decide therefore is whether, as a matter of law, the employment tribunal were entitled to hold that the case fell within regulation 8(2) [see now TUPE 2006 reg 7(2), (3)] in that the employers' reason for dismissal was a reason "entailing changes in the workforce" of the employers.

Mr Tabachnik, for the employers, does not persist in the argument which he unsuccessfully advanced at the appeal tribunal that the words "changes in the workforce" were wide enough to cover changes in the terms and conditions of the workforce. He accepts that what must be shown are changes in the number of the workforce or possibly changes in the job descriptions of the constituent elements of the workforce which, although involving no overall reduction in numbers, involves a change in the individual employees which together make up the workforce. But, says Mr Tabachnik, it is necessary to ask the question "what was the reason for dismissal" as at the date of the constructive dismissal, *i.e.*, 28 January 1983. At that date the reason for dismissal was not solely the employers' desire to standardise rates of pay, but also included the employee's refusal to accept the proposed change and his notice terminating his employment. Therefore, says Mr Tabachnik, the reason for dismissal entailed a change in the workforce since it entailed the constructive dismissal of the employee.

471

We do not accept these submissions. First, in our judgment, even in a case of constructive dismissal, [ERA s 98(1)] imposes on the employers the burden of showing the reason for dismissal, notwithstanding that it was the employee, not the employer, who actually decided to terminate the contract of employment. In our judgment, the only way in which the statutory requirements of the Act can be made to fit a case of constructive dismissal is to read [ERA s 98(1)] as requiring the employers to show the reasons for their conduct which entitled the employee to terminate the contract thereby giving rise to a deemed dismissal by the employers. We can see nothing in the decision in *Savoia* v *Chiltern Herb Farms Ltd* (1982) which conflicts with this view.

If that is right, when one turns to regulation 8(2) [see now TUPE 2006 reg 7(2), (3)] and asks the question, "What was the reason or principal reason for dismissing the employee?", in a case of constructive dismissal attention has to be focused on the employers' reasons for presenting the employee with the ultimatum changing his guaranteed rates of pay. It is the employers' reasons for its conduct not the employee's reaction to that conduct which is important. In the present case the reason for the employers' ultimatum was to produce standard rates of pay – not in any way to reduce the number in its workforce.

Then, in order to come within regulation 8(2) [see now TUPE 2006 reg 7(2), (3)], it has to be shown that *that* reason is an economic, technical or organisational reason entailing changes in the workforce. The reason itself (*i.e.*, to produce standardisation in pay) does not involve any change either in the number or the functions of the workforce. The most that can be said is that such organisational reason *may* (not must) lead to the dismissal of those employees who do not fall into line coupled with the filling of the vacancies thereby caused by new employees prepared to accept the conditions of service. In our judgment that is not enough. First, the phrase "economic, technical or organisational reason entailing changes in the workforce" in our judgment requires that the change in the workforce is part of the economic, technical or organisational reason. The employer's plan must be to achieve changes in the workforce. It must be an objective of the plan, not just a possible consequence of it.

Secondly, we do not think that the dismissal of one employee followed by the engagement of another in his place constitutes a change in the "workforce". To our minds, the word "workforce" connotes the whole body of employees as an entity: it corresponds to the "strength" or the "establishment". Changes in the identity of the individuals who make up the workforce do not constitute changes in the workforce itself so long as the overall numbers and functions of the employees looked at as a whole remain unchanged.

We are supported in this view by the fact that, if Mr Tabachnik is right, any case in which an employee is dismissed for an economic, technical or organisational reason will fall within regulation 8(2) [see now TUPE 2006 reg 7(2), (3)] and the words "entailing changes in the workforce" are otiose. Regulation 8(2) [see now TUPE 2006 reg 7(2), (3)] is dealing exclusively with cases where an employee has been dismissed for economic, technical or organisational reasons. Therefore, by definition there has, for a short while at least, been a reduction of one in the number of people employed. If that temporary reduction falls within the words "entailing changes in the workforce" then regulation 8(2) [see now TUPE 2006 reg 7(2), (3)] will cover every dismissal for an economic, technical or organisational reason and the words "entailing changes in the workforce" are given no effect whatsoever. That in our judgment could not be a proper construction of the regulation.

Mr Tabachnik points out that, if the construction we favour is correct, following a transfer of an undertaking employers will be precluded from imposing on the employees taken over necessary changes in their conditions of employment which, if there had been no transfer, could properly have been imposed on their existing workforce: see *Hollister* v *National Farmers' Union* (1979). This, says Mr Tabachnik, would be an undesirable result. We do not find this argument persuasive. Regulation 8(1) [see now TUPE 2006 reg 7(1)] will only render unfair a dismissal for failure to accept new conditions of service if the reason for dismissal is a reason connected with the transfer of the undertaking. If the reason for seeking to impose, say, standard conditions of service is connected with the transfer, it is far from clear that it was the intention of the legislature (or of Council Directive (77/187/EEC) which required the Regulations to be made) that immediately following a transfer the employees of the transferred undertaking could be made to accept new terms of service. The purpose of the directive was "the safeguarding of employees' rights in the event of transfers" and the regulations themselves include in their name the words "protection of employment". Amongst the most crucial rights of employees are their existing terms of service. We are not satisfied that there is a clear statutory intention to ensure that, following a transfer, the transferee company can insist on equating the terms and conditions of the "transferred" employees to those of his existing employees notwithstanding the fact that such alteration may constitute a detriment to the transferred employees.

For these reasons, which are much the same as those given by the appeal tribunal, we dismiss the appeal. It follows that under regulation 8(1) see now [TUPE 2006 reg 7(1)] the dismissal of the employee was unfair and, as the appeal tribunal directed, in default of agreement the amount of compensation must be remitted to the employment tribunal for assessment.'

Comment

(1) The judgment of the Court of Appeal in this case shows a welcome purposive approach to the interpretation of the Regulations, indicating that they provide an important protection for employees in the case of some kinds of restructuring, at any rate.

(2) The wording of TUPE 2006 differs from the 1981 TUPE Regulations in certain respects, but this does not affect the substance and authority of this decision.

CONSULTATION OVER REDUNDANCIES AND TRANSFERS

Both the Collective Dismissals Directive (98/59/EC) and the Acquired Rights Directive (2001/23/EC) require employers to consult with workers' representatives over redundancies and transfers. In British law this obligation was implemented by requiring consultation with recognised trade unions, which meant, of course, that where there was no recognised trade union, employees had no right to be consulted. In 1994, in *EC Commission* v *UK*, the ECJ confirmed that this was a breach of the directives. As a result the Collective Dismissals and Transfer of Undertakings (Protection of Employment) (Amendment) Regulations 1995 were passed, amending TULRCA and TUPE so as to require employers to consult with 'appropriate representatives' (who did not have to be trade union representatives, even if a trade union was recognised).

These provisions were criticised as inadequate because they made no provision for the method of electing employee representatives and because they did not even ensure that representatives would be elected: the employer needed only to give employees the opportunity to elect representatives, not to make sure that this happened. These points were addressed in further amendments to TULRCA and TUPE by the Collective Redundancies and Transfer of Undertakings (Protection of Employment) (Amendment) Regulations 1999, which also restored primacy to the trade union channel. If there is a recognised trade union, the employer should consult with it; if not, the consultation is with employee representatives.

Trade Union and Labour Relations (Consolidation) Act 1992

188 (1)   Where an employer is proposing to dismiss as redundant 20 or more employees at one establishment within a period of 90 days or less, the employer shall consult about the dismissals all the persons who are appropriate representatives of any of the employees who may be affected by the proposed dismissals or may be affected by measures taken in connection with those dismissals.

(1A)   The consultation shall begin in good time and in any event –

(a)   where the employer is proposing to dismiss 100 or more employees as mentioned in subsection (1), at least 90 days, and

(b)   otherwise, at least 30 days,

before the first of the dismissals takes effect.

(1B)   For the purposes of this section the appropriate representatives of any affected employees are –

(a)   if the employees are of a description in respect of which an independent trade union is recognised by their employer, representatives of the trade union, or

(b)   in any other case, whichever of the following employee representatives the employer chooses: –

(i)   employee representatives appointed or elected by the affected employees otherwise than for the purposes of this section, who (having regard to the purposes for and the method by which they were appointed or elected) have authority from those employees to receive information and to be consulted about the proposed dismissals on their behalf;

(ii)   employee representatives elected by the affected employees, for the purposes of this section, in an election satisfying the requirements of section 188A(1).

(2)   The consultation shall include consultation about ways of –

(a)   avoiding the dismissals,

(b)   reducing the numbers of employees to be dismissed, and

(c)   mitigating the consequences of the dismissals,

and shall be undertaken by the employer with a view to reaching agreement with the appropriate representatives . . .

Transfer of Undertakings (Protection of Employment) Regulations 2006

13   . . .

(2)   Long enough before a relevant transfer to enable the employer of any affected employees to consult the appropriate representatives of any affected employees, the employer shall inform those representatives of –

(a)   the fact that the transfer is to take place, the date or proposed date of the transfer and the reasons for it;

(b)   the legal, economic and social implications of the transfer for any affected employees;

(c)   the measures which he envisages he will, in connection with the transfer, take in relation to any affected employees or, if he envisages that no measures will be so taken, that fact; and

(d)   if the employer is the transferor, the measures, in connection with the transfer, which he envisages the transferee will take in relation to any affected employees who will become employees of the transferee after the transfer by virtue of regulation 4 or, if he envisages that no measures will be so taken, that fact.

(3)   For the purposes of this regulation the appropriate representatives of any affected employees are –

    (a)   if the employees are of a description in respect of which an independent trade union is recognised by their employer, representatives of the trade union; or

    (b)   in any other case, whichever of the following employee representatives the employer chooses –

        (i)   employee representatives appointed or elected by the affected employees otherwise than for the purposes of this regulation, who (having regard to the purposes for, and the method by which they were appointed or elected) have authority from those employees to receive information and to be consulted about the transfer on their behalf;

        (ii)   employee representatives elected by any affected employees, for the purposes of this regulation, in an election satisfying the requirements of regulation 14(1).

(4)   The transferee shall give the transferor such information at such a time as will enable the transferor to perform the duty imposed on him by virtue of paragraph (2)(d).

(5)   The information which is to be given to the appropriate representatives shall be given to each of them by being delivered to them, or sent by post to an address notified by them to the employer, or (in the case of representatives of a trade union) sent by post to the trade union at the address of its head or main office.

(6)   An employer of an affected employee who envisages that he will take measures in relation to an affected employee, in connection with the relevant transfer, shall consult the appropriate representatives of that employee with a view to seeking their agreement to the intended measures.

(7)   In the course of those consultations the employer shall –

    (a)   consider any representations made by the appropriate representatives; and

    (b)   reply to those representations and, if he rejects any of those representations, state his reasons.

(8)   The employer shall allow the appropriate representatives access to any affected employees and shall afford to those representatives such accommodation and other facilities as may be appropriate.

(9)   If in any case there are special circumstances which render it not reasonably practicable for an employer to perform a duty imposed on him by any of paragraphs (2) to (7), he shall take all such steps towards performing that duty as are reasonably practicable in the circumstances.

(10)   Where –

    (a)   the employer has invited any of the affected employees to elect employee representatives; and

    (b)   the invitation was issued long enough before the time when the employer is required to give information under paragraph (2) to allow them to elect representatives by that time,

the employer shall be treated as complying with the requirements of this regulation in relation to those employees if he complies with those requirements as soon as is reasonably practicable after the election of the representatives.

(11)   If, after the employer has invited any affected employees to elect representatives, they fail to do so within a reasonable time, he shall give to any affected employees the information set out in paragraph (2).

(12)   The duties imposed on an employer by this regulation shall apply irrespective of whether the decision resulting in the relevant transfer is taken by the employer or a person controlling the employer.

Comment

(1) The duties to consult under TULRCA s 188 and TUPE 2006 reg 13 are in parallel terms, but there are some important differences. Under TUPE 2006, the duty to consult applies to both transferor and transferee and the scope of the consultation is wider, covering the legal, economic and social implications of the transfer.

(2) Note that the employer still has no affirmative obligation to ensure that an election of representatives takes place. If affected employees who are not covered by a recognised trade union do not elect representatives, the employer is only required to furnish them with the relevant information individually – and not to consult with them as such. This applies to both kinds of consultation.

(3) For redundancy consultation, the obligation to consult now only arises where 20 or more are due to be made redundant over a 90-day period. Until the 1995 amendments, the obligation applied to every single redundancy. However, when it was obliged by the ECJ to amend TULRCA s 188, the then Conservative government took the opportunity to introduce this limitation, which is permitted by the Collective Dismissals Directive. The Labour government has not seen fit to restore the previous position.

(4) It is important to note also that the definition of redundancy has a special, extended meaning in relation to consultation over collective dismissals. TULRCA s 195 states as follows:

> (1) In this Chapter references to dismissal as redundant are references to dismissal for a reason not related to the individual concerned or for a number of reasons all of which are not so related.
> (2) For the purposes of any proceedings under this Chapter, where an employee is or is proposed to be dismissed it shall be presumed, unless the contrary is proved, that he is or is proposed to be dismissed as redundant.

(5) Note the difference in the timing of the two kinds of consultation: no specific period is laid down in TUPE 2006, as long as it is 'long enough before. . . ' TULRCA s 188 used to require consultation to begin 'at the earliest opportunity' but was also watered down by the 1995 Regulations. Under TUPE 2006 the duty to consult arises only when a transfer has been decided upon. Under TULRCA s 188, it is when the employer proposes to dismiss workers for redundancy. What is 'proposing to dismiss' and is this in accordance with the Collective Dismissals Directive?

Hough v Leyland Daf Ltd [1991] ICR 696 Employment Appeal Tribunal

The claimants had been employed as security staff by the company. In May 1987 the company accepted a report from its security manager recommending that security arrangements should be contracted out. The employees' union, APEX, was not informed until September 1987; the redundancies took effect at the end of December 1987. The employees claimed unfair dismissal (and were successful: this aspect of the case is not extracted), and their trade union complained of a failure to consult in breach of what is now TULRCA s 188.

KNOX J: '. . . It was submitted to us on behalf of Leyland that the requirements in [TULRCA s 188(4)] for disclosure of various matters indicated that the proposals will have reached a fairly advanced stage before the employer can be said to be "proposing" for the purposes of subsection (1) so as to be under an immediate duty to consult. We agree that [TULRCA s 188] read as a whole contemplates that matters should have reached a stage where a specific proposal has been formulated and that this is a later stage than the diagnosis of a problem and the appreciation that at least one way of dealing with it would be by declaring redundancies. Beyond that we doubt whether it is helpful to try and analyse conceptually the precise stage that an employer must have reached to be "proposing" for the purposes of subsection (1) because the section has to cover a large multiplicity of possible situations which would be susceptible of very widely differing types of treatment. In that state of affairs it seems to us better to stick to the words of the section . . .'

Comment

(1) In *R v British Coal ex parte Vardy* (1993) Glidewell LJ expressed the view that TULRCA s 188 did not properly implement the Collective Dismissals Directive:

> I say this because in the Directive consultation is to begin as soon as an employer contemplates redundancies, whereas under the Act it only needs to begin when he proposes to dismiss as redundant an employee. The verb 'proposes' in its ordinary usage relates to a state of mind which is much more certain and further along the decision-making process than the verb 'contemplate' . . .

His comments were *obiter*, but seem correct. It is perhaps surprising that this point was not taken up in the European Commission's infraction proceeding against the UK in *EC Commission v UK* (1994).

(2) In *MSF v Refuge Assurance* (2002) the EAT agreed with Glidewell LJ's comment in the Divisional Court that TULRCA s 188 was inconsistent with the directive on this point. The clearest indication of need for reform comes from the ECJ.

Junk v Kühnel [2005] IRLR 310 European Court of Justice

The company employing the claimant got into severe financial difficulties and appointed a liquidator. In due course the liquidator dismissed as redundant all the remaining employees of the company. The claimant challenged this on the ground that there had been no prior consultation as required by the Collective Dismissals Directive (98/59/EC). The German court referred two questions to the ECJ. First, whether 'redundancy' for the purposes of the Collective Dismissals Directive occurred on the issue of notice of dismissal for redundancy or at the later stage when the employment relationship was actually terminated. Secondly, if 'redundancy' meant the issue of notice of dismissal for redundancy, must the consultation process be complete before that happens?

JUDGMENT OF THE COURT: '. . . The object of the dispute in the main proceedings is to assess the lawfulness of a redundancy in the light of the consultation and notification procedures set out in Article 2 and in Articles 3 and 4 of the Directive respectively. For the purposes of that appraisal, it is necessary to determine at what point in time a redundancy occurs, that is to say, the point in time at which the event constituting redundancy takes place.

The resolution of the dispute in the main proceedings thus calls for clarification of the content of the concept of 'redundancy' within the meaning of the Directive.

Article 1(1)(a) of the Directive defines "collective redundancies" but fails to indicate the event triggering redundancy or to refer in this regard to the laws of the Member States.

In this connection, the need for uniform application of Community law and the principle of equality require that the terms of a provision of Community law which makes no express reference to the law of the Member States for the purpose of determining its meaning and scope must normally be given an autonomous and uniform interpretation throughout the Community, which must take into account the context of the provision and the purpose of the legislation in question (see, inter alia, *Linster* (2000), and *Commission v Portugal* (2005)).

That being so, the concept of "redundancy" referred to in Articles 2 to 4 of the Directive must be given an autonomous and uniform interpretation within the Community legal system.

The first question

By its first question, the Arbeitsgericht is in substance seeking to ascertain whether Articles 2 to 4 of the Directive are to be construed as meaning that the event constituting redundancy consists of the expression by the employer of his intention to put an end to the contract of employment or of the actual cessation of the employment relationship on the expiry of the period in the notices of redundancy.

. . . [I]it must be noted that Article 2(1) of the Directive imposes an obligation on the employer to begin consultations with the workers' representatives in good time in the case where he "is contemplating collective redundancies". Article 3(1) requires the employer to notify the competent public authority of "any projected collective redundancies".

The case in which the employer "is contemplating" collective redundancies and has drawn up a "project" to that end corresponds to a situation in which no decision has yet been taken. By contrast, the notification to a worker that his or her contract of employment has been terminated is the expression of a decision to sever the employment relationship, and the actual cessation of that relationship on the expiry of the period of notice is no more than the effect of that decision.

Thus, the terms used by the Community legislature indicate that the obligations to consult and to notify arise prior to any decision by the employer to terminate contracts of employment.

Finally, this interpretation is confirmed, in regard to the procedure for consultation of workers' representatives, by the purpose of the Directive, as set out in Article 2(2), which is to avoid terminations of contracts of employment or to reduce the number of such terminations. The achievement of that purpose would be jeopardised if the consultation of workers' representatives were to be subsequent to the employer's decision.

The answer to the first question must therefore be that Articles 2 to 4 of the Directive must be construed as meaning that the event constituting redundancy consists in the declaration by an employer of his intention to terminate the contract of employment.

The second question

By its second question, the Arbeitsgericht is seeking to ascertain whether an employer is entitled to carry out collective redundancies before the end of the consultation procedure set out in Article 2 of the Directive and of the notification procedure set out in Articles 3 and 4 of the Directive.

It follows already from the answer to the first question that an employer cannot terminate contracts of employment before he has engaged in the two procedures in question.

With regard to the consultation procedure, this is provided for, within the terms of Article 2(1) of the Directive, "with a view to reaching an agreement". According to Article 2(2), this procedure must, "'at least, cover ways and means of avoiding collective redundancies or reducing the number of workers affected, and of mitigating the consequences by recourse to accompanying social measures".

It thus appears that Article 2 of the Directive imposes an obligation to negotiate.

The effectiveness of such an obligation would be compromised if an employer was entitled to terminate contracts of employment during the course of the procedure or even at the beginning thereof. It would be significantly more difficult for workers' representatives to achieve the withdrawal of a decision that has been taken than to secure the abandonment of a decision that is being contemplated.

478

A contract of employment may therefore be terminated only after the conclusion of the consultation procedure, that is to say, after the employer has complied with the obligations set out in Article 2 of the Directive . . .'

The special circumstances defence

TULRCA s 188(7) and TUPE 2006 reg 13(9) provide an employer with a defence where special circumstances render prior consultation not reasonably practicable. When will this apply?

Clarks of Hove Ltd v *Bakers' Union* [1978] ICR 1076 Court of Appeal

The company, which had a bakery and retail business, found itself in serious financial trouble in late summer 1976. It sought a buyer for some of its shops in order to raise essential capital, but in October, its main prospect pulled out after seeing an auditor's report and on 24 October the last hope, in the shape of another buyer, also collapsed. The same day the directors put up a notice informing the employees that they were dismissed. The company argued that the financial situation amounted to special circumstances excusing their failure to consult.

GEOFFREY LANE LJ: '. . . What, then, is meant by "special circumstances"? Here we come to the crux of the case. In this aspect, also, decisions under the Road Traffic Acts appear to me to be unhelpful. The decisions are too well known to need reference. The basis of them all is probably *Whittall* v *Kirby* (1946) *per* Lord Goddard CJ,

> "A special reason . . . is one which is special to the facts of the particular case, that is, special to the facts which constitute the offence . . . A circumstance peculiar to the offender as distinguished from the offence is not a special reason . . ."

In so far as that means that the special circumstance must be relevant to the issue then that would apply equally here, but in these circumstances, the Employment Protection Act 1975 [now TULRCA s 188], it seems to me that the way in which the phrase was interpreted by the employment tribunal is correct. What they said, in effect, was this, that insolvency is, on its own, neither here nor there. It may be a special circumstance, it may not be a special circumstance. It will depend entirely on the cause of the insolvency whether the circumstances can be described as special or not. If, for example, sudden disaster strikes a company, making it necessary to close the concern, then plainly that would be a matter which was capable of being a special circumstance; and that is so whether the disaster is physical or financial. If the insolvency, however, was merely due to a gradual run-down of the company, as it was in this case, then those are facts on which the employment tribunal can come to the conclusion that the circumstances were not special. In other words, to be special the event must be something out of the ordinary, something uncommon; and that is the meaning of the word "special" in the context of this Act.

Accordingly it seems to me that the employment tribunal approached the matter in precisely the correct way. They distilled the problem which they had to decide down to its essence, and they asked themselves this question: do these circumstances, which undoubtedly caused the summary dismissal and the failure to consult the union as required by [TULRCA s 188] amount to special circumstances; and they went on, again correctly, as it seems to me, to point out that insolvency simpliciter is neutral, it is not on its own a special circumstance. Whether it is or is not will depend on the causes of the insolvency. They define "special" as being something out of the ordinary run of events, such as, for example, a general trading boycott – that is the passage which I have already read. Here, again, I think they were right . . .'

(Roskill LJ delivered a concurring judgment and Stephenson LJ agreed.)

Comment

(1) The decision that the reason for a sudden insolvency, and not merely its existence, is to be considered in deciding whether the circumstances are 'special' or not is of the first importance and has been widely applied since. Note that even if the full consultation period is impossible, employers should still strive, so far as feasible, to comply by engaging in consultation as soon as they can.

(2) It is common for counsel to argue the meaning of words in a statute by analogy with similar words in another statute, but the attempt to use the Road Traffic Acts by way of analogy seems singularly inappropriate.

(3) Under TULRCA s 189 the remedy for failure to consult is for the trade union (or employee representatives) to apply for a protective award on behalf of affected employees. The maximum award possible corresponds to the minimum consultation periods for multiple redundancies set out in TULRCA s 188. The remedy under TUPE 2006 reg 15 is similar, although here the maximum protective award is 13 weeks' pay (TUPE 2006 reg 16(3)). Where employees are entitled to protective awards under both pieces of legislation, they are awarded both: the protective awards are not set off against each other.

(4) TULRCA s 189(4)(b) and TUPE 2006 reg 16(3) both give tribunals discretion within the maximum limits to award an amount covering such a period as the tribunal considers to be 'just and equitable in all the circumstances having regard to the seriousness of the employer's default . . .'

Susie Radin Ltd v *GMB* [2004] IRLR 400 Court of Appeal

The company designed and manufactured clothing. In 2000 it decided to close down its factory in Durham, making 108 employees redundant. There was no prior consultation with the GMB, the recognised trade union. The employment tribunal found that the company had a fixed intention to close the factory and that therefore the dismissals for redundancy were inevitable. In these circumstances, they found that the lack of consultation with the workers did not make the dismissals unfair. However, the tribunal awarded the maximum possible protective award because there had been a total failure to consult as required by TULRCA s 188. This was upheld by the EAT and the company appealed.

This was the first time that the principles for making a protective award had been considered at Court of Appeal level.

PETER GIBSON LJ: '. . . it seems to me tolerably plain that the purpose of the protective award is to ensure that consultation in accordance with the requirements of s.188 takes place by providing a sanction against failure to comply with the obligations imposed on the employer. The potential severity of that sanction can be seen from the facts of the present case where the award, we are told, will cost the company some £250,000 by way of remuneration for the employees made redundant.

Whilst that sanction results in money being paid to the employees affected in the form of remuneration paid to them, there is nothing in the statutory provisions to link the length of the protected period to any loss in fact suffered by all or any of the employees. Their dismissals may not take effect at the same date. Their individual circumstances, for example whether another job immediately became available, may well differ. The required focus is not on compensating the employees but on the default of the employer and its seriousness. It is that seriousness which governs what is just and equitable in all the circumstances. I find it impossible to see how compensation for loss could be implied into the statutory provisions, given that the award, if one is to be made, is across the board for all employees falling within a particular description, as distinct from an individual award to each employee.

In *Association of Patternmakers & Allied Craftsmen* v *Kirvin Ltd* (1978), Lord McDonald, giving the judgment of a Scottish EAT, adverted to the punitive nature of the protective award when he said:

> "A tribunal, however, is specifically enjoined to determine the [protected] period and so the amount of the award by paying regard to the seriousness of the employer's default. This introduces a punitive element into the jurisdiction of an employment tribunal and in contrast with, eg, the calculation of a compensatory award which is based upon what is just and equitable having regard to the loss sustained."

. . . I cannot accept Mr Jones's submission that the futility of consultation is not only relevant to the issue of unfair dismissal and to the denial of any compensation but is also relevant to making no protective award or only a nominal award . . . [F]or the purpose of a protective award, as distinct from unfair dismissal, the required focus is on the seriousness of the employer's default in complying with the mandatory obligation to consult.

. . .

I suggest that employment tribunals, in deciding in the exercise of their discretion whether to make a protective award and for what period, should have the following matters in mind:

(1) The purpose of the award is to provide a sanction for breach by the employer of the obligations in TULRCA s 188: it is not to compensate the employees for loss which they have suffered in consequence of the breach.

(2) The employment tribunal have a wide discretion to do what is just and equitable in all the circumstances, but the focus should be on the seriousness of the employer's default.

(3) The default may vary in seriousness from the technical to a complete failure to provide any of the required information and to consult.

(4) The deliberateness of the failure may be relevant, as may the availability to the employer of legal advice about his obligations under TULRCA s 188.

(5) How the employment tribunal assesses the length of the protected period is a matter for the employment tribunal, but a proper approach in a case where there has been no consultation is to start with the maximum period and reduce it only if there are mitigating circumstances justifying a reduction to an extent which the employment tribunal consider appropriate.

. . . On the facts of this case I readily acknowledge that another employment tribunal might have taken a less serious view of the default given the relatively generous notice period. However, I find it impossible to say that the decision to make a protective award of the maximum period was perverse, given the findings that no consultation at all took place, although the company had been advised by its solicitor of the need for consultation, that on one occasion when consultation might have taken place, the company was merely going through the motions of what it considered to be consultation – a far cry from meaningful consultation with a view to reaching an agreement – and that none of the information required to be supplied in writing was supplied.

It follows that I would dismiss this appeal.'

(Laws and Longmore LJJ agreed.)

Comment

(1) The company in this case had given the employees 12 weeks' notice when they did not have to – but this was held to be beside the point: the purpose of the provision is to ensure that consultation takes place.

(2) This case was on the interpretation of TULRCA, but it seems likely that a similar approach would be taken to the interpretation of the parallel provision in TUPE 2006.

REFERENCES AND FURTHER READING

C Grunfeld (1989), *The Law of Redundancy*, 3rd ed, Sweet & Maxwell

J McMullen (ed) (2000), *Redundancy: the Law and Practice*, Sweet & Maxwell

J McMullen (2006), 'An Analysis of the TUPE Regulations 2006' 35 ILJ 113

B Napier (1993), *CCT, Market Testing and Employment Rights*, Institute of Employment Rights

D Pollard (2005), 'Pensions and TUPE' 34 ILJ 127

M Sargeant (2006), 'TUPE – the final round' [2006] JBL 549

Visit **http://www.mylawchamber.co.uk/pitt**
to access live web updates and web links to extend
your knowledge of Employment Law.

10

FREEDOM OF ASSOCIATION

FREEDOM OF ASSOCIATION AND THE STATE

Freedom of association is regarded as an aspect of human rights, since it covers freedom to belong not only to bodies like trade unions, but also to political parties, religious groups and other kinds of organisations. Hence a right to associate is to be found in many treaties on human rights, as well as in the Conventions of the International Labour Organization which are directly concerned with employment standards.

Treaties are addressed to states. Under international law, a state which ratifies a treaty has an obligation to change its municipal law to accord with it. Treaties do not generally apply directly.

Universal Declaration of Human Rights 1948

ARTICLE 20

1 Everyone has the right to freedom of peaceful assembly and association.
2 No one may be compelled to belong to an association.

Comment

(1) The Universal Declaration of Human Rights has achieved general acceptance and can be taken to represent international law. As it is both brief and general, it was intended that the standards should be filled out by later treaties. The International Covenant on Economic, Social and Cultural Rights, Art 8, and the International Covenant on Civil and Political Rights, Art 22, represent this next stage.

European Convention on Human Rights 1950

ARTICLE 11

1 Everyone has the right to freedom of peaceful assembly and to freedom of association with others, including the right to form and to join trade unions for the protection of his interests.
2 No restrictions shall be placed on the exercise of these rights other than such as are prescribed by law and are necessary in a democratic society in the interests of national security or public safety, for the prevention of disorder or crime, for the protection of health or morals or for the protection of the rights and freedoms of others. This Article shall not prevent the imposition of lawful restrictions on the exercise of these rights by members of the armed forces, of the police or of the administration of the State.

483

Comment

(1) Convention rights are enforceable in the United Kingdom by virtue of the Human Rights Act 1998 (see above, p 4). It remains possible for cases to be referred to the European Court of Human Rights for a definitive ruling on whether there has been a breach of the Convention, as recently happened in *ASLEF* v *UK* (2007) (below, p 510).

ILO Convention No 87 (1948) Freedom of Association and Protection of the Right to Organise

PART I: FREEDOM OF ASSOCIATION

Article 1

Each Member of the International Labour Organisation for which this Convention is in force undertakes to give effect to the following provisions.

Article 2

Workers and employers, without distinction whatsoever, shall have the right to establish and, subject only to the rules of the organisation concerned, to join organisations of their own choosing without previous authorisation.

Article 3

1   Workers' and employers' organisations shall have the right to draw up their constitutions and rules, to elect their representatives in full freedom, to organise their administration and activities and to formulate their programmes.
2   The public authorities shall refrain from any interference which would restrict this right or impede the lawful exercise thereof.

Article 4

Workers' and employers' organisations shall not be liable to be dissolved or suspended by administrative authority . . .

Article 9

1   The extent to which the guarantees provided for in this Convention shall apply to the armed forces and the police shall be determined by national laws or regulations.
2   In accordance with the principle set forth in paragraph 8 of Article 19 of the Constitution of the International Labour Organisation the ratification of this Convention by any Member shall not be deemed to affect any existing law, award, custom or agreement in virtue of which members of the armed forces or the police enjoy any right guaranteed by this Convention . . .

PART II: PROTECTION OF THE RIGHT TO ORGANISE

Article 11

Each Member of the International Labour Organisation for which this Convention is in force undertakes to take all necessary and appropriate measures to ensure that workers and employers may exercise freely the right to organise . . .

PART IV: FINAL PROVISIONS

Article 16

1   A Member which has ratified this Convention may denounce it after the expiration of ten years from the date on which the Convention first comes into force, by an act communicated to the Director-General of the International Labour Office for registration. Such denunciation shall not take effect until one year after the date on which it is registered.
2   Each Member which has ratified this Convention and which does not, within the year following the expiration of the period of ten years mentioned in the preceding paragraph, exercise the right of denunciation provided for in this Article, will be bound for another period of ten years and, thereafter, may denounce this Convention at the expiration of each period of ten years under the terms provided for in this Article.

ILO Convention No 98 (1949) Application of the Principles of the Right to Organise and to Bargain Collectively

Article 1

1   Workers shall enjoy adequate protection against acts of anti-union discrimination in respect of their employment.
2   Such protection shall apply more particularly in respect of acts calculated to –
    (a)   make the employment of a worker subject to the condition that he shall not join a union or shall relinquish trade union membership;
    (b)   cause the dismissal of or otherwise prejudice a worker by reason of union membership or because of participation in union activities outside working hours or, with the consent of the employer, within working hours.

Article 2

1   Workers' and employers' organisations shall enjoy adequate protection against any acts of interference by each other or each other's agents or members in their establishment, functioning or administration.
2   In particular, acts which are designed to promote the establishment of workers' organisations under the domination of employers or employers' organisations, or to support workers' organisations by financial or other means, with the object of placing such organisations under the control of employers or employers' organisations, shall be deemed to constitute acts of interference within the meaning of this Article.

Comment

(1) The provisions for coming into force and the denunciation of this Convention are the same as for Convention No 87.

(2) Note that states can make exceptions for the police and the armed forces – a permission taken up by the United Kingdom. The police may not belong to a trade union (Police Act 1996 s 64) and members of the armed forces may be discriminated against on grounds of union membership. The scope of protection under both the ILO Conventions and the European Convention on Human Rights was famously at issue in a dispute concerning civil servants at GCHQ in the 1980s.

Council of Civil Service Unions v Minister for the Civil Service
[1985] ICR 14 House of Lords

Government Communication Headquarters (GCHQ) at Cheltenham was responsible for ensuring the security of official and military communications and for monitoring foreign signals for the intelligence services. Employees belonged to various civil service unions which were members of the Council of Civil Service Unions (CCSU). In 1984 the Secretary of State announced without warning or consultation that all employees at GCHQ would have to cease being members of national trade unions. This was because they had taken part in a number of one-day strikes at their unions' behest between 1979 and 1981 which, in the view of the government, endangered national security. The CCSU challenged the decision because of the lack of prior consultation.

LORD FRASER:

. . . *'National security*

The issue here is not whether the minister's instruction was proper or fair or justifiable on its merits. These matters are not for the courts to determine. The sole issue is whether the decision on which the instruction was based was reached by a process that was fair to the staff at GCHQ. As my noble and learned friend Lord Brightman said in *Chief Constable of the North Wales Police* v *Evans* (1982), "Judicial review is concerned, not with the decision, but with the decision-making process."

I have already explained my reasons for holding that, if no question of national security arose, the decision-making process in this case would have been unfair. The respondent's case is that she deliberately made the decision without prior consultation because prior consultation "would involve a real risk that it would occasion the very kind of disruption [at GCHQ] which was a threat to national security and which it was intended to avoid". I have quoted from paragraph 27(i) of the respondent's printed case. Mr Blom-Cooper [counsel for the union] conceded that a reasonable minister could reasonably have taken that view, but he argued strongly that the respondent had failed to show that that was in fact the reason for her decision. He supported his argument by saying, as I think was conceded by Mr Alexander [counsel for the Government], that the reason given in paragraph 27(i) had not been mentioned to Glidewell J and that it had only emerged before the Court of Appeal. He described it as an "afterthought" and invited the House to hold that it had not been shown to have been the true reason.

The question is one of evidence. The decision on whether the requirements of national security outweigh the duty of fairness in any particular case is for the Government and not for the courts; the Government alone has access to the necessary information, and in any event the judicial process is unsuitable for reaching decisions on national security. But if the decision is successfully challenged, on the ground that it has been reached by a process which is unfair, then the Government is under an obligation to produce evidence that the decision was in fact based on grounds of national security. Authority for both these points is found in *The Zamora* (1916). The former point is dealt with in the well known passage from the advice of the Judicial Committee delivered by Lord Parker of Waddington,

"Those who are responsible for the national security must be the sole judges of what the national security requires. It would be obviously undesirable that such matters should be made the subject of evidence in a court of law or otherwise discussed in public."

The second point, less often referred to, appears where this passage occurs: "In their Lordships' opinion the order appealed from was wrong not because, as contended by the appellants, there is by international law no right at all to requisition ships or goods in the custody of the court, but because the judge had before him *no satisfactory evidence* that such a right was exercisable." (Emphasis added.)

. . . The evidence in support of this part of the respondent's case came from Sir Robert Armstrong in his first affidavit, especially at paragraph 16. Mr Blom-Cooper rightly pointed out that the affidavit does not in terms directly support paragraph 27(i). But it does set out the respondent's view that to have entered into prior consultation would have served to bring out the vulnerability of areas of operation to those who had shown themselves ready to organise disruption. That must be read along with the earlier parts of the affidavit in which Sir Robert had dealt in some detail with the attitude of the trade unions which I have referred to earlier in this speech. The affidavit, read as a whole, does in my opinion undoubtedly constitute evidence that the Minister did indeed consider that prior consultation would have involved a risk of precipitating disruption at GCHQ. I am accordingly of opinion that the respondent has shown that her decision was one which not only could reasonably have been based, but was in fact based, on considerations of national security, which outweighed what would otherwise have been the reasonable expectation on the part of the appellants for prior consultation. In deciding that matter I must with respect differ from the decision of Glidewell J but, as I have mentioned, I do so on a point that was not argued to him.

Minor matters

The judge held that had the prior consultations taken place they would not have been so limited that he could confidently say that they would have been futile. It is not necessary for me to reach a concluded view on this matter, but as at present advised I am inclined to differ from the learned judge, especially because of the attitude of two of the trade union members of CCSU which declared that they were firmly against any no-strike agreement.

The Court of Appeal considered the proper construction of certain international labour conventions which they cite. I respectfully agree with Lord Lane CJ who said that "the correct meaning of the material articles of the Conventions is by no means clear", but I do not propose to consider the matter as the Conventions are not part of the law in this country . . .'

(The unions' appeal over the failure to consult was dismissed. Lords Scarman, Diplock, Roskill and Brightman delivered concurring speeches.)

Comment

(1) The ILO's Committee of Experts decided in 1984 that removing the right of these civil servants to belong to a trade union was a breach of ILO Convention 87. However, the Conservative government of the time ignored this and ultimately dismissed those who still refused to give up their membership in 1988. See Ewing (1994) and Brown and McColgan (1992). One of the first acts of the Labour government elected in 1997 was to restore the right of GCHQ staff to belong to trade unions and to reinstate those who had been dismissed.

(2) While the ILO found in favour of the GCHQ staff, they lost their claim that this was a breach of ECHR Art 11, the case being rejected at the first stage by the European

Commission for Human Rights because of the proviso in Art 11(2) (*CCSU* v *UK* (1987)).

(3) Clearly, where states accept their obligations to guarantee freedom of association, they must limit the powers of employers to victimise employees because of union membership – otherwise the freedom is meaningless. This is examined in the next section.

FREEDOM OF ASSOCIATION AND THE EMPLOYER

Employees have had some form of protection from dismissal on grounds of union membership or participation in union activities since the action for unfair dismissal was introduced in 1972. Protection from adverse treatment for these reasons during employment was added by the Employment Protection Act 1975, along with a range of other positive employment protection rights. The last piece of the jigsaw fell into place when the Employment Act 1990 introduced a right not to be discriminated against in recruitment on grounds of union membership. However, this apparently complete protection for workers' freedom of association vis-à-vis the employer has given rise to significant difficulties of interpretation and has been substantially altered over the years, as we will see.

Dismissal and detriment on grounds of union membership

Scope of the protection

Trade Union and Labour Relations (Consolidation) Act 1992

146 (1) A worker has the right not to be subjected to any detriment as an individual by any act, or any deliberate failure to act, by his employer if the act or failure takes place for the sole or main purpose of –

(a) preventing or deterring him from being or seeking to become a member of an independent trade union, or penalising him for doing so,

(b) preventing or deterring him from taking part in the activities of an independent trade union at an appropriate time, or penalising him for doing so,

(ba) preventing or deterring him from making use of trade union services at an appropriate time, or penalising him for doing so, or

(c) compelling him to be or become a member of any trade union or of a particular trade union or of one of a number of particular trade unions.

(2) In subsection (1) 'an appropriate time' means –

(a) a time outside the worker's working hours, or

(b) a time within his working hours at which, in accordance with arrangements agreed with or consent given by his employer, it is permissible for him to take part in the activities of a trade union or (as the case may be) make use of trade union services;

and for this purpose 'working hours', in relation to a worker, means any time when, in accordance with his contract of employment (or other contract personally to do work or perform services), he is required to be at work.

. . .

(5) A worker or former worker may present a complaint to an employment tribunal on the ground that he has been subjected to a detriment by his employer in contravention of this section.

Comment

(1) TULRCA s 152 is in similar terms and states that it is automatically unfair to dismiss an employee on the same grounds. Note that TULRCA s 146 applies to the wider group of 'workers' rather than just 'employees' (a distinction discussed above, p 139). Only employees can claim unfair dismissal, but if a worker's contract was terminated on union membership grounds, this would be a detriment, thus giving rise to a claim under TULRCA s 146. Selection for redundancy on these grounds is also automatically unfair, although note the limitation shown up in *O'Dea v ISC Chemicals Ltd* (1996). There is no qualifying period of employment for dismissal contrary to TULRCA s 152.

(2) Originally TULRCA s 146 gave protection against 'action short of dismissal' on union membership grounds. That this was inadequate was demonstrated by the House of Lords decision in the first instalment of what has come to be known as 'the *Wilson/Palmer* litigation' (*Associated Newspapers* v *Wilson* (1995) and *Associated British Ports* v *Palmer* (1995) – joined appeals in the House of Lords). Both of these cases arose from the desire of employers to move employees on to individualised 'personal contracts' and away from collectively agreed terms and conditions of employment.

(3) In *Associated Newspapers* v *Wilson* the company terminated the collective agreement with the recognised trade union in April 1989. Employees who were willing to sign individual contracts were given a pay rise of 4.5 per cent from October 1989. Those (including Wilson) who declined and remained on the collectively agreed terms were told that they could expect no pay increase until the next salary review in October 1990. In later years they received pay increases, but never as much as the employees on individual contracts.

(4) In *Associated British Ports* v *Palmer* the company did not terminate collective bargaining but offered larger pay increases and other benefits to employees who opted for individual contracts. Palmer was one of those who elected to remain on collectively bargained terms. In both cases the claimants argued that the omission to give them a pay rise constituted action short of dismissal for the purpose of deterring their trade union membership.

(5) There were three issues in these cases:

(a) whether 'action short of dismissal' covered an omission to act – such as an omission to grant a pay rise;

(b) whether the employer could be said to be acting to deter union membership when this was a likely result of its actions, but not its only or main purpose;

(c) whether protection for union membership included protection for things incidental to union membership, such as making use of union representation and being represented for purposes of collective bargaining.

(6) The first issue was only argued in the House of Lords, since the lower courts were bound by the Court of Appeal's decision in *National Coal Board* v *Ridgeway* (1987) to hold that 'action short of dismissal' included an omission to act. On this novel point the House of Lords, by a majority of 3–2, held that 'action short of dismissal' did not include an omission to act. The claimants' cases therefore failed on this point. The opinions expressed on the other two issues were strictly *obiter*, but four of the five Law Lords indicated that they would have decided that in these circumstances the employer did not have the purpose of deterring trade union membership, nor that representation for collective bargaining was a necessary incident of union membership.

(7) The point that 'action short of dismissal' did not include an omission to act was dealt with by the Employment Relations Act 1999, which amended TULRCA ss 146 and 152 so that they now refer to a worker being 'subjected to a detriment' on union membership grounds. The other two issues formed the basis of Wilson's and Palmer's further claims to the European Court of Human Rights that the law breached ECHR Art 11 on freedom of association.

Wilson v UK; *Palmer v UK*; *Doolan v UK* [2002] IRLR 568
European Court of Human Rights

The facts of the case are given above.

JUDGMENT OF THE COURT:

'. . . A *Arguments of the parties*

39   The Government relied on the Court's case-law and submitted that there is no right inherent in Article 11 to collective bargaining or for individual trade union members to receive identical benefits to those agreed between an employer and other employees who decline to be represented by the union. If the Government were required to oblige employers to offer identical benefits to all employees, regardless of union membership, there would be no scope for different unions to engage in collective bargaining to achieve better terms and conditions for their members.

   The Government submitted that, under domestic law at the relevant time, trade unions had the freedom to take action to protect their members' interests. The essence of a voluntary system of recognition and collective bargaining, such as applied in the United Kingdom, was that it remained open to each side to persuade the other that recognition should be afforded and that collective bargaining on agreed issues should take place. Where a particular trade union was not recognised by the employer, it was open to the union to take steps, including strike action, to persuade the employer to recognise it for the purposes of collective bargaining (this would fall within the definition of a "trade dispute" under TULRCA s 219).

40   The applicants submitted that the right to union membership "for the protection of his interests" under Article 11 necessarily involved the rights of every employee (1) to be represented by his or her union in negotiations with the employer, and (2) not to be discriminated against for choosing to avail him or herself of the right to be represented. In this connection, the applicants referred to the findings and recommendations of the Committee of Experts under the European Social Charter and of the ILO's Committee on Freedom of Association, that the right of union representation is inherent in the right of union membership (as provided for in Article 5 of the Charter and in the ILO Convention).

   However, the House of Lords' judgment made it plain that domestic law protected only the right of union membership per se, and not any of the incidents of membership, such as collective representation in contract negotiations. Unless it could be shown that an employer acted with the intention to prevent, deter or penalise membership (per se) of a union, there was nothing to prevent the employer discriminating against an employee who chose to take advantage of one of the incidents of membership, such as collective representation.

B *The Court's assessment*

1   General principles
41   The Court observes at the outset that although the essential object of Article 11 is to protect the individual against arbitrary interference by public authorities with the exercise of the

rights protected, there may in addition be positive obligations to secure the effective enjoyment of these rights. In the present case, the matters about which the applicants complain – principally, the employers' de-recognition of the unions for collective-bargaining purposes and offers of more favourable conditions of employment to employees agreeing not to be represented by the unions – did not involve direct intervention by the State. The responsibility of the United Kingdom would, however, be engaged if these matters resulted from a failure on its part to secure to the applicants under domestic law the rights set forth in Article 11 of the Convention (see *Gustafsson* v *Sweden* (1996)).

42   The Court recalls that Article 11(1) presents trade union freedom as one form or a special aspect of freedom of association (see *National Union of Belgian Police* v *Belgium* (1975) and *Swedish Engine Drivers' Union* v *Sweden* (1976)). The words "for the protection of his interests" in Article 11(1) are not redundant, and the Convention safeguards freedom to protect the occupational interests of trade union members by trade union action, the conduct and development of which the Contracting States must both permit and make possible. A trade union must thus be free to strive for the protection of its members' interests, and the individual members have a right, in order to protect their interests, that the trade union should be heard (see *National Union of Belgian Police* and *Swedish Engine Drivers' Union*). Article 11 does not, however, secure any particular treatment of trade unions or their members and leaves each State a free choice of the means to be used to secure the right to be heard (see *National Union of Belgian Police* and *Swedish Engine Drivers' Union*).

2 Application of these principles to the present case

43   The Court notes that, at the time of the events complained of by the applicants, United Kingdom law provided for a wholly voluntary system of collective bargaining, with no legal obligation on employers to recognise trade unions for the purposes of collective bargaining. There was, therefore, no remedy in law by which the applicants could prevent the employers in the present case from de-recognising the unions and refusing to renew the collective bargaining agreements.

44   However, the Court has consistently held that although collective bargaining may be one of the ways by which trade unions may be enabled to protect their members' interests, it is not indispensable for the effective enjoyment of trade union freedom. Compulsory collective bargaining would impose on employers an obligation to conduct negotiations with trade unions. The Court has not yet been prepared to hold that the freedom of a trade union to make its voice heard extends to imposing on an employer an obligation to recognise a trade union. The union and its members must however be free, in one way or another, to seek to persuade the employer to listen to what it has to say on behalf of its members. In view of the sensitive character of the social and political issues involved in achieving a proper balance between the competing interests and the wide degree of divergence between the domestic systems in this field, the Contracting States enjoy a wide margin of appreciation as to how trade union freedom may be secured (see *Swedish Engine Drivers' Union*; *Gustafsson*; and *Schettini and others* v *Italy* (2000)).

45   The Court observes that there were other measures available to the applicant unions by which they could further their members' interests. In particular, domestic law conferred protection on a trade union which called for or supported strike action "in contemplation or furtherance of a trade dispute". The grant of the right to strike, while it may be subject to regulation, represents one of the most important of the means by which the State may secure a trade union's freedom to protect its members' occupational interests (see *Schmidt and Dahlström* v *Sweden* (1976) and *Unison* v *UK* (2002)). Against this background, the Court does not consider that the absence, under United Kingdom law, of an obligation on employers to enter into collective bargaining gave rise, in itself, to a violation of Article 11 of the Convention.

46   The Court agrees with the Government that the essence of a voluntary system of collective bargaining is that it must be possible for a trade union which is not recognised by an employer to take steps including, if necessary, organising industrial action, with a view to persuading the employer to enter into collective bargaining with it on those issues which the union believes are important for its members' interests. Furthermore, it is of the essence of the right to join a trade union for the protection of their interests that employees should be free to instruct or permit the union to make representations to their employer or to take action in support of their interests on their behalf. If workers are prevented from so doing, their freedom to belong to a trade union, for the protection of their interests, becomes illusory. It is the role of the State to ensure that trade union members are not prevented or restrained from using their union to represent them in attempts to regulate their relations with their employers.

47   In the present case, it was open to the employers to seek to pre-empt any protest on the part of the unions or their members against the imposition of limits on voluntary collective bargaining, by offering those employees who acquiesced in the termination of collective bargaining substantial pay rises, which were not provided to those who refused to sign contracts accepting the end of union representation. The corollary of this was that United Kingdom law permitted employers to treat less favourably employees who were not prepared to renounce a freedom that was an essential feature of union membership. Such conduct constituted a disincentive or restraint on the use by employees of union membership to protect their interests. However, as the House of Lords judgment made clear, domestic law did not prohibit the employer from offering an inducement to employees who relinquished the right to union representation, even if the aim and outcome of the exercise was to bring an end to collective bargaining and thus substantially to reduce the authority of the union, as long as the employer did not act with the purpose of preventing or deterring the individual employee simply from being a member of a trade union.

48   Under United Kingdom law at the relevant time it was, therefore, possible for an employer effectively to undermine or frustrate a trade union's ability to strive for the protection of its members' interests. The Court notes that this aspect of domestic law has been the subject of criticism by the Social Charter's Committee of Independent Experts and the ILO's Committee on Freedom of Association. It considers that, by permitting employers to use financial incentives to induce employees to surrender important union rights, the respondent State has failed in its positive obligation to secure the enjoyment of the rights under Article 11 of the Convention. This failure amounted to a violation of Article 11, as regards both the applicant trade unions and the individual applicants . . .'

Comment

(1) As a result of this decision, the relevant sections of TULRCA were further amended by the Employment Relations Act 2004. One amendment we have noted already – the extension of protection beyond employees to workers.

(2) The first crucial element of this decision is the ruling that failing to require employers to recognise trade unions is not in itself a breach of the Art 11 protection for freedom of association. However, as we saw in Chapter 5, since the Employment Relations Act 1999, a system for compulsory recognition of unions enjoying majority support has been introduced, thus dealing with a criticism made by the ILO's Committee on Freedom of Association, referred to in para 40 of the European Court of Human Rights' judgment.

(3) Secondly, however, the European Court of Human Rights holds (in paras 47–48) that allowing the employer to offer inducements to employees to give up collective representation does amount to a breach of Art 11. The Court is also clear, in para 46,

that the right to union membership must entail use of union services for representation. Hence the further amendments by the Employment Relations Act 2004, introducing TULRCA ss 145A–F.

Trade Union and Labour Relations (Consolidation) Act 1992

145A (1) A worker has the right not to have an offer made to him by his employer for the sole or main purpose of inducing the worker –

(a) not to be or seek to become a member of an independent trade union,

(b) not to take part, at an appropriate time, in the activities of an independent trade union,

(c) not to make use, at an appropriate time, of trade union services, or

(d) to be or become a member of any trade union or of a particular trade union or of one of a number of particular trade unions.

(2) In subsection (1) 'an appropriate time' means –

(a) a time outside the worker's working hours, or

(b) a time within his working hours at which, in accordance with arrangements agreed with or consent given by his employer, it is permissible for him to take part in the activities of a trade union or (as the case may be) make use of trade union services.

(3) In subsection (2) 'working hours', in relation to a worker, means any time when, in accordance with his contract of employment (or other contract personally to do work or perform services), he is required to be at work.

(4) In subsections (1) and (2) –

(a) 'trade union services' means services made available to the worker by an independent trade union by virtue of his membership of the union, and

(b) references to a worker's 'making use' of trade union services include his consenting to the raising of a matter on his behalf by an independent trade union of which he is a member.

(5) A worker or former worker may present a complaint to an employment tribunal on the ground that his employer has made him an offer in contravention of this section.

145B (1) A worker who is a member of an independent trade union which is recognised, or seeking to be recognised, by his employer has the right not to have an offer made to him by his employer if –

(a) acceptance of the offer, together with other workers' acceptance of offers which the employer also makes to them, would have the prohibited result, and

(b) the employer's sole or main purpose in making the offers is to achieve that result.

(2) The prohibited result is that the workers' terms of employment, or any of those terms, will not (or will no longer) be determined by collective agreement negotiated by or on behalf of the union.

(3) It is immaterial for the purposes of subsection (1) whether the offers are made to the workers simultaneously.

(4) Having terms of employment determined by collective agreement shall not be regarded for the purposes of section 145A (or section 146 or 152) as making use of a trade union service.

(5) A worker or former worker may present a complaint to an employment tribunal on the ground that his employer has made him an offer in contravention of this section.

Comment

(1) Claims under TULRCA ss 145A and 145B must be made to a tribunal within the usual three-month time limit (TULRCA s 145C). The employer has the burden of

proving what its purpose was in offering the inducement (TULRCA s 145D). Factors to be taken into account by tribunals in deciding what the employer's purpose was are set out in TULRCA s 145D(4):

(a) that when the offers were made the employer had recently changed or sought to change, or did not wish to use, arrangements agreed with the union for collective bargaining,
(b) that when the offers were made the employer did not wish to enter into arrangements proposed by the union for collective bargaining, or
(c) that the offers were made only to particular workers, and were made with the sole or main purpose of rewarding those particular workers for their high level of performance or of retaining them because of their special value to the employer.

If either of the first two situations exists, it suggests that the employer's main purpose was illegitimate. If the last exists, it suggests that the main purpose was permissible.

(2) If the claim is upheld, the tribunal must make a declaration and award the worker £2,900 – but, importantly, this also clears the way for the worker to make a detriment claim under TULRCA s 146. Any agreement to vary terms and conditions which is in breach of these sections will be unenforceable by either party – and if the employer has paid the employee a sum of money or provided some other inducement to get her acceptance, that benefit will be irrecoverable (TULRCA s 145E).

(3) Note that TULRCA s 145A(1)(c) specifically protects a union member's right to make use of trade union services, as defined by TULRCA s 145A(4). This is also included in TULRCA s 146(1)(ba) as a ground on which a worker must not be subjected to detriment and dismissal. It is limited in that the member must be doing this 'at an appropriate time' – the meaning of this is considered below.

(4) So do these amendments bring English law into line with ECHR Art 11? Doubt must still remain because the protection given by TULRCA ss 145A and 145B only applies where the employer's *sole or main purpose* in offering the inducement is to get the worker to give up union membership rights or collective bargaining. Thus if the employer has some other main purpose (eg retention of key workers, to use the government's example in its Explanatory Notes to ERelA 2004) then the inducement is permissible even if the employer has an explicit subsidiary purpose of weakening collective bargaining or making union membership less attractive. To this extent it seems possible that the protection offered by TULRCA is still not sufficient to satisfy the requirements of ECHR Art 11.

(5) This pessimistic view of the statutory protection is reinforced by *Department of Transport* v *Gallacher* (1994), where the Court of Appeal drew a distinction between purpose and effect, holding that the employer could not be said to have the *purpose* of deterring union activities even though that was the inevitable *effect* of its decision that the claimant would not be promoted unless he gave up his full-time union post and gained relevant managerial experience.

'As an individual . . .'
The worker's right not to be victimised under TULRCA s 146 is limited in that the detriment must be aimed at him 'as an individual'. The meaning of this is considered in the next case.

F W Farnsworth Ltd v McCoid [1999] IRLR 626 Court of Appeal

The company withdrew recognition of the appellant as an accredited shop steward for his trade union. This did not affect his terms and conditions of employment. The issue was whether or not this was detrimental treatment of him 'as an individual' for the purposes of TULRCA s 146. The EAT held that it was and the employers appealed.

LORD WOOLF MR: 'The employers read the opening words of [TULRCA s 146(1)] that their effect is that there has to be action short of dismissal taken against the employee as an individual by his employer, the words "as an individual" being interpreted as meaning "in his capacity as an employee". The employers say it is not sufficient if the action, short of dismissal, which was taken was in a capacity which only related to his position as here, a shop steward. That is an approach which I consider is inconsistent with the general intent of s 146(1)(b). The purpose of s 146(1)(b) is to allow an employee, who has as an individual, in the claim, been subject to victimisation, to put his allegation or complaint before an employment tribunal. If Mr McCoid cannot do that, because he was only affected in his office as a shop steward, that would involve inserting into the legislation words which do not appear, namely, "as an individual in his capacity as an employee" or such similar words to "as an individual employee". The addition would enable a distinction to be drawn between actions short of dismissal, in the capacity as an employee, and actions short of dismissal in the capacity of, for example, a shop steward.

The argument which has been skilfully developed by Mr Bowers on behalf of the employers would have had no prospect of success in my judgment but for the decision of the Court of Appeal in the case of *Ridgway* v *National Coal Board* (1987). That was a decision of this court by a majority, the majority consisting of Nicholls and Bingham LJJ with May LJ dissenting . . .

Under the heading "As an individual" Nicholls LJ recited the submission of the NCB that:

"When action is taken in a case where the true context is collective as opposed to individual, the action is not against the employee 'as an individual' even though he is affected. That is this case: the claimants were caught in the crossfire of an engagement between the UDM and the NUM."

As to that submission, Nicholls LJ says:

"I cannot accept this. It seems reasonably clear that the phrase 'as an individual' was included in s 53 of the Employment Protection Act 1975 (which was the forerunner of s 23 of the Employment Protection (Consolidation) Act of 1978 [now TULRCA s 146]) to exclude from the ambit of the right conferred on employees by that section conduct of the kind found in *Crouch* v *Post Office* (1973). There the Post Office refused facilities for trade union activities on its premises to one particular union, and Mr Crouch, who was a local branch organiser of that particular union, made a complaint under s 5 of the Industrial Relations Act 1971. Under s 5(2), it was an unfair industrial practice for an employer to 'discriminate against a worker' by reason of his exercising any of his statutory rights. The section contained no words corresponding to the phrase 'as an individual'.

Nevertheless it was argued that any discrimination there was against the union and not Mr Crouch personally.

That argument was rejected. Lord Reid said:

"It was argued that here any discrimination is against the TSA and not against Mr Crouch personally. But discrimination against a man's trade union generally affects him personally. The prejudice to the man himself may be so small as to be negligible. But where it is substantial and a necessary consequence of the discrimination against the trade union and this must have been known to the employer the employer has in fact so acted as to worsen the man's position in comparison with that of a man in another union against which there has been no discrimination. That appears to me to be well within the mischief against which this provision is directed and to come within its terms."

Nicholls LJ continues:

"Against that background it seems to me that the expression 'as an individual' in what is now s 23 of the Act of 1978 was intended to preclude adverse action taken against a union being treated ipso facto, on the reasoning adopted in the *Crouch* case, as action taken against the employee. Adverse action taken against a union is not, by reason only of any consequential effect it may have on members or officers of the union, to be treated as an action against individual employees. To be within the section the action has to affect the employee otherwise than merely qua member or officer of a union."

One can understand why Mr Bowers sees that paragraph as assisting his case. However, in my judgment, that paragraph of Nicholls LJ's judgment has to be understood in the context of the facts which he was considering. In that case, as in the case of the earlier decision of *Crouch v Post Office*, the action which had been taken had been taken against the union as a whole, not against an individual who was a union official. Before the words "as an individual" were inserted into the relevant section, Mr Crouch was entitled to a remedy but not afterwards. However, in this case, unlike *Ridgway v National Coal Board*, there was no action against the union, as a union; the only action was against Mr McCoid; who happened to be a shop steward. That was action against a person who is an individual and meets the requirements of the subsection which we are considering . . .

Turning to the judgment of Bingham LJ, he deals with the question of "as an individual". He indicates that both sides were agreed that the inclusion of those words was a legislative response to the decision in the *Crouch* case. He then adds this statement:

"The purpose of including the words 'as an individual' in s 53(1) of the Act of 1975 and then in s 23(1) of the Act of 1978 was, as I infer, to make plain that the action (short of dismissal) of which an employee is entitled to complain must be taken by his employer against him as an individual and that he cannot complain of action which only affects him in his capacity as a member of an organisation or body which is the subject of the action. It is to exclude indirect or derivative complaints . . .'"

(Otton and Ward LJJ delivered concurring judgments. The employer's appeal was dismissed.)

Comment

(1) It will be seen from the discussion in Lord Woolf MR's judgment that some version of the protection against discrimination on grounds of union membership has existed since the Industrial Relations Act 1971. The words 'as an individual' were introduced to prevent individuals being able to make claims about essentially collective disputes, as indicated.

(2) At the time of this case TULRCA s 146 protected against 'action short of dismissal' rather than 'detriment' – but this has no bearing on the issue in the case.

Union activities

What sort of union activities are protected? The dividing line between union activities which are protected and other kinds of activity which are not protected is not necessarily clear-cut.

Bass Taverns Ltd v Burgess [1995] IRLR 595 Court of Appeal

Burgess was employed as the manager of a public house owned by the company and was also a shop steward of his union, the National Association of Licensed House Managers. He had the status of trainer manager, which meant that he received extra pay for giving presentations on the company's training courses for new managers. On the first day of these courses, the company always allowed the union to make a presentation on its role, which could be a forum for recruitment. On one occasion Burgess made the union presentation, in the course of which he made disparaging remarks about the company, suggesting that only the union would fight on behalf of managers injured by inebriated customers and that the company was more interested in profits than the safety of its employees. The management took a dim view of this and decided that he should no longer be a trainer manager. The demotion meant a loss of pay as well. Burgess resigned and claimed that he had been constructively dismissed for his participation in trade union activities.

PILL LJ: '. . . Miss Slade QC for the company bases her submission upon the wording of [TULRCA s 152(1)(b)] and a limitation upon the consent given. It was permissible for the employment tribunal to conclude that the permission to recruit granted to the respondent had been exceeded. As the tribunal of fact they were entitled to conclude that the contents of the respondent's speech were, in the circumstances, outside the permitted scope of the meeting and that the consent had been exceeded. The circumstances relied upon were the context of the meeting, the first day of an induction course for trainee managers. Reliance is also placed upon the respondent's admission that he had "gone over the top". It is not suggested that the contents of the speech were dishonest or actuated by malice or that if delivered on a different trade union occasion, would have been other than taking part in the activities of an independent trade union. No malice or ill-feeling was involved, the employment tribunal found.

The consent was subject, it is submitted, to an implied limitation that the occasion would not be used to criticise the company or to undermine the company in the eyes of the trainees. The employment tribunal were entitled to conclude that the contents of the speech, as the tribunal found them to be, were outside the scope of the consent and therefore outside the scope of [TULRCA s 152(1)]. Miss Slade concedes that a finding in the company's favour depends upon the presence of an implied limitation upon the ambit of the consent given to the respondent. There was no evidence of any express limitation. While they were not referred to [TULRCA s 152(2)], the employment tribunal were entitled to and did find such a limitation . . .

The argument in relation to a limitation upon the consent is now augmented by reference to [TULRCA s 152(2)(b)]. No reference to that paragraph appears in the employer's written response to the original claim or in the evidence or submissions before the employment tribunal. The company's case has hitherto been put simply on the basis that the conduct of the respondent in addressing the trainee managers as he did should not be regarded as taking part in the activities of a trade union. The company were not legally represented before the employment tribunal. Having regard to their findings of fact, it was not, in my judgment, a permissible option for the employment tribunal to find that the dismissal was other than for taking part in trade union activities. The respondent was permitted to use the meeting as a "forum for recruitment". I will consider the alleged limitation on the consent later.

On the face of it, a consent to recruit must include a consent to underline the services which the union can provide. That may reasonably involve a submission to prospective members that in some respects the union will provide a service which the company does not. On the assumption that I am prepared to make that the life of a manager of licensed premises has its dangers and licensees are from time to time injured by members of the public, a union existing to protect the interests of licensees is entitled to claim that if such a situation arises it is the union and not the company which will fight the licensee's cause. Indeed, to bring a claim on behalf of members arising out of personal injuries is an important function of many trade unions and the service can properly be emphasised at a recruiting meeting.

In the findings of the employment tribunal as to what the respondent said, I find nothing beyond the rhetoric and hyperbole which might be expected at a recruiting meeting for a trade union or, for that matter, some other organisation or cause. Neither dishonesty nor bad faith are suggested. While harmonious relations between a company and a union are highly desirable, a union recruiting meeting cannot realistically be limited to that object. A consent which at the same time prevents the recruiter from saying anything adverse about the employer is no real consent. Given that there was consent to use the meeting as a forum for recruitment, it cannot be regarded as an "abuse of privilege" to make remarks to employees which are critical of the company. An employment tribunal may be surprised at the situation which developed, but it was the employers who, at the start of their induction course, put the respondent in the position of being both trainer manager and recruiter. Having put him in that position, they cannot reasonably expect his activities in the latter role to be limited by the fact that he also was performing the role of trainer manager.

It appears to me that the employment tribunal did base their decision on an implied term of the kind now contended for, albeit not in the same way. The company's case is not, in my judgment, improved by the present reliance upon an implied term that the recruiter should say nothing to criticise or disparage the company or upon the presence of the word "consent" and the word "permissible" in [TULRCA s 152(2)(b)]. One has only to consider the likely reaction if the company had attempted to make the term expressed. It is difficult to envisage any trade union official accepting a limitation upon his activities at a recruiting meeting that he should say nothing critical about his employer. Indeed, it is difficult to envisage a sensible employer attempting to require such a term. It is wholly unrealistic, in my judgment, to believe that such a term can be implied in the present context. The respondent's admission that he had "gone over the top" does not, in my judgment, provide a basis for a finding that during his speech he was not taking part in trade union activities. That is an expression sometimes used collo-quially in situation when that moderation and balance normally shown in social intercourse is perceived to have been exceeded. In the circumstances of the present case, however, it was not an admission that could form the basis for a conclusion that in law the contents of the speech were outside the scope of trade union activities. The Employment Appeal Tribunal correctly concluded that the employment tribunal had fallen into error . . .'

(Balcombe LJ and Sir Ralph Gibson agreed with Pill LJ.)

Comment

(1) It was held, therefore, that Burgess had been unfairly dismissed for trade union activities.

(2) Note the suggestion in argument that the status of the activity depended to some extent on the time at which it was done. This is the next element to consider.

'At an appropriate time . . .'

Zucker v *Astrid Jewels Ltd* [1978] ICR 1088 Employment Appeal Tribunal

The employee appealed against an employment tribunal's finding that her trade union activities had not been undertaken at an appropriate time.

PHILLIPS J: '. . . According to paragraph 3 of the employment tribunal's decision the matters primarily relied on by the employee as being the times when, as she said, she was engaged in trade union activities at an appropriate time, and in respect of which she was dismissed, are summarised as follows: talking with her colleagues about the question of trade union membership during the tea break in the morning from 10 to 10.20, during the tea break in the afternoon, and also at times like the lunch break. In addition to that she said that on the occasion of two lunch breaks she had left the premises, which she was allowed to do, and attended the office of her trade union in connection with her trade union activities. Over and above that, she said that while working on her machine, in the course of conversation with others working near her, she spoke of trade union matters and encouraged recruitment, and so on. No doubt the employers' case was that she engaged in these activities at unseasonable hours and in an unsuitable and disruptive manner. We do not know anything about that because there are no findings of fact about it.

But what the employment tribunal did, having referred themselves to the new definition in [TULRCA s 152(2)], was to say that it divided "appropriate time" into two, either time outside working hours, or time inside working hours when there had been an agreement; that as to the times mentioned it was within working hours because "'working hours' . . . means any time when, in accordance with his contract of employment, the employee is required to be at work". In effect they took the view that any time in respect of which the employee was paid, and when she was on the premises, was a time when she was required to be at work. The only exception they make is for what they call the "lunch half hour break", in respect of which not only was she not working, but also was not paid.

Well, now, the decision is only a satisfactory decision if those conclusions are right in point of law, and the employment tribunal correctly directed themselves. In our judgment they misdirected themselves. The relevant authority on the first point is *Post Office v Crouch* (1974) a decision of the House of Lords on the somewhat similar provision in section 5 of the Industrial Relations Act 1971. In his speech there, Lord Reid makes it quite clear that an employee is not necessarily required to be at work, and therefore, within the terms of the definition, is not within working hours, merely because he is on the premises, or, indeed, merely because he is on the premises during a time in respect of which he is being paid. It is not necessary to read it all, but his opinion makes it quite clear that it is not sufficient merely to be on the premises. He says, of the employee,

"He arrives at his employer's premises some time before he starts work. He leaves some time after his day's work is done. And I should think that in almost all cases he is not expected to work non-stop. There are recognised breaks for meals, and perhaps other purposes, during which he does and is expected to remain on his employer's premises."

He then goes on to explain the expression "in accordance with his contract", and concludes that paragraph by saying:

". . . in my judgment, the Act entitles a worker who is a member of a trade union to take part in the activities of his union while he is on his employer's premises but is not actually working."

To anticipate our conclusion, we find it necessary to remit the matter to be re-heard by a differently constituted employment tribunal. We do not wish to circumscribe their freedom, because they will decide the matter on the evidence which they have heard. But they will obviously guide themselves by the authority of the House of Lords in *Post Office v Crouch*. By way of further guidance we can say that on the facts so far as they appear in this decision, there seems every reason to suppose that the circumstances of the morning tea break, at all events (the circumstances of the afternoon tea break are not so clearly stated) seem to be such that that tea break, like the lunch half hour break, was a recognised break for a meal; and ordinarily one would have thought, therefore (though the final decision must rest with the employment tribunal upon the facts as they emerge), that those breaks would be times during which the employees, albeit they were being paid, were not required to be at work and therefore were not doing whatever they did "during working hours". But we repeat, the final decision must be for the employment tribunal.

There is another point where we think the employment tribunal misdirected themselves. It may be the case that some of the employee's activities took place, as we have already indicated, while she was working, in the course of conversation with others also working. The employment tribunal will want to consider all the circumstances in relation to that. But we do not think that it is a right conclusion, from *Post Office* v *Crouch*, to say that activities of that kind *cannot* be activities undertaken in accordance with arrangements agreed with or consent given by the employer. It is a question for the proper conclusion to be drawn from the evidence as it turns out . . . For example, if it be the case that the employees while working are permitted to converse upon anything they feel like conversing upon with fellow employees working nearby, there seems to be no reason why they should not, amongst other things, converse upon trade union activities; and if they were to do so, and if such conversation were generally allowed, to the extent that it did not interfere with the proper completion of the work or otherwise cause disruption, there seems no reason why an employment tribunal, in such circumstances, could not come to the conclusion that although there was no express arrangement, or express consent, there was implied consent or implied arrangements . . .'

Marley Tile Co v Shaw [1980] ICR 72 Court of Appeal

The employee was appointed as shop steward for the maintenance section at the factory despite having worked for the company for only two months. When he raised an issue over wage differentials with management, he was told that the company did not recognise him as a shop steward because he had not been there long enough. Annoyed by this, the employee responded that he was going at once to telephone his district official and call a meeting with the other five maintenance workers. The factory manager made no response to this. The employee made his telephone call and held his meeting, which resulted in an hour's stoppage of work. He was subsequently dismissed, and claimed it was because of his trade union activities. The employers argued that the activities were not protected because they had taken place during working hours without the employers' consent.

GOFF LJ: '. . . The matter then rests on the question of consent. It is not necessary to decide whether arrangements can only be express, because this was not something done pursuant to any general arrangement. The question turns on the word "consent". In my judgment in a proper case, consent may be implied but this is not such a case. I accept the view of the majority of the appeal tribunal, ". . . that the consent of the employers cannot be deduced from their silence", I add of Mr Wright, "when Mr Shaw announced that he was going to call a meeting of his members and telephone Mr Garwell". I accept the minority view of Mr Clement-Jones,

". . . unless there is a general agreement or arrangement which covers it, the shop steward unaccredited by the management at the relevant time cannot be taken to have implied permission to call such a meeting in working hours; particularly one which ends in an hour's stoppage of the shop floor workers, even if that was not intended by the shop steward. Furthermore, Mr Clement-Jones does not agree that an arrangement for the conduct of shop steward's duties can be reasonably assumed to exist either by extension from other factories in the Marley Group, or by having regard to custom and practice at their Dewsbury plant, inasmuch as it was found by the employment tribunal that neither had the AUEW hitherto nominated a shop steward nor had the TGWU done so for their membership on production in the factory."

Mr Rose [counsel for the employee] submitted that the calling out of the maintenance men to discuss the unexpected situation which had arisen was incidental to the original approach to the management to discuss the fitters' differential, which the company had agreed should be in working time, by giving the employee an appointment for that purpose and should, therefore, be treated as covered by that consent. I do not think that is right, because it was not necessary to do this in working time and because it involved a much more significant interference with the work of the factory in which all five men were involved and not the respondent only.

Alternatively, he relied on the speech of Lord Reid in *Post Office* v *Crouch* (1974) where, dealing with the precisely similar wording of s.5 of the Industrial Relations Act, 1971, his Lordship said:

"But again this must be applied reasonably. It is one thing to ask an employer to incur expense or submit to substantial inconvenience. That the worker may not do. But it is a different matter to use facilities which are normally available to the employers' workers or to ask him to submit to some trifling inconvenience. Men carrying on activities of their union on their employers' premises must do so in a manner which does not cause substantial inconvenience either to their employer or to fellow workers who are not members of their trade union – and employers must tolerate minor infringements of their strict legal rights which do them no real harm. In my view the employment tribunals are well fitted to deal with disputes about matters of that kind."

He argued that this applied to the present case and the employee's conduct was no more than that little inconvenience which employers must accept. In my judgment, however, it was much more than that, and I think the employment tribunal thought so too, when they said:

"Such a meeting must mean that the men are not as readily available for work as they would otherwise be, even if in this particular case these men were maintenance workers and would still be on call when in the canteen."

In my view there is no ground for inferring an implied consent to all the maintenance men being suddenly called from their place of work to a meeting, particularly one such as in the present case where the problem which had arisen did not call for a desperately urgent solution. In my judgment, therefore, even if the conduct for which the respondent was dismissed was taking part in trade union activities, which I have assumed, it was not at an appropriate time because it was carried out in working hours and was not in accordance with the arrangements agreed with or consent given by the company. For these reasons, I would allow this appeal, discharge the orders of the employment tribunal and the appeal tribunal and dismiss the employee's application.'

(Eveleigh and Stephenson LJJ agreed with Goff LJ.)

Comment

(1) These cases give guidance on what constitute protected union activities as well as the definition of 'appropriate time'. However, it is now necessary to note some important limitations on the protection for trade union activities.

Carrington v *Therm-A-Stor Ltd* [1983] ICR 208 Court of Appeal

The TGWU recruited some 60 of the 70 employees of the company and then approached the managing director, Mr Morris, seeking recognition. His reaction was to instruct his chargehands to select 20 employees – any 20 – for dismissal. As they had not been employed long enough to claim unfair dismissal on the usual grounds, the employees claimed that they had been dismissed for their union activities.

SIR JOHN DONALDSON MR: '. . . As I see it, the first question for consideration is whether the fact that the chargehands undertook the selection for dismissal means that the charge-hands' reason – probably last in, first out – was the reason for the men's dismissal. Mr Tabachnik [counsel for the employees] submits that so to conclude is to confuse the reason for dismissal with the basis for selection. As he rightly points out they are two quite different things and are so treated in [TULRCA s 153] in relation to redundancy. Where redundancy is the reason for the dismissal, the dismissal is not necessarily unfair. However the method of selection for dismissal can make the dismissal unfair. For my part I think that this is right and that the intervention of the chargehands can be disregarded as being concerned solely with selection and not with the reason for dismissal.

So far so good, but the four employees still have obstacles in their way. The employment tribunal did not find that the employers or Mr Morris decided to dismiss the group of 20 men because any or all of them had joined the union or proposed to do so or had taken part in union activities or proposed to do so. He decided to dismiss them by way of reaction to the union's letter seeking recognition. The reason for the dismissals was the union's plea for recognition . . .

Tempted as I am to provide the four employees with a remedy for what was an indefensible reaction to a simple request for union recognition, which could have been granted or politely refused, I cannot construe [TULRCA s 152] as being intended to deal with such a situation. The section is not concerned with an employer's reactions to a trade union's activities, but with his reactions to an individual employee's activities in a trade union context.

With regret, I would allow the appeal and restore the decision of the employment tribunal.'

(May and Watkins LJJ agreed.)

Comment

(1) The gap in protection revealed in *Carrington* v *Therm-A-Stor Ltd* arises from the fact that the remedy is provided for individuals yet the activities are likely to be collective in nature.

(2) See also *Chant* v *Aquaboats Ltd* (1978), where the dismissed employee had insti-gated a round-robin letter among union members about safety matters. As he was not a union official and the letter was not from the union to the employer, it was held that this was not a union activity and he was outside the protection of TULRCA s 152. In this situation today an employee could try to claim that his dismissal was contrary to ERA s 100 (dismissal on health and safety grounds), although it is not clear that the facts of this case would attract the protection of that section.

(3) What if action is taken against the employee, not because of union activities in this employment, but because of union activities in the past? This was the issue in the next case.

Fitzpatrick v *British Railways Board* [1992] ICR 221 Court of Appeal

The claimant was dismissed by BRB after working for them for only nine months, after a man-ager saw a report in the *Evening Standard* about union troubles at Ford Motors and British Telecom, which identified the claimant as a union activist having links with ultra-left Trotskyite groups, including Socialist Action. While she had disclosed her previous employment at British Telecom, she had deliberately not mentioned her brief employment at Ford on her application form for BRB, and she was ostensibly dismissed for this deceit. The employment tribunal found that the real reason for her dismissal was her previous union activities, which caused BRB to view her as a potential trouble-maker. However, the tribunal thought that this was not protected by TULRCA s 152.

WOOLF LJ: '. . . In the course of their decision the employment tribunal subjected the decision in *City of Birmingham District Council* v *Beyer* (1977) to careful scrutiny. It was the majority of the employment tribunal's understanding of the effect of that decision which caused them to come to the conclusion that the appellant did not fall within [TULRCA s 152(1)(b)]. The minority, the third member of the employment tribunal, came to the conclusion that the appellant fell within the language of the relevant part of that subsection.

Superficially the facts in the *Beyer* case are very similar to those on this appeal. Mr Beyer, who was the respondent before the Employment Appeal Tribunal, was a noted trade union activist. He had applied on two different occasions to the district council in order to obtain employment. On the first occasion he had used a false name and a bogus reference. When this was discovered he was summarily dismissed for gross misconduct. On the second occasion he did not disguise his identity but he was able to obtain employment on a site where he was unknown. When within a couple of hours the officials of the corporation discovered the true facts he was again dismissed on the grounds that he had grossly deceived the corporation when he made his previous application.

The employment tribunal held that "Mr Beyer had been dismissed for the inadmissible reason of his having taken part in trade union activities on the basis that he had to resort to deceit because he knew that his trade union activities in the past would bar him from employment and that therefore his act of deceit was a trade union activity". I draw particular attention to the basis of the employment tribunal's decision that the act of deceit by Mr Beyer was a trade union activity. On any showing, in my judgment, an act of deceit, of the sort that was being considered by the employment tribunal in the *Beyer* case, could not be considered to be a trade union activity.

In the Employment Appeal Tribunal, Mr Justice Kilner Brown started his judgment by reciting the facts. He then went on to say that:

". . . with some justification Mr Beyer feels deeply aggrieved, although he does not even now seem to appreciate that he is largely the author of his own misfortune. Anyway he has convinced himself that the deception which he practised was justifiable. He feels that he is blacklisted on account of his trade union activities, he is being victimised and unfair discrimination is exercised against him. This may well be true, but with the state of the law as it is at present there is nothing that he can lawfully and properly do about it."

Mr Justice Kilner Brown having referred to the relevant statutory provisions added:

"We find it surprising that the tribunal could have erred and misdirected themselves to the extent which they did. It ought to be obvious that the situation envisaged by the paragraph in question is some trade union activity [and I would add 'or proposed trade union activity'] after employment has commenced. It could not conceivably refer to activities outside and before the employment began. The matter if not previously clear is put beyond doubt by the definition of 'appropriate time' now introduced by [TULRCA s 152(2)]. We assume that the employment tribunal appreciated this and that is why they indulged in what appears to us to be defective reasoning."

Subject to a very minor caveat which I would make to what was said by Mr Justice Kilner Brown in relation to proposed activities, I find that paragraph of his judgment perfectly acceptable and as making clear that the activities referred to in [TULRCA s 152(1)(b)] are activities in the employment of the employee from which he or she alleges that he or she has been unfairly dismissed. It is not referring to a past employment from which he or she may have previously been dismissed. If there was any doubt as to that interpretation so far as [TULRCA s 152(1)] is concerned, in my judgment subsection (2) would remove that doubt.

I do not, however, regard the decision of the Employment Appeal Tribunal as meaning that what has happened in previous employment can have no relevance to whether or not a person has been unfairly dismissed, in accordance with [TULRCA s 152(1)] from a subsequent employment. What happened in a previous employment may form the reason for the dismissal in subsequent employment and therefore can be highly relevant to the question which a tribunal has to answer under [s 152(1)]. The effect of the *Beyer* case on [s 152] is to make clear that if an employee obtained an employment by deceit and the employer dismisses that employee for the deceit, that is not an employment which is terminated within the language of [s 152(1)(b)], albeit that the deceit was about previous trade union activities.

In this case British Rail purported to dismiss the appellant on the basis of her deceit in concealing her previous trade union activities. If the employment tribunal had accepted that it was her deceit which caused them to dismiss her, or if that was the primary reason for her dismissal, then the situation is that she would not have been able to bring herself within the language of [TULRCA s 152(1)(b)]. However, as already indicated, all three members of the employment tribunal accepted that it was not the deceit which was the operative cause for her dismissal.

What the majority concluded was, and I read here from paragraph 27 of the decision:

"It was the [appellant's] previous trade union (and possibly her political) activities, which gave her a reputation for being a disruptive force; and that was the prime reason for her dismissal."

That paragraph, in my judgment, discloses a failure on the part of the employment tribunal to answer the critical question. The fact that the appellant had a reputation with regard to trade union activities was, as Miss Booth in her argument made clear, only relevant to British Rail in so far as it would have an effect on what she did while she was employed by them. Miss Booth submits, clearly with justification, that British Rail did not suggest and would not in fact seek to dismiss the appellant merely in order to punish her for her previous trade union activities. Miss Booth submits that what the employment tribunal failed to do was to identify why it was that because of her previous trade union, and possibly political, activities British Rail decided to dismiss the appellant. If the tribunal had asked the question the answer would have been obvious. It would be that they would fear a repetition of the same conduct while employed by them.

The reason that the majority of the employment tribunal did not address the critical question is probably because of their understanding of the *Beyer* decision. They say, having examined that decision, that so far as proposed activities are concerned it must, and I quote: "involve some cogent and identifiable act and not some possible trouble in the future". In other words the employment tribunal are saying that in order to comply with the provisions of [TULRCA s 152(1)(b)] there must have been some activity on the part of the employee to which they took exception, which was not a mere possibility but something which was sufficiently precise to be identifiable in her present employment.

In my judgment, to adopt this approach is to read into the language of [s 152(1)(b)] a restriction which Parliament has not identified. To limit the language, in the way which the employment tribunal did, would prevent the actual reason for the dismissal in a case such as this from being considered by the employment tribunal. As long as the reason which motivated the employer falls within the words "activities that the employee . . . proposed to take part in", there is no reason to limit the language. The purpose of the subsection, in so far as (b) is concerned, is to protect those who engage in trade union activities and I can see no reason why that should not apply irrespective of whether the precise activities can be identified.

If an employer, having learnt of an employee's previous trade union activities, decides that he wishes to dismiss that employee, that is likely to be a situation where almost inevitably the employer is dismissing the employee because he feels that the employee will indulge in industrial activities of a trade union nature in his current employment. There is no reason for a rational and reasonable employer to object to the previous activities of an employee except in so far as they will impinge upon the employee's current employment . . .'

(Leggatt and Dillon LJJ agreed with Woolf LJ.)

Comment

(1) It was held, therefore, that the employee had been unfairly dismissed for proposing to take part in trade union activities.

(2) The difference between *Fitzpatrick* and *Beyer* is that in the former case, the tribunal found as a fact that the employee's deceit was not the true reason for the dismissal, whereas in the latter it was.

(3) At the time of *City of Birmingham* v *Beyer* (1977) there was nothing to prevent discrimination on grounds of union membership at the point of entry to employment. Some protection was introduced by the Employment Act 1990 and this is considered in the next section.

(4) Two further points to note before we leave detriment and dismissal on grounds of union membership or activities. First, if a claim for detriment is upheld, the tribunal must make a declaration and may award such compensation as is just and equitable, having regard to the loss suffered by the employee and the nature of the infringement of his or her right (TULRCA s 149). In *Cleveland Ambulance NHS Trust* v *Blane* (1997) the EAT held that this could include a sum for injury to feelings. If the tribunal finds that the employee has been unfairly dismissed for trade union membership or activities, a special regime of compensation applies, set out in TULRCA ss 155–156. In particular, the basic award cannot be less than £4,400.

(5) Secondly, it is worth noting that in *Doherty* v *British Midland Airways* (2006), the EAT held that there was no implied term in the contract of employment that employees should be free to engage in union membership and activities, coextensive with the statutory protection. This meant that the employee could not claim that she had been constructively dismissed when she resigned on the grounds that her employer was infringing her right to participate in union activities.

Refusal of employment on grounds of trade union membership

Protection for detriment and dismissal on grounds of trade union membership has existed since the 1970s. However, protection from discrimination in recruitment on grounds of union membership was introduced only in 1990. It may seem surprising at first sight that such protection should have been enacted by a Conservative government. The reason was that the Conservative government wanted to ban all manifestations of the closed shop – workplaces where trade union membership is a requirement of employment (discussed in the next section). To give a semblance of evenhandedness in their treatment of trade union members, rights given not to belong to a trade union were expressed in the same way as rights to belong and participate. Thus, if workers opposed to union membership were to have a right not to be discriminated against for that reason in getting a job, it was necessary to give a similar right to union members – and that is what the Employment Act 1990 established.

Trade Union and Labour Relations (Consolidation) Act 1992

137 (1) It is unlawful to refuse a person employment –
    (a) because he is, or is not, a member of a trade union, or
    (b) because he is unwilling to accept a requirement –
        (i) to take steps to become or cease to be, or to remain or not to become, a member of a trade union, or
        (ii) to make payments or suffer deductions in the event of his not being a member of a trade union.
  (2) A person who is thus unlawfully refused employment has a right of complaint to an employment tribunal . . .

Comment

(1) The protection enacted in 1990 and now found in TULRCA s 137 is not as extensive as the corresponding protection during employment. The major difference between TULRCA s 137 and ss 146 and 152 is that s 137 does not cover trade union activities. It is therefore critical to know how far the concept of membership can be stretched. We have seen that this problem was resolved in relation to detriment and dismissal through the introduction of TULRCA ss 145A–F and amendments to ss 146 and 152. However, there has been no parallel amendment of the point of entry protection.

(2) So would someone like Beyer have a remedy under TULRCA s 137? In the first reported case on TULRCA s 137, *Harrison* v *Kent CC* (1995), the claimant had been rejected because he was a union activist. The situation was much like *Fitzpatrick* v *BRB* or *City of Birmingham* v *Beyer*, save that he had not actually got the job. The EAT, relying on *Discount Tobacco* v *Armitage* (1990), held that the concept of union membership could embrace this situation also. The correctness of *Harrison* v *Kent CC* was put in doubt by the later decision of the House of Lords in *Associated Newspapers* v *Wilson* (1995), discussed above. However, in the light of the European Court of Human Rights decision in *Wilson* v *UK* (2002), it would seem that the wider reading of TULRCA s 137 accords better with ECHR Art 11.

(3) Another difference between s 137 and ss 146 and 152 is that protection against dismissal and detriment on union membership grounds applies only to members of independent trade unions, while s 137 applies to any trade union. This is unlikely to be significant in practice. The status of independent trade union is explained below (p 529).

(4) The Employment Relations Act 1999 s 3 gave power to the Secretary of State to make regulations to prevent the practice of blacklisting evident in cases like *Beyer*, and draft regulations were drawn up in 2003. However, in its 2003 consultation over the operation of the Employment Relations Act 1999, the government noted that: 'No respondent reported any evidence or knowledge of blacklisting taking place in recent years.' It therefore announced its intention to keep the regulations in reserve, to be legislated only if a change in circumstances made it necessary.

Contracts between employers

Trade Union and Labour Relations (Consolidation) Act 1992

144   A term or condition of a contract for the supply of goods or services is void in so far as it purports to require that the whole, or some part, of the work done for the purposes of the contract is done only by persons who are, or are not, members of trade unions or of a particular trade union.

Comment

(1) The main reason for introducing this provision (in the Employment Act 1982) was to deter contractual requirements that suppliers should only use unionised labour forces. It will be referred to again in the context of the closed shop.

FREEDOM OF ASSOCIATION AND TRADE UNIONS

In this context, the question is whether an individual should be able to rely on freedom of association as giving her a right to belong to an association even if the association does not want to admit her. Refer back to ILO Convention No 87 Arts 2 and 3, extracted above.

Faramus v *Film Artistes' Association* [1964] AC 925 House of Lords

Rule 4(2) of the union's rules provided that no one who had been convicted of an offence (other than a motoring offence not punishable by imprisonment) was eligible for membership. Faramus concealed his two convictions when he applied to join the union, and was treated as a member for eight years, even serving on the executive committee. When his convictions came to light, he was excluded.

LORD EVERSHED: 'My Lords, like the learned judge who tried this case at first instance and like all the judges in the Court of Appeal I find it indeed difficult not to be most sympathetic to the appellant in this case. True it is that in the year 1938, when aged seventeen years, he was convicted by a court of law in St Helier, where he was born, of the criminal offence of taking and driving away the motor cars of others without their consent; and for that offence he was sentenced to three months' imprisonment with hard labour. It is true also that two years later, during the period of the German occupation of Jersey, he was convicted by the local court of obtaining certain moneys by falsely stating that his wife was unemployed: and for this offence he was imprisoned for six months with hard labour. It appears that about the same time he was imprisoned for a further month for being in possession of propaganda literature. Indeed, for these last two offences he paid a penalty far more severe than the terms of imprisonment imposed on him, for he was deported to Germany and there suffered the appalling horrors of being placed in the concentration camp with the ill-omened name of Buchenwald, and other similar places, and was so adversely affected by this treatment that his weight was reduced to less than half its proper amount. Since that date, however, and more particularly since he came to this country and sought in the year 1950 to join the respondent union, his conduct, so far as is known, has been quite exemplary. Certainly there is no suggestion that during this latter period he has ever committed any criminal offence or ever been guilty of dishonest conduct. Yet if the respondent union's argument is right the appellant has not now, and never had, the necessary qualification for election to the union, so that his election was wholly void . . .'

LORD PEARCE: '... Since the respondent union have a monopoly, exclusion from membership prevents a man from earning his living in this particular profession. An absolute rule that so prevents any person who may have suffered a trivial conviction many years before is in restraint of trade and unreasonable. It is therefore void unless it is saved by s 3 of the Trade Union Act, 1871, which provides that: "The purposes of any trade union shall not, by reason merely that they are in restraint of trade, be unlawful so as to render void . . . any agreement or trust."

It is argued that this rule is not a "purpose of the union" and that therefore section 3 does not touch it. But the rule clearly helps to achieve one at least of the objects of the association. It would be detrimental to the position and status of film artistes if they had among their numbers persons convicted of serious or frequent crimes of fraud. Also it might create trouble between member and managers or between member and member if such dishonest persons could roam the changing rooms as of right. Rule 4 (2) in a more precise form is at least desirable for the objects of the association. Moreover, the evidence shows that one of the purposes of the union in support of their expressed objects is to cut down the number of persons engaged in this particular walk of life. For, if all who wished were admitted, there would not be an adequate living for any. This rule is partly directed to that purpose and it is no more unfair to keep out one man because he has been convicted albeit trivially and so to put another in his place, than to keep persons out simply because there is no room for them. Merely because a desirable rule is too far-reaching, it does not cease, in my opinion, to be one of the purposes of the union. The question here is, would the agreement (that is to say, the rules) or any part of it (or them) be void merely because the purpose of the union is in restraint of trade? If so, it is protected by s 3. In my opinion r 4 (2) would be void merely for that reason and for no other, and it is therefore protected . . .'

(Lords Reid, Hodson and Devlin concurred.)

Comment

(1) The modern version of the Trade Union Act 1871 s 3, which prevents trade union rules being held to be in restraint of trade, is TULRCA s 11.

(2) There are few cases about the legality of refusal of admission to trade unions at common law precisely because there are no obvious grounds on which a disappointed applicant can claim. Faramus thought he was claiming for wrongful expulsion, but it was held that he had never been validly admitted in the first place.

(3) Lord Denning led a campaign to give workers a right to appeal against exclusion from trade union membership where there was a closed shop in operation, based on an alleged right to work (see p 175 above; also *Nagle* v *Feilden* (1966) and *Edwards* v *SOGAT* (1981)). It was in the closed shop situation, where refusal of membership restricted job opportunities, that the issue was seen as really important, and in 1980 legislation was introduced to deal with the situation.

(4) The Employment Act 1980 provided that in closed shop situations, an employee should not be unreasonably excluded or expelled from a trade union. Compliance with the union's own rules was not considered to be conclusive proof of reasonableness.

(5) However, once the closed shop ceased to be enforceable the Conservative government turned its attention instead to the Bridlington Principles. The Bridlington Principles were adopted by the TUC at its 1939 Conference in Bridlington to deal with possible inter-union conflicts which could arise if more than one union was seeking to recruit the same group of workers.

(6) The Bridlington Principles provided that unions should not accept into membership someone who had previously belonged to another union without checking first that the former union did not object. They also stipulated that where one union already had a substantial presence in a business, another union should not try to muscle in and 'poach' the workers. Arguments between unions were referred to the TUC's Internal Disputes Committee.

(7) The Bridlington Principles could be regarded as limiting workers' choice as to which union they belonged to. This was how the Conservative government chose to present it, and in 1993 TURERA amended TULRCA in such a way as radically to transform the right of a union to choose who to admit.

Trade Union and Labour Relations (Consolidation) Act 1992

174 (1)   An individual shall not be excluded or expelled from a trade union unless the exclusion or expulsion is permitted by this section.

(2)   The exclusion or expulsion of an individual from a trade union is permitted by this section if (and only if) –

(a)   he does not satisfy, or no longer satisfies, an enforceable membership requirement contained in the rules of the union,

(b)   he does not qualify, or no longer qualifies, for membership of the union by reason of the union operating only in a particular part or particular parts of Great Britain,

(c)   in the case of a union whose purpose is the regulation of relations between its members and one particular employer or a number of particular employers who are associated, he is not, or is no longer, employed by that employer or one of those employers, or

(d)   the exclusion or expulsion is entirely attributable to conduct of his (other than excluded conduct) and the conduct to which it is wholly or mainly attributable is not protected conduct.

(3)   A requirement in relation to membership of a union is 'enforceable' for the purposes of subsection (2)(a) if it restricts membership solely by reference to one or more of the following criteria –

(a)   employment in a specified trade, industry or profession,

(b)   occupational description (including grade, level or category of appointment), and

(c)   possession of specified trade, industrial or professional qualifications or work experience.

(4)   For the purposes of subsection (2)(d) 'excluded conduct', in relation to an individual, means –

(a)   conduct which consists in his being or ceasing to be, or having been or ceased to be, a member of another trade union,

(b)   conduct which consists in his being or ceasing to be, or having been or ceased to be, employed by a particular employer or at a particular place, or

(c)   conduct to which section 65 (conduct for which an individual may not be disciplined by a union) applies or would apply if the references in that section to the trade union which is relevant for the purposes of that section were references to any trade union.

(4A)   For the purposes of subsection (2)(d) 'protected conduct' is conduct which consists in the individual's being or ceasing to be, or having been or ceased to be, a member of a political party.

509

(4B)   Conduct which consists of activities undertaken by an individual as a member of a political party is not conduct falling within subsection (4A).

(5)   An individual who claims that he has been excluded or expelled from a trade union in contravention of this section may present a complaint to an employment tribunal.

Comment

(1) Instead of stating certain reasons for which someone may not be excluded or expelled from a trade union, this section now starts from the other end and states that it is *only* if one of these reasons applies that a union may exclude someone who wishes to join or expel an existing member. The effect is virtually to remove a trade union's right to define its own identity through its membership rules.

(2) This section applies to expulsion from a trade union as well as exclusion – refusal to admit. There is therefore a considerable overlap with TULRCA s 65, dealing with unjustifiable discipline, which is explicitly referred to in s 174(4)(c). This aspect is considered in Chapter 11, below.

(3) The limitation on enforceable membership requirements in s 174(3) and the explicit statement in s 174(4) that membership of another union is not an acceptable ground for exclusion rendered the Bridlington Principles in their old form unenforceable. The latest version of the Principles, revised following the introduction of the statutory recognition procedure in 2000, still requires unions not to poach the members of other unions and not to compete where another union already has a substantial presence, but does not require them to exclude people who were until recently members of other unions.

(4) There is just one respect in which the present version of TULRCA s 174 is narrower than the previous formulation: there is no reference to reasonableness. Thus if a union refuses admission to someone in pursuance of an enforceable membership requirement, she or he would have no right to complain even if the union's decision was wholly unreasonable.

(5) Should trade unions be regulated so extensively as to who they admit? The ILO Committee of Experts on the Application of Conventions and Recommendations has expressed concern about the compatibility of TULRCA ss 65 and 174 with ILO Convention No 87 on a number of occasions. In the following case, the issue was referred to the European Court of Human Rights to consider compatibility with Art 11 of the ECHR.

ASLEF v United Kingdom [2007] IRLR 361 European Court of Human Rights

Lee, a member of the British National Party (formerly the National Front), joined ASLEF in February 2002. He stood as a BNP candidate in local elections and was involved in a number of BNP activities. Later that year the union decided to expel him on the grounds that his membership of the BNP was incompatible with membership with ASLEF, that he was likely to bring the union into disrepute and that he was against the objects of the union. Lee successfully challenged this before an employment tribunal, because this was not an enforceable membership requirement under TULRCA s 174. ASLEF complained to the ECtHR that the law preventing them from expelling Lee breached their rights under Art 11.

510

JUDGMENT OF THE COURT:

'A THE PARTIES' OBSERVATIONS

1 The Government

33   The Government accepted that TULRCA s 174 represented an interference with rights under Article 11 paragraph 1 in interfering with the autonomy which a trade union would otherwise possess in the matter of determining its membership. The restrictions imposed in respect of membership of a political party were, however, justified as necessary and proportionate. They relied on the importance of the countervailing rights of trade union members and prospective members to freedom of expression and freedom of association which would be engaged by expulsion from a trade union. Those rights were at the very foundation of democratic society, not least as the case concerned sanctions in respect of membership of a political party. They also claimed that a wide discretion remained for trade unions to expel or exclude on grounds of political activities. Section 174 only imposed a limited restriction on expelling those with views inimical to the trade union's objectives; it was only the applicant's own error in approach that led to a problem as there was ample conduct by Mr Lee, going beyond mere membership of the BNP, which the applicant could have relied on in order to found an entirely lawful decision to expel him.

34   The Government also emphasised the special status of trade unions which set them apart from other voluntary associations, pointing out that they play a potentially very important role in the working lives of individuals and exercising a direct influence over matters such as pay, holidays and other terms and conditions of employment, such that the Government were justified in imposing some limits on the applicant's power to confer or withhold the considerable benefits of membership. Finally, they relied on the wide margin of appreciation which applied when striking a balance between the autonomy of trade unions and the Articles 10 and 11 rights of individual members and prospective members.

2 The applicant

35   The applicant submitted that there was no justification for the interference with its right to determine its membership. There was no interference with Mr Lee's freedom of expression as expulsion did not interfere with his right to express his political views. In any event any sanction was minimal and did not take priority over its right, and its members' rights, to exercise their own freedom of association and expression. Mr Lee never claimed that he suffered any detriment from exclusion. It referred to Article 17 to the effect that Article 10 would not protect someone engaged in destroying other rights and freedoms. Since it was committed to opposing race discrimination, it would interfere with its rights, and its members, to be forced to admit into membership a person who was a member of such a right wing organisation. It did not accept that section 174 imposed a limited restriction, pointing out that it simply did not wish to associate with those whom they regarded as fascists or members of extreme right wing parties, whether active or not. It claimed that it had the right to dissociate itself from those whose political membership they abhorred. While Mr Lee's status as an activist might furnish greater reason to expel him, this did not touch on the fundamental issue. It would be acceptable if section 174 were framed so as to limit exclusion to membership of a party the objectives of which were contrary to the objectives of the trade union.

36   The applicant did not consider its role as a trade union was significant as alleged, since the collective bargaining that it was involved in applied to all, not just its members. There was nothing to suggest that Mr Lee lost any benefit in his working life from exclusion from ASLEF. Finally the applicant denied that there was a wide margin of appreciation as this was a situation

where domestic law ran counter to freedom of association and considered that the Court was not precluded from examining the proportionality of the measure and ensuring a fair balance was struck.

B THE COURT'S ASSESSMENT

1 General principles

37   The essential object of Article 11 is to protect the individual against arbitrary interference by public authorities with the exercise of the rights protected. The right to form and join trade unions is a special aspect of freedom of association which also protects, first and foremost, against State action. The State may not interfere with the forming and joining of trade unions except on the basis of the conditions set forth in Article 11 paragraph 2 (see *Young, James and Webster* v *United Kingdom* (1981)).

38   The right to form trade unions involves, for example, the right of trade unions to draw up their own rules and to administer their own affairs. Such trade union rights are explicitly recognised in Articles 3 and 5 of ILO Convention No 87, the provisions of which have been taken into account by the Convention organs in previous cases (see eg *Cheall* v *United Kingdom* (1986); *Wilson* v *United Kingdom* (2002)). *Prima facie* trade unions enjoy the freedom to set up their own rules concerning conditions of membership, including administrative formalities and payment of fees, as well as other more substantive criteria, such as the profession or trade exercised by the would-be member.

39   As an employee or worker should be free to join, or not join a trade union without being sanctioned or subject to disincentives (eg *Young, James and Webster* v *United Kingdom*, *mutatis mutandis*, *Wilson* v *UK*, cited above), so should the trade union be equally free to choose its members. Article 11 cannot be interpreted as imposing an obligation on associations or organisations to admit whosoever wishes to join. Where associations are formed by people, who, espousing particular values or ideals, intend to pursue common goals, it would run counter to the very effectiveness of the freedom at stake if they had no control over their membership. By way of example, it is uncontroversial that religious bodies and political parties can generally regulate their membership to include only those who share their beliefs and ideals. Similarly, the right to join a union "for the protection of his interests" cannot be interpreted as conferring a general right to join the union of one's choice irrespective of the rules of the union: in the exercise of their rights under Article 11 paragraph 1 unions must remain free to decide, in accordance with union rules, questions concerning admission to and expulsion from the union (*Cheall*, cited above; see also Article 5 of the European Social Charter and the Conclusions of the European Committee of Social Rights, Relevant International Materials, paragraphs 22–24 above) . . .

2 Application in the present case

47   The question that arises in the present case concerns the extent to which the State may intervene to protect the trade union member, Mr Lee, against measures taken against him by his union, the applicant.

48   It is accepted by the parties in this case that section 174 had the effect in this case of prohibiting the applicant from expelling Mr Lee as it barred unions from such action where it was motivated, at least in part, by membership of a political party. This constituted an interference with the applicant's freedom of association under the first paragraph of Article 11 which requires to be justified in the terms set out above.

49   In the context of the case, lawfulness is not an issue. Nor is it disputed that the measure had the aim of protecting the rights of individuals, such as Mr Lee, to exercise their various

political rights and freedoms without undue hindrance. The crucial question is whether the State has struck the right balance between Mr Lee's rights and those of the applicant trade union.

50   Taking due consideration of the Government's argument as to the importance of safeguarding fundamental individual rights, the Court is not persuaded however that the measure of expulsion impinged in any significant way on Mr Lee's exercise of freedom of expression or his lawful political activities. Nor is it apparent that Mr Lee suffered any particular detriment, save loss of membership itself in the union. As there was no closed shop agreement for example, there was no apparent prejudice suffered by the applicant in terms of his livelihood or in his conditions of employment. The Court has taken account of the fact that membership of a trade union is often regarded, in particular due to the trade union movement's historical background, as a fundamental safeguard for workers against employers' abuse and it has some sympathy with the notion that any worker should be able to join a trade union (subject to the exceptions set out in Article 11 paragraph 2 *in fine*). However, as pointed out by the applicant, ASLEF represents all workers in the collective bargaining context and there is nothing to suggest in the present case that Mr Lee is at any individual risk of, or is unprotected from, any arbitrary or unlawful action by his employer. Of more weight in the balance is the applicant's right to choose its members. Historically, trade unions in the United Kingdom, and elsewhere in Europe, were, and though perhaps to a lesser extent today are, commonly affiliated to political parties or movements, particularly those on the left. They are not bodies solely devoted to politically-neutral aspects of the well-being of their members, but are often ideological, with strongly held views on social and political issues. There was no hint in the domestic proceedings that the applicant erred in its conclusion that Mr Lee's political values and ideals clashed, fundamentally, with its own. There is no indication that the applicant had any public duty or role conferred on it, or has taken the advantage of state funding, such that it may reasonably be required to take on members to fulfil any other wider purposes.

51   As regards the Government's assertion that domestic law would have permitted the expulsion of Mr Lee if the applicant had restricted its grounds to conduct not related to his membership of the BNP, the Court would note that the Employment Tribunal found that the applicant's objections to Mr Lee were primarily based on his membership of the BNP. It does not find it reasonable to expect the applicant to have used the pretext of relying purely on Mr Lee's conduct which was largely carried out by him as a member of, and reflected his adherence to the aims of, the BNP.

52   Accordingly, in the absence of any identifiable hardship suffered by Mr Lee or any abusive and unreasonable conduct by the applicant, the Court concludes that the balance has not been properly struck and that the case falls outside any acceptable margin of appreciation.

53   There has, accordingly, been a violation of Article 11 of the Convention . . .'

Comment

(1) Before this case was decided, the government had accepted the evidence presented by trade unions that they were being infiltrated by political extremists. It was for this reason that the Employment Relations Act 2004 amended TULRCA s 174 to introduce subsections (4A) and (4B), the net effect of which was to make it lawful to expel someone for political *activities*, but not for mere membership of a political party. In the light of the ECtHR's judgment, the Employment Bill 2008 proposed to repeal these subsections.

(2) Is it justifiable to place any limitations on a union's power to exclude? What other possible benefits might someone excluded from the union be prevented from accessing? What sorts of limitations on a union's power to exclude would be compatible with Art 11?

The closed shop

Otto Kahn-Freund *Labour and the Law* (2nd ed 1977)

'. . . In many countries the freedom not to organise is put on a par with the freedom to organise. If everyone, so it is argued, has the fundamental right to join a union, he has the equally fundamental right not to do so. The law should not prevent anyone from being a union member, nor should it compel him to enter a union. But this is not enough. Just as the law must see that people can effectively exercise their freedom of association, and take positive steps to ensure this, so it is not enough to reject the principle of legally compulsory unionism (which in this country no one has ever advocated). The law must also protect people from being in fact constrained or pressed to join. No one must be exposed to the dilemma between joining a union he does not want to join, and not obtaining or holding a job he wants to obtain or to hold. This is as obnoxious as exposing him to the dilemma between getting or holding a job and joining or remaining in the union of his choice. For many people this reasoning appears to be intellectually attractive. Its symmetry is superficially satisfying . . .

There are strong arguments in favour of banning or at least restricting the closed shop – arguments far stronger than the shallow legalism of the reasoning from analogy with the freedom to organise. Access to jobs should be free. This is in the interest of the development of the economy and the optimal use of manpower. To exclude the non-unionist may mean to exclude the best man for the job. And if there are to be restrictions of access they should be imposed by organs of government responsible through democratic processes, and not by private organisations who are not publicly responsible. The closed shop is, if not a relic, then an image of the medieval guild organisation, or, if you like, of the Elizabethan Statute of Apprentices and it may produce job reservations for privileged minorities. This may not only restrict the supply of (especially skilled) labour, it may also, exactly like educational privileges, cause waste and frustration by robbing people of their opportunities, and it may subject the individual too much to the power of trade union officials. Where several unions compete, it may mean that minorities are suppressed by majorities, or the other way. In France the closed shop was banned in 1956, partly to protect minority unions against the powerful *Confédération Générale du Travail*. Lastly – the evidence received by the Donovan Commission was to this effect – there are small groups of people who have conscientious objections to joining unions, mainly on religious grounds . . .

The argument which is most frequently advanced in favour of the closed shop is "he who does not sow, neither shall he reap". The non-unionist enjoys the fruit of the union's negotiations with the employer – it is neither desirable nor practicable for the employer to differentiate between union members and others – but he does not pay his share of the cost. The main significance of this argument is that it is so widely held, and that it has an emotional appeal. It is not a very strong argument in itself because foreign experience (the "solidarity contribution" system in Switzerland, and the "agency shop" in America), shows that one can substitute for the obligation to join the union a contribution to its funds, not involving membership. Moreover, though the analogy may not be strong, it is, as McCarthy points out, a fact that people constantly reap the benefits of voluntary efforts to which they make no contribution: not only those who pay their annual subscription to the National Trust enjoy the scenery and the architecture it preserves.

The case for the closed shop can only be made in terms of the need for an equilibrium of power. It cannot be attacked or defended in terms of general ethical sentiments, but only in terms of social expediency. Moreover – and this is not the same point – the case for legislation against it can only be made in these terms: strictly in terms of utility and nothing else. It was for reasons of expediency that, after weighing the arguments *pro* and *contra*, the Donovan Commission decided not to recommend legislation against it. In the view of at least some employers it was in the mutual interest: it reduces friction on the shop floor and thus a whole range of causes of disputes and it ensures that the union represents the whole of the workforce. The scene of the struggle between groups among the workers, between militant and less militant wings is shifted away from the workplace. Further, there are branches of the economy where there can be no equilibrium without a closed shop, either because (as with seamen, road haulage workers and others) recruitment for membership is technically impossible, or because (as in large parts of the building industry) no collective regulation can be made effective without the entire work force being subject to union discipline. Even the Industrial Relations Act 1971, which on principle prohibited the closed shop, permitted it under very restricted conditions in order to take account of the needs of some of the unions facing the first of these situations.

What is (to me) perhaps the most powerful argument not in favour of the closed shop, but against legislation seeking to suppress it, is that formal closed shop arrangements are less frequent than informal arrangements. The experience made under the Industrial Relations Act 1971 has shown that the law cannot suppress practices based on informal and generally shared understandings of the workers, and for good reasons, tolerated, and sometimes even welcomed by employers.

There is a case for the closed shop, not necessarily the pre-entry closed shop, in the interest of creating or maintaining that equilibrium of power on which the system of labour relations rests. But there may be a case for it in the interest of management as well as of labour, and indeed of the public in general. This is especially the case where the closed shop prevents secession, the formation of breakaway unions . . .

Yet, it is said, the protection of human freedom comes first. If, during the Second World War, conscientious objectors were exempt from joining the Forces, then surely, whatever the general interest, no one should, as a condition for getting or holding a job be made to join a voluntary association if he does not wish to do so. No one has, I think, ever suggested that a closed shop agreement should be legally enforceable so as to order a worker into a union by means of a mandatory injunction. This would be absurd, and it is not the point. Compulsory unionism is as undesirable as compulsory voting at elections which exists in some countries, but will not, one hopes, ever be introduced here. The analogy is valid. In the occupational existence of most people trade unions are, as I have said, the equivalent of the franchise in their political existence. The law should encourage, but not compel, men and women to take an active part in determining the conditions in which they and their fellows live and work – to say the least it should neither discourage them nor allow others to do so. Conscientious objectors should be given the chance of staying outside without disadvantage but also without benefit to themselves, and as we shall see, the law takes account of this consideration. Beyond this, I cannot see that it is the office of the law, by suppressing the closed shop, to discourage union membership . . .'

Comment

(1) Draw up a table of Kahn-Freund's arguments for and against the closed shop. How would you categorise them? Arguments of principle, practical considerations, utilitarian arguments, economic or political claims? Do you find any of them compelling? Do they hold good in relation to modern employment relations, more than 30 years after Kahn-Freund wrote? If you think not, what has changed in the intervening period?

Report of the Royal Commission on Trade Unions and Employers' Associations 1965–1968 (the Donovan Commission) Cmnd 3623

588   We consider first the operation of the closed shop. This is a term with varying meanings. We use it in the sense in which it is used in Dr McCarthy's book on the subject, namely 'a situation in which employees come to realise that a particular job is only to be obtained and retained if they become and remain members of one of a specified number of trade unions'. Dr McCarthy shows that in 1964 about $3\frac{3}{4}$ million members of trade unions, that is about 2 out of every 5, worked in a closed shop. In some cases a person may have to be a member of a trade union before he can obtain the job he seeks. This is a 'pre-entry' closed shop. In other cases he may be obliged to join a trade union within a short time of beginning the job he has secured. This is the 'post-entry' closed shop. The pre-entry is less common than the post-entry closed shop, but at the time of Dr McCarthy's study it included about $3/4$ million workers . . .

589   Since 1964 the numbers employed in industries where the closed shop is common have gone down, but there is evidence that it has spread in other industries. The total extent of the closed shop therefore probably remains about the same today as when Dr McCarthy studied it.

590   A justification for the closed shop commonly put forward by trade unionists is that the benefits of agreements negotiated with employers apply to employees irrespective of whether they are union members or not. Consequently non-members, who pay no trade union subscriptions, are receiving benefits at the union's expense; they should therefore be obliged to contribute. However, as Dr McCarthy has shown, this is not the main reason for its existence. Admittedly some unions insist upon the closed shop wherever they have the strength to enforce it, but there are others which tolerate a minority of non-members even where they could take action to force them to join the union or lose their jobs.

591   Whether a closed shop will be imposed or not depends on the particular circumstances of the industry, and of the undertaking. If it seems possible that a closed shop will add considerably to the bargaining strength of the union or of a group of workers, then the closed shop is likely to be imposed. On the other hand, if non-unionists are not a serious source of weakness, then their presence will be tolerated.

THE CASE FOR THE CLOSED SHOP

592   The two most convincing arguments for the closed shop refer only to the first group of employments, and depend upon the close link between effective collective bargaining and strong trade unions. The first is that in some industries it is impossible or difficult for a union to establish effective and stable organisation without the help of the closed shop; the second is that even where membership can be recruited and retained without its assistance there are instances where it is needed to deploy the workers' bargaining strength to the full.

593   There are, however, other arguments which can apply even where these two lack force. London Transport told us that they see advantage in the closed shop, since, as they put it, it ensured that in dealings with the union they were meeting an organisation 'which does represent all your people'.

   A similar argument is that the closed shop helps to secure observance of agreements, since it adds to the power of the union to discipline those who ignore them.

594   It must not be supposed, however, that good industrial relations are the invariable accompaniment of the closed shop. On the contrary the closed shop is widespread in motor manufacturing, shipbuilding, coal-mining and the docks, the four industries in which strikes in breach of agreement have been most common in recent years.

THE CASE AGAINST THE CLOSED SHOP

595   Against the closed shop, it is argued that it reduces the individual's freedom in a number of ways. If he is to obtain or retain employment where there is a closed shop, he has no choice but to join the trade union and to pay a subscription. The trade union may refuse to accept him as a member, and is answerable to nobody for its decision. Once a member of the union, the individual has to comply with any relevant decisions it may make; if he does not he may be disciplined, and if things go too far he may eventually be expelled and lose his job in consequence. So far as he is concerned, therefore, the trade union is no longer a 'voluntary' organisation, at least in the normal sense, and he cannot register his disagreement with the union in the normal way open to members of voluntary organisations – by resignation – unless he is prepared also to face losing his job.

596   The importance of the loss of individual freedom is reinforced by the extent to which, as we show elsewhere, power in trade unions rests with work groups. Where matters are left to work groups to settle, they may need to support their decisions with some authority. Unions' disciplinary procedures designed with the needs of the branch in mind sometimes appear irrelevant to the work group when shop floor questions are at issue. As a result informal disciplinary measures, such as ostracism, may be used. Occasionally, trade union authority is wholly usurped; for example, there have been cases where the closed shop has been used to hound a man out of his job even where he had not formally been expelled, as in the case which reached the courts as *Huntley* v *Thornton* (1957).

597   The second principal objection advanced against the closed shop concerns its economic effects. Essentially, what is at issue here is entry to the skilled trades. It is argued that the craft unions use the closed shop to restrict to their own members, or certain classes of their own members, the right to do skilled work; and because they limit the number of entrants they will allow to be trained in the requisite skills, or refuse to recognise as eligible to do skilled work members who have not served apprenticeships, they cause shortages of skilled labour which are economically damaging . . .

Comment

(1) The references in both of the above extracts are to McCarthy's classic study, *The Closed Shop in Britain* (1964). Dunn and Gennard (1984) found that, by 1978, the number of employees covered by closed shop arrangements had risen to 5.2 million, or 23 per cent of the workforce. As total employment had declined in industries where the closed shop had traditionally been strong, the increase was the more significant. They found the most notable rises in the nationalised industries and in white collar employment.

(2) Both Kahn-Freund and the Donovan Commission (of which Kahn-Freund was a member) favoured restricting rather than abolishing the closed shop, by providing safeguards for individuals with genuine reasons for not joining. It is noticeable that one reason for not prohibiting it, put forward by both, is that it would be impossible to do so. This was to reckon without the determination to deal with the issue displayed by the Conservative government of the 1980s, who regarded it as a focal point of many of the things they deplored about trade unions. The Conservative government had already begun to legislate in the Employment Act 1980 against manifestations of the closed shop when it found itself in the odd position of defending the legislative position which had pertained under the previous Labour government before the European Court of Human Rights.

Young, James and Webster v *United Kingdom* [1981] IRLR 408
European Court of Human Rights

The three applicants had all been dismissed from their jobs with British Rail because of their refusal to join the appropriate trade union. At all times British Rail had operated a closed shop agreement with the rail unions which followed exactly the pattern permitted by the law of unfair dismissal as to who was exempt from the requirement to join. None of the claimants fell into an exempted category.

JUDGMENT OF THE COURT:

'. . . I *The existence of an interference with an Article 11 right*

51   A substantial part of the pleadings before the Court was devoted to the question whether Article 11 guarantees not only freedom of association, including the right to form and to join trade unions, in the positive sense, but also, by implication, a "negative right" not to be compelled to join an association or a union.

  Whilst the majority of the Commission stated that it was not necessary to determine this issue, the applicants maintained that a "negative right" was clearly implied in the text. The Government, which saw the Commission's conclusion also as in fact recognising at least a limited negative right, submitted that Article 11 did not confer or guarantee any right not to be compelled to join an association. They contended that this right had been deliberately excluded from the Convention and that this was demonstrated by the following passage in the *travaux préparatoires*:

> "On account of the difficulties raised by the 'closed-shop system' in certain countries, the Conference in this connection considered that it was undesirable to introduce into the Convention a rule under which 'no one may be compelled to belong to an association' which features in [Art 20 s 2 of] the United Nations Universal Declaration" (Report of 19 June 1950 of the Conference of Senior Officials, Collected Edition of the *Travaux Préparatoires*, vol IV, p 262).

52   The Court does not consider it necessary to answer this question on this occasion.

  The Court recalls, however, that the right to form and to join trade unions is a special aspect of freedom of association (see the *National Union of Belgian Police* (1975)); it adds that the notion of a freedom implies some measure of freedom of choice as to its exercise.

  Assuming for the sake of argument that, for the reasons given in the above-cited passage from the *travaux préparatoires*, a general rule such as that in Article 20 s 2 of the Universal Declaration of Human Rights was deliberately omitted from, and so cannot be regarded as itself enshrined in, the Convention, it does not follow that the negative aspect of a person's freedom of association falls completely outside the ambit of Article 11 and that each and every compulsion to join a particular trade union is compatible with the intention of that provision. To construe Article 11 as permitting every kind of compulsion in the field of trade union membership would strike at the very substance of the freedom it is designed to guarantee (see, *mutatis mutandis*, the *Belgian Linguistic* case (1979), *Golder* (1975) and *Winterwerp* (1979)).

53   The Court emphasises once again that, in proceedings originating in an individual application, it has, without losing sight of the general context, to confine its attention as far as possible to the issues raised by the concrete case before it (see, *inter alia, Guzzardi* (1980)). Accordingly, in the present case, it is not called upon to review the closed shop system as such in relation to the Convention or to express an opinion on every consequence or form of compulsion which it may engender; it will limit its examination to the effects of that system on the applicants.

54   As a consequence of the agreement concluded in 1975 the applicants were faced with the dilemma either of joining NUR (in the case of Mr James) or TSSA or NUR (in the cases of Mr Young and Mr Webster) or of losing jobs for which union membership had not been a requirement when they were first engaged and which two of them had held for several years. Each applicant regarded the membership condition introduced by that agreement as an interference with the freedom of association to which he considered that he was entitled; in addition, Mr Young and Mr Webster had objections to trade union policies and activities coupled, in the case of Mr Young, with objections to the political affiliations of the specified unions. As a result of their refusal to yield to what they considered to be unjustified pressure, they received notices terminating their employment. Under the legislation in force at the time, their dismissal was "fair" and, hence, could not found a claim for compensation, let alone reinstatement or re-engagement.

55   The situation facing the applicants clearly runs counter to the concept of freedom of association in its negative sense.

Assuming that Article 11 does not guarantee the negative aspect of that freedom on the same footing as the positive aspect, compulsion to join a particular trade union may not always be contrary to the Convention.

However, a threat of dismissal involving loss of livelihood is a most serious form of compulsion and, in the present instance, it was directed against persons engaged by British Rail before the introduction of any obligation to join a particular trade union.

In the Court's opinion, such a form of compulsion, in the circumstances of the case, strikes at the very substance of the freedom guaranteed by Article 11. For this reason alone, there has been an interference with that freedom as regards each of the three applicants.

56   Another facet of this case concerns the restriction of the applicants' choice as regards the trade unions which they could join of their own volition. An individual does not enjoy the right to freedom of association if in reality the freedom of action or choice which remains available to him is either non-existent or so reduced as to be of no practical value (see, *mutatis mutandis, Airey* (1979)).

The Government submitted that the relevant legislation not only did not restrict but also expressly protected freedom of action or choice in this area; in particular, it would have been open to the applicants to form or to join a trade union in addition to one of the specified unions. The applicants, on the other hand, claimed that this was not the case in practice, since such a step would have been precluded by British Rail's agreement with the railway unions and by the Bridlington Principles; in their view, joining and taking part in the activities of a competing union would, if attempted, have led to expulsion from one of the specified unions. These submissions were, however, contested by the Government.

Be that as it may, such freedom of action or choice as might have been left to the applicants in this respect would not in any way have altered the compulsion to which they were subjected since they would in any event have been dismissed if they had not become members of one of the specified unions.

57   Moreover, notwithstanding its autonomous role and particular sphere of application, Article 11 must, in the present case, also be considered in the light of Articles 9 and 10 (see, *mutatis mutandis, Kjeldsen, Busk Madsen and Pedersen* (1976)).

Mr Young and Mr Webster had objections to trade union policies and activities, coupled, in the case of Mr Young, with objections to the political affiliations of TSSA and NUR. Mr James' objections were of a different nature, but he too attached importance to freedom of choice and he had reached the conclusion that membership of NUR would be of no advantage to him.

The protection of personal opinion afforded by Articles 9 and 10 in the shape of freedom of thought, conscience and religion and of freedom of expression is also one of the purposes of freedom of association as guaranteed by Article 11. Accordingly, it strikes at the very substance of this Article to exert pressure, of the kind applied to the applicants, in order to compel some-one to join an association contrary to his convictions.

In this further respect, the treatment complained of – in any event as regards Mr Young and Mr Webster – constituted an interference with their Article 11 rights . . .'

Comment

(1) This was the decision of a majority of the Court. Six judges who concurred with the majority would have gone further and held that the right not to belong should in all respects be treated as on an equal footing with the right to belong. Three judges dissented, largely because it was clear from the *travaux préparatoires* that the drafters of the Convention had specifically intended to leave out the closed shop because of the lack of consensus between states on the issue.

(2) Until the law of unfair dismissal was introduced the courts had not been involved with the closed shop. Since an employer could dismiss for any reason (provided notice was given), a dismissal because someone refused to join a union was perfectly legitimate, as was refusing to recruit a worker on that ground.

(3) During the 1980s the Conservative government pursued salami tactics against the closed shop, introducing more and more exceptions to the basic rule that a dismissal in a closed shop situation was automatically fair, until the exceptions had virtually swallowed up the rule. In 1988 the basic rule was finally abolished by the Employment Act 1988 so that any dismissal for refusing to belong to a trade union became automatically unfair. This is now found in TULRCA s 152. Additionally, refusal to employ someone on grounds of non-membership and detrimental treatment of non-unionists during employment are prohibited by TULRCA ss 137 and 146, which treats non-membership as on a par with union membership protection rights. Thus, in the case of dismissal on this ground, the basic award cannot be less than £4,400 (TULRCA s 156). If the employer has bowed to pressure from a trade union in acting against a non-member, the union can be joined as a party to the proceedings and ordered to pay part or all of any compensation awarded (TULRCA ss 142, 150, 160).

(4) Thus while the closed shop is not illegal, it is no longer legally enforceable. A steep decline in trade union membership, coupled with the shrinkage of traditional industries and the antipathy to trade unions evinced by the Conservative government of the 1980s, means that the number of employees now covered in practice by closed shop arrangements is very small.

THE LEGAL STATUS OF TRADE UNIONS

The present legal status of trade unions is explicable to some extent in terms of their past; however, the history of trade unions is beyond the scope of this work. Pelling (1992) is a readable account.

In English law, two kinds of person are recognised: natural persons and legal persons. Legal persons are incorporated bodies: registered companies are the most obvious example of these. A company has a separate existence from its members and owns property, enters contracts, etc, in its own right. A trade union is not a corporate body: it is an unincorporated association of individual natural persons. However, in 1901 the House of Lords held in an historic decision that trade unions had certain quasi-corporate characteristics.

Taff Vale Railway v Amalgamated Society of Railway Servants
[1901] AC 426 House of Lords

The railway company sued for an injunction to prevent strike action being taken by the union. In an unprecedented move, the company sued the union in its own name. The union argued that, as an unincorporated association, it could not be sued as if it were a legal person. Farwell J found for the company, but his decision was reversed by the Court of Appeal. The company appealed to the House of Lords. In view of the references to Farwell J's judgment by members of the House of Lords, it is also extracted.

FARWELL J: 'The defendant society have taken out a summons to strike out their name as defendants, on the ground that they are neither a corporation nor an individual, and cannot be sued in a quasi-corporate or any other capacity. Failing this, they contend that no injunction ought to be granted against them. I reserved judgment last week on these two points, because the first is of very great importance, and counsel were unable to assist me by citing any reported case in which the question had been argued and decided.

Now it is undoubtedly true that a trade union is neither a corporation, nor an individual, nor a partnership between a number of individuals; but this does not by any means conclude the case. A trade union, as defined by s 16 of the Trade Union Act 1876 "means any combination, whether temporary or permanent, for regulating the relations between workmen and masters, or between workmen and workmen, or between masters and masters, or for imposing restrictive conditions on the conduct of any trade or business, whether such combination would or would not, if the principal Act had not been passed, have been deemed to have been an unlawful combination by reason of some one or more of its purposes being in restraint of trade". It is an association of men which almost invariably owes its legal validity to the Trade Union Acts 1871 and 1876 . . .

Now, the Legislature in giving a trade union the capacity to own property and the capacity to act by agents has, without incorporating it, given it two of the essential qualities of a corporation – essential, I mean, in respect of liability for tort, for a corporation can only act by its agents, and can only be made to pay by means of its property. The principle on which corporations have been held liable in respect of wrongs committed by its servants or agents in the course of their service and for the benefit of the employer – *qui sentit commodum sentire debet et onus* – (see *Mersey Docks Trustees v Gibbs* (1866)) is as applicable to the case of a trade union as to that of a corporation. If the contention of the defendant society were well founded, the Legislature has authorised the creation of numerous bodies of men capable of owning great wealth and of acting by agents with absolutely no responsibility for the wrongs that they may do to other persons by the use of that wealth and the employment of those agents. They would be at liberty (I do not at all suggest that the defendant society would so act) to disseminate libels broadcast, or to hire men to reproduce the rattening methods that disgraced Sheffield thirty or forty years ago, and their victims would have nothing to look to for damages but the pockets of the individuals, usually men of small means, who acted as their agents. That this is a consideration that may fairly be taken into account appears from the opinion of the judges given to the House of Lords in the *Mersey Docks Case*: "We cannot think that it was the intention of the Legislature to deprive a shipowner who pays dues to a wealthy trading company, such as the St Catherine's Dock Company for instance, of all recourse against it, and to substitute the personal liability of a harbour-master, no doubt a respectable person in his way, but whose whole means, generally speaking, would not be equal to more than a very small percentage of the damages, when there are any." The proper rule of construction of statutes such as these is that in the absence of express contrary intention the Legislature intends that the creature of the statute shall have the same duties, and that its funds shall be subject to the same liabilities as the general law would impose on a private individual doing the same thing. It would require very clear and express words of enactment to induce me to hold that the Legislature had in fact legalised the existence of such irresponsible bodies with such wide capacity for evil . . .'

EARL OF HALSBURY LC: 'My Lords, in this case I am content to adopt the judgment of Farwell J, with which I entirely concur; and I cannot find any satisfactory answer to that judgment in the judgment of the Court of Appeal which overruled it. If the Legislature has created a thing which can own property, which can employ servants, and which can inflict injury, it must be taken, I think, to have impliedly given the power to make it suable in a Court of Law for injuries purposely done by its authority and procurement.

I move your Lordships that the judgment of the Court of Appeal be reversed and that of Farwell J restored.'

LORD MACNAGHTEN: '. . . The substantial question, therefore, as Farwell J put it, is this: Has the Legislature authorised the creation of numerous bodies of men capable of owning great wealth and of acting by agents with absolutely no responsibility for the wrongs they may do to other persons by the use of that wealth and the employment of those agents? In my opinion, Parliament has done nothing of the kind. I cannot find anything in the Acts of 1871 and 1876, or either of them, from beginning to end, to warrant or suggest such a notion. It is perhaps satisfactory to find that nothing of the sort was contemplated by the minority of the members of the Royal Commission on Trade Unions, whose views found acceptance with the Legislature. In paragraph 4 of their report they say: "It should be specially provided that except so far as combinations are thereby exempted from criminal prosecution nothing should affect . . . the liability of every person to be sued at law or in equity in respect of any damage which may have been occasioned to any other person through the act or default of the person so sued." Now, if the liability of every person in this respect was to be preserved, it would seem to follow that it was intended by the strongest advocates of trade unionism that persons should be liable for concerted as well as for individual action; and for this purpose it seems to me that it cannot matter in the least whether the persons acting in concert be combined together in a trade union, or collected and united under any other form of association.

Then, if trade unions are not above the law, the only remaining question, as it seems to me, is one of form. How are these bodies to be sued? I have no doubt whatever that a trade union, whether registered or unregistered, may be sued in a representative action if the persons selected as defendants be persons who, from their position, may be taken fairly to represent the body . . .

The further question remains: May a registered trade union be sued in and by its registered name? For my part, I cannot see any difficulty in the way of such a suit. It is quite true that a registered trade union is not a corporation, but it has a registered name and a registered office. The registered name is nothing more than a collective name for all the members. The registered office is the place where it carries on business. A partnership firm which is not a corporation, nor, I suppose, a legal entity, may now be sued in the firm's name. And when I find that the Act of Parliament actually provides for a registered trade union being sued in certain cases for penalties by its registered name, as a trade union, and does not say that the cases specified are the only cases in which it may be so sued, I can see nothing contrary to principle, or contrary to the provisions of the Trade Union Acts, in holding that a trade union may be sued by its registered name.

I am, therefore, of opinion that the appeal should be allowed and the judgment of Farwell J restored with costs, here and below.'

(Lords Shand, Brampton and Lindley gave concurring opinions.)

Comment

(1) The policy reasons for deciding the case in this manner are obvious from the judgments. The impact of this decision in the field of industrial action is discussed below (p 599).

(2) Trade unions had been legalised by the Trade Union Act 1871 (amended 1876), which had provided the embryonic form of registration by which some store was set in the decision. The position is essentially the same today, with present definitions dating from the repeal of the Industrial Relations Act 1971 by TULRA 1974.

(3) The fact that trade unions are still not corporations with a legal personality separate from their members has two important consequences: first, they have to have certain quasi-corporate characteristics (like the right to own property) conferred on them by statute; secondly, they are defined in terms of their *purposes*, unlike companies, which are defined in terms of their *constitutions*.

Trade Union and Labour Relations (Consolidation) Act 1992

1   In this Act a 'trade union' means an organisation (whether temporary or permanent) –
    (a) which consists wholly or mainly of workers of one or more descriptions and whose principal purposes include the regulation of relations between workers of that description or those descriptions and employers or employers' associations; or
    (b) which consists wholly or mainly of –
       (i)   constituent or affiliated organisations which fulfil the conditions in paragraph (a) (or themselves consist wholly or mainly of constituent or affiliated organisations which fulfil those conditions), or
       (ii) representatives of such constituent or affiliated organisations,
      and whose principal purposes include the regulation of relations between workers and employers or between workers and employers' associations, or the regulation of relations between its constituent or affiliated organisations.
    . . .

10 (1) A trade union is not a body corporate but –
    (a) it is capable of making contracts;
    (b) it is capable of suing and being sued in its own name, whether in proceedings relating to property or founded on contract or tort or any other cause of action; and
    (c) proceedings for an offence alleged to have been committed by it or on its behalf may be brought against it in its own name.
   (2) A trade union shall not be treated as if it were a body corporate except to the extent authorised by the provisions of this Part.
   (3) A trade union shall not be registered –
    (a) as a company under the Companies Act 1985, or
    (b) under the Friendly Societies Act 1974 or the Industrial and Provident Societies Act 1965;
and any such registration of a trade union (whenever effected) is void.

Electrical, Electronic, Telecommunication and Plumbing Union v *Times Newspapers Ltd* [1980] 1 All ER 1097 Queen's Bench Division

The union sued the owners of *The Times* for libel in respect of statements defamatory of the union which had appeared in the newspaper. The issue before the court was whether a trade union could maintain an action for defamation.

O'CONNOR J: '. . . Now it is important to have clearly in mind that these issues are concerned with the law touching the action of defamation. The issues are in no way concerned with any of the law which may or may not touch on industrial disputes. It is the law of defamation with which I am concerned. As was said by Denning LJ in the Court of Appeal in his dissenting judgment in *Bonsor* v *Musicians' Union* (1954):

> "A libel is, of course, in its very nature, a wrong to the person, not a wrong to property; and it is apparent that it is only by attributing legal personality to a trade union that it can be permitted to sue for a libel on itself."

That is only applying to a trade union a much broader principle that the action for defamation is a personal matter because it is the reputation of the person which is defamed, and unless one can attach a personality to a body, it cannot sue for defamation . . .

Now where stands a trade union? It is not necessary for the purposes of this judgment to go into a detailed analysis of the history of trade unions in our law. It is well known that, before they were legalised, they ran foul of the law because they were unlawful combinations in the restraint of trade and suffered disabilities. But that is in the long and distant past. The Trade Union Acts since 1871 have recognised trade unions, but they were without question unincorporated associations, and as such one would have thought that they could neither sue in their own names, nor be sued, and as such could not be defamed in their proper name.

In 1901 in *Taff Vale Railway Co* v *Amalgamated Society of Railway Servants* the House of Lords got over this difficulty, but in circumstances which were disliked by the trade union movement, by introducing what has come to be called a quasi-corporation, or a near corporation. Quite shortly, what happened was this: looking at the registration of a trade union under the 1871 Act, and seeing the various matters dealt with in that statute, the House of Lords came to the conclusion that the trade union had a sufficient personality for that reason so that it could be sued in its own name and its funds charged in the action.

The reverse of that coin necessarily followed; if it could be sued so also it could maintain an action in its own name and, as we shall see in a moment, unions soon did so perfectly properly. The immediate effect of the *Taff Vale* decision was to call for a change in the law to give protection to trade unions (nothing whatever to do with actions of libel, but in their industrial capacity), and in 1906 Parliament passed the Trade Disputes Act in order to reverse the decision of the House of Lords in the *Taff Vale* case. That is, to reverse the decision which had enabled the claimants in that case to sue the union in tort. And in 1906, in the Trade Disputes Act, Parliament passed a blanket section relieving trade unions of liability in tort.

It left quite unaffected the decision of the House of Lords that this unincorporated body, because of the effect of the statute to which it was subject, had a quasi-corporate personality and thus we find that trade unions brought actions in their own name and, I have been told, that they sued for libel as early as 1913; but it is unnecessary to examine that because the matter was decided, in a decision which is binding on me, in 1945, that is *National Union of General and Municipal Workers* v *Gillian* . . .

In 1965 a Royal Commission was appointed to inquire into the position of the trade unions, under the chairmanship of Lord Donovan. In its report it considered the position of trade unions and it found that there were certain anomalies and recommended that the position be clarified by passing legislation requiring or saying that trade unions should be bodies corporate. It also made recommendations about the immunity in tort because there were all sorts of matters which were quite outside industrial relations, e.g. personal injuries that a visitor to union premises might suffer. It has got nothing whatever to do with the industrial capacity of the trade union. There were difficulties, which were set out in the report; and in the Industrial Relations Act 1971 effect was given certainly to the recommendation that unions should be bodies corporate. Now it is well known that that statute met with determined opposition from the trade unions and in due course it was repealed and replaced by the statute which governs their position today. It is unnecessary, other than the statement which I have made, to look further at the Act of 1971 because it has been repealed, and the present position, and the difficulty with which I am confronted, has been created by the Trade Union and Labour Relations Act 1974 [now repealed and replaced by TULRCA 1992] . . .

Section 2 [cf TULRCA s 10], the side note to which reads, "Status of trade unions", provides:

"(1) A trade union which is not a special register body shall not be, or be treated as if it were, a body corporate . . ."

In my judgment, those are absolutely clear words. One must remember the position in law at that time. At that time, trade unions if they were registered were not necessarily corporate bodies: they were made corporate bodies. If they were on the provisional register they had the attributes of corporate bodies and could properly be called quasi-corporate associations, and the whole background of the position of trade unions until 1971 was that they were quasi-corporate bodies. It was a matter which was as much in their interest as any possible disability. Nevertheless here we find Parliament telling us what a trade union may not be – it "shall not be, or be treated as if it were, a body corporate" . . .

If the words "or be treated as if it were" were not in [TULRCA s 10(2)], there would be absolutely no difficulty because all those powers which are attributed and given to trade unions make it quite clear that if they are, as the section would say, not a body corporate, they had the attributes of one and they were to be treated as one, so that they could possess the necessary personalities which they could protect by the action of defamation; but the words are there, and the words say that that is exactly what is not to be done. I do not find any ambiguity in them . . .

The tort of libel, as I have already demonstrated, must be founded on possession of a personality which can be libelled and [TULRCA s 10] has removed that personality from trade unions. I find nothing in the statute to show that those words are ambiguous. There are many attributes which, but for the presence of the words "or be treated as if it were" in [s 10(2)] would simply confirm that a trade union enjoyed a quasi-corporate personality and could bring an action in libel in its own name for the protection of its own reputation, and, as I have said, I am quite clear that apart from the law anybody would say that a trade union has a separate reputation and should be entitled to protect it; but there it is. Parliament has deprived the trade union of the necessary personality on which an action for defamation depends; and to the first question which I am asked, which is:

"Can a trade union (not being a special register body) maintain an action in its own name for damages for defamation in relation to its reputation as a legal entity whether or not such entity is separate and distinct from its individual members?"

the answer is, "No. It cannot."

As I have said, I regret that I have to arrive at that decision but, I repeat, it seems to me that I am driven to it by the clear words of the statute . . .'

Comment

(1) This illustrates that the 1974 definition of trade unions did not (as perhaps had been intended) simply return trade unions to the pre-Industrial Relations Act 1971 position.

(2) As will be seen, the total immunity in torts conferred on trade unions by the Trade Disputes Act 1906 has now been abolished (see Chapter 13).

(3) While the definition of a trade union is narrowed in that it must consist of 'workers' (thus excluding solicitors: *Carter* v *The Law Society* (1973)), on the whole it is a very wide definition. Trade unions may now incur extensive liabilities if they organise

industrial action, which gives considerable importance to the fact that the definition may include temporary organisations.

Midland Cold Storage v *Turner* [1972] ICR 230 National Industrial Relations Court

The company found that it had been made the subject of a blacking order (meaning that its goods would not be handled) made by a committee of shop stewards operating on the London docks. While the members of the committee were shop stewards of recognised trade unions, their committee had no official status in any of the unions and it was not recognised by the employers. Its activities were confined to the organisation and discontinuation of industrial action on the docks.

SIR JOHN DONALDSON: '. . . This brings us to the respondent committee. The habitual use of threatening notes over the name of the committee, the photograph of the chairman and the secretary visiting the picket line, and the complete absence of any repudiation by the committee of the pickets' authority, clearly point to the action of the pickets as being action taken on behalf of the committee. It must, therefore, seem strange that we are unable to make any order against the committee. The reason is this. The general law is that only individual men or women or corporations can be sued. Midland have taken proceedings against Mr Steer and Mr Turner as individuals but have not named any other individual members of the committee as being responsible for the threats of "blacking". Instead, they have taken proceedings against the committee as if it was a corporation, which it is not. Counsel for Midland admits that the committee is not a corporation, but he submits that s 154(2) of the 1971 Act justifies Midland in treating it as if it was, because it is an "organisation of workers". Section 154 certainly has that effect if the committee is an organisation of workers. But is it? An "organisation of workers" is defined in s 61(1) of the 1971 Act as,

> "an organisation (whether permanent or temporary) which either – (a) consists wholly or mainly of workers of one or more descriptions and is an organisation whose principal objects include the regulation of relations between workers of that description or those descriptions and employers or organisations of employers, or (b) is a federation of workers' organisations." [cf TULRCA s 1]

It follows that if Midland are to obtain an order against the committee they must satisfy us that (a) it is an organisation; (b) it consists wholly or mainly of workers; (c) its principal objects include the regulation of relations between workers of that description and employers.

We have no doubt at all that the committee exists and has great influence in the London docks. We have no evidence as to its composition, other than the fact that it has a chairman and secretary, and that, as we infer from its name and our general knowledge of organisation in the docks, it is composed wholly or mainly of trade union shop stewards. It is not recognised by employers, although they are well aware of its existence and may take account of its activities. Furthermore, there is no evidence that it seeks recognition by employers as a bargaining agent for any bargaining unit or as a representative body for or of any union or unions. It is proved to be an influential pressure group. Our general knowledge of the industry tells us that its activities are to some extent co-ordinated with those of other shop stewards' committees in other docks by a national dock shop stewards' committee, but that those other committees may have different compositions and functions. If we have to be able to point to evidence to confirm what as members of an industrial court we ought to know and do know, it was provided at a late stage in the hearing by the production of a printed leaflet, purporting to be issued by the committee, referring to support from the national committee. Its most apparent activity seems to consist of recommending the taking or abandonment of industrial action in the

London docks and organising any such action which may be decided on. Thereafter it does not seem to enter into negotiations with the employers but leaves this task to the established union machinery.

Against this background, we are satisfied that prima facie the committee is an organisation and that it consists wholly or mainly of workers as defined in the 1971 Act. However, we are not satisfied that there is a prima facie case for holding that its principal objects include the regulation of relations between workers of that description (namely registered dock workers) and employers. No body whose principal objects included such regulation could fail at least to seek recognition from employers and of such an attempt we have no evidence. Accordingly, we are unable to make any order against the committee as such . . .'

Comment

(1) Had the purposes of this ad hoc committee been different, it would have incurred liability. However, it is conceivable that there could be some scope for trade unions to delegate organisation of industrial action to non-union organisers in such a way as to avoid liability. It would be difficult, because of the wide canons of vicarious liability applied, but perhaps not impossible.

(2) While the union is able to own property in perpetuity by virtue of TULRCA s 12, it seems that according to the general law there is nothing to prevent branches owning their own funds separately. Now that union funds are frequently at risk when industrial action is taken, this could also be important, as the next case shows.

News Group Newspapers Ltd v Society of Graphical and Allied Trades 1982
[1986] ICR 716 Court of Appeal

In the wake of industrial action, a sequestration order was made against the funds of the union because of its contempt of court. While the union had over £5 million in its central funds, branch funds amounted to more than £6 million. This was an action by the sequestrator to get at the £279,297 held by the London branch.

LAWTON LJ: 'The union, which is registered under the Trade Union and Labour Relations Act 1974 was formed in 1982, being an amalgamation of two unions in the printing industry. It has about 200,000 members. Its objects are the usual ones of large trade unions, that is to say, collective bargaining, safeguarding working conditions and the provision of benevolent funds and services for its members. It is organised in branches. Every member has to belong to a branch and in every place of employment where two or more members work they have to form and join a chapel.

Each branch has a considerable degree of independence as rule 1(3) of SOGAT 1982's General Rules shows:

"For the convenience of members, branches shall be formed in such towns as may be found necessary. Each branch shall be at liberty to elect its own officers, conduct its own business, and be empowered to frame its own local, superannuation and distress fund rules and regulations, provided they are approved by the Executive Council and in conformity with the general rules."

Branches are empowered to "raise funds for local purposes": see rule 39(2). Rule 39(5) distinguishes between a branch's funds and property and the union's because there is a prohibition against any branch "disposing of the Society's funds or property otherwise than by these rules allowed". There is the same indication in rule 1(4) which envisages that on the secession or dissolution of a branch the union's funds, books and property shall be delivered to the General Secretary but the branch shall be entitled to keep "purely provident, local, superannuation and distress funds, books and properties".

All members of the union have to contribute to its funds and to branch funds, if there are any, and to chapel funds. By rule 41 local funds "'shall be the property of the branch". The branches are responsible to the union for the collection of the contributions to the union's funds. In practice members pay a composite sum at prescribed intervals which is made up of what is to go to the union and what to the local funds. Of that which is to go to the union, as a matter of convenience before forwarding it, the branches deduct 40 per cent which they use to help pay for the cost of administering the branches. In the case of the London branch this percentage is not enough to cover all their administrative expenses and is supplemented by payments out of its local funds. In the past the London branch has not differentiated in its bank accounts between what is due to the union and what it can keep as its local funds. Mr Mowbray on behalf of the London branch and the chapel, accepted that any identifiable sums in those accounts which belong to the union must be held to the order of the commissioners as must, as long as the order of sequestration is in operation, all contributions to union funds which its members may pay it. The rules of the London branch set out how its branch funds are to be spent, that is to say "to finance the activities and benefits of the branch", in specified ways which are all concerned with the activities and interests of its members, not of the union as such. As already recounted trustees of the funds and property have been appointed. Any decision relating to "the use, disbursement or investments of the assets of the branch is to be exclusively that of the branch committee to whose decision the trustees are bound to conform".

In my judgment, when the rules of both the union and the London branch are construed, not as if they were in a statute or deed but as the terms of a contract, the intention manifested by the words used was that the local funds of the London branch were to be used solely for the benefit of such of its members as it had at any one time, provided that any expenditure was for purposes in conformity with the objects of the union . . .

In my judgment the issue in this case is to be decided on the construction of the rules of the union and of the London branch. Since, as I adjudge, both sets of rules provide that the property and funds of the London branch are to be held for the benefit of that branch, it follows that its property and funds are not the property of the union and are not subject to the order of sequestration.

I would allow the appeal.'

(Lloyd and Glidewell LJJ delivered concurring judgments.)

LISTING AND INDEPENDENCE OF TRADE UNIONS

Listing

Trade Union and Labour Relations (Consolidation) Act 1992

2 (1) The Certification Officer shall keep a list of trade unions containing the names of –
   (a) the organisations whose names were, immediately before the commencement of this Act, duly entered in the list of trade unions kept by him under section 8 of the Trade Union and Labour Relations Act 1974, and
   (b) the names of the organisations entitled to have their names entered in the list in accordance with this Part.
   (2) The Certification Officer shall keep copies of the list of trade unions, as for the time being in force, available for public inspection at all reasonable hours free of charge.

(3) A copy of the list shall be included in his annual report.

(4) The fact that the name of an organisation is included in the list of trade unions is evidence (in Scotland, sufficient evidence) that the organisation is a trade union.

(5) On the application of an organisation whose name is included in the list, the Certification Officer shall issue it with a certificate to that effect.

(6) A document purporting to be such a certificate is evidence (in Scotland, sufficient evidence) that the name of the organisation is entered in the list.

Comment

(1) Registration under the Trade Union Act 1871, mentioned in the *Taff Vale* case, was replaced a hundred years later by registration under the Industrial Relations Act 1971. The consequences, however, were very different. Under the Industrial Relations Act, registered trade unions became corporate bodies, suable in tort and subject to a great deal of regulation of their internal affairs. Non-registration therefore became the rallying call of trade union opposition to that Act. In 1974, when the Industrial Relations Act was repealed, the word 'register' had too many unpleasant connotations to be used and so it was replaced by the more innocuous 'list'.

(2) There are certain minor tax advantages for trade unions in being listed; however, the main reason for seeking listing is that it is an essential first step before establishing the union's status as an independent and recognised trade union.

Independent trade unions

Trade Union and Labour Relations (Consolidation) Act 1992

5   In this Act an 'independent trade union' means a trade union which –

(a) is not under the domination or control of an employer or group of employers or of one or more employers' associations, and

(b) is not liable to interference by an employer or any such group or association (arising out of the provision of financial or material support or by any other means whatsoever) tending towards such control;

and references to 'independence', in relation to a trade union, shall be construed accordingly.

Comment

(1) A listed trade union may apply to the Certification Officer for a certificate of independence, which will be issued if the above definition is satisfied. An appeal from the Certification Officer's decision lies to the EAT.

(2) The reason for the emphasis on independence is to guard against employers encouraging what the Americans graphically term 'sweetheart unions'. A company may encourage workers to join an organisation in which it pulls the strings: it will then be entirely happy to grant exclusive negotiating rights to this body and will use it as an excuse to refuse to recognise any other union.

(3) The criteria used by the Certification Officer were described with approval by the EAT in the first appeal against a refusal to grant a certificate of independence.

Blue Circle Staff Association v Certification Officer [1977] ICR 224
Employment Appeal Tribunal

CUMMING-BRUCE J: '. . . In response to a question from the tribunal, the Certification Officer described his approach. He stated that he had found no nice clear yardstick which could be laid against each case, but that it was a case of looking at the factors and doing a balancing act. He then indicated certain criteria which he found useful. In view of the novelty and importance of the subject matter we set out these criteria as the witness described them, though we do not think it would give a fair impression of his evidence if we suggested that he presented them either as comprehensive, or of similar weight in any two cases.

1 *Finance*: If there is any evidence that a union is getting a direct subsidy from an employer, it is immediately ruled out.

2 *Other assistance*: The officer's inspectors see what material support, such as free premises, time off work for officials, or office facilities a union is getting from an employer, and attempt to cost them out.

3 *Employer interference*: If a union is very small and weak and gets a good deal of help, then on the face of it its independence must be in danger and liable to employer interference.

4 *History*: The recent history of a union, important in the case of Blue Circle Staff Association which before February 1976 was dominated by the employers, is considered. It was not unusual for a staff association to start as a "creature of management and grow into something independent". The staff association had started on this road but still had a way to travel.

5 *Rules*: The applicant union's rule book is scrutinised to see if the employer can interfere with or control it, and if there are any restrictions on membership. If a union is run by people near the top of a company it could be detrimental to rank and file members.

6 *Single company unions*: While they were not debarred from getting certificates, because such a rule could exclude unions like those of miners and railwaymen, they were more liable to employer interference. Broadly based multi-company unions were more difficult to influence.

7 *Organisation*: The Certification Officer's inspectors then examine the applicant union in detail, its size and recruiting ability, whether it is run by competent and experienced officers, the state of its finance, and its branch and committee structure. Again, if the union was run by senior men in a company, employer interference was a greater risk.

8 *Attitude*: Once the other factors had been assessed, inspectors looked for a "robust attitude in negotiation" as a sign of genuine independence, backed up by a good negotiating record. They may find a single company union with little resources which may have behaved in a robust or even militant way. It did not seem common sense to say that a union which has constantly caused trouble for an employer is dependent on that employer. However, that did not mean he favoured militancy, because, if a union dealt with a good, tactful and sensitive employer who paid well and its members had little to be militant about, it could be extremely difficult for it to demonstrate its robustness and militancy or, consequently, its independence . . .'

Squibb UK Staff Association v Certification Officer [1979] ICR 235 Court of Appeal

In 1973 white collar staff at E R Sqibb & Sons formed a staff association, which 231 out of a potential 290 employees joined. In 1976 it applied for a certificate of independence. The Certification Officer rejected the application because of the association's dependence on facilities provided free by the employer – free office and meetings accommodation, free stationery, telephone, photocopying, internal mailing and so on. Given the narrow membership base of the association and its limited resources, the Certification Officer thought that it would find it extremely difficult to function if these facilities were withdrawn. In consequence, he concluded that the association was 'liable to interference' within the meaning of TULRCA s 5.

LORD DENNING MR: '. . . The Certification Officer interpreted the words "liable to interference" as meaning "vulnerable to interference" or "exposed to the risk of interference" by the employer. Whereas counsel for the association suggested that it meant "likely" or "not unlikely" to be subjected to interference by the employer. The Employment Appeal Tribunal preferred Mr Irvine's interpretation [counsel for the association]. They said:

> "We feel that Mr Irvine's approach . . . is the better one and that the words must be construed as meaning that, in the circumstances and on the facts of each case, it is not unlikely that interference will take place and that, when it does, it is not unlikely to have the effect of some degree of control by the employer."

Applying that test, which I may call "the likelihood of interference" test, the appeal tribunal held that there should be a certificate of independence. They said:

> ". . . on the evidence we have heard and the documents we have read, there is no real likelihood either of the facilities being withdrawn, or, if they were, of this in any way affecting the independence of the union from employer interference, and that therefore the union has successfully rebutted the presumption."

So there it is. They decided because there was no real "likelihood of interference by the employer".

I agree that there are two possible meanings of the word "liable". It is a very vague and indefinite word. Having heard very good arguments on both sides, it seems to me that the Certification Officer's interpretation of "liable" is correct and the association's interpretation is not correct. One has to envisage the possibility that there may be a difference of opinion in the future between the employer and the staff association. It does not matter whether it is likely or not – it may be completely unlikely – but one has to envisage the possibility of a difference of opinion. It may be on the amount of pay; it may be on the question of a pension; it may be on the safeguards; and the like. Whatever it may be, there may be a difference of opinion. It may be a mere possibility. But when it arises, the questions have to be asked: what is the strength of the employers? What pressures could they bring to bear against the staff association? What facilities could they withdraw? [TULRCA s 5] contemplates that the association may be liable to interference arising out of "the provision of financial or material support or by any other means whatsoever".

The employers could take away the four facilities which the Certification Officer mentioned in his reasons. They could take away the facility of time off for meetings. They could take away the facility of free use of office accommodation, and so forth. Those are pressures which the employers could bring to bear on their side. On the other side, this association is rather weak. It has a narrow membership base. It has small financial resources. Weighing the two sides, one against the other, the Certification Officer came to the conclusion that the association was liable to interference in this way: the association was so weak that it was vulnerable, in that it was exposed to the risk of interference tending towards control by the employer.

The Employment Appeal Tribunal reversed the Certification Officer. It seems to me that it misdirected itself. It concentrated too much on the "likelihood of interference" whereas it should have had regard to the "vulnerability to interference". I would therefore allow the appeal and restore the decision of the Certification Officer. . . .'

(Shaw and Brandon LJJ agreed.)

Comment

(1) The main importance of gaining the status of independent trade union is in relation to the rights of recognised trade unions (dealt with in Chapter 5 above), many of which are granted only to independent trade unions.

(2) There are also advantages for workers in that the protection against detriment or dismissal on grounds of union membership or activities applies only to members of independent trade unions (TULRCA ss 146, 152; contrast s 137).

REFERENCES AND FURTHER READING

D Brown and A McColgan (1992), 'UK Employment Law and the ILO: the spirit of co-operation?' 21 ILJ 265

S Corby (1986), 'Limitations on Freedom of Association in the Civil Service and the ILO's response' 15 ILJ 161

B Creighton (1994), 'The ILO and Protection of Freedom of Association in the United Kingdom' in K Ewing, C Gearty and B Hepple (eds), *Human Rights and Labour Law*, Mansell

S Dunn and J Gennard (1984), *The Closed Shop in British Industry*, Macmillan

K Ewing (1994), *Britain and the ILO*, 2nd ed, Institute of Employment Rights

K Ewing (2003), 'The implications of *Wilson and Palmer*' 32 ILJ 1

K Ewing (2007), 'The implications of the *ASLEF* case' 36 ILJ 425

G Morris and T Archer (2000), *Collective Labour Law*, Hart Publishing

T Novitz (1998), 'Freedom of association and Fairness at Work: an assessment of the impact and relevance of ILO Convention No 87 on its fiftieth anniversary' 27 ILJ 169

T Novitz (2000), 'International promises and domestic pragmatism: to what extent will the Employment Relations Act 1999 implement international labour standards relating to freedom of association?' 63 MLR 37

H Pelling (1992), *A History of British Trade Unionism*, 5th ed, Penguin

Lord Wedderburn (1989), 'Freedom of Association and Philosophies of Labour Law' 18 ILJ 1

Lord Wedderburn (1991), 'Freedom of Association or Right to Organise? The Common Law and International Sources' in Wedderburn, *Employment Rights in Britain and Europe*, Lawrence and Wishart

For the Conservative government's arguments on the closed shop during the 1980s, see:

Removing Barriers to Employment, Cm 655 (1989) Chap 2

Trade Unions and Their Members, Cm 95 (1987) Chap 4

Working Paper for Consultations on Proposed Industrial Relations Legislation – Closed Shop (Department of Employment, July 1979)

11

TRADE UNIONS AND THEIR MEMBERS

Usually when you join an organisation, such as a club or a political party or the National Trust, you agree to abide by the rules of that organisation. If you don't like the rules, you have two choices: either don't join, or else join and work from the inside to persuade the necessary majority to your point of view. The law basically keeps out of the affairs of private organisations, except in so far as the law of trusts may regulate their financial affairs.

The position in relation to companies is entirely different. The basic principle behind English company law is that entrepreneurs should be free to get on with their business as they think fit – subject to their accountability to their shareholders. Thus, while the board of directors of a company has great discretion as to what business to pursue and how to pursue it, this is balanced against stringent obligations in relation to the formation and registration of companies, disclosure to shareholders and regular reporting on financial and other matters which are in the public domain.

Should trade unions be treated like private clubs or like companies? In a sense, neither model is wholly appropriate. While a trade union is a voluntary unincorporated association, like a club or a political party, it could be argued that it is too important in working life to be left outside legal regulation; also, it does have quasi-corporate characteristics, as we saw in the last chapter. But the model of the registered company is also inapt: companies are top-down organisations whose members have almost no interest either in its day-to-day affairs or in broad policy-making. Trade unions receive their direction from the grass roots, and members are not only closely involved in making policy, but are also affected by and participate in its day-to-day affairs.

Another important consideration is the requirement in ILO Convention No 87 on Freedom of Association that 'Workers' and employers' organisations shall have the right to draw up their constitution and rules, to elect their representatives in full freedom, to organise their administration and activities and to formulate their programmes' (Art 3, above, p 484). Too much interference by the state in the internal affairs of trade unions may infringe this Convention; this is something to consider particularly in relation to the increase in statutory intervention in trade union government.

In this chapter we will consider the law's regulation of the internal affairs of trade unions in three areas: first, the political activities of trade unions; secondly, common law supervision of trade union rules, and finally, the increasing statutory intervention in the relationship of union and member.

EXPENDITURE FOR POLITICAL PURPOSES

When trade unions were first legalised by the Trade Union Acts 1871–76, nothing was stated about the use of trade union funds for political purposes.

Amalgamated Society of Railway Servants v Osborne
[1910] AC 87 House of Lords

In 1903 the union added to its list of purposes: 'to secure parliamentary representation' and in 1906, it altered its rules to state that candidates sponsored by the union should be subject to the Labour Party whip. Members were to be charged 1 shilling and 1 penny a year towards the parliamentary representation fund. A member challenged the legality of these rules.

LORD ATKINSON: '. . . The contentions relied upon to establish the validity of the impeached rule are, as I understand it, first, that the definition contained in section 16 of the Trade Union Amendment Act of 1876 [definition of a trade union: cf now TULRCA s 1] is not, as it is said, exhaustive, and that therefore a trade union, though registered, may have amongst its objects, in addition to one or more of the objects named in the section, any object whatever not in itself illegal, and accordingly that, provided it be created to effect one or more of the objects named, it is in other respects in the same position as any individual or voluntary association of individuals, and is therefore at liberty to expend its funds to procure the return of members of Parliament, and to maintain them there, as freely as an individual or such an association of individuals is to devote his or its moneys to a like purpose; and, second, that, even if such a union be not free to aim at all legal objects not named in the section, parliamentary representation, on the conditions prescribed in the rule, is the most effective means of attaining the objects which are named, and may therefore be lawfully provided for in the mode prescribed . . .

Now it is not contended that it is a matter of necessity for registered trade unions to secure parliamentary representation on the lines indicated in this rule, or on any other lines. Their whole history refutes such a suggestion. But it is contended that it is only fair to imply that they have this power, because such a representation would afford the most effective means of accomplishing the objects mentioned in section 16, inasmuch as legislation might be introduced to help or hinder them in the prosecution of those objects, and that it is vital to their interests to have in Parliament members in sympathy with their views to support the one form of legislation and to oppose the other; and, further, that they cannot procure the return of such members unless they pay out of their funds the election expenses of chosen candidates, and by the same means maintain them if returned to Parliament.

The answer to that argument is, I think, this. Trade unions are in this respect in precisely the same position as all corporations, municipal or commercial, including in the latter all limited liability companies created under the Companies Act 1862. These bodies, like the trade unions, may by legislation be helped or hindered in carrying out the objects which they were formed to carry out. Their most vital interest may be seriously prejudiced by taxation which the Legislature may impose, or enabling statutes, general in character, may be introduced calculated to enlarge their powers, increase their privileges, or remove restraints upon their action, or again some of them may be under the necessity of promoting private Bills to meet their own special needs. If, despite all this, the intention never has been and cannot be imputed to the Legislature to confer upon such corporations as these power or authority to devote their funds to the procurement of parliamentary representation in the manner in this case contended for, how can such an intention be imputed to it in the case of quasi-corporations such as registered trade unions? And if this intention cannot be imputed to the Legislature in the case of registered trade unions, as in my view it cannot be, there can be no such thing as an implied grant of the desired powers, because an addition to a grant is only introduced by implication in order to carry out the presumed intention of the grantor. During the argument I asked to be informed on what principle the case of registered trade unions was to be differentiated from that of other corporations such as I have named, and why the former were to be permitted, by an alteration of their rules, to convert themselves into political organizations, while a similar privilege was to be denied to the latter. No satisfactory reply was given to me, because none could, I believe, be given. I know of no such principle myself.

It is not disputed that up to 1903, at all events, members of trade unions were not on joining required to subscribe to any political creed, or submit to any political test, no more than are persons who become shareholders in a railway company, and, for all that appears, there may be as great a diversity of political views amongst the members of the one class as of the other. Freedom of opinion was probably permitted amongst the members of both classes because it was not the business of either of the bodies to which they respectively belonged to support particular political parties or to promote a particular political policy. It would be as unjust and oppressive as, in my view, it is illegal to compel, by passing rules such as that impeached, a member of a trade union, who like the respondent joined in the days when freedom of action was permitted, either to contribute to the promotion of a political policy of which he might possibly disapprove, or be expelled from the union to which he belonged for so many years and forfeit all benefit from the money he had subscribed.

I am therefore of opinion that power and authority such as are in this case claimed for the appellants have not been conferred upon them expressly or by implication; that the impeached rule is ultra vires; that the decision appealed from was on this point right and should be upheld, and the appeal dismissed with costs . . .'

(The Earl of Halsbury and Lord Macnaghten delivered concurring speeches. Lord James concurred on a different ground and Lord Shaw expressly refrained from deciding this issue.)

Comment

(1) This decision and *Taff Vale* are probably the most famous cases in the annals of trade union history. Both were regarded as attacks on the trade union movement.

(2) Note the emphasis in the speech on the analogy with the position of registered companies. Yet for many years it was possible for companies to give money for political purposes without any serious suggestion that this was ultra vires. It was not until the Committee on Standards in Public Life, reporting in 1998, recommended that political expenditure should require shareholder approval that action was taken on this. The Political Parties, Elections and Referendums Act 2000 introduced new ss 347A–347K into the Companies Act 1985, making it a requirement for political donations or expenditure to be approved in advance by ordinary resolution. Such a resolution can remain in force for up to four years. When the Companies Act 2006 is brought fully into force, these provisions will be repealed and replaced by ss 362–379 of that Act – which will water down the requirement by allowing retrospective approval by shareholders of unauthorised political donations or expenditure.

(3) The Liberal government of the day took prompt action to reverse the effects of *ASRS v Osborne*. However, trade unions were not given a free hand to use their funds for political purposes, as long as this was within their objects. Rather, the Trade Union Act 1913 required that a separate political fund should be set up and political spending financed from this alone. These requirements were substantially modified by the Trade Union Act 1984. The present law is to be found in TULRCA Chapter VI.

Trade Union and Labour Relations (Consolidation) Act 1992

71 (1) The funds of a trade union shall not be applied in the furtherance of the political objects to which this Chapter applies unless –

(a) there is in force in accordance with this Chapter a resolution (a 'political resolution') approving the furtherance of those objects as an object of the union (see sections 73 to 81), and

(b) there are in force rules of the union as to –

    (i) the making of payments in furtherance of those objects out of a separate fund, and

    (ii) the exemption of any member of the union objecting to contribute to that fund,

which comply with this Chapter (see sections 82, 84 and 85) and have been approved by the Certification Officer . . .

72 (1) The political objects to which this Chapter applies are the expenditure of money –

(a) on any contribution to the funds of, or on the payment of expenses incurred directly or indirectly by, a political party;

(b) on the provision of any service or property for use by or on behalf of any political party;

(c) in connection with the registration of electors, the candidature of any person, the selection of any candidate or the holding of any ballot by the union in connection with any election to a political office;

(d) on the maintenance of any holder of a political office;

(e) on the holding of any conference or meeting by or on behalf of a political party or of any other meeting the main purpose of which is the transaction of business in connection with a political party;

(f) on the production, publication or distribution of any literature, document, film, sound recording or advertisement the main purpose of which is to persuade people to vote for a political party or candidate or to persuade them not to vote for a political party or candidate.

(2) Where a person attends a conference or meeting as a delegate or otherwise as a participator in the proceedings, any expenditure incurred in connection with his attendance as such shall, for the purposes of subsection (1)(e), be taken to be expenditure incurred on the holding of the conference or meeting . . .

73 (1) A political resolution must be passed by a majority of those voting on a ballot of the members of the trade union held in accordance with this Chapter.

(2) A political resolution so passed shall take effect as if it were a rule of the union and may be rescinded in the same manner and subject to the same provisions as such a rule.

(3) If not previously rescinded, a political resolution shall cease to have effect at the end of the period of ten years beginning with the date of the ballot on which it was passed . . .

Comment

(1) The requirement that there should be a re-ballot every ten years was introduced by the Trade Union Act 1984 in such a way that all unions which had a political fund at that time (most of which had been set up shortly after 1913) had to re-ballot within a year. All were endorsed by the members, and this has continued in subsequent re-ballots. This led the Better Regulation Task Force (set up in 1997 to advise the government on ways of reducing the burden of regulation) to suggest that the requirement should be repealed, given the costs involved in balloting. However, in its 2003 review of the operation of the Employment Relations Act 1999, the government decided not to change this.

(2) Members who are against the political fund in effect get counted twice: they can vote against setting up the fund in the ballot but, even if the ballot goes against them, they can choose not to contribute to the fund (TULRCA s 71(1)(b)(ii)).

(3) The secret ballot on establishing the political fund or continuing it must be conducted according to rules approved by the Certification Officer (TULRCA s 74) and must be fully postal (that is, ballot papers sent out and returned by post) (TULRCA s 77). There must be an independent, qualified scrutineer, whose name must appear on the ballot paper (TULRCA ss 75, 77(2)). All members of the union must be given the right to vote (TULRCA s 76). The scrutineer's report on the ballot, including information on the number of ballot papers sent out, votes, spoiled papers and so on, must be sent to all members (TULRCA s 76). A member who thinks that the ballot has been conducted in breach of these requirements may make an application to the Certification Officer or to the court (TULRCA ss 80, 81).

(4) The list of political objects which can only be financed out of the political fund was extended by the Trade Union Act 1984. Any activity which is outside the political objects can be financed from the union's general funds. However, if an activity is within the political objects, a union which does not have a political fund is prohibited from spending any money on it.

Paul and Fraser v *National and Local Government Officers' Association* [1987] IRLR 413 Chancery Division

NALGO ran a campaign called 'Make People Matter' in 1987 (which was designated by the TUC as Public Services Year). The campaign highlighted cuts in public services. Two members of the union claimed that the expenditure on the campaign was unlawful because the union did not have a political fund.

BROWNE-WILKINSON V-C: '. . . The next leaflets were not issued to the public until April of this year, that is to say a month before the local government elections. They each deal with a separate topic or sector of public service. The first says, "Decent public services make all the difference." On the back it says, "I used to catch a bus to the shops. Now I have to walk to the shops to get a bus." Then it refers to "cut-backs in day centres and the number of home helps make it harder for elderly people to cope . . . sheltered housing for those who need it has been cut too. More than 36,000 National Health Service beds – one in 10 of the total – have been cut since 1979. People are waiting longer and longer for treatment – some die before they reach the top of the queue." In another passage it refers to "private contractors, encouraged by the Government to compete to run services, cut corners in order to cut costs". Then they refer to it being a time to invest, and at one point say, "Spending on health and education creates five times as many jobs as tax cuts." At the bottom it says, "You have a voice. You have a vote. Make people matter." In a box against a pink background the nature of NALGO is described, and this passage (which also appears in all subsequent leaflets) appears: "NALGO is not affiliated to any political party and is not seeking or opposing the election of any particular candidate or group of candidates. NALGO is campaigning so people can judge for themselves how important our public services are – to themselves and to the country as a whole." I will refer to that as "the disclaimer". The next leaflet is headed on its front, "Getting the truth behind the promises. Questions to ask before you vote." At the back it starts: "It's election time! On 7 May council elections take place." It goes on to say that "every party will claim they are determined to improve your local services, and that the others have got it wrong. So who's telling the truth?" Then there are a number of specimen questions which the elector is invited to ask his candidate. "If I vote for you, will you publicly support the case for more investment in the NHS, public education, low-cost housing and public transport?" . . .

The question is not whether the purposes being pursued by NALGO in this campaign are political; by any conceivable standard they are obviously political. The question is whether they are involved in the publication and distribution of literature, the main purpose of which is to persuade people not to vote for a political party.

The claimants' case is that this literature, read in its context, can only be read as an attempt to persuade people to vote against the Conservative Party. I would for myself emphasise in (f) the use of the words "to vote for or not to vote for". A crucial feature of any political purpose within [TULRCA s 72(1)(f)] is an element of persuasion to vote. Mere persuasion of people's minds to a particular viewpoint unconnected with the exercise of a vote at an election is not covered by this. What is precluded is the attempt to persuade somebody to exercise a vote one way or the other. I am not dealing with a case where there is a publicity campaign disconnected from an election and without an invitation to vote. The facts of this case are much nearer the line than that. What the claimants have to show is that the *main* purpose was to persuade people not to vote for a particular party, namely the Conservative Party . . .

. . . I will now turn to consider the literature which is complained of in this case, the effect of which I have sought to summarise. I have no doubt whatsoever that one purpose of the literature, particularly the leaflets, is to persuade people not to vote for the Conservative Party. The burden of the literature is to criticise the record of the Conservative Government which is said to be the run-down of the public services. That censure on the Conservative Government is confined to the Conservative Government. Though Mr Monks said, as I am sure is the case, that NALGO have been complaining of government cut-backs since before 1979, it is notable that in no place in the literature is any reference made to any cut-backs earlier than 1979. Each leaflet refers to the Conservative Government only and each leaflet refers to its policies and the implementation of its policies unfavourably. It does not refer to any other government critically or unfavourably, and it contains nothing critical of any other party. What is more, it takes matters of policy which are known to be Conservative Party policy, such as privatisation, and decries them.

The leaflets then go on, having given that one-sided view of the effect of the Conservative policy and its non-coincidence with NALGO policy, to invite the electorate to think and then to vote. Every one of the leaflets complained of expressly invites the member receiving the leaflet to vote. The inference to my mind from the leaflet itself is really overwhelming. It says that the Government's policies since 1979 are bad, you have to think about it, and having thought about it you have to vote. The only rational message to be drawn from that is, "'If you accept the message of the leaflet vote against the Conservatives."

Each leaflet contains the disclaimer, saying we are not inviting you to vote this way or that. I think where a message is as clear as this one a disclaimer of that kind is no more effective to avoid liability than is a disclaimer where in a libel case it is said that nobody in this book bears any resemblance to anybody in real life. It is not effective to escape liability once one looks at the purpose of the document as a whole. Therefore I have no doubt that one purpose of the literature was to persuade people to vote against the Conservative Party . . .

To sum up, in my judgment what we have here is literature which gives one side of the political argument. It attributes a bad record to the Conservative Party (admittedly indirectly by calling it the Government). That literature is then timed to be published at the time of an election. The same literature invites people to vote, taking into account the one-sided version of the issues involved. In those circumstances it seems to me impossible to say that the main purpose was not to influence the voting. While I have no explanation as to how the reference to voting crept in the fact is that it did. In those circumstances in my judgment the expenditure was unlawful as being in breach of [TULRCA s 71] . . .

Finally I would like to say that nothing in this judgment should be taken as suggesting that a publicity campaign organised by a union at times other than an election and therefore at a time when neither directly nor indirectly can the union be inviting anybody to exercise a vote at the time, is unlawful, merely because it expresses disapproval of the Government's policy. Unions, like anybody else, are entitled to disapprove of government policy and to say so. The vice in this case to my mind is that they have linked this disapproval in a biased way with an invitation to vote at the time of an election . . .'

Comment

(1) Despite the statement in the last paragraph extracted, this judgment alarmed unions representing workers in the public sector and persuaded many that they needed to set up political funds in order to be able to campaign around issues of government policy affecting their members.

(2) Union members who opt out of paying the political subscription are protected from discrimination on that account by TULRCA s 82, which states that they shall not on that account be disadvantaged or excluded from any office, except in relation to the management or control of the political fund. The scope of this was tested in the next case.

Birch v National Union of Railwaymen [1950] Ch 602 Chancery Division

Rule 21(8) of the defendant union provided that members who did not contribute to the political fund would not be under any disability compared with other members, except that they could take no part in the control or management of that fund and would be ineligible for any office involving such control or management. The union's rules had been approved by the Registrar in this form.

Birch, who contracted out of contributing to the political fund, had been elected as branch chairman. The general secretary of the union ruled that he was ineligible for this office because it inevitably involved management of the political fund. Birch sought a declaration that this was in breach of the Act.

DANCKWERTS J: '. . . It is to be observed that, when first read, the rule appears to follow the requirements of that paragraph and confine discrimination and ineligibility to positions involving control or management of the political fund, which is the exception mentioned in the paragraph. It is not until it is discovered that an exempted member is disqualified from holding the office of chairman because that office involves control or management of the political fund as well as the general fund, that doubts begin to arise.

Sir Walter Monckton [counsel for the union] contended (as I understood his argument) that (1) as a matter of practical administration of the affairs of the branch it is necessary to combine the control and management of the general fund and the political fund in the hands of the same officials of the branch, and (2) accordingly, the exempted member must suffer the disability or disadvantage of exclusion from office by reason of the exception permitting disability or disadvantage where the control or management of the political fund is involved. There is, he said, no provision confining the exception to functions concerned with control or management of the political fund. This is an ingenious argument, but be it observed that the effect is to exclude an exempted member from any part in the affairs of his branch as an officer or a representative by reason of the fact that the same persons administer (as the rules are constituted) both the general and the political funds. This appears to me to be equivalent to the exception swallowing the provisions of [TULRCA s 82(1)(c)] which were primarily designed to prevent disability from being imposed on the exempted member. In other words, as long as the constitution of the union fails to separate the control and management of the political fund from other functions of the union, there is no limit to the area of the exception and an exempted member might find himself excluded from practically all the activities of his branch. I cannot believe that this is the result of an exception introduced into a provision designed to protect the exempted member. It is entirely reasonable that a non-contributor should be excluded from control or management of the political fund; it is quite another matter that he should be excluded from any office in his union or branch.

I reach the conclusion, therefore, that rule 21 (8) in conjunction with the other rules of the union, offends against the provisions of [TULRCA s 82(1)(c)] . . .'

Comment

(1) It appears from this that unions must take steps to ensure that control of the political fund is completely separate from any other office within the union.

(2) Members of the union must be informed what amount is payable to the political fund (TULRCA s 85). It remains the case that members must opt out of payment (rather than opting in if they want to make political contributions), so the forces of inertia favour the political fund. However, members are reminded of their right to opt out every time the political fund resolution comes up for renewal (TULRCA s 84(2)).

(3) Where the employer automatically deducts the employee's union subscription from pay and forwards it directly to the union (the check-off system), the employee may at any time give notice of exemption of liability to pay and the employer must implement this at once (TULRCA s 86). However, such a member remains liable to the union to pay the political subscription for the rest of the calendar year, unless she has opted out within a month of the original political resolution ballot (TULRCA s 84(4)). It will be virtually impossible for the union to collect in these circumstances.

(4) Employers may not deduct union subscriptions from pay (whether or not including the political contribution) without express authorisation in writing from the union member (TULRCA s 68). In 1993 TURERA altered the law so that such an authorisation would lapse after three years unless renewed (a requirement repealed in 1998 by the Deregulation (Deduction from Pay of Union Subscriptions) Order). The Conservative government at the time clearly hoped that this would undermine the check-off system. It did, but probably not in the way the government intended. Many unions persuaded their members to pay union subscriptions by direct debit instead. This has two major advantages for the union: first, it means that the employer cannot identify union members simply by looking at payroll information; secondly, it means that the union still gets its subscriptions even if the member is not being paid (eg, because he is on strike).

UNION RULES AT COMMON LAW

The rules of a trade union form a contract between the union and the member. There are two major ways in which the courts have exercised control over union rules: first, in relation to their interpretation; secondly, in insisting that the rules of natural justice apply in this situation.

Interpretation of the rule book

The often-quoted words of Lord Wilberforce should be borne in mind from the outset.

Heatons Transport v Transport and General Workers' Union
[1973] AC 15 House of Lords

The issue was the extent of shop stewards' authority under the rules of the trade union.

LORD WILBERFORCE: '. . . Turning now, first, to the rules: the original source of the shop stewards' authority is the agreement entered into by each member by joining the Transport and General Workers' Union. By that agreement each member joins with all other members in authorising specified persons or classes of persons to do particular kinds of acts on behalf of all the members, who are hereafter referred to collectively as the union. The basic terms of that agreement are to be found in the union's rule book. But trade union rule books are not drafted by parliamentary draftsmen. Courts of law must resist the temptation to construe them as if they were, for that is not how they would be understood by the members who are the parties to the agreement of which the terms, or some of them, are set out in the rule book, nor how they would be, and in fact were, understood by the experienced members of the court. Furthermore, it is not to be assumed, as in the case of a commercial contract which has been reduced into writing, that all the terms of the agreement are to be found in the rule book alone: particularly as respects the discretion conferred by the members upon committees or officials of the union as to the way in which they may act on the union's behalf. What the members understand as to the characteristics of the agreement into which they enter by joining a union is well stated in the section of the TUC Handbook on the Industrial Relations Act which gives advice about the content and operation of unions' rules. Paragraph 99 reads as follows:

"Trade union government does not however rely solely on what is written down in the rule book. It also depends upon custom and practice, by procedures which have developed over the years and which, although well understood by those who operate them, are not formally set out in the rules. Custom and practice may operate either by modifying a union's rules as they operate in practice, or by compensating for the absence of formal rules. Furthermore, the procedures which custom and practice lays down very often vary from workplace to workplace within the same industry, and even within different branches of the same union."'

Comment

(1) In the past few decades trade union rule books have been much revised and the effects of statute are such that custom and practice may have less of a place than once was the case. However, in an important modern decision *Heatons Transport v TGWU* (1973) was relied on to support a finding that the union had an *implied* power to discipline and expel members.

McVitae v Unison [1996] IRLR 33 Chancery Division

Unison came into existence on 1 July 1993 on the amalgamation of three public sector unions: COHSE, NALGO and NUPE. The four claimants, members of Unison, had previously been members of the Liverpool branch of NALGO. At the time of the amalgamation they were subject to internal disciplinary proceedings, which had not been completed, concerning allegations that they were guilty of intimidation and sexual harassment of other union members. After the amalgamation they were charged with offences under the Unison rule book instead. They argued that it was beyond the powers of Unison to take this disciplinary action against them in respect of events which occurred when they were NALGO members, because there was no rule which permitted this. The union argued, *inter alia*, for an implied rule to that effect.

HARRISON J: '. . . The main thrust of the argument between the parties centred on whether a disciplinary power relating to pre-inception conduct could be implied into the contract between the Unison members. If such a term were not to be implied there would, in effect, be an amnesty for all offences committed before the vesting day but which had not by that date resulted in a penalty being imposed . . .

Mr King drew my attention to the following passage in *Harvey on Industrial Relations and Employment Law*, volume II, paragraph M 2652, where it is stated:

"The power of a union to discipline a member depends upon the express terms of the rule-book. A power to discipline or expel will not be implied."

Three authorities are quoted for those propositions: *Dawkins* v *Antrobus* (1881), *Abbott* v *Sullivan* (1952) and *Spring* v *National Amalgamated Stevedores' and Dockers' Society* (1956). Mr Langstaff QC, who appeared on behalf of the defendant, submitted that the three cases are not authority for the propositions quoted in *Harvey*.

Mr King, on the other hand, told me that he had not been able to find any case where the court had implied a power to discipline. He reminded me that the evidence on behalf of the claimants was that if the charges were proved against them they may be deprived of their jobs and it would have a serious effect on their personal reputations and their future employability. He therefore relied on the following passage in the judgment of Sedley J:

". . . where disciplinary proceedings are concerned there is a limit to the amount of relaxation which the courts are prepared to allow of the close reading of their provisions. The reason for this is equally obvious: such provisions within the domestic context of a trade union are truly penal and need to be therefore read down rather than up and read with caution rather than with excessive liberality. This is a balance, therefore, that needs to be argued out at trial more fully than has been possible or appropriate today."

. . . Mr Langstaff submitted that common sense dictated that Unison should have the power to discipline, for instance, a dishonest official whose financial irregularity had come to light after the vesting day. He suggested that Sedley J, when dealing with that situation, had not dealt with the real purpose of the disciplinary rules, which is not to punish or to recover money but to regulate the people who are entitled to be members and officers of the union.

So far as the law is concerned, Mr Langstaff relied in particular on the well-known passage in the judgment of MacKinnon LJ, in *Shirlaw* v *Southern Foundries (1926) Ltd* (1939) when he stated:

"Prima facie that which in any contract is left to be implied and need not be expressed is something so obvious that it goes without saying; so that, if, while the parties were making their bargain, an officious bystander were to suggest some express provision for it in their agreement, they would testily suppress him with a common 'Oh, of course!'"

Reliance was also placed on the words of Lord Wilberforce in *Liverpool City Council* v *Irwin* (1977) when, in dealing with implied terms, he said:

"The present case, in my opinion, represents a fourth category, or I would rather say a fourth shade on a continuous spectrum. The court here is simply concerned to establish what the contract is, the parties not having themselves fully stated the terms. In this sense, the court is searching for what must be implied."

Mr Langstaff submitted that, whether it was the *Moorcock* test, the officious bystander test or Lord Wilberforce's test, the power of Unison to discipline members for pre-inception conduct complied with it. It was, he said, necessary to have an implied term for enabling Unison to have such a power, otherwise how else, he asked, could it discipline or expel a dishonest or racist member for conduct before the vesting day? . . .

I should say straight away that I recognise the force of the arguments that have been raised by both sides on the jurisdiction point. It is a difficult issue with much to be said on both sides. The starting point, it seems to me, must be to consider whether the statement in *Harvey on Industrial Relations and Employment Law* that a power of a union to discipline or expel a member will not be implied is correct because, if it is, it would effectively dispose of the point. I have considered those three cases cited in support of that proposition but I am not satisfied that they are authority for such a widely stated proposition. In the case of *Dawkins* v *Antrobus* the Court of Appeal refused to interfere with a decision of a members' club expelling a member from the club. I do not find anything in the judgments in the Court of Appeal in that case to justify the general assertion that a power to discipline or expel will not be implied. In the case of *Abbott* v *Sullivan* a committee of corn porters, which had no written constitution, resolved to remove the claimant's name from the register of corn porters for striking a trade union official. The Court of Appeal held that the resolution was invalid because there was no evidence of a contract, express or implied, to show that they had jurisdiction to take that action. In deciding whether or not the claimant could claim damages from members of the committee, the court, Denning LJ dissenting, held that there could not be implied a contract between the claimant and the committee that the members of the committee would not do anything which was beyond their jurisdiction. The claimant was not therefore entitled to claim damages for breach of contract. I do not find that case to be authority for the general proposition that there can be no implied power to discipline a trade union member. It was a case decided on its own facts involving a committee which had no written constitution but which existed as a matter of custom and practice.

Finally, in the case of *Spring* v *National Amalgamated Stevedores' and Dockers' Society* the claimant's union excluded him from membership of the union as a result of an award by the Trades Union Congress that the union should exclude those members, including the claimant, who had been admitted to the union in breach of the Bridlington Agreement dealing with the relationship between trade unions. The court refused to imply a term of the claimant's contract of membership of the union that the union should have the right to do anything necessary and proper to comply with the Bridlington Agreement because the claimant did not know of the Bridlington Agreement when he became a member of the union. Furthermore the Agreement contained no rules about what a trade union member should do or abstain from doing and it contained no power of expulsion. That again was a case decided on its own particular facts which I do not read as laying down any general proposition that there can be no implied power to discipline or expel.

I therefore conclude that the statement in *Harvey on Industrial Relations and Employment Law* that a power of a union to discipline or expel a member will not be implied is too broadly stated and is not supported by the three cases which are cited as authority for it. In my view, the court can imply such a disciplinary power, although the court's power to do so is one which should be exercised with care and only where there are compelling circumstances to justify it. The reason why the court should be slow to imply a disciplinary power is that it is penal and could include serious consequences affecting the reputation and livelihood of the union member . . .

Having decided that, as a matter of principle, the court can imply a power by a union to discipline a member, the next question is whether in the particular circumstances of this case, there can be implied a power by the defendant to discipline the claimants for their alleged conduct occurring before the amalgamation.

It is quite clear from the evidence that although there were extensive negotiations between the amalgamating unions prior to the amalgamation, the Unison rulebook did not cover all matters covering the relationship between the union and its members. In a complex amalgamation involving three large unions I do not find that surprising. The evidence showed that there were various matters, including the continuation in office of the shop stewards and branch secretaries after the vesting day, the continuation of representation and legal assistance and the inclusion of membership of a member's former union as qualifying for a member's benefits, which were not included in the Unison rulebook but which were to be implied because they were generally assumed to be authorised. It is therefore clear that the Unison rulebook does not contain the whole of the contract between the union and its members. The principle of some terms being implied must therefore be accepted. There is nothing unusual in that, as can be seen from the case of *Heatons Transport* v *TGWU*.

It is clear that the existence of an implied power to discipline for pre-inception conduct must depend on the presumed intention of the parties . . .

I cannot conceive that it was intended that there should be a complete amnesty for pre-inception conduct. There is certainly no evidence of such an intention and common sense suggests that it would not have been intended. It offends against common sense that a member who has, for instance, done something dishonest before amalgamation which contravenes both the rules of his former union and the rules of Unison should escape penalty simply as a result of the amalgamation. As a responsible union, Unison would be just as intent on ensuring that such conduct was disciplined as would have been the former union. It is not in the interests of Unison that they should be unable to regulate their membership or the holding of office in such circumstances. In my judgment, it would have been the expectation of members in such circumstances that the union should be able to take disciplinary action. If they had been asked about it, they would have said that it was so obvious that it must have been intended to form part of the agreement between Unison and its members.

Such a conclusion does not cause any prejudice to the claimants because they would have been subject to the disciplinary proceedings anyway under the Nalgo rules if the amalgamation had not taken place. A contrary conclusion would have meant that they would have been the lucky beneficiaries of a technicality. Those considerations in themselves are relevant to what must be presumed to have been the intention of members of the union.

Although, as I have said, the court should be slow to imply disciplinary powers, it should equally be slow to reach a decision which, on the face of it, is contrary to what both the members and common sense would have expected. I have come to the conclusion, for the reasons that I have given, that the particular circumstances of this case are sufficiently compelling to warrant a disciplinary power being implied in relation to pre-inception conduct . . .'

Comment

(1) This case bucks the trend of judicial decisions on the interpretation of union rules, especially those relating to discipline and expulsion, where the tendency is usually to construe the rules very strictly. It also illustrates the continuing relevance of the common law in this area, despite increased statutory regulation.

(2) In *AB* v *CD* (2001) the issue was how to resolve a tie in votes for a union post produced by the single transferable vote (STV) system. The union's rules were silent on the matter, but the Electoral Reform Society (who acted as the union's election scrutineer) had published rules saying that, in these circumstances, the candidate who scored the highest number of votes in an earlier round should be elected, and this was stated also in a paper produced by the union's Standing Orders Committee. In these circumstances, the High Court held that such a term could be implied into the union's

contract with its members, on the basis that the contract would otherwise be incomplete – similar reasoning to that employed in *McVitae* v *Unison*. However, an argument that the rule could be implied on the basis of custom and practice was rejected because the practice was not well known among the general membership.

(3) As the rules constitute a contract, the courts have the opportunity to say what the contract means.

Lee v Showmen's Guild of Great Britain [1952] 2 QB 329 Court of Appeal

A dispute arose between Lee and another member of the union as to which of them was entitled to a particular site at Bradford Fair for his Noah's Ark roundabout. An internal committee decided in favour of the other member but Lee refused to accept this and took the site instead. The union committee then found Lee guilty of unfair competition contrary to the union's rules and fined him £100. Lee sought to challenge this by way of an action for a declaration.

DENNING LJ: 'The jurisdiction of a domestic tribunal, such as the committee of the Showmen's Guild, must be founded on a contract, express or implied. Outside the regular courts of this country, no set of men can sit in judgment on their fellows except so far as Parliament authorises it or the parties agree to it. The jurisdiction of the committee of the Showmen's Guild is contained in a written set of rules to which all the members subscribe. This set of rules contains the contract between the members and is just as much subject to the jurisdiction of these courts as any other contract . . .

Although the jurisdiction of a domestic tribunal is founded on contract, express or implied, nevertheless the parties are not free to make any contract they like. There are important limitations imposed by public policy. The tribunal must, for instance, observe the principles of natural justice. They must give the man notice of the charge and a reasonable opportunity of meeting it. Any stipulation to the contrary would be invalid. They cannot stipulate for a power to condemn a man unheard. That appears, I think, from the judgments of Brett LJ in *Dawkins* v *Antrobus* (1881), of Kelly CB in *Wood* v *Woad* (1874) and of Lord Birkenhead LC in *Weinberger* v *Inglis* (1919), which are to be preferred to the dictum of Maugham J in *Maclean* v *The Workers' Union* (1929) to the contrary. Another limitation arises out of the well-known principle that parties cannot by contract oust the ordinary courts from their jurisdiction: see *Scott* v *Avery* (1856), *per* Alderson B and Lord Cranworth LC. They can, of course, agree to leave questions of law, as well as questions of fact, to the decision of the domestic tribunal. They can, indeed, make the tribunal the final arbiter on questions of fact, but they cannot make it the final arbiter on questions of law. They cannot prevent its decisions being examined by the courts. If parties should seek, by agreement, to take the law out of the hands of the courts and put it into the hands of a private tribunal, without any recourse at all to the courts in case of error of law, then the agreement is to that extent contrary to public policy and void.

The question in this case is: to what extent will the courts examine the decisions of domestic tribunals on points of law? This is a new question which is not to be solved by turning to the club cases. In the case of social clubs, the rules usually empower the committee to expel a member who, in their opinion, has been guilty of conduct detrimental to the club; and this is a matter of opinion and nothing else. The courts have no wish to sit on appeal from their decisions on such a matter any more than from the decisions of a family conference. They have nothing to do with social rights or social duties. On any expulsion they will see that there is fair play. They will see that the man has notice of the charge and a reasonable opportunity of being heard. They will see that the committee observe the procedure laid down by the rules; but they will not otherwise interfere: see *Labouchere* v *Earl of Wharncliffe* (1879) and *Dawkins* v *Antrobus*.

It is very different with domestic tribunals which sit in judgment on the members of a trade or profession. They wield powers as great as, if not greater than, any exercised by the courts of law. They can deprive a man of his livelihood. They can ban him from the trade in which he has spent his life and which is the only trade he knows. They are usually empowered to do this for any breach of their rules, which, be it noted, are rules which they impose and which he has no real opportunity of accepting or rejecting. In theory their powers are based on contract. The man is supposed to have contracted to give them these great powers; but in practice he has no choice in the matter. If he is to engage in the trade, he has to submit to the rules promulgated by the committee. Is such a tribunal to be treated by these courts on the same footing as a social club? I say no. A man's right to work is just as important to him as, if not more important than, his rights of property. These courts intervene every day to protect rights of property. They must also intervene to protect the right to work.

But the question still remains: to what extent will the courts intervene? They will, I think, always be prepared to examine the decision to see that the tribunal has observed the law. This includes the correct interpretation of the rules. Let me give an illustration. If a domestic tribunal is given power by the rules to expel a member for misconduct, such as here for "unfair competition", does that mean that the tribunal is the sole judge of what constitutes unfair competition? Suppose it puts an entirely wrong construction on the words "unfair competition" and finds a member guilty of it when no reasonable person could so find, has not the man a remedy? I think that he has, for the simple reason that he has only agreed to the committee exercising jurisdiction according to the true interpretation of the rules, and not according to a wrong interpretation . . .

My conclusion, therefore, is that the court has power in this case to intervene in the decision of the committee of the Showmen's Guild if no facts were adduced before them which could reasonably be considered to be "unfair competition" within rule 15 (c), which says that "no member of the guild shall indulge in unfair competition with regard to the renting, taking, or letting of ground or position". The facts are not in dispute. In May, 1949, the claimant and Shaw applied to the Bradford Corporation for a site on the fair ground for the Bradford Moor Fair. No allocations were made by the corporation before the two showmen arrived on the ground; but when they got there, the best position was allotted to the claimant. Shaw then claimed that, in accordance with a previous ruling of the guild, he was entitled to the position. The corporation thought that the claimant was entitled to it, but they were quite ready to allow the showmen to decide between themselves: but the claimant said that, as the corporation had allotted it to him, he was going to stand on it. The judge held that there was nothing of "unfair competition" in the claimant's conduct, and I agree with him. It may have been very reprehensible of him not to abide by the previous ruling of the guild. He should have given way to Shaw: but he can hardly be said to have been guilty of unfair competition. There was no undercutting or anything of that sort. He only accepted the position allotted to him and stood on it. Inasmuch as the facts are not reasonably capable of being "unfair competition" it follows that the committee had no jurisdiction to find him guilty of it . . .'

(Somervell and Romer LJJ delivered concurring judgments.)

Comment

(1) This is a classic Denning judgment, where the higher the principles expressed, the greater the novelty of the point being argued for. It is interesting to contrast the wide scope the court here claims for its powers to review the decision of a union committee compared with the infinitely more limited powers of an employment tribunal to review an employer's decision to dismiss and of the EAT to review the decision of an employment tribunal (see p 389, above).

(2) Note that there are several grounds on which intervention by the court is said to be justified: the other grounds will be examined later. The principal justification given, however, is the risk of loss of livelihood if a union member is expelled. It is worth noting that this risk is minimal today, as the closed shop may no longer be legally enforced. There are other reasons for belonging to a trade union, such as participation in collective bargaining, which would justify at least some control over a union's powers of discipline and expulsion, but it may be doubted whether the stark contrast drawn in the judgment between trade unions and social clubs is entirely justified. After all, many people join social clubs as much to gain some kind of business or social advantage as to enjoy the company of other members, and loss of membership may be extremely damaging to their professional reputation. Could it be that judges in 1952 – and even 50 and 60 years later – have more confidence in the kind of chaps who are members of the committees of social clubs?

Leigh v National Union of Railwaymen [1970] Ch 326 Chancery Division

The claimant's nomination for election as president of the union was rejected by the general secretary on the grounds that he was not a member of the Labour Party as required by the union rules. When the claimant challenged this decision, the union argued, among other things, that he had no right to take legal proceedings without exhausting internal remedies first.

GOFF J: '. . . Next, it was submitted on behalf of the defendants that the claimant is not entitled to relief because he has not exhausted or, indeed, embarked upon the domestic remedies afforded by the rules. On this point I extract from *White v Kuzych* in the Privy Council, and *Lawlor v Union of Post Office Workers* in this court, two propositions. The first is that even where there is an express provision in the rules that the claimant must first exhaust his domestic remedies, the court is not absolutely bound by that because its jurisdiction cannot be ousted but the claimant will have to show cause why it should interfere with the contractual position. This is consonant with the rule in the case of a submission to arbitration where the court always has a discretion whether to stay an action but cause must be shown why it should not. The second proposition is largely the converse of the first, namely, that in the absence of such a provision the court can readily, or at all events more readily grant relief without prior recourse to the domestic remedies, but may require the claimant to resort first to those remedies. Thus, in *Lawlor's* case Ungoed-Thomas J said,

> "Trade union rules clearly cannot oust the jurisdiction of the courts. Contracts, including a contract constituted by trade union rules, may provide that recourse to domestic tribunals shall be exhausted before there is recourse to the courts, and the courts may recognise and give effect to that contract; but that does not oust its jurisdiction. So in this case, the court has jurisdiction, and here there is no contractual provision requiring domestic remedies to be exhausted before resort to the courts. Should that jurisdiction be exercised now, or should it be withheld, in the circumstances, pending appeal to annual conference?
>   This case involves the construction of the rules of the trade union, and it is for the courts, and not a domestic body, to decide questions of construction, as matters of law. It involves questions of natural justice, which again are matters for the courts to decide."

The claimant's counsel concedes that he cannot, on the evidence on this motion, show cause why an express provision, if there be one, requiring that domestic remedies should be first utilised should be disregarded, and the defendants submit that the rules, and in particular rules 3(6) and 9(4), have that effect. I must therefore first determine whether this is so, and

I am not prepared to accept that submission. The rules purport to exclude the jurisdiction of the court altogether and to that extent are void on the authority of *Lee v Showmen's Guild of Great Britain*, but that is no reason for construing them as requiring recourse to the domestic tribunal first. The two things are inconsistent.

Then ought I, notwithstanding the absence of such a provision, to refuse relief because the domestic remedies have not been adopted? In my judgment, on the facts of this case, I ought not. It is true that *Lawlor's* case was one of expulsion and infringement of the rules of natural justice, and is therefore much stronger than the present. On the other hand, this is at least one of refusing the opportunity of election to an office of honour and profit, and it is one turning on construction, which, as Ungoed-Thomas J observed in the passage I have quoted, is peculiarly appropriate for the court. Moreover, having regard to the union's decision in Bowman's case, the claimant could not reasonably expect to succeed, if at all, by the domestic remedies, short of an appeal to the annual general meeting, which would have meant driving the matter up to the very meeting at which the election should take place, and so have left him virtually no chance of obtaining relief through the court until after the election. This would not, as a matter of law, prevent him from obtaining relief at all, because he could apply to set it aside and for an injunction restraining the union and the successful candidate from acting on the vote, but it might well prejudice his position in fact on a subsequent election.'

Comment

(1) There is now a limitation on rules requiring internal procedures to be exhausted first. If the member makes an application to the union and the matter is not wrapped up within six months, the member is entitled to go to the court without further delay (TULRCA s 63, introduced originally by the Employment Act 1988).

(2) It is no longer possible for the rules of a trade union to require that the president, general secretary or any member of the principal executive committee of the union should belong to a particular political party; however, it is possible to prescribe that they must *not* be members of a particular party or parties (TULRCA s 47, introduced by the Trade Union Act 1984).

Natural justice

The rules of natural justice have been developed in public law to lay down minimum standards of procedural justice for bodies carrying out quasi-judicial functions. There are essentially two elements: first, that you should know the charge against you and have an opportunity to counter it; secondly, that the body making the decision should be unbiased.

Stevenson v United Road Transport Union [1977] ICR 893
Court of Appeal

The claimant, a member of the union, was appointed as regional officer for an indefinite period from 1970. In 1974, friction arose between him and other officers and members of the union. It resulted in the general secretary writing to him on 10 June suspending him on full pay until a disciplinary hearing to be held on 9 July. The letter stated that the disciplinary hearing would be about allegations of non-co-operation and failure to carry out instructions contained in a report by the officer to whom he was responsible.

The union declined to send him a copy of the relevant report, saying that he knew what it was about. At the disciplinary hearing, at which the claimant was not permitted legal representation, the charges were presented. The claimant asked for a copy in writing in order to prepare his defence, and made no attempt at that hearing to give his side of the story. The committee nevertheless decided to serve him with three months' notice of termination.

Although the claimant was an employee of the union, he was also a member of it, and the court considered that the rules of natural justice applied.

BUCKLEY LJ: '. . . So, in our judgment, the learned judge was right in his conclusion that the executive committee was bound to comply with the rules of natural justice. He went on to consider whether they had sufficiently done so. He rejected a suggestion by the claimant that the committee were biased against him. This is not an issue on this appeal.

Mr Rose [counsel for the union] has submitted that cases to which the rules of natural justice apply can be divided into three categories: (1) cases in which the rules may be said to apply in their full rigour, so that the accused party is entitled to notice and full particulars of the charges against him, perhaps with discovery, and to a hearing with or without witnesses, and perhaps with professional representation; (2) cases in which the accused party is merely entitled to an opportunity to state his own case; and (3) cases in which the only requirement is that the tribunal must act fairly, honestly and without bias. It is true that what natural justice requires may vary according to the circumstances of each case, but we think that it is undesirable to attempt to classify them. In *Russell* v *Duke of Norfolk* (1949) Tucker LJ said:

> "The requirements of natural justice must depend on the circumstances of the case, the nature of the inquiry, the rules under which the tribunal is acting, the subject-matter that is being dealt with, and so forth. Accordingly, I do not derive much assistance from the definitions of natural justice which have been from time to time used, but, whatever standard is adopted, one essential is that the person concerned should have a reasonable opportunity of presenting his case. I think from first to last the claimant did have such an opportunity."

We gratefully adopt that statement. A case may be of so uncomplex a character and the issues may be so well known to all parties concerned that no more particular notice of any charges may be required, an opportunity for the party of whom complaint is made to state his case being sufficient. *Russell* v *Duke of Norfolk* was such a case: but the present one is not, for the learned judge found as a fact that on 9 July 1974 the claimant did not know, when the hearing began, what charges were to be made against him. Mr Rose accepted in this court that what occurred at the meeting between Mr Moore and the claimant on 23 May 1974 was not enough to tell the claimant in sufficient detail the nature of all the charges he had to meet.

As was pointed out in *Kanda* v *Government of Malaya* (1962) if the right to be heard is to be a real right which is worth anything, it must carry with it a right for the party of whom complaint is made to know the case which is made against him (and see *Ridge* v *Baldwin* (1964)): and, since the purpose of that requirement is to enable that party to defend himself or answer the complaint, it must follow that the notice must be sufficient to enable him adequately to prepare his defence or answer. We agree with the judge in thinking that the claimant should have been supplied with a fair statement, by which we mean a sufficiently specific statement, of the charges which it was proposed to lay before the executive committee a reasonable time before the meeting of 9 July. This was not done. The claimant then asked, as he was entitled to do, for the charges to be formulated and for a sufficient adjournment to enable him to prepare his defence. He was not allowed either. The learned judge found that the members of the executive committee assumed on 9 July that the claimant then knew with what he was charged, but this, although it may explain the denial of what the claimant was fairly entitled to, cannot excuse it. Consequently, in our judgment, the proceedings on 9 July did not conform to the requirements of natural justice and were defective . . .'

Comment

(1) It seems that the rules of natural justice do not require that the 'accused' should be entitled to legal representation (*Enderby FC* v *Football Association* (1971)).

Roebuck v National Union of Mineworkers (No 2) [1978] ICR 676 Chancery Division

TEMPLEMAN J: 'The following principal material facts are pleaded by the claimants and admitted by the union. In 1974 the president of the union, Mr Scargill, brought an action for libel against a newspaper. The libel action was commenced and conducted by Mr Scargill, on behalf of the union, pursuant to a resolution of the area council. At the trial of the libel action, Mr Roebuck and Mr O'Brien gave evidence for the newspaper. After a trial which lasted from March 8 to 24, 1976, Mr Scargill was awarded £3,000 damages for libel and he has since accounted for those damages to the union. Shortly after the conclusion of the trial of the libel action, Mr Scargill prepared and signed a report, which was dated March 29, 1976. . . .

The report expressed the belief of Mr Scargill that Mr Roebuck's actions were clearly detrimental to the interests of the union; that the actions of Mr O'Brien could only be described as a very serious offence; and were clearly detrimental to the interests of the union; and that both as regards Mr Roebuck and Mr O'Brien, the matters set out in the report were of such magnitude and seriousness that Mr Scargill would be failing in his duty if he did not reflect it to the area council and include it in the report.

In this court, counsel for the union submitted that the statement in the report that Mr Scargill believed the action of Mr O'Brien could only be described as a very serious offence and was clearly detrimental to the interests of the union (thus foreshadowing and echoing the words of rule 42) only amounted to an indication that Mr Scargill believed that a prima facie case had been established. I am bound to say that to me those words read more like judgment before trial.

On April 12, 1976, the area council met, under the chairmanship of Mr Scargill. Although Mr Scargill's report had not been considered by the executive committee, and if the executive committee took a certain course would inevitably, or probably, be referred to the area council for review, Mr Scargill read his report aloud to the area council. The area council then referred the actions of Mr Roebuck and Mr O'Brien to the area executive committee. The area executive committee held a meeting, under the chairmanship of Mr Scargill, and attended by Mr Roebuck; and they resolved to charge Mr Roebuck with conduct detrimental to the union, in that he gave a signed statement to the union solicitors, and yet when he appeared under subpoena at the Sheffield High Court he completely contradicted that statement. In doing this, the charge alleged, Mr Roebuck misled the union and his action was of assistance to the newspaper in its defence against the union in the libel action.

The area executive committee held another meeting under the chairmanship of Mr Scargill and resolved to charge Mr O'Brien with conduct detrimental to the union, in that he gave a voluntary statement to the solicitors acting on behalf of the newspaper, which was of assistance to the newspaper in their defence against the union in the libel action; and in that he allowed the solicitors acting on behalf of the newspaper to see private correspondence between the area president and a branch of the union, which was directly concerned with the libel action; and in the view of the executive committee these letters were of assistance to the newspaper, in their defence against the union, in the libel action.

At a subsequent meeting of the area executive committee, under the chairmanship of Mr Scargill, and attended by Mr O'Brien, first of all the charges against Mr O'Brien were found to be proved; and Mr O'Brien was suspended from his office as branch secretary for a period of two years. At that or at a subsequent meeting on the same day, the charges against Mr Roebuck were found to be proved and he was declared to be ineligible for any office or committee of the union, for a like period of two years.

The area council held a meeting on May 24, 1976, under the chairmanship of Mr Scargill. Mr Roebuck and Mr O'Brien attended. Mr Scargill read and explained to the delegates a statement of facts which was based on his report; and, in the case of Mr Roebuck, the statement of facts said, inter alia, that the statement that Mr Roebuck had made to the solicitors of the newspaper was clearly in contradiction of the statement he had made to the union's solicitors; and on the basis of the evidence presented by Mr Roebuck himself, it was clear that the charge had been proved. In the case of Mr O'Brien, the statement of facts said, inter alia, that it was clear that the charges which had been put to Mr O'Brien at the meeting of the executive committee had been proved, on the basis of Mr O'Brien's admissions to the executive committee. The area council affirmed the convictions and punishments of Mr Roebuck and Mr O'Brien.

At the relevant meetings of the executive committee and the area council, Mr Scargill participated in the questioning of Mr Roebuck and Mr O'Brien, and participated in the deliberations of the executive committee and the area council, in each case outside the presence of Mr Roebuck and Mr O'Brien; but it is common ground that when the relevant resolutions were voted upon by the executive committee and the area council, Mr Scargill did not cast a vote. I do not know whether he had a vote to cast in his position as president; but whether because he had no power to vote, or because he did not choose to vote, the admitted fact is that he did not vote.

Those are the admitted facts; and Mr Turner-Samuels who appeared on behalf of the union, submitted – as indeed is true – that it is a strong thing to find against a defendant on admissions in the pleadings and he submitted that the union were entitled to a full trial. The object of that trial, as I understood him, was to produce evidence that Mr Scargill was not biased against Mr Roebuck or Mr O'Brien; that the presence and conduct of Mr Scargill did not inhibit or hinder Mr Roebuck or Mr O'Brien in the conduct of their defence; that the members of the executive committee and the area council reached their conclusions freely, conscientiously, and independently; and, in short, that Mr Scargill's presence and conduct had no influence on the result.

But, in my judgment, all those matters, which may be capable of proof, and on which I cannot and do not express any concluded view, are irrelevant. Mr Roebuck and Mr O'Brien were entitled to be tried by a tribunal whose chairman did not appear to have a special reason for bias, conscious or unconscious, against them. True it is that all the members of the executive committee and the area council, in common with all members of a domestic tribunal where the interests of their own organisation are at stake, have a general inclination to defend that union and its officers against attack from any source; this fact, every trade unionist and every member of a domestic organisation knows and accepts.

But Mr Scargill had a special position, which clearly disqualified him from taking the part in the critical meetings of the executive committee and the area committee which he did take. I say that as a question of fact and not as a question of criticism. It is a fact that Mr Scargill, as claimant, had clearly borne the heat and burden of the libel action. It is clear from the admissions that his cross-examination had been complicated and made difficult by the actions of Mr Roebuck and Mr O'Brien. It is clear that Mr Scargill was a witness to what had happened and to what Mr Roebuck and Mr O'Brien had said and done in the course of the libel action in the High Court. Whether or not those actions of Mr Roebuck and Mr O'Brien, before and during the High Court proceedings, were detrimental to the interests of the union, it is quite plain that they must have been gall and wormwood to Mr Scargill before, during and after the trial. Mr Scargill was a claimant and a witness – an important witness – in the High Court proceedings. Then he

551

reappeared as the complainant, the pleader, the prosecutor, the advocate and the chairman in the union proceedings, which followed swiftly. It is impossible to know what would have happened if Mr Scargill had recognised his impossible position and had not acted as he did. But his presence as chairman, and his conduct (admitted conduct) undoubtedly gave the impression that the dice were loaded against Mr Roebuck and Mr O'Brien. No amount of evidence can remove that impression, or establish affirmatively that the end result was unaffected by natural resentment and prejudice in the mind of Mr Scargill for prolonging his cross-examination and jeopardising the success of the action which, true enough, affected the union, but in addition vitally affected Mr Scargill, as president of the union, and as a private individual, who had been libelled. Whether he recognised the fact or not, Mr Scargill must inevitably have appeared biased against Mr Roebuck and Mr O'Brien. The appearance of bias was inevitable; the exercise of bias, conscious or unconscious, was probable. I am content to rest my judgment on the ground that it was manifestly unfair to Mr Roebuck and Mr O'Brien that Mr Scargill should have acted as chairman, and should have played the part which he admits to have played at the relevant meetings of the executive committee and the area council . . .'

Comment

(1) These cases illustrate the requirements of natural justice. However, there may be exceptional circumstances where expulsion may be permitted without the necessity of complying with these rules. In *Cheall* v *APEX* (1983) it was argued that the claimant should not be expelled from the union without a hearing. However, the rules of the union expressly conferred on it a power to expel members in order to comply with a ruling of the TUC Disputes Committee. In these circumstances the House of Lords held that he had no claim on grounds of breach of natural justice.

(2) While decisions of the internal committees of trade unions are still subject to the supervision of the courts on the grounds discussed in this section, there has now been a great deal of statutory intervention in this area, which means that resort to the common law is more rare.

Enforcing the rules

The cases examined so far have involved the personal rights of members in relation to discipline and expulsion. If a union member seeks to enforce observance of other union rules which do not affect her as directly or particularly as a disciplinary decision, some difficulties will be encountered. The miners' strike 1984–85 gave rise to a number of cases where this area of law was explored; these cases also provide some explanation for some of the subsequent legislation on the internal affairs of trade unions.

Taylor and Foulstone v National Union of Mineworkers (Yorkshire Area) [1984] IRLR 445 Chancery Division

The National Union of Mineworkers was composed of a number of area unions, with members of the area unions also being members of the national union. In interlocutory proceedings the claimants, members of the Yorkshire Area union, sued both the area union and the National Union of Mineworkers, alleging that the strike had been called in breach of the national and area rules (rules 43 and 53 respectively) which required a ballot before strike action and a 55 per cent majority in favour. (Under national rule 41 there was also provision for the national executive of the union to sanction strike action in an area.)

In January 1981 there had been a ballot in the Yorkshire Area where over 85 per cent had voted in favour of strike action; subsequently there had been three national ballots where the required majority in favour had not been achieved. In March 1984 the national executive committee of the union stated that proposed strike action in Yorkshire would be official.

NICHOLLS J: '. . . Finally I come to the relief concerned with the claim that the strike in the Yorkshire Area is invalid. On this the claimants first seek, in short, injunctions restraining the defendant Unions from instructing or seeking to persuade the claimants or other members of the Yorkshire Union to strike or not to cross picket lines by describing the strike or picket lines as official or by threatening disciplinary action. That the strike is not lawful national action is self-evident; rule 43 has not been complied with. But can the strike be justified as lawful area action under Yorkshire Union rule 53 and NUM rule 41? The claimants submit in effect that although sought to be dressed up as area by area action, what the Yorkshire Union and the NUM have entered upon is, and is alone, national action. Hence it cannot be justified in Yorkshire under rule 41. Moreover, even considered on an area by area basis as the NUM would seek to do, the strike in the Yorkshire Area did not comply with rule 53: an Area ballot was needed and none was held, the 1981 ballot being too remote in time and there having been too much change in branch membership of the Area since then for that ballot to be capable of justifying a call to strike action two and a half years later.

This is not the trial of the action. Suffice it for me to say that in my view on the evidence that I have referred to above the claimants have a highly arguable case on these points in support of a claim that the strike is in breach of the rules and constitution of the two Unions and as such is unlawful.

Since what is at issue is the right of the claimants to go to work and earn their living, I have no hesitation in concluding that this is a proper case in which to grant injunctive relief as sought pending the trial. The claimants have been kept from working now for many months. They have constant police protection and their houses are surrounded by police officers. Conversely if, despite the injunction, the Unions wish to continue to describe the strike as official in the Yorkshire Area then, as was pointed out by Mr Burton for the claimants, they have a remedy in their own hands: ballot their members. The Unions can then let the majority votes determine their policy, as the NUM president said when successfully proposing a reduction in the majority required on a ballot in April this year.

But on this part of the case the claimants go further and ask for a mandatory order that the NUM do now conduct a national ballot. For me to grant such an order I would have to find in the rules of the NUM, expressly or impliedly, a positive legal obligation on the NUM to hold such a ballot, of which obligation it was currently in breach. The only relevant rule is rule 43. The relevant part of the rule is expressed in negative terms. It limits the circumstances in which if national action is proposed by the NUM a national strike may be entered upon. The limit, the pre-requisite of a valid national strike, is a ballot vote taken in pursuance of a resolution of Conference and (as recently amended) a simple majority of those voting on the ballot being in favour of such a strike. In short, a national strike shall not be declared unless the national ballot condition is satisfied. Thus if, in contravention of that rule, the NUM declares (or "enters upon") a national strike without the national ballot condition being satisfied, the NUM is acting beyond its powers and unlawfully, and it can be restrained from so doing. What for my part I at present do not see (and I choose my words bearing in mind that this is not the trial of the action and it is not for me on this motion to seek to decide the point) is how, if the NUM does act *ultra vires* and unlawfully, by calling for a national strike without a national ballot being held pursuant to an appropriate resolution of a NUM Conference, there then arises a positive obligation on the NUM to conduct such a ballot regardless of whether Conference has resolved that there be a ballot or not. The NUM's acts will not be lawful unless and until it does hold a national ballot which shows a majority in favour of the strike. But, as at present advised, I am unable to spell out of rule 43 by implication any such positive obligation entitling a member to compel the NUM to hold a ballot. The member's right under the Rules is confined to being able to insist that a national strike cannot lawfully be held without a national ballot; but he has no greater right than that in respect of a national ballot. The point is, I accept, arguable, but following the approach to the grant of a mandatory injunction which I have stated above, I do not think I should on this interlocutory application make a mandatory order for the NUM to hold a national ballot . . .'

Comment

(1) This shows that, at best, a member can exercise a negative restraint – by preventing action in breach of the rules – but cannot positively require the union to do something if there is no positive obligation in the rules.

(2) Union members now have a statutory right to restrain any kind of industrial action without a prior ballot, regardless of what is in the union's rules (TULRCA s 62, below, p 645) but it remains the case that there is no mechanism to force the union to hold a ballot.

(3) A further restraint is to be found in the rule in *Foss* v *Harbottle* (1843). This is a company law rule, derived from a nineteenth-century case. The rule states that where a wrong is done to the company, such as action being taken in breach of the company's own rules, then if the wrong is capable of being ratified, no individual member of the company may bring legal action to complain of it.

One rationale of the rule is that it would be pointless to allow an individual member to bring an action if a majority of the other members could simply pass a resolution to ratify the wrongful act and thus scupper the legal proceedings. Note that it is not necessary for the majority actually to carry out the ratification: the mere possibility is enough. The other rationale of the rule is practical: the company should be protected from unnecessary litigation. If the majority do not wish to take action, the company should not be at the mercy of an individual shareholder who does.

(4) There are two issues in relation to the rule in *Foss* v *Harbottle*: first, does this company law rule apply to trade unions, and if so, when are breaches of the rules non-ratifiable?

Taylor v National Union of Mineworkers (Derbyshire Area) (No 3)
[1985] IRLR 99 Chancery Division

Taylor (a different Taylor), who was a member of the Derbyshire Area union, had already obtained a declaration that the strike in Derbyshire had been called in breach of the union's rules. In this action he claimed that £1,700,000 spent by the Derbyshire Area union on the strike was *ultra vires* (beyond the powers of) the union, and was thus a misapplication of union funds.

VINELOTT J: '. . . The first question is whether the claimants are in a position to maintain an action against the individual defendants in effect on behalf of the Derbyshire Union whose members have not been consulted on the question whether proceedings should be brought against the individual defendants. A great wealth of authority has been cited on this issue. The position, in my view, is not open to serious doubt. I need only refer to two cases, both cases concerning the National Union of Seamen, *Cotter* v *National Union of Seamen* (1929) and *Edwards* v *Halliwell* (1950).

In *Cotter's* case the claimants, members of the union, commenced proceedings to restrain the union and its officers from making an interest-free loan of £10,000 to the Miners' Non-Political Movement and for a declaration that a special general meeting had been invalidly convened and that a resolution of that meeting to make the loan was accordingly invalid. It was held by Romer J and the Court of Appeal that it was within the power of the union to make the £10,000 loan, that an irregularity in calling the meeting and in passing the resolution could be cured by a confirmatory resolution passed at a meeting properly convened, and that in those circumstances the claimants as a minority of the union were not entitled to sue on behalf of the union. Thus the court applied to the union the principle known to company lawyers as the rule of *Foss* v *Harbottle* after the case of that name in 1843.

I do not propose to cite extensively from the judgments in *Cotter's* case. The point is made shortly in two passages in the judgment of Romer J, which was affirmed by the Court of Appeal. He said:

"The principle, as I understand it, [that is, the principle in *Foss* v *Harbottle*] does not depend upon the existence of a corporation. The reasoning of it surely applies to any legal entity which is capable of suing in its own name and which is composed of individuals bound together by rules which give the majority of them the power to bind the minority."

At that time trades union law was still governed by the principles laid down in the Trades Union Act 1871. Section 8 of that Act provided for the property of a union to be vested in trustees for "the use and benefit of the trade union and the members thereof". It had been held in the well-known case of *Taff Vale Railway Company* v *Amalgamated Society of Railway Servants* (1901) that the effect of the Act was that a union could be sued in its own name and that the effect of s 8 was that the property so held for the benefit of the union and its members was the property of the union which was the beneficial owner of it.

The principle so laid down was, of course, an essential step in the reasoning of Romer J and the Court of Appeal. The trade union was treated as analogous to a company for the purposes of the rule in *Foss* v *Harbottle* because as regards its property it was to be treated as a separate legal entity governed by the code constituted by its rules and could be sued and be made liable to the extent of its property in its name. The argument of the unsuccessful claimant in *Cotter's* case was that the concluding words of the passage in s 8 which I have cited preserved the members' beneficial interest in the funds of that union. So, it was said, as in the case of any other unincorporated society such as a club any member could restrain an application of the funds of the union made otherwise than in compliance with the rules of the union. That argument was rejected by both Romer J and the Court of Appeal.

In *Edwards* v *Halliwell* the claimant, a member of the same union, claimed that a resolution increasing the contributions of employed members was invalid. Under the rules such a resolution required a two-thirds majority obtained at a ballot vote. The purported resolution was passed without a ballot. The Court of Appeal held that the rule in *Foss* v *Harbottle* did not apply to bar the claimant's right to sue. The failure to hold a ballot was not a mere irregularity. Any member was entitled to refuse to pay an increased subscription unless made payable by a valid resolution. In a classic exposition of the rule in *Foss* v *Harbottle*, which is often cited but which I shall cite again, Jenkins LJ said:

"The rule in *Foss* v *Harbottle*, as I understand it, comes to no more than this. First the proper claimant in an action in respect of a wrong alleged to be done to a company or an association of persons is *prima facie* the company or the association of persons itself. Secondly, where the alleged wrong is a transaction which might be made binding on the company or association and on all its members by a simple majority of the members, no individual member of the company is allowed to maintain an action in respect of that matter for the simple reason that, if a mere majority of the members of the company or association is in favour of what has been done, then *cadit quaestio*. No wrong has been done to the company or association and there is nothing in respect of which anyone can sue. If, on the other hand, a simple majority of members of the company or association is against what has been done, then there is no valid reason why the company or association itself should not sue. In my judgment, it is implicit in the rule that the matter relied on as constituting the cause of action should be a cause of action properly belonging to the general body of corporators or members of the company or association as opposed to a cause of action which some individual member can assert in his own right.

The cases falling within the general ambit of the rule are subject to certain exceptions. It has been noted in the course of argument that in those cases where the act complained of is wholly *ultra vires* the company or association the rule has no application because there is no question of the transaction being confirmed by any majority. It has been further pointed out that where what has been done amounts to what is generally called in these cases a fraud on the minority and the wrongdoers are themselves in control of the company, the rule is relaxed in favour of the aggrieved minority who are allowed to bring what is known as a minority shareholders' action on behalf of themselves and all others. The reason for this is that, if they were denied that right, their grievance would never reach the court because the wrongdoers themselves, being in control, would not allow the company to sue. Those exceptions are not directly in point in this case, but they show, especially the last one, that the rule is not an inflexible one and it will be relaxed where necessary in the interests of justice."

I have read that passage in full, because Jenkins LJ makes it clear that the protection afforded by the rule in *Foss* v *Harbottle* to a company and a trade union does not extend to cases where the claimant seeks to prevent or remedy an application of the funds of the body which is outside the powers conferred by its constitution. The reason is that such an application cannot be ratified by a mere majority of the members or indeed by any majority, however large. Any member is entitled to insist that the funds of the body be used exclusively in furtherance of its objects, those objects to be inferred from its constitution . . .

It seems to me that if the rules of a union provide expressly for allowances to be made to members on what I will for convenience call an "official strike" – that is, one called in accordance with the procedures prescribed by the rules – it is impossible to imply consistently with that a power for officers to make a precisely similar allowance to members on "unofficial strike" – that is, one called or followed in breach of the rules of the union. Every member of the union, as he has an interest in preserving the funds of the union, is, it seems to me, entitled to prevent the funds of the union being used in that way. That was quite clearly the approach of the Court of Appeal and the House of Lords in *Howden* v *Yorkshire Miners' Association* (1903), and although there is no doubt that today a more liberal approach to the construction of the rules of a union is appropriate, that principle seems to me equally applicable.

If that is the right conclusion, then it seems to me that it must follow that any payment to a member on unofficial strike whether by way of weekly allowance or by way of intermittent payment or by meeting expenses directly or in any other way with a view to making good the wages lost by the member on unofficial strike must be equally impermissible. So also must payments to pickets be impermissible . . .'

(Despite finding that this was a wrong which could not be ratified, Vinelott J held that the union members could validly resolve not to take further action to remedy the wrong, and so declined to order the defendant union officials to reimburse the union.)

Comment

(1) This decision has attracted two quite separate criticisms. First, it is argued by Lord Wedderburn (1985) that since TULRA 1974 stated that a trade union is not, *and is not to be treated as if it were*, a body corporate (see now TULRCA s 10), the doctrine of *ultra vires*, which is a company law doctrine, should not be applied to it – by parity of reasoning with *EETPU* v *Times Newspapers Ltd* (1980) (above, p 523). Secondly, if the claimants had the right to take individual action in this case, because the wrong was non-ratifiable, then the judge really had no warrant for refusing to order reimbursement.

(2) Note the exceptions outlined in the judgment where the rule in *Foss v Harbottle* will not apply. Cases involving the discipline or expulsion of union members will always fall under the exception for personal rights: that is, it is the member's personal right which is infringed by discipline or expulsion in breach of the rules, not just a wrong to the union. However, in the most recent case where the issue was argued, *Wise v USDAW* (1996), Chadwick J seemed to imply that this exception applied to all breaches of the rules. In that case, the president of the union brought an action challenging two decisions which had been taken by the union's national executive council against her advice that they would be in breach of the rules. The decisions related to elections in which she had no personal interest, in that she was not standing as a candidate, and the union therefore argued that her claim was precluded by the rule in *Foss v Harbottle*. The judge said:

> . . . the basis upon which a member of the union . . . agrees to be bound by the decisions of the executive council . . . is that those decisions will be made and elections for those offices will be held in accordance with the rules . . . Accordingly, as it seems to me, the right of a member to complain of a breach of the rules is a contractual right which is individual to that member; although of course, that member holds the right in common with all members having the like right.

It seems, therefore, that it will be an exceptional case where the rule in *Foss v Harbottle* will prevent a member's action.

(3) In 1990 the Conservative government created a new official, the Commissioner for the Rights of Trade Union Members, whose role (at public expense) was to assist members in taking action against their unions for breach of common law or statutory obligations. This office was abolished by the Employment Relations Act 1999, but instead new powers were given to the Certification Officer to investigate and make a declaration and enforcement order on such matters.

Trade Union and Labour Relations (Consolidation) Act 1992

108A (1) A person who claims that there has been a breach or threatened breach of the rules of a trade union relating to any of the matters mentioned in subsection (2) may apply to the Certification Officer for a declaration to that effect, subject to subsections (3) to (7).

(2) The matters are –

(a) the appointment or election of a person to, or the removal of a person from, any office;

(b) disciplinary proceedings by the union (including expulsion);

(c) the balloting of members on any issue other than industrial action;

(d) the constitution or proceedings of any executive committee or of any decision-making meeting;

(e)   such other matters as may be specified in an order made by the Secretary of State.

(3)   The applicant must be a member of the union, or have been one at the time of the alleged breach or threatened breach.

. . .

(5)   No application may be made regarding –
   (a)   the dismissal of an employee of the union;
   (b)   disciplinary proceedings against an employee of the union.

(6)   An application must be made –
   (a)   within the period of six months starting with the day on which the breach or threatened breach is alleged to have taken place, or
   (b)   if within that period any internal complaints procedure of the union is invoked to resolve the claim, within the period of six months starting with the earlier of the days specified in subsection (7).

Comment

(1) Members can choose either to complain to the Certification Officer or to the court, but not both (TULRCA s 108A(14), (15)). The advantages of complaint to the Certification Officer are that the proceedings will be simpler, quicker (they should be resolved within six months: TULRCA s 108B) and cheaper. The disadvantages are that applications for interim relief or awards of damages can only be made to the court. Furthermore, complaints to the Certification Officer must be made within six months, whereas the limitation period for contract claims in the normal courts is six years.

(2) The Certification Officer may decline to hear a complaint unless satisfied that the member has taken all reasonable steps to resolve the complaint through the union's internal procedures (TULRCA s 108B(1)). There can be an appeal from the Certification Officer's decision, on a point of law only, to the EAT (TULRCA s 108C).

STATUTORY REGULATION OF TRADE UNION RULES

The miners' strike of 1984–85 provided the impetus, and many of the ideas, for the reform of trade unions' internal rules.

Financial affairs

Trade Union and Labour Relations (Consolidation) Act 1992

30   (1)   A member of a trade union has a right to request access to any accounting records of the union which are available for inspection and relate to periods including a time when he was a member of the union.
   In the case of records relating to a branch or section of the union, it is immaterial whether he was a member of that branch or section.

(2)   Where such access is requested the union shall –
   (a)   make arrangements with the member for him to be allowed to inspect the records requested before the end of the period of twenty-eight days beginning with the day the request was made,
   (b)   allow him and any accountant accompanying him for the purpose to inspect the records at the time and place arranged, and

(c)   secure that at the time of the inspection he is allowed to take, or is supplied with, any copies of, or of extracts from, records inspected by him which he requires . . .

Comment

(1) This provision can be traced to *Taylor v NUM (Derbyshire Area) (No 2)* (1985), where the claimant had attempted to inspect the union's accounts accompanied by an accountant. It was held that if the rules gave a member a right to inspect (which they did), this impliedly included the right to do so with a professional agent. As a result, the NUM altered its rules expressly to exclude the right to professional accompaniment. This is no longer allowed – although the accountant can be asked to give an undertaking of confidentiality.

(2) In 1990 allegations surfaced in the media about the possible misuse of NUM funds during the 1984–85 strike. The union appointed Gavin Lightman QC to investigate and he identified a number of improper dealings. Criminal proceedings were started, but the charges were dropped when the court held that evidence uncovered by the Lightman Inquiry was inadmissible. This gave the Conservative government the ammunition it needed to introduce further controls on union finances and to extend penalties for their breach.

(3) TURERA 1993 gave the Certification Officer power to investigate the financial affairs of a trade union or any of its branches. It introduced TULRCA s 37A, giving power to require production of documents, and TULRCA s 37B, allowing the Certification Officer to appoint an inspector to investigate and report in any cases where he suspects fraud, misfeasance or other misconduct or non-compliance with accounting and auditing requirements. TULRCA s 37C(8) specifically provides that any such report is admissible in criminal proceedings.

(4) TULRCA s 45A, also introduced by TURERA, provides a series of criminal offences which will be committed by any trade union official who obstructs any such inquiry and, under TULRCA s 45B, anyone convicted of such an offence will be disqualified from holding office as president, general secretary or national executive member for up to ten years.

(5) TULRCA s 32A, introduced by TURERA, requires unions to provide an annual return to all members summarising the union's financial affairs and including information about the exact amounts of remuneration being paid to the president, general secretary and members of the national executive of the union. While many of the rules now applying to the financial affairs of unions are comparable to those applying to companies, it should be noted that this is more information than shareholders are entitled to in respect of directors and senior managers of registered companies.

Discipline and expulsion

In Chapter 10 we examined TULRCA s 174, which greatly restricts the grounds on which a union can refuse to admit a member. As we noted then, s 174 applies to *expulsion* from a union as well as exclusion. One of the grounds on which expulsion or exclusion is permitted is misconduct. This links with TULRCA s 64, which gives union members a right not to be unjustifiably disciplined for certain kinds of conduct. TULRCA s 174 provides that expulsion or exclusion on these grounds is unlawful. The kinds of conduct protected are defined in TULRCA s 65.

Trade Union and Labour Relations (Consolidation) Act 1992

65 (2) This section applies to conduct which consists in –

(a) failing to participate in or support a strike or other industrial action (whether by members of the union or by others), or indicating opposition to or a lack of support for such action;

(b) failing to contravene, for a purpose connected with such a strike or other industrial action, a requirement imposed on him by or under a contract of employment;

(c) asserting (whether by bringing proceedings or otherwise) that the union, any official or representative of it or a trustee of its property has contravened, or is proposing to contravene, a requirement which is, or is thought to be, imposed by or under the rules of the union or any other agreement or by or under any enactment (whenever passed) or any rule of law;

(d) encouraging or assisting a person
  (i) to perform an obligation imposed on him by a contract of employment, or
  (ii) to make or attempt to vindicate any such assertion as is mentioned in paragraph (c);

(e) contravening a requirement imposed by or in consequence of a determination which infringes the individual's or another individual's right not to be unjustifiably disciplined;

(f) failing to agree, or withdrawing agreement, to the making from his wages (in accordance with arrangements between his employer and the union) of deductions representing payments to the union in respect of his membership;

(g) resigning or proposing to resign from the union or from another union, becoming or proposing to become a member of another union, refusing to become a member of another union, or being a member of another union;

(h) working with, or proposing to work with, individuals who are not members of the union or who are or are not members of another union;

(i) working for, or proposing to work for, an employer who employs or who has employed individuals who are not members of the union or who are or are not members of another union; or

(j) requiring the union to do an act which the union is, by any provision of this Act, required to do on the requisition of a member.
. . .

(5) This section does not apply to an act, omission or statement comprised in conduct falling within subsection (2), (3) or (4) above if it is shown that the act, omission or statement is one in respect of which individuals would be disciplined by the union irrespective of whether their acts, omissions or statements were in connection with conduct within subsection (2) or (3) above.

(6) An individual is not unjustifiably disciplined if it is shown –

(a) that the reason for disciplining him, or one of them, is that he made such an assertion as is mentioned in subsection (2)(c), or encouraged or assisted another person to make or attempt to vindicate such an assertion,

(b) that the assertion was false, and

(c) that he made the assertion, or encouraged or assisted another person to make or attempt to vindicate it, in the belief that it was false or otherwise in bad faith,

and that there was no other reason for disciplining him or that the only other reasons were reasons in respect of which he does not fall to be treated as unjustifiably disciplined . . .

Comment

(1) The most controversial thing included in this section is strike-breaking. This is traditionally seen as a most serious offence by trade unions, given the crucial import- ance of solidarity to the success of industrial action. However, courts have always been reluctant to uphold expulsions on such a ground (see, eg, *Esterman* v *NALGO* (1974)). During and after the miners' strike 1984–85, the union attempted to discipline mem- bers who continued to work and crossed picket lines: hence the introduction of this pro- vision by the Employment Act 1988. Of course, the strike in that case had been called in breach of the union's own rules – but this section prevents unions from disciplining members for strike-breaking even if the strike is official and has been called following the statutory requirements discussed in Chapter 12.

(2) Note that under TULRCA s 64(5), rights under this section are specifically stated to be additional to any other rights. Thus the member is free to pursue also any com- mon law claims.

(3) There is a clear overlap here with TULRCA s 174 (preventing unreasonable exclu- sion or explusion from a trade union). Where the disciplinary measure falls short of expulsion, only s 64 is applicable. Where the expulsion is for anything other than mis- conduct, only s 174 is applicable. However, in cases where a member is expelled for conduct coming within the definition of unjustifiable discipline in s 65, a claim under either section is possible. The limitation period for a claim under s 64 is three months, but it is six months for a s 174 claim.

(4) This overlap is dealt with by providing that an action may only be brought under one of the sections and, if successful, may not form the basis for a claim under the other. However, it must be doubted whether two provisions are needed, let alone justified in their current form. Remedies for breach of TULRCA ss64 and 174 are also similar: a declaration plus compensation, which may not be less than £6,900 (in 2008) if the union has refused to re-admit the member. The maximum amount which can be awarded is the same as the maximum unfair dismissal award: £72,900 in 2008 (TULRCA s 176).

(5) In *Bradley* v *NALGO* (1991) the EAT made a minimum award to eight claimants who had been expelled for strike-breaking, because, in the absence of a closed shop, their job prospects had not been affected detrimentally and any injury to feelings they had felt was caused by their colleagues' reactions to them rather than the expulsion by the union. The point that they were henceforth excluded from any participation in the collective bargaining process does not seem to have been considered.

(6) Note, however, that strike-breaking must be distinguished from acting contrary to the policy of the union, which is conduct for which a member may properly be expelled.

Knowles v *Fire Brigades Union* [1996] IRLR 617 Court of Appeal

The union was in dispute with employers over the use of 'retained firefighters'. Where a station was not permanently staffed, retained firefighters would be on standby duty. At one time, full- time firefighters did this in their spare time as a way of earning extra money. The union con- sidered that this drove down full-time wages (because the employers assumed that everyone was doing retained duties in their spare time) and that it was a safety risk. In 1977 the union was successful in getting employer councils to cease this practice. However, towards the end of the 1980s, councils started looking at this again, and in 1990 Shropshire County Council decided to reintroduce the use of retained firefighters.

The two claimants, who were full-time firefighters at a station which was not staffed at night, were offered jobs as retained firefighters for the same station during night time. They accepted. They were then expelled from the union for acting contrary to union policy. They claimed that they had been expelled for refusing to take part in industrial action and that this was unjustifiable discipline within the meaning of TULRCA s 65. An employment tribunal upheld their claim, but its decision was reversed by the EAT. The claimants appealed.

NEILL LJ: '. . . It was argued on behalf of the appellants that in the absence of any statutory definition the question of whether there was or was not "other industrial action" was a question of fact which an employment tribunal was particularly suited to determine.

Counsel for the appellants drew our attention to the decision of the Court of Appeal in *Power Packing Casemakers Ltd* v *Faust* (1983). In that case the Court of Appeal upheld the decision of the EAT, who had decided that employees who had refused a request by their employers to work overtime had taken part in "other industrial action" within the meaning of [TULRCA s 238].

The question in issue in that case was whether the employment tribunal had any jurisdiction to determine whether the dismissal was fair or unfair. In the course of his judgment, Stephenson LJ approved the refusal of the EAT to define the phrase "other industrial action" in [TULRCA s 238] and their decision that the matter should be left to the good sense of employment tribunals. Earlier in his judgment Stephenson LJ said:

"An employment tribunal and the lay members of the appeal tribunal may be trusted to recognise industrial action when they see it, and that was how both tribunals, as well as one appellant and one other witness, described the employees' refusal to work overtime."

. . . It was argued in the alternative on behalf of the appellants that, if the question of what was meant by "other industrial action" were to be more properly regarded as a mixed question of fact and law rather than a question of pure fact, the employment tribunal did not misdirect themselves and there was no proper basis for the intervention by the EAT. It was to be noted that the employment tribunal made specific reference to the decision in *Rasool* v *Hepworth Pipe Co Ltd (No 2)* (1980), and that they had distinguished it on the basis that the steps taken by the union were not, as in *Rasool's* case, merely acts preparatory to ascertaining the feelings of the employees towards industrial action.

In *Rasool* v *Hepworth Pipe Co Ltd* the EAT was concerned with an argument that the attendance of employees at an unauthorised mass meeting for the purpose of ascertaining the views of the workforce with regard to impending wage negotiations constituted "other industrial action" within the meaning of the predecessor to [TULRCA s 238]. Waterhouse J said:

"It is sufficient for us to say that it is probably incorrect to attempt to interpret the expression [other industrial action] narrowly in terms of specific intention and that the nature and effect of the concerted action are probably of greater importance. Nevertheless, in our judgment, attendance at an unauthorised meeting for the purpose indicated by the majority of the tribunal in the instant case falls short of 'other industrial action'. As the majority of the tribunal found, it is more properly regarded as trade union activity, even though a degree of disruption of the manufacturing process resulted."

In addition counsel drew our attention to a phrase in the judgment of Ralph Gibson LJ in *British Telecommunications plc* v *Ticehurst* (1992), where he referred to the fact that Mrs Ticehurst had participated in "the concerted action" devised by the union. It was said that in the present case the appellants had failed to participate in the concerted action which the union had devised, namely that full-time fire fighters should refuse to enter into retained contracts. A refusal to enter into retained contracts was analogous to a refusal to operate machines. Pressure was applied to the employers who suffered inconvenience and incurred the expense of employing new retained fire fighters.

On behalf of the union on the other hand it was argued that what constituted "other industrial action" was plainly a mixed question of law and fact. In reaching their conclusions the employment tribunal had failed to distinguish between:

(a)   acts preparatory to industrial action;
(b)   threats of industrial action; and
(c)   actual industrial action.

By failing to make this distinction they had reached a conclusion which was perverse on the facts found. It was important to note that the employment tribunal stated in their reasons that they had heard no evidence as to whether the policy of the union "might financially inconvenience the local authorities". On the findings the effect of the policy went no further than to prevent the local authorities from carrying out the reorganisation of the fire service in the manner in which they might wish to do. The union had done no more than seek to persuade the county council not to offer retained contracts to whole-time fire fighters. No "action" had been taken against the employers by the union nor had there been any threats of action.

It was accepted that a breach of contract was not a necessary prerequisite for a finding that there had been industrial action, though normally industrial action does amount to or involve a breach of contract. Counsel referred us to the decision of the EAT in *Midland Plastics* v *Till* (1983). In that case, the employers had been informed by a member of the works committee that if the demands for a specified minimum wage were not met in full it was the workers' intention to take industrial action as from 11.00 am that day. In the interval between the receipt of the letter and 11.00 am four employees were asked by the management what action they were going to take if the demands were not met.

They replied that they were going to abide by the wishes of the workforce. They were immediately dismissed. By a majority, the employment tribunal concluded that the letter and the surrounding circumstances did not amount to "other industrial action" within [TULRCA s 238]. The EAT dismissed the employers' appeal. Browne-Wilkinson J said:

> "The majority of the employment tribunal have referred to the actions which, in normal contemplation, might be thought of as industrial action: walk-out, go-slow, working to rule, banning of overtime, picketing. We are far from saying that that is a comprehensive list. But if the employers are to succeed, as it seems to us, they must be able to show that the threat of taking industrial action can itself amount to taking industrial action. We reject that view."

Later he continued:

> "Unfortunately a substantial factor in industrial relations negotiations in this country is a display of power by one side in response to which the other side either does or does not yield to the wishes of the person displaying such power. The actual taking of industrial action is the last stage and is quite distinct from the stage at which the threat of it is being used as a negotiating weapon. Throughout the period of a strike notice what is bearing upon the employer is the risk to his business. We can see no distinction between what occurred in this case and the ordinary strike notice. In neither case has the matter matured into taking part in industrial action."

CONCLUSION

I accept that the words "other industrial action" are not to be narrowly construed. But they have to be looked at in a context where the transition from negotiations to action may have far-reaching consequences. We are not dealing in the present case with Part V of the TULRCA 1992, which is concerned with industrial action, or with s 226 in Part V, which provides that an act done by a trade union to induce a person to take part in industrial action is not protected unless the industrial action has the support of a ballot. But it is to be noted that one of the rights conferred on trade union members by Ch V in Part I is the right to a ballot before industrial action takes place (see TULRCA s 62).

Industrial action can take many forms, but, in the absence of any statutory definition, I do not think that any attempt at a paraphrase is likely to be useful. In my judgment, the question of what is industrial action for the purposes of TULRCA s 65 is a mixed question of fact and law. In large measure it is a question of fact, but the facts have to be judged in the context of the Act which plainly contemplates that industrial action is a serious step.

It is necessary to look at all the circumstances. These circumstances will include the contracts of employment of the employees and whether any breach of or departure from the terms of the contract are involved, the effect on the employer of what is done or omitted and the object which the union or the employees seek to achieve.

In the present case it seems to me that the following factors are relevant.

(a) At the date when the appellants were expelled from the union the policy had been in force for over 18 months. The object to be achieved by the union's policy was to prevent a unilateral departure from the terms which had been agreed in 1977.

(b) The policy did not require full-time workers to break or to depart from the terms of their existing contracts. The policy merely required fire fighters not to undertake additional work under new contracts.

(c) There is no evidence to suggest that either the county council or the union contemplated that the "pressure" exerted by the union required the support of a ballot.

(d) There was some discussion at the hearing as to whether any of the other full-time fire fighters in Shropshire had actually refused offers of retained contracts. Even in the absence of express evidence to this effect, however, it is reasonable to assume that some of the 45 other fire fighters did so refuse. But their compliance with the union's policy does not seem to me on the facts of this case to amount to a clear indication that the union and its members had crossed the threshold into taking industrial action within the meaning of s 65.

(e) The evidence of Mr Bryant shows that negotiations were being continued and that although the union were making clear that they intended to adhere to their policy, the breakdown which is almost implicit in the taking of industrial action had not occurred. As Browne-Wilkinson J said in *Midland Plastics* v *Till*, in the passage which I have already cited, "the actual taking of industrial action is the last stage and is quite distinct from the stage at which the threat of it is being used as a negotiating weapon". One must also take account of the reaction of the lay members of the EAT in the present case to the suggestion that the mere fact that an employer may feel himself inhibited as a result of pressure applied to him means that industrial action has been taken.

In my judgment, the EAT were justified in concluding that the employment tribunal had misdirected themselves in treating pressure plus inhibition as a sufficient test of industrial action. Furthermore, I think that counsel for the union was correct in her submission that the employment tribunal failed sufficiently to distinguish between conduct which fell short even of a threat and actual "industrial action" within the meaning of TULRCA s 65.

Accordingly I would dismiss this appeal.'

(Millett and Phillips LJJ agreed with Neill LJ.)

Election of trade union officials

Which officials must be elected?

Trade unions typically have two kinds of officials. First, there are those active members who have volunteered or stood for election and take on trade union responsibilities alongside their duties as employees. This category includes all shop stewards and usually members of the union's executive committees and the president and vice-president. Secondly, there are those officials who carry out the day-to-day management of the union's affairs as area, regional or branch officials, who work full-time for the union. These are career trade unionists; they are employees of the union, and they usually include the general secretary.

In theory, policy-making is carried out in committees and conferences with a high involvement of members of the union. However, since policy-making often starts with a discussion paper and the best informed are the best able to influence policy, there is no doubt that full-time officials are likely to have a significant input into the direction of union policy, nor is this in any sense unhealthy.

Again, the traditional pattern has been that lay officials (those who are not full-time employees of the union) are elected to their positions, while full-time officials are appointed in the same way as any employee. Until 1984, these matters were seen as purely internal matters for the trade union to decide. However, the Conservative government of that time was concerned that some important union officials were either never elected or, once elected, held office indefinitely (the then president of the NUM, Arthur Scargill, being the example that sprang most readily to mind).

Trade Union and Labour Relations (Consolidation) Act 1992

46 (1) A trade union shall secure –
  (a) that every person who holds a position in the union to which this Chapter applies does so by virtue of having been elected to it at an election satisfying the requirements of this Chapter, and
  (b) that no person continues to hold such a position for more than five years without being re-elected at such an election.
(2) The positions to which this Chapter applies (subject as mentioned below) are –
  (a) member of the executive,
  (b) any position by virtue of which a person is a member of the executive,
  (c) president, and
  (d) general secretary.
(3) In this Chapter 'member of the executive' includes any person who, under the rules or practice of the union, may attend and speak at some or all of the meetings of the executive, otherwise than for the purpose of providing the committee with factual information or with technical or professional advice with respect to matters taken into account by the executive in carrying out its functions.

(4)   This Chapter does not apply to the position of president or general secretary if the holder of that position –

    (a)   is not, in respect of that position, either a voting member of the executive or an employee of the union,

    (b)   holds that position for a period which under the rules of the union cannot end more than 13 months after he took it up, and

    (c)   has not held either position at any time in the period of twelve months ending with the day before he took up that position.

(4A)   This Chapter also does not apply to the position of president if –

    (a)   the holder of that position was elected or appointed to it in accordance with the rules of the union,

    (b)   at the time of his election or appointment as president he held a position mentioned in paragraph (a), (b) or (d) of subsection (2) by virtue of having been elected to it at a qualifying election,

    (c)   it is no more than five years since –

        (i)   he was elected, or re-elected, to the position mentioned in paragraph (b) which he held at the time of his election or appointment as president, or

        (ii)   he was elected to another position of a kind mentioned in that paragraph at a qualifying election held after his election or appointment as president of the union, and

    (d)   he has, at all times since his election or appointment as president, held a position mentioned in paragraph (a), (b) or (d) of subsection (2) by virtue of having been elected to it at a qualifying election.

(5)   In subsection (4) a 'voting member of the executive' means a person entitled in his own right to attend meetings of the executive and to vote on matters on which votes are taken by the executive (whether or not he is entitled to attend all such meetings or to vote on all such matters or in all circumstances).

(5A)   In subsection (4A) 'qualifying election' means an election satisfying the requirements of this Chapter.

(5B)   The 'requirements of this Chapter' referred to in subsections (1) and (5A) are those set out in sections 47 to 52 below.

(6)   The provisions of this Chapter apply notwithstanding anything in the rules or practice of the union; and the terms and conditions on which a person is employed by the union shall be disregarded in so far as they would prevent the union from complying with the provisions of this Chapter.

Comment

(1) The original provision introduced by the Trade Union Act 1984 only required *voting* members of the national executive committee to offer themselves for re-election every five years. On the whole, this sufficed to bring in democracy while not requiring employees of the union to put their jobs at risk every five years. However, it could also be circumvented by an official giving up his right to vote – which is what the president of the NUM did. Hence the Employment Act 1988 introduced the so-called 'Scargill clause', extending the election requirement to non-voting members and to the president and general secretary.

(2) In 2002 the Better Regulation Task Force suggested that the requirement for a ballot for the president was unnecessary, since the president is almost always someone who has already been elected to the national executive committee. This was accepted by the government in its 2003 review of the working of the Employment Relations Act 1999,

with the result that the Employment Relations Act 2004 relaxed this rule through the introduction of TULRCA s 46(4A): the president need not be elected by ballot of all the members if he or she has been subject to such an election within the previous five years.

(3) Note that references to 'the executive' in TULRCA s 46 mean the 'principal committee of the union exercising executive functions' (TULRCA s 119) – this committee is called the national executive in most trade unions. Thus members of other influential committees need not be subject to election in this manner (see *Paul* v *NALGO* (1987)).

Candidates for office

Trade Union and Labour Relations (Consolidation) Act 1992

47 (1) No member of the trade union shall be unreasonably excluded from standing as a candidate.
(2) No candidate shall be required, directly or indirectly, to be a member of a political party.
(3) A member of a trade union shall not be taken to be unreasonably excluded from standing as a candidate if he is excluded on the ground that he belongs to a class of which all the members are excluded by the rules of the union.
  But a rule which provides for such a class to be determined by reference to whom the union chooses to exclude shall be disregarded.

Comment

(1) Unions commonly have rules that ensure that the executive committee represents all regions, or stipulate that candidates should have been members of the union for a certain minimum period of time. Such requirements are lawful under TULRCA s 47(3). In *Ecclestone* v *NUJ* (1999) the national executive committee refused to recognise the claimant as a candidate for the office of deputy general secretary on the grounds that mutual trust and confidence between him and them had broken down. The claimant had been deputy general secretary for 17 years before being dismissed after a dispute with the general secretary and the national executive. The court held that by excluding any candidate in whom the national executive did not have confidence, the union was effectively excluding a 'class . . . determined by reference to whom the union chooses to exclude' in breach of TULRCA s 47(3).

(2) The effect of TULRCA s 47(2) is that rules excluding members of the Communist Party or the BNP from standing for office (which are not uncommon) continue to be lawful, but the other rule which used to be common, requiring an officer to be a member of the Labour Party, is not.

(3) Before the Trade Union Act 1984 it was common for members of the national executive to be elected by the annual national conference of the union rather than by the whole membership directly. This process can be seen either as encouraging the perpetuation of a self-selecting oligarchy somewhat to the left of the general membership, or as a sensible method of indirect representative democracy which ensured that the electorate was knowledgeable about the candidates. It is clear that the Conservative government which introduced these requirements thought that it would result in more 'moderate' union governance.

(4) As candidates may now not be known to the membership, TULRCA s 48 provides that the union must circulate election addresses from each candidate and any facilities for producing such an address must be afforded equally to all candidates. The costs of circulation must be borne by the union.

(5) While direct democracy is now required for these posts, it appears that it is still lawful for the union to hold a ballot at its national conference and to inform the membership that these candidates are official, or endorsed by the conference (*Paul* v *NALGO* (1987)).

Conduct of the ballot

The ballot must be secret and fully postal – meaning that the ballot papers are sent out and returned by post at no cost to the member. It must be subject to the control of an independent scrutineer, who supervises the ballot and reports on it at the end of the process. Under TURERA, the role of the independent scrutineer was strengthened, by requiring the scrutineer to inspect the union's membership register according to which the ballot papers have been distributed, among other things to ensure that it is up to date.

As *Veness* v *NUPE* (1992) indicates, there may be advantages for the union in having to delegate the conduct of the election to an independent scrutineer. In that case, members complained that there was a breach of union rules because only 100 out of 1,150 members of one branch and only 11 out of 2,200 members of another branch had received ballot papers. The union had, as required by law, delegated the conduct of the ballot, including distribution of ballot papers, to the Electoral Reform Society. The members' claim against the union was therefore struck out as disclosing no cause of action.

Trade Union and Labour Relations (Consolidation) Act 1992

50 (1) Subject to the provisions of this section, entitlement to vote shall be accorded equally to all members of the trade union.

(2) The rules of the union may exclude entitlement to vote in the case of all members belonging to one of the following classes, or to a class falling within one of the following –

(a) members who are not in employment;

(b) members who are in arrears in respect of any subscription or contribution due to the union;

(c) members who are apprentices, trainees or students or new members of the union.

(3) The rules of the union may restrict entitlement to vote to members who fall within –

(a) a class determined by reference to a trade or occupation,

(b) a class determined by reference to a geographical area, or

(c) a class which is by virtue of the rules of the union treated as a separate section within the union,

or to members who fall within a class determined by reference to any combination of the factors mentioned in paragraphs (a), (b) and (c).

The reference in paragraph (c) to a section of a trade union includes a part of the union which is itself a trade union . . .

Comment

(1) If some members do not receive a ballot paper, the ballot is not automatically invalidated, since the requirement is that 'so far as is reasonably practicable' all members should be sent a ballot paper (TULRCA s 51(4)). Under TULRCA s 24, unions have a duty to keep an accurate register of members, so problems of this kind should not be on a large scale.

(2) When the election requirement was introduced in 1984 workplace voting was allowed, but the Employment Act 1988 changed the law so that all ballots had to be fully postal. Adopting another suggestion of the Better Regulation Task Force, the Employment Relations Act 2004 s 54 gives the Secretary of State power to make regulations for alternative methods of voting, which may mean a return of workplace ballots, or part-postal ballots. It also clears the way for innovations such as voting via the Internet.

(3) Where it is alleged that there has been a breach of the statutory election requirements, an aggrieved member has the choice of a complaint to the Certification Officer under TULRCA s 55 or to the court under TULRCA s 56. As noted already, a complaint to the Certification Officer is quicker and easier and should be resolved within six months. A decision of the Certification Officer can be appealed to the EAT, but only on a point of law.

REFERENCES AND FURTHER READING

K Ewing (1985), 'The Strike, the Courts and the Rule-Books' 14 ILJ 1 (on the litigation in the miners' strike 1984–85)

R Kidner (1984), 'Trade Union Democracy: Election of Trade Unions Officers' 13 ILJ 193 (on the Trade Union Act 1984)

Lord Wedderburn (1985), 'Ultra vires: out?' 14 ILJ 127

The thinking of the Conservative government over the 1980s on this area may be followed through its Green Papers preceding trade union law reform:

Democracy in Trade Unions, Cmnd 8778 (1983)

Industrial Relations in the 1990s, Cm 1602 (1991) Chaps 1, 2, 5, 6, 7

Removing Barriers to Employment, Cm 655 (1989)

Trade Unions and Their Members, Cm 95 (1987)

Visit **http://www.mylawchamber.co.uk/pitt** to access live web updates and web links to extend your knowledge of Employment Law.

 mylawchamber

12

INDUSTRIAL ACTION I

Why should workers be free to engage in industrial action if they have a dispute with their employer? Such action may cause financial loss to the business which is disproportionate to the importance of the dispute; it is likely also to interfere with the business of the employer's customers, even though they are not involved in the dispute; and it could affect innocent third parties such as the general public. Is there no better way of dealing with industrial disputes than allowing such disruptive action with its random harmful effects?

While such questions seem simple and obvious, the answer to them is not so straightforward. One answer could be that, if we prohibit workers from withdrawing their labour, then we are looking at a situation of forced labour, tantamount to slavery. Suppression of trade unions and abolition of the right to strike are usually among the first actions of repressive governments. On this basis, the answer to the question, 'why should workers be allowed to strike?' is that this is an aspect of human rights and should be guaranteed for that reason.

Charter of Fundamental Rights of the European Union (2000/C 364/01)

ARTICLE 5

Prohibition of slavery and forced labour

1   No one shall be held in slavery or servitude.
2   No one shall be required to perform forced or compulsory labour . . .

ARTICLE 28

Right of collective bargaining and action

Workers and employers, or their respective organisations, have, in accordance with Community law and national laws and practices, the right to negotiate and conclude collective agreements at the appropriate levels and, in cases of conflicts of interest, to take collective action to defend their interests, including strike action.

Unison v *UK* [2002] IRLR 497 European Court of Human Rights

JUDGMENT OF THE COURT: '. . . The Court recalls that, while Article 11 paragraph 1 [of the European Convention on Human Rights] includes trade union freedom as a specific aspect of freedom of association, this provision does not secure any particular treatment of trade union members by the State. There is no express inclusion of a right to strike or an obligation on employers to engage in collective bargaining. At most, Article 11 may be regarded as safe-guarding the freedom of trade unions to protect the occupational interests of their members. While the ability to strike represents one of the most important of the means by which trade unions can fulfil this function, there are others . . .'

Comment

(1) The EU's Charter of Fundamental Rights is a good example of the human rights approach to the right to strike. The Charter currently has no legal force, although it has persuasive influence in the ECJ and is symbolic of the values and aspirations of the European Union. The Treaty of Lisbon will incorporate some parts of the Charter in the Treaty of Rome from 2009, if ratified by the member states. However, this is unlikely to require any change to domestic law, given the high level and relatively unspecific nature of the expression of the right to take collective action.

(2) As can be seen from *Unison* v *UK* (2002), the right to strike is only indirectly protected by Art 11 of the European Convention on Human Rights, which guarantees freedom of association – and was ultimately found not to have been infringed in this case (see below, p 629).

(3) It will be noted that in Art 28 of the Charter of Fundamental Rights the right to strike is allied to the right to engage in collective bargaining. As long ago as 1942 Lord Wright said: 'the right of workmen to strike is an essential element in the principle of collective bargaining' (*Crofter Hand Woven Harris Tweed* v *Veitch* (1942)). This provides another justification for the right to take industrial action.

European Social Charter 1961

ARTICLE 6

The right to bargain collectively

With a view to ensuring the effective exercise of the right to bargain collectively, the Contracting Parties undertake:
1 to promote joint consultation between workers and employers;
2 to promote, where necessary and appropriate, machinery for voluntary negotiations between employers or employers' organisations and workers' organisations, with a view to the regulation of terms and conditions of employment by means of collective agreements;
3 to promote the establishment and use of appropriate machinery for conciliation and voluntary arbitration for the settlement of labour disputes;
and recognise:
4 the right of workers and employers to collective action in cases of conflicts of interest, including the right to strike, subject to obligations that might arise out of collective agreements previously entered into.

Comment

(1) The justification for the right to strike as an essential element of the collective bargaining process involves two related arguments. The equilibrium argument holds that the individual worker's subordination to the employer needs a balance and the power of the employer can be balanced by the power of workers acting collectively. An employer

may be able to ignore one person, but not all the workers united. The autonomy argument depends on the voluntary nature of collective bargaining in the United Kingdom. Since the law largely stays out of the collective bargaining process, it is argued it should stay out of the sanctions inherent in that process – whether this is by way of a lock-out, or a withdrawal of capital by the employer (cf *Moon* v *Homeworthy Furniture* (1977) above, p 442) or by way of industrial action by the workforce. Of course, the more that the law intervenes to regulate collective bargaining, the less the power of the autonomy argument (see Chapter 5 above).

(2) This also points to a possible answer to the question, is there not a better way of dealing with industrial disputes? It is common for collective bargains to stipulate procedures to be followed in case of disputes, to make industrial action a last resort, although it is very unusual for these to be in the form of legally binding agreements. However, where there is an impasse, it may require the flexing of industrial muscle on both sides to get some movement or resolution of the issue. Both employers and unions are reluctant to refer issues to be decided by some outside body: as we saw in Chapter 1, the voluntary arbitration jurisdiction of the CAC is now pretty much a dead letter.

(3) When industrial action is taken, the employer at whom it is aimed has two possible targets for legal action: the employees on strike and the organisers of the strike – usually a trade union. In this chapter we will consider, first, the position of individual employees who take part in strikes and other industrial action and then the potential liability in tort for trade unions who organise industrial action.

INDUSTRIAL ACTION AND INDIVIDUAL RIGHTS

Strikes and the contract of employment

The issue here is whether going on strike is a breach of an employee's contract of employment. Within that question is the subsidiary issue as to whether the answer is affected by the employees giving notice of their intention to strike.

Morgan v Fry [1968] 2 QB 710 Court of Appeal

The claimant sued the defendant, an official of the TGWU, for the tort of intimidation. The defendant had threatened the employer with strike action unless members of a breakaway union (including the claimant) were dismissed. A central question before the court was whether the threatened strike action would be a breach of contract for the employees involved.

LORD DENNING MR: '. . . This brings me, therefore, to the crux of the case: was the "strike notice" in this case the threat of a breach of contract? If it had been a full week's notice by the men to terminate the employment altogether, it would not have been a threat to commit a breach of contract. Every man was entitled to terminate his contract of employment by giving a week's notice. But the "strike notice" in this case was not a notice to terminate the employment. It was a notice that they would not work with non-unionists. That looks very like a threat of a breach of contract: and, therefore, intimidation. In *Stratford (J T) & Son Ltd* v *Lindley* (1965) I stated the argument in this way:

> "Suppose that a trade-union officer gives a 'strike notice'. He says to an employer: 'We are going to call a strike on Monday week unless you . . . dismiss yonder man who is not a member of the union.' . . . Such a notice is not to be construed as if it were a week's notice on behalf of the men to terminate their employment, for that is the last thing any of the men

would desire. They do not want to lose their pension rights and so forth by giving up their jobs. The 'strike notice' is nothing more nor less than a notice that the men will not come to work" – or, as in this case, that they will not do their work as they should – "In short, that they will break their contracts. . . . In these circumstances . . . the trade-union officer, by giving the 'strike notice', issues a threat to the employer. He threatens to induce the men to break their contracts of employment unless the employer complies with their demand. That is a threat to commit a tort. It is clear intimidation . . ."

It is difficult to see the logical flaw in that argument. But there must be something wrong with it: for if that argument were correct, it would do away with the right to strike in this country. It has been held for over 60 years that workmen have a right to strike (including therein a right to say that they will not work with non-unionists) provided that they give sufficient notice beforehand: and a notice is sufficient if it is at least as long as the notice required to terminate the contract.

There have been many cases where trade-union officials have given "strike notices" of proper length, and no one has suggested there was anything illegal about them . . .

What then is the legal basis on which a "strike notice" of proper length is held to be lawful? I think it is this: The men can leave their employment altogether by giving a week's notice to terminate it. That would be a strike which would be perfectly lawful. If a notice to terminate is lawful, surely a lesser notice is lawful: such as a notice that "we will not work alongside a non-unionist". After all, if the employers should retort to the men: "We will not accept this notice as lawful", the men can at once say: "Then we will give notice to terminate." The truth is that neither employer nor workmen wish to take the drastic action of termination if it can be avoided. The men do not wish to leave their work for ever. The employers do not wish to scatter their labour force to the four winds. Each side is, therefore, content to accept a "strike notice" of proper length as lawful. It is an implication read into the contract by the modern law as to trade disputes. If a strike takes place, the contract of employment is not terminated. It is suspended during the strike and revives again when the strike is over . . .'

(Davies and Russell LJJ concurred in the result, but on different grounds.)

Comment

(1) The judgment of Lord Denning that the contract is suspended where the strike notice is of equivalent length to that needed to terminate the contract was a novelty. Neither of the other judges in the Court of Appeal decided the case on those grounds. The argument was considered by the Donovan Commission in its contemporaneous report.

Report of the Royal Commission on Trade Unions and Employers' Associations 1965–1968 (the Donovan Commission) Cmnd 3623

936 Strikes may be preceded by no notice or some notice given by or on behalf of the employees concerned.

937 If no notice is given, then ignoring special cases such as engagement from day to day where no notice is required, a breach of the contract of employment will normally result. The same is true even if notice of the intention to strike is given, whether the notice be shorter, or longer, or the same length as the notice required by the contract for its termination.

938 If however the notice is in terms a notice to terminate the contract and is of the required length, and the employee works the notice out before ceasing work, no breach of contract occurs. On the contrary, the contract has been fulfilled according to its terms.

939 It is sometimes said that this situation does not reflect the true intentions of the parties. Where notice of a stoppage of work is given, not being a notice to terminate the contract, it is true that the employees concerned are in breach of the contract. Under that contract they are bound to go on rendering service until some event has occurred upon which it was agreed that the contract should end, as for example the giving of due notice to terminate it. Yet by ceasing to work without giving such a notice, the employees are not, it is argued, really intending to repudiate the contract altogether – they simply want it modified. Nor does the employer in such a case regard the cessation of work as a repudiation of the contract, entitling him to rescind it. He really wants the contract to continue and he hopes to be able to come to terms over the modification which his employees are seeking. Only if this hope is finally dashed will questions of repudiation and consequent rescission arise.

940 Similarly when due notice to end the contract is given prior to the strike, the notice being to the effect that the employee will cease work on its expiry, neither side, it is said, really wishes to put an end to the contract. One party simply wants different terms; the other hopes to come to some agreement about them.

941 It has accordingly been proposed by some that this situation should be reflected in the law and that, if the intention of the parties is simply to suspend the contract for the period of the strike, then the law of contract should produce that effect; for one of the purposes of the law, after all, is to give effect to the intentions of the contracting parties.

942 To this end it has been suggested that strikes should merely suspend the contract of employment without breaking it, or terminating it. In practice this would mean creating a new right of unilateral suspension, since either side to the contract of employment could exercise the right without the consent of the other, the employee by striking, the employer by locking out.

943 The concept is not as simple as it sounds: and before any such new law could be formulated problems of some difficulty would have to be faced and solved. They include the following:

(a) To what strikes would it apply? To unofficial and unconstitutional as well as to official strikes? How would strikes be defined for this purpose?

(b) Would it also apply to other industrial action such as a ban on overtime in breach of contract or to a 'go-slow'?

(c) Would it apply to 'lightning strikes' or only to strikes where at least *some* notice was given, though less than the notice required for the termination of the contract? If so, what length of notice should be required?

(d) Would the new law apply to the gas, water and electricity industries, which at present are subject to the special provisions of section 4 of the Conspiracy and Protection of Property Act 1875? What also would be the position under section 5 of the same Act [now TULRCA s 240]?

(e) Would the employer still be allowed instantly to dismiss an employee for grave misconduct during the course of the strike? (Note: this is the case under French law where strikes are treated as suspending the contract of employment.) If so, what kind of acts would constitute 'grave misconduct'?

(f) Would 'contracting out' of the new law be permissible, eg in collective bargains, or in individual contracts of employment?

(g) Would strikers be free to take up other employment while the contract was suspended? If so, would any obligations of secrecy in the suspended contract be suspended too?

(h) If all efforts to end the strike failed, upon what event would the suspension of the contract cease and be replaced by termination?

944   This list is not exhaustive, but is perhaps sufficient to show that considerable technical difficulties would be encountered if the doctrine of unilateral suspension of contracts of employment were to be made part of our law.

Comment

(1) In the light of more recent developments in the law – for example, the concept of the partially suspended contract of employment during maternity leave – it may be felt that the difficulties outlined in para 943 of the Donovan Commission Report are overstated. Courts have successfully dealt with questions as to whether industrial action is constitutional (ie, in accordance with the union's own rules or not) on a number of occasions, as seen in Chapter 11. For some years there has also been a statutory definition of what counts as unofficial industrial action in TULRCA ss 20 and 237, although it is controversial, as we will see. Can you think of how the other issues identified could be or have been dealt with by the law?

(2) The classic view expressed here by the Donovan Commission to the effect that a strike is a fundamental breach of contract whether or not notice has been given is generally preferred to the Denning approach (cf *Simmons* v *Hoover* (1977)). This means that, at common law, an employer would be entitled to dismiss strikers without notice.

(3) It is admitted on all sides, however, that if employees all give notice to *terminate* their contracts on the same day, then even if they are acting in concert in order to pressurise their employer, their actions will not be in breach of contract. But it must be clear that this is the true construction of the facts.

Boxfoldia v *National Graphical Association (1982)*
[1988] ICR 752 Queen's Bench Division

SAVILLE J: 'At a meeting held on 20 February 1985 the National Council of the National Graphical Association (1982) endorsed a recommendation made to them by Mr Harding, a national officer of this trade union, that 14 days' notice of withdrawal of labour should be served on Boxfoldia Ltd in respect of those employees of that company who were members of that trade union. By a letter dated 21 February 1985, Mr Harding wrote to the managing director of Boxfoldia Ltd in the following terms:

"Further to our meeting in your offices on Friday, 1 February, I gave a full report on the breakdown of our negotiations to our national council at its meeting on 20 February. Our council have taken the decision to fully support our members' aspirations as far as Boxfoldia are concerned. Therefore I have been instructed to write giving the company 14 days' notice of withdrawal of all NGA members' labour from the company as from Monday, 25 February. Therefore, this would become effective as of Monday, 11 March."

The NGA sent copies of this letter to their local branch and to the union chapel officials at Boxfoldia. It is common ground that by acting as they did, the NGA called for an official strike of its members working for this company to begin on 11 March 1985.

On that day 39 employees of Boxfoldia who were members of the NGA failed to report to work. Later on the same day the company wrote to each of those employees, stating in effect that those whose absence meant that they were taking part in the strike were dismissed with immediate effect. In truth, with two exceptions resulting from ill-health, the failure of those employees to report for work was indeed because they were taking part in the strike called by their union, and it is also common ground that the NGA, by calling an official strike, induced those employees to act as they did . . .

On behalf of the NGA, Mr Goudie's principal submission was that his clients had not induced the majority of the employees concerned to break their contracts of employment. He pointed out, as was the fact, that in the case of all but nine of the employees, the contracts of employment provided for two weeks' notice of termination; and his submission was that this contractual notice had been given on behalf of those employees by the NGA in their letter dated 21 February 1985. Thus, argued Mr Goudie, the NGA had done no more than to induce those employees to bring their contracts to a lawful end, something which it is accepted the union were perfectly entitled to do. As to the remaining nine employees, whose contracts provided for four weeks' notice of termination, Mr Goudie submitted that no loss was proved to have flowed from the termination of those contracts alone, a submission which Mr Mitting for the company did not seek to dispute.

In these circumstances, the central issue in the case is whether the letter of 21 February 1985 is properly to be treated as one written on behalf of the employees concerned giving contractual notice of the termination of their contracts of employment . . .

In my judgment, it would not be right to approach any given case on the basis that the one construction is automatically to be preferred to the other. Whether or not a strike notice is properly categorised as one giving notice of termination in accordance with the terms of the employment contracts depends in my view on the meaning and effect of the words used in the context in which they were used, that is to say by the application of the ordinary and well established rules of law developed to deal with contractual and other matters of this kind.

I turn, therefore, to consider the letter itself. This was written in the context of a long-standing and unresolved trade dispute between local officials of the NGA and the company over terms and conditions of employment of members of the NGA employed by the company. Indeed, for many months past the dispute had resulted from time to time in various forms of industrial action (short of a strike) against the company. The employer (the company) was anxious for the matter to be considered by the NGA at national level, but negotiations at this level which took place eventually at the beginning of February 1985 were not successful. This led to Mr Harding, who was the national officer of the NGA involved in the negotiations, to make a report and recommendations to the national council of the NGA. The result was the decision of the national council (who clearly constituted responsible persons within the meaning of s 15 of the Employment Act 1982 [see now TULRCA s 20]) to call the official strike.

In my judgment, the letter cannot be categorised as a notice given pursuant to the termination provisions of the respective contracts of employment, that at the end of the stipulated notice period the contracts of employment would come to an end. To have this effect it seems to me that the letter would have to be capable of being reasonably read and understood in its context as one written by the NGA as agent for the employees concerned, communicating the decision of those employees to implement the termination provisions and giving on their behalf the appropriate notice of termination. On its face the letter fulfils none of these requirements. It does not purport to be written on behalf of or as agent for those employees; it does not purport to communicate the decision of those employees to bring their contracts to an end; and it does not purport on their behalf to give the appropriate termination notice stipulated in their contracts. On the contrary, the material part of the letter on its face is written by Mr Harding on the instructions of the national council (not the employees) communicating the decision of that council (not the employees) to call an official strike on 14 days' notice. While I agree with Mr Goudie that the phrase "withdrawal of labour" is in itself theoretically capable of being read as referring to notice of contractual termination, in the context in which it was used in this case I consider that it cannot sensibly bear that meaning . . .

There is no evidence in the present case, nor is it suggested, that any of the members concerned gave any specific authority to the NGA to act as agent to give contractual notice of termination of the employment and contracts on their behalf. There is nothing in the union rules which vests the union with any such authority. On the contrary, rule 40(2) of the rules of the NGA provides that if a dispute cannot be settled by conciliatory means and where the sanction of the national council has been obtained, all members working in offices affected by the dispute and paying full subscriptions must give notice to terminate their engagements. Thus, so far from the NGA being authorised to give contractual (or other) notices of termination on behalf of and as agent for the members, it is the latter who by the rules have agreed to give such notice themselves if instructed by their union to do so. To my mind this provision, which forms part of the terms and conditions of the contract of union membership, is quite inconsistent with and indeed the antithesis of the authority which it is suggested was impliedly conferred on the union by its members . . .'

Comment

(1) This case involved the employer suing the union in tort for inducing employees to break their contracts of employment. As the union had not balloted its members before calling the strike, it did not have the usual immunity from tortious liability. But if it had been able successfully to argue that the employees had not broken their contracts of employment, it would not have been liable for the tort of inducing a breach.

(2) The case is also of interest in relation to the question of how far a trade union can be regarded as the agent of its members (see p 219).

Industrial action short of a strike

Go-slow

General Engineering Services v *Kingston and St Andrew Corporation* [1989] ICR 88 Privy Council

The advice of the Privy Council was delivered by LORD ACKNER:
'The claimant carries on the business of mechancial and electrical engineering and at all material times owned 27 Dunrobin Avenue, Kingston, St Andrew, where they stored specialised medical-electrical equipment and other material connected with their business. At about 5.45 am on 13 October 1977 Mrs Enid Holding, who lived at 29, Dunrobin Avenue, heard a slight crackling sound coming from no 27. On looking through her bedroom window she saw smoke and flames coming from a section of the building. She dialled the fire brigade at Half Way Tree, which is only one and a half miles away, involving a journey which normally takes the fire engine no more than 3 and a half minutes. When some 15 minutes later the fire brigade had not arrived, she telephoned again and was told the unit was on its way. It arrived shortly after the telephone call, having taken some 17 minutes to drive this short distance. It was common ground that if the fire brigade had arrived with its usual expedition, the fire would have been speedily extinguished and the complete destruction not only of the office and store room, but also of its contents involving a total loss of approximately $6.2 million, would have been avoided.

The reason why it took some five times longer for the fire brigade to reach this fire than normally was that the firemen, in furtherance of an industrial dispute, were operating a "go slow" policy in order to bring pressure on their employers to satisfy their grievances. Mrs Holding, who became very anxious at the non-arrival of the fire brigade after making her second telephone call, went up the road along which she was expecting them to arrive. She saw them turn the corner, enter Dunrobin Avenue and then noticed the fire engine slowly moving forward, then stopping, then moving slowly again and then once more stopping. Evidence was given by Mr Dixon, the claimant's managing director, who arrived at the scene of the fire about an hour later, that he asked the chief officer in charge of the fire brigade, "Why did you let the place burn down?" This question elicited the reply, "We are on a go-slow and, even if my mother was in there, it would have to burn down. I want my raise of pay." Although this reply was denied, Mr Cotran, on behalf of the claimant, did not seek to challenge that the clear inference from the facts was that the firemen had, in pursuance of their go slow policy, decided to take so long to get to the fire that by the time of their arrival the property would have been substantially destroyed.

On 17 August 1978 the claimant issued a writ against the defendant alleging that, under the Kingston and St Andrew Fire Brigade Act, the defendant had a statutory duty to extinguish this fire, that in breach of this duty, it failed to respond promptly to the emergency call and was vicariously responsible for the negligence of the members of the fire brigade. Had the defendant complied with its statutory duty and had the fire brigade travelled to the scene of the fire with due expedition, the fire, so it was alleged, would have been extinguished with minimal damage and loss to the claimant . . .

It is of course common ground that a master is not responsible for a wrongful act done by his servant unless it is done in the course of his employment. Further it is well established that the act is deemed to be so done if it is either (1) a wrongful act authorised by the master or (2) a wrongful and unauthorised mode of doing some act authorised by the master. Mr Cotran contended that the conduct of the members of the fire brigade could properly be categorised as a wrongful and unauthorised mode of doing some act, ie driving to the scene of a fire, which was authorised by the defendant, their employer . . .

Their Lordships have no hesitation in agreeing with the unanimous decision of the Court of Appeal, upholding that of Malcolm J that the members of the fire brigade were not acting in the course of their employment when they, by their conduct described above, permitted the destruction of the building and its contents. Their unauthorised and wrongful act was so to prolong the time taken by the journey to the scene of the fire, as to ensure that they did not arrive in time to extinguish it, before the building and its contents were destroyed. Their mode and manner of driving – the slow progression of stopping and starting – was not so connected with the authorised act, that is driving to the scene of the fire as expeditiously as reasonably possible, as to be a mode of performing that act . . .

Here the unauthorised and wrongful act by the firemen was a wrongful repudiation of an essential obligation of their contract of employment, namely the decision and its implementation not to arrive at the scene of the fire in time to save the building and its contents. This decision was not in furtherance of their employer's business. It was in furtherance of their industrial dispute, designed to bring pressure on their employer to satisfy their demands, by not extinguishing fires until it was too late to save the property. Such conduct was the very negation of carrying out some act authorised by the employer, albeit in a wrongful and unauthorised mode . . .'

Comment

(1) The issue here was whether the employer was vicariously liable for the action (or inaction) of its employees. For our purposes, the important point is that the Privy Council states clearly that a go-slow is a fundamental breach of contract: the corollary is that the employer would be justified at common law in summarily dismissing the employees on this ground.

Work-to-rule

Secretary of State v *ASLEF (No 2)* [1972] 2 QB 455 Court of Appeal

Under the Industrial Relations Act 1971 the Secretary of State for Employment had power to invoke emergency procedures in case of a strike, or industrial action short of a strike, thought to be injurious to the national economy. Three rail unions, ASLEF, NUR and TSSA had ordered their members to work strictly to rule and also to ban overtime and rest day working in pursuit of a pay claim. The Secretary of State in these proceedings sought to enforce the emergency procedures.

LORD DENNING MR: '. . . Now for the next requisite, "irregular industrial action short of a strike". Before any ballot is ordered, it must appear to the Secretary of State under [the Industrial Relations Act] s 141(1)(a) that "any irregular industrial action short of a strike has begun or is likely to begin". It is said that the Secretary of State has misdirected himself in the law on the meaning of the words "irregular industrial action" and that it could not reasonably appear to him that there was any irregular industrial action.

I turn, therefore, to the definition in the Act of "irregular industrial action short of a strike". It is contained in section 33(4). The primary requisite is that there should be a concerted course of conduct by a group of workers "with the intention of . . . interfering with the production of goods or the provision of services". That primary requisite is here fulfilled. The three unions have combined together to order the men to work to rule. They readily admit that their intention is to disrupt the railway service. But there is a further requisite, I will call it the secondary requisite, in section 33(4)(b). This requires that "in the case of some or all" of the group of workers the concerted course of conduct is carried on in "breach of their contracts of employment".

For this purpose, of course, we must consider what their contracts of employment are and see whether this conduct is in breach of those contracts. So we have been referred to the contracts of employment. They are contained in a series of collective agreements made by the Railways Board with the trade unions. The terms are set out in some books which have been put before us. They contain detailed provisions on all sorts of matters, such as hours of duty, meal times, rates of pay, rest days and so forth.

The rule book is entirely different. It has 280 pages and 239 rules with many sub-rules. Each man signs a form saying that he will abide by the rules. But these rules are in no way terms of the contract of employment. They are only instructions to a man as to how he is to do his work. Some of them are quite out of date, such as that the coal on the engine must not be stacked too high. Others contain trivial details, such as that the employees must on duty be neat in appearance. A few are important in this case, particularly rule 2 (1), which says that employees must see that the safety of the public is their chief care under all circumstances, a rule to which all would subscribe. Rule 126 (i), which was specially emphasised in the instructions to the men, says: "The driver and fireman MUST . . . satisfy themselves that the engine is in proper order". Rule 176 is a compendious rule which is worth noting: "Inspectors, shunters, guards, drivers, signalmen and all others concerned, must make every effort to facilitate the working of trains and prevent any avoidable delay."

Those rules are to be construed reasonably. They must be fitted in sensibly the one with the other. They must be construed according to the usual course of dealing and to the way they have been applied in practice. When the rules are so construed the railway system, as we all know, works efficiently and safely. But if some of those rules are construed unreasonably, as, for instance, the driver takes too long examining his engine or seeing that all is in order, the system may be in danger of being disrupted. It is only when they are construed unreasonably that the railway system grinds to a halt. It is, I should think, clearly a breach of contract first to construe the rules unreasonably, and then to put that unreasonable construction into practice . . .

[T]he principal discussion before us (and it is the most important discussion for the purposes of the case) was as to the general instruction to the men to "work to rule", or, as it is put more fully in the instructions, "Strictly observe all BRB rules". The meaning of that instruction is not in doubt. It is well known to everyone in the land. The instruction was intended to mean, and it was understood to mean, "Keep the rules of your employment to the very letter, but, whilst doing so, do your very utmost to disrupt the undertaking". Is that a breach of contract?

Now I quite agree that a man is not bound positively to do more for his employer than his contract requires. He can withdraw his goodwill if he pleases. But what he must not do is wilfully to obstruct the employer as he goes about his business. That is plainly the case where a man is employed singly by a single employer. Take a homely instance, which I put in the course of argument. Suppose I employ a man to drive me to the station. I know there is sufficient time, so that I do not tell him to hurry. He drives me at a slower speed than he need, with the deliberate object of making me lose the train, and I do lose it. He may say that he has performed the letter of the contract; he has driven me to the station; but he has wilfully made me lose the train, and that is a breach of contract beyond all doubt. And what is more, he is not entitled to be paid for the journey. He has broken the contract in a way that goes to the very root of the consideration; so he can recover nothing. Such a case is akin (it has been said we have had no authorities on the subject) to the many cases where there is an implied term not wilfully to prevent the carrying out of the contract . . .

So much for the case when a man is employed singly. It is equally the case when he is employed, as one of many, to work in an undertaking which needs the service of all. If he, with the others, takes steps wilfully to disrupt the undertaking, to produce chaos so that it will not run as it should, then each one who is a party to those steps is guilty of a breach of his contract. It is no answer for any one of them to say "I am only obeying the rule book", or "I am not bound to do more than a 40-hour week". That would be all very well if done in good faith without any wilful disruption of services; but what makes it wrong is the object with which it is done. There are many branches of our law when an act which would otherwise be lawful is rendered unlawful by the motive or object with which it is done. So here it is the wilful disruption which is the breach. It means that the work of each man goes for naught. It is made of no effect. I ask: Is a man to be entitled to wages for his work when he, with others, is doing his best to make it useless? Surely not. Wages are to be paid for services rendered, not for producing deliberate chaos. The breach goes to the whole of the consideration . . .'

BUCKLEY LJ: '. . . With regard to the direction to the men to work strictly in accordance with the rules, the contracts of employment between the board and the railwaymen are entered into as part of the board's commercial activity. Such contracts have commercial objectives and are based on commercial considerations. Just as, where a contract is entered into the performance of which requires the continued existence of a particular state of affairs, the wilful act of one party in bringing that state of affairs to an end so as to render the performance of the contract impossible constitutes a breach of an implied term of the contract, so, in my judgment, in the case of a contract of a commercial character the wilful act of one party which, although not, maybe, departing from the literal letter of the agreement, nevertheless defeats the commercial intention of the parties in entering into the contract, constitutes a breach of an implied term of the contract to perform the contract in such a way as not to frustrate that commercial objective.

Assuming in the appellants' favour that the direction to work to rule avoided any specific direction to commit a breach of any express term of the contract, the instruction was, nevertheless, directed, and is acknowledged to have been directed, to rendering it impossible, or contributing to the impossibility, to carry on the board's commercial activity upon a sound commercial basis, if at all. The object of the instruction was to frustrate the very commercial object for which the contracts of employment were made. It struck at the foundation of the consensual intentions of the parties to those contracts, and amounted, in my judgment, to an instruction to commit what were clearly breaches or abrogations of those contracts. These are or would be, in my judgment, breaches of an implied term to serve the employer faithfully within the requirements of the contract. It does not mean that the employer could require a man to do anything which lay outside his obligations under the contract, such as to work excess hours of work or to work an unsafe system of work or anything of that kind, but it does mean that within the terms of the contract the employee must serve the employer faithfully with a view to promoting those commercial interests for which he is employed. The contrary view is, in my opinion, one which proceeds upon much too narrow and formalistic an approach to the legal relations of employer and employee and is an approach which, I may perhaps add, seems to me to be unlikely to promote goodwill or confidence between the parties . . .'

ROSKILL LJ: '. . . The fact that under normal conditions railways operate satisfactorily when the rule book is interpreted as it clearly is normally interpreted suggests to me that over the years a course of dealing and common understanding in the performance of the instructions has arisen, from which an employee is not free arbitrarily to depart. Mr Wedderburn [counsel for the NUR] said this morning that there was no evidence of any such course of conduct. With respect, that seems to me to be wrong. There is ample evidence, for it is a matter of common knowledge that the railways work satisfactorily and efficiently in normal times when the rule book is observed as it normally is observed. An implied term can only be implied if it is both reasonable and necessary to make the implication so as to ensure that the contract works. The courts are rightly slow to write into contracts terms for which the parties have not themselves made provision. The courts do not, cannot, and must not re-write contracts so as to make them, as some may think, more reasonable than they are if they are construed as the parties have provided.

Mr Wedderburn this morning, in a happy phrase, said that the implication which the Crown and the Railways Board sought was designed not to make the contract work, but to make the workers work. If I thought that that aphorism accurately stated the position I would not hesitate to refuse to imply any such term. The courts will only imply a term when it is so clear that the only reason why it has not been expressly included is because the parties thought the need for the provision was self-evident. Mr Pain [counsel for ASLEF] has referred more than once, and again finally this morning, to the well-known illustration of the officious bystander. I have endeavoured, following Mr Pain's line of argument, to attempt to apply that test by imagining an officious bystander watching an interview between a responsible officer of the Railways Board about to engage a highly articulate and intelligent driver or guard and that driver or guard. I have imagined a copy of the rule book being handed over the table and the onlooker asking the former why he has not said to the latter: "You do understand, don't you, that you must not operate these instructions so as to disrupt the entire running of the railways system of the country?" Traditionally it is enough if the answer to that hypothetical question is a testy "of course". Were such a question put I doubt if the driver's or guard's response would have been limited, in MacKinnon LJ's famous phrase, to such a testy "Oh, of course". I think he might well have been forgiven if he had replied to such a question in more vigorous and less restrained language.

Notwithstanding the skill with which the contrary view has been urged upon us, I regard it as self-evident that each party to each service agreement must, as rational beings, be taken to have assumed as a matter of course, when each service contract was entered into, that the employee would never seek so to interpret and act upon the rules as to disrupt the entire railway system. Accordingly, I have no hesitation in implying a term into the contract of service that each employee will not, in obeying his lawful instructions, seek to obey them in a wholly unreasonable way which has the effect of disrupting the system, the efficient running of which he is employed to ensure. I prefer to rest my decision that work to rule is a breach of contract on this ground rather than on the alternative ground, clearly equally tenable, advanced by the Solicitor-General, that work to rule involves a breach of the positive obligation of faithful service owed by employee to his master . . .'

Comment

(1) Note that each judge gives a different reason for saying that the work-to-rule is a breach of contract. What is the *ratio decidendi* of this case?

(2) These judgments are also important in relation to the development of implied terms in contracts of employment (see Chapter 4).

(3) The final paragraph of Lord Denning's judgment seems to suggest that otherwise lawful action can become a breach of contract because of the motive with which it is done – a theme which appears also in *Ticehurst* v *British Telecom* (above, p 192). But this surely goes too far. If it were correct, every kind of industrial action would be a breach of contract, which would be contrary to general principle. This passage was considered by the Privy Council in the next case.

Burgess v *Stevedoring Services Ltd* [2002] IRLR 810 Privy Council

The issue was whether an overtime ban was a breach of contract.

LORD HOFFMANN: '. . . Mr Strachan [counsel for the employer] relies upon this passage [from Lord Denning's judgment in *Secretary of State* v *ASLEF (No 2)*] in support of a submission that, even if the employees were not under a contractual obligation to report for overtime duty, their failure to do overtime was a breach of contract because it was done wilfully to disrupt the business of their employer. But their Lordships do not think that Lord Denning MR intended to go so far. It seems clear from the examples which he gave that he had in mind that employees may legitimately perform their duties in a way which does not suit the employer (like keeping the train waiting while they check the engine) if they have a bona fide reason but not if their purpose is to be wilfully obstructive. But that does not mean that they are in breach for refusing to do things altogether outside their contractual obligations (like going to work on Sunday) merely because they do not have a bona fide reason for refusal. They do not have to have any reason at all.'

Blacking and part-performance

One way in which trade unionists have traditionally given support to other trade unionists engaged in a trade dispute is to 'black' – that is, refuse to handle – goods supplied by, or destined for, the employer in dispute. Blacking is thus usually a form of sympathy action.

Related to it, in the sense that it also involves employees not doing all their work, is part-performance, where the tactic used is to refuse to do certain duties while remaining ready and willing to do everything else. This is often resorted to where the dispute is over whether these duties can properly be regarded as part of the employees' work (cf *Cresswell* v *Board of Inland Revenue* (1984), p 170 above). However, it may be used in order to put pressure on the employer over some other matter, as in the following case.

Miles v *Wakefield MDC* [1987] ICR 368 House of Lords

LORD TEMPLEMAN: 'My Lords, the respondent claimant is the superintendent registrar of births, deaths and marriages for the district of Wakefield. The claimant was appointed by the appellant defendants, Wakefield Metropolitan District Council. The claimant is paid a salary by the council, and he works a 37-hour week. One of the most important functions of the claimant as superintendent registrar is to conduct civil wedding ceremonies, and the most popular time for such weddings is Saturday morning when the registry office provided by the council is open for three hours between nine o'clock and midday. On instructions from his trade union, NALGO, the claimant, by way of industrial action, refused to conduct weddings on Saturday morning. The object of the union was, by inconveniencing the public, to obtain publicity and support for the campaign conducted by the union in the interests of its members for a higher scale of salary to be paid to superintendent registrars. The claimant remained willing to work a 37-hour week and to work on Saturday but he refused to conduct weddings on Saturday. By a letter dated 8 October 1981, the council:

> "made it clear to the registration officers that whilst ever they are not prepared to undertake the full range of their duties on Saturdays they are not required to attend for work and accordingly will not be paid. If the registrars attend at their offices on Saturdays that is entirely a matter for them."

Thus the council treated the claimant as being under a duty to work three out of his 37 hours on Saturday morning for the purpose of conducting weddings if required. The claimant refused to conduct weddings on Saturday and the council treated him as working for only 34 hours. In refusing to conduct weddings on Saturday, the claimant, as he now frankly concedes, acted in breach of his duties as superintendent registrar. The council deducted $\frac{3}{37}$ ths of the salary of the claimant while he remained unwilling to conduct weddings on Saturday, between August 1981 and October 1982, when the salary dispute was settled. The claimant now seeks payment of the sums deducted, amounting to £774. Nicholls J decided against the claimant. The Court of Appeal by a majority (Parker and Fox LJJ) held that the claimant was entitled to be paid his full salary unless and until he was dismissed . . .

My Lords, industrial action involves a worker, in conjunction with all or some of his fellow workers, declining to work or declining to work efficiently in each case with the object of harming the employer so that the employer will feel obliged to increase wages or improve conditions of work or meet the other requirements put forward by the workers' representatives. The form of industrial action which consists of declining to work is a strike. The form of industrial action which consists of declining to work efficiently has many manifestations including the "go slow" and the refusal by the claimant to carry out some of his functions on Saturday. In essence, the claimant was employed by the public and his industrial action took the form of declining to work efficiently on Saturday with the object of inconveniencing the public and advancing the claim of his union for higher salaries. Industrial action is an effective method of enhancing the bargaining power of the workers' representatives. The courts are not competent to determine and are not concerned to determine whether a strike or other form of industrial action is justified or malicious, wise or foolish, provoked or exploited, beneficial or damaging; history has proved that any such determination is speculative and liable to be unsound. Any form of industrial action by a worker is a breach of contract which entitled the employer at common law to dismiss the worker because no employer is contractually bound to retain a worker who is intentionally causing harm to the employer's business . . .

Where industrial action takes the form of working inefficiently, the employer may decline to accept any work and the worker will not then be entitled to wages.

I agree with my noble and learned friend Lord Bridge of Harwich that industrial action can take many forms and that the legal consequences of industrial action will depend on the rights and obligations of the worker, the effect of the industrial action on the employer and the response of the employer. For my part, however, I take the provisional view that on principle a worker who, in conjunction with his fellow workers, declines to work efficiently with the object of harming his employer is no more entitled to his wages under the contract than if he declines to work at all . . .

My Lords, I would allow this appeal.'

(Lords Brightman, Brandon, Bridge and Oliver agreed that the Council's appeal should be allowed.)

Comment

(1) Lord Templeman's statement that 'any form of industrial action by a worker is a breach of contract . . .' would seem to be too wide, unless the courts are to take the view that the motive of a worker can turn otherwise lawful conduct into a breach of contract. However, refusing to carry out part of one's duties is clearly a breach, though it is open to an employer to waive it.

(2) In *Wiluszynski* v *Tower Hamlets LBC* (1989) the principle in this case was extended so as to deny any payment at all to local government officers who had refused to answer queries from local councillors during a trade dispute, although they continued to carry out all their other duties. In this case, the employer had not physically barred them from the premises in order to prevent them carrying out their other duties, but it had been made clear to them that part-performance was not acceptable and that any work they did while refusing to carry out some of their duties would be treated as having been done on a voluntary basis. Although answering queries was a small part of the claimant's work – at the end of the dispute, which lasted over a month, it took him only three hours to deal with the queries which had built up – the Court of Appeal held that he was not entitled to any pay for the period of the dispute. These decisions reduce the attractiveness of part-performance as a form of industrial action, which had initially looked like a tactic which could be used without employees losing as much pay as they would in an all-out strike.

(3) Whether or not blacking constitutes a breach of the contract of employment has not been the subject of any decision on individual contracts, but it has been treated without discussion as a breach in a number of cases dealing with trade union liability for organising industrial action (see, for example, *Thomson* v *Deakin* (1952)).

Overtime ban

National Coal Board v *Galley* [1958] 1 WLR 16 Court of Appeal

The defendant was employed as a pit deputy – in effect a kind of supervisor – at a mine in Derbyshire. His contract of employment stated that his terms and conditions were 'regulated by such national agreement and the county wages agreement for the time being in force . . .'. Galley's union, NACODS, had concluded an agreement replacing the previous overtime arrangement and providing that 'deputies shall work such days and part days in each week as may reasonably be required by the management in order to promote the safety and efficient working of the pit . . .'

All the deputies refused to work the Saturday morning shift following a dispute over levels of overtime. In the absence of proper supervision, the pit could not be operated and the entire morning's production output was therefore lost.

The judgment of the Court was given by PEARCE LJ: '. . . We come now to the central point in this appeal, namely, whether the defendant became in breach of his contract of employment when he refused to obey his employer's request to work the Saturday voluntary shift on June 16, 1956. He had already worked 11 shifts on the preceding 11 days. Could he reasonably be required to work a twelfth day before having two days off? In other words, was it reasonable to require him to work 12 days in the fortnight? It is, of course, clear that the court is in no way concerned with what are reasonable hours in the abstract. Its task is to consider the agreement made in 1952 and to determine on the evidence whether or not the defendant was being required to work in breach of that agreement. The only yardstick stated in the agreement is what is reasonably required by the management in order to promote the safety and efficient work of the pit and to comply with statutory requirements. But this clearly is not the only yardstick, since the hours of work a deputy could reasonably be required to work for these purposes would depend on the number of deputies employed. Ultimately the question must be whether the defendant himself was being required to work reasonable hours. If, of course, he was being required to work longer hours than other deputies, that, in the absence of some exceptional circumstances, would be evidence that the requirement made on him was unreasonable. There is, however, no suggestion of that in this case . . .

No complaint was made in regard to hours of work until Oct 31, 1955, and then only in regard to hours in excess of the six-shift week. It was not until May 18, 1956, that any suggestion was made to reduce the six-shift week; and it is to be observed that it was then put forward as an alternative to an increase in wages, since it was recognised that wages was a matter for agreement at the national and not the divisional level. We agree with the learned judge when he said:

> "I do not think it is relevant at all to the issues I have to decide in this case. It may be a matter for consideration when negotiating a new agreement, but it cannot, in my opinion, alter the plain meaning of the agreement which has been made."'

(The court held that the claimant's refusal to work the shift was a breach of contract.)

Comment

(1) In this case it was held that overtime was required by the contract of employment, so that failure to do it was a breach of contract. However, in the more common situation where overtime is voluntary, the employee would commit no breach of contract in refusing to do it and so could not be lawfully summarily dismissed at common law. Note that the position in relation to unfair dismissal is different: *Power Packing Casemakers* v *Faust* (1983), below, p 585.

(2) This case was unusual in that the employer sued the employees directly for damages for breach of contract, rather than following the ordinary course of suing the union for organising the industrial action. The employer claimed loss of profit on the pit's output – £545 – as the measure of damages, to be apportioned between the strikers. However, the Court of Appeal held that damages had to be assessed on the basis of the loss arising from each individual breach, ignoring the fact that they had acted in concert. The loss was therefore only the cost of employing a replacement – in other words, the pay they would have paid to a replacement – assessed at just £3 18s 2d per employee.

(3) One remedy which is never open to an employer is to get the court to order the employees back to work. This is related to the ban on forced labour, referred to at the beginning of this chapter, and is enshrined in TULRCA s 236.

(4) In *Burgess* v *Stevedoring Services Ltd* (2002) the Privy Council held that an overtime ban was not a breach of contract where the workers had an obligation to report for overtime when they were assigned to an overtime gang – but under the relevant collective agreement, it was the responsibility of the union to make up overtime gangs and the union had refused to do so. As the workers had not been called on to do overtime, they committed no breach of contract by not doing it.

Strikes and unfair dismissal

Special provision has always been made in unfair dismissal legislation for employees dismissed while taking part in strikes or other industrial action. For many years, the overriding principle was said to be one of neutrality – to keep the law out of adjudicating on the rights and wrongs of industrial disputes. However, this so-called neutrality took a rather strange form: provided that the employer dismissed everyone who was taking part in the industrial action, none of them could claim unfair dismissal! It was only if the employer dismissed some but not others that dismissed employees could claim – and then they might or might not be successful, depending on the employer's reason for choosing them.

The Conservative government tightened the position in the Employment Act 1990, introducing a concept of 'unofficial' industrial action – meaning action not authorised or endorsed by the union in accordance with statute. Employees dismissed while taking part in such action cannot claim unfair dismissal, even if the employer is selective and does not dismiss all of them.

This position was then changed radically by the Employment Relations Act 1999, which for the first time made it automatically unfair to dismiss employees for taking part in industrial action – provided stringent conditions were met.

There are thus three possibilities where employees are dismissed in relation to strikes and other industrial action:

- The employee has no claim, because the action was not authorised or endorsed by the union (TULRCA s 237).
- The dismissal is automatically unfair, because it falls within the conditions in TULRCA s 238A.
- The dismissal may be unfair, because it does not fall within either of the above two sections, and the employer has not treated all the strikers in the same manner (TULRCA s 238).

The first thing to look at is what kinds of activity constitute industrial action so as to bring these provisions into play. We must then work out the meaning of action authorised or endorsed by the union, and then see how these concepts apply in each of the three situations.

What is industrial action?

Trade Union and Labour Relations (Consolidation) Act 1992

246 In this Part – . . .
'strike' means . . . any concerted stoppage of work; . . .

Comment

(1) This definition was imported from the Trade Union Act 1984, where it was only used in relation to ballots before industrial action. It now applies to the whole of TULRCA Part V, the statutory provisions dealing with industrial action. TULRCA was meant to be a purely consolidating measure: arguably, the extension of this definition means that it goes beyond mere consolidation of the previous law.

(2) We have seen that not all forms of industrial action constitute a breach of contract at common law. Does lawful industrial action come within the statutory definition? This is addressed in the next case.

Power Packing Casemakers v *Faust* [1983] ICR 282 Court of Appeal

Three employees were dismissed for refusing to work overtime. The company, which only had 15 employees, had an important rush order to fulfil. It was clear that the refusal to work overtime was motivated by a dispute over wages. The employment tribunal found that the employees had no contractual obligation to work overtime.

STEPHENSON LJ: '. . . The employment tribunal were not addressing their minds to [TULRCA s 238] and the meaning of the words "industrial action" there. But I find that that makes the material provided by the evidence quoted, and the findings based on it, all the more impressive. An employment tribunal and the lay members of the appeal tribunal may be trusted to recognise industrial action when they see it, and that was how both tribunals, as well as one appellant and one other witness, described the employees' refusal to work overtime.

Now Mr Jones [counsel for the employees] submitted on the employees' behalf that they ought not to have described it so, because it was not a breach of contract. His point on construction is this: to constitute "industrial action", in the natural meaning of those words, on the part of an employee, there must be action in breach of his contract of employment. If he merely refuses to do something which he is not contractually bound to do, he cannot be taking part in industrial action. I would agree that if he refuses because he has a private commitment to visit a sick friend, or a personal preference for a football match, he is not taking industrial action. But that is not this case. If he refuses because he and others who refuse with him hope to extract an increase of wages out of his employers because their business will be disrupted if they do not grant it, that continued application of pressure is industrial action in the common sense of the words. I do not feel able to say any more about that argument of Mr Jones that that is not the natural meaning of "industrial action". And when the words come at the end of the phrase "taking part in a strike or other industrial action", they seem to me to cover even more clearly a refusal used as a bargaining weapon, whether it is a breach of contract or not . . .

Since the repeal in 1974 of the [Industrial Relations] Act 1971 there are no references in these statutory provisions to the requirement that the "other industrial action" should be "irregular" or in breach of contract, or, for that matter, "short of a strike"; and I respectfully agree with the view of Waterhouse J, giving the judgment of the appeal tribunal in *Rasool* v *Hepworth Pipe Co Ltd* (1980) that it is impermissible to import the earlier definition into the later provisions.

Why were those words left out? Why should they be put back? When they were put in, I agree with Mr Carr [counsel for the employer] that Parliament was thereby indicating that without them "other industrial action" extended to action involving no breach of contract or irregularity. I would assume that the qualifying words and the definition of them were not accidentally omitted, that there was some reason for deliberately omitting them. I cannot take the words now used as shorthand for the words no longer used or for the now absent definition, and I can find no compelling reason for putting those in after their four years' absence. Subsequent statutes of 1980 and 1982 have not reinserted them. I can infer that the words "short of a strike" were left out as unnecessary or otiose, but why leave out "irregular" or the restriction to breaches of contract? Why, furthermore, should the employment tribunal have to embark on an inquiry into the terms of a claimant's contract of employment, express and implied, in order to decide whether he was taking part in industrial action when he was dismissed?

Mr Jones submits that to give these words the extended (and what, contrary to his first sub-mission, I have held to be the natural) meaning which they bear if not confined to breaches of contract, would do injustice and defeat the purpose and object of [TULRCA s 238] and its predecessor in the Employment Protection Act 1975, namely, to deprive an employee of his right to complain to an employment tribunal of unfair dismissal if, and only if, he has been guilty of misconduct or has broken the terms of his contract. If Mr Jones's gloss – for such, contrary to his submission, it clearly is – upon the language of the section is rejected, unscrupulous employers will be allowed, so he submits, to dismiss unfairly and unjustly those who take legitimate industrial action, without any fear of the circumstances being investigated by the statutory tribunals, or of having to pay compensation or reinstate those unfairly dismissed employees. He calls attention to an obvious misunderstanding by the appeal tribunal of the effect of their interpretation of [TULRCA s 238] . . .

Mr Carr concedes that the criticisms of this part of May J's judgment are well founded, but counters the potential injustice relied on by Mr Jones by submitting that the purpose and object of the section is to avoid courts of law and tribunals being required to investigate the rights and wrongs, or to adjudicate on the merits, of trade disputes in the context of unfair dismissal appli-cations. He referred us to what Lord Scarman said, in *NWL Ltd* v *Woods* (1979) about the pol-icy of the Trade Union and Labour Relations Act 1974 to exclude trade disputes from judicial review by the courts and to substitute an advisory, conciliation and arbitration process; and he pointed out that such disputes are often complex and to give the determination of them to employment tribunals would defeat the legislative aim of providing cheap and speedy hearings of unfair dismissal complaints by such tribunals. These considerations must, he submitted, have outweighed, with the legislature, the potential injustice created by the statutory ban imposed not only on determining complaints by strikers or those engaged in industrial action by [TULRCA s 238(1)(b)], but imposed by [s 238(1)(a)] on determining complaints by employees locked out by employers at the date of dismissal.

I feel the force of these submissions, but no certainty as to the intention of the legislature in enacting this provision.

In threading my way from section and subsections to schedule and paragraphs, and from schedule back to section, I may have lost the way, or the thread, or sight of Parliament's aim and object, even if Parliament itself did not. But of this I have no doubt, that as there is no com-pelling reason why the words of the provision should not be given their natural and ordinary meaning, and good reason why they should not now be defined as once they were, we ought to give them that meaning and apply them, as the appeal tribunal did, to the undisputed facts of the case in favour of the employers. I would accordingly affirm their decision and dismiss this appeal.'

(Purchas LJ delivered a concurring judgment and Sir George Baker agreed.)

Comment

(1) This decision means that employees who manage to find a form of industrial action which does not break their contracts of employment are nonetheless at risk of being dis-missed without redress if their action does not fall within the conditions of TULRCA s 238A. Should this be the case? The difference between this case and *NCB* v *Galley* (1958) is that here overtime working was not obligatory under the contract, so that a refusal to work overtime was not a breach of contract.

(2) While it may not necessarily protect employees that their action is not a breach of contract, it does have implications for trade unions organising industrial action, as we will see.

(3) See also the discussion of 'other industrial action' in *Knowles* v *Fire Brigades Union* (1996) extracted on p 561.

(4) Not only industrial action taken by employees attracts the special regime in TULRCA ss 237, 238 and 238A. They can also apply where an employer takes industrial action, or responds to a threat of industrial action, in the form of a lock-out. This is where the employer either shuts the workplace (literally 'locks out' the workers) or otherwise refuses to let them work, in the context of an industrial dispute. It may occur where employees refuse to work normally (cf *Wiluszynski* v *Tower Hamlets LBC* (1989) (above, p 584) or where the employer is seeking to impose new terms and conditions on the workforce, which refuses to accept them. It will not escape readers' notice that the latter situation would be a fundamental breach of contract at common law by the employer, but the effect of TULRCA ss 238 and 238A is that employees' rights to claim unfair dismissal in these circumstances are limited. This is a strange encouragement to employers to be confrontational in introducing change.

Official and unofficial action

Originally, 'official' industrial action meant industrial action called in accordance with the union's own rules and constitution. The legal relevance of this was confined to the relationship between the union and its members: as we saw in the cases arising from the miners' strike in 1984–85, discussed in Chapter 11, it was possible at common law for members to sue the union if it called industrial action in breach of its own rules. However, whether the action was official or not in this sense was completely irrelevant in relation to the legal position of an employee dismissed for taking part in industrial action.

This was changed by the Conservative government in the Employment Act 1982, which introduced a statutory concept of 'unofficial' action – action which has not been authorised or endorsed by relevant trade union officials as set out in TULRCA s 20(2) (extracted below, p 662).

Unofficial industrial action and unfair dismissal

Trade Union and Labour Relations (Consolidation) Act 1992

237 (1) An employee has no right to complain of unfair dismissal if at the time of dismissal he was taking part in an unofficial strike or other unofficial industrial action.

. . .

(2) A strike or other industrial action is unofficial in relation to an employee unless –

(a) he is a member of a trade union and the action is authorised or endorsed by that union, or

(b) he is not a member of a trade union but there are among those taking part in the industrial action members of a trade union by which the action has been authorised or endorsed.

Provided that, a strike or other industrial action shall not be regarded as unofficial if none of those taking part in it are members of a trade union.

(3)   The provisions of section 20(2) apply for the purpose of determining whether industrial action is to be taken to have been authorised or endorsed by a trade union.

(4)   The question whether industrial action is to be so taken in any case shall be determined by reference to the facts as at the time of dismissal . . .

(6)   For the purposes of this section membership of a trade union for purposes unconnected with the employment in question shall be disregarded; but an employee who was a member of a trade union when he began to take part in industrial action shall continue to be treated as a member for the purpose of determining whether that action is unofficial in relation to him or another notwithstanding that he may in fact have ceased to be a member.

Comment

(1) Note that the effect of s 237(2) is that even non-unionists are prevented from claiming unfair dismissal if the action in which they take part is unofficial so far as the trade union members are concerned – unless the action is taking place at a wholly un-unionised organisation, where the concept of trade union authorisation has no meaning.

(2) The effect of s 237(6) is to stop union members trying to get round this section by all resigning from the union once the unofficial action has started and then claiming that it is an un-unionised workplace.

(3) It is also important to note that this section comes into play if *at the time of the dismissal* the employee was taking part in the unofficial action. The question for the tribunal is therefore a straightforward question of verifiable fact: when did the dismissal take place? The tribunal does not have to try and decide whether the *reason* for the dismissal was participation in industrial action.

(4) The Labour government declined to alter this section in its first legislation on unfair dismissal and industrial action. Instead, it built on the same concept of official and unofficial action to give employees a right to claim that dismissal in connection with industrial action would be automatically unfair in some circumstances, examined next.

Protected industrial action and unfair dismissal

Trade Union and Labour Relations (Consolidation) Act 1992

238A   (1)   For the purposes of this section an employee takes protected industrial action if he commits an act which, or a series of acts each of which, he is induced to commit by an act which by virtue of section 219 is not actionable in tort.

(2)   An employee who is dismissed shall be regarded for the purposes of Part X of the Employment Rights Act 1996 (unfair dismissal) as unfairly dismissed if –

(a)   the reason (or, if more than one, the principal reason) for the dismissal is that the employee took protected industrial action, and

(b)   subsection (3), (4) or (5) applies to the dismissal.

(3)   This subsection applies to a dismissal if the date of the dismissal is within the protected period.

(4)   This subsection applies to a dismissal if –

(a)   the date of the dismissal is after the end of that period, and

(b)   the employee had stopped taking protected industrial action before the end of that period.

(5)   This subsection applies to a dismissal if –

(a)   the date of the dismissal is after the end of that period,

(b)   the employee had not stopped taking protected industrial action before the end of that period, and

(c)   the employer had not taken such procedural steps as would have been reasonable for the purposes of resolving the dispute to which the protected industrial action relates.

(6)   In determining whether an employer has taken those steps regard shall be had, in particular, to –

(a)   whether the employer or a union had complied with procedures established by any applicable collective or other agreement;

(b)   whether the employer or a union offered or agreed to commence or resume negotiations after the start of the protected industrial action;

(c)   whether the employer or a union unreasonably refused, after the start of the protected industrial action, a request that conciliation services be used;

(d)   whether the employer or a union unreasonably refused, after the start of the protected industrial action, a request that mediation services be used in relation to procedures to be adopted for the purposes of resolving the dispute;

(e)   where there was agreement to use either of the services mentioned in paragraphs (c) and (d), the matters specified in section 238B.

(7)   In determining whether an employer has taken those steps no regard shall be had to the merits of the dispute.

(7A)   For the purposes of this section 'the protected period', in relation to the dismissal of an employee, is the sum of the basic period and any extension period in relation to that employee.

(7B)   The basic period is twelve weeks beginning with the first day of protected industrial action.

(7C)   An extension period in relation to an employee is a period equal to the number of days falling on or after the first day of protected industrial action (but before the protected period ends) during the whole or any part of which the employee is locked out by his employer.

(7D)   In subsections (7B) and (7C), the 'first day of protected industrial action' means the day on which the employee starts to take protected industrial action (even if on that day he is locked out by his employer) . . .

Comment

(1) TULRCA s 238A was introduced by the Employment Relations Act 1999 and amended by the Employment Relations Act 2004. The essential idea that it embodies is that, provided the industrial action is lawful, then the employer should not be able to dismiss workers engaging in it, for a reasonable period at any rate. If the dispute continues beyond a reasonable period, then the employer should be allowed to use dismissal as a weapon to bring the action to an end.

(2) There are two conditions for TULRCA s 238A to come into play. First, as stated in s 238A(1), the action must attract immunity from liability in tort under TULRCA s 219: this is examined later in this chapter. This entails the second condition, that the action must have been authorised or endorsed by relevant union officials in accordance with TULRCA s 20(2) (below, p 662). Industrial action which complies with these two conditions is referred to as 'protected industrial action' in the statute.

(3) Unlike TULRCA s 237, s 238A applies only if the *reason* (or principal reason) for the dismissal is the employee's participation in the industrial action: s 238A(2)(a). It

would appear that the burden of proof is on the employee to show this. It would have been simpler had this provision instead applied provided that the dismissal took place *at a time when* the employee was taking part in protected industrial action – the formulation used in TULRCA ss 237 and 238.

(4) The 'protected period' for protected industrial action is set out in s 238A(7A)–(7D). Originally it was set at eight weeks. In the 2003 review of the operation of the Employment Relations Act 1999, unions criticised this as too short, in that it encouraged employers to string out disputes beyond the eight-week period and also because it made no allowance for the fact that in some disputes, some or all of the eight-week period could be accounted for by the employer locking out the workforce rather than the employees having initiated the action. This happened in one dispute in Wales in 2001, at a factory belonging to Friction Dynamics, where workers were locked out for nine weeks and then dismissed. Employers, on the other hand, felt that the very existence of s 238A encouraged disputes and were opposed to any extension of the protected period.

(5) The government's response was initially to retain the eight-week period on the basis that their research showed that between April 2000 and August 2003, 93 per cent of disputes lasted for less than eight weeks. However, they acceded to the argument about lock-outs and proposed that days lost through a lock-out would not count against the protected period (which was implemented by s 238A(7C)). Between this response being published in December 2003 and the passage of the Employment Relations Act 2004, amending TULRCA s 238A, there was a change of heart and, as can be seen in s 238A(7B), the basic protected period was extended to 12 weeks.

(6) Note that the protection applies not only where the employee is dismissed during the protected period, but also in two other situations. The first is where the dismissal is outside the protected period, but the employee ceased taking part in the action during the protected period (s 238A(4)). The second, and more controversial, situation is where the employee was still taking action after the protected period, but the employer is judged not to have taken reasonable procedural steps to try and resolve the dispute (s 238A(5)).

(7) In the 2001 Friction Dynamics dispute, it was felt that the employer made only minimal efforts to engage in the conciliation process. As a result, the Employment Relations Act 2004 introduced TULRCA s 238B to be more specific about what genuine engagement in conciliation and mediation would look like: whether the parties were represented by appropriately senior personnel, whether they were co-operative in setting up meetings, whether they were prepared to answer questions, and so on.

(8) If TULRCA s 238A applies, the employee's dismissal will be automatically unfair. The remaining situation to consider is where the employees are taking part in official industrial action, but TULRCA s 238A does not apply.

Other industrial action dismissals

Trade Union and Labour Relations (Consolidation) Act 1992

238 (1) This section applies in relation to an employee who has a right to complain of unfair dismissal (the 'complainant') and who claims to have been unfairly dismissed, where at the date of the dismissal –

(a)   the employer was conducting or instituting a lock-out, or

(b)   the complainant was taking part in a strike or other industrial action.

(2)   In such a case an employment tribunal shall not determine whether the dismissal was fair or unfair unless it is shown –

(a)   that one or more relevant employees of the same employer have not been dismissed, or

(b)   that a relevant employee has before the expiry of the period of three months beginning with the date of his dismissal been offered re-engagement and that the complainant has not been offered re-engagement.

. . .

(2B)   Subsection (2) does not apply in relation to an employee who is regarded as unfairly dismissed by virtue of section 238A below.

(3)   For this purpose 'relevant employees' means –

(a)   in relation to a lock-out, employees who were directly interested in the dispute in contemplation or furtherance of which the lock-out occurred, and

(b)   in relation to a strike or other industrial action, those employees at the establishment of the employer at or from which the complainant works who at the date of his dismissal were taking part in the action.

Nothing in section 237 (dismissal of those taking part in unofficial industrial action) affects the question who are relevant employees for the purposes of this section . . .

Comment

(1) Section 238(2) does not mean that these dismissals are fair: simply that the tribunal does not have jurisdiction to investigate whether they are fair or not. This is meant to embody the neutrality principle. It must be admitted that the theoretical distinction might be lost on a striking worker whose dismissal falls within TULRCA s 238.

(2) Equally, in those cases where the tribunal does have jurisdiction, because the employer has not treated all strikers in the same way, it does not follow that the dismissal is bound to be unfair. The employer may be able to justify the dismissal of some but not all of the strikers: cf *Crosville Wales Ltd* v *Tracey (No 2)* (1997).

(3) Since TULRCA s 238 only applies where other 'relevant employees' have been treated differently from the complainant, the question of who are 'relevant employees' is critical.

H Campey & Sons Ltd v *Bellwood* [1987] ICR 311 Employment Appeal Tribunal

When employees refused to accept variations to their terms and conditions of employment, the employer locked them all out. A week later, the employer gave them an ultimatum to return to work the next day. Those who did not were dismissed. They claimed unfair dismissal on the basis that the employer had taken back those who complied with the ultimatum.

POPPLEWELL J: 'In *Stock* v *Frank Jones (Tipton) Ltd*, not dissimilar legislation had been considered. The House of Lords held that the fact that two employees, who had been on strike had returned to work before the complaining employees' dismissal rendered their dismissal unfair. The House of Lords decided that there was no justification for reading into the paragraph the words "at the date of the dismissal were taking part". No doubt as a result of that decision [TULRCA s 238(3)(b)] was amended in its present form.

The distinction as to time in sub-paragraphs [(a)] and [(b)] is very marked and has been emphasised by the amendment to sub-paragraph [(b)]. It is further emphasised by the absence of amendment as to time in relation to sub-paragraph [(a)].

In *Fisher* v *York Trailer Co Ltd* (1979), the facts were that the workforce were deliberately working slowly. By letter of 7 February 1978 the company sought from the workforce an undertaking that they would work at a normal pace. They were told if they did not give the undertaking by signing they would be suspended. There was a meeting. All but seven of the employees signed the undertaking and subsequently they were dismissed. It was held:

> "That on the true construction of the amended [TULRCA s 238(3)(a)] 'relevant employees' were not confined to those who were actually locked out, but included those employees who were directly interested in the trade dispute; that the lock-out in the present case occurred when the 34 employees were told that they would not be allowed to work and did not work on 8 February and, since none of them had signed the undertaking on that date, they were all directly interested in the dispute and, therefore, 'relevant employees' for the purposes of the paragraph and, as they had not all been dismissed, the tribunal had jurisdiction in accordance with [TULRCA s 238] to determine whether the six employees had been unfairly dismissed."

. . . We would, ourselves, on the language of [TULRCA s 238(3)(a)] without any further assistance have come to the same conclusion as the employment tribunal. We are however fortified in our view by the reasoning and judgment in the *Fisher* case. It is the practice of this appeal tribunal, in so far as it is possible, to follow our own decisions and if there is to be a conflict it is to be resolved by the Court of Appeal. The decision in the *Fisher* case seems to us to be right in law and logic. It has been followed without criticism so far as we are aware for a number of years. In the world of industrial relations it is even more important than elsewhere that decisions which have been consistently relied on by employers and employees and acted on should not lightly be overturned.

We are also fortified in our conclusion by the legislative changes that have occurred since. We have already observed that [TULRCA s 238(3)(b)] has been amended in order to identify the time in relation to a strike; no doubt to give effect to the observations of the House of Lords, that it was for Parliament to introduce legislation; to add words which previously had been missing. The absence of amendment to [TULRCA s 238(3)(a)] . . . lends substance to the view that Parliament, and those responsible for drafting the legislation, did not think that the *Fisher* case had misinterpreted what Parliament intended. Nothing would have been easier than to have added "at the complainant's date of dismissal" to subparagraph [(a)] as well as to subparagraph [(b)].

Mr Hand has observed that the effect of the decision, by widening those who are directly interested, may cause grave difficulties to employers in the same way that the decision in *Stock* v *Frank Jones (Tipton) Ltd* (1978) did. The answer to that may well lie in the argument that if an employer chooses to exercise his right of lock-out, then the consequences are on his own head. We should not seek to do what the House of Lords said we must not do in order to remedy an alleged defect, but should seek to interpret the Act in accordance with the intention of Parliament. For these reasons we are unable to say that the *Fisher* case was wrongly decided or that it can be distinguished; indeed the effect of subsequent amendments is to strengthen the decision of the *Fisher* case and not to weaken it.

Accordingly we take the view that the employment tribunal have properly directed themselves and their decision cannot be faulted.'

Comment

(1) This decision emphasises the different test for who is a relevant employee according to whether the dismissal took place in the context of a strike or a lock-out. In the case of a lock-out, all those originally locked out are 'relevant'. Thus if the employer

takes some of them back to work while dismissing the remainder, as happened in this case, those dismissed can maintain an action for unfair dismissal. In the case of a strike, however, it is only those still on strike at the time that this complainant was dismissed who are 'relevant' for purposes of comparison – not all the original strikers.

(2) The amendment to this effect was made to the law following the House of Lords decision in *Stock* v *Jones* (1978), as noted here. In that case, 35 employees went on strike, but two returned to work after a couple of weeks. The rest stayed out and, after three months, the employer dismissed them. They were allowed to bring unfair dismissal claims because two of the original strikers had been allowed back. This would not happen now, because those two were not still on strike at the time of the others' dismissal.

(3) The result of the present version of TULRCA s 238(3)(a) is that, in these circumstances, an employer can wait until some employees drift back to work and then give the rest an ultimatum. Anyone who does not then return may be safely dismissed.

(4) It may be that not all workers who fail to turn up for work are taking part in the strike: they may be ill or on holiday. How should tribunals approach this situation?

Coates v *Modern Methods & Materials Ltd* [1982] ICR 763 Court of Appeal

A dispute blew up at the employer's factory on 12 February over the compulsory transfer of workers. Coates and others were dismissed in March for taking part in industrial action. They claimed unfair dismissal, and argued that the tribunal had jurisdiction because Leith, another employee, had taken part in the strike but had not been dismissed.

Leith had arrived for work as usual on 12 February, but did not cross the picket line because she did not want to be subjected to the verbal abuse which the pickets meted out to those who did go in to work. The following day, her doctor certified her as unfit to work because of back trouble, a state of affairs which lasted until late April when she returned to work. During her absence she did not draw strike pay, but she attended some strike meetings 'to know what was going on'.

An employment tribunal held that Leith did take part in the strike and that therefore it had jurisdiction to hear the other employees' unfair dismissal claims. The EAT reversed that decision and the employees appealed.

STEPHENSON LJ: '. . . It is to be observed that the employment tribunal's decision rests partly on the view that there was no good reason why Mrs Leith should withhold her labour and that she decided not to break the strike or did not break it. They must have held that to refuse to pass the pickets because she did not want the abuse meted out to Mrs Jessop and to stay outside the works gates in consequence with the others – some 40 in number according to the evidence – instead of going in to work with Mrs Jessop and, according to the evidence, one other, constituted taking part in the strike. There is no reference in their decision to Mrs Leith's reason, expressed to Mr Brearley, for declining strike pay not because she was disqualified by certificated sickness but because she was not on strike. And the tribunal cannot have regarded that or her explanation for attending strike meetings as of importance, if indeed they accepted her evidence on those two matters.

Can Mrs Leith reasonably be said to have taken part in this strike by yielding to her fear of abuse, and so withholding her labour – a dignified paraphrase of "not working" – and not breaking the strike either by braving the pickets and going to work, or by some protest or expression of dissent? . . .

I have found this a difficult case. It ought to be easy to decide what "taking part in a strike" means and whether on proved or accepted facts a particular employee was or was not taking part in a strike. The employment tribunal seem to have found it easy, because they unanimously decided that Mrs Leith was taking part, and on an application for review the chairman thought the weight of the evidence showed that she was taking part and a review had no reasonable prospect of success. I know that the construction of a statute is a question of law; but the meaning of ordinary words is not, and the meaning of "taking part in a strike" seems to me to be just the sort of question which an industrial jury is best fitted to decide. No member of either tribunal has spelt out its meaning, perhaps because it was thought unwise or impossible to attempt a paraphrase of plain words. But I should be very reluctant to assume that any of them attributed to the words an unnatural meaning which they were incapable of bearing in their context, or to differ from their conclusion that Mrs Leith took part in the strike. Only the plainest error in law would enable me to differ from them on such a finding, particularly when the majority of the appeal tribunal, whose decision convicts them of such error, appear themselves to be influenced by an erroneous conception of their power to interfere with the employment tribunal's decision. On the other hand, I think that on the evidence without argument and reflection I should have taken the view which Mrs Leith's employer appears to have taken that she was not on strike or striking or taking part in the strike. That view takes into account her state of mind, her intention, her motive, her wishes. Some support for doing that is to be found in what Talbot J said in giving the judgment of the appeal tribunal in *McCormick* v *Horsepower Ltd* (1980) about Brazier not being motivated by fear in refusing to cross the picket line and withdrawing his labour to aid the strikers: and also in what Lawton LJ, in the passage I have quoted from his judgment in the same case said obiter about giving help generally and about Brazier not being shown to have had a common purpose with the striking boilermakers. Furthermore, it seems hard on an employer who takes the trouble to investigate an employee's motives and reasons for stopping work to be told "you were wrong to accept what she told you, you ought to have dismissed her and so prevented two other strikers from complaining to the employment tribunal of unfair dismissal". On the other side it was said that it would be intolerable to impose on employers the burden, which this employer undertook with one employee, of looking into the mind of every employee withholding his or her labour before deciding whether to dismiss, in order to see if each had some reason for stopping work unconnected with the object of the strike.

I have come to the conclusion that participation in a strike must be judged by what the employee does and not by what he thinks or why he does it. If he stops work when his workmates come out on strike and does not say or do anything to make plain his disagreement, or which could amount to a refusal to join them, he takes part in their strike. The line between unwilling participation and not taking part may be difficult to draw, but those who stay away from work with the strikers without protest for whatever reason are to be regarded as having crossed that line to take part in the strike. In the field of industrial action those who are not openly against it are presumably for it. This seems to be the thinking behind the employment tribunal's decision. If the words in question are capable of bearing that meaning, they are capable of being applied to Mrs Leith's actions on the morning of February 12, 1980, though her time outside the factory gates with the strikers was short and her reason for not entering the factory was accepted. In my judgment a reasonable tribunal could give that meaning to the statutory words and could apply them to Mrs Leith. The employment tribunal did not, therefore, go wrong in law and it was the majority of the appeal tribunal who did. I would accordingly allow the appeal, set aside the decision of the Employment Appeal Tribunal and restore the decision of the employment tribunal.'

(Kerr LJ delivered a concurring judgment; Eveleigh LJ dissented.)

P & O European Ferries (Dover) Ltd v *Byrne* [1989] ICR 779 Court of Appeal

MAY LJ: '. . . The brief circumstances of the case are these. Some time last year a substantial number of employees of the employer took industrial action in the form of a strike. As a consequence the employers' contention is that all those employees were dismissed. There were offers of re-engagement but we need not go into that in this appeal. All 1,025 employees concerned applied for compensation for unfair dismissal.

The particular employee who is the claimant in this case, Mr Byrne, was the first to make a claim to the appropriate employment tribunal and, when he did so, his employers countered by contending that the employment tribunal should not hear the complaint by virtue of the provisions of [TULRCA s 238] . . .

From what I have said it will be apparent that this is a case within [TULRCA s 238(1)], in that the employee concerned was dismissed at a time when he was taking part in a strike. Consequently, if there had been no discrimination amongst all the employees of the employer taking part in that strike, then subsection (2)(a) would be applicable and in those circumstances the employment tribunal would not have been entitled to determine Mr Byrne's application.

When the employers took this point in their pleading, the claimant in his turn countered by alleging that at least one "relevant employee" had not in fact been dismissed at the material time and accordingly there had in fact been discrimination, whether the employers intended it or not, and accordingly his claim for compensation was not barred by the provisions of [TULRCA s 238(2)(a)]. Understandably the employers at once asked for particulars of that allegation and especially for the identity of the single employee not dismissed, upon whose retention in employment the claimant relied to avoid the disqualification involved in [s 238(2)(a)]. Particulars giving the name of the one employee not dismissed have however been refused on the ground that to identify this employee would enable the employers, prior to the determination of the claimant's application by the employment tribunal, to ensure that what may have been discrimination in fact no longer inures, by the simple course of dismissing forthwith the one employee so identified. In those circumstances the employers sought an order for the particulars on the ground that it was essential for them to know the identity of the one employee to enable them adequately to deal with the employee's contention based, as I say, on [s 238(2)(a)].

When the application for these particulars came before the employment tribunal it refused to order them on the basis that it would indeed enable the employer to put matters right, from the employers' point of view, in the sense that I have indicated in so far as the present employee respondent is concerned, on one particular construction of [s 238(2)(a)]: in any event even on the alternative construction of the subsection, to give the particular sought would enable the employers to put matters right vis-à-vis the other 1,024 employees whose claims for compensation for unfair dismissal still have to be heard . . .

In so far as the reasons for not ordering particulars, which the employment tribunal gave and in which it was supported by the appeal tribunal, are concerned, I respectfully disagree with both tribunals. It was, I think, an improper exercise of the discretion of the tribunals below not to order such particulars on the ground that to do so would enable the employers to put matters right, if one relevant employee had got through the net and was not dismissed at the time when the remaining 1,025 employees were dismissed. It is true that a party to litigation is not entitled to particulars solely for the purpose of ascertaining the names of his opponent's witnesses. But a party is entitled to particulars to enable him to know what case he has to meet, even though giving those particulars will identify one or more of the potential witnesses on behalf of the other party . . .

The particular parts of [TULRCA s 238(2)] which require careful consideration are, first, the word "determine" in the earlier part of the subsection, and in the next line the words "unless it is shown". The use of the word "determine" is in my judgment arguably ambiguous. One speaks

597

of a determination in the litigious context both of the final decision of the issues in that litigation and also of the actual hearing itself. In one sense a court determines by a trial from the time that the case is called on until the time when the court gives its ultimate decision. But there is no such ambiguity in the words "unless it is shown". Those words necessarily direct one's attention to the conclusion of the relevant hearing before the employment tribunal and in my opinion require one to conclude that on its proper construction the material point in time is when the employment tribunal either determines the substantive hearing which involves determining the jurisdiction point as well, or alternatively determines the jurisdiction point on a preliminary hearing prior to going on, or not going on, as the case may be, with the substantive hearing for compensation.

That in my judgment is the clear and plain meaning of the statutory provision and although we were pressed on the one side not to and on the other side to insert words into the subsection and also to adopt what was said to be a purposive construction of [s 238(2)], to lead us to adopt a construction which looked to the start of the hearing rather than its conclusion as the material time, Mr Supperstone, who has said everything that could be said on behalf of the claimant with skill and cogency was in the end, as I think, almost bound to accept that the meaning of the statutory phrase was clear. When pressed to detail the respects in which he suggested that one should give the phrase a narrow rather than a wider construction, as he suggested at one point was the correct approach, he very properly and realistically found himself unable to do so.

I should just mention that Mr Supperstone also pointed to this potential difficulty if the construction for which he contended was not to be accepted and that is that in the circumstances the unknown Mr X is put in an invidious position. If he is called to give evidence to the effect that he was on strike but not dismissed, he would clearly know that the consequence would be that he would in fact immediately be dismissed so as to preclude the continuing existence of any discrimination under the provisions of [TULRCA s 238(2)(a)]. But this cannot affect what in my view is the clear and literal meaning of the subsection.

For my part I do not think that much more need be said on this appeal, although that is in no way intended to be disrespectful to the interesting arguments which counsel on both sides have addressed to the court. In my judgment the employment tribunal, and the appeal tribunal following it, erred in directing themselves that it was a legitimate reason for refusing to order particulars which the employers had to have in order to meet the case made against them, that to do so might prejudice not only the claimant's claim but also perhaps the claim of the other 1,024 people and indeed might have a deleterious effect on the continued employment prospects of the unknown Mr X. The allegation had been made against the employers that there had been discrimination in that Mr X had not been dismissed and they were entitled to know who he was so that they could meet that case. They were entitled to know that at that stage in the litigation, particularly having regard to the proper construction of [s 238(2)] which requires one to look to the end of the decision of the relevant determination by the employment tribunal and not the start.

In those circumstances I would allow this appeal and, subject to hearing further from counsel if necessary, make an order directing that the relevant particulars be given by the claimant to the employer.'

(Neill and Nourse LJJ delivered concurring judgments.)

Comment

(1) It may be doubted whether the legislation was intended to operate in the way that it did in the last case. It would seem sensible and fairer to amend the statute so that a

relevant employee was one who was still employed at the date of the claimant's dismissal, even if that person had been dismissed by the time the claimant made an application to the employment tribunal.

(2) The converse situation to *P & O Ferries* v *Byrne* occurred in *Bigham and Keogh* v *GKN Kwikform Ltd* (1992). All strikers, including B and K, were dismissed, but B later applied for and got a job with a different branch of the company. He made no attempt to conceal the fact of his earlier dismissal and made no untrue statements in his application. Four weeks later, the employers made the connection and dismissed him. He and others of the original strikers then claimed unfair dismissal based on selective re-engagement – the fact that B had, albeit briefly, been re-employed by the same employer. The EAT held that the employer should have known about his earlier employment history with them, and that in the absence of fraud, where an employer with actual or constructive notice of the earlier dismissal re-engages a dismissed striker, the others may bring unfair dismissal claims. B ultimately withdrew his appeal; it is unclear whether he could have claimed too.

(3) Note that where the claimant is relying on selective re-engagement, only an offer of re-engagement need be proved: however, it must have been made within three months of the relevant employee's original dismissal. It is all right for the employer to re-engage on a selective basis after three months.

(4) The usual three-month time limit for lodging an unfair dismissal claim is varied in relation to industrial action dismissals, since the right to claim may only be triggered by a selective re-engagement occurring some time after the claimant's dismissal. However, there is an overall time limit of six months from the claimant's dismissal (TULRCA s 239).

(5) Before the Employment Relations Act 1999 the ILO had concluded that UK law in relation to dismissals in connection with industrial action contravened ILO Convention No 87 on Freedom of Association. While the introduction of TULRCA s 238A is a big step forward, anomalies remain – including the fact that it is possible for a striker to have no claim for unfair dismissal where she is dismissed while taking part in industrial action which is not a breach of her contract of employment.

THE RIGHT TO ORGANISE INDUSTRIAL ACTION

Industrial action does not only involve workers breaking their contracts of employment. The organisers, whether individuals or trade unions, may also commit civil wrongs by bringing about those breaches and causing knock-on interference with the employer's commercial contracts. Until the House of Lords' decision in *Taff Vale* v *Amalgamated Society of Railway Servants* in 1901, it was thought to be practically impossible for technical reasons to sue trade unions in contract or tort. This meant that trade unions could organise industrial action with impunity. The individual trade union officials might be liable, but in practice no employer would bother suing for damages an individual who would probably have very limited means.

The pattern that grew up, therefore, was for employers who thought that they had an action in tort to sue for an injunction to get the action called off. As they could not sue the union, they sued the officials – usually choosing a top official such as the president or general secretary. While an injunction against an individual only binds that individual, in practice if the employer was successful, the union would accept the situation and treat it as awarded against the union.

All this changed following *Taff Vale*, for if unions could be sued, their property could be seized to pay damages claims. Given the huge financial costs which can quickly result from strike action, a union would risk swift bankruptcy whenever it became involved in industrial action. It is the belief that there should in some sense be a right to strike which justifies the law intervening to prevent that state of affairs.

The response to *Taff Vale* of the Liberal government in 1906 was to pass the Trade Disputes Act 1906, giving trade unions *total* immunity from any action in tort, and giving *partial* immunity to individuals: they would be immune from liability for some named torts provided that they were acting in contemplation or furtherance of a trade dispute. In 1982, the Conservative government abolished unions' immunity from tort actions and put them in the same position as individuals. Thus, today, unions and individuals have partial immunity from liability for some torts, as long as they are acting in contemplation or furtherance of a trade dispute. At the same time, from 1980 to 1993, the same government increasingly squeezed down the ambit of that immunity. There has been little change under the Labour government in power since 1997.

The result is that, today, the question of legal liability for organising industrial action must be looked at in three stages. First, would the action be unlawful at common law? If it is not tortious, no one is going to be liable for organising it or participating in it. Secondly, if the action does involve the commission of torts, is there *prima facie* statutory immunity for this? This entails two sub-questions: (a) is the alleged tort one which is covered by the statutory immunity, and, if so, (b) was the action 'in contemplation or furtherance of a trade dispute'? Finally, even if such immunity is established, there is a third stage: has the immunity been lost for one of the specific statutory reasons?

Each of these stages will be examined in turn in the rest of this chapter and the next.

Liability for the economic torts

Certain kinds of torts, known as the 'economic torts' because they cause economic rather than physical loss to the claimant, are particularly liable to occur during industrial disputes. Unions and individuals receive statutory immunity from some of these. Thus it is first necessary to see whether the tort alleged to have been committed is one for which there is statutory immunity. If not, the union and/or individuals involved in organising the industrial action will be liable for it. Employers and their advisers have become ever more creative over the years in outflanking the statutory immunity by identifying other torts which they say the industrial action has caused. The position in relation to the torts which are covered by the statutory immunity is also complicated as a result of the House of Lords groundbreaking decision in 2007 in *OBG* v *Allan*, which has to some extent rewritten history in the process of reclassifying the economic torts.

Inducing breach of contract

Lumley v *Gye* (1853) 2 E&B 216 Court of Queen's Bench

The claimant, manager of the Queen's Theatre in London, had hired the opera singer, Johanna Wagner, to sing exclusively at his theatre for three months. The defendant, knowing of this, offered her more money to come and sing in his theatre instead. This would be a breach of her contract with the claimant (see *Lumley* v *Wagner* (1852)) but as well as suing the singer in contract, the theatre manager also sued his rival in tort. The law at this time recognised a tort of enticing a servant away from a master, but it was doubtful that the singer could be regarded as the servant of the claimant.

CROMPTON J: '. . . The law as to enticing servants was said to be contrary to the general rule and principle of law, to be anomalous, and probably to have had its origin from the state of society when serfdom existed and to be founded upon, or upon the equity of, the Statute of Labourers. It was said that it would be dangerous to hold that an action was maintainable for persuading a third party to break a contract unless some boundary or limits could be pointed out; that the remedy for enticing away servants was confined to cases where the relation of master and servant, in a strict sense, subsisted between the parties; and that, in all other cases of contract, the only remedy was against the party breaking the contract.

Whatever may have been the origin or foundation of the law as to enticing of servants, and whether it be, as contended by the claimant, an instance and branch of a wider rule, or, as contended by the defendant, an anomaly and an exception from the general rule of law on such subjects, it must now be considered clear law that a person who wrongfully and maliciously, or, which is the same thing, with notice, interrupts the relation subsisting between master and servant by procuring the servant to depart from the master's service, or by harbouring and keeping him as servant after he has quitted it and during the time stipulated for as the period of service, whereby the master is injured, commits a wrongful act for which he is responsible at law. I think that the rule applies wherever the wrongful interruption operates to prevent the service during the time for which the parties have contracted that the service shall continue, and I think that the relation of master and servant subsists, sufficiently for the purpose of such action, during the time for which there is in existence a binding contract of hiring and service between the parties . . .'

ERLE J: '. . . If it is objected that this class of actions for procuring a breach of contract of hiring rests upon no principle and ought not to be extended beyond the cases heretofore decided, and that, as those have related to contracts respecting trade, manufactures, or household service, and not to performance at a theatre, therefore, they are no authority for an action in respect of a contract for such performance, the answer appears to me to be that the class of cases referred to rests upon the principle that the procurement of the violation of the right is a cause of action, and that when this principle is applied to a violation of a right arising upon a contract of hiring, the nature of the service contracted for is immaterial. It is clear that the procurement of the violation of a right is a cause of action in all instances where the violation is an actionable wrong, as in violations of a right to property, whether real or personal, or to personal security. He who procures the wrong is a joint wrongdoer, and may be sued, either alone or jointly with the agent, in the appropriate action for the wrong complained of. Where a right to the performance of a contract has been violated by a breach thereof, the remedy is upon the contract against the contracting party. If he is made to indemnify for such breach, no further recourse is allowed, and, as in case of the procurement of a breach of contract the action is for a wrong and cannot be joined with the action on the contract, and as the act itself is not likely to be of frequent occurrence nor easy of proof, therefore, the action for this wrong, in respect of other contracts than those of hiring, are not numerous, but still they seem to me sufficient to show that the principle has been recognised . . .'

(Wightman J delivered a concurring judgment; Coleridge J dissented.)

Comment

(1) This was seen at the time as a considerable extension of the existing (and archaic) tort of enticement of a servant, although it is important to notice that Erle J explains and justifies the tort by reference to a wider principle. This is picked up again by the House of Lords in *OBG v Allan* (2007).

(2) The applicability of inducing breach of contract to industrial action is obvious: the organisers of a strike are inducing employees who go on strike to break their contracts of employment. If they persuade the employer's commercial contacts, suppliers and customers, not to perform existing contracts with the employer, they will induce breaches of those commercial contracts. The elements of the tort of inducing breach of contract were authoritatively restated by the House of Lords in *OBG v Allan*.

OBG Ltd v Allan; Douglas and others v Hello! Ltd; Mainstream Properties Ltd v Young and others [2007] IRLR 608 House of Lords

LORD HOFFMANN: 'My Lords,

The three appeals

1   These three appeals are principally concerned with claims in tort for economic loss caused by intentional acts

(a)   In *OBG Ltd v Allan* the defendants were receivers purportedly appointed under a floating charge which is admitted to have been invalid. Acting in good faith, they took control of the claimant company's assets and undertaking. The claimant says that this was not only a trespass to its land and a conversion of its chattels but also the tort of unlawful interference with its contractual relations. It claims that the defendants are liable in damages for the value of the assets and undertaking, including the value of the contractual claims, as at the date of their appointment. Alternatively, it says the defendants are liable for the same damages in conversion.

(b)   In *Douglas v Hello! Ltd* the magazine *OK!* contracted for the exclusive right to publish photographs of a celebrity wedding at which all other photography would be forbidden. The rival magazine *Hello!* published photographs which it knew to have been surreptitiously taken by an unauthorised photographer pretending to be a waiter or guest. *OK!* says that this was interference by unlawful means with its contractual or business relations or a breach of its equitable right to confidentiality in photographic images of the wedding.

(c)   In *Mainstream Properties Ltd v Young* two employees of a property company, in breach of their contracts, diverted a development opportunity to a joint venture in which they were interested. The defendant, knowing of their duties but wrongly thinking that they would not be in breach, facilitated the acquisition by providing finance. The company says that he is liable for the tort of wrongfully inducing breach of contract . . .

Inducing breach of contract: elements of the Lumley v Gye *tort*

39   To be liable for inducing breach of contract, you must know that you are inducing a breach of contract. It is not enough that you know that you are procuring an act which, as a matter of

law or construction of the contract, is a breach. You must actually realise that it will have this effect. Nor does it matter that you ought reasonably to have done so. This proposition is most strikingly illustrated by the decision of this House in *British Industrial Plastics Ltd v Ferguson* (1940), in which the claimant's former employee offered the defendant information about one of the claimant's secret processes which he, as an employee, had invented. The defendant knew that the employee had a contractual obligation not to reveal trade secrets but held the eccentric opinion that if the process was patentable, it would be the exclusive property of the employee. He took the information in the honest belief that the employee would not be in breach of contract. In the Court of Appeal McKinnon LJ observed tartly that in accepting this evidence the judge had "vindicated [his] honesty . . . at the expense of his intelligence" but he and the House of Lords agreed that he could not be held liable for inducing a breach of contract.

40   The question of what counts as knowledge for the purposes of liability for inducing a breach of contract has also been the subject of a consistent line of decisions. In *Emerald Construction Co Ltd v Lowthian* (1966), union officials threatened a building contractor with a strike unless he terminated a sub-contract for the supply of labour. The defendants obviously knew that there was a contract – they wanted it terminated – but the court found that they did not know its terms and, in particular, how soon it could be terminated. Lord Denning MR said:

> "Even if they did not know the actual terms of the contract, but had the means of knowledge – which they deliberately disregarded – that would be enough. Like the man who turns a blind eye. So here, if the officers deliberately sought to get this contract terminated, heedless of its terms, regardless whether it was terminated by breach or not, they would do wrong. For it is unlawful for a third person to procure a breach of contract knowingly, or recklessly, indifferent whether it is a breach or not."

41   This statement of the law has since been followed in many cases and, so far as I am aware, has not given rise to any difficulty . . .

42   The next question is what counts as an intention to procure a breach of contract. It is necessary for this purpose to distinguish between ends, means and consequences. If someone knowingly causes a breach of contract, it does not normally matter that it is the means by which he intends to achieve some further end or even that he would rather have been able to achieve that end without causing a breach. Mr Gye would very likely have preferred to be able to obtain Miss Wagner's services without her having to break her contract. But that did not matter. Again, people seldom knowingly cause loss by unlawful means out of simple disinterested malice. It is usually to achieve the further end of securing an economic advantage to themselves. As I said earlier, the Dunlop employees who took off the tyres in *GWK Ltd v Dunlop Rubber Co Ltd* (1926) intended to advance the interests of the Dunlop company.

43   On the other hand, if the breach of contract is neither an end in itself nor a means to an end, but merely a foreseeable consequence, then in my opinion it cannot for this purpose be said to have been intended. That, I think, is what judges and writers mean when they say that the claimant must have been "targeted" or "aimed at" . . .

44   Finally, what counts as a breach of contract? In *Torquay Hotel Co Ltd v Cousins* (1969), Lord Denning said that there could be liability for preventing or hindering performance of the contract on the same principle as liability for procuring a breach. This dictum was approved by Lord Diplock in *Merkur Island Shipping Corporation* (1983). One could therefore have liability for interference with contractual relations even though the contracting party committed no breach. But these remarks were made in the context of the unified theory which treated procuring a breach as part of the same tort as causing loss by unlawful means. If the torts are to be separated, then I think that one cannot be liable for inducing a breach unless there has been a breach. No secondary liability without primary liability. Cases in which interference with contractual relations have been treated as coming within the *Lumley v Gye* tort (like *Dimbleby*

& Sons v *National Union of Journalists* (1984)) are really cases of causing loss by unlawful means . . .

69   In my opinion this case [ie, *Mainstream Properties Ltd* v *Young*] comes squarely within *British Industrial Plastics Ltd* v *Ferguson* (1940). On the finding of the judge, Mr De Winter [the defendant] honestly believed that assisting Mr Young and Mr Broad with the joint venture would not involve them in the commission of breaches of contract. Nor can Mr De Winter to be said to have been indifferent to whether there was a breach of contract or not, as in *Emerald Construction Co Ltd* v *Lowthian* (1966), or made a conscious decision not to inquire in case he discovered a disagreeable truth. He therefore did not intend to cause a breach of contract and the conditions for accessory liability under the *Lumley* v *Gye* tort are not satisfied . . .'

(Lords Nicholls and Walker, Baroness Hale and Lord Brown all delivered speeches agreeing with Lord Hoffmann on this issue.)

Comment

(1) The three essential elements identified by Lord Hoffmann for the tort of inducing breach of contract are thus:

(a) knowledge that the action will bring about a breach of contract;
(b) an intention to do this;
(c) an actual breach of contract.

(2) In relation to knowledge, note that wilful blindness as to whether the contract can be lawfully terminated or not will suffice: *Emerald Construction* v *Lowthian* (1966). It is a little surprising that Lord Hoffmann thinks that the test for knowledge of the contract does not give rise to difficulty. In *Timeplan Education Group Ltd* v *National Union of Teachers* (1997) the union was in dispute with the claimant company, which supplied temporary teachers to schools, over its wage rates. The company recruited most of its teachers from Australia and New Zealand. It placed some advertisements in the magazine of a New Zealand teachers' union, NZEI. The NUT wrote to NZEI expressing concern over the adverts, in view of the ongoing dispute, but the letter was delayed for two months. When they received the letter, NZEI faxed the NUT to ask if the dispute was still ongoing, and when told that it was, they suspended Timeplan's adverts, in breach of contract. The trial judge held the NUT liable for inducing breach of contract on the basis that the NUT must have realised that there was 'some sort of contractual relationship' between Timeplan and NZEI. The Court of Appeal reversed, holding that there was nothing to show that the NUT was aware of an existing contract between Timeplan and NZEI, and the fact that the magazine had carried Timeplan's adverts in the past did not necessarily indicate that they had a contract to do so in future. But see the next extract.

Merkur Island Shipping Corporation v *Laughton* [1983] ICR 490
House of Lords

LORD DIPLOCK: '. . . Such facts as it is necessary to recount in order to dispose of this appeal can be stated briefly. The respondents ("the shipowners") own the *Hoegh Apapa* ("the ship"), a Liberian registered ship, of which the majority of the crew were Filipinos. On July 15, 1982, she arrived at a dock in Liverpool for loading. ITF [the International Transport Workers' Federation] (of which the individual appellants are officials), having previously learnt that the shipowners were paying less than the rate of wages approved by ITF persuaded the tugmen employed by a company known as Rea Towing ("the tugowners") to refuse, in breach of their contract of employment with the tugowners, to move the ship out of the dock so as to enable her to sail.

The ship was let by the shipowners to Leif Hoegh and Co ("the charterers") under a time charter ("the charter") in the New York Produce Exchange form with certain additional clauses, to two of which it will be necessary to refer. The charterers in turn had sub-chartered the ship to Ned Lloyd under a six-month time charter ("the sub-charter") containing similar clauses. Both charter and sub-charter provided that the charterers thereunder should,

> "provide and pay for all . . . port charges, normal pilotages, agencies, commissions, consular charges . . . and all other usual expenses . . . but when the vessel puts into a port for causes for which the vessel is responsible, then all such charges incurred shall be paid by the owners."

Pursuant to this clause in the sub-charter, the sub-charterers, who have a running contract with the tugowners for the provision of tugs to all their vessels using the port of Liverpool, made through their agent a specific contract with the tugowners for the provision of tugs to take the ship into and out of the dock at which the ship was to be loaded. As a result of the blacking of the vessel, however, on completion of the loading on July 16 the tugmen employed by the tugowners, in breach of their contracts of employment, refused to move the ship except to a lay berth . . .

As respects knowledge, ITF had been given an actual copy of the charter on July 19, 1980, three days after the "blacking" started but two days before the application to Parker J was made. Quite apart from this, however, there can hardly be any one better informed than ITF as to the terms of the sort of contracts under which ships are employed, particularly those flying flags of convenience. I agree with what was said by the Master of the Rolls on the question of ITF's knowledge:

> "Whatever the precise degree of knowledge of the defendants at any particular time, faced with a laden ship which, as they well knew, was about to leave port, the defendants must in my judgment be deemed to have known of the almost certain existence of contracts of carriage to which the shipowners were parties. The wholly exceptional case would be that of a ship carrying the owner's own goods. Whether that contract or those contracts consisted of a time charter, a voyage charter or one or more bill of lading contracts or some or all of such contracts would have been immaterial to the defendants. Prima facie their intention was to immobilise the ship and in so doing to interfere with the performance by the owners of their contract or contracts of carriage – immobilising a laden ship which had no contractual obligation to move would have been a pointless exercise, since it would have brought no pressure to bear on the owners."

The last sentence of this citation deals also with intention. It was the shipowners upon whom ITF wanted to bring pressure to bear, because it was they who were employing seamen at rates of pay lower than those it was the policy of ITF to enforce. The only way in which income could be derived by the shipowners from the ownership of their ship was by entering into contracts with third parties for the carriage of goods under which a primary obligation of the shipowners would be to prosecute the contract voyages with the utmost dispatch, and their earnings from their ship would be diminished by its immobilisation in port. Diminishing their earnings under the contract of carriage was the only way in which pressure could be brought to bear on the shipowners . . .'

(Lords Edmund-Davies, Keith, Brandon and Brightman agreed with Lord Diplock.)

Comment

(1) Since the defendants had a copy of the contract, they could not argue ignorance of its contents; however, what is interesting is that the House of Lords was prepared to hold them liable on what, in their opinion, they 'must have known' without proof of actual knowledge. This position did not attract any criticism from the House of Lords in *OBG* v *Allan*. However, it bears out the argument that the point is hardly free from difficulty. Cf also *Dimbleby & Sons Ltd* v *NUJ* (1984), extracted below, p 627.

(2) It is common practice for employers in dispute to send the union copies of relevant contracts, as done here, in order to ensure that they cannot argue lack of requisite knowledge.

(3) Note also what is said in relation to intention in *OBG* v *Allan*: the fact that the person inducing the breach of contract has no intention to harm the claimant but essentially wants to advance his or her own interests is no defence, if that end can only be obtained by means of inducing the breach. However, as Lord Diplock notes in *Merkur Island*, in industrial disputes, the breach of contract is frequently the desired and intended outcome of the action.

(4) It is in discussing the need for there to be an actual breach of contract as a result of the defendant's inducement that the House of Lords in *OBG* v *Allan* makes a decisive break with the past in relation to this tort. Lord Hoffmann refers in para 44 of his speech to the 'unified theory'. This is the theory that the named economic torts, including inducing breach of contract, could all be regarded as specific examples of a more general tort of actionable interference with contractual rights. This theory was unanimously rejected by the House of Lords in *OBG* v *Allan*. They held instead that inducing breach of contract stands alone, alongside the second tort of causing loss by unlawful means. This second tort is capable of embracing at least some of the other named economic torts, but not inducing breach of contract. One of the main reasons for this is that in the *Lumley* v *Gye* situation, no unlawful means are used to bring about the breach of contract, except for the tort of inducing breach of contract itself – and to rely on that as unlawful means would involve circular reasoning.

(5) Another way of putting this point, also appearing in the speeches in *OBG* v *Allan*, is that the tort of inducing breach of contract involves accessory liability: the defendant can only be liable for inducing breach of contract if the contract-breaker has primary liability for breach of contract (as Johanna Wagner did in *Lumley* v *Gye*). And this accessory liability can therefore only occur if there is an actual breach of contract.

(6) It follows that *Torquay Hotel* v *Cousins* (1969), where the Court of Appeal held that it was tortious knowingly to interfere with the expected performance of a contract, even though not actually causing its breach, must now be regarded as wrongly decided, and the apparent approval of that principle by Lord Diplock in *Merkur Island Shipping Corporation* v *Laughton* (1983) (in a passage not extracted above) was also mistaken. As Lord Walker said in *OBG* v *Allan*: 'The decision of this House in *Merkur Island Shipping Corporation* v *Laughton* should not be followed, so far as it holds that inducing an actual breach of contract is not a necessary ingredient of the *Lumley* v *Gye* tort.'

(7) The House of Lords therefore rejected the appeals in *OBG* v *Allan* and *Douglas* v *Hello! Ltd* in relation to the claims for interference with contractual relations. The receivers in *OBG* v *Allan* made an honest mistake: they did not intend to induce breaches of contract nor to injure the claimant company. Thus essential elements of the

tort of inducing breach of contract and the tort of causing loss by unlawful means were lacking. In *Douglas v Hello! Ltd, Hello!* magazine had not used unlawful means to get the pictures. The photographer was a trespasser – but he was not *Hello!*'s agent: he sold them the photographs afterwards.

(8) As several members of the House of Lords pointed out, ever since *Allen v Flood* (1898), it has been a general principle of law that intentional injury to another person is not actionable in tort unless unlawful means are used. This fundamental principle is powerfully restated in *OBG v Allan*.

(9) One reason for the confusion which arose in relation to the economic torts is that in many cases, especially in relation to industrial disputes, it is possible for the same facts to give rise to both torts. As Lord Hoffmann put it in *OBG v Allan*:

> If A, intending to cause loss to B, threatens C with assault unless he breaks his contract with B, he is liable as accessory to C's breach of contract under *Lumley v Gye* and he commits the tort of causing loss to B by unlawful means. The areas of liability under the two torts may be intersecting circles which cover common ground. This often happened in 20th century industrial disputes, where, for example, a union would use unlawful means (inducing members to break their contracts of employment) to put pressure upon the employer to break his contract with someone else who was the union's real target.

We turn now to look at the elements of this second economic tort.

Causing loss by unlawful means

OBG Ltd v Allan; Douglas and others v Hello! Ltd; Mainstream Properties Ltd v Young and others [2007] IRLR 608 House of Lords

LORD HOFFMANN: '. . .

Causing loss by unlawful means

6   The tort of causing loss by unlawful means has a different history. It starts with cases like *Garret v Taylor* (1620), in which the defendant was held liable because he drove away customers of Headington Quarry by threatening them with mayhem and vexatious suits. Likewise, in *Tarleton v M'Gawley* (1793) Lord Kenyon held the master of the *Othello*, anchored off the coast of West Africa, liable in tort for depriving a rival British ship of trade by the expedient of using his cannon to drive away a canoe which was approaching from the shore. In such cases, there is no other wrong for which the defendant is liable as accessory. Although the immediate cause of the loss is the decision of the potential customer or trader to submit to the threat and not buy stones or sell palm oil, he thereby commits no wrong. The defendant's liability is primary, for intentionally causing the claimant loss by unlawfully interfering with the liberty of others.

7   These old cases were examined at some length by the House of Lords in *Allen v Flood* (1898) and their general principle approved. Because they all involved the use of unlawful threats to intimidate potential customers, *Salmond on Torts* 1st ed (1907) classified them under the heading of "Intimidation" and the existence of a tort of this name was confirmed by the House of Lords in *Rookes v Barnard* (1964). But an interference with the liberty of others by unlawful means does not require threats. If, for example, the master of the *Othello* in *Tarleton v M'Gawley* had deprived the claimant of trade by simply sinking the approaching vessel with its cargo of palm oil, it is unlikely that Lord Kenyon would have regarded this as making any difference. Salmond's tort of intimidation is therefore only one variant of a broader tort, usually

called for short "causing loss by unlawful means", which was recognised by Lord Reid in *J T Stratford & Son Ltd* v *Lindley* (1965):

> "the respondent's action [in calling a strike] made it practically impossible for the appellants to do any new business with the barge hirers. It was not disputed that such interference with business is tortious if any unlawful means are employed." . . .

Causing loss by unlawful means: elements of the tort

45   The most important question concerning this tort is what should count as unlawful means . . .

47   The essence of the tort therefore appears to be (a) a wrongful interference with the actions of a third party in which the claimant has an economic interest and (b) an intention thereby to cause loss to the claimant. The old cases of interference with potential customers by threats of unlawful acts clearly fell within this description. So, for the reasons I have given, did *GWK Ltd* v *Dunlop Rubber Co Ltd* (1926). Recent cases in which the tort has been discussed have also concerned wrongful threats or actions against employers with the intention of causing loss to an employee (as in *Rookes* v *Barnard* (1964)) or another employer (as in *J T Stratford & Son Ltd* v *Lindley* (1965)). In the former case, the defendants conspired to threaten the employer that unless the employee was dismissed, there would be an unlawful strike. In the latter, the union committed the *Lumley* v *Gye* tort of inducing breaches of the contracts of the employees of barge hirers to prevent them from hiring the claimant's barges . . .'

Comment

(1) This is where there is some rewriting of history. The general thesis of Lord Hoffmann's account of the economic torts is that recognition of these two can be traced back to *Allen* v *Flood* (1898) and the tort of causing loss by unlawful means was always there, albeit not always well recognised. However, in reality, the way the case law developed was quite different. In *Rookes* v *Barnard* (1964) the union threatened the employer that employees would strike (in breach of their contracts of employment) unless Rookes was dismissed. The employer dismissed Rookes lawfully as a result of this threat. Thus the union did not induce breaches of contract, and even if they had done, they would have been covered by the statutory immunity. It was regarded then and afterwards as a complete novelty for the tort of intimidation to be extended to a threat to break a contract, and the result of the House of Lords holding that the union had committed it meant that the union was liable because intimidation was not covered by the statutory immunity. As a result, the Trade Disputes Act 1965 was passed to give unions immunity from liability for threats to induce breaches of contract. There was no recognition that it was a species of causing loss by unlawful means.

(2) In *GWK Ltd* v *Dunlop Rubber Co Ltd* (1926) the claimants were car makers, who had contracted to fit all their new cars with tyres made by the ARM company, and to show them at trade exhibitions fitted with ARM tyres. On the night before a motor show in Glasgow, Dunlop employees changed the tyres on two cars to Dunlop tyres, intentionally putting GWK in breach of their contract with ARM. Lord Hoffmann describes this as 'a good example of intentionally causing loss by unlawful means', but, as he explains, this was not how it was treated at the time. In fact it was treated as a species of the *Lumley* v *Gye* tort, interference with contractual relations.

(3) In the highly influential later case of *D C Thomson & Co Ltd* v *Deakin* (1952) this concept was developed in a famous judgment of Jenkins LJ in the Court of Appeal. He

analysed the case law as showing two versions of the tort of inducing breach of contract: what he called direct inducement (as in *Lumley* v *Gye* itself) and indirect inducement, as in *GWK* v *Dunlop* where the tortfeasor *prevented* rather than *persuaded* the contract breaker not to perform a contract with the claimant. This analysis, characterised in *OBG* v *Allan* as 'the unified theory', held sway until the House of Lords decision in that case. It is now clear that the tort of inducing breach of contract can only be committed where the tortfeasor directly persuades the contract-breaker to breach the contract. Where there is prevention of performance, there is only liability if it comes within the parameters of causing loss by unlawful means.

(4) In *J T Stratford & Son Ltd* v *Lindley* (1965) the Watermen's Union instructed its members, who manned barges in the Port of London, not to handle barges belonging to the claimant company, with whose owner it was in dispute over recognition. The company's business was hiring out barges in the Port of London, so this action brought their business to a standstill. This is an example of the intersection of the two torts: as Lord Hoffmann points out, the union induced breaches of the barge employees' contracts of employment, and this constituted the unlawful means for the tort of causing loss by unlawful means committed against the claimant company, who was their intended target.

(5) As Lord Hoffmann states, the crucial question for the tort of causing loss by unlawful means is, what should count as unlawful means? This was a point on which the House of Lords in *OBG* v *Allan* did not agree. The majority, however, agreed with Lord Hoffmann.

OBG Ltd v Allan; Douglas and others v Hello! Ltd; Mainstream Properties Ltd v Young and others [2007] IRLR 608 House of Lords

LORD HOFFMANN: '. . .

49   In my opinion, and subject to one qualification, acts against a third party count as unlawful means only if they are actionable by that third party. The qualification is that they will also be unlawful means if the only reason why they are not actionable is because the third party has suffered no loss. In the case of intimidation, for example, the threat will usually give rise to no cause of action by the third party because he will have suffered no loss. If he submits to the threat, then, as the defendant intended, the claimant will have suffered loss instead. It is nevertheless unlawful means. But the threat must be to do something which *would* have been actionable if the third party had suffered loss. Likewise, in *National Phonograph Co Ltd* v *Edison-Bell Consolidated Phonograph Co Ltd* (1908) the defendant intentionally caused loss to the claimant by fraudulently inducing a third party to act to the claimant's detriment. The fraud was unlawful means because it would have been actionable if the third party had suffered any loss, even though in the event it was the claimant who suffered. In this respect, procuring the actions of a third party by fraud (*dolus*) is obviously very similar to procuring them by intimidation (*metus*).

50   *Lonrho plc* v *Fayed* (1990) was arguably within the same principle as the *National Phonograph Co* case. The claimant said that the defendant had intentionally caused it loss by making fraudulent statements to the directors of the company which owned Harrods, and to the Secretary of State for Trade and Industry, which induced the directors to accept his bid for Harrods and the Secretary of State not to refer the bid to the Monopolies Commission. The defendant was thereby able to gain control of Harrods to the detriment of the claimant, who wanted to buy it instead. In the Court of Appeal, Dillon LJ referred to the *National Phonograph* case as authority for rejecting an argument that the means used to cause loss to the claimant could not be unlawful because neither the directors nor the Secretary of State had suffered any

loss. That seems to me correct. The allegations were of fraudulent representations made to third parties, which would have been actionable by them if they had suffered loss, but which were intended to induce the third parties to act in a way which caused loss to the claimant. The Court of Appeal therefore refused to strike out the claim as unarguable and their decision was upheld by the House of Lords.

51   Unlawful means therefore consists of acts intended to cause loss to the claimant by interfering with the freedom of a third party in a way which is unlawful as against that third party and which is intended to cause loss to the claimant. It does not in my opinion include acts which may be unlawful against a third party but which do not affect his freedom to deal with the claimant.

52   Thus in *RCA Corporation v Pollard* (1983) the claimant had the exclusive right to exploit records made by Elvis Presley. The defendant was selling bootleg records made at Elvis Presley concerts without his consent. This was an infringement of section 1 of the Dramatic and Musical Performers' Protection Act 1958, which made bootlegging a criminal offence and, being enacted for the protection of performers, would have given Elvis Presley a cause of action: see Lord Diplock in *Lonrho Ltd v Shell Petroleum Co Ltd (No 2)* (1982). The Court of Appeal held that the infringement of the Act did not give RCA a cause of action. The defendant was not interfering with the liberty of the Presley estate to perform the exclusive recording contract which, as Oliver LJ noted was "no more than an undertaking that he will not give consent to a recording by anyone else". Nor did it prevent the Presley estate from doing any other act affecting the claimants. The bootlegger's conduct, said Oliver LJ:

> "merely potentially reduces the profits which [the claimants] make as the result of the performance by Mr Presley's executors of their contractual obligations." . . .

55   *Lonrho Ltd v Shell Petroleum Co Ltd (No 2)* (1982) was an attempt to found a cause of action simply on the fact that the conduct alleged to have caused loss was contrary to law. The defendant's conduct was alleged to be a criminal offence but not actionable by anyone. In this respect it was unlike *RCA v Pollard* and *Isaac Oren v Red Box Toy Factory Ltd*, in which it could at least be said that the conduct was a wrong against someone in contractual relations with the claimant. Lonrho owned and operated a refinery in Rhodesia supplied by a pipeline from the port of Beira. When Rhodesia declared independence in 1965, the UK imposed sanctions which made it unlawful for anyone to supply the country with oil. As a result, the refinery and pipeline stood idle until the independence regime came to an end. Lonrho alleged that Shell had prolonged the regime by unlawfully supplying Rhodesia with oil through other routes and thereby caused it loss. The House of Lords decided that the alleged illegality gave rise to no cause of action on which Lonrho could rely. Again, there was no allegation that Shell had intended to cause loss to Lonrho, but I cannot see how that would have made any difference. Shell did not interfere with any third party's dealings with Lonrho and even if it had done so, its acts were not wrongful in the sense of being actionable by such third party . . .'

Comment

(1) It may seem odd that, as in *Lonrho v Shell*, a criminal offence does not count as unlawful means for this tort, but note Lord Hoffmann's rationale. Baroness Hale and Lord Brown agreed with Lord Hoffmann on this point. Lord Nicholls took a different view and Lord Walker, while tending to agree with Lord Hoffmann, thought that 'neither is likely to be the last word on this difficult and important area of law'.

(2) *Lonrho v Shell* was also argued as a case of conspiracy. This aspect is dealt with below.

(3) The final issue in relation to the tort of causing loss by unlawful means is the element of intention.

OBG Ltd v Allan; Douglas and others v Hello! Ltd; Mainstream Properties Ltd v Young and others [2007] IRLR 608 House of Lords

LORD HOFFMANN: '. . .

62   Finally, there is the question of intention. In the *Lumley* v *Gye* tort, there must be an intention to procure a breach of contract. In the unlawful means tort, there must be an intention to cause loss. The ends which must have been intended are different. *South Wales Miners' Federation* v *Glamorgan Coal Co Ltd* (1905) shows that one may intend to procure a breach of contract without intending to cause loss. Likewise, one may intend to cause loss without intending to procure a breach of contract. But the concept of intention is in both cases the same. In both cases it is necessary to distinguish between ends, means and consequences. One intends to cause loss even though it is the means by which one achieved the end of enriching oneself. On the other hand, one is not liable for loss which is neither a desired end nor a means of attaining it but merely a foreseeable consequence of one's actions.

63   The master of the *Othello* in *Tarleton* v *M'Gawley* may have had nothing against the other trader. If he had gone off to make his fortune in other waters, he would have wished him well. He simply wanted a monopoly of the local trade for himself. But he nevertheless intended to cause him loss. This, I think, is all that Woolf LJ was intending to say in a passage in *Lonrho plc* v *Fayed* (1990) which has proved controversial:

> "Albeit that he may have no desire to bring about that consequence in order to achieve what he regards as his ultimate ends, from the point of view of the claimant, whatever the motive of the defendant, the damage which he suffers will be the same."

64   On the other hand, I think that Henry J was right in *Barretts & Baird (Wholesale) Ltd* v *Institution of Professional Civil Servants* (1987) when he decided a strike by civil servants in the Ministry of Agriculture in support of a pay claim was not intended to cause damage to an abattoir which was unable to obtain the certificates necessary for exporting meat and claiming subsidies. The damage to the abattoir was neither the purpose of the strike nor the means of achieving that purpose, which was to put pressure on the government . . .'

Comment

(1) In *South Wales Miners' Federation* v *Glamorgan Coal Co Ltd* (1905) the union argued that its action in calling on miners not to work on certain days (in breach of contract) was not intended to harm the company, because it was aimed at maintaining the market price of coal – which was in the coal company's interest too. But the union intended to cause breaches of employment contracts, even if they did not intend to cause loss.

(2) The approval of Henry J's decision in *Barretts & Baird* v *IPCS* (1987) suggests that the county court decision in *Falconer* v *ASLEF* (1986), to the effect that a commuter stranded by an unlawful rail strike could claim damages against the rail unions, was wrong.

(3) In summary, the effect of *OBG* v *Allan* (2007) on the economic torts is as follows:

(a)   Inducing breach of contract is a distinct tort for which liability in tort depends on the defendant having persuaded the third party actually to break a contract with the claimant.

(b)   The broader tort of causing loss by unlawful means encompasses the tort of intimidation in the *Rookes* v *Barnard* (1964) sense.

611

(c)   There is no tort of interference with contractual relations or interference with trade
or business absent unlawful means.

Conspiracy

Since trade unions are combinations of people, and since the organisation of industrial action will inevitably involve a number of people working together, it is not surprising to find charges of conspiracy, which depend on concerted action, being used
against them. Indeed, at the beginning of the nineteenth century, trade unions were
treated as criminal conspiracies. Criminal liability for conspiracy was effectively
removed by the Trade Union Act 1871, but there remained the *tort* of conspiracy,
which was used instead. There are two forms of the tort of conspiracy: conspiracy
to injure, and conspiracy to use unlawful means.

Conspiracy to injure

This tort consists of two or more people acting together with the intention of harming the claimant. It is actionable even if no unlawful means are used.

Lonrho Ltd v *Shell Petroleum (No 2)* [1982] AC 173 House of Lords

Following the illegal unilateral declaration of independence (UDI) by the Smith regime in
Rhodesia in 1965, oil shipments to Rhodesia were banned by statutory regulation, breach of
which was a criminal offence. Lonrho alleged that Shell and BP had continued to supply oil to
Rhodesia, thus prolonging the existence of the illegal government and damaging the business
of Lonrho. Lonrho had extensive business interests in Rhodesia, including oil supply, which
were suspended for as long as sanctions were applied. Lonrho's claim was either on what
Lord Diplock described as 'an innominate tort . . . of causing foreseeable loss by an unlawful
act' (now the tort of causing loss by unlawful means, discussed above) or alternatively, on
conspiracy.

LORD DIPLOCK: '. . . Question 5 (b), to which I now turn, concerns conspiracy as a civil tort.
Your Lordships are invited to answer it on the assumption that the purpose of Shell and BP in
entering into the agreement to do the various things that it must be assumed they did in contravention of the sanctions Order, was to forward their own commercial interests; *not* to injure
those of Lonrho. So the question of law to be determined is whether an intent by the defendants
to injure the claimant is an essential element in the civil wrong of conspiracy, even where the
acts agreed to be done by the conspirators amount to criminal offences under a penal statute.
It is conceded that there is no direct authority either way upon this question to be found in the
decided cases; so if this House were to answer it in the affirmative, your Lordships would be
making new law.
   My Lords, conspiracy as a criminal offence has a long history. It consists of "the agreement
of two or more persons to effect any unlawful purpose, whether as their ultimate aim, or only as
a means to it, and the crime is complete if there is such agreement, even though nothing is done
in pursuance of it". I cite from Viscount Simon LC's now classic speech in *Crofter Hand Woven
Harris Tweed Co Ltd* v *Veitch* (1942).
   Regarded as a civil tort, however, conspiracy is a highly anomalous cause of action. The gist
of the cause of action is damage to the claimant; so long as it remains unexecuted the agreement, which alone constitutes the crime of conspiracy, causes no damage; it is only acts done
in execution of the agreement that are capable of doing that. So the tort, unlike the crime,
consists not of agreement but of concerted action taken pursuant to agreement.

As I recall from my early years in the law first as a student and then as a young barrister, during its chequered history between Lord Coleridge CJ's judgment at first instance in *Mogul Steamship Co Ltd* v *McGregor, Gow & Co* (1888) and the *Crofter* case, the civil tort of conspiracy attracted more controversy among academic writers than success in practical application. Why should an act which causes economic loss to A but is not actionable at his suit if done by B alone become actionable because B did it pursuant to an agreement between B and C? An explanation given at the close of the 19th century by Bowen LJ in the *Mogul* case when it was before the Court of Appeal was:

"The distinction is based on sound reason, for a combination may make oppressive or dangerous that which if it proceeded only from a single person would be otherwise."

But to suggest today that acts done by one street-corner grocer in concert with a second are more oppressive and dangerous to a competitor than the same acts done by a string of supermarkets under a single ownership or that a multinational conglomerate such as Lonrho or oil company such as Shell or BP does not exercise greater economic power than any combination of small businesses, is to shut one's eyes to what has been happening in the business and industrial world since the turn of the century and, in particular, since the end of World War II. The civil tort of conspiracy to injure the claimant's commercial interests where that is the predominant purpose of the agreement between the defendants and of the acts done in execution of it which caused damage to the claimant, must I think be accepted by this House as too well-established to be discarded however anomalous it may seem today. It was applied by this House 80 years ago in *Quinn* v *Leathem* (1901), and accepted as good law in the *Crofter* case, where it was made clear that injury to the claimant and not the self-interest of the defendants must be the predominant purpose of the agreement in execution of which the damage-causing acts were done.

My Lords, in none of the judgments in decided cases in civil actions for damages for conspiracy does it appear that the mind of the author of the judgment was directed to a case where the damage-causing acts although neither done for the purpose of injuring the claimant nor actionable at his suit if they had been done by one person alone, were nevertheless a contravention of some penal law. I will not recite the statements in those judgments to which your Lordships have been referred by the appellants as amounting to dicta in favour of the view that a civil action for conspiracy does lie in such a case. Even if the authors' minds had been directed to the point, which they were not, I should still find them indecisive. This House, in my view, has an unfettered choice whether to confine the civil action of conspiracy to the narrow field to which alone it has an established claim or whether to extend this already anomalous tort beyond those narrow limits that are all that common sense and the application of the legal logic of the decided cases require.

My Lords, my choice is unhesitatingly the same as that of Parker J and all three members of the Court of Appeal. I am against extending the scope of civil tort of conspiracy beyond acts done in execution of an agreement entered into by two or more persons for the purpose not of protecting their own interests but of injuring the interests of the claimant. So I would answer Question 5 (b): "No" . . .'

(Lords Edmund-Davies, Keith, Scarman and Bridge agreed with Lord Diplock.)

Crofter Hand Woven Harris Tweed Co Ltd v *Veitch* [1942] AC 435 House of Lords

Only tweed woven on the Island of Lewis could be described as Harris Tweed. Crofters on the island, most of whom belonged to the TGWU, spun the yarn and wove the tweed, but found that their prices and their jobs were threatened by the activities of companies such as the appellants, who brought yarn spun on the mainland into the island for weaving, and sent the cloth back to the mainland for finishing. The respondents, who were officials of the trade union, called on their members who were dockers on the island to place an embargo on the import of yarn and the export of cloth. The appellants sought an order to stop the embargo.

VISCOUNT SIMON LC: '. . . However the origin of the rule may be explained, I take it to be clear that there are cases in which a combination of individuals to act in a certain way, resulting in deliberate damage to others, is actionable, even though the same thing, if done by a single individual without any element of combination, would not expose him to liability. In the present case, the evidence did not support an allegation that the defendants, or either of them, had procured a breach of contract, and if one of them, acting alone, had without employing unlawful means induced the dockers to refuse to handle the appellants' goods, I cannot see that any action would have lain against him. Everything turns, therefore, on whether the two respondents were engaged in a combination "to injure", in the sense in which that phrase is employed when liability results; it is to this question that I now address myself . . .

The question to be answered, in determining whether a combination to do an act which damages others is actionable, even though it would not be actionable if done by a single person, is not "did the combiners appreciate, or should they be treated as appreciating, that others would suffer from their action", but "what is the real reason why the combiners did it?" Or, as Lord Cave puts it, "what is the real purpose of the combination?" The test is not what is the natural result to the claimants of such combined action, or what is the resulting damage which the defendants realise or should realise will follow, but what is in truth the object in the minds of the combiners when they acted as they did. It is not consequence that matters, but purpose; the relevant conjunction is not ωστε, "so that . . ." but ινα "in order that".

Next, it is to be borne in mind that there may be cases where the combination has more than one "object" or "purpose". The combiners may feel that they are killing two birds with one stone, and, even though their main purpose may be to protect their own legitimate interests notwithstanding that this involves damage to the claimants, they may also find a further inducement to do what they are doing by feeling that it serves the claimants right. The analysis of human impulses soon leads us into the quagmire of mixed motives, and even if we avoid the word "motive", there may be more than a single "purpose" or "object". It is enough to say that if there is more than one purpose actuating a combination, liability must depend on ascertaining the predominant purpose. If that predominant purpose is to damage another person and damage results, that is tortious conspiracy. If the predominant purpose is the lawful protection or promotion of any lawful interest of the combiners (no illegal means being employed), it is not a tortious conspiracy, even though it causes damage to another person . . .

I am content to say that, unless the real and predominant purpose is to advance the defendants' lawful interests in a matter where the defendants honestly believe that those interests would directly suffer if the action taken against the claimants was not taken, a combination wilfully to damage a man in his trade is unlawful. Although most of the cases have dealt with trade rivalry in some form or other, I do not see why the proposition as to the conditions under which conspiracy becomes a tort should be limited to trade competition. Indeed, in its original sense, conspiracy as a tort was a combination to abuse legal procedure: see Winfield's *History of Conspiracy*, c. ii. I have used the word "directly" without seeking to define its boundaries as an indication that indirect gains, such as the subscription in the illustration above, would not provide a justification.

In the present case, the conclusion, in my opinion, is that the predominant object of the respondents in getting the embargo imposed was to benefit their trade-union members by preventing under-cutting and unregulated competition, and so helping to secure the economic stability of the island industry. The result they aimed at achieving was to create a better basis for collective bargaining, and thus directly to improve wage prospects. A combination with such an object is not unlawful, because the object is the legitimate promotion of the interests of the combiners, and because the damage necessarily inflicted on the appellants is not inflicted by criminal or tortious means and is not "the real purpose" of the combination. I agree with Lord Fleming when he says in his judgment that it is not for a court of law to consider in this connection the expediency or otherwise of a policy adopted by a trade union. Neither can liability be determined by asking whether the damage inflicted to secure the purpose is disproportionately severe: this may throw doubts on the bona fides of the avowed purpose, but once the legitimate purpose is established, and no unlawful means are involved, the quantum of damage is irrelevant. I move that this appeal be dismissed with costs.'

(Viscount Maugham and Lords Thankerton, Wright and Porter delivered concurring judgments.)

Comment

(1) The predominant purpose doctrine as here interpreted has meant that in most trade disputes, there will be no liability for conspiracy to injure. The defendants' motive will usually be predominantly the more or less ruthless pursuit of their own self-interest, which will not attract liability provided lawful means are used.

Conspiracy to use unlawful means

This tort is committed when two or more people combine to injure the claimant and use unlawful means to achieve their purpose.

Lonrho plc v *Fayed* [1991] 3 All ER 303 House of Lords

Lonrho's attempt to take over the House of Fraser (including Harrods) was referred to the Monopolies Commission by the Secretary of State. Lonrho gave an undertaking not to acquire more shares in the company before the Commission reported. While Lonrho was still bound by that undertaking, the Fayed brothers successfully bid for and bought the House of Fraser. Their bid was not referred to the Monopolies Commission. Lonrho sued the Fayeds, alleging that they had made fraudulent misrepresentations to the Secretary of State.

LORD BRIDGE: '... As against all the defendants, Lonrho's statement of claim pleads that their intention was both to benefit the Fayeds and Holdings by furthering their interest in the acquisition of HoF and to injure Lonrho by preventing them from acquiring HoF. Lonrho claims to have lost the opportunity to acquire HoF by bidding for the shares without competition from the Fayeds or Holdings and thereby to have suffered damage. Lonrho asserts that these facts are sufficient to establish a cause of action for the common law tort of interfering with business by unlawful means. But the statement of claim also relied additionally or alternatively on the same allegations of fact as establishing the tort of conspiracy to injure ...

Where conspirators act with the predominant purpose of injuring the claimant and in fact inflict damage on him, but do nothing which would have been actionable if done by an individual acting alone, it is in the fact of their concerted action for that illegitimate purpose that the law, however anomalous it may now seem, finds a sufficient ground to condemn their action as illegal and tortious. But when conspirators intentionally injure the claimant and use unlawful means to do so, it is no defence for them to show that their primary purpose was to further or protect their own interests; it is sufficient to make their action tortious that the means used were unlawful.

Did the House in *Lonrho Ltd* v *Shell Petroleum Co Ltd* (1982) depart from this reasoning and lay down for the first time a new principle that a claimant, seeking to establish the tort of conspiracy to injure, must in every case prove that the intention to injure him was the predominant purpose of the defendants, whether the means used were lawful or unlawful? ...

My Lords, I am quite unable to accept that Lord Diplock or the other members of the Appellate Committee concurring with him, of whom I was one, intended the decision in *Lonrho Ltd* v *Shell Petroleum Co Ltd* to effect, sub silentio, such a significant change in the law as it had been previously understood. The House, as is clear from the parties' printed cases, which we have been shown, had never been invited to take such a step. Moreover, to do so would have been directly contrary to the view of Lord Denning MR expressed in the judgment which the House was affirming and inconsistent with the dicta in what Lord Diplock described as 'Viscount Simon LC's now classic speech in *Crofter Hand Woven Harris Tweed Co Ltd* v *Veitch* (1942)'. I would overrule the *Metall* case in this respect.

It follows from this conclusion that Lonrho's acceptance that the pleaded intention on the part of the defendants to cause injury to Lonrho was not the predominant purpose of their alleged unlawful action is not necessarily fatal to the pleaded cause of action in conspiracy and therefore affords no separate ground for striking out that part of the pleading. If the defendants fail to establish that Lonrho's primary pleading asserting the tort of interference with business by unlawful means should be struck out, they are in no stronger position in relation to the pleaded cause of action in conspiracy. It is not, I think, necessary for present purposes to consider whether the pleaded conspiracy adds anything of substance or raises any significantly different issues from those on which the rest of the pleading depends. At this interlocutory stage it is sufficient to say that the two pleaded causes of action must stand or fall together. Either both should be struck out or both should go to trial . . .'

(Lords Brandon, Templeman, Goff and Jauncey agreed with Lord Bridge.)

Comment

(1) The decision makes clear the distinction between the two forms of tortuous conspiracy. In practice, conspiracy to use unlawful means is not of great significance, because it will either amount to causing loss by unlawful means (in which case it is not necessary to prove the element of combination) or it will not be actionable.

(2) The approach of the House of Lords to unlawful means in this case was referred to with approval by the House of Lords in *OBG* v *Allan* (2007). While conspiracy was not discussed by the House of Lords in that case, it seems likely that the test for intention used in that case would apply also in relation to conspiracy to use unlawful means.

The statutory immunity

Trade Union and Labour Relations (Consolidation) Act 1992

219 (1) An act done by a person in contemplation or furtherance of a trade dispute is not actionable in tort on the ground only –
   (a) that it induces another person to break a contract or interferes or induces another person to interfere with its performance, or
   (b) that it consists in his threatening that a contract (whether one to which he is a party or not) will be broken or its performance interfered with, or that he will induce another person to break a contract or interfere with its performance.
(2) An agreement or combination by two or more persons to do or procure the doing of an act in contemplation or furtherance of a trade dispute is not actionable in tort if the act is one which if done without any such agreement or combination would not be actionable in tort . . .

Comment

(1) The basic statutory immunity for torts occurring in industrial action is contained in TULRCA s 219. It applies provided the action is 'in contemplation or furtherance of a trade dispute' and provided that the immunity is not removed on some other ground. These two conditions are examined in the next chapter.

(2) From this it can be seen that the torts for which immunity is given are: (i) inducing breach of contract (TULRCA s 219(1)(a)); (ii) intimidation where the threat is to induce breaches of contract (TULRCA s 219(1)(b)), and (iii) conspiracy to injure (TULRCA s 219(2)). Importantly, the House of Lords held in *Hadmor Productions* v *Hamilton* (1982) that an act which is immune from liability under s 219 cannot be regarded as 'unlawful means' for the purposes of committing any other tort. It follows therefore that some forms of causing loss by unlawful means and conspiracy to use unlawful means will be protected, as long as the means used are within the statutory immunity.

(3) There is no statutory immunity for other torts committed in the course of industrial disputes. In the next section some of the torts most likely to arise in this context are considered.

Liability for other torts

If it can be shown that industrial action involves the commission of torts for which there is no immunity, it will be actionable. Hence the creativity shown by employers and their advisers in seeking to find new torts which outflank the statutory immunity.

Inducing breach of statutory duty

Meade v *Haringey LBC* [1979] ICR 494 Court of Appeal

LORD DENNING MR: 'On Monday, January 22, 1979 the caretakers at the schools in Haringey came out on strike. There were very few of them. Only one or two for a school of 500 or 600 children. Their duties were simple enough. To look after the buildings and the heating system. To unblock drains. To lock up at night and open up in the morning. And so forth. Yet by coming out on strike they succeeded in paralysing the educational system of the great London Borough of Haringey. The borough council closed over 100 schools for weeks on end. 37,000 children were deprived of the teaching they should have had. They were put back in their examinations and their careers. Some ran loose in the streets while their mothers were out working.

   The parents of the children were much upset by all this. They went to their lawyers to see if there was any way to get the schools reopened. The lawyers looked up the statute and found that it was the duty of the borough council under s 8(1) of the Education Act 1944 "to secure that there shall be available for their area sufficient schools . . . for providing . . . full-time education suitable to the requirements of [the] pupils" . . .

   Now comes the great question in this case: had the borough council any just cause or excuse for closing the schools as they did? On the evidence as it stands, the borough council were acting under the influence of the trade unions and indeed in combination with them. And the trade unions and their secretaries were, as I see it, acting quite unlawfully. They were calling on the local education authority to break their statutory duty – to close the schools instead of keeping them open as they should have done. Now [TULRCA s 219] gives them immunity if they induce a person to break a contract. But it gives them no immunity if they induce a local authority to break its statutory duty . . .

On the evidence as it stands before us, it appears that the trade unions were the dominating influence in requiring the schools to be closed – and not reopened: and the borough council closed them at the behest of the trade unions or in agreement with them. In so doing the borough council were breaking their statutory duty: and the trade unions' leaders were inducing them to break it. Such conduct was in my view unlawful: and the trade unions' leaders have no immunity in respect of it . . .'

(Eveleigh LJ and Sir Stanley Rees delivered concurring judgments.)

Comment

(1) There remains some doubt about the parameters and applicability of this tort in relation to industrial action. It was argued that it was committed in a dock strike in *Associated British Ports* v *TGWU* (1989), but the House of Lords was not prepared to accept easily that workers in breach of contract were also in breach of a statutory duty. The issue did not arise in *OBG* v *Allan* (2007), where Lord Nicholls expressly left open how far the *Lumley* v *Gye* principle could be held to apply to statutory obligations. It must also be doubtful how far this tort could be relied upon as unlawful means for the purposes of other torts, given the limits placed on that concept by Lord Hoffmann in *OBG* v *Allan*.

(2) Many jobs in the public sector are regulated by statute to some extent, so this tort may present risks for those organising industrial action among public sector workers.

Inducing breach of an equitable obligation

Prudential Assurance Co Ltd v *Lorenz* (1971) 11 KIR 78 Chancery Division

In furtherance of a trade dispute, the union representing insurance agents working for the claimant company called on them not to submit accounts to the company.

PLOWMAN J: 'Now, Mr Pain on behalf of the claimants puts the claimants' case in three ways. First of all he submits that the circular is an incitement to members to commit a breach of a duty to account which is implied by the general law independently of the agents' service agreement, with the consequence that notwithstanding the existence of a trade dispute in this case, [TULRCA s 219] affords no protection, and as authority for this proposition Mr Pain cited an unreported decision of Pennycuick J's of May 13, 1969 in a case called the *Co-operative Insurance Society Ltd* v *Quinlan* (1969) . . .

With regard to Mr Pain's first submission Mr Oliver submitted that the circular went no further than to suggest an interference with the contractual obligation of the claimants' agents to account, and he cited authority to show what an agent's liability to account, apart from express contract, is. However, as I understood it, he was constrained to admit that if he was right, the two *Co-operative Insurance Society* cases to which I have already referred must be wrong. But he pertinently pointed out that the authorities on which he relied, *Turner* v *Burkinshaw* (1867) and *The Earl of Hardwicke* v *Vernon* (1808) were not cited in the *Co-operative Insurance Society* cases. Well, it is certainly possible that Mr Oliver may be right in his submission and in due course the Court of Appeal may say so, but in this court I think that Mr Pain is entitled to rely on those two cases, at the very least to the extent of saying that they establish a sufficient prima facie case in his favour for the purposes of an interlocutory injunction . . .'

Comment

(1) While inducing a breach of an equitable obligation to account is here regarded as tortious, it must be remembered that in interlocutory proceedings points are not fully argued. It seems that this probably does not apply in relation to all breaches of equitable obligation. In *Metall und Rohstoff AG* v *Donaldson, Lufkin, Jenrette Inc* (1989) the Court of Appeal held that there was no such tort as inducing a breach of trust (the decision was overruled on a different point by the House of Lords in *Lonrho* v *Fayed* (1991)).

(2) In *Mainstream Properties* v *Young* (2007) there was an attempt to argue that the defendant had induced the two employees to commit a breach of their obligation of good faith towards their employer. This was rejected by Lord Hoffmann because the point had not been raised and argued in the lower courts. Lord Nicholls expressly left open whether or not the *Lumley* v *Gye* principle should apply in these circumstances.

Economic duress

Universe Tankships Inc of Monrovia v *International Transport Workers' Federation* [1982] ICR 262 House of Lords

The case arose out of the long-running campaign by the ITF against ships flying flags of convenience – that is, registered in countries which do not require their owners to observe internationally agreed standards, particularly in relation to the terms and conditions of employment of their crews.

The *Universe Sentinel* was blacked by the union on its arrival in Milford Haven and was thus unable to leave port. In order to get the blacking order lifted, the owners agreed to pay $6,480 to the union's welfare fund. Subsequently the owners tried to reclaim the money.

LORD DIPLOCK: '. . . My Lords, I turn to the second ground on which repayment of the $6,480 is claimed, which I will call the duress point. It is not disputed that the circumstances in which ITF demanded that the shipowners should enter into the special agreement and the typescript agreement and should pay the moneys of which the latter documents acknowledge receipt, amounted to economic duress upon the shipowners; that is to say, it is conceded that the financial consequences to the shipowners of the *Universe Sentinel* continuing to be rendered off-hire under her time charter to Texaco, while the blacking continued, were so catastrophic as to amount to a coercion of the shipowners' will which vitiated their consent to those agreements and to the payments made by them to ITF. This concession makes it unnecessary for your Lordships to use the instant appeal as the occasion for a general consideration of the developing law of economic duress as a ground for treating contracts as voidable and obtaining restitution of money paid under economic duress as money had and received to the claimants' use . . .

Commercial pressure, in some degree, exists wherever one party to a commercial transaction is in a stronger bargaining position than the other. It is not, however, in my view, necessary, nor would it be appropriate in the instant appeal, to enter into the general question of the kinds of circumstances, if any, in which commercial pressure, even though it amounts to a coercion of the will of a party in the weaker bargaining position, may be treated as legitimate and, accordingly, as not giving rise to any legal right of redress. In the instant appeal the economic duress complained of was exercised in the field of industrial relations to which very special considerations apply.

My Lords, so far as is relevant to this appeal, the policy of Parliament, ever since the Trade Disputes Act 1906 was passed to overrule a decision of this House, has been to legitimise acts done by employees, or by trade unions acting or purporting to act on their behalf, which would otherwise be unlawful wherever such acts are done in contemplation or furtherance of a dispute which is connected with the terms and conditions of employment of any employees. I can confine myself to the kind of acts and the particular subject matter of the trade dispute that was involved in the instant case, and I use the expression "legitimise" as meaning that the doer of the act is rendered immune from any liability to damages or any other remedy against him in a court of justice, at the suit of a person who has suffered loss or damage in consequence of the act; save only a remedy for breach of contract where the act is done in breach of a direct contract between the doer of the act and the person by whom the damage is sustained . . .

The use of economic duress to induce another person to part with property or money is not a tort per se; the form that the duress takes may, or may not, be tortious. The remedy to which economic duress gives rise is not an action for damages but an action for restitution of property or money exacted under such duress and the avoidance of any contract that had been induced by it; but where the particular form taken by the economic duress used is itself a tort, the restitutional remedy for money had and received by the defendant to the claimant's use is one which the claimant is entitled to pursue as an alternative remedy to an action for damages in tort.

In extending into the field of industrial relations the common law concept of economic duress and the right to a restitutionary remedy for it which is currently in process of development by judicial decisions, this House would not, in my view, be exercising the restraint that is appropriate to such a process if it were so to develop the concept that, by the simple expedient of "waiving the tort", a restitutionary remedy for money had and received is made enforceable in cases in which Parliament has, over so long a period of years, manifested its preference for a public policy that a particular kind of tortious act should be legitimised in the sense that I am using that expression.

It is only in this indirect way that the provisions of [TULRCA] are relevant to the duress point. The immunities from liability in tort provided by [TULRCA s 219] are not directly applicable to the shipowners' cause of action for money had and received. Nevertheless, these sections, together with the definition of trade dispute in [TULRCA s 244], afford an indication, which your Lordships should respect, of where public policy requires that the line should be drawn between what kind of commercial pressure by a trade union upon an employer in the field of industrial relations ought to be treated as legitimised despite the fact that the will of the employer is thereby coerced, and what kind of commercial pressure in that field does amount to economic duress that entitles the employer victim to restitutionary remedies . . .'

Comment

(1) The House of Lords here recognises an action for economic duress as grounds for restitution where illegitimate pressure is used. In the event, the case turned on whether the pressure used (the blacking of the *Universe Sentinel*) attracted the statutory immunity or not. By a majority, the House of Lords held it did not (see below, p 637); thus the shipowners could recover their money.

(2) Pressure which was lawful because it attracted immunity under TULRCA s 219 would not have been regarded as illegitimate. However, in *Dimskal Shipping v ITF* (1992) the House of Lords reduced this protection. The facts of the case were similar, but the money was paid in Sweden. The pressure used would have been lawful under Swedish law, although not under British law. Nonetheless, the shipowners were allowed to recover the money paid.

(3) We turn to the scope of the statutory immunity in the next chapter.

REFERENCES AND FURTHER READING

R Benedictus (1985), 'The Use of the Law of Tort in the Miners' Dispute' 14 ILJ 176

H Carty (2001), *An Analysis of the Economic Torts*, OUP

P Elias (1994), 'The Strike and Breach of Contract: a Reassessment' in K Ewing, C Gearty and B Hepple (eds), *Human Rights and Labour Law*, Mansell

K Ewing (1991), *The Right to Strike*, Clarendon Press

K Miller and C Woolfson (1994), 'Timex, Industrial Relations and the Use of the Law in the 1990s' 23 ILJ 209

B Napier (1987), 'Strikes and the Individual Worker', [1987] CLJ 287

T Novitz (2003), *International and European Protection of the Right to Strike*, OUP

G Pitt (1995), *The Limits of Industrial Action*, Institute of Employment Rights

R Rideout (1997), 'Industrial Relations: the empire strikes back', [1997] CLP 361

B Simpson (2007), 'Economic Tort Liability in Labour Disputes: the potential impact of *OBG v Allan*' 36 ILJ 468

M Sterling (1982), 'Actions for Duress, Seafarers and Industrial Disputes' 11 ILJ 156

13

INDUSTRIAL ACTION II

The three-stage approach to determining whether industrial action is lawful involves asking at Stage 1 whether or not the activity would be tortious at common law in the first place. If not, then there should be no problem – although see the provision about ballots on p 645. If it is tortious, then Stage 2 is to ask whether it comes within the basic immunity in TULRCA s 219. As noted in the last chapter, Stage 2 breaks down into two sub-questions: first, does s 219 cover the tort which has been committed; and, secondly, if it does, are the other conditions in s 219 met?

In Chapter 12 we looked at how far organising industrial action would involve torts at common law and also at what the basic immunity covered. It is now time to consider the other requirements before immunity can be claimed under TULRCA s 219.

IMMUNITY UNDER TULRCA s 219

Trade Union and Labour Relations (Consolidation) Act 1992

219 (1) An act done by a person in contemplation or furtherance of a trade dispute is not actionable in tort on the ground only –

(a) that it induces another person to break a contract or interferes or induces another person to interfere with its performance, or

(b) that it consists in his threatening that a contract (whether one to which he is a party or not) will be broken or its performance interfered with, or that he will induce another person to break a contract or interfere with its performance.

(2) An agreement or combination by two or more persons to do or procure the doing of an act in contemplation or furtherance of a trade dispute is not actionable in tort if the act is one which if done without any such agreement or combination would not be actionable in tort.

(3) Nothing in subsections (1) and (2) prevents an act done in the course of picketing from being actionable in tort unless it is done in the course of attendance declared lawful by section 220 (peaceful picketing).

(4) Subsections (1) and (2) have effect subject to sections 222 to 225 (action excluded from protection) and to sections 226 (requirement of ballot before action by trade union) and 234A (requirement of notice to employer of industrial action); and in those sections 'not protected' means excluded from the protection afforded by this section or, where the expression is used with reference to a particular person, excluded from that protection as respects that person.

Comment

(1) As noted in Chapter 12, this means that there is *prima facie* immunity for the torts of inducing breach of contract, intimidation where the threat is to induce breaches of contract and conspiracy to injure, provided that the other conditions in s 219 are met.

(2) Other forms of causing loss by unlawful means and conspiracy to use unlawful means are not directly protected, but if the unlawful means attract immunity, they cannot be relied on for these other torts.

(3) The major condition for s 219 to apply is that the torts must have been committed 'in contemplation or furtherance of a trade dispute'. This phrase was first used in the Conspiracy and Protection of Property Act 1875 and was conveniently dubbed 'the golden formula' by Lord Wedderburn. Its meaning has changed over recent decades, because of substantial amendment of the definition of a trade dispute.

Trade Union and Labour Relations (Consolidation) Act 1992

244 (1) In this Part a 'trade dispute' means a dispute between workers and their employer which relates wholly or mainly to one or more of the following –

  (a) terms and conditions of employment, or the physical conditions in which any workers are required to work;
  (b) engagement or non-engagement, or termination or suspension of employment or the duties of employment, of one or more workers;
  (c) allocation of work or the duties of employment between workers or groups of workers;
  (d) matters of discipline;
  (e) a worker's membership or non-membership of a trade union;
  (f) facilities for officials of trade unions; and
  (g) machinery for negotiation or consultation, and other procedures, relating to any of the above matters, including the recognition by employers or employers' associations of the right of a trade union to represent workers in such negotiation or consultation or in the carrying out of such procedures . . .

(3) There is a trade dispute even though it relates to matters occurring outside the United Kingdom, so long as the person or persons whose actions in the United Kingdom are said to be in contemplation or furtherance of a trade dispute relating to matters occurring outside the United Kingdom are likely to be affected in respect of one or more of the matters specified in subsection (1) by the outcome of the dispute.

(4) An act, threat or demand done or made by one person or organisation against another which, if resisted, would have led to a trade dispute with that other, shall be treated as being done or made in contemplation of a trade dispute with that other, notwithstanding that because that other submits to the act or threat or accedes to the demand no dispute arises.

(5) In this section –

'employment' includes any relationship whereby one person personally does work or performs services for another; and
'worker', in relation to a dispute with an employer, means –

  (a) a worker employed by that employer; or
  (b) a person who has ceased to be so employed if his employment was terminated in connection with the dispute or if the termination of his employment was one of the circumstances giving rise to the dispute.

An existing dispute

Bents Brewery Co Ltd v *Hogan* [1945] 2 All ER 570 Liverpool Assizes

The union, through its divisional officer, had sent a questionnaire to the managers of public houses seeking information about takings, staff costs, etc, which it wanted for collective bargaining purposes. As some of the information requested was confidential, the managers would have been in breach of their contracts of employment in disclosing it. Sued for inducing breach of contract, the union claimed that it was not liable because it was acting in contemplation or furtherance of a trade dispute.

LYNSKEY J: '. . . The next question I have to decide is whether the document was sent out by the defendant, or on his behalf, in contemplation or furtherance of a trade dispute. Long and detailed particulars were given by the defendant as to trade disputes alleged to be existing or in contemplation. I do not propose to go through these particulars or the evidence relating to them, as, in my opinion, they do not disclose any dispute either in being or imminent. The document was sent out to managers of brewery companies. No demand has been made for either better conditions or increased wages by any manager to any of the claimant brewery companies. No such demands had been made by the defendant, or his union, on behalf of such managers. The defendant in his evidence before me said he sent out the document containing the questionnaire to find out whether there was a trade dispute, and to find out whether the conditions and wages were satisfactory. In my opinion, a dispute cannot exist unless there is a difference of opinion between two parties as to some matter. There is no evidence before me that any dispute existed. The highest that it can be put on the evidence in favour of the defendant is that the document was sent out to obtain information which, after consideration of the information obtained, might lead to a request which, if not granted, might result in a dispute.

In *Conway* v *Wade* (1909), Lord Loreburn LC dealt with the meaning of the words "an act done in contemplation or furtherance of a trade dispute". In his speech he said:

> "I think they mean that either a dispute is imminent and the act is done in expectation of and with a view to it, or that the dispute is already existing, and the act is done in support of one side to it. In either case the act must be genuinely done as described and the dispute must be a real thing imminent or existing."

There was no dispute when the document was sent out which was a real thing, either imminent or existing. There was a possibility of a dispute at some future time, but no certainty that such a dispute would arise.

In my view there was no dispute existing at the time this questionnaire was sent and the result is that the protection given by [TULRCA s 219] does not help the defendant . . .'

University College London Hospital NHS Trust v *Unison*
[1999] ICR 204 Court of Appeal

The union balloted its members on taking industrial action. The hospital trust applied for an interim injunction on the basis that the strike would not be within the statutory immunity.

LORD WOOLF MR: '. . . The facts leading up to the dispute can be summarised shortly. The claimant hospital trust ("the trust") came in to existence in 1994. While it was initially only concerned with University College London Hospital, it subsequently became responsible for managing a group of hospitals which now employ over 5,000 staff. The defendants ("the union") represent many of the non-clinical staff and some of the nursing staff. The trust are in the process of negotiating with a consortium under the private finance initiative, an arrangement whereby private companies will first erect and then run for the trust a new hospital. This will result in members of the union, who are at present employed by the trust, being transferred to the employment of the consortium. The union are, as a matter of principle, against this method of financing the new hospital. The union would like to see a new hospital, but it would like to see it being built and run by the National Health Service and not being built and run by the private sector. The union regard what is intended to happen to the new hospital as being a form of privatisation . . .

The regional office, through Mr Thompson [the union's regional officer], was seeking to persuade the trust to enter into a contractual arrangement with the consortium. The arrangement was to ensure that members of the union who came to work for the consortium would be given a guarantee of equivalent terms and conditions of employment to those which existing employees who were not transferred to the consortium would obtain from the trust. The policy was designed to benefit not only employees who were transferred from the employment of the trust to the consortium, but also employees who were employed by the consortium who had not previously been employed by the trust.

I have used the term "consortium", but it is not clear who will actually constitute the consortium, nor is it clear who will be subcontractors of the consortium. Ideally, the union are seeking a policy which will achieve a guarantee on the lines already indicated for a period of up to 30 years. However, I have no doubt that something which approached that objective might well be acceptable to the union . . .

In the ballot paper it is possible to identify four different strands. First, what is sought to be achieved for existing staff where the existing terms are to continue to apply when they are transferred to a new employer; secondly, that staff who have not previously been employed by the trust are to have equal protection; and, thirdly, there should be the same collective bargaining arrangements. There is also a separate strand which refers to the employees having equally favourable conditions as the trust staff . . .

I now turn to TULRCA s 244, which I regard as critical to the outcome of this appeal . . . I draw attention to the fact that s 244 opens by referring to a dispute between workers and their employer. That can be said to be the first requirement of a trade dispute. The second requirement is that the dispute must relate wholly or mainly to one or more of the activities which are set out in subparagraphs (a) to (g), of which (a), and possibly (g), are relevant. The third requirement that can be identified is that the act for which protection is sought must be carried out in contemplation or furtherance of a trade dispute. This third requirement is not an issue on this appeal. It is the first and second requirements which are important . . .

I therefore turn to consider whether the more limited policy and objective of the union in this case falls within the requirements of s 244. In doing so, I note that the statutory categories of permitted purposes must be the predominant purpose. The dispute must relate wholly or mainly to those purposes. If it relates to them, that is not sufficient to fulfil the statutory requirement.

Together with the objectives of obtaining a guarantee for existing employees, the union is seeking to secure the same guarantee for employees who have never been employed by the trust. As the 30-year period for which the guarantee is at present being sought progresses, there is bound to be a situation which will arise where the great majority of the employees will never have been employed by the trust. I cannot see how it is possible to apply the language of s 244(1)(a) and (5) in a way which covers the terms and conditions of employment of employers of a third party who have never been employed by the employer who is to be the subject of the strike action. This in itself is fatal to the case which the defendants advance on this appeal.

In addition, so far as existing employees are concerned, the strike seeks to achieve protection for them in relation to employment with the so far unidentified future employer. Recognising that this does not readily fall within the language of s 244, Mr Hendy [for the union] submits that the obtaining of the future protection does relate wholly or mainly to the existing terms and conditions of the employees of the trust because it will provide those employees with a sense of security which they would not otherwise have . . .

As to that argument, I see its force. However, in my judgment, it does not assist Mr Hendy because, on the facts which are before the court, while it is true that a consequence of obtaining a guarantee would be to give the existing employees the additional security to which he refers, and therefore to that extent a matter which relates to their terms and conditions of employment, that is not the dispute which those employees are wholly or mainly concerned about. They are wholly or mainly concerned about the dispute with different employment; the employment with the so far unidentified new employer. For that reason, even with regard to the employees who are already employed by the trust, I consider that on the facts which are before the court, it is unlikely that the union could take advantage of the statutory immunity . . .

The third matter to which I draw attention is the different strands of the ballot paper. This refers to the subsequent staff. In view of what I have said about staff who have never been employed by the trust, it seems to me that that is an impermissible subject for the ballot. As it is impossible to identify the motives of those who voted in favour of strike action for doing so, it follows that this nullifies the ballot which took place. In addition, the ballot paper is very persuasive evidence as to what is the proposed purpose of the strike. The terms of the ballot paper support that it was for different purposes, one of which is clearly flawed.

The failure to meet the requirements of s 244, coupled with the defect in the ballot paper, means that this appeal must be dismissed. On the true approach to the statutory provisions to which I have referred, the only conclusion which a court could reach on the evidence which is before us is that the proposed strike is not subject to the protection of the Act . . .'

(Hutchison and Judge LJJ agreed with Lord Woolf.)

Comment

(1) Similar arguments were used in some of the cases involving the ITF's campaign against flags of convenience, where crews recruited from poor countries were often satisfied with their wages, even though they were below ITF rates: see *Star Sea Transport* v *Slater* (1978), for example.

(2) Unions are not required to state what the dispute is about on the ballot paper sent out to members, but it is usual to do so, as happened in *University College London Hospital* v *Unison*, and it is recommended in the *Code of Practice on Industrial Action Ballots* (2005) para 36. Where this happens, it is obviously compelling evidence of what the dispute is said to be about, and if it is more than one thing, they must all be existing dispute issues, as that case shows. See also *London Underground* v *NUR* (1989) (below, p 653).

'Workers and their employer'

Until amendment by the Employment Act 1982, a dispute could be between workers and employers generally (so that the dispute did not have to be with a worker's own employer) or between workers and workers. The limiting effect of the revised wording is demonstrated in the next case.

Dimbleby & Sons Ltd v *NUJ* [1984] ICR 386 House of Lords

The claimant company (referred to as 'Dimbleby' in the speech of Lord Diplock) published local newspapers ('the Dimbleby newspapers') and employed journalists who were members of the NUJ.

LORD DIPLOCK: '. . . The Dimbleby newspapers were printed not by Dimbleby themselves but by an associated company – an arrangement which your Lordships were informed is common in the case of publishers of provincial newspapers. That associated company, Dimbleby Printers Ltd, had been, and apparently still is, engaged in a trade dispute with a powerful trade union that enforces a "closed shop" in nearly all establishments engaged in the printing trade, the National Graphical Association ("NGA"). As a result of this trade dispute there was a strike by members of the NGA employed by Dimbleby Printers Ltd which stopped the Dimbleby newspapers from appearing after 19 August 1983. In order to resume publication of the Dimbleby newspapers, Dimbleby had to find an alternative printer for their newspapers who did not employ members of the NGA. It found one in TBF, which was an associated company of T Bailey Forman Ltd, the publishers of the *Nottingham Evening Post*, with whom the NUJ has been engaged in a trade dispute which started in 1979 and is still continuing. The two companies have parallel shareholding and are controlled by the same (third) company.

In the first week of October 1983, Dimbleby entered into an oral contract with TBF for the provision by Dimbleby to TBF Printers of copy for the Dimbleby newspapers and the printing of the necessary quantities of those newspapers by TBF. On learning of this the NUJ, who apparently at that stage did not know that TBF was a different company from T Bailey Forman Ltd, with which they were in long-standing dispute, instructed the NUJ journalists employed by Dimbleby to refuse to provide copy to Dimbleby for printing by TBF. With this instruction, given on 10 October 1983, the NUJ journalists complied. They refused to provide copy to their employer Dimbleby as their contracts of employment required them to do. As a result of that refusal, which they persisted in, they were suspended from their employment and so remain.

My Lords, since this is only an interlocutory appeal and from the evidence given at the trial there may emerge a picture of the facts of the case different from that which is disclosed by the affidavits and documents that were before the judge, I shall confine myself (1) to mentioning the main grounds on which it was contended by the NUJ that there was a likelihood that their defence, that their acts which were the subject of the suit, were done in contemplation or furtherance of a trade dispute, would succeed and that the balance of convenience lay in favour of refusing the injunction sought; and (2) to giving a brief indication of the reasons why, in my opinion, upon the evidence as it stands at present, none of these contentions is likely to succeed.

I start with the simplest argument advanced on behalf of the NUJ. This was: that the NUJ journalists' refusal, on the instructions of the NUJ, to provide copy to Dimbleby constituted in itself a trade dispute between workers and their employer as to the terms and conditions of their employment, within the meaning of [TULRCA s 244] . . .

There was, however, in the evidence before the judge no vestige of any claim by the NUJ itself or by the NUJ journalists that their current contracts of employment by Dimbleby – and it is only their *current* contracts that can be relevant to this argument – contained a term entitling them to refuse to comply with instructions given to them by Dimbleby to provide copy of the kind that they were employed to obtain, if they received instructions to the contrary from the NUJ. Indeed, it passes beyond the bounds of credibility that any responsible newspaper proprietor would agree to such a term in contracts of employment with his journalists. The evidence that was before the judge makes it perfectly clear that the NUJ journalists acknowledged that by refusing to provide copy for the Dimbleby newspapers so long as they were to be printed by TBF they were breaking their contracts, albeit they were doing so reluctantly on the instructions,

627

enforceable by disciplinary sanctions, that had been given to them by the NUJ. But for the fact that, contrary to the unanimous opinion of the Court of Appeal, the judge himself appears to have thought that there was a trade dispute between Dimbleby and the NUJ as to the terms and conditions of employment by Dimbleby of the NUJ journalists, I should not myself have thought that on this issue the evidence before the judge raised any arguable question to be tried but, having regard (as [TULRCA s 221(2)] commands me) to the likelihood of the NUJ's succeeding in this particular defence at the trial, I agree with the Court of Appeal that the like-lihood is minimal.

Your Lordships were also invited to consider an alternative ground on which it was sub-mitted that there existed a trade dispute between Dimbleby and the NUJ, viz "the allocation of work or the duties of employment as between workers or groups of workers" within the meaning of [TULRCA s 244(1)(c)], the allocation sought to be relied on being the allocation between workers employed by Dimbleby Printers Ltd (not Dimbleby itself) and workers employed by TBF.

This contention does not appear to have been advanced on behalf of the NUJ before either the judge or the Court of Appeal. Even if an argument to this effect could have been advanced with any degree of plausibility before the amendment of s 29 of the Trade Union and Labour Relations Act 1974 by s 18 of the Employment Act 1982, all vestige of plausibility is removed by the amended definitions of "trade dispute" and "worker" found in [TULRCA s 244(1) and (5)] respectively. The effect of subsection (1) is to redefine "trade dispute" as a dispute between workers and their employer wholly "or mainly related to" one or more of the matters listed in [TULRCA s 244(1)]. Subsection (5), so far as relevant, provides that "'worker', in relation to a trade dispute with an employer, means a worker employed by that employer".

So allocation of work or duties of employment between workers or groups of workers as a possible subject of a trade dispute is now limited to demarcation issues between workers or groups of workers employed by the same employer. The likelihood of the NUJ succeeding in this particular defence is, in my view, nil.

It is not now disputed that in October 1983 when the NUJ journalists refused to provide copy to be printed by T Bailey Forman Ltd there was still in existence a trade dispute between the NUJ and T Bailey Forman Ltd . . .'

(Lords Fraser, Scarman, Bridge and Brandon agreed with Lord Diplock.)

Comment

(1) There were three potential trade disputes in this case. The first was between the journalists and Dimbleby, their employer, over whether they should have to supply copy in contravention of their union's instructions. Lord Diplock effectively said that because they have no complaint about their own terms and conditions, they cannot say that there is a trade dispute just because they are breaking their contracts of employment. However, it could be argued that they were in dispute about whether there should be a *new* term in their contracts, that they should not have to disobey their union's instruc-tions. Lord Diplock impliedly negatived this, but without much by way of argument. This point will be returned to.

(2) The journalists argued, alternatively, that they were in dispute with Dimbleby over allocation of work, which is a trade dispute issue under TULRCA s 244(1)(c). How-ever, they were complaining about the allocation of work to TBF away from printers employed by a different employer, Dimbleby Printers Ltd. Because the printers did not work for the same employer as the journalists, the journalists could not be in dispute with *their* employer about them.

Dimbleby and Dimbleby Printers Ltd were, of course, associated companies with the same people controlling them: but legally they were different employers and the veil of incorporation is not lifted in these circumstances – which provides a clear incentive for employers to structure different parts of their business as separate companies.

(3) The second dispute was between the printers and their employer, Dimbleby Printers Ltd: the dispute which led to Dimbleby Printers Ltd switching the work to TBF in the first place. This was clearly a trade dispute, and before 1982 this would have sufficed for the journalists' action to come within the immunity. Even under the present wording, the journalists could have said that they were acting in contemplation or furtherance of this dispute even though it was not their own dispute. The present wording requires only that *somewhere* there is a trade dispute between workers and their own employer, and that the industrial action in question was organised in contemplation or furtherance of it. However, if the journalists were acting in furtherance of someone else's dispute, it would be sympathy action (secondary action) and, as we will see, immunity is lost in those circumstances.

(4) It is, however, worth noting that Lord Diplock accepts that demarcation disputes between groups of workers employed by the same employer will count as trade disputes. After the 1982 amendment this had been doubted by some commentators, who thought that such a dispute would be regarded as one between workers and workers only. But, as others have pointed out, the employer is virtually bound to get involved.

(5) The third dispute is between the NUJ and T Bailey Forman Ltd. This is admitted on all sides to be a trade dispute. However, there are two problems about immunity here. First, action in furtherance of it by the Dimbleby journalists is sympathy (secondary) action, which loses immunity on that account. Secondly, the company struck at was TBF – an associated company of T Bailey Forman Ltd, run by the same people, but having a separate identity in law. The House of Lords refused to treat them as effectively the same and consequently action taken against TBF was also secondary action and would therefore be deprived of immunity.

(6) This shows clearly that it is no longer sufficient to be able to point at some industrial dispute somewhere. The parties need to be identified with some precision if there is to be immunity.

(7) The compatibility of this position with the European Convention of Human Rights was tested in the next case.

Unison v United Kingdom [2002] IRLR 497 European Court of Human Rights

Following the decision in *University College London Hospital NHS Trust v Unison* (1999) the union challenged whether limiting lawful industrial action to current employees was an infringement of the right to freedom of association guaranteed by Art 11 of the European Convention of Human Rights. The Court had to decide whether the claim was admissible. After general observations on Art 11 and the right to strike the Court continued:

JUDGMENT OF THE COURT: '. . . 36   In the present case, the applicant trade union submits that the decision of the Court of Appeal prohibiting the strike against UCLH was a disproportionate interference with its right, under Article 11, to take effective action to protect its members' interests in light of the proposed transfer of part of the UCLH's functions to private companies. The Government dispute that Article 11 comes into play at all, considering that the strike did not concern the occupational interests of its members as it concerned protection of yet unidentified individuals to be employed by yet unidentified transferee companies. The Court observes that this was the approach taken by the domestic courts in applying the applicable legislation concerning "trade disputes". This is not a decisive consideration for the purposes of Article 11 of the Convention. It notes that UCLH was proposing to transfer part of its functions to private sector companies and that, potentially, members of the applicant would be affected by these transfers. Even if the guarantees sought by the applicant extend to protect hypothetical future employees, it appears that they would have provided its existing members with an additional protection, however slight or difficult to enforce, against any measures taken by a future transferee company which might affect their pay and conditions. The Court of Appeal considered that the guarantee if obtained by the union could have been of benefit to its members. The proposed strike must be regarded therefore as concerning the occupational interests of the applicant's members in the sense covered by Article 11 of the Convention.

37   The Court further considers that the prohibition of the strike must be regarded as a restriction on the applicant's power to protect those interests and therefore discloses a restriction on the freedom of association guaranteed under the first paragraph. It has examined, below, whether this restriction was in compliance with the requirements of Article 11 paragraph 2 of the Convention, namely whether it was "prescribed by law", pursued one or more legitimate aims under paragraph 2 and was "necessary in a democratic society" for the achievement of those aims.

38   It is not disputed that the measure, imposed by the Court of Appeal in application of domestic law, was "prescribed by law".

39   The applicant does dispute that it pursued any legitimate aim, considering that the measure was a consequence, not intended by Parliament, of the interpretation of domestic law adopted by the courts. The Government submitted that the measure pursued the aims of protecting the rights of others, namely the employer UCLH and the members of the public which would have been affected by any strike. To this, the applicant replied that the protection of the economic interest of UCLH in maintaining its freedom of contract with transferee companies was hardly a weighty consideration and that there was no evidence about any possible impact on the public of the strike. The Court recalls that the Court of Appeal had ruled that the latter element was irrelevant to the legal issues in the case. The importance of the former element is however a matter to be taken into account in assessing the proportionality of the restriction. The Court is satisfied that the employer UCLH could claim that its ability to carry out its functions effectively, including the securing of contracts with other bodies, might be adversely affected by the actions of the applicant and accordingly the measures taken to prevent the strike may be regarded as concerning the "rights of others", namely those of UCLH.

40   The necessity of the measure remains to be determined. The applicant argues that the Government are wrong to claim that their members' interests are adequately safeguarded by employment provisions and that it enjoys other means of protecting those interests. It points, inter alia, to the fact that although on transfer the employees' wages and conditions are maintained under TUPE this does not prevent a new employer giving notice of dismissal while offering new contracts on less advantageous terms and that, to the extent that a transferee company is bound by any existing recognition of the applicant or existing collective agreements, the transferee company would be able to repudiate them. As regards the former possibility, the Court notes that the transferee company would nonetheless face actions for unfair dismissal by any employee threatened with such a measure. As regards the latter, it appears that any employer, including the UCLH, has the ability, in appropriate circumstances, to de-recognise a union or repudiate a collective agreement, which has not been made legally enforceable. This therefore appears to be a risk that faces all trade unions and their members under the current legal framework. It does not derive per se from UCLH's alleged intransigence. Furthermore it appears that under legislation recently entering into force (Schedule A1 to the

1992 Act), the applicant could, if enjoying sufficient support from the work force and where other relevant conditions were complied with, compel an employer to recognise it for the purposes of collective bargaining.

41   The Court notes that the applicant objects strongly to the method, known as the Private Finance Initiative, which public bodies are encouraged by the Government to use in buying services from, or contracting out functions to, private companies. It is regarded as a way of providing public services at a lower cost and, the applicant argues, the principal saving inevitably derives from the private sector's policies of forcing wage cuts and reductions in the work force. The Court understands that employees faced with transfer from a public service to the private sector feel vulnerable and under threat. It is not for this Court however to determine whether this method of providing services is a desirable or damaging policy. It notes that the applicant trade union remains able to take strike action if the UCLH takes any step itself to dismiss employees or change their contracts prior to the transfer and that it could seek to take strike action against any transferee company that in the future threatened the employment of its members or to de-recognise the applicant. While the applicant points out that this might involve individual strike action against a number of different companies in the future, as opposed to one large hospital trust before the transfers commenced, the Court is not persuaded that this means that they are thereby deprived of the possibility of effective action in the future.

42   As regards the argument that the applicant's interests in protecting its members must weigh more heavily than the UCLH's economic interest, the Court considers that the impact of the restriction on the applicant's ability to take strike action has not been shown to place its members at any real or immediate risk of detriment or of being left defenceless against future attempts to downgrade pay or conditions. When, and if, its members are transferred, it may continue to act on their behalf as a recognised union and negotiate with the new employer in ongoing collective bargaining machinery. What it cannot claim under the Convention is a requirement that an employer enter into, or remain in, any particular collective bargaining arrangement or accede to its requests on behalf of its members. The Court therefore does not find that the respondent State has exceeded the margin of appreciation accorded to it in regulating trade union action.

43   In these circumstances, the prohibition on the applicant's ability to strike can be regarded as a proportionate measure and "necessary in a democratic society" for the protection of the rights of others, namely UCLH.

44   It follows that this part of the application is manifestly ill-founded and must be rejected pursuant to Article 35 paragraphs 3 and 4 of the Convention . . .'

Comment

(1) The ECtHR seems to accept that there must be some effect on the rights of existing members for Art 11 to be engaged. However, it also states that the fact that the strike aimed in part to protect unidentified future employees from unidentified future employers is not a decisive criterion, so far as Art 11 is concerned.

(2) In the end, the Court's assessment of proportionality and the availability of other means for Unison to pursue its aims means that it finds no breach of Art 11.

Subject matter of the dispute

In order to be protected, the dispute must be about one of the matters listed in TULRCA s 244(1). Disputes which put pressure on the government are often argued to be political rather than trade disputes.

National Sailors' and Firemen's Union v *Reed* [1926] Ch 536 Chancery Division

This is the only reported case arising from the General Strike in 1926. Miners took strike action because their employers were proposing to reduce wages and increase hours of work. They called on other unions to assist and the TUC called a general strike. The defendants, officials of the Tower Hill branch of the NSFU, passed a motion supporting the strike and called on members to withdraw their labour, without authority from the union executive.

ASTBURY J: '. . . According to the evidence before me certain members of the claimant Union have been misled and compelled in London by the defendants and their pickets to leave their ships and to suffer serious loss and damage, and have been placed in doubt as to their position as members of this Union. These acts on the part of the defendants have been done without the authority of the claimant Union and contrary to its rules and orders, and lastly, no strike has been called by the claimant Union, and no ballot of its members, as provided for by its rules, has been completed. In these circumstances the claimant Union seeks the injunction which I have referred to, and the learned counsel who has appeared for the Union bases his right to claim this injunction on two grounds: one, that the defendants have acted in breach of the rules and orders of the Union and are liable to be restrained as prayed, and secondly, that they have acted contrary to the common law of this country.

I will endeavour now to state what I apprehend is the law upon this matter. To take the more general ground first, it is evident from the facts above mentioned and from the rest of the evidence that has been filed that members of the claimant Union have been placed in a position of doubt and danger, and it is my duty, as I have been requested by the claimants and defendants to do, to state shortly their rights and those of their Union. The so-called general strike called by the Trades Union Congress Council is illegal, and persons inciting or taking part in it are not protected by the Trade Disputes Act, 1906. No trade dispute has been alleged or shown to exist in any of the unions affected, except in the miners' case, and no trade dispute does or can exist between the Trades Union Congress on the one hand and the Government and the nation on the other. The orders of the Trades Union Congress above referred to are therefore unlawful, and the defendants are acting illegally in obeying them, and accordingly (for the reason I shall state under the other head) can be restrained by their own Union from doing so. The claimants' counsel has contended that if the members of the claimant Union stay in their jobs and refuse to strike they cannot be deprived of their trade union benefits, and the defendants who have appeared before me have stated, and stated very properly, that it is important to them that their members should know their rights in this respect.

Now the law upon that matter is as follows. No member of the claimant Union or any other trade unionist in this country can lose his trade union benefits by refusing to obey unlawful orders, and the orders of the Trades Union Congress and the unions who are acting in obedience thereto in bringing about the so-called general strike are unlawful orders, and the claimant Union is entitled to have this fact made clear and brought to the attention of its members . . .'

Comment

(1) This judgment prompted a famous article by Goodhart (1926–27), which criticised the reasoning on two grounds. First, and most importantly, since every strike puts pressure on parties not directly involved, it should not be treated as political just because the third party affected was the government. Secondly, since Astbury J admitted that there was a genuine trade dispute between the miners and their employers, the others should have been within the immunity, as they were acting in furtherance of it. These arguments are still pertinent, although with regard to the second, sympathy (secondary) action now loses immunity, as we will see.

(2) What if actions of the government have a direct impact on terms and conditions of employment?

Sherard v *AUEW* [1973] ICR 421 Court of Appeal

The union called a one-day strike for 1 May 1973 in protest at the government's implementation of phase two of the Counter-Inflation (Temporary Provisions) Act 1972, which was to have the effect of imposing a pay freeze. Some members, employed at government installations, sought an injunction to stop the strike on the grounds (among other things) that it was political. At this time the Industrial Relations Act 1971 was in force, but its definition of an 'industrial dispute' did not differ for our purposes from the definition in TULRCA s 244.

LORD DENNING MR: '. . . I am of opinion that a dispute between the TUC, on the one hand, and the government, on the other hand, is not an industrial dispute. To that extent I would agree with the view expressed by Astbury J in *National Sailors' and Firemen's Union of Great Britain and Ireland* v *Reed* (1926). At first sight this did appear to be a dispute between the TUC and the government. But Mr Irvine [counsel for the union] asks us to say that there is a dispute between workers in the employ of the government on the one hand and the government as employers on the other hand. The government as employers have decided to enforce phase two, which has frozen wages against the will of the workers. The men in the government employ object to this freezing of their wages. They – or some of them – are in dispute with their employers about it.

I think that this point made by Mr Irvine is arguable. If it is good, it means that the whole dispute is an "industrial dispute" and, therefore, not within the cognisance of these courts.

In *Conway* v *Wade* (1909) Lord Loreburn LC said:

"A dispute may have arisen, for example, in a single colliery, of which the subject is so important to the whole industry that either employers or workmen may think a general lock-out or a general strike is necessary to gain their point. Few are parties to, but all are interested in, the dispute."

Seeing that this is arguably an industrial dispute, I do not think we should grant an interlocutory injunction . . .'

ROSKILL LJ: '. . . I ventured to ask Mr Campbell [counsel for the claimant] at an early stage of his argument when he meant by a "political strike". He replied "a strike which was not the subject of an accompanying industrial dispute". Although the phrase "political strike" has from time to time been used in reported cases, it is to my mind a phrase which should be used, at any rate in a court of law, with considerable caution, for it does not readily lend itself to precise or accurate definition. It is too easy for someone to talk of a strike as being a "political strike" when what that person really means is that the object of the strike is something of which he as an individual subjectively disapproves . . .

There is only one other matter to which I would refer. At the outset of his submission Mr Campbell founded part of his argument upon the well-known (some might call it notorious) decision in *National Sailors' and Firemen's Union of Great Britain and Ireland* v *Reed* (1926). He suggested when his attention was drawn to the fact that that case had been the subject of much extra-judicial criticism that that criticism had come from parties who might be regarded as not wholly disinterested. But, as Mr Irvine pointed out, that case was the subject of a very well-known article by Professor Goodhart over 45 years ago in (1927) 36 *Yale Law Journal*. I say no more than that. One day it may be necessary to reconsider in this court that decision of Astbury J. The present is not the occasion. I only mention the matter in deference to the arguments of counsel.

For the reasons I have given I too, would dismiss this appeal.'

Comment

(1) As these were interim proceedings, only two judges sat in the Court of Appeal.

(2) Lord Denning seems to have been swayed here by the argument that if employees of the government took part in the strike, they could definitely claim that it was a trade dispute, and then the rest would be able to say that they were acting in furtherance of it. Today, the others would be taking part in sympathy (secondary) action which would not be immune. Roskill LJ placed his decision on wider grounds.

(3) As the immunity was originally formulated, action was regarded as being in contemplation or furtherance of a trade dispute if it was 'connected with' one of the matters listed in TULRCA s 244(1). The Employment Act 1982 introduced the present wording, which requires that the dispute be 'wholly or mainly' about one of these matters. As the next case shows, this may increase the risks of a dispute being regarded as political.

Mercury Communications Ltd v *Scott-Garner* [1984] ICR 74 Court of Appeal

At the beginning of the 1980s the government decided to break the Post Office monopoly on telecommunications. It passed the British Telecommunications Act 1981, establishing British Telecom and also empowering the Secretary of State to license rival telecommunications services. The Post Office Engineering Union was opposed to this policy of 'liberalisation' and also feared that privatisation, to which it was also opposed, was on the horizon. When a license was granted to Mercury, the POEU instructed its members to disobey orders from their employer, British Telecom, to connect Mercury to the BT telecommunications system.

Mercury sought an injunction, claiming that the union's action did not enjoy the trade dispute immunity. The union argued that it was a dispute about termination of employment (cf TULRCA s 244(1)(b)), because they feared compulsory redundancies. Their evidence in this regard was undermined by the production, at a fairly late stage of the proceedings, of a Job Security Agreement concluded in 1980, whereby the employer had given a commitment that there would be no compulsory redundancies.

SIR JOHN DONALDSON MR: '. . . The most obvious way of finding out what a particular dispute is wholly or mainly about is to inquire what the men concerned – in this case primarily those who refuse to interconnect – said to management at the time. Unfortunately we have no evidence, but it is a fair inference from what we do know that they said that the interconnection was contrary to their union's instructions. This throws one back to what the dispute between the union and BT was wholly or mainly about. That was not, of course, a relevant dispute because the union is neither an employer nor a worker in this context, but the subject matter of the dispute between BT and its employees can legitimately be taken to be the same as that between the union and BT.

What the union's dispute with BT is about is the subject matter of paragraph 22 of Mr Stanley's first affidavit which I have already quoted:

"... BT have entered into an interconnection agreement with [Mercury]. It is over this that the union are in dispute with BT . . . BT . . . have . . . allowed a rival organisation to interconnect with its network. It is this fact which puts them at odds with my union . . . The action which BT is taking is inconsistent with the desire of my members to retain the traditional monopoly over telecommunications facilities within BT. Once BT embarked upon a course of seeking to facilitate and implement liberalisation, they embarked upon a course which can only lead to a dispute between them and the union."

Mr Stanley goes on to say that the *cause* of the dispute is that BT wished his members to take a step which his members regarded as putting their jobs at risk (my emphasis) and a few sentences later this suffers a further change when he states that the subject matter of the dispute is the risk to jobs.

Well; which is the subject matter – facilitating and implementing liberalisation, agreeing to interconnect, ordering interconnection or the risk to jobs? Only the latter would enable the dispute to qualify as a trade dispute. The evidence has to be looked at as a whole, but I find it impossible to conclude on the evidence at present available that the risk to jobs was a major part of what the dispute was about. I say that because I find it inconceivable that if the dispute was wholly or mainly about jobs, the union would not have approached BT asking for a guarantee of job security or a strengthening of the Job Security Agreement. Yet nothing of the sort appears to have happened and the union did not even think that this agreement was relevant to the present proceedings. On the other hand there is massive evidence that the union was waging a campaign against the political decisions to liberalise the industry and to privatise BT . . .'

(May and Dillon LJJ delivered concurring judgments.)

Comment

(1) Even with the 'wholly or mainly' test, there is some scope for recognising mixed motives. In *University College London Hospital NHS Trust* v *Unison* (1999) Lord Woolf said:

> As I have already indicated, there can be two strands to a policy. A union can have a policy of opposing a particular course of action root and branch which is seeking to achieve a political objective. At the same time it could have a more limited objective, namely to alleviate the adverse consequences which it anticipates could flow from the more general policy. That more limited objective can be the reason for taking strike action. That more limited policy can comply with the requirements of s 244.

See also *Wandsworth LBC* v *NAS/UWT* (1994) and *Westminster City Council* v *Unison* (2001).

British Broadcasting Corporation v Hearn [1977] ICR 685 Court of Appeal

The Association of Broadcasting Staff was proposing to prevent transmission of the Cup Final by satellite to South Africa, because they argued that it would be seen as showing support for the then South African policy of apartheid. The BBC sought an injunction to stop the union inducing breaches of contract by its staff on the grounds that this was not a trade dispute.

LORD DENNING MR: '. . . So I come to the words "in contemplation or furtherance of a trade dispute". There comes the rub. Was a trade dispute in contemplation? This has been discussed in the courts. As long ago as 1908 one of my predecessors, Cozens-Hardy MR in *Conway* v *Wade* (1908) said:

> "The words 'in contemplation' are difficult, but they must embrace an act done by a person with a view to bringing about a trade dispute. If, for example, a minister of religion says to an employer, 'If you do not tomorrow morning discharge all your workmen who are not of my sect, I will call out all my co-religionists', he may act with impunity."

That view was expressly rejected by the House of Lords. Lord Loreburn LC himself said he could not agree. And Lord Shaw of Dunfermline said that he "respectfully but totally" dissented from that view of the Master of the Rolls. Lord Shaw said:

"... I think the argument was well founded that the contemplation of such a dispute must be the contemplation of something impending or likely to occur, and that they do not cover the case of coercive interference in which the intervener may have in his own mind that if he does not get his own way he will thereupon take ways and means to bring a trade dispute into existence."

Adapting those words to the illustration given by Cozens-Hardy MR it means that if shop stewards – who object to a man's religious belief – say to an employer, "Dismiss this man or we will go out on strike", that is not a trade dispute. It is coercive interference with the man's freedom of religion and with the employer's business. Take the case which I put in the course of argument: if printers in a newspaper office were to say: "We don't like the article which you are going to publish about the Arabs – or the Jews – or on this or that political issue – you must withdraw it. If you do not do so, we are not going to print your paper." That is not a trade dispute. It is coercive action unconnected with a trade dispute. It is an unlawful interference with the freedom of the press. It is a self-created power of censorship. It does not become a trade dispute simply because the men propose to break their contracts of employment in doing it. Even if the men have a strong moral case, saying, "We have a conscientious objection to this article. We do not want to have anything to do with it", that does not turn it into a trade dispute. The dispute is about the publication of the article, not about the terms and conditions of employment.

Applying those considerations to this case, all that was happening was that the trade union, or its officers, were saying: "Stop this televising by the Indian Ocean satellite, stop it yourself. If you don't, we will ask our own people to stop it for you." That is not a trade dispute. They were hoping, I suppose, that the BBC would give in; but, if they did not give in, they were going to order their members to stop the broadcast. That does not seem to me to be a trade dispute. To become a trade dispute, there would have to be something of the kind which was discussed in the course of argument before us: "We would like you to consider putting a clause in the contract by which our members are not bound to take part in any broadcast which may be viewed in South Africa because we feel that is obnoxious to their views and to the views of a great multitude of people. We would like that clause to be put in, or a condition of that kind to be understood." If the BBC refused to put in such a condition, or refused to negotiate about it, that might be a trade dispute. That, I think, is rather the way in which the judge approached this case. Towards the end of his judgment he said, putting it into the mouths of members through their union:

"We wish it established as a condition of employment that we shall not be required to take part in broadcasts to South Africa so long as the South African Government pursues its policy of apartheid."

If that request had been made, and not acceded to, there might be a trade dispute as to whether that should be a condition of the employment. But the matter never reached that stage at all. It never reached the stage of there being a trade dispute. There was not a trade dispute "in contemplation". It was coercive interference and nothing more. If that is the right view, it means that the trade union and its officers are not exempt from the ordinary rule of law – which is that men must honour their contracts, and must not unlawfully interfere with the performance of them ...'

(Roskill and Scarman LJJ delivered concurring judgments.)

Comment

(1) The last part extracted from Lord Denning's judgment seems to offer considerable scope for turning what otherwise might not be trade dispute matters into disputes over

terms and conditions of employment. However, the House of Lords has shown some antipathy to this notion.

Universe Tankships of Monrovia v International Transport Workers Federation [1982] ICR 262 House of Lords

The facts of this case are given on p 619. The company was reclaiming money paid to the union welfare fund, arguing that it had been paid under duress. One issue was whether the action came within the trade dispute immunity.

LORD DIPLOCK: '. . . In my view, it is not enough in order to create the necessary connection between a dispute relating to terms and conditions of employment of employees of a particular employer, and a demand made upon that employer by a trade union acting on its own behalf and not on behalf of employees working for the employer, that the demand should be made at a time when the trade union is negotiating a collective agreement relating to the terms and conditions of employment of those employees, and the employer's yielding to that demand is made a condition precedent to the lifting of the blacking additional to the condition precedent that the employer should also agree to the terms of the collective agreement insisted on by the trade union. To take an extreme example, if a trade union were to demand as a condition precedent to lifting a blacking that the employer should make a contribution to a particular political party favoured by the union, or to a guerrilla group in some foreign country, such a demand whenever it was made would not, in my opinion, have the necessary connection with any dispute about terms or conditions of employment in furtherance of which the blacking was imposed . . .

In view of the difference of opinion between the members of this House upon the duress point it may be appropriate that before departing from the subject I should state that my opinion that the demand for a contribution to the welfare fund is not legitimised so as to deprive the shipowners of a restitutionary remedy would not necessarily be different if a requirement that the shipowners should make such a contribution were incorporated in the ITF Collective Agreement. [TULRCA ss 219 and 244] are not directly applicable to restitutional remedies; they are relevant only for such indications as they give of the public policy as to what kinds of demands ought to be regarded as legitimate in the field of industrial relations notwithstanding that compliance with them is induced by economic duress. The fact that ITF had also insisted that a term as to the requirement of payment to the welfare fund should be inserted in the ITF Collective Agreement would not, in my opinion, affect the public policy under which it is excluded from being legitimised . . .'

LORD CROSS: '. . . I would add, although on the facts of this case the point does not arise for decision, that I fully concur with the view expressed by my noble and learned friend in the concluding paragraph of his speech, that in the case supposed it would have made no difference to the right of the appellants to recover the payments to the guerrilla fund that ITF had insisted, as a condition of lifting the "blacking" of the vessel, that an undertaking by the appellants to make the payments should be inserted in the contracts of employment of each member of the crew and that the appellants had, under duress entered into such undertakings with each member. A trade union cannot turn a dispute which in reality has no connection with terms and conditions of employment into a dispute connected with terms and conditions of employment by insisting that the employer inserts appropriate terms into the contracts of employment into which he enters . . .'

(Lord Russell gave a speech agreeing with Lords Diplock and Cross; Lords Scarman and Brandon dissented on this point.)

Comment

(1) Lord Cross's remarks are *obiter*. Why should it be impossible to conjure up a trade dispute in this way? Dealing obliquely with the argument in *Dimbleby v NUJ* (1984), Lord Diplock said: '. . . it passes the bounds of credibility that any responsible newspaper proprietor would agree to such a term [that is, a term that they should not have to supply copy to a company blacked by their union] in contracts of employment with his journalists.' Yet the fact that an employer is most unlikely to agree to a term does not mean that there cannot be a dispute about whether the employer *should* agree to it (think of some of the more optimistic wage claims that unions have submitted . . .). Also, *Hadmor Productions v Hamilton* (1982) – another case in which Lord Diplock delivered the principal speech in the House of Lords – affords an example of an employer (Thames Television) which had agreed just such a clause with its union.

(2) Could the ABS have claimed that it was acting in contemplation or furtherance of a trade dispute between black South African workers and their employers? On these facts, no, because there was no evidence of any such dispute. It was rather a protest against the political system in South Africa at that time. However, even if there were such a dispute, note the restriction on immunity in respect of overseas disputes in TULRCA s 244(3). And there is the problem of sympathy (secondary) action.

(3) Not only political reasons take a dispute outside the 'trade dispute' formula. Compare *Huntley v Thornton* (1957), where it was held that action was not within the immunity because union officials were pursuing a private vendetta against a member.

LOSS OF IMMUNITY

Until 1980, consideration of the legality of industrial action stopped at the end of the last section. However, the strategy of the Conservative government which was in power from 1979–97 was to limit the ambit of lawful industrial action in two main ways. The first was to narrow the concept of trade dispute, and the effects of that were seen in the last section. The second was to introduce new conditions for lawful industrial action by providing that trade unions and individuals would forfeit immunity if they failed to comply with them.

Secondary action

The winter of 1978–79 was called 'the winter of discontent' by some sections of the press, because of a number of high-profile national strikes which had a great effect on the general public. The perceived failure of the then Labour government to deal effectively with the situation was a major reason for the Labour Party's defeat in the 1979 general election and its replacement by a Conservative government led by Margaret Thatcher.

Three important cases came to the Court of Appeal and the House of Lords around that time: *NWL v Woods* (1979), *Express Newspapers v McShane* (1979) and *Duport Steels v Sirs* (1980). In each of them the Court of Appeal (or, to be more accurate, Lord Denning) attempted to develop a concept of remoteness and to withdraw immunity from action regarded as 'too remote' from the original dispute. In each case, the House of Lords reversed the Court of Appeal's decision on the ground that there was no justification for such a gloss on the statute – although most members of the House of Lords evinced overt or covert sympathy for the general aim of restricting union power.

The following extract is from the Court of Appeal decision in one of those cases. It is given because it is a good example of the kind of action which was seen to be the problem, and also because Lord Denning's concept of secondary action was taken up by the Conservative government in its first piece of employment legislation, the Employment Act 1980.

Express Newspapers Ltd v *McShane* [1979] ICR 210 Court of Appeal

LORD DENNING MR: 'There are about 1,000 local newspapers published in this country. They are served by about 9,000 journalists of whom 8,500 belong to a trade union called the National Union of Journalists ("the NUJ"). Unfortunately there is a difference about their pay. The journalists feel that they are underpaid and that they ought to be paid more. The proprietors feel they cannot pay more because of the government's policy of the 5 per cent limit and their own financial situation. That difference has not been resolved. Feeling very upset about it, some journalists took disruptive action. The *Bolton Evening News* dismissed 105 NUJ members. In consequence the NUJ (through their national executive council) decided to take industrial action. The decision was taken by a majority vote of 14 to seven. It is the first time, we are told, in the 71 years of its existence that this union has called a strike. On 4th December 1978 ($2\frac{1}{2}$ weeks ago) the NUJ called a strike withdrawing all the services of their member journalists on the local newspapers, with the result that those journalists would not supply any news or copy for the local papers. That may be called the "primary" action taken by the NUJ. It brought pressure to bear directly on the employers.

But this strike did not put the local papers out of action altogether. Those papers do not depend solely on their journalists to feed them with news. They also get news copy through the important organisation called the Press Association. The Press Association have some 250 journalists on their staff. They collect news of all kinds (major and minor happenings, sporting items, Parliamentary items, items from these courts and the like). They send out these items in a continuous stream from their offices in Fleet Street by teleprinter to all the media in the country. It is sent to the national newspapers, the local newspapers, the broadcasters, and on tape to clubs, offices and institutions throughout the country.

In order to make the strike more effective, the NUJ wished to stop the news going out from the Press Association to the local newspapers. So they called on the journalists on the Press Association (many of whom are members of the union) to come out on strike as well. If they stopped work, it would mean that no news would be provided by the Press Association to anyone. It would affect not only the local newspapers with whom there was a dispute, but also the national newspapers, the media, clubs, and so forth, with whom there was no dispute. None of them would get their news from the Press Association. That may be called a "secondary" action taken by the union. It brought pressure to bear on the Press Association who were not involved in the dispute at all.

In order to induce the journalists on the Press Association to strike, the union promised to pay them £50 a week (much more than the hardship allowance paid to the provincial journalists). But even so many of the journalists on the Press Association were unwilling to strike. They did not wish to obey the orders of the national executive council. So they had a meeting to determine it. Out of the 250 journalists on the Press Association 162 attended. Eighty-six decided to ignore the call to strike. They stayed at work. Seventy-six came out on strike. The 86 were joined by others who were not members of the union. In rough figures, half the journalists on the Press Association remained at work and half came out on strike. The half who were still at work continued to send out news over the teleprinter to all the newspapers up and down the country and to all the media. So a good deal of news still got through to the local newspapers and enabled them to carry on, not fully, but partially.

At the same time the union took a further measure which may be described as a further "secondary" action. They had members working for the *Daily Express* and other national newspapers and also for the media. The union ordered these members to "black" the Press Association copy. That meant that they called on their members working for the *Daily Express* and other newspapers to refuse to use the copy which came through on the teleprinter from the Press Association. They told their members at the *Daily Express* not to handle it or make any use of it whatsoever. They allowed their members to get news from other sources. For instance, their members could telephone freelance journalists or other sources of information so as to get news for the *Daily Express*. But they were not to use any of the copy supplied by the Press Association. Their members were still to get their full pay from their employers, but were not to do their work properly . . .

At the outset I would say that it is clear that there was a "trade dispute" between the local newspapers and the journalists employed by them. It was a dispute about their pay. But there was no other trade dispute at all. There was no dispute between the Press Association and the union. There was no dispute between the *Daily Express* and the union. The only dispute was with the local provincial newspapers.

The "primary" action was certainly taken by the union "in furtherance of" that dispute. They called out on strike their members who were employed by the local newspapers. That would bring direct pressure on the local newspapers. The first "secondary" action may also be said to be "in furtherance of" the dispute. The union called out on strike their members at the Press Association. That would also bring pressure to bear on the local newspapers because, by stopping copy going out from the Press Association, it would hamper the production of local newspapers, even though it might hamper the national newspapers also.

But what about the further "secondary" action? The act of calling on the member journalists employed by the *Daily Express* to "black" the copy supplied by the Press Association? That would not affect the local newspapers in the slightest degree. It would not bring any pressure to bear on them. It would not affect the Press Association either. The only persons whom it would affect would be the *Daily Express* and put them to great trouble, difficulty and expense. But not the local newspapers. Can such an act be said to be "in furtherance of" the dispute?

Before dealing with this point, I would draw attention to the very great power which the leaders of the trade unions have over their members, especially when there are "closed shops" . . .

In this case there is no evidence that the "blacking" at the *Daily Express* of the Press Association copy has had any effect on the only trade dispute there is, the dispute of the provincial journalists with the local newspapers. It has had no practical effect on it at all. It has not induced any more men at the Press Association to come out on strike, nor has it affected the supply of news from the Press Association to its subscribers. It has been going on for 2½ weeks now. There is no evidence from any strikers or non-strikers at the Press Association that it has had any effect on them. As far as one knows they are still about half and half at the Press Association, half on strike and half still remaining at work. I have no doubt that the acts were done "in connection with" the trade dispute with the local newspapers, but they were not done "in furtherance of" it.

It seems to me that the leaders of trade unions have been reading these words "in furtherance of" in a wide sense as if they extended to any acts done "in connection with" or "in consequence of" a trade dispute. But as the judge said they are narrower words and are to be given a narrower construction. A wide construction would confer far too wide an immunity . . .'

(Lawton and Brandon LJJ delivered concurring judgments.)

Comment

(1) The action taken by journalists at the Press Association and in turn those employed by national newspapers was sympathy action: they had no particular dispute with their own employers at that time. However, previously this had been regarded as within the statutory immunity because it was in contemplation or furtherance of the primary dispute – here, the dispute between the provincial papers and their employees.

(2) Lord Denning described both the action at the Press Association and the action at the national papers as being 'secondary action'. However, it is notable that he thought that the action at the Press Association *was* capable of furthering the primary dispute – and would therefore be covered by the immunity. It is the secondary action (or tertiary action) at the national newspapers which, in his opinion, would have no effect one way or the other on the dispute.

(3) This is important, because it was this pattern which was adopted by the Conservative government in its first treatment of secondary action in the Employment Act 1980 s 17. Under that provision, the Press Association action would have been 'protected secondary action' – protected, because there was a contractual link between the Press Association and the employer in dispute. The action at the national newspapers would not have been protected, because there was no contractual link between the employers in dispute (the provincial papers) and the employer whose employees were being induced to break their contracts of employment (the national newspapers). This was known as the 'first customer/first supplier' exception.

(4) Under the Employment Act 1980 s 17, two other kinds of secondary action were protected: action taken against a company in the same group as the employer in dispute *provided* that the associated company was doing work which would normally have been done by the company in dispute. Thus, to a limited extent, a union could 'follow struck work' and attempt to make the strike effective by stopping the employer in dispute from switching production elsewhere.

(5) The other kind of protected secondary action was where it occurred in the context of lawful picketing. This will be considered in the section on picketing later in this chapter.

(6) In a Green Paper in 1989, the Conservative government gave its reasons for altering the law on secondary action.

Removing Barriers to Employment Cm 655 March 1989

[Paras 3.5–3.8 described the legal position as it then stood.]

3.9   The arrangements described above were framed in the light of circumstances in 1980, at a time when secondary action had been much more widespread than it has been in recent years. But it is now right to ask whether the immunities described in paragraphs 3.7 and 3.8 are still justified.

3.10 The Government believe that the following considerations indicate that the present law needs amendment:
- In general there is no good reason why employers who are not party to a dispute should be at risk of having industrial action organised against them;
- Secondary action may deter employers from starting up for the first time in this country, with harmful effects on new investment and on jobs. For example, there might be

a threat of secondary action being organised among workers of the new firm's customers or suppliers, with the aim of forcing the new enterprise to accept certain terms and conditions. This sort of threat was made when the American Ford Motor Company was planning to establish a new factory at Dundee. Regardless of whether they are lawful or unlawful under the present law, there is no good reason why any threats of this kind, or the organisation of action of this kind, should enjoy immunity.

– The law as it stands is complicated, and it could well be difficult for those involved to determine, in the absence of a court judgment, whether there would be immunity for organising certain secondary action. An example might be secondary action which involved a union inducing transport workers to refuse to move coal to power stations, in support of an industrial dispute between British Coal and its employees. If the coal was part of a shipment including other goods from other suppliers, it might be very difficult to know whether there would be immunity for refusal to move the shipment as a whole. The same would apply if the coal was unloaded and stored with coal from other suppliers, from which it could not be distinguished, and transport workers then refused to move any part of the coal.

Comment

(1) These were the arguments put forward to justify the complete removal of immunity from all forms of sympathy or solidarity action, the traditional strength of the trade union movement, and indeed, their *raison d'être* in the eyes of many. As well as the quaint references to coal and nationalised industries, note the complete absence of reference to international standards.

(2) The law was changed by the Employment Act 1990. The relevant provision is now found in TULRCA.

Trade Union and Labour Relations (Consolidation) Act 1992

224   (1)   An act is not protected if one of the facts relied on for the purpose of establishing liability is that there has been secondary action which is not lawful picketing.

(2)   There is secondary action in relation to a trade dispute when, and only when, a person –

(a)   induces another to break a contract of employment or interferes or induces another to interfere with its performance, or

(b)   threatens that a contract of employment under which he or another is employed will be broken or its performance interfered with, or that he will induce another to break a contract of employment or to interfere with its performance,

and the employer under the contract of employment is not the employer party to the dispute.

(3)   Lawful picketing means acts done in the course of such attendance as is declared lawful by section 220 (peaceful picketing) –

(a)   by a worker employed (or, in the case of a worker not in employment, last employed) by the employer party to the dispute, or

(b)   by a trade union official whose attendance is lawful by virtue of subsection (1)(b) of that section.

(4)   For the purposes of this section an employer shall not be treated as party to a dispute between another employer and workers of that employer; and where more than one employer is in dispute with his workers, the dispute between each employer and his workers shall be treated as a separate dispute.

In this subsection "worker" has the same meaning as in section 244 (meaning of "trade dispute").

(5)　An act in contemplation or furtherance of a trade dispute which is primary action in relation to that dispute may not be relied on as secondary action in relation to another trade dispute.

Primary action means such action as is mentioned in paragraph (a) or (b) of subsection (2) where the employer under the contract of employment is the employer party to the dispute.

(6)　In this section 'contract of employment' includes any contract under which one person personally does work or performs services for another, and related expressions shall be construed accordingly.

Comment

(1) Thus the position now is that sympathy action loses its immunity at Stage 3, with the exception of secondary action occurring in the context of lawful picketing. Note that the effect of s 224(4) is that a national strike across an industry with more than one employer will not be protected unless there is a dispute with each employer involved.

(2) In over ten years of Labour government there has been no change to this position. In its first White Paper on employment law reform, *Fairness at Work* (Cm 3968, 1997) the then Prime Minister, Tony Blair, made a virtue of this, saying in his Foreword:

> There will be no going back. The days of strikes without ballots, mass picketing, closed shops and secondary action are over. Even after the changes we propose, Britain will have the most lightly regulated labour market of any leading economy in the world.

This stance was reiterated in the DTI Review of the Employment Act (February 2003):

> 3.22　The Act left unchanged the essential features of pre-1997 law on industrial action. For example, the law on secondary industrial action and picketing was not altered, and the overall requirements to hold ballots and issue notices and sample ballot papers to the employer were retained. These features of the law are now well established and ensure that the inevitable disruption inherent in industrial action is confined as far as possible to those directly involved in an industrial dispute. **The Government therefore re-affirms its commitment to retain the essential features of the pre-1997 law on industrial action.**

Failure to hold a ballot

Before the Trade Union Act 1984, unions were entitled to agree their own rules for calling industrial action. Obviously no union is likely to call action where the members do not support it, because that would risk destroying their credibility. But not all unions had rules like those of the National Union of Mineworkers, which not only required a ballot of all the members, but also a special majority of 55 per cent before action could be called.

The Trade Union Act 1984 did not expressly require unions to ballot before industrial action, but indirectly compelled this by removing immunity from industrial action where a proper ballot had not been held. The requirements for a lawful ballot have become more complicated with subsequent legislation.

Trade Union and Labour Relations (Consolidation) Act 1992

226 (1)   An act done by a trade union to induce a person to take part, or continue to take part, in industrial action –

(a)   is not protected unless the industrial action has the support of a ballot, and

(b)   where section 226A falls to be complied with in relation to the person's employer, is not protected as respects the employer unless the trade union has complied with section 226A in relation to him.

In this section 'the relevant time', in relation to an act by a trade union to induce a person to take part, or continue to take part, in industrial action, means the time at which proceedings are commenced in respect of the act.

(2)   Industrial action shall be regarded as having the support of a ballot only if –

(a)   the union has held a ballot in respect of the action –

(i)   in relation to which the requirements of section 226B so far as applicable before and during the holding of the ballot were satisfied,

(ii)   in relation to which the requirements of sections 227 to 231 were satisfied, and

(iii) in which the majority voting in the ballot answered 'Yes' to the question applicable in accordance with section 229(2) to industrial action of the kind to which the act of inducement relates;

(b)   such of the requirements of the following sections as have fallen to be satisfied at the relevant time have been satisfied, namely –

(i)   section 226B so far as applicable after the holding of the ballot, and

(ii)   section 231B;

(bb) section 232A does not prevent the industrial action from being regarded as having the support of the ballot; and

(c)   the requirements of section 233 (calling of industrial action with support of ballot) are satisfied.

Any reference in this subsection to a requirement of a provision which is disapplied or modified by section 232 has effect subject to that section.

(3)   Where separate workplace ballots are held by virtue of section 228(1) –

(a)   industrial action shall be regarded as having the support of a ballot if the conditions specified in subsection (2) are satisfied, and

(b)   the trade union shall be taken to have complied with the requirements relating to a ballot imposed by section 226A if those requirements are complied with,

in relation to the ballot for the place of work of the person induced to take part, or continue to take part, in the industrial action.

(3A) If the requirements of section 231A fall to be satisfied in relation to an employer, as respects that employer industrial action shall not be regarded as having the support of a ballot unless those requirements are satisfied in relation to that employer.

(4)   For the purposes of this section an inducement, in relation to a person, includes an inducement which is or would be ineffective, whether because of his unwillingness to be influenced by it or for any other reason.

Comment

(1) It is important to notice that it is only trade unions who are subject to the balloting requirement. If non-union workers decide to engage in industrial action, it will not lose immunity solely on the ground that they did not conduct a ballot first.

(2) We have seen that not all industrial action necessarily involves breaches of contract, and thus not all organisation of industrial action necessarily involves the commission of

torts. If industrial action is lawful and does not involve torts, then a union has no need of immunity from action in tort and thus has no need to ballot – you might think. This was the case, until 1988.

Trade Union and Labour Relations (Consolidation) Act 1992

62   (1)   A member of a trade union who claims that members of the union, including himself, are likely to be or have been induced by the union to take part or to continue to take part in industrial action which does not have the support of a ballot may apply to the court for an order under this section . . .

(3)   Where on an application under this section the court is satisfied that the claim is well-founded, it shall make such order as it considers appropriate for requiring the union to take steps for ensuring –
  (a)   that there is no, or no further, inducement of members of the union to take part or to continue to take part in the industrial action to which the application relates, and
  (b)   that no member engages in conduct after the making of the order by virtue of having been induced before the making of the order to take part or continue to take part in the action . . .

Comment

(1) This provision was introduced by the Employment Act 1988. It only gives members a right to sue for an injunction, not for damages, but it applies to any industrial action, not just industrial action which involves the commission of torts. As no union can be absolutely sure than no single member will decide to challenge under this section, effectively a union which wants to call any industrial action must ballot first.

(2) In 1993 this idea was extended yet further.

Trade Union and Labour Relations (Consolidation) Act 1992

235A   (1)   Where an individual claims that –
  (a)   any trade union or other person has done, or is likely to do, an unlawful act to induce any person to take part, or to continue to take part, in industrial action, and
  (b)   an effect, or a likely effect, of the industrial action is or will be to –
    (i)   prevent or delay the supply of goods or services, or
    (ii)   reduce the quality of goods or services supplied,
    to the individual making the claim,
he may apply to the High Court or the Court of Session for an order under this section.

(2)   For the purposes of this section an act to induce any person to take part, or to continue to take part, in industrial action is unlawful –
  (a)   if it is actionable in tort by any one or more persons, or
  (b)   (where it is or would be the act of a trade union) if it could form the basis of an application by a member under section 62.

(3)   In determining whether an individual may make an application under this section it is immaterial whether or not the individual is entitled to be supplied with the goods or services in question.

(4)   Where on an application under this section the court is satisfied that the claim is well-founded, it shall make such order as it considers appropriate for requiring the person by whom the act of inducement has been, or is likely to be, done to take steps for ensuring –
  (a)   that no, or no further, act is done by him to induce any persons to take part or to continue to take part in the industrial action, and

(b) that no person engages in conduct after the making of the order by virtue of having been induced by him before the making of the order to take part or continue to take part in the industrial action.

(5) Without prejudice to any other power of the court, the court may on an application under this section grant such interlocutory relief (in Scotland, such interim order) as it considers appropriate.

(6) For the purposes of this section an act of inducement shall be taken to be done by a trade union if it is authorised or endorsed by the union; and the provisions of section 20(2) to (4) apply for the purposes of determining whether such an act is to be taken to be so authorised or endorsed.

Those provisions also apply in relation to proceedings for failure to comply with an order under this section as they apply in relation to the original proceedings.

Comment

(1) This is the so-called 'Citizens' Charter' right to get industrial action called off if it does not have immunity, introduced by the Trade Union Reform and Employment Rights Act 1993. Note the extended definition of 'unlawful' industrial action in s 235A, which thus allows restraint even of action which does not involve the commission of torts or breaches of contract.

(2) The numerous requirements for a valid ballot, referred to in TULRCA s 226, will be examined in turn. Reference should also be made to the government's *Code of Practice on Industrial Action Ballots and Notices to Employers* (2005).

Who votes?

Trade Union and Labour Relations (Consolidation) Act 1992

227 (1) Entitlement to vote in the ballot must be accorded equally to all the members of the trade union who it is reasonable at the time of the ballot for the union to believe will be induced by the union to take part or, as the case may be, to continue to take part in the industrial action in question, and to no others.

232A Industrial action shall not be regarded as having the support of a ballot if the following conditions apply in the case of any person –
(a) he was a member of the trade union at the time when the ballot was held,
(b) it was reasonable at that time for the trade union to believe he would be induced to take part or, as the case may be, to continue to take part in the industrial action,
(c) he was not accorded entitlement to vote in the ballot, and
(d) he was induced by the trade union to take part or, as the case may be, to continue to take part in the industrial action.

232B (1) If –
(a) in relation to a ballot there is a failure (or there are failures) to comply with a provision mentioned in subsection (2) or with more than one of those provisions, and
(b) the failure is accidental and on a scale which is unlikely to affect the result of the ballot or, as the case may be, the failures are accidental and taken together are on a scale which is unlikely to affect the result of the ballot,
the failure (or failures) shall be disregarded for all purposes (including, in particular, those of section 232A(c)).
(2) The provisions are section 227(1), section 230(2) and section 230(2B).

Comment

(1) The basic idea is that the members who will be required to put themselves on the line by actually taking part in the industrial action are the ones who ought to have a vote: they, and no others. This is expressed in TULRCA s 227. The effect of TULRCA s 232A is that if someone entitled to vote is denied that entitlement, the resulting industrial action loses its immunity.

(2) Two problems have arisen in relation to this. First, what happens if one or more union members are accidentally omitted from the ballot? Secondly, what if the 'constituency' changes between the ballot and the action, because either new people join the union or because new people come to work for the employer? The first problem was addressed by the House of Lords in the next case.

P v National Association of Schoolmasters/Union of Women Teachers
[2003] ICR 386 House of Lords

The claimant was a minor who had been expelled from school because he was disruptive in class and violent and abusive in the playground. He appealed to the school governors, who ordered that he should be reinstated from the autumn term. In that term there were more incidents of disruptive behaviour, leading the teachers to complain to their union, the NAS/UWT.

The union sent out ballot papers to 30 members who were teachers at the school; 26 voted in favour of action in the form of refusing to teach P alongside other children and none voted against. However, two teachers who were union members did not receive ballot papers. This was because they had only recently moved to the school and had not informed the union of their change of job.

P brought action under TULRCA s 235A alleging that the industrial action was not protected because these two teachers had been denied their entitlement to vote.

LORD HOFFMANN: '. . . In my opinion the key provision in section 232A is, for present purposes, condition (c). Is it the case that the two members were not accorded entitlement to vote in the ballot? For this purpose, one must consider what counts as being accorded entitlement to vote.

Before the 1999 amendments, the concept of being accorded entitlement to vote was already being used in section 227(1). That provided that entitlement to vote must be accorded equally to all members of the union whom it was reasonable to believe would be induced to take part in the industrial action. Section 227(2), which was repealed by the 1999 Act, provided:

"The requirement in subsection (1) shall be taken not to have been satisfied if any person who was a member of the trade union at the time when the ballot was held and was denied entitlement to vote in the ballot is induced by the union to take part . . . in the industrial action."

Here too, there were no exceptions. No one may be denied entitlement to vote. So the previous legislation also raised the question of what counted as being accorded entitlement to vote, or not being denied entitlement to vote. In particular, does the fact that one has not been sent a ballot paper mean that one has not been accorded entitlement to vote? If it did, then failure to send any person a ballot paper would have invalidated the ballot.

The answer to this question may be found in section 230(2), which provides that "so far as is reasonably practicable" every person who is entitled to vote must be sent a ballot paper. That provision in my opinion shows that, if it was not reasonably practicable, the omission to send a ballot paper to a person entitled to vote does not amount to a denial of his entitlement. Otherwise there would be no point in the qualifying words "so far as is reasonably practicable". . .'

(Lords Bingham, Hobhouse and Scott agreed with Lord Hoffmann; Lord Walker delivered a concurring opinion.)

Comment

(1) The House of Lords in effect draws a distinction between being given an *entitlement* to vote and being given an *opportunity* to vote. The union did not deny these teachers their entitlement to vote, even though it mistakenly failed to give them an opportunity to do so.

(2) This could now be dealt with by TULRCA s 232B, which excuses small accidental failures which would not have affected the outcome of the ballot. However, at the time of this case, s 232B did not excuse failures in relation to s 232A – because of a draftsman's mistake when those sections were introduced by the Employment Relations Act 1999. This was rectified by further amendment in the Employment Relations Act 2004.

(3) An example where the 'small accidental failures' exception could not be relied upon is *National Union of Rail, Maritime and Transport Workers* v *Midland Mainline Ltd* (2001), where the union failed to ballot 25 members and the industrial action was approved only by 25 votes to 17, with 49 members failing to record a vote.

(4) The second problem, a shift in the people making up the balloting constituency, arose in the next case.

London Underground Ltd v National Union of Rail, Maritime and Transport Workers [1995] IRLR 636 Court of Appeal

In the course of a trade dispute the union called on its members to take part in a series of one- and two-day strikes on the London Underground, following a ballot which had produced a vote in favour of this action. Between the date when the ballot closed, and the commencement of one series of strikes, the union recruited 692 new members among the London Underground workforce. Was the action protected if these new members were called on to take part, even though they had not been balloted?

MILLETT LJ: '. . . *The appeal: the 692*
The question here is whether a trade union, without losing its immunity from suit, can call on a significant number of members to take part in industrial action who have joined the union since the date of the ballot and who have therefore not had an opportunity to vote in the ballot. A subsidiary question is whether it makes any difference that the new members have not joined the union by natural accretion during a long dispute, but have been actively recruited in order to make the industrial action more effective. The claimant insists that those who have been balloted represent the constituency of those who can be called on to take part in the action. If more than a *de minimis* number of members who have not been balloted are called upon to take part in industrial action, it is submitted that the action does not have the support of a ballot and the immunity is lost. It does not matter that the members in question joined the union after the ballot and so could not have been balloted. The union must take care to confine its call to take part in industrial action to those of its members who were balloted . . .

What must have the support of a ballot is "the industrial action", that is to say, the industrial action referred to in the preceding line. That is not industrial action by a particular person (assuming for the moment that that is capable of being an accurate expression), but the industrial action in which a particular person has been induced to take part . . .

Industrial action is collective action. An individual does not take collective action; he takes part in it. Those who take part in it will normally be in breach of their contracts of employment. By inducing them to take part in it the union would be liable for the tort of inducing a breach of contract but for the immunity conferred by s 219. That immunity is withdrawn by the combined effect of s 219(4) and s 226(1) if the industrial action does not have the support of a ballot. But the participation of a particular individual in collective industrial action and the industrial action itself are two different things. It is the industrial action which must have the support of a ballot, not the participation of those who have been induced to take part in it.

This construction of the section is supported by the text of other provisions to be found in this part of the Act. Every person taking part in the ballot, for example, must be asked whether he is prepared to take part, or continue to take part, in industrial action (s 229(2)). If a majority of those who vote in the ballot answer "Yes", and the other requirements of the Act are satisfied, then "the industrial action shall be regarded as having the support of a ballot" (s 226(2)). The industrial action which is to be regarded as having the support of a ballot is not the industrial action of any particular individual, nor is it the action of those who voted "Yes". Even those who voted "No", but were outvoted, may be called upon to take part in the industrial action without the union losing its immunity. It is the industrial action in which a majority of those voting in the ballot have declared themselves prepared to take part. The collective action is treated as distinct from the participation of the individuals who are prepared to take part in it.

There is nothing in the very detailed requirements which Parliament has laid down for the conduct of the ballot which compels the union to restrict its call for industrial action to those of its members who were members at the date of the ballot and were given the opportunity to take part in it. Parliament must be taken to have appreciated that there would be constant changes in the membership of a large union, and that by normal accretion alone significant numbers of new members might join the union between the date of the ballot notice given to the employer under s 226A and the holding of the ballot, and between the holding of the ballot and the taking of industrial action. In the case of a lengthy dispute, the numbers in the latter case could be very large indeed . . .

The main thrust of the claimant's argument before us was that industrial action involving an additional 692 members or more is not the same industrial action as that upon which the members were balloted. I am unable to accept the submission. It is the same industrial action albeit calculated to be that much more effective . . .

I am satisfied that there is nothing in the wording of ss 226–235 of the Act to deprive a union of its statutory immunity by reason only of the fact that it has induced members to take part in industrial action who were not balloted because they did not become members until after the time when the ballot was held. This is supported by a consideration of the legislative purpose, and in particular of the mischief which it was the intention of Parliament to bring to an end. Before the balloting requirements were introduced in 1984, industrial action could be called by a militant executive committee of the union without consulting the membership, the majority of whom might be opposed to the taking of industrial action. Even when the membership was consulted, this was traditionally done by calling for a show of hands at a mass meeting attended by militant and vociferous members who made it clear that any failure to vote in favour of industrial action would be unwelcome. There was, to say the least, a risk that members who were privately opposed to the taking of industrial action might be cowed into giving their public and highly visible support.

Parliament's object in introducing the democratic requirement of a secret ballot is not to make life more difficult for trade unions by putting further obstacles in their way before they can call for industrial action with impunity, but to ensure that such action should have the genuine support of the members who are called upon to take part. The requirement has not been imposed for the protection of the employer or the public, but for the protection of the union's own members. Those who are members at the date of the ballot, and whom the union intends to call on to take industrial action, are entitled to be properly consulted without pressure or intimidation. There is no possible reason to extend the same protection to those who join the union after the ballot. They do so of their own volition and in the knowledge of the outcome of the ballot and of the imminence of industrial action in which they will be called upon to take part . . .

The immunities conferred by ss 219 and 220 are still in the widest terms. Sections 226–235, which introduce the balloting requirements, are concerned exclusively with the relationship between a union and its members and are intended for the protection of members. Non-members have no right to be consulted before a union calls on its members to take industrial action; indeed, as we have seen, the union must not include them in the ballot. But there is nothing in ss 226–235 to limit the union's right to seek to persuade non-members to support it by abstaining from work . . .

The judge may also have been influenced by the fact that the union has obtained a large influx of new members by an active recruiting campaign. I am unable to see what objection there can be to such activity. A union is plainly free to campaign actively for new members before it holds the ballot in the hope that such members will support industrial action. If they become members before the ballot, they must be balloted, even though their views may affect the result of the ballot. I am unable to see why activity which is unobjectionable before the ballot is objectionable after it.

I would allow the appeal . . .'

(Ward and Butler-Sloss LJJ agreed.)

Comment

(1) This interpretation is supported now by TULRCA s 232A(1)(a), which specifically refers to the entitlement to vote of those who were members *at the time* of the ballot. In *P* v *NAS/UWT* (2003) Lord Hoffmann pointed out that *London Underground* v *NURMT* (1995) strictly only dealt with existing employees joining after the ballot and not employees who had come to work for the employer after the ballot. He noted that the Explanatory Notes to the Employment Relations Act 1999 indicated that the new TULRCA s 232A was intended to close that perceived gap, and he so interpreted it. In approving the approach of Millett LJ, Lord Hoffmann also agreed that the contrary dictum of Lord Donaldson in *Post Office* v *Union of Communication Workers* (1990) was wrong.

(2) Note the important point in Millett LJ's judgment that there is nothing wrong with the union calling out non-members, who of course will not have been balloted.

(3) Millett LJ firmly characterises the purpose of the ballot provisions as being the protection of union members and 'not to make life more difficult for trade unions'. Trade union lawyers who have to grapple with the complexity of the ballot provisions might take a different view. You may care to think about this in looking through the rest of the ballot requirements.

(4) In *Shipping Company Uniform Inc* v *International Transport Workers' Federation* (1985) the union had not held a ballot for the very good reason that the ITF was a federation of unions and had no individual members; therefore, there was no one it could ballot. Rather than hold it was exempt from the requirement, Staughton J held that no ballot meant no immunity. The union would have to change its rules to allow members

of the federated unions to become direct members of the ITF so that ballots could be held in the future.

Notice to employers

Trade Union and Labour Relations (Consolidation) Act 1992

226A (1) The trade union must take such steps as are reasonably necessary to ensure that –
    (a) not later than the seventh day before the opening day of the ballot, the notice specified in subsection (2), and
    (b) not later than the third day before the opening day of the ballot, the sample voting paper specified in subsection (2F)

is received by every person who it is reasonable for the union to believe (at the latest time when steps could be taken to comply with paragraph (a)) will be the employer of persons who will be entitled to vote in the ballot.

    (2) The notice referred to in paragraph (a) of subsection (1) is a notice in writing –
    (a) stating that the union intends to hold the ballot,
    (b) specifying the date which the union reasonably believes will be the opening day of the ballot, and
    (c) containing –
        (i) the lists mentioned in subsection (2A) and the figures mentioned in subsection (2B), together with an explanation of how those figures were arrived at, or
        (ii) where some or all of the employees concerned are employees from whose wages the employer makes deductions representing payments to the union, either those lists and figures and that explanation or the information mentioned in subsection (2C).

(2A) The lists are –
    (a) a list of the categories of employee to which the employees concerned belong, and
    (b) a list of the workplaces at which the employees concerned work.

(2B) The figures are –
    (a) the total number of employees concerned,
    (b) the number of the employees concerned in each of the categories in the list mentioned in subsection (2A)(a), and
    (c) the number of the employees concerned who work at each workplace in the list mentioned in subsection (2A)(b).

(2C) The information referred to in subsection (2)(c)(ii) is such information as will enable the employer readily to deduce –
    (a) the total number of employees concerned,
    (b) the categories of employee to which the employees concerned belong and the number of the employees concerned in each of those categories, and
    (c) the workplaces at which the employees concerned work and the number of them who work at each of those workplaces.

(2D) The lists and figures supplied under this section, or the information mentioned in subsection (2C) that is so supplied, must be as accurate as is reasonably practicable in the light of the information in the possession of the union at the time when it complies with subsection (1)(a).

(2E) For the purposes of subsection (2D) information is in the possession of the union if it is held, for union purposes –
    (a) in a document, whether in electronic form or any other form, and
    (b) in the possession or under the control of an officer or employee of the union.

(2F)   The sample voting paper referred to in paragraph (b) of subsection (1) is –
  (a)   a sample of the form of voting paper which is to be sent to the employees con-
        cerned, or
  (b)   where the employees concerned are not all to be sent the same form of voting
        paper, a sample of each form of voting paper which is to be sent to any of them.
(2G)   Nothing in this section requires a union to supply an employer with the names of the
employees concerned.
(2H)   In this section references to the 'employees concerned' are references to those employees of the employer in question who the union reasonably believes will be entitled to
vote in the ballot . . .

Comment

(1) There are actually two requirements to give notice to employers: in addition to this
provision, giving notice of the ballot, TULRCA s 234A, which is in parallel terms,
requires notice to be given seven days before the action actually starts.

(2) This is the third version of the notice provisions. They evolved into their present
state as follows. The first version, introduced by TURERA, required the union to give
the employer a notice which 'describes (so he can readily ascertain them)' the employees
to be balloted or called out. In *Blackpool and the Fylde College v NATFHE* (1994) the
Court of Appeal interpreted this as obliging the union to produce a list of names of
relevant union members for the employer, although it had been denied in Parliament
that this would be required when TURERA was debated. The decision caused an outcry because named members would feel vulnerable to pressure or retaliatory action
from the employer, and also, if union members chose to keep their membership secret
by paying their subscriptions through a bank order rather than automatic deduction
from wages (the check-off system), this would compromise their right to privacy.

(3) Thus the Employment Relations Act 1999 amended TULRCA ss 226A and 234A
so that instead the union had to give the employer such information 'as would help the
employer to make plans and bring information to the attention of' the relevant employees. It also inserted a provision that failure to name these employees would not
make the notice non-compliant.

(4) Two cases on the amended provision revealed yet more problems. In *National
Union of Rail, Maritime and Transport Workers v London Underground Ltd* (2001) the
Court of Appeal held that it was insufficient for the union simply to say it was calling
out all its members working for London Underground, about 40 per cent of the total
17,000 workforce. The union was required to provide a matrix showing numbers in
each category of staff in each workplace – a far more onerous requirement than providing a list of names of union members. In *Westminster City Council v Unison* (2001) the
union gave notice that it would ballot its 45 members who paid union dues through the
check-off system. There were only 70 employees in total. Although the Court of Appeal
ultimately held that this was a sufficient identification for the purposes of TULRCA
s 226A, since the employer could find out the names of these employees by looking
at payroll records, the trial judge had held it was not enough.

(5) In its review of the Employment Relations Act 1999, the government accepted the
argument that the revised notice provisions were actually more onerous for trade unions
than the original version. It rejected arguments that the notice provisions should be
scrapped, or reduced to one, declaring that both notices served useful purposes.

Instead, it committed itself to simplifying the requirements. The amendments were carried through by the Employment Relations Act 2004 and the result is above. You can decide whether the government's aim was achieved.

The ballot paper

Trade Union and Labour Relations (Consolidation) Act 1992

229 (1)   The method of voting in a ballot must be by the marking of a voting paper by the person voting . . .
(2)   The voting paper must contain at least one of the following questions –
   (a)   a question (however framed) which requires the person answering it to say, by answering 'Yes' or 'No', whether he is prepared to take part or, as the case may be, to continue to take part in a strike;
   (b)   a question (however framed) which requires the person answering it to say, by answering 'Yes' or 'No', whether he is prepared to take part or, as the case may be, to continue to take part in industrial action short of a strike.
(2A)   For the purposes of subsection (2) an overtime ban and a call-out ban constitute industrial action short of a strike . . .
(4)   The following statement must (without being qualified or commented upon by anything else on the voting paper) appear on every voting paper –

'If you take part in a strike or other industrial action, you may be in breach of your contract of employment.
   However, if you are dismissed for taking part in strike or other industrial action which is called officially and is otherwise lawful, the dismissal will be unfair if it takes place fewer than twelve weeks after you started taking part in the action, and depending on the circumstances may be unfair if it takes place later.'

London Underground Ltd v National Union of Railwaymen
[1989] IRLR 341 Queen's Bench Division

In balloting its members, the union indicated that the dispute was about four issues, but asked only a single question as to whether or not members were in favour of a strike. The company argued that this invalidated the ballot because three of the issues were no longer the subject of negotiation.

SIMON BROWN J: '. . . Mr Lemon [counsel for the company] further argues that, even if all four issues are trade disputes, nevertheless it is impermissible and offensive to the scheme of [TULRCA ss 226–235] to wrap them all up together in a single question. That part of his submissions I cannot accept. Mr Hendy's submission, advanced on behalf of the defendant union, is that it is not fatal to his client's right to invoke the statutory immunity even if the three subsidiary issues are found not to be trade disputes. He submits that, even if only one of the four issues is a trade dispute, that is sufficient to give immunity. That submission equally I reject. I recognise that it is arguable, but to my mind that is certainly not the unambiguous purport and meaning of the Act, and it would be surprising if the argument were right. If it were, then a majority of the voters at the qualifying ballot could well support strike action in regard to issues that were not trade disputes and for which, in the ordinary way, no [TULRCA s 219] immunity would arise, and indeed be wholly against the notion of striking for the only issue capable of founding that immunity. Mr Hendy says that that is irrelevant: so long as members, for whatever reason, support a strike, then it is immaterial that that support is not in regard to the only legitimate reason, namely the trade dispute, for which the strike is called.

True, the only question that requires to be asked under [TULRCA s 229(2)] is a simple question involving a yes or no answer. True too, all that the statute expressly requires to appear on the voting paper is the cautionary sentence: 'If you take part in a strike . . . you may be in breach of your contract of employment.' But I am not inclined to construe [TULRCA s 226(2)(a)] as being satisfied where the ballot poses a question which, either wholly or in part, asks whether the member is prepared to participate in a strike by reference to issues other than trade disputes.

The result of those conclusions is this. The defendants, although asserting that all four issues here constituted trade disputes, at this point cannot, to my mind, show that more probably than not they will succeed in that assertion. Were they to do so, then, in line with Lord Diplock's approach in *NWL Ltd* v *Woods* (1979) and rejecting as I do Mr Lemon's wider submissions, I would refuse this application. As it is, however, it seems to me that the defendants are as likely to fail as to succeed in what I believe to be the necessary step in their argument for immunity of showing that all issues constitute trade disputes. That being so, and all other factors to be weighed in the balance of convenience to my mind very firmly supporting the maintenance of the *status quo* and thus the calling off of Monday's strike, I believe that this injunction must be granted.

I add only this. Although inevitably that is a decision which I am driven to take at this late hour and after insufficient argument and certainly insufficient consideration, I am to some degree comforted by the thought that it may well not be the last word on this obviously important and by no means straightforward issue. For my part, however, I believe that the application is well-founded and that the relief sought should be granted.'

Comment

(1) This case involved emergency interim proceedings held on a single day with judgment given late in the evening. It illustrates one of the endemic problems about the case law on industrial action: many never proceed beyond the interim stage, where they are heard in great haste, without time fully to explore the complex points arising. Thus decisions may not be as completely considered as would be desirable.

(2) That said, it seems that this judgment must accurately state the law. Presumably it is for the union to satisfy the court that all the issues are genuine trade dispute issues. There is no statutory requirement that the union should state on the ballot paper, or in literature sent out with it, what the dispute is about, although this is recommended in the *Code of Practice on Industrial Action Ballots* (2005) para 36.

(3) Note that ballot papers must contain the 'health warning' set out in TULRCA s 229(4). It is obviously intended to have a chilling effect on the workers' enthusiasm for action. The case above refers to the earlier version of the health warning. The second paragraph, beginning 'However . . .' was added by the Employment Relations Act 1999 to take account of the new provisions on unfair dismissal contained in TULRCA s 238A (discussed above, p 590). Do you think that a union member reading this would find this helpful in assessing his or her legal position?

(4) It is clear that s 229(2) requires two questions where the union is planning both strike action and action short of a strike (*Post Office* v *UCW* (1990)).

(5) In *West Midlands Travel* v *TGWU* (1994) the union asked separate questions on all-out strike action and action short of a strike. On strike action, 1,265 were in favour, 1,225 were against and 147 left the question blank. On action short of a strike, 1,059

were in favour, 1,156 were against and 427 left the question blank. Thus, overall, 2,642 votes had been cast and the employer argued that therefore a majority of 1,322 was necessary before action could lawfully be taken. However, the Court of Appeal held that 'majority' meant a majority on each question, discounting those who chose not to vote (otherwise their abstentions would effectively count as 'no' votes).

Conduct of the ballot

Trade Union and Labour Relations (Consolidation) Act 1992

230 (1) Every person who is entitled to vote in the ballot must –
  (a) be allowed to vote without interference from, or constraint imposed by, the union or any of its members, officials or employees, and
  (b) so far as is reasonably practicable, be enabled to do so without incurring any direct cost to himself.
  (2) Except as regards persons falling within subsection (2A), so far as is reasonably practicable, every person who is entitled to vote in the ballot must –
  (a) have a voting paper sent to him by post at his home address or any other address which he has requested the trade union in writing to treat as his postal address; and
  (b) be given a convenient opportunity to vote by post . . .
  (4) A ballot shall be conducted so as to secure that –
  (a) so far as is reasonably practicable, those voting do so in secret, and
  (b) the votes given in the ballot are fairly and accurately counted.
  For the purposes of paragraph (b) an inaccuracy in counting shall be disregarded if it is accidental and on a scale which could not affect the result of the ballot.

Comment

(1) Fully postal ballots have been required since TURERA. The Employment Relations Act 2004 s 54 gives the Secretary of State power to relax these rules, but there has been no move to do so to date.

(2) TURERA also extended the scrutiny provisions which had been used for political fund and union official elections to industrial action ballots. Under TULRCA s 226B a scrutineer must be appointed to monitor the ballot and report afterwards as to whether it complied with the law (s 231B). The scrutineer must be someone qualified to act as such within the meaning of the Trade Union Ballots and Elections (Independent Scrutineer Qualifications) Order 1993 as amended – essentially, solicitors, trade union auditors and bodies such as the Electoral Reform Society. There is an exception if no more than 50 people are to be balloted (s 226C).

(3) The *Code of Practice on Industrial Action Ballots* (2005) para 27 recommends that at least seven days should be allowed for a postal ballot where first class post is used, and at least 14 days for second class post. Many ballots are open for longer periods than this: the postal ballot requirement makes it harder for unions to strike while the iron is hot.

Separate workplaces

Trade Union and Labour Relations (Consolidation) Act 1992

228 (1) Subject to subsection (2), this section applies if the members entitled to vote in a ballot by virtue of section 227 do not all have the same workplace.

(2)   This section does not apply if the union reasonably believes that all those members have the same workplace.

(3)   Subject to section 228A, a separate ballot shall be held for each workplace; and entitlement to vote in each ballot shall be accorded equally to, and restricted to, members of the union who –

(a)   are entitled to vote by virtue of section 227, and

(b)   have that workplace.

(4)   In this section and section 228A 'workplace' in relation to a person who is employed means –

(a)   if the person works at or from a single set of premises, those premises, and

(b)   in any other case, the premises with which the person's employment has the closest connection.

228A   (1)   Where section 228(3) would require separate ballots to be held for each workplace, a ballot may be held in place of some or all of the separate ballots if one of subsections (2) to (4) is satisfied in relation to it.

(2)   This subsection is satisfied in relation to a ballot if the workplace of each member entitled to vote in the ballot is the workplace of at least one member of the union who is affected by the dispute.

(3)   This subsection is satisfied in relation to a ballot if entitlement to vote is accorded to, and limited to, all the members of the union who –

(a)   according to the union's reasonable belief have an occupation of a particular kind or have any of a number of particular kinds of occupation, and

(b)   are employed by a particular employer, or by any of a number of particular employers, with whom the union is in dispute.

(4)   This subsection is satisfied in relation to a ballot if entitlement to vote is accorded to, and limited to, all the members of the union who are employed by a particular employer, or by any of a number of particular employers, with whom the union is in dispute.

(5)   For the purposes of subsection (2) the following are members of the union affected by a dispute –

(a)   if the dispute relates (wholly or partly) to a decision which the union reasonably believes the employer has made or will make concerning a matter specified in subsection (1)(a), (b) or (c) of section 244 (meaning of 'trade dispute'), members whom the decision directly affects,

(b)   if the dispute relates (wholly or partly) to a matter specified in subsection (1)(d) of that section, members whom the matter directly affects,

(c)   if the dispute relates (wholly or partly) to a matter specified in subsection (1)(e) of that section, persons whose membership or non-membership is in dispute,

(d)   if the dispute relates (wholly or partly) to a matter specified in subsection (1)(f) of that section, officials of the union who have used or would use the facilities concerned in the dispute.

Comment

(1) The purpose of TULRCA s 228 is to stop unions defining the constituency of those entitled to take part in a strike ballot in such a way that a militant group can outweigh moderate voters. The original version of s 228 was obscurely drafted, so the Employment Relations Act 2004 replaced it with new ss 228 and 228A.

(2) While s 228 states the basic rule of separate ballots in separate workplaces, the exceptions in s 228A where a single ballot will be allowed are wide enough almost to swallow up the rule. In particular, s 228A(3) means that national balloting will still be

possible where there is a national dispute, as long as each employer can be said to be involved in that dispute. This gives statutory effect to the decision in *UCE* v *NALGO* (1993). Conversely, if employers move away from national collective bargaining to local bargaining, it becomes more likely that separate ballots will be necessary.

(3) The definition of 'workplace' in s 228(4) deals with the problem thrown up by *Intercity West Coast Ltd* v *RMT* (1996), where it was argued that train conductors, all of whom worked at Manchester Piccadilly station (belonging to Railtrack) but who had separate employers, Intercity West Coast Ltd and North West Regional Railways, had separate workplaces, because workplace was defined as 'premises occupied by the employer'. Under the new definition, the question of who owns or occupies the premises is no longer relevant.

Procedure after the ballot

After the ballot has been held, TULRCA s 231 requires the union to provide all those entitled to vote with a breakdown of the result. Following amendment by TURERA, s 231A means that they must also provide this information to every employer of members entitled to vote. TULRCA s 233 stipulates that subsequent industrial action will only be protected if the person specified on the ballot paper as having authority to call the action actually does so.

Tanks & Drums Ltd v Transport and General Workers' Union
[1992] ICR 1 Court of Appeal

The specified person on the ballot paper was Ron Todd, General Secretary of the TGWU. The employers claimed that the strike was not immune because it had in fact been called by two shop stewards. Mr Todd gave evidence that the usual procedure was for the regional officer to inform him of the ballot result and he would then authorise the action and ask the regional officer to inform the district organiser, who in turn should inform the members. In this case, word had gone down to the district organiser that the action could start if the employers' stance did not change at a final negotiating meeting which was due the next day. The district organiser informed the shop stewards of this. At the meeting, the employers asked for more time to consider their position and were given four days. However, later the same day the shop stewards formed the view that the employers were not serious about reconsidering their proposals. The shop stewards therefore called a meeting of the workforce at which it was decided to strike at once.

NEILL LJ: '. . . On behalf of the claimant in this court it has been argued that in [TULRCA s 233] the call for a strike which is there envisaged is an unequivocal call by the specified person and one which is free from any conditions. It was said that that is not only the natural meaning of the subsection but is also consistent with the mischief against which this legislation is aimed. If in fact it was possible to impose conditions, it would mean that somebody other than the specified person would have a discretion and authority to decide whether the conditions had been met. The plain purpose of this legislation is that it is only at the end of the road, when negotiations have really reached a make or break point, that the specified person, with all the facts in front of him, should have an opportunity to make up his mind whether or not at that stage to call for a strike. That is Mr Supperstone's [counsel for the employer] principal submission: he says that it meets the purpose of the Act.

For my part I am unable to accept that argument. Mr Supperstone was constrained to admit that in a case such as this if a specified person says "I call a strike" or "I call for industrial action" and then tells his subordinate union officers "If you have a successful meeting tomorrow you should not go ahead with the strike", that is something which is permissible and within the wording of the section, but what cannot be allowed is for the specified person to say "I call for or authorise a strike if the meeting tomorrow is not successful". It seems to me that such a distinction, which depends purely on the language which the specified person uses over the telephone, cannot be a proper distinction to be drawn on circumstances of this kind.

Clearly, as I see it, there must be a very close link in time between the call for a strike and the event; for example, an unsuccessful meeting, which precipitates the final action. Mr Hendy conceded that it certainly would not be within the purpose of this legislation if a general secretary or other specified person were to give a blanket authority for a local union official to go ahead with negotiations on the basis that a strike could then be treated as being authorised if things did not go well. It seems to me that, as was put in the course of argument, it is a question of fact and degree in each case. At the end of the day one has to answer the simple question: did the specified person call or not call for the industrial action? This union decided to make the general secretary the specified person. This may be regarded as an indication that the union treats the legislation seriously and regards the calling of a strike as a serious matter which, before it is authorised, has to go the highest level . . .

It seems to me that one has to look at this evidence as a whole. For my part I pay particular attention to what Mr Todd himself said in his affidavit. He was saying: "I call for a strike if the meeting which the local officers are having tomorrow is not successful". It was on that basis and only on that basis that a condition was imposed on the strike. It seems to me that in the field of industrial relations it would be impracticable to leave matters in such a way that there was no possibility for the exercise of judgment on the ground. Some matters must be left for the judgment of those on the ground who have to decide how and when as a matter of common sense the call for action is to be put into operation. Therefore for those reasons I would reject Mr Supperstone's two primary arguments . . .'

(Russell LJ delivered a concurring judgment and Leggatt LJ agreed.)

Comment:

(1) The ostensible purpose of the 'specified person' provision was to stop minor officials (like shop stewards) jumping the gun and starting action as soon as the result of the ballot was announced. However, as this case shows, it has the potential for being one more trap which may result in the loss of immunity. The Court of Appeal shows a welcome realism in this decision.

(2) Reference is made in the case to the time limit on the effectiveness of the ballot: TULRCA s 234 provides that the ballot ceases to be effective four weeks after the last day of the ballot, or for up to eight weeks if the employer and union agree. The possibility of extending the period to eight weeks by agreement was introduced by the Employment Relations Act 1999, recognising that it might impede negotiations to settle a dispute if the union had to ensure that it used its mandate within the limited statutory period.

(3) In most cases, however, the window within which action can be started is quite narrow and it becomes narrower with every requirement that has to be fulfilled before the action can begin. Under s 234A, no action can begin until the employer has been given seven days' notice of the start date – and that notice cannot be given until the result of the ballot has been announced, so that reduces the usual four-week window to three weeks from the outset. If a union were to follow the recommendation in the *Code of Practice on Industrial Action Ballots* (2005) para 49, to wait until the scrutineer's

report is received before calling the action, the room for manoeuvre would be almost non-existent.

(4) An anomaly in the original law was thrown up by *Associated British Ports* v *TGWU* (1989). The union, representing dockers, wanted to organise a dock strike in protest at the proposed deregulation of the docks which was at that time going through Parliament (it eventually became the Dock Work Act 1989). A majority voted in favour of action in a ballot, but the employer sued for an interim injunction on the grounds that the action was outside the trade dispute immunity. By the time the House of Lords found in favour of the union and discharged the injunction against them, the original four-week mandate had expired. By the time another ballot could be held, the bill had passed into law, and protest was too late. For this reason, what is now TULRCA s 234(2) was passed, so that in such circumstances the time limit can be extended – although the court has discretion as to whether or not to order this.

(5) What if the action produces fresh negotiations with the employer and the action is suspended? Does there have to be a fresh ballot before action can be recommenced?

Monsanto plc v *Transport & General Workers' Union*
[1987] ICR 269 Court of Appeal

There was a dispute at the company over the use of temporary labour. The union held a ballot on 6 May, and action started the day after a result in favour was announced. On 12 June the action was suspended because there were new meetings with management in an attempt to settle the dispute. There was no settlement, and so on 23 June the union resumed its industrial action.

DILLON LJ: '. . . Mr Goudie [counsel for the company] says first that once industrial action is discontinued, for whatever reason and even if it is only pending negotiations, it is spent and there must be a further ballot before it can legitimately be resumed . . .

In relation to Mr Goudie's first submission it seems to me that in the normal course of industrial relations where industrial action has been begun the employer is likely to say that he will not negotiate while the industrial action is continuing. The union may be prepared to suspend industrial action while negotiations take place, but the intention throughout would be that that is not a discontinuance of the industrial action but a temporary suspension for the purposes of negotiations so that the industrial action will be resumed if the negotiations fail. I do not for my part see that in such circumstances the statute or good industrial relations require a further ballot at each stage if there is a suspension for negotiations.

Proceeding from there it seems to me that as the matters which led to the outbreak of the further industrial action or the reimposition of it are matters within the scope of the settlement of the original dispute, the principle of which has not been answered either way – that is to say, the principle of the company's power as manager to employ temporary labour – this is a case in which on the facts, so far as we can discern them from the affidavit evidence in advance of the trial, the union is considerably more likely than not to succeed at the trial of the action.

That being so, I disagree with the view which I take Gatehouse J to have formed in relation to [TULRCA s 221(2)]. Having to balance the important factor of the union's prospects of success against the balance of convenience factors affecting the company which I mentioned earlier, I reach the conclusion, feeling free to exercise a discretion having regard to the judge's approach to [TULRCA s 221] that in the circumstances of this case the injunction ought not to be granted . . .'

(Neill LJ delivered a concurring judgment.)

Post Office v Union of Communication Workers [1990] ICR 258 Court of Appeal

LORD DONALDSON MR:

'The effect of discontinuity of industrial action

The intention of Parliament was quite clear that industrial action, whether taking the form of a strike or of industrial action short of a strike or both, should be begun, or its continuance endorsed, within a short period after the date of the ballot: see [TULRCA s 226(2)(c)]. The reason is clear. Industrial relations are essentially fluid and attitudes change quickly. Accordingly, authority obtained from a ballot may in fact, as distinct from law, become invalid within a relatively short time. Although the Act in terms only requires the action to be begun in the specified period of four weeks, it is implicit that, once begun, it shall continue without substantial interruption, if reliance is to continue to be placed upon the verdict of the ballot. This is a question of fact and degree, but the question which the court has to ask itself is whether the average reasonable trade union member, looking at the matter at or shortly after any interruption in the industrial action, would say to himself: "the industrial action has now come to an end", even if he might also say: "the union may want to call us out again if the dispute continues". This is to be contrasted with a situation revealed in *Monsanto plc* v *TGWU* (1986) where industrial action was "suspended" for a short period (14 days) in order to enable active negotiations to take place. The negotiations failed and any reasonable union member would have said, and this court did say, that the termination of the period of suspension restored the original and authorised industrial action.

On the facts of the present case, it is quite clear that the all out one day strike on 12 December 1988 ended the industrial action contemplated and authorised by the August 1988 ballot and that this is why no further such action took place for over nine months. Applying the analysis of the traditional firework display, various rockets and bangers were discharged between 12 October and 30 November 1988 with the set piece finale on 12 December 1988. This was followed by a complete change of tactics, namely the mounting of a public relations campaign, with a reversion to a policy of industrial action only in September 1989, even if a decision or tentative decision to adopt this course was taken in May 1989. This represented entirely new and disconnected action which needed the support of a fresh ballot . . .'

(Butler-Sloss LJ delivered a concurring judgment and Farquharson LJ agreed.)

Comment

(1) In *Post Office* v *UCW*, the union lost immunity on two grounds: the point discussed here, and also because it had asked just one question in relation to both strike action and action short of a strike. See also *Secretary of State for Scotland* v *Scottish Prison Officers' Association* (1991).

(2) It should be clear that the requirements to be met for a valid ballot are both numerous and complicated. Should a union fail anywhere along the line, the industrial action will lose its immunity and be actionable in tort.

(3) Ballots are not unmitigated bad news for unions, however. Getting a ballot result in favour of action can be a very powerful bargaining weapon which may well encourage an employer to settle a dispute. Perhaps it is for this reason that the *Code of Practice on Industrial Action Ballots* states in para 6 that 'A union should hold a ballot on industrial action only if it is contemplating the organisation of industrial action' – an injunction which is wholly without legal effect.

Action for prohibited reasons

The final strategy pursued by the Conservative government of the 1980s in order to reduce the ambit of lawful industrial action was to identify certain reasons for taking action as unlawful. Action for one of these reasons will then lose its immunity. These provisions sit rather oddly with TULRCA s 244(1), as in that section, these reasons are recognised as valid subject matter for a trade dispute.

Union membership and recognition requirements

Trade Union and Labour Relations (Consolidation) Act 1992

222 (1) An act is not protected if the reason, or one of the reasons, for which it is done is the fact or belief that a particular employer –
    (a) is employing, has employed or might employ a person who is not a member of a trade union, or
    (b) is failing, has failed or might fail to discriminate against such a person.
(2) For the purposes of subsection (1)(b) an employer discriminates against a person if, but only if, he ensures that his conduct in relation to –
    (a) persons, or persons of any description, employed by him, or who apply to be, or are, considered by him for employment, or
    (b) the provision of employment for such persons,
is different, in some or all cases, according to whether or not they are members of a trade union, and is more favourable to those who are.
(3) An act is not protected if it constitutes, or is one of a number of acts which together constitute, an inducement or attempted inducement of a person –
    (a) to incorporate in a contract to which that person is a party, or a proposed contract to which he intends to be a party, a term or condition which is or would be void by virtue of section 144 (union membership requirement in contract for goods or services), or
    (b) to contravene section 145 (refusal to deal with person on grounds relating to union membership) . . . .

Comment

(1) This means that industrial action taken to enforce the closed shop or to spread it to other employers will lose immunity.

(2) In similar vein, TULRCA s 225 removes immunity from action taken to enforce recognition requirements.

(3) The genesis of both ss 222 and 225 was the practice of Labour-controlled councils in the late 1970s to put union membership requirements into contracts offered for tender. That meant that firms wanting to gain local government contracts would have to undertake to maintain a closed shop or to use only union labour. When it was proposed to outlaw such requirements in the Employment Act 1982, some councils retaliated by inserting recognition requirements instead – requirements that the contractor would recognise the appropriate union for their workers. In addition to industrial action being unlawful if it is to enforce these kinds of stipulations, all such requirements are now void (see TULRCA ss 186–187).

(4) Compare TULRCA s 244(1)(e) and (g).

Reinstatement of unofficial strikers

Trade Union and Labour Relations (Consolidation) Act 1992

223   An act is not protected if the reason, or one of the reasons, for doing it is the fact or belief that an employer has dismissed one or more employees in circumstances such that by virtue of section 237 (dismissal in connection with unofficial action) they have no right to complain of unfair dismissal.

Comment

(1) The restrictions on lawful industrial action made unions reluctant to call official action, which led to an increase in unofficial action. We saw in Chapter 12 that workers dismissed for taking part in unofficial action have no claim for unfair dismissal in any circumstances. This provision takes this further and removes immunity from any industrial action taken with a view to getting them their jobs back.

(2) Note that the immunity is lost in this case (and under TULRCA ss 222 and 225) if only *one* of the reasons for action is a prohibited reason.

(3) Compare TULRCA s 244(1)(b).

Who represents the union?

Where organising industrial action results in tortious liability, the individuals who have actually done the organising are personally liable. However, the employer usually wants to claim against the union – either to get damages or to get the action called off. But who is the union for this purpose? Once the Employment Act 1982 removed the total immunity that unions had previously enjoyed and put them on the same footing as individuals, it became crucial to know the answer to this question. Unfortunately, there is not one answer, but two.

Trade Union and Labour Relations (Consolidation) Act 1992

20   (1)   Where proceedings in tort are brought against a trade union –
    (a)   on the ground that an act –
        (i)   induces another person to break a contract or interferes or induces another person to interfere with its performance, or
        (ii)   consists in threatening that a contract (whether one to which the union is a party or not) will be broken or its performance interfered with, or that the union will induce another person to break a contract or interfere with its performance, or
    (b)   in respect of an agreement or combination by two or more persons to do or to procure the doing of an act which, if it were done without any such agreement or combination, would be actionable in tort on such a ground,
then, for the purpose of determining in those proceedings whether the union is liable in respect of the act in question, that act shall be taken to have been done by the union if, but only if, it is to be taken to have been authorised or endorsed by the trade union in accordance with the following provisions.
(2)   An act shall be taken to have been authorised or endorsed by a trade union if it was done, or was authorised or endorsed –
    (a)   by any person empowered by the rules to do, authorise or endorse acts of the kind in question, or

(b) by the principal executive committee or the president or general secretary, or

(c) by any other committee of the union or any other official of the union (whether employed by it or not).

(3) For the purposes of paragraph (c) of subsection (2) –

(a) any group of persons constituted in accordance with the rules of the union is a committee of the union; and

(b) an act shall be taken to have been done, authorised or endorsed by an official if it was done, authorised or endorsed by, or by any member of, any group of persons of which he was at the material time a member, the purposes of which included organising or co-ordinating industrial action.

(4) The provisions of paragraphs (b) and (c) of subsection (2) apply notwithstanding anything in the rules of the union, or in any contract or rule of law, but subject to the provisions of section 21 (repudiation by union of certain acts) . . . .

(7) In this section 'rules', in relation to a trade union, means the written rules of the union and any other written provision forming part of the contract between a member and the other members.

Comment

(1) Note that by virtue of subsection (1), this statutory definition of vicarious liability applies only in relation to the torts for which immunity is given by virtue of TULRCA s 219. For all other purposes, normal common law principles of vicarious liability will apply.

(2) Subsection (2) lists the officials whose authorisation (ahead of action) or endorsement of it (after it has started) will make the union liable. Those mentioned in (a) and (b) are obvious: the top officials are the people who run the union and must therefore be taken to speak for it. If the rules give power to anyone else to authorise or endorse industrial action, it makes sense to add them too. Subsection (2)(c), however, goes much further: 'any other official' would cover every shop steward in the country, which in the case of the largest unions would run to thousands. Union liability was extended to this group by the Employment Act 1990.

(3) There is a let-out for the union where action is authorised or endorsed by these lesser officials. It can escape liability if it promptly repudiates the action. However, the conditions for a valid repudiation were made considerably more onerous by the Employment Act 1990.

Trade Union and Labour Relations (Consolidation) Act 1992

21 (1) An act shall not be taken to have been authorised or endorsed by a trade union by virtue only of paragraph (c) of section 20(2) if it was repudiated by the executive, president or general secretary as soon as reasonably practicable after coming to the knowledge of any of them.

(2) Where an act is repudiated –

(a) written notice of the repudiation must be given to the committee or official in question, without delay, and

(b) the union must do its best to give individual written notice of the fact and date of repudiation, without delay –

(i) to every member of the union who the union has reason to believe is taking part, or might otherwise take part, in industrial action as a result of the act, and

(ii) to the employer of every such member.

(3)   The notice given to members in accordance with paragraph (b)(i) of subsection (2) must contain the following statement –

'Your union has repudiated the call (or calls) for industrial action to which this notice relates and will give no support to unofficial industrial action taken in response to it (or them). If you are dismissed while taking unofficial industrial action, you will have no right to complain of unfair dismissal.'

(4)   If subsection (2) or (3) is not complied with, the repudiation shall be treated as ineffective.

(5)   An act shall not be treated as repudiated if at any time after the union concerned purported to repudiate it the executive, president or general secretary has behaved in a manner which is inconsistent with the purported repudiation.

(6)   The executive, president or general secretary shall be treated as so behaving if, on a request made to any of them within three months of the purported repudiation by a person who –

(a)   is a party to a commercial contract whose performance has been or may be interfered with as a result of the act in question, and

(b)   has not been given written notice by the union of the repudiation,

it is not forthwith confirmed in writing that the act has been repudiated.

(7)   In this section 'commercial contract' means any contract other than –

(a)   a contract of employment, or

(b)   any other contract under which a person agrees personally to do work or perform services for another.

Comment

(1)   The burdensome requirements in subsections (2)(b) and (3), to give individual written notices to affected members and employers, were introduced by the Employment Act 1990.

(2)   Subsection (6) was also introduced then. However, even before this, the courts had shown themselves astute to the possibility of a purported repudiation not being genuine: see *Express & Star Ltd* v *National Graphical Association (1982)* (1986).

Trade Union and Labour Relations (Consolidation) Act 1992

22   (1)   This section applies to any proceedings in tort brought against a trade union, except –

(a)   proceedings for personal injury as a result of negligence, nuisance or breach of duty;

(b)   proceedings for breach of duty in connection with the ownership, occupation, possession, control or use of property;

(c)   proceedings brought by virtue of Part I of the Consumer Protection Act 1987 (product liability).

(2)   In any proceedings in tort to which this section applies the amount which may be awarded against the union by way of damages shall not exceed the following limit—

Number of members of union	Maximum award of damages
Less than 5,000	£10,000
5,000 or more but less than 25,000	£50,000
25,000 or more but less than 100,000	£125,000
100,000 or more	£250,000

(3)   The Secretary of State may by order amend subsection (2) so as to vary any of the sums specified; and the order may make such transitional provision as the Secretary of State considers appropriate . . .

Comment

(1) These limits have not been raised since their introduction in 1982. TULRCA s 23 further provides that the union's political and benevolent funds (if any) will not be available for paying damages, provided that the rules of those funds prevent them from being used to finance industrial action.

(2) Note, however, that the limits apply only to actions in tort. In contempt proceedings, for example, there is no limit on the fines which may be levied for a union continuing action which the court has ordered to be called off. This happened during a number of industrial campaigns in the 1980s, when these provisions were still new, and fines of over £500,000 were imposed. The limits also apply only to each claim. If a number of employers were able to make claims, the union could face damages up to the limit in each action.

(3) As noted already, the statutory scheme of vicarious liability applies only to the torts specified in TULRCA s 20(1). For any other claims, common law principles of vicarious liability apply.

Thomas v National Union of Mineworkers (South Wales Area) [1985] ICR 886 Chancery Division

The case arose during the 1984–85 miners' strike. The claimants sought an injunction against mass picketing at the collieries where they worked, and picketing at the homes of working miners and other industrial premises. The action was brought against the South Wales area union, the national union, and named members of the national coordinating committee.

SCOTT J: '. . . I now come to the question whether the defendants, or any of them, can be held responsible in law for the colliery gates picketing.

I will deal first with the position of Mr Hendy's clients, the NUM and the members of the national co-ordinating committee. These defendants on the evidence I have seen played no part in organising the colliery gate picketing, or for that matter any other picketing within the South Wales area. They have no control over the picketing that goes on within the South Wales area. It follows that injunctions to control that picketing cannot be granted against any of them. Mr Blom-Cooper [counsel for the claimants], I think, accepted that that was so.

Next I want to deal with the position of the second to seventh defendants. The second, third and fourth defendants are, or were, the trustees of the South Wales union's funds. The fifth, sixth and seventh defendants are the union's principal officers. There was nothing in the evidence which links any of the trustees to the organisation of the colliery gate picketing. There is clearly no case for the grant of injunctions regarding colliery gate picketing against the second, third or fourth defendants. There is, however, some evidence that the three main officers of the union are responsible for the general picketing policy put into effect by the lodges . . .

The fifth, sixth and seventh defendants have the general control and management of the South Wales union. Each is an active officer. Each would in my view be responsible under the general law for taking appropriate steps to see that the union obeyed any order made against it. I propose therefore to leave their liability on that basis and not to make any order against them personally.

The real question concerns the responsibilities of the lodges and through them of the South Wales union. There is, as I have said, a real question on the evidence as to the responsibility of the lodges and their respective officers for the nature and manner of the colliery gate picketing that is taking place. But none of the lodge officers is a defendant, so unless responsibility can be imposed on the South Wales union for what is done by the lodge officers the claimants' claim in this action for injunctive relief to control the colliery gate picketing must fail.

The lodges are constituent parts of the South Wales union. I have already referred to rule 27 of the rules. There are many other rules which refer to the lodges and their officers, but, otherwise than in respect of funds, contributions, accounts and other like matters, there is no rule which sets out the powers or duties of the lodges. These powers and duties are obviously and sensibly enough left to practice and custom. The rules do, however, provide for the objects of the South Wales union itself. The objects include under paragraph 3 (b):

> "To advance and protect the interests of members in relation to questions of wages, hours, holidays, conditions of employment, safety, compensation and all other questions arising out of and/or in connection with the member's employment or occupation."

The object is plainly wide enough to cover the conduct of an official strike and, in my view, under the rules the overall responsibility for the conduct of any official strike rests with the union itself. The arrangements for local picketing at collieries and elsewhere may be left to the individual lodges, but in carrying out this function the lodges are, in my judgment, acting on behalf of the South Wales union for the purpose of enabling the union to pursue one of its own most important objects, namely the advancement of the interests of its members in connection with their employment.

Mr Scrivener [counsel for the South Wales Area union and its officials] referred me to *Heatons Transport (St Helens) Ltd* v *Transport and General Workers' Union* (1973) on this question of the union's vicarious responsibility for its lodges. The point in that case was whether a union against which an injunction had been granted was liable for contempt of court where one of its shop stewards had acted in breach of the order. The relationship between the union and its shop stewards was examined. The House of Lords, reversing the Court of Appeal, held the union liable, not on a vicarious footing for what the shop steward had done, but rather on the ground that the union had failed to take adequate steps to try and ensure that the order was obeyed. But as to the vicarious liability point Lord Wilberforce said:

> "In the Court of Appeal Lord Denning MR and Roskill LJ in considering the scope of the shop stewards' scope of authority placed considerable reliance on the fact that the shop stewards were agents rather than servants. But we think that is not an important factor in this case. No new development is involved in the law relating to the responsibility of a master or principal for the act of a servant or agent. In each case the test to be applied is the same: was the servant or agent acting on behalf of, and within the scope of the authority conferred by, the master or principal?: ... Usually a servant, as compared with an agent, has a wider authority because his employment is more permanent and he has a larger range of duties as he may have to exercise discretion in dealing with a series of situations as they arise. The agent in an ordinary case is engaged to perform a particular task on a particular occasion and has authority to do whatever is required for that purpose but has no general authority."

The application of the principle there expressed to the facts of the present case leads, in my judgment, to the conclusion that the South Wales union is responsible on ordinary principles of vicarious liability for what is done by the lodges and their officers in organising colliery gate and other local picketing on behalf of and in the name of the South Wales union. That leads me to the question of the responsibility of the lodges and their officers for the numbers who attend at the colliery gates and for the behaviour of those who attend.

Mr Scrivener impressed upon me that given the strength of the feelings in the South Wales mining towns and villages in support of the strike and of anger against those who are breaking the strike and returning to work, spontaneous attendance of large numbers at the collieries and

666

expressions of abuse, anger and sometimes violence, were all to be expected. I follow that sub-mission and it may very well be right. But it is reasonably clear that some degree of organisa-tion by the lodges does regularly take place. The extent and nature of the organising are likely to vary from lodge to lodge, but, as I understand the evidence, the lodge officers regard it as the duty of the lodge to see that the colliery gates are picketed, there is usually a lodge officer in attendance on the picket line and the officer in attendance has an authority, as evidenced by his selection of the six who stand close to the colliery gates, which is respected by those pres-ent. Further, there is a telling lack in the evidence of any suggestion that on any occasion any lodge officer has discouraged the attendance at the colliery gates of large numbers. Further, there are minutes of meetings of the South Wales union's area executive council which appear to establish a policy of picketing in large numbers. At a meeting on 6 November it was agreed that "picketing at collieries will be stepped up significantly". It is not to be expected that this policy was not made known to the lodges and required to be implemented by the lodges.

At this interlocutory stage of the case, with affidavit evidence and no cross-examination, I can and should come to no final conclusion as to the extent to which the picketing I regard as tortious has been arranged by the lodges. But that the lodges have played a significant part seems to me to be clear . . .'

Comment

(1) From 1971 until 1974 unions could be sued under the Industrial Relations Act 1971. *Heatons Transport* v *TGWU* (1973) arose at that time, and the House of Lords held that the union's rules, supplemented by custom and practice, had devolved the power to call strikes to shop stewards. It was accordingly liable for their actions.

(2) In the light of this, it is clearly essential for unions to keep under review the powers of officials under their own rules, and to ensure that the rules are complied with.

(3) The facts of *Thomas* v *NUM* (1985) leads us neatly to the next topic: picketing.

PICKETING

Establishing a picket line is frequently seen as essential to the successful prosecu-tion of industrial action, not only to make sure that people do not work, but also to ensure that supplies are not brought in and products are not got out. Since picket-ing involves face-to-face confrontation and feelings run high. it can be a volatile, potentially violent situation. Hence the criminal law as well as the civil law is fre-quently invoked against pickets. There is also a Code of Practice, drawn up by the Secretary of State, issued originally in 1980 and revised in 1992, which must be taken into account by courts and tribunals when it is relevant to do so.

Civil liability for picketing

If successful, pickets can induce breaches of contracts of employment (by persuad-ing people not to work) and breaches of commercial contracts (by, for example, stopping deliveries) and would thus potentially be liable in tort at Stage 1, if there were no immunity. However, they receive the basic immunity under TULRCA s 219 *provided* that the picketing is lawful under the terms of TULRCA s 220.

Trade Union and Labour Relations (Consolidation) Act 1992

220 (1) It is lawful for a person in contemplation or furtherance of a trade dispute to attend –
     (a) at or near his own place of work, or
     (b) if he is an official of a trade union, at or near the place of work of a member of the union whom he is accompanying and whom he represents,

for the purpose only of peacefully obtaining or communicating information, or peacefully persuading any person to work or abstain from working.

(2) If a person works or normally works –
     (a) otherwise than at any one place, or
     (b) at a place the location of which is such that attendance there for a purpose mentioned in subsection (1) is impracticable, his place of work for the purposes of that subsection shall be any premises of his employer from which he works or from which his work is administered.

(3) In the case of a worker not in employment where –
     (a) his last employment was terminated in connection with a trade dispute, or
     (b) the termination of his employment was one of the circumstances giving rise to a trade dispute,

in relation to that dispute his former place of work shall be treated for the purposes of subsection (1) as being his place of work.

(4) A person who is an official of a trade union by virtue only of having been elected or appointed to be a representative of some of the members of the union shall be regarded for the purposes of subsection (1) as representing only those members; but otherwise an official of a union shall be regarded for those purposes as representing all its members.

Comment

(1) The significant limitation of lawful picketing to picketing one's own place of work was introduced by the Employment Act 1980 to curb the use of 'flying pickets'.

(2) Picketing at other places will lose immunity – but of course, this does not matter if there is no tortious liability in the first place: see *Middlebrook Mushrooms Ltd* v *TGWU* (1993), for example.

(3) The special provision for workers who do not work in one place, or whose place of work is inaccessible, might indicate an intention that everyone should have a place to picket. However, this is not how it has been interpreted.

News Group Newspapers Ltd v SOGAT '82 (No 2)
[1987] ICR 181 Queen's Bench Division

The decision of Rupert Murdoch to move his newpaper business (including the *Sun*, the *News of the World*, *The Times* and the *Sunday Times* from Fleet Street to Wapping, together with the streamlined practices he intended to introduce, sparked a bitter war with the print unions, which intensified with the dismissal of 5,000 workers. As the operations had moved to Wapping, that is where the pickets went – but it was not where they had formerly been employed.

STUART-SMITH J: '. . . Mr Grabiner [counsel for the claimants] submits that three propositions are established on the evidence:

1. That those who attend at or near Wapping are not at or near their place of work.

I agree. Counsel on behalf of the defendants have submitted that because the dismissed workers previously did work in printing *The Sun*, *News of the World*, *The Times* and *Sunday Times* and that work has now been transferred to Wapping, Wapping has become their place of work. But it seems to me that place refers to a geographical location; and without special words in the section, a place where he has never worked cannot become one where he does. And this is made clear by [TULRCA s 220(3)] which provides:

> "In the case of a worker who is not in employment where – (a) his last employment was terminated in connection with a trade dispute, or (b) the termination of his employment was one of the circumstances giving rise to a trade dispute subsection (1) above shall in relation to that dispute have effect as if any reference to his place of work were a reference to his former place of work."

This subsection makes it clear that the place of work of the dismissed men within the meaning of the section is Bouverie Street or Gray's Inn Road, as the case may be.

It follows from this that even if they are acting peacefully, that is to say, not abusing or threatening people or creating an obstruction or nuisance, official pickets and others not employed there who attend at Wapping will be committing the tort of interference with contract if they induce other persons to break their contracts of employment . . .

2. That the conduct complained of committed by those who attend at or near Wapping demonstrates that they are not there for the purpose only of peacefully obtaining or communicating information or peacefully persuading any person to work or abstain from working.

I agree. The contrary has not been argued.

3. That all those taking part in official pickets, daily demonstrations, marches, rallies and other demonstrations are picketing.

There is no definition of picketing in the relevant legislation. As I understand his submission, Mr Grabiner sought to spell out a definition from [TULRCA s 220], the essential elements being a person who in contemplation or furtherance of a trade dispute attends at or near a place of work for the purpose of obtaining or communicating information or persuading any person to work or abstain from working. This definition accords with that in the *Oxford English Dictionary*, namely:

> "men acting in a body or singly who are stationed by a trades-union or the like, to watch men going to work during a strike or in non-union workshops, and to endeavour to dissuade or deter them."

Applying either of these tests it seems to me that there can be little doubt that the official pickets and daily demonstrators come within it. On the other hand I do not think that those who take part in marches and rallies, if they proceed peaceably along the Highway into Wellclose Square are picketing. The problem arises when they break ranks or disperse and commit the acts complained of to which I have referred. In my view the claimants do have an arguable case that such people are picketing. They are attending at or near the claimants' plant for the purpose, inter alia, of communicating information in the form of their views and abuse and persuading people to abstain from working.

These considerations are also relevant to the grant of interlocutory relief, since the court in exercising its discretion whether or not to grant the injunction must have regard to the likelihood of the defendants succeeding at the trial of the action in establishing the matter or matters which would, under the provisions of [TULRCA ss 219 and 220], afford a defence to the action: see [TULRCA s 221(2)]. For the two reasons which I have given I consider it unlikely that such defences will be established in relation to Wapping . . .'

Comment

(1) The Court of Appeal dealt with a similar situation in the same way in *Union Traffic Ltd* v *TGWU* (1989), where Bingham LJ said:

> . . . Underlying Mr Walker's submissions was, I thought, the premise that everyone must have somewhere where he can effectively picket. That is, in my judgment, not so, as a reading of

[TULRCA s 220] makes plain. One need only take the case of an employee who works, or normally works, at one place that is closed; it may then be futile to picket at that place, but it may nonetheless be the case that there are no other premises of his employer from which he works or from which his work is administered, and in that event there is nowhere he can effectively picket . . .

(2) In *Rayware* v *TGWU* (1989) the Court of Appeal held that pickets were at or near their employer's premises on a private industrial estate when they were on the public road at the entrance to the estate, some 1,230 yards from the actual workplace. They could not get closer because they would have been trespassing.

(3) Implicitly accepting this, the revised Code of Practice on picketing (1992) recommends that where the picket is taking place at a place of work of more than one employer, the pickets should ensure that the workers who are not involved in the dispute are not interfered with. It also states that where there is a choice of locations which could be regarded as 'at or near' the place of work picketing should be confined to the closest.

(4) The status of such pronouncements in the Code of Practice is problematic. While it is true that the Code should be taken into account in all relevant proceedings, yet it is also the case that its recommendations do not have the force of law. Therefore, it is submitted that if the picketing can properly be described as 'at or near', then it will not be rendered unlawful merely because it is not in fact at the nearest possible point.

(5) A similar issue arises in relation to the well-known recommendation in the Code that no more than six pickets should be necessary at any one entrance. This is frequently treated by police on duty to keep the peace as if it were a legal requirement.

(6) Pickets who are successful may persuade employees of employers other than the employer in dispute to break their contracts of employment. An obvious example would be if pickets persuaded lorry drivers not to deliver goods to the struck firm, thus inducing a breach of the lorry drivers' contracts of employment with their own employers and disrupting the commercial contract between the supplier and the employer in dispute. Under TULRCA s 224(2) this is secondary action. But by virtue of s 224(1), it is protected secondary action. This is the one and only situation where workers do not lose immunity while engaging in secondary action.

(7) Pickets who are lawful by the terms of TULRCA s 220 receive immunity from liability for the economic torts as provided by s 219. However, there are other torts which may be committed on the picket line and there is no immunity in respect of these. An extreme case, the Wapping dispute referred to above, provides an overview of the kind of liability which could be at issue.

News Group Newspapers Ltd v *SOGAT '82 (No 2)* [1987] ICR 181 Queen's Bench Division

The reasons for the dispute are set out on p 668.

STUART-SMITH J:

'. . . *The conduct complained of*

The conduct complained of consists of allegedly unlawful and tortious acts committed in the course of activities organised by the various defendants. It is necessary to describe these activities at the various sites with which I am concerned and the tortious acts alleged.

Wapping

Three forms of activity take place, which for convenience may be described as picketing, daily demonstrations, and marches, rallies and demonstrations. It should be emphasised that this is merely for ease of definition. It does not matter what people are called. What is relevant is what they do. The claimants submit that there is really no difference between the activities of any of those who attend at or near the plant: they are all picketing . . .

Pickets

These are sometimes described as official pickets. They are organised by the two defendant unions through the London District Council of SOGAT and the joint liaison committee of the unions. They consist of six pickets, two at least of whom are members of SOGAT and one at least NGA, together with a steward. They wear official armbands or other insignia. By agreement with the police they are stationed at the outer main gate. They are there 24 hours a day and have attended every day since the dispute began save perhaps for the first day or so. They change every four hours.

Daily demonstrators

Estimates of their numbers vary to some extent between 50 and 200. They tend to be at their maximum in the morning and evening when the bulk of the claimants' workforce are coming to and from work. In the main, they congregate on the north side of the Highway, behind crush barriers at a distance of some 80 yards from the main gate. There is a police presence at the north end of Virginia Street.

There is a dispute in the evidence as to whether or not the daily demonstrators are organised by the defendants or any of them, particularly the unions. This is denied by the defendants' deponents. It is said that they are in the main dismissed print workers and their families, who, having a great sense of grievance, come spontaneously each day to express their feelings. The claimants on the other hand allege that they are organised . . .

This is clearly an important issue of fact which cannot be resolved without oral evidence, cross-examination and discovery. But to my mind the claimants have at least a good arguable case that the daily demonstrators are, in fact, being organised by or on behalf of the defendant unions. Whatever may be the position in a remote mining village in South Wales, where it is not improbable that striking miners may assemble spontaneously and without organisation by their union at their pit at the beginning and end of a shift, I find it hard to believe that day after day for six months 50 to 200 dismissed print workers and some of their families assemble spontaneously from all over London and maybe further afield, at their own expense to signify by their presence the depth of their feelings, unless they are organised. Obviously it is not the same people who come each day, morning and evening, with lesser numbers during the rest of the day.

Rallies, marches and demonstrations

Every week on Wednesday and Saturday nights and sometimes at other times as well – for example, 1 and 5 May (the latter being apparently for the benefit of the local residents) – rallies, marches and demonstrations take place. They normally take the form of an assembly at some point, usually Tower Hill, then a procession to Wapping, where it moves into Wellclose Square and at this point is addressed by speakers who sympathise with the cause of the dismissed workers. Thereafter, those involved should disperse. That is what is supposed to happen. As will be seen, it seldom if ever works just like that. It is not disputed that these activities are organised by or on behalf of both unions. The numbers attending vary from about 700 or 800 to between 6,000 and 7,000. Generally there are more on Saturdays than on Wednesdays. Recently the numbers of those attending has tended to decrease . . .

All these activities are supposed to take place in an orderly and peaceful way with the pickets peaceably attempting to persuade those who work there not to do so or imparting information to them and the demonstrators showing by their presence that they have a grievance and a just cause and appealing to the consciences of those in work and the claimants' management for a more generous settlement of the dispute. That is the theory, and if that were the practice the claimants would have no cause to complain. In fact, it is very far from the practice.

It is necessary to examine the evidence in some detail in relation to each place and kind of activity, though I do not intend to lengthen the judgment with detailed description of all the incidents.

Pickets and daily demonstrations at Wapping

There is overwhelming evidence that those of the claimants' employees who pass both the pickets and daily demonstrators are almost invariably subjected to abuse and, frequently, to threats. They are called scabs, but that is the least of the insults. Vile and obscene language is used, particularly to women. Much of the abuse is of a personal nature, since many of the claimants' employees, and particularly the journalists, are known by name and sight. There are also threats, such as "We'll get you" and "You can't hide forever". To add point to their meaning there have been other touches. Earlier in the dispute a coffin was suspended from a lamp post in Virginia Street. Several witnesses speak of being photographed as they come and go at the gate and having the numbers of their cars taken. There was at one time a so-called roll of dishonour of those working, which gave their names and addresses. The significance of these matters will become clear later . . .

The marches and rallies

Very often, though not on every occasion, there have been incidents of violence and obstruction and not infrequently they have been of a serious nature. In the course of these forays journalists have been attacked in their cars and so have drivers of TNT lorries and vans. A particularly dangerous incident occurred when a sharpened stick was thrown through the back window of a car, showering the occupant of the back seat with glass. On another, 40 yards of the perimeter fence was knocked over. Rockets, flares and stones have been directed against the claimants' buildings. But in the main the violence has been directed against the police, who have had to be present in large numbers in order to try and protect the claimants' premises and employees. They have borne the brunt of the casualties. It is quite clear that on occasions some of those who have attended have come armed with an assortment of offensive weapons in order to make a concerted attack . . .

The claimants contend that the conduct complained of involves the commission of four separate torts – that is to say, nuisance, intimidation, harassment and interference with the performance of their commercial contracts. They then contend that the defendants are liable in respect of some or all of these torts . . .

Nuisance

A nuisance may be a public nuisance actionable at the suit of a particular claimant or a private nuisance.

(a) *Public nuisance*

Public nuisance is a criminal offence which for the purpose of this case may be defined as an unlawful act which endangers lives, safety, health, property or comfort of the public or by which the public are obstructed in the exercise or enjoyment of any right common to all Her Majesty's subjects. It must materially affect the reasonable comfort and convenience of a class of Her Majesty's subjects who come within the sphere or neighbourhood of its operation (see *per* Romer LJ in *Attorney-General* v *PYA Quarriers Ltd* (1957)). It is only actionable as a civil wrong if the claimant can show particular damage other than and beyond the general inconvenience suffered by the public. Such particular damage must be substantial, but it is not limited to special damage in the sense of probable pecuniary loss . . .

(b) *Private nuisance*

The owner of land adjoining the highway has a right of access to the highway from any part of his premises. Interference with this right is actionable; but where the interference is as here, alleged obstruction, it is subject to the same qualification that the obstruction must be an unreasonable use of the highway. It is submitted that the third claimants as owners of the land are entitled to sue at Wapping, the first and second at Bouverie Street and Gray's Inn Road, respectively, if the nuisance is thus made out.

How are these principles to be applied to the facts at the various places in question?

Wapping

I have no doubt that the conduct of the pickets and the daily demonstrators as described in the evidence amounts to an unreasonable obstruction of the highway. Moreover, it seems to me that unlike the working miners in *Thomas* v *National Union of Mineworkers (South Wales Area)* (1986), who were unable to establish special damage because they were driven into the pit in a bus provided by their employer and there was no other evidence of damage, both the seventh claimant and the other claimants can establish damage peculiar to them. The seventh claimant describes how she no longer feels able to leave the plant during the day for a meal or similar break. She has to go by taxi or mini-cab instead of on foot and how she feels drained by the constant pressure of having to come to work through the picket line. These are all matters in my view capable of being regarded as substantial damage.

So far as the other claimants are concerned, although it is not entirely clear who incurs the expense, the cost of busing their employees is £100,000 per month – by no means insubstantial damage. Moreover, Mr Wilson, the editor of *The Times*, has made it clear that the second claimants have both lost some journalists and failed to attract others because of the conduct of the pickets and daily demonstrators. Journalists are the life-blood of a newspaper, and, in my view, this is very serious damage.

The third claimants' cause of action in private nuisance is also established, it not being necessary to establish peculiar damage in that case.

So far as the twice-weekly marches, rallies and demonstrations are concerned, when they are peaceful and orderly no nuisance is created. But it is quite clear that on those occasions when the marches or demonstrations get out of control, attack the police, the employees of the claimants and TNT and obstruct the highway by masses of people, that is not a reasonable use of the highway and amounts to a nuisance . . .

Intimidation

The tort of intimidation is committed when A delivers a threat to B that he will commit an act or use means unlawful against B, as a result of which B does or refrains from doing some act which he is entitled to do, thereby causing damage either to himself or C. The tort is one of intention and the claimant, whether it be B or C, must be a person whom A intended to injure (see *Clerk & Lindsell on Torts*, 15th ed (1982), p 729) . . .

The defendants submit, rightly in my view, that abuse, swearing and shouting does not amount to a threat of violence. They further submit that the threat has to be express or implied that if the person threatened does not do what is required he will be subjected to violence and that such threats as have been made do not amount to this. I disagree. The words, "Scab, we will get you", or words to the same effect, could mean, "We will assault you because you have been working for the claimants." But, since the obvious intention is to dissuade people from continuing to work, the more likely meaning is, "We will get you if you do not stop working for the claimants." There is ample evidence of such threats at Wapping from both the pickets and daily demonstrators. There is also some evidence to this effect in relation to those who attend at Bouverie Street and Gray's Inn Road.

If a threat is little more than idle abuse and is not to be taken seriously, then it would not be sufficient to found an action for intimidation. Indeed, the tort is not complete unless the person threatened succumbs to the threat and damage is suffered. But it is clear that injunctive relief can be granted to restrain the unlawful act and also threats to commit the unlawful act: *Clerk & Lindsell on Torts*, p 743, footnote 42). But in order for an injunction to be granted the threat or threats must be serious and taken seriously by those who receive them. It is in this context that, in my view, the evidence of what has happened away from the claimants' premises is material. Where there is such an abundance of evidence of the employees being followed, molested, assaulted and subject to criminal damage to their cars and houses, to say nothing of the treatment meted out to TNT drivers, it is idle to suggest that the threats are not serious or to be taken seriously. The taking of photographs of employees, noting of numbers of their cars and the distribution of so-called rolls of dishonour is particularly significant in this context . . .

Harassment

In *Thomas v National Union of Mineworkers (South Wales Area)* (1986) Scott J, after holding that the conduct of the pickets at the colliery gates was intimidating in the ordinary sense of the word, said:

> "Nuisance is strictly concerned with, and may be regarded as confined to, activity which unduly interferes with the use or enjoyment of land or of easements. But there is no reason why the law should not protect on a similar basis the enjoyment of other rights. All citizens have the right to use the public highway. Suppose an individual were persistently to follow another on a public highway, making rude gestures or remarks in order to annoy or vex. If continuance of such conduct were threatened no one can doubt but that a civil court would, at the suit of the victim, restrain by an injunction the continuance of the conduct. The tort might be described as a species of private nuisance, namely unreasonable interference with the victim's rights to use the highway. But the label for the tort does not, in my view, matter.
>
> In the present case, the working miners have the right to use the highway for the purpose of going to work. They are, in my judgment, entitled under the general law to exercise that right without unreasonable harassment by others. Unreasonable harassment of them in the exercise of that right would, in my judgment, be tortious.
>
> A decision whether in this, or in any other similar case, the presence or conduct of pickets represents a tortious interference with the right of those who wish to go to work to do so without harassment must depend on the particular circumstances of the particular case. The balance to which I have earlier referred must be struck between the rights of those going to work and the rights of the pickets."

The defendants criticise this statement of the law. They submit that Scott J should not have invented a new tort and that it is not sufficient to found liability that there has been an unreasonable interference with the rights of others, even though when a balance is struck between conflicting rights and interests the scale comes down in favour of the claimants, unless those rights are recognised by the law and fall within some accepted head of tort.

I am bound to say that, with all respect to Scott J, I think there is force in these criticisms, especially where it does not appear that damage is a necessary ingredient of the tort. If, of course, damage peculiar to the claimant is established, then the tort is that of nuisance.

Since, in my view, the tort of nuisance is established and the tort of intimidation is threatened, it is unnecessary for me to express a final view on the question of harassment . . .'

Comment

(1) The judge also considered that the tort of causing loss by unlawful means was made out, given that the TULRCA s 219 immunity did not apply to the picketing. In any case, immunity would not extend to the torts discussed here which would be outside the statutory immunity: intimidation is only covered by s 219 when what is threatened is inducing breaches of contract.

(2) Note the debate ongoing at that time as to whether there was a distinct tort of harassment. This has now been overtaken to a large extent by the Protection from Harassment Act 1997, which created a statutory tort (as well as a crime) of harassment. The tort is committed by either pursuing a course of conduct which the defendant knows or ought to know amounts to harassment or which the defendant knows or ought to know causes fear of violence in another person. Conduct is defined so as to include speech, and a course of conduct means on more than one occasion. It is clear that this tort could be committed in the course of picketing.

(3) This case has been criticised on the ground that it makes the union liable for the activities of people it cannot possibly control: do you agree? See also *Gate Gourmet London Ltd* v *TGWU* (2005).

Criminal liability for picketing

Specific types of picketing have been criminal offences since the Conspiracy and Protection of Property Act 1875.

Trade Union and Labour Relations (Consolidation) Act 1992

241 (1) A person commits an offence who, with a view to compelling another person to abstain from doing or to do any act which that person has a legal right to do or abstain from doing, wrongfully and without legal authority –
    (a) uses violence to or intimidates that person or his spouse or civil partner or children, or injures his property,
    (b) persistently follows that person about from place to place,
    (c) hides any tools, clothes or other property owned or used by that person, or deprives him of or hinders him in the use thereof,
    (d) watches or besets the house or other place where that person resides, works, carries on business or happens to be, or the approach to any such house or place, or
    (e) follows that person with two or more other persons in a disorderly manner in or through any street or road.

(2)   A person guilty of an offence under this section is liable on summary conviction to imprisonment for a term not exceeding six months or a fine not exceeding level 5 on the standard scale, or both.

Comment

(1) Note that the activity in question must be independently wrongful before it becomes a criminal offence: *Ward Lock & Co Ltd* v *Operative Printers' Assistants' Society* (1906).

(2) These provisions were rarely used for a century, but a revival of interest came with the miners' strike 1984–85: see Wallington (1985).

(3) As noted already, in addition to the statutory tort of harassment, the Protection from Harassment Act 1997 also defines a criminal offence of harassment. Other statutory provisions which could well be applicable to pickets are contained in the Public Order Act 1986.

(4) In practice, the most common offences committed by pickets are obstruction of the highway and obstruction of a police officer in the execution of his duty. The next case examines the ambit of the latter offence.

Piddington v *Bates* [1960] 3 All ER 660 Queen's Bench Divisional Court

This was an appeal by way of case stated against the appellant's conviction for obstructing a police officer in the execution of his duty, contrary to what is now the Police Act 1996 s 89(2).

The police had been called to a printing works where a van containing about 18 people arrived to picket the two entrances. The police refused to allow more than two pickets at each entrance. What occurred next was reported as follows:

> 'The respondent told the appellant three times that, in his view, two pickets at each entrance were sufficient. The appellant said, "I'm going there and you can't stop me. I know my rights", and, "I can stand by the gate if I want to", and finally, "I'm going to join them. If you don't want me to you'd better arrest me." The appellant then pushed gently past the respondent and was gently arrested. There was no obstruction of the highway in the vicinity of the premises, nor any disorder, nor any violence, threatened or offered, by any of the pickets or other persons present. In para (k) of the Case Stated it was found that the respondent arrived at his view that two pickets at each entrance were enough, on the grounds that that number was sufficient for peaceful picketing in view of the number of persons who might then, or later, leave the premises, and that picketing by persons in excess of that number might lead to intimidation and a breach of the peace.
>
> It was contended on behalf of the appellant that in the peaceful circumstances of the picketing the respondent had no right in law to restrict the number of pickets on the doors to two and that, accordingly, the appellant was not guilty of the offence charged.'

LORD PARKER CJ: '. . . The question here is whether the constables were acting in the course of the execution of their duty when, so it is said, they were obstructed. The court has been referred to a great number of cases, both Irish and English, dealing with the position when a police constable can be said to contemplate a breach of the peace and to take action to preserve it, but I find it unnecessary to refer to those cases. It seems to me that the law is reasonably plain. First, the mere statement by a constable that he did anticipate that there might be a breach of the peace is clearly not enough. There must exist proved facts from which a constable could reasonably have anticipated such a breach. Second, it is not enough that his contemplation is that there is a remote possibility but there must be a real possibility of a breach of the peace. Accordingly, in every case it becomes a question whether, on the particular facts, there were reasonable grounds on which a constable charged with this duty reasonably anticipated that a breach of the peace might occur . . .'

(The judge held that in this case, the police officer had reasonable grounds for his belief and that the appellant was rightly convicted. Ashworth and Elwes JJ agreed.)

Comment

(1) In practice, the police have a lot of discretion in deciding how to regulate pickets and courts are reluctant to judge with hindsight that a decision taken on the spot was wrong. Note that the officer here considered that two pickets per entrance was sufficient. Since the Code of Practice on Picketing suggests a limit of six, many police officers tend to use that as if it were a rule of law.

(2) The appellant here was arrested even as he uttered the immortal words: 'I know my rights.' In *Hunt* v *Broome* (1974) the House of Lords made it clear that there is no positive right to engage in picketing – so pickets were not allowed to stop a vehicle to force the driver to listen to their pitch, even though no violence was used.

Tynan v *Balmer* [1967] 1 QB 91 Queen's Bench Divisional Court

This was an appeal by way of case stated against the appellant's conviction for obstructing a police officer in the execution of his duty.

WIDGERY J: '. . . The pickets in question on November 20 were walking round in a circle in the mouth of the main entrance, that circle being prescribed in the service road which is part of the public highway. An inspector of police was there, he told the appellant that he was not happy about this procedure but clearly did not feel able to press the matter further without reference to higher authority. On Monday, November 23, which is the day of the alleged offence, two police constables were on duty outside the factory and they saw the appellant leading about 40 strike pickets in the circular movement which I have already described. There is no dispute that the police officers heard the appellant instructing the pickets to form a circle in this way, and that he in fact led them out as the first man in the circle. Constable O'Hare requested the appellant to stop the pickets from circling, expressing the view that it was an obstruction and an intimidation. I need not pursue the suggestion that it was an intimidation because the recorder found that it was not, and that matter has not been re-opened before us.

The officer, however, expressed the view that the circle was an obstruction and requested the appellant to tell his men to desist. The appellant replied: "No, I am challenging your authority on this . . . we want to make a test case of it". He thereupon proceeded to lead the 40 pickets round the circle and Constable O'Hare arrested him, took him to the police station and charged him with the offence of obstruction . . .

In my judgment, the proper way to approach this question, and it is a way which may well have commended itself to the recorder also, is to ask whether the conduct of the pickets would have been a nuisance at common law as an unreasonable user of the highway. It seems, in my judgment, that it clearly would have been so regarded. One leaves aside for the moment any facilities enjoyed by those acting in furtherance of a trade dispute, and if one imagines these pickets as carrying banners advertising some patent medicine or advocating some political reform, it seems to me that their conduct in sealing off a part of the highway by this moving circle would have been an unreasonable user of the highway.

In so far as it is a question of fact, the recorder takes the same view, and has, as I read his judgment, found that it was an unreasonable user of the highway.'

(Widgery J concluded that as the police officer had reasonable grounds for believing the pickets to be obstructing the highway, he was entitled to tell them to stop. The appellant was therefore rightly convicted of obstructing a police officer in the execution of his duty. Sachs J and Lord Parker CJ agreed.)

Comment

(1) Thus this creative attempt to avoid liability for obstruction of the highway resulted in conviction for obstructing a police officer in the execution of his duty.

(2) The issue of what constitutes reasonable use of the highway was considered by the House of Lords in *DPP* v *Jones* (1999). The House of Lords held that a peaceful assembly which did not constitute a public or private nuisance was not necessarily trespassory, provided that it did not 'unreasonably' obstruct the highway. This was in the context of a demonstration at Stonehenge rather than an industrial dispute.

(3) A final legislative provision should be considered here, although its applicability is not confined to picketing.

Trade Union and Labour Relations (Consolidation) Act 1992

240 (1) A person commits an offence who wilfully and maliciously breaks a contract of service or hiring, knowing or having reasonable cause to believe that the probable consequences of his so doing, either alone or in combination with others, will be –
(a) to endanger human life or cause serious bodily injury, or
(b) to expose valuable property, whether real or personal, to destruction or serious injury.

(2) Subsection (1) applies equally whether the offence is committed from malice conceived against the person endangered or injured or, as the case may be, the owner of the property destroyed or injured, or otherwise.

(3) A person guilty of an offence under this section is liable on summary conviction to imprisonment for a term not exceeding three months or to a fine not exceeding level 2 on the standard scale or both . . .

Comment

(1) This section derives originally from the Conspiracy and Protection of Property Act 1875. Clearly, it could potentially be invoked in a wide range of industrial disputes – but curiously, it seems never to have been used.

REFERENCES AND FURTHER READING

S Auerbach (1987), 'Legal Restraint of Picketing: New Trends; New Tensions' 16 ILJ 227

S Auerbach (1988), 'Injunction Procedure in the Seafarers' Dispute' 17 ILJ 227

S Auerbach (1990), *Legislating for Conflict*, Clarendon Press

H Carty (1987), 'The Public Order Act 1986: Police Powers and the Picket Line' 16 ILJ 146

K Ewing and B Napier (1986), 'The Wapping Dispute and Labour Law' [1986] CLJ 285

A Goodhart (1926), 'The Legality of the General Strike' 36 Yale L Journal 464 (reprinted in Goodhart (1927), *Essays in Jurisprudence and the Common Law*, OUP)

G Lightman (1987), 'A Trade Union in Chains: Scargill Unbound – the Legal Constraints of Receivership and Sequestration' 40 CLP 25

P Wallington (1986), 'Injunctions and the Right to Demonstrate' [1986] CLJ 86

P. Wallington (1985), 'Policing the Miners' Strike' 14 ILJ 145

The thinking of the Conservative government over the 1980s on this area may be followed through its papers preceding trade union law reform:

Democracy in Trade Unions, Cmnd 8778 (1983), Chap 3

Industrial Relations in the 1990s, Cm 1602 (1991), Chaps 1–4

Removing Barriers to Employment, Cm 655 (1989), Chap 3

Review of Public Order Law, Cmnd 9510 (1985)

Trade Union Immunities, Cmnd 8128 (1981)

Unofficial Action and the Law, Cm 821 (1989)

Working Paper for Consultations on Proposed Industrial Relations Legislation – Picketing (Department of Employment, July 1979)

Working Paper on Secondary Industrial Action (Department of Employment, February 1980)

INDEX